NUMERICAL SIMULATIONS OF PHYSICAL AND ENGINEERING PROCESSES

Edited by **Jan Awrejcewicz**

Numerical Simulations of Physical and Engineering Processes
Edited by Jan Awrejcewicz

Published by InTech
Janeza Trdine 9, 51000 Rijeka, Croatia

Technical Editor Sonja Mujacic

Cover Designer InTech Design Team

Additional hard copies can be obtained from orders@intechopen.com

Numerical Simulations of Physical and Engineering Processes,
Edited by Jan Awrejcewicz
p. cm.
ISBN 978-953-307-620-1

For EU product safety concerns:
IN TECH d.o.o., Prolaz Marije Krucifikse Kozulić 3, 51000 Rijeka, Croatia,
info@intechopen.com or visit our website at intechopen.com.

Meet the editor

Jan Awrejcewicz (www.abm.p.lodz.pl) graduated from the Technical University of Lodz in 1977 (Mechanics) and from the University of Lodz in 1978 (Philosophy), Poland. He obtained PhD (Habilitation) in 1981 (1990), and became a Full Professor in 1997. He authored and/or co-authored: 39 monographs, 2 textbooks, 252 journal papers, 305 conference papers, 35 chapters in books, 13 journal special issues, edited 5 books and 13 conference proceedings, and supervised 17 PhD theses. He serves/ed in editorial boards of 38 journals, gave 80 invited seminars at international universities, delivered 28 plenary/keynote lectures and served as a member of scientific committees to 110 conferences. He carried out 10 years of research abroad supported by Fulbright Award (University of California, Berkeley), Kosciuszko Foundation Award (University of Illinois, Urbana), Research Centre for Advanced Science and Technology and Japanese Society for Promotion of Science (JSPS), Tokyo University, Alexander von Humboldt Foundation, The University of Braunschweig, TEMPRA and Région Rhône-Alpes (France), NATO Grant Award, Lyon, Central European University (Budapest), among other. He is a recipient of the HUMBOLDT RESEARCH AWARD, 2011; MASTER Grant Award, Foundation for Polish Science, 2010-2012; Golden Lamp Award (PGNiG) in Poland, 2006, and numerous awards of the Ministry of Science and Education of Poland.

Contents

Preface

The proposed book contains a lot of recent research devoted to numerical simulations of physical and engineering systems. It can be treated as a bridge linking various numerical approaches of two closely inter-related branches of science, i.e. physics and engineering. Since the numerical simulations play a key role in both theoretical and application-oriented research, professional reference books are highly required by pure research scientists, applied mathematicians, engineers as well post- graduate students. In other words, it is expected that the book serves as an effective tool in training the mentioned groups of researchers and beyond. The book is divided into two parts. Part 1 includes numerical simulations devoted to physical processes, whereas part 2 contains numerical simulations of engineering processes.

Part 1 consists of 14 chapters. In **chapter 1.1** a uniform distribution of particles in d for the computational modeling is assumed by M. I. Andriychuk and A. G. Ramm. Authors of this chapter have shown that theory could be used in many practical problems: some results on EM wave scattering problems, a number of numerical methods for light scattering are presented or even an asymptotically exact solution of the many body acoustic wave scattering are explored. The numerical results are based on the asymptotical approach to solving the scattering problem in a material with many small particles which have been embedded in it to help understand better the dependence of the effective field in the material on the basic parameters of the problem, and to give a constructive way for creating materials with a desired refraction coefficient.

Richard Bouma et al. in **chapter 1.2** analyzed an overview of simulations of deformation processes in energetic materials at the macro-, meso-, and molecular scales. Both non-reactive and reactive processes were considered. An important motivation for the simulation of deformation processes in energetic materials was the desire to avoid accidental ignition of explosives under the influence of a mechanical load, what required the understanding of material behavior at macro-, meso- and molecular scales. Main topics in that study were: the macroscopic deformation of a PBX, a sampling of the various approaches that could be applied for mesoscale modeling, representative simulations based on grain-resolved simulations and an overview of applications of molecular scale modeling to problems of thermal-mechanical-chemical properties prediction and understanding deformation processes on submicron scales.

In **chapter 1.3** Yi Chen et al. analysed EIT and EIT-based slow light in a Doppler-broadened six-level atomic system of ^{87}Rb D2 line. The EIT dip shift due to the existence of the neighbouring levels was investigated. Authors of this study offered a better comprehension of the slow light phenomenon in the complicated multi-level system. They also showed a system whose hyperfine states were closely spaced within the Doppler broadening for potential applications of optical and quantum information processing, such as multichannel all-optical buffer memories and slow-light-based enhanced cross-phase modulation. An N-type system and numerical simulation of slow light phenomenon in this kind of system were also presented. The importance of EIT and the slow light phenomenon in multilevel system was explained and it showed potential applications in the use of ultraslow light for optical information processing such as all-optical multichannel buffer memory and quantum gate based on enhanced cross-phase modulation owing to increased interaction time between two slow-light pulses.

In **chapter 1.4** coauthored by Dipti Gupta et al. a new class of electronic materials for thin film transistor (TFT) applications such as active matrix displays, identification tags, sensors and other low end consumer applications were illustrated. Authors explained the importance of two dimensional simulations in both classes of materials by aiming at several common issues, which were not clarified enough by experimental means or by analytical equations. It started with modeling of TFTs based on tris-isopropylsilyl (TIPS) – pentacene to supply a baseline to describe the charge transport in any new material. The role of metal was stressed and then the stability issue in solution processable zinc oxide (ZnO) TFTs was taken into consideration. To sum up, the important role of device simulations for a better understanding of the material properties and device mechanisms was recognized in TFTs and it was based on organic and metal oxide semiconductors. By providing illustrations from pentacene, the effect of physical behavior which was related to semiconductor film properties in relation to charge injection and charge transport was underlined, TIPS- pentacene and ZnO based TFTs. The device simulations brightened the complex device phenomenon that occurred at the metal-semiconductor interface, semiconductor-dielectric interface, and in the semiconductor film in the form of defect distribution.

The main subjects summarized by Wenlong He et al. of **chapter 1.5** were: the simulations and optimizations of a W-band gyro-BWO including the simulation of a thermionic cusp electron gun which generated an annular, axis-encircling electron beam. The optimization of the W-band gyro-BWO was presented by using the 3D PiC (particle-in-cell) code MAGIC. The MAGIC simulated the interaction between charged particles and electromagnetic fields as they evolved in time and space from the initial states. Fields in the three-dimensional grids were solved by Maxwell equations. The other points which were introduced were: the simulation of the beam-wave interaction in the helically corrugated interaction region and the simulation and optimization of an energy recovery system of 4-stage depressed collector.

Paul Horley et al. in **chapter 1.6** analyzed different representations (spherical, Cartesian, stereographic and Frenet-Serret) of the Landau-Lifshitz-Gilbert equation describing magnetization dynamics. The numerical method was chosen as an important point for the simulations of magnetization dynamics. The LLG which was shown required at least a second-order numerical scheme to obtain the correct solution. The scope was to consider various representations of the main differential equations governing the motion of the magnetization vector, as well as to discuss the main numerical methods which were required for their appropriate solution. It showed the modeling of the temperature influence over the system, which was usually done by adding a thermal noise term to the effective field, leading to stochastic differential equations that require special numerical methods to solve them. Authors summarized that in order to achieve more realistic results, it was necessary to allow the variation of the magnetization vector length, which could be realized, for example, in the Landau-Lifshitz-Bloch equation.

In **chapter 1.7** Antonio Jurado-Navas et al. focused on how to model the propagation of laser beams through the atmosphere with regard to line-of-sight propagation problems, i.e., receiver is in full view of the transmitter. The aim of this work was to show an efficient computer simulation technique to derive irradiance fluctuations for a propagating optical wave in a weakly inhomogeneous medium under the assumption that small-scale fluctuations modulated by large-scale irradiance fluctuations of the wave. A novel and easily implementable model of turbulent atmospheric channel was presented in this study and the adverse effect of the turbulence on the transmitted optical signal was also included. Authors used some techniques to reduce the computational load. Namely, to generate the sequence of scintillation coefficients of Clarke's method used, the continuous-time signal of the filter was sampled and a novel technique was applied to reduce computational load.

A novel statistical model for atmospheric optical scintillation was presented by Antonio Jurado-Navas et al. in **chapter 1.8** focusing on strong turbulence regimes, where multiple scattering effects were important. The aim was to demonstrate that authors' proposed model, which fitted in very well with the published data in the literature, generalized in a closed-form expression most of the developed pdf models that have been proposed by the scientific community for more than four decades. Authors' proposal appeared to be applicable for plane and spherical waves under all conditions of turbulence from weak to super strong in the saturation regime. It derived some of the distribution models most frequently employed in the bibliography by properly choosing the magnitudes of the parameters involving the generalized model. In the end, they performed several comparisons with published plane wave and spherical wave simulation data over a spacious range of turbulence conditions that included inner scale effects.

Tatsunosuke Matsui in **chapter 1.9** specified the computational procedure of (an auxiliary differential equation finite-difference time-domain) ADE-FDTD method for the analysis of lasing dynamics in CLC (Cholesterol liquid crystal) and also presented that this technique was quite useful for the analysis of EM field dynamics in and out of CLC laser cavity under lasing condition, which might cooperate with the deep comprehension of the underlying physical mechanism of lasing dynamics in CLC. The lasing dynamics in CLC as a 1D chiral PBG material by the ADE-FDTD approach, which connected FDTD with ADEs, such as the rate equation in a four-level energy structure and the equation of motion of Lorentz oscillator was also analyzed. The field distribution in CLC with twist-defect was rather different from that without any defect. Finally, it was established that to find more effective mechanism architecture for achieving a lower lasing threshold, the ADE-FDTD approach could be used.

In **chapter 1.10** Rafael Navarro and Justo Arines studied three different problems that one faces when implementing practical applications (either numerical or experimental): lack of completeness of ZPs (Zernike polynomials); lack of orthogonality of ZPs and lack of orthogonality of ZP derivatives. The aim was based on the study of these three problems and provided practical solutions, which were tested and validated through realistic numerical simulations. The next goal was to solve the problem of completeness (both for ZPs and ZPs derivatives), because if there was guaranteed completeness, then it would apply straightly to Gram-Schmidt (or related method) to obtain an orthonormal basis over the sampled circular pupil. Firstly, the basic theory was overwintered and then the study obtained the orthogonal modes for both the discrete Zernike and the Zernike derivatives transforms for different sampling patterns. Afterwards, the implementation and results of realistic computer simulations were described. The non redundant sampling grids presented above were found to keep completeness of discrete Zernike polynomials within the circle.

In **chapter 1.11** Ratno Nuryadi showed a numerical simulation of the single electron transistor using Maltab. The simulation was based on the Master equation, which was obtained from the stochastic process. The following aspects were mentioned: the derivation of the free energy change due to electron tunneling event, the flowchart of numerical simulation, which was based on Master equation and the Maltab implementation. The results produced the staircase behavior in the current-drain voltage characteristics and periodic oscillations in current-gate voltage characteristics. The result also recreated the previous studies of SET showing that the simulation technique achieved good accuracy.

Anatolii Shchedrin and Anna Kalyuzhnaya in **chapter 1.12.** reported systematic studies of the electron-kinetic coefficients in mixtures of helium and xenon with iodine vapors as well as in the He:Xe:I_2 mixture. An analysis of the distributions of the power into the discharge between the dominant electron processes in helium-iodine and xenon-iodine mixtures was performed. The numerical simulation yielded good agreement with experiment, which was testified to the right choice of the calculation model and elementary processes for numerical simulation. The numerical simulation of the discharge and emission kinetics in excimer lamps in mixtures of helium and xenon with iodine vapours allowed to determine the most important kinetic reactions having a significant effect on the population kinetics of the emitting states in He:I_2 and He:Xe:I_2 mixtures. The influence of the halogen concentration on the emission power of the excimer lamp and the effect of xenon on the relative emission intensities of iodine atoms and molecules were analyzed. Author stresses that the replacement of chlorine molecules by less aggressive iodine ones in the working media of excilamps represented an urgent task. Because the optimization of the output characteristics of gas-discharge lamps was based on helium-iodine and xenon-iodine mixtures, numerical simulation of plasma kinetics in a low-pressure discharge in the mentioned active media was carried out.

The recent progress in the management of the laser pulses by means of optical fibers with smoothly variable dispersion is described in **chapter 1.13** by Alexej A. Sysoliatin et al. Authors used numerical simulations to present and analyze solution and pulse dynamics in three kinds of fibers with variable dispersion: dispersion oscillating fiber, negative dispersion decreasing fiber. The studies focused mainly on the stability of solutions, where simulations showed that solution splitting into the pairs of pulses with upshifted and downshifted central wavelengths could be achieved by stepwise change of dispersion or by a localized loss element of filter. Authors emphasized that numerical simulation described in their work revealed solution dynamics and analysis of the solitonic spectra, which gave us a tool to optimize a fiber dispersion and nonlinearity or most efficient soliton splitting or pulse compression.

Tohru Tashiro and Tatekawa Takayuki constructed a theory in **chapter 1.14** which can explain the dynamics toward such a special steady state described by the King model especially around the origin. The idea was to represent an interaction by which a particle of the system is affected by the others by a special random force that originates from a fluctuation in SGS only (a self-gravitating system). A special Langevin equation was used which included the additive and the multiplicative noises. The study demonstrated how their numerical simulations were executed. Furthermore, a treatment for stochastic differential equations became precise, and so the analytical result derived by a different method changed a little. The authors also provided a brief explanation about the machine and the method which were used when the numerical simulations were performed. Then, the number of densities of SGS (a self-gravitating system) derived from their numerical simulations was investigated. Apart from that, the authors showed the densities, which were like that of the King model and both the exponent and the core radius. Finally, forces influencing each particle of SGS (a self-gravitating system) were modeled and by using these forces, Langevin equations were constructed.

Part 2 (Engineering Processes) includes thirteen chapters. In **chapter 2.1** coauthored by Sandra Constanzo and Giuseppe Di Massa the idea to recover far-field patterns from near-field measurements to face the problem of impractical far-field ranges is introduced and implemented as leading to use noise controlled test chambers with reduced size and costs. The accessibility relied on the acquisition of the tangential field components on a prescribed scanning surface, with the subsequent far-field evaluation essentially, which was based on a modal expansion inherent to the particular geometry. In connection to the above, two classes of methods are discussed in this study. The first one refers to efficient transformation algorithms for not canonical near-field surfaces, and the second one is relative to accurate far-field characterization by near-field amplitude-only (or phase less) measurements.

In **chapter 2.2** Edo D'Agaro studied fishing methods that attractive elements of fish such as light used in many parts of the world. The basic elements that were taken into consideration for those who were preparing to use a sea electric attraction system was the safety of operators and possible damage to fish. Streams which were used in electro-fishing could be continuous (DC), alternate (AC) or pulsed (PDC), depending on environmental characteristics (conductivity, temperature) and fish (species, size). The three types (DC, AC, PDC) produced different effects. Only DC and PDC caused a galvanotaxis reaction, as an active swim towards the anode. The main problem in sea water electro-fishing was the high electric current demand on the equipment caused by a very high concentration of salt water. The answer was to reduce the current demand as much as possible by using pulsed direct current, the pulses being as small as possible. The numerical simulations of a non homogeneous electric field (fish and water) permitted to estimate the current gradient in the open sea and to evaluate the attraction capacity of fish using an electro-fishing device. Tank simulations were carried out in a uniform electric field and were generated by two parallel linear electrodes. In practice, in the open sea situation, the efficiency of an electro-fishing system was stronger, in terms of attraction area. Numerical simulations that were carried out using a group of 30 fish, both in open sea and in the tank, showed the presence of a "group effect", increasing the electric field intensity in the water around each fish.

Chapter 2.3 coauthored by Jan Awrejcewicz and Larisa P. Dzyubak focuses on analysis of some problems related to rotor, which were suspended in a magneto-hydrodynamics field in the case of soft and rigid magnetic materials. 2-dof nonlinear dynamics of the rotor were analyzed, supported by the magneto-hydrodynamic bearing (MHDB) system in the cases of soft and rigid magnetic materials. 2–dof non–linear dynamics of the rotor, which were suspended in a magneto–hydrodynamic field were studied. In the case of soft magnetic materials, the analytical solutions were obtained using the method of multiple scales, but in the case of rigid magnetic materials, hysteresis were investigated using the Bouc–Wen hysteretic model. The significant obtained points: amplitude level contours of the horizontal and vertical vibrations of the rotor and phase portraits and hysteretic loops were in good agreement with the chaotic regions. Chaos was generated by hysteretic properties of the system considered.

Anselmo Buso and Monica Giomo in **chapter 2.4** show two different examples of expanding a mathematical model essential for two different complex chemical systems. The complexity of the system was related to the structure heterogeneity in the first case study and to the various physical-chemical phenomena, which was involved in the process in the second one. In addition, concentration on the estimation of the significant parameters of the process and finally the availability of a tool was shown as well as on the verified and validated (V&V) mathematical model, which could be used for simulation, process analysis, process control, optimization and design.

The conception of **chapter 2.5** coauthored by Aicha Elhsoumi et al. benefited from the use of Luenberger and Kalman observers for modeling and monitoring nonlinear dynamic processes. The aim of this study was to explore a system to monitor performance degradation in a chemical process involving a class of chemical reactions, which occur in a jacketed continuous reactor. The comparison between the measurements of variables set characterizing the behavior of the monitored system and the corresponding estimates predicted via the mathematical model of system were included in model-based methods. Apart from this, the generated fault indicators were related to a specific faults, which might affect the system. Finally, a note of Fault Detection and Isolation (FDI) in the chemical processes and basic proprieties of linear observers were introduced and the study also resented how the Luenberger and Kalman observers can be used for systematic generation of FDI algorithms.

C.A.F. Fernandes and José A.P. Morgado in **chapter 2.6** presented an example concerning the use of a numerical simulation method, designated by transfer-matrix-method (TMM) which was a numerical simulation tool especially adequate for the design of distributed feedback (DFB) laser structures in high bit rate optical communication systems (OCS) and represented a paradigmatic example of a numerical method related to heavy computational times. A detailed description of those numerical techniques makes the scope of this work. Matrix methods usually very heavy in terms of processing times were summarized and they should be optimized in order to improve their time computational efficiency. Authors concluded that the TMM, both in its static and dynamic versions, represents a powerful tool used in the important domain of OCS for the optimization of laser structures especially designed to provide (SLM) single-longitudinal mode operation.

Hiroshi Okumura and Akira Sano in **chapter 2.7** aimed to prove that a control method, which could selectively attenuate only unnecessary signals, is needed. In this chapter, the authors proposed a novel control scheme which could transmit necessary signals (Necs) and attenuate only unnecessary signals (Unecs). The control diagram was called Signal Selection Control (SSC) scheme. The aim of the authors was to explore two types of the SSC. First, the Necs-Extraction Controller which transmitted only signals set as Necs, and the other was Unecs-Canceling Controller which weakened only signals set as Unecs. Furthermore, four adaptive controllers were characterized. It was validated that the 2-degree-of-freedom Virtual Error controller had the best performance in the four adaptive controller. Consequently, effectiveness of both SSC was legalized in two numerical simulations of the Sound Selection Systems.

In **chapter 2.8** white-light interferometry was established as a method to measure the geometrical shape of objects by Pavel Pavlíček. In this chapter the influence of rough surface and shot noise on measurement uncertainty of white-light interferometry on rough surface was investigated and it showed that both components of measurement add uncertainty geometrically. Two influences that cause the measurement uncertainty were considered: rough surface and the shot noise of the camera. The numerical simulations proved that the influence of the rough surface on the measurement uncertainty was for usual values of spectral widths, sampling step and noise-to-signal ratio significantly higher than that of shot noise. The obtained results determined limits under which the conditions for white-light interferometry could be regarded as usual.

The aim of **chapter 2.9** coauthored by Leandro Prevosto et al. was to present a versatile study of the double-arcing phenomenon, which was one of the drawbacks that put limits to increasing capabilities of the plasma arc cutting process. There are some hypothesis in the literature on the physical mechanism that it had triggered the double-arcing in cutting torches. The authors carried out a study where the staring point was the analysis and interpretation of the nozzle current-voltage characteristic curve. A physical interpretation on the origin of the double-arcing phenomenon was presented and it explained why the double-arcing appeared for example at low values of the gas mass flow. A complementary numerical study of the space-charge sheath was also mentioned, which was formed between the plasma and the nozzle wall of a cutting torch. The numerical study corresponded to a collision-dominated model (ion mobility-limited motion) for the hydrodynamic description of the sheath adjacent to the nozzle wall inside of a cutting torch and a physical explanation on the origin of the transient double-arcing (the so-called non-destructive double-arcing) in cutting torches was reported. The authors presented a study of the arc plasma-nozzle sheath structure which was the area where the double-arcing had taken place and a detailed study of the sheath structure by developing a numerical model for a collisional sheath.

Yohei Saika illustrated in **chapter 2.10** both theoretical and practical aspects of inverse halftoning on the basis of statistical mechanics and its variant, which related to the generalized statistical smoothing (GSS) and for halftone images obtained by the dither and error diffusion methods. Furthermore, the statistical performance of the present method using both the Monte Carlo simulation for a set of snapshots of the Q-Ising model and the analytical estimate via infinite-range model was presented. From above studies, it was clear that statistical mechanics were applied to many problems in various fields, such as information, communication and quantum computation.

The studies in **chapter 2.11** coauthored by Rudolf Reinhard et al. proved that complexity in modern production processes increases continuously. The virtual planning of these processes simplified their realization extensively and decreased their implementation costs. The necessary matter was also to interconnect different specialized simulation tools and to exchange their resulting data. In this work authors introduced the architecture of a framework for adaptive data integration, which enabled the interconnection of simulation tools of a specified domain. Authors focused on the integration of data generated during the applications' usage, which could be handled with the help of modern middleware techniques. The development of the framework, which was shown in this study, could be regarded as an important step in the establishment of digital production, as the framework allows a holistic, step-by-step simulation of a production process by usage of specialized tools. With respect to the methodology used in this chapter, it was not necessary to adapt applications to the data model aforementioned.

Flavius Dan Surianu in **chapter 2.12.** emphasized the necessity to increase the number of the system elements whose mathematical modelling had to be examined in simulation in order that main components of the power system are included starting from the thermal, hydro and mechanical primary installations up to the consumers. Furthermore, the analysis of the simulation results presented compliance with the evolution of the dynamics of thermal and hydro-mechanic primary installations. Besides, it was established that the simulation realistically represents a physical phenomena both in pre- disturbance steady state and in the dynamic processes following the disturbances in the electric power system.

Hidenori Taga in **chapter 2.13.** illustrated the return-to-zero differential phase shift keying (RZ-DPSK) transmission system and the behavior at using the numerical simulations which showed that the conventional intensity-modulation direct-detection (IM-DD) system gives better performance near the system zero dispersion wavelength rather than the other wavelengths. Furthermore, a method of the numerical simulations was presented, where the results were obtained through the simulation and the transmission performance of the long-haul RZ-DPSK system using an advanced optical fibre was simulated, what completed the work.

I would like to thank all book contributors for their patience and improvement of their chapters. In addition, it is my great pleasure to thank Ms Ana Nikolic for her professional support during the book preparation.

Finally, I would like to acknowledge my working visit to Darmstadt, Germany supported by the Alexander von Humboldt Award which also allowed me time to devote to the book preparation.

Jan Awrejcewicz
Technical University of Łódź
Poland

Part 1

Physical Processes

1

Numerical Solution of Many-Body Wave Scattering Problem for Small Particles and Creating Materials with Desired Refraction Coefficient

M. I. Andriychuk[1] and A. G. Ramm[2]
[1]*Pidstryhach Institute for Applied Problems in Mechanics and Mathematics, NASU*
[2]*Mathematics Department, Kansas State University*
[1]*Ukraine*
[2]*USA*

1. Introduction

Theory of wave scattering by small particles of arbitrary shapes was developed by A. G. Ramm in papers (Ramm, 2005; 2007;a;b; 2008;a; 2009; 2010;a;b) for acoustic and electromagnetic (EM) waves. He derived analytical formulas for the S-matrix for wave scattering by a small body of arbitrary shape, and developed an approach for creating materials with a desired spatial dispersion. One can create a desired refraction coefficient $n^2(x,\omega)$ with a desired x,ω-dependence, where ω is the wave frequency. In particular, one can create materials with negative refraction, i.e., material in which phase velocity is directed opposite to the group velocity. Such materials are of interest in applications, see, e.g., (Hansen, 2008; von Rhein et al., 2007). The theory, described in this Chapter, can be used in many practical problems. Some results on EM wave scattering problems one can find in (Tatseiba & Matsuoka, 2005), where random distribution of particles was considered. A number of numerical methods for light scattering are presented in (Barber & Hill, 1990). An asymptotically exact solution of the many body acoustic wave scattering problem was developed in (Ramm, 2007) under the assumptions $ka << 1$, $d = O(a^{1/3})$, $M = O(1/a)$, where a is the characteristic size of the particles, $k = 2\pi/\lambda$ is the wave number, d is the distance between neighboring particles, and M is the total number of the particles embedded in a bounded domain $D \subset \mathbb{R}^3$. It was not assumed in (Ramm, 2007) that the particles were distributed uniformly in the space, or that there was any periodic structure in their distribution. In this Chapter, a uniform distribution of particles in D for the computational modeling is assumed (see Figure 1). An impedance boundary condition on the boundary S_m of the m-th particle D_m was assumed, $1 \leq m \leq M$. In (Ramm, 2008a) the above assumptions were generalized as follows:

$$\zeta_m = \frac{h(x_m)}{a^\kappa}, \qquad d = O(a^{(2-\kappa)/3}), \qquad M = O(\frac{1}{a^{2-\kappa}}), \qquad \kappa \in (0,1), \tag{1}$$

where ζ_m is the boundary impedance, $h_m = h(x_m)$, $x_m \in D_m$, and $h(x) \in C(D)$ is an arbitrary continuous in $\overline{D}$ function, $\overline{D}$ is the closure of D, $\text{Im}h \leq 0$. The initial field u_0 satisfies the Helmholtz equation in $\mathbb{R}^3$ and the scattered field satisfies the radiation condition. We assume in this Chapter that $\kappa \in (0,1)$ and the small particle D_m is a ball of radius a centered at the point $x_m \in D, 1 \leq m \leq M$.

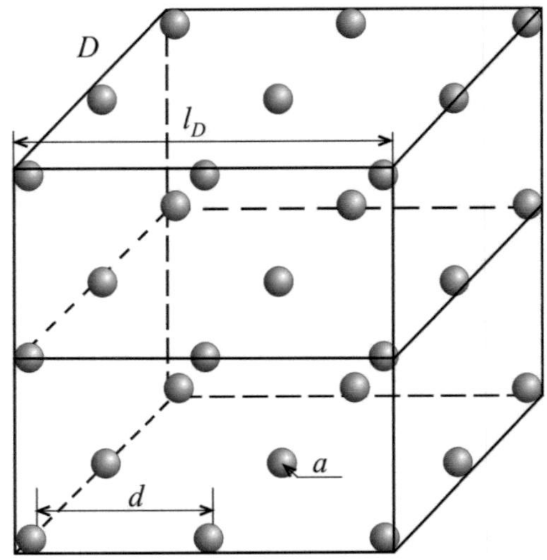

Fig. 1. Geometry of problem with $M = 27$ particles

2. Solution of the scattering problem

The scattering problem is

$$[\nabla^2 + k^2 n_0^2(x)]u_M = 0 \quad \text{in} \quad \mathbb{R}^3 \setminus \bigcup_{m=1}^{M} D_m, \tag{2}$$

$$\frac{\partial u_M}{\partial N} = \zeta_m u_M \quad \text{on} \quad S_m, 1 \leq m \leq M, \tag{3}$$

where

$$u_M = u_0 + v_M, \tag{4}$$

u_0 is a solution to problem (2), (3) with $M = 0$ (i.e., in the absence of the embedded particles) and with the incident field $e^{ik\alpha \cdot x}$. The scattered field v_M satisfies the radiation condition. The refraction coefficient $n_0^2(x)$ of the material in a bounded region D is assumed for simplicity a bounded function whose set of discontinuities has zero Lebesgue measure in $\mathbb{R}^3$, and $\text{Im}n_0^2(x) \geq 0$. We assume that $n_0^2(x) = 1$ in $D' := \mathbb{R}^3 \setminus D$. It was proved in (Ramm, 2008) that the unique solution to problem (2) - (4) exists, is unique, and is of the form

$$u_M(x) = u_0(x) + \sum_{m=1}^{M} \int_{S_m} G(x,y)\sigma_m(y)dy, \tag{5}$$

where $G(x,y)$ is Green's function of the Helmholtz equation (2) in the case when $M = 0$, i.e., when there are no embedded particles, and $\sigma_m(y)$ are some unknown functions. If these functions are chosen so that the boundary conditions (3) are satisfied, then formula (5) gives the unique solution to problem (2) - (4). Let us define the "effective field" u_e, acting on the m-th particle:

$$u_e(x) := u_e(x,a) := u_e^{(m)}(x) := u_M(x) - \int_{S_m} G(x,y)\sigma_m(y)dy, \tag{6}$$

where $|x - x_m| \sim a$. If $|x - x_m| >> a$, then $u_M(x) \sim u_e^{(m)}(x)$. The $\sim$ sign denotes the same order as $a \to 0$. The function $\sigma_m(y)$ solves an exact integral equation (see (Ramm, 2008)). This equation is solved in (Ramm, 2008) asymptotically as $a \to 0$, see formulas (12)-(15) in Section 3. Let $h(x) \in C(D)$, Im$h \leq 0$, be arbitrary, $\Delta \subset D$ be any subdomain of D, and $\mathcal{N}(\Delta)$ be the number of the embedded particles in Δ. We assume that

$$\mathcal{N}(\Delta) = \frac{1}{a^{2-\kappa}} \int_\Delta N(x)dx[1 + o(1)], \quad a \to 0, \tag{7}$$

where $N(x) \geqslant 0$ is a given continuous function in D. The following result was proved in (Ramm, 2008).

Theorem 1. There exists the limit $u(x)$ of $u_e(x)$ as $a \to 0$:

$$\lim_{a \to 0} ||u_e(x) - u(x)||_{C(D)} = 0, \tag{8}$$

and $u(x)$ solves the following equation:

$$u(x) = u_0(x) - 4\pi \int_D G(x,y)h(y)N(y)u(y)dy. \tag{9}$$

This is the equation, derived in (Ramm, 2008) for the limiting effective field in the medium, created by embedding many small particles with the distribution law (7).

3. Approximate representation of the effective field

Let us derive an explicit formula for the effective field u_e. Rewrite the exact formula (5) as:

$$u_M(x) = u_0(x) + \sum_{m=1}^{M} G(x,x_m)Q_m + \sum_{m=1}^{M} \int_{S_m} [G(x,y) - G(x,x_m)]\sigma_m(y)dy, \tag{10}$$

where

$$Q_m = \int_{S_m} \sigma_m(y)dy. \tag{11}$$

Using some estimates of $G(x,y)$ (see (Ramm, 2007)) and the asymptotic formula for Q_m from (Ramm, 2008), one can rewrite the exact formula (10) as follows:

$$u_M(x) = u_0(x) + \sum_{m=1}^{M} G(x,x_m)Q_m + o(1), \quad a \to 0, \quad |x - x_m| \geqslant a. \tag{12}$$

The numbers $Q_m, 1 \leq m \leq M$, are given by the asymptotic formula

$$Q_m = -4\pi h(x_m)u_e(x_m)a^{2-\kappa}[1+o(1)], \quad a \to 0, \tag{13}$$

and the asymptotic formula for σ_m is (see (Ramm, 2008)):

$$\sigma_m = -\frac{h(x_m)u_e(x_m)}{a^\kappa}[1+o(1)], \quad a \to 0. \tag{14}$$

The asymptotic formula for $u_e(x)$ in the region $|x - x_j| \sim a, 1 \leq j \leq M$, is (see (Ramm, 2008)):

$$u_e^{(j)}(x) = u_0(x) - 4\pi \sum_{m=1, m\neq j}^{M} G(x, x_m)h(x_m)u_e(x_m)a^{2-\kappa}[1+o(1)]. \tag{15}$$

Equation (9) for the limiting effective field $u(x)$ is used for numerical calculations when the number M is large, e.g., $M = 10^b, b > 3$. The goal of our numerical experiments is to investigate the behavior of the solution to equation (9) and compare it with the asymptotic formula (15) in order to establish the limits of applicability of our asymptotic approach to many-body wave scattering problem for small particles.

4. Reduction of the scattering problem to solving linear algebraic systems

The numerical calculation of the field u_e by formula (15) requires the knowledge of the numbers $u_m := u_e(x_m)$. These numbers are obtained by solving the following linear algebraic system (LAS):

$$u_j = u_{0j} - 4\pi \sum_{m=1, m\neq j}^{M} G(x_j, x_m)h(x_m)u_m a^{2-\kappa}, \quad j = 1, 2, ..., M, \tag{16}$$

where $u_j = u(x_j),\ 1 \leq j \leq M$. This LAS is convenient for numerical calculations, because its matrix is sometimes diagonally dominant. Moreover, it follows from the results in (Ramm, 2009), that for sufficiently small a this LAS is uniquely solvable. Let the union of small cubes Δ_p, centered at the points y_p, form a partition of D, and the diameter of Δ_p be $O(d^{1/2})$. For finitely many cubes Δ_p the union of these cubes may not give D. In this case we consider the smallest partition containing D and define $n_0^2(x) = 1$ in the small cubes that do not belong to D. To find the solution to the limiting equation (9), we use the collocation method from (Ramm, 2009), which yields the following LAS:

$$u_j = u_{0j} - 4\pi \sum_{p=1, m\neq j}^{P} G(x_j, x_p)h(y_p)N(y_p)u_p|\Delta_p|, \qquad p = 1, 2, ..., P, \tag{17}$$

where P is the number of small cubes Δ_p, y_p is the center of Δ_p, and $|\Delta_p|$ is volume of Δ_p. From the computational point of view solving LAS (17) is much easier than solving LAS (16) if $P << M$. We have two different LAS: one is (16), the other is (17). The first corresponds to formula (15). The second corresponds to a collocation method for solving equation (9). Solving these LAS, one can compare their solutions and evaluate the limits of applicability of the asymptotic approach from (Ramm, 2008) to solving many-body wave scattering problem in the case of small particles.

5. EM wave scattering by many small particles

Let D is the domain that contains M particles of radius a, d is distance between them. Assume that $ka \ll 1$, where $k > 0$ is the wavenumber. The governing equations for scattering problem are:

$$\nabla \times E = i\omega\mu H, \quad \nabla \times H = -i\omega\varepsilon'(x)E \text{ in } \mathbb{R}^3, \tag{18}$$

where $\omega > 0$ is the frequency, $\mu = \mu_0 = \text{const}$ is the magnetic constant, $\varepsilon'(x) = \varepsilon_0 = \text{const} > 0$ in $D' = \mathbb{R}^3 \backslash D$, $\varepsilon'(x) = \varepsilon(x) + i\frac{\sigma(x)}{\omega}$; $\sigma(x) \geq 0$, $\varepsilon'(x) \neq 0 \ \forall \ x \in \mathbb{R}^3$, $\varepsilon'(x) \in C^2(\mathbb{R}^3)$ is a twice continuously differentiable function, $\sigma(x) = 0$ in D', $\sigma(x)$ is the conductivity. From (18) one gets

$$\nabla \times \nabla \times E = K^2(x)E, \quad H = \frac{\nabla \times E}{i\omega\mu}, \tag{19}$$

where $K^2(x) = \omega^2\varepsilon'(x)\mu$. We are looking for the solution of the equation

$$\nabla \times \nabla \times E = K^2(x)E \tag{20}$$

satisfying the radiation condition

$$E(x) = E_0(x) + v, \tag{21}$$

where $E_0(x)$ is the plane wave

$$E_0(x) = \mathcal{E}e^{ik\alpha\cdot x}, \quad k = \frac{\omega}{c}, \tag{22}$$

$c = \omega\sqrt{\varepsilon\mu}$ is the wave velocity in the homogeneous medium outside D, $\varepsilon = \text{const}$ is the dielectric parameter in the outside region D', $\alpha \in S^2$ is the incident direction of the plane wave, S^2 is unit sphere in $\mathbb{R}^3$, $\mathcal{E} \cdot \alpha = 0$, $\mathcal{E}$ is a constant vector, and the scattered field v satisfies the radiation condition

$$\frac{\partial v}{\partial r} - ikv = o(\frac{1}{r}), \quad r = |x| \to \infty \tag{23}$$

uniformly in directions $\beta := x/r$. If E is found, then the pair $\{E, H\}$, where H is determined by second formula (19), solves our scattering problem. It was proved in (Ramm, 2008a), that scattering problem for system (18) is equivalent to solution of the integral equation:

$$E(x) = E_0(x) + \sum_{m=1}^{M} \int_{D_m} g(x,y)p(y)E(y)dy + \sum_{m=1}^{M} \nabla_x \int_{D_m} g(x,y)q(y) \cdot E(y)dy, \tag{24}$$

where M is the number of small bodies, $p(x) = K^2(x) - k^2$, $p(x) = 0$ in D', $q(y) = \frac{\nabla K^2(x)}{K^2(x)}$, $q(x) = 0$ in D', $g(x,y) = \frac{e^{ik|x-y|}}{4\pi|x-y|}$. Equation (24) one can rewrite as

$$E(x) = E_0(x) + \sum_{m=1}^{M} [g(x,x_m)V_m + \nabla_x g(x,x_m)v_m] + \sum_{m=1}^{M} (J_m + K_m), \tag{25}$$

where

$$J_m := \int_{D_m} [g(x,y) - g(x,x_m)p(y)E(y)dy, \tag{26}$$

$$K_m := \nabla_x \int_{D_m} [g(x,y) - g(x,x_m)q(y)E(y)dy. \tag{27}$$

Neglecting J_m and K_m, let us derive a linear algebraic system for finding V_m and v_m. If V_m and v_m , $1 \leq m \leq M$, are found, then the EM wave scattering problem for M small bodies is solved by the formula

$$E(x) = E_0(x) + \sum_{m=1}^{M} [g(x,x_m)V_m + \nabla_x g(x,x_m)v_m] \tag{28}$$

with an error $O(\frac{a}{d} + ka)$ in the domain $\min_{1\leq m\leq M} |x - x_m| := d \gg a$. To derive a linear algebraic system for V_m and v_m multiply (25) by $p(x)$, integrate over D_j, and neglect the terms J_m and K_m to get

$$V_j = V_{0j} + \sum_{m=1}^{M} (a_{jm}V_m + B_{jm}v_m), 1 \leq j \leq M, \tag{29}$$

where

$$V_{0j} := \int_{D_j} p(x)E_0(x)dx, \quad V_j := \int_{D_j} p(x)E(x)dx, \tag{30}$$

$$a_{jm} := \int_{D_j} p(x)g(x,x_m)dx, \tag{31}$$

$$B_{jm} := \int_{D_j} p(x)\nabla_x g(x,x_m)dx. \tag{32}$$

Take the dot product of (25) with $q(x)$, integrate over D_j, and neglect the terms J_m and K_m to get

$$v_j = v_{0j} + \sum_{m=1}^{M} (C_{jm}V_m + d_{jm}v_m), 1 \leq j \leq M, \tag{33}$$

where

$$v_{0j} := \int_{D_j} q(x) \cdot E_0(x)dx, \quad v_j := \int_{D_j} q(x) \cdot E(x)dx, \tag{34}$$

$$C_{jm} := \int_{D_j} q(x)g(x,x_m)dx, \tag{35}$$

$$d_{jm} := \int_{D_j} q(x) \cdot \nabla_x g(x,x_m)dx. \tag{36}$$

Equations (29) and (33) form a linear algebraic system for finding V_m and v_m, $1 \leq m \leq M$. This linear algebraic system is uniquely solvable if $ka \ll 1$ and $a \ll d$. Elements B_{jm} and C_{jm}

are vectors, and a_{jm}, d_{jm} are scalars. Under the conditions

$$\max_{1\le j\le M}\sum_{m=1}^{M}(|a_{jm}|+|d_{jm}|+||B_{jm}||+||C_{jm}||)<1 \tag{37}$$

one can solve linear algebraic system (29), (33) by iterations. In (37), $||B_{jm}||$ and $||C_{jm}||$ are the lengths of corresponding vectors. Condition (37) holds if $a \ll 1$ and M is not growing too fast as $a \to 0$, not faster than $O(a^{-3})$. In the process of computational modeling, it is necessary to investigate the solution of system (29), (33) numerically and to check the condition (37) for given geometrical parameters of problem.

6. Evaluation of applicability of asymptotic approach for EM scattering

One can write the linear algebraic system corresponding to formula (24) as follows (Ramm, 2008a)

$$\begin{aligned} &E_j = E_{0j} + \sum_{j\neq p,p=1}^{P} g(x_j,x_p)p(x_p)E(x_p) + \nabla_x \sum_{j\neq p,p=1}^{P} g(x_j,x_p)\,q(x_p)\cdot E(x_p),\\ &j=1,2,...,P,\ x_j,x_p\in D\ , \end{aligned} \tag{38}$$

where $E_j = E(x_j)$. Having the solution to (38), the values of $E(x)$ in all R^3 one can calculate by

$$E(x) = E_0(x) + \sum_{p=1}^{P} g(x,x_p)p(x_p)E(x_p) + \nabla_x \sum_{p=1}^{P} g(x,x_p)\,q(x_p)\cdot E(x_p). \tag{39}$$

The values $E(x_p)$ in (39) correspond to set $\{E(x_p), p = 1,...,P\}$, which is determined in (38), where P is number of collocation points. In the process of numerical calculations the integration over regions D_m in formula (24) is replaced by calculation of a Riemannian sum, and the derivative ∇_x is replaced by a divided difference. This allows one to compare the numerical solutions to system (38) with asymptotical ones calculated by the formula (28).

7. Determination of refraction coefficient for EM wave scattering

Formula (28) does not contain the parameters that characterize the properties of D, in particular, its refraction coefficient $n^2(x)$. In (Ramm, 2008a) a limiting equation, as $a \to 0$, for the effective field is derived:

$$E_e(x) = E_0(x) + \int_D g(x,y)C(y)E_e(y)dy, \tag{40}$$

and an explicit formula for refraction coefficient $n^2(x)$ is obtained. These results can be used in computational modeling. One has $E_e(x) := \lim_{a\to 0} E(x)$, and

$$C(x_m) = c_{1m}N(x_m). \tag{41}$$

Formula (41) defines uniquely a continuous function $C(x)$ since the points x_m are distributed everywhere dense in D as $a \to 0$. The function $C(x)$ can be created as we wish, since it is determined by the numbers c_{1m} and by the function $N(x)$, which are at our disposal. Apply the operator $\nabla^2 + k^2$ to (40) and get

$$[\nabla^2 + \mathrm{K}^2(x)]E_e = 0, \ \mathrm{K}^2(x) := k^2 + C(x) := k^2 n^2(x). \tag{42}$$

Thus, the refraction coefficient $n^2(x)$ is defined by the formula

$$n^2(x) = 1 + k^{-2}C(x). \tag{43}$$

The functions $C(x)$ and $n^2(x)$ depend on the choice of $N(x)$ and c_{1m}. The function $N(x)$ in formula (7) and the numbers c_{1m} we can choose as we like. One can vary $N(x)$ and c_{1m} to reduce the discrepancy between the solution to equation (40) and the solution to equation (39). A computational procedure for doing this is described and tested for small number of particles in Section 9.

8. Numerical experiments for acoustic scattering

The numerical approach to solving the acoustic wave scattering problem for small particles was developed in (Andriychuk & Ramm, 2010). There some numerical results were given. These results demonstrated the applicability of the asymptotic approach to solving many-body wave scattering problem by the method described in Sections 3 and 4. From the practical point of view, the following numerical experiments are of interest and of importance:
a) For not very large M, say, M=2, 5, 10, 25, 50, one wants to find a and d, for which the asymptotic formula (12) (without the remainder $o(1)$) is no longer applicable;
b) One wants to find the relative accuracy of the solutions to the limiting equation (9) and to the LAS (17);
c) For large M, say, $M = 10^5$, $M = 10^6$, one wants to find the relative accuracy of the solutions to the limiting equation (9) and of the solutions to the LAS (16);
d) One wants to find the relative accuracy of the solutions to the LAS (16) and (17);
e) Using Ramm's method for creating materials with a desired refraction coefficient, one wants to find out for some given refraction coefficients $n^2(x)$ and $n_0^2(x)$, what the smallest M (or, equivalently, largest a) is for which the corresponding $n^2_{M(x)}$ differs from the desired $n^2(x)$ by not more than, say, 5% - 10%. Here $n^2_{M(x)}$ is the value of the refraction coefficient of the material obtained by embedding M small particles into D accoring to the recipe described below.
We take $k = 1$, $\kappa = 0.9$, and $N(x) = \text{const}$ for the numerical calculations. For $k = 1$, and a and d, used in the numerical experiments, one can have many small particles on the wavelength. Therefore, the multiple scattering effects are not negligible.

8.1 Applicability of asymptotic formulas for small number of particles

We consider the solution to LAS (17) with 20 collocation points along each coordinate axis as the benchmark solution. The total number P of the collocation points is $P = 8000$. The applicability of the asymptotic formulas is checked by solving LAS (16) for small number M of particles and determining the problem parameters for which the solutions to these LAS are close. A standard interpolation procedure is used in order to obtain the values of the solution to (17) at the points corresponding to the position of the particles. In this case the number P of the collocation points exceeds the number M of particles. In Fig. 2, the relative errors of real (solid line) and imaginary (dashed line) parts, as well as the modulus (dot-dashed line) of the solution to (16) are shown for the case $M = 4$; the distance between particles is $d = a^{(2-\kappa)/3}C$, where C is an additional parameter of optimization (in our case $C = 5$, that yields the smallest error of deviation of etalon and asymptotic field components), $N(x) = 5$. The minimal relative error of the solution to (16) does not exceed 0.05% and is reached when $a \in (0.02, 0.03)$. The value of the function $N(x)$ influences (to a considerable degree) the quality of approximation. The relative error for $N(x) = 40$ with the same other parameters is shown in Fig. 3. The error is smallest at $a = 0.01$, and it grows when a increases. The minimal error that we were able to obtain for this case is about 0.01% . The dependence of the error on the distance d between

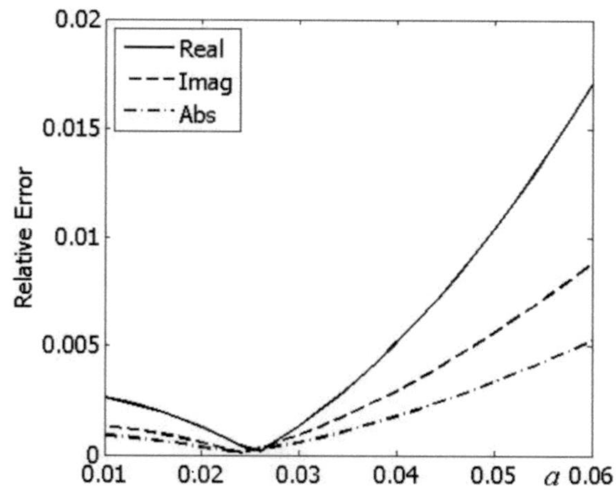

Fig. 2. Relative error of solution to (16) versus size a of particle, $N(x) = 5$

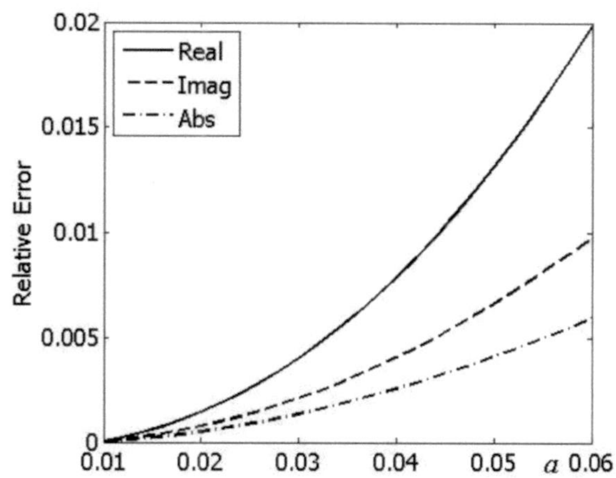

Fig. 3. Relative error of solution to (16) versus size a of particle, $N(x) = 40$

particles for a fixed a was investigated as well. In Fig. 4, the relative error versus parameter d is shown. The number of particles $M = 4$, the radius of particles $a = 0.01$. The minimal error

was obtained when $C = 14$. This error was 0.005% for the real part, 0.0025% for the imaginary part, and 0.002% for the modulus of the solution.
The error grows significantly when d deviates from the optimal value, i.e., the value of d for which the error of the calculated solution to LAS (16) is minimal. Similar results are obtained for the case $a = 0.02$ (see Fig. 5). For example, at $M = 2$ the optimal value of d is 0.038 for $a = 0.01$, and it is 0.053 for $a = 0.02$. The error is even more sensitive to changes of the distance d in this case. The minimal value of the error is obtained when $C = 8$. The error was 0.0078% for the real part, 0.0071% for the imaginary part, and 0.002% for the modulus of the solution.
The numerical results show that the accuracy of the approximation of the solutions to LAS

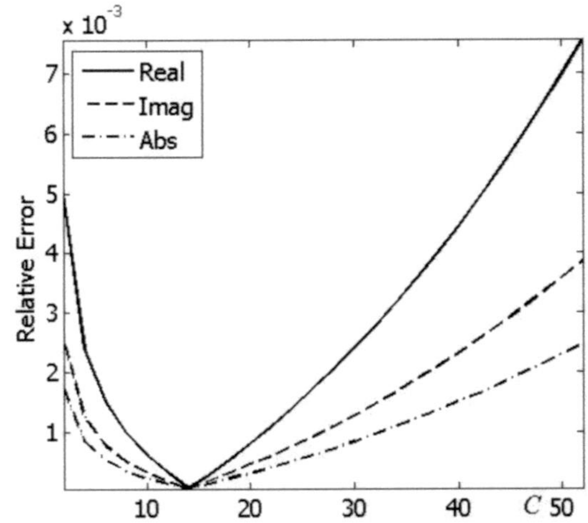

Fig. 4. Relative error of solution versus distance d between particles, $a = 0.01$

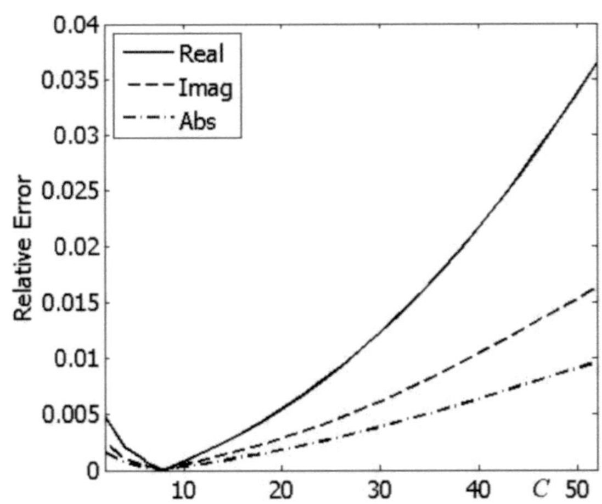

Fig. 5. Relative error of solution versus distance d between particles, $a = 0.02$

	M value			
	$M = 2$	$M = 4$	$M = 6$	$M = 8$
$a = 0.01$	0.038	0.025	0.026	0.027
$a = 0.02$	0.053	0.023	0.027	0.054

Table 1. Optimal values of d for small M

	M value			
	$M = 10$	$M = 20$	$M = 30$	$M = 40$
$a = 0.01$	0.011	0.0105	0.007	0.006
$a = 0.02$	0.016	0.018	0.020	0.023

Table 2. Optimal values of d for medium M

(16) and (17) depends on a significantly, and it improves when a decreases. For example, the minimal error, obtained at $a = 0.04$, is equal to 0.018%. The optimal values of d are given in Tables 1, and 2 for small and not so small M respectively. The numerical results show that the distribution of particles in the medium does not influence significantly the optimal values of d. By optimal values of d we mean the values at which the error of the solution to LAS (16) is minimal when the values of the other parameters are fixed. For example, the optimal values of d for $M = 8$ at the two types of the distribution of particles: $(2 \times 2 \times 2)$ and $(4 \times 2 \times 1)$ differ by not more than 0.5% . The numerical results demonstrate that to decrease the relative error of solution to system (16), it is necessary to make a smaller if the value of d is fixed. One can see that the quality of approximation improves as $a \to 0$, but the condition $d >> a$ is not valid for small number M of particles: the values of the distance d is of the order $O(a)$.

8.2 Accuracy of the solution to the limiting equation

The numerical procedure for checking the accuracy of the solution to equation (9) uses the calculations with various values of the parameters k, a, l_D, and $h(x)$, where l_D is diameter of D. The absolute and relative errors were calculated by increasing the number of collocation points. The dependence of the accuracy on the parameter ρ, where $\rho = \sqrt[3]{P}$, P is the total number of small subdomains in D, is shown in Fig. 6 and Fig. 7 for $k = 1.0$, $l_D = 0.5$, $a = 0.01$ at the different values of $h(x)$. The solution corresponding to ρ =20 is considered as "exact" solution (the number P for this case is equal to 8000). The error of the solution to equation (9) is equal to 1.1% and 0.02% for real and imaginary part, respectively, at $\rho = 5$ (125 collocation points), it decreases to values of 0.7% and 0.05% if $\rho = 6$ (216 collocation points), and it decreases to values 0.29% and 0.02% if $\rho = 8$ (512 collocation points), $h(x) = k^2(1-3i)/(40\pi)$. The relative error smaller than 0.01% for the real part of solution is obtained at $\rho = 12$, this error tends to zero when ρ increases. This error depends on the function $h(x)$ as well, it diminishes when the imaginary part of $h(x)$ decreases. The error for the real and imaginary parts of the solution at $\rho = 19$ does not exceed 0.01%. The numerical calculations show that the error depends much on the value of k. In Fig. 8 and Fig. 9 the results are shown for $k = 2.0$ and $k = 0.6$ respectively ($h(x) = k^2(1-3i)/(40\pi)$). It is seen that the error is nearly 10 times larger at $k = 2.0$. The maximal error (at $\rho = 5$) for $k = 0.6$ is less than 30% of the error for $k = 1.0$. This error tends to zero even faster for smaller k.

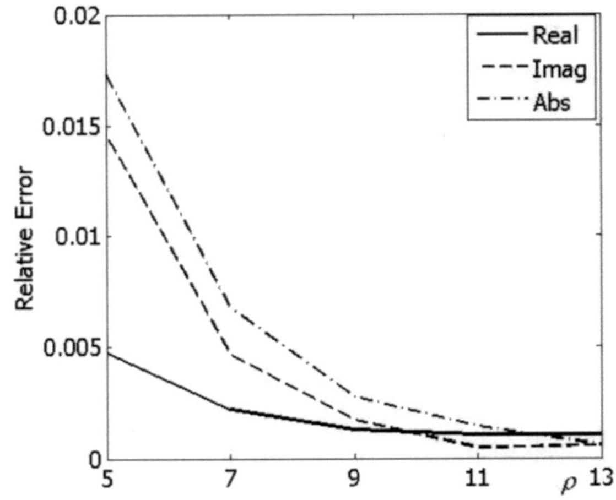

Fig. 6. Relative error versus the ρ parameter, $h(x) = k^2(1-7i)/(40\pi)$

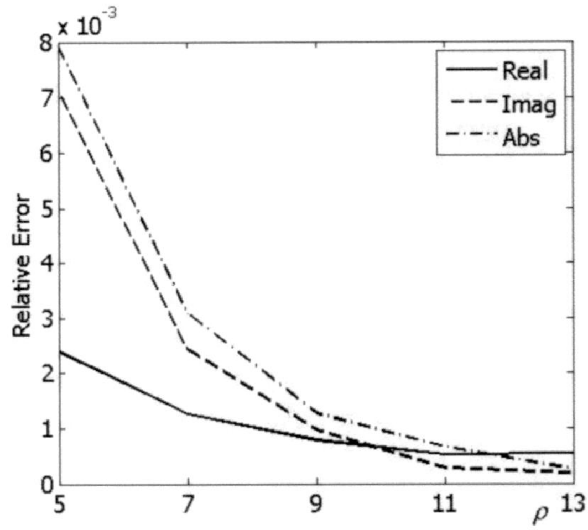

Fig. 7. Relative error versus the ρ parameter, $h(x) = k^2(1-3i)/(40\pi)$

8.3 Accuracy of the solution to the limiting equation (9) and to the asymptotic LAS (16)

As before, we consider as the "exact" solution to (9) the approximate solution to LAS (17) with $\rho = 20$. The maximal relative error for such ρ does not exceed 0.01% in the range of problem parameters we have considered ($k = 0.5 \div 1.0$, $l_D = 0.5 \div 1.0$, $N(x) \geq 4.0$). The numerical calculations are carried out for various sizes of the domain D and various function $N(x)$. The results for small values of M are presented in Table 3 for $k = 1$, $N(x) = 40$, and $l_D = 1.0$. The second line contains the values of a_{est}, the estimated value of a, calculated by formula (7), with the number $\mathcal{N}(\Delta_p)$ replacing the number M. In this case the radius of a particle is calculated as

$$a_{est} = (M/\int_{\Delta_p} N(x)dx)^{1/(2-\kappa)}. \tag{44}$$

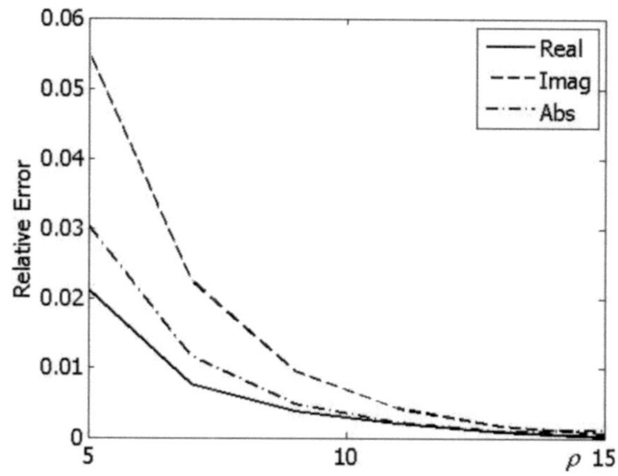

Fig. 8. Relative error versus the ρ parameter, $k = 2.0$

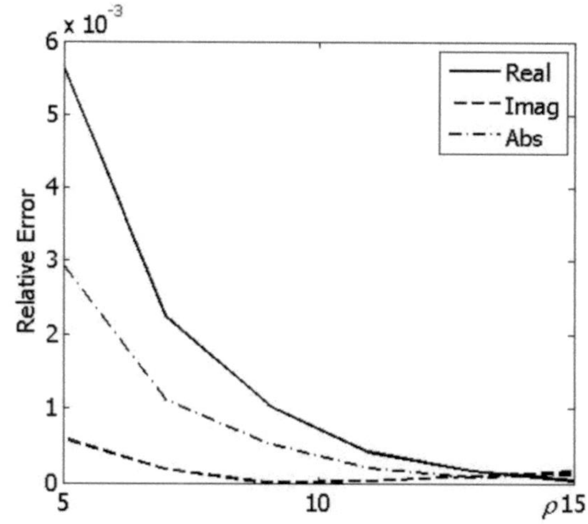

Fig. 9. Relative error versus the ρ parameter, $k = 0.6$

The values of a_{opt} in the third line correspond to optimal values of a which yield minimal relative error of the modulus of the solutions to equation (9) and LAS (16). The fourth line contains the values of the distance d between particles. The maximal value of the error is obtained when $\mu = 7$, $\mu = \sqrt[3]{M}$ and it decreases slowly when μ increases. The calculation results for large number of μ with the same set of input parameters are shown in Table 4. The minimal error of the solutions is obtained at $\mu = 60$ (total number of particles $M = 2.16 \cdot 10^5$. Tables 5 and 6 contain similar results for $N(x) = 4.0$, other parameters being the same. It is seen that the relative error of the solution decreases when number of particles M increases. This error can be decreased slightly (on 0.02%-0.01%) by small change of the values a and l_D as well. The relative error of the solution to LAS (16) tends to the relative error of the solution to LAS (17) when the parameter μ becomes greater than 80 ($M = 5.12 \cdot 10^5$). The relative error of the solution to LAS (17) is calculated by taking the norm of the difference of the solutions

μ	7	9	11	13	15
a_{est}	0.1418	0.0714	0.0413	0.0262	0.0177
a_{opt}	0.1061	0.0612	0.0382	0.0261	0.0172
d	0.1333	0.1105	0.0924	0.0790	0.0688
$Rel.error$	2.53%	0.46%	0.45%	1.12%	0.81%

Table 3. Optimal parameters of D for small μ, $N(x) = 40.0$

μ	20	30	40	50	60
a_{est}	0.0081	0.0027	0.0012	6.65×10^{-4}	4.04×10^{-4}
a_{opt}	0.0077	0.0025	0.0011	6.6×10^{-4}	4.04×10^{-4}
d	0.0526	0.0345	0.0256	0.0204	0.0169
$Rel.error$	0.59%	0.35%	0.36%	0.27%	0.19%

Table 4. Optimal parameters of D for big μ, $N(x) = 40.0$

μ	7	9	11	13	15
a_{est}	0.0175	0.0088	0.0051	0.0032	0.0022
a_{opt}	0.0179	0.0090	0.0052	0.0033	0.0022
d	0.1607	0.1228	0.0990	0.0828	0.0711
$Rel.error$	1.48%	1.14%	1.06%	1.05%	0.91%

Table 5. Optimal parameters of D for small μ, $N(x) = 4.0$

μ	20	30	40	50	60
a_{est}	9.97×10^{-4}	3.30×10^{-4}	1.51×10^{-4}	8.20×10^{-5}	4.98×10^{-5}
a_{opt}	1.02×10^{-3}	3.32×10^{-4}	1.50×10^{-4}	8.21×10^{-5}	4.99×10^{-5}
d	0.0542	0.0361	0.0265	0.0209	0.0172
$Rel.error$	0.21%	0.12%	0.11%	0.07%	0.03%

Table 6. Optimal parameters of D for big μ, $N(x) = 4.0$

to (17) with P and $2P$ points, and dividing it by the norm of the solution to (17) calculated for $2P$ points. The relative error of the solution to LAS (16) is calculated by taking the norm of the difference between the solution to (16), calculated by an interpolation formula at the points y_p from (17), and the solution of (17), and dividing the norm of this difference by the norm of the solution to (17).

8.4 Investigation of the relative difference between the solution to (16) and (17)

A comparison of the solutions to LAS (16) and (17) is done for various values of a, and various values of the number ρ and μ. The relative error of the solution decreases when ρ grows and μ remains the same. For example, when ρ increases by 50% , the relative error decreases by 12% (for $\rho = 8$ and $\rho = 12$, $\mu = 15$). The differences between the real parts, imaginary parts, and moduli of the solutions to LAS (16) and (17) are shown in Fig. 10 and Fig. 11 for $\rho = 7$, $\mu = 15$. The real part of this difference does not exceed 4% when $a = 0.01$, it is less than 3.5% at $a = 0.008$, less than 2% at $a = 0.005$; $d = 8a$, $N(x) = 20$. This difference is less than 0.08% when $\rho = 11$, $a = 0.001$, $N = 30$, and $d = 15a$ (μ remains the same). Numerical calculations for wider range of the distance d demonstrate that there is an optimal value of d, starting

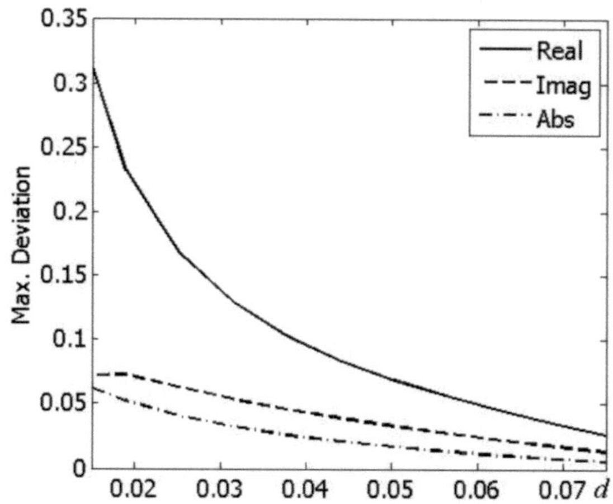

Fig. 10. Deviation of component field versus the distance d between particles, $N(x) = 10$

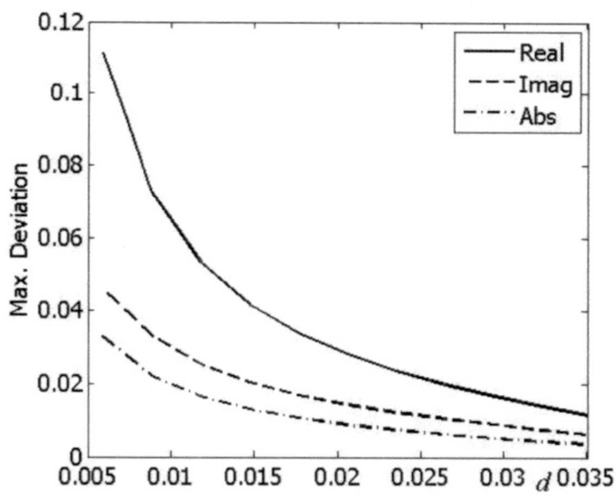

Fig. 11. Deviation of component field versus the distance d between particles, $N(x) = 30$

from which the deviation of solutions increases again. These optimal values of d are shown in Table 7 for various $N(x)$. The calculations show that the optimal distance between particles increases when the number of particles grows. For small number of particles (see Table 1 and Table 2) the optimal distance is the value of the order a. For the number of particles $M = 15^3$, i.e. $\mu = 15$, this distance is about $10a$.

The values of maximal and minimal errors of the solutions for the optimal values of distance d are shown in Table 8.

One can conclude from the numerical results that optimal values of d decrease slowly when the function $N(x)$ increases. This decreasing is more pronounced for smaller a. The relative error of the solution to (16) also smaller for smaller a.

	$N(x)$ value				
	$N(x) = 10$	$N(x) = 20$	$N(x) = 30$	$N(x) = 40$	$N(x) = 50$
$a = 0.005$	0.07065	0.04724	0.04716	0.04709	0.04122
$a = 0.001$	0.08835	0.07578	0.06331	0.06317	0.05056

Table 7. Optimal values of d for various $N(x)$

	$N(x)$ value				
	$N(x) = 10$	$N(x) = 20$	$N(x) = 30$	$N(x) = 40$	$N(x) = 50$
$a = 0.005$	0.77/0.12	5.25/0.56	0.52/0.1	0.97/0.12	0.32/0.05
$a = 0.001$	2.47/0,26	1.7/0.3	0.5/0.1	2.7/0,37	1.5/0.2

Table 8. Relative error of solution in % (max/min) for optimal d

8.5 Evaluation of difference between the desired and obtained refraction coefficients

The recipe for creating the media with a desired refraction coefficient $n^2(x)$ was proposed in (Ramm, 2008a). It is important from the computational point of view to see how the refraction coefficient $n_M^2(x)$, created by this procedure, differs from the one, obtained theoretically. First, we describe the recipe from (Ramm, 2010a) for creating the desired refraction coefficient $n^2(x)$. By $n_0^2(x)$ we denote the refraction coefficient of the given material.

The recipe consists of three steps.

Step 1. Given $n_0^2(x)$ and $n^2(x)$, calculate

$$\bar{p}(x) = k^2[n_0^2(x) - n^2(x)] = \bar{p}_1(x) + i\bar{p}_2(x). \tag{45}$$

Step 1 is trivial from the computational and theoretical viewpoints.

Using the relation

$$\bar{p}(x) = 4\pi h(x)N(x) \tag{46}$$

from (Ramm, 2008a) and equation (45), one gets the equation for finding $h(x) = h_1(x) + ih_2(x)$, namely:

$$4\pi[h_1(x) + ih_2(x)]N(x) = \bar{p}_1(x) + i\bar{p}_2(x). \tag{47}$$

Therefore,

$$N(x)h_1(x) = \frac{\bar{p}_1(x)}{4\pi}, \quad N(x)h_2(x) = \frac{\bar{p}_2(x)}{4\pi}. \tag{48}$$

Step 2. Given $\bar{p}_1(x)$ and $\bar{p}_2(x)$, find $\{h_1(x), h_2(x), N(x)\}$.

The system (48) of two equations for the three unknown functions $h_1(x)$, $h_2(x) \le 0$, and $N(x) \ge 0$, has infinitely many solutions $\{h_1(x), h_2(x), N(x)\}$. If, for example, one takes $N(x)$ to be an arbitrary positive constant, then h_1 and h_2 are uniquely determined by (48). The condition $\mathrm{Im}n^2(x) > 0$ implies $\mathrm{Im}\bar{p} = \bar{p}_2 < 0$, which agrees with the condition $h_2 < 0$ if $N(x) \ge 0$. One takes $N(x) = h_1(x) = h_2(x) = 0$ at the points at which $\bar{p}_1(x) = \bar{p}_2(x) = 0$. One can choose, for example, N to be a positive constant:

$$N(x) = N = \text{const}, \tag{49}$$

$$h_1(x) = \frac{\bar{p}_1(x)}{4\pi N}, \quad h_2(x) = \frac{\bar{p}_2(x)}{4\pi N}. \tag{50}$$

Calculation of the values $N(x)$, $h_1(x)$, $h_2(x)$ by formulas (49)-(50) completes *Step 2* our procedure.
Step 2. is easy from computational and theoretical viewpoints.
Step 3. This step is clear from the theoretical point of view, but it requires solving two basic technological problems. First, one has to embed many (M) small particles into D at the approximately prescribed positions according to formula (7). Secondly, the small particles have to be prepared so that they have prescribed boundary impedances $\zeta_m = h(x_m)a^{-\kappa}$, see formula (1).
Consider a partition of D into union of small cubes Δ_p, which have no common interior points, and which are centered at the points $y^{(p)}$, and embed in each cube Δ_p the number

$$\mathcal{N}(\Delta_p) = \left[\frac{1}{a^{2-\kappa}} \int_{\Delta_p} N(x)dx \right] \tag{51}$$

of small balls D_m of radius a, centered at the points x_m, where $[b]$ stands for the integer nearest to $b > 0$, $\kappa \in (0,1)$. Let us put these balls at the distance $O(a^{\frac{2-\kappa}{3}})$, and prepare the boundary impedance of these balls equal to $\frac{h(x_m)}{a^\kappa}$, where $h(x)$ is the function, calculated in Step 2 of our recipe. It is proved in (Ramm, 2008a) that the resulting material, obtained by embedding small particles into D by the above recipe, will have the desired refraction coefficient $n^2(x)$ with an error that tends to zero as $a \to 0$.
Let us emphasize again that Step 3 of our procedure requires solving the following technological problems:
(i) How does one prepare small balls of radius a with the prescribed boundary impedance? In particular, it is of practical interest to prepare small balls with large boundary impedance of the order $O(a^{-\kappa})$*, which has a prescribed frequency dependence.*
(ii) How does one embed these small balls in a given domain D, filled with the known material, according to the requirements formulated in Step 3 ?
The numerical results, presented in this Section, allow one to understand better the role of various parameters, such as a, M, d, ζ, in an implementation of our recipe. We give the numerical results for $N(x) = \text{const}$. For simplicity, we assume that the domain D is a union of small cubes (subdomains) Δ_p ($D = \bigcup_{p=1}^{P} \Delta_p$). This assumption is not a restriction in practical applications. Let the functions $n_0^2(x)$ and $n^2(x)$ be given. One can calculate the values h_1 and h_2 in (50) and determine the number $\mathcal{N}(\Delta_p)$ of the particles embedded into D. The value of the boundary impedance $\frac{h(x_m)}{a^\kappa}$ is easy to calculate. Formula (51) gives the total number of the embedded particles. We consider a simple distribution of small particles. Let us embed the particles at the nodes of a uniform grid at the distances $d = O(a^{\frac{2-\kappa}{3}})$. The numerical calculations are carried out for the case $D = \bigcup_{p=1}^{P} \Delta_p, P = 8000$, D is cube with side $l_D = 0.5$, the particles are embedded uniformly in D. For this P the relative error in the solution to LAS (16) and (17) does not exceed 0.1%. Let the domain D be placed in the free space, namely $n_0^2(x) = 1$, and the desired refraction coefficient be $n^2(x) = 2 + 0.01i$. One can calculate the value of $\mathcal{N}(\Delta_p)$ by formula (51). On the other hand, one can choose the number μ, such that

$M = \mu^3$ is closest to $\mathcal{N}(\Delta_p)$. The functions $\tilde{n}_1^2(x)$ and $\tilde{n}_2^2(x)$, calculated by the formula

$$\tilde{n}_1^2(x) = -\frac{4\pi h_1(x)N}{k^2} + n_0^2, \quad \tilde{n}_2^2(x) = -\frac{4\pi h_2(x)N}{k^2}, \tag{52}$$

differ from the desired coefficients $n_1^2(x)$ and $n_2^2(x)$. In (52), $N = \frac{Ma^{2-\kappa}}{V_D}$, V_D is volume of D, $\kappa < 1$ is chosen very close to 1, $\kappa = 0.99$. To obtain minimal discrepancy between $n_j^2(x)$ and $\tilde{n}_j^2(x)$, $j = 1,2$, we choose two numbers μ_1 and μ_2 such that $M_1 < \mathcal{N}(\Delta_p) < M_2$, where $M_1 = \mu_1^3$ and $M_2 = \mu_2^3$. Hence, having the number $\mathcal{N}(\Delta_p)$ for a fixed a, one can estimate the numbers M_1 and M_2, and calculate the approximate values of $n_1^2(x)$ and $n_2^2(x)$ by formula (52). In Fig. 12, the minimal relative error of the calculated value $\tilde{n}^2(x)$ depending on the radius a of particle is shown for the case $N(x) = 5$ (the solid line corresponds to the real part of the error, and the dashed line corresponds to the imaginary part of the error in the Figs. 12-14). These results show that the error depends significantly on the relation between the

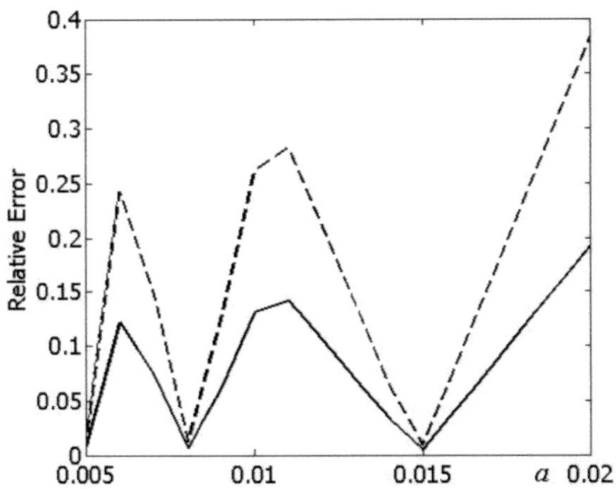

Fig. 12. Minimal relative error for calculated refraction coefficient $\tilde{n}^2(x), N(x) = 5$

numbers M_1, M_2, and $\mathcal{N}(\Delta_p)$. The error is smallest when one of the values M_1 and M_2 is sufficiently close to $\mathcal{N}(\Delta_p)$. The error has quasiperiodic nature with growing amplitude as a increases (this is clear from the behavior of the function $\mathcal{N}(\Delta_p)$ and values M_1 and M_2). The average error on a period increases as a grows. Similar results are shown in Fig. 13 and Fig. 14 for $N = 20$ and $N = 50$ respectively. The minimal error is attained when $a = 0.015$, and this error is 0.51%. The error is 0.53% when $a = 0.008$, and it is equal to 0.27% when $a = 0.006$ for $N(x) = 20, 50$ respectively. Uniform (equidistant) embedding small particles into D is simple from the practical point of view. The results in Figs. 12-14 allow one to estimate the number M of particles needed for obtaining the refraction coefficient close to a desired one in a given domain D. The results for $l_D = 0.5$ are shown in Fig. 15. The value $\mu = \sqrt[3]{M}$ is marked on the y axes here. Solid, dashed, and dot-dashed line correspond to $N(x) = 5, 20, 50$, respectively. One can see from Fig. 15 that the number of particles decreases if radius a increases. The value $d = O(a^{(2-\kappa)/3})$ gives the distance d between the embedded particles. For example, for $N(x) = 5$, $a = 0.01$ d is of the order 0.1359, the calculated d is equal to 0.12 and to 0.16 for

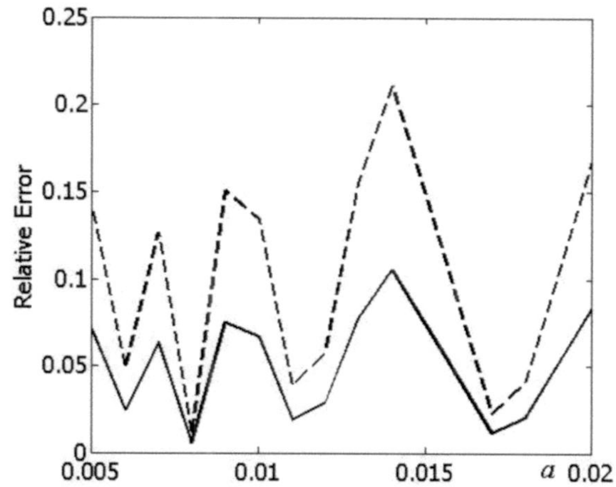

Fig. 13. Minimal relative error for calculated refraction coefficient $\tilde{n}^2(x), N(x) = 20$

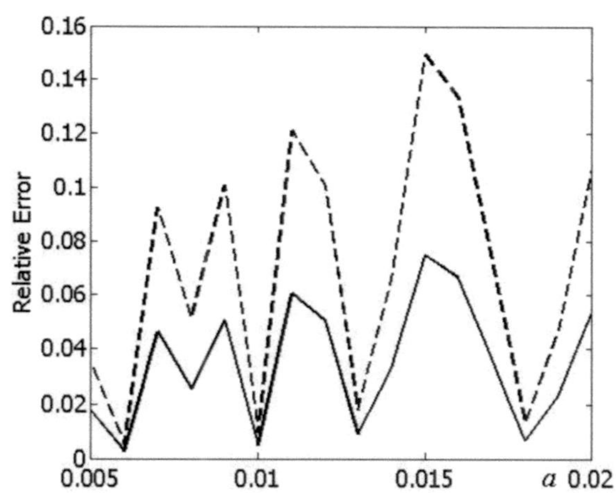

Fig. 14. Minimal relative error for calculated refraction coefficient $\tilde{n}^2(x), N(x) = 50$

$\mu = 5$ and $\mu = 4$, respectively. The calculations show that the difference between the both values of d is proportional to the relative error for the refraction coefficients. By the formula $d = O(a^{(2-\kappa)/3})$, the value of d does not depend on the diameter l_D of D. This value can be used as an additional optimization parameter in the procedure of the choice between two neighboring μ in Tables 9, 10. On the other hand, one can estimate the number of the particles embedded into D using formula (51). Given $\mathcal{N}(\Delta_p)$, one can calculate the corresponding number M of particles if the particles distribution is uniform. The distance between particles is also easy to calculate if l_D is given. The optimal values of $\mu, \mu = \sqrt[3]{M}$ are shown in the Tables 9 and 10 for $l_D = 0.5$ and $l_D = 1.0$ respectively.
The numerical calculations show that the relative error of $\tilde{n}^2(x)$ for respective μ can be decreased when the estimation of d is taken into account. Namely, one should choose μ from Tables 9 or 10 that gives value of d close to $(a^{(2-\kappa)/3})$.

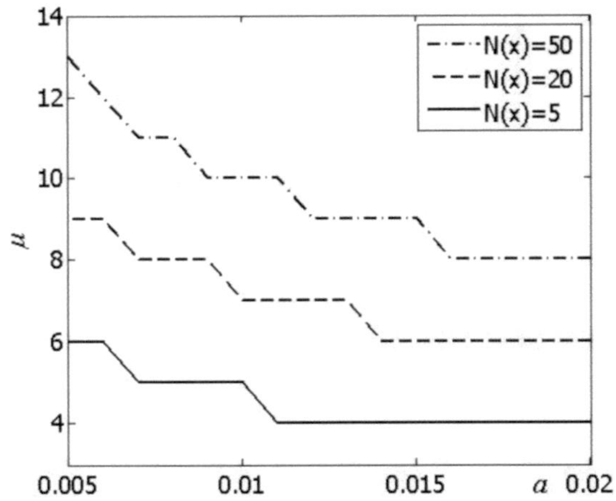

Fig. 15. Optimal value of μ versus the radius a for various $N(x)$

a	$\mathcal{N}(\Delta_p)$	Optimal μ
0.02	96.12	$4 \leq \mu \leq 5$
0.01	204.05	$4 \leq \mu \leq 5$
0.008	245.62	$6 \leq \mu \leq 7$
0.005	416.17	$7 \leq \mu \leq 8$
0.001	2442.1	$13 \leq \mu \leq 14$

Table 9. Optimal values of μ for $l_D = 0.5$

a	$\mathcal{N}(\Delta_p)$	Optimal μ
0.02	809.25	$9 \leq \mu \leq 10$
0.01	1569.1	$11 \leq \mu \leq 12$
0.008	1995.3	$12 \leq \mu \leq 13$
0.005	3363.3	$15 \leq \mu \leq 16$
0.001	19753	$27 \leq \mu \leq 28$

Table 10. Optimal values of μ for $l_D = 1.0$

9. Numerical results for EM wave scattering

Computing the solution by limiting formula (28) requires much PC time because one computes $3-D$ integrals by formulas (30)-(32) and (34)-(36). Therefore, the numerical results, presented here, are restricted to the case of not too large number of particles ($M \leq 1000$). The modeling results demonstrate a good agreement with the theoretical predictions, and demonstrate the possibility to create a medium with a desired refraction coefficient in a way similar to the one in the case of acoustic wave scattering.

9.1 Comparison of "exact" and asymptotic solution

Let $\alpha = e_3$, where e_3 is unit vector along z axis, then the condition yields $E \cdot \alpha = 0$, that vector E is placed in the xOy plane, i. e. it has two components E_x and E_y only. In the case

M	$a = 0.1$	$a = 0.2$	$a = 0.3$	$a = 0.4$
8	0.351	0.798	0.925	1.457
27	0.327	0.825	0.956	1.596
64	0.315	0.867	1.215	1.691
125	0.306	0.935	1.454	1.894

Table 11. Minimal values of d guaranteeing the convergence of iterative process (29), (33)

if domain D is placed symmetrically to axis z and $\alpha = e_3$ one can consider the component E_x or E_y because of symmetry (this restriction is valid if $x-$ and $y-$components in E_0 are the same). The applicability of asymptotic approach was checked by comparison of solution by the limiting formula (28) and solution determined by the formula (39). The first solution implies the knowledge of vectors V_j and numbers v_j which are received from the solutions to LAS (29), (33). The second solution requires the values $\{E(y_p), p = 1, ..., P\}$, which are received as solution to LAS (38) by the collocation method (Ramm, 2009). We consider the solution to LAS (38) with 15 collocation points along each coordinate axis as a benchmark or "exact" solution. The total number P of the collocation points is $P = 3375$ and relative error of solution does not exceed 0.5% in the range of considered values a, d, and M. The LAS (29), (33) is solved by iterations and condition (37) superimposes considerable restriction on the relation d to a. The analytical estimation gives $d \sim 15a$ and greater. It means that dimensions of D at big number of M are very large that can not satisfy the engineering requirements. Therefore, the knowledge of minimal values d at which the iterative process for solution to system (29), (33) is still converged has a practical importance. In Table 11, the minimal values of d for several a at fixed number of particles M are shown.
One can see that allowable distance d is order $d \sim 4a$ that is less three times than theoretical estimation.
The investigation of the amplitude field deviation for the both solutions depending on the radius a of particle was performed for points in the middle and far zone at $M = 125$, $k = 0.1$, and $d = 1$. In Fig. 16, the results are presented for the far zone of D ($d_f = 15$, where d_f is distance from center of D to far zone). The thick curves correspond to the case of the same amplitude distribution of $x-$ and $y-$components of the field $E_0(x)$, and thin curves correspond to the case of various $x-$ and $y-$components. In the middle zone the solutions differ in the limits of 20% and greater at the small values of a, this difference grows if a increases. The results for the far zone are in good correspondence with theoretical condition, i. e., the asymptotical solution tends to "exact" one as $a \to 0$. The maximum deviation of field components is observed at $a = 0.05$ and it is equal to 5%, and it is equal to 25% if a grows to 0.5. The relative error can be decreased in the considerable extent if the value of d to icrease. In the above example the relation d/a is equal to 2 only, and it is complicate situation for our asymptotical approach.

9.2 Creating the desired refraction coefficient

In Section 7, the formula for refraction coefficient $n^2(x)$ for domain D with $\mathcal{N}(\Delta)$ embedded particles of radius a was derived. If $n^2(x)$ is presribed, one can easy to determine the parameters of D that can provide the desired value of refraction coefficient. Similarly to

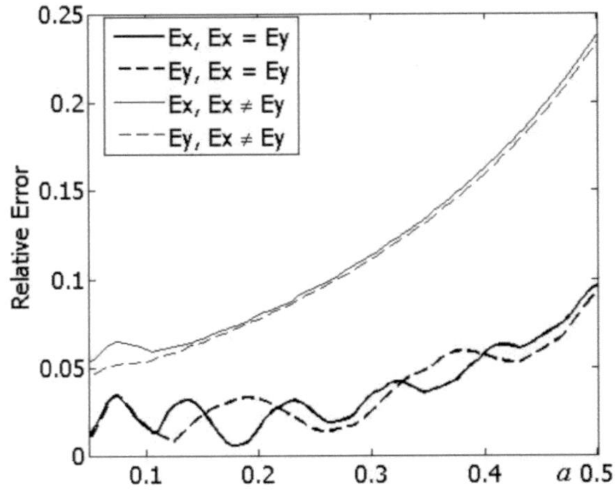

Fig. 16. Relative error of solution to limiting equation (28) for differing $E_0(x)$

M	$N(x)$	c_{1m}	γ_m	$\max\|p(x)\|$	Relative error
8	0.7407	0.0675	2.0250	64.4578	0.0005
27	0.5400	0.0912	2.7360	87.0896	0.0009
64	0.4665	0.1072	3.2154	102.1494	0.0023

Table 12. Optimal parameters of D for $n^2(x) = 1.2$

the case of acoustic wave scattering, we formulate constructive recipe to create the media with desired refraction coefficient. Let us denote the refraction coefficient of medium without embedded particles $n_0^2(x) = 1$. We develop a method to create a desired refraction coefficient $n^2(x)$. To do this, we impose some mild restrictions on the function $N(x)$ and $p(x)$. Let the domain D be a cube with M embedded particles. If one assumes that $N(x) = \text{const}$ in D, then $N(x) = Ma^2/(d+2a)^3$. Having the prescribed $n^2(x)$ and known $N(x)$, one can find c_{1m} from the relation $C(x) = c_{1m}N(x)$, and number γ_m by the formula $\gamma_m = 30c_{1m}$ (see (Ramm, 2008a)). In order to derive the limiting equation of the form (40), the function $p(x)$ is chosen as follows:

$$p(r) = p(r,a) = \begin{cases} \frac{\gamma_m}{4\pi a^\kappa}(1-t)^2, & 0 \le t \le 1, \\ 0, \ t > 1; \ t := \frac{r}{a}, & \kappa = \text{const} > 0. \end{cases} \quad (53)$$

The values of various parameters, calculated by above procedure, are presented in Tables 12 and 13. The relative error of the asymptotic solution is presented in the last columns in these Tables. This error is minimal at the value of $\max p(x)$ presented in the neighboring column.
In order to obtain greater $n^2(x)$ it is necessary to increase $p(x)$ remaining the same of rest parameters.
The dependence of $n^2(x)$ on a for the various d is shown in Fig. 17 at $M = 125$ and Fig. 18 at $M = 1000$. At the small values of a the scattering from D is negligible, therefore $n^2(x) \to n_0^2(x)$ as $a \to 0$. If a grows, then $n^2(x)$ decreases and differs considerably from $n_0^2(x)$.
The relative error of the solution to limiting equation (40) is shown in Fig. 19. The error gets smaller as $a \to 0$. The numerical results show that the relative error for various d gets larger if a approaches $d/3$.

M	$N(x)$	c_{1m}	γ_m	$\max\|p(x)\|$	Relative error
8	0.7407	0.1350	4.0500	128.9155	0.0008
27	0.5400	0.1825	5.4750	174.2747	0.0012
64	0.4665	0.2144	6.4309	204.7019	0.0033

Table 13. Optimal parameters of D for $n^2(x) = 1.4$

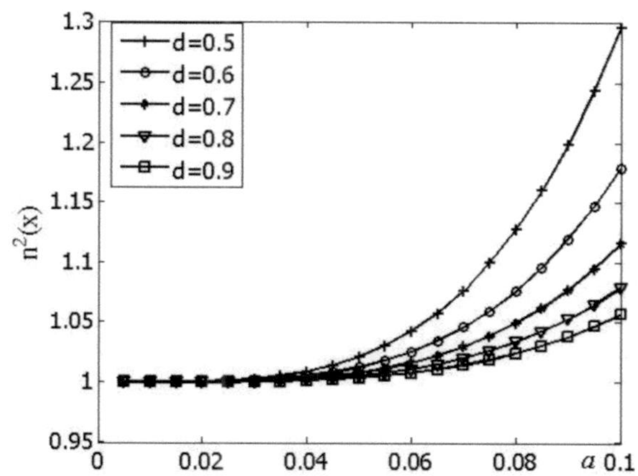

Fig. 17. The refraction coefficient $n^2(x)$ at $M = 125$

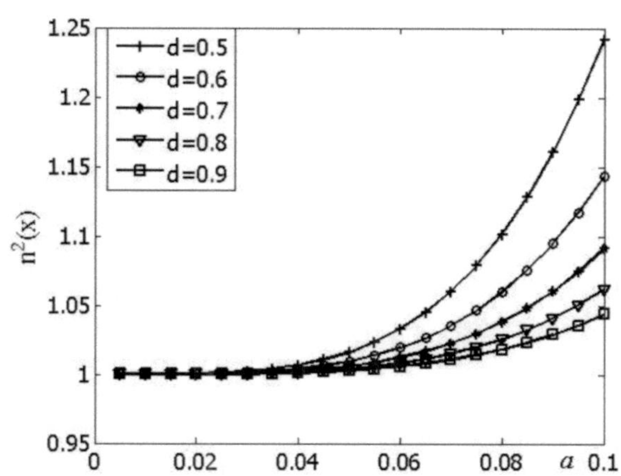

Fig. 18. The refraction coefficient $n^2(x)$ at $M = 1000$

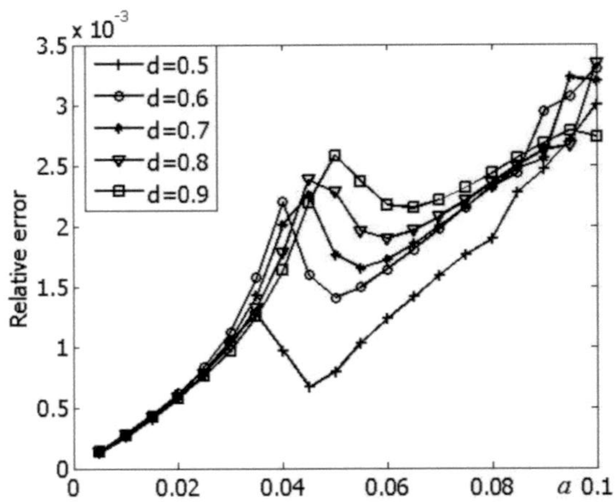

Fig. 19. The relative error of solution to limiting equation (40) for various d

10. Conclusions

The numerical results based on the asymptotical approach to solving the scattering problem in a material with many small particles embedded in it help to understand better the dependence of the effective field in the material on the basic parameters of the problem, namely, on $a, M, d, \zeta_m, N(x)$, and $h(x)$, and to give a constructive way for creating materials with a desired refraction coefficient $n^2(x)$, see (Ramm, 2009a), (Ramm, 2010), (Ramm, 2010a).

For acoustic wave scattering, it is shown that, for small number M of particles there is an optimal value of a, for which the relative error to asymptotic solution is minimal. When $a \to 0$ and M is small ($M < 100$) the matrix of (16) is diagonally dominant and the error goes to 0. This is confirmed by the numerical results as well. The relative error can be decreased by changing function $N(x)$ or by decreasing a, d being fixed, but the condition $d >> a$ is not necessary if M is small.

The accuracy of the solution to the limiting equation (9) depends on the values of k, a, and on the function $h(x)$. The accuracy of the solution improves as the number P increases.

The relative error of the solution to asymptotic LAS (16) depends essentially on the function $N(x)$ which is at our disposal. In our numerical experiments $N(x) = \text{const}$. The accuracy of the solution is improved if $N(x)$ decreases, while parameters M, a, and d are fixed. The error of the solution decreases if M grows, while d is fixed and satisfying condition $d \gg a$.

The relative difference between the solutions to LAS (16) and (17) can be improved by changing the distance d between the particles, a being fixed. The optimal values of d change slowly in the considered range of function $N(x)$. The relative error is smaller for smaller a.

A constructive procedure, described in Section 8, for prescribing the function $N(x)$, calculating the numbers μ, and determining the radius a, allows one to obtain the refraction coefficient approximating better the desired one.

These results help to apply the proposed technique for creating materials with a desired refraction coefficient using the recipe, formulated in this paper. Development of methods for embedding many small particles into a given domain D according to our recipe, and for preparing small balls with the desired large impedances $\zeta = \frac{h(x)}{a^\kappa}$, especially if one wants

to have function $h(x, \omega)$ with a desired frequency dependence, are two basic technological problems that should be solved for an immediate practical implementation of our recipe.
For EM wave scattering it is shown that, for convergence of iterative procedure (29), (33) condition (37) is not necessary, but only sufficient: in many examples we had convergence, but condition was voilated. Altough theoretically we assumed $d > 10a$, our numerical results show that the proposed method gives good results even for $d = 3a$ in many cases.
The relative error between the "exact" solution corresponding to equation (39) and limiting solution (28) depends essentially on the ratio d/a. For example, for fixed M and a, ($M = 125, a = 0.05$) this difference changed from 2.3% to 0.7% if d/a decreases twice.
As in the case of acoustic wave scattering, a simple constructive procedure for calculation of desired refraction coefficient $n^2(x)$ is given. The numerical experiments show that in order to change the initial value $n_0^2(x)$ one increases radius a while the number M is fixed and not too large, or increases M and decreases a if M is very large. The second way is more attractive, because it is in correspondence with our theoretical background.
The extension of the developed numerical procedures for very large M, $M \geq O(10^5)$, and their applications to solving real-life engineering problems is under consideration now.

11. References

Andriychuk M. I. and Ramm A. G. (2010). Scattering by many small particles and creating materials with a desired refraction coefficient, *Int. J. Computing Science and Mathematics*, Vol. 3, No. 1/2, pp.102–121.

Barber, P. W., Hill, S. C. (1990) *Light scattering by particles: computational methods.* World Scientific, Singapore.

Hansen, R. C. (2008). Negative refraction without negative index, *Antennas and Propagation, IEEE Transactions on*, vol. 56 (2), pp. 402–404.

Ramm, A. G. (2005). *Wave scattering by small bodies of arbitrary shapes,* World Scientific, Singapore.

Ramm, A. G. (2007). Many body wave scattering by small bodies and applications. *J. Math. Phys.* Vol. 48, No 10, p. 103511.

Ramm, A. G. (2007). Distribution of particles which produces a "smart" material, *J. Stat. Phys.*, 127, N5, pp.915-934.

Ramm, A. G. (2007). Distribution of particles which produces a desired radiation pattern, *Physica B*, 394, N2, pp. 145-148.

Ramm, A. G. (2008). Wave scattering by many small particles embedded in a medium. *Physics Letters A.* 372, pp. 3064–3070.

Ramm, A. G. (2008). Electromagnetic wave scattering by small bodies, *Phys. Lett. A*, 372/23, (2008), 4298-4306.

Ramm, A. G. (2009). A collocation method for solving integral equations. *Intern. Journ. of Computing Science and Mathematics.* Vol. 2, No 3, pp. 222–228.

Ramm, A. G. (2009). Preparing materials with a desired refraction coefficient and applications, in Skiadas, C. at al., *Topics in Chaotic Systems: Selected Papers from Chaos 2008 International Conference*, World Sci.Publishing, Singapore, 2009, pp.265–273.

Ramm, A. G. (2010). Electromagnetic wave scattering by many small bodies and creating materials with a desired refraction coefficient, *Progress in Electromag. Research,* M, Vol. 13, pp. 203–215.

Ramm, A. G. (2010). Materials with a desired refraction coefficient can be created by embedding small particles into the given material, *International Journal of Structural Changes in Solids (IJSCS)*, 2, N2, pp. 17-23.

Ramm, A. G. (2010). Wave scattering by many small bodies and creating materials with a desired refraction coefficient *Afrika Matematika*, 22, N1, pp. 33-55.

Rhein, von A., Pergande, D., Greulich-Weber, S., Wehrspohn, R. B. (2007). Experimental verification of apparent negative refraction in low-epsilon material in the microwave regime, *Journal of Applied Physics*, vol. 101, No 8, pp. 086103–086103-3.

Tateiba, M., Matsuoka, T., (2005) Electromagnetic wave scattering by many particles and its applications, *Electronics and Communications in Japan (Part II: Electronics)*, vol. 88 (10), pp. 10–18.

2

Simulations of Deformation Processes in Energetic Materials

R.H.B. Bouma[1], A.E.D.M. van der Heijden[1],
T.D. Sewell[2] and D.L. Thompson[2]
[1]TNO Technical Sciences
[2]University of Missouri
[1]The Netherlands
[2]USA

1. Introduction

The sensitivity of energetic materials has been studied extensively for more than half a century, both experimentally and numerically, due to its importance for reliable functioning of a munition and avoidance or mitigation of accidents (Bowden & Yoffe, 1952). While the shock initiation of an explosive under nominal conditions is relatively well understood from an engineering perspective, our understanding of initiation due to unintended stimuli (weak shock or fragment impact, fire, damaged explosive charge) is far less complete. As an example, one cannot exclude the ignition of an explosive due to mechanical deformation, potentially leading to low- or even high-order explosion/detonation as a consequence of mechanical stimuli with strain rates and pressures well below the shock sensitivity threshold. During the last two decades there has been an increased interest in the scientific community in understanding initiation sensitivity of energetic materials to weak insults.

A relationship between energy dissipation and rate of plastic deformation has been developed for crystalline energetic materials (Coffey & Sharma, 1999). Chemical reactions are initiated in crystalline solids when a crystal-specific threshold energy is exceeded. In this sense, initiation is linked to the rate of plastic deformation. However, practical energetic materials are usually heterogeneous composites comprised of one or more kinds of energetic crystals (the filler, for which the mass fraction can exceed 90%) bound together with a binder matrix that often consists of several different polymer, plasticizer, and stabilizer materials. Clearly, the mechanical behavior of these polymer-bonded (plastic-bonded) explosives (PBXs) is far more complicated than for neat crystals of high explosive. It is necessary in realistic constitutive modeling of energetic compositions to incorporate features reflecting the complex, multiphase, multiscale structural, dynamical, and chemical properties; see, for example, Bennett et al., 1998, and Conley & Benson, 1999. The goal in constitutive modeling is to bridge the particulate nature at the mesoscale to the mechanical properties at the macroscale.

The macroscale deformations applied to PBX composites in experiments are generally not the same as the local deformation fields in a component crystal within the composite. This has been demonstrated using grain-resolved mesoscale simulations wherein the individual grains and binder phases in a PBX are resolved within a continuum simulation framework.

Baer & Trott (2002) studied the spatial inhomogeneities in temperature and pressure that result when a shock wave passes through a sample of material. The statistical properties of the shocked state were characterized using temporal and spatial probability distribution functions of temperature, pressure, material velocity and density. The results showed that reactive waves in composite materials are distinctly different from predictions of idealized, traditional models based on singular jump state analysis.

Energy and stress localization phenomena culminating in rapid, exothermic chemistry are complex processes, particularly for shocks near the initiation threshold, for which subvolumes of material corresponding to the tails of the distribution functions of temperature and pressure are where initiation will begin. Therefore, a detailed understanding of composite energetic materials initiation requires knowledge of how thermal and mechanical energies are transferred through the various constituents and interfaces of a PBX; how the distributed energy causes structural changes associated with plasticity or phase transformations; and, when these processes (among others) lead to sufficiently high localization of energy, how and at what rate chemical reactions occur as functions of the local stress, temperature, and thermodynamic phase in the material. Each of these can in principle be studied by using molecular dynamics (MD) simulations. Distributions of field variables available from mesoscale simulations can be sampled to provide input to MD simulations; alternatively, results obtained from MD simulations can be used to guide the formulation of, and determine parameters for, improved mesoscale descriptions of the constituent materials in the PBX, for structurally perfect materials as well as ones containing various kinds of crystal lattice defects, voids, crystal surface features, and material interfaces (Kuklja & Rashkeev 2009; Sewell, 2008; Strachan et al., 2005; Shi & Brenner, 2008).

This chapter gives an overview of simulations of deformation processes in energetic materials at the macro-, meso-, and molecular scales. Both non-reactive and reactive processes are considered. Macroscale simulations are usually developed to mimic real life situations (for example, munitions performance under intended conditions or response under accident scenarios) or are used in the development of small-scale experiments designed to elucidate fundamental properties and behaviors. Because macroscale simulations lack detailed information concerning microscopic physics and chemistry, their use for predicting energetic materials initiation is generally limited to engineering applications of the types mentioned above. For many applications, however, the macroscopic treatment is sufficient to characterize and explain the deformation behavior of PBXs. At the other extreme of space and time scales, MD can be used to simulate the fine-scale details of deformation, including detailed mechanisms of phase changes, chemistry, and processes that occur at material interfaces or other spatial heterogeneities. Mesoscale simulation and theory is required to bridge the gap between these limiting cases.

The outline of the remainder of the chapter is as follows: First, the macroscopic deformation of a PBX, treated as a homogeneous material, is discussed. Specific examples are provided in which experimental data and simulation results are compared. Next, a sampling of the various approaches that can be applied for mesoscale modeling is presented. Representative simulations based on grain-resolved simulations are discussed. Finally, an overview of applications of molecular scale modeling to problems of thermal-mechanical-chemical properties prediction and understanding deformation processes on submicron scales is given, with specific references to the literature to highlight current capabilities in these areas.

2. Simulation of deformation at the macroscale: Plastic-bonded explosives treated as homogeneous material

The low-velocity impact vulnerability of energetic materials is typically studied by using simulations of deformations at the macroscale. For example, the engineering safety margin for acceptable crush-up limits of an encased energetic material is the most widely-used parameter in modern barrier design to prevent sympathetic detonation in ammunition storage sites. The accidental detonation of a storage module will lead to blast, ground shock, and propulsion of the barriers placed around that storage module. These accelerated barriers can impact adjacent storage modules and crush the munitions contained therein. The development of munition-specific acceptance criteria (Tancreto et al., 1994), and the comparison of double flyer-plate impact and crush-test results with simulation results (Malvar, 1994) helped advance the successful design of the so-called High Performance Magazine (Hager et al., 2000). Munitions are nowadays categorized into sensitivity groups based on robustness and sensitivity. The initiation threshold of a sensitivity group is expressed as the required kinetic energy and impulse per unit area from an impacting barrier to cause a reaction in munitions of that sensitivity group.
The concept of sensitivity groups allows for the design of other storage configurations through engineering models. One example is the simulation of barrier propulsion by the detonation of a single storage module containing 5 ton TNT equivalent of explosives, for which simulated results have been verified experimentally (Bouma et al., 2003; van Wees et al., 2004); see Fig. 1. However, design parameters related to the barrier do not describe the processes that may lead to ignition, and certainly do not help in formulating insensitive explosive compositions.

Fig. 1. Left: Experiment prior to detonation of 5 ton TNT equivalent of explosives in the central 24 ft container, which is surrounded by four different barrier designs and four munition storage modules. Right: The simulated results illustrate the pressure contours 5 ms after the detonation of 5 ton TNT equivalent of explosives, and the disintegration and movement of the trapezoid-shaped barrier in the photograph towards an adjacent storage module.

Many experimental tests, including the Susan impact test and friability test (UN, 2008), Steven impact test (Chidester et al., 1998), set-back generator (Sandusky et al., 1998), spigot intrusion (Wallace, 1994), drop-weight and projectile impact, and split Hopkinson pressure bar (Siviour et al., 2004), study the response of a PBX under mechanical loading conditions that are specific to particular accident scenarios. Collectively, these tests span a wide range of geometric complexity and data richness. For some of them the results are expressed in relatively qualitative terms; for example, the Steven test where the severity of the mechanical insult to a stationary target with high explosive is based on the impact velocity of a projectile, and reaction violence is based on criteria such as amount of PBX recovered, damage to the target containment, and blast pressure at some distance from the location of projectile/target impact. In other tests more sophisticated experimental methods and highly instrumented diagnostics allow the detailed mechanical behavior to be inferred from the data; for example, the split Hopkinson pressure bar. In many cases simulations are required to aid in the interpretation of the data; specific examples for the split Hopkinson pressure bar, Steven impact, and LANL impact tests can be found in (Bailly et al., 2011; Gruau et al., 2009; Scammon et al., 1998).

The ballistic impact chamber is a specific drop-weight impact test designed to impose a shear deformation in a cylindrical sample of explosive (Coffey, 1995). (The name drop-weight impact test originates with the fact that the impact velocity depends on the height from which the weight is dropped onto the sample.) If a relationship between energy dissipation and rate of plastic deformation is known, the deformation rate can be used to define a mechanical initiation threshold (Coffey & Sharma, 1999). A drop-impact load impinges on the striker, which loads a cylindrical sample between the striker and an anvil (see Fig. 2) The cylinder is compressed along the cylinder axis and expands radially. The shear rate in the ballistic impact chamber is described by

$$\frac{d\gamma}{dt} \approx \frac{r_{t=0}}{h^2}\sqrt{\frac{h_{t=0}}{h}}\frac{dh}{dt}, \tag{1}$$

with r and h the radius and the height of the sample, respectively, γ the shear, and t the time. The shear rate is largest near the perimeter of the cylinder. Initiation is detected by photodiodes. Knowing the striker velocity dh/dt and the time of initiation, the required shear rate for initiation $d\gamma/dt$ can be calculated. Measured shear rate thresholds are given by Namkung & Coffey (2001).

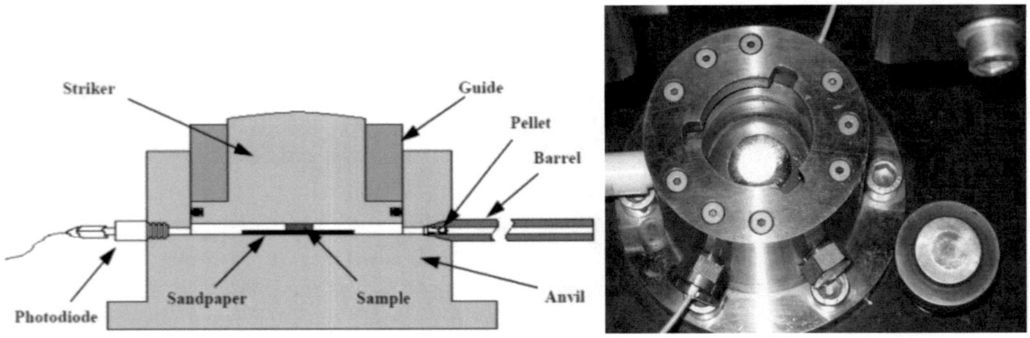

Fig. 2. Left: Schematic cross section of the ballistic impact chamber. Right: Top view of the chamber. The sample can be seen in the center of the chamber. Attached to the side are two fiber optic cables and a pressure transducer. The striker is located to the right of the chamber assembly.

The deformation of energetic materials in the ballistic impact chamber according to equation 1 has been verified by simulations of a cylindrical sample of PBXN-109 (64 wt% cyclotrimethylene trinitramine, 20 wt% aluminium and 16 wt% polybutadiene-based binder), 6.35 mm in diameter and 1.75 mm in height (Meuken et al., 2006). In this example, the drop weight had an impact velocity of 3 $m \cdot s^{-1}$, and the striker achieved an initial velocity of $\approx$ 6 $m \cdot s^{-1}$ due to elastic collision. The simulation was carried out using the ANSYS Autodyn software suite, a versatile explicit analysis tool for modeling the nonlinear dynamics of solids, fluids, gases and interactions among them. (Autodyn provides, for example, finite element solvers for computational structural dynamics and mesh-free particle solvers for high velocities, large deformation and fragmentation (Autodyn, Birnbaum et al., 1987).) The resulting shear rate in PBXN-109 as a function of time is shown in the right-hand panel of Fig. 3. The maximum shear rate of approximately 8×10^5 s^{-1} is reached shortly before the end of the negative acceleration of the striker, at a radial distance about 70% of the sample radius (Bouma et al., 2007). The shear rate values from equation 1 and the Autodyn simulation are comparable, except the rise in shear rate in the simulation occurs at a longer time since impact. The deformation is complex - there are small oscillations visible in Fig. 3 due to the shock and reflection waves that travel through the striker and anvil. Evaluation of the shear sensitivity according to equation 1 is non-trivial, and simulations are key to interpreting this "simple" cylindrical compression experiment. The analysis requires that the sample not resists compression by the striker prior to initiation and that an accurate value of the striker velocity is known. In the example discussed here the first requirement is satisfied so long as the time to reaction is less than 90% of the original sample height divided by twice the drop weight velocity at the moment of impact. The experimentally determined shear initiation threshold in the ballistic impact chamber of PBXN-109 is 1.7×10^5-2.0×10^5 s^{-1}. A simulation that approximates the experimental conditions and which includes chemical reaction yields an ignition time of 180 μs. The chemical reaction model used in the simulation is limited to an Arrhenius-type ignition term; a more sophisticated treatment of chemistry that includes, for instance, the Lee-Tarver (Lee & Tarver, 1980) growth term has not been performed (Zerilli et al., 2002).

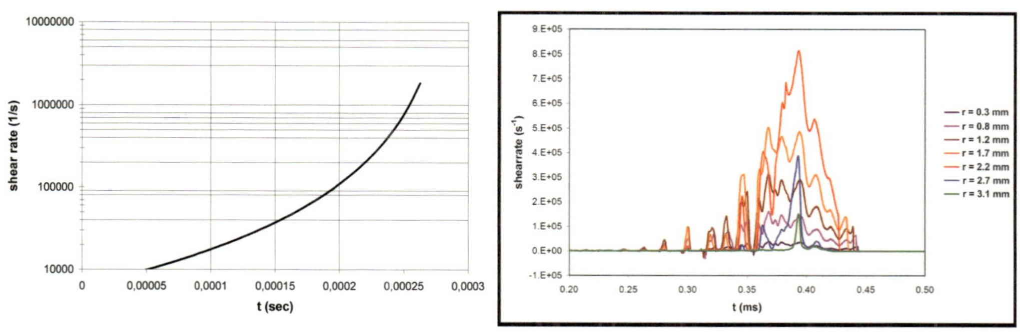

Fig. 3. Left: Shear rate vs. time, calculated using equation 1. The deformation starts at $t = 0$ and is monitored until the height of the sample is equal to 10% of the initial height. Right: Same as the left-hand panel except the result is obtained from an Autodyn simulation. Results in the right-hand panel are shown for points near the sample-anvil interface and originally located at radial distances r = 0.3, 0.8, 1.2, 1.7, 2.2, 2.7, and 3.1 mm from the center of the sample; deformation of the sample starts at t = 0.07 ms.

The shear-rate threshold just discussed should also apply to other experimental configurations. For example, PBXN-109 has been subjected to an explosion-driven deformation (Meuken et al., 2006). Steel cylinders were filled with PBXN-109 and a layer of 3.0, 4.0, or 5.0 mm plastic explosive, covering one-third of the circumference of the steel cylinder, was detonated; the results are shown in Fig. 4. In the 3-mm layer case the PBXN-109 was slightly extruded from the deformed steel cylinder without any sign of reaction. In the 4-mm layer case there was a mild reaction, as shown by the slightly expanded steel cylinder. In the 5-mm layer case a violent reaction of the PBXN-109 was observed, resulting in fragmentation of the steel cylinder.

Figure 5 shows the 2-D simulation set-up of the deformation experiment (left panel); as well as the shear rate (right panel) in the PBXN-109, calculated close to the inner surface of the steel cylinder as a function of the angle (where angle θ=0° corresponds to the center of the deformation layer). The maximum shock pressure is ≈0.5 GPa, which is well below the 2.2-5.2 GPa initiation pressure of PBXN-109 in the large scale gap test (Doherty & Watt, 2008). The maximum shear rates in Fig. 5 are 0.72×10^5, 1.19×10^5, and 1.51×10^5 s^{-1}, respectively, for the 3-, 4-, and 5-mm layer experiments. The initiation threshold in this deformation test resembles the threshold in the ballistic impact chamber.

Fig. 4. Explosion-driven deformation of steel-cased PBXN-109 charges. The deformation results from the detonation of a layer of plastic explosive that partially surrounds the PBX-N109 charges (see Fig. 5). Results are shown for plastic explosive layer thicknesses of 3 mm (left), 4 mm (middle) and 5 mm (right).

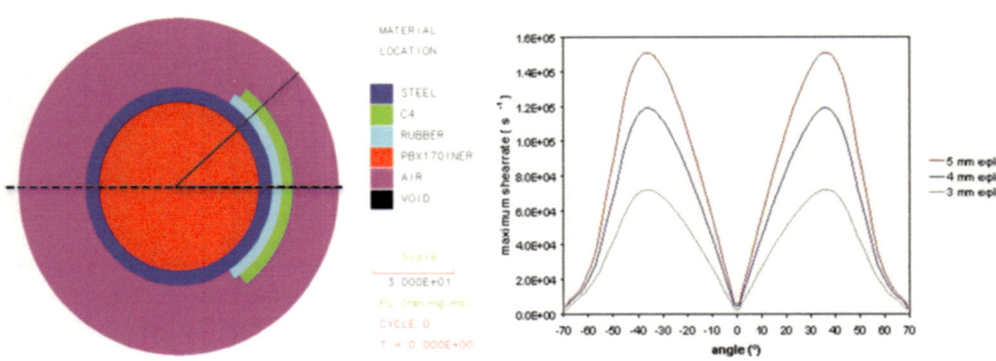

Fig. 5. Left: Schematic configuration for 2-D Autodyn simulation of an explosive deformation test. Right: Maximum shear rates in PBXN-109 as functions of the angle θ when deformed by explosive layers of thickness 3 mm (green), 4 mm (blue), and 5 mm (red).

The maximum shear rate depends on the test configuration. The friability test (UN, 2008) and the LANL impact test (Bennett et al., 1998) have been simulated for the explosive PBXN-109, and the Steven impact test (Vandersall et al., 2006) for explosive composition C4, to correlate the severity of mechanical deformation to initiation of the explosive, see table 1 (Bouma & Meuken, 2004). Permanent deformation and extensive fracturing of the PBX in the friability test, in which a flat-ended cylindrical projectile is fired into a rigid steel target, are evident in Fig. 6 (left-hand panel, from Bouma, 1999) as well as the simulated evolution of shear rate (right-hand panel). The largest calculated shear rate, ~0.45×10^5 s^{-1}, occurs near the edges of the ∅18 mm sample. The experimental result in the left-hand panel of Fig. 6 shows that this rate is too low to cause initiation; this is qualitatively consistent with the threshold maximum shear rates discussed in connection with Figs. 3-5. The extensive fracture of the material, which is deliberately induced in this test, has not been modeled.

Fig. 6. Left: Permanent deformation and fracture of a PBX containing 80% HMX at 91, 110, 121, and 154 m·s^{-1} impact velocity in a friability test. Right: The evolution of shear rate at various radial distances from the sample in the friability test and near the explosive/steel interface for PBXN-109 at 150 m·s^{-1} impact velocity. The maximum shear rate develops near the outer radius.

The Steven impact test has been simulated near the experimental initiation thresholds for explosives PBX 9404 and PBX 9501, respectively 31-34 m·s^{-1} and 39-54 m·s^{-1} (Chidester et al., 1998). Again, the calculated shear rates of ≈10^5 s^{-1} confirm experimental initiation thresholds. Note that the experimental threshold for C4 is an impact velocity of more than 195 m·s^{-1} (Vandersall et al., 2006), resulting in a shear rate of at least 1.8×10^5 s^{-1}. In the LANL impact test a pusher impacts a thin rectangular slab of explosive of the same thickness (Bennett et al., 1998). The violence of reaction depends on the diameter and shape of the pusher (result not shown). The calculated peak shear rate of 16×10^5 s^{-1} is large but is very localized, within 1 mm of the edge of the ∅10 mm pusher, and has duration <1μs.

An analytical model has been developed that links mechanical properties and particle sizes with the thermal ignition of an explosive. This micro-structural model (Browning, 1995) is based on 1) Hertz contact stress between two particles of the same diameter in relation to the applied normal pressure, 2) mechanical work due to sliding motion under a normal pressure, and 3) thermo-chemical decomposition due to an applied and local heat flux (the latter originating from the mechanical work in the Hertzian contact points). The ignition criterion in the model requires the evaluation of the pressure and the shear rate at the macroscale (Browning, 1995; Gruau et al., 2009; Scammon et al., 1998). Scammon et al. (1998) evaluate the parameter

$$p^{2/3}\left(\frac{d\gamma}{dt}\right)_{max}^{1.27} t_{ign}^{1/4} \qquad (2)$$

Configuration, explosive	Test specifics	Shear rate / s^{-1}	Experimental observation
Explosion driven deformation, PBXN-109	3 mm deformation layer 4 mm deformation layer 5 mm deformation layer	Max. 0.72×10^5 Max. 1.19×10^5 Max. 1.51×10^5	No reaction Burn Violent reaction
Ballistic Impact Chamber, PBXN-109		1.7×10^5-2.0×10^5 at initiation	Initiation
Friability test, PBXN-109	18 mm Ø, 9 gram, 150 $m{\cdot}s^{-1}$ impact velocity	Max. 0.4×10^5-0.5×10^5	No reaction
LANL impact test, PBXN-109	10 mm blunt steel pusher at 196 $m{\cdot}s^{-1}$ into 25 mm ×20 mm sample	Max. 16×10^5	Not available
Steven impact test, C4	50 $m{\cdot}s^{-1}$ impact velocity 100 $m{\cdot}s^{-1}$ impact velocity 157-195 $m{\cdot}s^{-1}$ impact velocity	Max. 0.5×10^5 Max. 1.8×10^5	No reaction

Table 1. Comparison of shear rates calculated in simulation of various test configurations of PBXN-109 and explosive composition C4 to experimental results.

with time to ignition t_{ign}, assuming that pressure p and shear rate $d\gamma/dt$ are constant. Ignition is associated with the parameter exceeding an explosive-specific value. The underlying thermo-chemical model has been analyzed in detail for HMX only. However, equation 2 (or the corresponding expression for variable pressure and shear strain rate loading histories (Browning & Scammon, 2001; Gruau et al., 2009)), may not be directly applicable to non-HMX PBXs. The thermo-chemical decomposition in the above model requires a thermo-chemical simulation of the ignition time as a function of thermal energy fluence through a crystal-crystal contact surface area, and involves explosive-specific decomposition chemistry that can be measured, for example, in a one-dimensional time-to-explosion (ODTX) test (Hsu et al., 2010). This may lead to different exponents in eq. 2 for non-HMX PBXs.

As shown in this section, a macroscopic treatment is generally sufficient to characterize and explain the deformation behavior of PBXs. However, since macroscopic models treat the PBX as a homogeneous material, their use for predicting energetic materials initiation is rather limited. As a first step to a more detailed description of the deformation and initiation behavior of energetic materials, mesoscale simulations can be performed that include the influence of the particulate nature of PBX formulations.

3. Simulation of deformation at the mesoscale: The influence of particulate nature of plastic-bonded explosives

The influence of the particulate nature at the mesoscale can be accounted for in different ways. One can 1) fit a continuum model with particle-specific features to experimental data; 2) simulate the mechanical behavior of a representative volume element with the mechanical properties of its constituents and determine the collective mechanical behavior; or, 3) when sufficient computer resources are available, simulate the mechanical behavior with spatially resolved explosive grains and binder.

An example of the first approach is based on the statistical crack mechanics model (Dienes, 1985) in combination with a five-component Maxwell visco-elasticity model, fitting the parameters to experimental Young's moduli spanning eight orders of magnitude of relaxation times (Bennett et al., 1998). Constitutive equations are obtained for implementation into the DYNA3D nonlinear, explicit finite element code for solid and structural mechanics (DYNA3D). An example of the second approach is the construction of a continuum constitutive model based on homogenization procedures applied to realistic 2-D or 3-D representative volume element microstructures obtained, for instance, from digital images of cross sections (De & Macri, 2006) or X-ray microtomography (Bardenhagen et al., 2006) of a PBX. An example of the third approach is the direct simulation at the mesoscale of the propagation of a shock wave through randomly packed crystal ensembles (Baer & Trott, 2002). Probabilistic distribution functions of wave field variables such as pressure, density, particle velocity, chemical composition, and temperature are studied to gain insight into the initiation and growth of reactions in heterogeneous materials. For additional studies of grain-resolved systems see Baer (2002), Reaugh (2002), and Handley (2011); the latter is a recent Ph.D. dissertation that includes a thorough review of mesoscale simulations and theory applied to PBXs.

During mechanical deformation of a PBX interfacial de-bonding can occur and crystals may even crack. Figure 7 contains a scanning electron micrograph of HMX crystals in a hydroxy-terminated-polybutadiene binder. A cylindrical sample of this explosive, 9 grams in weight and 18 mm in diameter, has been impacted at 92 $m \cdot s^{-1}$ against a steel plate. The micrograph corresponds to a section near the impact site in the friability test and demonstrates interfacial de-bonding as well as crystal cracking (Scholtes et al., 2002). These phenomena can also be simulated. Figure 8 gives the principal stress in uniaxial compression of PBX 9501 at 2% overall strain. The computational model is 0.465 mm $\times$ 0.495 mm and contains 25 particles. De-bonding occurs when the work applied perpendicular or tangential to an interface exceeds the normal or shear cohesive energy, respectively. The cohesive energies used to generate the left- and right-hand panels of Fig. 8 are, respectively, below and above the experimentally derived values. The extent of interfacial de-bonding decreases with increasing cohesive energy between the particle and binder phases. The increase in cohesive energy results in a large stress localization within crystals, which increases the probability for cracks to develop within the crystal (Yan-Qing & Feng-Lei, 2009). Note that the peak shear rates in the impact experiment of Fig. 7 are of the order of 10^3 s^{-1}, whereas the simulation results shown in Fig. 8 are for a strain rate of 1.2×10^{-3} s^{-1}.

The particulate nature of most energetic materials and the imperfection of the component crystals (for example, grain boundaries, seeding crystals, voids, cracks, lattice defects, solvent inclusions) not only influence the deformation behaviour of the PBX but also the sensitivity to shock (Doherty & Watt, 2008; van der Heijden & Bouma, 2004a, 2004b, 2010). Examples of imperfections are shown in Figs. 9 and 10. On the left is an optical micrograph of a cross section of an RDX crystal. The crystal outer surface is irregular, grains have grown into each other, and there are multiple defects with sizes of the order of 10 μm. On the right a scanning electron micrograph of the cross section of an RDX crystal from the same lot (RDX type II obtained from Dyno) is shown. At this magnification, one can see voids with sizes on the order of hundreds of nm, as well as a string of voids extending vertically across the image; note that this latter structure is not a grain boundary. Fig. 10 shows two confocal scanning laser micrographs with a Dyno Type II RDX crystal at the left and a BAe Royal Ordnance RDX crystal at the right. By using a confocal scanning laser microscope in reflection mode it is possible to make optical slices from a transparent object down to a thickness of about 0.5 μm. In this way, local differences in the refractive index inside a crystal will be revealed as bright spots on a dark background. The images are recorded with a Leica TCS SL confocal system using a DM6000 B microscope equipped with a 40X objective, zoom factor setting of 2. The spots indicate locations with a different refractive index from the surrounding area and correspond most likely to small inclusions present in the crystal. Also of interest are the "diffuse" areas within the crystals in the left-hand panel of Fig. 10. The differences in spot density for the two RDX lots obtained from different producers are assumed to be correlated with the difference in mechanical sensitivity (Thompson et al., 2010) and shock sensitivity (Doherty & Watt, 2008).

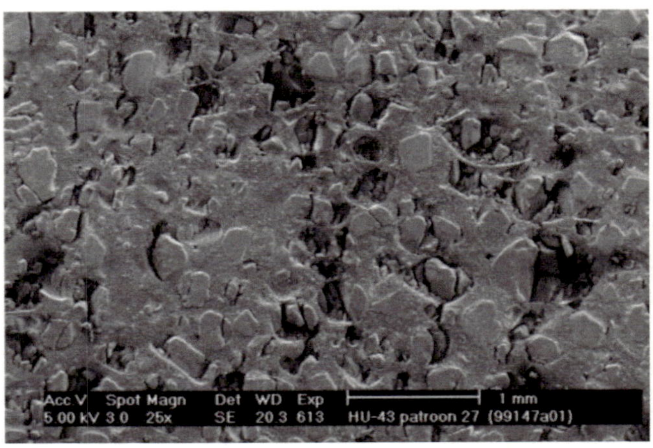

Fig. 7. Interfacial debonding and crystal cracking in a friability test (Scholtes et al., 2002).

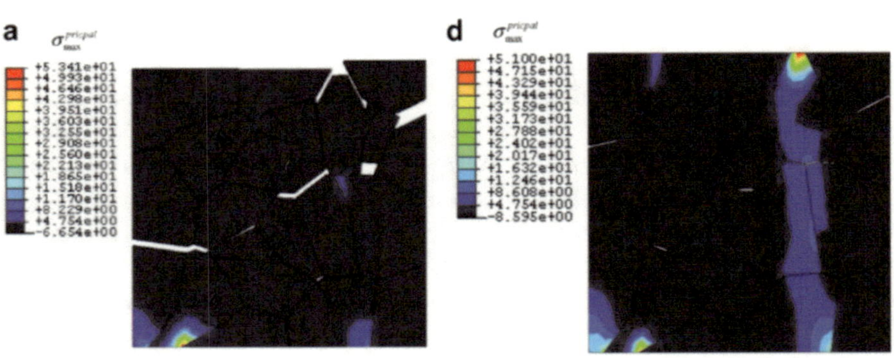

Fig. 8. Maximum principal stress in uniaxial compression of PBX 9501 (Reprinted from Yan-Qing & Feng-Lei, 2009, © 2008, with permission from Elsevier). The two simulations are identical except that the particle/binder cohesive energy used to generate the right-hand panel is four times that used to generate the left-hand panel.

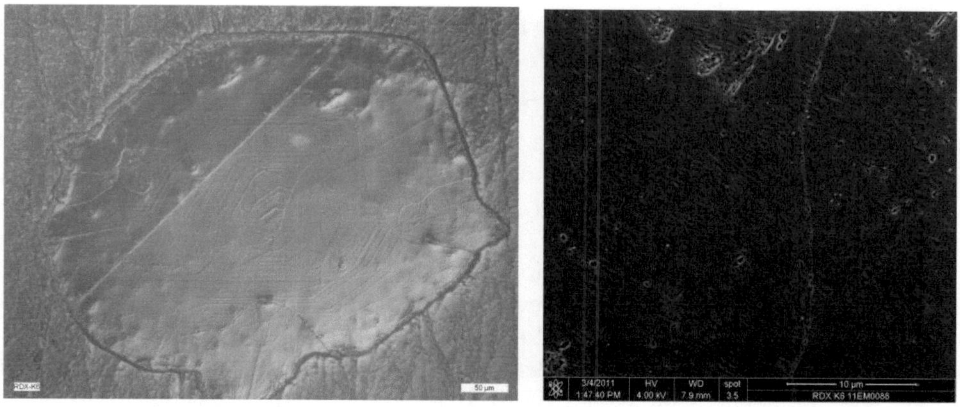

Fig. 9. Optical micrograph (left) and scanning electron micrograph (right) of a cross-section of a crystal of Dyno type II RDX (Thompson et al., 2010).

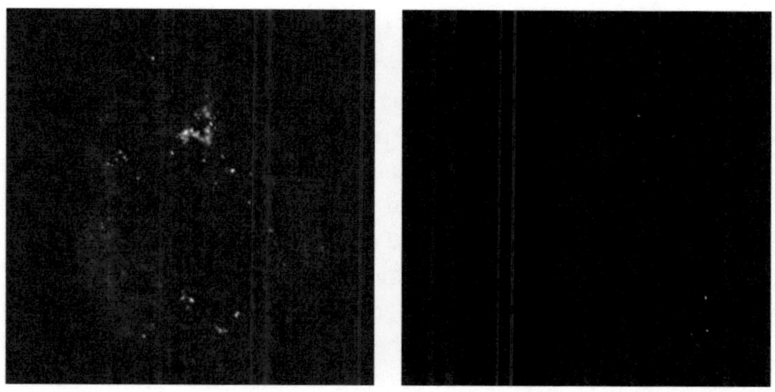

Fig. 10. Confocal scanning laser micrographs for two different qualities of RDX crystals, produced at a focal plane below the surface. Left: 93.5 μm × 93.5 μm image of Dyno type II RDX. Right: a 375 μm × 375 μm image of BAe Royal Ordnance RDX (Thompson et al., 2010).

Ideally, a simulation at the meso- or molecular-scale should incorporate microstructural features such as grain boundaries, packing of particles, defects, and voids. A new method to create a computational set-up with a random pack of arbitrary shapes of particles has been applied to "typical" HMX crystals by Stafford & Jackson (2010). Armstrong (2009) has reviewed dislocation mechanics modeling of energetic materials. The review covers experimental mechanics studied through indentation-hardness properties, impact properties in various test geometries, and granular compaction. The thermal dissipation of energy is associated with individual dislocation motions, which may induce a strong adiabatic heating through dislocation pile-up avalanches. Lei and Koslowski (2010) have published a phase field dislocation dynamics model for low-symmetry organic crystals. Using only information about the crystallography and elastic constants they were able to predict the onset of plastic deformation in sucrose and paracetamol. (Although these are not energetic materials, the fundamental physics and materials science developed by Lei and Koslowski would apply equally well to energetic crystals.) Lei and Kowslowski identified several properties that could be provided from atomic-scale simulations. The use of MD simulations as a means of providing input to, or guiding the formulation of, mesoscale models will be discussed in the next section.

4. Simulation of deformation at the molecular scale: Structural changes and chemical reactions near lattice defects, voids, and interfaces

Atomic-level simulation methods – MD and Monte Carlo (MC) – in which individual atoms or chemical functional groups are treated explicitly can be used to understand and predict the equilibrium and dynamic properties of energetic crystals, binders, and interfaces between them. In MD a set of classical (e.g., Newton's) equations of motion are solved in terms of the interatomic forces, possibly with additional terms corresponding to coupling of the system to an external thermostat (Hoover, 1985; Nosé, 1984), barostat (Martyna et al., 1996; Parrinello et al., 1981), or other constraint such as to sample a Hugoniot state of a material (Maillet & Stoltz, 2008; Ravelo et al., 2004; Reed et al., 2003) to confine the simulation to a particular ensemble, leading to a trajectory (time history) of particle positions and momenta from which physical properties can be calculated in terms of appropriate statistical averages or time correlation functions (Tuckerman, 2010). The interatomic forces required for MD can be obtained from a parameterized empirical force field or from electronic structure calculations wherein the forces are obtained directly from the instantaneous electronic wave function of the system.

Monte Carlo sampling of configuration space is usually performed using a random walk based on a Markov chain constructed to satisfy microscopic reversibility and detail balance in an appropriate statistical ensemble. (See, for example: Frenkel & Smit, 2002; Wood, 1968.) Because the sequence of states in a Markov chain does not comprise a dynamical trajectory, only properties that can be expressed as averages of some microscopic function of configuration in phase space that does not explicitly involve the time can be computed. Metropolis MC (Metropolis et al., 1953), the version of MC most frequently used in molecular simulations, does not require evaluation of forces but rather only differences in potential energy between adjacent states (configurations) sampled by the Markov chain. Although in many cases MC and MD can be used equally effectively, in practice Monte Carlo is not used as widely as MD in simulations of energetic materials; therefore here we focus on MD.

Electronic structure calculations are sometimes used to study the structures, energies, charge distributions and higher multipole moments, spectroscopy, and reaction pathways. These properties can be calculated for isolated molecules, clusters, or periodic structures, usually at zero Kelvin; however, the effects of finite temperature can be incorporated, for example, by using the quasi-harmonic approximation (for example, Zerilli & Kukla, 2007), explicitly from MD trajectories, (Manaa et al., 2009; Tuckerman & Klein, 1998) or using an appropriate MC sampling scheme (Coe et al., 2009a, 2009b). Most practical electronic structure calculations for energetic materials are performed using methods based on the Kohn-Sham density functional theory (DFT) (Koch & Holthausen, 2001), although *ab initio* methods are used in some cases (Molt et al., 2011).

The advantage of atomic-level simulation methods is the detailed information they can provide. For instance, a MD simulation provides the time histories of the phase space coordinates along a trajectory, from which any classical property of the system, including detailed reaction chemistry can, in principle, be computed. The main obstacle to the use of atomic methods in practical multi-scale simulation frameworks is the small spatiotemporal scales that can be studied – approximately tens of millions of atoms for time scales of nanoseconds or less – and the requirement, at least for accurate studies rather than ones designed to examine basic qualitative features of the material response, to have a reliable description of the inter-atomic forces within the given thermodynamic regime of interest.

(While the development of parallel, linear scaling algorithms for electronic structure studies of condensed phase systems has considerably increased the numbers of atoms that can be studied (see, for example, Bock et al., 2011; Kresse et al., 2011), system sizes and simulation times tractable based on electronic structure theory calculations are far smaller than those using analytical force fields.) A more fundamental question in the case of MD or MC simulations is that of the applicability of classical statistical mechanics or dynamics for the study of molecular phenomena.

In the following we discuss ways by which atomic-scale information can be incorporated within a multiscale simulation framework, providing specific examples relevant to energetic materials. The focus of most MD simulations of energetic materials has been on predicting physical properties in the absence of chemistry. A major (and ongoing) hurdle to reliably treating complex chemistry in MD simulations is the difficulty of describing the forces for the variety of electronic structures that would be explored at the high temperatures and pressures corresponding to the von Neumann spike or Chapman-Jouguet state of a detonating explosive. Currently, the methods to do this are plane-wave DFT or parameterized analytic representations such as the ReaxFF (van Duin et al., 2001; Strachan et al., 2005) or AIREBO (Stuart et al., 2000; Liu & Stuart, 2007) force fields. Han et al. (2011) have recently published simulations of the thermal decomposition of condensed phase nitromethane studied using ReaxFF.

In general, there are two approaches to the multiscale problem. The arguably simpler approach is a sequential (or "handshaking") one in which specific physical properties required in mesoscale or macroscopic simulations — for example, thermal, transport, or mechanical properties — are calculated as functions of temperature and pressure and used directly in the larger-scale simulations. Assuming the validity of classical mechanics, the major challenge to obtaining reliable predictions for such quantities is the need to realistically account for defect structures that can be of sizes that exceed the limited MD spatiotemporal scales. Reliable predictions of properties or structures of rate-dependent materials or ones with extended interfaces are also difficult to model due to the large time and space scales associated with them; for example, binders in energetic materials are usually based on polymers (often with other additives such as plasticizers or stabilizers) that exhibit both viscoelastic behavior and in some cases complex microphase-segregated morphologies and non-negligible concentration gradients in the neighborhood of interfaces. Such simulations are quite challenging within a MD framework; see, for example, Jaidann et al. (2009). Nevertheless, in some instances it is possible to regard MD predictions as comprising bounding cases (for example, limit of perfect crystals). Moreover, for many properties of interest experimental data either do not exist for conditions away from room temperature/atmospheric pressure or have large apparent uncertainties based on disparate results obtained for a given property using different experimental techniques. In such instances the results of atomic simulations can be used to extend the intervals over which needed parameter values can be estimated or to discriminate among inconsistent data sets.

Examples are included in Table 2, which includes the results of various measurements or calculations of the second-order elastic tensors for PETN, α-RDX, and β-HMX; and Table 3 which contains the pressure and temperature dependence of the bulk and shear moduli of crystalline TATB for the Reuss (uniform stress) and Voigt (uniform strain) bounds. Note the wide variation in some of the experimentally determined values, particularly for RDX and HMX. In each case, the MD results - based on force fields that were not parameterized using elasticity data - yield predictions in good agreement with the most recent, and presumably most accurate, experimental data based on impulsive stimulated thermal scattering.

A difficulty with direct application of sequential approaches is that, even if a given property appears in a mesoscopic theory and can be calculated directly and accurately using atomic methods, possibly including temperature and pressure dependencies, use of those accurate property values which are treated as adjustable parameters in mesoscale simulations may lead initially to decreased predictive capability compared to experimental results; that is, an improved subgrid model or more accurate physically-based parameter specification may disrupt the overall calibration of the mesoscale model.

The other general approach to multiscale simulation of energetic materials is the concurrent method in which two different levels of material description are included simultaneously within a single simulation domain. One example where such an approach would be useful is grain-resolved mesoscale simulations wherein regions of atomically resolved material are contained within a larger volume of material treated using continuum mechanics. Such an approach would be particularly useful for mesoscopic studies of the effects of intra-crystal defects (dislocations, grain boundaries, voids) or intermaterial interfaces (crystal-binder, High Explosive (HE)-metal) where localization of temperature, stress, or microscopic strain rate might be large leading to large gradients in the material (often called *hot spots*) wherein chemical reactions are likely to occur. In addition to theoretical difficulties with formulating a single simulation method in which particles and continuum regions are treated seamlessly, concurrent methods are difficult to implement due to the high degree of time sub-cycling required given the large difference between the time step in a MD simulation (~0.01-1 fs) compared to the time step in even a high resolution mesoscale simulation (~0.1 ns). Other possibilities for progress based on concurrent approaches include using different levels of description (and, tacitly assumed, different accuracies of forces) within a single MD computational domain; for example, use within a limited region such as the neighborhood of an interface of a force description based on electronic structure or empirically-calibrated force fields that include chemical reaction surrounded by a (typically much larger) region of material represented by a less accurate but computationally cheaper model (for instance one with fixed intramolecular connectivity that does not treat chemical reaction). Applications of the *computational materials design facility* (for example, Jaramillo-Botero et al., 2011 and references therein) illustrate the potential of such methods.

Another approach to extending the space and time scales accessible to molecularly-detailed methods that has been used with increasing frequency is particle-based coarse-graining in which chemical functional groups or entire molecules or collections of molecules are treated as effective particles, with corresponding effective potentials. As an example, Desbiens et al. (2007, 2009) have developed a model for nitromethane in which the four atoms of the methyl group are treated as a single particle. This simplified model has been parameterized using a MC optimization approach, and shown to yield good agreement with several measured quantities, including second shock temperatures. Gee and co-workers (Gee et al., 2006; Lin et al., 2007) have developed a coarse-grained description for PETN in which individual PETN molecules are represented by a five-bead model (nominally the tetramethyl carbon and the four nitrate pendent groups) (Gee et al., 2006), and have used this model to study surface diffusion of PETN molecules on different PETN crystal faces (Lin et al., 2007). Izvekov et al. (2010) have developed a formalism for systematic coarse-graining of molecular materials and applied it to nitromethane; both a one-site model, in which the molecules are treated as single particles, and a two-site model, in which the methyl group and nitro groups are treated as distinct particles, were developed. The approach, which is based on a systematic calibration of effective coarse-grained particle-particle interactions using potential-of-mean-force calculations for fully atomic systems, was shown in the case of a density-dependent potential formulation to reproduce the nitromethane liquid structure and shock Hugoniot locus. Lynch et al. (2008) have developed a simplified model for α-HMX in which individual molecules are treated as single particles; a novel aspect of this reduced dimensionality "mesodynamics" (Strachan & Holian, 2005) potential function is that it includes the effects of intramclecular vibrational degrees of freedom through incorporation of implicit degrees of freedom. The model, which is only intended to provide a schematic representation of HMX, has been used to study spall behavior in the shocked crystals. With all coarse-graining or multiscale methods, a key requirement is to capture the dominant features of the physics at the finer scale when passing from one scale to the next larger one, and to minimize the amount of non-essential information that is carried along. The specific requirements will vary depending on the material type, the thermodynamic and mechanical loading regime of interest, and the fidelity of the higher-scale model in which the finer-scale results are to be used.

	C_{11}		C_{33}	C_{44}		C_{66}	C_{12}	C_{13}					
PETN													
Ultrasonics[a]	17.22		12.17	5.04		3.95	5.44	7.99					
ISTS[b]	17.12		12.18	5.03		3.81	6.06	7.98					
MD/MC[c]	17.6		10.5	4.66		4.92	4.7	6.65					
	C_{11}	C_{22}	C_{33}	C_{44}	C_{55}	C_{66}	C_{12}	C_{13}	C_{23}				
RDX													
MC[d]	26.9	24.1	17.7	8.4	5.3	7.6	6.27	5.68	6.32				
Ultrasonics[e]	25.02	19.6	17.93	5.17	4.07	6.91	8.2	5.8	5.9				
Brillouin[f]	36.67	25.67	21.64	11.99	2.72	7.68	1.38	1.67	9.17				
RUS[g]	25.6	21.3	19.0	5.38	4.27	7.27	8.67	5.72	6.4				
ISTS[b]	25.15	20.08	18.21	5.26	4.06	7.10	8.23	5.94	5.94				
Energy Minimized[h]	25.0	23.8	23.4	3.1	7.7	5.2	10.6	7.6	8.8				
	C_{11}	C_{22}	C_{33}	C_{44}	C_{55}	C_{66}	C_{12}	C_{13}	C_{23}	C_{15}	C_{25}	C_{35}	C_{46}
β-HMX													
ISLS[i]	20.8	---	18.5	---	6.1	---	---	12.5	---	-0.5	---	1.9	---
Brillouin[j]	18.41	14.41	12.44	4.77	4.77	4.46	6.37	10.50	6.42	-1.10	0.83	1.08	2.75
ISTS[k]	20.58	19.69	18.24	9.92	7.69	10.67	9.65	9.75	12.93	-0.61	4.89	1.57	4.42
MD/MC[l]	22.2	23.9	23.4	9.2	11.1	10.1	9.6	13.2	13.0	-0.1	4.7	1.6	2.5

a. Winey & Gupta, 2001.
b. Sun et al., 2008. ISTS: Impulsive stimulated thermal scattering.
c. Borodin et al., 2008. Composite MD/MC simulations using flexible molecules.
d. Sewell and Bennett, 2000. MC simulations using rigid molecules.
e. Haussuhl, 2001. The crystal axes used in the original publication have been transformed to coincide with that used here.
f. Haycraft et al., 2006.
g. Schwarz et al., 2006. RUS: Resonant ultrasound spectroscopy.
h. Munday et al., 2011. Molecular mechanics using flexible molecules.
i. Zaug, 1998. Partial determination. ISLS: Impulsive stimulated light scattering.
j. Stevens & Eckhardt, 2005.
k. Sun et al., 2009.
l. Sewell et al., 2003.

Table 2. Second-order elastic coefficients of PETN, RDX, and β-HMX determined using various methods. Units are GPa.

Pressure (GPa)	K_{Reuss}	K_{Voigt}	G_{Reuss}	G_{Voigt}
0.0	13.2	20.3	1.8	11.5
4.0	46.1	62.7	5.2	27.9
8.0	73.3	97	6.5	37.9

Table 3. Calculated pressure-dependent Reuss average and Voigt average bulk and shear moduli for TATB crystal. Units are GPa. The temperature is $T = 300$ K. (Adapted from Bedrov et al., (2009).)

Menikoff & Sewell (2002) have reviewed the physical properties and processes needed for mesoscale simulations of HMX. Among the properties required that can be reliably computed for pure materials using atomic-level modeling methods are the thermodynamic phase boundaries between the polymorphic forms of the crystal and the melting point as a function of pressure; the coefficients of thermal expansion and isothermal compression; the heat capacity as a function of temperature and, in general, pressure; the modal and volumetric Gruneisen coefficient; the elastic tensor and derived isotropic moduli as functions of temperature and pressure; the elastic-plastic yield surface, which in general is temperature and stress dependent, and may also exhibit a strain-rate dependence; and thermal conductivity and shear viscosity as functions of pressure and temperature. A number of these properties have been computed for HMX and used in continuum simulations: the elastic tensor (Sewell et al., 2003; Barton et al., 2009; Zamiri & De, 2010), the temperature-dependent shear viscosity of the liquid (Bedrov et al., 2000; Dienes et al., 2006), the temperature-dependent specific heat (Goddard et al., 1998; Sewell & Menikoff, 2004), Other properties discussed by Menikoff and Sewell that must be considered in a realistic simulation are the "damage" state of the material, for instance size and distributions of cracks; the nature and density of defects within the crystals; and the effects of material interfaces on the composite behavior. Bedrov et al. (2003) have discussed how some of these properties can be obtained from MD simulations. More recently, Rice and Sewell (2008) reviewed atomic-scale simulations of physical properties in energetic materials, with a focus on predictions of properties for systems in thermal equilibrium.

Single-crystal plasticity of RDX has been studied using atomic-level simulation methods and, in some cases, compared to experimental results. Cawkwell and co-workers (Cawkwell et al., 2010; Ramos et al. 2010) have used MD simulations of the shock response of initially defect-free (111)- and (021)-oriented RDX single crystals to interpret the "anomalous" elastic-plastic response observed in flyer plate experiments for that orientation, wherein the evolution with increasing impact strength of VISAR velocity profiles for the (111) orientation transforms from a clear two-wave elastic-plastic structure to a nearly-overdriven structure over an interval of shock pressures that is narrow compared to the results obtained for other crystal orientations. The MD results show that, above a well-defined threshold shock strength, stacking faults nucleate homogeneously in the material then rapidly propagate, leading to mechanical hardening consistent with the abrupt transition from a two-wave structure to a nearly overdriven one (Cawkwell et al., 2010). Based on the results for the (111)-oriented crystal, Ramos et al. (2010) predicted that similar behavior should arise for shocks in (021)-oriented RDX, a result that was confirmed both from MD simulations and flyer plate experiments. Chen et al. (2008) performed large-scale MD simulations of nanoindentation of (100)-oriented RDX crystal by a diamond indenter using a version of the ReaxFF reactive force field (van Duin et al., 2001; Strachan et al., 2005). They observed localized damage in the region of the indenter, and calculated a material hardness that is consistent with experimental data. They concluded that dominant slip occurs in the (210) plane along the $[\bar{1}20]$ direction. Ramos et al. (2009) have reported atomic-force microscopy/nanoindentation experiments for oriented RDX crystals. Because Ramos et al. did not study indentation for the (100) surface, a direct comparison between their data and the MD results of Chen et al. is not possible.

Energetic material crystals (and organic crystals generally) often crystallize into low-symmetry space groups, exhibit polymorphism (*c.f.*, the multiple crystal phases of HMX (see Refs. 2-5 in Sewell et al., 2003) and RDX (Millar et al. (2010), and references therein; and Munday et al. (2011))), and are often highly anisotropic in terms of thermal, mechanical, and surface properties (the graphitic-like stacking of layers in TATB crystal provides an extreme case (Kolb & Rizzo, 1979; Bedrov et al., 2009). This can lead to anisotropic elastic-plastic shock response (Hooks et al., 2006; Menikoff et al., 2005; Winey & Gupta, 2010) and even anisotropic shock initiation thresholds, as has been shown by (Dick, 1984; Dick et al., 1991, 1997) for the case of PETN crystal.

A number of MD studies have been performed to assess shock-induced phase transitions, anisotropic shock response, and effects of crystal surface properties on polymer adhesion properties. Thompson and co-workers have studied melting in RDX, and noted a structural transition that occurs for temperatures just below the melting point (Agrawal et al, 2006). Thompson and co-workers have also studied the melting (Agrawal et al., 2003; Zheng et al., 2006; Siavosh-Haghighi, 2006) and crystallization (Siavosh-Haghighi et al., 2010) of nitromethane using a non-reactive force field (Sorescu et al., 2000; Agrawal et al., 2003), including a prediction of the pressure dependence of the melting point, $T_m = T_m(P)$ (Siavosh-Haghighi & Thompson, 2011; see Fig. 11). Using that same force field Thompson and coworkers have studied the shock strength dependence for (100)-oriented crystals (Siavosh-Haghighi et al., 2009; Dawes et al. 2009). They found that considerable disordering occurs for shock strengths of 2.0 km·s^{-1} and greater. By projecting the instantaneous kinetic energy of individual molecules in the system onto the normal mode eigenvectors for a single molecule in the explicit crystal field they characterized the detailed energy transfer between the shock and molecular translational, rotational, and vibrational modes of the molecule. The results showed that, among the vibrational modes, shock excitation first excites the low-frequency modes; subsequent excitation of higher frequency vibrations occurs on longer time scales, with an approximately monotonic dependence between the frequency of a given mode and the time required for it to reach a steady-fluctuating energy in the shocked state. Further, the detailed energy transfer pathways differ for molecules that are impacted "methyl end first" versus "nitro end first" in the (100) shock orientation. (This latter point is interesting in light of the observation by Nomura et al. (2007a) for the case of reactive ReaxFF (van Duin et al., 2001; Strachan et al., 2005) shocks propagating along [100] in RDX that molecules belonging to the two distinct orientations in the crystal respond differently to the shock; one group of molecules undergoes chemical reaction while the other exhibits flattening and rotation without chemistry.)

He et al. (2011) studied shocks in oriented nitromethane crystals impacted at 2.0 km·s^{-1} using MD with the same force field as Dawes et al. (2009). They observed significant differences in the responses to shocking along the [100], [010], and [001] directions. Jaramillo et al. (2007) studied the shock response of (100)-oriented α-HMX using a non-reactive force field model (Smith & Bharadwaj, 1999; Bedrov et al., 2002) for impact strengths between 0.5 and 2.0 km·s^{-1}. They observed a clear transition between elastic, elastic-plastic, and overdriven behavior in the crystals. Their results show that at lower pressures plasticity is mediated by the nucleation and spread of crystallographic dislocations, whereas at higher pressures there is a transition from dislocations to the formation of nanoscale shear bands in the material. They noted that regions of material associated with these defects had larger local temperatures. Eason and Sewell (2011) have used a non-reactive force field (Borodin et al., 2008) to study the shock response of (100)- and (001)-oriented PETN. These orientations were found to be insensitive and sensitive, respectively, to shock initiation in the experiments by Dick and coworkers (Dick, 1984; Dick et al., 1991, 1997). For 1.0 km·s^{-1} shocks, Eason and Sewell (2011) observed the formation of defects in (110) planes for (100)-oriented shocks, but only elastic compression for (001)-oriented shocks; see Fig. 12.

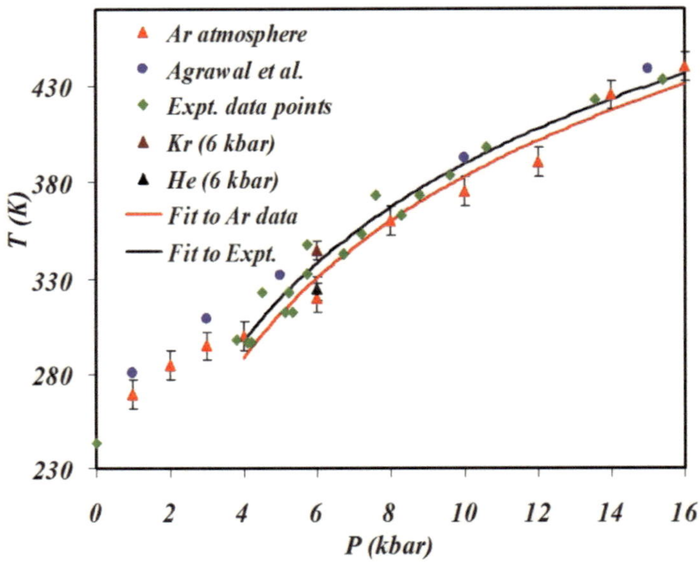

Fig. 11. Computed and experimental melting curves for nitromethane. The MD simulation results were obtained using the SRT force field (Sorescu et al., 2003). See Siavosh-Haghighi & Thompson (2011) and references therein.

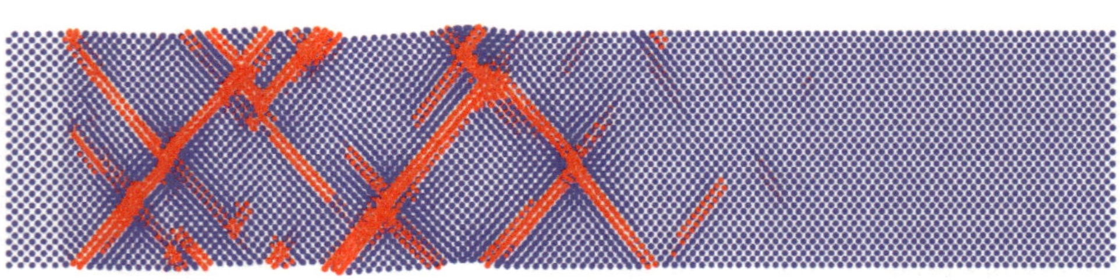

Fig. 12. Snapshot from a MD simulation of a shock wave propagating along [100] in PETN crystal. Only molecular centers of mass are shown. At the left end of the system is a rigid piston; the shock wave propagates from left to right. The snapshot corresponds to the instant of maximum compression (that is, the time when the shock front reaches the right-hand end of the sample). Blue corresponds to the piston, unshocked material, or elastically shock-compressed material. Red corresponds to molecules that have undergone locally inelastic compression.

Zybin and coworkers (Budzien et al. 2009; Zybin et al., 2010) studied the reactive dynamics of PETN using the ReaxFF force field. Budzien et al. studied the onset of chemistry for shocks propagating along [100] with impact velocities of 3 or 4 km·s^{-1}. Zybin et al. (2010) studied the anisotropic initiation sensitivity of PETN in conjunction with a compress-and-shear model. By imposing rapid compression followed by rapid shear, with specific combinations of those two deformation types chosen to emulate the possible interactions between oriented shocks and probable slip systems, they were able to correlate the buildup of stresses, local temperatures, and onset of chemistry with the experimentally observed initiation anisotropy.

Atomic-level simulations of shock waves interacting with pre-existing defects or interfaces have been performed. Various models ranging in complexity from highly schematic ($2AB \rightarrow A_2 + B_2 + \Delta H$) to relatively realistic (RDX → small molecule products) have been used. Shi and Brenner (2008), using a reactive force field model for the schematic energetic material nitrogen cubane (overall stoichiometry $N_8(s) \rightarrow 4N_2(g)$), have studied the effects of faceted interfaces on energy localization and detonation initiation. These simulations are of particular interest because of discussions of whether, or to what extent, the relative shock insensitivity of certain RDX formulations can be attributed to smoothed crystal edges obtained by treatment by surfactants or mechanical milling. Shi and Brenner identified shock focusing and local compression of the facets as two mechanisms for hotspot formation; which one dominates in a given situation depends on the shock impedance mismatch between the binder and energetic crystal. Using a version of the ReaxFF reactive force field (van Duin, 2001; Strachan, 2005), Nomura et al. (2007b) studied the collapse of single 8-nm diameter cylindrical voids in RDX crystal for the case of shock propagation along the [100] direction, with piston impact velocities of 1 and 3 km·s^{-1} (shock velocities of ~3 and ~9 km·s^{-1}, respectively). They observed the formation of nanojets during void collapse, which led to energy focusing when the jet impinged on the downstream wall of the void. For the weaker shock the local heating from jet impact on the downstream wall remained largely localized near the collapsed jet/wall interface stagnation zone, whereas for the stronger shock a conical region of material extending into the downstream wall underwent vibrational heating. For the stronger shock the dominant reaction during void closure was N-N bond cleavage; smaller reaction products (N_2, H_2O, HONO) were rapidly generated once the nanojet reached the downstream wall. Cawkwell and Sewell (2011) have performed preliminary studies of void collapse in various oriented single crystals of RDX. Figure 13 contains a snapshot, taken when the shock wave reached the far end of the simulation cell, of the molecular centers of mass of an RDX crystal subsequent to the passage of a shock wave with piston impact speed 0.5 km·s^{-1} over a 20 nm cylindrical void in a (210) shock. Molecules initially on the surface of the cylindrical void are colored blue; all others are colored red. The results indicate considerable structural complexity in the shock response, including regions of intense plastic deformation, stacking faults, and a stress-induced phase transition. Note also the large asymmetry of the void collapse process; for the crystal orientation and impact speed chosen, lateral jets form from the top and bottom of the void and collide near the geometric center of the original void. Using a reactive force field for the model reactive diatomic material $2AB \rightarrow A_2 + B_2 + \Delta H$, Herring *et al.* (Herring *et al.*, 2010) performed a detailed study, in 2-D, of the effects of void size and geometrical arrangement on thresholds for initiation. They considered a number of geometric arrangements of circular voids including single voids, voids on square and triangular lattices, and randomly arranged voids. Although the AB system is a highly idealized model, it captures many features of reactive waves in real materials (Heim, 2007, 2008a, 2008b).

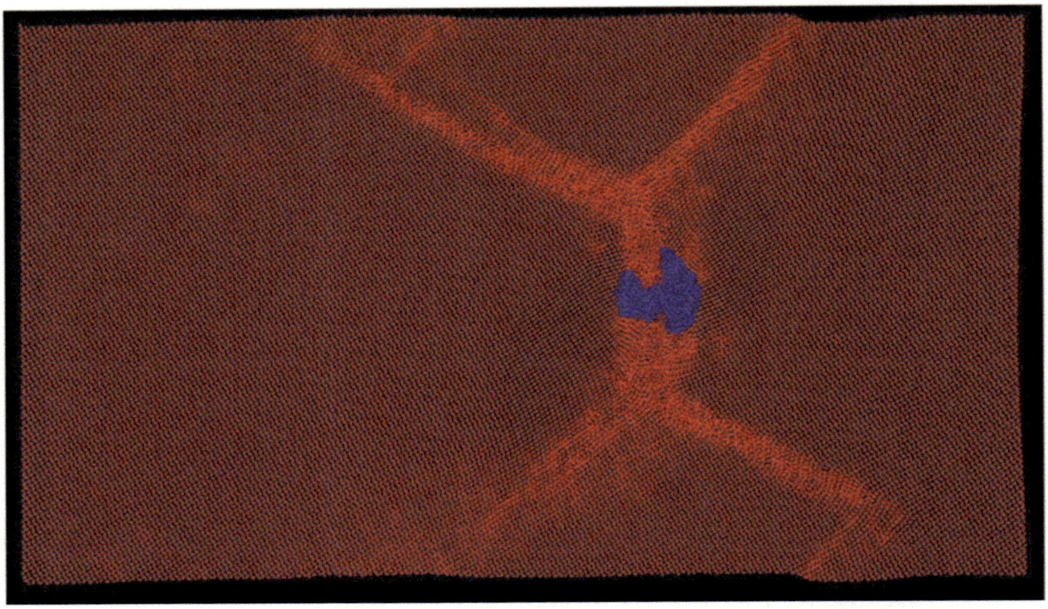

Fig. 13. Snapshot from a MD simulation of void collapse in (210)-oriented RDX. Only molecular centers of mass are shown. (Cawkwell & Sewell, 2011.)

As illustrated by the preceding discussion, MD simulations of energetic materials constituent materials and structures can be used in a variety of ways with objectives that range from near-quantitative predictions of spectroscopic or thermo-mechanical properties needed directly within existing constitutive or reactive burn models but currently unavailable, sparse, or unreliable with present-day experimental methods; to ones designed to reveal or refine existing understanding of fundamental dynamical processes associated with material dynamics (inelastic deformation, stress-induced phase transitions); to more qualitative ones designed to answer basic questions about, for example, material response in the presence of seeded defects and how material response changes with variations in the geometric features of those defects or how the morphology of a heterogeneous system affects the shock-induced localization of energy.

5. Conclusions

An important motivation for the simulation of deformation processes in energetic materials is the desire to avoid accidental ignition of explosives under the influence of a mechanical load. This requires the understanding of material behavior at macro-, meso- and molecular scales.

Experimental methods to determine the sensitivity of energetic materials to an external stimulus can be directly interpreted in terms of test severity in order to rank explosives. Simulation at the macroscale facilitates interpretation of experimental results; for example, by exceeding certain threshold values the ignition of a specific explosive composition is anticipated. Presented thresholds are related to 1) shear rate, 2) a pressure-, shear-rate- and load-duration-dependent parameter, and 3) a parameter incorporating time-varying pressure and shear-rate loading. The latter two approaches are based on a micro-structural model. Unfortunately, results are applied only to PBX9501 or similar HMX-containing explosive compositions. Starting from the same micro-structural model however, one may arrive at a threshold parameter for PBXs containing energetic crystals other than HMX.

Simulations of PBXs including features from the mesoscale can be categorized as follows. First, one can use continuum models with particle-specific features that are fitted to experimental data and use those continuum models as input for simulations at the macroscale. Secondly, one can determine the collective mechanical behavior by simulation of a representative volume element with the mechanical properties of all individual constituents. And thirdly, one can simulate the mechanical behavior in deformation processes directly at the mesoscale, and interpret the results in terms of probabilistic distribution functions of wave field variables.

Atomic-level simulations of energetic materials can be used to predict physical properties such as equations of state, transport coefficients, and spectroscopic features, and to study fundamental processes such as energy transfer, inelastic deformation, phase transitions, and reaction chemistry. These are among the properties needed for the development and parameterization of improved mesoscale models. Depending on the accuracy of the force field used, these predictions can be expected to be semi-quantitative or to reveal general features of materials behavior in complicated polyatomic materials. Studies of the effects of defects, voids, or material interfaces on the physical properties and dynamic response can be studied in detail; although the results must be interpreted with caution if the goal is to link directly to the mesoscale, due to the disparity between defect sizes or number densities that can be simulated using MD and those that occur in real materials.

6. Acknowledgments

The authors acknowledge support from the U. S. Defense Threat Reduction Agency. R.H.B.B. and A.E.D.M.H. acknowledge support from The Netherlands Ministry of Defence. T.D.S. acknowledges support from the U. S. Office of Naval Research and the Los Alamos National Laboratory LDRD program. T.D.S and D.L.T. acknowledge support from a DOD MURI grant managed by the U. S. Army Research Office.

7. References

Agrawal, P.M., Rice, B.M., Zheng, L., & Thompson, D.L. (2006). Molecular dynamics simulations of hexahydro-1,3,5-trinitro-1,3,5-s-triazine (RDX) using a combined Sorescu-Rice-Thompson AMBER force field. *Journal of Physical Chemistry B* 110, 26185.

Agrawal, P.M., Rice, B.M. & Thompson, D.L. (2003). Molecular dynamics studies of the melting of nitromethane. *Journal of Chemical Physics* 119, 9617.

Armstrong, R. W. (2009). Dislocation mechanics aspects of energetic material composites. In: *Reviews on Advanced Materials Science 19*, Ovid'ko, I.A., (Ed), pp. 14-34.

Autodyn, http://www.ansys.com/Products/Simulation+Technology/Explicit+Dynamics/ANSYS+AUTODYN.

Baer, M.R. & Trott, W.M. (2002). Theoretical and experimental mesoscale studies of impact-loaded granular explosive and simulant materials. *Proceedings of 12th International Detonation Symposium*, San Diego, USA, August 2002.

Baer, M.R. (2002). Modeling heterogeneous energetic materials at the mesoscale. *Thermochimica Acta* 384, 351.

Bailly, P., Delvare, F., Vial, J., Hanus, J. L., Biessy, M. & Picart, D. (2011). Dynamic behavior of an aggregate material at simultaneous high pressure and strain rate: SPHB triaxial tests. *International Journal of Impact Engineering*, 38, (2011), pp. 73-84.

Bardenhagen, S.G., Brydon, A.D., Williams, T.O. & Collet, C. (2006). Coupling grain scale and bulk mechanical response for PBXs using numerical simulations of real microstructures. *AIP Conference Proceedings*, 845 (2006), pp. 479-482.

Barton, N.R., Winter, N.W. & Reaugh, J. E. (2009). Defect evolution and pore collapse in crystalline energetic materials. *Modelling and Simulation in Materials Science and Engineering*, 17, 035003.

Bedrov, D., Smith, G.D. & Sewell, T.D. (2000). Temperature-dependent shear viscosity coefficient of octahydro-1,3,5,7-tetranitro-1,3,5,7-tetrazocine (HMX): A molecular dynamics simulation study. *Journal of Chemical Physics* 112, 7203.

Bedrov, D., Ayyagari, C., Smith, G.D., Sewell, T.D., Menikoff, R. & Zaug, J.M. (2001). Molecular dynamics simulations of hmx crystal polymorphs using a flexible molecule force field, *Journal of Computer-Aided Materials Design* 8, 77.

Bedrov, D., Smith, G.D. & Sewell, T.D. (2003). Thermodynamic and mechanical properties from atomistic simulations, in *Energetic Materials, Volume 12: Part 1. Decomposition, Crystal, and Molecular Properties (Theoretical and Computational Chemistry)*, Murray, J.S. and Politzer, P. Eds. (Elsevier, Amsterdam).

Bedrov, D., Borodin, O., Smith, G.D., Sewell, T.D., Dattelbaum, D.M. & Stevens, L.L. (2009). A molecular dynamics simulation study of crystalline 1,3,5-triamino-2,4,6,trinitrobenzene as a function of pressure and temperature. *Journal of Chemical Physics* 131, 224703.

Bennett, J.G., Haberman, K.S., Johnson, J.N., Asay, B.W. & Henson, B.F. (1998). A constitutive model for the non-shock ignition and mechanical response of high explosives. *J. Mech. Phys. Solids*, 46, (1998), pp. 2302-2322.

Birnbaum, N.K., Cowler, M.S., Itoh, M., Katayama, M. & Obata, H. (1987). AUTODYN - an interactive nonlinear dynamic analysis program for microcomputers through supercomputers. *Proceedings of 9th Int. Conf. on Structural Mechanics in Reactor Technology*, Lausanne, Switzerland, 1987.

Bock, N., Challacombe, M., Gan, C.-K., Henkelman, G., Nemeth, K., Niklasson, A.M.N., Odell, A., Schwegler, E., Tymczak, C.J. & Weber, V. (2011). FreeON. Los Alamos National Laboratory (LA-CC 01-2, LA-CC-04-086) http://freeon.org.

Borodin, O., Smith, G.D., Sewell, T.D., and Bedrov, D. (2008). Polarizable and nonpolarizable force fields for alkyl nitrates. *Journal of Physical Chemistry* B 112, 734.

Bouma, R.H.B., Courtois, C., Verbeek, H.J. & Scholtes, J.H.G. (1999). Influence of mechanical damage on the shock sensitivity of plastic bonded explosives. *Proceedings of Insensitive Munitions & Energetic Materials Technology Symposium*, Tampa, USA, November 1999.

Bouma, R.H.B., Verbeek, H.J. & van Wees, R.M.M. (2003). Design of barriers for the prevention of sympathetic detonation in out-of-area munition storage. *Proceedings of 30th International Pyrotechnics Seminar*, Saint Malo, France, June 2003.

Bouma, R.H.B. & Meuken, B. (2004). Explosive and mechanical deformation of PBXN-109. *Proceedings of workshop on shear stress evaluation and contribution to the ignition of PBX*, Institut für Chemische Technologie, Pfinztal, Germany, June 2004.

Bouma, R.H.B., Meuken, B. & Verbeek, H.J. (2007). Shear initiation of Al/MoO3-based reactive materials. *Propellants, Explosives, Pyrotechnics*, 32, (2007), pp. 447-453.

Bowden, F.P. & Yoffe, Y.D. (1952). *Initiation and growth of explosion in liquids and solids*, Cambridge University Press, ISBN 0 521 31233 7, Cambridge, United Kingdom.

Browning, R.V. (1995). Microstructural model of mechanical initiation of energetic materials. *Proceedings of APS Conference on Shock Compression of Condensed Matter*, Seattle, USA.

Browning, R.V. & Scammon, R.J. (2001). Microstructural modal of ignition for time varying loading conditions, *Proceedings of APS Conference on Shock Compression of Condensed Matter*, CP620, 987-990.

Browning, R.V. & Scammon, R.J. (2002). Influence of mechanical properties on non-shock ignition. *Proceedings of 12th Int. Detonation Symposium*, San Diego, USA, August 2002.

Budzien, J., Thompson, A.P. & Zybin, S.V. (2009). Reactive molecular dynamics simulations of shock through a single crystal of pentaerythritol tetranitrate. *Journal of Physical Chemistry B* 113, 13142.

Cawkwell, M.J., Sewell, T.D., Zheng. L & Thompson, D.L. (2008). Shock-induced shear bands in an energetic molecular crystal: Application of shock-front absorbing boundary conditions to molecular dynamics simulations, *Physical Review B* 78, 014107.

Cawkwell, M.J., Ramos, K.J., Hooks, D.E. & Sewell, T.D. (2010). Homogeneous dislocation nucleation in cyclotrimethylene trinitramine under shock loading. *Journal of Applied Physics* 107, 063512.

Cawkwell, M.J. and Sewell, T.D. (2011). Unpublished results.

Chen, Y.-C., Nomura, K.-i., Kalia, R.K., Nakano, A. & Vashishta, P. (2008). Molecular dynamics nanoindentation simulation of an energetic material. *Applied Physics Letters* 93, 171908.

Chidester, S.K., Tarver, C.M. & Garza, R. (1998). Low amplitude impact testing and analysis of pristine and aged solid high explosives. *Proceedings of 11th Int. Detonation Symposium*, Snowmass, USA.

Coe, J.D., Sewell, T.D. & Shaw, M.S. (2009). Optimal sampling efficiency in Monte Carlo simulation with an approximate potential. *Journal of Chemical Physics* 130, 164104.

Coe, J.D., Sewell, T.D. & Shaw, M.S. (2009). Nested Markov chain Monte Carlo sampling of a density functional theory potential: Equilibrium thermodynamics of dense fluid nitrogen. *Journal of Chemical Physics* 131, 074105.

Coffey, C.S. (1995). Impact testing of explosives and propellants. *Propellants, Explosives, Pyrotechnics*, 20, (1995), pp. 105-115.

Coffey, C.S. & Sharma, J. (1999). Plastic deformation, energy dissipation, and initiation of crystalline explosives. *Physical Review B – Condensed Matter and Materials Physics*, 60, (1999), pp. 9365-9371.

Conley, P.A. & Benson, D.J. (1999). An estimate of the linear strain rate dependence of octahydro-1,3,5,7-tetranitro-1,3,5,7-tetrazocine. *Journal of Applied Physics*, 939. (199), pp. 6717-6728.

Dawes, R., Siavosh-Haghighi, A., Sewell, T.D. & Thompson, D.L. (2009). Shock-induced melting of (100)-oriented Nitromethane: Energy partitioning and vibrational mode heating. *Journal of Chemical Physics* 131, 224513.

De, S. & Macri, M. (2006). Modeling the bulk mechanical response of heterogeneous explosives based on microstructural information. *Proceedings of 13th Int. Detonation Symposium* 373., Norfolk, USA.

Desbiens, N., Bourasseau, E. & Maillet, J.-B. (2007). Potential optimization for the calculation of shocked liquid nitromethane properties, *Molecular Simulation* 33, 1061.

Desbiens, N., Bourasseau, E., Maillet, J.-B. & Soulard, L. (2009). Molecular based equation of state for shocked liquid nitromethane. *Journal of Hazardous Materials* 166, 1120.

Dick, J.J. (1984). Effect of crystal orientation on shock initiation sensitivity of pentaerythritol tetranitrate explosive. *Applied Physics Letters* 44, 859.

Dick, J.J., Mulford, R.N., Spencer, W.J., Pettit, D.R., Garcia, E. & Shaw, D.C., (1991). Shock response of pentaerythritol tetranitrate single crystals. *Journal of Applied Physics* 70, 3572.

Dick, J.J. (1997). Anomalous shock initiation of detonation in pentaerythritol tetranitrate crystals. *Journal of Applied Physics* 81 601.

Dienes, J.K. (1985). A statistical theory of fragmentation processes, *Mechanics of Materials*, Vol 4, 325-335.

Dienes, J.K., Zuo, Q.H. & Kersher, J.D. (2006). Impact initiation of explosives and propellants via statistical crack mechanics. *Journal of the Mechanics and Physics of Solids* 54, 1237.

Doherty, R.M. & Watt, D.S. (2008). Relationship between RDX properties and sensitivity. *Propellants, Explosives, Pyrotechnics*, 33, (2008), pp. 4-13.

DYNA3D (2005). User Manual, Available from https://www-eng.llnl.gov/pdfs/mdg_dyna3d.pdf

Eason, R.M. and Sewell, T.D. (2011). Unpublished results.

Frenkel, D. & Smit. B. (2002) *Understanding Molecular Simulation*, 2nd Ed. (Academic Press, San Diego.)

Gee, R.H., Wu, C. & Maiti, A. (2006). Coarse-grained model for a molecular crystal. *Applied Physics Letters* 89, 021919.

Goddard, W.A., Meiron, D.I., Ortiz, M., Shepherd, J.E. & Pool, J. (1998). *Technical Report 032, Center for Simulation of Dynamic Response in Materials*, California Institute of Technology. http://www.cacr.caltech.edu/ASAP/publications/cit-asci-tr/cit-asci-tr032.pdf.

Goldman, N., Reed, E.J. & Fried, L.E. (2009). Quantum mechanical corrections to simulated shock Hugoniot temperatures. *Journal of Chemical Physics* 131, 204103.

Gruau, C., Picart, D., Belmas, R., Bouton, E., Delmaire-Sizes, F., Sabatier, J. & Trumel, H. (2009). Ignition of a confined high explosive under low velocity impact. *International Journal of Impact Engineering*, 36, (2009), pp. 537-550.

Hager, K., Tancreto, J. & Swisdak, M. (2000). High Performance Magazine non-progation wall design criteria. *Proceedings of 29th DDESB Seminar*, New Orleans, USA, July 2000.

Han, S.-p., van Duin, A.C.T., Goddard, W.A. III & Strachan, A. (2011) Thermal decomposition of condensed-phase nitromethane from molecular dynamics from ReaxFF reactive dynamics. *Journal of Physical Chemistry B* 115, 6534.

Handley, C.A. (2011). Numerical modeling of two HMX-based plastic-bonded explosives at the mesoscale. Ph. D. thesis, St. Andrews University. Available from http://research-repository.st-andrews.ac.uk

Haussühl, S. (2001). Elastic and thermoelastic properties of selected organic crystals: acenaphthene, trans-azobenzene, benzophenone, tolane, trans-stilbene, dibenzyl, diphenyl sulfone, 2,20-biphenol, urea, melamine, hexogen, succinimide, pentaerythritol, urotropine, malonic acid, dimethyl malonic acid, maleic acid, hippuric acid, aluminium acetylacetonate, iron acetylacetonate, and tetraphenyl silicon. *Z. Kristallogr.* 216, 339.

Haycraft, J.J., Stevens, L.L., & Eckhardt, C.J. (2006). The elastic constants and related properties of the energetic material cyclotrimethylene trinitramine (RDX) determined by Brillouin scattering, *Journal of Chemical Physics*, 124, 024712.

He, L. Sewell, T.D. & Thompson, D.L. (2011). Molecular dynamics simulations of shock waves in oriented nitromethane single crystals. *Journal of Chemical Physics* 134, 124506.

Heim, A.J., Grønbech-Jensen, N., Germann, T.C., Holian, B.L., Kober, E.M. & Lomdahl, P.S. (2007). Influence of interatomic bonding potentials on detonation properties. *Physical Review E* 76, 026318.

Heim, A.J., Grønbech-Jensen, N., Kober, E.M., Erpenbeck, J.J. & Germann, T.C. (2008a). Interaction potential for atomic simulations of conventional high explosives. *Physical Review E* 78, 046709.

Heim, A.J., Grønbech-Jensen, N. Kober, E.M. & Germann, T.C. (2008b). Molecular dynamics simulations of detonation instability. *Physical Review E* 78, 046710.

Hooks, D.E., Ramos, K.J. & Martinez, A.R. (2006). Elastic-plastic shock wave profiles in oriented single crystals of cyclotrimethylene trinitramine (RDX) at 2.25 GPa. *Journal of Applied Physics* 100, 024908.

Hoover, W.G. (1985). Canonical dynamics: Equilibrium phase-space distributions. *Physical Review A* 31, 1695.

Hsu, P.C., Hust, G., Howard, M. & Maienschein, J.L. (2010). The ODTX system for thermal ignition and thermal safety study of energetic materials, *Proceedings of the 14th Int. Detonation Symposium*, Coeur D'Alene, USA

Izvekov, S., Chung, P.W. & Rice, B.M. (2010). The multiscale coarse-graining method: Assessing its accuracy and introducing density dependent coarse-grain potentials. *Journal of Chemical Physics* 133, 064109.

Jaidann, M., Lussier, L.-S., Bouamoul, A., Abou-Rachid, H. & Brisson, J. (2009). Effects of interface interactions on mechanical properties in RDX-based PBXs HTPB-DOA: Molecular dynamics simulations. In *Lecture Notes in Computer Science* 5545 (Proceedings of the ICCS, 2009, Part II). Allen, G. et al. (Eds.) (Springer-Verlag, Berlin) 131.

Jaramillo, E., Sewell, T.D. & Strachan, A. (2007). Atomic-level view of inelastic deformation in a shock loaded molecular crystal. *Physical Review B* 76, 064112.

Jaramillo-Botero, A., Nielsen, R., Abrol, R., Su, J. Pascal, T., Mueller, J. & Goddard, W.A. III (2011). First-principles-based multiscale, multiparadigm molecular mechanics and dynamics methods for describing complex chemical processes. *Top. Curr. Chem.* DOI: 10.1007/128_2010_114 (Springer-Verlag, Heidelberg).

Koch, W. & Holthausen, M.C. (2001). *A Chemist's Guide to Density Functional Theory,* 2nd Ed. (Wiley-VCH, Wenheim).

Kolb, J.R. & Rizzo, H.F. (1979). Growth of 1,3,5-triamino-2,4,6-trinitrobenzene (TATB) I. Anisotropic thermal expansion. *Propellants, Explosives, and Pyrotechnics* 4, 10.

Kresse, G. et al. (2011). Vienna *Ab Initio* Simulation Package (VASP), Department of Computational Physics, Universität Wien, Wien, Austria, http://cms.mpi.univie.ac.at/vasp/.

Kuklja, M. & Rashkeev, S.N. (2009). Interplay of decomposition mechanisms at shear-strain interface. *The Journal of Physical Chemistry C* 113, pp. 17-20.

Lee, E.L. & Tarver, C.M., Phenomenological model of shock initiation in heterogeneous explosives. *Physics of Fluids*, Vol. 23 (1980), p. 2362.

Lei, L. & Koslowski, M., (2011). Mesoscale modeling of dislocations in molecular crystals. *Philosophical Magazine* 91, 865.

Lin, P.-H., Khare, R., Weeks, B.L. & Gee, R.H. (2007). Molecular modeling of diffusion on a crystalline pentaerythritol tetranitrate surface. *Applied Physics Letters* 91, 104107.

Liu, A. & Stuart, S.J. (2008). Empirical bond-order potential for hydrocarbons: Adaptive treatment of van der Waals interactions. *Journal of Computational Chemistry* 29, 601.

Lynch, K., Thompson, A. & Strachan, A. (2009) Coarse-grain modeling of spall failure in molecular crystals: Role of intra-molecular degrees of freedom. *Modelling and Simulation in Materials Science and Engineering* 17, 015007.

Maillet, J.-B. & Stoltz, G. (2008). Sampling constraints in average: The example of Hugoniot curves. *Applied Mathematics Research eXpress* 2008, abn004.

Malvar, L.J. (1994). Development of HPM nonpropagation walls: test results and Dyna3D predictions of acceptor response. *Proceedings of 26th DDESB Seminar*, New Orleans, USA, August 1994.

Manaa, M.R., Reed, E.J., Fried, L.E. & Goldman, N. (2009). Nitrogen-rich heterocycles as reactivity retardants in shocked insensitive explosives. *Journal of the American Chemical Society* 131, 5483.

Martyna, G.J., Tuckerman, M.E., Tobias, D.J. & Klein, M.L. (1996). Explicit reversible integration algorithms for extended systems dynamics. *Molecular Physics* 87, 1117.

Menikoff, R. & Sewell, T.D. (2002). Constituent properties of HMX needed for mesoscale simulations. *Combustion Theory and Modeling* 6, 103.

Menikoff, R., Dick, J. J. & Hooks, D. E.(2005). Analysis of wave profiles for single-crystal cyclotetramethylene tetranitramine. *Journal of Applied Physics* 97, 023529.

Menikoff, R. (2008). Comparison of constitutive models for plastic-bonded explosives. *Combustion Theory and Modeling* 12, 73.

Menikoff, R. (2011). Hot spot formation from shock reflections. *Shock Waves* 21, 141.

Metropolis, N. Rosenbluth, A.W., Rosenbluth, M.N., Teller, A.H. & Teller, E. (1953). Equation of state calculations by fast computing machines. *Journal of Chemical Physics* 21, 1087.

Meuken, B., Martinez Pacheco, M., Verbeek, H.J., Bouma, R.H.B. & Katgerman, L. (2006). Shear initiated reactions in energetic and reactive materials. *Mater. Res. Soc. Symp. Proc. Vol. 896,* (2006) 0896-H06-06, pp. 1-6.

Millar, D.I.A., Oswald, I.D.H., Barry, C., Francis, D.J., Marshall, W.G., Pulham, C.R. & Cumming, A.S. (2010). Pressure-cooking of explosives – the crystal structure of ε-RDX as determined by X-ray and neutron diffraction. *Chemical Communications* 46, 5662.

Molt, R.W. Jr., Watson, T. Jr., Lotrich, V.F. & Bartlett, R.J. (2011). RDX geometries, excited states, and revised energy ordering of conformers via MP2 and CCSD(T) methodologies: Insights into decomposition mechanism. *Journal of Physical Chemistry A* 115, 884.

Munday, L. B., Chung., P. W., Rice, B. M., and Solares, S. D. (2011). Simulations of high-pressure phases in RDX. *Journal of Physical Chemistry B* 115, 4378.

Namkung, J. & Coffey, C.S. (2001). Plastic deformation rate and initiation of crystalline explosives. *Proceedings of Shock Compression of Condensed Matter,* Furnish, M.D., Thadhani, N.N. & Horie, Y. (Eds), CP620, (2001), pp. 1003-1006.

Nomura, K.-i., Kalia, R.K., Nakano, A. & Vashishta, P. (2007a). Dynamic transition in the structure of an energetic crystal during chemical reactions at shock front prior to detonation. *Physical Review Letters* 99, 148303.

Nomura, K.-i., Kalia, R.K., Nakano, A. & Vashishta, P. (2007b). Reactive nanojets: Nanostructure-enhanced chemical reactions in a defected energetic crystal. *Applied Physics Letters,* 91, 183109.

Nosé, S. (1984). A unified formulation of the constant temperature molecular dynamics methods. *Journal of Chemical Physics* 81, 511.

Parrinello, M. & Rahman, A. (1981). Polymorphic transitions in single crystals: A new molecular dynamics method. *Journal of Applied Physics* 52, 7182.

Ramos, K.J., Hooks, D.E. & Bahr, D.F. (2009). Direct observation of plasticity and quantitative hardness measurements in single crystal cyclotrimethylene trinitramine by nanoindentation. *Philosophical Magazine* 89, 2381.

Ramos, K.J., Hooks, D.E., Sewell, T.D. & Cawkwell, M.J. (2010). Anomalous hardening under shock compression in (021)-oriented cyclotrimethylene trinitramine single crystals. *Journal of Applied Physics* 108, 066105.

Ravelo, R., Holian, B.L., Germann, T.C. & Lomdahl, P.S. (2004). Constant-stress Hugoniostat method for following the dynamical evolution of shocked matter. *Physical Review B* 70, 014103.

Reaugh, J.E. (2002). Grain-scale dynamics in explosives, Lawrence Livermore National Laboratory Unclassified Report UCRL-ID-150388.

Reed, E.J., Fried, L.E. & Joannopoulos, J.D. (2003). A method for tractable dynamical studies of single and double shock compression. *Physical Review Letters* 90, 235503.

Rice, B.M. & Sewell, T.D. (2008). Molecular dynamics simulations of energetic materials at thermodynamic equilibrium, in *Energetic Materials at Static High Pressures,* Piermarini G. and Peiris, S.M., Eds. (Springer-Verlag, Heilderberg).

Sandusky, H.W., Paul Chamber, G. & Carlson, V.J. (1998). Setback simulation of fielded and candidate explosive fill for 5"/54 guns. *Proceedings of 1998 JANNAF Propulsion Systems Hazards Subcommittee Meeting,* CPIA Publ. 681, Vol. II, p. 137-145.

Scammon, R.J., Browning, R.V., Middleditch, J., Dienes, J.K., Haberman, K.S. & Bennett, J.G. (1998). Low amplitude insult project: structural analysis and prediction of low order reaction. *Proceedings of 11th Int. Detonation Symposium,* Snowmass, USA, August 1998.

Scholtes, J.H.G., Bouma, R.H.B., Weterings, F.P., & van der Steen, A.C. (2002). Thermal and mechanical damage of PBXs. *Proceedings of 12th International Detonation Symposium*, San Diego, USA, August 2002.

Schwarz, R.B., Hooks, D.E., Dick, J.J., Archuleta, J.I., and Martinez, A.R. (2005). Resonant ultrasound spectroscopy measurement of the elastic constants of cyclotrimethylene trinitramine. *Journal of Applied Physics* 98, 056106.

Sewell, T. D., and Bennett, C. M. (2000). Monte Carlo calculations of the elastic moduli and pressure-volume-temperature equation of state for hexahydro-1,3,5-trinitro-1,3,5-triazine. *Journal of Applied Physics* 88, 88.

Sewell, T.D. (2008). Atomistic-based mesoscopic constitutive models for high explosive constituent materials. *Final report for project 49449-EG*, (2008).

Sewell, T.D., Menikoff, R., Bedrov, D. & Smith, G.D. (2003). A molecular dynamics simulation study of elastic properties of HMX. *Journal of Chemical Physics* 119, 7417.

Shane Stafford, D. & Jackson, T.L. (2010). Using level sets for creating virtual random packs of non-spherical convex shapes. *Journal of Computational Physics* 229, (2010), 3295-3315.

Shi, Y. & Brenner, D.W. (2008). Molecular simulation of the influence of interface faceting on the shock sensitivity of a model plastic bonded explosive, *Journal of Physical Chemistry B* 112, 14898.

Siavosh-Haghighi, A., & Thompson, D.L. (2006). Molecular dynamics simulations of surface-initiated melting of nitromethane. *Journal of Chemical Physics* 125, 184711.

Siavosh-Haghighi, A., Dawes, R., Sewell, T.D. & Thompson, D.L. (2009). Shock-induced melting of (100)-oriented nitromethane: Structural relaxation. *Journal of Chemical Physics* 131, 064503.

Siavosh-Haghighi, A., Sewell, T.D., and Thompson, D.L. (2010). Molecular dynamics study of the crystallization of nitromethane from the melt. *Journal of Chemical Physics* 133, 194501.

Siavosh-Haghighi, A. and Thompson, D.L. (2011). Unpublished results.

Siviour, C.R., Williamson, D.M., Grantham, S.G., Palmer, S.J.P., Proud, W.G. & Field, J.E. (2004), Split Hopkinson bar measurements of PBXs, In: *Shock Compression of Condensed Matter*, Furnish, M.D., Gupta, Y.M. & Forbes, J.W. (eds.), CP706, American Institute of Physics.

Smith, G. D. & Bharadwaj, R.K. (1999). Quantum chemistry based force field for simulations of HMX. *Journal of Physical Chemistry B* 103, 3570.

Sorescu, D.C., Rice, B.M. & Thompson, D.L. (2000). Theoretical studies of solid nitromethane. *Journal of Physical Chemistry B* 104, 8406.

Stevens, L.L., & Eckhardt, C. J. (2005). The elastic constants and related properties of β-HMX determined by Brillouin scattering, *Journal of Chemical Physics* 122, 174701.

Strachan, A. & Holian, B.L. (2005). Energy exchange between mesoparticles and their internal degrees of freedom. *Physical Review Letters* 94, 014301.

Strachan, A., Kober, E.M., van Duin, A.C.T., Oxgaard, J. & Goddard III, W.A. (2005). Thermal decomposition of RDX from reactive molecular dynamics. *The Journal of Chemical Physics*, 122, 054502.

Stuart, S.J., Tutein, A.B., & Harrison, J.A. (2000). A reactive potential for hydrocarbons with intermolecular interactions. *Journal of Chemical Physics* 112, 6472.

Sun, B., Winey, J.M., Hemmi, N., Dreger, Z.A., Zimmerman, K.A., Gupta, Y.M., Torchinsky, D.H., & Nelson, K.A. (2008). Second-order elastic constants of pentaerythritol tetranitrate and cyclotrimethylene trinitramine using impulsive stimulated thermal scattering, *Journal of Applied Physics* 104, 073517.

Sun, B., Winey, J. M, Gupta, Y. M., & Hooks, D. E. (2009). Determination of second-order elastic constants of cyclotetramethylene tetranitramine (β-HMX) using impulsive stimulated thermal scattering. *Journal of Applied Physics* 106, 053505.

Swantek, A.B. & Austin, J.M. (2010). Collapse of void arrays under stress wave loading. *Journal of Fluid Mechanics* 649, 399.

Tancreto, J., Swisdak, M. & Malvar, J. (1994). High Performance Magazine acceptor threshold criteria. *Proceedings of 26th DDESB Seminar*, Miami, USA, August 1994.

Thompson, D., Sewell, T., Bouma, R.H.B. & van der Heijden, A.E.D.M. (2010). Investigation of fundamental processes and crystal-level defect structures in metal-loaded high-explosive materials under dynamic thermo-mechanical loads and their relationships to impact survivability of munitions. Project HDTRA1-10-1-0078.

Tuckerman, M.E. (2010). *Statistical Mechanics: Theory and Molecular Simulation* (Oxford University Press, U.S.A.)

Tuckerman, M.E. & Klein, M.L. (1998). Ab initio molecular dynamics study of solid nitromethane. *Chemical Physics Letters* 283, 147.

UN (2008). *Recommendations on the transport of dangerous goods, Manual of tests and criteria.* Available from https://unp.un.org/Details.aspx?pid=17299.

Van Duin, A.C.T., Dasgupta, S., Lorant, F. & Goddard, W. A. III (2001). ReaxFF: A reactive force field for hydrocarbons. *Journal of Physical Chemistry A* 105, 9396.

Van der Heijden, A.E.D.M. & Bouma, R.H.B. (2004). Crystallization and characterization of RDX, HMX and Cl-20. *Crystal Growth and Design*, 4, (2004), 999-1007.

Van der Heijden, A.E.D.M., Bouma, R.H.B. & van der Steen, A.C. (2004). Physicochemical parameters of nitramines determining shock sensitivity. *Propellants, Explosives, Pyrotechnics* 29 (2004) 304-313.

Van der Heijden, A.E.D.M. & Bouma, R.H.B. (2010). Energetic Materials: Crystallization and Characterization, in: *Handbook of Material Science Research*, eds. René, C. & Turcotte, E., 2010, ISBN 978-1-60741-798-9.

Vandersall, K.S., Switzer, L.L. & Garcia, F. (2006). Threshold studies on TNT, Composition B, C-4 and ANFO explosives using the Steven impact test. *Proceedings of 13th Int. Detonation Symposium*, Norfolk, USA, July 2006.

Van Wees, R.M.M., van Dongen, Ph. & Bouma, R.H.B. (2004). The participation of the Netherlands in the UK/AUS defense trial 840. Study of barricades to prevent sympathetic detonation in field storage. *Proceedings of 31th DoD Explosives Safety Seminar*, San Antonio, USA, August 2004.

Wallace, I.G. (1994). Spigot Intrusion. *Proceedings of 26th DoD Explosives Safety Seminar*, Miami, USA.

Winey, J.M. & Gupta, Y.M. (2001). Second-order elastic constants for pentaerythritol tetranitrate single crystals. Journal of Applied Physics 90, 1669.

Winey, J.M. & Gupta, Y.M. (2010). Anisotropic material model and wave propagation simulations for shocked pentaerythritol tetranitrate single crystals. *Journal of Applied Physics* 107, 103505.

Wood, W.W. (1968) in *Physics of Simple Fluids*, edited by Temperley, H.N.V., Rowlinson, J.S., and Rushbrooke G.S. (North-Holland, Amsterdam), Ch. 5, p. 115.

Yan-Qing, W. & Feng-Lei, H. (2009). A micromechanical model for predicting combined damage of particles and interface debonding in PBX explosives. *Mechanics of Materials*, 41, (2009), 27-47.

Zamiri, A.R. & De, S. (2010). Deformation distribution maps of β-HMX molecular crystals. *Journal of Physics D: Applied Physics* 43, 035404.

Zaug, J. M. (1998). Elastic constants of β-HMX and tantalum, equations of state of supercritical fluids and mixtures and thermal transport determinations. *Proceedings of the 11th International Detonation Symposium*, Snowmass, CO, Aug 31-Sept 4, 498.

Zerilli, F.J., Guirguis, R.H. & Coffey, C.S. (2002). A burn model based on heating due to shear flow: proof of principle calculations. *Proceedings of 12th Int. Detonation Symposium*, San Diego, USA, August 2002.

Zerilli, F.J. & Kuklja, M.M. (2007). *Ab initio* equation of state of an organic molecular crystal: 1,1-diamino-2,2-dinitroethylene. *Journal of Physical Chemistry A* 111, 1721.

Zheng, L., Luo, S.-N., & Thompson, D.L. (2006). Molecular dynamics simulations of melting and the glass transition in nitromethane. *Journal of Chemical Physics* 124, 154504.

Zybin, S.V., Goddard III, W.A., Xu, P., van Duin, A.C.T. & Thompson, A.P. (2010). Physical mechanism of anisotropic sensitivity in pentaerythritol tetranitrate from compressive-shear reaction dynamics simulations. *Applied Physics Letters* 96, 081918.

3

Numerical Simulation of EIT-Based Slow Light in the Doppler-Broadened Atomic Media of the Rubidium D2 Line

Yi Chen[1], Xiao Gang Wei[2] and Byoung Seung Ham[3]
[1]*Institute of Atomic and Molecular Physics, Jilin University*
[2]*College of Physics, Jilin University*
[3]*School of Electrical Engineering, Inha University*
[1,2]*China*
[3]*South Korea*

1. Introduction

Quantum coherence and interference effects (Scully & Zubairy, 1997) in atomic systems have attracted great attention in the last two decades. With quantum coherence, the absorption and dispersion properties of an optical medium can be extremely modified, and can lead to many important effects such as coherent population trapping (CPT) (Arimondo & Orriols, 1976; Alzetta et al., 1976; Gray et al., 1978), lasing without inversion (LWI) (Harris, 1989; Scully et al., 1989; Padmabandu et al., 1996), electromagnetically induced transparency (EIT) (Boller et al., 1991; Harris, 1997; Ham et al., 1997; Phillips et al., 2003; Fleischhauer et al., 2005; Marangos, 1998), high refractive index without absorption (Scully, 1991; Scully & Zhu, 1992; Harris et al., 1990), giant Kerr effect (Schmidt & Imamoglu, 1996), slow and fast light (Boyd & Gauthier, 2002), light storage (Phillips et al., 2001), and other effects. In particular, EIT plays an important role in the quantum optics area.

EIT, named by Harris and his co-workers, has been extensively studied both experimentally and theoretically since it was proposed in 1990 (Harris et al., 1990). Harris et al. first experimentally demonstrated EIT in Sr atomic vapour in 1991 (Boller et al., 1991), providing the basis for further EIT works. Subsequently, M. Xiao and co-workers successfully observed the EIT effect in Rb vapor by using continuous wave (CW) diode lasers (Xiao et al., 1995; Li & Xiao, 1995). This work simplified EIT research, and attracted related research. With the growth of EIT technique, the researchers also realized EIT in several solid state materials and semiconductors (Serapoglia et al., 2000; Zhao et al., 1997; Ham et al., 1997). These works provide a firm foundation for EIT-based applications.

One of EIT applications is slow light. Due to the steep dispersion property within the EIT transparency window, EIT can be used to control the group velocity of light. In the past decade, ultraslow group velocity based on EIT (Harris et al., 1992) has drawn much attention to quantum optical applications, such as quantum memories (Liu et al., 2001; Turukhin et al., 2002; Julsgaard et al., 2004), quantum entanglement generations (Lukin & Hemmer, 2000; Petrosyan & Kurizki, 2002; Paternostro et al., 2003), quantum routing (Ham, 2008), and quantum information processing (Nielsen & Chuang, 2000). So far EIT-based slow light has been observed in many media. In 1995, S. E. Harris and co-workers observed group velocity as slow as c /165 in Pb vapour (Kasapi et al., 1995). In 1999, Hau et al. obtained the famous ultraslow group velocity 17 m/s in Bose-Einstein condensate of Na (Hau et al., 1999). In the same year, Scully et al. reported the group velocity of 90 m/s in hot rubidium gas (360 K) (Kash et al., 1999). In 2002, the light speed of 45 m/s was demonstrated in an optically dense crystal of Pr doped Y_2SiO_5 by B. S. Ham et al. (Turukhin et al., 2002).

Based on deeply investigated EIT and slow light in simple three-level system, recently, researchers have turned their interests to multi-level system, which may render more interesting phenomena and closer to the realistic situations. In this chapter, we will study EIT and EIT-based slow light in a Doppler-broadened six-level atomic system of the rubidium D2 line. This research work may offer a clearer understanding of the slow light phenomenon in the complicated multi-level system, and also present a system whose hyperfine states are closely spaced within the Doppler broadening for potential applications of optical and quantum information processing, such as multichannel all-optical buffer memories and slow-light-based enhanced cross-phase modulation (Petrosyan & Kurizki, 2002; Paternostro et al., 2003).

This chapter is organized as following: In section 2, we brief review EIT in a three-level system and discuss EIT in a Doppler-broadened multi-level atomic system of the rubidium D2 line. In section 3, based on the results we obtained in section 2, we study EIT-based slow light in the same atomic system. In section 4, we introduce an N-type system, and numerically simulate slow light phenomenon in such kind of system. Finally, section 5 offers conclusions.

2. EIT in the Doppler-broadened multi-level atomic system of ^{87}Rb D2 line

2.1 Brief review of EIT in a three-level system

EIT is one of the most important quantum coherent effects, and also serves as the foundation of this chapter. We will first review the optical properties of EIT in a three-level system. Fig. 1 shows the most famous three types of EIT scheme: lambda, ladder, and vee. Among these three EIT types, the lambda type is the best candidate to obtain EIT and EIT-related effects. For this reason, we will illustrate the EIT phenomenon by using the lambda configuration.

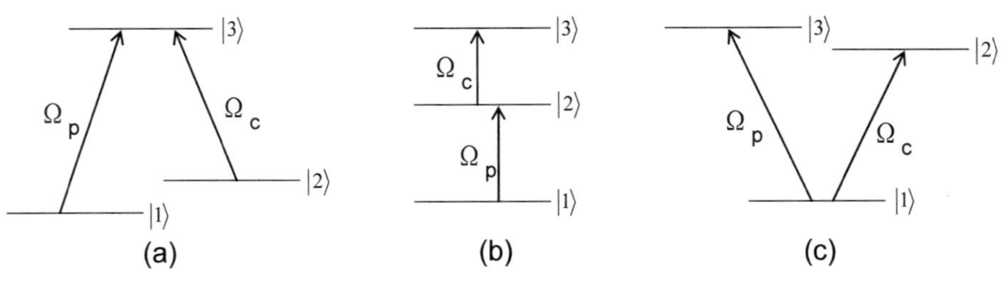

Fig. 1. Schematic of EIT in (a) lambda, (b) ladder, and (c) vee-type schemes.

In the absence of the coupling field Ω_c, absorption of the probe field is described by the blue curve in Fig. 2(a). When the probe frequency is resonant with the transition |1> – |3>, the probe field is strong absorbed by the medium. When we add a coupling field to the system, the strong absorbed peak of the probe disappears at the resonant frequency due to this coupling field (red curve in Fig. 2(a)). This means that the coupling field can modify the absorption property of the medium, and make the optically medium transparent. The transparent position depends on the detuning of the coupling field, and the transparent degree is determined by the Rabi frequency of the coupling field. The physics underlying the EIT can be clearly explained by the dressed state theory (Scully & Zubairy, 1997): almost zero absorption at the resonant frequency is due to the destructive interference between two channels. Except for making the opaque media transparent, the steep dispersion characteristic at the resonant region (see red curve in Fig. 2(b)) is another important feature of EIT. This steep dispersion characteristic allows for control of the group velocity of the light, and opens up a series of promising applications.

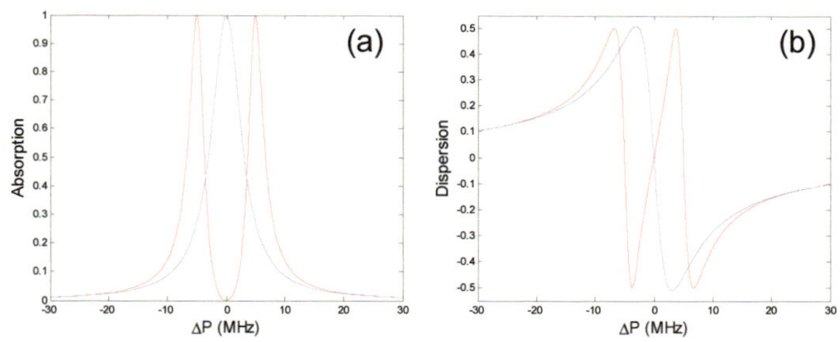

Fig. 2. (a) Absorption and (b) dispersion of probe field as a function of probe detuning for a three-level lambda system.

2.2 EIT in the multi-level atomic system of ^{87}Rb D2 line

Based on the theory of EIT in a three-level system, now we can study the EIT phenomenon in a multi-level atomic system.

2.2.1 Model and theory

An energy level diagram of the ^{87}Rb D2 line is shown in Fig. 3. It shows a six-level atomic system, where F=1 (|1>) and F=2 (|2>) of $5S_{1/2}$ form two ground levels and F′=0, 1, 2, 3 (|3>, |4>, |5>, |6>) of $5P_{3/2}$ form excited levels. The coupling field with frequency ω_c and amplitude E_c couples the levels |4> and |2>, while the probe field with frequency ω_p and amplitude E_p couples the levels |4> and |1>. The frequency detuning of the coupling and probe is given by $\Delta_c = \omega_c - \omega_{42}$ and $\Delta_p = \omega_p - \omega_{41}$, respectively. Thus, a typical Λ-type EIT scheme can be satisfied.

In the framework of semiclassical theory, the Hamiltonian for this scheme is given by $H=H_0+H_1$, where H_0 and H_1 represent the unperturbed and interaction parts of the Hamiltonian, respectively. The interaction Hamiltonian H_1 can be written as:

$$H_1 = -\frac{\hbar}{2}(\Omega_{p31}e^{-i\omega_p t}|3\rangle\langle 1| + \Omega_{p41}e^{-i\omega_p t}|4\rangle\langle 1| + \Omega_{p51}e^{-i\omega_p t}|5\rangle\langle 1| \\ + \Omega_{c42}e^{-i\omega_c t}|4\rangle\langle 2| + \Omega_{c52}e^{-i\omega_c t}|5\rangle\langle 2| + \Omega_{c26}e^{-i\omega_c t}|6\rangle\langle 2| + H.C.) \tag{1}$$

where $\Omega_{pi1} = \mu_{i1}E_p / \hbar$ is the Rabi frequency of the probe field for the transition |i> – |1> (i =3,4,5), and $\Omega_{Cj2} = \mu_{j2}E_C / \hbar$ is the Rabi frequency of the coupling field for the transition |j> – |2> (j =4,5,6). For the ^{87}Rb D2 line, the transitions $5S_{1/2}$, F=2→$5P_{3/2}$, F′=0 and $5S_{1/2}$, F=1→$5P_{3/2}$, F′=3 are forbidden.

Under the rotating-wave approximation, the density matrix equation of motion for the interaction Hamiltonian is described by:

$$\dot{\rho} = -\frac{i}{\hbar}[H_I, \rho] - \frac{1}{2}\{\Gamma, \rho\}. \quad (2)$$

The susceptibility $\chi(\Delta_p) = \chi' + i\chi''$ can be obtained by solving this density matrix equation numerically under the steady state condition, where χ' and χ'' represent dispersion and absorption, respectively. Under the Doppler broadening which resulted from the random motions of atoms, the total susceptibility for all excited levels becomes:

$$\chi_{Dop}(\Delta_P) = \int_{-\infty}^{\infty} \chi(\Delta_P, v) \frac{N}{v_p\sqrt{\pi}} e^{-v^2/v_p^2} dv \quad (3)$$

where N is the atom density, $v_p = \sqrt{2kT/m} = \sqrt{2RT/M}$ is the most probable atom velocity, k is the Boltzmann constant, R is the gas constant, and T is the temperature of the atomic system. In Eq. (3), Δ_P and Δ_C are substituted by $\Delta_P - \omega_{41}v/c$ and $\Delta_C - \omega_{42}v/c$, respectively.

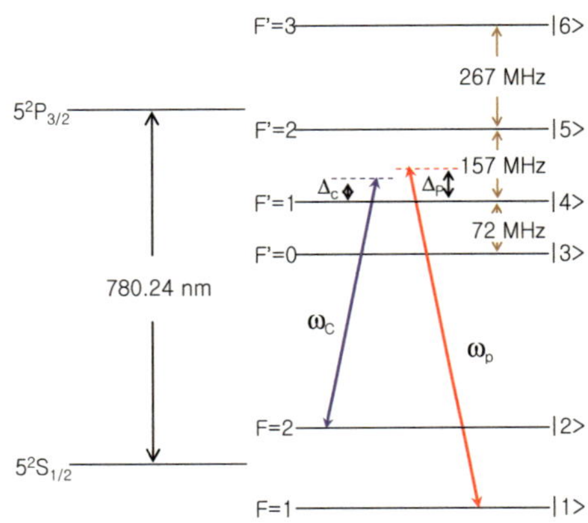

Fig. 3. Schematic diagram of a six-level ^{87}Rb (D2 line) atomic system for EIT.

2.2.2 Numerical simulations and discussion

We consider the following cases:

Case I: The coupling laser is resonant with the transition $5S_{1/2}$, F=2→$5P_{3/2}$, F′=1 (|2> – |4>);
Case II: The coupling laser is resonant with the center line between the level $5P_{3/2}$, F′=1 and $5P_{3/2}$, F′=2 from level $5S_{1/2}$, F=2;
Case III: The coupling laser is resonant with the transition $5S_{1/2}$, F=2→$5P_{3/2}$, F′=2 (|2> – |5>);
Case IV: The coupling laser is resonant with the center line between the level $5P_{3/2}$, F′=1 and $5P_{3/2}$, F′=3 from level $5S_{1/2}$, F=2;
Case V: The coupling laser is resonant with the center line between the level $5P_{3/2}$, F′=2 and $5P_{3/2}$, F′=3 from level $5S_{1/2}$, F=2;
Case VI: The coupling laser is resonant with the transition $5S_{1/2}$, F=2→$5P_{3/2}$, F′=3 (|2> – |6>).

Based on the density matrix equations obtained in the previous subsection, we can numerically calculate the Doppler-broadened absorption (Fig. 4(a)) and dispersion (Fig. 4(b)) of the probe for a particular transition with different Rabi frequencies of the coupling field, where the coupling (probe) is tuned to the transition |4> – |2> (|4> – |1>) in case I. The parameters used in Fig. 4 are T=50°C, $\Gamma_{21} = 0.3$ MHz, $\Gamma_{31} = 6$ MHz, $\Gamma_{41} = 5$ MHz, $\Gamma_{51} = 3$ MHz, $\Gamma_{42} = 1$ MHz, $\Gamma_{52} = 3$ MHz, $\Gamma_{62} = 6$ MHz, $\Omega_{C42} = \sqrt{1/20}\,\Omega_C$, $\Omega_{C52} = 1/2\Omega_C$, $\Omega_{C62} = \sqrt{7/10}\,\Omega_C$, $\Delta_{34} = 72$ MHz, $\Delta_{45} = 157$ MHz, $\Delta_{56} = 267$ MHz, and $\Delta_c = 0$ MHz.

Unlike the Doppler-free case in an ideal three-level system, where EIT line center locates at two-photon resonance frequency, EIT detuning exists in the multilevel system of Fig. 3, even with a small coupling Rabi frequency much less than the separation between the nearest neighboring state |3> (see the inset of Fig. 4(a)). When the Rabi frequency of the coupling increases, the EIT linewidth becomes wider. In particular, the EIT position is variable for different Rabi frequencies, whereas in a three-level system, it is not. As the Rabi frequency of the coupling field increases, the EIT position becomes more red-shifted, due to the extra interactions with the neighboring excited levels and the different dipole moment between different transitions.

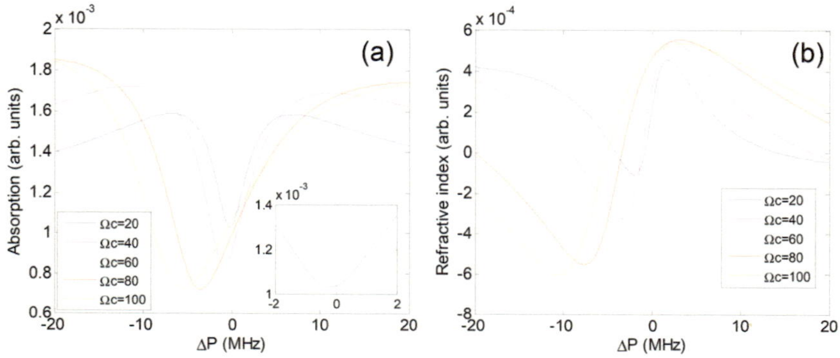

Fig. 4. The absorption (a) and dispersion spectra (b) for a six-level Doppler-broadened system (Case I).

In exploring this phenomenon further, we neglect the level |6> in the structure shown in Fig. 3 and assume that the transition |3> – |2> is allowed for the coupling field. Furthermore, we assume the neighboring levels are symmetrically distributed ($\triangle_{34}$=$\triangle_{45}$=72 MHz). By setting the same decay rates and the same dipole moments for all transitions ($\Omega_{C32} = \Omega_{C42} = \Omega_{C52} = 40$ MHz), the system becomes symmetrical. There is no EIT detuning in this system, as shown in Fig. 5(a). In the ^{87}Rb D2 line, the level $5P_{3/2}$, F'=0 is much nearer the level $5P_{3/2}$, F'=1 than the level $5P_{3/2}$, F'=2 ($\triangle_{34}$=72 MHz, $\triangle_{45}$=157 MHz). Under this condition, and keeping all the decay rates and dipole moments the same, we find that the EIT position becomes red shifted (Fig. 5(b)). However, if we assume unbalanced dipole moments ($\mu_{52} = 2\mu_{32} = 2\mu_{42}$, $\Omega_{C32} = \Omega_{C42} = \Omega_{C52}/2 = 40$ MHz) for the neighboring levels symmetrically distributed ($\Delta_{34} = \Delta_{45} = 72$ MHz), we also find that the EIT position is red shifted as shown in Fig. 5(c). If we use another unbalanced dipole moments condition ($\mu_{32} = 2\mu_{52} = 2\mu_{42}$), then the EIT position becomes blue shifted as shown in Fig. 5(d).

By using the parameters in the ^{87}Rb D2 line, for Cases I through VI (I: $\triangle_c$=0 MHz; II: $\triangle_c$ =157/2 MHz; III: $\triangle_c$=157 MHz; IV: $\triangle_c$=157+267/2 MHz; V: $\triangle_c$= (157+267)/2 MHz; VI: $\triangle_c$ =157+267 MHz), we calculate the Doppler broadened absorption of the probe field as a function of one-photon detuning for corresponding $\triangle_c$. As shown in Fig. 6, EIT red detuning always occurs, because in the ^{87}Rb D2 line, the relative dipole matrix elements are $\sqrt{1/20}$, 1/2, $\sqrt{7/10}$ for the transitions |2> – |4>, |2> – |5> and |2> – |6>, and the neighboring levels are unsymmetrically distributed ($\triangle_{34}$=72 MHz, $\triangle_{45}$=157 MHz, $\triangle_{56}$=267 MHz). In Fig. 6, the Rabi frequency of the coupling field is $\Omega_C = 80$ MHz, and other parameters are same as those in Fig. 4.

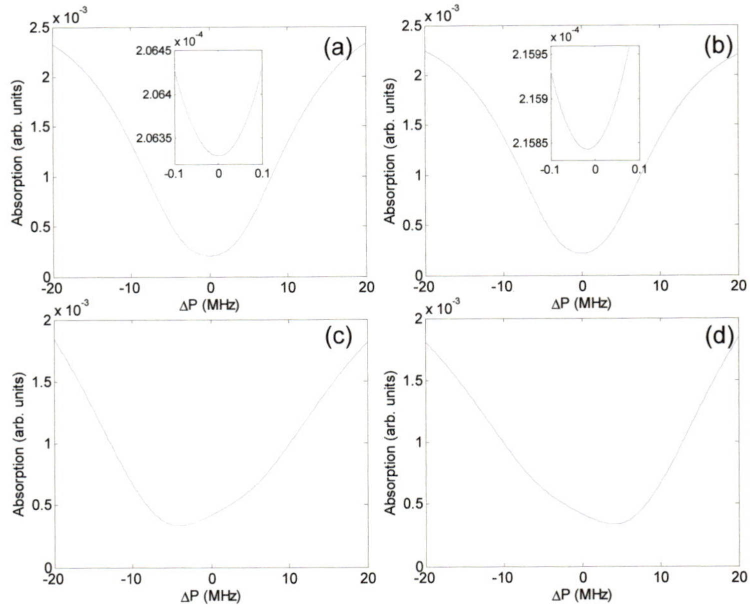

Fig. 5. The absorption spectra for a five-level Doppler-broadened system.

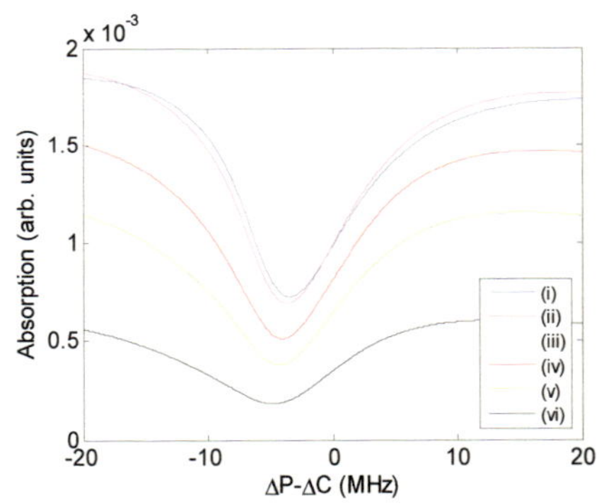

Fig. 6. The absorption spectra for a six-level Doppler-broadened system for Cases I ~ VI.

3. EIT-based slow light in the multi-level atomic system of ^{87}Rb D2 line

Because of the steep dispersion spectrum directly resulting from the narrower EIT window according to the Kramers Kronig relation, the group velocity of the probe pulse can be much smaller than the group velocity in vacuum. The group velocity and the group delay are given by:

$$v_g = \frac{c}{n + \omega \dfrac{dn}{d\omega}} \tag{4}$$

$$\tau_g = L\left(\frac{1}{v_g} - \frac{1}{c}\right) \tag{5}$$

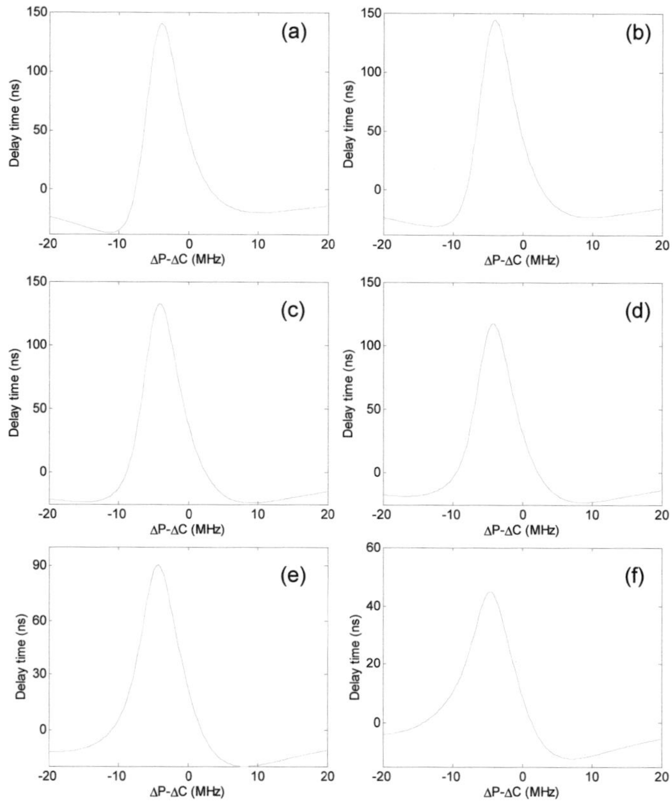

Fig. 7. Group delay time of the probe as a function of the probe detuning for Cases I ~ VI.

where L is the length of the medium, c is the speed of light in vacuum, and n is given by $n = \sqrt{1+\chi'}$.

The neighboring excited-state-modified Doppler broadened atoms affect on the EIT line center shifted, resulting in the so-called detuned slow light phenomenon. In Fig. 7 we numerically calculate the group delay of each case mentioned in above, using reasonable parameters according to the actual experimental condition. (Here we choose the same parameters as those in Fig. 6, and let L=7.5 cm).

For all cases, the probe shows a red shift to the slow light. In Fig. 7 (a), for instance, the maximum group delay is red-shifted for the resonant transition by ~ 4 MHz. When the coupling field is tuned to the crossover transitions as shown in Figs. 7(b), 7(d), and 7(e), first, the slow light phenomenon also exists; and second, the maximum group delay position is also detuned from the crossover line center. Even when the coupling field is resonant with the transition |2> – |6> (Case VI) (transition |2> – |6> is forbidden to the probe), there also exists slow light and group delay detuning, due to the EIT effects from levels |4> and |5>. For more detail information and experimental results see Ref. (Chen et al., 2009).

4. Slow light in N-type system of ^{87}Rb D2 line

In this section, we investigate coherent control of the four-level N-type scheme in a Doppler-broadened six-level atomic system of the ^{87}Rb D2 line (Chen et al., 2009). With limited spectral distribution of the excited hyperfine states in the ^{87}Rb D2 line, which is confined by the Doppler broadening, each hyperfine state can be used for individual optical channels for optical quantum information processing. For this application we choose nonelectromagnetically induced absorption (EIA) schemes for the investigation of reduced absorption spectra resulting in Mollow sideband-like enhanced transparency windows across the EIT line center. Unlike a double-EIT system satisfied by rigid (uncontrollable) two coupling fields applicable only for a single slow-light channel, the present scheme uses a fixed coupling field with a variable control field, where group velocity control and multiple slow-light channels are applicable.

N-type scheme in a Doppler-broadened six-level atomic system of the ^{87}Rb D2 line is shown in Fig. 8. It is similar to EIT situation, but with a third coherent field (the control field) at a frequency ω_S with an amplitude E_S couples the transition |3> – |1> ($5S_{1/2}$, F=1 → $5P_{3/2}$, F′=0) with a detuning of Δ_S ($\Delta_S = \omega_{31} - \omega_S$).

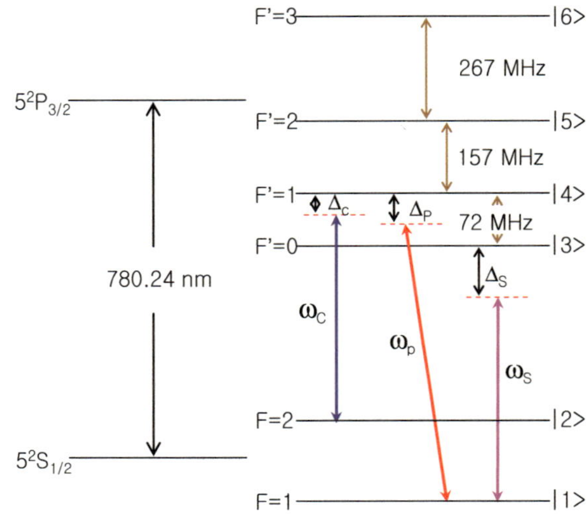

Fig. 8. Schematic of a Doppler-broadened six-level atomic system of the ^{87}Rb D2 line interacting with three coherent fields.

In a framework of the semiclassical theory, under the rotating-wave approximation, we obtain the following density matrix equations of motion for the interaction Hamiltonian:

$$\dot{\rho}_{11} = \frac{i}{2}\Omega_{S31}(\rho_{31} - \rho_{13}) + \frac{i}{2}\Omega_{S41}(\rho_{41} - \rho_{14}) + \frac{i}{2}\Omega_{S51}(\rho_{51} - \rho_{15}) + \Gamma_{31}\rho_{33} + \Gamma_{41}\rho_{44} + \Gamma_{51}\rho_{55} + \Gamma_{21}\rho_{22} - \Gamma_{21}\rho_{11},$$

$$\dot{\rho}_{12} = (i\Delta_S + i\Delta_{34} - i\Delta_C - \gamma_{12})\rho_{12} + \frac{i}{2}\Omega_{S31}\rho_{32} + \frac{i}{2}\Omega_{S41}\rho_{42} + \frac{i}{2}\Omega_{S51}\rho_{52} - \frac{i}{2}\Omega_{C42}\rho_{14} - \frac{i}{2}\Omega_{C52}\rho_{15} - \frac{i}{2}\Omega_{C62}\rho_{16},$$

$$\dot{\rho}_{13} = (i\Delta_S - \gamma_{13})\rho_{13} + \frac{i}{2}\Omega_{S31}(\rho_{33} - \rho_{11}) + \frac{i}{2}\Omega_{S41}\rho_{43} + \frac{i}{2}\Omega_{S51}\rho_{53},$$

$$\dot{\rho}_{14} = (i\Delta_S + i\Delta_{34} - \gamma_{14})\rho_{14} + \frac{i}{2}\Omega_{S31}\rho_{34} + \frac{i}{2}\Omega_{S41}(\rho_{44} - \rho_{11}) + \frac{i}{2}\Omega_{S51}\rho_{54} - \frac{i}{2}\Omega_{C42}\rho_{12},$$

$$\dot{\rho}_{15} = (i\Delta_S + i\Delta_{35} - \gamma_{15})\rho_{15} + \frac{i}{2}\Omega_{S31}\rho_{35} + \frac{i}{2}\Omega_{S41}\rho_{45} + \frac{i}{2}\Omega_{S51}(\rho_{55} - \rho_{11}) - \frac{i}{2}\Omega_{C52}\rho_{12},$$

$$\dot{\rho}_{16} = (i\Delta_S + i\Delta_{36} - \gamma_{16})\rho_{16} + \frac{i}{2}\Omega_{S31}\rho_{36} + \frac{i}{2}\Omega_{S41}\rho_{46} + \frac{i}{2}\Omega_{S51}\rho_{56} - \frac{i}{2}\Omega_{C62}\rho_{12}$$

$$\dot{\rho}_{22} = \frac{i}{2}\Omega_{C42}(\rho_{42} - \rho_{24}) + \frac{i}{2}\Omega_{C52}(\rho_{52} - \rho_{25}) + \frac{i}{2}\Omega_{C62}(\rho_{62} - \rho_{26}) + \Gamma_{42}\rho_{44} + \Gamma_{52}\rho_{55}$$
$$+ \Gamma_{62}\rho_{66} + \Gamma_{21}\rho_{11} - \Gamma_{21}\rho_{22},$$

$$\dot{\rho}_{23} = (i\Delta_C - i\Delta_{34} - \gamma_{23})\rho_{23} + \frac{i}{2}\Omega_{C42}\rho_{43} + \frac{i}{2}\Omega_{C52}\rho_{53} + \frac{i}{2}\Omega_{C62}\rho_{63} - \frac{i}{2}\Omega_{S31}\rho_{21},$$

$$\dot{\rho}_{24} = (i\Delta_C - \gamma_{24})\rho_{24} + \frac{i}{2}\Omega_{C42}(\rho_{44} - \rho_{22}) + \frac{i}{2}\Omega_{C52}\rho_{54} + \frac{i}{2}\Omega_{C62}\rho_{64} - \frac{i}{2}\Omega_{S41}\rho_{21},$$

$$\dot{\rho}_{25} = (i\Delta_C + i\Delta_{45} - \gamma_{25})\rho_{25} + \frac{i}{2}\Omega_{C52}(\rho_{55} - \rho_{22}) + \frac{i}{2}\Omega_{C42}\rho_{45} + \frac{i}{2}\Omega_{C62}\rho_{65} - \frac{i}{2}\Omega_{S51}\rho_{21},$$

$$\dot{\rho}_{26} = (i\Delta_C + i\Delta_{46} - \gamma_{26})\rho_{26} + \frac{i}{2}\Omega_{C62}(\rho_{66} - \rho_{22}) + \frac{i}{2}\Omega_{C42}\rho_{46} + \frac{i}{2}\Omega_{C52}\rho_{56},$$

$$\dot{\rho}_{33} = \frac{i}{2}\Omega_{S31}(\rho_{13} - \rho_{31}) - \Gamma_{31}\rho_{33},$$

$$\dot{\rho}_{34} = (i\Delta_{34} - \gamma_{34})\rho_{34} + \frac{i}{2}\Omega_{S31}\rho_{14} - \frac{i}{2}\Omega_{S41}\rho_{31} - \frac{i}{2}\Omega_{C42}\rho_{32},$$

$$\dot{\rho}_{35} = (i\Delta_{35} - \gamma_{35})\rho_{35} + \frac{i}{2}\Omega_{S31}\rho_{15} - \frac{i}{2}\Omega_{S51}\rho_{31} - \frac{i}{2}\Omega_{C52}\rho_{32},$$

$$\dot{\rho}_{36} = (i\Delta_{36} - \gamma_{36})\rho_{36} + \frac{i}{2}\Omega_{S31}\rho_{16} - \frac{i}{2}\Omega_{C62}\rho_{32},$$

$$\dot{\rho}_{44} = \frac{i}{2}\Omega_{S41}(\rho_{14} - \rho_{41}) + \frac{i}{2}\Omega_{C42}(\rho_{24} - \rho_{42}) - (\Gamma_{41} + \Gamma_{42})\rho_{44},$$

$$\dot{\rho}_{45} = (i\Delta_{45} - \gamma_{45})\rho_{45} + \frac{i}{2}\Omega_{S41}\rho_{15} + \frac{i}{2}\Omega_{C42}\rho_{25} - \frac{i}{2}\Omega_{S51}\rho_{41} - \frac{i}{2}\Omega_{C52}\rho_{42},$$

$$\dot{\rho}_{46} = (i\Delta_{46} - \gamma_{46})\rho_{46} + \frac{i}{2}\Omega_{S41}\rho_{16} + \frac{i}{2}\Omega_{C42}\rho_{26} - \frac{i}{2}\Omega_{C62}\rho_{42},$$

$$\dot{\rho}_{55} = \frac{i}{2}\Omega_{S51}(\rho_{15} - \rho_{51}) + \frac{i}{2}\Omega_{C52}(\rho_{25} - \rho_{52}) - (\Gamma_{51} + \Gamma_{52})\rho_{55},$$

$$\dot{\rho}_{56} = (i\Delta_{56} - \gamma_{56})\rho_{56} + \frac{i}{2}\Omega_{S51}\rho_{16} + \frac{i}{2}\Omega_{C52}\rho_{26} - \frac{i}{2}\Omega_{C62}\rho_{52},$$

$$\rho_{ij} = \rho_{ji}, \quad \rho_{11} + \rho_{22} + \rho_{33} + \rho_{44} + \rho_{55} + \rho_{66} = 1 \tag{6}$$

where $\Omega_{Si1} = \mu_{i1}E_S / \hbar$ is the Rabi frequency of the control field for the transition | i > – |1> (i = 3,4,5). $\Gamma_{ij}(\gamma_{ij})$ stands for the population (phase) decay rate from state |i> to |j>, where Γ_{i1} and Γ_{j2} are the population decay rates from levels |i> to |1> (i = 3,4,5), and levels |j> to |2> (j = 4,5,6), respectively.

In order to calculate the probe absorption spectrum, the density matrix equations (6) can be rewritten in the following form:

$$\frac{d\Psi(t)}{dt} = L\Psi(t) + I \tag{7}$$

where

$$\Psi=(\rho_{11},\rho_{12},\rho_{13},\rho_{14},\rho_{15},\rho_{16},\rho_{21},\rho_{22},\rho_{23},\rho_{24},\rho_{25},\rho_{26},\rho_{31},\rho_{32},\rho_{33},\rho_{34},\rho_{35},\rho_{36},\\ \rho_{41},\rho_{42},\rho_{43},\rho_{44},\rho_{45},\rho_{46},\rho_{51},\rho_{52},\rho_{53},\rho_{54},\rho_{55},\rho_{56},\rho_{61},\rho_{62},\rho_{63},\rho_{64},\rho_{65})^T,$$

and

$$I=(0,0,0,0,0,0,0,\Gamma_{62},0,0,0,i\Omega_{C62}/2,0,0,0,0,0,0,0,0,0,0,0,0,0,0,0,0,0,0,0,-i\Omega_{C62}/2,0,0,0).$$

The solution of Eq. (7) is given by:

$$\Psi(t)=e^{L(t-t_0)}\Psi(t_0)+\int_{t_0}^{t}e^{L(t'-t0)}I\,dt' \tag{8}$$

According to the linear response theory, the steady state absorption spectrum of the weak probe laser can be written as:

$$A(\Delta_P)=\mathrm{Re}\left(\int_0^{\infty}\lim_{t\to\infty}\langle[P^-(t+\tau),P^+(t)]\rangle e^{i\Delta_P\tau}d\tau\right) \tag{9}$$

where $P^-=\mu_{31}|1\rangle\langle 3|+\mu_{41}|1\rangle\langle 4|+\mu_{51}|1\rangle\langle 5|$
and $P^+=\mu_{31}|3\rangle\langle 1|+\mu_{41}|4\rangle\langle 1|+\mu_{51}|5\rangle\langle 1|$ are the atomic polarization operators, with μ_{i1} being the dipole matrix elements of transition $|i\rangle-|1\rangle$ (i = 3,4,5). By using the quantum regression theory, we further obtain the absorption and refraction spectra of the probe field:

$$\begin{aligned}A(\Delta_P)=\mathrm{Re}[\sum_{i=3}^{5}\mu_{i1}(&M_{i,i}\rho_{11}(\infty)+M_{i,6+i}\rho_{21}(\infty)+M_{i,12+i}\rho_{31}(\infty)+M_{i,18+i}\rho_{41}(\infty)\\ &+M_{i,24+i}\rho_{51}(\infty)+M_{i,30+i}\rho_{61}(\infty)-(M_{i,1}\rho_{i1}(\infty)+M_{i,2}\rho_{i2}(\infty)\\ &+M_{i,3}\rho_{i3}(\infty)+M_{i,4}\rho_{i4}(\infty)+M_{i,5}\rho_{i5}(\infty)+M_{i,6}\rho_{i6}(\infty)))]\end{aligned} \tag{10-1}$$

$$\begin{aligned}B(\Delta_P)=\mathrm{Im}[\sum_{i=3}^{5}\mu_{i1}{}^2(&M_{i,i}\rho_{11}(\infty)+M_{i,6+i}\rho_{21}(\infty)+M_{i,12+i}\rho_{31}(\infty)+M_{i,18+i}\rho_{41}(\infty)\\ &+M_{i,24+i}\rho_{51}(\infty)+M_{i,30+i}\rho_{61}(\infty)-(M_{i,1}\rho_{i1}(\infty)+M_{i,2}\rho_{i2}(\infty)+M_{i,3}\rho_{i3}(\infty)\\ &+M_{i,4}\rho_{i4}(\infty)+M_{i,5}\rho_{i5}(\infty)+M_{i,6}\rho_{i6}(\infty)))],\end{aligned} \tag{10-2}$$

where $M=(i\Delta_s+i\Delta_{34}-i\Delta_p-L)^{-1}$ and $\rho_{ij}(\infty)\big|_{i,j=1\to 35}$ are the steady state solutions of Eq. (6).

The effects of Doppler broadening due to the atom's thermal velocity v can be considered by substituting Δ_P, Δ_S and Δ_C with $\Delta_P-\omega_{41}v/c$, $\Delta_S-\omega_{31}v/c$, and $\Delta_C-\omega_{42}v/c$, respectively. Then the total absorption and refraction coefficients of the weak probe are:

$$A(\Delta_P)=\int_{-\infty}^{\infty}A(\Delta_P,v)\frac{N}{v_p\sqrt{\pi}}e^{-v^2/v_p{}^2}dv, \tag{11-1}$$

$$B(\Delta_P) = \int_{-\infty}^{\infty} B(\Delta_P, v) \frac{N}{v_p\sqrt{\pi}} e^{-v^2/v_p^{\,2}} dv, \tag{11-2}$$

where N is the total number of atoms, $v_p = \sqrt{2kT/m} = \sqrt{2RT/M}$ is the most probable atomic velocity, k is the Boltzmann constant, R is the gas constant, and T is the temperature of the atomic system.

Similar as in section 2, we consider the following six types of four-level N-type systems:

Type I: The coupling light is resonant with the transition |2> – |4> ($5S_{1/2}$, F=2→$5P_{3/2}$, F′=1), while the control light is resonant with the transition |1> – |3> ($5S_{1/2}$, F=1→$5P_{3/2}$, F′=0).

Type II: The coupling light is resonant with the transition |2> – |4> ($5S_{1/2}$, F=2→$5P_{3/2}$, F′=1), while the control light is resonant with the transition |1> – |5> ($5S_{1/2}$, F=1→$5P_{3/2}$, F′=2).

Type III: The coupling light is resonant with the transition |2> – |5> ($5S_{1/2}$, F=2→$5P_{3/2}$, F′=2), while the control light is resonant with the transition |1> – |4> ($5S_{1/2}$, F=1→$5P_{3/2}$, F′=1).

Type IV: The coupling light is resonant with the transition |2> – |5> ($5S_{1/2}$, F=2→$5P_{3/2}$, F′=2), while the control light is resonant with the transition |1> – |3> ($5S_{1/2}$, F=1→$5P_{3/2}$, F′=0)

Type V: The coupling light is resonant to the center line between states |4> and |5> from state |2>, while the control light is resonant with the transition |1> – |3> ($5S_{1/2}$, F=1→$5P_{3/2}$, F′=0) with a small detuning δ_1.

Type VI: The coupling light is resonant to the center line between states |5> and |6>from state |2>, while the control light is resonant with the transition |1> – |5> ($5S_{1/2}$, F=1→$5P_{3/2}$, F′=2) with a small detuning δ_2.

Figs. 9 (a), 9 (b), 9 (c), and 9 (d) show the numerical simulation of probe absorption spectra for Type I, Type II, Type III, and Type IV, respectively. Figs. 9(e) ~ 9(h) are energy level diagrams corresponding to Figs. 9(a) ~ 9(d), respectively. The number in parentheses of the coupling C and control S stands for relative transition strength of Rabi frequency.

The parameters used in the simulations are T=25°C, $\Gamma_{21} =$ 0.01 MHz, $\Gamma_{31} = \Gamma_{62} =$ 6 MHz, $\Gamma_{41} = 5$ MHz, $\Gamma_{42} = 1$ MHz, $\Gamma_{51} = \Gamma_{52} = 3$ MHz,$\triangle_{34}$=72 MHz,$\triangle_{45}$=157 MHz,$\triangle_{56}$=267 MHz, $\Omega_S =$ 10 MHz, $\Omega_{C42} = \sqrt{1/20}\Omega_C$, $\Omega_{S41} = \Omega_{S51} = \sqrt{5/12}\Omega_S$, $\Omega_C =$ 30 MHz, $\Omega_{S31} = \sqrt{1/6}\Omega_S$, $\Omega_{C52} = \Omega_C / 2$ and $\Omega_{C62} = \sqrt{7/10}\Omega_C$. The calculations include all level transitions in Fig. 8. The N-type configuration yields interesting results when two-photon resonance is satisfied between the probe and the coupling for (a) $\triangle_p$= 0 MHz, (b) $\triangle_p$=0 MHz, (c) $\triangle_p$=-157 MHz, (d) $\triangle_p$=-157 MHz, (e) $\triangle_p$=-78.5 MHz, and (f) $\triangle_p$=-290.5 MHz.

In Figs. 9(a) and 9(b), the applied coupling Rabi frequency is much weaker than in Figs. 9(c) and 9(d) by a factor of $\sqrt{5}$. In Figs. 9(a) and 9(d), the Rabi frequency of the control field is weaker than in Figs. 9(b) and 9(c) by a factor of $\sqrt{5/2}$. Thus, Fig. 9(c) is for the strongest pump fields, and a symmetric pair of reduced absorption lines across the EIT line center is obtained (the dotted circle and two arrows indicate the reduced absorption lines): Mollow sideband-like transparency windows. The center transparency is much higher than the satellite transparencies. The symmetric sideband absorption bandwidth is comparable to the EIT linewidth or the spectral hole width. The generation of these absorption-reduced sidebands is due to dynamic energy splitting incurred by the control field acting on the coupling field according to dressed state interactions (Kong et al., 2007):

$$|D\rangle = \pm\frac{\Omega'_C}{2} \pm \frac{\Omega'_S}{2} \tag{12}$$

where |D> is the newly developed dressed states by the interaction of the coupling and control fields, and Ω'_C and Ω'_S are effective Rabi frequencies of the coupling and control fields, respectively, including an atom velocity factor (kv). Fig. 9(d) is similar to Fig. 9(c), also shows double sideband transparency windows. For the rest of the combinations of Figs. 9(a) and 9(b), no distinct change is obtained for the Mollow sideband-like transparency windows because of a weak field limit.

In comparison with Fig. 3(c) of Ref. (Kong et al., 2007), where the probe gain results in, rather than the Mollow sideband-like transparency, Fig. 9(c) here needs to be analyzed in more detail (see Fig. 11). Moreover the origin of the Mollow sideband-like effects which appeared in Fig. 4(a) of Ref. (Kong et al., 2007) for the case of $F_e = F_g+1$ by using D2 transition for the coupling but using D1 transition for the control, is the same as in Fig. 9(c) of the present chapter for the case of $F_e \leq F_g$ by using only D2 transition for both fields under the EIT condition. This condition will be discussed in Fig. 11 below.

According to Eq. (12), EIA-like enhanced absorption should be possible if $\Omega_C = \Omega_S$ (see Fig. 11(c)), owing to degenerate dressed states at the EIT line center. The sub-Doppler ultranarrow double transparency windows obtained in Fig. 9(c) have the potential of using double ultraslow light pulses for optical and quantum information processing such as Schrödinger's cat generation or quantum gate operation. For enhanced cross-phase modulation, double EIT-based ultraslow light is required. Multichannel all-optical buffer memory is another potential application.

Fig. 10 shows numerical simulation results of an absorption spectrum when the coupling laser Ω_C is tuned to crossover lines, which is a line center between levels |4> and |5> for Fig. 10(a) and |5> and |6> for Fig. 10(b): Types V and VI, respectively. In each case the Mollow sideband-like transparency windows appear. The control is purposely detuned by 6 MHz for Fig. 10 (a) for the transition |1> ↔ |3> ($5S_{1/2}$, F=1→$5P_{3/2}$, F′=0), and 30 MHz for Fig. 10 (b) for |1> ↔ |5> ($5S_{1/2}$, F=1→$5P_{3/2}$, F′=2). As shown in Fig. 10, the results are very similar to Fig. 9(c). The Mollow sideband-like reduced absorption lines and the hole-burning peak also appears on the right.

We now analyze Fig. 10 as follows, using the velocity selective atoms phenomenon. The original model of Fig. 10(a) can be divided into two models, as shown in the energy level diagram just below Fig. 10. The first row is for Fig. 10(a), and the second row is for Fig. 10(b). The left column is for the original level transition, and the right two columns are decomposed for purposes of analysis. For these two columns of energy-level diagrams, blue-Doppler-shifted atoms (middle column) and red-Doppler-shifted atoms (right column) by $\Delta_1 = 78.5$ MHz or $\Delta_2 = 133.5$ MHz are considered.

In the first row (for Fig. 10(a)) for blue-Doppler-shifted atoms (middle column), the blue shift $\triangle$ ($\triangle$=157/2 = 78.5 MHz) makes both the coupling field (C) and the control field (S) (see the middle column) resonant. This result occurs because initially the control field is red detuned by δ_1 (6 MHz); thus the total shift is 72.5 MHz (78.5 - 6), which is nearly resonant to the transition of |1> ↔ |4>. This outcome is the same as in Fig. 9(c). The right column, however, does not form an N-type model because of a big detuning of $\Delta_1 + \delta_1$. The EIT window cannot be affected by the detuning $\Delta_1 + \delta_1$ if two-photon resonance is satisfied. Actually, signal reduction and line narrowing result, but do not affect the line shape of Fig. 10(a). Therefore, the result of Fig. 10(a) must be the same as for Fig. 9(c).

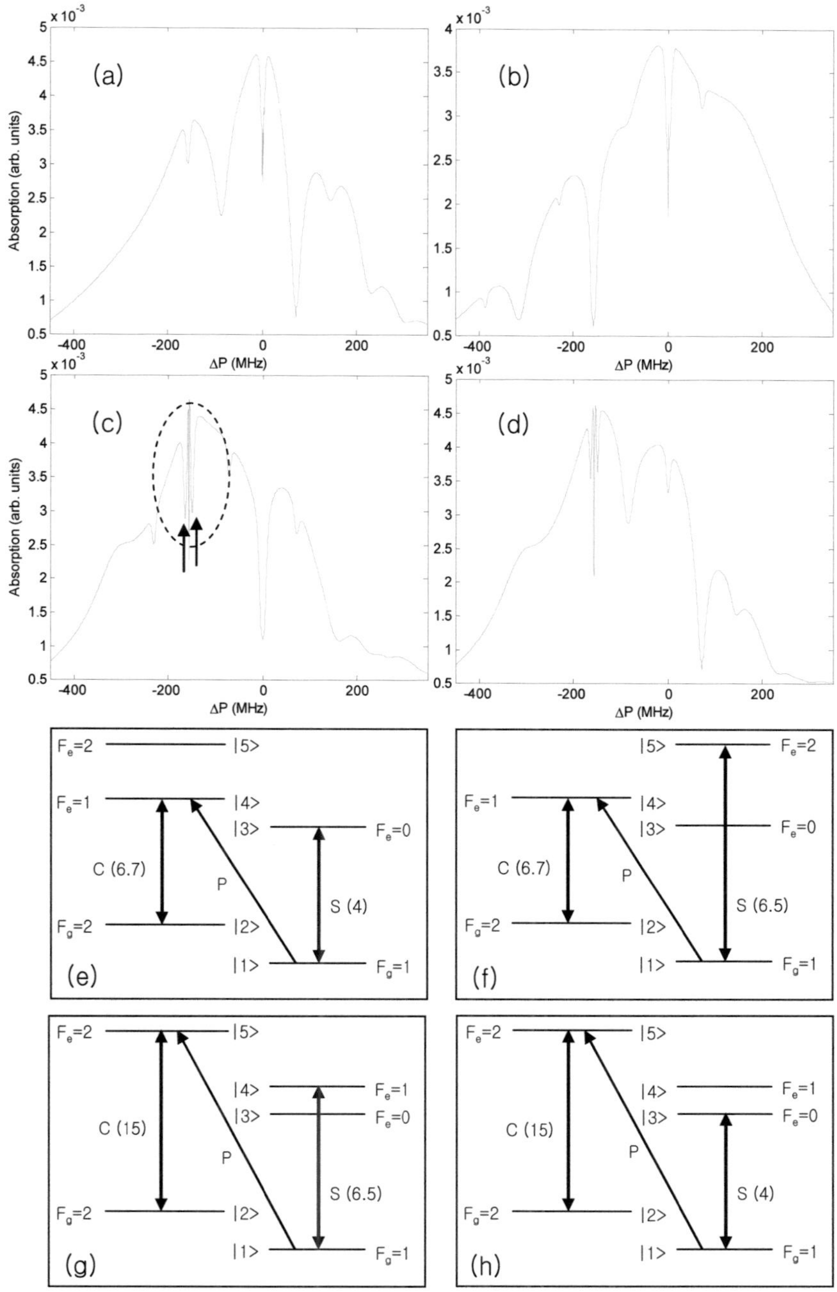

Fig. 9. Numerical calculations for the probe absorption for Type I, Type II, Type III, and Type IV.

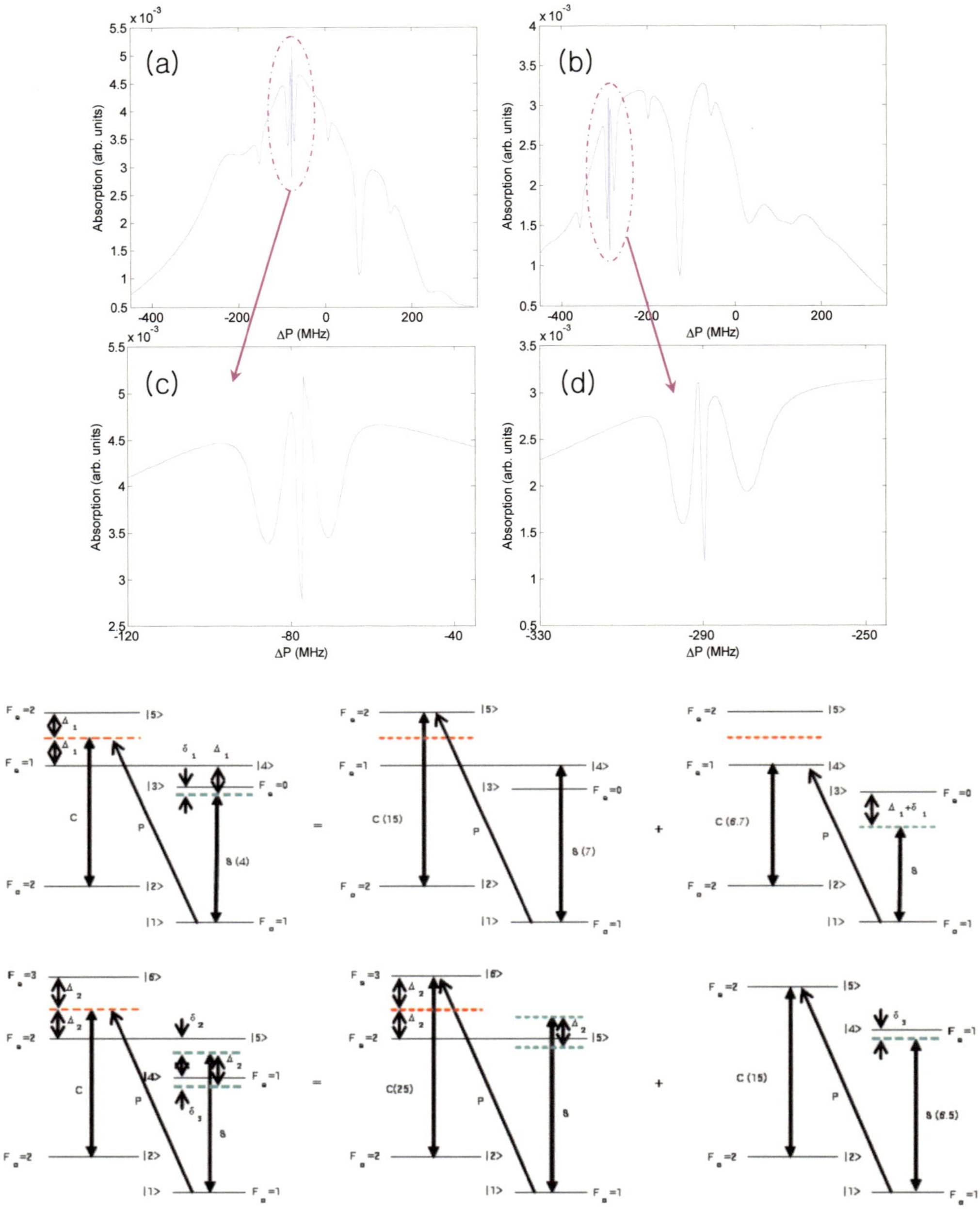

Fig. 10. Numerical calculations for the probe absorption for (a) Type V and (b) Type VI. (c) and (d) are for the extended feature of (a) and (b) , respectively.

In the second row (for Fig. 10(b)), for red-Doppler-shifted atoms (right column), the red shift $\triangle$ ($\triangle$=-267/2=-133.5 MHz) makes the coupling field (C) resonant, but blue detuned to the control field (S) by 23.5 MHz. However, the control field is set to be red detuned by δ_2 (30 MHz) initially; the net detuning is δ_3 (6.5 MHz) to the control, which is red detuned from the transition of |1> ↔ |4>. The two sidebands across the EIT line center are asymmetric. The blue-Doppler-shifted atoms (middle column) do not contribute anything on the sideband transparency windows as discussed for the first row because of too much detuning of the control field to form an N-type model.

Figs. 10(c) and 10(d) represent expanded absorption spectra of Figs. 10(a) and 10(b), respectively. As discussed in above, Fig. 10(c) is for resonant transition, and Fig. 10(d) is for off-resonant transition to the control field. As shown, the off-resonant case generates asymmetric Mollow sideband-like transparency windows with unequal window linewidth. Hence each probe light group velocity at each sideband can be controlled effectively with on-demand detuning of the control field. For the cross-phase modulation, this controllability is important to induce on-demand π phase shift (Petrosyan & Kurizki, 2002; Paternostro et al., 2003).

Fig. 11 represents the probe absorption spectrum versus the control (S) Rabi frequency for a fixed coupling (C) Rabi frequency and population decay rate Γ_{42} (from the excited state |4> to the ground state |2>) in a closed N-type model of Fig. 9(g). In the closed N-type model of Fig. 9(g), the atom flow rate of circulation at the probe line center should depend on both Γ_{42} and the control field strength. For a fast (slow) Γ_{42}, the probe experiences fast circulation and has more change on the probe spectrum. On the other hand, as seen in Fig. 11(c), the dressed state interactions at a low decay rate of $\Gamma_{42} = 1$ MHz results in enhanced absorption at the probe line center when the coupling and the control Rabi frequencies are equal (Kong et al., 2007). As shown in Figs. 11(a) ~ 11(c) for a weak decay rate, the probe gain may not be possible regardless of the control field strength because no population inversion between states |5> and |1> can be obtained. Applying moderate control strength (see the center column), however, one can obtain the probe gain once the system is ready for a fast atom flow rate, for example, with a high decay rate of $\Gamma_{42} = 10$ MHz (see Fig. 11(h)). Thus, the probe gain or EIT-like absorption must be understood in terms of system parameters of both control field strength and the medium's decay rate.

For balanced Rabi frequency between the coupling and the control, the EIA-like enhanced absorption can be obtained in Fig. 11(c). However, this enhanced absorption feature, which resulted from degeneracy of the dressed states (see Eq. (12)), changes into a probe gain if the atom flow rate increases as shown in Fig. 11(f) (see also Fig. 3(c) of Ref. (Kong et al., 2007)). The observation in Fig. 9(b) is for the intermediate case: $\Omega_C \sim \Omega_S$ and 1 MHz < Γ_{52} = 3 MHz < 5 MHz (see Fig. 9(f)). The decay rate falling between Figs. 11(c) and 11(f) explains a transient feature from the EIA-like absorption to the probe gain as seen in Fig. 9(b). We think that the broadened linewidth of the red line at Δ_P=0 in Fig. 9(b), may be caused by this intermediate feature with laser jitter as well as a weak control field. As numerically demonstrated in Fig. 11, the probe gain may not be possible in any types of the ^{87}Rb D2 line in Fig. 9 because the atom flow rate is not fast enough (see $\Gamma_{42} = 1$ MHz in Fig. 9(c)) unless a very strong control field is applied. The formation of Mollow sideband-like transparency windows in Fig. 4 of Ref. (Kong et al., 2007) and Fig. 9(c) of this chapter shows a very similar feature based on the dressed state interactions. However, Ref. (Kong et al., 2007) is not for EIT, while the present scheme is.

By using the Eq. (11-2), we can get the refraction coefficient of the probe. Because of the steep dispersion spectrum resulting from EIT window and sideband-like transparency windows, we can get slow light in three channels. The group velocity is given by Eq. (4).

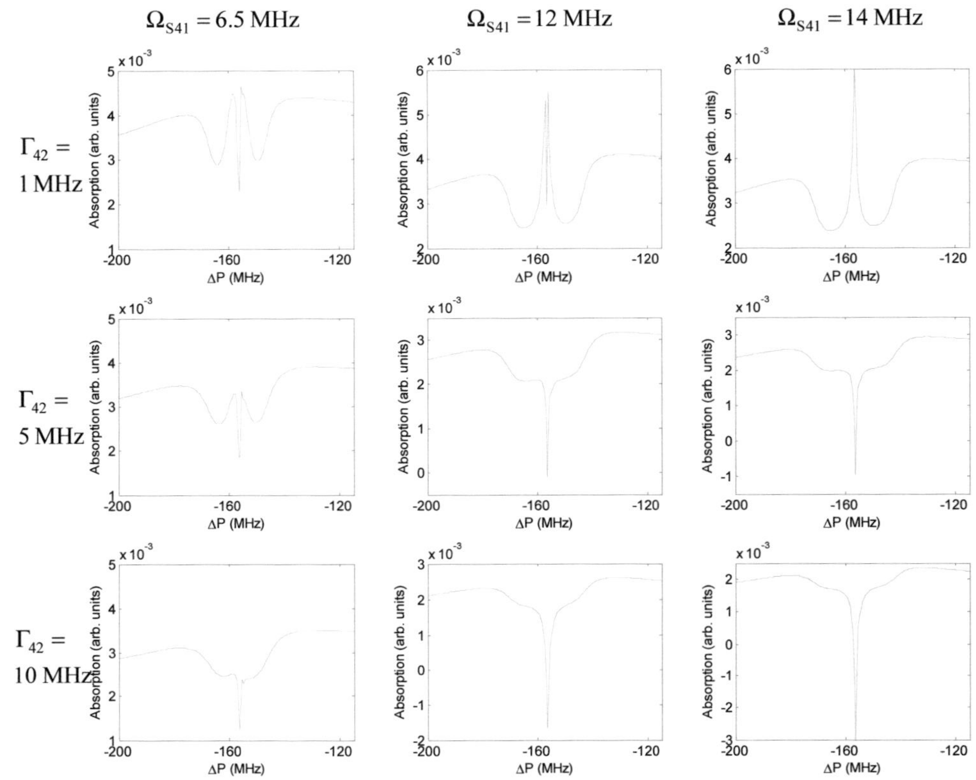

Fig. 11. Probe absorption spectra versus Γ_{42} and Ω_S for the case of Fig. 9(g). (a) The expanded feature of Fig. 9(c). (c) EIA-like enhanced absorption. (f), (h), (i): probe gain.

For the fixed atomic density, the width and depth of EIT widow are mainly depending on the intensity (Rabi frequency) of the coupling laser. The dipole moment of transition $|2\rangle \leftrightarrow |5\rangle$ is larger than the dipole moment of transition $|2\rangle \leftrightarrow |4\rangle$ by a factor $\sqrt{5}$, this means we have large slow light when the coupling laser resonant with transition $|2\rangle \leftrightarrow |4\rangle$. However, as shown in previous part, we can get more obviously multichannel slow light phenomena when coupling light resonant with the transition $|2\rangle \leftrightarrow |5\rangle$ due to the dipole moment and decay rate relationship in ^{87}Rb D2 line. Fig. 12 shows the refractive index and group index as a function of the detuning of the probe for different Rabi frequency of the control field. As seen in Fig. 11 and Fig. 12, the separation between two peaks of the Mollow sideband-like transparency windows is invariant for the control field intensity, which means the coupling Rabi frequency C□determines the splitting. The linewidth of the transparency windows, however, is controllable by adjusting the control field intensity or its detuning (see Figs 10(c) and 10(d)). Thus, the group velocity of the probe light at the sidebands is also controllable. That means double slow light-based enhanced cross-phase modulation is applicable in a much simpler scheme than the scheme suggested in Ref. (Kong et al., 2007). By the way, applications of the enhanced cross-phase modulation are also applicable to the EIT center line and the spectral hole-burning line.

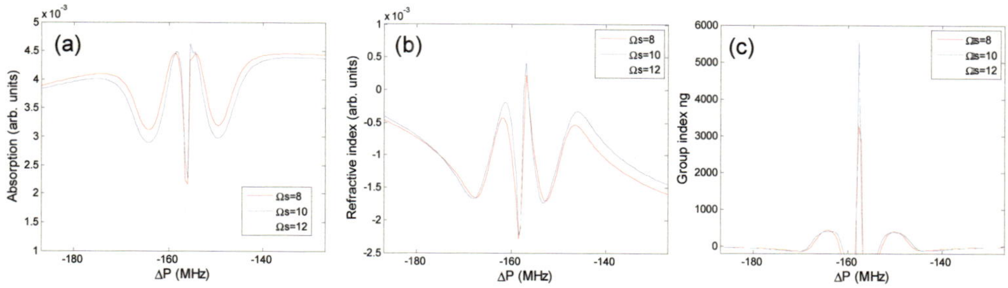

Fig. 12. (a) Absorption, (b) dispersion and (c) group index of the probe as a function of the detuning of the probe for Type III for different Rabi frequency of control light. $N=10^{10}cm^{-3}$.

5. Conclusions

We have investigated EIT and EIT-based slow light in a Doppler-broadened six-level atomic system of ^{87}Rb D2 line. The EIT dip shift due to the existence of the neighbouring levels has been numerically analyzed. When the coupling field is tuned to the different transition, we have shown the dependence of group delay of the one-photon detuning of the probe. Based on the EIT study, we also have discussed several N-type schemes in such system. The obtained Mollow sideband-like transparency windows across the EIT line centre are sub-Doppler broadened and controllable by adjusting the control field intensity or detuning. The work in this chapter may deepen the understanding of EIT and the slow light phenomenon in multilevel system and lead to potential applications in the use of ultraslow light for optical information processing such as all-optical multichannel buffer memory and quantum gate based on enhanced cross-phase modulation owing to increased interaction time between two slow-light pulses.

6. Acknowledgements

This work was supported by the Fund of Jilin University and also supported by the Creative Research Initiative program (Center for Photon Information Processing) of MEST via KOSEF.

7. References

Alzetta, G.; Gozzini, A.; Moi, L. & Oriols, G. (1976). An experimental method for the observation of r.f. transitions and laser beat resonances in oriented sodium vapor. *Nuovo Cimento B*, Vol. 36, 5-20.

Arimondo, E. & Orriols, G. (1976). Nonabsorbing atomic coherences by coherent two-photon transitions in a three-level optical pumping. *Nuovo Cimento Letters*, Vol. 17, No. 6, 333-338.

Boller, K. -J; Imamolu, A. & Harris, S. E. (1991). Observation of electromagnetically induced transparency. *Phys. Rev. Lett.*, Vol. 66, No. 20, 2593-2596, ISSN 0031-9007.

Boyd, R. W. & Gauthier, D. J. (2002). 'Slow' and 'fast' light. *Progress in Optics* 43, edited by E. Wolf, Chap. 6, 497 (Elsevier, Amsterdam).

Chen, Y.; Wei, X. G. & Ham, B. S. (2009). Detuned slow light in the Doppler broadened multi-level D2 line of Rubidium. *Optics Express*, Vol. 17, No. 3, 1781-1788.

Chen, Y.; Wei, X. G. & Ham, B. S. (2009). Optical properties of an N-type system in Doppler-broadened multilevel atomic media of the rubidium D2 line. *J. Phys. B: At. Mol. Opt. Phys.*, Vol. 42, 065506.

Fleischhauer, M.; Imamoglu, A. & Marangos, J. P. (2005). Electromagnetically induced transparency: optics in coherent media. *Rev. Mod. Phys.*, Vol. 77, No. 2, 633-673, ISSN 0034-6861.

Gray, H. R.; Whitley, R. M. & Stroud, Carlos R., Jr. (1978). Coherent trapping of atomic populations. *Opt. Lett.*, Vol. 3, 218-220, ISSN 0146-9592.

Ham, B. S. (2008). Observation of delayed all-optical routing in a slow-light regime. *Phys. Rev. A*, Vol. 78, 011808 (R).

Ham, B. S.; Hemmer, P. R. & Shahriar, M. S. (1997). Efficient electromagnetically induced transparency in a rare-earth doped crystal. *Opt. Commun.*, Vol. 144, 227-230, ISSN 0030-4018.

Harris, S. E. (1989). Lasers without inversion: Interference of lifetime-broadened resonances. *Phys. Rev. Lett.*, Vol. 62, No. 9, (1989) 1033-1036, ISSN 0031-9007

Harris, S. E. (1997). Electromagnetically induced transparency. *Phys. Today*, Vol. 50, No. 7, 36-42; ISSN 0031-9228.

Harris, S. E.; Fieldm, J. E. & Imamoglu, A. (1990). Nonlinear optical processes using electromagnetically induced transparency. *Phys. Rev. Lett.*, Vol. 64, No. 10, 1107-1110, ISSN 0031-9007.

Harris, S. E.; Fieldm, J. E. & Kasapi, A. (1992). Dispersive properties of electromagnetically induced transparency. *Phys. Rev. A*, Vol. 46, R29-32.

Hau, L. V.; Harris, S. E; Dutton, Z. & Behroozi. (1999). Light speed reduction to 17 metres per second in an ultracold atomic gas. *Nature*, Vol. 397, 594-598, ISSN 0028-0836.

Julsgaard, B.; Sherson, J.; Cirac, J. I.; Fiurasek, J. & Polzik, E. S. (2004). Experimental demonstration of quantum memory for light. *Nature*. Vol. 42, 482.

Kasapi, A.; Jain, M.; Yin, G. Y. & Harris, S. E. (1995). Electromagnetically induced transparency: propagation dynamics. *Phys. Rev. Lett.*, Vol. 74, No. 13, 2447-2450, ISSN 0031-9007.

Kash, M. M.; Sautenkov, V. A.; Zibrov, A. S.; Hollberg, L.; Welch, G. R.; Lukin, M. D.; Rostovtsev, Y.; Fry, E. S. & Scully, M. O. (1999). Ultraslow group velocity and enhanced nonlinear optical effects in a coherently driven hot atomic gas. *Phys. Rev. Lett.*, Vol. 82, 5229, ISSN 0031-9007.

Kong, L. B.; Tu, X. H.; Wang, J. ; Zhu, Y. F.& Zhan, M. S. (2007). Sub-Doppler spectral resolution in a resonantly driven four-level coherent medium. *Opt. Commun.*, Vol. 269, 362.

Liu, C.; Dutton, Z.; Behroozi, C. H.; Hau, L. V. & Harris, S. E. (2001). Observation of coherent optical information storage in an atomic medium using halted light pulses. *Nature*, Vol. 409, 490-493, ISSN 0028-0836.

Lukin, M. D. & Hemmer, P. R. (2000). Quantum entanglement via optical control of atom-atom interactions. *Phys. Rev. Lett.*, Vol. 84, 2818.

Marangos, J. P. (1998). Topical review electromagnetically induced transparency. *J. Modern Opt.*, Vol. 45, No. 3, 471-503, ISSN 0950-0340.

Nielsen, M. A. & Chuang, I. L. (2000). *Quantum Computation and Quantum Information*. Cambridge University Press, Cambridge, ISBN 0521635039.

Padmabandu, G. G.; Welch, G. R.; Shubin, I. N.; Fry, E. S.; Nikonov, D. E.; Lukin, M. D. & Scully, M. O. (1996). Laser oscillation without population inversion in a sodium atomic beam. *Phys. Rev. Lett.*, Vol. 76, No. 12, 2053-2056, ISSN 0031-9007.

Paternostro, M.; Kim, M. S. & Ham, B. S. (2003). Generation of entangled coherent states via cross-phase-modulation in a double electromagnetically induced transparency regime. *Phys. Rev. A*, Vol. 67, 023811.

Petrosyan, D. & Kurizki, G. (2002). Symmetric photon-photon coupling by atoms with Zeeman-split sublevels. *Phys. Rev. A*, Vol. 65, 033833.

Phillips, D. F.; Fleischhaueer, A.; Mair, A. & Walsworth, R. L. (2001). Storage of light in atomic vapor. *Phys. Rev. Lett.*, Vol. 86, 783, ISSN 0031-9007.

Phillips, M. C.; Wang, H. L.; Rumyantsev, I.; Kwong, N. H.; Takayama, R. & Binder, R. (2003). Electromagnetically induced transparency in semiconductors via biexcition coherence. *Phys. Rev. Lett.*, Vol. 91, No. 18, 183602, ISSN 0031-9007.

Serapiglia, G. B.; Paspalakis, E.; Sirtori, C.; Vdopyanov, K. L. & Phillips, C. C. (2000). Laser-induced quantum coherence in a semiconductor quantum well. *Phys. Rev. Lett.*, Vol. 84, 1019, ISSN 0031-9007.

Schmidt, H. & Imamoglu, A. (1996). Giant Kerr nonlinearities obtained by electromagnetically induced transparency. *Opt. Lett.*, Vol. 21, 1936-1938, ISSN 0146-9592.

Scully, M. O.; Zhu, S. Y. & Gravrielides, A. (1989). Degenerate quantum-beat laser: Lasing without inversion and inversion without lasing. *Phys. Rev. Lett.*, Vol. 62, No.24, 2813-2816, ISSN 0031-9007.

Scully, M. O. (1991). Enhancement of the index of refraction via quantum coherence. *Phys. Rev. Lett.*, Vol. 67, No. 14, 1855-1858, ISSN 0031-9007.

Scully, M. O. & Zhu, S. Y. (1992). Ultra-large index of refraction via quantum interference. *Opt. Commun.*, Vol. 87, 134-138, ISSN 0030-4018.

Scully, M. O. & Zubairy, M. S. (1997). *Quantum Optics*. Cambridge University Press, Cambridge, England, ISBN 0521435951.

Turukhin, A. V.; Sudarshanam, V. S; Shahriar, M. S.; Musser, J. A.; Ham, B. S. & Hemmer, P. R. (2002). Observation of ultraslow and stored light pulses in a solid. *Phys. Rev. Lett.*, Vol. 88, No. 2, 023602, ISSN 0031-9007.

Xiao, M. & Li, Y. Q. (1995). Electromagnetically induced transparency in a three-level lambda type system in rubidium atoms. *Phys. Rev. A*, Vol. 51, R2703-2706.

Xiao, M.; Li, Y. Q.; Jin, S. Z. & Gea-Banacloche, J. (1995). Measurement of dispersive properties of electromagnetically induced transparency in rubidium atom. *Phys. Rev. Lett.*, Vol. 74, 666-669, ISSN 0031-9007.

4

Importance of Simulation Studies in Analysis of Thin Film Transistors Based on Organic and Metal Oxide Semiconductors

Dipti Gupta[1], Pradipta K. Nayak[2], Seunghyup Yoo[3], Changhee Lee[1] and Yongtaek Hong[1]

[1]Seoul National University
[2]Universidade Nova de Lisboa
[3]Korea Advanced Institute of Science and Technology
[1,3]S. Korea
[2]Portugal

1. Introduction

Organic semiconductors and metal oxides (such as ZnO) have recently been recognized as a new class of electronic materials for thin film transistor (TFT) applications such as active matrix displays, identification tags, sensors and other low end consumer applications (Campbell et al, 2007; Fortunato et al, 2008; Masuda et al, 2003; Nelson et al, 1998; Sandberg et al, 2002). Owing to their low cost, large area coverage, and at par or better performance, these materials are also considered to have enormous potential to replace amorphous silicon for use in existing and new electronic device applications. From the device technology and fabrication point of view, there have been rapid developments in this area over the past decade, but the field is still very much nascent in gaining the fundamental understanding, both, at the material and the device physics level. For example, whereas, vanderwal bonded organic semiconductors often suffers from spatial and energetic disorder (Pope et al, 1999), ZnO has very rich defect chemistry (Özgür et al, 2005; McCluskey et al 2009). Additionally, they tend to have complex interaction with several surfaces, which often results in phenomenon difficult to explain by classical theories. It is therefore critical that the research in this area is necessarily be coupled with theoretical perspective in order to resolve several of the important issues, which will help in further enhancing its progress. In traditional electronics, device modelling and simulation has proven to be of great help in not only understanding the detailed device operation but has also served as a powerful tool to design and improve devices. The physics based device simulation is also becoming beneficial to the research area of organic and metal oxide semiconductors TFTs, where it is effectively predicting the device behaviour, giving insight into the underlying microscopic mechanisms and providing intuitive information about the performance of a new material (Bolognesi, 2002; Gupta et al, 2008, 2009, 2010; Hill, 2007; Hossain, 2003; Scheinert, 2004). Its continued involvement for explaining various device phenomenons will certainly be of great use for future developments.

In this chapter, we show the importance of two dimensional simulations in both the classes of materials by addressing several common issues which are often vaguely explained by experimental means or by analytical equations. Pentacene and tris-isopropylsilyl (TIPS) - pentacene are taken as examples in the class of organic semiconductors, while solution processed ZnO and Li- doped ZnO served as illustrations in the metal- oxide category. Pentacene is a small molecule organic semiconductor and has unarguably been considered as a high mobility material for TFT applications (Jackson). (TIPS) - pentacene, on the other hand is a novel functionalized derivative of pentacene that incorporates the best properties of pentacene moiety together with the solution processibility, which pentacene lacks (Anthony). We begin with modelling of TFTs based on tris-isopropylsilyl (TIPS) - pentacene to provide a baseline for describing the charge transport in any new material. We completely model its electrical characteristics by considering all the aspects of contact barrier effect, field-dependent mobility, and traps/ interface trapped charges (Gupta et al, 2008). We then highlighted the role of metal - semiconductor contacts and the effect of dielectric- semiconductor interface structure on the device characteristics of pentacene based TFTs, which are two of the major concerns in organic TFT (OTFT) operation. Next we consider the stability issue in solution processible zinc oxide (ZnO) TFTs, in which we investigated the problem of change in device characteristics when subjected to electrical stress or exposed to air for a prolonged time. ZnO has several merits like substantially high mobility as compared to amorphous silicon or organic semiconductors, better structural homogeneity than polycrystalline silicon, high transparency, low cost, and ease of processing by wet chemical routes. However, its device degradation with respect to electrical stress and air exposure may inhibit its full exploitation due to instability and reliability problems. We deal with this issue by considering the rich and undefined defect states in pure and Li-doped ZnO [10], and build a physical degradation model based on the changes in density of states (DOS) of active layers, which effectively explains the degradation phenomenon in ZnO. In each of the examples, by providing a detailed description of the modelling scheme, we systematically approach the problem underhand and verify the simulated results with the experimentally obtained device characteristics.

2. Device simulation procedure

The simulator used for device modeling in this chapter is Silvaco's ATLAS (Silvaco). ATLAS is a two-dimensional semiconductor device simulator which incorporates the physics that govern charge carrier transport and applies it to the dimensions of the device being studied. For simulation, the commercial device simulator Silvaco-Atlas® is used, which predicts the electrical characteristics associated with a specified physical structure and bias conditions by solving systems of Poisson's equation and continuity equation that are a set of coupled, partial differential equations as shown by Eqs. 1 and 2 below:

$$\varepsilon\nabla^2\psi = -q(p - n + N_D^+ - N_A^-) \tag{1}$$

$$-\frac{\partial p}{\partial t} = \frac{1}{q}\nabla \cdot J_p + G_p - R_p \tag{2a}$$

$$\frac{\partial n}{\partial t} = \frac{1}{q}\nabla \cdot J_n + G_n - R_n \tag{2b}$$

where ε is the dielectric constant, ψ is the potential, p is hole density, n is electron density, p refers to holes, n refers to electrons, q is the fundamental electronic charge, G is the charge generation rate, R is the charge recombination rate, and J is the current density which is given considering its drift and diffusion components by Eq.3:

$$J_p = qp\mu_p F + qD_p \nabla p \tag{3a}$$

$$J_n = qp\mu_n F + qD_n \nabla n \tag{3b}$$

where μ is mobility, F is the local electric field, and D is the diffusion coefficient. This simulator was primarily developed for silicon devices and, therefore, its applicability to organic materials is limited. However, the simulator can still predict the qualitative device characteristics correctly, as demonstrated by available literature [18, 26-29] on simulation of organic devices.

To account for the trapped charge, Poisson's equations are modified by adding an additional term Q_T, representing trapped charge. The trapped charge may consist of both donor - like and acceptor-like states across the forbidden energy gap, where the acceptor-like states act as electron traps and donor-like states act as hole traps. The density of defect states, g(E), is defined as a combination of four components. Two tail bands with an exponentially decreasing function are specified to contain large numbers of defect states at the conduction band (acceptor-like traps) and valence band (donor-like traps) edges, respectively. In addition, two deep-level bands for acceptor-and donor-like defects are defined that are modeled using a Gaussian distribution. The equations describing these terms are given as follows:

$$g_{TA}(E) = N_{TA} \exp\left(\frac{E - E_C}{W_{TA}}\right) \tag{4a}$$

$$g_{TD}(E) = N_{TD} \exp\left(\frac{E_V - E}{W_{TD}}\right) \tag{4b}$$

$$g_{GA}(E) = N_{GA} \exp\left[-\left(\frac{E - E_{GA}}{W_{GA}}\right)^2\right] \tag{4c}$$

$$g_{GD}(E) = N_{GD} \exp\left[-\left(\frac{E - E_{GD}}{W_{GD}}\right)^2\right] \tag{4d}$$

where E is the trap energy , E_C is conduction band energy, E_V is valence band energy, and the subscripts T, G,A, D stand for tail, Gaussian (deep level), acceptor and donor states respectively. The exponential distribution of DOS is described by conduction and valence band intercept densities (N_{TA} and N_{TD}), and by its characteristic decay energy (W_{TA} and W_{TD}). For Gaussian distributions, the DOS is described by its total density of states (N_{GA} and N_{GD}), its characteristic decay energy (W_{GA} and W_{GD}), and its peak energy/peak distribution (E_{GA} and E_{GD}).

2.1 Material parameters

In order to perform the simulations, it is necessary to define the required parameters for a particular material. The important material parameters required for a semiconductor as an input for the device simulation are band gap (E_g), electron affinity (E_A), effective density of states (N_C for conduction band and N_V for valence band) and permittivity. Table 1 summarizes the selected values of these parameters for pentacene, TIPS-pentacene and ZnO, as reported in the literature, including both theoretically calculated and experimentally measured values. Figure 1 shows the chemical structure of pentacene and TIPS-pentacene.

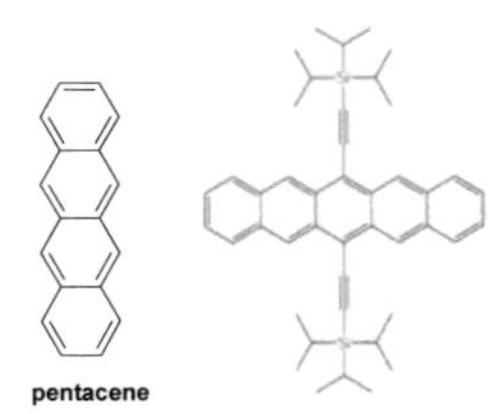

Fig. 1. Chemical structure of (a) pentacene and (b) TIPS- pentacene molecule.

Parameter	Pentacene	TIPS-Pentacene	ZnO	Ref.
Band Gap (eV)	2.2	2.2	3.4	Gupta et al, 2009; Hossain et al 2003
Electron Affinity (eV)	2.8	2.8	4.29	"
N_C (cm^{-3})	$2x10^{21}$	$2x10^{21}$	$4.5x10^{24}$	"
N_V (cm^{-3})	$2x10^{21}$	$2x10^{21}$	$9x10^{24}$	"
Permittivity	4	4	8.5	"

Table 1. Material parameters for pentacene, TIPS- pentacene and ZnO.

3. Device modelling of TFTs made of TIPS-pentacene

TIPS- pentacence based OTFTs were fabricated in bottom contact geometry on a 100 nm thick SiO_2 layer thermally grown on heavily doped n-Si wafers that also function as the gate (G) electrode (Gupta et al, 2008). The source (S) and drain (D) electrodes consist of 5 nm titanium adhesion layer and 100 nm gold layer onto which a solution of 2 wt% TIPS-pentacene in toluene was drop-cast. The solution was then allowed to dry slowly in a solvent-rich environment at 50°C to promote ordered molecular arrangement. The morphology of TIPS-pentacene films typically consist of platelet-like structures each of which may be regarded crystalline. The channel width W is 1.5 mm and length L is 50 µm, respectively.

Figure 2 shows the experimental output characteristics (dotted lines) in the forward sweep (off to on) at gate voltage (V_G) from 0 to -40 V in a step of -10 V. The curves exhibit saturation behavior at high drain voltages (V_D), but one can easily observe a non-ohmic behavior of the drain current (I_D) in the linear region at low V_D, which is often called as "current crowding". This may be explained mainly by a limited carrier injection from metal contacts to semiconductors due to an existing contact barrier Φ_B (Hill, 2007; Tessler et al, 2001). Φ_B is defined as the difference between the metal workfunction (Φ_S) and valence band maximum (E_v) of the semiconductor. Theoretically, Ti/Au contacts provide a proper energy level alignment with TIPS-pentacene, as the workfunction of gold lies between 4.7-5.0 eV.

However, in literature, it is many times quoted that an interfacial electrical dipole may be formed which can effectively change the work-function of the metal in the close proximity of the organic semiconductor. The reasons for the formation of this interfacial dipole is often debatable, but is believed to be the result of charge transfer, screening, or hybridization effects caused by the complex chemical interaction between the organic semiconductor and metal (Ishii et al, 1999; Kahn et al, 2003).

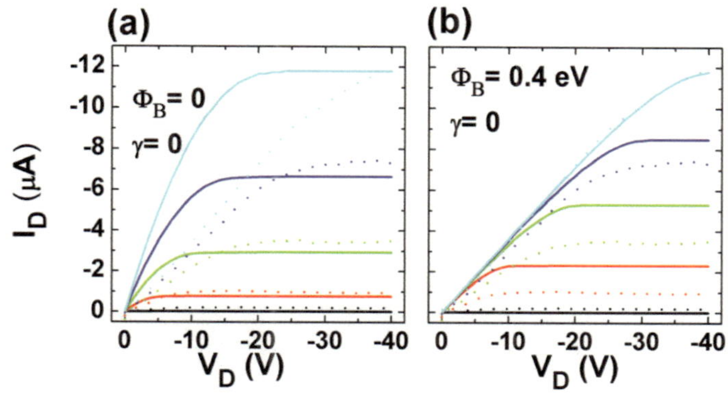

Fig. 2. Output characteristics of TIPS-pentacene TFTs: experimental (dotted) vs. numerical simulation (solid) results. (a) Simulated characteristics with $\Phi_B = 0$ and $\gamma = 0$ (no field-dependence) and (b) Simulated characteristics with $\Phi_B = 0.4$ eV and $\gamma=0$. In (a) and (b), the mobility value is scaled to match the value of $I_D(V_D$=-40V) for V_G=-40V. V_{GS} in (a) and (b) is varied from 0 to -40V in -10V steps. (Reprinted from *Organic Electronics*, vol.9, D.Gupta, N. Jeon, S. Yoo, "Modeling the electrical characteristics of TIPS-pentacene thin-film transistors: Effect of contact barrier, field-dependent mobility, and traps", p.1026, 2008, *with permission from Elsevier)*

On the basis of the above discussion, we investigated several values of effective contact barrier (Φ_B=0 to 0.4eV) to reproduce the output characteristics at low drain voltages in the output curves. However, we found that none of the values of Φ_B can reproduce the whole output characteristics in both linear and saturation regions over the range of V_{GS} used in this study. For example, the simulated device characteristics with Φ_B=0 (Fig. 2a) resulted in an ohmic behavior in the linear region, while Φ_B=0.4 eV (Fig. 2b) causes large reduction in drain current and requires adjustment of mobility towards a larger value. Therefore, field dependence of mobility in addition to contact barrier which has previously been shown to result in non-linear characteristics of the output curves is invoked. The presence of field-dependent mobility in TIPS-pentacene OTFTs is shown by extracting field-effect mobility of devices with L of 10, 20, and 50 μm at several values of V_{DS} in linear region and plotted it as a function of $(V_D/L)^{0.5}$, as shown in Figure 3a (Cherian et al, 2004; Wang et al, 2003). The logarithmic variation of mobility with $(V_D/L)^{0.5}$ for a series of channel lengths suggests that it follows the Poole-Frenkel (PF)-type field-dependence given by:

$$\mu = \mu_o \exp\left(\gamma\sqrt{F}\right) \tag{4}$$

where μ_0 is the zero-field mobility, F is the electric field and γ is the characteristic parameter for the field-dependence. A linear fit [dashed line in Fig. 4] to the data yielded field-dependent parameters of μ_o= 0.035 cm^2/Vs and γ =1.7×10^{-3} (cm/V)$^{0.5}$. It is noted that this PF field-dependence is often observed in disordered organic semiconductors. In this respect, the field-dependence of mobility given by Eq.4 is incorporated, in addition to the contact barrier effect, into the numerical simulation. Line curves in Fig. 3b shows the simulated output curves which take into account both the PF mobility and contact barriers. The best fit to the experimental data was obtained with Φ_B of 0.38 eV, μ_o of 0.061 cm^2/Vs, and γ of 1.8×10^{-3} (cm/V)$^{0.5}$, respectively.

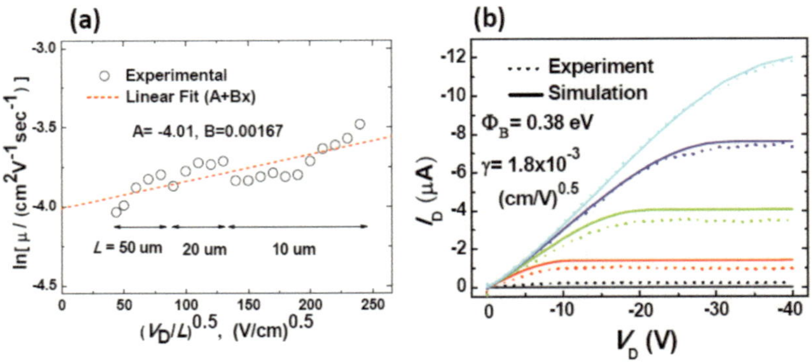

Fig. 3. (a) Natural logarithm of field-effect mobility as a function of $(V_D/L)^{0.5}$. Dashed line is a linear fit with which the field-dependent parameters are estimated to be μ_o= 0.035 cm^2/Vs and γ=1.7×10^{-3} (cm/V)$^{0.5}$. (b) Output characteristics of TIPS-pentacene TFTs: experimental (dotted) vs. numerical simulation (solid) results. Simulation was done in consideration of both a contact barrier height Φ_B of 0.38 eV, μ_o= 0.061 cm^2/Vs and γ=1.8×10^{-3} (cm/V)$^{0.5}$. V_G is varied from 0 to -40V in -10V steps. (Reprinted from *Organic Electronics*, vol.9, D.Gupta, N. Jeon, S. Yoo, "Modeling the electrical characteristics of TIPS-pentacene thin-film transistors: Effect of contact barrier, field-dependent mobility, and traps", p.1026, 2008, *with permission from Elsevier)*

The incorporation of contact barrier and PF dependence of mobility show a reasonable match to the output curves, but transfer curves still suffers from a significant deviation at low $|V_G|$ (curve 1 in Fig. 4a), which signifies include additional factors based on traps to complete the TFT model. Moreover, a hysteresis loop in the I_{DS}-V_{GS} transfer curve shown in Fig. 4(a), when scanned V_{GS} from 0 to -40 V and then back from -40 to 0 V again indicate about the existence of traps, which may come from dielectric-semiconductor interface or from structural defects in TIPS-pentacene films (Alam et al, 1997; Scheinert et al, 2004). This trap-related phenomenon is simulated by assuming a spatially uniform density of trap states in TIPS-pentacene films that is modeled by an exponential distribution of acceptor-like traps as in Eq. 4a and 4b. It was previously discussed that oxygen is the chemical origin of acceptor-like traps in pentacene and that acceptor-like traps provide extra hole current in the subthreshold region in pentacene OTFTs (Alam et al, 1997; Knipp et al, 2003; Scheinert et al, 2004; Street et al, 2002). Additionally, a positive interface trapped charge (N_{it}) is included, which may arise due to impurities such as moisture, oxygen or mobile charges in the dielectric. It was observed that the forward sweep (curve 2) can be better reproduced with N_{TA} = 1.0×10^{18} cm^{-3}eV^{-1}, W_{TA} = 0.55 eV and N_{it} = 8.0×10^{11} cm^{-2}, while reverse sweep (curve 3) requires N_{TA} = 8.0×10^{17} cm^{-3}eV^{-1}, W_{TA} = 0.55 eV, N_{it} = 2.0×10^{12} cm^{-2}, and μ_o = 0.058

cm^2/Vs. The increase in N_{it} in the reverse sweep is a result of discharging of the trap states that is relatively slow when compared to the sweep speed (= 5V/sec) used in this study and is mainly responsible for the shift in threshold voltage. The output curves were also well simulated with the additional incorporation of traps in TIPS- pentacene films, as shown in Fig. 4b. Thus, this work is helpful in building an integral picture of injection, transport, and traps in TIPS-pentacene in a context of OTFT operation, and will serve as a starting point for further performance optimization and baseline for simulation of TFT made of any new semiconductor.

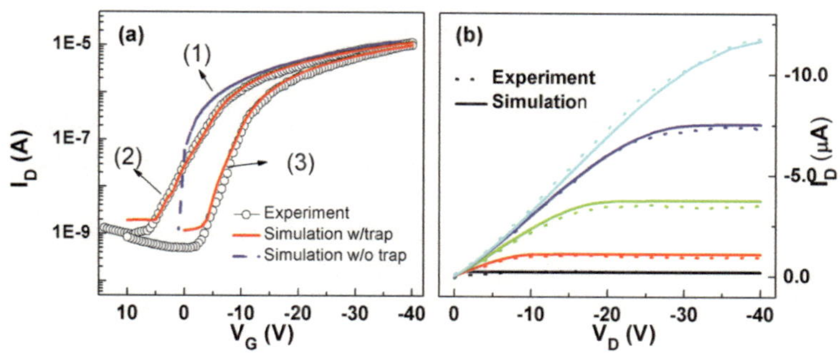

Fig. 4. (a) Numerical fit to the transfer curves (curve 1 is without traps, while curves 2 and 3 are plotted using trap distribution given by Eq. 4 and interface charges in forward (2) and reverse (3) bias sweep. (b) Output curves with DOS distribution and contact barrier height of 0.38 eV, μ_o= 0.052 cm^2/Vs and γ=1.8×10^{-3} $(cm/V)^{0.5}$ (Reprinted from *Organic Electronics*, vol.9, D.Gupta, N. Jeon, S. Yoo, "Modeling the electrical characteristics of TIPS-pentacene thin-film transistors: Effect of contact barrier, field-dependent mobility, and traps", p 1026, 2008, *with permission from Elsevier)*

4. Effect of device design of OTFT

In OTFTs, there is a common issue of difference in device performance of OTFTs fabricated in top contact and bottom contact device configurations (Gundlach et al, 2006; Gupta et al 2009; Roichman et al, 2002; Street et al, 2002). The process difference between the two device designs is that in top contact OTFT, semiconductor is deposited prior to depositing source and drain electrodes, while this is vice versa in bottom contact OTFT. From fabrication point of view, bottom contact OTFT is preferred because in this design the soft organic semiconductor can be protected from harsh chemicals, high temperatures and metal penetration. However, usually bottom contact OTFT show inferior performance, the reasons for which is provided on the basis of large metal-semiconductor contact resistance, irregular deposition or poor morphology of the semiconductor films around the source and drain contacts (Kang et al, 2003; Kymissis et al, 2001; Koch et al, 2002; Lee et al 2006, Schroeder et al, 2003). In the bottom contact OTFT, it is possible that both the contact barrier and the structural inhomogenities in the semiconductor play important role in affecting the charge injection and transport characteristics. However, separating one from the other and finding the dominant role of one of the effects is necessary to properly understand the device operation mechanisms.

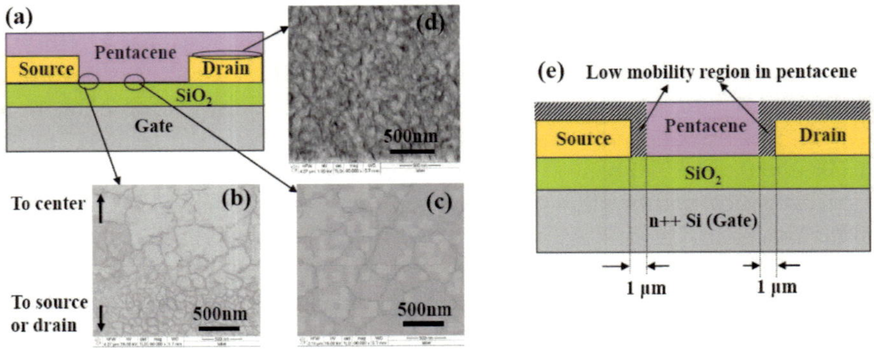

Fig. 5. (a) Schematic of the bottom contact device showing different region of pentacene morphology. Scanning electron micrograph of pentacene on gold contact (b) near gold contact edge on SiO_2, (c) far away from gold contact edge on SiO_2, (d) on gold contacts, and (e) Schematic of the 1μm wide low-mobility-region near the source and drain contact edges and above the contacts in bottom contact devices. (Reprinted from *Organic Electronics, Vol. 10, No. 1,* D. Gupta, M.Katiyar, Deepak, "An analysis of difference in device behavior of top and bottom contact devices using device simulation", *pp. 775-784, 2009, with permission from Elsevier)*

The experimental devices consist of n+ Si as gate, 40 nm gold as source and drain electrodes, 200 nm SiO_2 as gate insulator, and pentacene as the organic semiconductor. Pentacene films with thicknesses of 50 nm are deposited by thermal evaporation at the rate of 0.03-0.04 nm/sec at substrate temperature of 65°C. The channel length (L) for both top and bottom contact devices is 30 μm and their widths (W) are 1mm and 3.6mm, respectively. The experimentally obtained data in the output curves were also corrected in order to remove the effects of gate leakage and contact resistances (Gupta et al, 2009). To correct for the gate leakage, half of the gate current is added to the obtained drain current at each gate voltage. In order to correct the device characteristics for the metal-semiconductor contact resistance, device parasitic resistance (R_P) is calculated as a function of gate voltage following the procedures provided in the well- known transmission line method (TLM). R_P estimated by TLM method is then used to correct the drain currents to their equivalent values in a device with no metal-semiconductor contact resistance. From the as measured curves, the extracted field effect mobility for top and bottom contact devices are 0.125 cm^2/Vs and $1.74x10^{-3}$ cm^2/Vs, respectively, in the saturation region. After the gate leakage and contact resistance correction, an effective mobility of 0.14 cm^2/Vs and $3.2x10^{-3}$ cm^2/Vs is obtained for the top and bottom contact devices, respectively.

The simulation data obtained from the top and bottom contact device structures overlay on each other, which implies that device structure by itself is not responsible for causing any difference in the two device structures. The other factors then must lay down to the differences in the manner that two devices are fabricated. In bottom contact devices, it is possible that a shadow cast by metal during evaporation of pentacene could lead to unfilled corners at the source/drain contacts, which in turn could result in lower effective device mobility. This kind of situation in the simulation is incorporated by adding a vacuum layer of dimensions 50 nm x 40 nm adjacent to the source and drain electrodes. However, the resultant drain currents are only slightly affected by the unfilled corners, as the current find a way of charge injection/extraction through the top surface of the source and drain electrodes, respectively. The next possibility, i.e. the effect of morphology of pentacene is then deeply investigated in order to find out the reasons for inferior performance of bottom contact devices. The investigation of pentacene morphology in the different regions of the bottom contact device showed a marked variation in grain sizes. From the scanning electron micrograph of the device in Fig. 5, one can clearly see that the large grain structure far away from the source/drain contact edges changes into a small grain structure as one move closer to the edge of the channel, near the gold electrodes. On SiO_2, the average grain size is 0.57 µm and on the source and drain contacts, the grain size is 0.15 µm. The reason for such a difference in morphology is attributed to the difference in surface energies of metal and dielectric layers.

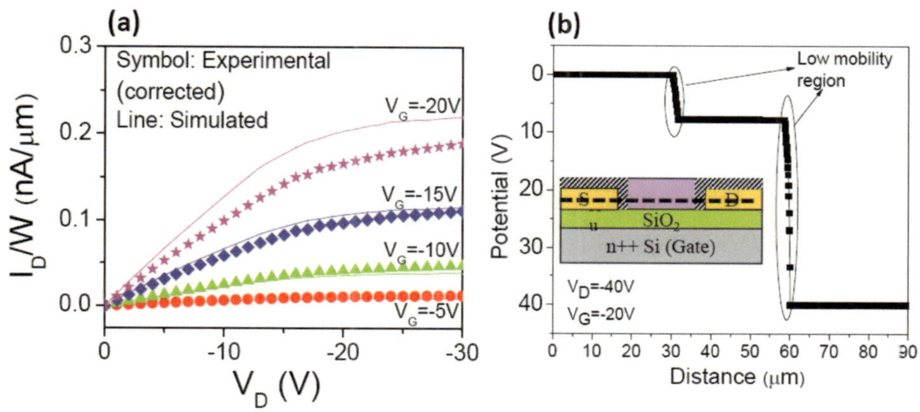

Fig. 6. (a) Comparison of the experimental (gate leakage and contact corrected) and the simulated output curves. The mobility of the low-mobility-region is 1.5x10-4 cm/#'/Vs and bulk mobility of pentacene is 0.14 cm^2/Vs. (b) Surface potential profile 1 nm above the dielectric surface (source, drain and channel lie between 0-30 µm, 60-90 µm and 30-60 µm, respectively). (Reprinted from *Organic Electronics, Vol. 10, No. 1,* D. Gupta, M.Katiyar, Deepak, "An analysis of difference in device behavior of top and bottom contact devices using device simulation", *pp. 775-784, 2009, with permission from Elsevier)*

The above mentioned structural features are then incorporated in the simulation model (as depicted in Fig. 5) where a low-mobility-region near the source and drain contact edges and above the contacts is defined in the bottom contact device. The low-mobility-region has lower mobility as compared to the rest of the pentancene, and the reason for such an assignment is attributed to the significantly lower grain size as compared to the bulk film. Keeping the bulk mobility as 0.14 cm^2/Vs, several values of mobility of the low-mobility-region are tried and a mobility value of $1.5x10^{-4}$ cm^2/Vs yields a good comparison with the measured data, as shown in Fig. 6a. The effective mobility calculated from this structure is $1.8x10^{-4}$ cm^2/Vs, which closely matches with the experimental value. In order to analyze the effects of low-mobility-region, potential profiles between the source and drain contacts at 1 nm above the dielectric interface (along a horizontal dashed line in the inset of Fig. 7b) are taken. Figure 6b shows that almost all the applied potential is accommodated in the low-mobility-region, forcing its effect on the overall device characteristics. The current density profiles (Fig. 7a) taken across the bottom contact device depicts that charge injection and extraction takes place from the lower region of metal contacts (within 5 nm region from the insulator) forcing the current to pass through the low-mobility region and causing a large potential drop. As an analogy, the low-mobility-region in the top contact devices is also introduced below the source and drain electrodes, which spans across the full thickness of pentacene. As an example, a mobility value of $1x10^{-3}cm^2/Vs$ for the low mobility region is taken, but no significant change in the device behaviour could be observed. The reason for this can be understood from the current density profile in Fig. 7b, which clearly indicates that charge is injected from the side/corner of the contacts, bypassing the low-mobility-region. Thus top contact devices would be less susceptible to morphological variations. Therefore, the simulation determines that the possible cause of differences observed in bottom and top contact devices could be due to differences in pentacene morphology leading to low mobility regions near the contacts.

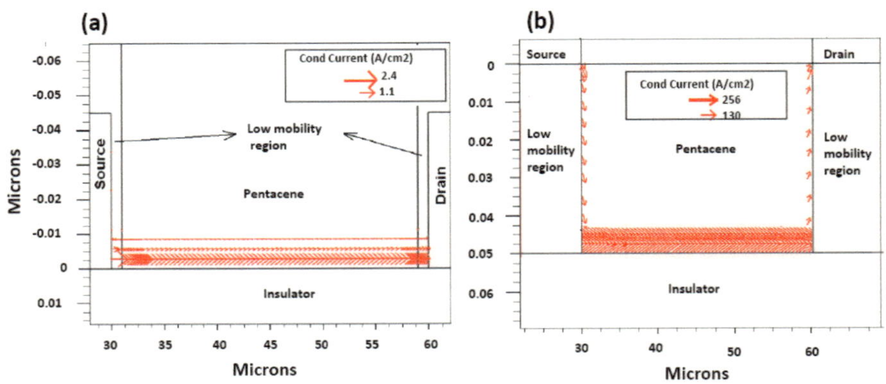

Fig. 7. Schematic diagram for the path of the current flow in pentacene film (line with the arrow) in a (a) bottom contact device having a low-mobility region adjacent to and above the source and drain contacts and in a (b) top contact device having a low-mobility-region under the source and drain contacts. (Reprinted from *Organic Electronics, Vol. 10, No. 1,* D. Gupta, M.Katiyar, Deepak, "An analysis of difference in device behavior of top and bottom contact devices using device simulation", *pp. 775-784, 2009, with permission from Elsevier)*

5. Effect of pentacene thickness

The next issue of interest is dependence of device performance on the semiconductor thickness. Theoretically, the device mobility should be independent of semiconductor thickness in TFTs, because the field effect causes all the charges to be accumulated in few nanometers of the semiconductor near the insulator, thus nullifying the effect of the rest of the film (Dinelli et al, 2004; Horowitz et al 2003). However, practically, this is a common observation and the reasons for such an occurrence are explained in terms of organic semiconductor morphology, semiconductor-insulator interfaces, and access resistances (Dodabalapur et al, 2005; Granstrom et al, 1999; Kiguchi et al, 2005; Schroeder et al 2003). Figure 8 shows the mobility dependence of top contact OTFTs based on pentacene for pentacene thicknesses of 10, 20, 35, 50, 80 and 100 nm, respectively. The source and drain electrodes are made of gold, gate is n+ silicon, insulator is 200 nm thick SiO_2, channel width W is 1.5 mm and length L is 30 µm, respectively. According to the experiments, the mobility increases until a pentacene thickness of 35 nm, and then it decreases. However, the simulated device characteristics are only very slightly affected by pentacene thickness (Fig. 8a), and not to the extent of experimental observations. Since there is a sufficient mobility variation with pentacene thickness experimentally, it is imperative to incorporate additional features in the simulation in order to model the device characteristics accurately. In the simulation, the physical behavior related to charge transport in the first few layers adjacent to the dielectric is not modeled. However, it is important to note that the first few layers, where most of the charge transport occurs, may have different electronic properties as compared to the bulk film. In literature, it has been demonstrated that the pentacene film near the dielectric may have several structural defects, discontinuities, low surface coverage and may also be affected by charge-surface phonon interaction caused by the polar oxide dielectric (Houilli et al 2006; Kiroval et al, 2003; Puntambekar et al, 2005; Sandberg et al, 2002; Stassen et al, 2004; Steudel et al, 2004; Ruiz et al 2005; Veres et al, 2002). Apart from this, inter layer surface potential between the pentacene layers and polarization interaction energy of the charge in the dielectric may force the mobile carriers more towards the vicinity of the dielectric (Houilli et al 2006; Kiroval et al, 2003; Puntambekar et al, 2005). Based on this discussion, following two points emerge (Gupta et al, 2009):

a. A monolayer of pentacene may have low mobility in comparison to the bulk pentacene. Hereafter this layer is referred as low mobility layer.
b. Mobile charge, for reasons not precisely understood, is preferentially forced to this low mobility region.

These effects are then systematically introduced in the simulation model for a better match with the experimental data. To evaluate the effect of the low mobility layer at the insulator surface, 1.5 nm thick layer (roughly the thickness of a monolayer of pentacene) at the dielectric interface is incorporated, as depicted in the inset of Fig. 8b. The simulations were performed while keeping the bulk mobility value of 0.28 cm^2/Vs, and lowering the mobility of the low-mobility-layer down to several decades. However, the extracted mobility from the simulation increases until pentacene thickness of 35 nm and then becomes almost constant (Fig. 8b). This simulated behaviour is significantly different than the experimental results and thus the second effect, ie charge confinement towards dielectric is investigated subsequently.

Since the commercial simulator in use here does not contain any models to physically simulate the carrier confinement, an energy band offset between the low mobility layer and bulk pentacene is intentionally introduced in the simulation model in such a way that it facilitates the charge migration towards the low mobility layer. Figure 9a shows the energy band diagram of pentacene film depicting the energy band offset between the low mobility layer and the bulk pentacene. To force the mobile charge towards the low mobility layer, the electron affinity (E_A) value of the low mobility layer (E_{A1}) is reduced in comparison to its value in the bulk pentacene (E_{A2}), while keeping the band gap (E_g) value same for both the regions. The combined effect of low-mobility-layer and the charge confinement induced by the above mentioned method is such that the effective mobility of the device reduces significantly as compared to the bulk mobility value. For example, for a pentacene thickness of 50nm, a bulk mobility value of 0.28 cm^2/Vs, a low-mobility-value of 0.014 cm^2/Vs and an energy band-offset of 0.1 eV produce an effective mobility value of 0.09 cm^2/Vs. With several trials and errors, it was observed that the quantitative behavior of mobility up to 35 nm is better matched for an energy band offset value of 0.11 eV, the mobility of low mobility layer as ~1x10^{-4} cm^2/Vs and bulk mobility as 1.3 cm^2/Vs (Fig. 9b). However, as shown in Fig. 9b, after 35 nm, no match could be obtained, which is discussed based on the pentacene morphology variation with thickness, in the next paragraph.

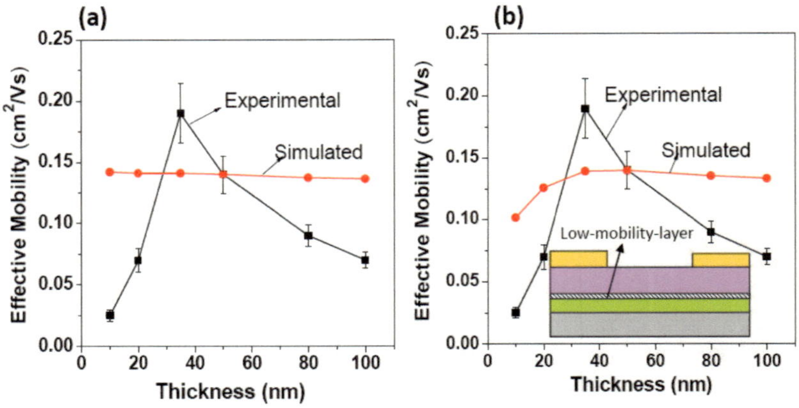

Fig. 8. (a) A comparison of the mobility values for the experimental and the simulated devices and (b) between experimental and simulated devices on incorporating the low-mobility-layer as a function of pentacene thickness. (Reprinted from *Organic Electronics, Vol. 11,* D. Gupta, Y. Hong, "Understanding the effect of semiconductor thickness on device characteristics in organic thin film transistors by way of two dimensional simulations", *pp. 127-136, 2010, with permission from Elsevier)*

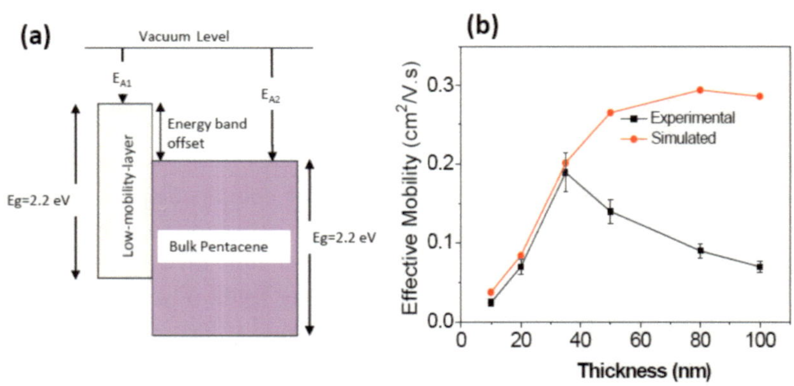

Fig. 9. (a) Schematic diagram of the energy levels in the low mobility layer and bulk of the pentacene film (b) Comparison of experimental and simulated mobility value as a function of pentacene thickness. The mobility of the low-mobility-layer is 1x10^{-4} cm^2/Vs and bulk mobility is 1.3 cm^2/Vs. The energy band offset value is 0.11 eV. (Reprinted from *Organic Electronics, Vol. 11,* D. Gupta, Y. Hong, "Understanding the effect of semiconductor thickness on device characteristics in organic thin film transistors by way of two dimensional simulations", *pp. 127-136, 2010, with permission from Elsevier)*

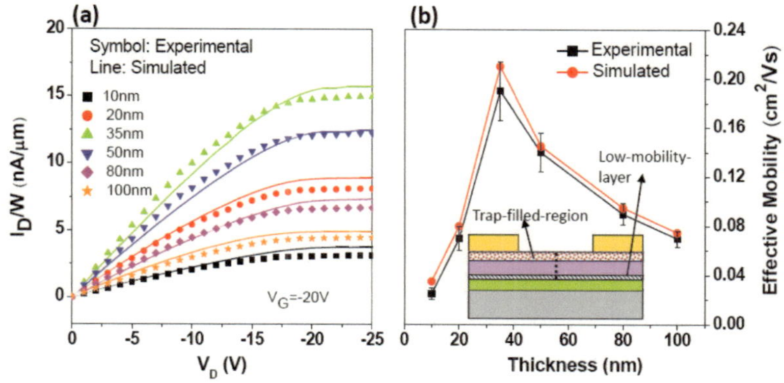

Fig. 10. A comparison of simulated and experimental (a) output curves and (b) mobility value as a function of pentacene thickness. The mobility of the low-mobility-layer and bulk pentacene is taken as 1×10^{-4} cm^2/Vs and 1.3 cm^2/Vs, respectively. The energy band offset value is 0.11 eV. The trap concentration is taken as 4×10^{16} cm^{-3} for 50 nm thick film and 6×10^{16} cm^{-3} for 80 and 100 nm thick films, respectively. (Reprinted from *Organic Electronics, Vol. 11,* D. Gupta, Y. Hong, "Understanding the effect of semiconductor thickness on device characteristics in organic thin film transistors by way of two dimensional simulations", *pp. 127-136, 2010, with permission from Elsevier)*

The investigation of morphology of pentacene films revealed that grain size and crystal structure varies as a function of thickness. It is found that until pentacene thickness of 35 nm, the average grain size remains ~0.85 µm. After further increasing the film thickness, the grain size reduces and reaches to 0.15 µm for the 100 nm thick pentacene films. The reduction in grain size causes more grain boundaries to appear, which acts as trapping centers for the mobile charge. The bulk traps in the region above 35 nm of pentacene thickness are then introduced, as illustrated in the inset of Fig. 10b. It was found that the donor type traps with a trap level of 0.4eV, produces a reasonable match between the experimental and simulated curves, if bulk donor trap concentration of 4×10^{16} cm^{-3} for 50 nm thick film and 6×10^{16} cm^{-3} for 80 and 100 nm thick films, respectively, are chosen. Figure 10a and 10b show the superimposed experimental and simulated results of the output curves and mobility values, respectively. Therefore, this study indicates that OTFT devices face several non-regularities, which are expressed in the form of low-mobility of the pentacene layers that are associated with the dielectric, existence of energy band offset between the interface layers and the bulk, and the bulk traps due to the structural defects like grain boundaries. The combined effect of these features causes the extracted mobility to depend on the film thickness, which in an ideal case should have been absent. It also signifies the importance of optimizing the thickness of organic semiconductor in order to have enhanced as well as reliable device performance.

6. Device stability of solution processed ZnO TFTs under electrical stress

Device stability of TFTs under electrical stress is highly important in view of practicality, which is not only important in estimating the device lifetime but also in understanding the instability mechanisms. Electrical instability in TFTs is typically measured by threshold voltage (V_T) shift that occurs when the device is subjected to constant voltage or drain current for certain duration (Wehrspon et 2003, Jahinuzzaman et al, 2005). During constant gate bias, the channel charge and hence the on current continuously decreases to eventually saturate the V_T shift. On the other hand, during constant current stress the applied gate bias continually adjusts itself in time to keep the drain current constant. Also important is the post-stress relaxation characteristics of the device, where V_T shift occurring during the stress state is recovered in the off-state. From a practical point of view, this situation occurs in displays or integrated circuits where the device is temporarily switched on, and then switched off.

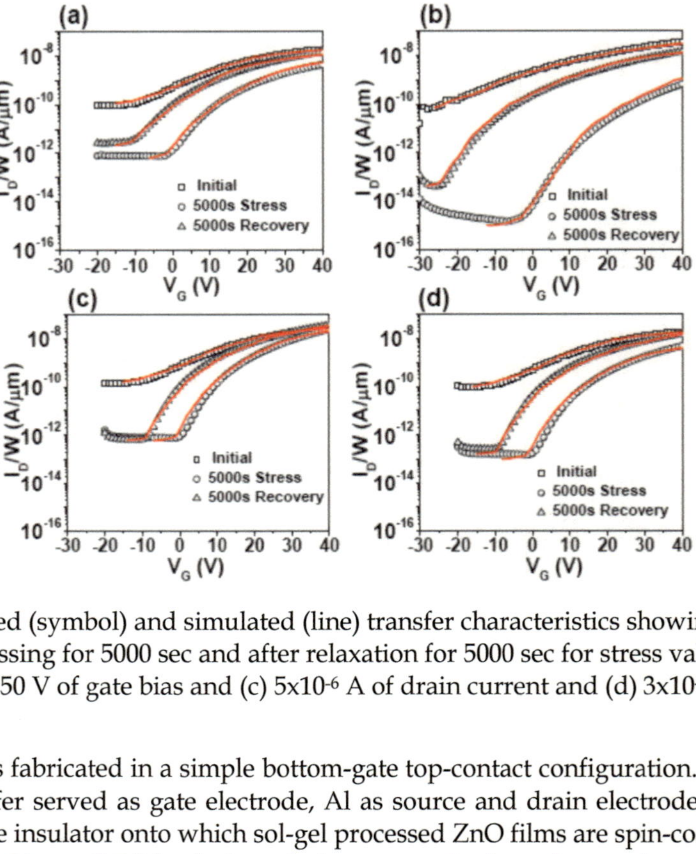

Fig. 11. Measured (symbol) and simulated (line) transfer characteristics showing initial curve, after stressing for 5000 sec and after relaxation for 5000 sec for stress values of (a) 20 V of gate bias, (b) 50 V of gate bias and (c) 5×10^{-6} A of drain current and (d) 3×10^{-5} A of drain current.

The ZnO-TFT is fabricated in a simple bottom-gate top-contact configuration. In this device, n++ silicon wafer served as gate electrode, Al as source and drain electrode, 100 nm-thick SiO_2 film as gate insulator onto which sol-gel processed ZnO films are spin-coated. The sol is prepared by making a 0.5 M solution of zinc acetate in the solvent mixture of DMF and methoxy-ethanol (volume ratio=3:2) (Gupta et al, 2008) and then spin-coated twice on the wafer. The films were pyrolyzed at 500°C for 1 hour, yielding polycrystalline films with an average grain size of 300 nm. The channel width is 1.0 mm and channel length is 50 μm, respectively. During electrical stress measurements in bias stress mode, a voltage is applied only to the gate while keeping the source and drain grounded in order to create a uniform electric field across the channel interface. During the current stressing, a constant current was applied to the drain keeping the gate and drain connected in a diode-connected configuration, while keeping the source grounded. This measurement configuration allows automatic adjustment of the gate/drain to source voltage (V_{GS}=V_{DS}) to achieve a constant drain current. The relaxation characteristics are measured soon after the stressing period of 5000 sec, while keeping all three terminals grounded. Figure 11a – 11d shows the obtained stress- recovery characteristics of the device in the gate bias (gate bias value = 20V and 50V) and current stress (current stress value= 5x10^{-6} A and 3x10^{-5} A) mode, respectively. As shown in Fig. 11, for both the gate bias and current stress, the on- current decreases and transfer curves shift to more positive gate voltages leading to a positive threshold voltage shift. Additionally, off- currents (V_G = -30 V) are reduced to a greater extent than the on current (V_G = 40V) in the stressing period of 5000 sec, which causes an improvement in the on/off ratio of the device. Also, to be noted is that in the first 2x10^3 sec of the stressing period approximately, the change in the off current and subthreshold slope (S) is maximum, after which this variation is not that significant. However, under both the voltage and current stress conditions, the transfer curves keep on shifting to the higher positive gate voltage values without change in S value. The mobility values, on the other hand, continue to decrease for the whole stress period. During the recovery period, the transfer curves shift in a parallel way towards negative value for approximately 2000 s, and then S/off-current values increase slowly on relaxing the devices subsequently. However, the initial on drain-current values could not be fully recovered in the measured period of 5000 sec.

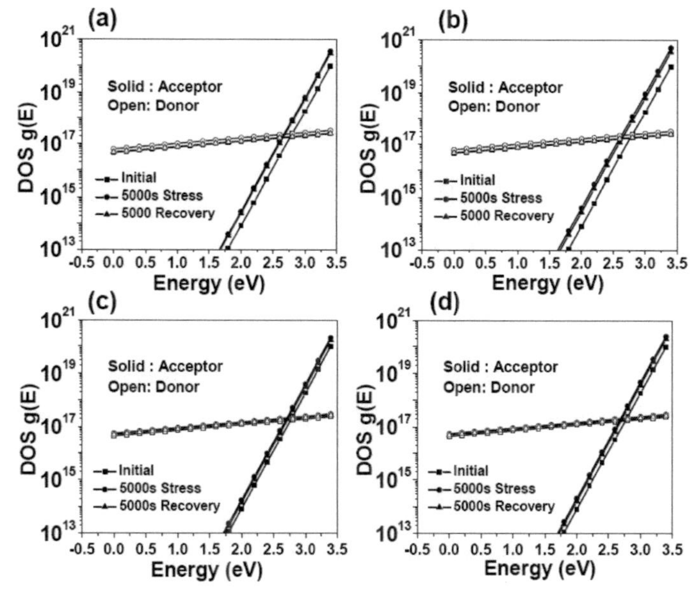

Fig. 12. Variation in density of states (DOS) during stress and recovery period for stress values of (a) 20 V of gate bias, (b) 50 V of gate bias and (c) 5x10^{-6} A of drain current and (d) 3x10^{-5} A of drain current.

In order to investigate deeply into the microscopic details of the instability mechanisms, we performed two dimensional device simulations by modelling ZnO films with a continuous and spatially uniform density of states (DOS) throughout its volume. This assumption is based on the fine grain structure of sol-gel ZnO films, which can be considered as composed of small crystalline grains embedded in an amorphous matrix. This kind of structure may produce a large defect density within the grain boundaries as well as in the grains. The total density of states g(E) is assumed to have exponential distribution of donor (D) like and acceptor (A) like defects that follow the equations 4a and 4c, respectively. This DOS model is attractive because of its simplicity and accuracy and has been used as the basis for many studies on metal oxide based TFTs (Hossain et al, 2003, 2004; Fung et al, 2009; Ming et al, 2009) . Additionally, traps at the semiconductor – dielectric interface are assumed, which are defined by their concentration (N_{it}) and energy level (E_{it}). Also shown in Fig. 11 are the simulated transfer characteristics using the above mentioned DOS model during stress and recovery. The obtained DOS distribution is shown in Fig. 12, and the values of N_{it} and E_{it} are listed in Table 2. It is to be noted that since off-current region in the transfer curves invariably exists in the negative gate voltage region, donor states have to be kept near conduction band edge (above mid-gap) in order to reproduce the observed behavior. The donor-like states near the mid-gap tend to be a recombination-generation center, helping electrons jump to the conduction band and increasing the leakage current. The acceptor states, on the other hand, extend far below the conduction band and reach up to the mid-gap, which signifies the importance of deep lying defect states in affecting the transfer curves during the stress measurements. Also, important is the role of deep donor traps (1.0 -1.2 eV from the conduction band) at the semiconductor-dielectric interface, which better reproduce the simulated behavior of the off-state leakage currents. On the basis of this model, N_{it} increases by approximately 24 - 30% after stressing the devices for a period of 5000 sec from the virgin state, but is not affected much during the recovery period of 5000 sec.

	Initial		Stress (5000 sec)		Recovery (5000 sec)	
	N_{it} (cm^{-2})	E_{it} (eV)	N_{it} (cm^{-2})	E_{it} (eV)	N_{it} (cm^{-2})	E_{it} (eV)
20V	8.4×10^{11}	1.13	1.1×10^{12}	1.16	1.0×10^{12}	1.16
50V	9.3×10^{11}	1.05	1.2×10^{12}	1.03	1.1×10^{12}	1.05
5×10^{-6} A	7.3×10^{11}	1.09	9.1×10^{11}	1.1	8.9×10^{11}	1.1
3×10^{-5} A	8.1×10^{11}	1.09	9.3×10^{11}	1.08	8.3×10^{11}	1.08

Table 2. Simulated values of N_{it} and E_{it} of the donor- like traps at semiconductor-dielectric interface for the initial state, after stressing for 5000 sec, and after relaxation for 5000 sec for different gate bias and drain current stress conditions.

The obtained DOS, as in Fig. 12, indicates that acceptor and donor states both vary from virgin to stress state and from stress to recovery state , however, acceptor like defect states are higher in density than the donor like defect states in the region near the conduction band (approximately 0.7 eV from the conduction band). The acceptor like defects also have pronounced effect in this region and affects the transfer curves significantly. Further, it was observed that the variation in N_{TA} and N_{TD} values from virgin to stress state and from stress to recovery state has more dominant effect than the change in slope values (W_{TA} and W_{TD}). An estimate of change in values of N_{TA} and N_{TD} from virgin to stress state and from stress to recovery state revealed that N_{TA} increases approximately 40% more than N_{TD} after stressing the device for a period of 5000 sec from the virgin state, for all the gate bias and current stress levels. This variation in N_{TA} is also significantly more than donor-like states during the recovery period. These results make it clear that acceptor like defects are substantially influential in affecting both the stress and recovery characteristics. This also explains the decrease in S value, positive V_T shift and relatively larger reduction in off currents on stressing the devices, because acceptor like defects strongly affects both the subthreshold and above threshold region.

Based on the simulation results, it is possible to correlate the electrical stress effect to the inherent defect chemistry of ZnO, ambient and to the ZnO-dielectric interface. In ZnO crystals and films, oxygen vacancies and zinc interstitials are identified as the two most common metastable defects (Ashrafi et al, 2007; Özgür et al, 2005). Whereas, positively charged oxygen vacancies can behave as acceptor-like traps, zinc interstitials act as donor defects. The oxygen vacancies tend to trap free electron carriers by a long-range coulomb interaction, which causes a positive shift of the transfer curves. Additionally, oxygen or water may get adsorbed on the surface of films, which predominantly create acceptor-like states in zinc oxide based materials (Chen et al, 2010; Li et al, 2005). Though further detailed studies are needed to distinguish between the operating mechanisms affecting the instability, we can say that the main degradation mechanism is the trapping by acceptor-like defects in upper half of the bandgap of solution processed ZnO, and donor-like trap generation at the semiconductor-dielectric interface.

7. Effect of Li- doping on environmental stability of ZnO TFTs

In solution processed Li-doped ZnO TFTs, Al serves as source and drain electrodes, ITO as gate electrode, and 215nm thick aluminium-tin-oxide (ATO) as insulator. The channel length (L) is 50 µm and width (W) is 1000 µm, respectively. Li-ZnO is coated from a precursor solution following thermal pyrolysis (Nayak et al, 2009). The investigated Li concentrations were 0%, 15% and 25%, and the device characteristics were checked in fresh state and after 7 days of exposure. First, the similar methodology developed in section 6 was adopted that used density of states as exponential distribution of both acceptor and donor -like traps. However, for any set of values of N_{TA}, N_{TD}, W_{TA} and W_{TD}, it was observed that simulated results using this DOS model was only partially successful for ach amount of Li doping. More specifically, the subthreshold region which is highly dependent on donor like traps showed a large amount of deviation in the exposed states. Therefore, another model which Gaussian distribution of both acceptor and donor - like traps is adopted to define the DOS states in these devices. This model too cannot reproduce the experimental device characteristics fully. Based on the above observations, a DOS model that combines exponential distribution of acceptor (A) like defects and Gaussian distribution of donor (D) like defects are employed that follow the expressions in Eq. 4.
Figure 13a and 13b shows the optimized fittings to the experimental transfer characteristics, using the DOS model in Eq. 4, for 0%, 15% and 25% Li-doped ZnO, respectively, in the fresh state and after 7 days of air exposure. The fitting parameters are listed in Table 3 and the obtained DOS distribution is shown in Fig. 14. As can be seen from Fig. 14, the density of acceptor states near the conduction band tail edge is higher, while they are significantly lower as one goes deep down the bandgap, for the devices with 25% Li- doping in comparison to devices without Li-doping. This arises due to the different slope values (W_{TA}) for devices with and without Li-doping. On the other hand, the donor states are significantly lesser in the devices with 25% Li-doping as compared to the devices without doping, in both the fresh and exposed states. Also, in the devices without Li-doping, both the donor and acceptor states increase on exposing the devices to the environment. However, in the case of devices with 25% Li-doping, the donor states showed a slight increase, while acceptor states decrease slightly, on exposing the devices. This might also arise due to some error in fitting parameters. On the whole, however, the devices with 25% Li-doping are not significantly affected by the environmental exposure.

Therefore, these results can partially explain the better performance of Li-doped TFTs in terms of improved subthreshold slope, better on/off ratio and improved air stability than the undoped ones. Also, it can be clearly said that Li- doping is effective in controlling the defect states in ZnO TFTs, which helps in improving its stability when exposed to the air for a prolonged period of time.

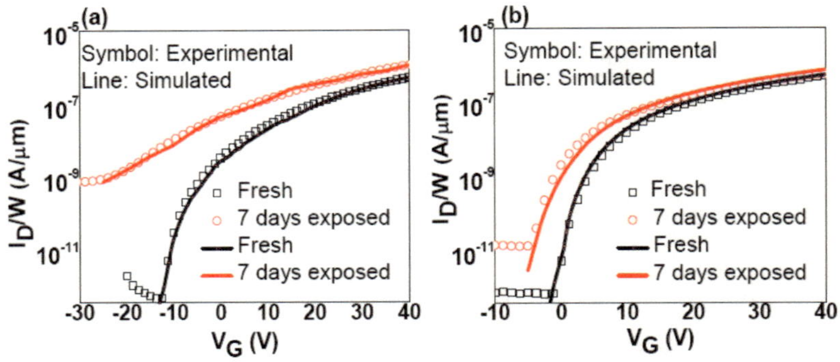

Fig. 13. Comparison of simulated and experimental transfer curves for (a) undoped and (b) 25% Li- doped ZnO TFTs in fresh state and after 7 days of air exposure at drain voltage of 40 V.

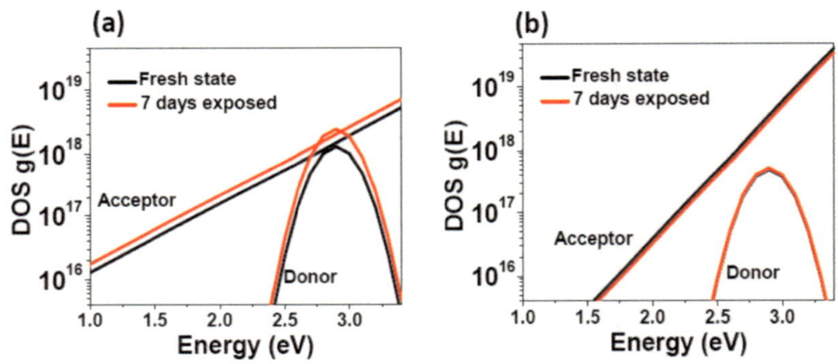

Fig. 14. The obtained density of states (DOS) distribution in the fresh state and after 7 days of air exposure for (a) undoped and (b) 25% Li- doped ZnO TFTs

	0% Li		**25 % Li**	
	Fresh	***Exposed***	***Fresh***	***Exposed***
N_{TA} *(cm⁻³)*	$5.2x10^{18}$	$7x10^{18}$	$4.2x10^{19}$	$3.5x10^{19}$
W_{TA} *(eV)*	0.4	0.4	0.2	0.2
N_{GD} *(cm⁻³)*	$1.3x10^{18}$	$2.4x10^{18}$	$4.8x10^{17}$	$5.1x10^{17}$
E_{GD} *(eV)*	0.5	0.5	0.5	0.5
W_{GD} *(eV)*	0.2	0.2	0.2	0.2

Table 3. List of fitting parameters for undoped and 25 % Li -doped ZnO TFTs

8. Conclusion

In conclusion, the important role of device simulations in a better understanding of the material properties and device mechanisms is recognized in TFTs based on organic and metal oxide semiconductors. The effect of physical behaviour related to semiconductor film properties in relation to charge injection and charge transport is underlined by providing illustrations from pentacene, TIPS- pentacene and ZnO based TFTs. The device simulations significantly help in explaining the complex device phenomenon that occur at the metal-semiconductor interface, semiconductor-dielectric interface, and in the semiconductor film in the form of defect distribution.

9. References

Alam, M. A., Dodabalapur, A. & Pinto, M. R. (1997), "A two-dimensional simulation of organic transistors." *Ieee Transactions on Electron Devices,* Vol. 44, No. 8, pp. 1332-1337, ISSN 0018-9383

Ashrafi, A. & Jagadish, C. (2007), "Review of zincblende ZnO: Stability of metastable ZnO phases." *Journal of Applied Physics,* Vol. 102, No. 7, pp. 71101-71113, ISSN 0021-8979

Bolognesi, A., Di Carlo, A.&Lugli, P. (2002), "Influence of carrier mobility and contact barrier height on the electrical characteristics of organic transistors." *Applied Physics Letters,* Vol. 81, No. 24, pp. 4646-4648, ISSN 0003-6951

Scott, J. C. & Bozano, L. D. (2007), "Nonvolatile memory elements based on organic materials." *Advanced Materials,* Vol. 19, No. 11, pp. 1452-1463, ISSN 0935-9648

Cherian, S., Donley, C., Mathine, D., LaRussa, L., Xia, W. & Armstrong, N. (2004), "Effects of field dependent mobility and contact barriers on liquid crystalline phthalocyanine organic transistors." *Journal of Applied Physics,* Vol. 96, No. 10, pp. 5638-5643, ISSN 0021-8979

Chen, Y. C., Chang, T. C., Li, H. W., Chen, S. C., Lu, J., Chung, W. F., Tai, Y. H. & Tseng, T. Y. (2010), "Bias-induced oxygen adsorption in zinc tin oxide thin film transistors under dynamic stress." *Applied Physics Letters,* Vol. 96, No. 26, pp. 262104-262107, ISSN 0003-6951

Dinelli, F., Murgia, M., Levy, P., Cavallini, M., Biscarini, F. & de Leeuw, D. M. (2004), "Spatially correlated charge transport in organic thin film transistors." *Physical Review Letters,* Vol. 92, No. 11, pp. 116802 -, ISSN 0031-9007

Dodabalapur, A., Torsi, L. & Katz, H. E. (1995), "Organic Transistors - 2-Dimensional Transport and Improved Electrical Characteristics." *Science,* Vol. 268, No. 5208, pp. 270-271, ISSN 0036-8075

Fortunato, E., Correia, N., Barquinha, P., Pereira, L., Goncalves, G.&Martins, R. (2008), "High-performance flexible hybrid field-effect transistors based on cellulose fiber paper." *Ieee Electron Device Letters,* Vol. 29, No. 9, pp. 988-990, ISSN 0741-3106

Fung, T. C., Chuang, C. S., Chen, C., Abe, K., Cottle, R., Townsend, M., Kumomi, H.&Kanicki, J. (2009), "Two-dimensional numerical simulation of radio frequency sputter amorphous In-Ga-Zn-O thin-film transistors." *Journal of Applied Physics,* Vol. 106, No. 8, pp. 84511-84521, ISSN 0021-8979

Granstrom, E. L. & Frisbie, C. D. (1999), "Field effect conductance measurements on thin crystals of sexithiophene." *Journal of Physical Chemistry B,* Vol. 103, No. 42, pp. 8842-8849, ISSN 1089-5647

Gundlach, D. J., Zhou, L., Nichols, J. A., Jackson, T. N., Necliudov, P. V.&Shur, M. S. (2006), "An experimental study of contact effects in organic thin film transistors." *Journal of Applied Physics,* Vol. 100, No. 2, pp. 024509-024512, ISSN 0021-8979

Gupta, D., Anand, M., Ryu, S. W., Choi, Y. K.&Yoo, S. (2008), "Nonvolatile memory based on sol-gel ZnO thin-film transistors with Ag nanoparticles embedded in the ZnO/gate insulator interface." *Applied Physics Letters,* Vol. 93, No. 22, pp. 224106-224108, ISSN 0003-6951

Gupta, D., Jeon, N.&Yoo, S. (2008), "Modeling the electrical characteristics of TIPS-pentacene thin-film transistors: Effect of contact barrier, field-dependent mobility, and traps." *Organic Electronics,* Vol. 9, No. 6, pp. 1026-1031, ISSN 1566-1199

Gupta, D.&Hong, Y. (2010), "Understanding the effect of semiconductor thickness on device characteristics in organic thin film transistors by way of two-dimensional simulations." *Organic Electronics,* Vol. 11, No. 1, pp. 127-136, ISSN 1566-1199

Gupta, D., Katiyar, M.&Gupta, D. (2009), "An analysis of the difference in behavior of top and bottom contact organic thin film transistors using device simulation." *Organic Electronics,* Vol. 10, No. 5, pp. 775-784, ISSN 1566-1199

Hill, I. G. (2005), "Numerical simulations of contact resistance in organic thin-film transistors." *Applied Physics Letters,* Vol. 87, No. 16, pp. 63514-63516, ISSN 0003-6951

Horowitz, G. (2003), "Tunneling current in polycrystalline organic thin-film transistors." *Advanced Functional Materials,* Vol. 13, No. 1, pp. 53-60, ISSN 1616-301X

Hossain, F. M., Nishii, J., Takagi, S., Ohtomo, A., Fukumura, T., Fujioka, H., Ohno, H., Koinuma, H. & Kawasaki, M. (2003), "Modeling and simulation of polycrystalline ZnO thin-film transistors." *Journal of Applied Physics,* Vol. 94, No. 12, pp. 7768-7777, ISSN 0021-8979

Hossain, F. M., Nishii, J., Takagi, S., Sugihara, T., Ohtomo, A., Fukumura, T., Koinuma, H., Ohno, H.&Kawasaki, M. (2004), "Modeling of grain boundary barrier modulation in ZnO invisible thin film transistors." *Physica E-Low-Dimensional Systems & Nanostructures,* Vol. 21, No. 2-4, pp. 911-915, ISSN 1386-9477

Houili, H., Picon, J. D., Zuppiroli, L.&Bussac, M. N. (2006), "Polarization effects in the channel of an organic field-effect transistor." *Journal of Applied Physics,* Vol. 100, No. 2, pp. 23702-23706, ISSN 0021-8979

Jahinuzzaman, S. M., Sultana, A., Sakariya, K., Servati, P.&Nathan, A. (2005), "Threshold voltage instability of amorphous silicon thin-film transistors under constant current stress." *Applied Physics Letters,* Vol. 87, No. 2, pp. 23502-23505, ISSN 0003-6951

Ishii, H., Sugiyama, K., Ito, E.&Seki, K. (1999), "Energy level alignment and interfacial electronic structures at organic metal and organic organic interfaces." *Advanced Materials,* Vol. 11, No. 8, pp. 605-+, ISSN 0935-9648

Kahn, A., Koch, N.&Gao, W. Y. (2003), "Electronic structure and electrical properties of interfaces between metals and pi-conjugated molecular films." *Journal of Polymer Science Part B-Polymer Physics,* Vol. 41, No. 21, pp. 2529-2548, ISSN 0887-6266

Kang, J. H.&Zhu, X. Y. (2003), "Pi-stacked pentacene thin films grown on Au(111)." *Applied Physics Letters,* Vol. 82, No. 19, pp. 3248-3250, ISSN 0003-6951

Kiguchi, M., Yoshikawa, G., Ikeda, S.&Saiki, K. (2005), "Electronic properties of metal-induced gap states formed at alkali-halide/metal interfaces." *Physical Review B,* Vol. 71, No. 15, pp. 353321-353324, ISSN 1098-0121

Kirova, N.&Bussac, M. N. (2003), "Self-trapping of electrons at the field-effect junction of a molecular crystal." *Physical Review B,* Vol. 68, No. 23, pp. 235312 -235316, ISSN 1098-0121

Koch, N., Ghijsen, J., Johnson, R. L., Schwartz, J., Pireaux, J. J.&Kahn, A. (2002), "Physiscrption-like interaction at the interfaces formed by pentacene and samarium." *Journal of Physical Chemistry B,* Vol. 106, No. 16, pp. 4192-4196, ISSN 1520-6106

Knipp, D., Street, R. A., Volkel, A.&Ho, J. (2003), "Pentacene thin film transistors on inorganic dielectrics: Morphology, structural properties, and electronic transport." *Journal of Applied Physics,* Vol. 93, No. 1, pp. 347-355, ISSN 0021-8979

Kymissis, I., Dimitrakopoulos, C. D.&Purushothaman, S. (2001), "High-performance bottom electrode organic thin-film transistors." *Ieee Transactions on Electron Devices,* Vol. 48, No. 6, pp. 1060-1064, ISSN 0018-9383

Lee, K. S., Smith, T. J., Dickey, K. C., Yoo, J. E., Stevenson, K. J.&Loo, Y. L. (2006), "High-resolution characterization of pentacene/polyaniline interfaces in thin-film transistors." *Advanced Functional Materials,* Vol. 16, No. 18, pp. 2409-2414, ISSN 1616-301X

Li, Q. H., Gao, T., Wang, Y. G.&Wang, T. H. (2005), "Adsorption and desorption of oxygen probed from ZnO nanowire films by photocurrent measurements." *Applied Physics Letters,* Vol. 86, No. 12, pp. 123117-123120, ISSN 0003-6951

Masuda, S., Kitamura, K., Okumura, Y., Miyatake, S., Tabata, H.&Kawai, T. (2003), "Transparent thin film transistors using ZnO as an active channel layer and their electrical properties." *Journal of Applied Physics,* Vol. 93, No. 3, pp. 1624-1630, ISSN 0021-8979

Zhou, Y. M., He, Y. G., Lu, A. X.&Wan, Q. (2009), "Simulation of grain boundary effect on characteristics of ZnO thin film transistor by considering the location and orientation of grain boundary." *Chinese Physics B,* Vol. 18, No. 9, pp. 3966-3969, ISSN 1674-1056

McCluskey, M. D.&Jokela, S. J. (2009), "Defects in ZnO." *Journal of Applied Physics,* Vol. 106, No. 7, pp. -, ISSN 0021-8979

Nayak, P. K., Jang, J., Lee, C.&Hong, Y. (2009), "Effects of Li doping on the performance and environmental stability of solution processed ZnO thin film transistors." *Applied Physics Letters,* Vol. 95, No. 19, pp. 71101-71113, ISSN 0003-695

Nelson, S. F., Lin, Y. Y., Gundlach, D. J.&Jackson, T. N. (1998), "Temperature-independent transport in high-mobility pentacene transistors." *Applied Physics Letters,* Vol. 72, No. 15, pp. 1854-1856, ISSN 0003-6951

Ozgur, U., Alivov, Y. I., Liu, C., Teke, A., Reshchikov, M. A., Dogan, S., Avrutin, V., Cho, S. J.&Morkoc, H. (2005), "A comprehensive review of ZnO materials and devices." *Journal of Applied Physics,* Vol. 98, No. 4, pp. 41301-41404, ISSN 0021-8979

Ostroverkhova, O., Cooke, D. G., Hegmann, F. A., Tykwinski, R. R., Parkin, S. R.&Anthony, J. E. (2006), "Anisotropy of transient photoconductivity in functionalized pentacene single crystals." *Applied Physics Letters,* Vol. 89, No. 19, pp. -, ISSN 0003-6951

Park, S. K., Jackson, T. N., Anthony, J. E.&Mourey, D. A. (2007), "High mobility solution processed 6,13-bis(triisopropyl-silylethynyl) pentacene organic thin film transistors." *Applied Physics Letters,* Vol. 91, No. 6, pp. 63514 -63516, ISSN 0003-6951

Pesavento, P. V., Puntambekar, K. P., Frisbie, C. D., McKeen, J. C.&Ruden, P. P. (2006), "Film and contact resistance in pentacene thin-film transistors: Dependence on film thickness, electrode geometry, and correlation with hole mobility." *Journal of Applied Physics,* Vol. 99, No. 9, pp. 94504-94508, ISSN 0021-8979

Pope, M. & Swenberg, C. E. (1999) Electronic Processes in Organic Crystals and Polymers ~Oxford University Press, New York

Puntambekar, K., Dong, J. P., Haugstad, G.&Frisbie, C. D. (2006), "Structural and electrostatic complexity at a pentacene/insulator interface." *Advanced Functional Materials,* Vol. 16, No. 7, pp. 879-884, ISSN 1616-301X

Roichman, Y.&Tessler, N. (2002), "Structures of polymer field-effect transistor: Experimental and numerical analyses." *Applied Physics Letters,* Vol. 80, No. 1, pp. 151-153, ISSN 0003-6951

Ruiz, R., Papadimitratos, A., Mayer, A. C.&Malliaras, G. G. (2005), "Thickness dependence of mobility in pentacene thin-film transistors." *Advanced Materials,* Vol. 17, No. 14, pp. 1795-+, ISSN 0935-9648

Sandberg, H. G. O., Frey, G. L., Shkunov, M. N., Sirringhaus, H., Friend, R. H., Nielsen, M. M.&Kumpf, C. (2002), "Ultrathin regioregular poly(3-hexyl thiophene) field-effect transistors." *Langmuir,* Vol. 18, No. 26, pp. 10176-10182, ISSN 0743-7463

Scheinert, S.&Paasch, G. (2004), "Fabrication and analysis of polymer field-effect transistors." *Physica Status Solidi a-Applied Research,* Vol. 201, No. 6, pp. 1263-1301, ISSN 0031-8965

Schroeder, P. G., France, C. B., Park, J. B.&Parkinson, B. A. (2003), "Orbital alignment and morphology of pentacene deposited on Au(111) and SnS2 studied using photoemission spectroscopy." *Journal of Physical Chemistry B,* Vol. 107, No. 10, pp. 2253-2261, ISSN 1520-6106

Schroeder, R., Majewski, L. A.&Grell, M. (2003), "A study of the threshold voltage in pentacene organic field-effect transistors." *Applied Physics Letters,* Vol. 83, No. 15, pp. 3201-3203, ISSN 0003-6951

Sebastian, L., Weiser, G.&Bassler, H. (1981), "Charge-Transfer Transitions in Solid Tetracene and Pentacene Studied by Electro-Absorption." *Chemical Physics,* Vol. 61, No. 1-2, pp. 125-135, ISSN 0301-0104

Sheraw, C. D., Jackson, T. N., Eaton, D. L.&Anthony, J. E. (2003), "Functionalized pentacene active layer organic thin-film transistors." *Advanced Materials,* Vol. 15, No. 23, pp. 2009-2011, ISSN 0935-9648

Silinsh, E.A. and Čápek, V. (1980) Organic Molecular Crystals. Their Electronic States., New York

Silinsh, E. A., Klimkans, A., Larsson, S.&Capek, V. (1995), "Molecular Polaron States in Polyacene Crystals - Formation and Transfer Processes." *Chemical Physics,* Vol. 198, No. 3, pp. 311-331, ISSN 0301-0104

Stassen, A. F., de Boer, R. W. I., Iosad, N. N.&Morpurgo, A. F. (2004), "Influence of the gate dielectric on the mobility of rubrene single-crystal field-effect transistors." *Applied Physics Letters,* Vol. 85, No. 17, pp. 3899-3901, ISSN 0003-6951

Steudel, S., De Vusser, S., De Jonge, S., Janssen, D., Verlaak, S., Genoe, J.&Heremans, P. (2004), "Influence of the dielectric roughness on the performance of pentacene transistors." *Applied Physics Letters,* Vol. 85, No. 19, pp. 4400-4402, ISSN 0003-6951

Street, R. A.&Salleo, A. (2002), "Contact effects in polymer transistors." *Applied Physics Letters,* Vol. 81, No. 15, pp. 2887-2889, ISSN 0003-6951

Street, R. A., Knipp, D.&Volkel, A. R. (2002), "Hole transport in polycrystalline pentacene transistors." *Applied Physics Letters,* Vol. 80, No. 9, pp. 1658-1660, ISSN 0003-6951

Tessler, N.&Roichman, Y. (2001), "Two-dimensional simulation of polymer field-effect transistor." *Applied Physics Letters,* Vol. 79, No. 18, pp. 2987-2989, ISSN 0003-6951

Veres, J., Ogier, S. D., Leeming, S. W., Cupertino, D. C.&Khaffaf, S. M. (2003), "Low-k insulators as the choice of dielectrics in organic field-effect transistors." *Advanced Functional Materials,* Vol. 13, No. 3, pp. 199-204, ISSN 1616-301X

Wang, L. A., Fine, D., Basu, D.&Dodabalapur, A. (2007), "Electric-field-dependent charge transport in organic thin-film transistors." *Journal of Applied Physics,* Vol. 101, No. 5, pp. 54515-54519, ISSN 0021-8979

Wehrspohn, R. B., Powell, M. J.&Deane, S. C. (2003), "Kinetics of defect creation in amorphous silicon thin film transistors." *Journal of Applied Physics,* Vol. 93, No. 9, pp. 5780-5788, ISSN 0021-8979

5

Numerical Simulation of a Gyro-BWO with a Helically Corrugated Interaction Region, Cusp Electron Gun and Depressed Collector

Wenlong He, Craig R. Donaldson, Liang Zhang, Kevin Ronald, Alan D. R. Phelps and Adrian W. Cross
SUPA, Department of Physics, University of Strathclyde, Glasgow, G4 0NG Scotland, UK

1. Introduction

The gyrotron backward wave oscillator (gyro-BWO) is an efficient source of frequency-tunable high-power coherent radiation in the microwave to the terahertz range. It has attracted significant research interest recently due to its potential applications in many areas such as remote sensing, medical imaging, plasma heating and spectroscopy. A gyro-BWO using a helically corrugated interaction region (HCIR) has achieved an even wider frequency tuning range and higher efficiency compared with a conventional gyro-BWO with a smooth-bore cavity. This is due to the existence of an "ideal"eigenwave in the HCIR with a large and constant group velocity when the axial wave number is small.

The eigenwave has a TE_{21}-like cross-sectional electric field distribution. For such a field structure it is favourable to use the second harmonic of the electron cyclotron frequency of an axis-encircling electron beam to interact with the wave. The advantage being that it lowers the required magnetic field strength by a factor of two whilst avoiding undesired parasitic oscillations. Therefore a cusp gun was used to produce an annular, axis-encircling electron beam with high velocity ratio, α (ratio of transverse velocity to axial velocity) for the gyro-BWO. This has inherent advantages over a solid beam for energy recovery due to the reduced beam power density in the collector surface making high power ($\sim$ kWs) continuous wave (CW) operation of a gyro-BWO more feasible. The overall efficiency of the gyro-BWO is further improved by using a four-stage depressed collector which recovers the energy from the spent electrons of the gyro-BWO.

The 3D particle-in-cell (PiC) code MAGIC was used to simulate the electron beam trajectories, beam-wave interaction and wave growth in the gyro-BWO. The trajectories of the electrons were simulated including their emission from the cathode, acceleration in the cusp gun region, transportation and interaction in the helical interaction region and deceleration in the depressed collector. Through the simulations a thermionic cusp electron gun was optimized to produce a 40 keV, 1.5 A, large-orbit, electron beam with an axial velocity spread $\Delta v_z/v_z$ of $\sim$8% and a relative α spread $\Delta\alpha/\alpha$ of $\sim$10% at an α value of 1.65. When driven by such a beam the gyro-BWO was simulated to have a 3 dB frequency bandwidth of 84–104 GHz, output power of 10 kW with an electronic efficiency of 17%. The optimization of the shape and dimensions of each stage of the depressed collector using a genetic algorithm achieved an overall recovery efficiency of about 70%, with a minimized back-streaming rate of 4.9% and maximum heat density on the electrodes of 240 W/cm^2. An overall efficiency of 40% was therefore simulated for the gyro-BWO.

A number of gyro-BWOs have been investigated both in theory and experiments. Two such experiments at the Naval Research Laboratory (Park et al., 1990) and the National Tsing Hua University (Kou et al., 1993) operating at the fundamental cyclotron harmonic and the fundamental mode of a smooth cylindrical waveguide demonstrated impressive voltage and frequency tuning up to 5% and 13%, respectively with a very high efficiency of nearly 20% at power levels of up to 100 kW at Ka-band frequencies. High-power, high-frequency, coherent radiation sources, especially in the range of mm and sub-mm wavelengths, have attracted significant research interest recently due to their desirable applications in many areas such as remote sensing (Manheimer et al., 1994), medical imaging (Arnone et al., 1999), plasma heating (Imai et al., 2001) and spectroscopy (Smirnova et al., 1995). Gyro-devices are promising candidates to fulfill such a demand due to the advantages of their characteristic fast wave interaction.

A HCIR has been demonstrated with a wave dispersion that has a near constant group velocity in the region of small axial wavenumber (Burt et al., 2005; 2004; McStravick et al., 2010; Samsonov et al., 2004). This allows broadband microwave amplification to be achieved in a gyrotron traveling wave amplifier (gyro-TWA) and wide frequency tuning in a gyro-BWO without compromising interaction efficiency and output power when compared with its counterparts using cylindrical smooth-bore waveguides (Bratman et al., 2007; 2000). Previous experiments using such a microwave system at Ka-band achieved an output power of ~1 MW, an efficiency of 10%, a frequency tuning band of 15% using a 20 ns, 300 keV electron beam (Bratman et al., 2001). Recently a relative frequency-tuning band of 17% at X-band with 16.5% electronic efficiency was achieved (Denisov et al., 1998; He et al., 2005) at the second harmonic of the electron cyclotron mode using a three-fold HCIR and an axis-encircling electron beam. Research projects involving a W-band gyro-BWO using a HCIR are in progress at the University of Strathclyde. The setup of the device is shown in Fig. 1.

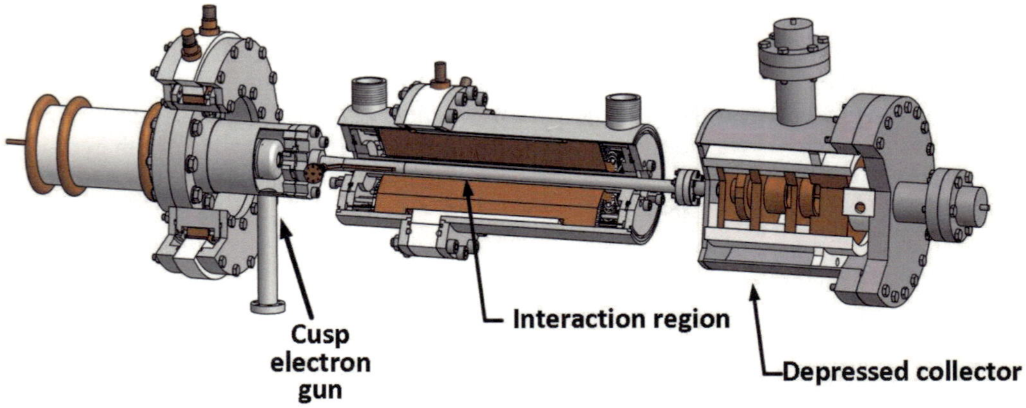

Fig. 1. The experimental setup of the W-band gyro-BWO.

Presented in this chapter is the simulation and optimization of the W-band gyro-BWO by using MAGIC (Goplen et al., 1995; Ludeking et al., 2003), (MAGnetic Insulation Code) by

Mission Research Laboratory. MAGIC simulates the interaction between charged particles and electromagnetic fields as they evolve in time and space from their initial states. Time and three-dimensional space are divided into finite grids. For each time step, the electromagnetic fields in the three-dimensional grids are solved from the Maxwell equations which are discretized with centered difference approximations. Then the complete Lorentz force equation was used to advance the momenta and coordinates of all charged particles in the simulation under the solved electromagnetic fields. The continuity equation is solved to map charge and current densities onto the grid, which are then used as sources for Maxwell's equations on the next time step. Self consistently solving Maxwell equations, the Lorentz equation and the continuity equation provided a basis for simulating beam field interaction problems.

The simulation and optimization of a thermionic cusp electron gun which generates an annular, axis-encircling electron beam is discussed in section 2. The simulation of the beam-wave interaction in the HCIR is presented in section 3. The simulation and optimization of an energy recovery system through a 4-stage depressed collector is given in section 4. Although it is possible that the integral system of the gyro-BWO, including the electron emissions from the thermionic cathode, beam acceleration in the cusp gun region, propagation in the beam-wave interaction region and deceleration in the depressed collector region and the beam-wave interaction itself can be simulated in one run, the time required to run the whole simulation would be too long. However the total simulation time can be reduced significantly by dividing it into three separate simulations as the system requires different coordinate resolution at different stages.

2. Simulation of the cusp electron gun

2.1 Introduction

The electron gun choice, design and quality of the transported beam is a very important aspect of any gyro-device. Designing the ideal diode is a complicated process taking into account many different factors including: space-charge forces, the magnetostatic and electrostatic fields and electron emission process. This section discusses the design of a cusp electron gun with numerical and analytical analysis of the cathode and electron beam.

2.2 Electron guns

There are a number of electron gun types but in gyro-devices there are three which are most common; the Magnetron Injection Gun (MIG), Pierce-like gun with "kicker"and the cusp electron gun. The MIG gun produces an annular electron beam where the electrons have small orbits each having its own axis, shown in Fig. 2(a). This type of gun is ideal for gyrotrons operating at the fundamental waveguide mode but operation with a harmonic mode is prone to parasitic oscillations. Many high-frequency gyro-devices operate at harmonics (Cooke et al., 1996; Idehara et al., 2004; Wang et al., 2000; 1994) to allow for the use of a larger cavity diameter and to decrease magnetic field strength by a factor of s, the harmonic number. An axis-encircling electron beam is ideal for harmonic gyro-devices due to its good mode selectivity as the beam-wave coupling requires that the azimuthal index of the waveguide mode, m to be equal to s (Chu, 1978). There are two such electron guns that can generate this type of beam, the Pierce-like gun with a "kicker"and the cusp electron gun. The Pierce-like gun with a "kicker"produces a solid pencil beam which travels through a magnetic "kicker"that induces azimuthal rotation so the beam will travel in a helical path through the interaction region as illustrated in Fig. 2(b). The disadvantages of this electron gun is that operation in the CW mode is difficult and the spent solid beam would cause a "bright spot"on the collector surface and hence damage the system. The cusp electron gun can generate an axis-encircling annular electron beam (see Fig. 2(c)), through a mechanism of beam generation which supports CW operation and allows the α of the beam to be controllable by changing the magnetic field strength at the cathode.

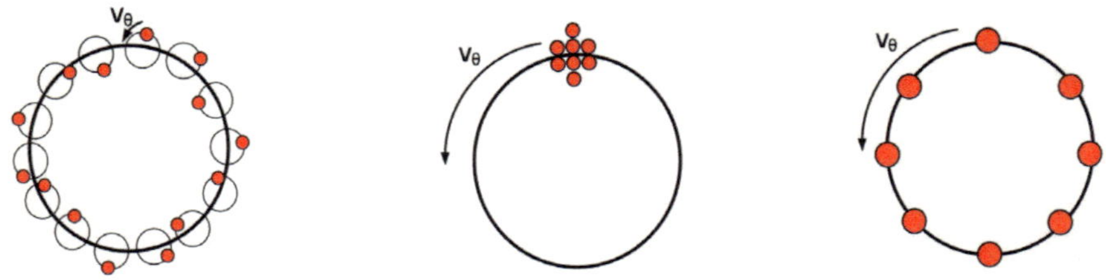

(a) MIG gun beam (b) Pierce-like gun beam with a "kicker" (c) Cusp gun produced beam

Fig. 2. Electron beam profile of various electron gun types.

2.3 Principle of the cusp electron gun

The cusp electron gun operates by utilizing two solenoids, one at the cavity region the other, with an opposite direction, just behind the cathode. The combination of magnetic fields results in a cusped magnetic field region in front of the cathode. When the electron beam passes through the cusp, the canonical angular momentum, described in Eq. 1, must be conserved. However, the vector potential A_θ is related to the amplitude of the magnetic field so the equation would then become unbalanced. In order to conserve the momentum, v_θ must change and so the electron beam will rotate around the axis of symmetry.

$$P_\theta = m v_\theta r + q r A_\theta \tag{1}$$

where r is the radius of the electrons, m is the electron mass, q is electron charge, A_θ is the vector potential.

It is possible to show (He et al., 2008) that the value of α can be described approximately through Eq. 2.

$$\alpha = \frac{v_\perp}{v_z} = \sqrt{\frac{r_c^2|\omega_c|\omega_0}{V_0^2 - r_c^2|\omega_c|\omega_0}} \tag{2}$$

where V_0 is the total electron velocity, $\omega = eB/\gamma m_e$, subscript "c" and "0" denote the cathode and the downstream uniform magnetic region. γ is the Lorentz factor of the electrons at the downstream region, and e and m_e are the charge and rest mass of the electron respectively.

The radius of the electrons in the cavity magnetic field region can be calculated by using Eq. 3 (Chen, 1974).

$$r_0 = \frac{r_c}{\sqrt{B_0/\,|B_c|}} \tag{3}$$

2.4 Previous research on cusp electron guns

Initially, transport of an electron beam through opposing magnetic fields (so called "magnetic cusp") was investigated in the 1960's (Schmidt, 1962; Sinnis & Schmidt, 1963) for plasma confinement applications. Schmidt described a threshold for magnetic mirroring of an electron stream and the effect on the electron trajectory passing through the cusp region. The main conclusion of this paper, with respect to microwave devices, is that the electrons gain azimuthal velocity around the axis of symmetry due to conservation of canonical angular momentum. This theoretical prediction was proven through experimental measurement (Sinnis & Schmidt, 1963). Building on the work of Schmidt et al., continuous efforts and progress have been made through both theoretical analysis and experimental study in the generation of the cusp-based electron beam sources (Destler & Rhee, 1977; Rhee & Destler, 1974). Special attention was paid to methods which can produce an ideal sharp cusp shape by using complex arrays of magnetic coils, magnetic poles and possibly magnetic material inside the cathode (Jeon et al., 2002; Nguyen et al., 1992; Scheitrum et al., 1989; Scheitrum & True, 1981). This culminated in a "state-of-the-art" cusp gun in 2000 by Northrop Grumman (Gallagher et al., 2000) which generated an electron beam of energy 70 kV, current 3.5 A and velocity ratio 1.5 with a small axial velocity spread of 5% at a magnetic field of ~0.25 T. Recently gyro-devices have begun to adopt cusp guns as their electron beam sources notably in lower frequency harmonic gyro-devices (McDermott et al., 1996).

A cold cathode cusp gun was developed for an X-Band gyro-TWA at the University of Strathclyde in 2007 (Cross et al., 2007). The methodology of the design was validated through results from numerical simulations, from MAGIC (MAGIC, 2002), agreeing well with the experimental results. A thermionic cusp gun was subsequently designed and numerically optimized based on this proven methodology. The MAGIC script used in this chapter is a derivative of the previous successful numerical code.

MAGIC allows different models of electron emission, for instance thermionic and explosive emission. The thermionic emission process was modeled using the Richardson-Dushman equation in Eq. 4.

$$J_e = A_e T_c^2 e^{\frac{-\phi_w}{k_B T_c}} \tag{4}$$

where T_c is the temperature of the emission surface and k_B is the Boltzmann constant. The work function, ϕ_w, was chosen to be 1.5 eV – the value found for previous cathodes using a tungsten cathode impregnated with barium.

2.5 Application requirements and design goals

Two primary goals of the design of the cusp electron gun were: a) to produce an electron beam of suitable quality to drive the gyro-BWO over the required magnetic field range; and b) to produce a design simple enough that this could be manufactured with fewer complications compared with usual electron guns. Consideration of the construction of the diode played an important role in the design process, as the cathode would be small radially and thus sensitive to manufacturing tolerances. The aim was that a good quality electron beam would be produced even with some imperfections in cathode shape. The gyro-BWO parameters as-well-as electron beam power, voltage, current and α were found through beam-wave interaction simulation of the interaction region and analytical calculations of the dispersion profile (see section 3). The targeted performances of the electron gun and gyro-BWO are given in Table 1. The axial velocity spread target of approximately less than 15% was chosen from previous investigation on the effect of velocity spread in helical waveguide gyro-devices (Denisov et al., 1998) where the velocity spread from 0% to 15% had little effect on the performance.

Beam parameter targets		Gyro-BWO	
Beam power	60 kW	Max power (CW)	10 kW
Accelerating voltage	40 kV	Efficiency	17%
Beam current	1.5 A	Frequency band	W-band
Velocity ratio (α)	1 to 2	B-field range	1.65 – 2.1 T
Axial velocity spread	<15%	Frequency tuning range	84 – 104 GHz

Table 1. Performance targets for the cusp electron gun and gyro-BWO.

The beginning of the design process focused on the emitting strip design and from this the focus electrodes and anode can be shaped around it. A schematic diagram of the general cathode geometry can be seen in Fig. 3, with some dimensions highlighted that are used in this discussion. The required dimensions of the emitter are: radial thickness of the strip, the average radius and the inclination of the surface. When a very narrow strip is chosen, a high quality beam can be produced, as the magnetic field variation – one of the leading causes of velocity and α spread – across the emission surface can be reduced at the expense of current density. Excessive current density, > 10A/cm^2, can lead to a vastly reduced cathode lifetime; therefore, the thickness of the strip is chosen to produce a current density less than this limit. In this initial design stage this value was chosen to be approximately 8A/cm^2.

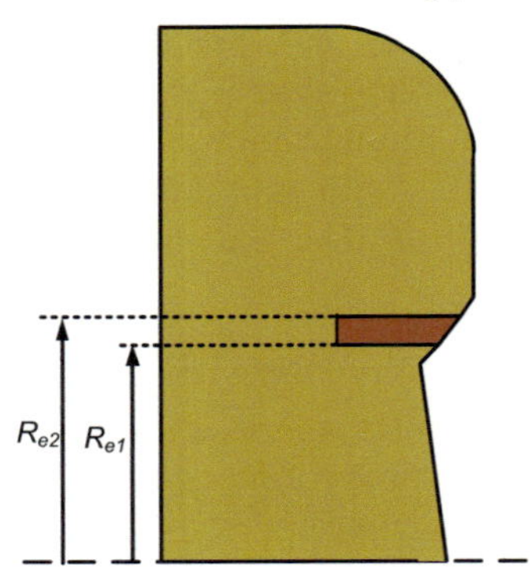

Fig. 3. Schematic diagram of the cusp electron gun cathode.

The emitting strip is inclined at an angle, as shown in Fig. 3. The average radius of the emitter can be chosen through the desired α value required. This is given through Eq. 5.

$$r_c = \frac{\alpha V_0}{\sqrt{(\alpha^2+1)}\,|\omega_c|\,\omega_0} \qquad (5)$$

The final design has the values of R_{e1}=5.79 mm, R_{e2}=6.29 mm and emission current density J_c=6 A/cm^2. A schematic diagram of the cusp gun geometry is shown in Fig. 4 with the Pierce principles (Pierce, 1954).

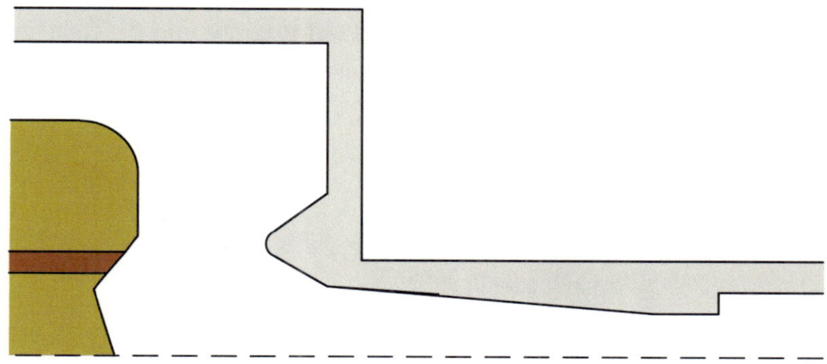

Fig. 4. Schematic of the simulation setup.

2.6 Numerical simulations

2.6.1 Simulation parameters

The geometry of the diode is simulated on a discrete spatial grid so this can lead to slight inaccuracies in the modeling when the mesh is not fine enough; however, if the system is meshed properly the results should be very accurate. The cathode can be visualized in both 2D, Fig. 5(a), and the full 3D, Fig. 5(b).

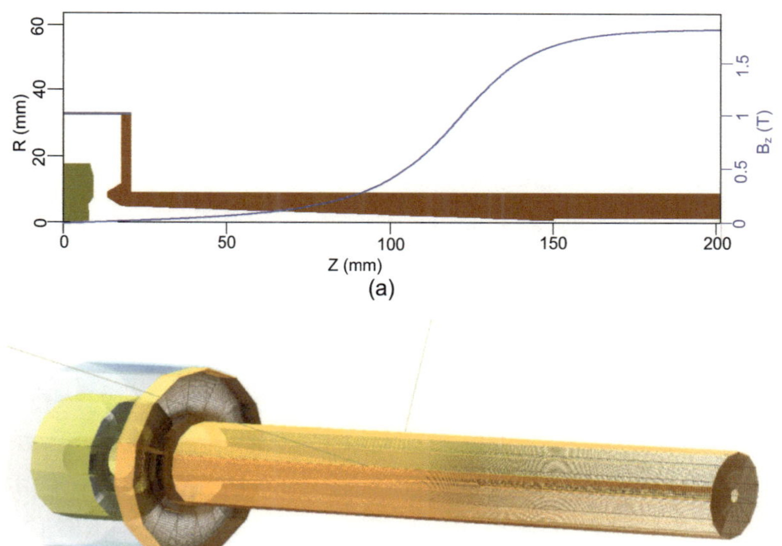

(a)

(b)

Fig. 5. Geometry of the cusp electron gun (a) 2D image with magnetic field profile overlaid and (b) 3D image.

It should be noted that although the simulation is 3D, to decrease the run-time the electron beam was only emitted from 4 points around the 360 degree axis. This still yields accurate results, as the system is axially symmetrical. In Fig. 5(a), the magnetic field is overlaid showing the position of the cusp point in relation to the geometry of the cathode and anode. In Fig. 6 a more detailed view of the cathode, focusing electrodes and anode is shown. It should be noted that at the cathode there are two small gaps above and below the emitting surface (coloured brown). These gaps stop contact between the cathode and the focus electrodes, so that the barium in the cathode would not migrate into the focusing electrodes. Such migration could lead to unwanted electron emission from the focusing electrodes.

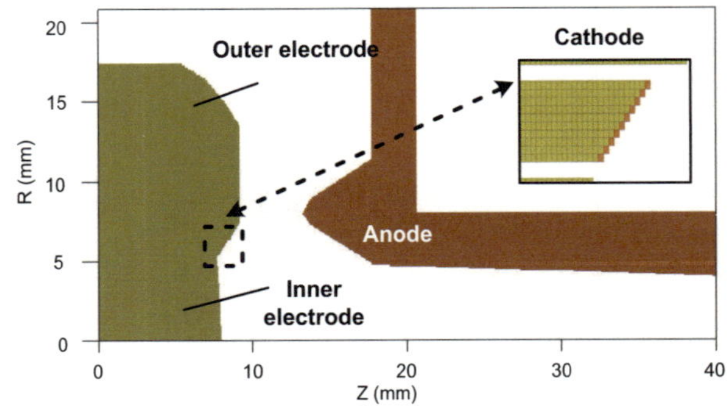

Fig. 6. A close-up view of the diode as illustrated by MAGIC.

2.6.2 Simulation of B-field profile

The magnetic coils defined in MAGIC are an approximation formed by a single line of coils at the average radius. The initial coil position is defined and then through a "do-loop" each subsequent coil is created. The magnetic field profile is critical to the operation of a cusp electron gun and the quality of the electron beam. An extra coil, so-called "shim coil", was added to each end of the cavity solenoid. The shim coils sharpen the magnetic field profile and reduce the total length of the solenoid and lower the electrical power consumption. The parameters of the solenoids are given in Table 2.

	Reverse coil	Cavity coil	1st Shim coil	2nd Shim coil
Start position	-6 cm	12.3 cm	12.3 cm	31.6 cm
Average radius	8 cm	2.84 cm	4.92cm	4.92 cm
Wire width	2.2 mm	2.2 mm	2.2 mm	2.2 mm
Number of turns	10	103	15	15
Coil current	713.28 A	3257.8 A	465.4 A	465.4 A

Table 2. Properties of the solenoids defined in MAGIC simulation code

It is important to note that while the current of the reverse coil is equal to 713.28 A in each turn, in practical terms, this would be distributed over a 4 layer coil with 178.32 A per layer. Similarly, for the cavity coil 3257.8 A is equal to 14 layers of 232.7 A per layer. The region of the flat top magnetic field strength has to match the length of the helically corrugated waveguide. The full magnetic field profile of the solenoid is shown in Fig. 7.

The magnetic fields at the cathode and the cavity solenoids are adjustable factors that determine the α value of the electron beam in the beam-wave interaction region. The spread of magnetic field over the emission surface is one of the biggest factors that contributes to velocity spread in the electron beam. The magnetic field vectors in the cusp region are shown in Fig. 8. This shows the direction and amplitude of the magnetic field that the electrons travel through from the cathode to the anode aperture. It also shows the position of the cusp point, in this case, at 4.3 mm from the middle point of the front face of the emitter.

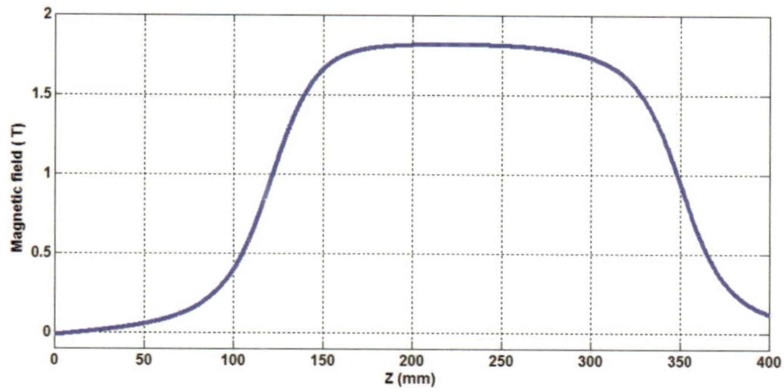

Fig. 7. Axial magnetic field (B_{max} = 1.82 T) along axis of symmetry as calculated by MAGIC.

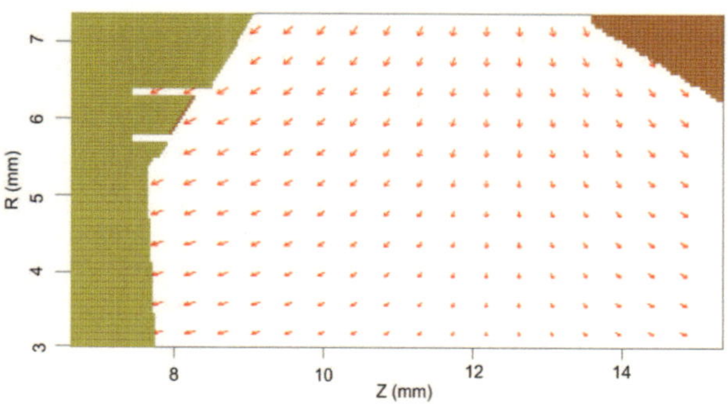

Fig. 8. Magnetic field vectors in the cathode-anode region.

2.6.3 Equipotential surfaces and electric field enhancement

The electron beam is focused as a result of the shape of the equipotentials in the diode region. The equipotentials are controlled through the shape of the focusing electrodes and the anode. The equipotentials in the diode region, Fig. 9(a), show us how the electrons are focused by the shape of the anode and cathode surface. The inner and outer focusing electrodes are used to convey the electron beam into the anode aperture.

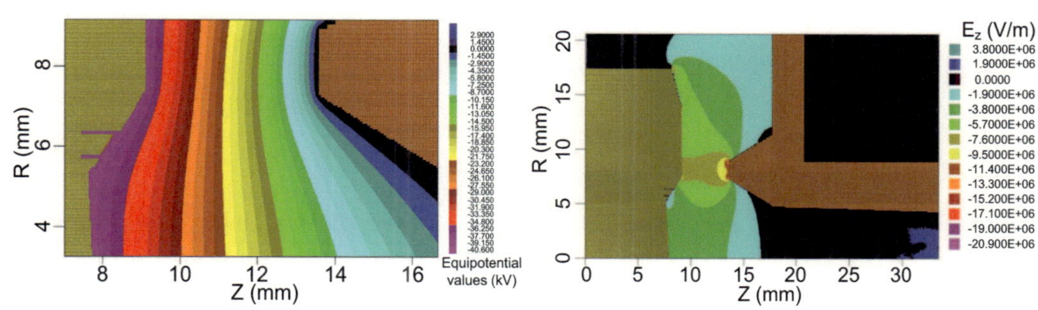

(a) Equipotentials (b) E_z

Fig. 9. Electric field profile in the cathode-anode region.

The magnitude of the electric field at the cathode and anode gap is a concern for electron gun design due to the possibility of electric field breakdown. The electric field at the cathode surface is required to be lower than the breakdown threshold in vacuum in order to ensure the cathode is not damaged during operation. The axial electric field (E_z) when the accelerating voltage is at its maximum 40 kV was recorded and is shown in Fig. 9(b). This field was below the breakdown threshold of 10 MV/cm. When the cathode is constructed the sharp edges would be rounded and so the areas of high electric field would be reduced.

2.7 Simulated electron trajectories

The electron trajectories after emission from the cathode are one of the most important diagnostic tools as these show if the electrons pass through the beam tube, where possible interception may occur, the thickness of the electron beam at the plateau magnetic field region and if the electron beam can pass through the backstop filter (the smallest diameter area of the tube). The electron trajectories through the diode and into the downstream uniform B-field region are shown in Fig. 10(a). These pictures show that the electrons pass through the waveguide geometry and form an axis-encircling beam, a view of which is clear to see in Fig. 10(b). There is small quantity of reflected electrons shown in this trajectory plot. These electrons amount to less than 1 mA, compared to the electron current of 1.5 A. At the end of the beam tube the thickness of the electrons beam can be calculated from the electron trajectories at the point of maximum magnetic field. The exact properties of this beam can be seen in Table 3. This shows that this beam has a thickness of ~0.2 mm corresponding to a spread of 60%.

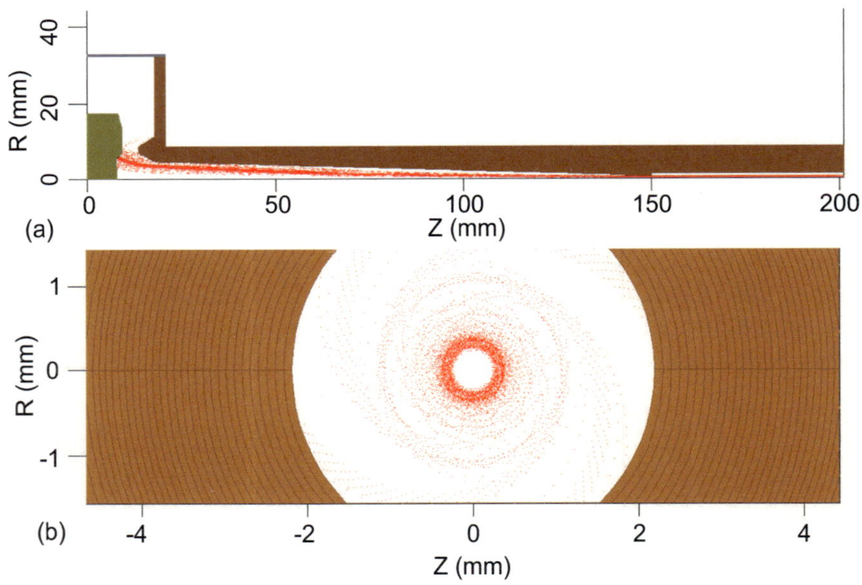

Fig. 10. MAGIC simulated electron trajectories at 1.82 T cavity field showing (a) the beam in the $r - z$ plane with the full geometry and (b) cross-sectional shape at the downstream region.

2.7.1 Electron beam current and voltage

The design of the waveguide interaction region determined the required electron beam current and energy. Simulation of these properties along the waveguide allows one to measure the beam power produced by the electron gun and compare that to the ideal target set for the electron gun. In the simulation a slowly rising accelerating voltage pulse was applied to the cathode and focusing electrodes. The rise time of the pulse was 1 ns with a steady voltage

Minimum radius	0.229 mm
Maximum radius	0.421 mm
Average radius	0.325 mm
Radius spread ($\Delta r/r$)	59.2%
Envelope ripple	15%

Table 3. Properties of the electron trajectories at the magnetic field plateau region, B_z = 1.82 T.

after that time. The current emitted from the cathode was simulated to be 1.57 A. This value was found to be 1.5 A emitted from the face of the emitter and 0.07 A from inside the gap between the emitting surface and the focusing electrode, which was not transported along the beam tube. The electron beam current at the downstream uniform magnetic field is a vital diagnostic as this allows calculation of the transported electron beam current to show what percentage of the electron beam is reflected or transmitted. The measured current downstream corresponded to 99.9% of the beam emitted.

2.7.2 Pitch angle and axial velocity spread

The two parameters of the electron beam that determine the interaction strength and efficiency of the gyro-BWO are the spreads in α, and axial velocity. The α value of the electron beam is a measure of the ratio of perpendicular to parallel velocity $\alpha = v_\perp / v_\parallel$ (He et al., 2001). Since it is only the transverse velocity, that participates in the interaction, this is a measure of the amount of the electron beam energy that is available for the interaction. The axial velocity spread will result in broadening of the electron cyclotron frequency and therefore excessive axial velocity spread will give rise to low beam-wave interaction efficiency.
The α value sought is variable between 1 and 2 but centered on $\sim$1.65. The α value as a function of the axial length along the beam tube was observed in the simulation and is shown in Fig. 11. Clearly shown here is the rise in the α value along the waveguide tube due to the rise in magnetic field. There are two stray beam lines shown here with a very large α value. These are emitted from inside the cathode gap and for the purpose of these calculations are not taken into consideration when estimating the average α value, and its spread. The calculated α values can be seen in Table 4 showing a spread of 10.7%.

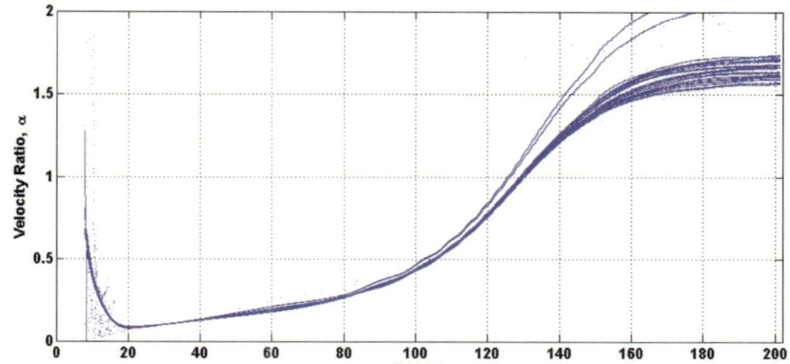

Fig. 11. Simulated α of the electron beam as a function of axial position. Measured with a magnetic field at the uniform downstream region of B_z = 1.82 T.

The axial momentum of the electrons (normalized to the electron rest mass m_e) along the axial ordinate is shown in Fig. 12. This shows the trajectories of the two electron beamlets with a

Minimum α value	1.56
Maximum α value	1.74
Average α value	1.65
α spread $(\Delta\alpha/\alpha)$	10.7%

Table 4. Simulated α values at B_z = 1.82 T.

much lower axial momentum than the rest of the electron beam consistent with the simulated results for α. If it is assumed that there is a negligible difference in electron mass from the lower and upper values of the momentum then the axial velocity spread can be found from Eq. 6.

$$\frac{\Delta v_z}{v_{z,av}} = \frac{\Delta m v_z}{m v_{z,av}} = \frac{\Delta P_z}{P_{z,av}} \tag{6}$$

where P_z is axial momentum, $P_{z,av}$ is average axial momentum, v_z is axial velocity and $v_{z,av}$ is average axial velocity.

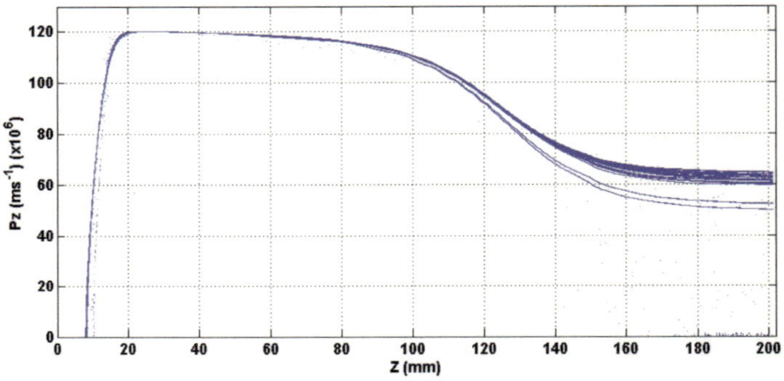

Fig. 12. Simulated axial momentum of the electron beam as a function of axial position.

Analysis of the axial momentum at the maximum magnetic field allows calculation of the axial velocity spread and the values obtained are given in Table 5. The axial velocity spread is within the design target.

Minimum axial velocity value	$5.97\text{x}10^7$ ms^{-1}
Maximum axial velocity value	$6.47\text{x}10^7$ ms^{-1}
Average axial velocity	$6.22\text{x}10^7$ ms^{-1}
Axial velocity spread ($\Delta v_z/v_z$)	8.1%

Table 5. Values of axial momentum and corresponding axial velocity spread at the plateau magnetic field region, B_z = 1.82 T.

2.7.3 Variation of magnetic field and different combinations of electron beam properties

The interaction frequency can be tuned through adjusting parameters of the electron beam such as accelerating voltage, α as well as the cavity magnetic field strength. In order to change the α values of the electron beam, the magnetic field at the cathode can be varied. The α value as a function of magnetic field at the cathode is shown in Fig. 13 at a fixed cavity magnetic field of 1.82 T. The α value can be analytically calculated through Eq. 3 and agrees well with the simulated value. The effect of varying the α value changes the electron beam dispersion line so different interaction frequencies can be achieved.

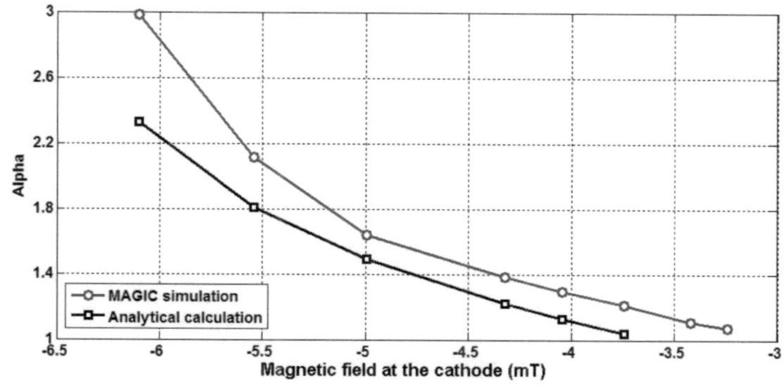

Fig. 13. α value as a function of magnetic field at the cathode surface. The cavity magnetic field is kept constant at $B_z = 1.82$ T.

While the cathode magnetic field is adjusted in order to change the value of α over the range of 1 to 3, the electron beam qualities (α and axial velocity spreads) will be affected. This can be seen in Fig. 14 where the optimum electron beam qualities are obtained at the designed cathode magnetic flux density of -4.97 mT corresponding to an α of 1.65.

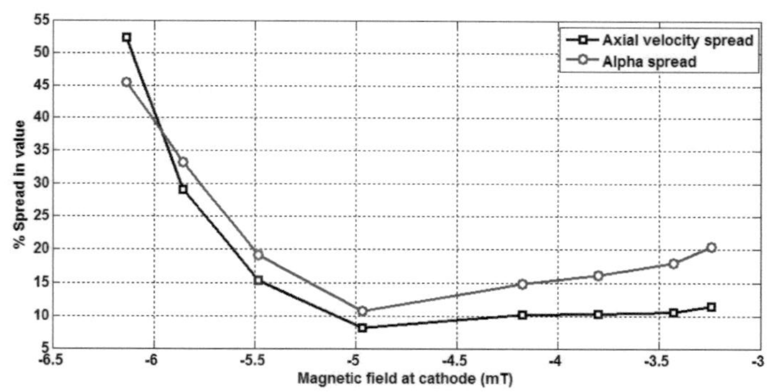

Fig. 14. Simulated values of axial velocity and α spreads as a function of cathode magnetic field strength.

The designed beam voltage is 40 kV but the gyro-BWO is tunable in frequency when the voltage changes so the electron gun had to transport the beam through the drift tube with an acceptable beam quality over a range of voltages. It was found that when the beam voltage varied from 35 – 45 kV the large orbit beam was still fully transported to the downstream cavity region. However, with a constant magnetic field configuration the beam α would be different and so some adjustment in the reverse coil strength would have to be made through the range of voltages. The α value was 2.46 and 1.35 for 35 kV and 45 kV respectively.
The electron beam quality also varies over this voltage range, as shown in Fig. 15. The plateau of the electron beam quality curve is centered on the designed voltage of 40 kV showing the optimized electron gun design. Throughout the range of voltages the electron beam maintained an acceptable quality, defined by the axial velocity and α spreads.

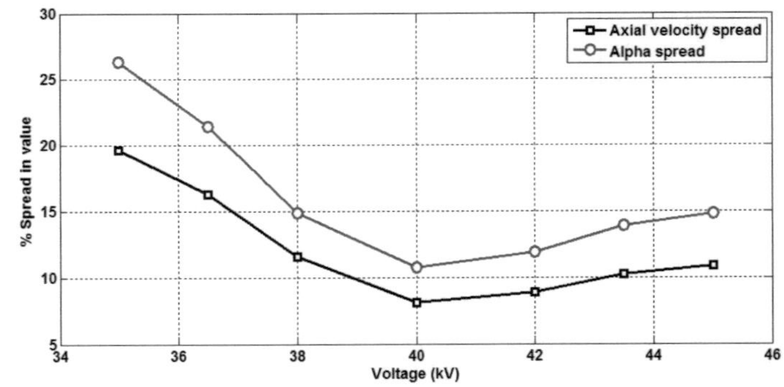

Fig. 15. Simulated axial velocity and α spreads as a function of the beam voltage. The average α and cavity magnetic field is kept constant at 1.65 and 1.82 T respectively.

If a constant α value is required when the voltage is changed the cathode magnetic field, and so reverse coil current, would have to be adjusted for each value of accelerating voltage. The range of cathode magnetic field that kept α at 1.65 with a cavity magnetic field of 1.82 T is shown in in Fig. 16.

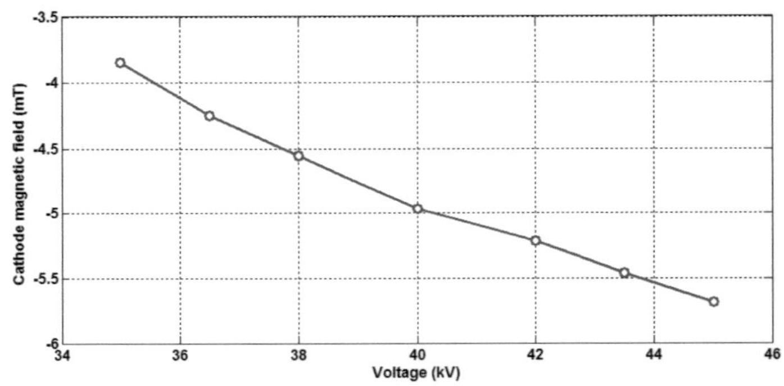

Fig. 16. Variation in cathode magnetic field required to keep a constant α (= 1.65) as the applied voltage is swept from 35 kV to 45 kV.

Changing the cavity magnetic field strength allows the frequency of interaction to be changed to any desired frequency over the full range of the gyro-BWO interaction, 84 – 104 GHz. This has a stronger effect on the electron beam line than any other method of frequency adjustment. The axial velocity and α spreads were simulated in the operating cavity magnetic field region and is shown in Fig. 17. Since the geometry of the cusp electron gun was optimised for the centre frequency of 94 GHz i.e. at a magnetic field of 1.82 T, the simulation at a different magnetic field would be an un-optimised setup so by changing some of the variables such as the reverse coil position, cavity coil position and applied voltage these results can be improved.

To obtain a constant value of α in the gyro-BWO operating regime which required a cavity magnetic field of 1.65 T – 2.1 T the cathode magnetic field must be changed in accordance with the change in the cavity magnetic field. The value of the magnetic field at the cathode as a function of the cavity magnetic field required to generate an α value of 1.65 is shown in Fig. 18.

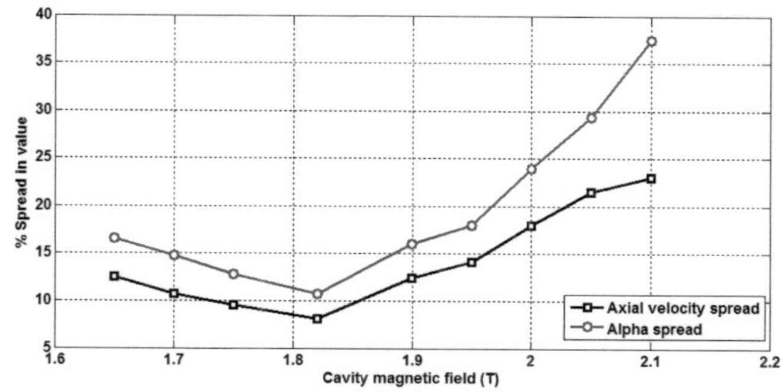

Fig. 17. α and axial velocity spreads as the cavity magnetic field is swept from 1.65 T – 2.1 T. The magnetic field at the cathode is adjusted in order to keep the α constant at 1.65.

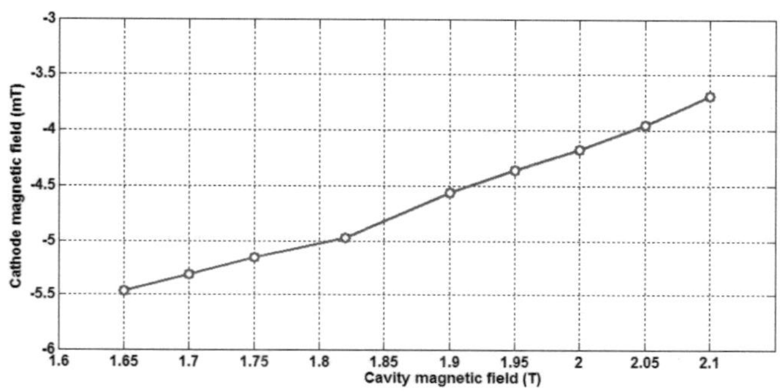

Fig. 18. Values of the magnetic field at the cathode required to keep a constant α (= 1.65) as the cavity magnetic field strength is changed.

2.8 Summary

In this section the cusp electron gun was designed, simulated and optimized to produce an axis-encircling annular beam of 40 kV, 1.5 A with an α of 1.65. The design was originally simulated in MAGIC and optimized through changing the diode geometry (Donaldson et al., 2010). The optimized design produced an electron beam with low axial velocity and α spreads at the center magnetic field strength with acceptable quality over the full magnetic field tuning range. Other factors were investigated for instance the scope for tuning α in the range of 1 to 2 and the potential for voltage tuning of the output frequency. In each case the electron beam passed through the beam tube without scraping or mirroring and had tolerable spreads in axial velocity and α spreads. The optimized electron gun design produced an electron beam of high enough quality in order to drive the beam-wave interaction within the gyro-BWO (Donaldson et al., 2009; Li et al., 2010).

3. Beam-wave interaction in gyro-BWO

3.1 Background

The surface of the helically grooved waveguide of the gyro-BWO can be represented in cylindrical coordinates r, ϕ, z as follows

$$r(\phi, z) = r_0 + l\cos(\bar{m}\phi + \bar{k}z) \qquad (7)$$

where r_0 is the waveguide mean radius, l, $\bar{m}$ and $\bar{k} = 2\pi/d$ are the amplitude, azimuthal and axial numbers of the corrugation respectively, and d is the corrugation period. If a three-fold helical waveguide is used ($\bar{m} = 3$) the corrugation would provide effective coupling of the TE_{21} near cut-off mode and the TE_{11} traveling mode if the corrugation period is chosen so that the Bragg conditions

$$\bar{k} \approx k_{11}, m_A + m_B = \bar{m} \tag{8}$$

are satisfied, where k_{11} is the axial wavenumber of the TE_{11} mode at the cutoff frequency of the TE_{21} mode and m_A and m_B are the azimuthual index of the near cutoff and traveling modes respectively.

The resonant coupling of the waves corresponds to the intersection of their dispersion curves or, more exactly the intersection between the TE_{21} mode and the first spatial harmonic of the TE_{11} mode (Fig. 19) and would result in an eigenwave with a TE_{21}-like cross-sectional electric field distribution. For such a field structure it is favourable to use the second harmonic of the electron cyclotron frequency for beam-wave interaction, which has the advantage of lowering the required magnetic field strength by a factor of two. The axis-encircling beam resonantly excites only co-rotating TE_{nm} modes with azimuthal indices equal to the cyclotron harmonic number, $\bar{m} = s$. The helical symmetry allows transformation of a selected direction of azimuthal rotation to a selected axial direction, in this case a wave which is propagating in a counter direction with respect to the electrons' axial velocity. The electron beam's linear dispersion characteristic can be adjusted with respect to the wave dispersion over a rather broad frequency range by changing either the axial guide magnetic field or the electron accelerating potential.

3.2 Dispersion and linear theory

The resonant coupling of the waves corresponds to the intersection of their dispersion curves. If the amplitude of the corrugation is small compared with the wavelength, the dispersions of the resultant eigenwaves, i.e. w_1 and w_2 in the helical waveguide, can be calculated approximately by the following equation from analytical perturbation theory (Denisov et al., 1998)

$$(h^2 - 2\delta)(h - \Delta_g + \delta/h_0) + 2\sigma^2 \Big/ h_0 = 0 \tag{9}$$

where all the symbols (also those that appear later) retain the meanings defined in ref. (Denisov et al., 1998). One of the eigenwaves, i.e. w_1, having a near constant negative group velocity and small axial wavenumbers in the designed operating frequency range, is the operating eigenwave of the interaction.

The electron cyclotron mode, normalized in a manner consistent with Denisov et al 1998, can be written as

$$\delta - h\beta_{z0} = s\Delta_H \tag{10}$$

The output frequency of the gyro-BWO interaction can therefore be calculated from the intersection of the dispersions of the eigenwaves and the beam cyclotron mode (Fig. 20).

For the highest interaction efficiency the gyro-BWO should be operated in a region of small axial wavenumber so that the detrimental effect of the Doppler broadening of the electron cyclotron line because of spread in axial electron velocity is minimized. Therefore a larger gradient of the eigenwave w_1 is favourable for increasing the interaction efficiency and frequency tuning range. For a gyro-BWO using a smooth cylindrical waveguide, the backward wave exists only in the negative half of the axial wavenumber, but for the

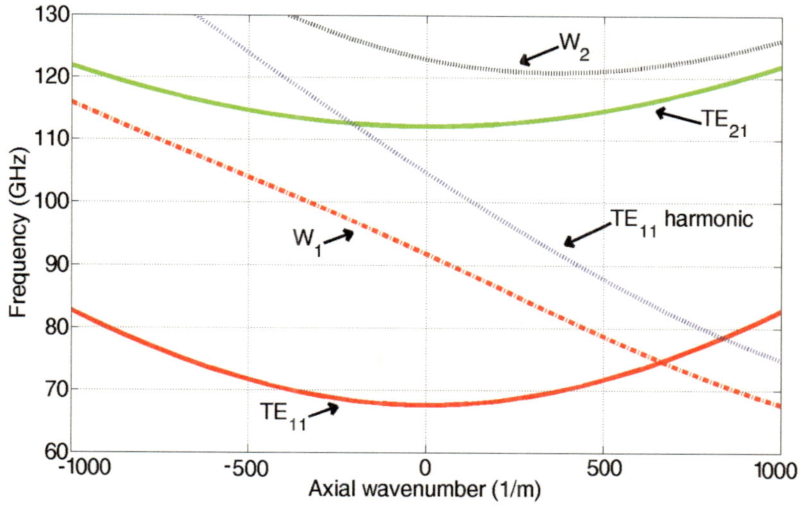

Fig. 19. Mode coupling between the spatial harmonic TE_{11} mode and TE_{21} mode.

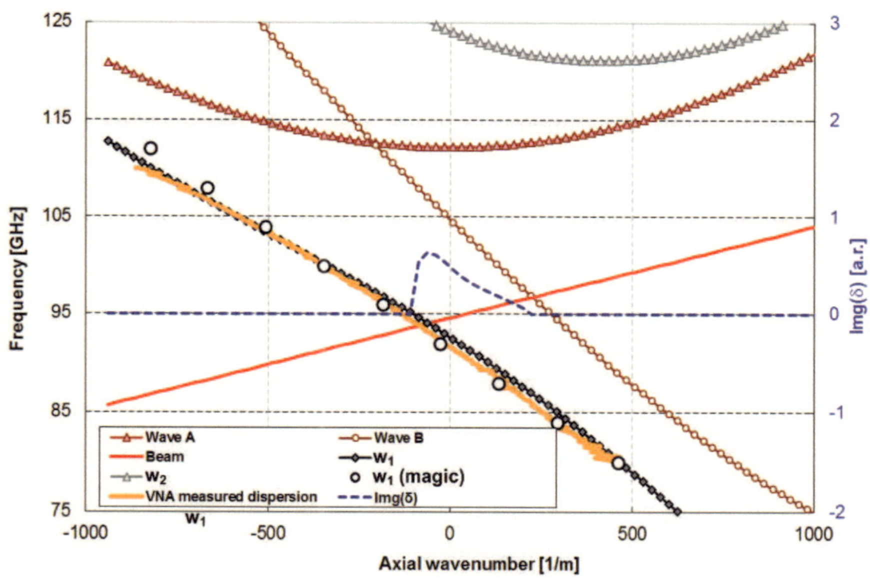

Fig. 20. The operating dispersion of the helical waveguide.

eigenwave w_1 in the helical waveguide the backward wave exists in both the negative and positive range of wavenumbers. Therefore the frequency tuning range of a gyro-BWO using a helical waveguide would have much wider frequency tuning range compared with its smooth-bore counterpart. The gradient of w_1 can be adjusted by altering the period and the corrugation amplitude of the helical waveguide.

In analogy to gyrotron interactions and ref. (Denisov et al., 1998), it is possible for one to derive the gyro-BWO beam-wave dispersion

$$\begin{aligned} &[(h^2 - 2\delta)(h - \Delta_g + \delta/h_0) + 2\sigma^2/h_0][h - (\delta - \Delta_H)/\beta_{z0}]^2 \\ &= C^3(h - \Delta_g + \delta/h_0)\{1 + \tfrac{2s}{\alpha_0{}^2\beta_{z0}}[h - (\delta - \Delta_H)/\beta_{z0}]\} \end{aligned} \tag{11}$$

where α_0 and β_{z0} are the beam initial pitch angle and relative velocity in the longitudinal direction respectively. The interaction frequency of the gyro-BWO can be calculated by solving the uncoupled beam-wave equation by setting $C = 0$ in Eq. 11, i.e. the intersection of the eigenwave w_1 and the beam dispersion line. In a general case, Eq. 11 has four $\delta(h)$ roots, with two real roots being the "hot" (electron beam present) eigenwaves, and a pair of conjugate complex roots, which are degenerates of the electron cyclotron mode due to the CRM interaction at and near the intersection when the beam parameters are suitably chosen. The negative imaginary number of the solution (Fig. 20, dashed line showing one such interaction for the gyro-BWO) gives rise to the oscillation that grows with time in the cavity and hence allows the starting condition and the small signal growth of the oscillation to be analyzed.
The dispersion of the operating eigenwave can be found by measuring the phase evolution of a counter-rotating circularly polarized wave when it propagates through the waveguide by using a vector network analyzer (VNA). It can also be measured by detecting the polarization angle of a linearly polarized wave when it propagates through the waveguide by using a scalar network analyzer (SNA)(Burt et al., 2004). In Fig. 20 the measured results using the VNA method are shown and compared with the results simulated by MAGIC using the same operating eigenwave. In the simulation using the MAGIC code, a left-polarized circular wave of one frequency was injected into the right-hand helical waveguide, and a component of the electric field inside the waveguide was measured along the axial direction. The measured field was then numerically analyzed and the axial wavenumber of the eigenwave was therefore obtained for that frequency (He et al., 2011).

3.3 Simulation of the beam-wave interaction

The dimensions of the helical structure used in this simulation were designed to support an operating eigenwave of a higher group velocity to achieve a higher electronic efficiency and wider frequency tuning range. MAGIC simulation of the performance of the gyro-BWO using this helical waveguide as the interaction region when driven by an electron beam of energy 40 keV, current 1.5 A and α 1.65 are presented.
The radiation of the gyro-BWO can be coupled out at two positions; One from an output coupler at the upstream side of the corrugated waveguide, the other through an output window at the downstream end. In the latter case the output window will act as a boundary of the cavity and therefore some reflection from the window (which can be as low as 1%) is desirable for the oscillation to start. Both the simulations and previous experiments at X-band (He et al., 2005) confirmed that the performance of the gyro-BWO is the same when using the two different output methods. In the simulation of the W-band gyro-BWO, the output power resulted from the beam-wave interaction in the helical waveguide region which was absorbed by a "microwave absorber"at the upstream location. This was achieved by defining a region of finite conductance as shown in Fig. 21. The output power of the gyro-BWO could therefore be simulated by measuring the total ohmic loss in this conductive volume. It was found in the simulation that the electron beam parameters are unaffected by this region.
An electron beam with parameters similar to that simulated and measured in the experiment was used, i.e. beam energy, current and beam pitch angle, guided by a magnetic field of

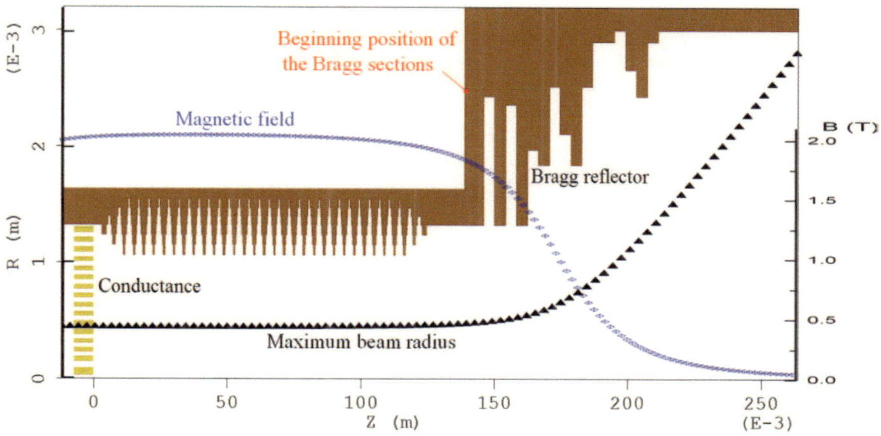

Fig. 21. The geometry used to simulate the beam-wave interaction.

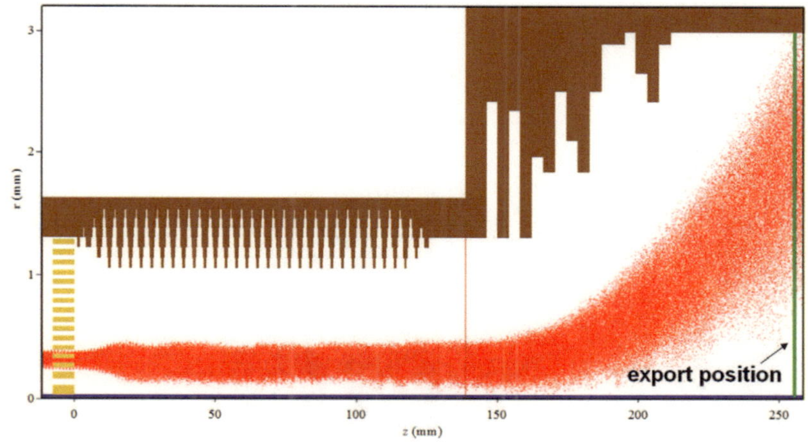

Fig. 22. The electron beam trajectories of an axis-encircling solid beam.

about 2.1 T in a beam tube of radius 1.3 mm in which the lowest order mode was cut-off and propagating in the downstream (right) direction. For the gyro-BWO to oscillate, the electron beam should rotate in the opposite direction to the helical structure. At the downstream end, a Bragg reflector was used to completely reflect any microwave signal back into the interaction region. At the same time the spent electron beam can pass through the Bragg reflector region. The electron beam (with all its physical parameters and the electromagnetic wave (with all its parameters) were then recorded at the cross-sectional plane located downstream from the Bragg reflector. This allowed the simulation of the depressed collector for energy recovery purpose as discussed in the later sections. A snap shot of the simulation showing the geometry and electron beam trajectories of the axis-encircling solid beam that was used in the experiment is shown in Fig. 22. When the magnetic field was 1.82 T, electron beam energy 40 keV, current 1.5 A, pitch α 1.65, a simulated power of 10 kW and frequency of 94 GHz were obtained. A typical simulated output spectrum and mode pattern are shown in Fig. 23. The simulated output power as a function of frequency is shown in Fig. 24. A 3 dB tuning range of 84–104 GHz was predicted from the simulation of the W-band gyro-BWO.

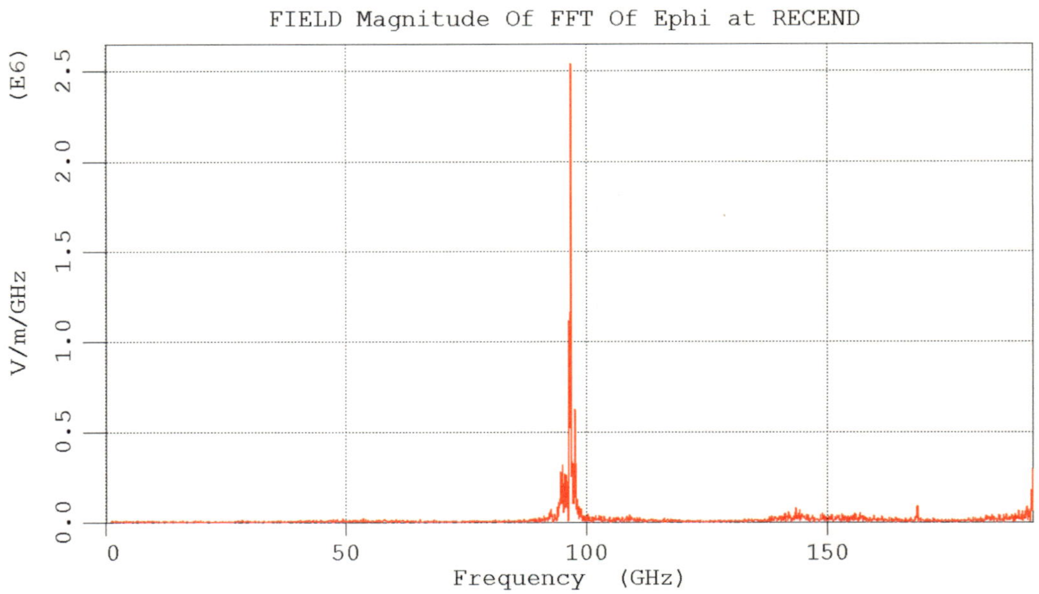

(a) Output spectrum of the gyro-BWO.

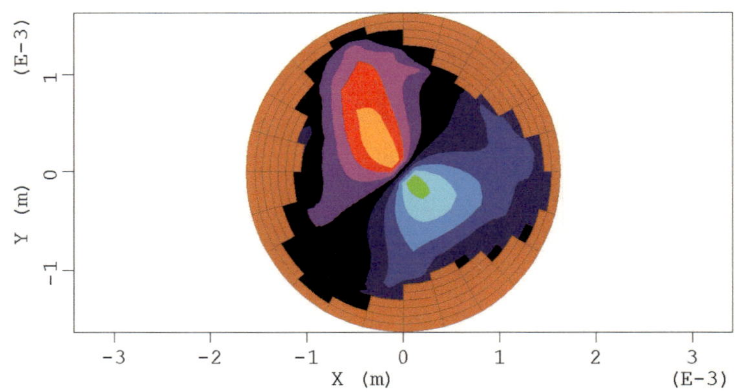

(b) E-field distribution inside the HCIR.

Fig. 23. Characteristic of microwave output from the gyro-BWO.

4. Simulation of the depressed collector

4.1 Principle of the depressed collector

The overall efficiency is an important parameter for high-power microwave sources. For a given RF output power, higher efficiency means less primary power is needed. Microwave sources with higher efficiency have less heat dissipation which means smaller cooling systems are needed. High efficiency is essential in space applications and some ground-based applications, such as deep space communication and mobile installations.

Several methods have been developed to improve the efficiency of the beam-wave interaction. One is to change the profile of the waveguide to obtain a higher electronic efficiency, such as employing a slot structure, helical structure as used in this chapter, slice structure, and so

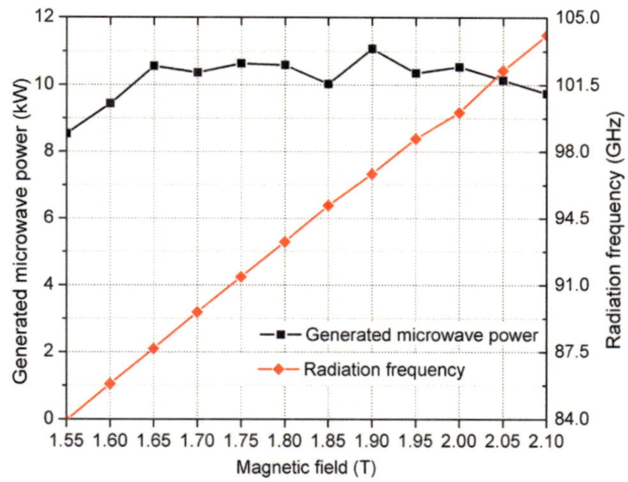

Fig. 24. The output powers and frequencies at different cavity magnetic fields.

on. The other way is to use a tapered magnetic field or tapered wall radius instead of the constant ones. (Ganguly & Ahn, 1989; Nusinovich & Dumbrajs, 1996; Sprangle & Smith, 1980; Walter et al., 1996) Another option for enhancing the efficiency is to recover energy from the spent beam using single or multi-stage depressed collectors. It has been shown that this is an effective way to improve the overall efficiency of microwave tubes, such as conventional klystrons, BWOs and TWTs (Neugebauer & Mihran, 1972; Wilson et al., 2007).

Depressed collectors are passive converters that can transfer the kinetic energy of the spent electrons into potential electric energy. "Depressed"means that the collector has a depressed potential as compared with the main body of the tube. The electrons lose their kinetic energy when passing through the retarding electrostatic field and finally land on the collector surface with a significant reduction in kinetic energy. They produce a loop current which results in a power recovery from the spent electrons (Sterzer & Princeton, 1958).The collected power by a depressed collector can be written as

$$P_{col} = \sum_{n=1}^{N} V_n I_n \tag{12}$$

Here N is the number of stages and V_n, I_n are the potentials and collected current on the nth-stage electrode, respectively. For a given energy distribution of the spent electrons, increasing the number of stages results in the collection of more power. However, the design of depressed collectors becomes more complex and the cost increases as the number of stages increases.

By introducing a depressed collector with a collection efficiency of $\eta_{col} = P_{col}/P_{spent\_beam}$ and output efficiency ε_{out} which is the ratio of P_{out} and the total microwave power in the cavity, the overall efficiency of the microwave tube with an electronic efficiency η_e can be calculated using

$$\eta_{tot} = \frac{P_{out}}{P_b - P_{col}} = \frac{\varepsilon_{out}\eta_e}{1 - \eta_{col}(1 - \eta_e)} \tag{13}$$

For those inherently low efficiency high power microwave devices, depressed collectors with efficiencies higher than 80% can significantly improve the overall efficiencies. For a moderately efficient source with an electronic and collection efficiency of 30% and 80%, respectively, with the use of depressed collection the overall efficiency could be increased to 61.4% when $\varepsilon_{out} = 0.9$, increasing the overall efficiency by a factor of 2.
To design a depressed collector with high efficiency, several issues need to be considered before commencing simulations.
a) Determining the potentials and the geometry of the electrodes to reach optimum collection efficiency. b) Secondary electrons. c) Heat dissipation on the electrodes.

4.2 Potentials on the electrode

In the design of the energy recovery system, the energy distribution of the electron beam was exported from the simulation of the gyro-BWO using MAGIC, as shown in Fig. 25. Table 6 shows the optimum potentials and the collection efficiency when a different number of stages are used. In this calculation, it was assumed that all the electrons were collected on the electrodes without consideration of secondary emissions. The minimum electrode potential was set to be the minimum energy of electrons to avoid backstreaming and the maximum potential was set to be the electron beam voltage which was 40 kV in the gyro-BWO device. It was found that when the number of stages increased beyond four, the collection efficiency did not significantly increase. Four stages were therefore chosen as a compromise between the collection efficiency and complexity of the system.

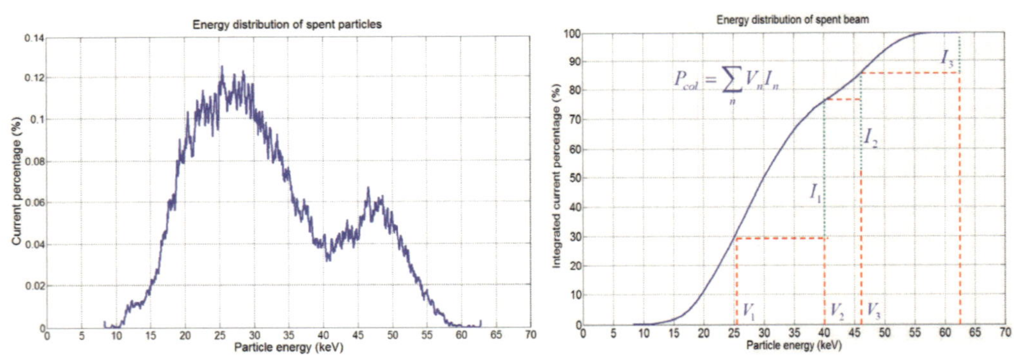

(a) Energy distribution of the spent beam (b) Recovered energy from the spent electrons

Fig. 25. Energy distribution of the spent beam under the condition of 40 kV electron beam voltage, 1.5 A beam current, beam α of 1.6, with a cavity magnetic field of 1.75 T.

4.3 Geometry of the depressed collector and optimization process

The collection efficiency calculated in section 4.2 assumed that all the spent electrons were sorted by the electric and magnetic field in the collection region. In practice, the distribution of the electric field is determined by the geometry of the electrodes. Proper design of the electrode geometry not only acts to sort the electrons with different kinetic energies, but also to decrease the possibility of secondary emission and to avoid the backstreaming of the electrons in the collector. One way to choose a good geometry is to use a searching algorithm such as a random walk and genetic algorithm to optimize the parameters (Ghosh & Carter, 2007).

No.	Potentials on electrodes (kV) (relative to ground voltage)							Collection efficiency
1	-9.24	–	–	–	–	–	–	28.8%
2	-9.24	-25.70	–	–	–	–	–	63.6%
3	-9.24	-22.14	-36.57	–	–	–	–	75.7%
4	-9.24	-19.55	-27.31	-40.00	–	–	–	82.5%
5	-9.24	-18.86	-24.96	-30.78	-40.00	–	–	85.7%
6	-9.24	-16.98	-22.14	-27.22	-32.66	-40.00	–	87.5%
7	-9.24	-16.82	-21.33	-25.47	-29.53	-34.23	-40.00	88.7%

Table 6. Collection efficiency for different number of stages.

An optimization program integrating a genetic algorithm was developed to optimize the depressed collector geometry parameters by controlling the MAGIC code without the need to know the source code. The optimization program firstly created an input file by inserting the new set of parameters to the template input file for MAGIC. Then MAGIC was invoked to simulate the new geometry and the result was read by the optimization program to evaluate the parameters. The flow diagram of this process is shown as Fig. 26 (Zhang et al., 2009a).

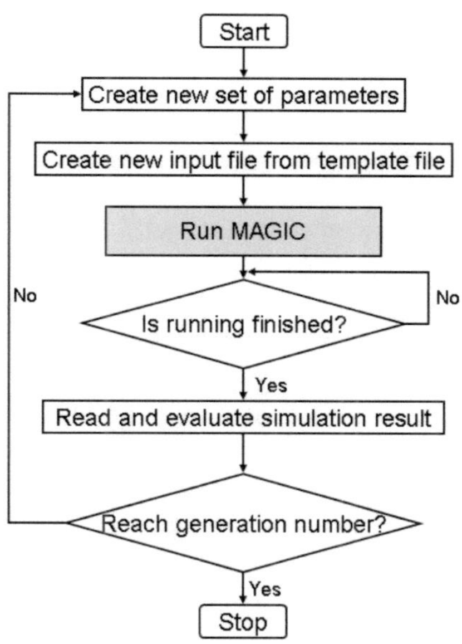

Fig. 26. Flow diagram of the optimization program.

The basic geometry of an electrode is shown in Fig. 27. It is determined completely by 4 parameters, the length of the electrode (*Li*), the height of the electrode (*Hi*), the offset from the Z axis (*Oi*) and the tilt angle (*Ai*). There should be 16 parameters in a 4-stage collector. However, the outer radius of the depressed collector was restricted to 60 mm, and the overall length was restricted to be 150 mm. Thus 14 parameters were to be optimized. Before the optimization, many simulations were carried out to find a proper range for each parameter to ensure the searching range was as small as possible.

The full geometry of the 4-stage depressed collector is shown in Fig. 28. A gap of 10 mm between the end of the collection region and the first stage of the collector was left to isolate

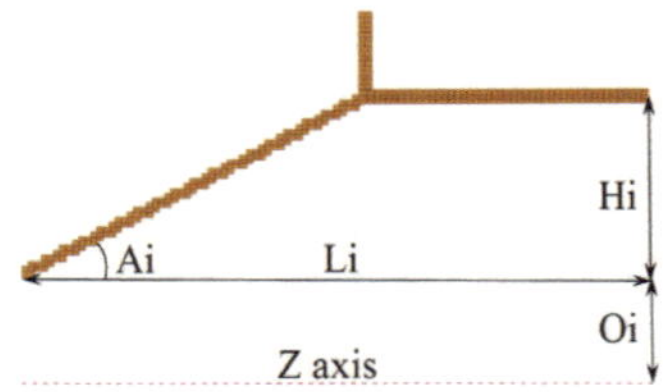

Fig. 27. Geometry of an electrode.

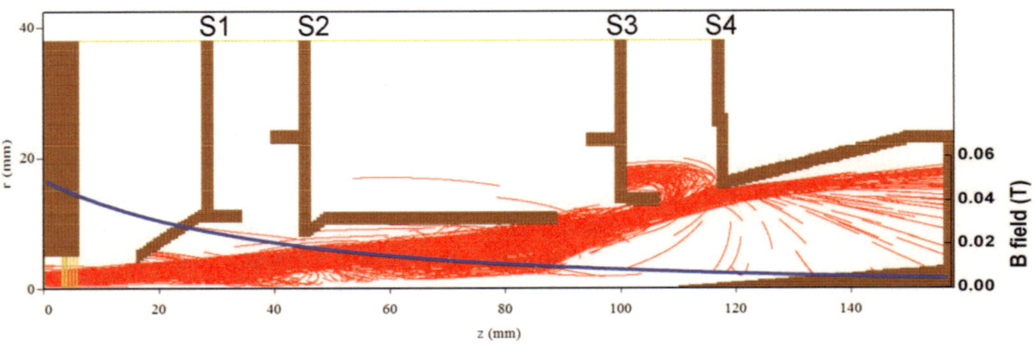

Fig. 28. Full geometry of 4-stage depressed collector.

the high voltage between them. The electrode shapes were modified as shown in S1, S2, S3 and S4 to avoid potential distortion in the simulation when the electric field was applied to the electrodes.

The potentials on each electrode were consistent with Table 6. After each simulation, the average current collected by each collector was read from a MAGIC output data file. Then the collected power was calculated from Eq. 12. The average power of the spent beam was calculated by counting all the energy from the spent electrons. The collection efficiency calculated by the collected power and power of the spent beam was used to evaluate the optimum geometric parameters. The crossover probability, mutation probability, and population size of the genetic algorithm were set to be 0.85, 0.05 and 12, respectively. The evaluation function is

$$\eta_{eva} = \eta_{col} - W\eta_{back} \tag{14}$$

where η_{back} was the percentage of the backstreaming electrons, and W was the weight. In our calculation, W was chosen as 1.5. The optimization was run with the magnetic field of 1.75 T. After 756 iterations, an optimum collection efficiency of 78.7% was achieved. It was 3.8% lower than the ideal collection efficiency calculated in the preceding section which assumed all the spent electrons were sorted perfectly. That was because not all the electrons were recovered by the optimum electrode and a small proportion were observed to backstream in the simulation. The trajectories of the spent electrons are also shown in Fig. 28.

By applying the optimum depressed collector with collection efficiency of 78.7%, the overall efficiency of the gyro-BWO was enhanced

$$\eta_{tot} = \frac{0.150}{1 - 0.787 \times (1 - 0.167)} \times 100\% = 43.6\% \tag{15}$$

The overall efficiency was greatly improved by using the energy recovery system. The spent electron beams for different magnetic fields were also simulated and the collection efficiencies were about 78.0%–82.0% under their optimum potentials.

4.4 Simulation with secondary electron emission

The secondary electrons have several negative effects on high power microwave devices. First of all, secondary electrons carrying velocities with opposite direction to the primaries will be accelerated by the electrostatic field in the collection region and some of them will backstream. The secondary electrons absorb energy from the electrostatic field and decrease the collection efficiency. Secondly, the backstreaming electrons enter into the RF interaction region, which will generate noise on the microwave output and decrease the performance of the microwave tube. Thirdly, in high average power devices, the backstreaming may contribute an additional thermal power on the thermally stressed waveguide structure (Ling et al., 2000). Thus in depressed collectors, it is essential to reduce the current of secondary electrons to be as low as possible.

Secondary electrons are generally divided into three classes, including the true secondary electrons (TSEs), the rediffused electrons, and the backscattered elastic electrons (Furman & Pivi, 2002). In our simulation, the rediffused electrons and the backscattered elastic electrons were treated by a uniform model for they had the same physical nature. Generally, the term of "backscattered electrons "(BSEs) was used to indicate these two types of secondary electrons. In MAGIC, the numbers, the energies and the angles of the emitted TSEs were sampled from the probability function of the yield, the energy distribution and the angular distribution by using a Monte Carlo algorithm. Therefore the true secondary yield (SEY), the emitted angular distribution and the emitted-energy spectrum are considered as important quantities in the simulation. Data about the SEY, the emitted angle distribution and the emitted-energy spectrum can be obtained from experiments, and several semiempirical formulas have been developed to fit the experimental data, such as Vaughan's, Furman's and Thomas's equations (Furman & Pivi, 2002; MAGIC, 2002; Vaughan, 1993).

The scattering process of the BSEs in MAGIC is carried out by ITS (The integrated TIGER Series of Coupled Electron/Photon Monte Carlo Transport Codes) code and it has been proved that the simulation results of the ITS code were in good agreement with the experiments (Halbleib et al., 1992). The "BACKSCATTER"option in MAGIC allows ITS to be invoked automatically to simulate the emission of both the rediffused and backscattered elastic electrons. The TSE and BSE models used in the MAGIC simulations were discussed in detail in ref. (Zhang et al., 2009b).

The optimization simulation was run once again with the secondary electrons considered. Copper was chosen as the material of the electrodes. The collected power taking account of the secondary electrons was revised as

$$
\begin{aligned}
&P_{col} = \sum_{n}^{N} V_n I_n + \sum_{n}^{N}\sum_{j}^{N} \mathrm{SIGN}(n-j) I_{nj}(V_n - V_j) - \sum_{n}^{N} V_n I_{Bn} \\
&SIGN(n-j) = \begin{cases} -1, n \leq j \\ 1, n > j \end{cases}
\end{aligned}
\tag{16}
$$

where N is the number of stages V_n , I_n and are the potentials and the collected primary current on the nth-stage electrode, respectively. I_{nj} is the current of the secondary electrons emitted

from the nth-stage electrode and collected on the jth-stage electrode. I_{Bn} is the backstreaming current by the secondary electrons emitted from the nth-stage electrode.
In the previous optimum geometry without considering the secondary electrons, a collection efficiency of 78.7% was obtained in the conditions of beam current of 1.5 A, beam voltage of 40 kV, magnetic field of 1.75 T, and the operation frequency of 91.4 GHz. When taking account of the secondary electron emission using Vaughan's true secondary emission model, the collection efficiency was reduced from 78.7% to 69.2% and the backstreaming increased from 4.5% to 9.4%. The backstreaming was large thus modifications in the geometry were required and the optimization process was carried out once again. After 552 iterations, an optimum collection efficiency of 69.0% was achieved when using Vaughan's true secondary emission model, whilst the backstreaming was reduced from 9.4% to 4.9%. Table 7 presents the predicted collection efficiency and the percentage of the backstreaming current for a range of secondary electron models. From the simulation results, by carefully designing the geometry of the depressed collector, the backstreaming could be reduced to a relatively low level.

Cases	True secondary model	Collection efficiency	Percentage of backstreaming
without TSEs, without BSEs	–	75.7%	4.79%
with TSEs, without BSEs	Vaughan	71.1%	4.79%
	Furman	68.9%	4.80%
	Thomas	73.0%	4.80%
without TSEs, with BSEs	–	73.9%	4.89%
with TSEs, with BSEs	Vaughan	69.0%	4.89%
	Furman	66.8%	4.91%
	Thomas	71.0%	4.90%

Table 7. The collection efficiency and the backstreaming rate in different cases.

From the simulation results, the backstreaming caused by the primary electrons was 4.79%, while TSEs and BSEs only contributed about 0.1%. Between BSEs and TSEs, the backstreaming was mostly composed by BSEs, as the BSEs had a higher energy than the TSEs thus they were better able to overcome the radial electric field and return to the interaction region. Fig. 29 shows the trajectories of the primary electrons, the true secondary electrons and the backscattered electrons in the designed depressed collector when using Vaughan's formula.
The reduction of the collection efficiency caused by the three different models of true secondary emission yield did not show a great difference and was about 4%. Each secondary emission model generated a different number of the true secondary electrons and impacted the second and third terms of Eq. 16. The second term was much smaller than the first term since $V_i - V_j$ was much smaller than V_i. In the simulation, the potentials on each electrode were -9.24 kV, -19.55 kV, -27.31 kV, -40.00 kV, respectively. From the trajectories of the true secondary electrons in Fig. 29(b), most of the true secondary electrons emitted from the forth, third and second electrodes were collected by the third, second, and first electrode, respectively. That made the second term of Eq. 16 a small value. Since the difference between the collection efficiency and backstreaming rate associated with the different true secondary emission models were found to be small, in subsequent calculations, we only used Vaughan's formula because it has been widely accepted in the literature.
The output frequency of the W-band gyro-BWO can be tuned by adjusting the amplitude of the cavity magnetic field. However the spent beam parameters were also affected by this

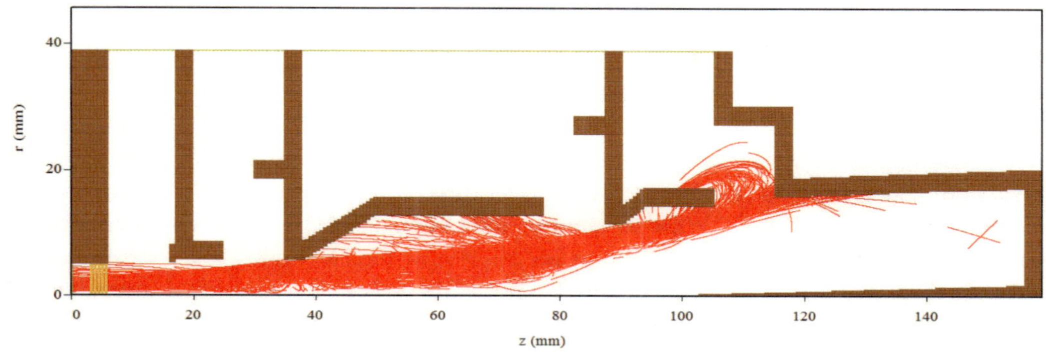

(a) Trajectories of the primary electrons

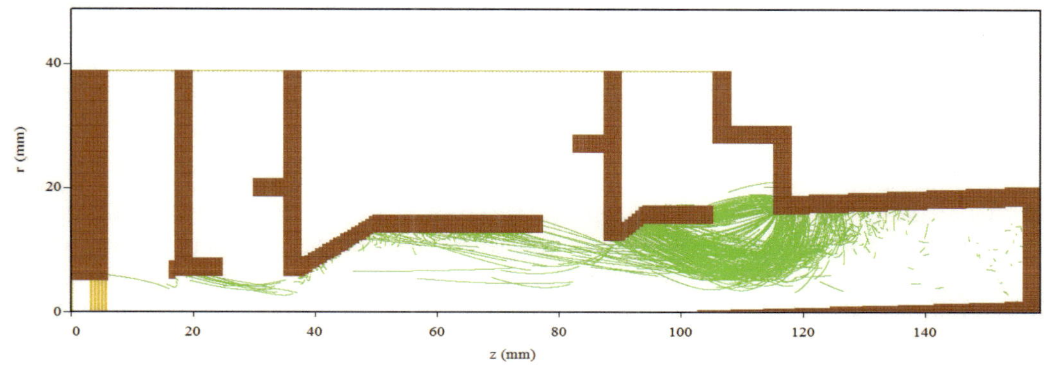

(b) Trajectories of the true secondary electrons

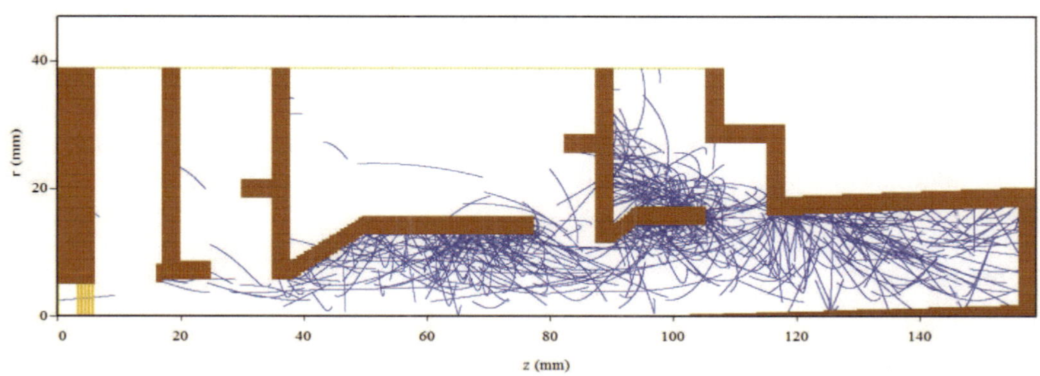

(c) Trajectories of the backscattered electrons

Fig. 29. Trajectories of the electrons in the depressed collector (using Vaughan's formulas).

tuning. The collection efficiencies and the backstreaming rate of the W-band gyro-BWO were therefore simulated in the whole frequency tuning range for the optimized configuration of the four-stage depressed collector. The collection efficiencies achieved were simulated to be about 70% and the backstreaming rate was lower than 7% in the working frequency band.

4.5 Heat power density distribution on the collector

To design an effective cooling system for the collector electrodes, the distribution of the heat power dissipated on the surface of the electrodes needs to be evaluated. In MAGIC, there is no way to obtain the heat power on the electrodes directly. However, it provides a command "OBSERVE COLLECTED POWER"to monitor the overall heat dissipation on a conductor. To obtain the heat power distribution on the surface of the electrodes, the four electrodes were divided into a large number of small conductors both in the azimuthal direction and the z direction and the heat power dissipated in each of these conductors was individually recorded, thus an approximate heat power distribution was obtained. The greater the number of conductors, the higher the resolution of the heat power distribution that could be achieved. The heat power densities on the conductors could be calculated by dividing the heat power by the area of the conductors'surface. In the simulation, the maximum heat density was $\sim$240W/cm^2. It is lower than the thermal stress threshold of the copper material thus the generation of "hot spots"can be avoided.

5. Conclusion

In this chapter, the simulations and optimizations of a W-band gyro-BWO including the simulation of a thermionic cusp electron gun which generates an annular, axis-encircling electron beam, the simulation of the beam-wave interaction in the helically corrugated interaction region and the simulation and optimization of an energy recovery system of a 4-stage depressed collector were presented.

The annular-shaped axis-encircling electron beam produced by the cusp electron gun had a beam current of 1.5 A at an acceleration potential of 40 kV, an optimized axial velocity spread $\Delta v_z / v_z$ of 8%, and a relative α spread $\Delta\alpha/\alpha$ of 10% at an α value of 1.65. When driven by such a beam the gyro-BWO was simulated to have a 3 dB frequency bandwidth of 84-104 GHz, output power of 10 kW with an electronic efficiency of 17%. The optimization of the shape and dimensions of each stage of the depressed collector using a genetic algorithm achieved an overall recovery efficiency of about 70%, with a minimized back-streaming rate of 4.9%. With the addition of a four stage depressed collector an overall efficiency of 40% was simulated for the gyro-BWO.

6. References

Arnone, D. D., Ciesla, C. M., Corchia, A., Egusa, S., Pepper, M., Chamberlain, J. M., Bezant, C., Linfield, E. H., Clothier, R. & Khammo, N. (1999). Applications of terahertz (THz) technology to medical imaging, *in* J. M. Chamberlain (ed.), *Society of Photo-Optical Instrumentation Engineers (SPIE) Conference Series*, Vol. 3828, pp. 209–219.

Bratman, V. L., Denisov, G. G., Samsonov, S. V, Cross, A. W., Phelps, A. D. R. & He, W. (2007). High-efficiency wideband gyro-TWTs and gyro-BWOs with helically corrugated waveguides, *Radiophys. and Quantum Elect.* **50**: 95–107.

Bratman, V. L., Denisov, G. G., Manuilov, V. N., Samsonov, S. V. & Volkov, A. B. (2001). Development of helical-waveguide gyro-devices based on low-energy electron beams, *Digest of Int. Conf. Infrared and Millimeter Waves, Toulouse, France* pp. 5–105.

Bratman, V. L., Cross, A. W., Denisov, G. G., He, W., Phelps, A. D. R., Ronald, K., Samsonov, S. V., Whyte, C. G. & Young, A. R. (2000). High-gain wide-band gyrotron traveling wave amplifier with a helically corrugated waveguide, *Phys. Rev. Lett.* **84**(12): 2746–2749.

Burt, G., Samsonov, S. V., Phelps, A. D. R., Bratman, V. L., Ronald, K., Denisov, G. G., He, W., Young, A., Cross, A. W. & Konoplev, I. V. (2005). Microwave pulse compression using a helically corrugated waveguide, *IEEE Trans. Plasma Sci.* **33**(2): 661–667.

Burt, G., Samsonov, S. V., Ronald, K., Denisov, G. G., Young, A. R., Bratman, V. L., Phelps, A. D. R., Cross, A. W., Konoplev, I. V., He, W., Thomson, J. & Whyte, C. G. (2004). Dispersion of helically corrugated waveguides: Analytical, numerical, and experimental study, *Phys. Rev. E* **70**(4): 046402.

Chen, F. F. (1974). *Introduction to Plasma Physics*, Plenum Press, New York.

Chu, K. R. (1978). Theory of electron cyclotron maser interaction in a cavity at the harmonic frequencies, *Phys. Fluids* **21**(12): 2354–2364.

Cooke, S. J., Cross, A. W., He, W. & Phelps, A. D. R. (1996). Experimental operation of a cyclotron autoresonance maser oscillator at the second harmonic, *Phys. Rev. Lett.* **77**(23): 4836–4839.

Cross, A. W., He, W., Phelps, A. D. R., Ronald, K., Whyte, C. G., Young, A. R., Robertson, C. W., Rafferty, E. G. & Thomson, J. (2007). Helically corrugated waveguide gyrotron traveling wave amplifier using a thermonic cathode electron gun, *Appl. Phys. Lett.* **90**: 253501.

Denisov, G. G., Bratman, V. L., Cross, A. W., He, W., Phelps, A. D. R., Ronald, K., Samsonov, S. V. & Whyte, C. G. (1998). Gyrotron traveling wave amplifier with a helical interaction waveguide, *Phys. Rev. Lett.* **81**(25): 5680–5683.

Denisov, G. G., Bratman, V. L., Phelps, A. D. R. & Samsonov, S. V. (1998). Gyro-TWT with a helical operating waveguide: New possibilites to enhance efficiency and frequency bandwidth, *IEEE Trans. Plasma Sci.* **26**(3): 508–518.

Destler, W. W. & Rhee, M. J. (1977). Radial and axial compression of a hollow electron beam using an asymmetric magnetic cusp, *Phys. Fluids* **20**(9): 1582–1584.

Donaldson, C. R., He, W., Cross, A. W., Li, F., Phelps, A. D. R., Zhang, L., Ronald, K., Robertson, C. W., Whyte, C. G. & Young, A. R. (2010). A cusp electron gun for millimeter wave gyrodevices, *Appl. Phys. Lett.* **96**(14): 141501.

Donaldson, C. R., He, W., Cross, A. W., Phelps, A. D. R., Li, F., Ronald, K., Robertson, C. W., Whyte, C. G., Young, A. R. & Zhang, L. (2009). Design and numerical optimization of a cusp-gun-based electron beam for millimeter-wave gyro-devices, *IEEE Trans. Plasma Sci.* **37**(11): 2153–2157.

Furman, M. A. & Pivi, M. T. (2002). Probabilistic model for the simulation of secondary electron emission, *Phys. Rev. Spec. Top., Accel. Beams* **5**(12): 124404.

Gallagher, D. A., Barsanti, M., Scafuri, F. & Armstrong, C. (2000). High-power cusp gun for harmonic gyro-device applications, *IEEE Trans. Plasma Sci.* **28**(3): 695–699.

Ganguly, A. K. & Ahn, S. (1989). Non-linear analysis of the gyro-BWO in three dimensions, *Int. J. Electronics* **67**(2): 261–276.

Ghosh, T. K. & Carter, R. G. (2007). Optimization of multistage depressed collectors, *IEEE Trans. Electron Devices* **54**(8): 2031–2039.

Goplen, B., Ludeking, L., Smithe, D. & Warren, G. (1995). User-configurable MAGIC for electromagnetic PIC calculations, *Comput. Phys, Commun,* **87**: 54–86.

Halbleib, J. A., Kensek, R. P., Valdez, G. D., Mehlhorn, T. A., Seltzer, S. M. & Berger, M. J. (1992). ITS: The integrated TIGER series of electron/photon transport codes – Version 3.0, *IEEE Trans. Nucl. Sci.* **39**(4): 1025–1030.

He, W., Cooke, S. J., Cross, A. W. & Phelps, A. D. R. (2001). Simultaneous axial and rotational electron beam velocity measurement using a phosphor scintillator, *Rev. Sci. Inst.* **72**(5): 2268–2270.

He, W., Ronald, K., Young, A. R., Cross, A. W., Phelps, A. D. R., Whyte, C. G., Rafferty, E. G., Thomson, J., Robertson, C. W., Speirs, D. C., Samsonov, S. V., Bratman, V. L. & Denisov, G. G. (2005). Gyro-BWO experiments using a helical interaction waveguide, *IEEE Trans. Electron Devices* **52**(5): 839 – 844.

He, W., Whyte, C. G., Rafferty, E. G., Cross, A. W., Phelps, A. D. R., Ronald, K., Young, A. R., Robertson, C. W., Speirs, D. C. & Rowlands, D. H. (2008). Axis-encircling electron beam generation using a smooth magnetic cusp for gyrodevices, *Appl. Phys. Lett.* **93**: 121501.

He, W., Donaldson, C. R., Li, F., Zhang, L., Cross, A. W., Phelps, A. D. R., Ronald, K., Robertson, C. W., Whyte, C. G. & Young, A. R. (2011). W-band gyro-devices using helically corrugated waveguide and cusp gun: design, simulation and experiment, *TST* **4**(1): 9 – 19.

Idehara, T., Ogawa, I., Mitsudo, S., Iwata, Y., Watanabe, S., Itakura, Y., Ohashi, K., Kobayashi, H., Yokoyama, T., Zapevalov, V. E., Glyavin, M. Y., Kuftin, A. N., Malgin, O. V. & Sabchevski, S. P. (2004). A high harmonic gyrotron with an axis-encircling electron beam and a permanent magnet, *IEEE Trans. Plasma Sci.* **32**(3): 903–909.

Imai, T., Kobayashi, N., Temkin, R., Thumm, M., Tran, M. Q. & Alikaev, V. (2001). Iter R & D: Auxiliary systems: Electron cyclotron heating and current drive system, *Fusion Eng. Des.* **55**(2-3): 281 – 289.

Jeon, S. G., Baik, C. W., Baik, D. H., Kim, D. H., Park, G. S., Sato, N. & Yokoo, K. (2002). Study on velocity spread for axis-encircling electron beams generated by single magnetic cusp, *Appl. Phys. Lett.* **80**: 3703.

Kou, C. S., Chen, S. H., Barnett, L. R., Chen, H. Y. & Chu, K. R. (1993). Experimental study of an injection-locked gyrotron backward-wave oscillator, *Phys. Rev. Lett.* **70**(7): 924–927.

Li, F., He, W., Cross, A. W., Donaldson, C. R., Zhang, L., Phelps, A. D. R. & Ronald, K. (2010). Design and simulation of a ~390 GHz seventh harmonic gyrotron using a large orbit electron beam, *J. Phys. D: Appl. Phys.* **43**(15): 155204.

Ling, G., Piosczyk, B. & Thumm, M. (2000). A new approach for a multistage depressed collector for gyrotrons, *IEEE Trans. Plasma Sci.* **28**(3): 606–613.

Ludeking, L., Smithe, D. & Gray, T. (2003). *Introduction to MAGIC*, Mission Research Corporation.

MAGIC (2002). *MAGIC User's Manual*, Mission Research Corporation.

Manheimer, W. M., Mesyats, G. & Petelin, M. I. (1994). *Applications of High-power Microwaves*, Artech House.

McDermott, D. B., Balkcum, A. J. & Luhmann Jr., N. C. (1996). 35-GHz 25-kW CW low-voltage third-harmonic gyrotron, *IEEE Trans. Plasma Sci.* **24**(3): 613–629.

McStravick, M., Samsonov, S. V., Ronald, K., Mishakin, S. V., He, W., Denisov, G. G., Whyte, C. G., Bratman, V. L., Cross, A. W., Young, A. R., MacInnes, P., Robertson, C. W. & Phelps, A. D. R. (2010). Experimental results on microwave pulse compression using helically corrugated waveguide, *J. Appl. Phys.* **108**(5): 054908–054908–4.

Neugebauer, W. & Mihran, T. G. (1972). A ten-stage electrostatic depressed collector for improving klystron efficiency, *IEEE Trans. Electron Devices* **19**(1): 111–121.

Nguyen, K. T., Smithe, D. N. & Ludeking, L. D. (1992). The double-cusp gyro-gun, *IEDM Tech. Dig.* pp. 219–222.

Nusinovich, G. S. & Dumbrajs, O. (1996). Theory of gyro-backward wave oscillators with tapered magnetic field and waveguide cross section, *IEEE Trans. Plasma Sci.* **24**(3): 620–629.

Park, S. Y., Kyser, R. H., Armstrong, C. M., Parker, R. K. & Granatstein, V. L. (1990). Experimental study of a Ka-band gyrotron backward-wave oscillator, *IEEE Trans. Plasma Sci.* **18**(3): 321 –325.

Pierce, J. R. (1954). *Theory and Design of Electron Beams*, Van Nostrand.

Rhee, M. J. & Destler, W. W. (1974). Relativistic electron dynamics in a cusped magnetic field, *Phys. Fluids* **17**(8): 1574–1581.

Samsonov, S. V., Phelps, A. D. R., Bratman, V. L., Burt, G., Denisov, G. G., Cross, A. W., Ronald, K., He, W. & Yin, H. (2004). Compression of frequency-modulated pulses using helically corrugated waveguides and its potential for generating multigigawatt rf radiation, *Phys. Rev. Lett.* **92**(11): 118301.

Scheitrum, G. P., Symons, R. S. & True, R. B. (1989). Low velocity spread axis-encircling electron beams forming system, *IEDM Tech. Dig.* pp. 743–746.

Scheitrum, G. P. & True, R. (1981). A triple pole piece magnetic field reversal element for generation of high rotational energy beam, *IEDM Tech. Dig.* **27**: 332–335.

Schmidt, G. (1962). Nonadiabatic particle motion in axialsymmetric fields, *Phys. Fluids* **5**(8): 994–1002.

Sinnis, J. & Schmidt, G. (1963). Experiment trajectory analysis of charged particles in a cusped geometry, *Phys. Fluids* **6**(6): 841–845.

Smirnova, T. I., Smirnov, A. I., Clarkson, R. B. & Belford, R. L. (1995). W-Band (95 GHz) EPR spectroscopy of nitroxide radicals with complex proton hyperfine structure: Fast motion, *J. Phys. Chem.* **99**(22): 9008–9016.

Sprangle, P. & Smith, R. A. (1980). The nonlinear theory of efficiency enhancement in the electron cyclotron maser (gyrotron), *J. Appl. Phys.* **51**(6): 3001–3007.

Sterzer, F. & Princeton, N. J. (1958). Improvement of traveling-wave tube efficiency through collector potential depression, *IRE Trans. Electron Devices* **5**(4): 300–305.

Vaughan, M. (1993). Secondary emission formulas, *IEEE Trans. Electron Devices* **40**(4): 830.

Walter, M. T., Gilgenbach, R. M., Luginsland, J. W., Hochman, J. M., Rintamaki, J. I., Jaynes, R. L., Lau, Y. Y. & Spencer, T. A. (1996). Effects of tapering on gyrotron backward-wave oscillators, *IEEE Trans. Plasma Sci.* **24**(3): 636–647.

Wang, Q. S., Huey, H. E., McDermott, D. B., Hirata, Y. & Luhmann Jr., N. C. (2000). Design of a W-band second-harmonic TE_{02} gyro-TWT amplifier, *IEEE Trans. Plasma Sci.* **28**(6): 2232–2237.

Wang, Q. S., McDermott, D. B., Chong, C. K., Kou, C. S., Chu, K. R. & C., L. J. N. (1994). Stable 1 MW, third-harmonic gyro-TWT amplifier, *IEEE Trans. Plasma Sci.* **22**(5): 608–615.

Wilson, J. D., Wintucky, E. G., Vaden, K. R., Force, D. A., Krainsky, I. L., Simons, R. N., Robbins, N. R., Menninger, W. L., Dibb, D. R. & Lewis, D. E. (2007). Advances in space traveling-wave tubes for NASA missions, *Proc. IEEE* **95**(10): 1958–1967.

Zhang, L., He, W., Cross, A. W., Phelps, A. D. R., Ronald, K. & Whyte, C. G. (2009a). Design of an energy recovery system for a gyrotron backward-wave oscillator, *IEEE Trans. Plasma Sci.* **37**(3): 390–394.

Zhang, L., He, W., Cross, A. W., Phelps, A. D. R., Ronald, K. & Whyte, C. G. (2009b). Numerical Optimization of a Multistage Depressed Collector With Secondary Electron Emission for an X-band Gyro-BWO, *IEEE Trans. Plasma Sci.* **37**(12): 2328 – 2334.

6

Numerical Simulations of Nano-Scale Magnetization Dynamics

Paul Horley[1], Vítor Vieira[2], Jesús González-Hernández[1], Vitalii Dugaev[2,3] and Jozef Barnas[4]

[1]Centro de Investigación en Materiales Avanzados, Chihuahua / Monterrey
[2]CFIF, Instituto Superior Técnico, Universidade Técnica de Lisboa, Lisboa
[3]Department of Physics, Rzeszów University of Technology, Rzeszów
[4]Department of Physics, Adam Mickiewicz University
[1]México
[2]Portugal
[3,4]Poland

1. Introduction

The discovery of the giant magnetoresistance (Baibich et al., 1988) attracted much scientific interest to the magnetization dynamics at the nano-scale, which eventually led to the formation of a new field - spintronics - aiming to join the conventional charge transfer electronics with spin-related phenomena. The characteristics of spintronic devices (Žutic, Fabian & Das, 2004) are very attractive, including extremely small size (nanometer scale), fast response time and high operating frequencies (on the GHz domain), high sensitivity and vast spectrum of possible applications ranging from magnetic memories (based on magnetization reversal) to microwave generators (involving steady magnetization precession) (Kiselev et al., 2003). The design of these devices, together with the resolution of many problems required for full harvest of spin transport effects in traditional silicon-based semiconductor electronics, is greatly aided by theoretical studies and numerical simulations. For these, one should use adequate models describing magnetization dynamics at the desired scale. If we go down to atomic level, the modelling from first-principles is obligatory. Despite a huge progress in this field (and significant improvement of the computational power of modern equipment), these calculations are far from being real-time and can embrace only a limited amount of particles. Increasing the size of the computational cell to several nanometers, it is possible to introduce the micromagnetic modelling technique, for which every ferromagnetic particle is characterized by an average magnetic moment **M**. These moments can interact with each other by short and long range forces due to exchange coupling and dipole-dipole interactions. The evolution of the individual particle is governed by the Landau-Lifshitz-Gilbert (LLG) equation – a semi-classical approximation allowing to represent the time evolution of the magnetization vector **M** depending on applied magnetic fields and spin-polarized currents passing through the particle.

Micromagnetics is a rapidly-developing field allowing tackling many serious problems (Fidler & Schrefl, 2000; Berkov & Gorn, 2006). It is far simpler to implement in comparison with first principles calculations, so that modern computers can be efficiently used even for 3D micromagnetic simulations of large systems (Scholz et al., 2003; Vukadinovic & Boust, 2007). The amount of calculations required strongly depends on the space discretization of the modelled object. For maximum accuracy, the volume of the magnetic body is divided into a set of triangular prisms according to different tessellation algorithms. The system thus becomes represented by a set of magnetization vectors $\mathbf{M}_i$ corresponding to the nodes of the resulting mesh. The evolution of the system can be obtained by solving the LLG equation using finite element methods (Koehler & Fredkin, 1992; Szambolics et al., 2008), which may involve re-structurization of the mesh to account for variation of the magnetization distribution inside the sample. These calculations require considerable computational resources and thus are usually performed on multi-processor computers or clusters thereof.

The calculations can be optimized for the case of regular meshes, with the simplest numerical procedures available for cubic (3D) and square (2D) grids. In this case, the cumbersome finite element methods can be substituted by simpler finite difference methods, which benefit from pre-calculated coefficients for the derivatives required in the calculation of near and far range interactions between the magnetic particles. The most time consuming part of micromagnetic simulations concerns long-range interactions contributing to the demagnetizing field. As this is formed by every particle belonging to the object, one should calculate a complete convolution for every magnetic moment $\mathbf{M}_i$. In the case of uniform grids, these calculations can be much simplified recalling that convolution in normal space correspond to multiplication in the Fourier space. Thus, one has to Fast Fourier Transform (FFT) the components of the demagnetizing field (Schabes & Aharoni, 1987) and $\mathbf{M}_i$ for every grid point, multiply them and inverse-FFT the result to obtain the demagnetizing field. The other option is to use the fast multipole algorithm (Tan, Baras & Krishnaprasad, 2000), which can be also accelerated with the Fast Fourier Transform (Liu, Long, Ong & Li, 2006). The downside of uniform square grids is the complication to represent non-rectangular objects. Even at small grid step the curves or lines that are not perpendicular to the grid directions generate the staircase structure, which is artificial and has no counterpart in the modelled ferromagnetic objects. This staircase acts as a nucleation source of magnetization vortices, which may lead to incorrect simulation data suggesting vortex-assisted magnetization dynamics (García-Cervera, Gimbutas & Weinan, 2003) while the real systems may display coherent magnetization rotation. To solve this issue (and to retain the benefits of fast calculation of demagnetizing fields using FFT) one can introduce corrections for the boundary cells (Parker, Cerjan & Hewett, 2000; Donahue & McMichael, 2007), allowing to take into account the real shapes in place of its cubic or square cells.

However, the general methodology of solving the LLG equation can be discussed for simpler models without the need to consider convolution, tessellation or grid discretization errors for smooth contours. Actually, we can consider a single magnetic moment obeying the LLG equation, which is the situation that can be found on a larger scale - thin magnetic films with dimensions of dozens of nanometers. Stacking several ferromagnetic films together and separating them by a non-magnetic spacer, one can obtain the simplest spintronic device, a spin valve. The layers composing the valve serve different purposes and because of this should have different thickness. The thicker layer is bulk enough to preclude re-orientation of its magnetization vector by an applied magnetic field. To improve its stability, it is usually linked with an anti-ferromagnetic interaction with yet another substrate layer. The role of this fixed layer consists in aligning the magnetic moments of the passing carriers, so that the current injected into the second, much thinner analyzer layer, will be spin-polarized. The analyzer layer, on the contrary, can be easily influenced by the applied magnetic field, and it will manage to change its magnetization as a whole – thus representing a *macrospin* (Xiao, Zangwill & Stiles, 2005). The experimental studies of spin valves successfully confirmed the theoretical predictions made in the macrospin approximation, including precessional and ballistic magnetization reversal, two types of steady magnetization oscillations – in-plane and out-of-plane, as well as magnetization relaxation to an intermediate canted state.

The detailed discussion of the magnetization dynamics is out of the scope of this chapter; however, it is imperative to consider various representations of the main differential equations governing the motion of the magnetization vector, as well as to discuss the numerical methods for their appropriate solution. In particular, the modelling of the temperature influence over the system, which is usually done adding a thermal noise term to the effective field, leading to stochastic differential equations that require special numerical methods to solve them.

2. Landau-Lifshitz-Gilbert equation

Let us consider a magnetic particle characterized by a magnetization vector **M**, and subjected to the action of an effective magnetic field **H** and spin-polarized current **J**, rendering magnetic torques on the system. The changes of magnetization with time are governed by the Landau-Lifshitz-Gilbert equation:

$$\frac{d\mathbf{M}}{dt} = -\gamma \mathbf{M}\times\mathbf{H} + \frac{\gamma}{M_S}\mathbf{M}\times(\mathbf{M}\times\mathbf{J}) + \frac{\alpha}{M_S}\mathbf{M}\times\frac{d\mathbf{M}}{dt} \tag{1}$$

The first term in the right side of the equation corresponds to the Larmor precession around the magnetic field direction, featuring a gyromagnetic ratio $\gamma = 2.21\times10^5$ m/(As). The second term, proposed by Slonczewski (1996), describes the spin torque rendered by the injected current **J**. The third term was introduced by Gilbert (2004); it presents a phenomenological description of magnetization damping, caused by dissipation of the macrospin energy due to lattice vibrations, formation of spin waves and so on (Saradzhev et al., 2007). Thus, in the absence of energy influx (provided by injected current), the system should relax to a stable state. As the magnetic motion is effectively controlled by the interplay of driving and damping forces, it is natural to suggest a model of viscous damping with a coefficient α multiplied by the rate of change of the magnetization. On the other hand, it is unclear if a constant damping coefficient is sufficient to reproduce accurately the magnetization dynamics (Mills & Arias, 2006), which may require additional tweaking such as making α dependent on the orientation of the magnetization vector (Tiberkevich & Slavin, 2007).

An essential feature of the LLG equation is that unconditionally preserves the length of the magnetization vector, which corresponds to the saturation magnetization M_S of the material. All possible magnetization dynamics is thus confined to the re-orientation of **M**, which can be visualized as a phase trajectory formed by the motion of the tip of the magnetization vector over the sphere with radius M_S. The effective magnetic field

$$\mathbf{H} = \mathbf{H}_{EXT} - (C_{DEM}M_X\mathbf{e}_X - C_{ANI}M_Z\mathbf{e}_Z)\,/\,M_S \tag{2}$$

is composed of applied external field $\mathbf{H}_{EXT}$, demagnetization field with a constant C_{DEM} (valid for thin film approximation), and anisotropy field with coefficient $C_{ANI} = 2K_1/\mu_0 M_S$

with easy axis anisotropy constant K_1. For the case of very thin ferromagnetic films the easy magnetization axis will be located in the film plane, while the demagnetizing field will penalize deviations of the magnetization from this plane. Therefore, in our case the ferromagnetic film is set in the plane *YZ*, with an easy magnetization axis directed along the axis *Z*. The injected spin-polarized current is scaled with $\hbar\eta / 4eVK_1$, with spin polarization degree η and volume of the analyzer layer *V*.

Taking a cross product of the LLG equation with $d\mathbf{M}/dt$, re-arranging the terms, and introducing the torque-inducing vectors $\mathbf{\Lambda} = \mathbf{H} + \alpha\mathbf{J}$ and $\mathbf{\Delta} = \mathbf{J} - \alpha\mathbf{H}$, one can transform the equation into the Landau explicit form, with the time derivative $d\mathbf{M}/dt$ on the r.h.s. only:

$$\frac{1}{\gamma_1}\frac{d\mathbf{M}}{dt} = -\mathbf{M}\times\mathbf{\Lambda} + \frac{1}{M_S}\mathbf{M}\times(\mathbf{M}\times\mathbf{\Delta}) \tag{3}$$

with a re-normalized gyromagnetic ratio $\gamma_1 = \gamma/(1+\alpha^2)$. For the calculations illustrated in this paper, we have used the common parameters for Co/Cu/Co spin valves (Kiselev et al., 2003): analyzer layer with dimensions 91×50×6 nm^3, C_{ANI} = 500Oe, $4\pi M_S$ = 10kOe, and α = 0.014. The main dynamic modes that can be obtained from the LLG equation include magnetization reversal between the stationary states $M_Z = \pm M_S$, relaxation of the magnetization to intermediate canted states, and steady magnetization precession. To illustrate the ranges of variables H and J for which these states take place, it is useful to construct a dynamic diagram of the system (Fig. 1). The task can be simplified by choosing the proper numerical characteristics allowing clear distinction between the corresponding states. The situation with up/down and canted orientation of **M** is easily resolved by monitoring the average value of the magnetization component along the easy axis, $\langle M_Z \rangle$. In this way one can easily discover low-field and high-field magnetization switching. The former occurs when the applied field overcomes the anisotropy constant C_{ANI}, which is marked with a thick horizontal line in Fig. 1. Below it, the magnetization vector remains in the initial state pointing down. Above this line, the magnetization points upwards (Fig. 1a). Under high fields and applied currents, it is also possible to obtain magnetization pointing down (Fig. 1g). The transition between these two states comes through slow magnetization reversal with phase trajectories practically covering the entire sphere (Fig. 1h). Lowering the field, one can shift the stable point from the stationary states $M_Z = \pm M_S$, reaching a canted state (Fig. 1e-g). The variation of current "opens" the canted state into a periodic trajectory (Fig. 1d). At this point, the observation of $\langle M_Z \rangle$ does not suffice to distinguish between oscillating and non-oscillating states, because the average for a cyclic orbit gives a position of its centre, as if the system converges to the canted state. The situation becomes more complicated for complex phase portraits that contain several loops (Fig. 1b). To solve this problem, it is useful to calculate the Hausdorff dimension (Lichtenberg & Lieberman, 1983):

$$D_H = -\lim_{\varepsilon\to 0}\frac{\log N}{\log\varepsilon} \tag{4}$$

where *N* is the number of cubes with side ε required to cover the phase portrait. If we are considering the stationary state, when the magnetization vector is fixed, the corresponding phase portrait will be a point with D_H = 0. When the system performs magnetization oscillations along a fixed trajectory, the Hausdorff dimension will be equal or above unity. The higher values of D_H will be achieved for higher number of loops, and when these will eventually cover the whole sphere, the dimension should reach the value of 2.

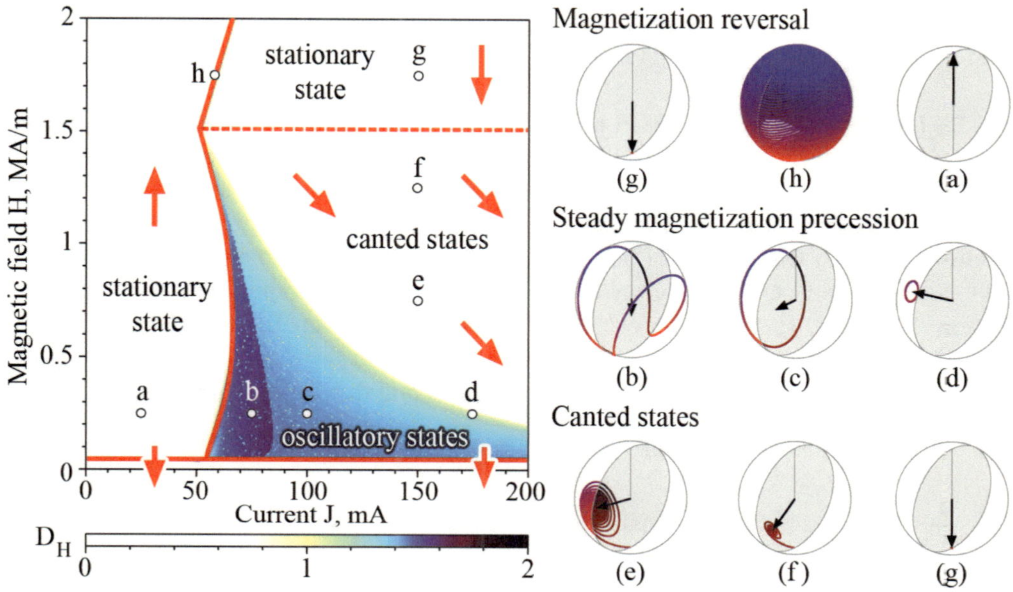

Fig. 1. Dynamic diagram of macrospin system for different applied magnetic field and injected spin-polarized current. The right panel shows the characteristic phase portraits with grey oval corresponding to film plane *YZ*, and an arrow denoting averaged magnetization.

The macrospin model features two types of steady oscillations. In the simplest case, the magnetization vector precesses around the canted axis, considerably deviating from the film plane (Fig. 1c, d), hence the name - out-of-plane precession (OPP). For lower values of injected current, the precession cycle splits into a butterfly-shaped curve (Fig. 1b), symmetric regarding the film plane. Thus, despite magnetization vector deviates from the film plane for certain periods, the average over the whole oscillation cycle will remain parallel to the axis *Z*, so that this type of phase portrait is called in-plane precession (IPP). The dynamic diagram shows how efficient is the use of the Hausdorff dimension for visual separation of the parameter areas where in-plane and out-of-plane precession takes place; it also works fine for complicated cases of multi-loop phase portraits triggered by pulsed fields and currents (see Horley et al., 2008). Now, having the idea of what to expect from the solution of the LLG equation, let us discuss in detail its different representations (including strengths and weaknesses thereof from the computational point of view), as well as numerical methods required for the most efficient and accurate solution of this equation.

2.1 Cartesian projection

As we are studying the evolution of the magnetization in three-dimensional space, it is straightforward to re-write the LLG for the Cartesian system as a set of ordinary differential equations regarding the individual components of the magnetization vector M_X, M_Y and M_Z:

$$\begin{aligned}
\frac{dM_X}{dt} &= -\gamma_1(M_Y\Lambda_Z - M_Z\Lambda_Y - M_X\Xi + M_S\Delta_X) \\
\frac{dM_Y}{dt} &= -\gamma_1(M_Z\Lambda_X - M_X\Lambda_Z - M_Y\Xi + M_S\Delta_Y) \\
\frac{dM_Z}{dt} &= -\gamma_1(M_X\Lambda_Y - M_Y\Lambda_X - M_z\Xi + M_S\Delta_Z)
\end{aligned} \tag{5}$$

with $\Xi = (\mathbf{M}\cdot\Delta)/M_S$. The Cartesian representation of the LLG is very easy to implement; since it uses only basic arithmetic operations, ensuring very fast calculations. However, the length of the magnetization vector is not unconditionally preserved in the straightforwardly discretized version of these equations, so that even with a small integration step the system will diverge after a few dozens of iterations. The common methodology to keep the length of $\mathbf{M}$ constant consists in re-normalization of the magnetization after some (or each) iteration. However, such an approach is often criticized: when the magnetization vector goes out of the sphere with radius M_S, it becomes difficult to say if it is adequate to solve the situation only by re-scaling of the vector without resorting to re-orientation of $\mathbf{M}$.

In fact, the condition $\mathbf{M}^2 = M^2$ imposes a series of conditions starting with $\mathbf{M}\cdot\frac{d\mathbf{M}}{dt}=0$ and $\mathbf{M}\cdot\frac{d^2\mathbf{M}}{dt^2} = -\left(\frac{d\mathbf{M}}{dt}\right)^2$. In the renormalization procedure one has

$$\mathbf{M}(t+\Delta t) \approx \frac{\mathbf{M}(t)+\frac{d\mathbf{M}}{dt}\Delta t}{\sqrt{1+\frac{1}{M^2}(\frac{d\mathbf{M}}{dt})^2(\Delta t)^2}} \approx \mathbf{M}(t) + \frac{d\mathbf{M}}{dt}\Delta t - \frac{1}{2}\frac{1}{M^2}(\frac{d\mathbf{M}}{dt})^2\mathbf{M}(t)(\Delta t)^2 \tag{6}$$

so that the requirement of second order restriction is automatically implemented, fixing the component $\frac{1}{2}\frac{d^2\mathbf{M}}{dt^2}\Delta t^2$ along the direction of $\mathbf{M}(t)$ itself; however, it is not fixed completely, as we will see in section 2.4. Thus, one will need reasonably small time steps (below pico-second level) to replicate the experimental system behaviour with an acceptable precision.

2.2 Spherical projection

The constant length of the magnetization vector invites to use spherical coordinates, describing the orientation of the magnetization vector with zenith and azimuth angles θ and φ. The LLG equation in this projection has the following form:

$$\begin{aligned}
\frac{d\theta}{dt} &= \gamma_1[-\Lambda_X\sin\varphi + \Lambda_Y\cos\varphi - \cos\theta(\Delta_X\cos\varphi + \Delta_Y\sin\varphi) + \Delta_Z\sin\theta] \\
\sin\theta\frac{d\varphi}{dt} &= -\gamma_1[\cos\theta(\Lambda_X\cos\varphi + \Lambda_Y\sin\varphi) - \Lambda_Z\sin\theta - \Delta_X\sin\varphi + \Delta_Y\cos\varphi]
\end{aligned} \tag{7}$$

Despite the system is comprised only of two equations, it includes numerous trigonometric functions. As one immediately sees, the quantities $\sin\theta$, $\sin\varphi$, $\cos\theta$ and $\cos\varphi$ enters several times into the equations, calling for obvious optimization by calculating these quantities only once per iteration. However, as we need to take into account magnetic anisotropy as well as demagnetizing field, the equations corresponding to (1) in the spherical coordinates representation would be loaded with trigonometric functions, which require a considerable calculation time. Additionally, one may want to obtain the projections of the magnetization vector (e.g., for visualization of the phase portrait):

$$\begin{aligned} M_X &= M_S \sin\theta \cos\varphi \\ M_Y &= M_S \sin\theta \sin\varphi \\ M_Z &= M_S \cos\theta \end{aligned} \tag{8}$$

Such pronounced use of trigonometric functions slows down the calculation process considerably. In comparison with the Cartesian coordinate representation (including re-normalization of magnetization vector on every step), the numerical solution of the LLG in the spherical representation is about six times slower (Horley et al., 2009).

2.3 Stereographic projection

Aiming to optimize the calculation time, one seeks to keep the LLG equation reduced to the lower number of components and avoiding, if possible, the use of special functions. One solution to this problem is the use of the stereographic projection mapping the sphere into a plane with the complex variable $\zeta = \tan(\frac{1}{2}\theta)e^{i\varphi}$. The LLG equation has the following form in the stereographic projection (Horley et al., 2009):

$$\frac{2}{1+\zeta^*\zeta} = \gamma_1[-(J_{S+} + i\varsigma H_{S+}) + \alpha(H_{S+} - i\varsigma J_{S+})] \tag{9}$$

The quantities marked with subscript "S₊" correspond to spherical components of the vector **H** (and similarly **J**) in a rotated basis, defined by a rotation transforming $\mathbf{e}_Z$ into $\mathbf{e}_r$, so that $H_{S+} = (H_+ - \zeta^2 H_- - 2\varsigma\alpha H_0)/(1+\zeta^*\zeta)$. The variables H_+, H_- and H_0 represent the irreducible spherical components of a Cartesian tensor (Normand & Raynal, 1982). If the magnetization trajectory is limited only to the upper or to the lower hemisphere, the task of choosing the proper projector pole is trivial. However, if we want to study the magnetization reversal with the phase point passing from one pole to another, the corresponding equation written for a single projection pole will cause numerical overflow. The situation can be solved by dynamical switching of the projector pole. The variable $\varsigma = \pm 1$ denotes the projector pole (lower or upper). It is important to mention that for $\varsigma = 1$ the upper pole will correspond to $\zeta = 0$, while the lower (projector) pole will cause $\zeta \to \infty$. Switching the projector pole to upper one ($\varsigma = -1$), one should recalculate the projection variable as $\zeta' = 1/\zeta^*$, after which the value $\zeta = 0$ will correspond to the lower, and $\zeta \to \infty$ to the upper pole. Thus, for phase portraits situated in the upper and lower hemisphere one will have two projections that merge at the equatorial line. It is convenient to present both projections in different colours (depending on the projection pole used) in the same plot, as it is illustrated in Figure 2 for the case of IPP and OPP cycles. This approach simplifies the visualization of the phase portraits, offering a useful "recipe" for obtaining a clear 2D plot of a 3D magnetization curve. The superimposed plots may become complicated for phase portraits composed of numerous loops, but this situation does not occur in a system subjected to constant fields and currents (Horley et al., 2008).

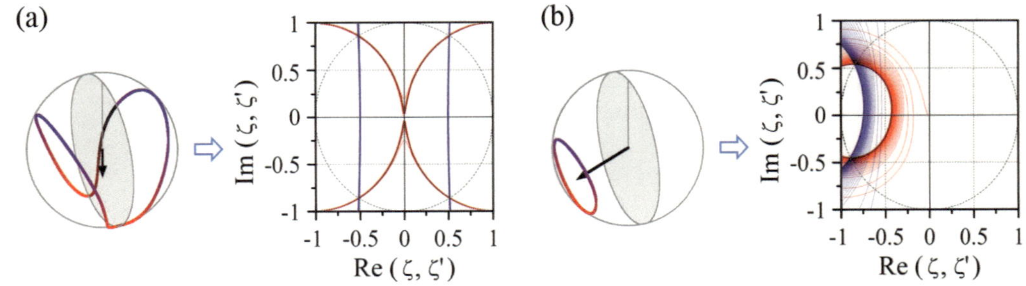

Fig. 2. Stereographic projection of in-plane (a) and out-of-plane (b) steady precession of a macrospin. Red curves show the projection from the upper pole, blue curves correspond to projection from the lower pole. The dotted grey circle represents the equator of the sphere $|\mathbf{M}|$ = *const*, normalized over saturation magnetization M_S.

To improve the calculation performance for the LLG equation written in the stereographic projection, it is important to optimize the procedure for projector pole switching. Our previous studies have shown that it is not productive to switch the pole each time the magnetization trajectory crosses the equator (Horley et al., 2009). A more useful approach consists in the introduction of a certain threshold value $|\zeta|_S$, after crossing which the pole switching should be performed. Our numerical tests shown that threshold values of $|\zeta|_S$ = 1000 (corresponding to the zenith angle θ = 0.99936π) boosts the calculation performance, allowing to achieve five-time speed-up of the simulation comparing with the spherical representation of the LLG equation. Increase of $|\zeta|_S$ by five orders of magnitude does not lead to any further improvement of calculation speed.

2.4 Frenet-Serret projection

Another representation of a curve in three-dimensional space can be made in the Frenet-Serret reference frame consisting of tangent vector **T**, normal **N** and binormal **B** = **T** × **N**. The equations governing the variation of these vectors for a curve parameterized by the arc length s are the following

$$\frac{d\mathbf{T}}{ds} = \chi \mathbf{N}, \qquad \frac{d\mathbf{N}}{ds} = -\chi \mathbf{T} + \tau \mathbf{B}, \quad \frac{d\mathbf{B}}{ds} = -\tau \mathbf{N} \tag{10}$$

where χ and τ are the curvature and torsion of the curve, given by

$$\chi = \frac{\left| \frac{d\mathbf{M}}{dt} \times \frac{d^2\mathbf{M}}{dt^2} \right|}{\left| \frac{d\mathbf{M}}{dt} \right|^3}, \qquad \tau = \frac{\left(\frac{d\mathbf{M}}{dt} \times \frac{d^2\mathbf{M}}{dt^2} \right) \cdot \frac{d^3\mathbf{M}}{dt^3}}{\left| \frac{d\mathbf{M}}{dt} \times \frac{d^2\mathbf{M}}{dt^2} \right|^2} \tag{11}$$

They depend on higher order derivatives (second or second and third), putting more demanding requirements on the precision of the numerical integration method used. It is interesting to use these two scalars (χ and τ) for characterization of the LLG solutions. Using the above equations one can write the lowest terms in the time development of the magnetization vector as

$$\mathbf{M}(t+\Delta t)=\mathbf{M}(t)+\frac{ds}{dt}\mathbf{T}\Delta t+\frac{1}{2}\left(\frac{d^2s}{dt^2}\mathbf{T}+\chi\left(\frac{ds}{dt}\right)^2\mathbf{N}\right)(\Delta t)^2+\cdots \tag{12}$$

The tangent component of the second order correction vanishes if one uses the arc length instead of time in the curve parameterization. Since the vectors **T**, **N** and **B** form a complete basis, the vector **M** is, at each time, a linear combination of the vectors **N** and **B**. Using the Frenet-Serret equations one finds that

$$\mathbf{M}=-\frac{1}{\chi}\mathbf{N}+\frac{\chi'}{\chi^2\tau}\mathbf{B} \tag{13}$$

where the prime denotes differentiation with respect to the arc length, together with the condition $\left(\frac{\chi'}{\chi^2\tau}\right)'=\frac{\tau}{\chi}$, which also follows from the constraint $\mathbf{M}^2 = const$. One sees that the second order condition $\mathbf{M}\cdot\frac{d^2\mathbf{M}}{dt^2}=-\left(\frac{d\mathbf{M}}{dt}\right)^2$ is automatically satisfied since the parallel components of **M** and $\frac{d^2\mathbf{M}}{dt^2}$ in the Frenet-Serret reference frame (i.e. along **N)** are inversely proportional. Alternatively, one can say that the renormalization of the magnetization vector fixes the component of $\frac{d^2\mathbf{M}}{dt^2}$ along **M**, but that it misses to fix the component along the direction orthogonal to **M** and **T**.

The analytical expressions of the curvature and torsion in the absence of applied current are

$$\chi=\frac{\sqrt{\gamma_1^2+\lambda^2+\zeta^2}}{\sqrt{\gamma_1^2+\lambda^2}} \tag{14}$$

$$\tau=\frac{\sqrt{\gamma_1^2+\lambda^2}}{\gamma_1^2+\lambda^2+\zeta^2}\frac{d\zeta}{ds} \tag{15}$$

Equations (14) and (15) use re-normalized gyromagnetic ratio $\gamma_1 = \gamma/\,(1+\alpha^2)$, $\lambda=\alpha\gamma_1$ and the variable ζ given by the formula

$$\zeta=\frac{1}{|\mathbf{m}\times\mathbf{H}|}\left[\gamma_1(\mathbf{m}\cdot\mathbf{H})+\sqrt{\gamma_1^2+\lambda^2}\left(\mathbf{m}_1\cdot\frac{d\mathbf{H}}{ds}\right)\right]. \tag{16}$$

Its derivative along the trajectory can be found as

$$\begin{aligned}\frac{d\zeta}{ds}=\frac{\sqrt{\gamma_1^2+\lambda^2}}{|\mathbf{m}\times\mathbf{H}|}\Bigg[&\frac{\lambda}{\gamma_1^2+\lambda^2}(\zeta\,\mathbf{m}-\gamma_1\mathbf{m}_2)\cdot\mathbf{H}\\&+\frac{2}{\sqrt{\gamma_1^2+\lambda^2}}(\gamma_1\,\mathbf{m}+\zeta\,\mathbf{m}_2)\cdot\frac{d\mathbf{H}}{ds}+\left(\mathbf{m}_1\cdot\frac{d^2\mathbf{H}}{ds^2}\right)\Bigg]\end{aligned} \tag{17}$$

The quantities $\mathbf{m}$, $\mathbf{m}_1$ and $\mathbf{m}_2$ entering equations (16) and (17) are defined as

$$\mathbf{m} = \frac{\mathbf{M}}{M_S}, \quad \mathbf{m}_1 = \frac{\mathbf{m}\times\mathbf{H}}{|\mathbf{m}\times\mathbf{H}|}, \quad \mathbf{m}_2 = \mathbf{m}\times\frac{\mathbf{m}\times\mathbf{H}}{|\mathbf{m}\times\mathbf{H}|} \tag{18}$$

It is worth noting that formulas (14) and (15) are derived for the case when macrospin is subjected only to an external magnetic field. This model can be easily extended to include the Slonczewski torque term into the LLG equation by noticing that the spin-polarized current torque in (1) can be formally incorporated into the precession term, which will result in replacement of the applied field $\mathbf{H}$ by the effective field $\mathbf{H}_{EFF}$:

$$\mathbf{H}_{EFF} = \mathbf{H} - \frac{\mathbf{M}}{M_S}\times\mathbf{J} \tag{19}$$

In a similar manner, the equation (3) can be rewritten for the case of the injected spin-polarized current with the same effective field replacement according to formula (19). This methodology can be used to incorporate the Slonczewski torque into the formulas (14) and (15) for torsion and curvature. Due to simplicity of this replacement, it was deemed unnecessary to present the modified versions of formulas (14) and (15) here.

The Frenet-Serret frame allows analysis of the magnetization curve properties, shown in Figs. 3 and 4 for in-plane and out-of-plane precession cases, respectively. To be able to carry out the comparison, it was necessary to adequate the phase portraits that are characterized by different precession frequencies. To do this, we separated a single precession cycle using the following algorithm:

1. for each magnetization component m_i, find the local minimum at time a_i;
2. find the second local minimum at time b_i;
3. find the estimated period as $c_i = b_i - a_i$;
4. choose the variable with the largest c_i and consider the portion of a phase portrait formed by the data limited by time moments a_i and b_i.

To visualize the values of velocity, curvature and torsion (VCT) directly on the phase portrait, we faced the following difficulty. It is possible to code these quantities as colours, but it may be quite complicated to interpret them as, for example, the torsion can be positive or negative. Thus, it would be preferable to show the corresponding quantities as vectors. As they give the local characteristics of the curve, it would be impractical to show them as a tangent vector of varying length. On the contrary, plotting the corresponding quantities along the normal or binormal would be more understandable. It resulted that namely plotting VCT along the normal offered a more straightforward intuitive interpretation. Thus, if the local torsion is positive, it would be plotted as a vector pointing inside the curve; if the torsion is negative, the corresponding vector will point outside of the curve. To visualize the smooth variation of VCT along the phase portrait, it proved considerably useful to plot an enveloping curve for every calculated phase point, introducing only several reference vectors denoting the behaviour of the local velocity, curvature and torsion.

The resulting plots allow clear analysis and interpretation of the VCT parameters. The largest rate of magnetization variation (velocity of the phase point) is observed at the upper part of the "wings" of the butterfly-shaped phase portrait (Fig. 3a, point A). This is understandable as the stationary solutions of the LLG include upper and lower poles of the

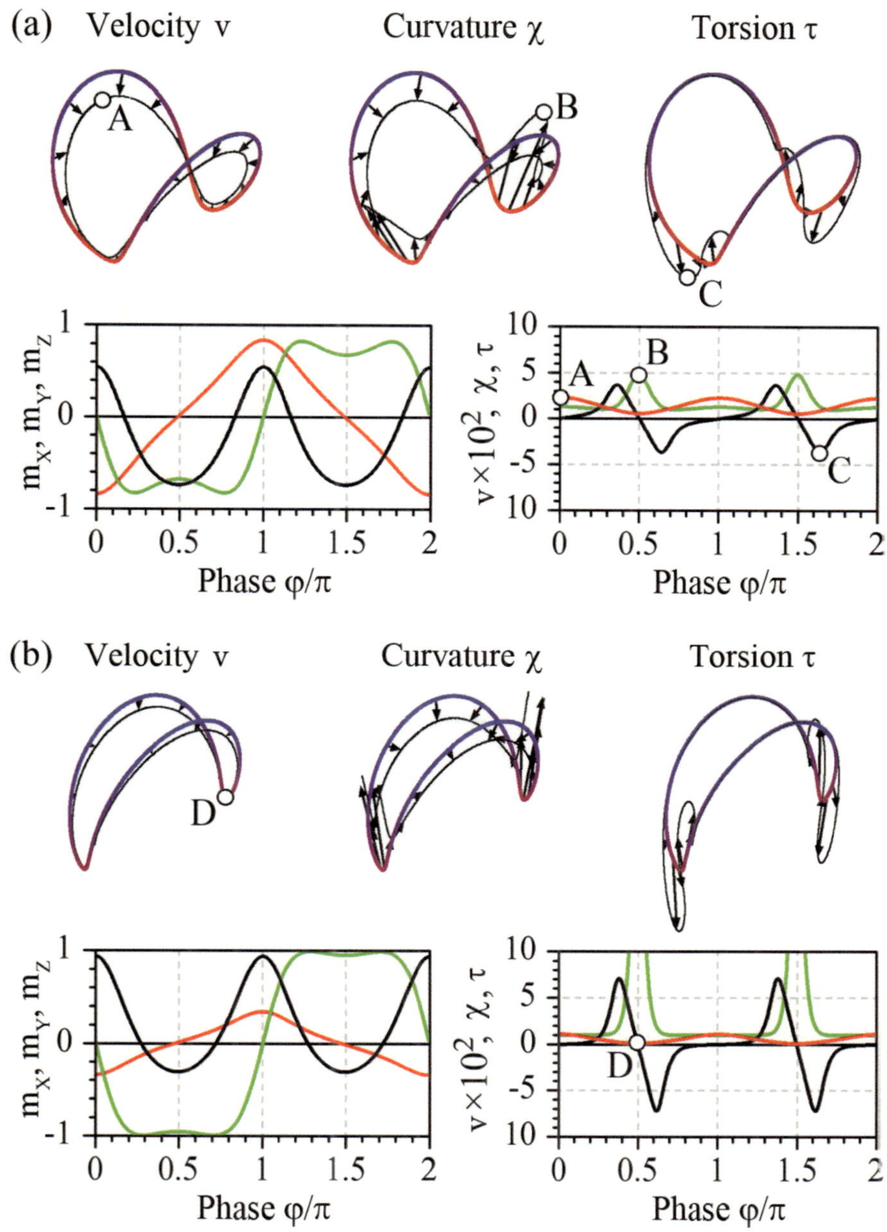

Fig. 3. Velocity, curvature and torsion of in-plane precession phase portrait calculated for a) H = 0.4 MA/m, J = 69mA; b) H = 0.53 MA/m, J = 64mA. The curve characteristics are plotted as vectors directed along the normal to the curve, not to scale with the phase portrait. The enveloping curve is shown as thin black line. The panels below presents the distribution of normalized magnetization components $m_i = M_i/M_S$ (red - m_X, green - m_Y and black - m_Z) as well as velocity, curvature and torsion (red, green and black, respectively). The characteristic points are marked with letters: A) large velocity; B) large curvature; C) large torsion and D) small velocity and torsion

sphere and canted states, which are located outside of the easy magnetization plane. Thus, passing along the upper part of the trajectory, the phase point travels through the area well away from the stationary points, where the energy gradient is high, causing fast reorientation of the magnetization. Upon approaching to the folding point, the phase point travels closer to the stationary point, resulting in a much slower magnetization variation (Fig. 3b, point D). As the two wings of the phase portrait join at the easy magnetization plane, the curvature of the trajectory will increase significantly (Fig. 3a, point B), becoming higher for smaller separation between the wings (Fig. 3b). At the peak of the curvature and minimum velocity, the torsion changes sign, becoming negative after passing the point with maximum curvature (Fig. 3a, point C). It is worth mentioning that, because the curvature of the phase portrait is always positive, the period of the VCT curves constitutes a half of the total period of in-plane precession oscillations. Thus, one cannot use VCT plots to distinguish between the left and right "wings" of the magnetization curve.

In the case of out-of-plane precession cycle (Fig. 4), the behaviour of the VCT is similar, because the phase point moves in the same energy landscape. When we consider the large precession cycle (Fig. 4a) that corresponds to one of the wings of in-plane precession cycle, one can observe increase of the magnetization precession velocity upon approaching the upper part of the cycle. The lower part, while looking quite smooth, features increase of curvature representing a "relic" of butterfly-shaped phase portrait corresponding to in-plane precession. The small "splash" of torsion is also observable in this part of the phase trajectory. However, if the phase portrait represents a cycle set well away from the easy magnetization plane, the velocity of the phase point will be considerably uniform (Fig. 4b). The curvature becomes constant and the torsion is vanishing, proving that this phase portrait approaches to a circle lying in a plane, for which, as we know, the curvature is equal to the inverse of the radius and the torsion is zero. Namely this type of oscillations, despite of their modest amplitude, is most promising for microwave generator use, because the time profiles of its magnetization components approach the harmonic signal (Fig. 4b).

3. Numerical methods

A proper choice of the numerical method for the solution of the LLG equation is very important. The straightforward solution to obtain the most accurate results is to apply a higher-order numerical scheme to the equations written in one of the coordinate systems that ensures unconditional preservation of the magnetization vector length. However, depending on the complexity of the system, this approach may require many hours of computer time. The opposite approach consists in the choice of the simplest (first order) numerical method applied to the fastest-to-calculate representation of LLG - the Cartesian coordinates. In this way, the speed of simulations will increase up to an order of magnitude - but alas, the results will be completely flawed even using reasonably small values of the integration step h. Additional problems appear if we want to include the temperature into the model - the resulting LLG equation is stochastic, and correct results can be achieved only using numerical methods converging to the Stratonovich solution. All these details should be taken into account in search of a balance between calculation speed and accuracy.

We will focus here on explicit numerical schemes, which are simpler for implementation as they offer direct calculation of the next point using the current value of the function. Writing the ordinary differential equation as

$$y' = f(t, y(t)), \tag{20}$$

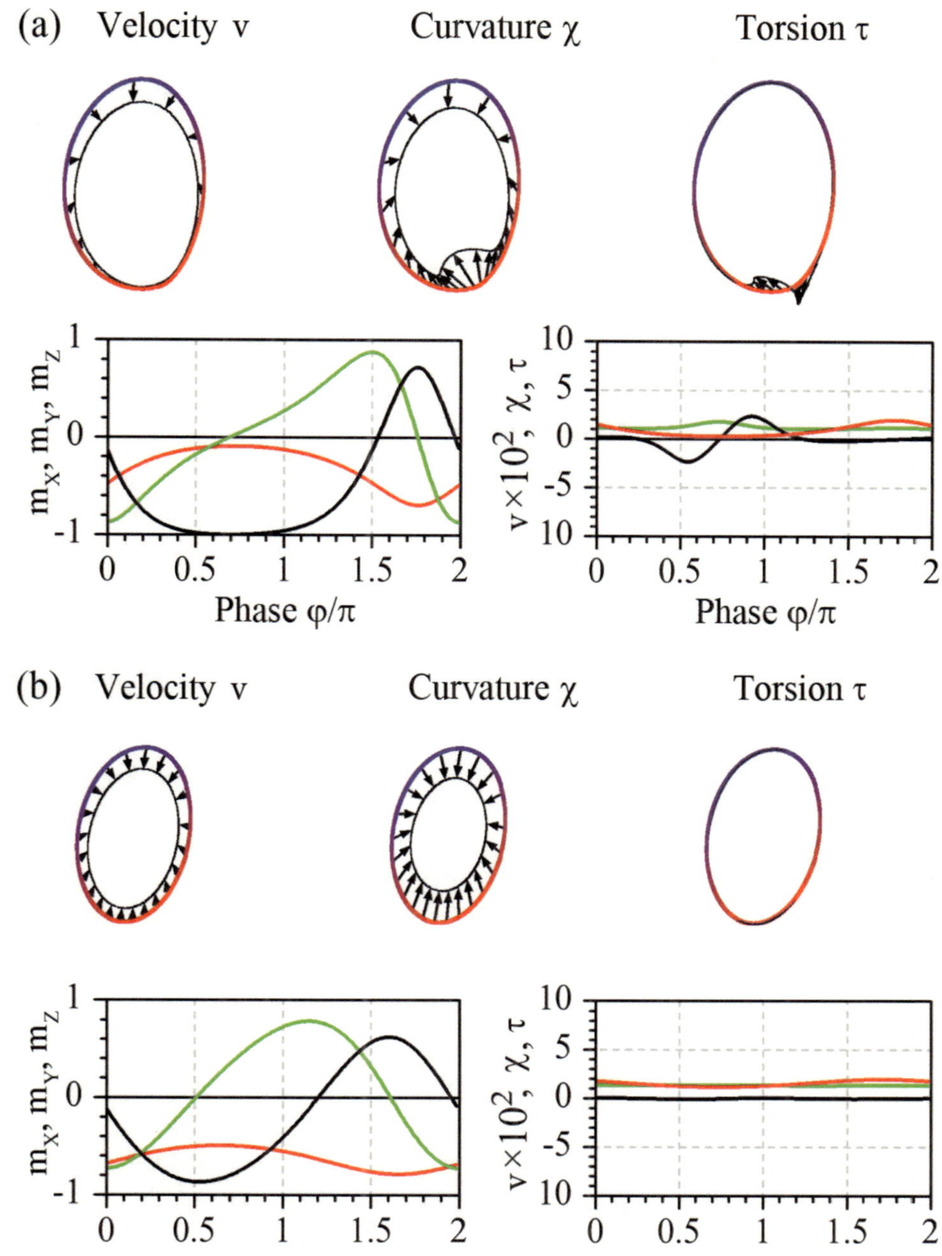

Fig. 4. Velocity, curvature and torsion of out-of-plane phase portrait calculated for a) H = 0.2 MA/m, J = 87mA; b) H = 0.18 MA/m, J = 136mA. Similarly to Fig. 3, the thin black curve envelops the vectors corresponding to aforementioned characteristics of the phase portrait, set along the normal to the curve. The time distribution of normalized magnetization $m_i = M_i/M_S$ (red - m_X, green - m_Y and black - m_Z) and velocity, curvature and torsion (red, green and black, respectively) are given in the bottom panels.

one can obtain the value of the derivative for the point t. Depending on the accuracy required, this value can be used as is or improved introducing intermediate points. Knowing the initial value of the function (Cauchy boundary condition), one can thus obtain the next point and then iterate from there. For simplicity, we will consider here single-step methods that require only information about a single point for the integration of the system.

3.1 First order methods

The simplest integration formula, suggested by Leonhard Euler, straightforwardly uses Eq. (20) to calculate the value of the function in the next point y_{n+1} basing on its current value y_n:

$$y_{n+1} = y_n + hf(t_n, y_n) \tag{21}$$

This approach suffers from the fact that the value of the derivative in the point (y_n, t_n) does not hold for the whole integration step h, resulting in an error $O(h)$. While it can be acceptable for other systems, in the case of the LLG the situation is special due to the fact that the first order methods are insufficient for accurate solution (see discussion after equation (13)). Accumulation of these errors distorts the results, leading to significantly different time evolution of the magnetization. This situation is illustrated in Fig. 5 showing solutions of the LLG calculated with the Euler method and 4th order Runge-Kutta method.

As one can see from the figure, starting from the first peak (t ~ 115ps) the curve obtained with the Euler method deviates; upon reaching the first minimum (t ~ 150ps) the difference with the curve integrated with the Runge-Kutta method already becomes significant. It is necessary to emphasize that the curves shown in Fig. 5 feature different amplitude and frequencies - that is, the solution obtained with the Euler method is much distinct and should be regarded as inadequate. Due to this accuracy issue, the first-order methods should not be used at all for the numerical solution of the LLG equation.

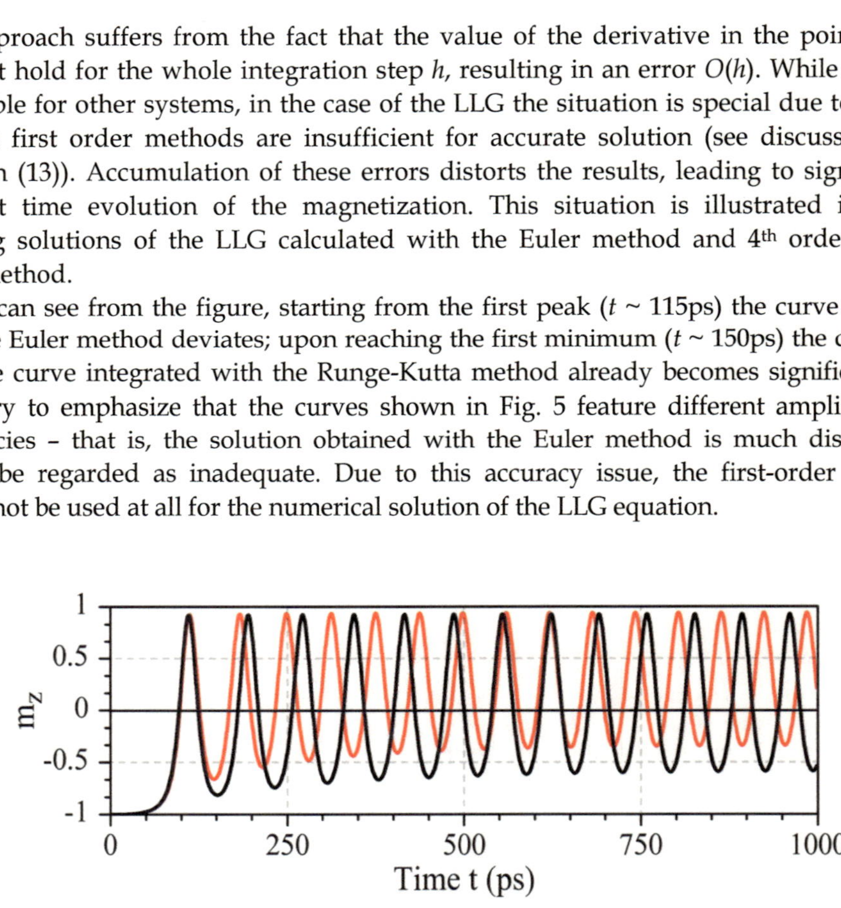

Fig. 5. Comparison of time evolution of normalized magnetization component $m_z = M_Z/M_S$: red curve - integrated with Euler method; black curve - integrated with 4th order Runge-Kutta method. Parameter values: applied magnetic field H = 60kA/m, injected spin-polarized current J = 0.07A, integration step h = 0.5 ps.

3.2 Higher order methods

The simplest way to improve the accuracy of the Euler method is to observe that

$$\begin{aligned} y(t+h) &= y(t) + h\frac{dy}{dt} + \tfrac{1}{2}h^2\frac{d^2y}{dt^2} + O(h^3) \\ &= y(t) + hf(t,y(t)) + \tfrac{1}{2}h^2\left(\frac{\partial f}{\partial t} + \frac{\partial f}{\partial y}f\right) + O(h^3) \\ &= y(t) + h\left[f(t,y(t)) + \tfrac{1}{2}h\left(\frac{\partial f}{\partial t} + \frac{\partial f}{\partial y}f\right)\right] + O(h^3) \\ &= y(t) + hf\left[t + \tfrac{1}{2}h, y(t) + \tfrac{1}{2}hf(t)\right] + O(h^3) \end{aligned} \tag{22}$$

A similar second order integrator is the "modified Euler method" or "Heun method":

$$\hat{y}_{n+1} = y_n + hf(t_n, y_n), \qquad y_{n+1} = y_n + \tfrac{1}{2}h\big(f(t_n, y_n) + f(t_{n+1}, \hat{y}_{n+1})\big) \tag{23}$$

which can be interpreted as an predictor-corrector method. It can be obtained formally integrating the differential equation and using then the trapezoidal method to correct the values of the derivative. Higher order integration methods are usually derived choosing a specific form of the integrator with a certain number of points and some free weights which are then chosen to obtain the desired accuracy.

In the framework of the generalization proposed by Carl Runge and Martin Kutta, the Heun method can be classified as a second order Runge-Kutta method. It already has an acceptable accuracy, at the same time featuring considerable calculation speed. The precision of the integrator can be improved by using more intermediate points, leading to the most commonly-used 4th order Runge-Kutta method with total accumulated error $O(h^4)$:

$$\begin{aligned} k_1 &= f(t_n, y_n), \\ k_2 &= f(t_n + \tfrac{1}{2}h, y_n + \tfrac{1}{2}hk_1), \\ k_3 &= f(t_n + \tfrac{1}{2}h, y_n + \tfrac{1}{2}hk_2), \\ k_4 &= f(t_n + h, y_n + hk_3), \\ y_{n+1} &= y_n + \tfrac{1}{6}h(k_1 + 2k_2 + 2k_3 + k_4) \end{aligned} \tag{24}$$

To compare the performance of the different numerical methods and projections of the LLG, we calculated a dynamical diagram of the system in H-J parameter space, using a 300×300 grid. For each pair of parameters, the LLG equation was integrated with the time step 0.5 ps, reconstructing a phase portrait of the system containing 50,000 points. The initial 40,000 points were discarded to consider the steady motion of the magnetization vector without any transitional effects. The Hausdorff dimension was calculated for resulting 10,000 points using the same algorithm. The obtained dynamical diagrams are illustrated in Fig. 6. Therefore, the difference in calculation times will be attributed only to the choice of the numerical method used to solve the equation and the particular representation of the LLG. The comparison of calculation times is given in the table.

As one can see from the table, the projection of the LLG equation has a pronounced influence on the calculation times, leading to a seven-time speed gain for the Cartesian and a five-time speed gain for the stereographic projection in comparison with the LLG calculations in spherical coordinates. Within the same projection type, the variation of the calculation times is less impressive - the 1st order Euler method scores about 40-50%, and the 2nd order Heun method - 60-80% relative to the 4th order Runge-Kutta method.

Method / Projection	Euler	Heun	4th order Runge-Kutta
Cartesian	17^m58^s / (7%)	23^m57^s / (10%)	31^m43^s / (13%)
Spherical	$1^h40^m38^s$ / (42%)	$2^h28^m01^s$ / (61%)	$4^h1^m19^s$ / (100%)
Stereographic	20^m20^s / (8%)	26^m52^s / (11%)	46^m08^s / (19%)

Table 1. Calculation times for different integration methods and representations of LLG equation. The numbers in parenthesis give the (rounded) percentage, assigning 100% to spherical LLG calculated with 4th order Runge Kutta method (grey cell).

Let us analyze the dynamical diagrams presented in Fig. 6. At a first glance, the results obtained by the Euler method are drastically different from those obtained with higher-order methods. The IPP/OPP boundary is shifted to larger currents, but the difference does not consist in mere scaling - the data obtained by the Euler method features distinct oscillation modes (such as precession around the easy axis), which has no correspondence for the case of Runge-Kutta or Heun integration. One may argue that such low accuracy is caused by the fact that re-normalization of the magnetization vector **M** in the Cartesian system is not enough, since it does not take into account second order changes of the orientation of the magnetization vector. However, the very same situation takes place for the dynamical diagrams calculated with the Euler method using the spherical and stereographic projections, which reduce the number of degrees of freedom and automatically satisfy the condition of constant length of the magnetization vector **M**.

Curiously, the distortion of the dynamic diagrams slightly improves (so that the division line between IPP and OPP modes is shifted to lower currents) - perhaps, because the two-dimensional projection somewhat "lowers" the accumulated calculation error. In any case, the dynamic diagrams obtained with the Euler method are definitely wrong - for example, LLG written in the stereographic projection displays three IPP/OPP boundaries in the dynamic diagram, while the calculation made with a 2nd order method clearly show that there should be only *one* such boundary.

Therefore, comparison of accuracy and performance suggests that the Heun method is the most recommendable for fast and reliable solution of the LLG equation in different representations. To improve precision one should use the 4th order Runge-Kutta method, which, however, will mean at least doubled calculation times.

3.3 Stochastic case

The deterministic LLG equation, considered above, is applicable only for T=0K. At higher temperatures, the system is affected by thermal fluctuations due to the interaction of the magnetic moment with phonons, nuclear spins, etc. Due to this, the description of the magnetization dynamics becomes probabilistic, and can be found by solving the Fokker-Planck equation for the non-equilibrium distribution of the probability $P(M, t)$. This approach is very useful to magnetization reversal studies, allowing obtaining the probability

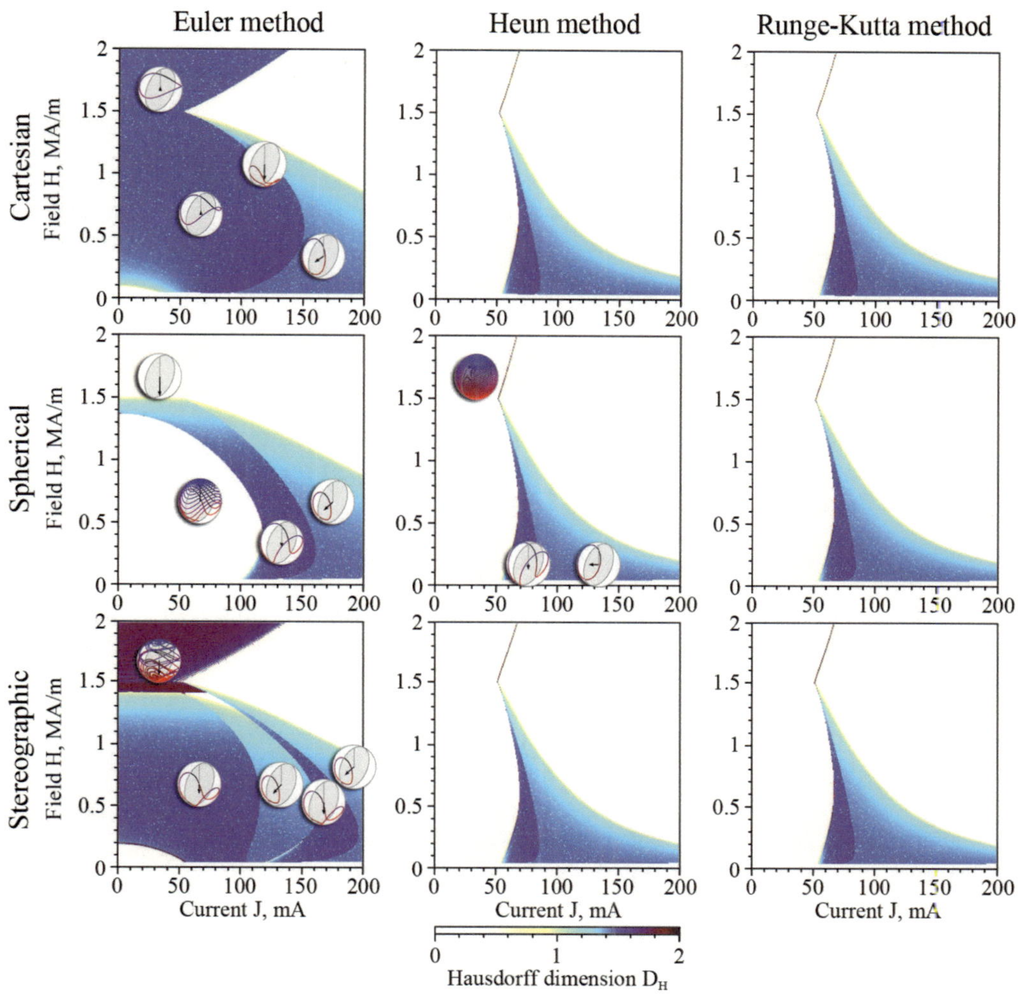

Fig. 6. Dynamic diagrams (based on the Hausdorff dimension D_H) calculated using 1st order Euler, 2nd order Heun and 4th order Runge-Kutta methods in Cartesian, spherical and stereographic projections. Integration step for all cases is 0.5 ps.

of switching under a given applied magnetic field, injected spin-polarized current *and* finite temperature, which is undoubtedly important for the development of magnetic memory devices. At the same time, for studies of magnetization precession it is desirable to have access to the time evolution of the magnetization vector, studying the phase portraits of the system as was done in the deterministic LLG case (García-Palacios & Lázaro 1998, Sukhov & Berakdar 2008). To do this, one should introduce the noise term to the effective field:

$$H_t = \sqrt{\frac{2\alpha kT}{\gamma_1 \mu_0 V M_S \Delta t}} W_t . \tag{25}$$

Here k is Boltzmann constant, T is temperature, V is the volume of magnetic particle and Δt is integration step for the time (referred above as h). The quantity W_t is the random variable corresponding to a Wiener process with zero mean value and constant standard deviation. The noise term transforms the LLG into a stochastic differential equation (SDE)

$$\frac{1}{\gamma_1}\frac{d\mathbf{M}}{dt} = -\mathbf{M}\times(\mathbf{H}+\mathbf{H}_t+\alpha\mathbf{J})+\frac{1}{M_S}\mathbf{M}\times(\mathbf{M}\times(\mathbf{J}-\alpha(\mathbf{H}+\mathbf{H}_t)) \tag{26}$$

As one can see, the current-induced torque does not contribute to the noise term, while the field-induced torque does. As vector products are distributive over addition, one can separate deterministic and noise parts of the equation

$$\frac{1}{\gamma_1}\frac{d\mathbf{M}}{dt} = \left[-\mathbf{M}\times\mathbf{\Lambda}+\frac{1}{M_S}\mathbf{M}\times(\mathbf{M}\times\mathbf{\Delta})\right]-\left[\mathbf{M}\times\mathbf{H}_t+\frac{1}{M_S}\mathbf{M}\times(\mathbf{M}\times\alpha\mathbf{H}_t)\right] \tag{27}$$

Here torque-inducing vectors $\mathbf{\Lambda}$ and $\mathbf{\Delta}$ are the same as those introduced for equation (3). The general form of such a SDE can be written as a sum of a drift (deterministic) and diffusion (noise) terms $f(y)$ and $g(y)$, respectively

$$dy = f(y)dt + g(y)dW_t\,. \tag{28}$$

This is a Langevin equation with multiplicative noise, because the noise term g depends on the phase variable $y \equiv \mathbf{M}$. To find the increment of the function during a finite time step dt the equation (28) should be integrated

$$dy = \int_t^{t+dt} f(y(t'),t')dt' + \int_t^{t+dt} g(y(t'),t')dW_{t'}dt'\,. \tag{29}$$

The deterministic integral is easy to find as the function $f(t)$ is a regular function. The situation with the stochastic term is radically different, because the function $g(y)$ includes a Wiener process that is non-differentiable. In the simplest case, one can estimate the value of the integral by evaluating $g(y)$ at the beginning of a small dt interval, assume it constant, and thus obtain the integral as multiplication $W_t dt^{1/2}$, because dW_t is proportional to the square root of the integration time step dt. Under these assumptions, one will obtain the Itô interpretation of the stochastic differential equation:

$$dy(t) = f(y(t),t)dt + g(y(t),t)W_t\sqrt{dt}\,. \tag{30}$$

The other option is to evaluate the diffusion term at an intermediate point belonging to the time interval $[t,\ t + dt]$ that would give rise to an additional drift term. If one chooses the intermediate point to be the midpoint of the aforementioned interval which, from the discussion of eq. (22) gives a second order algorithm, the stochastic equation can be rewritten as:

$$dy(t) = \left[f(y(t),t)+\tfrac{1}{2}g'(y(t),t)g(y(t),t)\right]dt + g(y(t),t)W_t\sqrt{dt}\,. \tag{31}$$

with the partial derivative $g'(y) = \partial g(y,t)/\partial y$. The latter formula corresponds to the Stratonovich interpretation of the SDE, where the usual chain rule of integration remains valid. As equations (30) and (31) are different, they will naturally lead to distinct solutions. One should then use the drift term appropriate to the interpretation being used (the Fokker-

Planck equation for the probability distribution is the same in both interpretations). The Itô interpretation is widely used for mathematical problems and for financial applications, in particular. It has the advantage that only requires information about past events. The Stratonovich interpretation is appropriate for physical and engineering systems (Kloeden & Platen, 1999), where Langevin equations are derived from microscopic models by a coarse-graining process. Therefore, to simulate magnetization dynamics governed by a stochastic LLG equation, one need to ensure that: 1) the appropriate method for the solution of the deterministic part of the LLG (i.e. at least a second-order numerical method) will be used; 2) this method will converge to the Stratonovich solution of the SDE; 3) the integration will be performed with a proper integration step so that $dt \sim dW^2$, requiring a smaller step for the case of higher temperatures; and 4) the random numbers used to generate the noise term of the stochastic equation will meet the requirements of a Wiener process.
The straightforward re-mapping of the Euler method to the stochastic case is known as the Euler-Maruyama method (Mahony, 2006):

$$y_{n+1} = y_n + \Delta_t f(y_n) + \Delta_{Wn} g(y_n) \,. \tag{32}$$

Similarly to the case of ODE, this method is easy to implement, but it gives unreliable results if the drift and diffusion terms vary significantly (which includes the case of magnetization dynamics simulations). The stochastic Euler method converges to the Itô solution (Kloeden & Platen 1999). To obtain the Stratonovich solution, one may introduce the additional drift term into the first-order numerical scheme, leading to the Milstein method (Mahony, 2006):

$$y_{n+1} = y_n + \Delta_t f(y_n) + \Delta_{Wn} g(y_n) + \tfrac{1}{2} g(y_n) g'(y_n)(\Delta_{Wn}^2 - \Delta_t) \tag{33}$$

This approach allows to increase the convergence order to unity, which is still insufficient for the LLG SDE. As we have shown before, the numerical method should be at least of the second order to allow proper treatment of the deterministic LLG. Therefore, the basic choice also points to the stochastic Heun method (Burrage, Burrage & Tian, 2004):

$$\bar{y}_n = y_n + \Delta_t f(y_n) + \Delta_W g(y_n) \quad y_{n+1} = y_n + \tfrac{1}{2}\Delta_t (f(y_n) + f(\bar{y}_n)) + \tfrac{1}{2}\Delta_{Wn}(g(y_n) + g(\bar{y}_n)) \tag{34}$$

It converges to the Stratonovich solution and is convenient for implementation as no additional drift term is necessary. Further precision improvement can be achieved by use of stochastic Runge-Kutta methods, such as second-order method (Mahony, 2006):

$$\bar{y}_n = y_n + \tfrac{2}{3}\Delta_t f(y_n) + \tfrac{2}{3}\Delta_{Wn} g(y_n)$$

$$y_{n+1} = y_n + \Delta_t (\tfrac{1}{4} f(y_n) + \tfrac{3}{4} f(\bar{y}_n)) + \Delta_{Wn}(\tfrac{1}{4} g(y_n) + \tfrac{3}{4} g(\bar{y}_n)) \tag{35}$$

The Runge-Kutta methods also converge to the Stratonovich solution and do not require insertion of any additional drift terms.
The next important question is to ensure the proper characteristics of the noise. The basic generators of random numbers available in BASIC, FORTRAN, C or Pascal actually represent pseudo-random numbers, which repeat after a certain large number of steps. For the solution of stochastic differential equations, we should generate random numbers corresponding to a Wiener process, i.e., characterized by zero mean and constant dispersion.

One of the useful approaches is the Ziggurat method proposed by Marsaglia and Tsang (2000). It consists in binning of the area below the desired distribution curves with rectangles of the same area, the lowest of which tails to the infinity. Upon generation of an integer random number, its rightmost bits are counted as an index to the bin. If the random number fits below the distribution curve, it is used as an outcome of the algorithm; in the opposite case, the number becomes transformed until this condition is satisfied. By storing several arrays of coefficients describing the binning applied, it is possible to achieve fast generation of random numbers obeying the required decreasing distribution. Comparison of the Ziggurat method with other fast generators of random numbers show a considerable performance gain, requiring three-times less time than Ahrens-Dieter and 5.5 times - than Leva method (Marsaglia & Tsang, 2000).

For a three-dimensional system, one should use a 3D Wiener process for the thermal field. This means that we should create three independent sets of random numbers modifying the effective field components H_X, H_Y and H_Z. However, for practical application it is computation-costly to re-generate a whole set of random numbers if one is going to calculate the dynamic diagrams composed of dozens of thousands of points; additionally, as thermal fluctuations should be taken into account from a probabilistic point of view, it will be necessary to average over several different realizations of the stochastic process to obtain the required statistical data about the system. We suggest to improve this situation by pre-generating several sets of Wiener processes (which can be saved into a file for further use), and then to generate three non-repeating random numbers to pick independent stochastic "channels". This approach allows $P(n,k) = n!/(n-k)!$ permutations for channel number n grouped in $k = 3$ subsets. In our studies, n=20 pre-calculated channels were used, giving 6840 possible types of 3D Wiener processes. Increasing the number of pre-calculated channels to 50, one easily obtains over 10^5 possible combinations.

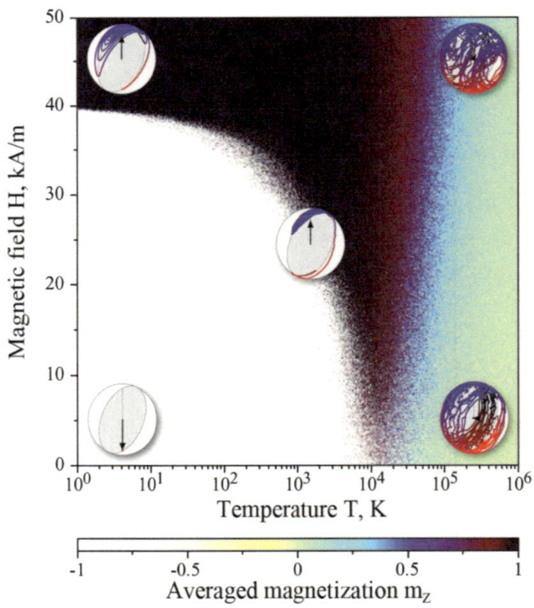

Fig. 7. The dynamic diagram of macrospin reversal with temperature. The plot is averaged over 20 realizations of Wiener process. The characteristic phase portraits are shown.

To illustrate the influence of the temperature on the macrospin dynamics, we present in Fig. 7 the dynamical diagram, averaged over 20 realizations of the stochastic process, for a macrospin in the parameter space (*H*, *T*). Here we focus on magnetization reversal, observing the change of normalized magnetization component $m_Z = M_Z / M_S$ allowing clear distinction between up / down magnetization states. As it is natural to expect, for the low temperatures ($T < 10$K) the border between $m_Z = \pm 1$ states is very sharp. The transition occurs upon application of magnetic field overcoming easy axis anisotropy, which is responsible for "holding" the magnetization in its stationary state. With increase of the temperature, the thermal fluctuations intensify and help the macrospin to overcome the potential barrier. At a certain temperature the fluctuations are so strong that the potential barrier created with the easy axis anisotropy is insufficient to separate the states with $m_Z = \pm 1$. Above this temperature the system becomes paramagnetic.

The overall qualitative behaviour of the system as illustrated in Fig. 7 is physically sound; however, a quantitative picture is far from perfect. One would expect the transition temperature to correspond to the Curie temperature, which for the model material (Co) is 1404K; the simulation plot shows that the loss of ferromagnetism occurs for temperatures about one order of magnitude higher. These unrealistic temperatures are a known problem with macrospin simulations (Xiao, Zangwill, & Stiles, 2005). They can be partially explained by the fixed length of the magnetization vector, while in real-life ferromagnetics the saturation magnetization decreases for increasing temperature. Therefore, the macrospin model is unrealistically "tough" to repolarise in the high-temperature mode, yielding an unrealistic Curie temperature. Indeed, if the magnetization vector is allowed to change its length – the approach used in the Landau-Lifshitz-Bloch equation – the simulation of the magnetization dynamics becomes more realistic at high temperatures (Chubykalo-Fesenko et al., 2006).

4. Conclusion

We analyzed different representations (spherical, Cartesian, stereographic and Frenet-Serret) of the Landau-Lifshitz-Gilbert equation describing magnetization dynamics. The fastest calculations are achieved for the equation written in Cartesian coordinates, which, however, requires re-normalization of the magnetization vector at every integration step. The use of spherical coordinates, despite being the straightforward approach for the system with constant **M**, is laden with trigonometric functions and requires larger calculation times.

The choice of the numerical method is also an important point for the simulations of magnetization dynamics. It was shown that the LLG *requires* at least a second-order numerical scheme to obtain the correct solution. Analysis of calculation performance suggests that the Heun method is a reasonable choice in terms of producing adequate results under acceptable calculation times.

For the case of finite-temperature modelling, the LLG becomes a stochastic equation with multiplicative noise, which makes it important to select the proper interpretation of the stochastic differential equation. Since this is a physical problem, it is usually more natural and favourable to consider the physical system in the framework of the Stratonovich interpretation, where the usual chain rule is still valid. The set of numerical methods suitable for its solution is then narrowed down. On the other hand, since it is possible to convert the SDE to the Itô interpretation, it is also possible to use the Itô integration as well, as we are dealing with the white thermal noise. Aiming to use minimally second-order method for the deterministic LLG equation, we return to the suggestion that the Heun's scheme offers a reasonable accuracy. At the same time, the imposition of constant length of the magnetization vector (as it appears in the LLG) makes the system unrealistically stable at high temperatures, which results in a non-physical value of the Curie temperature. In order to achieve more realistic results, it is necessary to allow the variation of the magnetization vector length, which can be realized, for example, in the Landau-Lifshitz-Bloch equation.

5. Acknowledgment

The authors gratefully acknowledge the support by the grants of CONACYT as Basic Science Project # 129269 (México) and FCT Project PTDC/FIS/70843/2006 (Portugal).

6. References

Baibich, M.N.; Broto, J.M.; Fert, A.; Nguyen Van Dau, F.; Petroff, F.; Eitenne, P.; Creuzet, G.; Friederich A. & Chazelas J. (1988). Giant magnetoresistance of (001)Fe/(001)Cr magnetic superlattices, *Physical Review Letters*, Vol. 61, pp. 2472–2475, ISSN 0031-9007

Berkov, D.V. & Gorn, N.L. (2006). Micromagnetic simulations of the magnetization precession induced by a spin-polarized current in a point-contact geometry, *Journal of Applied Physics*, Vol. 99, 08Q701, ISSN 0021-8979

Burrage, K.; Burrage P.M., & Tian, T. (2004). Numerical methods for strong solutions of SDES, *Proceedings of the Royal Society, London*, Vol. 460, pp. 373–402, ISSN 0950–1207

Chubykalo-Fesenko, O.; Nowak, U.; Chantrell, R.W. & Garanin, D. (2006). Dynamic approach for micromagnetics close to the Curie temperature, *Physical Review B*, Vol. 74, 094436, ISSN 1098-0121

Donahue, M.J. & McMichael, R.D. (2007). Micromagnetics on curved geometries using rectangular cells: error correction and analysis, *IEEE Transactions on Magnetics*, Vol. 43, pp. 2878-2880, ISSN 0018-9464

Fidler, J. & Schrefl, T. (2000). Micromagnetic modelling—the current state of the art. *Journal of Physics D: Applied Physics*, Vol. 33, pp. R135–R156, ISSN 0022-3727

García-Cervera, C.J.; Gimbutas, Z. & Weinan, E. (2003). Accurate numerical methods for micromagnetics simulations with general geometries, *Journal of Computational Physics*, Vol. 184, pp. 37–52, ISSN 0021-9991

García-Palacios, J.L. & Lázaro, F.J. (1998). Langevin-dynamics study of the dynamical properties of small magnetic particles, *Physical Review B*, Vol. 58, pp. 14937–14958, ISSN 1098-0121

Gilbert T.L. (2004). A phenomenological theory of damping in ferromagnetic materials, *IEEE Transactions on Magnetics*, Vol. 40, pp. 3443-3449, ISSN 0018-9464

Horley, P.P.; Vieira, V.R.; Gorley, P.M.; Dugaev, V.K.; Berakdar, J. & Barnaś, J. (2008). Influence of a periodic magnetic field and spin-polarized current on the magnetic dynamics of a monodomain ferromagnet, *Physical Review B*, Vol. 78, pp. 054417, ISSN 1098-0121

Horley, P.P.; Vieira, V.R.; Sacramento, P.D. & Dugaev, V.K. (2009). Application of the stereographic projection to studies of magnetization dynamics described by the Landau–Lifshitz–Gilbert equation, *Journal of Physics A: Mathematical and Theoretical*, Vol. 42, 315211, ISSN 1751-8113

Kiselev, S.I.; Sankey, J.C.; Krivorotov, I.N.; Emley, N.C.; Schoelkopf, R.J.; Buhrman, R.A. & Ralph, D.C. (2003). Microwave oscillations of a nanomagnet driven by a spin-polarized current, *Nature*, Vol. 425, pp. 380–383, ISSN 0028-0836

Kloeden, P.E. & Platen, E. (1999). *Numerical solution of stochastic differential equations*, Springer Verlag, ISBN 3-540-54062-8, Berlin

Koehler, T.R. & Fredkin D.R. (1992). Finite element method for micromagnetics, *IEEE Transactions on Magnetics,* Vol. 28, pp. 1239-1244, ISSN 0018-9464

Lichtenberg, A.J. & Lieberman, M.A. (1983). *Regular and stochastic motion.* Springer-Verlag, ISBN 3-540-90707-6, Berlin-Heidelberg-New York

Liu, Z.J.; Long, H.H.; Ong, E.T., & Li, E.P. (2006). A fast Fourier transform on multipole algorithm for micromagnetic modeling of perpendicular recording media, *Journal of Applied Physics*, Vol. 99, 08B903, ISSN 0021-8979

Mahony, C.O. (2006). The numerical analysis of stochastic differential equations, Available from http://citeseerx.ist.psu.edu/viewdoc/summary?doi=10.1.1.117.8043

Marsaglia, G. & Tsang, W.W. (2000). The Ziggurat method for generating random variables, *Journal of Statistical Software*, Vol. 5, pp. 1–7, ISSN 1548-7660

Mills, D.L. & Arias, R. (2006). The damping of spin motions in ultrathin films: Is the Landau–Lifschitz–Gilbert phenomenology applicable? *Physica B*, Vol. 384, pp. 147–151, ISSN 0921-4526

Normand, J.M. & Raynal, J. (1982). Relations between Cartesian and spherical components of irreducible Cartesian tensors, *Journal of Physics A: Mathematical and General*, Vol. 15, pp. 1437–1461, ISSN 0305-4470

Parker, G.J.; Cerjan, C., & Hewett, D.W. (2000). Embedded curve boundary method for micromagnetic simulations, *Journal of Magnetism and Magnetic Materials*, Vol. 214, pp. 130-138, ISSN 0304-8853

Saradzhev, F.M.; Khanna, F.C.; Sang Pyo Kim & de Montigny, M. (2007). General form of magnetization damping: Magnetization dynamics of a spin system evolving nonadiabatically and out of equilibrium, *Physical Review B*, Vol. 75, 024406, ISSN 1098-0121

Schabes, M.E. & Aharoni, A. (1987). Magnetostatic interaction fields for a three-dimensional array of ferromagnetic cubes, *IEEE Transactions on Magnetics,* Vol. MAG-23, pp. 3882-3888, ISSN 0018-9464

Scholz, W.; Fidler, J.; Schrefl, T.; Suess, D.; Dittrich, R.; Forster, F. & Tsiantos, V. (2003). Scalable parallel micromagnetic solvers for magnetic nanostructures, *Computational Materials Science*, Vol. 28, pp. 366–383, ISSN 0927-0256

Slonczewski, J.C. (1996). Current-driven excitation of magnetic multilayers, *Journal of Magnetism and Magnetic Materials*, Vol. 159, pp. L1-L7, ISSN 0304-8853

Sukhov, A. & Berakdar, J. (2008). Temperature-dependent magnetization dynamics of magnetic nanoparticles, *Journal of Physics: Condensed Matter*, Vol. 20, 125226, ISSN 0953-8984

Szambolics, H.; Buda-Prejbeanu, L.D.; Toussaint, J.C. & Fruchart, O. (2008). A constrained finite element formulation for the Landau–Lifshitz–Gilbert equations, *Computational Materials Science*, Vol. 44, pp. 253–258, ISSN 0927- 0256

Tan, X.; Baras, J.S. & Krishnaprasad P.S. (2000). Fast evaluation of demagnetizing field in three dimensional micromagnetics using multipole approximation, *Proceedings SPIE*, Vol. 3984, pp. 195-201, ISSN 0277-786X

Tiberkevich, V. & Slavin, A. (2007). Nonlinear phenomenological model of magnetic dissipation for large precession angles: Generalization of the Gilbert model, *Physical Review B*, Vol. 75, 014440, ISSN 1098-0121

Vukadinovic, N. & Boust, F. (2007). Three-dimensional micromagnetic simulations of magnetic excitations in cylindrical nanodots with perpendicular anisotropy, *Physical Review B*, Vol. 75, 014420, ISSN 1098-0121

Xiao, J.; Zangwill, A. & Stiles, M.D. (2005). Macrospin models of spin transfer dynamics, *Physical Review B*, Vol. 72, 014446, ISSN 1098-0121

Žutic, I.; Fabian J. & Das, S. (2004). Spintronics: fundamentals and applications, *Reviews of Modern Physics*, Vol. 76, pp. 323–410, ISSN 0034-6861

7

A Computationally Efficient Numerical Simulation for Generating Atmospheric Optical Scintillations

Antonio Jurado-Navas, José María Garrido-Balsells,
Miguel Castillo-Vázquez and Antonio Puerta-Notario
Communications Engineering Department, University of Málaga
Campus de Teatinos
Málaga, Spain

1. Introduction

Atmospheric optical communication has been receiving considerable attention recently for use in high data rate wireless links (Juarez et al., 2006; Zhu & Kahn, 2002). Considering their narrow beamwidths and lack of licensing requirements as compared to microwave systems, atmospheric optical systems are appropriate candidates for secure, high data rate, cost-effective, wide bandwidth communications. Furthermore, atmospheric free space optical (FSO) communications are less susceptible to the radio interference than radio-wireless communications. Thus, FSO communication systems represent a promising alternative to solve the last mile problem, above all in densely populated urban areas. Then, applications that could benefit from optical communication systems are those that have platforms with limited weight and space, require very high data links and must operate in an environment where fiber optic links are not practical. Also, there has been a lot of interest over the years in the possibility of using optical transmitters for satellite communications (Nugent et al., 2009). This chapter is focused on how to model the propagation of laser beams through the atmosphere. In particular, it is concerned with line-of-sight propagation problems, i.e., the receiver is in full view of the transmitter. This concern is referred to situations where if there were no atmosphere and the waves were propagating in a vacuum, then the level of irradiance that a receiver would observe from the transmitter would be constant in time, with a value determined by the transmitter geometry plus vacuum diffraction effects. Nevertheless, propagation through the turbulent atmosphere involves situations where a laser beam is propagating through the clear atmosphere but where very small changes in the refractive index are present too. These small changes in refractive index, which are typically on the order of 10^{-6}, are related primarily to the small variations in temperature (on the order of 0.1-1°C), which are produced by the turbulent motion of the atmosphere. Clearly, fluctuations in pressure of the atmosphere also induces in refractive index irregularities. Thus, the introduction of the atmosphere between source and receiver, and its inherent random refractive index variations, can lead to power losses at the receiver and eventually it produces spatial and temporal fluctuations in the received irradiance, i.e. turbulence-induced signal power fading (Andrews & Phillips, 1998); but this random variations in atmospheric refractive index along the optical path also produces fluctuations in other wave parameters such as phase, angle of arrival and frequency. Such fluctuations can produce an increase in the

link error probability limiting the performance of communication systems. In this particular scenario, the turbulence-induced fading is called scintillation.
The goal of this chapter is to present an efficient computer simulation technique to derive these irradiance fluctuations for a propagating optical wave in a weakly inhomogeneous medium under the assumption that small-scale fluctuations are modulated by large-scale irradiance fluctuations of the wave.

2. Turbulence cascade theory

Temperature, pressure and humidity fluctuations, which are close related to wind velocity fluctuations, are primarily the cause of refractive index fluctuations transported by the turbulent motion of the atmosphere. In fact, all these effects let the formation of unstable air masses that, eventually, can be decomposed into turbulent eddies of different sizes, initiating the turbulent process. This atmospheric turbulent process can be physically described by Kolmogorov cascade theory (Andrews & Phillips, 1998; Brookner, 1970; Frisch, 1995; Tatarskii, 1971). Thus, turbulent air motion represents a set of eddies of various scales sizes. Large eddies become unstable due to very high Reynolds number and break apart (Frisch, 1995), so their energy is redistributed without loss to eddies of decreasing size until the kinetic energy of the flow is finally dissipated into heat by viscosity. The scale sizes of these eddies extend from a largest scale size L_0 to a smallest scale size l_0. Briefly, the largest scale size, L_0, is smaller than those at which turbulent energy is injected into a region. It defines an effective outer scale of turbulence which near the ground is roughly comparable with the height of the observation point above ground. On the contrary, the smallest scale size, l_0, denotes the inner scale of turbulence, the scale where the Reynolds number approaches unity and the energy is dissipated into heat. It is assumed that each eddy is homogeneous, although with a different index of refraction. These atmospheric index-of-refraction variations produce fluctuations in the irradiance of the transmitted optical beam, what is known as *atmospheric scintillation*.
It is widely accepted two further assumptions: the assumption of local homogeneity and the assumption of local isotropy. The first of them, the local homogeneity assumption, implies that the velocity difference statistics depend only on the displacement vector, $\mathbf{r}$. Hence, we may write the random variation of the refractive index as (Clifford & Strohbehn, 1970):

$$n(\mathbf{r}) = n_0 + n_1(\mathbf{r}), \tag{1}$$

where $\mathbf{r}$ is the displacement vector, $n_0 \cong 1$ is the ensemble average of n (its free space value), whereas $n_1(\mathbf{r}) \ll 1$ is a measure of the fluctuation of the refractive index from its free space value.
The second assumption is the supposition of local isotropy, which implies that only the magnitude of $\mathbf{r}$ is important. On the other hand, for locally homogeneous and isotropic turbulence, a method of analysis involving structure functions is successful in meeting such problem (Strohbehn, 1968). Hence, we can define the structure function for the refractive index fluctuations, $D_n(r)$, as:

$$D_n(r) = E\left[\left(n(\mathbf{r_1}) - n(\mathbf{r_1}+r)\right)^2\right] = 2\left[B_n(0) - B_n(r)\right], \tag{2}$$

where $E[\cdot]$ is the ensemble average operator, $B_n(r)$ is the covariance function of the refractive index and $r = |\mathbf{r}|$. By applying the Fourier transform to $B_n(r)$, we can obtain the spatial power spectrum of refractive index, $\Phi_n(\kappa)$. Then, we consider now that the outer scale, L_0, and the inner scale, l_0, of turbulence satisfy the following conditions (Tatarskii, 1971) :

$$L_0 \gg \sqrt{(\lambda L)}, \quad \text{and} \quad l_0 \ll \sqrt{(\lambda L)}, \qquad [m], \tag{3}$$

where λ is the optical wavelength in meters and L is the transmission range, also expressed in meters. Hence, the result is the easiest of the expressions to describe $\Phi_n(\kappa)$, given by

$$\Phi_n(\kappa) = 0.033 C_n^2 \kappa^{-11/3}, \qquad \frac{1}{L_0} \ll \kappa \ll \frac{1}{l_0}; \tag{4}$$

that it is usually named as *Kolmogorov spectrum* (Andrews & Phillips, 1998). This power spectrum of refractive index represents the energy distribution of turbulent eddies transported by the turbulent motion. In the last expression, κ is the spatial wave number and C_n^2 is the refractive-index structure parameter, which is altitude-dependent.

3. Wave propagation in random media

There is an extensive literature on the subject of the theory of line-of-sight propagation through the atmosphere (Andrews & Phillips, 1998; Andrews et al., 2000; Fante, 1975; Ishimaru, 1997; Strohbehn, 1978; Tatarskii, 1971). One of the most important works was developed by Tatarskii (Tatarskii, 1971). He supposed a plane wave that is incident upon the random medium (the atmosphere in this particular case). It is assumed that the atmosphere has zero conductivity and unit magnetic permeability and that the electromagnetic field has a sinusoidal time dependence (a monochromatic wave). Under these circumstances, Maxwell's equations take the form:

$$\nabla \cdot \mathbf{H} = 0, \tag{5}$$

$$\nabla \times \mathbf{E} = jk\mathbf{H}, \tag{6}$$

$$\nabla \times \mathbf{H} = -jkn^2\mathbf{E}, \tag{7}$$

$$\nabla \cdot (n^2\mathbf{E}) = 0; \tag{8}$$

where $j = \sqrt{-1}$, $k = 2\pi/\lambda$ is the wave number of the electromagnetic wave with λ being the optical wavelength; whereas $n(\mathbf{r})$ is the atmospheric index of refraction whose time variations have been suppressed and being a random function of position, $\mathbf{r}$. The ∇ operator is the well-known vector derivative $(\partial/\partial x, \partial/\partial y, \partial/\partial z)$. The quantities $\mathbf{E}$ and $\mathbf{H}$ are the vector amplitudes of the electric and magnetic fields and are a function of position alone. The assumed sinusoidal time dependence is contained in the wave number, k.
Thus, if we take the curl of Eq. (6) and, after substituting Eq. (7), then the following expression is obtained:

$$-\nabla^2\mathbf{E} + \nabla(\nabla \cdot \mathbf{E}) = k^2 n^2 \mathbf{E}, \tag{9}$$

where the ∇^2 operator is the Laplacian $(\partial^2/\partial x^2 + \partial^2/\partial y^2 + \partial^2/\partial z^2)$.
Equation (8) is expanded and solved for $\nabla \cdot \mathbf{E}$, and the result inserted into Eq. (9) so that we can obtain the final form of the vector wave equation:

$$\nabla^2\mathbf{E} + k^2 n^2(\mathbf{r})\mathbf{E} + 2\nabla\left(\mathbf{E} \cdot \nabla \log n(\mathbf{r})\right) = 0, \tag{10}$$

where $\mathbf{r} = (x, y, z)$ denotes a point in space. In Eq. (10) we have substituted the gradient of the natural logarithm for $\nabla n/n$. Equation (10) can be simplified by imposing certain characteristics of the propagation wave. In particular, since the wavelength λ for optical radiation is much smaller than the smallest scale of turbulence, l_0, (Strohbehn, 1968) the maximum scattering angle is roughly $\lambda/l_0 \approx 10^{-4}$ rad. As a consequence, the last term on the left-hand side of Eq. (10) is negligible. Such a term is related to the change in polarization of the wave as it propagates (Strohbehn, 1971; Strohbehn & Clifford, 1967). This conclusion permit us to drop the last term, and Eq. (10) then simplifies to

$$\nabla^2 \mathbf{E} + k^2 n^2(\mathbf{r})\mathbf{E} = 0. \tag{11}$$

Because Eq. (11) is easily decomposed into three scalar equations, one for each component of the electric field, **E**, we may solve one scalar equation and ignore the vector character of the wave until the final solution. Therefore if we let $U(\mathbf{r})$ denote one of the scalar components that is transverse to the direction of propagation along the positive x-axis (Andrews & Phillips, 1998), then Eq. (11) may be replaced by the scalar stochastic differential equation

$$\nabla^2 U + k^2 n^2(\mathbf{r})U = 0. \tag{12}$$

The index of refraction, $n(\mathbf{r}) = n_0 + n_1(\mathbf{r})$, fluctuates about the average value $n_0 = E[n(\mathbf{r})] \cong 1$, whereas $n_1(\mathbf{r}) \ll 1$ is the fluctuation of the refractive index from its free space value. Thus

$$\nabla^2 U + k^2(n_0 + n_1(\mathbf{r}))^2 U = 0. \tag{13}$$

For weak fluctuation, it is necessary to obtain an approximate solution of Eq. (13) for small n_1. This can be done in two ways: one is to expand U in a series:

$$U = U_0 + U_1 + U_2 + ..., \tag{14}$$

and the other is to expand the exponent of U in a series:

$$U = \exp(\psi_0 + \psi_1 + \psi_2 + ...) = \exp(\psi). \tag{15}$$

In Eq. (14), U_0 is the unperturbed portion of the field in the absence of turbulence and the remaining terms represent first-order, second-order, etc., perturbations caused by the presence of random inhomogeneities. It is generally assumed that $|U_2(\mathbf{r})| \ll |U_1(\mathbf{r})| \ll |U_0(\mathbf{r})|$. In this sense, in Eq. (15), ψ_1, ψ_2 are the first-order and second-order complex phase perturbations, respectively, whereas ψ_0 is the phase of the optical wave in free space.
The expansion of Eq. (14) is the Born approximation, and has the important inconvenient that the complex Gaussian model for the field as predicted by this model does not compare well with experimental data. The other expansion given by Eq. (15) is called the Rytov solution. This technique is widely used in line-of-sight propagation problems because it simplifies the procedure of obtaining both amplitude and phase fluctuations and because its exponential representation is thought to represent a propagation wave better than the algebraic series representation of the Born method. From the Rytov solution, the wave equation becomes:

$$\nabla^2 \psi + (\nabla\psi)^2 + k^2(n_0 + n_1(\mathbf{r}))^2 = 0. \tag{16}$$

This is a nonlinear first order differential equation for $\nabla\psi$ and is known as the Riccati equation. Consider now a first order perturbation, then

$$\psi(L, \mathbf{r}) = \psi_0(L, \mathbf{r}) + \psi_1(L, \mathbf{r}); \tag{17a}$$

$$n(\mathbf{r}) = n_0 + n_1(\mathbf{r}); \qquad n_0 \cong 1. \tag{17b}$$

Operating, assuming that $|\nabla\psi_1| \ll |\nabla\psi_0|$, due to $n_1(\mathbf{r}) \ll 1$, neglecting $n_1^2(\mathbf{r})$ in comparison to $2n_1(\mathbf{r})$, and equating the terms with the same order of perturbation, then the following expressions are obtained:

$$\nabla^2\psi_0 + (\nabla\psi_0)^2 + k^2 n_0^2(\mathbf{r}) = 0; \tag{18a}$$

$$\nabla^2\psi_1 + 2\nabla\psi_0\nabla\psi_1 + 2k^2 n_1(\mathbf{r}) = 0. \tag{18b}$$

The first one is the differential equation for $\nabla\psi$ in the absence of the fluctuation whereas turbulent atmosphere induced perturbation are found in the second expression. The resolution of Eq. (18) is detailed in (Fante, 1975; Ishimaru, 1997). For the particular case of a monochromatic optical plane wave propagating along the positive x-axis, i.e., $U_0(L,\mathbf{r}) = \exp(jkx)$, this solution can be written as:

$$\psi_1(L,\mathbf{r}) = \frac{k^2}{2\pi}\iiint_V n_1(\mathbf{r}')\frac{\exp\left(jk\left[|\mathbf{r}-\mathbf{r}'| - |L-x'|\right]\right)}{|\mathbf{r}-\mathbf{r}'|}d^3\mathbf{r}', \tag{19}$$

where the position $(L,\mathbf{r})$ denotes a position in the receiver plane (at $x = L$) whereas $(x',\mathbf{r}')$ represents any position at an arbitrary plane along the propagation path. The mathematical development needed to solve Eq. (19) can be consulted in (Andrews & Phillips, 1998; Ishimaru, 1997). Furthermore, the statistical nature of $\psi_1(L,\mathbf{r})$ can be deduced in an easy way. Equation (19) has the physical interpretation that the first-order Rytov perturbation, $\psi_1(L,\mathbf{r})$ is a sum of spherical waves generated at various points $\mathbf{r}'$ throughout the scattering volume V, the strength of each sum wave being proportional to the product of the unperturbed field term U_0 and the refractive-index perturbation, n_1, at the point $\mathbf{r}'$ (Andrews & Phillips, 1998). Thus it is possible to apply the central limit theorem. According to such a theorem, the distribution of a random variable which is a sum of N independent random variables approaches normal as $N \to \infty$ regardless of the distribution of each random variable. Application of the central limit theorem to this integral equation leads to the prediction of a normal probability distribution for ψ. Since we can substitute $\Psi = \chi + jS$, where χ and S are called the log-amplitude and phase, respectively, of the field, then application of the central limit theorem also leads to the prediction of a Gaussian (normal) probability distribution for both χ and S, at least up to first order corrections (χ_1 and S_1).

Accordingly, under this first-order Rytov approximation, the field of a propagating optical wave at distance L from the source is represented by:

$$U = \exp(\psi) = U_0(L,\mathbf{r})\exp(\psi_1). \tag{20}$$

Hence, the irradiance of the random field shown in Eq. (20) takes the form:

$$I = |U_0(L,\mathbf{r})|^2 \exp(\psi_1 + \psi_1^*) = I_0 \exp(2\chi_1), \qquad [w/m^2] \tag{21}$$

where, from now onwards, we denote χ_1 as χ for simplicity in the notation. Hence,

$$I = I_0 \exp(2\chi), \qquad [w/m^2]. \tag{22}$$

In Eq. (21), operator $*$ denotes the complex conjugate, $|U_0|$ is the amplitude of the unperturbed field and I_0 is the level of irradiance fluctuation in the absence of air turbulence that ensures that the fading does not attenuate or amplify the average power, i.e., $E[I] = |U_0|^2$. This may be thought of as a conservation of energy consideration and requires the choice of $E[\chi] = -\sigma_\chi^2$, as was explained in (Fried, 1967; Strohbehn, 1978), where $E[\chi]$ is the ensemble average of log-amplitude, whereas σ_χ^2 is its variance depending on the structure parameter, C_n^2. With all of these expressions, we have modeled the irradiance of the random field, I, in the space at a single instant in time. Now, because the state of the atmospheric turbulence varies with time, the intensity fluctuations will also be temporally correlated. Then, Eq. (22) can be expressed as:

$$I = \alpha_{sc}(t) \cdot I_0, \tag{23}$$

whereas $\alpha_{sc}(t) = \exp(2\chi(t))$ is the temporal behavior of the scintillation sequence and represents the effect of the intensity fluctuations on the transmitted signal. In Section 5.1.1, the space-to-time statistical conversion needed to derive Eq. (23) will be conveniently explained by assuming the well-known Taylor's hypothesis of frozen turbulence (Tatarskii, 1971; Taylor, 1938). The generation of this scintillation sequence is treated in detail further in this chapter. As analyzed before, and by the central limit theorem, the marginal distribution of the log-amplitude, χ, is Gaussian. Thus,

$$f_\chi(\chi) = \left(\frac{1}{2\pi\sigma_\chi^2}\right)^{1/2} \exp\left[-\frac{(\chi - E[\chi])^2}{2\sigma_\chi^2}\right]. \tag{24}$$

Hence, from the Jacobian statistical transformation (Papoulis, 1991),

$$f_I(I) = \frac{f_\chi(\chi)}{\left|\frac{dI}{d\chi}\right|}, \tag{25}$$

the probability density function of the intensity, I, can be identified to have a lognormal distribution typical of weak turbulence regime. Then:

$$f_I(I) = \left(\frac{1}{2I}\right)\left(\frac{1}{2\pi\sigma_\chi^2}\right)^{1/2} \exp\left[-\frac{(\ln I - \ln I_0)^2}{8\sigma_\chi^2}\right]. \tag{26}$$

Theoretical and experimental studies of irradiance fluctuations generally center around the scintillation index. It was evaluated in (Mercier, 1962) and it is defined as the normalized variance of irradiance fluctuations:

$$\sigma_I^2 = \frac{E[I^2]}{(E[I])^2} - 1. \tag{27}$$

With this parameter it is possible to define the weak turbulence regimes as those regimes for which the scintillation index given in Eq. (27) is less than unity. From the following property given in (Fried, 1966)

$$E[\exp(a \cdot g)] = \exp\left[aE[g] + \frac{1}{2}a^2 E[(g - E[g])^2]\right], \tag{28}$$

obeyed by any independent Gaussian random variable, g, with a being a constant, we can employ Eq. (28) to obtain the first and second order moments (mean value and variance, respectively) of the irradiance fluctuation. So,

$$E[I(\mathbf{r}, L)] = E[I_0(\mathbf{r}, L)\exp[(2\chi(\mathbf{r}, L)] = I_0(\mathbf{r}, L)\exp(2E[\chi(\mathbf{r}, L) + 2\sigma_\chi^2]), \tag{29}$$

where, as mentioned before, σ_χ^2 is the variance of log-amplitude of the scintillation. From energy-conservation consideration (Fried, 1967; Strohbehn, 1978), $E[I(\mathbf{r},L)] = I_0(\mathbf{r},L)$. Then, inserting this result into Eq. (29), we obtain:

$$E[\chi(\mathbf{r},L)] = -\sigma_\chi^2. \tag{30}$$

By repeating the same process to the root mean square of the irradiance, I, then:

$$E[I^2(\mathbf{r},L)] = E[(I_0(\mathbf{r},L)\exp[(2\chi(\mathbf{r},L))^2] = I_0^2(\mathbf{r},L)\exp(4\sigma_\chi^2). \tag{31}$$

If we insert Eqs. (29)-(31) into Eq. (27), the scintillation index is finally derived as:

$$\sigma_I^2 = \frac{E[I^2]}{\left(E[I]\right)^2} - 1 = \exp(4\sigma_\chi^2) - 1 \cong 4\sigma_\chi^2 \quad \text{if } \sigma_I^2 \ll 1, \tag{32}$$

depending on σ_χ^2. It can be seen (Andrews & Phillips, 1998; Andrews et al., 2001), that the derived expression for the scintillation index is proportional to the Rytov variance for a plane wave given by:

$$\sigma_1^2 = 1.23 C_n^2 k^{7/6} L^{11/6}, \tag{33}$$

where, again, C_n^2 ($\mathrm{m}^{-2/3}$) is the index of refraction structure parameter, $k = 2\pi/\lambda$ (m^{-1}) is the optical wave number, λ (m) is the wavelength, and L (m) is the propagation path length between transmitter and receiver. The Rytov variance represents the scintillation index of an unbounded plane wave in weak fluctuations based on a Kolmogorov spectrum as the shown in Eq. (4), but is otherwise considered a measure of optical turbulence strength (Andrews et al., 2001).

4. Generation of scintillation sequences

Any kind of mechanism to model the behavior of the turbulent atmosphere as a time-varying channel is necessary. Let the transmitted instantaneous optical power signal defined by

$$s(t) = \sum_i a_i \cdot P_{peak} \cdot p_n(t - iT_b) \qquad i \in \mathbf{Z} \tag{34}$$

where the random variable a_i takes the values of 0 for the bit "0" (off pulse) and 1 for the bit "1" (on pulse), P_{peak} the peak optical power transmitted each bit period, T_b, with active pulse; and $p_n(t)$ is the pulse shape having normalized amplitude. In this manner, the received signal will consist, in a generic channel, of two terms: the first one is the line-of-sight (LOS) contribution, and the second one is due to energy which is scattered to the receiver. This fact will be thought as a multipath channel. Every contribution (the LOS component and each multipath contribution) will travel through different paths in the atmosphere, each of them with a different propagation delay, $\tau_n(t)$. Thus, the expression for the received signal can be written as:

$$y(t) = \sum_n \alpha_{sc_n}(t) s(t - \tau_n(t)), \tag{35}$$

where $\alpha_{sc_n}(t)$ is the time-varying scintillation sequence representing the effect of the intensity fluctuations on the nth-multipath component. As discussed in (Fante, 1975; Ishimaru, 1997; Kennedy, 1968), dispersion and beam spreading due to turbulent atmosphere can be neglected. Only for the very short pulses less than 100 ps proposed for high-data rate communications systems, or in extreme scenarios such as the one detailed in (Ruike et al., 2007), where sand and dust particles are likely present, pulse spreading owing to turbulent atmosphere must be included. For this latter case, physically, two possible causes exist for this pulse spreading: scattering (dispersion) and pulse wander (fluctuations in arrival time), although it is found that, under the condition of weak scattering, pulse wandering dominates the contribution to the overall broadening of the pulse (Jurado-Navas et al., 2009; Young et al., 1998).

Nonetheless, a general scenario where dispersion and beam spreading can be neglected is assumed in this chapter. Hence, the channel impulse response, $h(\tau_n;t)$, can be obtained by substituting $s(t) = \delta(t)$ into Eq. (35). Then,

$$h(\tau_n;t) = \sum_n \alpha_{sc_n}(t)\delta(t - \tau_n(t)). \tag{36}$$

Some channel models assume a continuum of multipath delays, in which case the sum in Eq. (36) becomes an integral which simplifies to a time-varying complex amplitude associated with each multipath delay, τ, as indicated in (Goldsmith, 2005):

$$h(\tau;t) = \int \alpha_{sc}(\xi;t)\delta(\tau - \xi)d\xi = \alpha_{sc}(\tau;t), \tag{37}$$

by using the definition of the Dirac delta function, $\delta(t)$. Note that $h(\tau;t)$ has two time parameters: the time t when the impulse response is observed at the receiver, and the time $t - \tau$ when the impulse is launched into the channel relative to the observation time, t. Hence, $h(\tau;t)$ is the response of the system to a unit impulse applied at time t.

An important characteristic of a multipath channel is the time delay spread, T_m, it causes to the received signal. This delay spread equals the time delay between the arrival of the first received signal component (LOS or multipath) and the last received signal component associated with a single transmitted pulse. In these atmospheric optical communication systems, the delay spread is small compared to the inverse of the signal bandwidth, as commented above, then there is little time spreading in the received signal. Of course, the propagation delay associated with the i-th multipath component is $\tau_i \leq T_m \not\forall\ i$ so that $s(t - \tau_i) \approx s(t) \not\forall\ i$, and then, Eq. (35) can be expressed as:

$$y(t) = s(t) \sum_n \alpha_{sc_n}(t). \tag{38}$$

As the propagation delay is very small, then the corresponding multipath scintillation sequences will be received in the same bit interval and having the same magnitude. Finally,

$$y(t) = s(t)\alpha_{sc}(t). \tag{39}$$

Then, the received light intensity is compounded of the transmitted instantaneous optical power signal, $s(t)$, initially transmitted, and affected in a multiplicative manner by the scintillation sequence, $\alpha_{sc}(t)$. This latter one represents the intensity fluctuations due to the effect of the atmospheric turbulence on the transmitted signal, $s(t)$.

Finally, a characteristic of $\alpha_{sc}(t)$ is its time-varying nature. This time variation arises from the turbulent motion of the atmosphere described by Kolmogorov cascade theory (Tatarskii, 1971). The component of the wind velocity transverse to the propagation direction, $u_{\perp}$, characterizes the average fade duration.

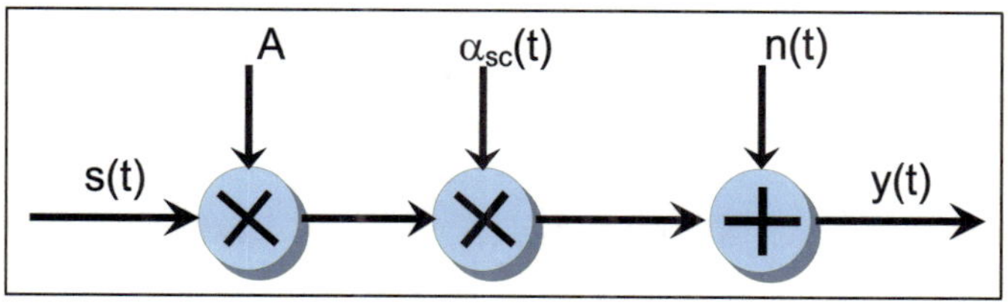

Fig. 1. Scheme model of the turbulent atmospheric optical model.

Obviously, the lognormal atmospheric channel model employed in the previous section and represented by Eqs. (22)-(23) is consistent with Eq. (39) derived here. Hence, the atmospheric channel model must be consisted of a multiplicative noise model that enhances the effect of the atmospheric turbulence on the propagation of the transmitted optical signal. Clearly, accordingly to Eqs. (22)-(23) and Eq. (39), an appropriate channel model for describing these effects is shown in Fig. 1. This scalar model assumes the transmitted field to be linearly polarized (no polarization modulation). This fact is realistic because the depolarization effects of the atmospheric turbulence are negligible (Strohbehn, 1968; 1971; Strohbehn & Clifford, 1967) and because it is reasonable to assume that the relevant noise has statistically independent polarization components (Kennedy, 1968).
In Fig. 1 the real process $s(t)$ represents the instantaneous optical power transmitted, and given by Eq. (34). The additive white Gaussian noise is represented by $n(t)$ and it is assumed to include any shot noise caused by ambient light that may be much stronger than the desired signal as well as any front-end receiver thermal noise in the electronics following the photodetector. On the other hand, the factor A involves any weather-induced attenuation caused by rain, snow, and fog that can also degrade the performance of atmospheric optical communication systems in the way shown in (Al Naboulsi & Sizun, 2004; Muhammad et al., 2005), but it is not considered in this chapter ($A = 1$). Finally, the process $\alpha_{sc}(t) = \exp(2\chi(t))$ denotes the temporal behavior of the scintillation sequence and represents the effect of the intensity fluctuations on the transmitted signal, in the same way as Eq. (39) or Eq. (23).

5. Turbulent atmospheric channel model

The goal of this section is to obtain the time-varying scintillation sequence, denoted as $\alpha_{sc}(t)$ in Fig. 1, that represents the fluctuations of the intensity on the transmitted signal owing to the adverse effect of the turbulent atmosphere. To achieve this purpose, we start with the channel model proposed in (Jurado-Navas et al., 2007). Thus, to generate the $\alpha_{sc}(t)$ coefficients, a scheme based on Clarke's method (Rappaport, 1996) is implemented.
In brief, Clarke's model is based on a low-pass filtering of a random Gaussian signal, $z(t)$, as it is shown in Fig. 2. Hence, the output signal, $\chi(t)$, keeps on being statistically Gaussian, but shaped in its power spectral density by the $H_{sc}(f)$ filter. The output signal, $\chi(t)$, is the log-amplitude perturbation of the transmitted optical wave, as explained in previous sections. Next, $\chi(t)$ is passed through a nonlinear device which converts its probability distribution from Gaussian to lognormal, according to Eq. (26), typical of a weak turbulence regime, the scenario that has been considered through this chapter.

5.1 Covariance function: weak fluctuations

The first task we need to achieve is to obtain the shape of the filtering stage displayed in Fig. 2. In this respect, the theoretical Kolmogorov theory requires to solve the following expression

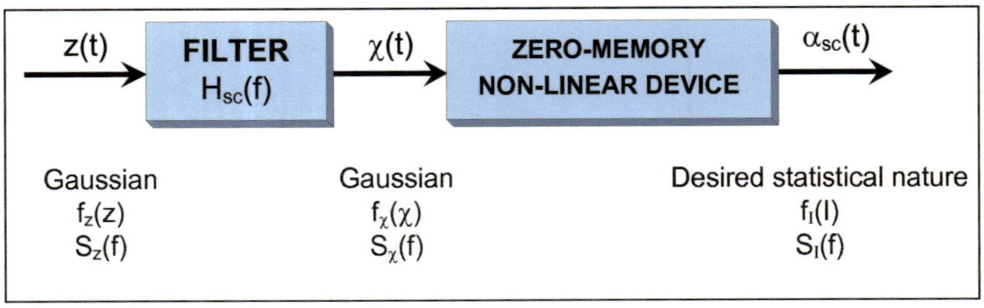

Fig. 2. Block diagram to generate the scintillation sequence, $\alpha_{sc}(t)$.

for the covariance function for irradiance fluctuations, $B_I(r, L)$:

$$B_I(r,L) = 8\pi^2 k^2 L \int_0^1 \int_0^\infty \kappa \Phi_n(\kappa) J_0(\kappa r) \left(1 - \cos \frac{L\kappa^2 \xi}{k}\right) d\kappa d\xi, \tag{40}$$

where κ is the spatial wave number, $\Phi_n(\kappa)$ denotes the spatial power spectrum of refractive index, k is the wave number, L represents the propagation path length whereas $J_0(\cdot)$ is the Bessel function of the first kind and 0th order. In Eq. (40), an homogeneous and isotropic random medium has been assumed in addition to a conversion to cylindrical coordinates since B_I is a function of the transverse distance r (Ishimaru, 1997; Tatarskii, 1971). The obtention of such an expression is conveniently treated in (Ishimaru, 1997; Lawrence & Strohbehn, 1970) and will be the starting point to generate the filter $H_{sc}(f)$. Nevertheless, Eq. (40) requires a high computational complexity when any theoretical model for the spatial power spectrum of refractive index, $\Phi_n(\kappa)$, is employed. This feature is a critical point; in this respect, we develop an efficient approximation to calculate such an integration that will be detailed below in Subsection 5.1.2. Anyway, and by the Wiener-Khintchine theorem, we can obtain the resulting temporal spectrum of irradiance fluctuations from which the filter frequency response, $H_{sc}(f)$, is obtained.

5.1.1 Taylor's hypothesis of frozen turbulence

A useful property in turbulent media is the well-known Taylor's hypothesis of frozen turbulence (Jurado-Navas & Puerta-Notario, 2009; Tatarskii, 1971; Taylor, 1938). Modeling the movement of atmospheric eddies is extremely difficult and a simplified "frozen air" model is normally employed. Thus under this hypothesis, the collection of atmospheric eddies will remain frozen in relation to one another, while the entire collection is transported as a whole along some direction by the wind. When a narrow beam propagating over a long distance is assumed, the refractive index fluctuations along the direction of propagation will be well-averaged and will be weaker than those along the transverse direction to propagation. Hence, consider the case when the atmospheric inhomogeneities move at constant velocity, $u_\perp$, perpendicular to the propagation direction. Taylor's frozen-in hypothesis can be expressed as (Lawrence & Strohbehn, 1970):

$$n(\mathbf{r}, t + \tau) = n(\mathbf{r} - u_\perp \tau, t). \tag{41}$$

Accordingly, a space-to-time conversion of statistics can be accomplished assuming the use of Taylor's hypothesis. The turbulence correlation time is therefore

$$\tau_0 = \frac{d_0}{u_\perp}, \qquad [s]; \tag{42}$$

where d_0 is the correlation length of intensity fluctuations. When the propagation length, L satisfies the condition $l_0 < \sqrt{\lambda L} < L_0$, with λ being the optical wavelength and with l_0 and L_0 being the inner and outer scale of turbulence, respectively, then d_0 can be approximated by (Andrews & Phillips, 1998; Tatarskii, 1971)

$$d_0 \approx \sqrt{\lambda L}, \qquad [m]. \tag{43}$$

5.1.2 Shaping a Gaussian temporary spectrum of irradiance

As explained at the begining of this subsection, to obtain the filter frequency response, $H_{sc}(f)$, needed to generate the time-varying nature of scintillation sequence, $\alpha_{sc}(t)$, (see Fig. 2), the covariance function of irradiance fluctuations, B_I, must be employed. Under the assumption of weak irradiance fluctuations ($\sigma_\chi^2 \ll 1$), the covariance functions of I and χ are related by $B_I(r) \simeq 4B_\chi(r)$, in a similar reasoning to obtain Eq. (32), where r denotes separation distance between two points on the wavefront. Taking this latter relationship into account, the filter, $H_{sc}(f)$, employed in the scheme and displayed in Fig. 2 corresponds, for simplicity, to the log-amplitude fluctuations. Furthermore, based on the Taylor frozen turbulence hypothesis, spatial statistics can be converted to temporal statistics by knowledge of the average wind speed transverse to the direction of propagation. In the case of a plane wave, this is accomplished by setting $r = u_\perp \tau$, where $u_\perp$ is the wind velocity transverse to the propagation direction in meters per second, and τ is in seconds. Now, taking into account an approximation developed by Andrews and Phillips (Andrews & Phillips, 1998), Eq. (40), in the case of a plane wave, reduces to

$$B_I(\tau, L) = 3.87\sigma_1^2 \mathrm{Re}\left[j^{5/6}\, {}_1F_1\left(-\frac{5}{6};1;\frac{jk(u_\perp \tau)^2}{2L}\right) - 0.60\left(\frac{k(u_\perp \tau)^2}{L}\right)^{5/6}\right], \tag{44}$$

with ${}_1F_1(a;b;v)$ being the confluent hypergeometric function of the first kind whereas σ_1^2 is the Rytov variance for a plane wave, as expressed in Eq. (33) that, under weak fluctuation, can also be written as $\sigma_1^2 \cong \sigma_I^2$. Even so, Eq. (44) still suffers from significant numerical complexity, especially if we try to solve the power spectral density (PSD), so an easier approach is proposed by the authors in (Jurado-Navas et al., 2007). Hence, suppose small separation distances in Eq. (44) so that $l_0 \ll r \ll \sqrt{\lambda L}$, and assume $B_I(r) \simeq 4B_\chi(r)$. Now, if we consider the following approximation for the hypergeometric function:

$$ {}_1F_1(a;b;-v) \approx 1 - \frac{av}{b} \qquad |v| \ll 1; \tag{45}$$

then

$$R_\chi(\tau) = E[\chi(t)\chi^*(t-\tau)] = \sigma_\chi^2 \exp\left[-\left(\frac{\tau}{\tau_0}\right)^2\right] = B_\chi(u_\perp \tau), \tag{46}$$

where $R_\chi(\tau)$ is the autocorrelation function of the process $\chi(t)$. We must remark that, in Eq. (46), it has been assumed a weak fluctuation regime so that we can state that $(E[\chi])^2 = \sigma_\chi^4 \approx 0$. Thus $R_\chi(\tau) \cong B_\chi(\tau)$, with $B_\chi(\tau)$ being the covariance function of the log-amplitude perturbation.

5.2 Design of the filter frequency response

From Eq. (46), the resulting temporal spectrum of log-amplitude perturbation, $\chi(t)$, can be obtained (Ishimaru, 1997; Tatarskii, 1971) as:

$$S_\chi(f) = 4\int_0^\infty B_\chi(\tau)\cos 2\pi f\tau d\tau. \tag{47}$$

Since assumed a weak irradiance fluctuations regime, $R_\chi(\tau) \cong B_\chi(\tau)$ so that we can apply the Wiener-Khintchine theorem to solve Eq. (47). Thus the power spectral density of χ is given by:

$$|H_{sc}(f)|^2 = \int_{-\infty}^{\infty} R_\chi(\tau)\exp(-j2\pi f\tau)d\tau = \sigma_\chi^2\tau_0\sqrt{\pi}\exp\left[-(\pi\tau_0 f)^2\right]. \tag{48}$$

To corroborate the Gaussian approximation regarding to the theoretical zero inner-scale ($l_0 = 0$) Kolmogorov spectrum, both of them have been plotted in Figure 3 with a remarkable resemblance between them. As an interesting feature, the Kolmogorov spectrum was obtained after s

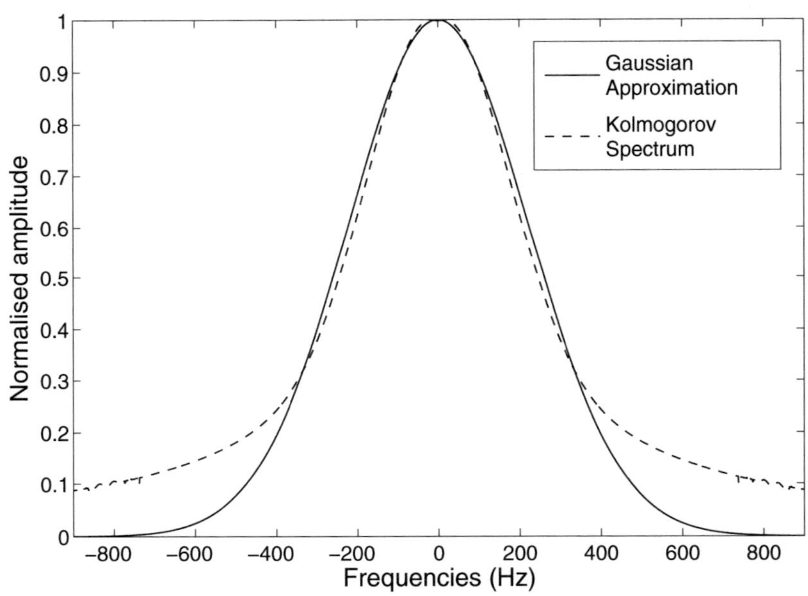

Fig. 3. Zero inner-scale model of Kolmogorov spectrum (Andrews et al., 2001) against Gaussian approximation conformed spectrum (Jurado-Navas et al., 2007).

To obtain the filter $H_{sc}(f)$, we assume a causal channel. This fact is desirable and so, the output sequence value of the system at the instant time $t = t_0$ depends only on the input sequence values for $t \leq t_0$. This implies that the system is nonanticipative (Oppenheim, 1999). Thus if the system is causal, zero phase is not attainable, and consequently, some phase distortion must be allowed. To design the nature of the filter phase it is sufficient to mention two concepts: first, a nonlinear phase can have an important effect on the shape of a filtered signal, even when the frequency-response magnitude is constant; and second, the effect of linear phase with integer slope is a simple time shift. It seems to be desirable to design systems to have exactly or approximately linear phase owing to the hard effort made to obtain the modulus of the filter.

Hence the filter frequency response is designed to have a linear phase:

$$H_{sc}(f) = |H_{sc}(f)| \exp(-j2\pi f\alpha), \tag{49}$$

where α is the delay introduced by the system. The magnitude of α will be established to half the length, M, of the filter impulse response, $H_{sc}(f)$. Consequently, the final expression for the behavior of the filter included in Figure 2 is:

$$H_{sc}(f) = \left(\sigma_{\chi}^{2}\tau_0\sqrt{\pi}\right)^{1/2} \exp\left[-\frac{1}{2}(\pi\tau_0 f)^2\right] \exp\left[-j2\pi f\alpha\right]. \tag{50}$$

The procedure to accomplish from now onwards is the following: for the time domain method, we first determine the impulse response of the filter, $h_{sc}(t) = \mathfrak{F}^{-1}\{H_{sc}(f)\}$, but represented in its discrete-time version: $h_{sc}[n], 0 \leq k \leq M-1$, with M being the length of the filter impulse, whereas $\mathfrak{F}^{-1}\{\cdot\}$ is the inverse Fourier transform operator. In this respect, we initially select a sampling rate, F_s, that is five times the maximum bandwidth of the filter which is proportional to the inverse of the turbulence correlation time, τ_0, such that:

$$F_s\tau_0 \approx 5. \tag{51}$$

Ultimately, the scintillation will be interpolated up to a much higher sample rate as will be discussed subsequently. This fact let us achieve a great reduction of computational load. We denote $\hat{\chi}[n]$ as the discrete output sequence value of the filter at a frequency rate of $F_s = 5/\tau_0$ whereas $\chi[n]$ represents the discrete log-amplitude scintillation with the proper bandwidth for its power spectral density, as a consequence of the interpolation process that fills in the missing samples of $\hat{\chi}[n]$.

5.3 Continuous-to-discrete time conversion

At this point, and as just commented, it is necessary to sample the continuous-time signal of the filter converting it in a discrete time signal because of their advantages in realizations. Hence we will obtain $\alpha_{sc}[n]$.

The chosen sampling frequency is F_s inversely proportional to the turbulence correlation time, τ_0. We initially choose $F_s\tau_0 \approx 2-5$, depending on the computer's memory. This initial value is not very relevant since the scintillation sequence will be interpolated later up to a much higher sample rate. However, this fact let the discrete Fourier transform (DFT) computation time be remarkably reduced. The election of the F_s magnitude must satisfy the Nyquist sampling theorem and should help avoid aliasing, should improve resolution and should reduce noise, removing the possibility of obtaining a very oversampled signal with very few useful samples of information (Oppenheim, 1999).

The $N-$point discrete version of the filter, denoted by $H_{sc}[k]$, is given by

$$\begin{aligned} H_{sc}[k] = H_{sc}(e^{j\omega}), \qquad & 0 \leq k \leq N-1, \\ & \omega = \frac{2\pi k}{N}; \end{aligned} \tag{52}$$

where it is employed a $N-$point DFT, with ω being the discrete frequency in rads. In Eq. (52), $H_{sc}(e^{j\omega})$ is the Fourier transform of $h_{sc}[n]$, being this latter one the sequence of samples of the continuous-time impulse response $h_{sc}(t)$, whereas $H_{sc}[k]$ is obtained by sampling $H_{sc}(e^{j\omega})$ at frequencies $\omega_k = \frac{2\pi k}{N}$. Consequently, from (Oppenheim, 1999), and substituting Eq. (50) into

Eq. (52):

$$H_{sc}[k] = F_s\left(\sigma_\chi^2 \tau_0 \sqrt{\pi}\right)^{1/2} \exp\left[-\frac{1}{2}\left(\pi\tau_0\frac{kF_s}{N}\right)^2\right] \exp\left[-j2\pi\frac{M}{2}\frac{kF_s}{N}\right], \qquad 0 \le k \le N/2. \tag{53}$$

Since the desired impulse response, $h_{sc}[k]$ $0 \le k \le M-1$, is a real sequence, by applying the Hermitian symmetry property it follows that

$$\begin{aligned} H_{sc}[k] &= H_{sc}(e^{j\omega}), \quad 0 \le k \le N/2, \quad \omega = \frac{2\pi k}{N}; \\ H_{sc}[N-k] &= H_{sc}^*[k], \quad 1 \le k \le N/2 - 1. \end{aligned} \tag{54}$$

By applying the inverse-DFT (IDFT) of $H_{sc}[k]$, we can obtain $h_{sc}[n] = \mathfrak{F}^{-1}\{H_{sc}[k]\}$. Consider $h_{sc}[n]$ as a finite-length sequence, i.e. a finite impulse response (FIR) system. Accordingly, one of the simplest method of FIR filter design is called the *window method*, explained in (Oppenheim, 1999). The method consists in defining a new system with impulse response $h_{wsc}[n]$. This impulse response is the desired causal FIR filter given by

$$h_{wsc}[n] = \begin{cases} h_{sc}[n]w[n], & 0 \le n \le M, \\ 0, & \text{otherwise.} \end{cases} \tag{55}$$

In Eq. (55), $w[n]$ is the finite-duration window. In this paper, we use a M-points Hamming window symmetric about the point $M/2$ of the form

$$w[n] = \begin{cases} 0.54 - 0.46\cos(2\pi n/M), & 0 \le n \le M, \\ 0, & \text{otherwise;} \end{cases} \tag{56}$$

owing to it is optimized to minimize the maximum (nearest) side lobe. As a result, the definitive expression for $h_{wsc}[n]$ is:

$$h_{wsc}[n] = \frac{1}{N} w[n] \sum_{k=0}^{N-1} H_{sc}[k] \exp\left\{j\frac{2\pi kn}{N}\right\}, \qquad 0 \le n \le M-1. \tag{57}$$

Consequently, the output sequence without being upsampled, $\hat{\chi}[n]$, accomplished with the filter stage of Fig. 2, is of the form:

$$\hat{\chi}[n] = \beta \sum_{k=0}^{M-1} h_{wsc}[k] z[n-k], \tag{58}$$

where β is the scaling constant chosen to yield the desired output variance, σ_χ^2, with $z[n]$ representing the discrete version of $z(t)$, this latter being a random unit variance Gaussian input signal to be filtered by $H_{sc}(f)$, as it is shown in Figure 2. We must remind that $\hat{\chi}[n]$ is a Gaussian version of the scintillation sequence without being upsampled, i.e., at $F_s = 5/\tau_0$, whereas $\chi[n]$ is the upsampled and accuracy version of $\hat{\chi}[n]$.

Equation (58), however, makes reference to a linear convolution between two finite-duration sequences: $h_{wsc}[n]$, M samples in extent; and $z[n]$, N samples in extent. Since we want the product to represent the DFT of the linear convolution of $h_{wsc}[n]$ and $z[n]$, which has length $M+N-1$, the DFTs that we compute must also be at least that length, i.e., both $h_{wsc}[n]$ and $z[n]$ must be augmented with sequence values of zero amplitude. This process is referred to as zero-padding (Oppenheim, 1999) and it is necessary to adopt it to compute such a linear convolution by a circular convolution avoiding time-aliasing of the first $M-1$ samples. With the purpose of employing fast Fourier transform (FFT) algorithms to compute all values of the DFTs, it is required that we first zero-pad N samples of the white, unit variance random Gaussian input sequence $z[n]$ and M samples of $h_{wsc}[n]$ out to $2N$ samples and compute the FFT of each (zero-padded) sequence. As an interesting remark, for the computation of all N values of a DFT using the definition, the number of arithmetical operations required is approximately N^2, while the amount of computation is approximately proportional to $N \log_2 N$ for the same result to be computed by an FFT algorithm (Oppenheim, 1999). Even more, when N is a power of 2, the well-known decimation-in-time radix-2 Cooley-Tukey algorithm can be employed and then, the computational load is reduced to only $(N/2)\log_2 N$. Such an algorithm is based on a divide and conquer technique by breaking a length-N DFT into two length-N/2 DFTs followed by a combining stage consisting of many size-2 DFTs called "butterfly" operations, so-called because of the shape of the data-flow diagrams (Oppenheim, 1999). Thus, according to these criteria, the zero-pad versions of $z[n]$ and $h_{wsc}[n]$, denoted as $z_{zp}[n]$ and $h_{wsc;zp}[n]$ respectively, are:

$$z_{zp}[n] = \begin{cases} z[n], & 0 \le n \le N-1, \\ 0, & N \le n \le 2N-1; \end{cases} \tag{59}$$

and

$$h_{wsc;zp}[n] = \begin{cases} h_{wsc}[n], & 0 \le n \le M-1, \\ 0, & M \le n \le 2N-1. \end{cases} \tag{60}$$

Hence, after computing an FFT of length $2N$ to the sequences written in Eqs. (59)-(60), we can obtain the following expressions:

$$Z_{zp}[k] = \sum_{n=0}^{2N-1} z_{zp}[n] e^{-j2\pi kn/(2N)}, \tag{61}$$

and

$$H_{wsc;zp}[k] = \sum_{n=0}^{2N-1} h_{wsc;zp}[n] e^{-j2\pi kn/(2N)}. \tag{62}$$

Now, the inverse FFT of the product, $Z_{zp}[k] \cdot H_{wsc;zp}[k]$ is then computed and the first N samples of the result are retained, i.e.

$$\hat{\chi}[n] = \frac{1}{2N} \sum_{k=0}^{2N-1} Z_{zp}[k] H_{wsc;zp}[k] e^{j2\pi kn/(2N)}, \quad 0 \le n \le N-1, \tag{63}$$

Thus, once this latter expression were multiplied by the scaling constant, β, the result will coincide with the first N samples of the linear convolution between $h_{wsc}[n]$ and $z[n]$.

5.4 Increasing the sampling rate

Up until now, the temporal behavior of a Gaussian-amplitude scintillation sequence was modeled. Nevertheless, this sequence lacks the right value of the temporal frequency of the amplitude and, consequently, its adequate temporal variability. Such a temporal frequency will be achieved including the frequency content of the intensity fluctuation power spectral density. Fante, in (Fante, 1975), observed that the power spectral density bandwidth of the intensity fluctuations under weak turbulence is:

$$f_c = \frac{1}{\tau_0} = \frac{u_\perp}{\sqrt{\lambda L}}, \tag{64}$$

as a direct result of the atmospheric motion, with λ being the optical wavelength, L is the propagation path length and $u_\perp$ denotes the wind velocity transverse to the propagation direction. By including this bandwidth reported in Eq. (64), we will be able to increase the sampling rate by a factor of P. The way of yielding this is:

$$\begin{cases} F_s = \frac{i}{\tau_0} = i \cdot f_c, & i \in [2-5] \\ P = \frac{R}{F_s}; \end{cases} \tag{65}$$

where R is the desired bit rate in bits/s; and F_s is the sampling frequency. Thus, and found P, the output samples of the filter H_{sc}, are upsampled by linear interpolation:

$$\chi[n] = \hat{\chi}[i] + \left\{\hat{\chi}[i+1] - \hat{\chi}[i]\right\}\left(\frac{n - i \cdot P}{P}\right), \text{ if } \mathrm{i{\cdot}P} \leq \mathrm{n} \leq \mathrm{(i{+}1){\cdot}P{-}1}, \quad 0 \leq \mathrm{i} \leq \mathrm{N{-}1}; \tag{66}$$

where, as we said before, $\chi[n]$ is the upsampled version of $\hat{\chi}[n]$ shown in Eq. (58).

5.5 Changing the statistical description

At this point, we have modeled the known random log-amplitude of the scintillation, χ, with a statistically Gaussian PDF, $f_\chi(\chi)$. Next, its PDF is converted from Gaussian to a lognormally distributed one that is generally accepted for the irradiance fluctuations, I, under weak turbulence conditions; or to a gamma-gamma PDF, a K PDF or even a Beckmann probability density (Hill & Frehlich, 1997) that much more accurately reflects the statistics of the intensity scintillations if Rytov variance (Andrews & Phillips, 1998) increases even beyond the limits of the weak turbulence regime. The resulting PDF is here denoted as $f_{\alpha_{sc}}(\alpha_{sc})$.

The statistical conversion is carried out with the zero-memory nonlinear device that was shown in Fig. 2. According to (Gujar & Kavanagh, 1968), this nonlinear device is just a one-to-one transformation between χ and α_{sc} of the form:

$$f_\chi\left(\chi - \frac{\delta\chi}{2}\right)|\delta\chi| = f_{\alpha_{sc}}\left(\alpha_{sc} - \frac{\delta\alpha_{sc}}{2}\right)|\delta\alpha_{sc}|, \tag{67}$$

where $f_{\alpha_{sc}}(\alpha_{sc})$ is the PDF typical of the scintillation coefficients sequence (lognormal, gamma-gamma or Beckmann, for instance). This $f_{\alpha_{sc}}(\alpha_{sc})$ PDF is identical to the probability density function of the irradiance fluctuations, I. Consequently, for any point (χ, α_{sc}) in the transformation, the probability of $\chi(t)$ being in the range $(\chi - \delta\chi)$ to χ is equal to the probability that $\alpha_{sc}(t)$ is in the corresponding range of $(\alpha_{sc} - \delta\alpha_{sc})$ to α_{sc}, where $\delta\chi$ and $\delta\alpha_{sc}$ are small increments beyond the points of study (χ_0, α_{sc_0}) in every moment. The known initial points are given by the mean values of the sequences χ and I, whose values are given by (Huang et al., 1993; Zhu & Kahn, 2002):

$$\begin{aligned} \chi_0 &= -\sigma_\chi^2, \\ E[I] &\equiv \alpha_{sc_0}; \end{aligned} \tag{68}$$

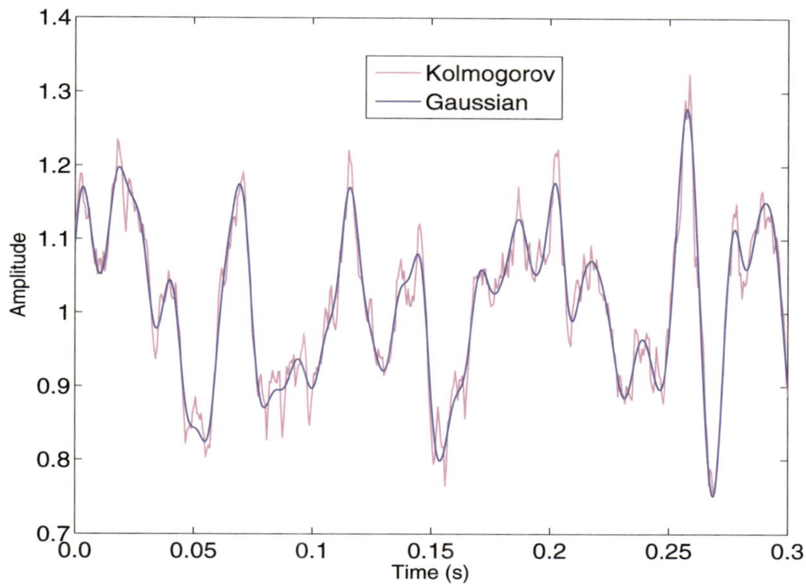

Fig. 4. Comparison of time series realizations characterized by the Kolmogorov (magenta) and Gaussian (blue) spectra.

where $E[\cdot]$ denotes an ensemble average or, equivalently with the assumption of ergodicity, a long-time average; and σ_I^2 is the normalized irradiance variance.
To illustrate the effect of a Gaussian spectrum, Figure 4 shows segments of time series realizations generated by the process of filtering white Gaussian noise with the proposed Gaussian spectrum given in Eq. (48). This realization is compared with another obtained by using the theoretical Kolmogorov spectrum.

6. Numerical results

To study the performance of both Kolmogorov and the proposed Gaussian spectra under identical conditions of simulation, IM/DD links are assumed operating through a 250 m horizontal path at a bit rate of 50 Mbps and transmitting pulses with on-off keying (OOK) formats under the assumption of equivalent bandwidth of 50 MHz. The criterion of constant average optical power is adopted, being one of the most important features of IM/DD channels (Jurado-Navas et al., 2010). In relation to the detection procedure, a maximum likelihood (ML) detection and a soft-decision decoding are considered respectively. A 830-nm laser wavelength is employed. All these features are included in the system model proposed in Figure 5 so that the spectra under study (Kolgomorov and Gaussian) can be compared under identical conditions of simulation. Thus its remarkable elements are: first, the channel model depicted in this chapter corresponding to a turbulent atmospheric environment, where the component of the wind velocity transverse to the propagation direction, $u_\perp$ is taken to be 8 m/s. This average wind velocity is a typical magnitude, at least in southern Europe being the main reason to employ this concrete magnitude. On the other hand, the values of turbulence strength structure parameter, C_n^2 were set to 1.23×10^{-14} and 1.23×10^{-13} m$^{-2/3}$ for $\sigma_\chi^2 = 0.01$ and 0.1, respectively and for plane waves. As a second remarkable element of Figure 5, a three-pole Bessel high-pass filter with a -1 dB cut-off frequency of 500 kHz for natural (solar) light suppression is designed. However, this is an optional stage that can be

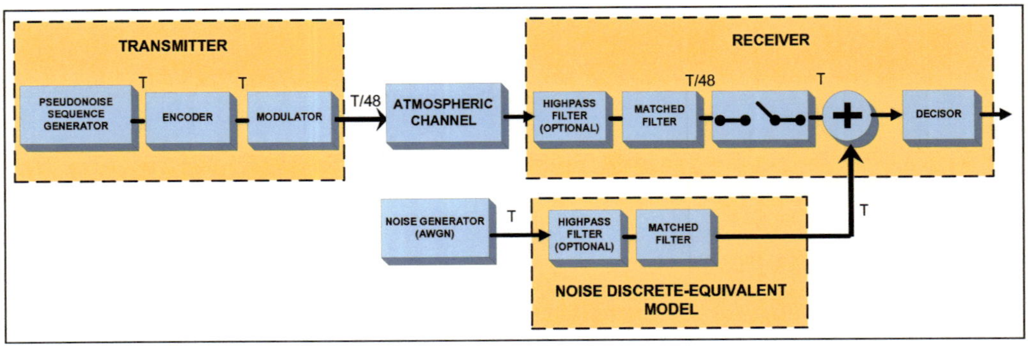

Fig. 5. Atmospheric optical system model with Monte-Carlo bit error rate estimation.

suppressed. Finally, a five-pole Bessel low-pass filter employed as a matched filter constitutes the third main stage of Figure 5. The receivers employed here are point receivers whereas the weather-induced attenuation is neglected so that we concentrate our attention on turbulence effects. Furthermore, the atmospheric-induced beam spreading that causes a power reduction at the receiver is also neglected because we are considering a terrestrial link where beam divergence is typically on the order of 10 μRad.

As a remarkable comment, with the inclusion of a wind speed, concretely 8 m/s as was said before, we can study the effect of the channel coherence in terms of burst error rate (Jurado-Navas et al., 2007) so that we obtain highly reliable link performance predictions. In addition, in urban atmospheres, especially near or among roughness elements, strong wind shear is expected to create high turbulent kinetic energy, as was detailed in (Christen et al., 2007). In such assumptions, we could have employed a higher magnitude for the wind speed without loss of generality. This fact even avoids a higher numerical complexity when we generate the lognormal scintillation sequence. Finally, and for simplicity, we assume that the wind direction is entirely transverse to the path of propagation. For special scenarios where Taylor's hypothesis may not be fully satisfied (scenarios affected by strong wind shear, urban environments or tropical areas), the procedure needed to generate the scintillation pattern may be modified as detailed in (Jurado-Navas & Puerta-Notario, 2009). In such cases, scintillation sequences registered by a receiver will not be identical to the patterns seen by another receiver except for a small shift in time, but the entrance of new structures into the optical propagation path may introduce new fluctuations into the received irradiance. Although Taylor's hypothesis is a good estimate for many cases, and for mathematical convenience this Taylor's hypothesis is assumed to be fully satisfied in this paper, however, the corrections proposed in (Jurado-Navas & Puerta-Notario, 2009) may be very useful to obtain more realistic results in particular environments.

The obtained performance for an OOK format with a 25% duty cycle are presented in terms of burst error rate average, as displayed in Figure 6 (Jurado-Navas et al., 2007). Hence, the impact of the atmospheric channel coherence on the behavior of the different signalling schemes can be taking into account, as was indicated in (Jurado-Navas et al., 2007), due to burst error rate average represents a second order of statistics and so, the temporal variability of the received irradiance fluctuations can influence on such metric of performance. However, this fact is not considered simply by doing a bit error rate analysis since bit error rate does not change with the variable wind speed, i.e., bit error rate is the first order of statistics and, consequently, it is just a function of the lognormal channel variance. Accordingly such bursts of errors are affected by the temporal duration of the turbulence-induced fadings, as it was already contemplated in Eq. (48), that was depending on τ_0 and consequently, from Eq. (42),

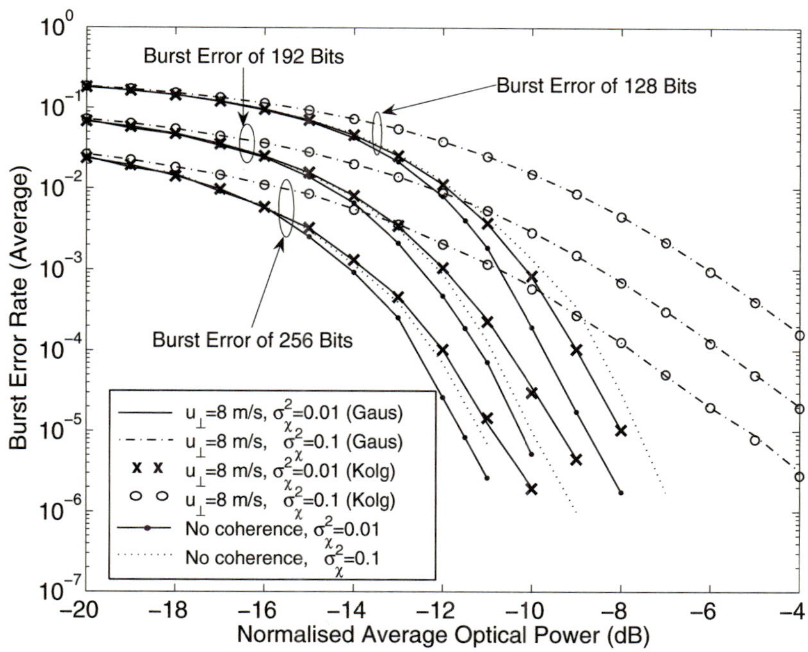

Fig. 6. Burst error rate against normalized average optical power for OOK format with a 25 % duty cycle for $\sigma_\chi^2 = 0.1$ and 0.01 and for $u_\perp = 8$ m/s and no coherence ($u_\perp \to \infty$). The burst error length is established to 256, 192 and 128 bits (Jurado-Navas et al., 2007).

in inverse proportion to $u_\perp$. Concretely, two time-varying scintillation sequences, $\alpha_{sc}(t)$ are represented in Figure 7 for two different average wind speed transverse to the direction of propagation. Hence, different temporal variabilities in such scintillation sequences must entail different performance in any atmospheric optical link.

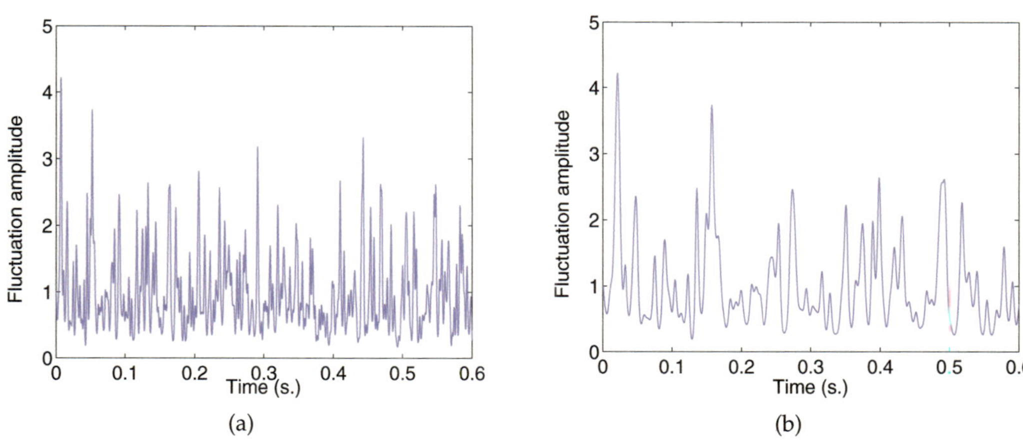

Fig. 7. Time-varying atmospheric scintillation sequence, $\alpha_{sc}(t)$ generated for an average wind speed transverse to the direction of propagation of a) $u_\perp = 8$ m/s. b) $u_\perp = 2.5$ m/s.

To include these atmospheric coherence effects, we followed Deutsch and Miller's (Deutsch & Miller, 1981) definition of a burst error with lengths of 256, 192 and 128 bits

respectively for the particular case of Figure 6, not containing more than $L_b - 1$ consecutive correct bits ($L_b = 5$ as explained in (Deutsch & Miller, 1981)) any sequence of burst error. An excellent agreement between our proposed channel model and the theoretical model can be observed from the results included in such a figure.
Additionally, the main conclusion we can deduce from Figure 7 is the vulnerability to the coherence of the channel in FSO communications, specially if the variance of the log-amplitude of the intensity, σ_χ^2, increases. Thus, for instance, if comparing both the curves where channel coherence has been taking into account to the ideal curves without the adverse effect of the coherence, we can achieve a cut in average optical power requirements above 0.8 and 5.9 optical dB at a burst error rate of 10^{-5} for $\sigma_\chi^2 = 0.01$ and 0.1, respectively, assuming a burst error with length of 256 bits. In this sense, the consideration of the atmospheric coherence may be a key factor to value a much more realistic performance of these systems in order to obtain a more detailed information about the design of a specific FSO link.
A wide set of results can be consulted in (Jurado-Navas et al., 2010) for different transmission schemes including repetition coding, pulse-position modulation (PPM) or even an alternative rate-adaptive transmission techniques based on the use of variable silence periods and on-off keying (OOK) formats with memory.

7. Conclusion

In this chapter, we have presented a novel easily implementable model of turbulent atmospheric channel in which the adverse effect of the turbulence on the transmitted optical signal is included. We adopt some of the ideas proposed in (Brookner, 1970) that represent the starting point for our investigation. Thus a locally homogeneous and locally isotropic atmosphere is supposed through which a plane wave is transmitted under a weak fluctuation regime. Under these assumptions, a time-varying atmospheric scintillation sequence is generated and included in a multiplicative model. Some useful techniques have also been employed to reduce the computational load: so, first, to generate the sequence of scintillation coefficients, it has been chosen to adapt to optical environments the Clarke's method, so frequently used in fading channels in radiofrequency. It consists on filtering a random statistically Gaussian signal. Hence, the output signal, i.e. $\chi(t)$, keeps on being statistically Gaussian, but shaped in its power spectral density by the filter, $H_{sc}(f)$, employed in this method. This $H_{sc}(f)$ filter is forced to have a linear phase to minimize any effect on the modulus of the filter. Second, the continuous-time signal of the filter is sampled, converting it in a discrete time signal because of their advantages in realizations. In this respect, we initially select a very low sampling rate, F_s, to obtain a first and decimated version of the atmospheric scintillation sequence. This fact let the computation time be remarkably reduced. The election of the F_s magnitude must satisfy the Nyquist sampling theorem and should help avoid aliasing, should improve resolution and should reduce noise, removing the possibility of obtaining a very oversampled signal with very few useful samples of information. At the end of the process, the scintillation sequence will be interpolated later up to a much higher sample rate, which provides it with the adequate temporal variability.
As a third useful technique employed to reduce the computational load, the $H_{sc}(f)$ filter is proposed to be as a causal FIR filter. For this purpose, a window method is considered, employing a Hamming window owing to it is optimized to minimize the maximum side lobe. Then, a zero-padding process to compute a linear convolution by a circular convolution avoiding time-aliasing is implemented. A fast Fourier algorithm is employed to compute all values of the DFTs so that the number of arithmetical operations required will be substantially

reduced. In this respect, the number of samples of any FFT is a power of two. Thus the well-known decimation-in-time radix-2 Cooley-Tukey algorithm is implemented.
However, the most important decision taken to reduce the computational load is the proposal of a second-order Gaussian statistical model that substitutes the theoretical Kolmogorov spectrum, offering a great analytical simplicity. The integration time involved in such process is reduced 12-15 times in a DELL computer (8 Gb RAM, 8 CPU processors at 2.66 GHz each one).
On another note, the model shown in (Gujar & Kavanagh, 1968) is taken into account. Hence it makes the statistical conversion from Gaussian to the desired statistical nature (lognormal, gamma-gamma, Beckmann, etc.) much easier and better modularized in structure due to its well differentiated stages.
Finally, we must remark that a great accuracy in results using the approximation proposed in Eq. (46) instead of the theoretical model is achieved and, secondly, we have demonstrated the need to include consideration of channel coherence as a key factor to fully evaluate the performance of atmospheric optical communication systems.

8. Acknowledgment

This work was supported by the Spanish Ministerio de Ciencia e Innovación, Project TEC2008-06598.

9. Nomenclature

$B_I(\tau)$, $B_\chi(\tau)$	Covariance function of irradiance and log-amplitude, respectively.
C_n^2	Refractive-index structure parameter.
$D_n(r)$	Index of refraction structure function.
d_0	Correlation length of intensity fluctuations.
$\mathbf{E}$	Vector amplitude of the electric field.
f_c	Power spectral density bandwidth of the intensity fluctuations.
$f_\chi(\chi)$	Probability density function of random log-amplitude scintillation.
$f_I(I)$	Probability density function of intensity fluctuations ($=f_{\alpha_{sc}}(\alpha_{sc})$).
${}_1F_1(a;c;v)$	Confluent hypergeometric function of the first kind.
$\mathbf{H}$	Vector amplitude of the magnetic field.
$h_{sc}(t)$	Impulse response of the filter $H_{sc}(f)$.
$h_{sc}[n]$	Discrete version of the impulse response of the filter $H_{sc}(f)$.
$h_{wsc}[n]$	$h_{sc}[n]w[n]$.
$h_{wsc;zp}[n]$	Zero pad version of $h_{wsc}[n]$.
$H_{sc}(f)$	Filter frequency response.
$H_{sc}[k]$	Discrete version of the filter frequency response.
I	Irradiance of the random field.
I_0	Level of irradiance fluctuation in the absence of air turbulence.
$J_v(\cdot)$	Bessel function of order v.
k	Wave number of beam wave ($=2\pi/\lambda$).
L	Propagation path length.
l_0	Inner scale of turbulence.
L_0	Outer scale of turbulence.
$n(\mathbf{r})$	Index of refraction.
n_0	Average value of index of refraction.

n_1	Fluctuations of the refractive index.
$p_n(t)$	Pulse shape having normalized amplitude.
$\mathbf{r}$	Transverse position of observation point.
r	Magnitude of the transverse distance between two points.
S	Random phase of the field.
$S_\chi(\omega)$	Temporal spectrum of log-amplitude perturbation.
$U_0(\mathbf{r}, z)$	Complex amplitude of the field in free space.
$U_1(\mathbf{r}, z)$, $U_2(\mathbf{r}, z)$,	First and second order perturbations of the complex amplitude of the field.
$U(\mathbf{r}, z)$	Complex amplitude of the field in random medium.
$u_\perp$	Component of the wind velocity transverse to the propagation direction.
$w[n]$	Hamming window.
$\alpha_{sc}(t)$	Time-varying atmospheric scintillation sequence.
$\chi(t)$	Log-amplitude fluctuation of scintillation.
$\chi[n]$	Discrete version of log-amplitude fluctuation of scintillation.
$\hat{\chi}[n]$	$\chi[n]$ at a lower frequency rate.
κ	Scalar spatial wave number.
λ	Wavelength.
$\Phi_n(\kappa)$	Power spectrum of refractive index.
$\psi(\mathbf{r}, L)$	Phase perturbations of Rytov approximation.
$\psi_0(\mathbf{r}, L)$	Phase of the optical wave in free-space.
$\psi_1(\mathbf{r}, L)$, $\psi_2(\mathbf{r}, L)$	First and second order phase perturbations of Rytov approximation.
σ_1^2	Rytov variance for a plane wave.
σ_I^2	Scintillation index (normalized irradiance variance).
σ_χ^2	Log-amplitude variance.
τ_0	Turbulence correlation time.
ω	Discrete frequency (in rads.).

10. References

Al Naboulsi, M. & Sizun, H. (2004). Fog Attenuation Prediction for Optical and Infrared Waves. *SPIE Optical Engineering,* Vol. 43, No. 2 (February 2004), pp. 319 – 329, ISSN 0091-3286.

Andrews, L. C. & Phillips, R. L. (1998). *Laser Beam Propagation Through Random Media,* SPIE - The International Society for Optical Engineering, ISBN 081942787x, Bellingham, Washington.

Andrews, L. C.; Phillips, R. L. & Hopen, C. Y. (2000). Aperture Averaging of Optical Scintillations: Power Fluctuations and the Temporal Spectrum. *Waves in Random Media,* Vol. 10, No. 1 (2000), pp. 53 – 70, ISSN 1745-5049.

Andrews, L. C.; Phillips, R. L. & Hopen, C. Y. (2001). *Laser Beam Scintillation with Applications,* SPIE - The International Society for Optical Engineering, ISBN 0-8194-4103-1, Bellingham, Washington.

Brookner, E. (1970). Atmosphere Propagation and Communication Channel Model for Laser Wavelengths. *IEEE Transactions on Communication Technology,* Vol. 18, No. 4 (August 1970), pp. 396 – 416, ISSN 0018-9332.

Christen, A.; van Gorsel, E. & Vogt, R. (2007). Coherent Structures in Urban Roughness Sublayer Turbulence. *International Journal of Climatology,* Vol. 27, No. 14 (November 2007), pp. 1955–1968, ISSN 1097-0088.

Clifford, S. & Strohbehn, J. W. (1970). The theory of microwave line-of-sight propagation through a turbulent atmosphere. *IEEE Transactions on Antennas and Propagation*, Vol. 18, No. 2, (March 1970), pp. 264–274, ISSN 0018-926X.

Deutsch, L. J. & Miller, R. L. (1981). Burst Statistics of Viterbi Decoding, In: *The Telecommunications and Data Acquisition Progress Report*, TDA PR 42-64 (May and June 1981), pp. 187-193, Jet Propulsion Laboratory, California Institute of Technology, Pasadena, California.

Fante, R. L. (1975). Electromagnetic Beam Propagation in Turbulent Media. *Proceedings of the IEEE*, Vol. 63, No. 12 (December 1975), pp. 1669–1692, ISSN 0018-9219.

Fried, D. L. (1966). Optical Resolution Through a Randomly Inhomogeneous Medium for Very Long and Very Short Exposures. *Journal Optical Society of America*, Vol.56, No. 10, (October 1966), pp. 1372– 1379, ISSN 0030-3941.

Fried, D.L. (1967). Aperture Averaging of Scintillation. *Journal Optical Society of America*, Vol. 57, No. 2 (February 1967), pp. 169–175, ISSN 0030-3941.

Frisch, U. (1995)*Turbulence. The legacy of A.N. Kolmogorov*, Cambridge University Press, ISBN 0-521-45103-5, Cambridge, UK.

Goldsmith, A. (2005). *Wireless Communications*. Cambridge University Press, ISBN 0-521-83716-2, New York, USA.

Gujar, U.G. & Kavanagh, R.J. (1968). Generation of Random Signals with Specified Probability Density Functions and Power Density Spectra. *IEEE Transactions on Automatic Control*, Vol. 13, No. 6 (December 1968), pp. 716 – 719, ISSN 0018-9286.

Hill, R. J. & Frehlich, R. G. (1997). Probability distribution of irradiance for the onset of strong scintillation. *Journal Optical Society America A* Vol. 14, No. 7 (July 1997), pp. 1530–1540, ISSN 0740-3232.

Huang, W.; Takayanagi, J.; Sakanaka, T. & Nakagawa, M. (1993) Atmospheric Optical Communication System using Subcarrier PSK Modulation. *IEICE Transactions on Communications*, Vol. E76-B, No. 9 (September 1993), pp. 1169 – 1176, ISSN 0916-8516.

Ishimaru, A. (1997) *Wave Propagation and Scattering in Random Media*, IEEE Press and Oxford University Press, Inc. vol. 1-2, ISBN 0-7803-4717-X, New York, USA.

Juarez, J. C.; Dwivedi, A.; Hammons, A. R.; Jones, S. D.; Weerackody, V. & Nichols, R.A. (2006). Free-Space Optical Communications for Next-Generation Military Networks. *IEEE Communications Magazine*, Vol. 44, No. 11 (November 2006), pp. 46–51, ISSN 0163-6804.

Jurado-Navas, A.; García-Zambrana, A. & Puerta-Notario A. (2007). Efficient Lognormal Channel Model for Turbulent FSO Communications. *IEE Electronics Letters*, Vol. 43, No. 3 (February 2007), pp. 178 – 180, ISSN 0013-5194.

Jurado-Navas, A. & Puerta-Notario, A. (2009). Generation of Correlated Scintillations on Atmospheric Optical Communications. *Journal of Optical Communications and Networking*, Vol. 1, No. 5 (October 2009), pp. 452–462, ISSN 1943-0620.

Jurado-Navas, A.; Garrido-Balsells, J.M..; Castillo-Vázquez, M. & Puerta-Notario A. (2009). Numerical Model for the Temporal Broadening of Optical Pulses Propagating through Weak Atmospheric Turbulence. *OSA Optics Letters*, Vol. 34, No. 23 (December 2009), pp. 3662 – 3664, ISSN 0146-9592.

Jurado-Navas, A.; Garrido-Balsells, J.M..; Castillo-Vázquez, M. & Puerta-Notario A. (2010). An Efficient Rate-Adaptive Transmission Technique using Shortened Pulses for Atmospheric Optical Communications. *OSA Optics Express*, Vol. 18, No. 16 (August 2010), pp. 17346–17363, ISSN 1094-4087.

Kennedy, R. (1968). On the Atmosphere as an Optical Communication Channel. *IEEE Transactions on Information Theory,* Vol. 14, No. 5 (September 1968), pp. 716–724, ISSN 0018-9448.

Lawrence, R. & Strohbehn, J. W. (1970). A Survey of Clear-Air Propagation Effects Relevant to Optical Communications. *Proceedings of the IEEE,* Vol. 58, No. 10 (October 1970), pp. 1523–1545, ISSN 0018-9219.

Mercier, F.P. (1962). Diffraction by a Screen Causing Large Random Phase Fluctuations. *Mathematical Proceedings of the Cambridge Philosophical Society,* Vol. 58, No. 2 (April 1962), pp. 382–400, ISSN 0305-0041.

Muhammad, S.S.; Kohldorfer, P. & Leitgeb, E. (2005). Channel Modeling for Terrestrial Free Space Optical Links. *Proceedings of 2005 7th International Conference on Transparent Optical Networks,* IEEE, Barcelona, Spain, pp. 407–410, ISBN 0-7803-9236-1.

Nugent, P. W.; Shaw, J. A. & Piazzolla, S. (2009) Infrared Cloud Imaging in Support of Earth-Space Optical Communication. *OSA Optics Express*, Vol. 17, No. 10 (May 2009), pp. 7862–7872, ISSN 1094-4087.

Oppenheim, A. V. (1999). *Discrete-Time Signal Processing* (2nd edition), Prentice-Hall, ISBN 0-13-754920-2, Upper Saddle River, New Jersey, USA.

Papoulis, A. (1991). *Probability, Random Variables, and Stochastic Processes* (3rd edition), McGraw-Hill, ISBN 0070484775, New York, USA.

Rappaport, T. S. (1996). *Wireless Communications - Principles and Practice*. Prentice Hall, ISBN 0-13-375536-3, Upper Saddle River, New Jersey, USA.

Ruike, Y.; Xiange, H; Yue, H. & Zhongyu, S. (2007). Propagation Characteristics of Infrared Pulse Waves through Windblown Sand and Dust Atmosphere. *International Journal of Infrared and Millimeter Waves,* Vol. 28, No. 2 (February 2007), pp. 181–189, ISSN 0195-9271.

Strohbehn, J.W. (1968) Line-of-Sight Wave Propagation through the Turbulent Atmosphere. *Proceedings of the IEEE*, Vol. 56, No. 8 (August 1968), pp. 1301–1318, ISSN 0018-9219.

Strohbehn, J.W. (1971) Optical Propagation through the Turbulent Atmosphere. in *Progress in Optics*, Vol. 9, pp. 73 – 122, ISBN 0720415098, edited by E. Wolf (North-Holland, Amsterdam, 1971).

Strohbehn, J.W. (1978)*Laser Beam Propagation in the Atmosphere,* Springer, Topics in Applied Physics Vol. 25, ISBN 3-540-08812-1, New York, USA.

Strohbehn, J.W. & Clifford, S.F. (1967) Polarization and Angle-of-Arrival Fluctuations for a Plane Wave Propagated through a Turbulent Medium. *IEEE Transactions on Antennas and Propagation,* Vol. 15, No. 3 , (May 1967), pp. 416–421, ISSN 0018-926X.

Tatarskii, V. I. (1971). *The Effects of the Turbulent Atmosphere on Wave Propagation,* McGraw-Hill, ISBN 0 7065 06804, New York, USA.

Taylor, G.I. (1938). The Spectrum of Turbulence. *Proceeding of the Royal Society of London. Series A, Mathematical and Physical Sciences,* Vol. 164, No. 919 (February 1938), pp. 476–490.

Young, C. Y.; Andrews, L. C. & Ishimaru, A. (1998). Time-of-Arrival Fluctuations of a Space-Time Gaussian Pulse in Weak Optical Turbulence: an Analytic Solution. *Applied Optics*, Vol. 37, No.33, (November 1998), pp. 7655-7660, ISSN 0003-6935.

Zhu, X. & Kahn, J.M. (2002). Free-space Optical Communication through Atmospheric Turbulence Channels. *IEEE Transactions on Communications,* Vol. 50, No.8, (August 2002), pp. 1293-1300, ISSN 0090-6778.

8

A Unifying Statistical Model for Atmospheric Optical Scintillation

Antonio Jurado-Navas, José María Garrido-Balsells, José Francisco Paris and Antonio Puerta-Notario
Communications Engineering Department, University of Málaga
Campus de Teatinos
Málaga, Spain

1. Introduction

Atmospheric optical communication has been receiving considerable attention recently for use in high data rate wireless links (Juarez et al., 2006)-(Zhu & Kahn, 2002). Considering their narrow beamwidths and lack of licensing requirements as compared to microwave systems, atmospheric optical systems are appropriate candidates for secure, high data rate, cost-effective, wide bandwidth communications. Furthermore, atmospheric free space optical (FSO) communications are less susceptible to the radio interference than radio-wireless communications. Thus, FSO communication systems represent a promising alternative to solve the last mile problem, above all in densely populated urban areas.

However, even in clear sky conditions, wireless optical links may experience fading due to the turbulent atmosphere. In this respect, inhomogeneities in the temperature and pressure of the atmosphere lead to variations of the refractive index along the transmission path. These random refractive index variations can lead to power losses at the receiver and eventually to fluctuations in both the intensity and the phase of an optical wave propagating through this medium (Andrews & Phillips, 1998). Such fluctuations can produce an increase in the link error probability limiting the performance of communication systems. In this particular scenario, the turbulence-induced fading is called scintillation.

The reliability of an optical system operating in an environment as the mentioned above can be deduced from a mathematical model for the probability density function (pdf) of the randomly fading irradiance signal. For that reason, one of the goals in studying optical wave propagation through turbulence is the identification of a tractable pdf of the irradiance under all irradiance fluctuation regimes.

The purpose of this chapter is to develop a new tractable pdf model for the irradiance fluctuations of an unbounded optical wavefront (plane and spherical waves) propagating through a homogeneous, isotropic turbulence to explain the focusing and strong turbulence regimes where multiple scattering effects are important. Hence, the desired theoretical solution can be useful in studying the performance characteristics of any optical communication system operating through a turbulent atmosphere. We demonstrate through this chapter that our proposed model fits very well to the published data in the literature, and it generalizes in a closed-form expression most of the developed pdf models that have been proposed by the scientific community for more than four decades.

2. Background: distribution models

2.1 Limiting cases of weak turbulence and far into saturation regime.

Over the years, many irradiance pdf models have been proposed with varying degrees of success. Under weak irradiance fluctuations it has been well established that the Born and Rytov perturbation methods (Andrews & Phillips, 1998) predict results consistent with experimental data, but neither is applicable in moderate to strong fluctuations regimes.

The Born approximation (de Wolf, 1965) is a perturbation technique and remains valid only as long as the amplitude fluctuations remain small. This approximation assumes that the field at the receiver can be calculated as a sum of the original incident field, $U_0 = A_0 \exp[j\phi_0]$, plus the field scattered one time from a turbulent blob, $U_1 = A_1 \exp[jS_1]$. It is assumed that the real and imaginary parts of U_1 are uncorrelated and have equal variances, so U_1 is said to be circular complex Gaussian. Thus, from the first-order Born approximation, the irradiance of the field along the optical axis, I, has, from (Andrews & Phillips, 1998), a pdf given by the modified Rice-Nakagami distribution,

$$f_I(I) = \frac{1}{2b_0} \exp\left[-\frac{(A_0^2 + I)}{2b_0}\right] I_0\left(\frac{2A_0}{2b_0}\sqrt{I}\right), \qquad I > 0, \tag{1}$$

where $2b_0 = E[A_1^2]$ and the operator $E[\cdot]$ stands for ensemble average, being $I_0(\cdot)$ the modified Bessel function of the first kind and order zero. As shown above, the Born approximation includes only single scattering effects. However, for many problems in line-of-sight propagation, multiple scattering effects cannot be ignored and so, the results based on the Born approximation have a limited range of applicability, particularly at optical wavelengths. Due to the problems associated to the Born approximation, greater attention was focused on the Rytov method for optical wave propagation. Rytov's method is similar to the Born approximation in that it is a perturbation technique, but applied to a transformation of the scalar wave equation (Andrews & Phillips, 1998; de Wolf, 1965). It does satisfy one of the mentioned objections to the Born approximation in that it includes multiple scattering effects (Heidbreder, 1967). However, these effects are incorporated in an inflexible way which does not depend on the turbulence or other obvious factors. The method does contain both the Born approximation and geometrical optics as special cases, but does not extend the limitations on these methods as much as originally claimed. In this approach, the electric field is written as a product of the free-space field, U_0, and a complex-phase exponential, $\exp(\Psi)$. Based on the assumption that the first-order Born approximation, U_1, is a circular complex Gaussian random variable, it follows that so is the first-order Rytov approximation, $\Psi = \chi + jS$, where χ and S denote the first-order log-amplitude and phase, respectively, of the field. Then, the irradiance of the field at a given propagation distance can be expressed as:

$$I = |U_0|^2 \exp(\Psi + \Psi^*) = I_0 \exp(2\chi), \tag{2}$$

as was written in (Andrews & Phillips, 1998). In Eq. (2), $I_0 = |A_0|^2$ is the level of irradiance fluctuation in the absence of air turbulence that ensures that the fading does not attenuate or amplify the average power, i.e., $E[I] = |A_0|^2$. This may be thought of as a conservation of energy consideration and requires the choice of $E[\chi] = -\sigma_\chi^2$, as was explained in (Fried, 1967; Strohbehn, 1978), where $E[\chi]$ is the ensemble average of log-amplitude, whereas σ_χ^2 is its variance. By virtue of the central limit theorem, the marginal distribution of the log-amplitude is Gaussian distributed. Hence, from the Jacobian statistical transformation, the probability density function of the intensity can be identified to have a lognormal distribution

$$f_I(I) = \frac{1}{2I}\frac{1}{\sqrt{2\pi\sigma_\chi^2}}\exp\left(-\frac{\left[\ln(I/I_0)+2\sigma_\chi^2\right]^2}{8\sigma_\chi^2}\right), \qquad I>0, \tag{3}$$

as indicated in (Andrews & Phillips, 1998). Nevertheless, it has also been observed that the lognormal distribution can underestimate both the peak of the pdf and the behavior in the tails as compared with measured data (Churnside & Frehlich, 1989; Hill & Frehlich, 1997).
As the strength of turbulence increases and multiple self-interference effects must be taken into account, greater deviations from lognormal statistics are present in measured data. In fact, it has been predicted that the probability density function of irradiance should approach a negative exponential in the limit of infinite turbulence (Fante, 1975; de Wolf, 1974). The negative exponential distribution is considered a limit distribution for the irradiance and it is therefore approached only far into the saturation regime.

2.2 Modulated probability distribution functions

Early theoretical models developed for the irradiance fluctuations were based on assumptions of statistical homogeneity and isotropy. However, it is well known that atmospheric turbulence always contains large-scale components that usually destroy the homogeneity and isotropy of the meteorological fields, causing them to be non-stationary. This non-stationary nature of atmospheric turbulence has led to model optical scintillations as a conditional random process (Al-Habash et al., 2001; Churnside & Clifford, 1987; Churnside & Frehlich, 1989; Fante, 1975; Hill & Frehlich, 1997; Strohbehn, 1978; Wang & Strohbehn, 1974; de Wolf, 1974), in which the irradiance can be written as a product of one term that arises from large-scale turbulent eddy effects by a second term that represent the statistically independent small-scale eddy effects.
One of the first attempts to gain wide acceptance for a variety of applications was the K distribution (Abdi & Kaveh, 1998; Jakerman, 1980) that provides excellent models for predicting irradiance statistics in a variety of experiments involving radiation scattered by turbulent media. The K distribution can be derived from a mixture of the conditional negative exponential distribution and a gamma distribution. In particular, in this modulation process, the irradiance is assumed governed by the conditional negative exponential distribution:

$$f_1(I|b) = \frac{1}{b}\exp\left(-\frac{I}{b}\right), \qquad I>0, \tag{4}$$

as written in (Andrews & Phillips, 1998); whereas the mean irradiance, $b = E[I]$, is itself a random quantity assumed to be characterized by a gamma distribution given by

$$f_2(b) = \frac{\alpha(\alpha b)^{\alpha-1}}{\Gamma(\alpha)}\exp\left(-\alpha b\right), \qquad b>0, \quad \alpha>0. \tag{5}$$

In Eq. (5), $\Gamma(\cdot)$ is the gamma function and α is a positive parameter related to the effective number of discrete scatterers. The unconditional pdf for the irradiance is obtained by calculating the mixture of the two distributions presented above, and the resulting distribution is given by:

$$f_I(I) = \int_0^\infty f_1(I|b)f_2(b)\mathrm{d}b = \frac{2\alpha}{\Gamma(\alpha)}(\alpha I)^{\frac{(\alpha-1)}{2}}K_{\alpha-1}(2\sqrt{\alpha I}), \qquad I>0, \quad \alpha>0; \tag{6}$$

as detailed in (Andrews & Phillips, 1998). In Eq. (6), $K_p(x)$ is the modified Bessel function of the second kind and order p. The normalized variance of irradiance, commonly called the scintillation index, predicted by the K distribution satisfies $\sigma_I^2 = 1 + 2/\alpha$, which always exceeds unity but approaches it in the limit $\alpha \to \infty$. This fact restricts the usefulness of this distribution to moderate or strong turbulence regimes; even where it can be applied it tends to underestimate the probability of high irradiances (Churnside & Clifford, 1987) and, thus, to underestimate higher-order moments. Certainly, it is not valid under weak turbulence for which the scintillation index is less than unity. One attempt at extending the K distribution to the case of weak fluctuations led to the homodyned K (HK) (Jakerman, 1980) and the I-K distribution (Andrews & Phillips, 1985; 1986), this latter with a behavior very much like the HK distribution (Andrews & Phillips, 1986), but it did not generally provide a good fit to the experimental data in extended turbulence (Churnside & Frehlich, 1989).

With respect to other models based on modulation process, Wang and Strohbehn (Wang & Strohbehn, 1974) proposed a distribution, called log-normal Rician (LR) or also Beckmann's pdf, which results from the product of a Rician amplitude and a lognormal modulation factor. Thus, the observed field can be expressed, from (Churnside & Clifford, 1987), as:

$$U = (U_C + U_G)\exp(\chi + jS), \tag{7}$$

where U_C is a deterministic quantity and U_G is a circular Gaussian complex random variable, with χ and S being the log-amplitude and phase, respectively, of the field, assumed to be real Gaussian random variables. The irradiance is therefore given by $I = |U_C + U_G|^2 \exp(2\chi)$, where $|U_C + U_G|$ has a Rice-Nakagami pdf and the multiplicative perturbation, $\exp(2\chi)$, is lognormal. Then, the pdf is defined by the integral:

$$f_I(I) = \int_0^\infty f(I|\exp[2\chi])\, f(\exp[2\chi])\mathrm{d}[\exp(2\chi)], \tag{8}$$

where $f(I|\exp[2\chi])$ is the conditional probability density function of the irradiance given the perturbation $\exp(2\chi)$, governed by a Rician distribution; whereas $f(\exp[2\chi])$ denotes the lognormal pdf for the multiplicative perturbation. Then, Eq. (8) can be expressed as (Al-Habash et al., 2001):

$$f_I(I) = \frac{(1+r)\exp(-r)}{\sqrt{2\pi}\sigma_z} \int_0^\infty I_0\left\{2\left[\frac{(1+r)rI}{z}\right]^{1/2}\right\} \exp\left\{-\frac{(1+r)I}{z} - \frac{[\ln z + (1/2)\sigma_z^2]^2}{2\sigma_z^2}\right\}\frac{\mathrm{d}z}{z^2}, \tag{9}$$

where $r = |U_C|^2/|U_G|^2$ is the coherence parameter, z and σ_z^2 represent the irradiance modulation factor, $\exp(2\chi)$, and its variance, respectively, and $I_0(\cdot)$ is the zero-order modified Bessel function of the first kind. Although it provides an excellent fit to various experimental data, the LR pdf has certain impediments, for instance, a closed-form solution for this integral is unknown or its poor convergence properties that makes the LR model cumbersome for numerical calculations.

Under strong fluctuations, the LR model reduces to the lognormally modulated exponential distribution (Churnside & Hill, 1987), but this latter distribution is valid only under strong fluctuation conditions.

Finally, in a recent series of papers on scintillation theory (Al-Habash et al., 2001; Andrews et al., 1999), Andrews et al. introduced the modified Rytov theory and proposed the gamma-gamma pdf as a tractable mathematical model for atmospheric turbulence. This model is, again, a two-parameter distribution which is based on a doubly stochastic theory of scintillation and assumes that small scale irradiance fluctuations are modulated by large-scale irradiance fluctuations of the propagating wave, both governed by independent gamma distributions. Then, from the modified Rytov theory (Andrews et al., 1999), the optical field is defined as $U = U_0 \exp(\Psi_x + \Psi_y)$, where Ψ_x and Ψ_y are statistically independent complex perturbations which are due only to large-scale and small-scale atmospheric effects, respectively. Then, the irradiance is now defined as the product of two random processes, i.e., $I = I_x I_y$, where I_x and I_y arise, respectively, from large-scale and small-scale atmospheric effects. Moreover, both large-scale and small-scale irradiance fluctuations are governed by gamma distributions, i.e.:

$$f_x(I_x) = \frac{\alpha(\alpha I_x)^{\alpha-1}}{\Gamma(\alpha)} \exp(-\alpha I_x), \qquad I_x > 0, \quad \alpha > 0, \tag{10}$$

$$f_y(I_y) = \frac{\beta(\beta I_y)^{\beta-1}}{\Gamma(\beta)} \exp(-\beta I_y), \qquad I_y > 0, \quad \beta > 0. \tag{11}$$

To obtain the unconditional gamma-gamma irradiance distribution, we can form:

$$f_I(I) = \int_0^\infty f_y(I|I_x) f_x(I_x) \mathrm{d}I_x = \frac{2(\alpha\beta)^{(\alpha+\beta)/2}}{\Gamma(\alpha)\Gamma(\beta)} I^{(\alpha+\beta)/2-1} K_{\alpha-\beta}(2\sqrt{\alpha\beta I}), \qquad I > 0, \tag{12}$$

where $K_a(\cdot)$ is the modified Bessel function of the second kind of order a. In Eq. (12), the positive parameter α represents the effective number of large-scale cells of the scattering process, larger than that of the first Fresnel zone or the scattering disk whichever is larger (Al-Habash et al., 2001); whereas β similarly represents the effective number of small-scale cells, smaller than the Fresnel zone or the coherence radius. This gamma-gamma pdf has been suggested as a reasonable alternative to Beckmann's pdf because makes computations easier in comparison with this latter distribution.

Now, through this chapter, we propose a new and generic propagation model and, from it, and assuming a gamma approximation for the large-scale fluctuations, we obtain a new and unifying statistical model for the irradiance fluctuations. The proposed model is valid under all range of turbulence conditions (weak to strong) and it is found to provide an excellent fit to the experimental data, as will be shown through Section 5. Furthermore, the statistical model presented in this chapter can be written in a closed-form expression and it contains most of the statistical models for the irradiance fluctuations that have been proposed in the bibliography.

3. Generation of a new distribution: the $\mathcal{M}$ distribution

As was pointed out before, the Rytov theory is the conventional method of analysis in weak-fluctuations regimes, as shown in Eq. (2). Extensions to such theory were developed in (Churnside & Clifford, 1987; Wang & Strohbehn, 1974) to obtain the LR model; and in (Al-Habash et al., 2001) to generate the gamma-gamma pdf as a plausible and easily tractable approximation to Beckmann's pdf. Both models, of course, approximate the behavior of optical irradiance fluctuations in the turbulent atmosphere under all irradiance fluctuation regimes. In fact, the LR model can be seen as a generic model because includes the lognormal distribution which can be employed under weak turbulence; the lognormally modulated exponential distribution used in strong path-integrated turbulence and, moreover, it can be reduced to the negative exponential pdf in extremely strong turbulence regimes (Churnside & Frehlich, 1989). On this basis, we propose a more generic distribution model that includes, as special cases, almost all valid models and theories that have been previously proposed in the bibliography, unifying them in a more general closed-form formulation. Thus, among others, the Rice-Nakagami, the lognormal, the K and the HK distribution, the gamma-gamma and the negative-exponential models are contained and, as we detail through this chapter, a gamma-Rician distribution can be derived from our proposed model as a very accurate alternative to the LR pdf for its simple closed-form representation (we must remark that a closed-form solution for the LR pdf is still unknown).

3.1 The model of propagation including a new scattering component coupled to the line-of-sight contribution

Assume an electromagnetic wave is propagating through a turbulent atmosphere with a random refractive index. As the wave passes through this medium, part of the energy is scattered and the form of the irradiance probability distribution is determined by the type of scattering involved. In the physical model we present in this chapter, the observed field at the receiver consists of three terms: the first one is the line-of-sight (LOS) contribution, U_L, the second one is the component which is quasi-forward scattered by the eddies on the propagation axis, U_S^C and coupled to the LOS contribution; whereas the third term, U_S^G, is due to energy which is scattered to the receiver by off-axis eddies, this latter contribution being statistically independent from the previous two other terms. The inclusion of this coupled to the LOS scattering component is the main novelty of the model and it can be justified by the high directivity and the narrow beamwidths of laser beams in atmospheric optical communications. The model description is depicted in Fig. 1.

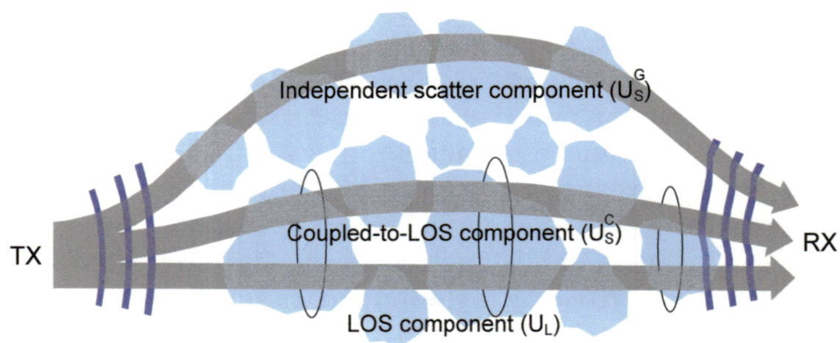

Fig. 1. Proposed propagation geometry for a laser beam where the observed field at the receiver consists of three terms: first, the line-of-sight (LOS) component, U_L; the second term is the coupled-to-LOS scattering term, U_S^C, whereas the third path represents the energy scattered to the receiver by off-axis eddies, U_S^G.

Mathematically, we can write the total observed field as:

$$U = \left(U_L + U_S^C + U_S^G\right) \exp\left(\chi + jS\right) \tag{13}$$

where

$$U_L = \sqrt{G}\sqrt{\Omega}\exp\left(j\phi_A\right), \tag{14}$$

$$U_S^C = \sqrt{\rho}\sqrt{G}\sqrt{2b_0}\exp\left(j\phi_B\right), \tag{15}$$

$$U_S^G = \sqrt{(1-\rho)}U_S'; \tag{16}$$

being U_S^C and U_S^G statistically independent stationary random processes. Of course, U_L and U_S^G are also independent random processes. In Eq. (13), G is a real variable following a gamma distribution with $E[G] = 1$. It represents the slow fluctuation of the LOS component. Following the same notation as (Abdi et al., 2003), the parameter $\Omega = E[|U_L|^2]$ represents the average power of the LOS component whereas the average power of the total scatter components is denoted by $2b_0 = E[|U_S^C|^2 + |U_S^G|^2]$. ϕ_A and ϕ_B are the deterministic phases of the LOS and the coupled-to-LOS scatter components, respectively. On another note, $0 \leq \rho \leq 1$ is the factor expressing the amount of scattering power coupled to the LOS component. This ρ factor depends on the propagation path length, L, the intensity of the turbulence, the optical wavelength, λ, the beam diameter, the average scale of inhomogeneities ($l = \sqrt{\lambda L}$), the beam divergence due to the atmospheric-induced beam spreading, and the distance between the different propagation paths (line of sight component and scattering components), due to if the spacing between such paths is greater than the fading correlation length, then turbulence-induced fading is uncorrelated. Finally, U_S' is a circular Gaussian complex random variable, and χ and S are, again, real random variables representing the log-amplitude and phase perturbation of the field induced by the atmospheric turbulence, respectively.

As an advance, the proposed model, with the inclusion of a random nature in the LOS component in addition to a new scattering contribution coupled to the LOS component, offers a highly positive mathematical conditioning due to its obtained irradiance pdf can be expressed in a closed-form expression and it approaches as much as desired to the result derived from the LR model, for which a closed-form solution for its integral is still unknown. Moreover, it has a high level of generality due to it includes as special cases most of the distribution models proposed in the bibliography until now.

From Eq. (13), the irradiance is therefore given by:

$$\begin{aligned} I =& \left|U_L + U_S^C + U_S^G\right|^2 \exp(2\chi) = \\ =& \left|\sqrt{G}\sqrt{\Omega}\exp(j\phi_A) + \sqrt{\rho}\sqrt{G}\sqrt{2b_0}\exp(j\phi_B) + \sqrt{(1-\rho)}U_S'\right|^2 \exp(2\chi). \end{aligned} \tag{17}$$

As indicated in (Churnside & Clifford, 1987), the larger eddies in the atmosphere produce the lognormal statistics and the smaller ones produce the shadowed-Rice model analogous to the one proposed in (Abdi et al., 2003).

As was explained in (Wang & Strohbehn, 1974), there is no strong physical justification for choosing a particular propagation model and different forms could be chosen equally well. However, there exists some points to support our proposal: so if we assume the conservation of energy consideration, then $E[I] = \Omega + 2b_0$ and requires the choice of $E[\chi] = -\sigma_\chi^2$, as was detailed in (Fried, 1967; Strohbehn, 1978). Finally, a plausible justification for the coupled-to-LOS scattering component, U_S^C, is provided in (Kennedy, 1970). There, it is said that if the turbulent medium is so thin that multiple scattering can be ignored, the multipath delays of the scattered radiation collected by a diffraction-limited receiver will usually be small relative to the signal bandwidth. Then the scattered field will combine coherently with the unscattered field and there will be no-"interfering" signal component of the field, in a similar way as U_S^C combines with U_L in our proposed model. Of course, when the turbulent medium becomes so thick, then the unscattered component of the field can be neglected.

3.2 Málaga ($\mathcal{M}$) probability density function

From Eq. (17), the observed irradiance of our proposed propagation model can be written as:

$$I = \left| U_L + U_S^C + U_S^G \right|^2 \exp(2\chi) = YX,$$
$$\begin{cases} Y \triangleq \left| U_L + U_S^C + U_S^G \right|^2 & \text{(small-scale fluctuations)} \\ X \triangleq \exp(2\chi) & \text{(large-scale fluctuations)}, \end{cases} \tag{18}$$

where the small-scale fluctuations denotes the small-scale contributions to scintillation associated with turbulent cells smaller than either the first Fresnel zone or the transverse spatial coherence radius, whichever is smallest. In contrast, large-scale fluctuations of the irradiance are generated by turbulent cells larger than that of either the Fresnel zone or the so-called "scattering disk", whichever is largest. From Eq. (13), we rewrite the lowpass-equivalent complex envelope as:

$$R(t) = \left(U_L + U_S^C + U_S^G \right) = \sqrt{G}\left(\sqrt{\Omega} \exp(j\phi_A) + \sqrt{\rho}\sqrt{2b_0} \exp(j\phi_B) \right) + \sqrt{(1-\rho)} U_S', \tag{19}$$

so that we have the identical shadowed Rice single model employed in (Abdi et al., 2003), composed by the sum of a Rayleigh random phasor (the independent scatter component, U_S') and a Nakagami distribution ($\sqrt{G}$, used for both the LOS component and the coupled-to-LOS scatter component). The other remaining terms in Eq. (19) are deterministics. Then, we can apply the same procedure exposed in (Abdi et al., 2003) consisting in calculating the expectation of the Rayleigh component with respect to the Nakagami distribution and then deriving the pdf of the instantaneous power. Hence, the pdf of Y is given by:

$$f_Y(y) = \frac{1}{\gamma} \left[\frac{\gamma\beta}{\gamma\beta + \Omega'} \right]^{\beta} \exp\left[-\frac{y}{\gamma} \right] {}_1F_1\left(\beta; 1; \frac{1}{\gamma} \frac{\Omega'}{(\gamma\beta + \Omega')} y \right), \tag{20}$$

where $\beta \triangleq (E[G])^2/\mathrm{Var}[G]$ is the amount of fading parameter with $\mathrm{Var}[\cdot]$ as the variance operator. We have denoted $\Omega' = \Omega + \rho 2b_0 + 2\sqrt{2b_0\Omega\rho}\cos(\phi_A - \phi_B)$ and $\gamma = 2b_0(1-\rho)$. Finally, ${}_1F_1(a; c; x)$ is the Kummer confluent hypergeometric function of the first kind.

Otherwise, the large-scale fluctuations, $X \triangleq \exp(2\chi)$, is widely accepted to be a lognormal amplitude (Churnside & Clifford, 1987) but, however, as in (Abdi et al., 2003; Al-Habash et al., 2001; Andrews & Phillips, 2008; Phillips & Andrews, 1982), this distribution is approximated by a gamma one, this latter with a more favorable analytical structure. This latter distribution can exhibit characteristics of the lognormal distribution under the proper conditions, avoiding the infinite-range integral of the lognormal pdf. Then, the gamma pdf is given by:

$$f_X(x) = \frac{\alpha^{\alpha}}{\Gamma(\alpha)} x^{\alpha-1} \exp(-\alpha x), \tag{21}$$

where α is a positive parameter related to the effective number of large-scale cells of the scattering process, as in (Al-Habash et al., 2001). Now, the statistical characterization of the model presented in Eq. (17) will be formally accomplished.S

Definition: *Let I=XY be a random variable representing the irradiance fluctuations for a propagating optical wave. It is said that I follows a generalized $\mathcal{M}$ distribution if X and Y are random variable distributions according to Eqs. (21) and (20), respectively. That the distribution of I is a generalized $\mathcal{M}$ distribution can be written in the following notation: $I \sim \mathcal{M}^{(G)}(\alpha, \beta, \gamma, \rho, \Omega')$, being α, β, γ, ρ, Ω' the real and positive parameters of this generalized $\mathcal{M}$ distribution. And for the pivotal case of β being a natural number, then it is said that I follows an $\mathcal{M}$ distribution and it is denoted by $\mathcal{M}(\alpha, \beta, \gamma, \rho, \Omega')$.*

Lemma 1: *Let $I \sim \mathcal{M}^{(G)}(\alpha,\beta,\gamma,\rho,\Omega^{'})$. Then, its pdf is represented by:*

$$f_I(I) = A^{(G)} \sum_{k=1}^{\infty} a_k^{(G)} I^{\frac{\alpha+k}{2}-1} K_{\alpha-k}\left(2\sqrt{\frac{\alpha I}{\gamma}}\right), \tag{22}$$

where

$$\begin{cases} A^{(G)} \triangleq \dfrac{2\alpha^{\frac{\alpha}{2}}}{\gamma^{1+\frac{\alpha}{2}}\Gamma(\alpha)}\left(\dfrac{\gamma\beta}{\gamma\beta+\Omega^{'}}\right)^{\beta}; \\ a_k^{(G)} \triangleq \dfrac{(\beta)_{k-1}(\alpha\gamma)^{\frac{k}{2}}}{\left[(k-1)!\right]^2\gamma^{k-1}(\Omega^{'}+\gamma\beta)^{k-1}}. \end{cases} \tag{23}$$

In Eq. (22), $K_\nu(\cdot)$ is the modified Bessel function of the second kind and order ν whereas $\Gamma(\cdot)$ is the gamma function.
Otherwise, let $I \sim \mathcal{M}(\alpha,\beta,\gamma,\rho,\Omega^{'})$, i.e., β is a natural number; then, its pdf is given by:

$$f_I(I) = A \sum_{k=1}^{\beta} a_k I^{\frac{\alpha+k}{2}-1} K_{\alpha-k}\left(2\sqrt{\frac{\alpha\beta I}{\gamma\beta+\Omega^{'}}}\right) \tag{24}$$

where

$$\begin{cases} A \triangleq A^{(G)}\left(\dfrac{\gamma\beta}{\gamma\beta+\Omega^{'}}\right)^{\frac{\alpha}{2}}; \\ a_k \triangleq \dbinom{\beta-1}{k-1}\dfrac{1}{(k-1)!}\left(\dfrac{\Omega^{'}}{\gamma}\right)^{k-1}\left(\dfrac{\alpha}{\beta}\right)^{\frac{k}{2}}\left(\gamma\beta+\Omega^{'}\right)^{1-\frac{k}{2}}. \end{cases} \tag{25}$$

In Eq. (24), $K_\nu(\cdot)$ is, again, the modified Bessel function of the second kind and order ν. Moreover, in Eq. (25), $A^{(G)}$ was one of the parameters defined in Eq. (23), whereas $\binom{\beta}{k}$ represents the binomial coefficient. In the interest of clarity, the proof of this lemma is moved to Appendix A.
To conclude this subsection, we can point out that the pdf functions given in Eq. (22) and Eq. (24) can be expressed as a discrete mixture and a finite discrete mixture, respectively (see Chap. 7 of Ref. (Charalambides, 2005)) involving a resized irradiance variable, I', in the form: $f_{I'}(I') = \sum_k \omega_k \cdot f_{GG}(I')$, being the mixed distribution, $f_{GG}(I')$, a gamma-gamma pdf whereas the weight function, ω_k, satisfies that $\sum_k \omega_k = 1$ due to $\int_0^\infty f_{I'}(y)dy = \sum_k \omega_k \cdot \int_0^\infty f_{GG}(y)dy = 1$ by definition and $\int_0^\infty f_{GG}(y)dy=1$ also by definition.

3.3 Moments of the $\mathcal{M}$ probability distribution

In this subsection, the kth moment of the $\mathcal{M}$ probability distribution is obtained.
Lemma 2: *Let I the randomly fading irradiance signal following a generalized $\mathcal{M}$ distribution and expressed as $I \sim \mathcal{M}^{(G)}(\alpha,\beta,\gamma,\rho,\Omega^{'})$. Then, its centered moments, denoted by $m_k^{(G)}(I)$, are given by:*

$$m_k^{(G)}(I) \triangleq E\left[I^k\right] = \frac{\Gamma(\alpha+k)}{\Gamma(\alpha)\alpha^k}\left(\frac{\gamma\beta}{\gamma\beta+\Omega^{'}}\right)^{\beta}\gamma^k\Gamma(k+1)\,{}_2F_1\left(k+1,\beta;1;\frac{\Omega^{'}}{\gamma\beta+\Omega^{'}}\right), \tag{26}$$

where ${}_2F_1(a,b;c;x)$ is the Gaussian hypergeometric function. In addition, if the intensity signal now follows an $\mathcal{M}$ distribution, $I \sim \mathcal{M}(\alpha,\beta,\gamma,\rho,\Omega^{'})$, with β being a natural number, then its centered *moments are given by:*

$$m_k(I) = \frac{\Gamma(\alpha+k)}{\Gamma(\alpha)\,\alpha^k}\frac{1}{\gamma}\left(\frac{\gamma\beta}{\gamma\beta+\Omega'}\right)^{\beta}\sum_{r=0}^{\beta-1}\binom{\beta-1}{r}\frac{1}{r!}\left(\frac{\Omega'}{\gamma(\gamma\beta+\Omega')}\right)^{r}\frac{\Gamma(k+r+1)}{\left(\frac{\beta}{\gamma\beta+\Omega'}\right)^{k+r+1}}. \tag{27}$$

For the sake of clarity of the whole chapter, the proof of this lemma is, again, moved and extensively explained in Appendix B.

3.4 Cumulative distribution function (cdf) of the $\mathcal{M}$ probability distribution

In this subsection, the cumulative distribution function (cdf) of the $\mathcal{M}$ probability distribution is obtained.

Lemma 3: *Let I the randomly fading irradiance signal following a generalized $\mathcal{M}$ distribution and expressed as $I \sim \mathcal{M}^{(G)}(\alpha,\beta,\gamma,\rho,\Omega')$. Then, its cdf is given by:*

$$P(I \le I_T) = \int_0^{I_T} f_I(I)\mathrm{d}I = \frac{A^{(G)}}{I_T^{\frac{\alpha}{2}+1}}\times$$

$$\sum_{k=1}^{\infty}\frac{a_k^{(G)}}{I_T^{\frac{k}{2}}}\left\{2^{-(\alpha-k)-1}\left(2I_T^{-1/2}\sqrt{\frac{\alpha}{\gamma}}\right)^{-(\alpha-k)}\frac{\Gamma(\alpha-k)}{k+1}\,{}_1F_2\left(k+1;1-\alpha+k,k+2;\frac{\alpha}{\gamma I_T}\right)+\right.$$

$$\left.+2^{1-(\alpha-k)}\left(2I_T^{-1/2}\sqrt{\frac{\alpha}{\gamma}}\right)^{(\alpha-k)}\frac{\Gamma(k-\alpha)}{\alpha+1}\,{}_1F_2\left(\alpha+1;1+\alpha-k,\alpha+2;\frac{\alpha}{\gamma I_T}\right)\right\}, \tag{28}$$

where I_T is a threshold parameter, $A^{(G)}$ and $a_k^{(G)}$ are defined in Eq. (23) and ${}_1F_2(a;c,d;x)$ deno-tes a generalized hypergeometric function. Nevertheless, if the irradiance signal now follows an $\mathcal{M}$ distribution, $I \sim \mathcal{M}(\alpha,\beta,\gamma,\rho,\Omega')$, with β being a natural number, then its cdf is given by:

$$P(I \le I_T) = \int_0^{I_T} f_I(I)\mathrm{d}I = \frac{A}{I_T^{\frac{\alpha}{2}+1}}\times$$

$$\sum_{k=1}^{\beta}\frac{a_k}{I_T^{\frac{k}{2}}}\left\{2^{-(\alpha-k)-1}\left(\frac{2I_T^{-\frac{1}{2}}}{k+1}\sqrt{\frac{\alpha\beta}{\gamma\beta+\Omega'}}\right)^{-(\alpha-k)}\Gamma(\alpha-k)\,{}_1F_2\left(k+1;1-\alpha+k,k+2;\frac{\alpha\beta}{(\gamma\beta+\Omega')\,I_T}\right)+\right.$$

$$\left.+2^{1-(\alpha-k)}\left(\frac{2I_T^{-\frac{1}{2}}}{\alpha+1}\sqrt{\frac{\alpha\beta}{\gamma\beta+\Omega'}}\right)^{(\alpha-k)}\Gamma(k-\alpha)\,{}_1F_2\left(\alpha+1;1+\alpha-k,\alpha+2;\frac{\alpha\beta}{(\gamma\beta+\Omega')\,I_T}\right)\right\}, \tag{29}$$

where, again, I_T is a threshold parameter and A and a_k are defined in Eq. (25). The proof of this lemma is treated in Appendix C.

4. Derivation of existing distribution models

In this section, we derive, from our proposed generalized distribution, $\mathcal{M}^{(G)}(\alpha,\beta,\gamma,\rho,\Omega')$, (or from $\mathcal{M}(\alpha,\beta,\gamma,\rho,\Omega')$, if its β parameter is a natural number) most of the existing distribution models that have been proposed for atmospheric optical communications in the bibliography.

4.1 Rice-Nakagami and lognormal distribution functions

Consider the propagation model presented in this chapter and written in Eq. (17). Thus, starting with the first models proposed in the bibliography for weak turbulence regimes, we indicated in Section 2 that, from the first-order Born approximation, the irradiance, I, has a pdf governed by the modified Rice-Nakagami distribution (see Eq. (1)). From Eq. (17), if we assume both $\rho = 0$ and Var$[|U_L|]$= 0, where Var$[\cdot]$ represents the variance operator, then U_L becomes a constant random variable where $E[|U_L|] = \sqrt{\Omega}$ since $E[G] = 1$, as was pointed out in Section 2. If we consider that χ is a zero mean random variable (strictly speaking, $E[\chi] = -\sigma_\chi^2$ due to conservation energy consideration (Fried, 1967; Strohbehn, 1978)) and Var$[\chi]$=Var$[S] = 0$, then, from (Andrews & Phillips, 1998), Eq.(17) becomes:

$$I = \left|\sqrt{G}\sqrt{\Omega}\exp\left(j\phi_A\right) + U'_S\right|^2. \tag{30}$$

Equation (30) represents the first-order Born approximation, as indicated in (Andrews & Phillips, 1998). As $U'_S = A'_S \exp\left(jS'_S\right)$ is a circular Gaussian complex random variable where $E[|U'_S|^2] = 2b_0 = \gamma$ owing to $\rho = 0$; and if we denote $A_0 = \sqrt{G}\sqrt{\Omega}$, then the irradiance, I, of the field along the optical axis has a modified Rice-Nakagami distribution given by:

$$f_I(I) = \frac{1}{\gamma}\exp\left[-\frac{(A_0^2 + I)}{\gamma}\right] I_0\left(\frac{2A_0}{\gamma}\sqrt{I}\right), \qquad I > 0, \tag{31}$$

identical to Eq. (1). Thus, the Rice-Nakagami distribution is included in our proposed $\mathcal{M}$ distribution. Moreover, as indicated in (Strohbehn, 1978), when $A_0^2/\gamma \to \infty$, then the Rice-Nakagami distribution leads to a lognormal distribution, one of the most widely employed distributions for weak turbulence regimes and derived by the used of the Rytov method and the application of the central limit theorem.

4.2 Rytov model

Thus, consider now the following different perturbational approach, the Rytov approximation, again restricted to weak fluctuation conditions. In this case, as was commented above, the pdf for the irradiance fluctuations is the lognormal distribution shown in Eq. (3). We can deduce this model from our proposed perturbation model written in Eqs. (13) and (17). Thus, lets assume again Var$[|U_L|]$= 0, so U_L becomes a constant random variable where $E[|U_L|]=\sqrt{\Omega}$ since $E[G]=1$ as was discussed in Section 2. If the average power of the total scatter components is established to $2b_0 = 0$ (no scattering power, $U_S^C = U_S^G = 0$), then Eq. (17) reduces to:

$$I = |U_L|^2 \exp\left(2\chi\right) = \left|\sqrt{G}\sqrt{\Omega}\exp\left(j\phi_A\right)\right|^2 \exp\left(2\chi\right). \tag{32}$$

If we identify $I_0 = \left|\sqrt{G}\sqrt{\Omega}\exp\left(j\phi_A\right)\right|^2$ as the irradiance fluctuation in the absence of air turbulence and we assume the conservation of energy consideration $E[\chi] = -\sigma_\chi^2$, then we have the same conditions exposed in Eq. (2) so that the pdf of the intensity could be identified to have a lognormal distribution, as in Eq. (3). However, we have approximated the behavior of the large-scale fluctuations, $X = \exp\left(2\chi\right)$, by a gamma distribution due to it is proven that lognormal and gamma distributions can closely approximate each other (Clark & Karp, 1970). Thus, the behavior of the classical first-order Rytov approximation is included in our proposed propagation model.

4.3 Generation of existing modulated probability density functions

4.3.1 K, HK and negative exponential distribution

Now, to obtain the modulated probability distribution functions that have been widely employed in the bibliography, we must start calculating the moment generating function (MGF) of the random processes X and Y defined in Eq. (18). The MGF for a generic function, $f_Z(z)$, is defined by $M_Z(s) \triangleq \mathcal{L}\{f_Z(z);-s\}$, where $\mathcal{L}[\cdot]$ denotes the Laplace transform. Hence, from Eqs. (2.68) and (2.22) of Ref. (Simon & Alouini, 2005), we have:

$$M_Y(s) \triangleq \mathcal{L}[f_Y(y);-s] = \left(\frac{\gamma\beta}{\gamma\beta+\Omega'}\right)^{\beta} \frac{(1-\gamma s)^{\beta-1}}{\left(1-\frac{\Omega'}{\gamma\beta+\Omega'}-\gamma s\right)^{\beta}}, \tag{33}$$

$$M_X(s) \triangleq \mathcal{L}[f_X(x);-s] = \frac{1}{(1-\frac{s}{\alpha})^{\alpha}}; \tag{34}$$

for $f_Y(y)$ and $f_X(x)$ given in Eqs. (20) and (21), respectively. Now, if $\Omega = 0$ (no LOS power) and $\rho = 0$ (no coupled-to-LOS scattering power, U_S^C), i.e., $\Omega' = 0$, then Eq. (33) is reduced to:

$$M_Y(s) = (1-\gamma s)^{-1}, \tag{35}$$

and Eq. (20) is, obviously, reduced to an exponential distribution:

$$f_Y(y) = \frac{1}{\gamma}\exp\left[-\frac{y}{\gamma}\right]. \tag{36}$$

In addition, we can obtain this exponential distribution when β is unity in Eq. (33), and Eq. (36) would be written in the same form, replacing γ parameter by $\gamma+\Omega'$. Anyhow, as was detailed in (Andrews & Phillips, 1998), with a negative exponential distribution for $f_Y(y)$ and a gamma distribution for $f_X(x)$, the unconditional pdf for the irradiance is obtained by calculating the mixture of these two latter distributions in the same form indicated in Eq. (6), leading to the K-distribution model. Of course, as the effective number of discrete scatterer cells, α, becomes unbounded (a huge thick turbulent medium), i.e., $\alpha \to \infty$, the K distribution tends to the negative exponential distribution as the gamma distribution that governs X approaches a delta function (Andrews et al., 2001). So the K distribution and the exponential one are also included in our proposed statistical model. Finally, a generalization of the K distribution, the homodyned K (HK) distribution is also included (Andrews & Phillips, 1986). This HK model is composed by a Rice-Nakagami distribution and a gamma distribution. The Rice-Nakagami model can be deduced in a similar way as Eq. (31). However, the gamma model needed to build the unconditional HK pdf is the distribution function of the fluctuating average irradiance of the random field component (U_S^G since U_S^C=0 as ρ=0 for deriving the Rice-Nakagami model from our $\mathcal{M}$ distribution). Thus, we have to identify the large-scale fluctuations, X, given in Eq. (18) with the parameter γ=$2b_0$=$E[|U_S^G|^2]$ so that $x \triangleq \gamma$ in Eq. (21). Then, the HK distribution is also contained in our proposed model as a special case of the $\mathcal{M}$ distribution.

4.3.2 Gamma-gamma model

On the other hand, and returning again to our original model given in Eqs. (20) and (21) with their MGFs calculated in Eqs. (33) and (34), we now take $\rho = 1$, i.e., there only exists LOS component, U_L, and coupled-to-LOS scattering component, U_S^C, in our propagation model given in Eq. (17). If $\rho = 1$ then $\gamma = 0$ so Eq. (33) becomes:

$$M_Y(s) = \lim_{\gamma \to 0} \left\{ \left(\frac{\gamma\beta}{\gamma\beta + \Omega'} \right)^{\beta} \frac{(1-\gamma s)^{\beta-1}}{\left(1 - \frac{\Omega'}{\gamma\beta+\Omega'} - \gamma s\right)^{\beta}} \right\} = \left(\Omega'\right)^{-\beta} \left(\frac{1}{\Omega'} - \frac{s}{\beta} \right)^{-\beta}. \tag{37}$$

If we fix $\Omega' = 1$, then Eq. (37) is reduced to:

$$M_Y(s) = \left(1 - \frac{s}{\beta}\right)^{-\beta}. \tag{38}$$

This last expression is the MGF of a gamma function so that we can identify that the small-scale fluctuations, Y, are governed by a gamma distribution. As the behavior of large-scale fluctuations, X were approximated to follow a gamma distribution, then the unconditional pdf for the irradiance is obtained by calculating the mixture of these two gamma distributions in the same form as indicated in Eq. (12). Then, the gamma-gamma model presented in (Al-Habash et al., 2001) is also included in our $\mathcal{M}$ model by, first, canceling the U_S^G component, i.e., the energy which is scattered to the receiver by off-axis eddies; and, secondly, normalizing the Ω component at 1. In this particular case, α represents the effective number of large-scale cells of the scattering process and β similarly represents the effective number of small-scale effects, in the same form as was explained in (Al-Habash et al., 2001).

4.3.3 Gamma-Rician model approximating to lognormal-Rician (LR) model

Finally, and again returning to our original model given in Eqs. (20) and (21) and in Eqs. (33) and (34), we can approximate our $\mathcal{M}$ distribution to the LR model proposed in Eq. (9). For this purpose, we only need to take $\beta \to \infty$; then, from the definition of $e = (1 + 1/x)^x$, $x \to \infty$, and from L'Hopital's rule, the MGF of Y is given by:

$$M_Y(s) = \lim_{\beta \to \infty} \left\{ \left(\frac{\gamma\beta}{\gamma\beta + \Omega'} \right)^{\beta} \frac{(1-\gamma s)^{\beta-1}}{\left(1 - \frac{\Omega'}{\gamma\beta+\Omega'} - \gamma s\right)^{\beta}} \right\} = (1-\gamma s)^{-1} \exp\left[\frac{\Omega' s}{1-\gamma s} \right], \tag{39}$$

according to Eq. (2.17) of Ref. (Simon & Alouini, 2005), where its associated pdf is, from Eq. (20), rewritten as:

$$f_Y(y) = \frac{1}{\gamma} \exp\left[-\frac{y + \Omega'}{\gamma} \right] I_0 \left(\frac{2\sqrt{\Omega' y}}{\gamma} \right). \tag{40}$$

Equation (40) represents a Rice pdf (Abdi et al., 2003). As the behavior of large-scale fluctuations, X were approximated to follow a gamma distribution as indicated in Eq. (21), then the unconditional pdf for the irradiance, I, is obtained by calculating the mixture of these two gamma distributions in the form:

$$f_I(I) = \int_0^\infty f_Y(I|x)\, f_X(x)\mathrm{d}x =$$
$$= \frac{1}{\gamma}\frac{\alpha^\alpha}{\Gamma(\alpha)}\exp\left(-\frac{\Omega'}{\gamma}\right)\sum_{k=0}^{\infty}\frac{(-1)^k\left(\Omega' I\right)^k}{k!\Gamma(k+1)\gamma^{2k}}\int_0^\infty x^{\alpha-2-k}\exp\left(-\frac{I}{x\gamma}-\alpha x\right)\mathrm{d}x, \tag{41}$$

where we have expanded the modified Bessel function, $I_0(\cdot)$, by its series representation:

$$I_p(z) = \sum_{k=0}^{\infty}\frac{(-1)^k (z/2)^{2k+p}}{k!\Gamma(k+p+1)}, \qquad |z| < \infty; \tag{42}$$

as indicated in (Andrews, 1998). Now, using again Eq. (3.471-9) of Ref. (Gradshteyn & Ryzhik, 2000), written in this chapter in Eq. (52), and substituting it into Eq. (41), we can derive:

$$f_I(I) = \frac{1}{\gamma}\frac{\alpha^\alpha}{\Gamma(\alpha)}\exp\left(-\frac{\Omega'}{\gamma}\right)\sum_{k=1}^{\infty}\frac{(-1)^{k-1}\left(\Omega' I\right)^{k-1}}{(k-1)!\Gamma(k)\gamma^{2k-2}}\left(\frac{I}{\alpha\gamma}\right)^{\frac{\alpha-k}{2}} K_{\alpha-k}\left(2\sqrt{\frac{\alpha I}{\gamma}}\right). \tag{43}$$

On the other hand, Eq. (43) can be expressed as:

$$f_I(I) = \hat{A}\sum_{k=1}^{\infty}\hat{a_k} I^{\frac{\alpha+k}{2}-1}K_{\alpha-k}\left(2\sqrt{\frac{\alpha I}{\gamma}}\right), \tag{44}$$

where

$$\begin{cases} \hat{A} \stackrel{\Delta}{=} \dfrac{2\alpha^{\frac{\alpha}{2}}}{\gamma^{1+\frac{\alpha}{2}}\Gamma(\alpha)}\exp\left(-\dfrac{\Omega'}{\gamma}\right); \\ \hat{a_k} \stackrel{\Delta}{=} \dfrac{(-1)^{k-1}\Omega'^{k-1}(\alpha\gamma)^{\frac{k}{2}}}{(k-1)!\Gamma(k)\gamma^{2k-2}}. \end{cases} \tag{45}$$

Then, the distribution directly derived from our proposed $\mathcal{M}$-distribution when $\beta \to \infty$ and presented in Eq. (43) is a gamma-Rician model. Of course, this gamma-Rician distribution is suggested to approximate the LR model detailed in (Churnside & Clifford, 1987), in which the large-scale fluctuations, X, are assumed to follow a lognormal distribution. But, as was discussed in Section 3.2., a lognormal distribution is well approximated by a gamma one (Abdi et al., 2003; Al-Habash et al., 2001; Andrews & Phillips, 2008). So this gamma-Rician approximation to the LR model will provide an excellent fit to experimental data avoiding the impediments of the LR model; thus, the gamma-Rician approximation provides a closed-form solution whereas the solution to the integral in the LR model is unknown and, moreover, its integral form undergoes a poor convergence making the LR pdf cumbersome for numerical calculations. In addition, the gamma-Rician approximation derived from our proposed $\mathcal{M}$ distribution has directly identified the α parameter, related to the large-scale cells of the scattering process, as in the gamma-gamma distribution (Abdi et al., 2003); whereas the other parameters can be calculated by using the heuristic theory of Clifford *et al.*, (Clifford et al., 1974), Hill and Clifford, (Hill & Clifford, 1981) and Hill (Hill, 1982).

Distribution model	Generation	Distribution model	Generation
Rice-Nakagami	$\rho = 0$ $\mathrm{Var}[\lvert U_L \rvert] = 0$	Lognormal	$\rho = 0$ $\mathrm{Var}[\lvert U_L \rvert] = 0$ $\gamma \to 0$
Gamma	$\rho = 0$ $\gamma = 0$	K distribution	$\Omega = 0$ and $\rho = 0$ or $\beta = 1$
HK distribution	$\mathrm{Var}[G] = 0$ $\rho = 0$ $X = \gamma$	Exponential distribution	$\Omega = 0$ $\rho = 0$ $\alpha \to \infty$
Gamma-gamma distribution	$\rho = 1$, then $\gamma = 0$ $\Omega' = 1$	Gamma-Rician distribution	$\beta \to \infty$
Shadowed-Rician distribution	$\mathrm{Var}[\lvert X \rvert] = 0$		

Table 1. List of existing distribution models for atmospheric optical communications and generation by using the proposed $\mathcal{M}$ distribution model.

4.4 Summary

To conclude this section, all the approximations involved in deriving the different distribution models that, until now, had been proposed in the bibliography are summarize in Table 1. Finally, Fig. 2 displays, as an example, the K distribution and the gamma-gamma one as special cases of the $\mathcal{M}$ distribution, showing the transition between them corresponding to various values of the factor ρ representing the amount of scattering power coupled to the LOS component. In such example, we have fixed $\Omega = 0$, $2b_0 = 1$ and $\phi_A - \phi_B = \pi/2$.

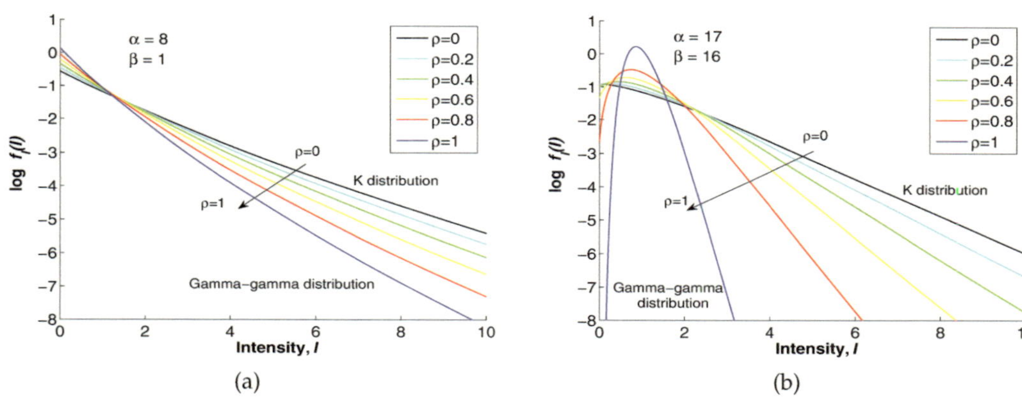

Fig. 2. Log-pdf of the irradiance (Subfigs. (a) and (b)) for different values of ρ, showing the transition from a K distribution ($\rho = 0$) to a gamma-gamma distribution ($\rho = 1$) using the proposed $\mathcal{M}$ distribution, in the case of strong irradiance fluctuations (a) and weak irradiance fluctuations (b). In both figures, $\Omega = 0$, $2b_0 = 1$ and $\phi_A - \phi_B = \pi/2$.

5. Comparison with experimental plane wave and spherical wave data

Flatté et al. (Flatté et al., 1994) calculated the pdf from numerical simulations for a plane wave propagated through homogeneous and isotropic atmospheric turbulence and compared the results with several pdf models. On the other hand, Hill et al. (Hill & Frehlich, 1997) used numerical simulation of the propagation of a spherical wave through homogeneous and isotropic turbulence that also led to pdf data for the log-irradiance fluctuations. In this section, we compare our $\mathcal{M}$ distribution model with some of the published numerical simulation data plots in (Flatté et al., 1994) and (Hill & Frehlich, 1997) of the log-irradiance pdf, covering a range of conditions that extends from weak irradiance fluctuations far into the saturation regime characterized by a Rytov variance, σ_1^2, of 25, where σ_1^2=$1.23C_n^2k^{7/6}L^{11/6}$, In that expression, k=$2\pi/\lambda$ is the optical wave number, λ is the wavelength, C_n^2 is the atmospheric refractive-index structure parameter and L is the propagation path length between transmitter and receiver. For values less than unity, the Rytov variance is the scintillation index (normalized variance of irradiance) of a plane wave in the absence of inner scale effects and for values greater than unity it is considered a measure of the strength of optical fluctuations. The $\mathcal{M}$ distribution model employed in this section to fit with the experimental numerical data is intentionally restricted to have its β parameter as a natural number in all cases. Hence, the infinite summation included in the closed form expression obtained for the generalized $\mathcal{M}$ distribution (Eq. (22)) can be avoided. This fact let us offer an even more evident analytical tractability by directly employing Eq. (24), with a finite summation of β terms, and maintaining an extremely high accuracy.

For the current case of a plane wave propagated through turbulent atmosphere the simulation parameters that determine the physical situation are only l_0/R_F and σ_1^2, as explained in (Flatté et al., 1994), where l_0 is the inner scale of turbulence. The quantity $R_F = \sqrt{L/k}$ is the scale size of the Fresnel zone.

Thus, we plot in Figs. 3 (a)-(c) the predicted log-irradiance pdf associated with the $\mathcal{M}$ distribution (black solid line) for comparison with some of the simulation data illustrated in Figs. 4, 5 and 7 of (Flatté et al., 1994). The simulation pdf values are plotted as a function of $(\ln I - < \ln I >)/\sigma$, as in (Flatté et al., 1994), where $< \ln I >$ is the mean value of the log-irradiance and $\sigma = \sqrt{\sigma^2_{\ln I}}$, the latter being the root mean square (rms) value of $\ln I$. The simulation pdf's were displayed in this fashion in the hope that it would reveal their salient features. For sake of brevity, and as representative of typical atmospheric propagation, we only use the inner scale value $l_0 = 0.5R_F$ so we can include the effect of l_0 in our results. We also plot the gamma-gamma pdf (red dashed line) obtained in (Al-Habash et al., 2001) for the sake of comparison. In Fig. 3 (a) we use a Rytov variance $\sigma_1^2 = 0.1$ corresponding to weak irradiance fluctuations, in Fig. 3 (b) we employ $\sigma_1^2 = 2$ corresponding to a regime of moderate irradiance fluctuations whereas in Fig. 3 (c), σ_1^2 was established to 25 for a particular case of strong irradiance fluctuations.

Values of the scaling parameter σ required in the plots for the $\mathcal{M}$ pdf are obtained from Andrews' development (Andrews et al., 2001) in the presence of inner scale. From such development, the model for the refractive-index spectrum, $\Phi_n(\kappa)$, used is the effective atmospheric-spectrum defined by:

$$\Phi_n(\kappa) = 0.033C_n^2\kappa^{-11/3}\left[f(\kappa, l_0)\exp\left(-\frac{\kappa^2}{\kappa_x^2}\right) + \frac{\kappa^{11/3}}{(\kappa^2+\kappa_y^2)^{11/6}}\right], \tag{46}$$

where κ is the scalar spatial wave number. In Eq. (46), the inner-scale factor, $f(\kappa l_0)$, describes the spectral bump and dissipation range at high wave numbers and, from (Andrews et al.,

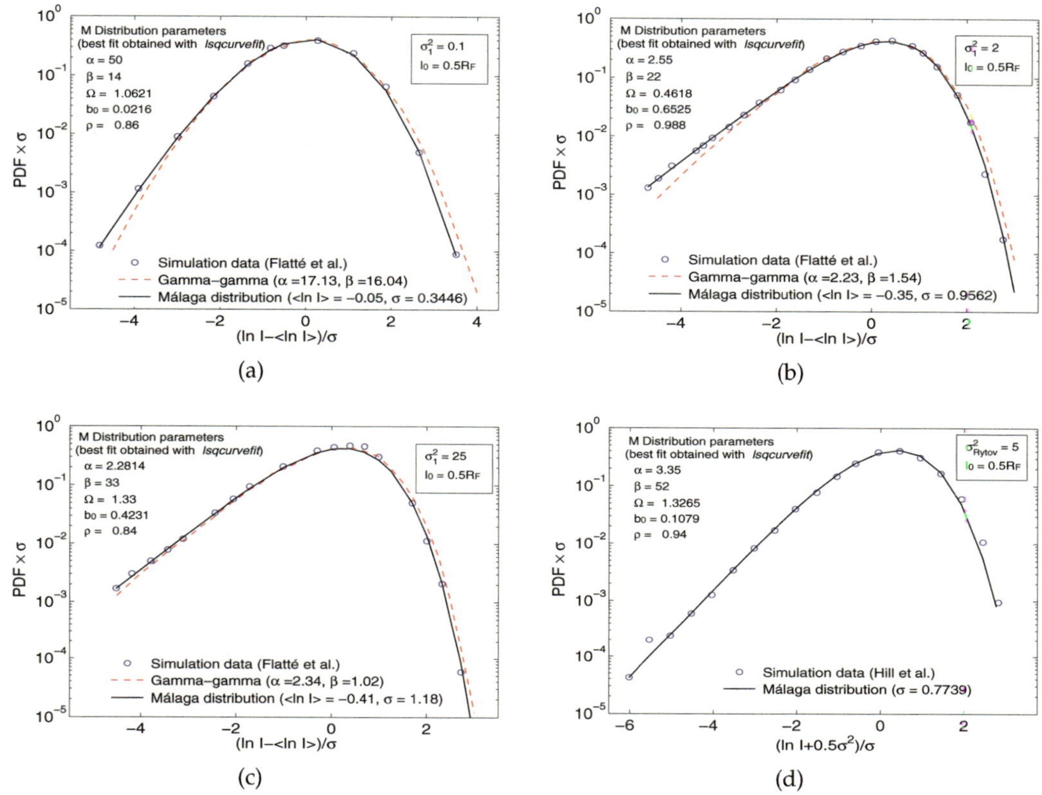

Fig. 3. The pdf of the scaled log-irradiance for a plane wave (Figures (a), (b) and (c)) and a spherical wave (Figure (d)) in the case of: (a) weak irradiance fluctuations ($\sigma_1^2 = 0.1$ and $l_0/R_F = 0.5$); (b) moderate irradiance fluctuations ($\sigma_1^2 = 2$ and $l_0/R_F = 0.5$); (c) strong irradiance fluctuations ($\sigma_1^2 = 25$ and $l_0/R_F = 0.5$); and (d) strong irradiance fluctuations ($\sigma_{Rytov}^2 = 5$ and $l_0/R_F = 0.5$). The blue open circles represent simulation data, the dashed red line is from the gamma-gamma pdf with α and β predicted in (Flatté et al., 1994) and the solid black line is from our $\mathcal{M}$ distribution model. In all subfigures, $\phi_A - \phi_B = \pi/2$.

2001), it is defined by:

$$f(\kappa, l_0) = \exp\left(-\frac{\kappa}{\kappa_l^2}\right)\left[1 + 1.802\left(\frac{\kappa}{\kappa_l}\right) - 0.254\left(\frac{\kappa}{\kappa_l}\right)^{7/6}\right], \qquad \kappa_l = \frac{3.3}{l_0}, \tag{47}$$

where it depends only on the dimensionless variable, κl_0. The limit $\kappa l_0 \to 0$ gives the inertial-range formula for $\Phi_n(\kappa)$ because $f(0) = 1$. The quantity κ_l identifies the spatial wave number associated with the inner scale, l_0 (m) of the optical turbulence. Finally, in Eq. (46), κ_x and κ_y represent cutoff spatial frequencies that eliminate mid-range scale size effects under moderate-to-strong fluctuations. Thus, if we invoke the *modified Rytov theory* then

$$\sigma = \sqrt{\sigma_{\ln_I}^2} = \sqrt{\ln\left(\sigma_I^2 + 1\right)}, \tag{48}$$

where σ_I^2 is the scintillation index. From these expressions, σ is obtained and for its calculated magnitude, the other scaling parameter, $< \ln I >$, required in the plots were directly extracted from the Figure 1 in (Flatté et al., 1994). Now, with Eq. (48) we can calculate the set of parameters $(\alpha, \beta, \gamma, \rho, \Omega')$ with the constraint imposed by Eq. (27), and taking into account that we had imposed β parameter will be a natural number. Such set of parameters were obtained by running the function *lsqcurvefit* in MATLAB (Mathworks, 2011) in order to solve this nonlinear data-fitting problem. The $\mathcal{M}$ pdf curves in Figs 3 (a)-(c) provide excellent fits with the simulation data, even better than the provided by the gamma-gamma model, for all conditions of turbulence, from weak irradiance fluctuations far into the saturation regime. In particular, in Fig. 3 (a), (b) and (c) we use the simulation values $\sigma_1^2 = 0.1$, $l_0 = 0.5R_F$, $\sigma_1^2 = 2$, $l_0 = 0.5R_F$ and $\sigma_1^2 = 25$, $l_0 = 0.5R_F$ and the predicted σ from Andrews's work (Eq. (48)) is found to be $\sigma = 0.3427$, $\sigma = 0.9332$ and $\sigma = 1.0192$. The obtained values from the $\mathcal{M}$ distribution produce a "best fitting" curve with a calculated σ of: $\sigma = 0.3446$, $\sigma = 0.9562$ and $\sigma = 1.18$, respectively. Only the value obtained for $\sigma_1^2 = 25$, $l_0 = 0.5R_F$ is a bit higher than the one predicted by Andrews's work so his developments can be used as a good starting-point to obtain the set of parameters of the $\mathcal{M}$ distribution.
Finally, in Fig. 3 (d) we have obtained a very good fitting to the simulation data for a spherical wave in the case of strong irradiance fluctuations. Following Hill's representation (Hill & Frehlich, 1997), the simulation pdf data and pdf values predicted by the $\mathcal{M}$ distribution are displayed as a function of $(\ln I + 0.5\sigma^2)/\sigma$, where σ was defined in Eq. (48). In this particular case of propagating a spherical wave, various additional parameters are needed: first, the Rytov parameter, σ^2_{Rytov}, defined as the weak fluctuation scintillation index in the presence of a finite inner scale. Thus: $\sigma^2_{Rytov}=\beta_0^2\tilde{\sigma}^2(l_0/R_F)$, as indicated in (Al-Habash et al., 2001; Andrews et al., 2001), where the quantity β_0^2 is the second additional parameter used in the analysis of the numerical simulation data for a spherical wave. Concretely, this latter parameter is the classic Rytov scintillation index of a spherical wave in the limit of weak scintillation and a Kolmogorov spectrum, defined by: $\beta_0^2 = 0.4\sigma_1^2 = 0.496C_n^2k^{7/6}L^{11/6}$.
For the particular case displayed in Fig. 3 (d), the gamma-gamma pdf does not fit with the simulation data and, even more, the Beckmann pdf did not lend itself directly to numerical calculations and so are omitted. Nevertheless, the $\mathcal{M}$ pdf shows very good agreement with the data once again, with the advantage of a simple functional form, emphasized by the fact that its β parameter is a natural number, which leads to a closed-form representation.

6. Concluding remarks

In this chapter, a novel statistical model for atmospheric optical scintillation is presented. Unlike other models, our proposal appears to be applicable for plane and spherical waves under all conditions of turbulence from weak to super strong in the saturation regime. The proposed model unifies in a closed-form expression the existing models suggested in the bibliography for atmospheric optical communications. In addition to the mathematical expressions and developments, we have introduced a different perturbational propagation model, indicated in Fig. 1, that gives a physical sense to such existing models. Hence, the received optical intensity is due to three different contributions: first, a LOS component, second, a coupled-to-LOS scattering component, as a great novelty in the model, that includes the fraction of power traveling very closed to the line of sight, and eventually suffering from almost the same random refractive index variations than the LOS component; and third, the scattering component affected by refractive index fluctuations completely different to the other two components. The first two components are governed by a gamma distribution whereas the scattering component is depending on a circular Gaussian complex random variable. All of them let us model the amplitude of the irradiance (small-scale fluctuations), while the multiplicative perturbation that represents the large-scale fluctuations, X, and depending of the log-amplitude scintillation, χ, is approximated for a gamma distribution.

Therefore, we have derived some of the distribution models most frequently employed in the bibliography by properly choosing the magnitudes of the parameters involving the generalized $\mathcal{M}^{(G)}$ model (or, directly, $\mathcal{M}$, if β is a natural number). Then, the Rice-Nakagami distribution is obtained when U_L becomes a constant random variable while the coupled-to-LOS scattering is eliminated. As indicated in (Strohbehn, 1978), it is straightforward to obtain a lognormal distribution from this model. If we now eliminate the two components representing the scattering power, U_S^C and U_S^G, and taking again U_L as a constant, then the gamma model is derived.

To obtain the K distribution function, both the LOS component and the coupled-to-LOS scattering component must be eliminated from the model. If the effective number of discrete scatterers is unbounded then the K distribution tends to the negative exponential distribution as the gamma distribution that governs the large-scale fluctuations approaches a delta function.

To generate the gamma-gamma model, we must eliminate U_S^G. Then, this model is obtained when the LOS component and the coupled-to-LOS scattering component take part in the propagation model, i.e., the scattering contribution is, in fact, connected to the line of sight.

To close the fourth section of this chapter, we have taken the lognormal-Rician pdf as the model that provides the best fit to experimental data (Andrews et al., 2001; Churnside & Clifford, 1987). To derive such model from the $\mathcal{M}$ distribution presented in this chapter, we have suggested the gamma-Rician pdf obtained in this current work as a reasonable alternative to the LR pdf for a number of reasons. First, the gamma distribution itself has often been proposed as an approximation to the lognormal model. It is desirable to use the gamma distribution as an approximation to the lognormal pdf because of its simple functional form, which leads to a closed-form representation of the gamma-Rician pdf given by Eq. (43). This makes computations extremely easy in comparison with LR pdf. Second, parameter value α is directly related to calculated values of large-scale scintillation that depend only on values of atmospheric parameters. Third, and perhaps most important, the cumulative distribution function (cdf) for the $\mathcal{M}^{(G)}$ and the $\mathcal{M}$ pdf's can also be found in closed form, as was shown in Eqs. (28), (29). For practical purposes, it is the cdf that is of greater interest than the pdf since the former is used to predict probabilities of detection and fade in an optical communication or radar system.

Hence, knowing the physical and/or meteorological parameters of a particular link, it is at the discretion of researchers to determine, to choose or to switch among the different statistical natures offered by the closed-form analytical model presented in this work. So, in conclusion, the $\mathcal{M}$ distribution model unifies most of the proposed statistical model for the irradiance fluctuations derived in the bibliography,

Finally, we have made a number of comparisons with published plane wave and spherical wave simulation data over a wide range of turbulence conditions (weak to strong) that includes inner scale effects. The $\mathcal{M}$ distribution model is intentionally restricted to have its β parameter as a natural number for the sake of a simpler analytical tractability. The $\mathcal{M}$ distribution model is found to provide an excellent fit to the simulation data in all cases tested.

Again, we must remark that all the results shown in section 5 are obtained with β being a natural number so that the number of terms in the summation included in Eq. (24) is finite (limited, precisely, by β). This feature provides a more remarkable analytical tractability to the proposed $\mathcal{M}$ distribution that, in addition, was already written in a closed form expression.

7. Appendix A: proof of lemma 1

Starting with the pdf of the generalized distribution, $\mathcal{M}^{(G)}$, written in Eq. (22), we can proceed as follows: first, the confluent hypergeometric function of the first kind employed in Eq. (20) can be expanded by its series representation:

$$ {}_1F_1\left(a;c;z\right) = \sum_{k=1}^{\infty} \frac{(a)_{k-1}}{(c)_{k-1}} \frac{z^{k-1}}{(k-1)!}, \qquad |z| < \infty; \tag{49} $$

as indicated in (Andrews, 1998), where $(a)_k$ represents the Pochhammer symbol. Then, Eq. (20) can be expressed as:

$$ f_Y\left(y\right) = \frac{1}{\gamma}\left(\frac{\gamma\beta}{\gamma\beta+\Omega'}\right)^{\beta} \exp\left(-\frac{y}{\gamma}\right) \sum_{k=1}^{\infty} \frac{(\beta)_{k-1}}{[(k-1)!]^2} \frac{y^{k-1}\left(\Omega'\right)^{k-1}}{\gamma^{k-1}\left(\Omega'+\gamma\beta\right)^{k-1}}. \tag{50} $$

To obtain the unconditional generalized distribution, $\mathcal{M}^{(G)}$, and from Eqs. (21) and (50), we can form:

$$ \begin{aligned} f_I(I) = \int_0^{\infty} f_Y(I|x) f_X(x) \mathrm{d}x = \frac{1}{\gamma}\frac{\alpha^{\alpha}}{\Gamma\left(\alpha\right)}\left(\frac{\gamma\beta}{\gamma\beta+\Omega'}\right)^{\beta} \\ \sum_{k=1}^{\infty} \frac{(\beta)_{k-1}}{[(k-1)!]^2} \frac{I^{k-1}\left(\Omega'\right)^{k-1}}{\gamma^{k-1}\left(\Omega'+\gamma\beta\right)^{k-1}} \int_0^{\infty} x^{\alpha-1-k} \exp\left(-\frac{I}{\gamma x}-\alpha x\right) dx, \end{aligned} \tag{51} $$

having integrated term by term as the radius of convergence of Eq. (50) is infinity. Now, using Eq. (3.471-9) of Ref. (Gradshteyn & Ryzhik, 2000),

$$ \int_0^{\infty} x^{\nu-1} \exp\left(-\frac{\beta}{x}-\gamma x\right) dx = 2\left(\frac{\beta}{\gamma}\right)^{\frac{\nu}{2}} K_{\nu}\left(2\sqrt{\beta\gamma}\right), \tag{52} $$

and substituting it into Eq. (51), we obtain:

$$ f_I\left(I\right) = \frac{1}{\gamma}\frac{\alpha^{\alpha}}{\Gamma\left(\alpha\right)}\left(\frac{\gamma\beta}{\gamma\beta+\Omega'}\right)^{\beta} \sum_{k=1}^{\infty} \frac{(\beta)_{k-1}}{[(k-1)!]^2} \frac{I^{k-1}\left(\Omega'\right)^{k-1}}{\gamma^{k-1}\left(\Omega'+\gamma\beta\right)^{k-1}} 2\left(\frac{I}{\alpha\gamma}\right)^{\frac{\alpha-k}{2}} K_{\alpha-k}\left(2\sqrt{\frac{\alpha I}{\gamma}}\right). \tag{53} $$

Finally, Eq. (53) can be rewritten as:

$$ f_I\left(I\right) = A^{(G)} \sum_{k=1}^{\infty} a_k^{(G)} I^{\frac{\alpha+k}{2}-1} K_{\alpha-k}\left(2\sqrt{\frac{\alpha I}{\gamma}}\right), \tag{54} $$

where

$$\begin{cases} A^{(G)} \triangleq \dfrac{2\alpha^{\frac{\alpha}{2}}}{\gamma^{1+\frac{\alpha}{2}}\Gamma(\alpha)}\left(\dfrac{\gamma\beta}{\gamma\beta+\Omega'}\right)^{\beta}; \\ a_k^{(G)} \triangleq \dfrac{(\beta)_{k-1}(\alpha\gamma)^{\frac{k}{2}}}{[(k-1)!]^2\gamma^{k-1}(\Omega'+\gamma\beta)^{k-1}}; \end{cases} \tag{55}$$

as was already indicated in Eqs. (22) and (23).

In reference of the $\mathcal{M}(\alpha,\beta,\gamma,\rho,\Omega')$ distribution, where the β parameter represents a natural number, the way to prove the lemma is something different. In this respect, we can obtain the Laplace transform, $\mathcal{L}[f_Y(y);s]$, of the shadowed Rice single pdf, $f_Y(y)$, written in Eq. (20), in a direct way, with the help of Eq. (7) of Ref. (Abdi et al., 2003), since the moment generating function (MGF) and the Laplace transform of the pdf $f_Y(y)$ are related by $M[f_Y(y);-s]=\mathcal{L}[f_Y(y);s]$:

$$\mathcal{L}[f_Y(y);s]=\left(\frac{\gamma\beta}{\gamma\beta+\Omega'}\right)^{\beta}\frac{(1+\gamma s)^{\beta-1}}{\left(\frac{\gamma\beta}{\gamma\beta+\Omega'}+\gamma s\right)^{\beta}}=\frac{1}{\gamma}\left(\frac{\gamma\beta}{\gamma\beta+\Omega'}\right)^{\beta}\frac{\left(\frac{1}{\gamma}+s\right)^{\beta-1}}{\left(\frac{\beta}{\gamma\beta+\Omega'}+s\right)^{\beta}}. \tag{56}$$

Now, let us consider the following Laplace-transform pair

$$\Gamma(\nu+1)(s-\lambda)^n(s-\mu)^{-\nu-1}\Leftrightarrow n!t^{\nu-n}e^{\mu t}L_n^{\nu-n}[(\lambda-\mu)t], \qquad \mathrm{Re}(\nu)>n-1; \tag{57}$$

given in (Elderlyi, 1954), Eq. (4) in pp. 238, where the minor error in the sign of the argument of the Laguerre polynomial found and corrected in (Paris, 2010) has already taken into account. If we denote $\lambda=-\frac{1}{\gamma}$, $\mu=-\frac{\beta}{\gamma\beta+\Omega'}$, $n=\beta-1$ and $\nu=\beta-1$, then

$$(\beta-1)!\left(s+\frac{1}{\gamma}\right)^{\beta-1}\left(s+\frac{\beta}{\gamma\beta+\Omega'}\right)^{-\beta}\Leftrightarrow(\beta-1)!e^{-\frac{\beta}{\gamma\beta+\Omega'}t}L_{\beta-1}\left[\frac{-\Omega'}{\gamma\beta+\Omega'}\frac{t}{\gamma}\right], \tag{58}$$

where $L_n[\cdot]$ is the Laguerre polynomial of order n. If we substitute Eq. (58) into Eq. (56), then the pdf of Y can be expressed as:

$$f_Y(y)=\frac{1}{\gamma}\left(\frac{\gamma\beta}{\gamma\beta+\Omega'}\right)^{\beta}\exp\left(-\frac{\beta}{\gamma\beta+\Omega'}y\right)L_{\beta-1}\left[\frac{-\Omega' y}{(\gamma\beta+\Omega')\gamma}\right]. \tag{59}$$

Now, to obtain the unconditional $\mathcal{M}$ distribution, from Eqs. (21) and (59), we can form:

$$\begin{aligned} f_I(I) &= \int_0^\infty f_Y(I|x)f_X(x)\mathrm{d}x = \\ &= \frac{\alpha^\alpha}{\gamma\Gamma(\alpha)}\left(\frac{\gamma\beta}{\gamma\beta+\Omega'}\right)^{\beta}\int_0^\infty\frac{1}{x}\exp\left(-\frac{\beta}{\gamma\beta+\Omega'}\frac{I}{x}\right)L_{\beta-1}\left[\frac{-\Omega'}{\gamma\beta+\Omega'}\frac{I}{\gamma x}\right]x^{\alpha-1}\exp(-\alpha x)\,dx. \end{aligned} \tag{60}$$

By expressing the Laguerre polynomial in a series,

$$L_n[x]=\sum_{k=0}^{n}(-1)^k\binom{n}{k}\frac{x^k}{k!}, \tag{61}$$

as was shown in Eq. (8.970-1) of Ref. (Gradshteyn & Ryzhik, 2000), it follows that Eq. (60) becomes

$$f_I(I) = \frac{\alpha^\alpha}{\Gamma(\alpha)}\frac{1}{\gamma}\left(\frac{\gamma\beta}{\gamma\beta+\Omega'}\right)^\beta \sum_{k=1}^{\beta}(-1)^{k-1}\binom{\beta-1}{k-1}\frac{1}{(k-1)!}\left(\frac{-\Omega'}{\gamma\beta+\Omega'}\frac{1}{\gamma}\right)^{k-1} I^{k-1} \\ \cdot\int_0^\infty \exp\left(-\frac{\beta}{\gamma\beta+\Omega'}\frac{I}{x}\right)x^{\alpha-1-k}\exp(-\alpha x)\,dx. \tag{62}$$

Now, we denote by G_k the integral:

$$G_k = \int_0^\infty x^{\alpha-1-k}\exp\left(-\frac{\beta}{\gamma\beta+\Omega'}\frac{I}{x}-\alpha x\right)dx. \tag{63}$$

Again, using Eq. (52), we can solve G_k:

$$G_k = 2\left(\frac{\beta}{\alpha(\gamma\beta+\Omega')}\right)^{\frac{\alpha-k}{2}} I^{\frac{\alpha-k}{2}} K_{\alpha-k}\left(2\sqrt{\frac{\beta I}{\gamma\beta+\Omega'}\alpha}\right). \tag{64}$$

Employing this latter result and inserting it into Eq. (62), we find the pdf of I in the form:

$$f_I(I) = A^{(G)}\left(\frac{\gamma\beta}{\gamma\beta+\Omega'}\right)^{\frac{\alpha}{2}} \sum_{k=1}^{\beta} a_k I^{\frac{\alpha+k}{2}-1} K_{\alpha-k}\left(2\sqrt{\frac{\alpha\beta I}{\gamma\beta+\Omega'}}\right), \tag{65}$$

where, again, we can identify $A^{(G)}$ and a_k parameters as the ones given by Eq. (25). □

8. Appendix B: proof of lemma 2

As indicated in Eq. (18), the observed irradiance, I, of our proposed propagation model can be expressed as: $I = XY$, where the pdf of variables X and Y were written in Eqs. (21) and (20), respectively. Based on assumptions of statistical independence for the underlying random processes, X and Y, then:

$$m_k(I) = E\left[X^k\right]E\left[Y^k\right] = m_k(X)\,m_k(Y). \tag{66}$$

From Eq. (2.23) of Ref. (Simon & Alouini, 2005), the moment of a Nakagami-m pdf is given by:

$$m_k(X) = \frac{\Gamma(\alpha+k)}{\Gamma(\alpha)\alpha^k}; \tag{67}$$

and, from Eq. (2.69) of Ref. (Simon & Alouini, 2005), the moment of the Rician-shadowed distribution is given by:

$$m_k(Y) = \left(\frac{\gamma\beta}{\gamma\beta+\Omega'}\right)^\beta \gamma^k\Gamma(k+1)\,{}_2F_1\left(k+1,\beta;1;\frac{\Omega'}{\gamma\beta+\Omega'}\right). \tag{68}$$

When performing the product of Eq. (67) by Eq. (68), we finally obtain the centered moments for the generalized distribution, $\mathcal{M}^{(G)}$, as was written in Eq. (26).

On the other hand, in reference to the $\mathcal{M}(\alpha, \beta, \gamma, \rho, \Omega^{'})$ distribution, where the β parameter is restricted to be a natural number for this particular case, we can proceed as follows: from Eq. (59), we can obtain the moment of the Rician-shadowed distribution, given by:

$$
\begin{aligned}
m_k(Y) &= \frac{1}{\gamma}\left(\frac{\gamma\beta}{\gamma\beta+\Omega^{'}}\right)^{\beta}\int_0^{\infty} y^k \exp\left(-\frac{\beta y}{\gamma\beta+\Omega^{'}}\right) L_{\beta-1}\left[\frac{-\Omega^{'} y}{\gamma\left(\gamma\beta+\Omega^{'}\right)}\right] dy \\
&= \frac{1}{\gamma}\left(\frac{\gamma\beta}{\gamma\beta+\Omega^{'}}\right)^{\beta}\sum_{r=0}^{\beta-1}\binom{\beta-1}{r}\frac{1}{r!}\left(\frac{\Omega^{'}}{\gamma\left(\gamma\beta+\Omega^{'}\right)}\right)^{r}\int_0^{\infty} y^{k+r}\exp\left(-\frac{\beta y}{\gamma\beta+\Omega^{'}}\right) dy.
\end{aligned}
\tag{69}
$$

Now, from Eq. (3.381-4) of Ref. (Gradshteyn & Ryzhik, 2000),

$$
\int_0^{\infty} x^{\nu-1}\exp(-\mu x)dx = \frac{1}{\mu^{\nu}}\Gamma(\nu), \qquad [\mathrm{Re}(\mu) > 0, \quad \mathrm{Re}(\nu) > 0], \tag{70}
$$

we can express Eq. (69) as:

$$
m_k(Y) = \frac{1}{\gamma}\left(\frac{\gamma\beta}{\gamma\beta+\Omega^{'}}\right)^{\beta}\sum_{r=0}^{\beta-1}\binom{\beta-1}{r}\frac{1}{r!}\left(\frac{\Omega^{'}}{\gamma\left(\gamma\beta+\Omega^{'}\right)}\right)^{r}\frac{\Gamma(k+r+1)}{\left(\frac{\beta}{\gamma\beta+\Omega^{'}}\right)^{k+r+1}}. \tag{71}
$$

Finally, when performing the product of Eq. (67) by Eq. (71), we certainly obtain Eq. (27). □

9. Appendix C: proof of lemma 3

For both cases, when I follows a generalized distribution, $\mathcal{M}^{(G)}$, or directly an $\mathcal{M}$ distribution if its β parameter is a natural number, then we need to solve the same integral. Thus, from Eq. (6.592.2) of Ref. (Gradshteyn & Ryzhik, 2000),

$$
\begin{aligned}
&\int_0^1 x^{\lambda}(1-x)^{\mu-1}K_{\nu}\left(a\sqrt{x}\right)dx = \\
&2^{-\nu-1}a^{-\nu}\frac{\Gamma(\nu)\Gamma(\mu)\Gamma\left(\lambda+1-\frac{1}{2}\nu\right)}{\Gamma\left(\lambda+1+\mu-\frac{1}{2}\nu\right)}\,{}_1F_2\left(\lambda+1-\frac{1}{2}\nu;1-\nu,\lambda+1+\mu-\frac{1}{2}\nu;\frac{a^2}{4}\right)+ \\
&+2^{-1-\nu}a^{\nu}\frac{\Gamma(-\nu)\Gamma\left(\lambda+1+\frac{1}{2}\nu\right)\Gamma(\mu)}{\Gamma\left(\lambda+1+\mu+\frac{1}{2}\nu\right)}\,{}_1F_2\left(\lambda+1+\frac{1}{2}\nu;1+\nu,\lambda+1+\mu+\frac{1}{2}\nu;\frac{a^2}{4}\right), \\
&\qquad\qquad \mathrm{Re}(\lambda) > -1+\frac{1}{2}|\mathrm{Re}(\nu)|, \qquad \mathrm{Re}(\mu) > 0;
\end{aligned}
\tag{72}
$$

and by making the following change of variables: $x' = I_T \cdot x$, then $dx' = I_T dx$; and identifying $\mu = 1$, $\lambda = (\alpha+k)/2$, $\nu = \alpha - k$, where $a = 2\sqrt{\alpha/(\gamma I_T)}$ and $a = 2\sqrt{\alpha\beta/([\gamma\beta+\Omega^{'}]I_T)}$ for the $\mathcal{M}^{(G)}$ and the $\mathcal{M}$ distribution, respectively; thus, the cdf associated with the $\mathcal{M}^{(G)}$ and the $\mathcal{M}$ distribution is readily found to be the expressions indicated in Eqs. (28) and (29). □

10. Acknowledgment

This work was fully supported by the Spanish Ministerio de Ciencia e Innovación, Project TEC2008-06598.

11. References

Abdi, A. & Kaveh, M. (1998). K Distribution: an appropriate substitute for Rayleigh-lognormal distribution in fading-shadowing wireless channels. *IEE Electronics Letters*, Vol. 34, No. 9, (April 1998), pp. 851–852, ISSN 0013-5194.

Abdi, A.; Lau, W.C.; Alouini, M.-S. & Kaveh, M.A. (2003). A new simple model for land mobile satellite channels: first- and second-order statistics. *IEEE Transactions on Wireless Communications*, Vol. 2, No. 3 (May 2003), pp. 519–528, ISSN 1536-1276.

Al-Habash, M.A.; Andrews, L.C. & Phillips, R.L. (2001). Mathematical model for the irradiance probability density function of a laser beam propagating through turbulent media. *Optical Engineering*, Vol. 40, No. 8 (August 2001), pp. 1554–1562, ISSN 0091-3286.

Andrews, L.C. & Phillips, R.L. (1985). I-K distribution as a universal propagation model of laser beams in atmospheric turbulence. *Journal of the Optical Society of America A*, Vol. 2, No. 2 (February 1985), pp. 160–163, ISSN 0740-3232.

Andrews, L.C. & Phillips, R.L. (1986). Mathematical genesis of the I-K distribution for random optical fields. *Journal of the Optical Society of America A*, Vol. 3, No. 11 (November 1986), pp. 1912–1919, ISSN 0740-3232.

Andrews, L.C. (1998) *Special Functions of Mathematics for Engineers* (2nd edition), SPIE - The International Society for Optical Engineering, ISBN 0819426164, Bellingham, Washington, USA.

Andrews, L. C. & Phillips, R. L. (1998). *Laser Beam Propagation Through Random Media*, SPIE - The International Society for Optical Engineering, ISBN 081942787x, Bellingham, Washington, USA.

Andrews, L.C.; Phillips, R.L.; Hopen, C.Y. & Al-Habash, M.A. (1999). Theory of optical scintillation. *Journal of the Optical Society of America A*, Vol. 16, No. 6 (June 1999), pp. 1417–1429, ISSN 0740-3232

Andrews, L. C.; Phillips, R. L. & Hopen, C. Y. (2001). *Laser Beam Scintillation with Applications*, SPIE - The International Society for Optical Engineering, ISBN 0-8194-4103-1, Bellingham, Washington, USA.

Andrews, L.C. & Phillips, R.L. (2008). Recent results on optical scintillation in the presence of beam wander. *Proceedings of SPIE, Conference on Atmospheric Propagation of Electromagnetic Waves II*, Vol. 6878, pp. 1–14, ISBN 978-0-8194-7053-9, San Jose, CA, January 2008, SPIE-int Soc. Optical Engineering, Bellingham, Washington, USA.

Charalambides, C.A. (2005). *Combinatorial Methods in Discrete Distributions*, John Wiley & Sons, ISBN 978-0-471-68027-7, Wiley, West Sussex, UK.

Clark, J.R. & Karp, S. (1970) Approximations for lognormally fading optical signals. *Proc. of the IEEE*, Vol 58, No. 12 (December 1970), pp. 1964–1965, ISSN 0018-9219.

Clifford, S.F.; Ochs, G.R. & Lawrence, R.S. (1974). Saturation of optical scintillation by strong turbulence. *Journal of the Optical Society of America*, Vol. 64, No. 2 (February 1974), pp. 148–154, ISSN 0030-3941.

Churnside, J. H. & Clifford, S.F. (1987). Log-normal Rician probability-density function of optical scintillations in the turbulent atmosphere. *Journal of the Optical Society of America A*, Vol. 4, No. 10 (October 1987), pp. 1923–1930, ISSN 1084-7529.

Churnside, J. H. & Hill, R.J. (1987). Probability density of irradiance scintillations for strong path-integrated refractive turbulence. *Journal of the Optical Society of America A*, Vol. 4, No. 4 (April 1987), pp. 727–733, ISSN 1084-7529.

Churnside, J. H. & Frehlich, R. G. (1989) Experimental evaluation of lognormally modulated Rician and IK models of optical scintillation in the atmosphere. *Journal of the Optical Society of America A*, Vol. 6, No. 1 (November 1989), pp. 1760–1766, ISSN 1084-7529.

Elderlyi, A. (1954). *Table of Integral Transforms, Vol. I*, McGraw-Hill, New York, USA.

Fante, R. L. (1975). Electromagnetic Beam Propagation in Turbulent Media. *Proceedings of the IEEE*, Vol. 63, No. 12 (December 1975), pp. 1669–1692, ISSN 0018-9219.

Flatté, S.M.; Bracher, C. & Wang, G.-Y. (1994). Probability-density functions of irradiance for waves in atmospheric turbulence calculated by numerical simulation. *Journal of the Optical Society of America A*, Vol. 11, No. 7 (July 1994), pp. 2080–2092, ISSN 0740-3232.

Fried, D.L. (1967). Aperture Averaging of Scintillation. *Journal of the Optical Society of America*, Vol. 57, No. 2 (February 1967), pp. 169–175, ISSN 0030-3941.

Gradshteyn, I. S. & Ryzhik, I.M. (2000). *Table of Integrals, Series and Products* (6th edition), Academic Press, ISBN 0-12-294757-6, New York, USA.

Heidbreder, G. R. (1967). Multiple scattering and the method of Rytov. *Journal of the Optical Society of America*, Vol. 57, No. 12 (December 1967), pp. 1477–1479, ISSN 0030-3941.

Hill, R. J. & Clifford, S. F. (1981). Theory of saturation of optical scintillation by strong turbulence for arbitrary refractive-index spectra. *Journal of the Optical Society of America*, Vol. 71, No. 6 (June 1981), pp. 675–686, ISSN 0030-3941.

Hill, R. J. (1982). Theory of saturation of optical scintillation by strong turbulence: plane-wave variance and covariance and spherical-wave covariance. *Journal of the Optical Society of America*, Vol. 72, No. 2 (February 1982), pp. 212–222, ISSN 0030-3941.

Hill, R. J. & Frehlich, R. G. (1997). Probability distribution of irradiance for the onset of strong scintillation. *Journal of the Optical Society of America A*, Vol. 14, No. 7 (July 1997), pp. 1530–1540, ISSN 0740-3232.

Jakerman, E. (1980). On the statistics of K-distributed noise. *Journal of Physics A*, Vol. 13, No. 1 (January 1980), pp. 31–48, ISSN 0305-4470.

Juarez, J. C.; Dwivedi, A.; Hammons, A. R.; Jones, S. D.; Weerackody, V. & Nichols, R.A. (2006). Free-Space Optical Communications for Next-Generation Military Networks. *IEEE Communications Magazine*, Vol. 44, No. 11 (Nov. 2006), pp. 46–51, ISSN 0163-6804.

Jurado-Navas, A. & Puerta-Notario, A. (2009). Generation of Correlated Scintillations on Atmospheric Optical Communications. *Journal of Optical Communications and Networking*, Vol. 1, No. 5 (October 2009), pp. 452–462, ISSN 1943-0620.

Jurado-Navas, A.; Garrido-Balsells, J.M..; Castillo-Vázquez, M. & Puerta-Notario A. (2009). Numerical Model for the Temporal Broadening of Optical Pulses Propagating through Weak Atmospheric Turbulence. *OSA Optics Letters*, Vol. 34, No. 23 (December 2009), pp. 3662 – 3664, ISSN 0146-9592.

Jurado-Navas, A.; Garrido-Balsells, J.M..; Castillo-Vázquez, M. & Puerta-Notario A. (2010). An Efficient Rate-Adaptive Transmission Technique using Shortened Pulses for Atmospheric Optical Communications. *OSA Optics Express*, Vol. 18, No. 16 (August 2010), pp. 17346–17363, ISSN 1094-4087.

Kennedy, R.S. (1970). Communication through optical scattering channels: an introduction. *Proceedings of the IEEE* Vol. 58, No. 10 (October 1970), pp. 1651–1665 ISSN 0018-9219.

MathWorks. R2010b Documentation → Optimization Toolbox: lsqcurvefit, In: *Mathworks: accelerating the pace of engineering and science*, February 2011, Available from http://www.mathworks.com/help/toolbox/optim/ug/lsqcurvefit.html

Paris, J.F. (2010). Closed-form expressions for Rician shadowed cumulative distribution function. *Electronics Letters*, Vol 46, No. 13 (June 2010), pp. 952 –953, ISSN 0013-5194.

Phillips, R.L. & Andrews, L.C. (1982). Universal statistical model for irradiance fluctuations in a turbulent medium. *Journal of the Optical Society of America*, Vol. 72, No. 7 (July 1982), pp. 864–870, ISSN 0030-3941.

Simon, M.K. & Alouini, M.S. (2005). *Digital Communications over Fading Channels*, (2nd edition), Wiley-Interscience, ISBN 0-471-64953-8, New Jersey, USA.

Strohbehn, J. W. (1978). Modern theories in the propagation of optical waves in a turbulent medium, In: *Laser Beam Propagation in the Atmosphere*, J.W. Strohbehn ed., pp. 45–106, Springer-Verlag, ISBN ,3-540-08812-1 New York, USA.

Wang, T. & Strohbehn, J.W. (1974). Perturbed log-normal distribution of irradiance fluctuations. *Journal of the Optical Society of America*, Vol. 64, No. 7 (July 1974), pp. 994–999, ISSN 0030-3941.

de Wolf, D. A. (1965). Wave propagation through quasi-optical irregularities. *Journal of the Optical Society of America*, Vol. 55, No. 7 (July 1965), pp. 812–817, ISSN 0030-3941.

de Wolf, D. A. (1974). Waves in turbulent air: a phenomenological model. *Proceedings of the IEEE*, Vol. 62, No. 11 (November 1974), pp. 1523–1529, ISSN 0018-9219.

Zhu, X. & Kahn, J.M. (2002). Free-space Optical Communication through Atmospheric Turbulence Channels. *IEEE Transactions on Communications*, Vol. 50, No.8, (August 2002), pp. 1293-1300, ISSN 0090-6778.

9

Numerical Simulation of Lasing Dynamics in Choresteric Liquid Crystal Based on ADE-FDTD Method

Tatsunosuke Matsui
Mie University
Japan

1. Introduction

Liquid crystals (LCs) are categorized in one class of condensed materials which show both character of liquids and solids (crystals). Liquid-like fluidic character of LCs allows them to show dynamic response to external stimuli such as electrical, optical and magnetic fields. Anisotropic characters of LCs like crystals show determines the way how they respond to external stimuli and also how they appear (de Gennes & Prost, 1995). These characteristics are widely utilized in LC display devices. LCs are further categorized in subgroups (phases) in terms of their degrees of order (orientational and positional) as shown in Fig. 1.

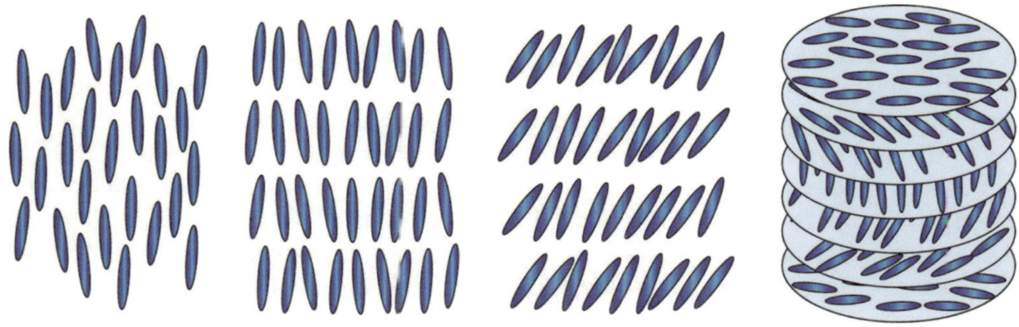

Fig. 1. Schematics of several liquid crystal phases.

Cholesteric liquid crystal (CLC) is one of these sub-phases of LCs and the self-organized formation of periodic helical structure is the most significant characters of this phase from the viewpoint of device application. In case the pitch of the helix of CLCs is in the range of the wavelength of visible light, they selectively reflect part of incident light in a certain manner determined by their refractive index and the sense of helix. Figure 2 shows the simulated transmission and reflection spectra of right-handed-circularly-polarized light normally incident on CLC. Transmission/reflection band (stop band) can be recognized. The central frequency and the bandwidth of the band are dependent on both refractive indices and pitch of helix of CLC.

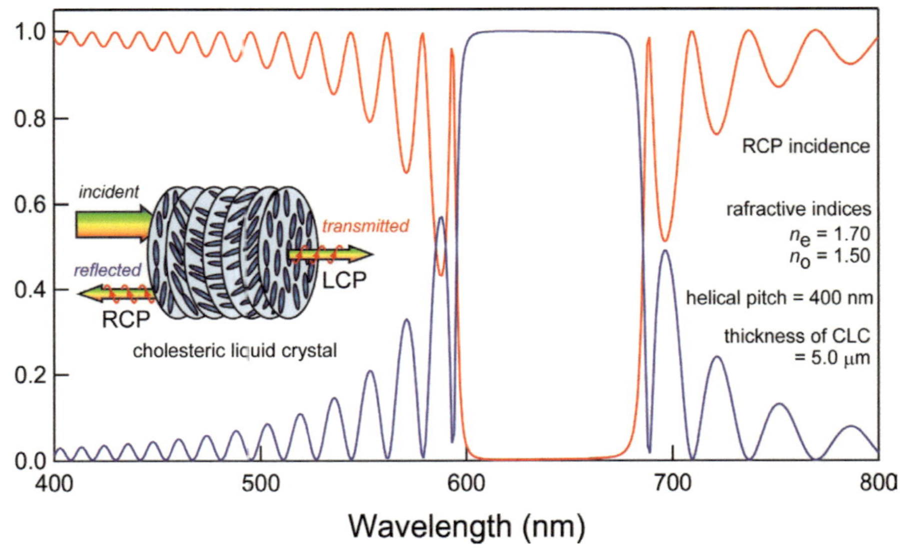

Fig. 2. Transmission and reflection spectra simulated by Berreman's 4 × 4 transfer matrix method. Right-handed circularly polarized light is supposed to normally incident on 5 μm-thick CLC with 400 nm-pitch right-handed helix. Extraordinary and ordinary refractive indices are 1.70 and 1.50, respectively. (Inset) schematic representation of selective reflection by CLC with right-handed helix. As an incident light, linearly or randomly polarized and in the photonic band wavelength is assumed.

So many studies have been made to utilize this so-called "selective reflection" character of CLC to make the reflection type display, or in other words, electronic paper. Recently, CLCs are also extensively studied as a photonic band gap (PBG) material or photonic crystal (PC). In 1987, Yablonovitch (Yablonovitch, 1987) and John (John, 1987) put forward the basic concept of PBG and since then so many studies have been carried out. Electromagnetic (EM) wave (photons) propagating in PCs composed of periodic stacking of dielectric materials with different dielectric permittivity behaves just like de Broglie wave (electrons) travelling in periodic Coulomb potential in crystals. Long dwell time of photon at PBG edge energy allows strong light-matter interaction and low threshold lasing may be obtained in such PBG system with optical gain introduced (Dowling et al, 1994). Introducing defect states in PC can induce photon localization in PC (Joannopoulos et al., 1995).

Periodic helical structure of CLC can also work as PBG material. In 1998, Kopp and his coworkers succeeded in obtaining band-edge lasing from dye-doped CLC (Kopp et al., 1998). Since their pioneering work, numerous studies have been carried out from the viewpoint of academic interest and technical applications (Coles & Morris, 2010). The introduction of various types of defects has also been attempted in CLC as schematically summarized in Fig. 3. Yang and his coworkers showed, based on numerical analysis, that introduction of isotropic thin layer as a defect in the middle of CLC layer (Fig. 3 (a)) creates the defect state (narrow transmission band) in the stop band, which can be tuned via altering thickness or refractive index of the defect layer (Yang et al., 1999). Kopp and Genack have numerically demonstrated that twist-defect, discontinuous phase shift of the helical twist of CLC molecules (Fig. 3 (b)), could indeed function as a defect (Kopp & Genack, 2002). This type of defect is unique in CLC with optical anisotropy. Lasing from twist-defect has been experimentally attained utilizing photopolymerized CLC polymer films (Ozaki et al., 2003; Schmidtke et al., 2003). It has been also shown that introducing defect can contribute to reduce lasing threshold. Other types of defects have also been introduced. It has been numerically shown that local modulation of helical pitch of CLC as schematically shown in Fig. 3 (c) can also introduce defect states in the stop band (Matsui et al., 2004). Multi-layer of CLCs with different helical pitch as shown in Fig. 3 (d) has been experimentally realized, which have been successful to achieve reduced lasing threshold (Ozaki et al., 2006; Takanishi et al., 2007).

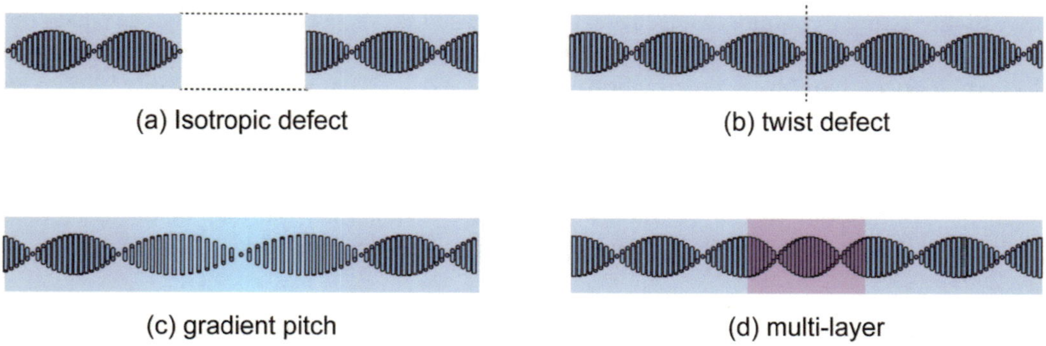

Fig. 3. Schematic representations of proposed defects in CLC PCs. (a) isotropic defect (b) twist defect (c) locally modulated pitch (d) multi-layer system.

Refining device architecture may realize further lowering of the lasing threshold, which motivated us to develop numerical simulation technique for the development of the more efficient laser device architectures. We have recently reported on numerical simulation of lasing dynamics in CLCs (Matsui & Kitaguchi, 2010). We have employed an auxiliary differential equation finite-difference time-domain (ADE-FDTD) method, which was first applied to the analysis of random lasing in one-dimensional (1D) random system (Jiang & Soukoulis, 2000). We have successfully reproduced circularly-polarized lasing in CLC at the energy of the edge of the stop band. Moreover, as will be discussed later, we have also shown that our computational scheme can also be utilized to search for more efficient device architecture with reduced lasing threshold. Here we will summarize the computational procedure of ADE-FDTD method for the analysis of lasing dynamics in CLC and show that this technique is quite useful for the analysis of EM field dynamics in and out of CLC laser cavity under lasing condition, which might contribute to the deep understanding of the underlying physical mechanism of lasing dynamics in CLC.

2. Numerical simulations

In this section, numerical simulation techniques employed in this study (1) ADE-FDTD method for the analysis of lasing dynamics and (2) Berreman's 4×4 transfer matrix method for the analysis of transmission and reflection spectra are summarized. As will be discussed, ADE-FDTD approach enables us to analyze lasing dynamics in CLC from various viewpoints such as time-dependent EM fields, Fourier-transformed emission spectra and snapshots of spatial-distributions of EM fields. Berreman's 4×4 transfer matrix method is traditionally employed to simulate transmission and reflection spectra in rather simpler way.

2.1 ADE-FDTD based numerical simulation of lasing dynamics

In this subsection, overview of ADE-FDTD approaches for the analysis of lasing dynamics in various types of micro- and nano-laser systems made so far will be given first, and then detailed numerical procedure will be given.

2.1.1 Overview of ADE-FDTD approach for the analysis of lasing dynamics in micro- and nano-photonics systems

FDTD has been widely utilized to numerically simulate the propagation and/or localization of EM waves in micro- and nano-photonic media (Taflove & Hagness, 2005). In order to investigate lasing dynamics, ADE-FDTD approaches have also been developed, in which the FDTD method is usually coupled with the rate equation in a four-level energy structure and the equation of motion of polarization (Nagra & York, 1998) as schematically shown in Fig. 4. As discussed above, Jiang and Soukoulis have employed ADE-FDTD method for the analysis of random lasing in 1D random system (Jiang & Soukoulis, 2000). Numerous groups have followed them to investigate lasing dynamics in various kinds of laser cavities such as 2D random media (Vanneste & Sebbah, 2001), PCs (Bermel et al., 2006; Shi & Prather, 2007), and distributed Bragg reflectors (Chang & Taflove, 2004; Redding et al., 2008).

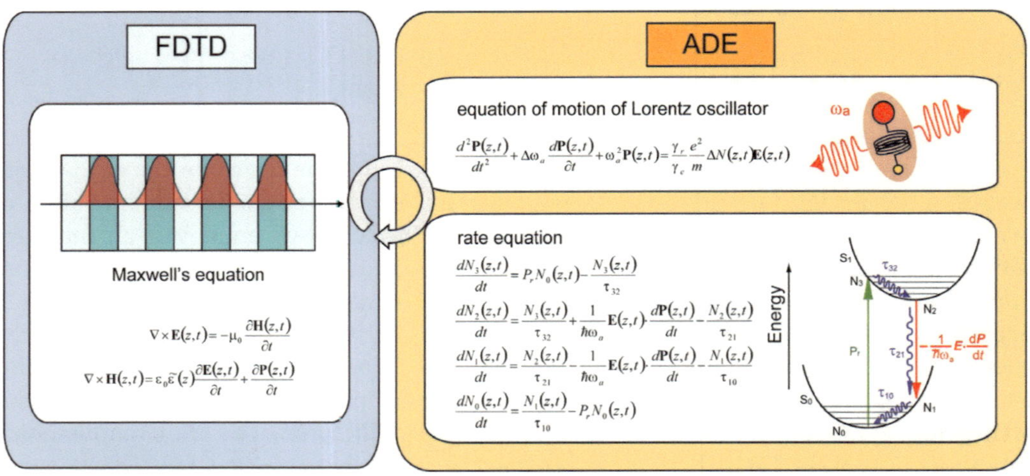

Fig. 4. Schematic representation of ADE-FDTD simulation scheme.

2.1.2 ADE-FDTD method for the analysis of lasing dynamics in CLCs

Here numerical procedures for the ADE-FDTD analysis of lasing dynamics will be given. Here we deal with a 1D system, where the time-dependent EM field propagating along the z-axis is simulated using Yee's FDTD algorithm (Yee, 1966) to solve the following Maxwell's equations:

$$\nabla \times \mathbf{E}(z,t) = -\mu_0 \frac{\partial \mathbf{H}(z,t)}{\partial t} \tag{1}$$

$$\nabla \times \mathbf{H}(z,t) = \varepsilon_0 \varepsilon(z) \frac{\partial \mathbf{E}(z,t)}{\partial t} + \frac{\partial \mathbf{P}(z,t)}{\partial t} \tag{2}$$

where ε_0 and μ_0 are the dielectric permittivity and the magnetic permeability in vacuum, respectively. $\varepsilon(z)$ is dielectric permittivity of the medium and should be tensor for LCs and will be given later. $\mathbf{P}(z, t)$ is the polarization density, which provides a gain mechanism in the laser system. On the basis of the classical electron oscillator (Lorentz) model, one can obtain the following equation of motion of $\mathbf{P}(z, t)$ in the presence of an electric field

$$\frac{d^2\mathbf{P}(z,t)}{dt^2}+\Delta\omega_a\frac{d\mathbf{P}(z,t)}{\partial t}+\omega_a^2\mathbf{P}(z,t)=\frac{\gamma_r}{\gamma_c}\frac{e^2}{m}\Delta N(z,t)\mathbf{E}(z,t) \tag{3}$$

where $\Delta\omega_a = 1/\tau_{21} + 2/T_2$ is the full width at half-maximum (FWHM) linewidth of the atomic transition. T_2 is the mean time between dephasing events and ω_a (= $2\pi c/\lambda_a$) is the central frequency of emission. $\Delta N(z, t)$ (= $N_1(z, t) - N_2(z, t)$) is the difference between electron numbers at levels 1 and 2 (Fig. 4), $\gamma_r = 1/\tau_{21}$ and $\gamma_c = (e^2/m)[\omega_a^2/(6\pi\varepsilon_0 c^3)]$ is the classical rate, e is the electron charge, m is the electron mass and c is the speed of light in vacuum.
The electron numbers at each energy level, $N_0(z, t)$, $N_1(z, t)$, $N_2(z, t)$ and $N_3(z, t)$ obey the following rate equations.

$$\frac{dN_3(z,t)}{dt}=P_rN_0(z,t)-\frac{N_3(z,t)}{\tau_{32}} \tag{4}$$

$$\frac{dN_2(z,t)}{dt}=\frac{N_3(z,t)}{\tau_{32}}+\frac{1}{\hbar\omega_a}\mathbf{E}(z,t)\cdot\frac{d\mathbf{P}(z,t)}{dt}-\frac{N_2(z,t)}{\tau_{21}} \tag{5}$$

$$\frac{dN_1(z,t)}{dt}=\frac{N_2(z,t)}{\tau_{21}}-\frac{1}{\hbar\omega_a}\mathbf{E}(z,t)\cdot\frac{d\mathbf{P}(z,t)}{dt}-\frac{N_1(z,t)}{\tau_{10}} \tag{6}$$

$$\frac{dN_0(z,t)}{dt}=\frac{N_1(z,t)}{\tau_{10}}-P_rN_0(z,t) \tag{7}$$

where τ_{32}, τ_{21}, and τ_{10}, are the lifetimes at each energy levels, and P_r is the pumping rate of electrons from ground state (level 0) to upper energy level (level 3) and is a controlled variable that should be tuned by the pumping intensity in the real experiment. By coupling these equations (1) - (7), numerical simulation of lasing dynamics can be made as schematically shown in Fig. 4. Flow chart of ADE-FDTD algorithm for the analysis of lasing dynamics is summarized in Fig. 5.
In order to deal with anisotropic medium like LC, dielectric permittivity should be represented as tensor. Assuming that LC molecules are uniaxial with optical major axis (director) along y-axis and that extraordinary and ordinary refractive indices of LCs are n_e and n_o, respectively, then the dielectric tensor of LCs should be represented as

$$\tilde{\varepsilon}(z)=\begin{bmatrix}\varepsilon_{xx}(z) & \varepsilon_{xy}(z) & \varepsilon_{xz}(z)\\ \varepsilon_{yx}(z) & \varepsilon_{yy}(z) & \varepsilon_{yz}(z)\\ \varepsilon_{zx}(z) & \varepsilon_{zy}(z) & \varepsilon_{zz}(z)\end{bmatrix}=\mathbf{R}[-\theta(z)]\begin{bmatrix}n_o^2 & 0 & 0\\ 0 & n_e^2 & 0\\ 0 & 0 & n_o^2\end{bmatrix}\mathbf{R}[\theta(z)] \tag{8}$$

where $\mathbf{R}[\theta(z)]$ is a rotation matrix about the z-axis and should be expressed as follows,

$$\mathbf{R}\left[\theta(z)\right]=\begin{bmatrix}\cos\theta(z) & -\sin\theta(z) & 0\\ \sin\theta(z) & \cos\theta(z) & 0\\ 0 & 0 & 1\end{bmatrix} \tag{9}$$

where $\theta(z)$ is the rotated angle from y-axis. By changing $\theta(z)$ gradually as a linear function of z, modeling CLC with a helix can be made. Introduction of various types defects as summarized in Fig. 3 can be easily made by modulating this $\theta(z)$ appropriately.

In order to excite the system, a short seed pulse should be launched. E_x and E_y fields are monitored at a point in the glass until the system reaches a steady state. By Fourier-transforming time domain signals, emission spectra can be analyzed in frequency domain.

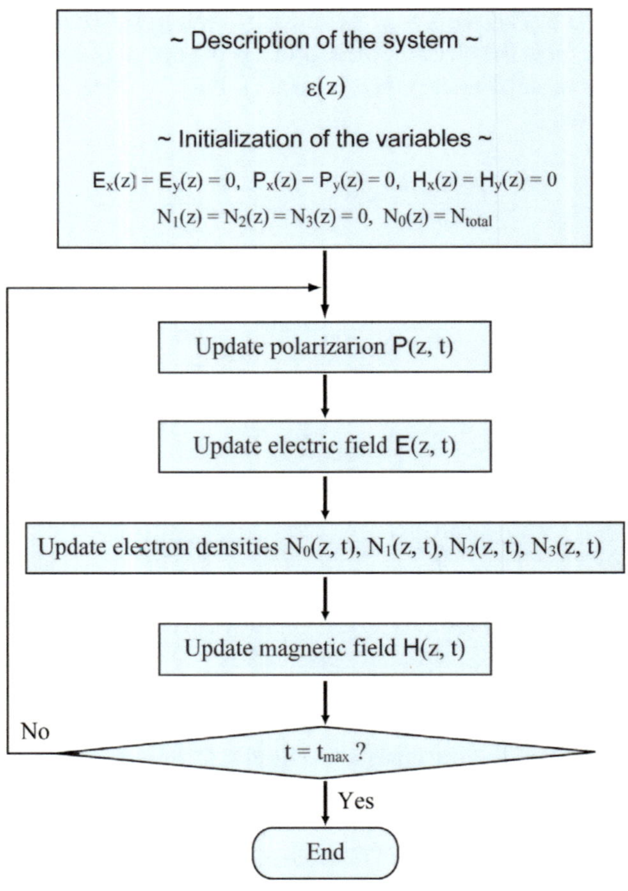

Fig. 5. Flow chart of ADE-FDTD algorithm for the analysis of lasing dynamics.

2.2 Berreman's 4 × 4 matrix for the analysis of transmission and reflection spectra of CLCs

Berreman's 4 × 4 transfer matrix has been widely utilized for the numerical analyses of the optical transmission and reflection spectra in CLC with helical structure (Berreman, 1970). EM fields propagating along the z-axis with frequency ω are given by

$$\frac{d\mathbf{\Psi}(z)}{dz} = \frac{i\omega}{c}\mathbf{D}(z)\mathbf{\Psi}(z) \tag{10}$$

where $\mathbf{\Psi}(z) = [E_x(z), H_y(z), E_y(z), H_x(z)]^T$ and $\mathbf{D}(z)$ is a derivative propagation matrix which should be expressed as follows,

$$\mathbf{D}(z) = \begin{bmatrix} -\frac{\varepsilon_{zx}(z)}{\varepsilon_{zz}(z)}\frac{ck}{\omega} & 1-\frac{1}{\varepsilon_{zz}(z)}\left(\frac{ck}{\omega}\right)^2 & -\frac{\varepsilon_{zy}(z)}{\varepsilon_{zz}(z)}\frac{ck}{\omega} & 0 \\ \varepsilon_{xx}(z)-\frac{\varepsilon_{xz}(z)\varepsilon_{zx}(z)}{\varepsilon_{zz}(z)} & -\frac{\varepsilon_{xz}(z)}{\varepsilon_{zz}(z)}\frac{ck}{\omega} & \varepsilon_{xy}(z)-\frac{\varepsilon_{xz}(z)\varepsilon_{zy}(z)}{\varepsilon_{zz}(z)} & 0 \\ 0 & 0 & 0 & -1 \\ \frac{\varepsilon_{yz}(z)\varepsilon_{zx}(z)}{\varepsilon_{zz}(z)}-\varepsilon_{yx}(z) & -\frac{\varepsilon_{yz}(z)}{\varepsilon_{zz}(z)}\frac{ck}{\omega} & \left(\frac{ck}{\omega}\right)^2-\varepsilon_{yy}(z)+\frac{\varepsilon_{yz}(z)\varepsilon_{zy}(z)}{\varepsilon_{zz}(z)} & 0 \end{bmatrix} \tag{11}$$

where c is the speed of light in vacuum, k and ω are wave number and frequency of light, respectively. ε_{ij} ($i, j = x, y$ or z) are dielectric permittivity of LC.

3. Results and discussion

In this chapter, our results will be given. In Fig. 6, one of the analyzed CLC laser system with twist defect is schematically represented as an example. A CLC layer is sandwiched between two glass substrates. Physical parameters used in our simulation such as thickness of CLC t_{CLC} and glass substrates t_g, extraordinary and ordinary refractive indices of LCs n_e, n_o, refractive index of the glass substrate n_g, the helical pitch of CLC p are summarized in Table. 1.

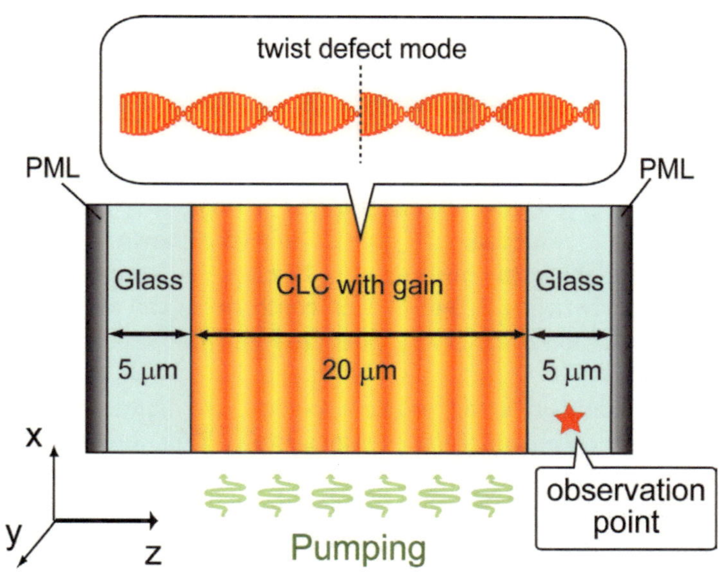

Fig. 6. Schematic representation of CLC laser cavity system with twist-defect at the middle of CLC layer.

Here we assume that a gain material with a four-level energy structure is introduced in the CLC. The lifetimes at each energy levels, τ_{32}, τ_{21}, and τ_{10}, are chosen to be similar to those of laser dyes such as coumarine or rhodamine. The total electron density at each point $N_{total} = N_0(z, t) + N_1(z, t) + N_2(z, t) + N_3(z, t)$ should be a constant, and initially, all of them are assumed to be at the ground state, namely, $N_0(z, 0) = N_{total}$ and $N_1(z, 0) = N_2(z, 0) = N_3(z, 0) = 0$. These values are also given in Table. 1.

In order to model an open system, appropriate absorbing boundary conditions should be employed. We have employed perfectly matched layer (PML) (Berenger, 1994). The space increment Δx and the time increment Δt are chosen to be 10 nm, 0.02 fs, respectively.

thickness of CLC: t_{CLC}	20 μm
thickness of glass substrates: t_g	5 μm
extraordinary refractive index of LCs: n_e	1.70
ordinary refractive index of LCs: n_o	1.50
refractive index of the glass substrate: n_g	1.50
helical pitch of CLC: p	400 nm
central wavelength of oscillation of Lorentz oscillator: λ_a	600 nm
lifetime at energy level 3: τ_{32}	1.0×10^{-13} s
lifetime at energy level 2: τ_{21}	1.0×10^{-9} s
lifetime at energy level 1: τ_{10}	1.0×10^{-11} s
total electron density: N_{total}	$5.5\times6.02\times10^{23}$

Table 1. Physical parameters of materials and dimensions of device of our model

3.1 Lasing dynamics

In Fig. 7, transient responses of electric fields and Fourier-transformed emission spectrum for the case without any defect are summarized. In Fig. 7 (a), transient responses of E_x and E_y fields monitored at a point in glass are shown. The pumping rate ($P_r = 1.0\times10^{10}$ s^{-1}) is well above the threshold for the lasing. After a short time (~ 3 ps), rapid evolution of both E_x and E_y fields are observed, and after several oscillations, they reach a steady state. In Fig. 7 (b), the steady-state responses of E_x and E_y fields are shown. A sinusoidal response, which might be due to sharp (monochromatic) lasing emission, is observed. A quarter-wavelength phase shift between E_x and E_y field components can also be recognized. This implies that lasing emission is circularly polarized and this reproduces experimentally observed results well.

Time-windowed time-domain steady-state responses are Fourier-transformed for the evaluation of the power spectrum of the emission. In Fig. 7 (c), the emission spectrum and the transmission spectrum are summarized. A sharp lasing peak appears above the threshold pumping at 600 nm which corresponds to the higher energy edge of the stop band. In Fig. 7 (d), the emission intensity at the peak wavelength (λ_a = 600 nm) is shown as a function of pumping rate P_r. The threshold pumping rate for lasing can be identified. As discussed above, this can be utilized to pursue the more efficient CLC laser device with reduced lasing threshold.

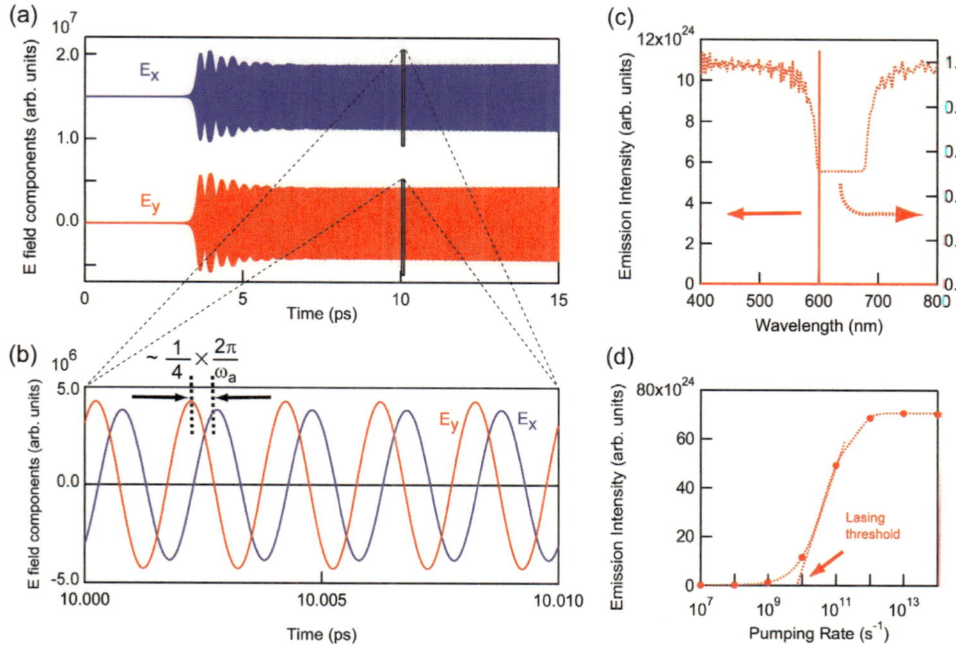

Fig. 7. (a) Transient responses of E_x and E_y field components observed at the glass. Pumping rate P_r is 1.0×10^{10} s^{-1}. (b) Steady-state response at around 10 ps. (c) Fourier-transformed emission spectrum and transmittance of CLC with 400 nm helical pitch. (d) Emission intensity at the lasing peak wavelength (λ_a = 600 nm) as a function of pumping rate P_r.

3.2 Field distribution

ADE-FDTD scheme is also suitable to visualize time-dependent spatial distribution of EM fields. This might offer further understanding of underlying physics of CLC lasers. Fig. 8 (a) shows a snapshot of field distribution of E_x and E_y field components under lasing condition ($P_r = 1.0\times10^{10}$ s^{-1} and at 10 ps). As can be seen, both E_x and E_y fields have higher amplitude in the middle of CLC layer, which implies that EM fields are more strongly confined in the middle part of CLC. In our model no gain was introduced in glass, however, both E_x and E_y fields can be seen and they have almost the same amplitude (envelope) in the whole range in the glass. They might be attributed to the laser emission emitted from CLC laser cavity.

In Fig. 8 (b), magnified snapshots of E_x and E_y fields in the glass (from 2.0 to 2.6 μm) at different timings around 10 ps are shown. It can be recognized that both E_x and E_y fields are propagating towards left, and also there is a quarter-wavelength phase shift between E_x and E_y field oscillations. These facts clearly indicate that a circularly polarized lasing emission is obtained from CLC laser cavity. On the other hand, time-dependent magnified snapshots of E_x and E_y fields in the CLC (from 15.0 to 15.6 μm) show different characteristics as shown in Fig. 8 (c). Both E_x and E_y fields do not propagate and they form a standing wave. This also manifests that CLC is working as a distributed feedback laser cavity. There is also a quarter-wavelength shift between E_x and E_y fields, which shows that a standing wave in CLC laser cavity is also circularly polarized and this might explain why circularly polarized lasing is achieved in CLC lasers. In Fig. 8 (d), the angle of oscillation of electric field in the x-y plane

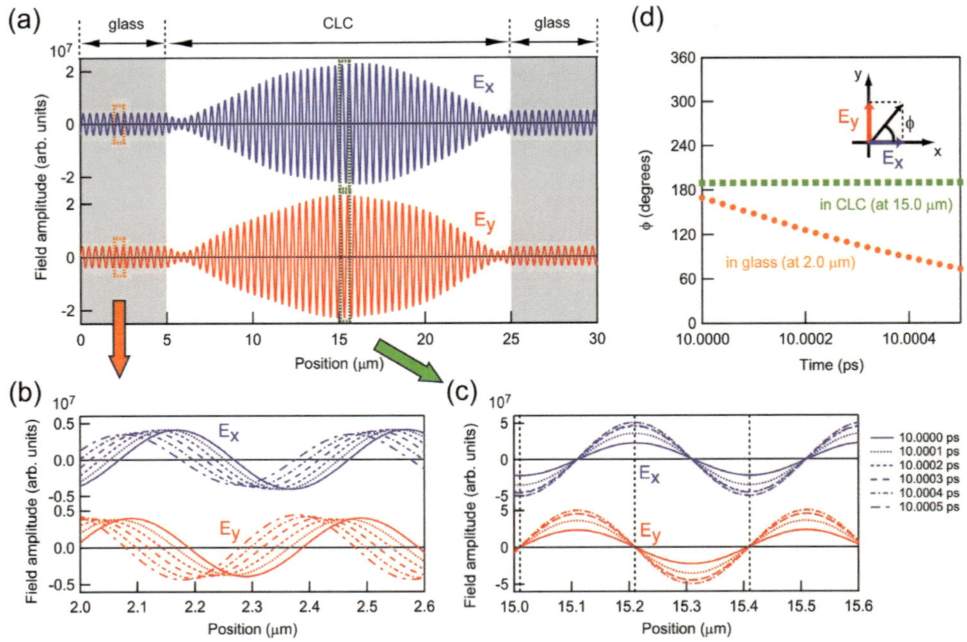

Fig. 8. (a) Spatial distribution of E_x and E_y field components in CLC and glass at 10 ps. Pumping rate P_r is 1.0×10^{10} s^{-1}. Time-dependent spatial distribution of E_x and E_y field components in (b) glass and (c) CLC at around 10 ps. (d) the angle of oscillation of electric field in x-y plane ϕ as function of time. Inset: the definition of ϕ.

$\phi(z, t)$ is shown as function of time at a point in glass (2.0 μm) and in CLC (15.0 μm). The definition of the angle $\phi(z, t)$ is schematically shown in the inset of Fig. 8 (d) and can be deduced as follows.

$$\phi(z,t) = \arctan\left[\frac{E_y(z,t)}{E_x(z,t)}\right] \tag{12}$$

In CLC, the angle $\phi(z = 15.0\ \mu m, t)$ does not change at all, which agrees well with the fact that electric field forms a standing wave in CLC. Moreover, it can also be shown that the angle is perpendicular to the director of liquid crystal molecules in the case lasing occurs at the higher edge of the stop band (data is not shown). On the other hand, the angle $\phi(z = 2.0\ \mu m, t)$ changes linearly with time, which show the angle ϕ rotates at a same rate and the value of this rate evaluated from the slope of the plot is roughly equal to the central frequency of lasing emission ω_a. This also manifests that electric fields observed in glass is lasing emission emitted from CLC laser cavity and this is circularly polarized.

3.3 Twist-defect-mode-lasing

As discussed above, introduction of various types of defects have been proposed and tested. One of these defects, twist-defect (Fig. 3 (b)), is analyzed here. Most of the conditions for the simulation are kept the same except the thickness of CLC is 10 μm here. In Fig. 9 (a) transmission and reflection spectra analyzed by Berreman's 4×4 transfer matrix are shown.

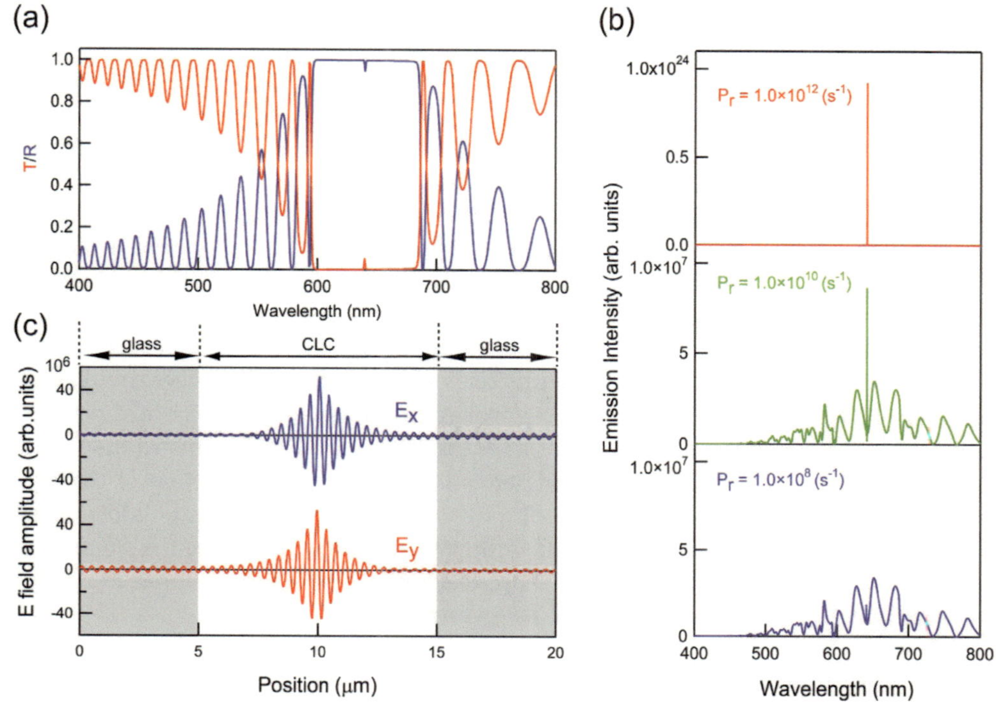

Fig. 9. (a) Transmission and reflection spectra simulated by 4 × 4 matrix method. Right-handed circularly polarized light is supposed to normally incident on 10 μm-thick CLC with 400 nm-pitch right-handed helix and with a twist-defect in the middle. Extraordinary and ordinary refractive indices are 1.70 and 1.50, respectively. (b) Fourier-transformed emission spectra at various pumping rates. Pumping rates P_r are 1.0×10^8 s^{-1}, 1.0×10^{10} s^{-1}, 1.0×10^{12} s^{-1} from bottom to top. (c) Spatial distribution of E_x and E_y field components in CLC with twist-defect in the middle and glass.

It can be recognized that a sharp transmission/reflection peak appears in the middle of the stop band at around 640 nm. In Fig. 9 (b) Fourier-transformed emission spectra at various pumping rates are summarized. In this case, the central frequency of Lorentz oscillator ω_a was set to be $2\pi c/(\lambda_a$ = 620 nm) such that band edge lasing (~ 600 nm) and twist-defect-mode lasing (~ 640 nm) can be assumed under similar pumping conditions with similar gain. Above certain threshold pumping around $P_r = 1.0\times10^{10}$ s^{-1}, sharp lasing peak appears at around 640 nm, which corresponds to the energy of introduced twist-defect state. When pumping rate is increased further, another lasing peak appears at around 600 nm which corresponds to higher energy edge of the stop band (data is not shown). These results imply that lasing at twist-defect-mode can be obtained with lowered threshold than that at the edge of the stopband and also shows that the introduction of defect is quite effective for the reduction of lasing threshold.

Fig. 9 (c) shows a snapshot of field distribution of E_x and E_y field components under lasing condition. Field distribution (envelope) in CLC with twist-defect is quite different from that without a defect (Fig. 8 (a)). Electric fields are strongly localized at the site where the twist-defect is introduced. This strong confinement of EM fields might enable strong light-matter interaction and result in lower lasing threshold.

4. Conclusions

In conclusion, we numerically investigated the lasing dynamics in CLC as a 1D chiral PBG material by the ADE-FDTD approach which couples FDTD with ADEs such as the rate equation in a four-level energy structure and the equation of motion of Lorentz oscillator. This technique enables us to analyze lasing dynamics from various viewpoints such as time-dependent emission dynamics, Fourier-transformed emission spectra and time-dependent field distributions. Band edge circularly polarized lasing was successfully reproduced above threshold pumping. Through the analysis of time-dependent EM field distributions, it is shown that circularly polarized lasing emission is obtained from CLC laser cavity. It is also shown that standing wave with quarter-wavelength phase shift between orthogonal field components is obtained in CLC, which might explain CLC works as distributed feedback laser cavity for circularly polarized lasing emission. With the introduction of twist-defect, lasing emission at defect-mode energy with lower lasing threshold was obtained. It is also shown that the field distribution in CLC with twist-defect is introduced is quite different from that without any defect. ADE-FDTD approach might be utilized to find more efficient device architecture for obtaining a lower lasing threshold.

5. Acknowledgment

The presented works have been done with one of former graduate students of our research group, Mr. Masahiro Kitaguchi.

6. References

Berenger, J.-P. (1994). A perfectly matched layer for the absorption of electromagnetic waves. *Journal of Computational Physics*, Vol.114, No.2, pp.185-200.

Bermel, P., Lidorikis, E., Fink, Y. & Joannopoulos, J. D. (2006). Active materials embedded in photonic crystals and coupled to electromagnetic radiation. *Physical Review B*, Vol.73, No.16, pp.165125-1-8.

Berreman, D. W. & Scheffer, T. J. (1970). Bragg reflection of light from single-domain cholesteric liquid-crystal films. *Physical Review Letters*, Vol.25, No.9, pp.577-581.

Chang, S.-H. & Taflove, A. (2004). Finite-difference time-domain model of lasing action in a four-level two-electron atomic system. *Optics Express*, Vol.12, No.16, pp.3827-3833.

Coles, H. & Morris, S. (2010). Liquid-crystal lasers. *Nature Photonics*, Vol.4, No.10, pp.676–685.

de Gennes, P. G. & Prost, J. (1995). *The Physics of Liquid Crystals* (2nd ed.), Oxford University Press, ISBN 9780198517856, New York.

Dowling, J. P., Scalora, M., Bloemer. M. J., Bowden, C. M. (1994). The Photonic Band-edge Laser - A New Approach to Gain Enhancement. *Journal of Applied Physics*, Vol.75, No.4, pp.1896-1899.

Jiang, X. & Soukoulis, C. M. (2000). Time Dependent Theory for Random Lasers. *Physical Review Letters*, Vol.85, No.1, pp.70-73.

Joannopoulos, J. D., Meade, R. D. & Winn, J. N. (1995). *Photonic Crystals: Molding the Flow of Light*, Princeton University Press, ISBN 0691037442, New Jersey

John, S. (1987). Strong localization of photons in certain disordered dielectric superlattices. *Physical Review Letters*, Vol.58, No.23, pp.2486-2489.

Kopp, V. I., Fan, B., Vithana, H. K. & Genack, A. Z. (1998). Low-threshold lasing at the edge of a photonic stop band in cholesteric liquid crystals. *Optics Letters*, Vol.23, No.21, pp.1707-1709.

Kopp, V. I. & Genack, A. Z. (2002). Twist defect in chiral photonic structures. *Physical Review Letters*, Vol.89, No.3, pp.033901-1-4.

Matsui, T., Ozaki, M. & Yoshino, K. (2004). Tunable photonic defect modes in a cholesteric liquid crystal induced by optical deformation of helix. *Physical Review E*, Vol.69, No.6, pp.061715-1-4.

Matsui, T. & Kitaguchi, M. (2010). Finite-Difference Time-Domain Analysis of Laser Action in Cholesteric Photonic Liquid Crystal. *Applied Physics Express*, Vol.3, No.6, pp.061701-1-3.

Nagra, A. S. & York, R. A. (1998). FDTD Analysis of Wave Propagation in Nonlinear Absorbing and Gain Media. *IEEE Transactions on Antennas and Propagation*, Vol.46, No.3, pp.334-340.

Ozaki, M., Ozaki, R., Matsui, T. & Yoshino, K. (2003). Twist-Defect-Mode Lasing in Photopolymerized Cholesteric Liquid Crystal. *Japanese Journal of Applied Physics*, Vol.42, No.5A, pp.L472-L475.

Ozaki, R., Sanda, T., Yoshida, H., Matsuhisa, Y., Ozaki, M. & Yoshino, K. (2006). Defect Mode in Cholesteric Liquid Crystal Consisting of Two Helicoidal Periodicities. *Japanese Journal of Applied Physics*, Vol.45, No.1B, pp.493-496.

Redding, B., Shi, S., Creazzo, T. & Prather, D. W. (2008). Electromagnetic modeling of active silicon nanocrystal waveguides. *Optics Express*, Vol.16, No.12, pp. 8792-8799.

Schmidtke, J., Stille, W. & Finkelmann, H. (2003). Defect mode emission of a dye doped cholesteric polymer network. *Physical Review Letters*, Vol.90, No.8, pp.083902-1-4.

Shi, S. & Prather, D. W. (2007). Lasing dynamics of a silicon photonic crystal microcavity. *Optics Express*, Vol.15, No.16, pp.10294-10302.

Takanishi, Y., Tomoe, N., Ha, N. Y., Toyooka, T., Nishimura, S., Ishikawa, K. & Takezoe, H. (2007). Defect-mode lasing from a three-layered helical cholesteric liquid crystal structure. *Japanese Journal of Applied Physics*, Vol.46, No.6A, pp.3510–3513.

Taflove, A., & Hagness, S. C. (2005). *Computational Electrodynamics: The Finite-Difference Time-Domain Method* (3rd ed.), Artech House, ISBN 1580538320, Norwood, MA.

Vanneste, C. & Sebbah, P. (2001). Selective Excitation of Localized Modes in Active Random Media. *Physical Review Letters*, Vol.87, No.18, pp.183903-1-4.

Yablonovitch, E. (1987). Inhibited spontaneous emission in solid-state physics and electronics. *Physical Review Letters*, Vol.58, No.20, pp.2059-2062.

Yang, Y.-C., Kee, C.-S., Kim, J.-E., Park., H.-Y., Lee. J.-C. & Jeon., Y.-J. (1999). Photonic defect modes of cholesteric liquid crystals. *Physical Review E*, Vol.60, No.6, pp.6852–6854.

Yee, K. S. (1966). Numerical solution of initial boundary value problems involving maxwell's equations in isotropic media. *IEEE Transactions on Antennas and Propagation*, Vol.14, No.3, pp.302-307.

10

Complete Modal Representation with Discrete Zernike Polynomials - Critical Sampling in Non Redundant Grids

Rafael Navarro[1] and Justo Arines[2]
[1]*ICMA, Consejo Superior de Investigaciones Científicas & Universidad de Zaragoza*
[2]*Universidade de Santiago de Compostela*
Spain

1. Introduction

Zernike polynomials (ZPs) form a complete orthogonal basis on a circle of unit radius. This is useful in optics, since a great majority of lenses and optical instruments have circular shape and/or circular pupil. The ZP expansion is typically used to describe either optical surfaces or distances between surfaces, such as optical path differences (OPD), wavefront phase or wave aberration. Therefore, applications include optical computing, design and optimization of optical elements, optical testing (Navarro & Moreno-Barriuso, 1999), wavefront sensing (Noll, 1978)(Cubalchini, 1979), adaptive optics (Alda & Boreman, 1993), wavefront shaping (Love, 1997) (Vargas-Martin et al., 1998), interferometry (Kim, 1982)(Fisher et al., 1993)(van Brug, 1997)(Chen & Dong, 2002), surface metrology topography (Nam & Rubinstein, 2008), corneal topography (Schwiegerling et al., 1995)(Fazekas et al., 2009), atmospheric optics (Noll, 1977) (Roggemann, 1996), etc. This brief overview shows that the modal description provided by ZPs was highly successful in a wide variety of applications. In fact, ZPs are embedded in many technologies such as optical design software, large telescopes, ophthalmology, communications , etc.
The modal representation of a function (wavefront, OPD, surface, etc.) over a circle in terms of ZPs is:

$$W(\rho,\theta) = \sum_{n,m} c_n^m Z_n^m(\rho,\theta) \tag{1}$$

where c_n^m are the coefficients of the expansion; (ρ,θ) are polar coordinates with origin at the pupil centre. The radial coordinate is normalized to the physical (real) radius of the circle $\rho = r/R$, since the ZPs are orthogonal only within a circle of unit radius. The usefulness and importance of ZPs is associated to two main properties, completeness and orthogonality (Mahajan, 2007). However, in real applications one is constrained to work with discrete (sampled) arrays of data rather than with continuous functions, and then the discrete (sampled) Zernike polynomials loose these two essential properties, namely orthogonality and completeness (Wang & Silva, 1980)(Navarro et al., 2009). For this reason different authors have proposed alternative basis functions, such as Fourier series, splines or Chebyshev-polynomials (Ares & Royo, 2006)(Soumelidis, 2005).

The estimation of the coefficients of the Zernike expansion is still an open problem, which has attracted the interest of many researchers. In particular, different studies had shown the decisive influence of the type of sampling pattern on the quality of the reconstructions (Voitsekhovich, 2001)(Diaz-Santana et al., 2005)(Pap & Shipp, 2005). For instance, orthogonal discrete ZPs were introduced for wavefront fitting (Malacara et al., 1990) (Fisher et al., 1993); random patterns provided enhanced performance (Soloviev & Vdovin, 2005); and Albrecht grids have the property of keeping the orthoganilty of ZPs (Rios et al., 1997). Nevertheless, apart of the lack of completeness and orthogonality of discrete ZPs, there is an additional issue, which affect several important applications, such as optical design (ray tracing), wavefront sensing and surface metrology. In all these applications the modal description of the wavefront is not reconstructed from wavefront samples but from (measure or computation of) wavefront slopes (Southwell, 1980) (Bará, 2003) (Liang et al., 1994) (Solomon, 1998) (Primot, 2003). The third problem arises because in order to reconstruct the wavefront, one fit the data (slopes) to the slopes, i.e. partial derivatives, of ZPs, and these partial derivatives are not orthogonal even for the ideal continuous polynomials.

In summary, there are three different problems that one has to face when implementing practical applications (either numerical or experimental): (1) Lack of completeness of ZPs; (2) Lack of orthogonality of ZPs and (3) Lack of orthogonality of ZP derivatives. To overcome these limitations, the general standard procedure is to apply a strong oversampling (redundancy) and reconstruct the wavefront by standard least squares fit. The advantage of a strong redundancy is to minimize the reconstruction noise, but it has two main disadvantages. When one reconstructs fewer modes than measures, then there is a high probability of having cross coupling and aliasing in the modal wavefront estimation (Herrmann, 1981). In addition, oversampling necesarily implies that the wavefront reconstruction is not invertible. This means that it is not possible to recover the initial measures (or samples) from the reconstructed wavefront. This complicates or can even preclude some applications involving iterative processes, inverse problems, etc.

Our goal in this work was to study these three problems and provide practical solutions, which are tested and validated through realistic numerical simulations. Our approach was to start studying and eventually solve the problem of completeness (both for ZPs and ZPs derivatives), because if we can guarantee completeness, then it is straightforward to apply Gram-Schmidt (or related method) to obtain an orthonormal basis over the sampled circular pupil (Upton et al., 2004). Furthermore, completeness in the discrete domain, means that Eq.1 can be expressed as a matrix-vector product, where the matrix is square and has an inverse. This means that we have the same number of samples and coefficients and that we should be able to pass one set to the other and viceversa. However, orthogonality becomes important, especially for large matrices, because in that case the inverse transform (matrix) is equal to its transpose, which guarantees numerical stability of matrix inversion. Our approach to guarantee completeness is based on the intuitive idea of avoiding any redundancy in the sampling pattern. This means that the coordinates of the sampling points never repeat: that is $\theta_i \neq \theta_k$ and $\rho_i \neq \rho_k \ \forall i,k$ in the sampling grid. We confirmed empirically, with different sampling patterns (regular, random and randomly perturbed regular), that these non-redundant sampling schemes keep completeness of both ZPs and ZP derivatives. This permits to work with invertible square matrices, which can be orthogonalized through the classic QR factorization. In the following Sections, we first overview the basic theory (Section 2); then we obtain the orthogonal modes for both the discrete Zernike and the Zernike derivatives transforms for different sampling patterns (Section 3); in Section 4 we describe the implementation and results of realistic computer simulations; and the main conclusions are given in Section 5.

2. Theory

Zernike polynomials are separable into radial polynomial and an angular frequency. According to the ANSI Z80.28 standard the general expression is:

$$Z_n^m(\rho,\theta) = \begin{Bmatrix} N_n^m R_n^{|m|}(\rho)\cos m\theta & \text{for} \quad m \geq 0 \\ -N_n^m R_n^{|m|}(\rho)\sin m\theta & \text{for} \quad m < 0 \end{Bmatrix} \tag{2}$$

where the radial polynomial is:

$$R_n^{|m|}(\rho) = \sum_{s=0}^{(n-|m|)/2} \frac{(-1)^s (n-s)!}{s!\left[0.5(n+|m|)-s\right]!\left[0.5(n-|m|)-s\right]!}\rho^{n-2s} \tag{3}$$

and orthonormality is guaranteed by the normalization factor N:

$$N_n^m = \sqrt{\frac{2(n+1)}{1+\delta_{m0}}} \tag{4}$$

where δ_{m0} is the Kronecker delta function. The radial order n is integer positive, and the angular frequency m can only take values $-n$, $-n + 2$, $-n + 4$, ... n. For practical implementation, sampled signals and discrete polynomials, we shall use vector-matrix formulation, and hence it is useful to merge n and m indexes into a single one $j = \left(n(n+2)+m\right)/2$ (ANSI Z80.28 standard).

2.1 Critical sampling and invertible transform

The classical problem to represent a function as an expansion such as that of Eq. 1 is to obtain the coefficients $c_n^m = c_j$. The orthogonality of ZPs implies that we can compute the coefficients as the projections (inner product) of the function W on each basis function:

$$c_n^m = \int_0^1 \int_0^{2\pi} W(\rho,\theta) Z_n^m(\rho,\theta) \rho d\theta d\rho \tag{5}$$

but this expression can be hardly applied when we only have a discrete set of samples of W, and the discrete polynomials are not orthogonal.

The discrete version of Eq. 1 is **w** = **Zc**. Now, **w** is a column vector whose components are the I samples of $W(\rho,\theta)$; **c** is another column vector formed by J expansion coefficients $c_j = c_n^m$; and **Z** is a matrix, $Z_{i,j}$, whose columns are sampled Zernike polynomials. Matrix Z is rectangular, but for a given sampling pattern, the number of coefficients (modes) has to be less or equal to the number of samples ($J \leq I$). The case $J = I$ corresponds to critical sampling. To obtain the coefficients one can solve **w** = **Zc** for **c**, but for doing that **Z** must have an inverse so that one can apply **c** = $\mathbf{Z}^{-1}$**w**. The inverse $\mathbf{Z}^{-1}$ exists only if (1) it is square (critical sampling) and (2) its determinant $Det(\mathbf{Z}) \neq 0$. In other words the rank of this IxJ matrix has to be $Rank(\mathbf{Z}) = I = J$. As we will see below, $Rank(\mathbf{Z}) < I$ for most common sampling patterns, and $\mathbf{Z}^{-1}$ does not exist. The standard way to overcome this problem is to apply a strong oversampling to the wavefront W and estimate a number of coefficients much lower than the number of samples (J<< I). Provided that, $Rank(\mathbf{Z}) \geq J$, then the coefficients can be estimated computing the Moore-Penrose pseudoinverse of $\mathbf{Z}$:

$$\hat{\mathbf{c}} = \left(\mathbf{Z}^T\mathbf{Z}\right)^{-1}\mathbf{Z}^T\mathbf{w} \tag{6}$$

This is a standard (linear) least squares fit. The tilde means estimated, since the wavefront expansion is approximated. This estimation is optimal under a least squares criterion (minimum RMS error). However it may not be exact due to mode coupling and aliasing (Herrmann, 1980) (Herrmann, 1981) and always requires a highly redundant sampling. As a consequence, Eq. 6 is not invertible, in the sense that one recovers estimates $\hat{\mathbf{w}} = \mathbf{Z}\hat{\mathbf{c}}$ rather than the true original samples $\mathbf{w}$. In Section 3 we show that non redundant patterns keep completeness of the ZPs basis, which permits to work with critical sampling, and guarantee the existence of both direct and inverse transfoms:.

$$\mathbf{w} = \mathbf{Zc} \text{ and } \mathbf{c} = \mathbf{Z}^{-1}\mathbf{w} \tag{7}$$

2.2 Critical sampling of Zernike polynomial derivatives

There is a variety of applications where the measurements (samples) are slopes or gradient of the surface (surface metrology) or wavefront (numerical ray tracing or wavefront sensing) (Wyant & Creath, 1992) (Welsh et al., 1995). In the last case, the original samples at points (ρ_i, θ_i), i = 1,… I are transverse aberrations, proportional to the wavefront slopes, components of the wavefront gradient:

$$(x'_i, y'_i) = f'/R \;\nabla W(\rho_i, \theta_i) \tag{8}$$

where R is the total pupil radius and f′ is the focal length of the lens (or microlens array) of the measuring instrument (Navarro & Moreno-Barriuso, 1999). To recover the wavefront W one has to integrate the gradient, and to this end it is convenient to apply some expansion of W in terms of some derivable basis functions. For circular pupils, Zernike polynomials (ZPs) seem an appropriate basis even though ZP derivatives are not orthogonal. In terms of ZPs derivatives, we can express the gradient of W as a column vector, and using the expansion of Eq. 1 we arrive to the expression of a normalized i-th measure vector $\mathbf{m}_i$, formed by the normalized measurements along the x and y axes:

$$\mathbf{m}_i = {R_{pup}}\Big/{f'}\begin{pmatrix} x'_i \\ y'_i \end{pmatrix} = \sum_{j=1}^{J} c^j \begin{pmatrix} Z'^{\,j}_X \\ Z'^{\,j}_Y \end{pmatrix} \tag{9a}$$

where $Z'^{\,j}_X$, $Z'^{\,j}_Y$ are the partial derivatives of the j-th ZP at point i. It is important to note that we exclude the constant piston term j = 0 since the partial derivatives are zero.For the complete set of samples in vector-matrix notation we obtain:

$$\mathbf{m} = \begin{pmatrix} \mathbf{Z}'_X \\ \mathbf{Z}'_Y \end{pmatrix}\mathbf{c} = \mathbf{Dc} \tag{9b}$$

This expression **m** = **Dc** is similar to the discrete version of Eq. 1 (**w** = **Zc**) before, but now the columns of matrix **D** are concatenated partial derivatives of ZPs. This means that **D** has double $2I$ rows. As in the preceding Subsection, the usual strategy is to apply a strong oversampling, $J << I$, and then compute the least squares solution, i.e. the pseudo inverse, so that the coefficients are estimated as $\hat{\mathbf{c}} = \left(\mathbf{D}^{\mathrm{T}}\mathbf{D}\right)^{-1}\mathbf{D}^{\mathrm{T}}\mathbf{m}$. Again, in case that we could guarantee completeness, it would be possible to apply critical sampling, so that **D** is square $J = 2I$; as before, completeness means that $Det(\mathbf{D}) \neq 0$ or equivalently $Rank(\mathbf{D}) = 2I = J$.

It is worth remarking that critical sampling in this case means to recover double number of modes than sampling points, J=2I, simply applying $\mathbf{c} = \mathbf{D}^{-1}\mathbf{m}$. This possibility is plausible since we have two measures (two partial derivatives in $\mathbf{m}_i$) at each point, provided that there is no redundancy (Navarro et al., 2011). This would be similar to the Hermite interpolation, where one has the function and its first derivative at each point and recovers J=2I coefficients. Regarding completeness, the intuitive hypothesis is that if the original basis **Z** is complete, and able to represent any continuous (derivable) function W within a circular support, then we would expect that the set formed by their derivatives **D** should provide a complete representation for the derivatives (gradient) of W. As shown in the next Section, this hypothesis was verified empirically for a variety of families of non redundant sampling patterns.

2.3 Orthogonalization

As we said above, our main empirical finding was that different types of non redundant sampling patterns on the circle keep completeness of both the discrete ZPs and discrete (sampled) derivatives. However, orthogonality is lost in both cases after sampling. One of the most important problems caused by the lack of orthogonality is a bad condition number of matrix **Z** (or **D**), which makes the inversion ($\mathbf{Z}^{-1}$ or $\mathbf{D}^{-1}$) to be numerically unstable (Navarro et al., 2011) (Zou & Rolland, 2006). The consequence is noise amplification when one tries to estimate the coefficients, using either $\mathbf{c} = \mathbf{Z}^{-1}\mathbf{w}$ or $\mathbf{c} = \mathbf{D}^{-1}\mathbf{m}$. The condition number (CN), ratio between the highest and lowest singular value of the matrix, is the main metric for the expected numerical instability, and also provides an initial prediction of the level of expected noise amplification when passing from the measures (samples) to the coefficients. The ideal value is CN = 1 since then the noise amplification factor is 1 as well; that is no amplification. Orthogonality implies that the inverse matrix equals its transpose. As matrix transpose is a trivial transform, thus for orthogonal matrices CN =1. If that is not the case, CN tends to increase with the size of the matrix. For the typical sizes used in practical applications it can take huge values (from 10^2 up to 10^5 in the cases analyzed in the next Section), which means that the numerical implementation with real data will be ineffective.

The Gram-Schmidt orthogonalization (and further enhanced versions) method permits us to decompose the initial matrix into a product **Z** = **QR** (also known as QR factorization), where **Q** is the matrix formed with the new orthonormal basis vectors, so that $\mathbf{Q}^{-1} = \mathbf{Q}^{T}$; and **R** is an upper triangular matrix passing from the **Q** to the **Z** basis. (Of course we can apply $\mathbf{D} = \mathbf{Q}_d\mathbf{R}_d$ as well). If the initial matrix was square and $Det(\mathbf{Z}) \neq 0$ (complete basis), then we can express both the **Q** direct and inverse transform (the Discrete Zernike Transform):

$$\mathbf{w} = \mathbf{Q}\mathbf{c}_{\mathrm{q}} \text{ and } \mathbf{c}_{\mathrm{q}} = \mathbf{Q}^{\mathrm{T}}\mathbf{w} \tag{10a}$$

and similarly for the Zernike derivatives:

$$\mathbf{m} = \mathbf{Q}_d\mathbf{c}_d \text{ and } \mathbf{c}_d = \mathbf{Q}_d{}^T\mathbf{m} \tag{10b}$$

Nothe that $\mathbf{Q}$ and $\mathbf{Q}_d$ are new basis, and the new coefficients will be different. To pass from former to the new basis we simply apply $\mathbf{R}$: $\mathbf{c}_q = \mathbf{Rc}$ and $\mathbf{c}_d = \mathbf{R}_d\mathbf{c}$ respectively. Also, we can pass from $\mathbf{Q}_d$ to $\mathbf{Q}$: $\mathbf{c}_d = \mathbf{R}_d\mathbf{R}^{-1}\mathbf{c}_q$ and vice versa. This is a crucial point because the condition number of matrix $\mathbf{R}$ is the same as that of the initial basis $\mathbf{Z}$. If we want to recover the original coefficients $\mathbf{c}$, then we have to invert $\mathbf{R}$: $\mathbf{c} = \mathbf{R}^{-1}\mathbf{c}_q$ and then we will have the deleterious effects of noise amplification again. In other words, orthogonalization makes sense only if the new Q basis has a clear physical meaning and the coefficients of the transform $\mathbf{c}_q$ are useful to us. In the case of $\mathbf{Z}$ and $\mathbf{Q}$, the physical meaning of $\mathbf{R}$ is to pass from the continuous to the discrete domain. When we adopt the $\mathbf{Q}$ basis we are giving up knowing the wavefront outside the sampling points. That is, we can recover the exact values of the samples from the coefficients $\mathbf{c}_q$, but we can not interpolate between them. In order to interpolate, to know the continuous wavefront, then we have to apply $\mathbf{R}^{-1}$ with the potential danger of noise amplification. In other words, we get an important gain: an exact and fully invertible transform, with a maximum number of coefficients (critical sampling), which in turns minimizes the effects of spectral overlapping and avoids noise amplification. The cost is the constraint to work within the discrete domain, without trying to reconstruct a continuous version of the wavefront. This (somehow optional) cost is fully assumable in most applications where the final interpolation is not necessary. In fact this is totally equivalent to the discrete Fourier transform (DFF) in signal processing, where one always work within the discrete domain.

In the case of the Zernike derivatives basis, the physical meaning of $\mathbf{R}_d$ is different because now, that basis change implies two transforms: passing from the continuous to the discrete domain, but also differentiating to pass from the wavefront to the derivatives. This means that the range of applications of the $\mathbf{Q}_d$ basis is lower. It can be highly useful to have a complete orthogonal basis for spot diagrams, but $\mathbf{Q}_d$ is not a particularly useful basis for wavefront sensing or applications where the main goal is to integrate.

Finally, we want to remark that the DZT basis $\mathbf{Q}$ is going to change not only with the number of samples I, but also with the sampling scheme. For each sampling scheme, we will have a different $\mathbf{Z}$ matrix and hence a different basis change operator $\mathbf{R}$ and sampling-distinctive direct $\mathbf{Q}$ and inverse $\mathbf{Q}^T$ discrete Zernike transform DZT.

3. Construction of orthogonal basis

In this Section we apply the above theory to construct the complete basis and to obtain orthogonal modes.

3.1 Complete sampling patterns

Our starting point is to analyze the rank of matrix $\mathbf{Z}$ (and $\mathbf{D}$) for different regular sampling patterns chosen among the most used in the literature (redundant) and types of non redundant patterns proposed here. The rank measures the dimension of the subspace covered by the basis functions, so that the case $Rank(\mathbf{Z}) = I$ means that the basis is complete. The rank was computed always for critical sampling (square matrix) and for different numbers of sampling points.

3.1.1 Non redundant sampling patterns: Random, perturbed and regular

Random patterns (i) were generated as follows. Each sampling point is obtained by adding a random displacement to the coordinates of the previous sampling element. These displacements have a Gaussian distribution with zero mean and standard deviation equal to the diameter of the sampling element. Non-overlapping between samples and total inclusion of the sampling element into the measured pupil were imposed. Several masks were generated and compared in terms of the condition number of the **Z** matrix obtained for each of them, in order to choose the best realization.

The perturbed regular sampling patterns (ii) were implemented by adding small random Cartesian displacements ($\varepsilon_x, \varepsilon_y$) to the sampling points of regular grids. These perturbations have a Gaussian distribution with zero mean, and their magnitude is determined by the standard deviation σ. We have performed simulations with perturbations ranging from 10^{-8} to 10^{-2} in pupil radius (R) units. To be effective we found that σ has to be equal or grater than $10^{-3} R$.

Finally, we designed regular (deterministic) non redundant sampling patterns (iii). Regular sampling patterns are commonly obtained by convolution of the function to be sampled with a Dirac comb. Let us start with the angular coordinate. To sample the interval $[0, \theta_{max}]$ with I equally spaced samples, the interval will be $\delta\theta = \theta_{max}/(I-1)$. Now, we could apply a similar sampling to ρ. If the comb is 2D (2-dimensional) we obtain a pure polar sampling, which is redundant in both coordinates. A way to avoid redundancy is to apply 1D Dirac combs to both coordinates; or in other words to make ρ proportional to θ and set $\theta_{max} = 2\pi N_C$. In this way we obtain a rolled 1D pattern, which is a spiral with N_C cycles covering a circular area with radius $\rho_{max} \propto \theta_{max}$. To completely avoid redundancy, we have to be careful with the periodicity of the angular variable, i.e. we need to guarantee that the number of samples per cycle $NSPC = 2\pi/\delta\theta$ is non integer. The difference between polar and spiral patterns is that the former is a purely 2-dimensional whereas the spiral is obtained by rolling a 1D pattern. Despite their different nature, both can adequately cover a circular domain. The linear spiral, however, has the problem that the density of samples per unit of area is high at the centre and decreases towards the edge. One way to avoid that problem is to use an array of spirals to form an helical pattern (Mayall & Vasilevskis, 1960). Here, however, the goal was to avoid redundancy, and we implemented different spirals controlling the density of samples. The general expression for the radial coordinate was $\rho(\theta) = \sqrt[p]{\theta/\theta_{max}}$, which ensures that $\rho \le 1$. For p = 2 we obtain the Fermat or parabolic spiral, in which the density of samples is nearly constant when the angle is sampled uniformly. We also tried other values of p. In particular for p = 4 the density of samples shows a quadratic increase of density towards the periphery, which improves the orthogonality, and hence the condition number for inverting the transform.

For the Fermat spiral, constant density of samples occurs, in a first approximation, when the total number of cycles is proportional to the square root of the number of samples $N_c \approx \sqrt{I/\pi}$. Usually N_c is chosen to be integer, but in some cases this could result in a redundant sampling. If that happens (see below) we add 1/2 to break periodicity: Thus, we have different cases $N_c = \text{int}\left(\sqrt{I/\pi}\right)$ or $N_c = \text{int}\left(\sqrt{I/\pi}\right) + 0.5$ where "int" means nearest integer. In terms of the number of cycles $\delta\theta = 2\pi N_c/(I-1)$. By definition, the radial coordinate ρ is never repeated, and with the additional condition that the sampling is not

periodic in 2π (i.e. the number of samples per cycle is not integer, $NSPC = 2\pi/\delta\theta = (I-1)/N_c \neq i$), then we avoid any redundancy in both radial and angular coordinates. The examples implemented here correspond to maximum orders of ZPs $n = 7$ and $n = 12$, and represent the two possible cases of N_c integer or non integer. In the first case we have $J = I = 36$; then $N_c = 3$, $\delta\theta = 0.5386$ radians and $NSPC = 11.667$. Since this is not an integer number, the sampling is non redundant. In the second example, $N = 12$ and $I = J = 91$. If we choose an integer value $N_c = 5$, $\delta\theta = 0.349$ but then we will have $NSPC = 18$ and the sampling would be periodic in θ, i.e. redundant. We can avoid that redundancy by adding 0.5 cycles so that $N_c = 5.5$, then $\delta\theta = 0.384$ radians and $NSPC = 16.36$.
Finally, the last sample of the spiral has to strictly meet the condition $\rho_I < 1$ to avoid partial occlusion of the marginal samples by the pupil. One possible criterion is to keep the area covered by this last sample equal to the average. As an approximation, here we impose the radial distance of the last sample to the pupil edge to be equal to half the width of the last cycle: $1-\rho_I = 1/2(\rho_I - \rho_{I-NSPC})$; solving for $\rho_I = 2/3 + 1/3\rho_{I-NSPC}$; and in terms of N_c: $\rho_I = 2/3 + 1/3\sqrt{(N_c-1)/N_c}$. (In the examples $\rho_{I=36} = 0.9388$ for $I = 36$ and $\rho_{I=91} = 0.9682$ respectively.) Now, the sampling grid is fully determined by $\theta_i = \delta\theta/k + (i-1)\delta\theta$ with $i = 1, 2, \ldots I$ and $\rho_i = \rho_I\sqrt{\theta_i/\theta_I}$. Therefore, given a maximum order N of Zernike polynomials, we want as many samples as Zernike modes, $I = J = 1 + N(N+3)/2$; then assign a number of cycles (first option N_c integer when $NSPC$ is non integer; or add 0.5 to avoid periodicity if $NSPC$ integer). Finally choose a value for k to have the spiral sampling completely determined.
The above computation of the number of cicles N_c and last value of ρ corresponds to the Fermat spiral, $p = 2$, but the same analysis can be applied for different spirals. We found that $p = 2$ was optimal to get homogeneous density, but $p = 4$ was optimal in terms of minimum condition number.
Figure 1 shows some of the sampling patterns analyzed here, for the case of I = 91 samples (order n = 12), hexagonal (H91), hexagonal perturbed (HR91), hexapolar (HP91), random (R91), spiral (S91) and spiral with quadratic density (SQ91). The ranks obtained for the different patterns are summarized in Table 1. Three (left) columns correspond to three standard (redundant) patterns (square, hexagonal and hexapolar), and three (right) columns to the non-redundant patterns proposed here (hexagonal perturbed, random and spirals). Only random and spiral patterns permit to set an arbitrary number of samples which provides total flexibility to match the number of samples to any (maximum) order n of Zernike polynomials. This is the reason why some rows in Table 1 are incomplete. The 2D regular patterns considered here are centred at the origin (i.e. they include the central sample) and they can only match determined orders, except for the case n=7 (I=36), where we had to remove the central sample, otherwise we had 37 samples. This Table shows that non-redundant patterns (except for the case perturbed hexapolar not included in Table) provide maximum rank (completeness), whereas regular 2D patterns yield lower ranks. Among them, square and hexagonal seem equivalent, but the hexapolar shows the lowest value for 36 samples.
In summary, the completeness of sampled Zernike polynomial basis is strongly dependent on sampling pattern. The above results support the relationship between redundancy, low efficiency of sampling and lack of completeness. Taking into account the symmetry of ZPs where radial and angular parts are separable, polar (or hexapolar) sampling schemes are expected to have the highest redundancy in the **Z** matrix, which is confirmed by the lower

values both in rank and condition number of **Z**. Non-polar sampling (square, hexagonal) has an intermediate level of redundancy, which can be improved by introducing small perturbations to the regular sampling grid. On the other hand either fully random or spiral patterns seem to guarantee completeness. The later has the advantage of being deterministic and regular. Nevertheless, completeness does not ensure an accurate inversion in practice.

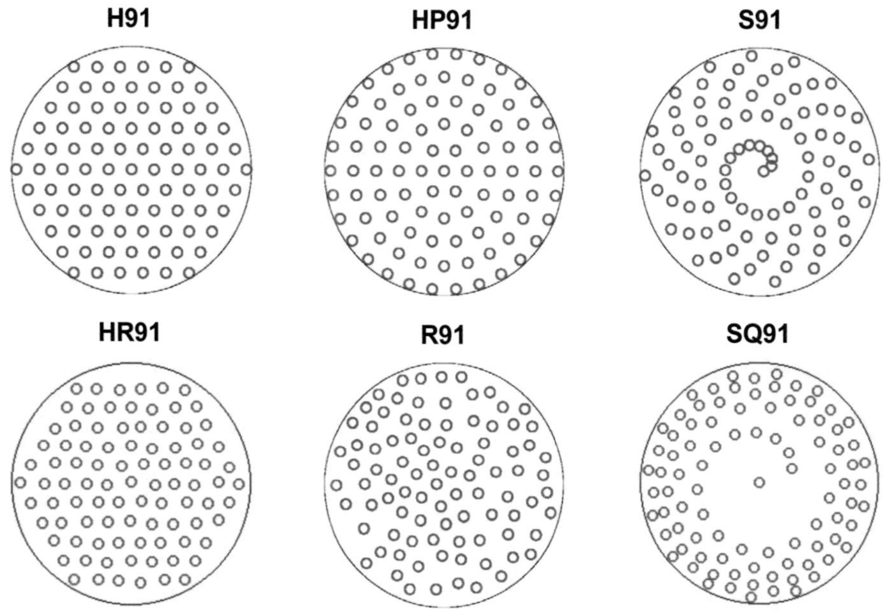

Fig. 1. Examples of sampling patterns with 91 points providing singular **Z** (hexagonal and hexapolar) and invertible (hexagonal perturbed, random and spirals).

The same non redundant sampling patterns, which guarantee completeness of the ZPs, namely random, perturbed regular, and spirals (especially Fermat and quadratic ones), do also guarantee completeness of the **D** basis (Navarro et al., 2011). In other words, the 2 sampled partial derivatives of ZPs form a complete basis for the set of measurements **m**. The size of the matrix is $2IxJ$ with $2I = J$. For the particular case of I = 91 and critical sampling, $J = 182$ and **D** is a 182x182 square matrix. The rank was always maximum, 182 for this case and for all non-redundant samplings. Surprisingly, the rank was much lower (by a factor of two approximately) and always lower than I for the rest of redundant sampling patterns: for example the rank was 89 < I for the hexagonal case. This suggests the possibility of implementing wavefront sensing with critical sampling to recover $2J$ modes of the wavefront.

	Square	Hexagonal	Hexapolar	Random	Perturbed	Spirals
I=36 (n=7)	34	34	30	36	36	36
I=91 (n=12)	-	87	88	91 (H)	91	91
I=120 (n=14)	112	-	-	120 (Sq)	120	120

Table 1. Rank of matrix **Z** for different sampling schemes (rows) and number of samples (columns). Square (Sq), Hexagonal (H).

The main limitation is that the condition number of **Z** (and **D**) strongly increases with matrix size. For I=36, CN is between 10^3 and 10^2 for the complete sampling patterns, and increases up to 10^5 for S1, 10^4 for random and keeps above 10^2 for quadratic spiral S2, all the cases with I=91. The high CN (obtained for the S1 and random sampling grids) mean that the estimation of $\mathbf{Z}^{-1}$ (or $\mathbf{D}^{-1}$) could be highly noisy, getting worse in general as the number of samples increases. In fact, when I is of the order of 10^2 or higher, matrix inversion will be numerically instable, so that completeness alone is insufficient for effective practical implementation. In this context, orthogonalization is the way to optimize CN and matrix inversion.

3.2 Orthogonal modes

In the next paragraph we analyze the resulting orthonormal basis functions after applying the QR factorization. The Zernike modes are highly significant in optics since each mode corresponds to a type of aberration: piston (n=0, m=0), tilt (n=1, m= ±1), defocus (n=1, m=0), and so on. Each mode corresponds to a Zernike polynomial defined on a continuous circle of unit radius. Sampled polynomials do not form an orthogonal basis anymore, but if we apply a complete (non redundant) critical sampling scheme and apply orthogonalization, then the resulting columns of matrix Q will be the new Zernike modes in the discrete domain (see figure 2).

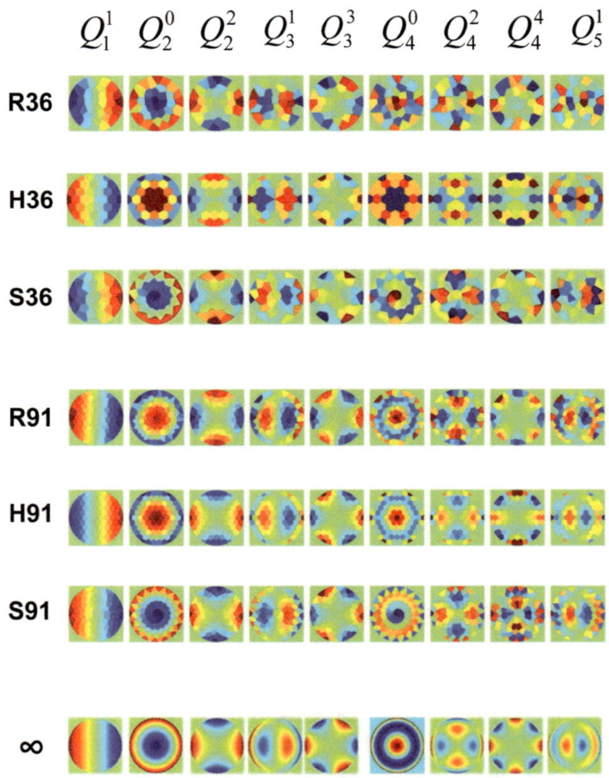

Fig. 2. a (left). Modes (m ≥ 0) of the DZT for different sampling schemes: random (R), perturbed hexagonal (H) and spiral (S). The three upper rows correspond to I = 36 samples and the three lower rows to I = 91. Bottom row represents the continuous (I = ∞) Zernike modes.

Fig. 2. b (right).

3.2.1 Discrete wavefront modes

Figure 2 compares the resulting discrete modes of the orthonormal DZT for the three types of non redundant sampling patterns: random, R, perturbed hexagonal (with perturbation $\sigma = 10^{-3}$) H and Fermat spiral, S. The three upper rows correspond to 36 ($n \leq 7$) samples, and the lower rows to 91 ($n \leq 12$) samples. The bottom row (∞ number of samples) shows the original continuous Zernike polynomials. (For the case H36 the central sample was removed, otherwise we would have 37 sampling points). On ly modes with non-negative angular frequency ($m \geq 0$) are shown up to radial order n=7. If we compare the discrete and continuous (bottom row) modes we can see clear differences. Many times we observe change of polarity (sign reversals) of different modes, depending on the sampling pattern and number of samples. For instance, tilt, $\mathbf{Q}_1^1$ shows a sign reversal for random and spiral patterns for the low sampling rate (36), but for 91 samples there are no reversals (except for the hexagonal one). In general, similarities between discrete and continuous modes increase with the number of samples (as expected). The differences tend to increase with the order of polynomials. This is patent for the highest order modes n=7 in the upper rows.

These discrete Zernike modes do change with the sampling pattern, which has physical consequences. For example, the spherical aberration of a standard (continuous) lens (Z_4^0, bottom row in Fig. 2) is different from that of a segmented mirror. If one has a mirror with 36 hexagonal facets the spherical aberration looks different: Q_4^0 for H36. The same applies for defocus, astigmatism and the rest of aberration modes. In fact, the aberration modes change both with the sampling type and the sampling rate, especially the highest orders. In other words, the **Q** basis may have a real physical meaning as wave aberration modes of segmented (or faceted) optical systems, such as compound eyes, large telescopes, lenslet arrays, spatial light modulators, etc.

3.2.2 Discrete modes of wavefront gradient

The same analysis can be applied to the partial derivatives (gradient) of the wavefront to obtain the complete orthogonal basis $\mathbf{Q}_d$. As we said before, the physical nature of the gradient modes is totally different, as the gradient is proportional to the transverse aberrations. These are the coordinates x'_i, y'_i of the impact of rays, normal to the wavefront. For this reason, $\mathbf{Q}_d$ contains the modes of the spot diagrams, which are the initial set of raw data in many optical computations (ray tracing) and measurements (wavefront sensing, etc.) Spot diagrams are essentially discrete in nature as they contain a finite number of spots. As before, we can obtain the modes for any non redundant pattern, but as we explain below, we obtained a much higher performance (lower CN) for the quadratic spiral (or spiral 2), with $p = 4$, so that the density of samples increases towards the periphery with ρ^2. Figure 3 shows the spot diagram modes for that spiral sampling and $I = 91$. The three columns represent the initial basis **D** (left); the same basis, but after normalizing the ZP derivatives (center), as an intermediate stage in the orthonormalization process, $\mathbf{D}_n$; and the final orthonormal modes, $\mathbf{Q}_d$ (right). The axis of the plots were adjusted for visualization, being an scaling factor of 10^2 between the axis used for representing **D** and those used fot $\mathbf{D}_n$ and $\mathbf{Q}_d$. The plot of the column of **D** corresponding to the pair (8,8) is incomplete, some of the impact rays were not represented because they are out of range, causing the difference in the aspect with the plot of $\mathbf{D}_n$.

4. Implementation and results of computer simulations

We implemented the above sampling patterns and basis functions and conducted different realistic computer simulations to test the possibilities of practical application.

4.1 Wavefronts

In the simulations we used ocular wavefront aberration data taken from an experimental data set used in a recent study (Arines et al., 2009). We implemented the different sampling patterns proposed so far, always with $I = 91$ samples. Two types of initial wavefronts having either 91 or 182 Zernike modes (non cero coefficients) were tested. Coefficients for higher orders were assumed to be zero. Different levels of noise (0%, 1%, 3% and 5%) were added to the initial samples. The metric used was always RMS errors (differences) or values. First of all, we compared standard least squares estimation (Eq. 6) and the inverse DZT ($\mathbf{Q}^T$) (Eq. 10a) to estimate the continuous and discrete coefficients (first and second rows in Table 2). From them, we reconstructed the wavefront (3rd and 4th rows). For the sake of simplicity, we only show results for regular (unperturbed) hexagonal (H), random (R) and spiral (S) patterns. The original RMS wavefront was 2.5 μm.

The results by standard least squares ($\mathbf{c}-\hat{\mathbf{c}}_Z$, first row,) are bad for the hexagonal pattern, even for the ideal case (left columns). The result is better for complete sampling schemes (R and S), but even then, the results are strongly affected by aliasing due to the presence of

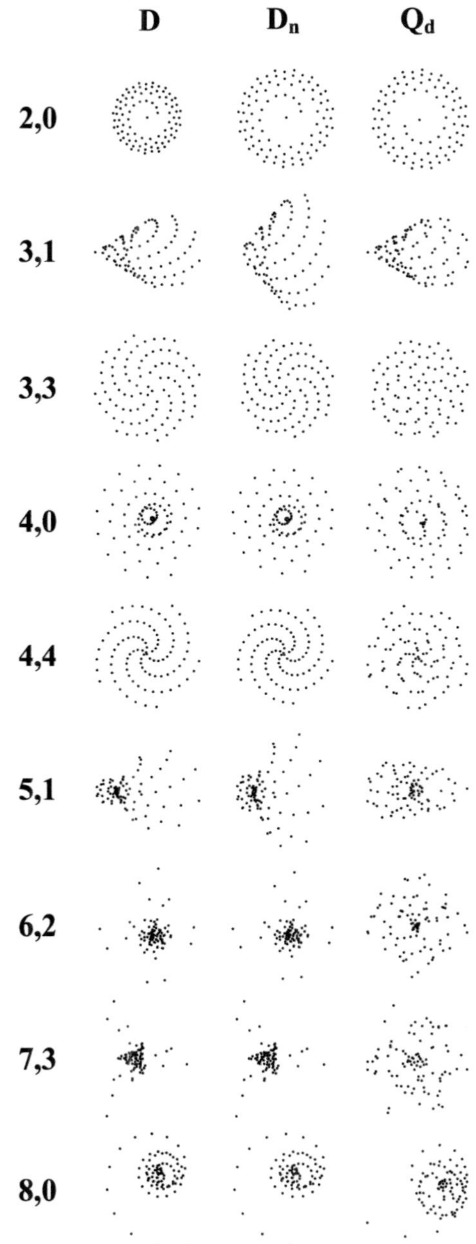

Fig. 3. Initial (**D**), normalized (**D$_n$**) and orthonormal modes (**Q$_d$**) of wavefront gradient (spot diagram) for the quadratic spiral of 91 samples. Pair numbers are the (n,m) index of ZPs.

higher order modes (i.e. undersampling; central columns). The right column shows huge errors in the presence of noise. Therefore, the standard method of Eq. 6 can not be applied with critical sampling in practice. This is the reason why standard modal estimation requires redundancy with I >> J. Using the DZT (and the non redundant schemes R and S), the results (second row in Table 2) are greatly improved (the errors are now residual, of the order of 10^{-14} μm). Note that now we applied matrix **R** to the continuous original coefficients to compute the RMS error in the discrete **Q** basis. Using the DZT, the error also increases with the presence of higher order modes and noise, but improves by one (182 modes, central columns) or three (noise, right columns) orders of magnitude compared to the standard method. If we now reconstruct the wavefront from the estimated coefficients, we observe that the standard method (third row in Table 2) is affected by both aliasing and noise, but the DZT, Q transform (bottom row in Table 2) is basically unaffected, and hence the initial measurements are recovered with high fidelity.

	91 modes; 0% noise			182 modes; 0% noise			91 modes; 3% noise		
RMS error	H	R	S	H	R	S	H	R	S
$\mathbf{c}-\hat{\mathbf{c}}_Z$	2.717	4.3x10-6	1.6x10-6	2.53	0.066	0.003	1.6x104	2.0 x103	1.2 x103
$\mathbf{Rc}-\hat{\mathbf{c}}_Q$		3.1x10-14	1.1x10-14		3.8x10-4	3.8x10-4		0.61	0.64
$\mathbf{w}-\mathbf{Z}\hat{\mathbf{c}}_Z$	2.4x10-8	2.0x10-10	1.3x10-10	4.5x10-5	1.5x10-10	1.3x10-10	0.13	2.7x10-7	9.5x10-8
$\mathbf{w}-\mathbf{Q}\hat{\mathbf{c}}_Q$		2.1x10-14	1.1x10-14		1.5x10-14	1.4x10-14		1.8x10-14	1.4x10-14

Table 2. RMS errors obtained with standard (**Z**) and discrete (**Q**) Zernike basis for coefficients (**c**) and in wavefront (**w**) for hexagonal (H), random (R) and Fermat spiral (S) sampling patterns. All values are in micrometers.

4.2 Wavefront reconstruction from wavefront slopes

The problem of wavefront reconstruction from its slopes is totally different, since here the reconstruction requires to integrate the gradient. If we apply $\mathbf{Q}_d^T$ we are not integrating, and therefore to recover the wavefront coefficients, we have to apply either $\mathbf{R}_d^{-1}$ or $\mathbf{D}^{-1}$ directly. This means that we have especial care with the condition number of these matrices to avoid excesive noise amplification. We studied the problem of potential noise amplification in two ways. First, we obtained the singular value decomposition of matrix **D** as a metric to predict the amplification of noise. The condition numbers obtained for the square 182x182 **D** matrices (I = 91) improve progressively: ∞ for H (hexagonal); 4.3x10^7 for P (perturbed H); 1.6x10^7 for S1 (homogeneous sampling spiral); 4x10^6 for R (random); and 1.71$0^5$ for S2 (quadratic sampling spiral). This has important consequences. In the presence of noise, noise amplification will preclude to work with critical sampling, but on the other hand we should expect that spiral S2 is going to provide better reconstructions.

To have a more realistic estimation of the performance, including the effects of noise amplification, we conducted a series of computer simulations. Now the task is to reconstruct different number of modes, starting from J = 1 (maximum redundancy) and progressively increasing up to the critical value J = 2I (zero redundancy). Now we will use standard least squares ($\hat{\mathbf{c}} = \left(\mathbf{D}^T\mathbf{D}\right)^{-1}\mathbf{D}^T\mathbf{m}$), except for the last case (critical sampling) where **D** is square. We applied the QR factorization to **D** to improve its condition number (typically by a factor of 2.) Our criterion for the best reconstruction is that of minimum RMS reconstruction error. We used the same data set as before, but now we always considered wavefronts with 182 Zernike modes. This means that now we only have the effect of noise, while we assume that the number of modes 182 is large enough to avoid aliasing (spectral overlapping.) Now the initial wavefront has an RMS value of 0.54 μm (~ 1 λ). For each condition, 30 different measurements **m** were simulated using the expression $\mathbf{m}_k = \mathbf{Dc} + \mathbf{n}_k$ for the k-th realization, where $\mathbf{n}_k$ is a column vector containing (Gaussian zero-mean) random noise. Then we computed the mean and standard deviation (error bars) over the 30 realizations. The noise variance was adjusted to simulate different levels of signal-to-noise ratio (SNR) from 1 to ∞ (zero noise). We computed the SNR as $SNR = \langle|\mathbf{m}|\rangle / \langle\sigma_{\mathbf{m}}\rangle_k$ the ratio between the average absolute measurements value among all the noise-free measurements, and the mean standard deviation of the noise (where *k* referes to the different realizations).

The results for the different sampling patterns are plotted in Figure 4, for the case of SNR = 30. That SNR is within the range of typical values in ocular aberrometers (Rodriguez et al., 2006). The vertical axis represents the RMS difference between the original (ideal) wavefront and that reconstructed from the noisy measurements; and the horizontal axis represents the number of modes *J* considered in the matrix **D**. As we can see, all the sampling patterns show a similar performance for $J \leq 62$, but for $J > 62$ the noise amplification increases rapidly for the redundant H pattern. This particular line ends when we reach the maximum rank of **D**. For the non redundant sampling patterns (R, P, S1 and S2) the effect of noise amplification becomes patent for higher values of *J*; as *J* increases S2 shows the best behaviour. For this sampling pattern, and SNR = 30, the optimal performance is obtained for $J \approx 122$, significantly greater than $I = 91$. This optimal number of modes (best reconstruction) is roughly double than 62 obtained for standard redundant patterns. For the ideal noise free case (SNR =∞) the best reconstruction corresponds to $J = Rank(\mathbf{D})$. This is $J = 89$ for standard (hexagonal) and $J = 182$ for non redundant sampling patterns respectively. The results for different SNR= 1, 10, 30, 100 and ∞, confirm the same type of behaviour as in Fig. 4. As the SNR increases, then the absolute minimum is lower and moves to the right (the optimum value of *J* increases) and conversely. Random and spiral curves are better in all cases and tend to show a rather flat valley indicating that the optimal value of number of modes, *J* is not critical. This behaviour is opposite to standard and perturbed sampling grids where the minimum is much more marked. This means that the number of modes is critical and that the least squares fit is less robust. Finally, the quadratic spiral S2 always provides the best reconstruction.

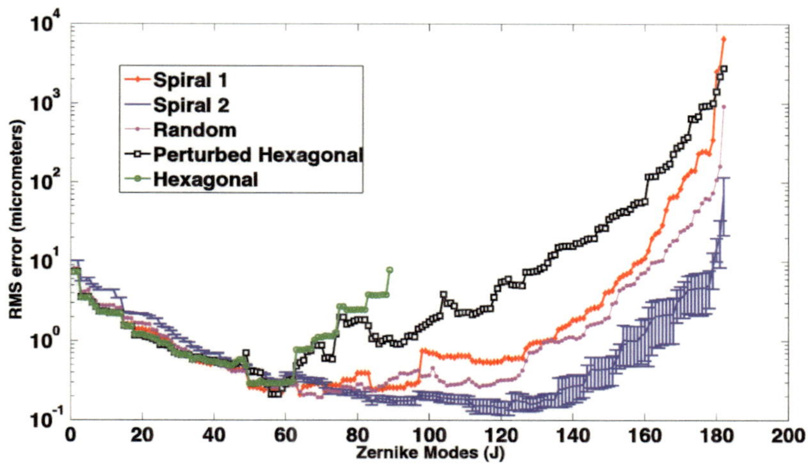

Fig. 4. RMS error of the reconstructed wavefront for different sampling patterns.

5. Conclusion

In conclusion, the non redundant sampling grids proposed above are found to keep completeness of discrete Zernike polynomials within the circle. This has important consequences both in theoretical and practical aspects. Now it is feasible to implement direct and inverse discrete Zernike transforms (DZT) for these sampling patterns. Furthermore, we found that when the discrete ZPs basis is complete, then the basis formed by their (equally sampled) gradients is complete as well. This is true for all non redundant grids tested so far, but spiral 2, with a quadratic increase of sampling density from the centre to the periphery, seems to be especially well adapted to the symmetry of ZPs. In fact, it provides the lowest CN. On the other hand, orthogonality is lost either by sampling or by differentiation in all cases studied. We can recover this property and construct an orthogonal basis **Q**, through QR factorization, but at the cost of loosing some information contained in **R**. In the case of the DZT, the **Q** basis implies to work in the discrete domain. Thus, we lose the interpolation ability of continuous polynomials. In the case of gradients, we loose the information both for interpolation and for integration. It is possible to apply $\mathbf{R}^{-1}$ but then there is the concern of noise amplification.

There are many practical implications of completeness. For standard redundant sampling grids, and realistic values of the SNR of the input data, the optimal number of modes providing the best reconstruction is about $J = I/2$. In wavefront sensing or ray tracing, where one has two measures at each point, J can be somewhat higher (0.6 or 0.7 times I). Our results suggest that by using non redundant sampling patterns, one can reconstruct double number of modes. This has a double effect in improving the reconstruction by decreasing the reconstruction error due to noise, but also due to potential spectral overlapping. Furthermore, both completeness and lower redundancy can help to save costs in many applications, ranging from numerical ray tracing to modal wavefront control by deformable mirrors (adaptive optics). In the first case one can save computing time, and in the second case one can save mechanical actuators.

We believe that the discrete orthogonal modes of Figures 2 and 3, for discrete wavefronts and for spot diagrams, respectively, have a clear physical meaning for optical systems, measurements or computations which are discrete intrinsically. Fig. 2 shows examples of wave aberration modes in segmented optics (arrays of facets, mirrors, microlenses, etc.) with determined geometries (hexagonal, random, or spiral). It is clear that these aberration modes change both with the array geometry and with the number of facets (samples), especially higher orders. The physical meaning of the modes of spot diagrams (Fig. 3) is even more obvious, since ray tracing or wavefront gradient measurements are essentially discrete.

Regarding practical applications, sampling grids with inhomogeneous densities, such as quadratic spiral, or random (irregular) are difficult to implement in conventional monolithic microlens arrays used in Hartmann-Shack sensors, segmented mirrors, etc. However there are highly flexible and re-configurable (almost in real time) devices such as liquid crystal spatial light modulators (Arines et al. 2007) or laser ray-tracing methods (Navarro & Moreno-Barriuso, 1999) which can easily implement almost any possible sampling grid.

6. Acknowledgment

This work was supported by the CICyT, Spain, under grant FIS2008-00697; J. Arines acknowledges support by the program Isidro Parga Pondal (Xunta de Galicia 2009). We thank Prof. Jesús M. Carnicer, Universidad de Zaragoza for highly useful advises on linear algebra.

7. References

Alda, J. & Boreman, G. D. (1993). Zernike-based matrix model of deformable mirrors: optimization of aperture size. *Appl. Opt.* Vol. 32, pp 2431-38

Ares, M. & Royo, S. (2006). Comparison of cubic B-spline and Zernike-fitting techniques in complex wavefront reconstruction. *App. Opt.* Vol. 45, pp 6954-64

Arines, J. , Durán, V., Jaroszewicz, Z. , Ares, J., Tajahuerce, E., Prado, P., Lancis, J., Bará, S., & Climent, V. (2007). Measurement and compensation of optical aberrations using a single spatial light modulator. *Opt. Express* Vol. 15, pp 15287-15292

Arines, J. , Pailos, E., Prado, P., & Bara, S. (2009). The contribution of the fixational eye movements to the variability of the measured ocular aberration. *Ophthalm. Physiol. Opt.* Vol. 29, pp 281-287

Bara S. (2003). Measuring eye aberrations with Hartmann-Shack wave-front sensors: Should the irradiance distribution across the eye pupil be taken into account?. *J. Opt. Soc. Am. A*, Vol. 20(12), pp 2237-2245

Cubalchini, R. (1979). Modal wave-front estimation from phase derivative measurements. *J. Opt. Soc. Am.* Vol. 69, pp 972-977

Diaz-Santana, L., Walker, G., & Bara, S. (2005). Sampling geometries for ocular aberrometry: A model for evaluation of performance. *Opt. Express* Vol. 13, pp 8801-18

Fazekas Z., Soumelidis A., & Schipp F. (2009). Utilizing the discrete orthogonality of Zernike functions in corneal measurements. *Proceedings of the World congress on Engineering 2009 Vol I WCE 2009, July London U.K.*, pp 1-3

Fischer, D. J., O'Bryan, J. T., Lopez, R., & Stahl, H. P. (1993).Vector formulation for interferogram surface fitting. *Appl. Opt.* Vol. 32, 4738-43

Herrmann, J. (1980). Least-squares wave front errors of minimum norm. *J. Opt. Soc. Am.* Vol. 70, pp 28-35

Herrmann, J. (1981). Cross coupling and aliasing in modal wave-front estimation. *J. Opt. Soc. Am.*, Vol. 71, pp 989-992

Kim, C.J. (1982). Polynomial fit of interferograms. *Appl. Opt.* Vol. 21, pp 4521–4525

Love, G. D. (1997). Wave-front correction and production of Zernike modes with a liquid-crystal spatial light modulator. *Appl. Opt.* Vol. 36, pp 1517–24

Liang, J. , Grimm, B., Goelz, S., Bille, J.F. (1994).Objective measurement of wave aberrations of the human eye with the use of a Hartmann-Shack wave-front sensor. *J. Opt. Soc. Am. A.* Vol. 11(7), pp 1949-1957

Mahajan, V. N. (2007). Zernike polynomials and wavefront fitting. *Optical Shop Testing,* 3rd ed., D. Malacara, ed. Wiley (New York).

Malacara, D., Carpio-Valadéz, J. M. , & Sanchez, J.J. (1990). Wavefront fitting with discrete orthogonal polynomials in a unit radius circle. *Opt. Eng.* Vol. 29, pp 672-675

Mayall, N. U. & Vasilevskis, S. (1960). Quantitative tests of the Lick Observatory 120-Inch mirror. *Astron. J.* Vol. 65, pp 304-317

Nam, J. & Rubinstein, J. (2008). Numerical reconstruction of optical surfaces. *J.Opt.Soc.Am. A* Vol. 25, pp 1697-1709

Navarro, R., & Moreno-Barriuso, E. (1999). A laser ray tracing method for optical testing. *Opt. Lett.* Vol.24, pp 951-953

Navarro, R., Arines, J., & Rivera, R. (2009). Direct and Inverse Discrete Zernike Transform. *Opt. Express* Vol.17, pp 24269-24281

Navarro, R. , Arines, J., & Rivera, R. (2011). Wavefront sensing with critical sampling. *Opt. Letters* Vol. 36, pp 433-435

Noll, R. J. (1976). Zernike polynomials and atmospheric turbulence. *J. Opt. Soc. Am.* Vol. 66, pp 207–211

Noll, R. J. (1978). Phase estimates from slope–type wave–front sensors. *J. Opt. Soc. Am.* Vol. 68, pp 139–140

Pap, M., & Schipp, F., *Discrete orthogonality of Zernike functions*, Mathematica Pannonica, Vol. 1, pp. 689-704, 2005

Primot J. (2003). Theoretical description of Shack-Hartmann wave-front sensor. *Opt. Comm,* Vol. 222, pp 81-92

Qi, B., Chen, H. & Dong, N. (2002). Wavefront fitting of interferograms with Zernike polynomials. *Opt. Eng.* Vol. 41, pp 1565–69

Rios, S., Acosta, E., & Bara, S. (1997).Hartmann sensing with Albrecht grids. *Opt. Comm.* Vol. 133, pp 443-453

Rodriguez, P., Navarro, R., Arines, J., & Bará, S. (2006).A New Calibration Set of Phase Plates for Ocular Aberrometers. *J. Refract. Surg.* Vol. 22, pp 275-284.

Roggemann M.C., & B. Welsh, Imaging through turbulence, Ed. CRC Press, Boca Raton, 1996.

Soumelidis, A., Fazekas, Z., & Schipp, F. (2005). Surface description for cornea topography using modified Chebyshev-polynomials. 16th IFAC World Congress, Prague, Czech Republic, pp. Fr-M19-TO/5

Schwiegerling, J. , Greivenkamp, J., & Miller, J. (1995). Representation of videokeratoscopic height data with Zernike polynomials. *J. Opt. Soc. Am. A*, Vol. 12, pp 2105-13

Solomon, C., Rios, S., Acosta, E. & Bará, S. (1998) Modal wavefront projectors of minimum error norm. *Opt. Comm.* Vol. 155, 251-254

Soloviev, O. & Vdovin, G. (2005). Hartmann - Shack test with random masks for modal wavefront reconstruction. *Opt. Express* Vol. 13, pp 9570-84

Southwell, W. H. (1980).Wave–front estimation from wave–front slope measurements. *J. Opt. Soc. Am* Vol. 70, pp 998-1006

Upton, R. & Ellerbroek, B. (2004). Gram-Schmidt orthogonalization of the Zernike polynomials on apertures of arbitrary shape, Opt. Lett. Vol 29 (24), pp 2840-2842

van Brug, H. (1997). Zernike polynomials as a basis for wave-front fitting in lateral shearing interferometry. *Appl. Opt.* Vol. 36, pp 2788–90

Vargas-Martín, F., Prieto,P.M., & Artal, P. (1998). Correction of the aberrations in the human eye with a liquid-crystal spatial light modulator: limits to performance. J. Opt. Soc. Am. A, Vol. 15(9), pp 2552- 2562

Voitsekhovich, V. , Sanchez, L., Orlov, V. & Cuevas, S. (2001). Efficiency of the Hartmann Test with Different Subpupil Forms for the Measurement of Turbulence-Induced Phase Distortions. *Appl. Opt.* Vol. 40, pp 1299-1304

Wang, J.Y. & Silva, D.E. (1980). Wave-front interpretation with Zernike polynomials," *Appl. Opt.* Vol. 19, pp 1510-1518

Welsh, B. M., Roggemann M.C., Ellerbroek, B.L.,& Pennington, T L. (1995).Fundamental performance comparison of a Hartmann and a shearing interferometer wave-front sensor. App. Opt., Vol. 34(21), pp. 4186-4195

Wyant J.C., & Creath, K. (1992). Basic Wavefront Aberration theory for optical metrology, Ed. Academic Press, Inc., Applied Optics and Optical Engineering Vol XI, Cap. 1.

Zou, W., & Rolland, P. (2006). Quantifications of error propagation in slope-based wavefront estimations. *J. Opt. Soc. Am. A.* Vol. 23(10), pp 2629-2638

11

Master Equation - Based Numerical Simulation in a Single Electron Transistor Using Matlab

Ratno Nuryadi
Center for Material Technology
Agency for Assessment and Application of Technology, Jakarta
Indonesia

1. Introduction

Recent modern fabrication technology allows us for the fabrication of nanometer-scaled devices, which is possible to observe single electronic or single electron tunneling phenomena (Averin & Likharev, 1991; Likharev, 1988; Likharev, 1999; Hanna et al., 1991; Tucker, 1992). On the other hand, MOSFET (metal-oxide-semiconductor field effect transistor) devices with channel length below 20 nanometer (nm) are no more properly operated because the down-scaling of MOS devices causes a large statistical fluctuation of the threshold voltage. A possible approach to overcome this problem is to use the single electron devices for future VLSI (very large scale integrated circuit) (Takahashi et al., 1995; Saitoh et al., 2001).

Nanometer scale single electron devices have the following features, i.e., low power consumption and small size. These are key features to realize ultra high density circuits. Single electron circuits with new architecture are also possible because the basic operation of single electron devices is quite different from that of conventional semiconductor devices.

There are two major requirements for single electron tunneling phenomena (Coulomb blockade) to occur (Averin & Lhikarev, 1991; Likharev, 1988; Likharev, 1999). Firstly, thermal energy k_BT must be much smaller than elemental charging energy $e^2/2C$. This ensures that the transport of charges is in fact governed by the Coulomb charging energy. This condition can be fulfilled either by lowering the temperature or by decreasing the capacitance which means to reduce the island size. Usually, experiments are performed at temperatures of a few mK and for structures with island sizes of a few hundred nanometers. Second requirement is related to tunnel resistance which must exceed the quantum resistance ($h/4e^2 \approx 6.5$ kΩ). This condition ensures that the wave functions of excess electrons between the barriers are basically localized. On the other word, in the case of lower tunnel resistance, excess charges extend over the barriers so that no single electron tunneling event can be possible.

There are several types of circuits where the single electron tunneling phenomena are being explored, such as single electron box (Likharev, 1999), single electron transistor (SET) (Tucker, 1992; Takahashi et al., 1995; Saitoh et al., 2001; Wolf et al., 2010; Sun et al., 2011; Lee et al., 2009), single electron pump (Ono et al., 2003), single electron turnstile (Moraru et al., 2011) and single electron circuits with several junctions (1D and 2D arrays) (Nuryadi et al., 2003; Nuryadi et al., 2005). A double junction system is most important single electron circuit because of a basic component of SET. At small applied voltage, the system remains in the Coulomb blockade state, and no current flows through the double junctions. On the other hand, at higher applied voltage, the Coulomb blockade is defeated and the electrons can tunnel through the junctions and finally the current flows. If the island between two tunnel junctions is electrostatically controlled by the gate capacitance, the system became single electron transistor. This device is reminiscent of a MOSFET, but with a small island (dot) embedded between two tunnel capacitors/junctions, instead of the usual inversion channel.

It is well known that a numerical simulation of the devices could help a great deal in their understanding of the devices. However, although so far several groups have reported the simulation and modeling of single electron tunneling devices (Amman et al., 1991; Kirihara et al., 1994; Fonseca et al., 1997; Wasshuber et al., 1997; Nuryadi et al., 2010), numerical simulation with detail explanation and easy examples is still needed, especially for beginners in the field of single electron devices. Basically there are two methods to simulate the single electron phenomena, i.e., master equation (Amman et al., 1991; Nuryadi et al., 2010) and Monte Carlo methods (Kirihara et al., 1994; Fonseca et al., 1997; Wasshuber et al., 1997).

The goal of this chapter is to simulate numerically current-voltage characteristics in the single electron transistor based on master equation. A master equation for the probability distribution of electrons in the SET dot (see Fig. 1) is obtained from the stochastic process, allowing the calculation of device characteristics. First, I will start with an introduction of the basic equations in Master equation (section II). Next, the derivation of free energy change due to electron tunneling event is discussed in section III. The flowchart of numerical simulation based on Master equation and the Matlab implementation will be discussed in section IV and V, respectively. The examples of simulation resuls are presented in section V. Finally, section VI is conclusion.

2. Basic equations in master equation based simulation

Figure 1 shows the SET circuit consisting of a dot between the source and drain electrodes separated by tunnel capacitors C_1 and C_2. Both tunnel capacitors C_1 and C_2 have tunnel resistances R_1 and R_2, respectively. The dot is also coupled to the gate electrode with capacitor C_G in order to control the current flow. The total capacitance between the dot and the outer environment can be writen as C_Σ, where

$$C_\Sigma = C_1 + C_2 + C_G. \tag{1}$$

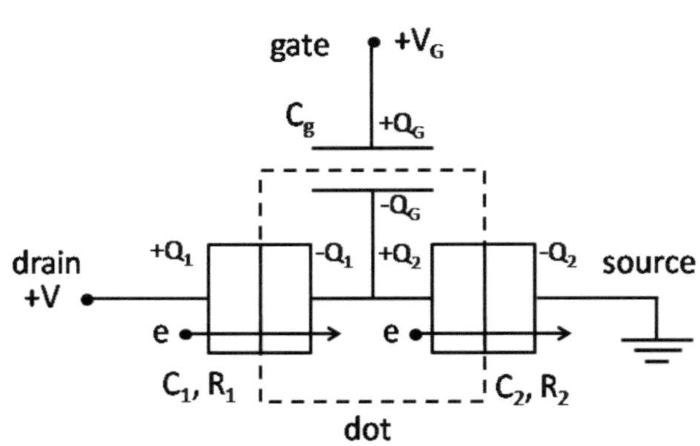

Fig. 1. Single electron transistor has a structure of the dot in the center coupled by two tunnel capacitors (C_1 and C_2) and a gate capacitor C_G. Source is connected to a ground, where drain and gate are applied by voltages V and V_G (Tucker, 1992).

There are four main equations for current-voltage characteristics of single electron circuits, i.e., free energy change ΔF, tunneling probability/rate Γ, steady state master equation and current equation I, as follows.

Free energy change:

$$\Delta F_1^{\pm}(n_1, n_2) = \frac{e}{C_\Sigma}\left\{\frac{e}{2} \pm (Ne - Q_0) \mp (C_G + C_2)V \pm C_G V_G\right\} \tag{2a}$$

$$\Delta F_2^{\pm}(n_1, n_2) = \frac{e}{C_\Sigma}\left\{\frac{e}{2} \mp (Ne - Q_0) \mp C_1 V \mp C_G V_G\right\} \tag{2b}$$

Tunneling probability/rate:

$$\Gamma_1^{\pm}(N) = \frac{1}{R_1 e^2}\left[\frac{-\Delta F_1^{\pm}}{1 - exp\left[\Delta F_1^{\pm}/k_B T\right]}\right] \tag{3a}$$

$$\Gamma_2^{\pm}(N) = \frac{1}{R_j e^2}\left[\frac{-\Delta F_2^{\pm}}{1 - exp\left[\Delta F_2^{\pm}/k_B T\right]}\right] \tag{3b}$$

Steady State Master equation:

$$\rho(N)[\Gamma_2^-(N) + \Gamma_1^+(N)] = \rho(N+1)[\Gamma_2^+(N+1) + \Gamma_1^-(N+1)] \tag{4}$$

Current equation:

$$I(V) = e\textstyle\sum_{N=-\infty}^{\infty}\rho(N)[\Gamma_1^+(N) - \Gamma_1^-(N)] = e\sum_{N=-\infty}^{\infty}\rho(N)[\Gamma_2^+(N) - \Gamma_2^-(N)] \tag{5}$$

where e is the elemental charge, k_B is the Boltzmann constant, T is the temperature, N is the number of electrons in the dot, n_1 and n_1 are a number of electrons flows through the capacitor C_1 and capacitor C_2, respectively, Q_0 is the background charge and +/- express that the electron tunnels through the capacitor with the direction from left to the right and from right to the left, respectively.

Equations (2a) and (2b) are used to calculate the free (electrostatic) energy change ΔF of the system due to the one electron tunneling event. It is important to be noted that only tunneling events decreasing the electrostatic energy (and dissipating the difference) are possible.

The values ΔF from equations (2a) and (2b) are used to calculate electron tunneling probability in the equations (3a) and (3b), respectively. The tunneling of a single electron through a particular tunnel junction is always a random event, with a certain rate Γ (i.e., probability per unit time) which depends solely on the ΔF. Equation (4) expresses the Master equation in steady state, resulting the value of $\rho(N)$, which is necessary to be used for the current calculation in equation (5).

3. Derivation of free energy change in single electron transistor circuit

As explained above that the free energy change of the system before and after tunnel event plays a key role on the occurrence of the electron tunneling, i.e., whether the tunneling event occurs or dot. Therefore, the origin of the free energy change in SET system is important to be reviewed. The free energy of voltage-biased single electron transistor is defined by the difference in electrostatic energy stored in the circuit (total charging energy) and work done by the external voltage source due to tunnel events.

3.1 Total charging energy

In order to calculate total charging energy, it is necessary to determine the voltage applied on the tunnel capacitor C_1 (V_1) and tunnel capacitor C_2 (V_2) using the following step. The configuration of the charges on each capacitor in the single-electron transistor circuit (Figure1) can be expressed as (Tucker, 1992),

$$Q_1 = C_1 V_1 = C_1(V - V_2), \tag{6a}$$

$$Q_2 = C_2 V_2, \tag{6b}$$

$$Q_G = C_G(V_G - V_2). \tag{6c}$$

It is noted that the V_2 is also subjected to the voltage in the dot. Charge in the dot is given by,

$$Q = Q_2 - Q_1 - Q_G = Ne - Q_0. \tag{7}$$

Here, $N = n_1 - n_2$ is a number of electrons in the dot.
If the equations (6a), (6b) and (6c) are inserted into an equation (7), it can be obtained the V_2 as a function of drain voltage V and gate voltage V_G, as follows,

$$C_2 V_2 - C_1(V - V_2) - C_G(V_G - V_2) = Q,$$

$$V_2 = \frac{1}{C_\Sigma}(C_1 V + C_G V_G + Q) \tag{8}$$

From equation (8) and relationship of $V_1 + V_2 = V$, it can be obtained the value of voltage on capacitor C_1, as follows,

$$V_1 = V - \frac{1}{C_\Sigma}(C_1 V + C_G V_G + Q)$$

$$V_1 = \frac{1}{C_\Sigma}[(C_2 + C_G)V - C_G V_G - Q] \tag{9}$$

Note that both V_1 and V_2 are a function of N, which is the number of electrons in the dot because of $Q = Ne - Q_0$.
Next, total charging energy on the SET system can be calculated as follows,

$$E_c = \frac{Q_1^2}{2C_1} + \frac{Q_2^2}{2C_2} + \frac{Q_G^2}{2C_G}$$

$$E_c = \frac{1}{2C_\Sigma}[C_G C_1 (V - V_G)^2 + C_1 C_2 V^2 + C_G C_2 V_G^2 + Q^2] \tag{10}$$

Since the values of external power supply V and V_G is constant, the effect on electron tunneling process only influences the term of $Q^2/2C_\Sigma$.

3.2 Work done by external voltage source due to tunnel event

There are two types of tunnel events, i.e., electron tunnels through the capacitor C_1 and the electron tunnels through the capacitor C_2. The amount of the work done by external voltage source is different from one event to another one. Therefore, the detail explanation of the work done for these two types is discussed. Figure 3 shows the charge flow enter/exit from the voltage source when the electron tunnel through the capacitor C_1 (right direction).

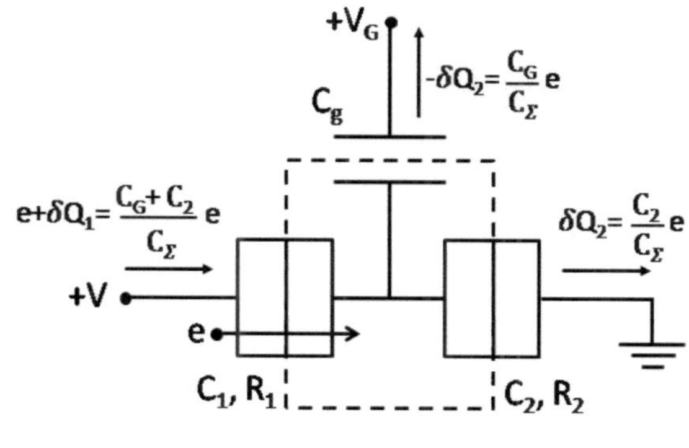

Fig. 3. The charge flow in the single electron transistor circuit when one electron through the capacitor C_1 (Tucker, 1992).

Work done by the power supply when the electron tunnel through the capacitor $C_1$is formulated as follows:

1. Change in charge when one electron tunnels through capacitor $\boldsymbol{C_1}$ $(\boldsymbol{n_1 \longrightarrow n_1+1})$

Change of dot potential due to this electron tunneling ($Q \longrightarrow Q+e$ or $N \longrightarrow N+1$) is $\delta V_2 = V_2^{after} - V_2^{before}$, thus:

$$\delta V_2 = \frac{1}{C_\Sigma}\big(C_1V + C_GV_G + (Q+e)\big) - \left[\frac{1}{C_\Sigma}(C_1V + C_GV_G + Q)\right]$$

$$\delta V_2 = \frac{e}{C_\Sigma} \tag{11}$$

It is noted that V_2^{after} and V_2^{before} express the values of V_2 after and before tunneling, respectively.

Change of charge in capacitor C_1 is $\delta Q_1 + e$, where $\delta Q_1 = Q_1^{after} - Q_1^{before}$. Consider the equation (6a) it is obtained the below relationship,

$$\delta Q_1 = C_1\big(V - V_2^{after}\big) - C_1\big(V - V_2^{before}\big),$$

$$\delta Q_1 = -C_1\delta V_2. \tag{12}$$

By inserting equation (11) into equation (12), it is obtained

$$\delta Q_1 = -\frac{C_1}{C_\Sigma}\mathrm{e}$$

Therefore, total change of the charge in capacitor C_1 is,

$$\delta Q_1 + e = -\frac{C_1}{C_\Sigma}\mathrm{e} + \mathrm{e}$$

$$\delta Q_1 + e = \frac{C_2 + C_G}{C_\Sigma}e \tag{13}$$

Change of charge in capacitor C_2 is $\delta Q_2 = Q_2^{after} - Q_2^{before}$. Consider the equation (6b) δQ_2 becomes,

$$\delta Q_2 = C_2 V_2^{after} - C_2 V_2^{before},$$

$$\delta Q_2 = C_2 \delta V_2,$$

$$\delta Q_2 = \frac{C_2}{C_\Sigma} e \tag{14}$$

Change of charge in capacitor C_G is $\delta Q_G = Q_G^{after} - Q_G^{before}$. Consider the equation (6c) δQ_G becomes,

$$\delta Q_G = C_G\left(V_G - V_2^{after}\right) - C_G\left(V_G - V_2^{before}\right),$$

$$\delta Q_G = -C_G \delta V_2,$$

$$\delta Q_G = -\frac{C_G}{C_\Sigma} e \tag{15}$$

2. Work done when one electron tunnel through capacitor $\boldsymbol{C_1}$ $(\boldsymbol{n_1 \rightarrow n_1 + 1})$

Work done by power supply is a sum of multiplication between charge change in each terminal and a given power supply voltage. Thus, when one electron tunnel through the capacitor C_1, the work becomes,

$$W_S(n_1) = n_1[(e + \delta Q_1)V + (\delta Q_G)V_G + (\delta Q_2) \times 0],$$

$$W_S(n_1) = n_1\left[\frac{C_G + C_2}{C_\Sigma} eV - \frac{C_G}{C_\Sigma} eV_G\right] \tag{16}$$

The same calculation can be done when the single electron tunnel through the capacitor C_2, as shown in Figure 3.

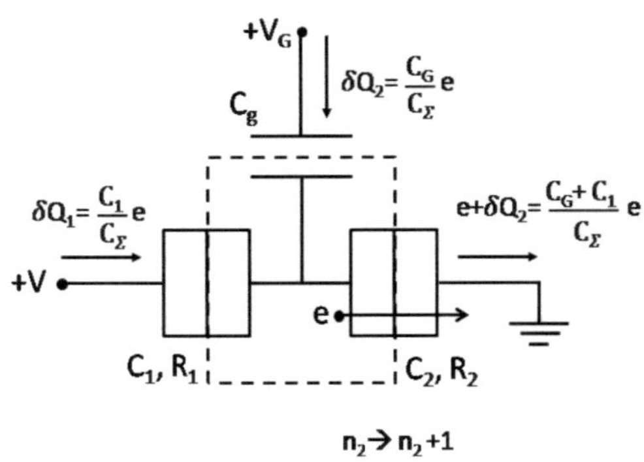

Fig. 3. The charge flow in the single electron transistor circuit when an electron tunnels through the capacitor C_2.

1. Change in charge when an electron through the capacitor $\boldsymbol{C_2}$ $(\boldsymbol{n_2 \rightarrow n_2 + 1})$

Change of potential in the dot due to electron tunneling ($Q \rightarrow Q - e$ or $N \rightarrow N - 1$) is $\delta V_2 = V_2^{after} - V_2^{before}$, thus :

$$\delta V_2 = \frac{1}{C_\Sigma}(C_1 V + C_G V_G + (Q - e)) - \left[\frac{1}{C_\Sigma}(C_1 V + C_G V_G + Q)\right],$$

$$\delta V_2 = -\frac{e}{C_\Sigma} \tag{17}$$

Change in charge on a capacitor C_1 is $\delta Q_1 = Q_1^{after} - Q_1^{before}$. Consider the equation (6a), δQ_1 becomes,

$$\delta Q_1 = C_1\left(V - V_2^{after}\right) - C_1\left(V - V_2^{before}\right),$$

$$\delta Q_1 = -C_1 \delta V_2,$$

$$\delta Q_1 = \frac{C_1}{C_\Sigma}\mathrm{e} \tag{18}$$

Change in the charge on a capacitor C_2 is $\delta Q_2 + e$, where $\delta Q_2 = Q_2^{after} - Q_2^{before}$. Consider the equation (6b), δQ_2 becomes,

$$\delta Q_2 = C_2 V_2^{after} - C_2 V_2^{before},$$

$$\delta Q_2 = C_2(\delta V_2),$$

$$\delta Q_2 = -\frac{C_2}{C_\Sigma}\mathrm{e}$$

So the total change in charge on the capacitor C_2 is,

$$\delta Q_2 + e = -\frac{C_2}{C_\Sigma}\mathrm{e} + \mathrm{e},$$

$$\delta Q_2 + e = \frac{C_1 + C_G}{C_\Sigma} e \tag{19}$$

Changes in the charge on a capacitor C_G is $\delta Q_G = Q_G^{after} - Q_G^{before}$. Consider equation (6c), δQ_G becomes,

$$\delta Q_G = C_G\left(V_G - V_2^{after}\right) - C_G\left(V_G - V_2^{before}\right),$$

$$\delta Q_G = -C_G \delta V_2,$$

$$\delta Q_G = \frac{C_G}{C_\Sigma}\mathrm{e} \tag{20}$$

2. Work done when one electron through the capacitor $\boldsymbol{C_2}$ $(\boldsymbol{n_2 \longrightarrow n_2 + 1})$

From the above calculation, the work done by the power supply when the electrons tunnels through the capacitor C_2 becomes

$$W_S(n_2) = n_2[(\delta Q_1)V + (\delta Q_G)V_G + (e + \delta Q_2) \times 0],$$

$$W_S(n_2) = n_2\left[\frac{C_1}{C_\Sigma} eV + \frac{C_G}{C_\Sigma} eV_G\right] \tag{21}$$

3.3 Free energy

The most important requirement for the accurence of single electron tunneling is that the total energy of the transistor system must decrease due to one electron tunneling. In the other word, the electron tunneling will not occur if the total energy of the system increases due to the electron tunneling. This condition is called as Coulomb blockade. The free energy is defined by the difference in the total charging energy and total work done by the power supply, as follows:

$$F(n_1,n_2) = E_c - W_S^{total},$$

$$F(n_1,n_2) = \frac{Q^2}{2C_\Sigma} - \left\{n_1 e\left[\frac{C_G+C_2}{C_\Sigma}V - \frac{C_G}{C_\Sigma}V_G\right] + n_2 e\left[\frac{C_1}{C_\Sigma}V + \frac{C_G}{C_\Sigma}V_G\right]\right\} + constant \tag{22}$$

3.4 Change in free energy due to tunnel event

Change in free energy after and before electron tunneling will determine whether the electron tunneling occurs or not. If the system becomes more stable (energy decreases) when the electron tunnels, electron tunneling will occur. Let's look at the conditions when the electron tunnels through the capacitor C_1. The free energy change after and before tunneling can be calculated as follows:

$$\Delta F_1^{\pm}(n_1,n_2) = F(n_1\pm 1,n_2) - F(n_1,n_2),$$

$$\Delta F_1^{\pm}(n_1,n_2) = \left\{\frac{(Q\pm e)^2}{2C_\Sigma} - \left\{(n_1\pm 1)e\left[\frac{C_G+C_2}{C_\Sigma}V - \frac{C_G}{C_\Sigma}V_G\right] + n_2 e\left[\frac{C_1}{C_\Sigma}V + \frac{C_G}{C_\Sigma}V_G\right]\right\}\right\}$$
$$-\left\{\frac{Q^2}{2C_\Sigma} - \left\{n_1 e\left[\frac{C_G+C_2}{C_\Sigma}V - \frac{C_G}{C_\Sigma}V_G\right] + n_2 e\left[\frac{C_1}{C_\Sigma}V + \frac{C_G}{C_\Sigma}V_G\right]\right\}\right\}$$

$$\Delta F_1^{\pm}(n_1,n_2) = \frac{e}{C_\Sigma}\left\{\frac{e}{2} \pm Q \mp (C_G+C_2)V \pm C_G V_G\right\} \tag{23}$$

By inserting $Q = Ne - Q_0$ into equation (23), the equation (2a) is obtained.
On the other hand, when the electron tunnels through the capacitor C_2, the free energy change when the after and before tunneling is calculated as follows:

$$\Delta F_2^{\pm}(n_1,n_2) = F(n_1,n_2\pm 1) - F(n_1,n_2),$$

$$\Delta F_2^{\pm}(n_1,n_2) = \left\{\frac{(Q\mp e)^2}{2C_\Sigma} - \left\{n_1 e\left[\frac{C_G+C_2}{C_\Sigma}V - \frac{C_G}{C_\Sigma}V_G\right] + (n_2\pm 1)e\left[\frac{C_1}{C_\Sigma}V + \frac{C_G}{C_\Sigma}V_G\right]\right\}\right\}$$
$$-\left\{\frac{Q^2}{2C_\Sigma} - \left\{n_1 e\left[\frac{C_G+C_2}{C_\Sigma}V - \frac{C_G}{C_\Sigma}V_G\right] + n_2 e\left[\frac{C_1}{C_\Sigma}V + \frac{C_G}{C_\Sigma}V_G\right]\right\}\right\}$$

$$\Delta F_2^{\pm}(n_1,n_2) = \frac{e}{C_\Sigma}\left\{\frac{e}{2} \mp Q \mp C_1 V \mp C_G V_G\right\} \tag{24}$$

By inserting $Q = Ne - Q_0$ into equation (24), the equation (2b) is obtained.

4. Master equation

Figure 4 shows the numerical simulation step to calculate IV curve based on Master equation method. First, the values of the physical constants (Boltzmann constant and elemental charge) and device parameters (C_1, C_2, C_G, R_1 and R_2) are defined. Then, the external parameters (V, V_G, Q_0 and T) are given. Next, the free energy change of the system ΔF when the electron tunnels across the tunnel capacitance, is calculated. The ΔF depends on the number of excess electrons N in the dot, as expressed in equations (23) and (24).

$$\Delta F_1^{\pm}(n_1, n_2) = \frac{e}{C_\Sigma}\left\{\frac{e}{2} \pm (Ne - Q_0) \mp (C_G + C_2)V \pm C_G V_G\right\} \tag{25a}$$

$$\Delta F_2^{\pm}(n_1, n_2) = \frac{e}{C_\Sigma}\left\{\frac{e}{2} \mp (Ne - Q_0) \mp C_1 V \mp C_G V_G\right\} \tag{25b}$$

Using the values of ΔF, single electron tunneling rates across each of two junctions is determined. Each rate depends on both the tunneling resistance of the junction and the total energy change of the system due to the tunneling event. On the other words, for single electron transistor circuit simulation, each electron tunneling has to be carefully monitored. The electron tunneling rate, which is represented by $\Gamma^{\pm}$, can be easily obtained from the basic golden-rule calculation (Averin & Lhikarev, 1991),

$$\Gamma_1^{\pm}(N) = \frac{1}{R_1 e^2}\left[\frac{-\Delta F_1^{\pm}}{1 - exp\left[\Delta F_1^{\pm}/k_B T\right]}\right] \tag{26a}$$

$$\Gamma_2^{\pm}(N) = \frac{1}{R_j e^2}\left[\frac{-\Delta F_2^{\pm}}{1 - exp\left[\Delta F_2^{\pm}/k_B T\right]}\right] \tag{26b}$$

Next, a stochastic process in SET circuit is considered. The island charge e will change by the tunneling of electrons from or to the island as described by the master equation.

$$\frac{\partial \rho(N,t)}{\partial t} = \rho(N+1)[\Gamma_2^{+}(N+1) + \Gamma_1^{-}(N+1)] - \rho(N)[\Gamma_2^{-}(N) + \Gamma_1^{+}(N)] \tag{27}$$

Here, the dc characteristics is investigated, therefore the steady state solution of equation (27) is desired. The steady state master equation is found by setting the time derivative of the probability distribution function equal to zero. Therefore, equation (27) becomes (Hanna et al., 1991)

$$\rho(N)[\Gamma_2^{-}(N) + \Gamma_1^{+}(N)] = \rho(N+1)[\Gamma_2^{+}(N+1) + \Gamma_1^{-}(N+1)]. \tag{28}$$

In this condition, it is necessary to calculate $\rho(N)$ for all of possible charge state N. By inserting N from $-\infty$ to ∞ into equation (28), the following equations are obtained.

$$\rho(-\infty)[\Gamma_2^{-}(-\infty) + \Gamma_1^{+}(-\infty)] = \rho(-\infty+1)[\Gamma_2^{+}(-\infty+1) + \Gamma_1^{-}(-\infty+1)]$$

$$\rho(-1)[\Gamma_2^{-}(-1) + \Gamma_1^{+}(-1)] = \rho(0)[\Gamma_2^{+}(0) + \Gamma_1^{-}(0)]$$

$$\rho(0)[\Gamma_2^{-}(0) + \Gamma_1^{+}(0)] = \rho(1)[\Gamma_2^{+}(1) + \Gamma_1^{-}(1)]$$

$$\rho(1)[\Gamma_2^-(1)+\Gamma_1^+(1)]=\rho(1)[\Gamma_2^+(2)+\Gamma_1^-(2)]$$

$$\rho(n)[\Gamma_2^-(n)+\Gamma_1^+(n)]=\rho(n+1)[\Gamma_2^+(n+1)+\Gamma_1^-(n+1)]$$

$$\rho(\infty-1)[\Gamma_2^-(\infty-1)+\Gamma_1^+(\infty-1)]=\rho(\infty)[\Gamma_2^+(\infty)+\Gamma_1^-(\infty)] \quad (29)$$

To solve equations above, the $\rho(n)$ must satisfy the standard boundary conditions, i.e.

$$\rho(N)\rightarrow 0, \text{ as } N\rightarrow \pm\infty. \quad (30)$$

Using this condition, all of the $\rho(N)$ can be found. However, the $\rho(N)$ here is not normalized, so that $\rho(N)$ requires the normalization as follows:

$$\sum_{N=-\infty}^{\infty}\rho(N)=1. \quad (31a)$$

For this, the following transformation is need.

$$\rho(N)\rightarrow\frac{\rho(N)}{\sum_{N=-\infty}^{\infty}\rho(N)} \quad (31b)$$

Finally, the current can be calculated by,

$$I(V)=e\sum_{N=-\infty}^{\infty}\rho(N)[\Gamma_1^+(N)-\Gamma_1^-(N)]. \quad (32a)$$

Here, the multiplication of the probability and the difference of rate $\Gamma_1^+(N)-\Gamma_1^-(N)$ describes the net current flowing through the first junction. In addition, the current may also expressed in the terms of the rates at second junction, as follows.

$$I(V)=e\sum_{N=-\infty}^{\infty}\rho(N)[\Gamma_2^+(N)-\Gamma_2^-(N)]. \quad (33b)$$

5. Matlab implementation

The above equations can be easily implemented in MATLAB. As explained in previous section, the flowchart of numerical simulation is as follows. In the first step, the following physical constant and device parameters are defined as follows.

```
% Matlab program source for numerical simulation of Master equation
% in single electron transistor
% This program code is made by Dr. Ratno Nuryadi, Jakarta, Indonesia
clear all;
% Definition of Physical constant
q=1.602e-19;            % electronic charge (C)
kb=1.381e-23;           % Boltzman constant (J/K)
% Definition of Device parameters
c1=1.0e-20;             % tunnel capacitor C1 (F)
c2=2.1e-19;             % tunnel capacitor C2 (F)
cg=1.0e-18;             % gate capacitor Cg (F)
ctotal=c1+c2+cg;        % total capacitance (F)
mega=1000000;           % definition of mega=10^6
r1=15*mega;             % tunnel resistance R1 (Ohm)
r2=250*mega;            % tunnel resistance R2 (Ohm)
```

Second, the values of external parameters (V, V_G, Q_0 and T) is given. Here, the V_G, Q_0 and T are kept a constant while the V is varied from V_{min} to V_{max}, as follows:

```
Vg=0;                        % gate voltage (V)
q0=0;                        % background charge q0 is assumed to be zero
temp=10;                     % temperature T (K)

vmin=-0.5;                   % drain voltage minimum Vmin (V)
vmax=0.5;                    % drain voltage maximum Vmax (V)
NV=1000;                     % number of grid from Vmin to Vmax
dV=(vmax-vmin)/NV;           % drain voltage increment of each grid point
for iv=1:NV                  % loop start for drain voltage
V(iv)=vmin+iv*dV;            % drain voltage in each grid point
% Note that loop end for drain voltage is located in the end of this
program source
```

Third step is calculation of ΔF, as follows:

```
Nmin=-20;                    % minimum number of N (charge number in dot)
Nmax=20;                     % maximum number of N (charge number in dot)
for ne=1:Nmax-Nmin           % loop start for N
    n=Nmin+ne;               % N charge number in dot
% Calculation of ΔF in equations (25a) and (25b)
    dF1p=q/ctotal*(0.5*q+(n*q-q0)-(c2+cg)*V(iv)+cg*Vg);
    dF1n=q/ctotal*(0.5*q-(n*q-q0)+(c2+cg)*V(iv)-cg*Vg);
    dF2p=q/ctotal*(0.5*q-(n*q-q0)-c1*V(iv)-cg*Vg);
    dF2n=q/ctotal*(0.5*q+(n*q-q0)+c1*V(iv)+cg*Vg);
% Noted that loop end for N is located after calculation of Γ
```

Forth, the values of ΔF are identified and then used for the calculation of Γ. If ΔF is negative, Γ will be calculated by equations (26a) and (26b(. However, if the ΔF is positive, Γ is set to be closed to the zero (very small). Note that the value of Γ is always positive. These identifications are done for four conditiond of ΔF.

```
    if dF1p<0
        T1p(ne)=1/(r1*q*q)*(-dF1p)/(1-exp(dF1p/(kb*temp)));
                                    % Γ positive in equation (26a)
    else
        T1p(ne)=1e-1;               % Γ positive is assumed to be very small
    end
    if dF1n<0
        T1n(ne)=1/(r1*q*q)*(-dF1n)/(1-exp(dF1n/(kb*temp)));
                                                 % Γ negative in equation (26a)
    else
        T1n(ne)=1e-1;               % Γ negative is assumed to be very small
    end
    if dF2p<0
        T2p(ne)=1/(r2*q*q)*(-dF2p)/(1-exp(dF2p/(kb*temp)));
                                    % Γ positive in equation (26b)
    else
        T2p(ne)=1e-1;               % Γ positive is assumed to be very small
    end
```

```
    if dF2n<0
        T2n(ne)=1/(r2*q*q)*(-dF2n)/(1-exp(dF2n/(kb*temp)));
                                             % Γ negative in equation (26b)
    else
        T2n(ne)=1e-1;                        % Γ negative is assumed to
                                               be very small
    end
end                                          % loop end for N
```

Fiveth, the $\rho(N)$ of equation (28) is calculated. For this, normalization of equation (31a) must be satisfied. Here, the values of ρ(Nmin) and ρ(Nmax) is assumed to be 0.01.

```
p(1)=0.001;                        % ρ(N_min) is assumed to be 0.01
p(Nmax-Nmin)=0.001;                % ρ(N_max) is assumed to be 0.01
```

Sixth, normalization of ρ is done. Here, $\sum_{N=-\infty}^{\infty}\rho(N)$ is calculated.

```
sum=0;                         % sum=0 is initial value to calculate ρ
for ne=2:Nmax-Nmin
    p(ne)=p(ne-1)*(T2n(ne-1)+T1p(ne-1))/(T2p(ne)+T1n(ne));
                               % calculation of ρ(N) in equation (28)
% The conditions below are used to avoid divergence of Matlab
calculation
    if p(ne)>1e250
        p(ne)=1e250;
    end
    if p(ne)<1e-250
        p(ne)=1e-250;
    end
% ----------------------
    sum=sum+p(ne);
end

for ne=2:Nmax-Nmin
    p(ne)=p(ne)/sum;           % Normalization in equation (31b)
end
```

Finally, the current is computed as follows:

```
sumI=0;                                      % sumI=0 is initial condition
                                               for current calculation
for ne=2:Nmax-Nmin
    sumI=sumI+p(ne)*(T2p(ne)-T2n(ne));
end
I(iv)=q*sumI;                                % I in equation (32b)
end                                          % end of drain voltage loop
plot(V,I);                                   % plot of I vs V

for iv=1:NV-1
    dIdV(iv)=(I(iv+1)-I(iv))/dV;             % calculation of dIdV
end
figure;
plot(V(1,1:NV-1),dIdV);                      % plot of dIdV vs V
```

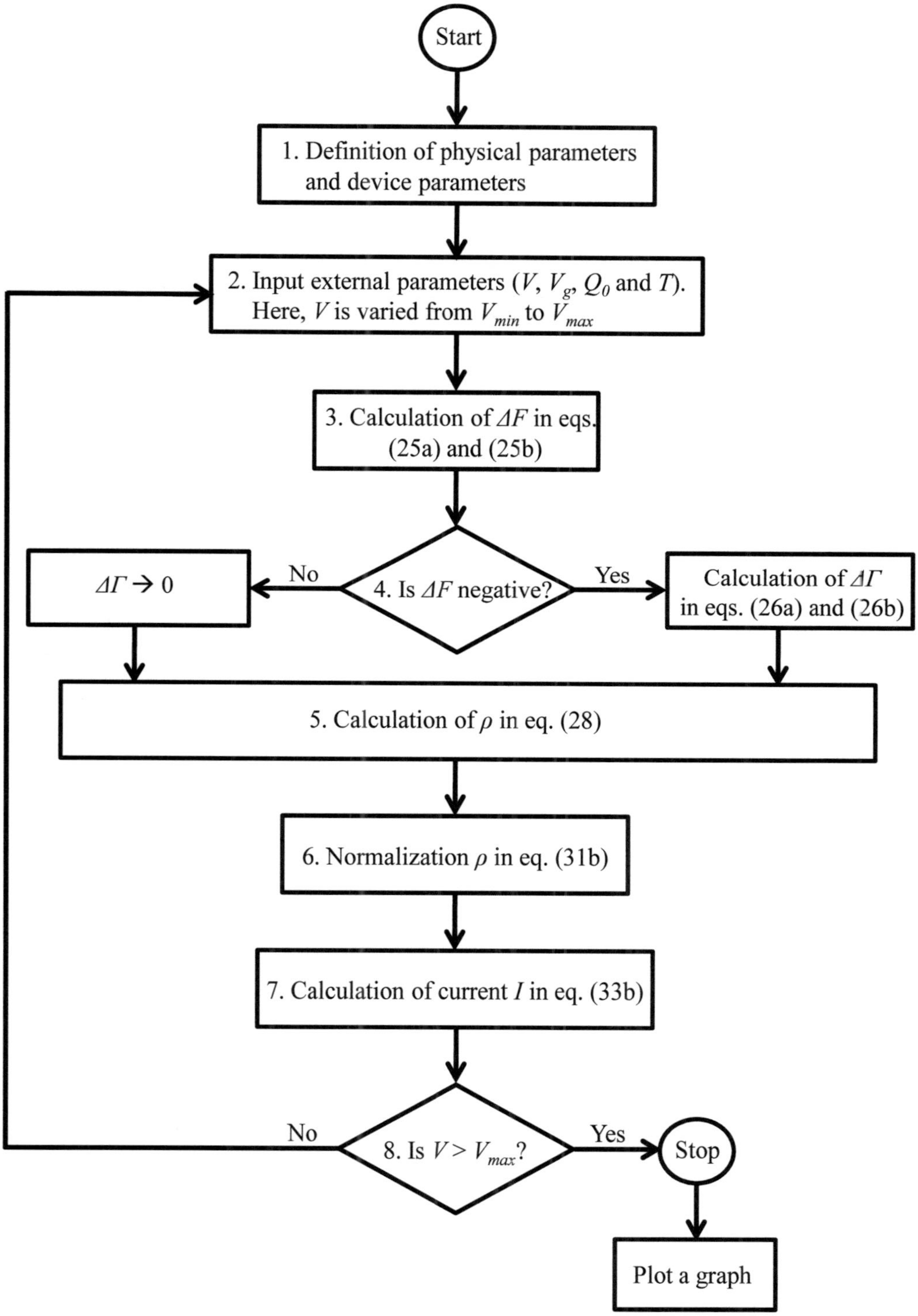

Fig. 4. Flow diagram of the Matlab program used to solve Master equation.

6. Examples of simulated results

Two examples will be used to demonstrate the numerical solution of Master equation in single electron transistor.

Example 1:

Figures 5(a) dan (b) shows current-drain voltage characteristic of the SET and its dI/dV curve. The parameter values are C_1= 1.0x10^{-20} F, C_2= 2.1x10^{-19} F, C_G= 1.0x10^{-18} F, R_1= 15 MΩ and R_2=250 MΩ. The calculation was carried out for an operating temperature of 10 K, V_G= 0 V and Q_0= 0. As shown in Fig. 5(a), at small source-drain voltage V there is no current, indicating the suppression of the current which is known as the Coulomb blockade. In this region, any tunneling event would lead to an increase of the total energy and also the tunneling rate is exponentially low. There is also evident that the I-V curve has staircase shape, which is called as Coulomb staircases.

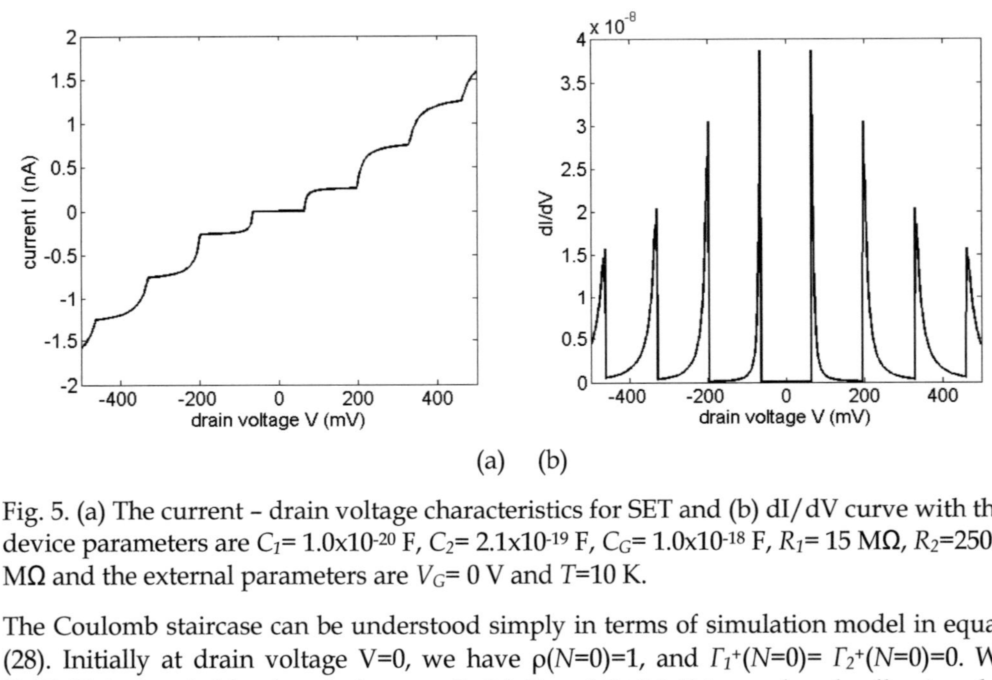

(a) (b)

Fig. 5. (a) The current - drain voltage characteristics for SET and (b) dI/dV curve with the device parameters are C_1= 1.0x10^{-20} F, C_2= 2.1x10^{-19} F, C_G= 1.0x10^{-18} F, R_1= 15 MΩ, R_2=250 MΩ and the external parameters are V_G= 0 V and T=10 K.

The Coulomb staircase can be understood simply in terms of simulation model in equation (28). Initially at drain voltage V=0, we have ρ(N=0)=1, and Γ_1^+(N=0)= Γ_2^+(N=0)=0. When V=V_t (V_t is threshold voltage), the rates Γ_1^+(N=0) and Γ_2^+(N=0) jump sharply allowing charge to flow through the junction capacitances, so that ρ(n=1)>0. When V=V_t+e/2C_Σ there is jump in Γ_1^+(N=1) producing the next another step in I-V characteristics. Such steps happen due to each increase of V by e/2C_Σ. Simulation result in Fig. 5 has values of C_2>C_1 and R_2>R_1. According to Fig. 5(b), the width of the steps is ~131 mV, which is determined by e/2C_Σ.

Example 2:

The current-gate voltage characteristics of SET is plotted in Fig. 6. The parameter values are C_1= 4.2x10^{-19} F, C_2= 1.9x10^{-18} F, C_G= 1.3x10^{-18} F, R_1= 150 MΩ, R_2=150 MΩ, T=10 K and V= 10 mV. The program source for this I-V curve can be seen below, which is modified from the previous source.

```
V=0.01;                      % drain voltage (V)
q0=0;                        % background charge q0 is assumed to be
zero
temp=10;                     % temperature T (K)

vgmin=-0.4;                  % gate voltage minimum Vmin (V)
vgmax=0.4;                   % gate voltage maximum Vmax (V)
NVg=800;                     % number of grid from Vgmin to Vgmax
dVg=(vgmax-vgmin)/NVg;       % gate voltage increment of each grid point
for iv=1:NVg                 % loop start for gate voltage
Vg(iv)=vgmin+iv*dVg;         % drain voltage in each grid point
% Note that loop end for drain voltage is located in the end of this
program source

Nmin=-20;                    % minimum number of N (charge number in dot)
Nmax=20;                     % maximum number of N (charge number in
dot)
for ne=1:Nmax-Nmin           % loop start for N
    n=Nmin+ne;               % N charge number in dot
% Calculation of ΔF in equations (25a) and (25b)
    dF1p=q/ctotal*(0.5*q+(n*q-q0)-(c2+cg)*V+cg*Vg(iv));
    dF1n=q/ctotal*(0.5*q-(n*q-q0)+(c2+cg)*V-cg*Vg(iv));
    dF2p=q/ctotal*(0.5*q-(n*q-q0)-c1*V-cg*Vg(iv));
    dF2n=q/ctotal*(0.5*q+(n*q-q0)+c1*V+cg*Vg(iv));
% Noted that loop end for N is located after calculation of Γ
```

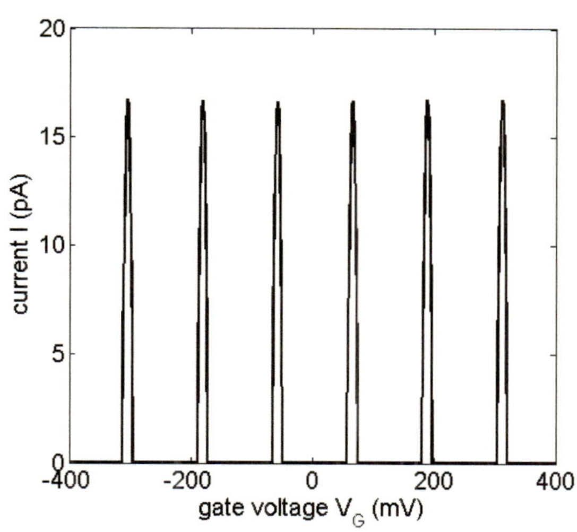

Fig. 6. The current – gate voltage characteristics for SET with the parameter values are C_1= 4.2x10^{-19} F, C_2= 1.9x10^{-18} F, C_G= 1.3x10^{-18} F, R_1= 150 MΩ, R_2=150 MΩ and T=10 K.The drain voltage is 10 mV.

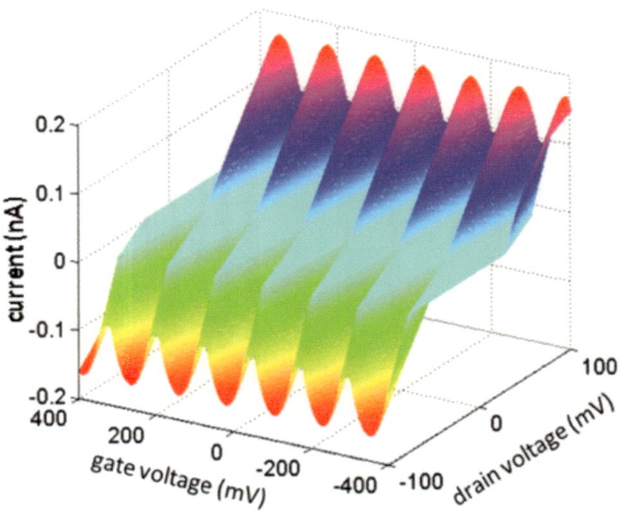

Fig. 7. 3D current - voltage characteristics for the SET. The range of source-drain voltage is from -100 mV to 100 mV and gate voltage is from -400 mV to 400 mV.

The current is a periodic function of the gate voltage V_G because the tunneling of one electron in or out of the dot is induced by the gate voltage. This periodic oscillations, which is also known as Coulomb oscillation, is the basis of the SET operation. In order to understand the overall of I-V characteristics, 3D plot is made as shown in Fig. 7. The Coulomb blockade region appears at very low source-drain voltage. The Coulomb blockade can be removed by the changing of gate voltage from inside Coulomb blockade to the outside. Outside the Coulomb blockade region, a current can flow the between the source and drain. At a given source-drain voltage V, the SET current can be modulated by gate voltage V_g. By sweeping the gate voltage, the currents oscillate between zero (Coulomb blockade) and non-zero (no Coulomb blockade), as shown in Fig. 6. The periodicity of the current is e/C_g along the gate voltage axis. Simulation results presented here reproduce the previous studies of the SET (Takahashi et al., 1995; Saitoh et al., 2001; Wolf et al., 2010; Sun et al., 2011; Lee et al., 2009), indicating that the simulation technique can be used to explain the basis of the SET.

7. Conclusion

This chapter has presented a numerical simulation of the single electron transistor using Matlab. This simulation is based on the Master equation method and is useful for both educational and research purposes, especially for beginners in the field of single electron devices. Simulated results produce the staircase behavior in the current-drain voltage characteristics and periodic oscillations in current-gate voltage characteristics. These results reproduce the previous studies of the SET, indicating that the simulation technique achieves good accuration. The resulting program can be also integrated into an engineering course on numerical analysis or solid-state physics.

8. References

Amman, M.; Wilkins, R.; Ben-Jacob, E.; Maker, P.D.; & Jaklevic, R.C. (1991). Analytic solution for the current-voltage characteristic of two mesoscopic tunnel junctions coupled in series, *Phys. Rev. B*, 43, pp. 1146-1149.

Averin, D.V. & Likharev, K.K. (1991). *Mesoscopic phenomena in Solids*, edited by B.L. Altshuler, P.A. Lee, and R.A. Webb (Elsevier, Amsterdam), pp. 173-271.

Fonseca, L.R.C.: Korotkov, A.N.: Likharev, K.K.; & Odintsov, A.A. (1997). A numerical study of the dynamics and statistics of single electron systems, *J. Appl. Phys.* 78 (5), pp. 3238-3251.

Hanna, A.E. & Tinkham, M. (1991). Variation of the Coulomb staircase in a two-junction system by fractional electron charge, *Phys. Rev. B*, 44, pp. 5919-5922.

Kirihara, M.; Kuwamura, N.; Taniguchi, K.; & Hamaguchi, C. (1994). Monte Carlo study of single-electronic devices, *Proceedings of the International Conference on Solid State Devices and Materials*, Yokohama, Japan, pp. 328-330.

Likharev, K.K. (1988). Correlated discrete transfer of single electrons in ultrasmall junctions, *IBM J. Res. Develop.* 32(1), pp. 144-157.

Likharev, K.K. (1999). Single-electron devices and their applications, *Proceedings of the IEEE*, 87, pp. 606-632.

Lee, D.S.; Yang, H.S.; Kang, K.C.; Lee, J.E.; Lee, J.H.; Park, S.H.; & Park, B.G. (2009). Silicon-Based Dual-Gate Single-Electron Transistors for Logic Applications", Jpn. J. Appl. Phys. 48, p. 071203.

Moraru, D.; Yokoi, K.; Nakamura, R.; Mizuno, T.; & Tabe, M. (2011). Tunable single-electron turnstile using discrete dopants in nanoscale SOI-FETs, *Key Engineering Materials*, 470, pp. 27-32.

Nuryadi, R.; Ikeda, H.; Ishikawa, Y.; & Tabe, M. (2003). Ambipolar coulomb blockade characteristics in a two-dimensional Si multidot device, *IEEE Trans. Nanotechnol.* 2, pp. 231-235.

Nuryadi, R.; Ikeda, H.; Ishikawa, Y.; & Tabe, M. (2005). Current fluctuation in single-hole transport through a two-dimensional Si multidot, *Appl. Phys. Lett.*, 86, p. 133106.

Nuryadi, R.: & Haryono, A. (2010). Numerical simulation of single electron transistor using master equation, *Proc. SPIE (Southeast Asian International Advances in Micro/Nanotechnology)*, Vol. 7743, p. 77430L.

Ono, Y.; & Takahashi, Y. (2003). Electron pump by a combined single-electron/field-effect-transistor structure, *Appl. Phys. Lett.*, 82 (8), pp. 1221–1223.

Saitoh, M.; Saito, T.; Inukai, T.; & Hiramoto, T. (2001). Transport spectroscopy of the ultrasmall silicon quantum dot in a single-electron transistor, *Appl. Phys. Lett.*, Vol. 79, No. 13, pp. 2025 - 2027.

Sun, Y.; Rusli & Singh, N. (2011). Room-Temperature Operation of Silicon Single-Electron Transistor Fabricated Using Optical Lithography, *IEEE Trans. Nanotechnology*, 10(1), pp. 96-98.

Takahashi, Y.; Nagase, M.; Namatsu, H.; Kurihara, K.; Iwadate, K.; Nakajima, Y.; Horiguchi, S.; Murase, K. & Tabe, M. (1995). Fabrication technique Si single electron transistor operating at room temperature, *Electron. Lett.*, Vol. 31, No. 2, pp. 136–137.

Tucker, J.R. (1992). Complementary digital logic based on the "Coulomb blockade", *J. Appl. Phys.*, 72 (9), pp. 4399-4413.

Wasshuber, C.; Kosina, H.; & Selberherr, S. (1997). SIMON-A simulator for single-electron tunnel devices and circuits, *IEEE Transactions on Computer-Aided Design of Integrated Circuits and Systems*, 16 (9), pp. 937 - 944.

Wolf, C.R.; Thonke, K.; & Sauer, R. (2010). Single-electron transistors based on self-assembled silicon-on-insulator quantum dots, *Appl. Phys. Lett.* 96, p. 142108.

12

Numerical Simulation of Plasma Kinetics in Low-Pressure Discharge in Mixtures of Helium and Xenon with Iodine Vapours

Anatolii Shchedrin and Anna Kalyuzhnaya
Institute of Physics, National Academy of Sciences of Ukraine
Ukraine

1. Introduction

Due to ecological problems related to the utilization of gas-discharge ultraviolet (UV) mercury vapour lamps widely used in lighting technology, photochemistry, and photomedicine, there arises a need for developing new mercury-free sources of UV radiation using electron bands of rare-gas monohalides and halogen molecules as well as spectral lines of their atoms (Lomaev et al., 2003). The most high-power mercury-free lamps are UV emitters with "chlorine - noble gas" active media emitting on transitions of the excimer molecules XeCl (308 nm) and KrCl (222 nm). The use of aggressive chlorine molecules in the gas mixtures of such emitters results in a comparatively low mixture life (1-100 hours), which impedes their wide application in various optical technologies. It is mainly due to the absorption of chlorine by open metal electrodes (especially strongly heated cathode) and its heterophase chemical reaction with a quartz discharge tube accompanied by the formation of polymer compounds (chlorosiloxanes).

That is why the replacement of chlorine molecules by less aggressive iodine ones in the working media of excilamps represents an urgent task. Ultraviolet radiation of glow discharge plasma in mixtures of helium with iodine vapours that is still transparent to air is mainly concentrated in the spectral ranges 175-210 nm and 320-360 nm. The mixture life of such lamps reaches 10^3 hours (Lomaev & Tarasenko, 2002; Shuaibov et al., 2005a, 2005b). The use of the He-Xe-I_2 active medium in a glow discharge lamp also allows one to obtain emission of the excimer molecule XeI(B-X) (253 nm) (Shuaibov, 2004 et al.). Moreover, of special interest is the fact that the wavelength of this transition is close to that of the most intense spectral line of the mercury atom in low-pressure gas-discharge lamps, which is used in a number of optical technologies. The basic spectral lines of the iodine atom (183.0, 184.5, 187.6, and 206.2 nm) (Liuti & Mentall, 1968) are also close to those of the mercury atom (184.9, 194.2, 202.7, and 205.3 nm) now used in the corresponding low pressure UV emitters.

In this connection, it is important to optimize output characteristics of helium-iodine and xenon-iodine gas discharge emitters. The kinetics of plasmachemical processes in the gas discharge plasma in mixtures of noble gases with iodine molecules was till now studied only for high-pressure emitters excited by a barrier discharge (BD) in krypton-iodine and xenon-iodine mixtures (Zhang & Boyd, 1998, 2000). The conditions of BD plasmachemical reactions that lead to the formation of excited iodine atoms and molecules as well as xenon iodide molecules differ substantially from those in a longitudinal low-pressure glow discharge. Therefore, the results of these calculations cannot be used to analyze the efficiency and physics of the processes taking place in excimer glow discharge lamps. The parameters and kinetics of plasmachemical processes in low-pressure plasma in mixtures of noble gases with iodine vapors were not studied till now.

In order to optimize the output characteristics of gas-discharge lamps based on helium-iodine and xenon-iodine mixtures, we have carried out numerical simulation of plasma kinetics in a low-pressure discharge in the mentioned active media. This chapter reports on systematic studies of the electron-kinetic coefficients in mixtures of helium and xenon with iodine vapors as well as in the He:Xe:I_2 mixture. The mean electron energies and drift velocities in the discharge are calculated. A comparative analysis of the distributions of the power introduced into the discharge between the dominant electron processes in helium-iodine and xenon-iodine mixtures is performed. The rates of electron-molecular processes were computed based on the numerical solution of the Boltzmann equation in the two-term approximation that provides a good description of the electron energy distribution function in the case where the electron thermal velocity considerably exceeds the drift one (which is true in all experiments).

The plasma kinetics in the active medium of the excimer UV emitter was numerically simulated by solving a system of kinetic equations for neutral, excited, and charged components together with the Boltzmann equation for the electron energy distribution function and the supply circuit equation. The kinetic model used in the calculation included more than 60 elementary processes. The simulation of the plasma kinetics allowed us to obtain the relation between the emission intensities of atomic and molecular iodine in the helium-iodine mixture as well as to analyze the effect of xenon on the relation between the emission intensities of iodine atoms and molecules as well as xenon iodide molecules in the mixture including xenon.

Based on the analysis of plasmachemical processes running in the active medium of the helium-iodine excimer lamp, we studied the dependences of the emission intensities of atomic and molecular iodine on the total pressure of the mixture and revealed the basic mechanisms of the pressure influence on the population kinetics of the emitting levels. The effect of the halogen concentration on the emission intensity of atomic and molecular iodine is investigated and the main factors resulting in the decrease of the emission intensity with varying halogen content are found.

The performed numerical simulation yielded good agreement with experiment, which first of all testifies to the right choice of the calculation model and elementary processes for numerical simulation.

2. Numerical simulation

2.1 Electron energy distribution function

The electron energy distribution function is of major importance for understanding processes running in the active medium of a gas discharge. It determines parameters significant for the analysis of the plasma kinetics, such as rates of elementary electron-impact processes in the discharge, mean electron energy and mobility. In the case of not too strong fields, where the thermal electron velocity considerably exceeds their drift velocity, the distribution function can be expanded in terms of the parameter characterizing its anisotropy. Restricting oneself to two terms of such an expansion and considering elastic and inelastic collisions of electrons with neutral particles, one arrives at the Boltzmann equation in the two-term approximation (Golant, 1980):

$$\frac{1}{n_e N}\sqrt{\frac{m}{2e}}\varepsilon^{1/2}\frac{\partial(n_e f)}{\partial t}-\frac{1}{3}\left(\frac{E}{N}\right)^2\frac{\partial}{\partial\varepsilon}\left(\frac{\varepsilon}{\sum\limits_i \frac{N_i}{N}Q_{Ti}}\frac{\partial f}{\partial\varepsilon}\right)-\frac{\partial}{\partial\varepsilon}\left[2\sum_i\frac{N_i}{N}\frac{m}{M_i}Q_{Ti}\varepsilon^2\left(f+T\frac{\partial f}{\partial\varepsilon}\right)\right]=S_{eN}. \quad (1)$$

Here, f stands for the symmetric part of the electron energy distribution function, ε, n_e, and m and the electron energy, density, and mass, correspondingly, E is the electric field in the discharge, T denotes the gas temperature (eV), N is the total gas concentration, N_i, M_i, and Q_{Ti} are the concentrations of atoms or molecules, their masses and momentum-transfer cross sections, and e=1.602·10^{-12} Erg/eV. The function $f(\varepsilon)$ is normalized by the condition

$$\int_0^\infty \varepsilon^{1/2} f(\varepsilon)d\varepsilon = 1. \quad (2)$$

The integral S_{eN} describing inelastic electron collisions with atoms and molecules has the form

$$S_{eN}=\sum_i\frac{N_j}{N}\left[(\varepsilon+\varepsilon_i)Q_i(\varepsilon+\varepsilon_i)f(\varepsilon+\varepsilon_i)-\varepsilon Q_i(\varepsilon)f_0(\varepsilon)\right]-\frac{N_{at}}{N}\varepsilon Q_{at}(\varepsilon)f(\varepsilon), \quad (3)$$

where Q_i and ε_i denote the cross sections and energy thresholds of the processes of electron-impact excitation, ionization, or dissociation of neutral species, correspondingly, while Q_{at} is the cross section for electron attachment to electronegative molecules.

The solution of Eq.(1) was obtained using the Thomas algorithm for tridiagonal matrices. Electron-electron collisions were not taken into account when calculating the distribution function due to the fact that their effect on the electron distribution at low electron densities ($n_e/N > 10^{-6}$) is negligible (Soloshenko et al., 2007).

A considerable part of iodine molecules in a gas discharge dissociates into atoms (Barnes & Kushner, 1998). That is why the Boltzmann equation for the electron energy distribution function was solved under the assumption that the halogen component in the discharge is presented by I_2 molecules (50%) and I atoms (50%) in the ground state.

One of the difficulties accompanying numerical modeling of the plasma kinetics in iodine-containing mixtures is the absence of both experimental and theoretical data on electron-impact excitation cross sections of iodine molecules. This fact is confirmed, in particular, by the bibliographic study of data on electron collisions with halogen molecules published in the 20th century performed by the National Institute for Fusion Science (Hayashi, 2003). That is why it is now generally accepted to allow for these processes using approximations of various kinds. For example, in (Avdeev et al., 2007), where the authors investigated the kinetics in the krypton-iodine mixture, the cross sections for inelastic electron collisions with iodine molecules were approximated based on general theories described in (Smirnov, 1967). In (Boichenko & Yakovlenko, 2003), the rates of electron-impact excitation and step ionization of iodine molecules were assumed to be the same as the corresponding rates for its atoms.

The solution of the Boltzmann equation and the simulation of the plasma kinetics in the active medium of an UV emitter were carried out with regard for three excited levels of the iodine molecule. As will be shown below, they play the key role in the formation of emitting iodine atoms and molecules. The excitation cross sections for these levels were introduced as those similar to the excitation cross section of the emitting state of the iodine atom shifted by the excitation threshold for each specific level of the iodine molecule. The cross section for electron dissociative attachment to iodine molecules was taken from (Tam & Wong, 1978), whereas the cross sections of the other electron collisions with iodine atoms and molecules were analogous to those used in (Avdeev et al., 2007). The processes of electron interactions with noble gas atoms are well studied. The cross sections for elastic and inelastic electron collisions with helium atoms are presented in (Rejoub et al., 2002; Saha, 1989; Cartwright & et al., 1992) and those with xenon atoms can be found in (Rejoub et al., 2002; NIFS; Hyman, 1979).

Knowing the electron energy distribution function, it is possible to analyze the distribution of the power introduced into the discharge among the most important electron processes. As was shown in (Soloshenko, 2009), the power spent for an electron-impact inelastic process with the threshold energy ε_{ei} can be presented as

$$W_{ei} = \sqrt{\frac{2e}{m}} n_e N_i \varepsilon_i \int_0^{\infty} \varepsilon Q_{ei}(\varepsilon) f(\varepsilon) d\varepsilon , \quad (4)$$

where Q_{ei} is the cross section of the corresponding inelastic process. The power spent for gas heating is described by the relation

$$W_i = \frac{2m}{M_i} \sqrt{\frac{2e}{m}} n_e N_i \int_0^{\infty} \varepsilon^2 Q_{Ti}(\varepsilon) f(\varepsilon) d\varepsilon , \quad (5)$$

where Q_{Ti} is the momentum-transfer cross section for electron scattering by atoms and molecules of the mixture. So, the specific power spent for an electron process has the form

$$\eta_i = \frac{W_{ei}}{\sum_j W_{ej} + \sum_j W_j} . \quad (6)$$

2.1 Plasma kinetics in mixtures of helium and xenon with iodine vapours

The time evolution of the concentrations of neutral, charged, and excited particles in the active medium of the excimer UV emitter was found by solving the system of kinetic equations

$$\frac{dN_i}{dt} = \sum_{ij} k_{ij} N_j + \sum_{ijl} k_{ijl} N_j N_l + \ldots , \quad (7)$$

where N_i are the concentrations of the corresponding components of the mixture and k_{ij}, k_{ijl} are the rates of kinetic reactions. In this case, the rates of inelastic electron-impact processes represent variable quantities due to their dependence on the electron energy distribution function:

$$k_{ie} = \sqrt{\frac{2e}{m}} \int_0^\infty \varepsilon Q_i(\varepsilon) f(\varepsilon) d\varepsilon. \tag{8}$$

In turn, the electron energy distribution is determined by the electric field in the discharge. That is why the construction of a self-consistent model of kinetic processes in the excimer-lamp medium requires the joint solution of the supply circuit equation, the Boltzmann equation, and the system of kinetic equations for the components of the medium.
The plasma kinetics was calculated for an excimer lamp operating on the helium-iodine and xenon-iodine mixtures as well as the ternary helium-xenon-iodine mixture in the pressure range 1-10 Torr. The diagram of the experimental set-up whose parameters were used for the numerical simulation will be given in what follows. It was assumed that the UV emitter is supplied by a constant voltage circuit with the ballast resistance R_b=10^4 Ohm and the charging voltage U_0=6 kV. The discharge resistance represents a variable quantity depending on the electron density in the discharge n_e and their mobility μ:

$$R = \frac{1}{\sigma}\frac{d}{S} = \frac{1}{en_e\mu_e}\frac{d}{S}, \tag{9}$$

where σ stands for the conductivity of the active medium, d is the interelectrode distance, and S is the electrode area.
The emission of UV lamps based on helium-iodine mixtures includes a spectral line corresponding to the electron transition of iodine atoms with a wavelength of 206 nm and the I_2(D′→A′) molecular band with a wavelength of 342 nm. The diagram of the energy levels of atomic and molecular iodine is presented in Fig.1 (Barnes & Kushner, 1996). Solid lines mark the states taken into account in the described kinetic model.
It was already noted that, due to the absence of experimental or theoretical data on electron excitation cross sections of iodine molecules, they were introduced as those of the emitting state of the iodine atom shifted by the excitation threshold for each specific level of the I_2* molecule. The effect of the inaccuracy in the values of these cross sections was estimated by means of test calculations of the plasma kinetics with the use of the cross sections twice larger and lower than those accepted in the kinetic model. It was found out that the variation of the excitation cross section of the I_2(D) state does not considerably influence the emission power of both atomic and molecular iodine – their change is less than 1%. The variation of the excitation cross section of the I_2(D′) level results in the 8% and 35% change of the emission powers of atomic and molecular iodine, correspondingly. In the case of variation of the excitation cross section of the I_2(B) level, the emission powers of atomic and molecular iodine change by 35% and 13%, correspondingly. Such a result is acceptable with regard for the fact that the general behavior of the theoretical curves did not change in the case of variation of the cross sections.
Molecular iodine effectively dissociates into atoms due to a number of elementary processes. Its recovery to the molecular state takes place at the walls of the discharge chamber (Barnes & Kushner, 1998). That is why the kinetic model takes into account the diffusion of iodine atoms to the walls. For this purpose, we include an additional process of conversion of atomic iodine to the molecular form taking place with the rate equal to the diffusion loss frequency of iodine atoms. The diffusion loss frequency was estimated as D/Λ^2 (Raizer,

1991), where D is the diffusion coefficient and Λ is the characteristic length scale. For a discharge tube representing a long cylinder with radius r_0, $\Lambda = r_0/2.4$ (Raizer, 1991). The diffusion coefficient in the mixture He-I_2 = 130-130 Pa was taken equal to 100 cm^2/s. In the case of variation of the quantitative composition of the active medium, the diffusion coefficient changed proportionally to the mean free path of iodine atoms in the mixture.

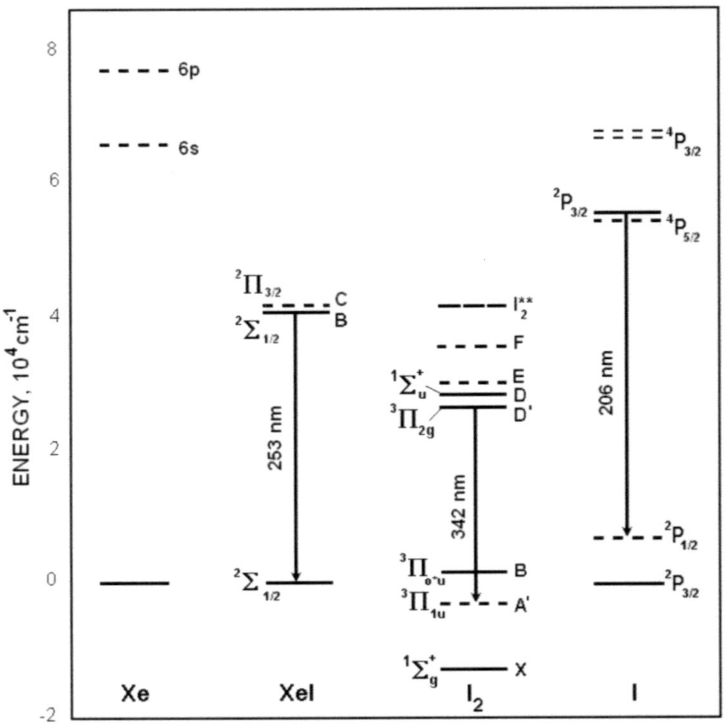

Fig. 1. Energy level diagram in the UV emitter

The full set of reactions used for the simulation of the plasma kinetics in the mixture of helium with iodine vapours is presented in Table 1 (Shuaibov et al., 2010a). As was already noted, the rates of electron-impact processes 1-11 were calculated at every time moment from the electron energy distribution function. The rates of ion-ion recombination (reactions 24-25) were calculated as functions of the pressure according to the Flannery formulas (McDaniel & Nighan, 1982). The rates of the other reactions used in the kinetic scheme were taken from (Avdeev et al., 2007; Boichenko & Yakovlenko, 2003; Kireev & Shnyrev, 1998; Stoilov, 1978; Baginskii et al., 1988).

The addition of xenon to the active medium of a helium-iodine UV-emitter results in the appearance of an additional radiation band at 253 nm corresponding to the B→X transition of XeI* excimers (Fig.1). Excimer molecules of rare gas halides (RX*) are generated in the discharge due to two basic algorithms. One of them is the ion-ion recombination (R^++X^-) that runs in the presence of a third body and is therefore of minor importance under the used low-pressure conditions and the other is the so-called harpoon reaction between an excited rare gas atom and a halogen molecule (R^*+X_2). However, as was shown by detailed studies (Barnes & Kushner, 1996, 1998), the harpoon reaction does not play a significant role in the formation of XeI* excimers. The main channel of their generation at pressures ≤ 5 Torr is the reverse harpoon reaction between a xenon atom in the ground state and a highly excited I_2^{**} levels. The specific iodine levels participating in the reverse harpoon process were not identified. Nevertheless, it is clear that neither of the states considered in our kinetic scheme has enough energy to provide the excitation of the XeI* molecule.

№	Reaction	Rate, cm^6/s, cm^3/s, s
1	e+He > He*+e	Calculated from the Boltzmann equation
2	e+He > He^++e+e	
3	e+I_2 > I_2(B)+e	
4	e+I_2 > I_2(D)+e	
5	e+I_2 > I_2(D′)+e	
6	e+I_2 > I_2^++e+e	
7	e+I_2 > I^-+I	
8	e+I_2 > I+I+e	
9	e+I > I*+e	
10	e+I > I^++e+e	
11	e+I* > I^++e+e	
12	I_2(B)+He > I+I+He	1.0e-11
13	I_2(D)+He > I_2(D′)+He	1.0e-12
14	I_2(D)+I_2 > I_2(D′)+I_2	1.5e-11
15	I_2(D)+I > I_2(D′)+I	1.5e-11
16	I_2(D)> I_2+hv	1.6e-8
17	I_2(D′)+He > I_2 +He	1.0e-12
18	I_2(D′)+ I_2 > I_2 + I_2	1.0e-11
19	I_2(D′)+I > I_2 +I	1.0e-11
20	I_2(D′)> I_2+hv (342 nm)	7.0e-9
21	I* > I + hv (206 nm)	3.5e-9
22	I+I+M > I_2+M	3.0e-33
23	I*+I_2 > I_2(D)+I	1.3e-9
24	I^++I^-+M > I_2(D′)+M	Calculated by the Flannery formulas
25	I_2^++I^-+M > I_2(D′)+I+M	
26	He*+2He > He_2^*+He	4.3e-34
27	He^++2He > He_2^++He	8.0e-32
28	He*+He* > He^++He+e	2.0e-10
29	He_2^*+He_2^* > He_2^++2He+e	5.0e-10
30	He_2^* > He+He	3.6e8
31	He_2^*+e > He+He+e	3.8e-9
32	He_2^++e > He+He	1.3e-11
33	2I > I_2	k_{diff}

Table 1. Kinetic reactions in the He-I_2 mixture

Thus, there are no ideas about both the levels of molecular iodine whose excitation contributes to the formation of XeI* and the rate of the reverse harpoon reaction. That is why, when calculating the kinetics in the He:Xe:I_2 medium, we introduced an additional excited level I_2** with the energy sufficient to excite the XeI molecule that took part in the reverse harpoon reaction (Fig. 1). Its rate was taken equal to the characteristic rate of the harpoon reaction (1.0e-9 cm^3/s) (Rhodes, 1979), whereas the excitation cross section of the I_2** level was chosen so that to provide the fraction of emission in the XeI*(B→X) band close to the experimental one. Such an approach allows us to analyze the effect of xenon on the emission intensities of atomic and molecular iodine. The set of reactions with participation of xenon is listed in Table 2. The used literature sources were the same as in Table 1.
Numerical simulation of the plasma kinetics in mixtures of helium and xenon with iodine vapours allowed us to obtain the relation between the emission intensities of iodine atoms and molecules, to calculate their dependences on the buffer gas pressure and halogen concentration, and to analyze the effect of xenon on the emission intensity of the medium.

3. Results of numerical simulation

3.1 Electron energy distribution function and electron-kinetic coefficients

Figure 2 presents the electron energy distribution functions calculated in the He-I_2-I= 800-50-50 Pa and Xe-I_2-I= 800-50-50 Pa mixtures at various values of the reduced electric field in the discharge E/N (50-300 Td) (Shuaibov et al., 2009).

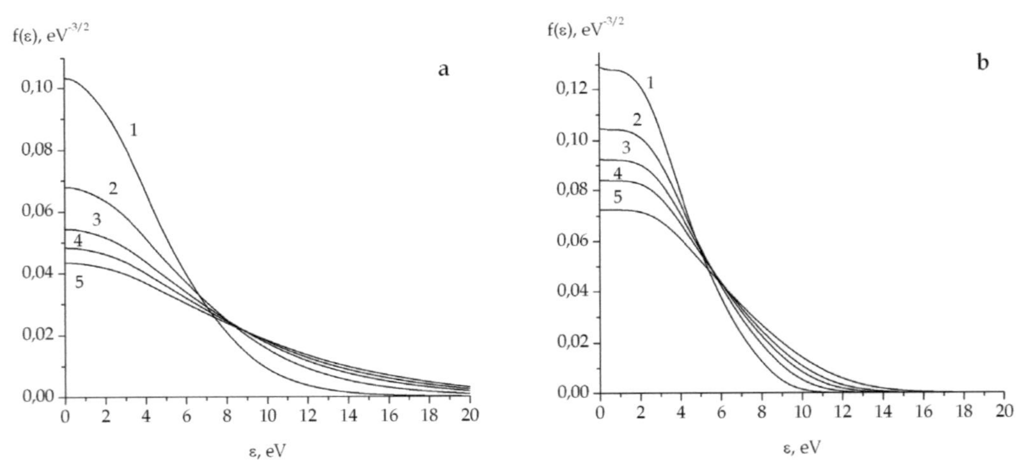

Fig. 2. Electron energy distribution functions calculated in the He-I_2-I= 800-50-50 Pa (a) and Xe-I_2-I= 800-50-50 Pa (b) mixtures at E/N = 50 (1), 100 (2), 150 (3), 200 (4), and 300 (5) Td

One can see that the replacement of the helium buffer gas by xenon results in the decrease of the portion of high-energy electrons in the discharge. It is due to the fact that the excitation and ionization thresholds of xenon atoms (8.3 eV and 12.1 eV, correspondingly) are significantly lower than those of helium (19.8 eV and 22.5 eV), therefore the tail of the distribution function in the xenon mixture is cut off at lower energies.
The drift velocities and the mean electron energies calculated as functions of the electric field in the discharge in the studied mixtures are shown in Fig.3 (Shuaibov et al., 2009). One can see that the increase of the reduced field from 50 to 300 Td results in the linear growth of the drift

№	Reaction	Rate, cm^6/s, cm^3/s, s
1	$e+Xe > Xe^*+e$	Calculated from the Boltzmann equation
2	$e+Xe > Xe^++e+e$	
3	$e+Xe^* > Xe^++e+e$	
4	$e+ I_2 > I_2^{**}+e$	
5	$I_2(B)+Xe > I+I+Xe$	2.0e-10
6	$I_2(D)+Xe > I_2(D')+Xe$	6.0e-12
7	$I_2(D')+Xe > I_2+Xe$	1.0e-12
8	$I_2^{**}+He > I_2+He$	1.0e-12
9	$I_2^{**}+ I_2> I_2+ I_2$	1.0e-12
10	$I_2^{**}+I > I_2+I$	1.0e-12
11	$I_2^{**}+Xe > XeI^*+ I$	1.0e-10
12	$Xe^++ I^-+M > XeI^*+M$	4.0e-26
13	$XeI^*+ I_2 > Xe+ I_2+I$	5.0e-10
14	$XeI^*+Xe > Xe+Xe+I$	9.2e-12
15	$XeI^* > Xe+I+hv$ (253 nm)	1/1.2e-8
16	$Xe^++Xe > Xe_2^+$	1.0e-31
17	$Xe_2^++e > Xe^*+Xe$	2.44e-7
18	$Xe_2^++e > Xe^++Xe+e$	2.44e-7
19	$Xe^*+I > Xe+ I^*$	1.0e-10
20	$Xe_2^*+I > Xe+Xe+ I^*$	1.0e-10
21	$XeI^*+I_2 > Xe + 3I$	1.0e-9
22	$Xe^++He+Xe > Xe_2^++He$	1.3e-31
23	$Xe^++Xe+Xe > Xe_2^++Xe$	3.6e-31
24	$He^++He+Xe > He_2^++Xe$	1.1e-31
25	$Xe^*+Xe^* > Xe+ Xe^++e$	5.0e-10
26	$Xe^*+Xe^* > Xe_2^++e$	1.1e-9
27	$He^*+Xe > Xe^++He+e$	7.5e-11
28	$He^++Xe > Xe^++He$	1.0e-11
29	$Xe^*+Xe+Xe > Xe_2^*+Xe$	8.0e-32
30	$Xe^*+Xe+He > Xe_2^*+He$	1.4e-32
32	$Xe_2^*> Xe+Xe$	6.0e7
33	$Xe_2^*+ I_2> Xe+Xe+ I_2(D')$	2.0e-10
34	$Xe^*+ I_2> Xe+ I_2(D')$	2.0e-10
35	$2I > I_2$	k_{diff}

Table 2. Kinetic reactions with participation of xenon in the He-Xe-I_2 mixture

velocity in the He-I_2-I medium in the range 10^7 – $5{\cdot}10^7$ cm/s, while in the Xe-I_2-I discharge, it changes in the interval $2{\cdot}10^6$ – $8{\cdot}10^6$ cm/s. In this case, the mean electron energy increases from 5.3 to 8.8 eV (He-I_2-I mixture) and from 4.2 to 7.5 eV (Xe-I_2-I mixture). The highest mean energies are observed in the helium medium characterized by a pronounced high-energy tail of the electron energy distribution function. The replacement of helium by xenon results in the abrupt cut-off the electron distribution at energies close to the xenon excitation threshold and, correspondingly, reduction of the mean electron energy in the discharge.

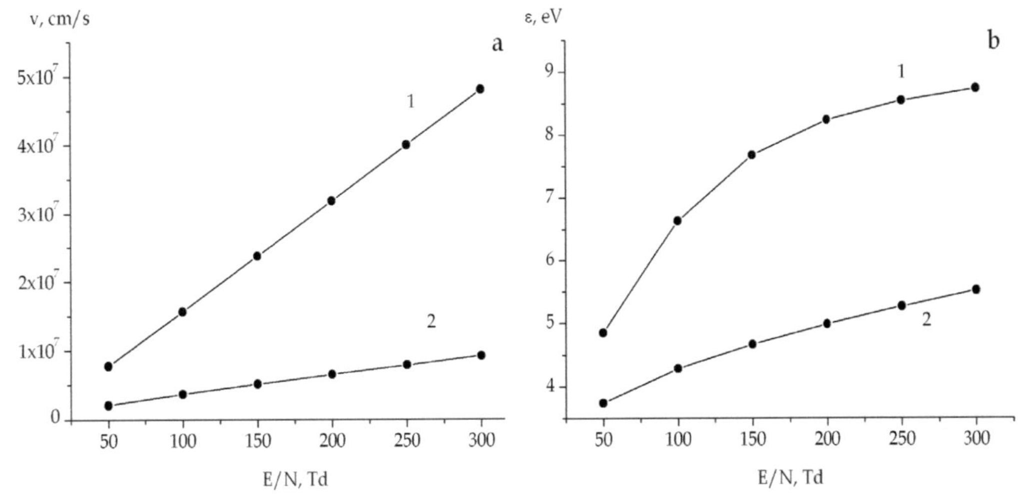

Fig. 3. Drift velocities (a) and mean energies (b) of electrons in the He:I_2-I= 800-50-50 Pa (1) and Xe:I_2-I= 800-50-50 Pa (2) mixtures as functions of the electric field in the discharge

The maximum electron drift velocities are also reached in the helium mixture and fall when passing to xenon. This fact is explained by a more intense electron scattering by xenon (the values of the momentum-transfer cross section for electron scattering by xenon atoms in the energy range 0-25 eV are one-two orders of magnitude higher than the corresponding characteristics of helium). The more intense electron scattering in xenon results in the decrease of the velocity of directed motion in this gas.

Tables 3-4 demonstrate the distribution of the power introduced into the discharge among the most important electron processes (Shuaibov et al., 2010b). They are the reactions of excitation and ionization of the rare gases, halogen atoms and molecules as well as dissociation and dissociative attachment of electrons to iodine molecules. The processes of stepwise ionization of the rare gases and iodine were neglected. It is explained by the facts that the concentrations of excited atoms and molecules strongly depend on the time and that their values are several orders of magnitude smaller than the concentrations of the primary components of the mixture (He, Xe, I_2, and I).

One can see that, due to very high excitation and ionization thresholds of helium atoms, the prevailing portion of the power in the He-I_2-I mixture is spent for reactions with participation of the halogen. Insignificant power costs for the process of electron attachment to iodine molecules are explained by the very low threshold energy of this process close to zero. An increase of the electric field results in the growth of the number of fast electrons and the rising role of the processes of ionization of iodine as well as excitation and ionization of helium.

In the xenon-based mixture, the portion of the power spent for excitation and ionization of the rare gas is much higher. The comparable thresholds of the processes with participation of xenon and iodine result in the fact that, at low electric fields, the power is distributed among them nearly equally. An increase of the electric field results in the growth of the portion of the power spent for processes with participation of the rare gas.

The highest rate is observed for the process with the smallest threshold (stepwise ionization of xenon), while the reactions with the lowest rates are those of helium and xenon ionization. The rates of all the processes grow with increasing electric field. The only

E/N, Td	He excitation	He ionization	I_2 excitation	I_2 attachment	I_2 dissociation	I_2 ionization	I excitation	I ionization
50	0.45	8.28e-5	12.9	9.56e-2	42	9.14	10	25.1
100	1.99	5.18e-4	7.6	3.01e-2	32	17	7.55	33
150	2.72	7.55e-4	6.37	2.08e-2	29	20	6.72	35
200	3.04	8.63e-4	5.92	1.79e-2	28	20.8	6.4	36
250	3.20	9.19e-4	5.71	1.66e-2	27	21.3	6.25	36
300	3.30	9.51e-4	5.6	1.59e-2	27	21.6	6.16	36

Table 3. Relative power costs for electron processes in the mixture He-I_2-I = 800-50-50 Pa (%)

E/N, Td	Xe excitation	Xe ionization	I_2 excitation	I_2 attachment	I_2 dissociation	I_2 ionization	I excitation	I ionization
50	58	0.163	17	0.44	17.6	1.12e-2	6.52	0.48
100	70	2.68	7.66	0.11	13.7	0.14	4.12	1.57
150	72	6.8	4.75	5.05e-2	10.7	0.33	3.0	2.22
200	71	10.8	3.38	2.88e-2	8.83	0.49	2.36	2.59
250	70,1	14.3	2.59	1.87e-2	7.52	0.65	1.95	2.80
300	68.6	17.3	2.09	1.31e-2	6.56	0.78	1.66	2.94

Table 4. Relative power costs for electron processes in the mixture Xe-I_2-I = 800-50-50 Pa (%)

exclusion is the dissociative attachment of electrons to iodine molecules that has the practically zero threshold and, correspondingly, does not depend on the number of fast electrons in the discharge.

The variation of the electric field in the range 50-300 Td results in the growth of the majority of the reaction rates within one order of magnitude. However, the helium ionization rate increases by four orders of magnitude owing to its strong dependence on the number of high-energy electrons.

The excitation and ionization rates of the rare gas in the xenon-iodine mixture are evidently higher than in the helium-iodine one due to lower threshold energies of these processes in xenon. As regards the reactions with participation of molecular and atomic iodine, their rates in the helium mixture are noticeably larger than in the xenon-based medium. It is explained by a much higher number of fast electrons in the discharge in helium that provide effective excitation, ionization, and dissociation of iodine.

Tables 5 and 6 present the values of the rates of the most important electron processes in the considered mixtures calculated as functions of the electric field in the discharge using Eq.(8) (Shuaibov et al., 2010b).

E/N, Td	50	100	150	200	250	300
He excitation	9.91e-13	1.36e-11	2.73e-11	3.6e-11	4.12e-11	4.44e-11
He ionization	1.62e-16	3.11e-15	6.66e-15	8.99e-15	1.04e-14	1.13e-14
I_2 excitation	1.77e-9	3.22e-9	3.97e-9	4.35e-9	4.56e-9	4.69e-9
I_2 attachment	6.71e-10	6.5e-10	6.61e-10	6.70e-10	6.76e-10	6.8e-10
I_2 dissociation	3.57e-9	8.45e-9	1.12e-8	1.26e-8	1.34e-8	1.39e-8
I_2 ionization	5.35e-10	3.09e-9	5.25e-9	6.51e-9	7.24e-9	7.7e-9
I excitation	1.08e-9	2.41e-9	3.16e-9	3.54e-9	3.76e-9	3.88e-9
I ionization	1.69e-9	6.9e-9	1.07e-8	1.29e-8	1.41e-8	1.49e-8

Table 5. Rates of electron processes in the mixture He-I_2-I= 800-50-50 Pa

E/N, Td	50	100	150	200	250	300
Xe excitation	7.42e-11	3.35e-10	7.33e-10	1.24e-9	1.84e-9	2.52e-9
Xe ionization	1.44e-13	8.81e-12	4.76e-11	1.29e-10	2.58e-10	4.37e-10
Xe stepwise ionization	2.3e-7	2.68e-7	2.92e-7	3.11e-7	3.26e-7	3.39e-7
I_2 excitation	2.30e-7	2.68e-7	2.92e-7	3.11e-7	3.26e-7	3.39e-7
I_2 attachment	7.51e-10	7.1e-10	6.84e-10	6.66e-10	6.52e-10	6.41e-10
I_2 dissociation	3.66e-10	1.05e-9	1.76e-9	2.47e-9	3.18e-9	3.88e-9
I_2 ionization	1.59e-13	7.61e-12	3.69e-11	9.54e-11	1.88e-10	3.17e-10
I excitation	1.65e-10	3.88e-10	6.01e-10	8.06e-10	1.0e-9	1.20e-9
I ionization	7.82e-12	9.54e-11	2.88e-10	5.72e-10	9.37e-10	1.37e-9

Table 6. Rates of electron processes in the mixture Xe-I_2-I= 800-50-50 Pa

3.2 Dependence of the emission intensities on the rare gas pressure

The analysis of the plasma kinetics in the mixture of rare gases with iodine vapours performed with regard for the described regularities makes it possible to study the effect of the buffer gas pressure on the emission intensities of molecular and atomic iodine. The results of the calculations performed for the helium-iodine mixture at the iodine concentration equal to 130 Pa are shown in Fig.4 (Shuaibov et al., 2010a).

One can see that the emission intensities of the 206-nm spectral line and the 342-nm molecular band of iodine depend on the helium pressure in the opposite ways. The emission intensity in the molecular band decreases with increasing rare gas pressure, while that in the 260-nm atomic line grows.

Excited iodine molecules $I_2(D')$ are generated in the discharge due to direct electron impact excitation. The rate of this process is determined by the electron energy distribution function and grows with increasing parameter *E/N*. Thus, an increase of the pressure of the mixture results in the decrease of the rate of formation of emitting $I_2(D')$ molecules in the discharge.

As was demonstrated in (Sauer, 1976; Baboshin, 1981), another important channel of generation of $I_2(D')$ molecules is the excitation transfer from the above-lying level $I_2(D)$ colliding with atoms and molecules of the active medium. However, at the considered pressures, the probability of radiation decay of the $I_2(D)$ state is much higher than the probability of its collision with other particles, that is why this channel makes practically no contribution to the formation of emitting $I_2(D')$ molecules.

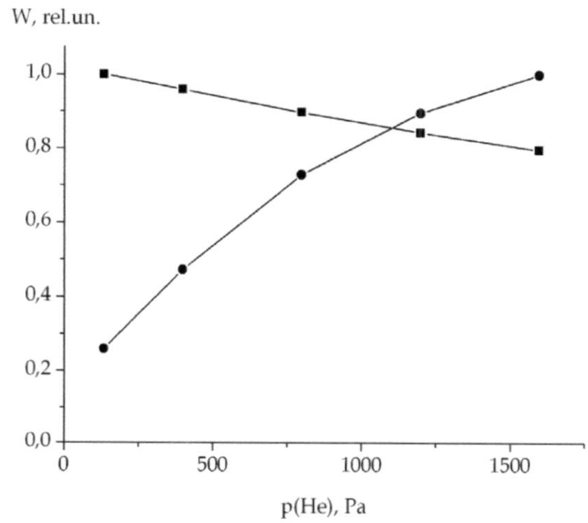

Fig. 4. Emission intensities of the 206-nm spectral line (•) and 342-nm molecular band (■) of iodine as functions of the helium pressure

A considerable part of iodine exists in the discharge in the dissociated state, which is confirmed by a high intensity of the 206-nm spectral line registered in a number of works (Avdeev, 2007; Shuaibov et al., 2005b; Zhang & Boyd, 2000). Measurements performed in (Barnes & Kushner, 1996, 1998) for Xe-I_2 mixture at pressures close to those used in our work have demonstrated that the fraction of iodine molecules dissociating in the discharge exceeds 90%. Moreover, the minimum concentration of I_2 molecules was registered at the axis of the discharge tube and the maximum one - close to the walls where iodine recovered to the molecular state.

Molecular iodine decays into atoms mainly owing to the processes of direct electron-impact dissociation (Table 1, reaction 8) and predissociation of the excited $I_2(B)$ state due to collisions with particles of the mixture (Table 1, reaction 12). The rate of the former reaction is determined by the form of the electron energy distribution function and decreases with increasing rare gas pressure, whereas the effectiveness of the latter process grows in direct proportion to the pressure.

Thus, an increase of the helium pressure in the He-I_2 glow discharge has a multiple effect on the efficiency of production of iodine atoms. The rate of electron-impact dissociation of the ground state of the iodine molecule falls due to the change of the electron energy distribution function. The rate of formation of the $I_2(B)$ excited state also decreases. At the same time, the efficiency of collisional predissociation of the $I_2(B)$ level abruptly increases, which appears determinative for the resulting effect.

Another important consequence of the increase of the rare gas pressure is the deceleration of the diffusion motion of iodine atoms to the walls of the discharge chamber, which results in the less efficient recovery of molecular iodine. Thus, with increasing pressure in the working medium of the halogen lamp, the relation between the concentrations of excited iodine molecules and atoms (and consequently powers of emission from the levels $I_2(D')$ and I^*) changes in favor of the latter.

3.3 Dependence of the emission intensities on the halogen pressure

With variation of the iodine concentration in the mixture, the emission intensities in the atomic 206-nm line and the 342-nm molecular band pass through a maximum (Fig.5). At $p(I_2) < 200$ Pa, the emission intensities grow with increasing halogen concentration, while at $p(I_2) > 200$-230 Pa, they sharply fall to zero.

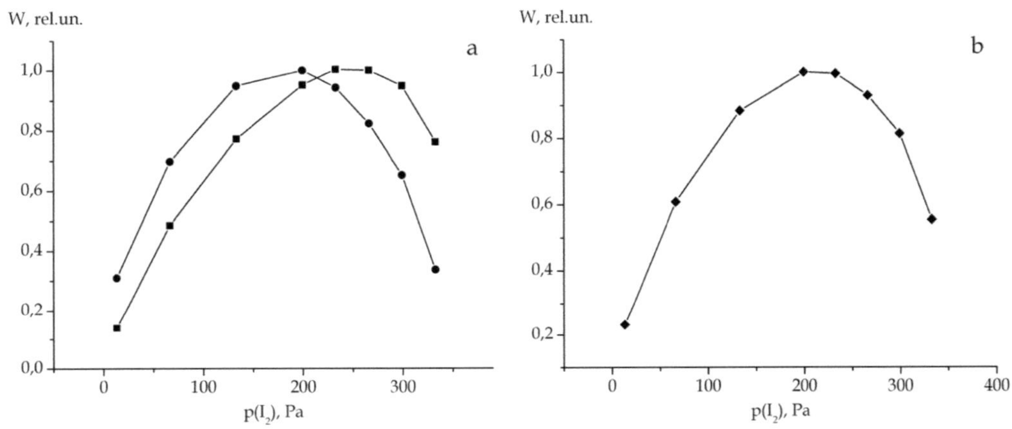

Fig. 5. Emission intensities of the spectral line of atomic iodine at 206 nm (•) and molecular band at 342 nm $I_2(D'\rightarrow A')$ (■) (a) and total emission intensity (b) as functions of the iodine concentration in the He-I_2 mixture at p(He)= 400 Pa

An increase of the iodine concentration is accompanied by the rise of the discharge voltage and reduction of the electron density in the discharge. This fact is caused by the effect of iodine on the electron energy distribution function. At low iodine concentrations, the distribution function is determined by the helium buffer gas characterized by large thresholds of excitation and ionization (19.8 eV and 22.5 eV, correspondingly). The addition of iodine to the active medium results in the cut-off of the distribution function at lower energies due to the smaller thresholds of its excitation and ionization as well as the increase of the total pressure of the mixture. Moreover, the rate of dissociative attachment of electrons to I_2 molecules (with a near-zero threshold) weakly depends on the iodine concentration, while the ionization rate determined by the tail of the distribution function sharply falls with increasing iodine content (Fig.6). The discharge voltage is determined by the balance of the ionization and attachment processes. That is why in order to maintain a discharge in a medium with a heightened halogen content, one should apply a larger voltage, which results in the decrease of the discharge current and, correspondingly, electron density.

The decrease of the electron concentration reduces the efficiency of generation of radiating particles in the discharge resulting in the decrease of the emission intensities both in the atomic line and in the molecular band of iodine. As one can see from Fig.5, the emission maximum in the case of the 342-nm band is reached at higher iodine pressure ≈ 230 Pa, whereas the emission intensity of atomic iodine starts falling already at $p(I_2) > 200$ Pa. It is explained by the fact that the generation of excited iodine atoms is more sensitive to the electron density in the medium because it runs via two electron processes - electronic excitation of iodine molecules to the $I_2(B)$ level followed by decay into atoms (or direct electron-impact dissociation of molecular iodine) and consequent excitation of iodine atoms to the radiating level. Radiating $I_2(D')$ molecules are formed due to direct electronic excitation of molecular iodine. If the iodine concentration in the mixture exceeds 400 Pa, then the voltage falling across the discharge gap appears insufficient for the breakdown and the emission intensities abruptly fall to zero. The maximum of the summary emission intensity is reached at the iodine pressure equal to 200 Pa.

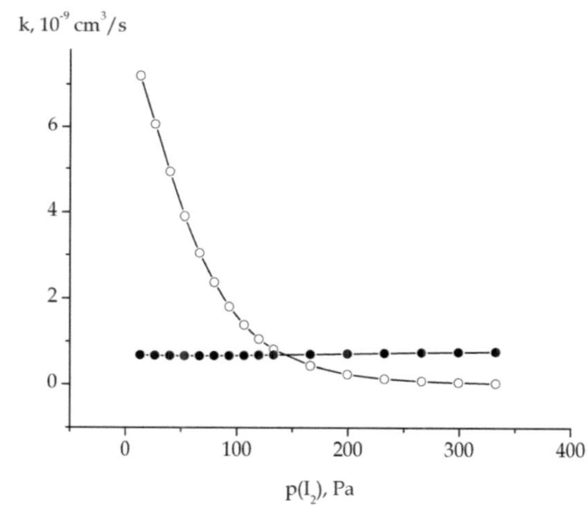

Fig. 6. Rates of dissociative attachment (•) and ionization (○) of iodine molecules as functions of the iodine concentration in the He-I_2 mixture at p(He)= 400 Pa and E = 150 V/cm

Taking into account the fact that the emission intensities of atomic and molecular iodine reach a maximum at different iodine concentrations, it is evident that the variation of its content in the mixture will result in the change of the relation between the emission intensities at 342 and 206 nm. With increasing iodine concentration, the relative emission intensity in the molecular band grows, and in the atomic line - falls. The calculated curve is given in Fig.7.

3.4 Effect of xenon on the emission of the excimer lamp

The presence of xenon in the active medium of the helium-iodine UV emitter results in the appearance of the additional emission band at 253 nm corresponding to the B→X transition of the XeI* excimer. As was already noted, XeI* molecules are generated in the discharge owing to the reverse harpoon reaction between a xenon atom in the ground state and some highly excited level I_2^{**} (Table 2, reaction 11). For today, the levels of molecular iodine participating in the reverse harpoon reaction are not identified. However, the analysis of the energy state diagram in the Xe:I_2:I mixture (Fig.1) testifies to the fact that neither of the states important for the kinetics in the helium-iodine medium has enough energy to excite the XeI* excimer molecule. It means that the addition of xenon does not result in the appearance of

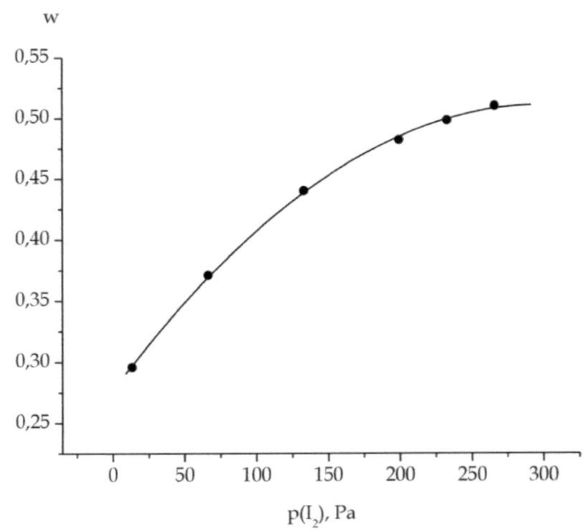

Fig. 7. Relative emission intensity in the 342-nm molecular band as a function of the iodine concentration in the He-I_2 mixture at p(He)= 400 Pa

additional channels of decay of the $I_2(D')$ and $I_2(B)$ states and influences their kinetics only through the electron distribution function. That is why, introducing a highly excited I_2^{**} state with the minimum energy sufficient for the formation of the XeI* molecule and choosing its excitation cross section so that to provide the fraction of the emission intensity in the XeI*(B→X) band close to that observed experimentally, it is possible to analyze the effect of the xenon admixture on the emission intensities of atomic and molecular iodine.

The addition of xenon changes the plasma kinetics in three ways. The first one is the variation of the electron energy distribution function, namely, the decrease of the number of fast electrons in the discharge. The smaller number of high-energy electrons results in the reduction of the rates of the electron processes responsible for the formation of both excited atoms and molecules of iodine. However, the other two factors facilitate the generation of atomic iodine. One of them is the increase of the efficiency of decay of the excited $I_2(B)$ level in its collisions with buffer gas atoms. The rate of this process in xenon is higher than in helium by a factor of 20. The second process is the decrease of the diffusion rate of iodine atoms to the walls of the discharge chamber due to the fact that the larger radius of xenon atoms as compared to helium ones provides the decrease of the mean free path of iodine atoms in the helium-xenon medium. These two factors result in the increase of the concentration of excited iodine atoms in the discharge.

According to the results of numerical simulations, the relation between the emission intensities of atomic and molecular iodine in He-I_2=400:130 Pa mixture amounts to W(206.2 nm)-W(342 nm) = 56-44%, whereas in the He-Xe-I_2=400:130:130 Pa medium, it changes to W(206.2 nm)-W(342 nm)=55:31%. Thus, the addition of xenon results in the decrease of the relative emission intensity of the 342-nm molecular band.

The dependences of the emission intensities on the concentration of iodine vapours in the mixture including xenon (p(He)-p(Xe) = 400-130 Pa) are qualitatively the same as those calculated for the He-I_2 medium. The maximum emission power in the 206-nm spectral line is reached at p(I_2)=230 Pa, while in the 342-nm band - at p(I_2)=170 Pa. Moreover, the maximum iodine concentration, at which the discharge is still initiated, is lower than in helium and amounts to 240 Pa. Such a difference is related to the fact that the ionization rates in the helium-iodine mixture at equal iodine concentration are lower than in the helium one, that is why the maintenance of the discharge requires higher voltages.

4. Comparison with experiment

The results of numerical simulations were compared to the data of experimental studies reported in a cycle of works (Shuaibov et al., 2004, 2005b, 2009).
A longitudinal glow discharge in helium and xenon rare gases was initiated in a cylindrical discharge tube made of quartz transparent to λ = 190 nm. The distance L between the cylindrical nickel electrodes was equal to 50 cm. The thickness of the tube walls and its inner diameter amounted to 1 mm and 1.4 cm, correspondingly. Crystalline iodine of high purity was located in a special appendix behind the anode of the discharge tube. The diagram of the experimental set-up is shown in Fig.8.

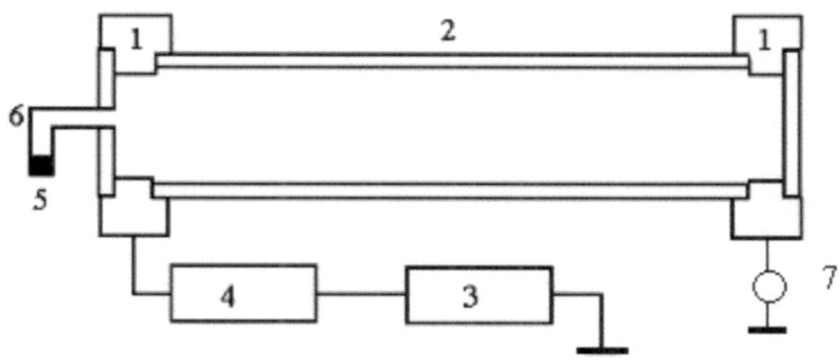

Fig. 8. Experimental set-up used for obtaining the glow discharge in mixtures of rare gases with iodine vapours: 1 - electrodes, 2 - quartz discharge tube, 3 - high-voltage rectifier, 4 - ballast resistor, 5 - iodine crystals, 6 - container for iodine, 7 - ammeter

The emission spectrum of the helium-iodine discharge included the spectral line of atomic iodine at 206 nm and a molecular band I_2 (D'-A') at 342 nm. At the partial helium pressure equal to 400 Pa, the emission intensities related as W(206.2 nm)-W(342nm) = 52-48 %. These values are in good agreement with the calculation results: W(206.2 nm)-W(342nm) = 56-44%.
The addition of xenon to the active medium of the UV emitter resulted in the appearance of the emission band at 253 nm, corresponding to the B→Xtransition of the XeI* molecule. At p(He)-p(Xe)=400-130 Pa, the emission intensities related as W(206.2 nm)-W(253 nm)-W(342 nm)=54-9-37%. In this case, the numerical computations yield the relation W(206.2 nm)-W(342 nm)=55:31%. Thus, both experimental and theoretical results testify to the fact that the addition of xenon to the active medium of the excimer lamp results in the decrease of the relative emission intensity of the I_2 (D'-A') molecular band, while that of the 206-nm line remains practically the same.

The experimentally obtained dependences of the registered emission intensities on the helium pressure in the He-I_2 mixture are presented in Fig.9. One can see that, with increasing helium pressure, the intensity of the molecular band decreases and that of the atomic line - grows. Such a behavior completely agrees with the results obtained by numerical simulation of the discharge kinetics in the UV emitter.

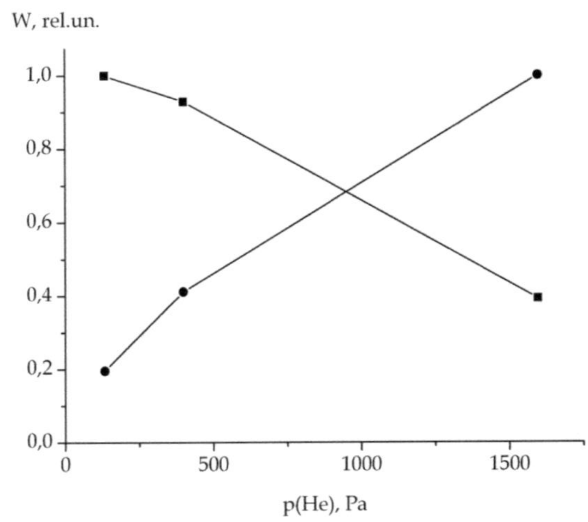

Fig. 9. Experimentally measured emission intensities of 206-nm spectral line (•) and 342-nm molecular band (■) of iodine as functions of the helium pressure

5. Conclusion

The numerical simulation of the discharge and emission kinetics in excimer lamps in mixtures of helium and xenon with iodine vapours allowed us to determine the most important kinetic reactions having a significant effect on the population kinetics of the emitting states in He:I_2 and He:Xe:I_2 mixtures. The opposite behavior of the dependences of the emission intensities of atomic and molecular iodine on the buffer gas pressure is explained. The influence of the halogen concentration on the emission power of the excimer lamp is investigated. The effect of xenon on the relative emission intensities of iodine atoms and molecules is analyzed. The calculation results are in good agreement with data of experimental studies, which is an evidence of the right choice of the calculation model and elementary processes for numerical simulation.

6. References

Avdeev, S.M.; Zvereva G.N., & Sosnin, E.A. (2007). Investigation of the conditions of efficient I^*_2 (342 nm) luminescence in a barrier discharge in a Kr-I2 mixture. *Optics and Spectroscopy*. Vol. 103, pp. 910-919

Baboshin, V.N., Mikheev, L.D., Pavlov, A.B., Fokanov, V.P., Khodorkovskii, M.A., & Shirokikh, A.P. (1981). Investigation of the luminescence and excitation spectrum of molecular iodine. *Soviet Journal of Quantum Electronics*. Vol. 11, pp. 683-686

Baginskii, V.M., Vladimirov, V.V., Golovinskii, P.M, & Shchedrin, A.I. (1988). *Optimization and stability of discharge in He/Xe/HCl excimer lasers*. Preprint of Acad. of Sci. of UkrSSR, Kyiv

Barnes P.N. & Kushner M.J. (1996). Formation of XeI(B) in low pressure inductive radio frequency electric discharges sustained in mixtures of Xe and I2. *Journal of Applied Physics*. Vol. 80, pp. 5593-5595

Barnes P.N. & Kushner M.J. (1998). Reactions in the afterglow of time modulated inductive discharges of Xe and I_2 mixtures. *Journal of Applied Physics*. Vol. 84, pp. 4727-4730

Boichenko, A.M. & Yakovlenko, S.I. (2003). Simulation of Xe/I2 Lamp Kinetics upon Capacitive Discharge Excitation. *Laser Physics*. Vol. 13, pp. 1461–1466

Cartwright, D.C., Csanak, G., Trajmar, S., & Register, D.F. (1992). Electron-impact excitation of the n1P levels of He. *Physical Review A* . Vol. 45, pp. 1602-1624

Golant, V.E., Zhilinsky A.P., & Sakharov I.E. (1980) *Fundamentals of Plasma Physics*, Wiley, ISBN 0-471-04593-4, New York

Hayashi, M. (2003) Bibliography of Electron and Photon Cross Sections with Atoms and Molecules Published in the 20th Century. Halogen Molecules, Available from: <www.nifs.ac.jp/report/NIFS-DATA-081.pdf>

Hyman, H.A. (1979). Electron-impact ionization cross sections for excited states of rare gases (Ne, Ar, Kr, Xe), cadmium, and mercury. *Physical Review A*. Vol. 20, pp. 855–859

Kireev, S.V. & Shnyrev, S.L. (1998). Collisional Predissociation of Vibrational Levels of the *B* state in I_2 Excited by 633-nm Radiation of a He–Ne Laser. *Laser Physics*. Vol. 8, pp. 483–486

Liuti G. & Mentall J.L. (1968). Monochromatic Iodine Lamp. *Review of Scientific Instruments*. Vol. 39, pp. 1767-1768

Lomaev, M.I., Skakun, V.S., Sosnin E.A., Tarasenko V.F., Shitts D.V., & Erofeev M.V. (2003). Excilamps: efficient sources of spontaneous UV and VUV radiation. *Physics-Uspekhi*, Vol. 46, pp. 193–209

Lomaev M.I. & Tarasenko V.F. (2002). Xe(He) I2-Glow and Capacitive Discharge Excilamps. *Proceedings of SPIE*. Vol. 4747, pp. 390-396

McDaniel, E.W. & Nighan, W.L. (Eds.). (1982). *Applied Atomic Collision Physics. Vol. 3. Gas Lasers*. Academic Press, ISBN 0-12-478803-3, New York

National Institute for Fusion Science. (n.d.). Xenon. Recommended electron collision cross sections, Available from: < dpc.nifs.ac.jp/DB/IEEJ/datafiles/Xe/Xe.pdf>

Raizer, Yu.P. (1991). *Gas Discharge Physics*, Springer, ISBN 978-3540194620, Berlin

Rejoub, R., Lindsay, B.G., & Stebbings, R.F. (2002). Determination of the absolute partial and total cross sections for electron-impact ionization of the rare gases. *Physical Review A*. Vol.65, 042713

Rhodes, C.K. (Ed.). (1984). *Excimer Lasers*, Springer-Verlag, ISBN 978-3540130130, Berlin

Saha, H.P. (1989). Accurate ab initio calculation on low-energy elastic scattering of electrons from helium. *Physical Review A*. Vol. 40, pp. 2976-2990

Sauer, M.C., Mulac, W.A., Cooper, R.F., & Grieser, F. (1976). Fast excited state formation and decay in the pulse radiolysis of gaseous argon–iodine systems. *Journal of Chemical Physics*. Vol. 64, pp. 4587-4591

Shuaibov, A.K. & Grabovaya, I.A. (2004). Electric-Discharge He/Xe/I2 excimer-halogen lamp. *Technical Physics*. Vol. 49, pp. 443-446

Shuaibov, A.K. & Grabovaya, I.A. (2005). A continuously emitting electric discharge UV lamp. *Instruments and Experimental Techniques*. Vol. 48, pp. 102-104

Shuaibov, A.K. & Grabovaya, I.A. (2005). Emission characteristics of a glow discharge in a mixture of heavy inert gases with iodine vapor. *Optics and Spectroscopy*. Vol. 98, pp. 510-513

Shuaibov, A.K., Minya, A.I., Gomoki, Z.T., Kalyuzhnaya, A.G. & Shchedrin, A.I. (2009). Output characteristics and parameters of the plasma from a gas-discharge low-pressure ultraviolet source on helium-iodine and xenon-iodine mixtures. *Technical Physics*. Vol. 54, pp. 1819-1824

Shuaibov, A.K., Gomoki, Z.T., Kalyuzhnaya, A.G. & Shchedrin, A.I. (2010). Radiative characteristics and kinetics of processes in low-pressure gas-discharge lamps on a mixture of helium and iodine vapors. *Optics and Spectroscopy*. Vol. 109, pp. 669-673

Shuaibov, A.K., Minya, A.I., Gomoki, Z.T., Kalyuzhnaya, A.G. & Shchedrin, A.I. (2010). Ultraviolet gas-discharge lamp on iodine molecules. *Technical Physics*. Vol. 55, pp. 1222-1225

Smirnov, B.M. (1967). *Atomic Collisions and Elementary Processes in Plasmas*, Atomizdat, Moscow

Soloshenko, I.A., Tsiolko, V.V., Pogulay, S.S., Terent'yeva, A.G., Bazhenov, V.Yu., Shchedrin, A.I., Ryabtsev, A.V., & Kuzmichev, A.I. (2007). The component content of active particles in a plasma-chemical reactor based on volume barrier discharge. *Plasma Sources Science and Technology*. Vol.16, pp. 56-66

Soloshenko, I.A., Tsiolko, V.V., Pogulay, S.S., Kalyuzhnaya, A.G., Bazhenov, V.Yu., & Shchedrin, A.I. (2009). Effect of water adding on kinetics of barrier discharge in air. *Plasma Sources Science and Technology*. Vol. 18, 045019

Stoilov, Yu. Yu. (1978). Characteristics of short-pulse iodine laser amplifier. *Soviet Journal of Quantum Electronics*. Vol. 8, pp. 223-226

Tam, Wing-Cheung & Wong, S.F. (1978). Dissociative attachment of halogen molecules by 0–8 eV electrons. *Journal of Chemical Physics*. Vol. 68, pp. 5626-5630

Zhang, J.-Y. & Boyd, I.W. (1998). Efficient XeI* excimer ultraviolet sources from a dielectric barrier discharge. *Journal of Applied Physics*. Vol. 84, pp. 1174-1178

Zhang, J.-Y. & Boyd, I.W. (2000). Multi-wavelength excimer ultraviolet sources from a mixture of krypton and iodine in a dielectric barrier discharge. *Applied Physics B*. Vol. 71, pp. 177-179

13

Dynamics of Optical Pulses Propagating in Fibers with Variable Dispersion

Alexej A. Sysoliatin[1], Andrey I. Konyukhov[2] and Leonid A. Melnikov[3]
[1]*Fiber Optics Research Center, Vavilov Street 38, Moscow*
[2]*Saratov State University, Astrakhanskaya 83, Saratov*
[3] *Saratov State Technical University, Politehnicheskaya 77, Saratov*
Russia

1. Introduction

The book chapter describes recent progress in the management of laser pulses by means of optical fibers with smoothly variable dispersion. Nonlinear Schrödinger equation based numerical simulations give powerful mathematics for optimizing of fiber dispersion for given task. In the book chapter we use numerical simulations to describe and analyse soliton and pulse dynamics in three kind of fibers with variable dispersion: i) dispersion oscillating fiber; ii) negative dispersion decreasing fiber. Optical pulse compression techniques are important for the generation of subpicosecond and femtosecond optical pulses. Dispersion decreasing fibers are useful for high quality, pedestal-free optical pulse compression.
The classical soliton concept was developed for nonlinear and dispersive systems that have been autonomous; namely, propagation distance has only played the role of the independent variable and has not appeared explicitly in the nonlinear Schrödinger equation (NLSE) (Ablowitz et al., 1981; Agraval, 2001; Akhmanov et al., 1991). Under condition of harmonical dispersion and nonlinearity nonautonomous solitons interact elastically and generally move with varying amplitudes, speeds, and spectra (Serkin et al., 2007).
High-order soliton propagating in a fiber with fixed dispersion and nonlinearity is reshaped periodically after propagation distance equal to the soliton period $0.16\pi|\beta_2|^{-1}T^2_{\text{FWHM}}$ (Agraval, 2001; Akhmanov et al., 1991), where β_2 is second order dispersion coefficient, T_{FWHM} is the full-width at half-maximum (FWHM) pulse duration. In a fiber with periodically modulated core diameter, the dispersion oscillates periodically along the fiber length. When the oscillation period approaches the soliton period, the soliton splits into few pulses. Simulations show that second-order soliton splits into two pulses, which carrier frequencies are located symmetrically with respect to the initial pulse frequency (Bauer et al., 1995; Hasegava et al., 1991). A sequence of second-order solitons transmitted through dispersion oscillating fiber (DOF) will produce a pulse train with alternate carrier frequency.
Nonlinear pulse propagation in periodic transmission lines with multisegmented fibers was investigated extensively. The dispersion managed soliton (Malomed, 2006; Smith et al., 1996), split-step soliton (Driben et al., 2000), and stationary rescaled pulse (Inoue et al., 2005) have been discovered. The studies were focused mainly on the stability of solitons.

Simulations show that soliton splitting into the pairs of pulses with upshifted and downshifted central wavelengths can be achieved by a stepwise change of dispersion or by a localized loss element or filter (Lee et al., 2003). The maximum spectral separation occurs at locations that correspond to a half of soliton period for second-order soliton and to 0.225 of soliton period for third-order soliton. In a fiber that consists of a few segments, the multiple breakups of each soliton can generate Cantor set fractals (Sears et al., 2000). Theoretical studies (Bauer et al., 1995; Hasegava et al., 1991; Lee et al., 2003; Sears et al., 2000) consider the soliton splitting without effect of stimulated Raman scattering or high-order dispersion. The fission of high-order soliton can be stimulated by self-steepening (Golovchenko et al., 1985), Raman scattering (Dianov et al., 1985; Tai et al., 1988), and cubic dispersion (Wai et al., 1986). These effects are not negligible for few-picosecond pulses.

Splicing losses and transient processes that arise due to a stepwise change of the dispersion restrict the application of multisegmented fibers for soliton splitting. These disadvantages of multisegmented fibers are surmountable in a fiber with a smooth modulation of the core diameter. We considered the soliton splitting in a fiber with a sine-wave variation of the fiber diameter (DOF).

Optical pulse compression techniques are important for the generation of sub-ps and fs optical pulses. Dispersion decreasing fibers (DDF) are useful for high-quality, pedestal-free optical pulse compression. There are several techniques to compress optical pulses, in particular it is possible to utilize soliton effects. Earlier research focused on using the compression of high-order solitons. This can provide rapid compression but suffers from residual pedestal. Furthermore, the pulse quality at the optimum point of compression is poor, since a significant proportion of the pulse energy is contained in a broad pedestal. A less rapid technique but with better pulse quality is adiabatic amplification of fundamental solitons. To avoid pulse distortion the amplification per soliton period cannot be too big. The method to vary dispersion along the fiber length can be used to obtain the same effect as adiabatic amplification, but the effect can be achieved in a passive fiber.

High pulse quality with minimal or no pedestal component can be achieved by the adiabatic compression technique using dispersion decreasing fibers. Improved quality pulse compression is possible and the input power requirements are significantly lower than that for soliton-effect compression. For a DDF with length L the ratio of input to output dispersion determines the maximum pulse compression factor for the case of no fiber loss and a constant nonlinearity coefficient:

$$W_{eff} = \frac{\beta_2(0)}{\beta_2(L)} \tag{1}$$

The maximum compression factor is determined by the ratio of input to output dispersion and could be over 50. Using DDF with optimum dispersion profile it is possible to obtain pedestal-free pulses of less than 200 fs duration using technique of adiabatic soliton compression (Pelusi et al., 1997). In the case of short (< 3 ps) solitons it is necessary to take into account the higher-order nonlinear and dispersive effects. In particular intrapulse Raman scattering results to the shift of the soliton mean frequency. This frequency shift leads to the change in GVD due to third-order dispersion β_3. These effects result to the soliton corruption. However the stable compression of ultrashort solitons in DDF can take place in the presence of the Raman effect and third order dispersion. Taking these effects into account it is possible to generate high quality pulses of 30 fs duration.

A tunable source can be based on the supercontinuum generation (Haus et al., 2000) and on the Raman conversion of the carrier frequency of the optical soliton (Dianov et al., 1985). Last method could be high efficient especially whether smooth tuning in some frequency range is required. Recently an efficient optical scheme has been proposed capable to generate 30 fs pulses at MHz pulse repetition rates, smoothly tuned in the telecommunication range using a high nonlinear dispersion decreasing fiber (Andrianov et al., 2007). The smooth tuning is based on the Raman frequency conversion of ultrashort pulses. However, until now nobody was able to build up the L-band tunable GHz ps source well synchronized with basic clock.
A high-repetition-rate broadband source is attractive both for high-capacity fiber transmission systems and in optical spectroscopy and metrology. The task to generate the broadband spectra in the nearby region of 1550 nm window was of remarkable interest from 1990 and since then the essential research efforts have been carried out in this area. Dense wavelength-division multiplexing is an efficient and practical method to increase the capacity of lightwave transmission systems. As the number of channels increases for such systems, the required number of lasers becomes large if each channel has its own transmitter. Under these conditions spectral slicing of a single coherent broadband transmitter has attracted attention, especially for gigabit-per-second systems in which external modulators are used. So far, spectral slicing has been limited to laboratory trials. However, the fiber transmission window has been expanded to 400 nm with the removal of the water absorption peak.
Spectral slicing may then become attractive in real systems, especially if a single source can cover the entire fiber transmission window (1300–1700 nm). Thus, a gigahertz-repetition-rate (rep-rate) broadband source can be important for high-capacity light-wave transmission systems. To achieve such a source a high-rep-rate mode-locked laser is used either as the seed for further external spectrum generation or as the source itself. Actively mode-locked lasers can provide high-rep-rate, good noise performance and can easily be locked to external clocks through their intracavity modulator. However, even with soliton pulse shortening these lasers produce only picosecond pulses. Further spectral broadening with these lasers has resulted only in limited spectral widths, even in the supercontinuum regime. Passively mode-locked lasers can provide short pulses directly and a very large externally generated bandwidth but at a low rep rate. Although passive harmonic mode locking or external time-division multiplexing can increase the rep rate of such lasers, they require extensive stabilization and (or) suffer from poor timing jitter and poor supermode suppression.

2. Pulse propagation in single mode fibers

This section covers some fundamental concepts for modelling of pulse propagation in fibers. The section describes numerical approaches used for modelling of the pulse propagation in single-mode fibers with variable dispersion. For this aim nonlinear Schrödinger equation (NLS) (or complex Ginzburg-Landau equation) is used. Split-step method with time-frequency Fourier transform is applied for solving the NLS equation. We examine the method of inverse scattering transform in application to numerical analysis of solitons dynamics in presence of variable dispersion, pulse self-steepening and stimulated Raman scattering. Numerical approaches used for solving and analysis of NLS equation are described in sections below.

2.1 Propagation equation

We assume that the incident light is polarized along a principal axis (for example chosen to coincide with the x axis). In time-domain the pulsed optical field can be presented as superposition of monochromatic waves

$$E_t(r,\phi,z) = \int_{-\infty}^{\infty} d\omega \mathcal{A}_\omega \psi(r,\phi,\omega) \exp\left[-i\omega t + i\beta(\omega)z\right] + \text{c.c.} \simeq$$

$$\psi(r,\phi,\omega_0) \int_{-\infty}^{\infty} d\omega \mathcal{A}_\omega \exp\left[-i\omega t + i\beta(\omega)z\right] + \text{c.c.}, \tag{2}$$

where ω is the field frequency, (r,ϕ) are transverse coordinates, z is the propagation distance, $A(\omega)$ is the mode amplitude, $\beta(\omega)$ is called propagation constant which is z-component of wavevector, "c.c." is complex conjugate, $\psi(r,\phi,\omega)$ describes transverse distribution of the mode field. The optical field is assumed to be quasi-monochromatic, i.e., the pulse spectrum, centered at ω_0, is assumed to have a spectral width $\Delta\omega \ll 1$. Thus the frequency dependence of ψ in (2) can be neglected and $\psi(r,\phi,\omega) \simeq \psi(r,\phi,\omega_0)$ where ω_0 is the pulse central frequency For weakly guiding step-profile fiber the function $\psi(r,\phi)$ gives transverse field distribution for LP_{01} mode (see section 12-11 in (Snyder et al., 1983))

$$\psi(r,\phi) = \begin{cases} \frac{J_0(ur/a)}{J_0(u)}, & r \leq a, \\ \frac{K_0(wr/a)}{K_0(w)}, & r > a \end{cases}, \tag{3}$$

where J_0 and J_1 are Bessel functions of the first kind, K_0 and K_1 are modified Bessel functions of the second kind, a is fiber core radius. Frequency dependent functions $u(\omega)$, $w(\omega)$ are defined from eigenvalue equation

$$u\frac{J_1(u)}{J_0(u)} = w\frac{K_1(w)}{K_0(w)}, \tag{4}$$

where $u^2 + w^2 = V^2$. Propagation constant can be found as $\beta^2 = k^2 n_c^2 - u^2/a^2$, where $k = \omega/c$ is wavenumber, n_c is the fiber core refractive index.

For optical fibers having complex transverse distribution of refractive index the propagation constant $\beta(\omega)$ can be calculated numerically. Different methods for Bragg fibers (Yeh et al., 1978),(Guo et al., 2004), photonic crystal fibers and microstructure fibers (Poli et al., 2007), (Lourtioz et al., 2005), (Brechet et al., 2000) are proposed.

Equation (2) is inverse Fourier transform. At $z = 0$ integral (2) gives Fourier transformation of input pulse $E_t(r,\phi,z) = \psi(r,\phi,\omega_0)A(t)$, where slowly varying pulse amplitude

$$A(t) = \int_{-\infty}^{\infty} d\omega \mathcal{A}_\omega e^{-i\omega t}, \tag{5}$$

$$\mathcal{A}_\omega = \frac{1}{2\pi}\int_{-\infty}^{\infty} dt A(t) e^{i\omega t}. \tag{6}$$

$$\mathcal{E}_\omega(r,\phi,z) = \mathcal{A}_\omega \psi(r,\phi,\omega_0) \exp\left[-i\omega_0 t + i\beta(\omega)z\right] + \text{c.c.}, \tag{7}$$

Taylor series of $\beta(\omega)$ about the central pulse frequency ω_0 is

$$\beta(\omega) = \beta(\omega_0) + \frac{1}{v_g}\Omega + \frac{\beta_2}{2}\Omega^2 + \sum_{m=3} \frac{\beta_m}{m!}\Omega^m \tag{8}$$

where v_g is the group velocity, $\Omega = \omega - \omega_0$

$$\frac{1}{v_g} = \frac{d\beta}{d\omega}\bigg|_{\omega=\omega_0}, \qquad \beta_m = \frac{d^m\beta}{d\omega^m}\bigg|_{\omega=\omega_0}. \tag{9}$$

Parameter β_2 represents dispersion of the group velocity and is responsible for pulse broadening. This phenomenon is known as the group-velocity dispersion (GVD), and β_2 is the GVD parameter (Agraval, 2001). For modelling femtosecond pulse propagation in microstructure fiber up to six-order dispersion coefficients can be used (Washburn et al., 2002). With large number terms ($m > 10$) the Taylor series (8) roughly approximate dispersion due to computing errors grows.
Pulse propagation in single mode fibers described by so-called generalized nonlinear Schrödinger equation (NLS) or generalized complex Ginzburg-Landau equation. Detailed derivation of this equation can be found in literature (Agraval, 2001), (Akhmanov et al., 1991), (Kivshar et al., 2003). Including high-order dispersion terms β_m the NLS equation takes form

$$\frac{\partial A}{\partial z} + \frac{\alpha}{2} + i\frac{\beta_2}{2}\frac{\partial^2 A}{\partial \tau^2} - i\sum_{m=3} i^m \frac{\beta_m}{m!}\frac{\partial^m A}{\partial \tau^m} = i\left(P_{NL} + i\frac{2}{\omega_0}\frac{\partial P_{NL}}{\partial \tau}\right). \tag{10}$$

where $\tau = t - z/v_g$ is the local time in coordinate system moving with the pulse at the group velocity v_g, α describes the effects of fiber losses, P_{NL} is nonlinear media polarization

$$P_{NL}(z,\tau) = \gamma|A|^2 A + \gamma_R Q(z,\tau)A(z,\tau). \tag{11}$$

The media polarization P_{NL} includes both the electronic and vibrational (Raman) contributions. The term $\gamma|A|^2 A$ describes instantaneous Kerr nonlinearity, $\gamma_R Q(z,t)A(z,t)$ associated with stimulated Raman scattering. The time derivative appearing on the right-hand side of Eq. (10) is responsible for self-steepening and shock formation (Akhmanov et al., 1991) at a pulse edge.
Nonlinear parameter γ in eq. (11) is defined as

$$\gamma = \frac{\omega_0 n_2}{c A_{\text{eff}}}, \tag{12}$$

In scalar approach the effective area is

$$A_{\text{eff}} = \frac{\left(\int_0^{2\pi}\int_0^{\infty} |\psi(r,\phi)|^2 r dr d\phi\right)^2}{\int_0^{2\pi}\int_0^{\infty} |\psi(r,\phi)|^4 r dr d\phi}, \tag{13}$$

In (Lægsgaard et al., 2003) modified formula for effective area is proposed

$$A_{\text{eff}} = \left(\frac{n_1}{n_0^g}\right)^2 \frac{\left(\int (\vec{E}\cdot\vec{D}) r dr d\phi\right)^2}{\int_{\text{SiO}_2} |\vec{E}\cdot\vec{D}|^2 r dr d\phi}, \tag{14}$$

where $\vec{D}$ is electric flux density of fundamental mode, n_0^g is effective group index of the mode, n_1 is the refractive index of silica in the limit of zero field. Note that the integration in the denominator is restricted to the silica parts fiber that contains air holes running along its length. Eq. (14) was applied for calculating of effective mode area in silica-based photonic bandgap fibers (Lægsgaard et al., 2003). This formula has been derived without making assumptions about the field energy distribution and is therefore applicable even in the case conventional fibers that guide light in silica or other materials.

Considering a mean value of the Raman gain efficiency $\bar{g}_R$ in the fiber cross-section, the relation between the Raman gain coefficient and the Raman effective area can be expressed as $\gamma_R = \bar{g}_R / A_{\text{eff}}^R$ (see for example Chapter 5 in (Poli et al., 2007)). Nonlinear parameter γ_R is responsible for Raman gain in (11). Notice that the coefficient $\bar{g}_R$ represents a total value of the Raman gain efficiency associated with the fiber, which takes into account the materials that compose the fiber and their spatial distribution. If the interacting signals have the same frequency, the Raman effective area coincides with that given by the "classical" definition (13). Nonlinear susceptibility $Q(z,\tau)$ in equation (11) for media polarization can be expressed as convolution

$$Q(z,\tau) = \int_{-\infty}^{\infty} h_R(t')|A(z,\tau-t')|^2 dt', \tag{15}$$

where

$$h_R(\tau) = \frac{T_1^2 + T_2^2}{T_1 T_2^2} \exp(-\tau/T_2) \sin(\tau/T_1). \tag{16}$$

Parameters T_1 and T_2 are two adjustable parameters and are chosen to provide a good fit to the actual Raman-gain spectrum. Their appropriate values are T_1=12.2 fs and T_2=32 fs. The Fourier transform $\tilde{h}_R(\omega)$ of $h_R(\tau)$ can be written as

$$\tilde{h}_R(\omega) = \frac{T_1^2 + T_2^2}{T_2^2 + T_1^2(1 - i\omega T_2^2)^2}. \tag{17}$$

Using Fourier transform $\mathcal{F}(|A(z,\tau)|^2)$ at the given plane z the function $Q(z,\tau)$ can be calculated as

$$Q(z,\tau) = \mathcal{F}^{-1}\left[\tilde{h}_R(\omega)\cdot\mathcal{F}(|A(z,\tau)|^2)\right], \tag{18}$$

where $\mathcal{F}^{-1}$ denote inverse Fourier transform.

Another approach for description of Raman delayed response is based on the approximation of $Q(z,\tau)$ by damping oscillations (Belenov et al., 1992):

$$\frac{\partial^2 Q}{\partial t^2} + \frac{2}{T_2}\frac{\partial Q}{\partial t} + \frac{1}{T_1^2} Q(z,t) = \frac{1}{T_1^2}|A(z,t)|^2. \tag{19}$$

Under assumption $T_1 \ll T_2$ eq. (19) can be reduced to eq.(15). Calculation of $Q(\tau)$ for the given $A(z,\tau)$ at the fixed plane z can be done by finite-difference scheme for (19). Such scheme can be somewhat convenient than inverse Fourier transform (18).

2.2 Numerical methods

For modelling of the pulse propagation in single mode fiber split-step Fourier method was applied (Agraval, 2001), (Malomed, 2006). Figure 1 shows numerical scheme applied for single propagation step Δz. Functions $Q(\tau)$ and $\partial P_{NL}/\partial\tau$ are calculated under a periodic boundary condition that imposed upon discrete Fourier transform. Use of periodic boundary condition for the given temporal frame allows to simulate the propagation of pulse train generated by a modelocked laser. For picosecond pulses which central frequency ω_0 is far from zero of the group velocity dispersion two dispersion terms β_2 and β_3 are sufficient. For z-dependent dispersion and nonlinearity coefficients $\beta_m(z)$, $\gamma(z)$ and $\gamma_R(z)$ should be evaluated for each z. The scheme (fig. 1) is performed repeatedly until fiber end is reached.

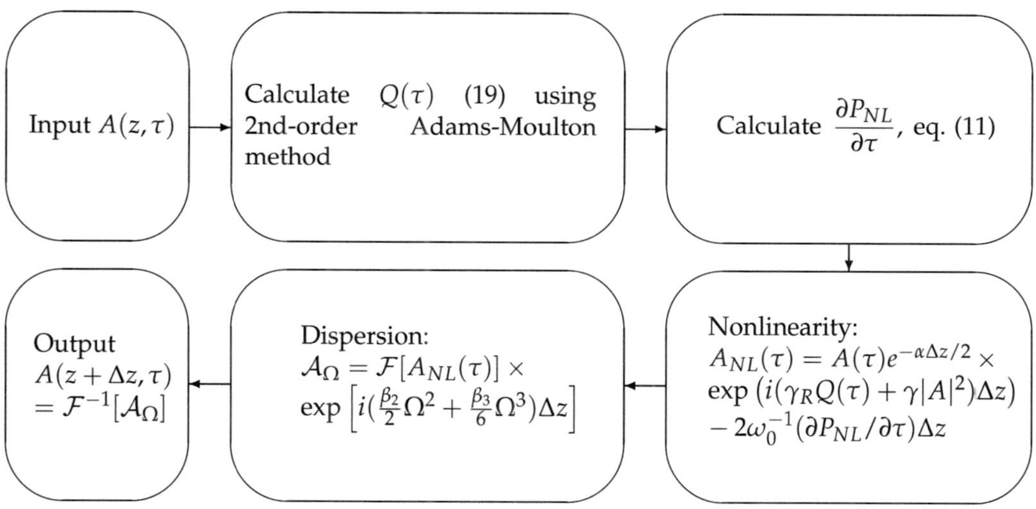

Fig. 1. Numerical scheme for the pulse propagation from plane z to the plane $z+\Delta z$. $\mathcal{F}$ is the fast forward Fourier transform (FFT), $\mathcal{F}^{-1}$ is the fast inverse Fourier transform (IFT).

2.3 Optical solitons

Optical solitons arize due to interplay between anomalous dispersion ($\beta_2 < 0$) and Kerr self-phase modulation. The solitons are solutions of nonlinear Schrödinger equation (NLS)

$$\frac{\partial A}{\partial z} + i\frac{\beta_2}{2}\frac{\partial^2 A}{\partial \tau^2} = i\gamma|A|^2 A(z,\tau). \tag{20}$$

Eq. (20) obtained from (10) neglecting by high-order dispersion terms ($\beta_m = 0$, $m = 3,4,5\ldots$), by stimulated Raman scattering ($\gamma_R = 0$) and by self-steepening ($\partial P_{NL}/\partial\tau = 0$).
NLS (20) has specific pulselike solutions that either do not change along fiber length or follow a periodic evolution pattern – such solutions are known as optical solitons. Their properties

were understood completely using inverse scattering method (Ablowitz et al., 1981). Details of the inverse scattering method in application to the optical solitons are available in literature (Agraval, 2001; Akhmanov et al., 1991; Malomed, 2006).
Initial field

$$A(0,\tau) = N\sqrt{\frac{|\beta_2|}{\gamma\tau_0}}\,\mathrm{sech}\left(\frac{\tau}{\tau_0}\right) \tag{21}$$

where τ_0 is initial pulse width. For integer N (21) give so-called N-soliton solution,
The first-order soliton ($N = 1$) corresponds to fundamental soliton It is referred to as the fundamental soliton because its shape does not change on propagation in the fiber with fixed dispersion. In the fiber with variable dispersion nonautonomous optical solitons propagate with varying amplitudes, speeds, and spectra. Analytical solution for fundamental nonautonomous solitons in (Serkin et al., 2007) is given.
Higher-order solitons are also described by the general solution of Eq. (20)

$$A(z,\tau) = \sum_{j=1}^{N} A_j\,\mathrm{sech}\left[\frac{u_j}{2}\left(\tau - zv_j\right)\right]\exp\left[i\left(\phi_0 + \frac{v_j}{2}\tau + \frac{u_j^2 - v_j^2}{4}z\right)\right], \tag{22}$$

where $A_j = 2\tau_0(|\beta_2|/\gamma)^{1/2} Im(\lambda_j)$, $v_j = 2\tau_0^{-1}Re(\lambda_j)$, $u_j = 2\tau_0^{-1}Im(\lambda_j)$, λ_j are roots of scattering matrix element of $a(\lambda) = 0$. Parameters λ_j give solitonic spectrum. The scattering matrix is

$$M(\lambda) = \begin{pmatrix} a(\lambda) & -b^*(\lambda) \\ b(\lambda) & a^*(\lambda) \end{pmatrix} =$$

$$\lim_{\tau\to\infty} \exp\left\{i\frac{\lambda}{2}\begin{pmatrix} \tau & 0 \\ 0 & -\tau \end{pmatrix}\right\} \exp\left\{i\int_{-\tau}^{\tau}\sqrt{\frac{\gamma}{|\beta_2|}}\begin{pmatrix} 0 & A^* \\ A & 0 \end{pmatrix}\right\} \exp\left\{i\frac{\lambda}{2}\begin{pmatrix} \tau & 0 \\ 0 & -\tau \end{pmatrix}\right\} \tag{23}$$

Numerical procedure for calculating (23) is described in (Akhmanov et al., 1991). The scattering matrix is calculated as product

$$M(\lambda) = \prod_{l=1,K} M_j(\lambda) = \prod_{l=1,K} \begin{pmatrix} a_l(\lambda) & -b_l^*(\lambda) \\ b_l(\lambda) & a_l^*(\lambda) \end{pmatrix} \tag{24}$$

where $M_l(\lambda)$ is partial scattering matrix, associated with temporal step $\Delta\tau = T/K$. The local time $\tau_l = -T/2 + l\Delta\tau, l = 1, \ldots, K$, K is the total number of time points,

$$a_l(\lambda) = e^{-i\lambda\Delta\tau}\left[\cos(d_l\Delta\tau) + i\lambda\frac{\sin(d_l\Delta\tau)}{d_l}\right] \tag{25}$$

$$b_l(\lambda) = ie^{i\lambda\Delta\tau}A^*(\tau_l)\sqrt{\frac{\gamma}{|\beta_2|}}\frac{\sin(d_l\Delta\tau)}{d_l}, \tag{26}$$

where $d_l = (\lambda^2 + |A(\tau_l)|^2\gamma|\beta_2|^{-1})^{1/2}$.
This procedure can be applied to numerical solution of (20) or (10). It allows to separate out amplitudes and phases of solitons.

Physically, parameters A_j and v_j in (22) represent amplitude and frequency shift respectively. Parameter u_j determines width of soliton. For the pulse (21)

$$\lambda_j = i(j - 1/2), \qquad j = 1, N \tag{27}$$

Higher-order solitons $(N > 1)$ show periodical evolution during propagation. Pulse shape is repeated over each section of length z_0 (fig.2 a).

$$z_0 = \pi\tau_0^2|2\beta_2|^{-1} \tag{28}$$

Figure 2 shows dynamics of second-order soliton. Note that soliton parameters $Im(\lambda)$ and $Re(\lambda)$ remain unchanged (fig.2 b).

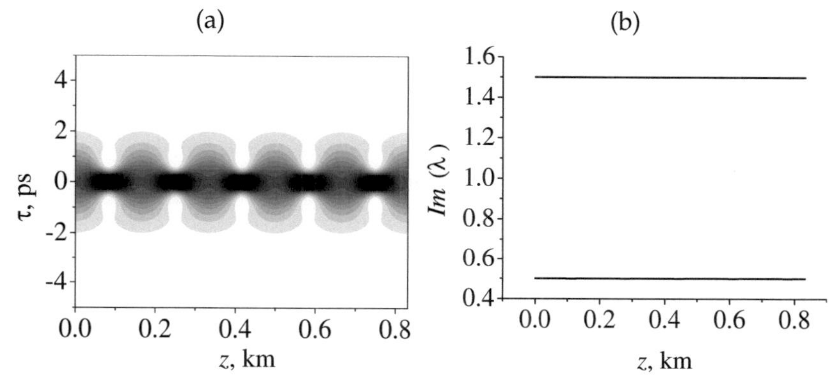

Fig. 2. Temporal evolution over five soliton periods for the second-order soliton. (a) Pulse dynamics. Black color corresponds to high intensity. (b) Soliton parameters $Im(\lambda)$. $N = 2$, $\beta_2 = -12.76\,\text{ps}^2/\text{km}$, $\gamma = 8.2\,\text{W km}^{-1}$, $z_0 = 0.166$ km.

2.4 Soliton fission due to harmonic modulation of the local dispersion

In this section we consider soliton dynamics governed by nonlinear Schrödinger equation with variable second-order dispersion coefficient

$$\frac{\partial A}{\partial z} + i\frac{\beta_2(z)}{2}\frac{\partial^2 A}{\partial \tau^2} = i\gamma|A|^2 A(z,\tau). \tag{29}$$

where

$$\beta_2(z) = \langle\beta_2\rangle\left(1 + 0.2\,\sin(2\pi\, z/z_m + \varphi_m)\right), \tag{30}$$

In the case of the harmonic periodic modulation of the local GVD coefficient, one may expect resonances between intrinsic vibrations of the free soliton. When the period of modulation of the fiber dispersion approaches the soliton period z_0, the soliton splits into pulses propagating with different group velocities (fig. 3a).

At $z = 0$ amplitudes of fundamental solitons are different $Im(\lambda_1) = 0.5$, $Im(\lambda_2) = 1.5$. But the group velocity associated with frequency shift is the same $Re(\lambda_1) = Re(\lambda_2) = 0$ (fig.3b). After single modulation period $z = z_0$ solitons acquire the same amplitudes $Im(\lambda_1) = Im(\lambda_2) = 0.987$, but different group velocities $Re(\lambda_1) = 0.411$, $Re(\lambda_2) = -0.411$. As the pulses propagates along the fiber imaginary part of λ decreases. After five modulation

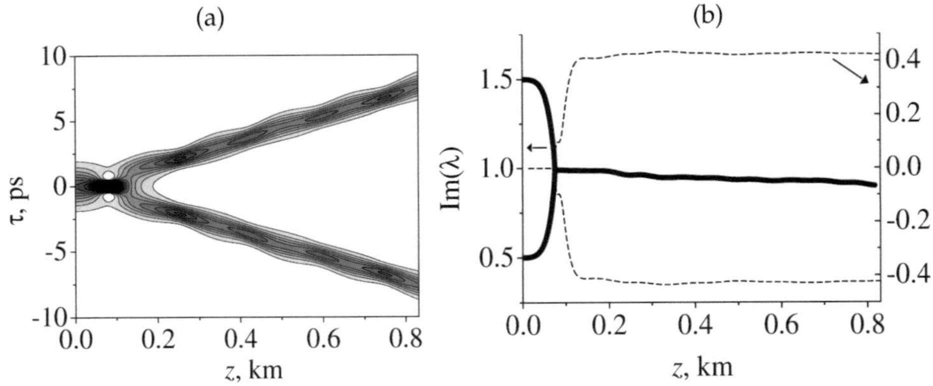

Fig. 3. A typical example of the splitting of a second-order soliton $N = 2$ into two fundamental solitons in the NLS equation with the sinusoidal modulation of the local dispersion coefficient (30). (a) Pulse dynamics; (b) $Im(\lambda)$ (solid curve, left axis) and $Im(\lambda)$ (dashed curve, right axis) $\langle\beta_2\rangle = -12.76\,\text{ps}^2/\text{km}$, $\varphi_m = \pi$ other parameters are the same as in Fig. 2.

periods ($z = 0.83\,\text{km}$) $Im(\lambda_1) = Im(\lambda_1) = 0.89$. Decrease of $Im(\lambda(z))$ connected with emerging of dispersive wave under harmonic modulation of the group-velocity-dispersion coefficient $\beta_2(z)$.
Regime shown in fig.3 corresponds to the fundamental resonance between small vibrations of the perturbed soliton and the periodic modulation of the local GVD. Change of modulation period z_m or modulation phase φ_m can degrade the soliton split (Malomed, 2006). In the fig.4 the pulse performs a few number of irregular oscillations, but finally decay into two fundamental solitons with opposite group velocities. For $\varphi_m = 0$ (fig.4b) group velocity of output pulses is less by half than the same for $\varphi_m = \pi$ (fig.3b).

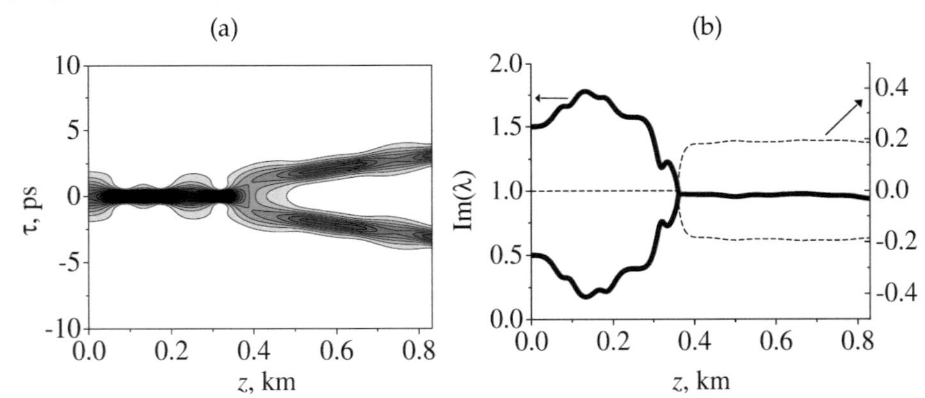

Fig. 4. Splitting of a second-order soliton into two fundamental solitons. (a) Pulse dynamics; (b) $Im(\lambda)$ (solid curve, left axis) and $Im(\lambda)$ (dashed curve, right axis) $\langle\beta_2\rangle = -12.76\,\text{ps}^2/\text{km}$, $z_m = z_0 = 0.166\,\text{km}$, $\varphi_m = 0$ other parameters are the same as in Fig. 2.

For $\varphi_m = \pi/4$ and $N = 2$ the width of input pulse performs a large number of irregular oscillations without splitting into fundamental solitons in spite of resonant conditions $z_m = z_0 = 0.166\,\text{km}$.

The parameter $N = 1.8$ corresponds to input pulse ($z = 0$) which consists of two fundamental solitons (22) having $\lambda_1 = i0.3$ and $\lambda_2 = i1.3$. The solitons remains propagating with the same group velocity (fig.5). For the constant GVD parameter $\beta_2(z) = \langle\beta_2\rangle$ the input pulse ($N = 1.8$) performs four periods of oscillations at the propagation distance ($z = 0.83$ km).

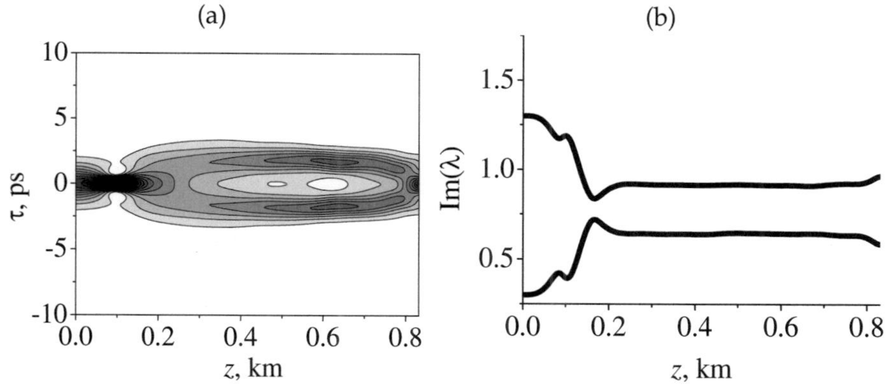

Fig. 5. Propagation of the pulse with $N = 1.8$. other parameters are the same as in Fig. 2. During propagation $Re(\lambda_1(z)) = Re(\lambda_2(z)) = 0$

3. Fission of optical solitons in dispersion oscillating fibers

Dispersion oscillating fibers have a periodic or quasi-periodic variation of the core diameter (Sysoliatin et al., 2008). Fission of second-order solitons or high-order solitons occurs due to longitudinal oscillation of the fiber dispersion and nonlinearity. In this section the results of numerical simulations of soliton fission in dispersion oscillating fiber are presented. Comparative analysis of experimental results and results of modified nonlinear Schrödinger equation based model is given. Effect of stimulated Raman scattering on the soliton fission is discussed.

3.1 Experimental confirmation

The solitons splitting described by the nonlinear Schrödinger equation with periodic perturbation was analysed in (Hasegava et al., 1991) published in 1991. However, the lack of a suitable fibers delayed experimental observation. Soliton splitting in dispersion-oscillating fiber was first observed in an experiment (Sysoliatin et al., 2008) that used a mode-locked laser (PriTel UOC) capable of emitting picosecond optical pulses near 1.55 μm, a wavelength near which optical fibers exhibit anomalous GVD together with minimum losses. Pulse repetition rate was 10 GHz. The pulses were amplified by erbium-doped fiber amplifier (EDFA) up to W =350 mW average power. The time bandwidth product for amplified pulses is found to be about $T_{\text{FWHM}}\Delta\nu = 0.304$, where $T_{\text{FWHM}} = 1.76\tau_0$ is a pulse duration and $\Delta\nu$ is the FWHM spectral pulse width. After EDFA, the pulses were launched into the DOF through fusion splicing with a single mode fiber. After propagation in 0.8-km length of DOF pulses were analyzed by intensity autocorrelator "Femtochrome" with the large scan range exceeding 100 ps and "Ando AQ6317" optical spectrum analyzer with a resolution bandwidth of 0.02 nm (fig.6).

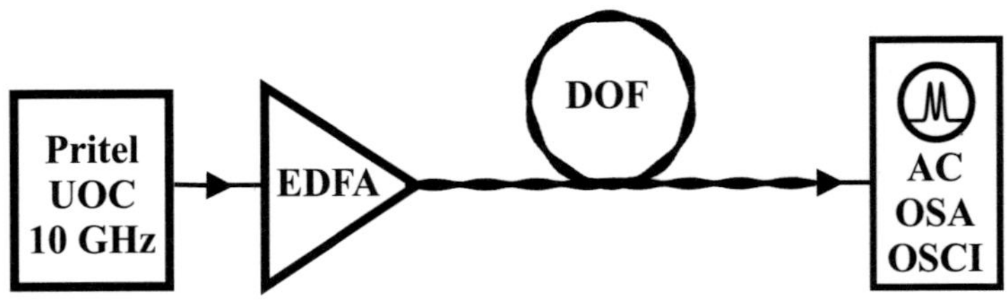

Fig. 6. Experimental setup: Pritel UOC, picosecond pulse source; EDFA, Er-doped fiber amplifier; DOF, dispersion oscillating fiber; AC, autocorrelator; OSA, optical spectrum analyzer, OSCI, wide-bandwidth oscilloscope.

The DOF was drawn in Fiber Optics Research Center (Moscow, Russia) from the preform with W-profile of refractive index. The manufactured DOF has linear loss 0.69 dB/km at 1550 nm. The fiber diameter varied slightly during the drawing in accordance with prearranged law. The variation of outer diameter of the fiber along its length is described by the sine-wave function

$$d(z) = d_0(1 + d_m \sin(2\pi z/z_m + \varphi_m)), \tag{31}$$

where $d_0 = 133\,\mu$m, $d_m = 0.03$ is the modulation depth, $z_m = 0.16$ km is the modulation period, φ_m is the modulation phase. For 0.8-km length of DOF in these experiments, $\varphi_m = 0$ at one fiber end and $\varphi_m = \pi$ at other fiber end, according to eq.(31). Thus, the modulation phase will be different for pulses launched into opposite fiber-ends.

With the average power of input pulse train below 120 mW the pulses transmitted through DOF were not split. The autocorrelation trace of output pulses have a shape typical for a train of single pulses separated by 100 ps interval. When average input power was increased, the autocorrelation trace of output pulses demonstrated three peaks (see Fig.7). Normalized intensity autocorrelation is given by:

$$C(\tau) = \left(\int |E(t)|^2 |E(t-\tau)|^2 dt\right) \left(\int |E(t)|^4 dt\right)^{-1}, \tag{32}$$

where $E(t)$ is electric field, t is the time, τ is autocorrelation delay time. Autocorrelations shown in Fig.7 correspond to two pulses $E(t) = A_1(t - T/2) + A_2(t + T/2)$ separated by temporal interval T. The value of T can be found measuring the distance between central and lateral peaks of autocorrelation function as it was shown in Fig.7(a).

The pulse splitting arises due to the fission of second order soliton. In the fiber with longitudinal variation of dispersion the second-order soliton decays into two pulses propagating with different group velocities. One of the pulses has red carrier frequency shift while the other has blue shift with respect to the initial pulse carrier frequency. The temporal separation between pulses depends on the difference between group velocities which are determined by pulse frequency shifts. In Fig.7 the pulse splitting dependence on the modulation phase and input pulse width is demonstrated. For $\varphi_m = \pi$ (Fig.7(a)(c)) the temporal interval T between pulse peaks is higher than the same for $\varphi_m = 0$ (Fig.7(b)(d)). Accordingly the largest frequency shift corresponds to the case shown in Fig.7(a)(c).

At time delay $\tau = \pm T$ the intensity autocorrelation (32) is given by

$$C(\pm T) = I_{12}/(1 + I_{12}^2), \tag{33}$$

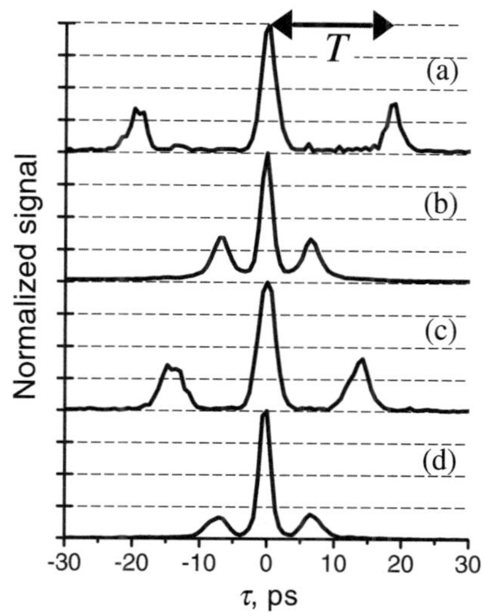

Fig. 7. Intensity autocorrelation traces of output pulses after propagation 0.8-km DOF. (a) The input average power is $P = 147.3$ mW. The input pulse width is $T_{\text{FWHM}} = 1.75$ ps. Modulation phase is $\varphi_m = \pi$. (b) $P = 150.5$ mW, $T_{\text{FWHM}} = 1.75$ ps, $\varphi_m = 0$. (c) $P = 167.4$ mW, $T_{\text{FWHM}} = 2.05$ ps, $\varphi_m = \pi$. (d) $P = 167.4$ mW, $T_{\text{FWHM}} = 2.05$ ps, $\varphi_m = 0$. The temporal interval between the peaks of output pulses T is given by the distance between peaks of autocorrelation trace as it shown in Fig.7(a).

where $I_{12} = |A_1(0)|^2/|A_2(0)|^2$ if $|A_1(0)|^2 < |A_2(0)|^2$ and $I_{12} = |A_2(0)|^2/|A_1(0)|^2$ if $|A_1(0)|^2 > |A_2(0)|^2$, $|A_1(0)|^2$ and $|A_2(0)|^2$ are peak intensities of output pulses. When the input pulse splits symmetrically ($I_{12} = 1$) the autocorrelation become $C(\pm T) = 0.5$. For autocorrelation trace shown in Fig.7(a) $C(T) = 0.38$, $C(T) = 0.33$ (Fig.7(b)), $C(T) = 0.41$ (Fig.7(c)), $C(T) = 0.19$ (Fig.7(d)). The value of $C(T)$ is underestimated due to the insufficient sensitivity of second harmonic generation (SHG) autocorrelator. However, it can be seen that for the same input power the value of $C(T)$ is higher for $\varphi_m = \pi$ (Fig.7(a)(c)) in comparison with the case $\varphi_m = 0$ (Fig.7(b)(d)). That means the case $\varphi_m = \pi$ is preferable for generation of pulse pairs with nearly identical peak intensity ($|A_1(0)|^2 \simeq |A_2(0)|^2$).

The splitting of second-order solitons produces two fundamental solitons (Bauer et al., 1995; Hasegava et al., 1991). The soliton spectrum is not broadened due to self-phase modulation because the last is balanced by negative dispersion. Spectral broadening shown in Fig.8 arises mainly due to the opposite frequency shifts of two pulses.

In time domain, the pulses are well separated (Fig.7), while in frequency domain the spectra are overlapped. Interference between these spectra leads to the modulation of the envelope of output spectrum (Fig.8(a)(b)). To a first approximation, the intensity of output spectrum can be expressed as follows:

$$\begin{aligned} F(\omega) &= |\mathcal{A}_1(\omega)e^{-i\omega(t-T/2)} + \mathcal{A}_2(\omega)e^{i\omega(t+T/2)}|^2 \\ &= |\mathcal{A}_1|^2 + |\mathcal{A}_2|^2 + 2|\mathcal{A}_1||\mathcal{A}_2|\cos[\omega T - \phi_1(\omega) + \phi_2(\omega)], \end{aligned} \tag{34}$$

where $F(\omega)$ is the spectral intensity at DOF output, $\mathcal{A}_{1,2}$ are the spectra of the first and second pulse, $\phi_{1,2} = \arg(\mathcal{A}_{1,2})$ are spectral phases. Eq. 34 shows that output spectrum is modulated

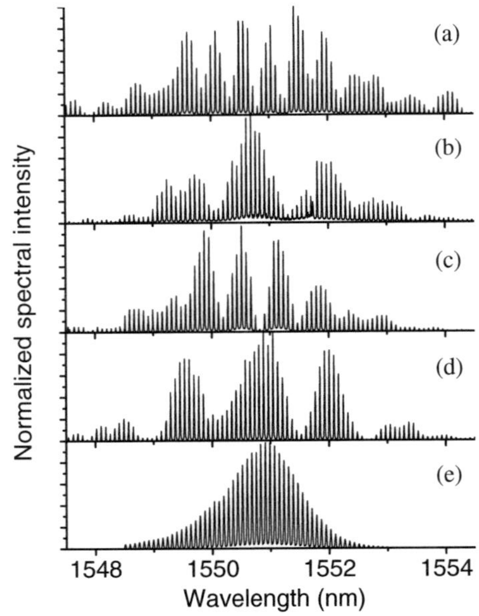

Fig. 8. Pulse train spectra. (a),(b),(c),(d) are the spectra of the output pulses, which autocorrelation traces are shown in Fig.7(a),(b),(c),(d) correspondingly. (e) the spectrum of input pulse train; FWHM spectral width of input pulses is 1.38 nm (0.172 THz).

T estimated by eq. 34	T measured
17. ps (from Fig.8(a))	18.3 ps (Fig.7(a))
6.3 ps (from Fig.8(b))	6.6 ps (Fig.7(b))
13. ps (from Fig.8(c))	14. ps (Fig.7(c))
6.3 ps (from Fig.8(d))	6.8 ps (Fig.7(d))

Table 1. Temporal interval between the peaks of output pulses.

by cosine function which period depends on the temporal interval T between two pulses. In the Table 1 the temporal interval between peaks of output pulses T is listed. The first column contains values of T estimated from spectra (Fig.8) by means of eq.(34). The second column contains the values directly measured from autocorrelation traces (Fig.7). In eq.(34) functions $\phi_{1,2}(\omega)$ are not known and assumed to be constant. This leads to underestimation of the value of T obtained from spectrum.

At large average power of input pulses train the autocorrelation trace (Fig.9(a)) and spectrum (Fig.9(b)) become more complicated. Initial pulse splits into a few low-intensity pulses and one high-intensity pulse which carrier frequency has a large red shift due to Raman scattering (Dianov et al., 1985). In Fig.9(b) the spectrum of Raman shifted pulse is located in wavelength range between 1554 nm and 1559 nm.

3.2 Modelling of soliton propagation in dispersion oscillating fibers

This section deals with solitons in the practically important model of the fibers with periodically modulated dispersion. Numerical model includes z-dependent second order and third-order dispersion coefficients $\beta_2(z)$, $\beta_3(z)$, stimulated Raman scattering and pulse self-steepening (eq. 10).

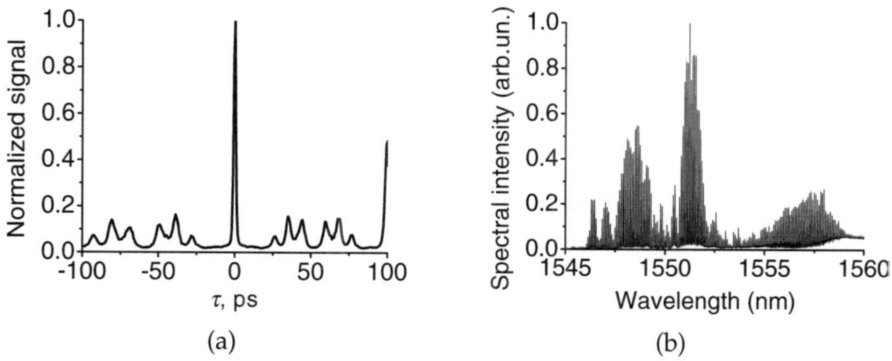

Fig. 9. High power pulse transmission through DOF. (a) Autocorrelation trace. (b) pulse train spectrum. Width of initial pulse is $T_{\text{FWHM}} = 2.05$ ps, The input average power is $P = 258.9$ mW. The phase of modulation is $\varphi = 0$.

For manufactured DOF which diameter is given by (31) the longitudinal variation of dispersion coefficients β_2 and β_3 can be expressed with the following approximation

$$\beta_2(z) = \langle\beta_2\rangle\,[1 + \beta_{2m}\ \sin(2\pi\ z/z_m + \varphi_m)]\,, \tag{35}$$

$$\beta_3(z) = \langle\beta_3\rangle\,[1 + \beta_{3m}\ \sin(2\pi\ z/z_m + \varphi_m)]\,, \tag{36}$$

where $\langle\beta_2\rangle = -12.76\,\text{ps}^2\text{km}^{-1}$, $\langle\beta_3\rangle = 0.0761\,\text{ps}^3\text{km}^{-1}$, $\beta_{2m} = 0.2$, $\beta_{3m} = 0.095$. The dispersion coefficients (35,36) were evaluated from the measurements of the dispersion of three fibers with the fixed outer diameter: 128 μm, 133 μm and 138 μm. All of three fibers and DOF are manufactured from the same preform.

Nonlinear medium polarization includes the Kerr effect and delayed Raman response $P_{NL}(z,t) = \gamma(z)|A|^2A + \gamma_R(z)QA(z,t)$, where $\gamma(z)$ and $\gamma_R(z)$ are nonlinear coefficients:

$$\gamma(z) = \langle\gamma\rangle\,[1 - \gamma_m\ \sin(2\pi\ z/z_m + \varphi_m)]\,, \tag{37}$$

$$\gamma_R(z) = \langle\gamma_R\rangle\,[1 - \gamma_m\ \sin(2\pi\ z/z_m + \varphi_m)]\,, \tag{38}$$

$\langle\gamma\rangle = 8.2\,\text{W}^{-1}\text{km}^{-1}$ and $\langle\gamma_R\rangle = 1.8\,\text{W}^{-1}\text{km}^{-1}$, $\gamma_m = 0.028$. These coefficients are obtained by calculating of effective area of fundamental mode.

The equation (10) was solved using standard split-step Fourier algorithm (see section 2.2). Simulations were carried out with hyperbolic secant input pulses. In simulations, we characterize the input pulses by the soliton number (order) N. The number of pulses that arise due to the splitting of high-order soliton is determined primarily by N (Bauer et al., 1995; Hasegava et al., 1991; Malomed, 2006).

The pulse splitting is most efficient in resonant regime when the modulation period z_m is equal to the soliton period $z_0 = 0.16\pi|\langle\beta_2\rangle|^{-1}T^2_{\text{FWHM}}$ (Hasegava et al., 1991; Tai et al., 1988). For initial pulse width $T_{\text{FWHM}} = 2.05$ ps (Fig.10) the soliton period $z_0 = 0.166$ km is close to the modulation period $z_m = 0.160$ km. For $\varphi_m = \pi$ only one modulation period of DOF is necessary for the soliton fission (Fig.10(a)). After propagation of 0.8 km of DOF the temporal separation between resulting pulses become $T = 14$ ps. The same value was obtained in experiment (Fig.7(c)). For $\varphi_m = 0$ the soliton fission arises after propagation of 0.6 km in DOF

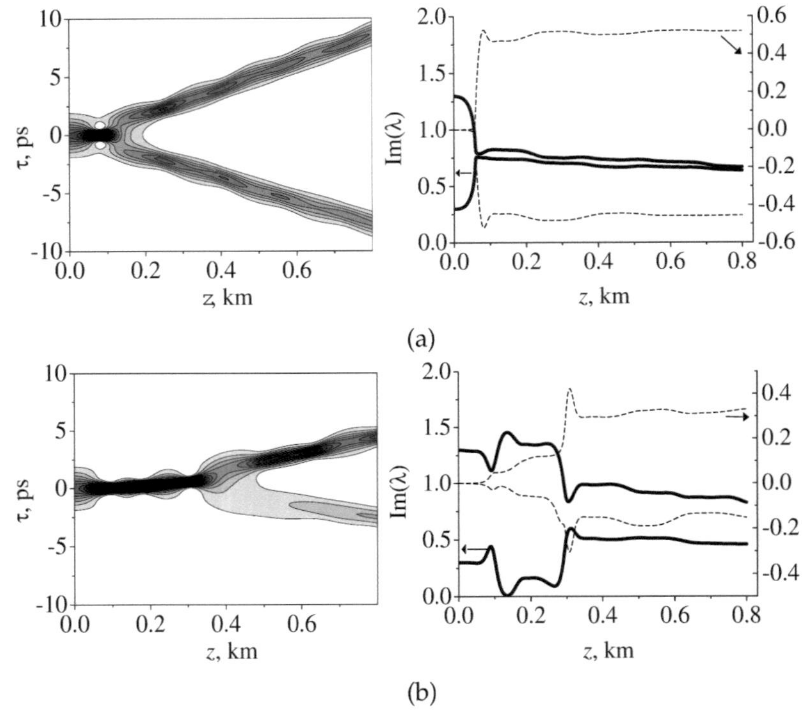

Fig. 10. Numerical simulation of the pulse evolution in DOF. Width of initial pulse is $T_{\text{FWHM}} = 2.05\,\text{ps}$, The pulse has soliton order $N = 1.8$. (a) $\varphi = \pi$. (b) $\varphi = 0$.

(Fig.10(b)). The temporal separation between output pulses is $T = 6.2\,\text{ps}$ that is agree well with experiment (Fig.7(d)).

For the initial pulse width $T_{\text{FWHM}} = 1.75\,\text{ps}$ the soliton period is $z_0 = 0.126\,\text{km}$. This value does not obey the resonant condition $z_0 = z_m$. However for input pulse width $T_{\text{FWHM}} = 1.75\,\text{ps}$ the temporal separation between pulses (Fig.7(a)) is higher than the same for resonant conditions $(T_{\text{FWHM}} = 2.05\,\text{ps},\ z_0 = 0.166\,\text{km} \simeq z_m)$ (Fig.7(c)). Experimental observation is in agreement with calculations. Numerical simulations show that such effect arises due to the simultaneous action of the periodical modulation of the fiber dispersion and stimulated Raman scattering. The frequency red shift due to the Raman scattering is inversely proportional to the fourth power of the pulse width (Tai et al., 1988). As result the change of the pulse group velocity and correspondent temporal separation between pulses will be higher for the shorter pulse width $(T_{\text{FWHM}} = 1.75\,\text{ps})$.

The input soliton decays into pulses with different peak intensities (Fig.10). Such asymmetry arises due to stimulated Raman scattering. For $\varphi_m = \pi$ (Fig.10(a)) the ratio of the peak of low-intensity pulse to the peak of high-intensity pulse is $I_{12} = 0.9$. For $\varphi_m = 0$ (Fig.10(b)) we obtain $I_{12} = 0.21$. Numerical calculations confirm our conclusions (Section 3.1) that the case $\varphi_m = \pi$ is preferable for the symmetrical splitting of input pulse. Note that without stimulated Raman scattering and third-order dispersion term the pulse with $N = 1.8$ does not split (see fig. 5).

The pulses become propagating with different group velocities (Fig.10) due to the shift of the carrier frequency. For the modulation phase $\varphi_m = \pi$ instantaneous frequency shift of output pulses is shown in Fig.11(a). The first pulse has blue shifted carrier frequency $(\nu_0 - \langle\nu\rangle_1) = -0.105$ THz while for the second pulse the frequency is red shifted $(\nu_0 - \langle\nu\rangle_2) = 0.120$ THz, where $\langle\nu\rangle_{1,2}$ are mean-weighted carrier frequencies of the first and second pulses correspondingly. Pulses are separated well in time domain. This allows to calculate their spectra separately (Fig.11(b)). The first pulse has the central wavelength $\lambda_1 = 1549.60$ nm while the second has $\lambda_2 = 1551.48$ nm. The difference $(\lambda_2 - \lambda_1) = 1.88$ nm is large enough to process the pulses in frequency domain separately using narrow-bandwidth fiber Bragg grating (Othonos et al., 1999), liquid crystal modulator array (Weiner, 1995) or arrayed waveguide grating (Oda et al., 2006), for example. To simulate effect of spectral filtering on the pulses (Fig.11(a,b)) the field after stopband filters $f_+(\omega)$ and $f_-(\omega)$ (39) was calculated.

$$f_\pm(\omega) = 1 - \tanh[(1.5 - (\omega - \omega_0 \pm \Delta))/0.08]/2 - \tanh[(1.5 + (\omega - \omega_0 \pm \Delta))/0.08]/2, \quad (39)$$

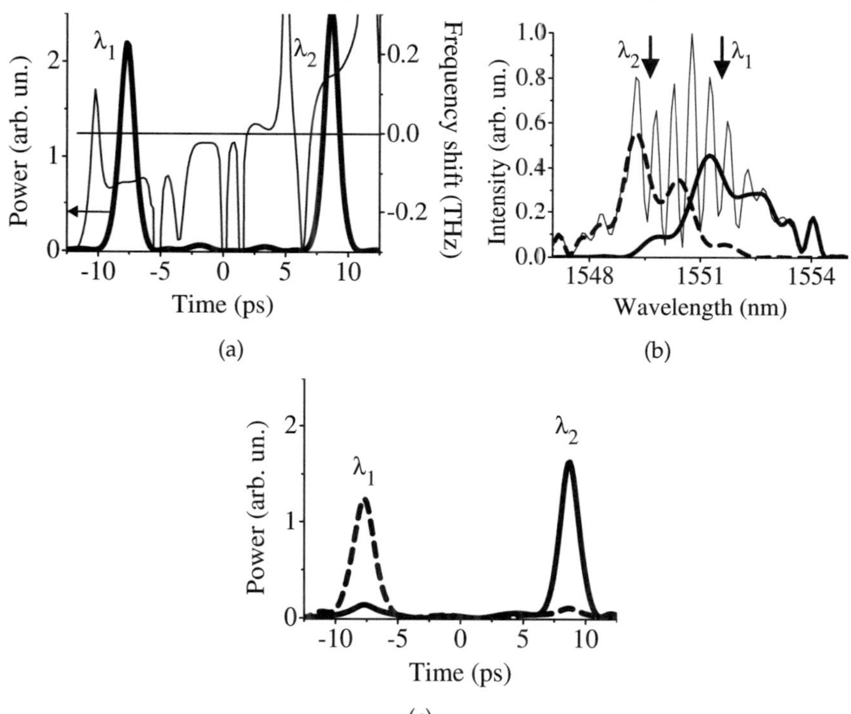

Fig. 11. Simulation of pulse characteristics after propagation in 0.8 km of DOF with $\varphi_m = \pi$. (a) Output intensity (left axis, thick curve) and instantaneous frequency shift (right axis, thin curve). (b) Thick solid curve shows spectrum of the first pulse. Thick dashed curve shows spectrum of the second pulse. Arrows mark central wavelengths λ_1 and λ_2 of the first and second pulses correspondingly. Thin solid curve is the spectrum envelope of the pulse train consists from pair of pulses shown in Fig.(a). The frequency shift was calculated as derivative $\partial \arg(A)/\partial t$. (c) Dashed curve is the pulse after stopband filter f_+ (39) solid curve is the pulse after stopband filter f_-. Simulation parameters are the same as in Fig.10(a)

where $\omega_0 = 2\pi\nu_0$, $\Delta = 1\,\text{ps}^{-1}$. After spectral filtering each half still remains a well defined pulse (Fig.11(c)).
The envelope of the spectrum of the train of output pulse pairs is modulated (Fig.11(b), thin solid curve) due to the interference between pulses. This is in agreement with experimental observations (see Section 3.1).

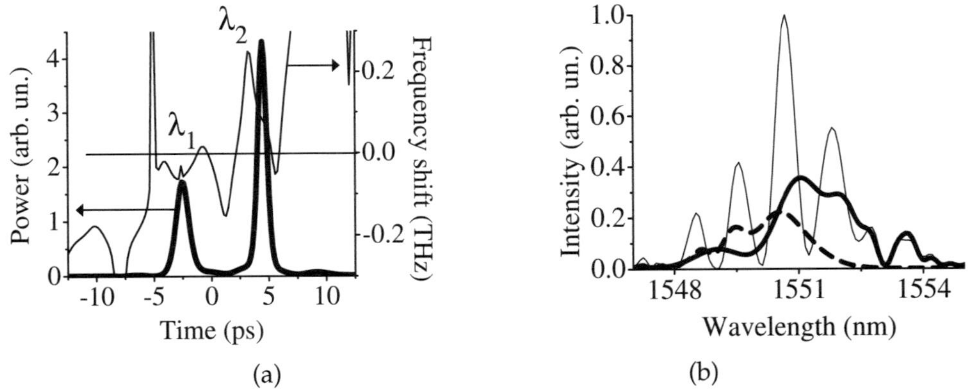

Fig. 12. Simulation of pulse characteristics after propagation in 0.8 km of DOF with $\varphi_m = 0$. (a) Output intensity (left axis, thick curve) and instantaneous frequency shift (right axis, thin curve). (b) Thick solid curve shows spectrum of the first pulse. Thick dashed curve shows spectrum of the second pulse. Thin solid curve is the spectrum envelope of the pulse train consistent from the pulse pairs shown in Fig.(a). Simulation parameters are the same as in Fig.10(b)

For $\varphi_m = 0$ output pulses are shown in Fig.12. The temporal interval between pulses is $T = 5.9\,\text{ps}$ (Fig.12(a)). While for the $\varphi_m = \pi$ the value $T = 13.8\,\text{ps}$ was obtained. The correspondent decrease of the temporal interval between pulse peaks with the change φ_m was observed in experiments (Fig.7). For $\varphi_m = 0$ output pulses are overlapped both in time domain and in frequency domain. Fig.12 demonstrated that deep oscillations of spectrum envelope (thin curve) arise only in region of overlapping of pulse spectra ($1549.0\,\text{nm} < \lambda < 1541.5\,\text{nm}$). The frequency shift for the first pulse is $(\nu_0 - \langle\nu\rangle_1) = -0.041\,\text{THz}$ ($\lambda_1 = 1549.75\,\text{nm}$) while for the second pulse $(\nu_0 - \langle\nu\rangle_2) = 0.093\,\text{THz}$ ($\lambda_2 = 1551.35\,\text{nm}$). The difference between central wavelengths of considered pulses is $(\lambda_2 - \lambda_1) = 1.08\,\text{nm}$. The value $(\lambda_2 - \lambda_1)$ is approximately half the same obtained for $\varphi_m = \pi$ (Fig.11). Overlapping of pulse spectra does not allow to process pulses in frequency domain separately.

4. Pulse propagation in dispersion-decreasing fibers

The fibers with dispersion varying along length have important applications in optical signal processing such as high-quality optical pulse compression, coherent continuum generation, nonlinear dynamic dispersion compensation and other applications (Sysoliatin et al., 2010). This section describes effect of the pulse compression in dispersion-decreasing fibers.
Our experimental setup (Fig.13) includes an actively mode-locked fiber laser operating at 10 GHz as a source of 2.6 ps pulses at central wavelength $\lambda_0 = 1552\,\text{nm}$, high power fiber amplifier, DFDDF (dispersion flattened dispersion decreasing fiber), filter at 1610 nm after the fiber. To analyze the pulse propagation a spectrum analyzer, autocorrelator and power meter

are used. The measurements have been carried out for different levels of EDFA pump current.

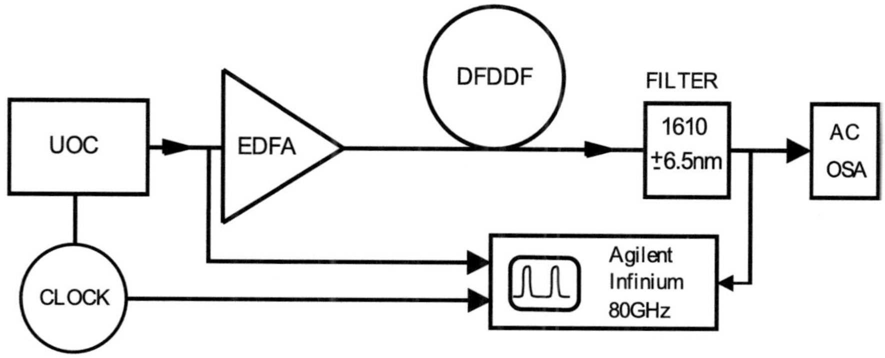

Fig. 13. Experimental setup: Pritel UOC, picosecond pulse source; EDFA, Er-doped fiber amplifier; DFDDF, 42 m length of dispersion flattened dispersion decreasing fiber; AC, autocorrelator "Femtochrome"; OSA, optical spectrum analyzer 'Ando AQ6317"; "Agilent Infinium", sampling scope with 80 GHz bandwidth; "FILTER", WDM filter

The DFDDF fiber has convex dispersion function vs wavelength (Fig.14). In experiments 42 m-length fiber was used. Outer diameter of the fiber decreases from 148 μm to 125 μm, and chromatic dispersion from 10 ps $nm^{-1}km^{-1}$ to -2 ps $nm^{-1}km^{-1}$. Group velocity dispersion is zero at $z = 40$ m.

Spectrum obtained after propagation of 2.6 ps pulses in DFDDF indicate a red-shifted sideband (fig.15(a)) due to the stimulated Raman scattering (Dianov et al., 1985; Tai et al., 1988). Using commercially available WDM bandpass filter we produce 0.9 ps pulses at 1610 nm. These pulses are synchronized with the input (Fig.15(b)). For a high pulse energies a broadband continuum radiation was observed. However it is essential that the input pulse

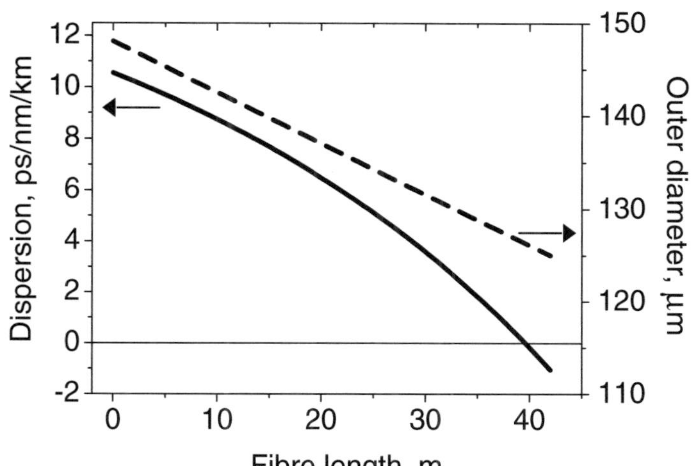

Fig. 14. Dispersion (solid curve) and outer diameter (dashed curve) of DFDDF versus fiber length.

energy should not exceed some critical value to obtain the high quality fully synchronized output pulses at 1610 nm after the filter.

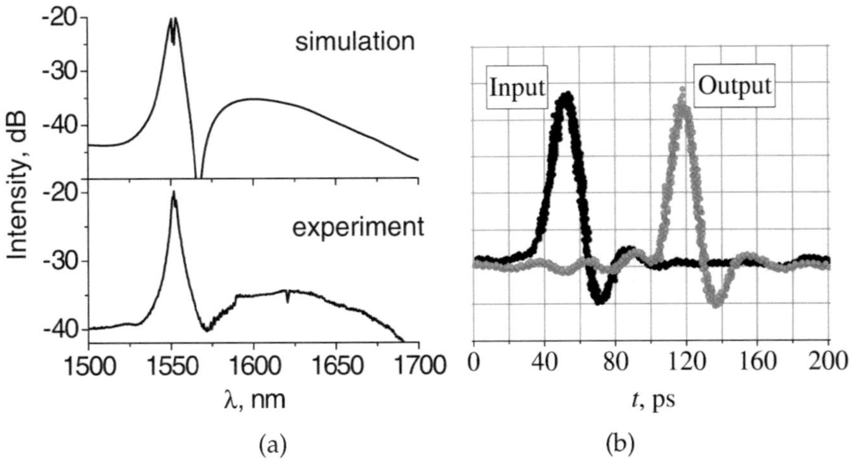

Fig. 15. Output of the DFDDF fiber. (a) Optical spectra obtained by simulation (top) and experimentally (bottom); (b) Sampling scope trace of the pulse at DFDDF input (black color) and output signal of 1610 nm filter (gray color). Input pulse energy is 140 nJ. Pulse repetition rate is 5.37 GHz.

The numerical simulations which model pulse propagation in the DDF are based on the nonlinear Schrödinger equation (10). For manufactured fiber linear absorption coefficient $\alpha = 0.08\,\text{km}^{-1}$, which corresponds to 0.35 dB/km measured loss. Dispersion coefficients $\beta_m(z)$, $(m = 2,3,4,5,6,7)$ take into account longitudinal variation of the fiber dispersion. The approximation $\beta_m(z) = \sum_{k=-2}^{k=3} a_{mk} d(z)^k$ was used. Where $d(z)$ is the DDF outer diameter. Effective area for nonlinear coefficients γ and γ_R (12) is approximated by $A_{\text{eff}} = a_0 + \sum_{j=1,2,3} \left[a_j d^j(z) + b_j d^{-j}(z) \right]$.

Due to the decreasing of the absolute value of the dispersion the initial solitonic pulse is strongly compressed (fig.16(a)). After compression the pulse envelope becomes modulated. As result the generation of Raman red-shifted radiation become efficient. Simulation shows that broadband red-shifted Raman component (Fig.16(b)) appears after the propagation distance $z = 35$ m.

Initial pulse $(z = 0)$ corresponds to four solitons $(N = 4.14)$. There are four solutions λ_j (fig.16(c,d)). The solitonic spectrum (fig.16(c,d)) is plotted up to $z = 40\,\text{m}$. Because for $z > 40\,\text{m}$ GVD is normal. After $z = 15\,\text{m}$ new solutions emerged. (fig.16(d)). The soliton amplitude associated with $Im(\lambda_j)$ (22). While the group velocity associated with $Re(\lambda_j)$. Up to $z = 25$ m all solitons propagate with the same group velocity, because $Re(\lambda_j) = 0$ (fig.16(c)). At $z = 35$ m the pulse is strongly compressed (fig.16(a)) and the soliton splitting appears (fig.16(c,d)). The soliton having maximum amplitude shown by thick solid curve (fig.16(c,d)). This soliton is responsible for generation of broad red-shifted sideband at fiber end (fig.16(b)).

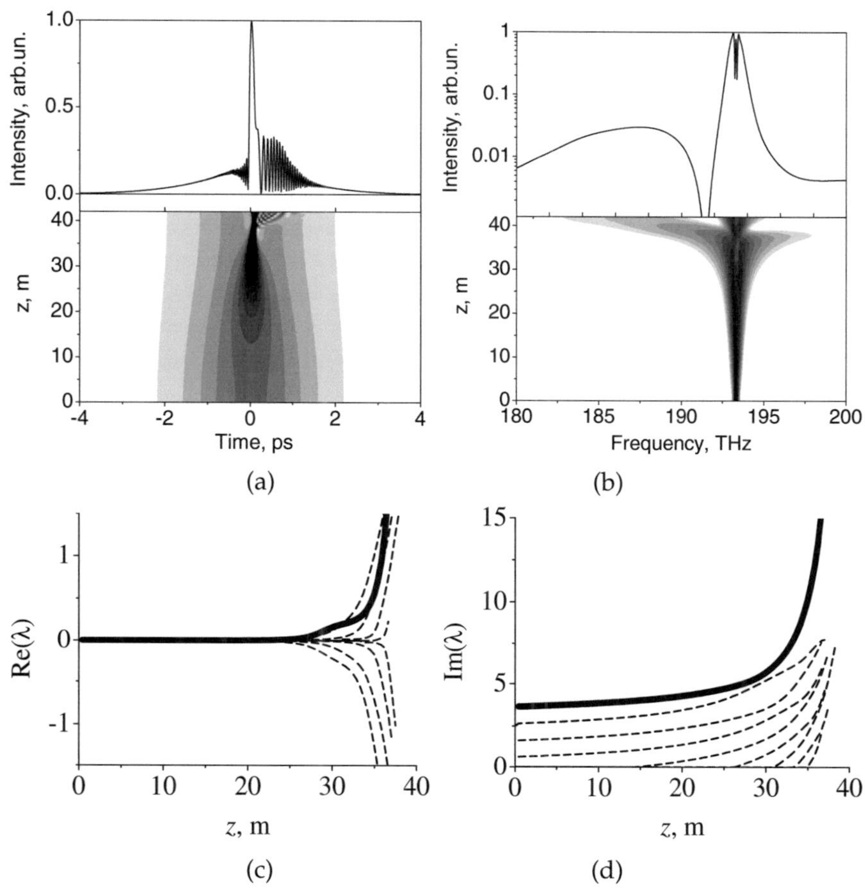

Fig. 16. Simulation of the pulse compression and red-shifted sideband generation. (a) Pulse dynamics. (b) Spectrum dynamics. Top inserts show the the intensity after 42 m propagation in DFDDF. In density plots black color corresponds to higher intensity. (c) Real part of λ_j. (d) Imaginary part of λ_j. Input pulse energy is 140 nJ.

5. Conclusion

The fibers with varying along length chromatic dispersion are of essential interest for nonlinear fiber optics. The fiber parameters variations can be treated as an effective loss or gain. The additional benefit is that the spontaneous emission noise is not amplified in such passive fiber. There are applications of such fibers as the high-quality soliton compression, soliton splitting, stable continuum generation, nonlinear dynamic dispersion compensation in optical network, widely tunable GHz repetition rate all-fiber laser and other.

Using a single-wavelength picosecond pulse laser and dispersion oscillating fiber, the generation of a train of picosecond pulses with alternate carrier frequency was demonstrated. Experimental observations are in agreement with numerical simulations. The model includes the Raman self-frequency shift, third-order dispersion, and nonlinear dispersion as well as the modulation of other fiber parameters. The pulses with different carrier frequencies are obtained due to the soliton splitting in the fiber with variable dispersion. We focus on the splitting of second-order solitons, because stimulated Raman scattering essentially complicates the dynamics of high-order solitons propagated in manufactured DOF. In this case, high-order soliton splits into a series of low-intensity pulses and a single high-intensity pulse with a large red shift of the carrier frequency. Second-order soliton transmitted through the DOF splits into two pulses with different amplitudes. For various applications, it is preferable to obtain the pulses with the same peak power. For second-order solitons, the difference between the peak powers of output pulses can be reduced by the appropriate choice of the phase of the periodical modulation of the core diameter of the fiber. The split pulses propagate with different group velocities. Transmitting pulses through a fiber with appropriate length, it is possible to achieve the doubling of the repetition rate of input pulse train.

The DOF can be used in principle for the splitting of high-order solitons. The effect of Raman scattering on the soliton splitting depends mainly on the pulse peak power. The peak power of solitons is reduced in a fiber with a small second-order dispersion β_2 . To achieve the splitting of third-or fourth-order solitons without significant effect of Raman scattering, one can use a dispersion oscillating fiber with reduced mean-weighted dispersion. Splitting of high-order solitons will allow increasing the frequency separation of output pulses and building up the efficient multiwavelength optical clock.

Using dispersion decreasing fiber we have demonstrated generation of pulse sideband having large frequency red-shift. The sideband is coherent. It allows to generate picosecond pulses using spectral filtering of this sideband. Such technique was applied to construct L-band tunable GHz repetition rate fiber laser. The novel efficient optical scheme allows to generate high quality 0.9 ps pulses at 1610 nm pulses, fully synchronized with basic clock at multi gigahertz pulse repetition rate.

Numerical simulations described in presented chapter reveal the solitons dynamics. Analysis of solitonic spectra (λ_j) give us a tool to optimize fiber dispersion and nonlinearity for most efficient soliton splitting or pulse compression.

6. Acknowledgement

The authors acknowledge the contribution of Dr. K.V. Reddy to this work.

7. References

Ablowitz, M.; Segur, H. (1981) *Solitons and the Inverse Scattering Transform*, SIAM, Philadelphia

Agrawal, G. P. (2001). *Nonlinear Fiber Optics*, 3-rd edition, Academic Press.

Akhmanov, S. A.; Vysloukh, V. A. & Chirkin, A. S. (1991). *Optics of femtosecond laser pulses*, American Institute of Physics.

Andrianov, A. V.; Muraviev, S. V.; Kim, A. V. & Sysoliatin, A. A. (2007). DDF-Based All-Fiber Optical Source of Femtosecond Pulses Smoothly Tuned in the Telecommunication Range. *Laser Physics*, Vol. 17, 1296-1302

Belenov, E. M.; Nazarkin, A. V. & Prokopovich, I. P. (1992) Dynamics of an intense femtosecond pulse in a Raman-active medium, *JETP Letters*, vol. 55, 218-222

Bauer, R. G. & Melnikov L. A. (1995). Multi-soliton fission and quasi-periodicity in a fiber with a periodically modulated core diameter. *Optics Communications*, Vol. 115, 190-195

Brechet, F.; Marcou, J.; Pagnoux, D. & Roy P. (2000). Complete Analysis of the Characteristics of Propagation into Photonic Crystal Fibers by the Finite Element Method. *Optical Fiber Technology*, Vol. 6, 181-191

Dianov, E. M.; Karasik, A. Ya.; Mamishev, P. V.; Prokhorov, A. M.; Serkin, V. N.; Stelmah, M. F. & Fomichev, A. A. (1985). Stimulated-Raman conversion of multisoliton pulses in quartz optical fibers. *JETP Letters*, Vol. 41, 294-297

Driben, R. & Malomed, B. A. (2000). Split-step solitons in long fiber links, *Optics Communications*, Vol. 185, 439-456

Golovchenko, E. A.; Dianov, E. M.; Prokhorov, A. M. & Serkin, V. N. (1985). Decay of optical solitons. *JETP Letters*, Vol. 42, 87-91

Guo, S. & Albin, S. (2004). Comparative analysis of Bragg fibers. *Optics Express*, Vol. 12, No. 1, 198-207

Hasegawa, A. & Kodama Y. (1991) Guiding center solitons. *Physical Review Letters*, Vol. 66, 161-164

Yu, C. X.; Haus, H. A.; Ippen, E. P.; Wong, W. S. & Sysoliatin, A. A. (2000). Gigahertz-repetition-rate mode-locked fiber laser for continuum generation. *Optics Letters*, Vol. 25, 1418-1420

Inoue, T.; Tobioka, H. & Namiki, S. (2005). Stationary rescaled pulse in alternately concatenated fibers with O(1)-accumulated nonlinear perturbations. *Physical Review E*, vol. 72, 025601(R)

Kivshar, Yu. S. & Agrawal, G. P. (2003). *Optical solitons : from fibers to photonic crystals*, San Diego, CA: Academic Press

Lee, K. & Buck, J. (2003). Wavelength conversion through higher-order soliton splitting initiated by localized channel perturbations. *Journal of Optical Society of America B*, Vol. 20, 514-519

Lourtioz, J. M.; Benisty, H.; Berger, V.; Gerard, J. M.; Maystre, D.; Tchelnokov, A. (2005) *Photonic Crystals. Towards Nanoscale Photonic Devices*, Springer-Verlag, Berlin, Heidelberg

Lægsgaard, J.; Mortensen, N. A. & Bjarklev, A. (2003). Mode areas and field-energy distribution in honeycomb photonic bandgap fibers. *Journal of Optical Society of America B*, Vol. 20, No. 10, 2037-2045

Malomed, B. A. (2006). *Soliton management in periodic systems*, Springer.

Oda, S. & Maruta, A. (2006). Two-bit all-optical analog-to-digital conversion by filtering broadened and split spectrum induced by soliton effect or self-phase modulation in fiber. *IEEE Journal of Selected Topics in Quantum Electronics*, Vol. 12, No. 2, 307-314

Othonos, A. & Kalli, K. (1999). *Fiber Bragg Gratings: Fundamentals and Applications in Telecommunications and Sensing*, Boston, Artech House

Pelusi M. D. & Liu H. F. (1997). Higher order soliton pulse compression in dispersion-decreasing optical fibers. *IEEE Journal of Quantum Electronics*, Vol. 33, 1430-1439

Poli, F.; Cucinotta, A.; Selleri, S. (2007). *Photonic Crystal Fibers. Properties and Applications*, Springer Series in Materials Science, Vol. 102

Sears, S; Soljacic, M.; Segev, M.; Krylov, D. & Bergman, K. (2000). Cantor set fractals from solitons. *Physical Review Letters*, Vol. 84, 1902-1905

Smith, N. J.; Knox, F. M.; Doran, N. J., Blow, K. J. & Benion, I. (1996). Enhanced power solitons in optical fibers with periodic dispersion management. *Electronics Letters*, Vol. 32, 54-55

Serkin, V. N.; Hasegawa, A. & Belyaeva, T. L. (2007). Nonautonomous Solitons in External Potentials *Physical Review Letters*, Vol. 98, No. 7, 074102

Snyder, A. W. & Love, J. D. (1983) *Optical waveguide theory*, London, Chapman and Hall Ltd.

Sysoliatin, A.; Belanov, A.; Konyukhov, A.; Melnikov, L. & Stasyuk, V. (2008). Generation of Picosecond Pulse Train With Alternate Carrier Frequencies Using Dispersion Oscillating Fiber, *IEEE Journal of Selected Topics in Quantum Electronics*, Vol. 14, 733-738

Sysoliatin, A.; Konyukhov, A.; Melnikov, L. & Stasyuk, V. (2010). Subpicosecond optical pulse processing via fiber dispersion management. *International journal of microwave and optical technology*, Vol. 5, No. 1, 47-51

Tai, K.; Hasegawa, A. & Bekki N. (1988). Fission of optical solitons induced by stimulated Raman effect. *Optics Letters,* Vol. 13, 392-394

Wai, P. K.; Menyuk, C. R.; Lee, Y. C. & Chen, H. H. (1986) Nonlinear pulse propagation in the neighborhood of the zero dispersion wavelength of monomode optical fibers. *Optics Letters,* Vol. 11, 464-466

Washburn, B. R.; Ralph, S. E. & Windeler, R. S. (2002). Ultrashort pulse propagation in air-silica microstructure fiber. *Optics Express*, Vol. 10, No. 13, 575-580

Weiner, A. M. (1995). Femtosecond optical pulse shaping and processing. *Progress in Quantum Electronics*, Vol. 19, 161-137

Yeh, P.; Yariv, A. & Marom, E. (1978). Theory of Bragg fiber. *Journal of Optical Society of America*, Vol. 68, 1196-1201

14

Stochastic Dynamics Toward the Steady State of Self-Gravitating Systems

Tohru Tashiro[1] and Takayuki Tatekawa[2]
[1]*Ochanomizu University*
[2]*Center for Computational Science and e-Systems, Japan Atomic Energy Agency*
Japan

1. Introduction

A self-gravitating system (SGS) is a system where many particles interact via the gravitational force. When we shall explain a distribution of SGS in phase space, the Boltzmann-Gibbs statistical mechanics is not useful. This is because the statistical mechanics is constructed under the condition of the additivity of the energy: as well known, the total energy of several SGSs is not equal to the sum of the energy of each system. In fact, SGS does not have a tendency to become a state characterized with a temperature.
If we use the statistical mechanics assuming that the state of the SGS with an equal mass m becomes isothermal with the temperature T and that the particles of the system are distributed spherically symmetrically, what kind of distribution can be obtained? Then, the structure in phase space can be determined using the Maxwell-Boltzmann distribution. For example, the number density at a radial distance r in real space is given by

$$n_{\rm MB}(r) \propto e^{-\frac{m}{k_{\rm B}T}\Phi(r)}, \tag{1}$$

where $\Phi(r)$ is the mean gravitational potential per mass generated by this whole system at r and $k_{\rm B}$ is the Boltzmann constant. This potential should satisfy a relation with number density by the Poisson equation,

$$\frac{{\rm d}^2\Phi(r)}{{\rm d}r^2} + \frac{2}{r}\frac{{\rm d}\Phi(r)}{{\rm d}r} = 4\pi G m n_{\rm MB}(r), \tag{2}$$

where G is the gravitational constant. A special solution to Eq. (1) and this Poisson equation is $n_{\rm MB}(r) = k_{\rm B}T/2\pi G m^2 r^2$, known as the singular isothermal sphere (Binney & Tremaine, 1987). However, this solution has two problems: infinite density at $r = 0$ and infinite total mass. Even though we solve the equations with a finite density at $r = 0$, the solutions behave $\propto r^{-2}$ at a large r, and so we cannot avoid the infinite total mass problem. In either case, the solutions are unrealistic.
Of course, real examples of SGS in the universe, e.g., globular clusters and galaxies, have various structures with a finite radius. As for most globular clusters, it is known that their number densities in real space have a flat core and behave as a power law outside this core. King interpreted these profiles by introducing the new distribution function in phase space,

known as the *lowered Maxwellian;*

$$f(r,v) \propto \begin{cases} e^{-\beta(E-m\Phi_t)} - 1 & \text{for } E \le m\Phi_t\,, \\ 0 & \text{for } E > m\Phi_t\,, \end{cases} \tag{3}$$

in which E is the total energy of a particle belonging to a globular cluster. This distribution becomes zero when the total energy is greater than $m\Phi_t$, and so Φ_t can be understood as a potential energy per mass at the surface of the globular cluster. Because the velocity of the particle must be in the range of $0 \le v \le \sqrt{2\{\Phi_t - \Phi(r)\}}$, the number density $n_{\text{KM}}(r)$ can be obtained integrating $f(r,v)$ as

$$n_{\text{KM}}(r) \propto \int_0^{\sqrt{2\{\Phi_t-\Phi(r)\}}} \mathrm{d}v 4\pi v^2 f(r,v)\,. \tag{4}$$

Moreover, using a dimensionless potential $W(r) \equiv -m\beta\{\Phi_t - \Phi(r)\}$ and integrating by parts, the number density becomes

$$n_{\text{KM}}(r) \propto e^{W(r)} \int_0^{W(r)} \mathrm{d}\zeta e^{-\zeta}\zeta^{3/2}\,. \tag{5}$$

As mentioned before, the potential energy and the number density has a relation through the Poisson equation. Thus, $W(r)$ must satisfy the following equation:

$$\frac{\mathrm{d}^2 W(r)}{\mathrm{d}r^2} + \frac{2}{r}\frac{\mathrm{d}W(r)}{\mathrm{d}r} = -\frac{9}{a^2}\frac{n_{\text{KM}}(r)}{n_{\text{KM}}(0)}\,, \tag{6}$$

where $a \equiv \sqrt{9/\{4\pi G m^2 \beta n_{\text{KM}}(0)\}}$ corresponds to the core radius. The number density satisfying Eqs. (5) and (6) can be calculated numerically as shown in Fig. 1. This is called the King model (King, 1966). When $W(0)$ is larger than about 5, the number density around the origin can be represented by the following approximation:

$$n_{\text{KM}}(r) \propto \frac{1}{(1 + r^2/a^2)^{3/2}}\,, \tag{7}$$

which is shown as the red curve in Fig. 1.

Since King put forward this model, this number density has been applied to fitting for the surface brightness of many globular clusters, for example as in Ref. (Peterson & King, 1975; Chernoff & Djorgovski, 1989; Trager & King, 1995; Lehmann & Scholz, 1997; Meylan et al., 2001), that is, most exponents of power law outside the core of globular clusters are similar to -3 which cannot be explained by the model with the isothermal assumption. But, it is not easy to see what kind of dynamics occurred in the system, because his procedure was done to the distribution function in the steady state.

So, we will construct a theory which can explain the dynamics toward such a *special* steady state described by the King model especially around the origin. The idea is to represent an interaction by which a particle of the system is affected from the others by a *special* random force described by a position-dependent intensity noise, in other words the multiplicative noise, that originates from a fluctuation only in SGS. That is, we will use a *special* Langevin equation, just as the *normal* Langevin equation with a constant-intensity noise, in other

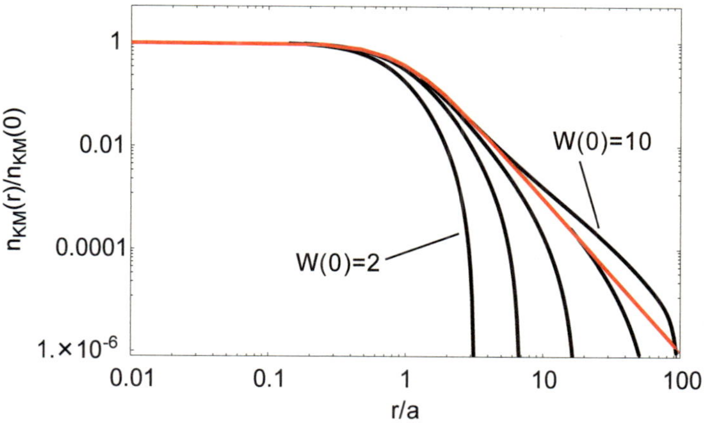

Fig. 1. Black curves denote the number density of the King model $n_{KM}(r)$ as a function of the radius normalized with the core radius, r/a, for several $W(0)$. As the curve changes from left to right, $W(0)$ gets larger from 2 to 10 in steps of 2. The red curve means the approximated formula, $1/(1+r^2/a^2)^{3/2}$, for larger $W(0)$.

words the additive noise, can unveil the dynamics toward the steady state described by the Maxwell-Boltzmann distribution. However, we cannot introduce the randomness into the system without any evidence. Then, we must confirm that each orbit is random indeed. Of course, it is impossible to understand orbits of stars in globular clusters from observations. Thus, we must use numerical simulations.

From the numerical simulations of SGS, the ground that we can use the random noise becomes clear. The *special* Langevin equation includes additive and multiplicative noises. By using this stochastic process, we derive that non-Maxwell-Boltzmann distribution of SGS especially around the origin. The number density can be obtained through the steady state solution of the Fokker-Planck equation corresponding to the stochastic process. We exhibit that the number density becomes equal to the density profiles around the origin, Eq. (7), by adjusting the friction coefficient and the intensity of the multiplicative noise.

Moreover, we also show that our model can be applied in the system which has a heavier particle (5-10 times as heavy as the surrounding particle). The effect of the heavier particle in SGS, corresponding to a black hole in a globular cluster, has been studied for long time. If the black hole is much heavier than other stars, a cusp of the density distribution appears at the center of a cluster (Peebles, 1972; Bahcall & Wolf, 1976; 1977). The observations which suggest that intermediate mass black hole (IMBH, $\sim 10^2 - 10^3 M_{\odot}$) is in the globular cluster in recent years are accomplished one after another (Clark et al., 1975; Newell et al., 1976; Djorgovski & King, 1984; Gebhardt et al., 2002; Gerssen et al., 2002; Noyola et al., 2008). Although these studies are very interesting, our model does not treat these situations: in our model, the heavier particle is too lighter than IMBH. Our model corresponds small globular cluster (10^4 stars) with only a stellar black hole ($\simeq 1 - 10 M_{\odot}$).

Here, note that we have reported similar results in our previous letter (Tashiro & Tatekawa, 2010). In this paper, however, we demonstrate how we executed our numerical simulations. Moreover, a treatment for stochastic differential equations becomes precise, and so the analytical result derived by a different method changes a little.

This paper is organized as follows. In Sec. 2.1, and Sec. 2.2, we provide brief explanations about a machine and a method we used when we did numerical simulations, respectively. In Sec. 2.3, we investigate number densities derived from our numerical simulations where all particles of SGS with a mass m and a particle with a mass M interact via the gravitational force. Then, we show the densities are like that of the King model and both the exponent and the core radius are dependent on M. In Sec. 3.1, forces influencing each particle of SGS are modeled. Then, using these forces, Langevin equations are constructed in Sec. 3.2. Section 3.3 makes it clear that the steady state solution of the corresponding Fokker-Planck equation gives the same result with the King model. In Sec. 4, we discuss our results and make the relation between King's procedure and our idea clear. Section 5 gives a summary of this work.

2. Numerical simulations of SGS using GRAPE

2.1 GRAPE

SGSs require quite long time for relaxation. Furthermore, because only attractive force is exerted on particles in SGS and the gravitational potential is asymptotically flat, we must compute interaction of all particle pairs. When we treat N particles, the computation of interaction becomes $O(N^2)$ by direct approach. By these reasons, we require huge computation for numerical simulation of the evolution of SGS.

For time evolution of SGS, many improvements of algorithm and hardware have been carried out. First, we consider integrator for simulation. For long-time evolution, both the local truncation error and the global truncation error are noticed. These error occur deviation of the conservation physical quantities such as total energy. For compression of the global truncation error, symplectic integrator has been developed. The symplectic integrator conserves the total energy for long-time evolution. We apply 6th-order symplectic integrator for the time evolution of SGS. Secondly, we apply special-purpose processor for the computation of the interaction. Most of the computation of the time evolution in SGS is 2-body interaction. As special-purpose processors, GRAPE system has been developed (Sugimoto et al., 1990). GRAPE system can compute 2-body interaction from position and mass of particles quickly. In our study, we apply GRAPE-7 chip, which consists of Field-Programmable Gate Array (FPGA) for computation of the interaction (Kawai & Fukushige, 2006). GRAPE-7 chip implements GRAPE-5 compatible pipelines [1]. The performance of GRAPE-7 chip is approximately 100 GFLOPS and is almost equal to a processor of present supercomputers, but the energy consumption of the chip is only 3 Watts. Using sophisticated integrator and special-purpose processor, we have analyzed time evolution of SGS.

2.2 Symplectic integrator

For time evolution, we must choose reasonable integrator for simulation. For long-time evolution, not only the local truncation error but also the global truncation error is noticed. For example, 4th-order Runge-Kutta method has been applied for time evolution of physical systems (Press et al., 2007). Although its local truncation error is $O\left((\Delta t)^5\right)$, because its error accumulates, the global truncation error increases during time evolution. For example, we

[1] GRAPE-5 computes low-accuracy 2-body interaction. If we treat collisional systems, i.e., the effect of 2-body relaxation cannot be neglected, we should use high-accuracy chip such as GRAPE-6 (Makino et al., 2003). As we will mention later, because our simulation notices until 100 t_{ff}, we can simulate the systems with GRAPE-7 chip.

apply 4th-order Runge-Kutta method for the harmonic oscillation.

$$H = \frac{p^2}{2} + \frac{q^2}{2}. \tag{8}$$

Using exact solutions, the orbit of the harmonic oscillation in the phase space draws a circle. Of course, the total energy is conserved. On the other hand, when we apply 4th-order Runge-Kutta method for time evolution, the total energy is decreased monotonically.

$$H(t) = \frac{1}{2}\left[1 - \frac{1}{72}(\Delta t)^6 + O\left((\Delta t)^7\right)\right]\left(p^2 + q^2\right). \tag{9}$$

The orbit of the harmonic oscillation in the phase space draws a spiral and it converges to origin ($p = q = 0$). When we consider long-time evolution, 4th-order Runge-Kutta method is not reasonable integrator. If Hamiltonian of physical system is given, we can apply symplectic integrator which based on canonical transformation (Ruth, 1983; Feng & Qin, 1987; Suzuki, 1992; Yoshida, 1993). This method suppresses increase of the global truncation error. In generic case, the symplectic integrator is implicit method. If Hamiltonian is divided to coordinate parts and momentum parts, the integrator becomes explicit method. The procedure of low-order integration becomes easy more than Runge-Kutta method. The simplest integrator is called "leap-flog method" (2nd-order integrator).

$$p\left(t + \frac{\Delta t}{2}\right) = p(t) + \frac{\Delta t}{2}\dot{p}\left(x(t)\right), \tag{10}$$

$$x(t + \Delta t) = x(t) + \Delta t \cdot p\left(t + \frac{\Delta t}{2}\right), \tag{11}$$

$$p(t + \Delta t) = p\left(t + \frac{\Delta t}{2}\right) + \frac{\Delta t}{2}\dot{p}\left(x(t + \Delta t)\right). \tag{12}$$

Using leap-flog method for the harmonic oscillator, the following equation is satisfied.

$$\frac{1}{2}(p^2 + q^2) + \frac{\Delta t}{2}pq = \text{const.}. \tag{13}$$

Therefore the orbit in the phase space draws an oval. The deviation from the exact solution is suppressed. To suppress the local truncation error, higher-order symplectic integrators have been developed. We apply 6th-order symplectic integrator for time evolution of SGS (Yoshida, 1990).

$$p_i = q_{i-1} + c_i \Delta t \dot{p}(q_{i-1}) \quad (1 \le i \le 8), \tag{14}$$

$$q_j = p_{j-1} + d_j \Delta t p_j \quad (1 \le j \le 7), \tag{15}$$

where $p_0 = p(t), q_0 = q(t), p_8 = p(t + \Delta t), q_7 = q(t + \Delta t)$. The coefficients c_j, and d_j are shown in Tab. 1.

The symplectic integrator conserves the total energy and the symplectic structure in generic cases. When we use n-th order symplectic integrator, the local truncation error of the total energy becomes $O\left((\Delta t)^{n+1}\right)$. Furthermore, the global truncation error is not accumulated (Sanz-Serna, 1988).

i	c_i	d_i
1	0.39225680523878	0.78451361047756
2	0.510043411918458	0.0235573213359357
3	−0.471053385409757	−1.17767998417887
4	0.06875316825252	1.31518632068391
5	0.06875316825252	−1.17767998417887
6	−0.471053385409757	0.0235573213359357
7	0.510043411918458	0.78451361047756
8	0.39225680523878	

Table 1. Coefficients of 6th-order symplectic integrator (Solution A in (Yoshida, 1990)).

In SGS, because the interaction at zero distance diverges, the local truncation error would diverge in long-time evolution. For avoidance of this divergence, some kind of softening parameter has been introduced to gravitational interaction. When the nature of the pure gravity is analyzed, the regularization procedure of interaction is required (Kustaanheimo & Stiefel, 1965; Aarseth, 2003).

2.3 Steady number density in numerical simulation

Now, we investigate the steady number density (SND) of the SGS with a mass m including a particle with a mass M by numerical simulation. In particular, we show that SNDs have a core and behave as a power law outside the core.

The system is composed of $N = 10000$ particles. At $t = 0$, all velocities of the particles are zero and they are distributed by $n_0(r) \propto (1 + r^2/a_p{}^2)^{-5/2}$ $(0 \leq r \leq 4a_p)$, which is the density in real space of Plummer's solution (Binney & Tremaine, 1987). In this SGS, we put *another particle* with a mass M in the origin at $t = 0$. We shall change the mass as $M/m = 1, 5$, and 10. Throughout this paper, we adopt a unit system where the core radius of Plummer's solution a_p, the initial free fall time t_{ff}, and the total mass $N \cdot m$ are unity.

We started the numerical simulation under these conditions. For dynamical evolution, we used GRAPE-7 at Center for Computational Astrophysics, CfCA, of National Astronomical Observatory of Japan. For the computation of gravitational force, we applied Plummer's softening: the potential energy between the ith and jth particles separated by a distance r_{ij} is $-Gm^2/\sqrt{r_{ij}{}^2 + \varepsilon_s{}^2}$, where ε_s is the softening parameter. We set $\varepsilon_s = 10^{-3}$. For time evolution, we used 6th-order symplectic integrator (Yoshida, 1990). The time step for the simulation is defined as $\Delta t = 10^{-5}$. We carried out simulations until $t = 100\ t_{ff}$. During simulations, the error in total energy was less than 0.1%.

First, most particles collapse into the origin within several t_{ff}. After approximately 20 t_{ff}, the distribution becomes stable and the system reaches the steady state. Of course, we can confirm whether the system becomes steady or not from the profile of the number density. However, furthermore we also focus on the number of particles inside a sphere. Figure 2 shows the change of the number inside the sphere with a radius 1 in time. During the collapse, the number becomes large. After that, the number decreases, which means that many particles with positive energy evaporated from inside of the sphere, and so the number becomes about 6000 on average. For other radii, similar changes of the number in time can be seen.

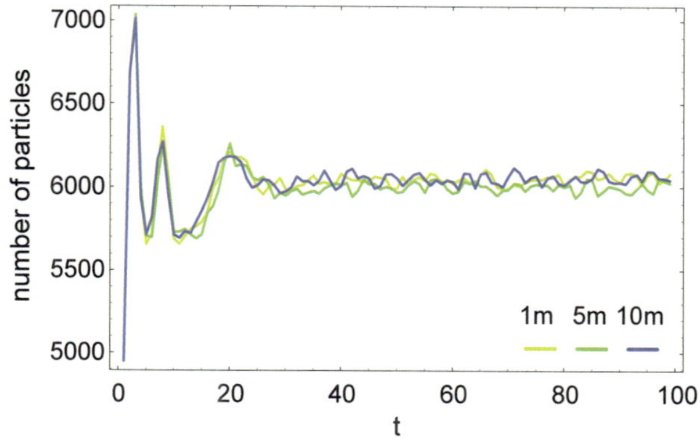

Fig. 2. Change of the number of particles inside a sphere with a radius 1 in time for $M/m = 1, 5$, and 10.

SND is calculated by taking the time average during the steady state. In Fig. 3, we show the logarithm of SND as a function of $\log r$ for $M/m = 1$, 5, and 10. For each M, the SND has a core and behaves as a power law at r larger than the core radius. Here, we fit SNDs around the core by $n_{\text{fit}}(r) = C/(1 + r^2/a^2)^{\kappa}$. The results are summarized in Tab. 2. For $M/m = 1$ and 5, $\kappa \simeq 3/2$, which is similar to the exponent of the King model. The density at the origin C increases as M increases, which is simply understood to be a result of many particles being attracted by the heavier particle.

M/m	$a \times 10^2$	κ	$C \times 10^{-5}$
1	6.20 ± 0.22	1.46 ± 0.03	7.06 ± 0.14
5	6.06 ± 0.18	1.46 ± 0.02	7.57 ± 0.13
10	5.68 ± 0.14	1.43 ± 0.02	8.13 ± 0.12

Table 2. Best-fit parameters of the function $C/(1 + r^2/a^2)^{\kappa}$ for steady number densities shown in Fig. 3

3. Simple model

3.1 Forces acting on each particle of SGS

As shown in the last section, SND is the King-like profile even though the system includes the heavier particle. In this section, in order to explain these results and derive this non-Maxwell-Boltzmann distribution around the origin, we demonstrate a simple model based on stochastic process, which is quite different from the King model.

The reason why stochastic process appears in the SGS is as follows. After the collapse, the density around the origin becomes high. Thus, the particles around the region disturb the

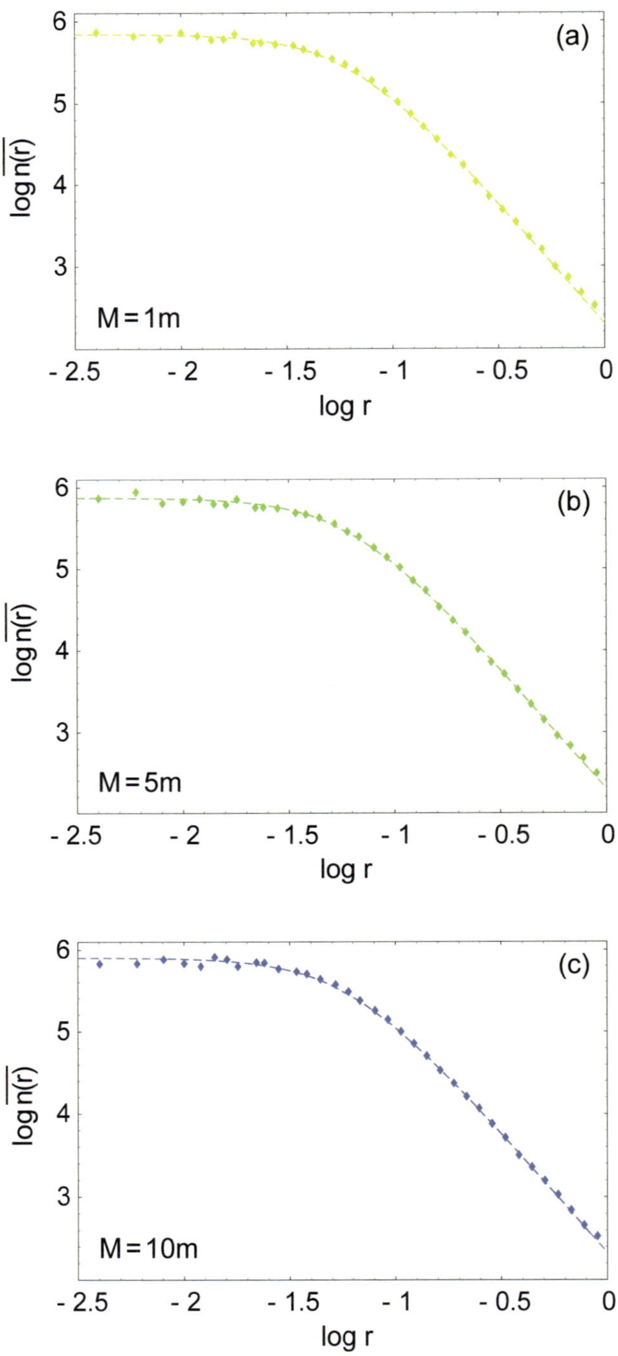

Fig. 3. Logarithm of the steady number density derived from our numerical simulation, $\overline{n(r)}$, as a function of $\log r$ for (a) $M/m = 1$, (b) $M/m = 5$, and (c) $M/m = 10$. In each figure, the dashed curve and symbols denote a fitting curve $\overline{n_{\rm fit}(r)} = C/(1 + r^2/a^2)^\kappa$ and the result of our numerical simulation, respectively.

orbits of other particles repeatedly, so that their movements become random [2]. As the time at which this disturbance occurs, we introduce the local 2-body relaxation time $t_{\rm rel}$ (Spitzer, 1987):

$$t_{\rm rel}(r) = \frac{0.065\sigma(r)^3}{G^2\overline{n(r)}m^2\ln(1/\varepsilon_s)}\,, \tag{16}$$

where $\sigma(r)$ is the standard deviation of the velocity at r; we adopted $\ln(1/\varepsilon_s)$ as the Coulomb logarithm.

Figure 4 shows the logarithm of $t_{\rm rel}$, which is calculated using the $\sigma(r)$ and $\overline{n(r)}$ during the steady state obtained from our numerical simulation, as a function of $\log r$. As expected, $t_{\rm rel}$ around the origin is short. Our simulation continues after the collapse at about 80 t_{ff}, which is sufficiently longer than the $t_{\rm rel}$ around the core. As radius increases, however, $t_{\rm rel}$ becomes longer than the rest of our simulation time, which means that no stochastic motion occurs at a large r. Therefore, note that our model is valid only in the neighborhood of the core.

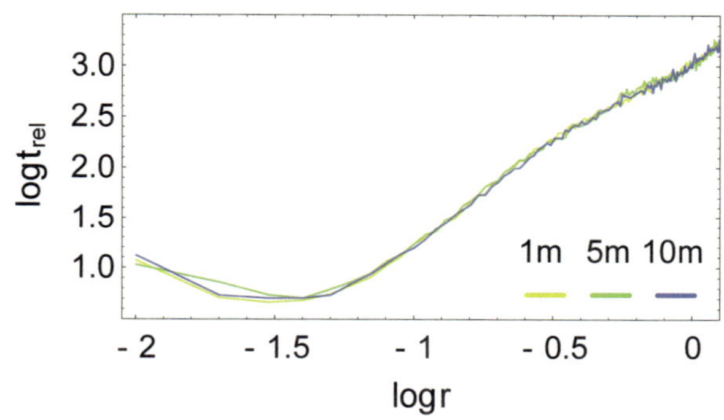

Fig. 4. Logarithm of the local 2-body relaxation time $t_{\rm rel}$ as a function of $\log r$ for $M/m = 1, 5$, and 10.

When constructing our model, the following points are premised: the model describes the stochastic dynamics near the steady state and the mean distribution is spherically symmetric. As is well known, the gravitational force at r arising from such a spherically symmetric system depends only on the particles existing inside a sphere with a radius r, and this attractive force acts along the radial direction. In other words, this mean force $-F(r)$ is the gradient of the mean potential: $-F(r) = -m\partial\Phi(r)/\partial r$ (< 0). Indeed, $\lim_{r\to 0} F(r) = 0$. Hence, $F(r)$ can be expanded around the origin as

$$F(r) = c_0 r + O(r^3)\,. \tag{17}$$

It will be clarified later that the lowest exponent must be 1 and the coefficient c_0 is related to the number density at the origin C as

$$c_0 = 4\pi G m^2 C/3\,. \tag{18}$$

[2] Generally, a particle going into a region where the gravitational potential is deep, e.g. the core of SGS, attains a high velocity. Because of many disturbances around the core, however, the mean velocity of the particle decreases, which is, naively speaking, the *dynamical friction* (Binney & Tremaine, 1987). Therefore, even though the heavier particle at the origin of the system makes the gravitational potential deeper, there are few particles that can escape from the core smoothly. Then more particles are drawn toward the heavier particle.

For $M/m = 1$, we can identify *another particle* together with the other particles. Contrary to this, we must consider the effect of the particle in the case $M/m \neq 1$. Now, we suppose that the heavier particle exists at the origin. Then, the attractive force by this particle at r is $-\mathscr{F}(r) = -GmM/r^2$. We can estimate $F(r)$ around this region as $F(r) \sim c_0 r = 4\pi G m^2 C r/3$, where we used Eq. (18). Thus, $\mathscr{F}(r)/F(r) \sim 3Mr^{-3}/4\pi C m$. This ratio becomes significant when $r \lesssim 10^{-2}$, since $C \sim 10^6$ as shown in Tab. 2. Therefore, if r is smaller than the radius, particles are influenced by not only $F(r)$ but also $\mathscr{F}(r)$, so that the core disappears. In fact, we have performed a numerical simulation with the heavier particle fixed at the origin, where this result is confirmed. On the other hand, Miocchi improved the King model in order to describe the steady state of a globular cluster including an IMBH and reported that the density becomes cuspy as the mass of the black hole increases (Miocchi, 2007). The nature of a globular cluster when a massive black hole is much heavier than the surrounding star, have been studied as mentioned in Introduction. In this case, the massive black hole stays at the center mostly. Then, a cusp of the density distribution at the center appears. Because the heavier particles in our numerical simulation are not very heavy, the particles are not trapped at the origin. Therefore, we do not consider the effect of heavier particles explicitly and we suppose that the particles influence SGS through the density at the origin C: as M becomes larger, it attracts more particles and C increases, as shown in Tab. 2. Thus, c_0 is an increasing function of M.

It is natural to consider that the distribution fluctuates around the mean because of the many disturbances. In fact, as shown in Fig. 2, the number of particles existing inside the sphere with a radius 1 fluctuates around the mean value. The fluctuating part of the distribution should not be spherically symmetric, so that this produces forces along not only the radial direction, but also other directions. We assume that they are random forces and set their intensity at r $2H(r)$. In addition to such random forces resulting from the fluctuating distribution, a particle at r is expected to be influenced by random forces generated from neighboring particles. We set the intensity $2D$, which is independent of position.

3.2 Langevin equations

Stochastic dynamics under the above assumptions is described by the following Langevin equations in spherical coordinates: the radial direction

$$ma_r + m\gamma\dot{r} = -F(r) + \sqrt{2H(r)}\eta_r(t) + \sqrt{2D}\xi_r(t)\,, \tag{19}$$

the elevation direction

$$ma_\theta + m\gamma r\dot{\theta} = \sqrt{2H(r)}\eta_\theta(t) + \sqrt{2D}\xi_\theta(t)\,, \tag{20}$$

and the azimuth direction

$$ma_\phi + m\gamma r\sin\theta\dot{\phi} = \sqrt{2H(r)}\eta_\phi(t) + \sqrt{2D}\xi_\phi(t)\,, \tag{21}$$

where a_r, a_θ, and a_ϕ are accelerations along those directions; γ is the coefficient of dynamical friction in the low velocity limit, independent of velocity (Binney & Tremaine, 1987). In the Chandrasekhar dynamical friction formula, the coefficient is more complicated (Binney & Tremaine, 1987; Chandrasekhar, 1943). However, we use the coefficient in such a limit, because the density around the core is so high that particles around there move slowly.

Now, we focus on the overdamped limit of these equations, because we have interests in the stochastic dynamics near the steady state. In the case of the *normal* Langevin equation with a constant-intensity noise, we only neglect the inertial term. But, as for *special* Langevin equations with noises whose intensity depends on a position, the new force $-\nabla H(\mathbf{r})/2m\gamma$ should be considered additionally [3]. Thus, the Langevin equations in the overdamped limit becomes as follows:

$$\text{radial direction}: m\gamma\dot{r} = -F(r) + \sqrt{2H(r)}\eta_r(t) + \sqrt{2D}\xi_r(t) - \frac{1}{2m\gamma}H'(r)\,, \tag{22}$$

$$\text{elevation direction}: m\gamma r\dot{\theta} = \sqrt{2H(r)}\eta_\theta(t) + \sqrt{2D}\xi_\theta(t)\,, \tag{23}$$

$$\text{azimuth direction}: m\gamma r\sin\theta\dot{\phi} = \sqrt{2H(r)}\eta_\phi(t) + \sqrt{2D}\xi_\phi(t)\,, \tag{24}$$

where the prime indicates a derivative with respect to r. The noises in each Langevin equation, $\xi_i(t)$ and $\eta_j(t)$ $(i,j = r,\theta,\text{and }\phi)$, are zero-mean white Gaussian and correlate only with themselves. Indeed, the correlation function is the Dirac delta function [4].
Here, revisit the position-dependent intensity noise. We have introduced such a noise in order to represent a random force originating from the fluctuation of the distribution around the mean value which yields the mean force $-F(r)$. Thus, the first and the second terms on the right-hand side of Eq. (22) must denote that the mean force acting along radial direction is fluctuating. As a minimal formulation describing this situation, we propose the following one:

$$-F(r)\{1 - \sqrt{2\epsilon}\eta_r(t)\}\,, \tag{25}$$

in which ϵ is a positive constant. This can be realized by setting

$$H(r) = \epsilon F(r)^2\,. \tag{26}$$

Note that this *fluctuating mean force* is the essential feature for SGS. Since the gravitational force is a long-range one, each particle is influenced from the whole system. The mean force is produced by the mean potential which is decided by the number density in the steady state through the Poisson equation. Obviously, this number density determines only the mean positions of the particles, and they do not remain stationary at those positions: they fluctuate. Then, the mean force also fluctuates. ϵ indicates the extent of fluctuations. If ϵ is 0, that is, means the mean force does not fluctuate, the stochastic dynamics of each particle is governed only by the constant-intensity random force originating from the neighboring particles. Then, the Maxwell-Boltzmann distribution is obtained as the steady solution, by which the number density of globular clusters cannot be explained as written in Introduction.

---

[3] This force is necessary in order to interpret products in theses Langevin equations as Storatonovich ones in the corresponding stochastic differential equations. See details in Ref. (Sekimoto, 1999).

[4] It may not be natural that correlations of the random forces generated from the gravity are described by the Dirac delta function. But in this paper, for simplicity, the correlation times are assumed to be negligible. In other words, the time resolution of our simple model in the over-damped limit is assumed to be much longer than the correlation times.

3.3 Fokker-Planck equation and the asymptotic steady solution around the origin

From the Langevin equations (22), (23), and (24), we obtain the Fokker-Planck equation governing the spherically symmetric probability distribution function (PDF) $P(r,t)$

$$\frac{\partial}{\partial t}P(r,t) = \frac{D}{(m\gamma)^2}\left\{\frac{\partial^2}{\partial r^2}+\frac{2}{r}\frac{\partial}{\partial r}\right\}P(r,t)+\frac{1}{m\gamma}\frac{1}{r^2}\frac{\partial}{\partial r}r^2F(r)P(r,t)$$
$$+\frac{\epsilon}{(m\gamma)^2}\left\{\frac{\partial^2}{\partial r^2}F(r)^2+\frac{2}{r}\frac{\partial}{\partial r}F(r)^2\right\}P(r,t)\,,$$

in which we have replaced $H(r)$ by $F(r)$ using Eq. (26). Then, the PDF with the Jacobian $\rho(r,t)\equiv 4\pi r^2P(r,t)$ satisfies the following Fokker-Planck equation.

$$\frac{\partial}{\partial t}\rho(r,t) = \frac{D}{(m\gamma)^2}\left\{\frac{\partial^2}{\partial r^2}-\frac{\partial}{\partial r}\frac{2}{r}\right\}\rho(r,t)+\frac{1}{m\gamma}\frac{\partial}{\partial r}F(r)\rho(r,t)$$
$$+\frac{\epsilon}{(m\gamma)^2}\left\{\frac{\partial^2}{\partial r^2}-\frac{\partial}{\partial r}\frac{2}{r}\right\}F(r)^2\rho(r,t) \qquad (27)$$

This equation is useful when integrating with respect to r.

The steady state solution $\rho_{\rm st}(r)$ satisfies Eq. (27) with the left-hand side zero. By integrating the equation with respect to r, we have

$$\left\{\frac{D}{(m\gamma)^2}+\frac{\epsilon}{(m\gamma)^2}F(r)^2\right\}\rho'_{\rm st}(r)$$
$$-\left[\frac{D}{(m\gamma)^2}\frac{2}{r}-\frac{\epsilon}{(m\gamma)^2}\left\{2F(r)F'(r)-\frac{2}{r}F(r)^2\right\}-\frac{F(r)}{m\gamma}\right]\rho_{\rm st}(r)=\text{const.}\,. \qquad (28)$$

Now, we impose the binary condition that $P_{\rm st}(r)\equiv\rho_{\rm st}(r)/(4\pi r^2)$ and the derivative do not diverge at the origin. Then, when $r\to 0$,

$$\rho_{\rm st}(r)=O(r^2)\,, \qquad (29)$$

and

$$\lim_{r\to 0}\rho'_{\rm st}(r)=\lim_{r\to 0}4\pi(2rP_{\rm st}(r)+r^2P'_{\rm st}(r))=0\,, \qquad (30)$$

by which the constant on the right-hand side of Eq. (28) is decided and we obtain

$$r\left\{D+\epsilon F(r)^2\right\}\rho'_{\rm st}(r)=-\left[rF(r)\left\{2\epsilon F'(r)+m\gamma\right\}-2\left\{D+\epsilon F(r)^2\right\}\right]\rho_{\rm st}(r)\,. \qquad (31)$$

Thus, if $F(r)$ is obtained, $\rho_{\rm st}(r)$ can also be obtained. Here, $F(r)$ relates with SND, $n_{\rm st}(r)$, through the following relation, since $-F(r)=-m\Phi'(r)$.

$$F'(r)+\frac{2}{r}F(r)=4\pi Gm^2n_{\rm st}(r) \qquad (32)$$

Incidentally, the SND can be obtained by multiplying PDF in the steady state by total number N:

$$n_{\rm st}(r)=NP_{\rm st}(r)=\frac{N\rho_{\rm st}(r)}{4\pi r^2}\,. \qquad (33)$$

Therefore, equation (32) can be represented as

$$F'(r) + \frac{2}{r}F(r) = \frac{GNm^2\rho_{\rm st}(r)}{r^2}\,. \tag{34}$$

In short, $\rho_{\rm st}(r)$ and $F(r)$ are closely connected with each other through Eqs. (31) and (34). Here, we focus on the asymptotic behaviors of them around the origin, since our model is valid around there as mentioned before. Furthermore, due to this approach, we can treat them analytically.

Assume that $F(r)$ can be expanded around the origin with the lowest exponent k as follows.

$$F(r) = r^k \sum_{l=0}^{\infty} c_l r^l \tag{35}$$

Substituting this expression into Eq. (34), we find that $\rho_{\rm st}(r)$ can also be expanded like

$$\rho_{\rm st}(r) = \frac{r^{k+1}}{GNm^2}\sum_{l=0}^{\infty} c_l(k+l+2)r^l\,. \tag{36}$$

After substituting both Eqs.(35) and (36) into Eq.(31), we can obtain

$$\begin{aligned}
&\left\{D + \epsilon r^{2k}\left(\sum_{l=0}^{\infty} c_l r^l\right)^2\right\}\frac{r^{k+1}}{GNm^2}\sum_{l=0}^{\infty} c_l(k+l+1)(k+l+2)r^l \\
&= -\left[r^{k+1}\sum_{l=0}^{\infty} c_l r^l\left\{2\epsilon r^{k-1}\sum_{s=0}^{\infty} c_s(k+s)r^s + m\gamma\right\} - 2\left\{D + \epsilon r^{2k}\left(\sum_{l=0}^{\infty} c_l r^l\right)^2\right\}\right] \\
&\times \frac{r^{k+1}}{GNm^2}\sum_{l=0}^{\infty} c_l(k+l+2)r^l\,.
\end{aligned} \tag{37}$$

Firstly, we compare the lowest order terms on the both hand sides of Eq. (37), so that the following relation can be seen:

$$D\frac{r^{k+1}}{GNm^2}c_0(k+1)(k+2) = 2D\frac{r^{k+1}}{GNm^2}c_0(k+2)\,. \tag{38}$$

Therefore, we can conclude that $k = 1$. Secondly, compare the next lowest order terms proportional to r^3 and we get

$$D\frac{r^2}{GNm^2}c_1\cdot 3\cdot 4\cdot r = 2D\frac{r^2}{GNm^2}c_1\cdot 4\cdot r\,, \tag{39}$$

and so $c_1 = 0$. Lastly, selecting only terms proportional to r^4 from Eq. (37), we can find

$$\epsilon r^2 {c_0}^2\frac{r^2}{GNm^2}c_0\cdot 2\cdot 3 + D\frac{r^2}{GNm^2}c_2\cdot 4\cdot 5\cdot r^2 = -r^2 c_0 m\gamma\frac{r^2}{GNm^2}c_0\cdot 3 + 2D\frac{r^2}{GNm^2}c_2\cdot 5\cdot r^2\,, \tag{40}$$

from which the following relation can be obtained:

$$\frac{5}{3}\frac{c_2}{c_0} = -\frac{\epsilon {c_0}^2}{D}\left(1 + \frac{m\gamma}{2\epsilon c_0}\right) . \tag{41}$$

Without going into detail, we can see that $c_3 = 0$ by comparison with terms containing r^5. So, $\rho_{\rm st}(r)$ becomes as follows:

$$\begin{aligned}\rho_{\rm st}(r) &= \frac{r^2}{GNm^2}\left(3c_0 + 5c_2 r^2\right) + O(r^6)\\ &= \frac{3c_0 r^2}{GNm^2}\left(1 + \frac{5}{3}\frac{c_2}{c_0}r^2\right) + O(r^6)\\ &= \frac{3c_0 r^2}{GNm^2}\left\{1 - \frac{\epsilon {c_0}^2}{D}\left(1 + \frac{m\gamma}{2\epsilon c_0}\right) r^2\right\} + O(r^6) .\end{aligned} \tag{42}$$

Here, if we set [5]

$$a^2 \equiv \frac{D}{\epsilon {c_0}^2} \quad \text{and} \quad \kappa \equiv 1 + \frac{m\gamma}{2\epsilon c_0} , \tag{43}$$

$\rho_{\rm st}(r)$ can be expressed around the origin like

$$\rho_{\rm st}(r) \sim \frac{3c_0}{GNm^2}\frac{r^2}{(1 + r^2/a^2)^\kappa} , \tag{44}$$

which yields

$$n_{\rm st}(r) = \frac{N}{4\pi r^2}\rho_{\rm st}(r) \sim \frac{3c_0}{4\pi Gm^2}\frac{1}{(1 + r^2/a^2)^\kappa} . \tag{45}$$

Thus, we can derive the number density around the origin of SGS from the model using stochastic dynamics.

The relation (18) is easily obtained by setting $r = 0$ on Eq. (45), that is,

$$C = n_{\rm st}(0) = \frac{3c_0}{4\pi Gm^2} . \tag{46}$$

4. Discussion

In this section, we investigate the results derived in the preceding section and understand the roles of two noises and the heavier particle in Eq. (45). Additionally, we discuss the difference between the King model and our model.

As in Eq. (43), the exponent κ must be larger than 1, which does not contradict our numerical simulation shown in Tab. 2. In order for Eq. (45) to correspond completely to the King model, $\kappa = 3/2$ or $\gamma = \epsilon c_0/m = 4\pi Gm\epsilon C/3$ must hold. We can regard this relation between the friction coefficient γ and the intensity of the multiplicative noise ϵ as a kind of *fluctuation-dissipation relation* (Kubo et al., 1991), which usually plays an important role when a stochastic process with a constant-intensity noise goes to the equilibrium state described by the Maxwell-Boltzmann distribution.

[5] The dimension of $\sqrt{D/\epsilon {c_0}^2}$ is a length and $m\gamma/2\epsilon c_0$ is dimensionless. See Appendix A.

The core radius a is proportional to a square root of the intensity of the additive noise D owing to Eq. (43). Then, this intensity spreads the region where the density is almost constant. This is recognized as the effect of this noise, which makes a system homogeneous and isothermal. The existence of the core at globular clusters shows that such a diffusive effect does not disappear even for the system with long-range force. In other words, all statistical mechanical features observed in a system with short-range force, that is, *normal* system, does not change drastically in SGS and this effect is still universal. Our model makes it clear that the special distribution can be obtained just considering the fluctuation of mean force.

Now, let us examine the role of the mass of the heavier particle, M, in this system by a naive discussion. As mentioned previously, c_0 is an increasing function of M. c_0 exists in the denominators of a and κ. Then, both values should be reduced when M is increased if other parameters are independent of M. These theoretical expectations are consistent with our numerical results shown in Tab. 2.

How the *special* distribution (45) changes if we do not consider the fluctuating mean force? The steady state solution of Eq. (27) with $\epsilon = 0$ is

$$P_{st}(r) \propto e^{-\frac{m^2\gamma}{D}\Phi(r)} . \tag{47}$$

Therefore, our result goes to a singular isothermal sphere, as discussed at the beginning of this paper, by which the number density of globular clusters cannot be explained.

Here, we examine the relationship between the King model and our model. King transformed the distribution function in the phase space in order to avoid a singular isothermal sphere. In our model, we introduce the multiplicative noise into the system influenced by the mean force and the additive noise whose PDF becomes Maxwellian in the steady state, as shown in Eq. (47), so that the non-Maxwell-Boltzmann distribution (45) is derived. In short, although these procedures seem to be different, they may have the same meaning at least around the origin. However, we emphasize that the stochastic dynamics around there near the steady state becomes clear owing to Eqs. (19), (20), and (21).

5. Conclusion

In conclusion, the non-Maxwell-Boltzmann distribution (45) has been obtained using the stochastic dynamics with the fluctuating mean force and the additive white noise. This number density can be the same as that of the King model around the origin by controlling friction coefficient and the intensity of multiplicative noise. Furthermore, our model can describe the SGS having a heavier particle. Of course, these results are consistent with our numerical simulation. We can say that such a stochastic dynamics occurs behind the background of the King model. In short, the diffusive effect, which is represented by the additive noise, is universal even in SGS, and it is particular to SGS that the fluctuation of the distribution around the mean value producing the mean force makes influence on each particle of this system, which our simple model can describe.

Finally, note that our result is available only in the neighborhood of the origin. Therefore, we must derive the density globally by further extended model and investigate the difference between the model and the King model.

Appendix A. Dimensions of $\sqrt{D/\epsilon c_0{}^2}$ and $m\gamma/2\epsilon c_0$

From now on, $[\bullet]$ represents a dimension of $\bullet$. Since the correlation function of the random noises $\xi_i(t)$ and $\eta_j(t)$ $(i, j = r, \theta, \text{and } \phi)$ is the Dirac delta function with argument t,

$$[\xi_i(t)] = [\eta_j(t)] = \text{time}^{-1/2}\,. \tag{A.1}$$

Thus, from the expression (25) whose dimension is a force, we can see that

$$[\epsilon] = \text{time}\,. \tag{A.2}$$

Furthermore, from $\sqrt{2D}\xi_r(t)$ whose dimension is also a force, the dimension of D can be clear like

$$[D] = \text{force}^2 \cdot \text{time} = \text{mass}^2 \cdot \text{length}^2 \cdot \text{time}^{-3}\,. \tag{A.3}$$

Owing to Eqs. (17) or (18), the dimension of c_0 equals a force per length:

$$[c_0] = \text{force} \cdot \text{length}^{-1} = \text{mass} \cdot \text{time}^{-2}\,. \tag{A.4}$$

As well known, the dimension of the damping constant, γ, is an inverse of time: $[\gamma] = \text{time}^{-1}$. Thereby,

$$\left[\sqrt{\frac{D}{\epsilon c_0{}^2}}\right] = \sqrt{\frac{\text{mass}^2 \cdot \text{length}^2 \cdot \text{time}^{-3}}{\text{time} \cdot \text{mass}^2 \cdot \text{time}^{-4}}} = \text{length}\,, \tag{A.5}$$

and

$$\left[\frac{m\gamma}{\epsilon c_0}\right] = \frac{\text{mass} \cdot \text{time}^{-1}}{\text{time} \cdot \text{mass} \cdot \text{time}^{-2}} = 1\,. \tag{A.6}$$

6. Acknowledgement

We would like to thank Prof. Masahiro Morikawa, Dr. Osamu Iguchi, and members of Morikawa laboratory for extensive discussions. All numerical computations were carried out on the GRAPE system at the Center for Computational Astrophysics, CfCA, of National Astronomical Observatory of Japan. The page charge of this paper is partly supported by CfCA. This work was supported by the Grant-in-Aid for Scientific Research Fund of the Ministry of Education, Culture, Sports, Science and Technology, Japan (Young Scientists (B) 21740188).

7. References

Binney, J. & Tremaine, S. (1987). *Galactic Dynamics*, Princeton University Press, ISBN 978-0-6910-8445-9, Princeton.

King, I. R. (1966). The structure of star clusters. III. Some simple dynamical models. *Astron. J.*, Vol.71, No.1, 64-75.

Peterson, C. J. & King, I. R. (1975). The structure of star clusters. VI. Observed radii and structural parameters in globular clusters. *Astron. J.*, Vol.80, No.6, 427-436.

Chernoff, D. F. & Djorgovski, S. (1989). An analysis of the distribution of globular clusters with postcollapse cores in the galaxy. *Astrophys. J.*, Vol.339, 904-918.

Trager, S. C.; King, I. R. & Djorgovski, S. (1995). Catalogue of galactic globular-cluster surface-brightness profiles. *Astron. J.*, Vol.109, No.1, 218-241.

Lehmann, I. & Scholz, R.-D. (1997). Tidal radii of the globular clusters M5, M12, M13, M15, M53, NGC5053 and NGC5466 from automated star counts. *Astron. Astrophys.* Vol.320, 776-782.

Meylan, G.; Sarajedini, A.; Jablonka, P.; Djorgovski, S. G.; Bridges, T. & Rich, R. M. (2001). Mayall II=G1 in M31: giant globular cluster or core of a dwarf elliptical galaxy? *Astron. J.*, Vol.122, 830-841.

Peebles, P. J. E. (1972). Star Distribution Near a Collapsed Object. *Astrophys. J.* Vol.178, 371-376.

Bahcall, J. N. & and Wolf, R. A. (1976). Star distribution around a massive black hole in a globular cluster. *Astrophys. J.* Vol.209, 214-232.

Bahcall, J. N. & and Wolf, R. A. (1977). The star distribution around a massive black hole in a globular cluster. II Unequal star masses. *Astrophys. J.* Vol.216, 883-907.

Tashiro, T. & and Tatekawa, T. (2010). Brownian Dynamics around the Core of Self-Gravitating Systems. *J. Phys. Soc. Jpn.* Vol.79, 063001-1-063001-4.

Clark, G. W.; Markert, T. H.; Li, F. K. (1975). Observations of variable X-ray sources in globular clusters. *Astrophys. J.* Vol.199, L93-L96.

Newell, B; Da Costa, G. S.; Norris, J. (1976). Evidence for a Central Massive Object in the X-Ray Cluster M15. *Astrophys. J.* Vol.208, L55-L59.

Djorgovski, S. & King, I. R. (1984). Surface photometry in cores of globular clusters. *Astrophys. J.* Vol.277, L49-L52.

Gebhardt, K.; Rich, R. M.; Ho, L. C. (2002). A 20,000 M_{solar} Black Hole in the Stellar Cluster G1. *Astrophys. J.* Vol.578 L41-L45.

Gerssen, J. *et al.* (2002). Hubble Space Telescope Evidence for an Intermediate-Mass Black Hole in the Globular Cluster M15. II. Kinematic Analysis and Dynamical Modeling. *Astron. J.* Vol.124, 3270-3288.

Noyola, E.; Gebhardt, K.; Bergmann, M. (2008). Gemini and Hubble Space Telescope Evidence for an Intermediate-Mass Black Hole in ω Centauri. *Astrophys. J.* Vol.676, 1008-1015.

Sugimoto, D.; Chikada, Y.; Makino, J.; Ito, T.; Ebisuzaki, T; Umemura, M. (1990). A special-purpose computer for gravitational many-body problems. *Nature*, Vol.345, 33-35.

Kawai, A. & Fukushige, T. (2006). $158/GFLOPS astrophysical N-body simulation with reconfigurable add-in card and hierarchical tree algorithm. *Proceedings of the 2006 ACM/IEEE conference on Supercomputing*, No.48.

Makino, J.; Fukushige, T.; Koga, M.; Namura, K. (2003). GRAPE-6: Massively-Parallel Special-Purpose Computer for Astrophysical Particle Simulations *Pub. Astron. Soc. Japan*, Vol.55, 1163-1187.

Press, W. H.; Teukolsky, S. A.; Vetterling, W. T. & Flannery, B. P. (2007). *Numerical Recipes 3rd edition*, Cambridge University Press, ISBN 978-0-5218-8068-8, Cambridge.

Ruth, R. (1983). A canonical integration technique. *IEEE Transactions on Nuclear Science*, Vol.30, 2669-2671.

Feng, K. & Qin, M.-Z. (1987). The symplectic methods for the computation of Hamiltonian equations. *Lecture Notes in Mathematics*, Vol.1297, 1-37

Suzuki, M. (1992). General theory of higher-order decomposition of exponential operators and symplectic integrators. *Phys. Lett. A*, Vol.165, 387-395.

Yoshida, H. (1990). Construction of higher order symplectic integrators. *Phys. Lett. A* Vol.150, 262-268.

Yoshida, H. (1993). Recent progress in the theory and application of symplectic integrators. *Celes. Mech. Dyn. Astron.* Vol.56, 27-43.

Sanz-Serna, J. M. (1988). Runge-Kutta schemes for Hamiltonian systems. *BIT* Vol.28, 877-883.

Kustaanheimo, P. & Stiefel, E. (1965). Perturbation theory of Kepler motion based on. spinor regularization. *J. Reine Angw. Mathematik* Vol.218, 204-219.

Aarseth, S. (2003). *Gravitational N-body simulations,* Cambridge University Press, ISBN 978-0-5211-2153-8, Cambridge.

Spitzer, L. (1987). *Dynamical Evolution of Globular Clusters,* Princeton University Press, ISBN 978-0-6910-8460-2, Princeton.

Miocchi, P. (2007). The presence of intermediate-mass black holes in globular clusters and their connection with extreme horizontal branch stars. *Not. R. Astron. Soc.* Vol.381, 103-116.

Chandrasekhar, S. (1943). Dynamical Friction. I. General Considerations: the Coefficient of Dynamical Friction. *Astrophys. J.,* Vol.97, 255-262.

Sekimoto, K. (1999) Temporal coarse graining for systems of Brownian particles with non-constant temperature. *J. Phys. Soc. Jpn.* Vol.68, 1448-1449.

Kubo, R.; Toda, M. & Hashitsume, N (1991). *Statistical Physics II: Nonequilibrium Statistical Mechanics,* Springer-Verlag, ISBN 978-3-5405-3833-2, Berlin.

Part 2

Engineering Processes

15

Advanced Numerical Techniques for Near-Field Antenna Measurements

Sandra Costanzo and Giuseppe Di Massa
University of Calabria
Italy

1. Introduction

The evaluation of antenna radiation features requires the accurate determination of its far-field pattern, whose direct measurement imposes to probe the field at a distance proportionally related to the ratio between the squared dimension *D* of the antenna aperture and the excitation wavelength (Fig.1). As a consequence of this, the direct evaluation of antenna far-field pattern could require prohibitive distances in the presence of electrically large radiating systems, with increasing complexity and cost of the measurement setup in order to minimize interfering effects.

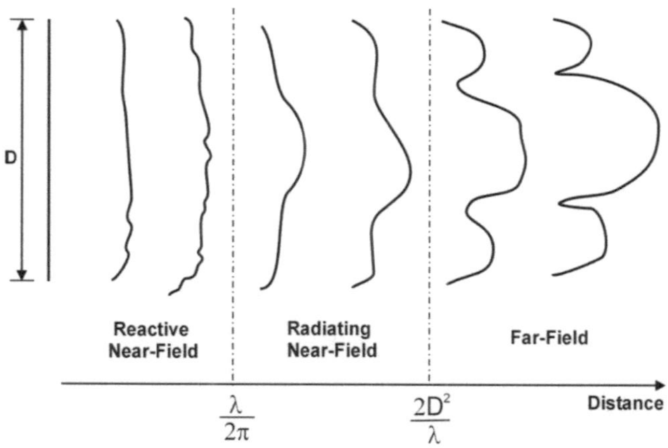

Fig. 1. Antenna field regions.

To face the problem of impractical far-field ranges, the idea to recover far-field patterns from near-field measurements (Johnson et al., 1973) has been introduced and is largely adopted today, as leading to use noise controlled test chambers with reduced size and costs. The near-field approach relies on the acquisition of the tangential field components on a prescribed scanning surface, with the subsequent far-field evaluation essentially based on a modal expansion inherent to the particular geometry (Yaghajian, 1986). The accuracy and performances of near-field methods are strictly limited by the effectiveness of the related transformation algorithms as well as by the measurement accuracy of available input data, and in particular of near-field phase, which is very difficult to obtain at high operating frequencies. In relation to the above aspects, two classes of methods are discussed in this chapter, the first one concerning efficient transformation algorithms for not canonical near-field surfaces, and the second one relative to accurate far-field characterization by near-field amplitude-only (or phaseless) measurements.

2. Efficient near-field to far-field transformations on strategic scanning surfaces

Near-field to far-field (NF-FF) transformation algorithms, taking also into account for the presence of non-ideal probes, have been developed in literature for the most common scanning surfaces of planar, cylindrical and spherical type (Yaghajian, 1986). All these canonical near-field geometries have their own features, limiting in some way the applicability of the related near-field technique. Due to its intrinsic simplicity, from both the analytical and the computational viewpoints, the planar (Fig. 2(a)) near-field configuration (Wang, 1988) results to be the most attractive one, suffering however of a limited spatial resolution which allows an efficient application only in the presence of highly directive antennas with pencil beam patterns. Slightly greater computational efforts are required by the near-field cylindrical (Fig. 2(b)) scanning (Leach and Paris, 1973), leading to obtain a complete far-field azimuth pattern, with the only exclusion of elevation angles equal to 0 and 180 degrees, for which the Hankel function is not defined (Johnson et al., 1973). A full pattern reconstruction is assured by the near-field spherical (Fig. 2(c)) scanning (Ludwig, 1971), which however requires a complicated measurement setup and a time consuming transformation algorithm for the computation of the relative expansion coefficients.

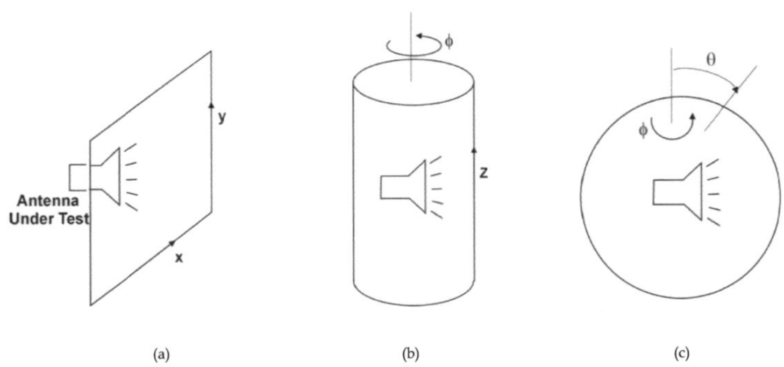

Fig. 2. Canonical near-field scannings: (a) planar, (b) cylindrical, (c) spherical.

In order to reduce the acquisition time as well as to enlarge the scan area, innovative configurations have been proposed in recent years as variant to the most common planar and cylindrical scannings. These new acquisition geometries, namely the helicoidal (Costanzo and Di Massa, 2004), plane-polar (Costanzo and Di Massa, 2006 a), bi-polar (Costanzo and Di Massa, 2006 b) and spiral ones (Costanzo and Di Massa, 2007), give a simpler, more compact and less expensive scanning setup, by imposing a continuous motion of the antenna under test (AUT) and the measuring probe. However, due to the non-standard location of the near-field data points, these innovative configurations strongly complicate, in principle, the NF-FF transformation process, as a conversion to a rectangular data format, in the case of plane-polar, bi-polar and spiral geometries, or to a cylindrical format, in the case of helicoidal scanning, is generally required to enable the application of standard NF-FF planar or cylindrical transformations. In some recent papers (Costanzo and Di Massa, 2004; 2006 a;b; 2007), direct NF-FF algorithms have been proposed to obtain the far-field pattern from near-field data acquired on the above strategic geometries, by properly apply the fast Fourier transform (FFT) and the related shift property (Bracewell, 2000) to avoid any kind of intermediate interpolation. The theoretical details of the above efficient NF-FF transformation procedures are discussed in the next sections.

2.1 Helicoidal NF-FF transformation

In the helicoidal scanning configuration (Fig. 3), near-field data are acquired on a cylindrical helix of radius r_o at sample points $P_e\,(r_o, \phi_o, z_o)$, by imposing a simultaneous linear movement (along z-axis) of the probe and an azimuthal rotation of the AUT (Costanzo and Di Massa, 2004).

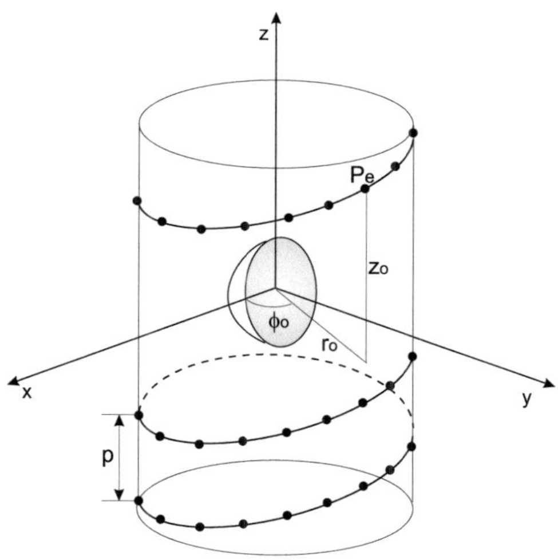

Fig. 3. Helicoidal near-field scanning.

The tangential field components on the helicoidal surface can be expressed in terms a cylindrical modal expansion (Leach and Paris, 1973), with coefficients a_n, b_n given by the expressions:

$$b_n(h)\frac{\Lambda^2}{k}H_n^{(2)}\left(\Lambda r_o\right) = \frac{1}{4\pi^2}\int_{-\infty}^{+\infty}\int_{-\pi}^{+\pi} E_z(\phi_o, z_o)e^{-jn\phi_o}e^{jhz_o}d\phi_o dz_o \tag{1}$$

$$b_n(h)\frac{nh}{kr_o}H_n^{(2)}\left(\Lambda r_o\right) - a_n(h)\frac{\partial H_n^{(2)}}{\partial r}(\Lambda r)|_{r=r_o} = \frac{1}{4\pi^2}\int_{-\infty}^{+\infty}\int_{-\pi}^{+\pi} E_\phi(\phi_o, z_o)e^{-jn\phi_o}e^{jhz_o}d\phi_o dz_o \tag{2}$$

where k is the free-space propagation factor, $\Lambda = \sqrt{k^2 - h^2}$ and $H_n^{(2)}(..)$ is the Hankel function of the second kind and order n (Abramowitz and Stegun, 1972).
In the standard case of a near-field acquisition on a cylinder of radius r_o, integrals appearing into equations (1) and (2) are efficiently evaluated by a two-dimensional FFT, by assuming sampling spacings $\Delta\phi = \frac{\lambda}{2a}$ and $\Delta z = \frac{\lambda}{2}$, a being the radius of the smallest cylinder completely enclosing the AUT. The far-field is finally obtained in terms of asymptotic evaluation of cylindrical wave expansion (Leach and Paris, 1973) as:

$$E_\theta(\theta, \phi) = j sin\theta \sum_{n=-\infty}^{+\infty} j^n b_n(kcos\theta)e^{jn\phi} \tag{3}$$

$$E_\phi(\theta, \phi) = sin\theta \sum_{n=-\infty}^{+\infty} j^n a_n(kcos\theta)e^{jn\phi} \tag{4}$$

In the case of helicoidal near-field acquisition as illustrated in Fig. 3, the azimuthal and z-axis coordinates are related by the equation:

$$z_o = p\frac{\phi_o}{2\pi} \tag{5}$$

where p is the helix step, i.e. the distance between adjacent points along a generatrix. By imposing $p = \frac{\lambda}{2}$, near-field data on the cylindrical helix can be arranged into a matrix $\underline{\underline{A}} \in C^{MxN}$, M being the number of helicoidal revolutions and N the number of azimuthal samples for each revolution. Data distributed on the $i-th$ column of matrix $\underline{\underline{A}}$ are shifted with respect to the first column by a quantity $i\Delta z_\phi$, where $\Delta z_\phi = p\frac{\Delta\phi}{2\pi}$. This particular data arrangement leads to efficiently solve integrals involved in the computation of modal expansions coefficients $a_n(h)$,$b_n(h)$ as given by equations (1) and (2). If we consider the numerical implementation of integral:

$$I_n(h) = \frac{1}{4\pi^2}\int_{-\infty}^{+\infty}\int_{-\infty}^{+\infty} E_z\left(\phi_o, z_o\right) e^{-jn\phi_o} e^{jhz_o} d\phi_o dz_o \tag{6}$$

which appears into equation (1), after some manipulations (Costanzo and Di Massa, 2004) we can write:

$$I_n(h) = \sum_{r=0}^{N-1} \widetilde{E}_{zs}\left(r\Delta\phi, h\right) e^{-j\frac{2\pi nr}{N}} \tag{7}$$

where the term:

$$\widetilde{E}_{zs}\left(r\Delta\phi, h\right) = \widetilde{E}_z\left(r\Delta\phi, h\right) e^{-j\frac{2\pi hr\Delta z_\phi}{M}} \tag{8}$$

represents the discrete Fourier transform (DFT) (Bracewell, 2000) of the sequence $E_z\left(r\Delta\phi, s\Delta z\right)$, axially translated by a quantity $r\Delta z_\phi$ through the application of the Fourier transform shift property (Bracewell, 2000).
The computation procedure for integral (6), described by equation (7), can be summarized by the following steps:

1. given the tangential component E_z on the helicoidal surface, perform FFT on each column of matrix data $\underline{\underline{A}}$;
2. apply the Fourier transform shift property to the transformed columns obtained from step 1;
3. perform FFT on the rows to obtain the final result in (7);

The outlined procedure can be obviously repeated for the computation of integral appearing into equation (2), which involves the component E_ϕ. Combined results are finally used to determine the expansion coefficients $a_n(h)$, $b_n(h)$, giving the far-field pattern components (3), (4).
The far-field reconstruction process from helicoidal near-field data is validated by performing numerical simulations on a linear array of z-oriented 37 elementary Huyghens sources, $\lambda/2$ spaced along z-axis (Costanzo and Di Massa, 2004). Near-field samples are collected on a cylindrical helix of radius $r_o = 21.5\lambda$ and height equal to 120λ, with an azimuthal sampling step $\Delta\phi = 2.38^o$. The effectiveness of the helicoidal NF-FF transformation procedure is demonstrated under Fig. 4, where the computed far-field pattern for the dominant E_θ component is successfully compared with that obtained from a standard cylindrical NF-FF transformation on a cylindrical surface having the same radius and height as those relative to the helicoidal acquisition curve.

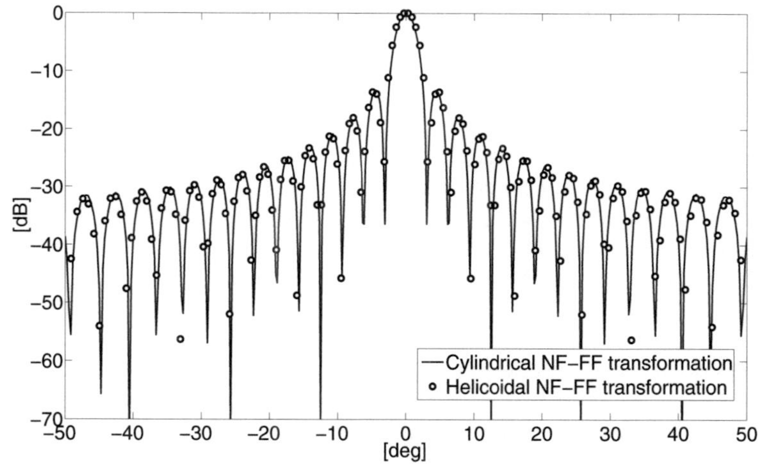

Fig. 4. Far-field amplitude (E_θ component) for linear array of z-oriented 37 elementary Huyghens sources: comparison between cylindrical and helicoidal NF-FF transformations.

2.2 NF-FF transformations on innovative planar-type geometries

The coordinate system relevant to the acquisition scheme for the planar-type geometries is illustrated in Fig. 5, where the measuring probe moves on the $z = 0$ plane to collect the near-field coming from a test antenna mounted on the z-axis.

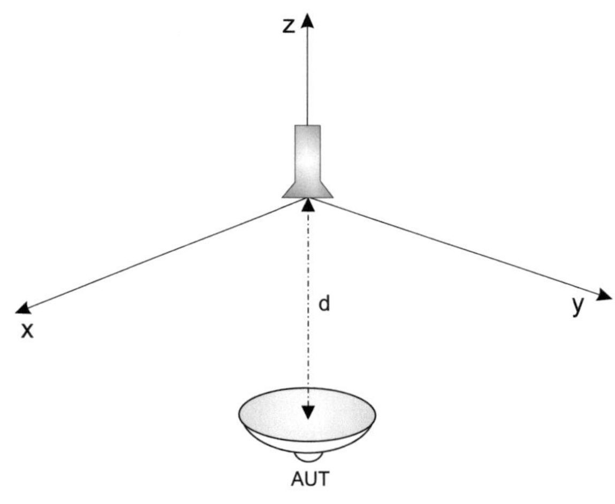

Fig. 5. Coordinate system relevant to the near-field planar-type acquisition scheme.

The mathematical relationship between the antenna field and the probe equivalent aperture currents can be easily found by applying Lorentz reciprocity (Costanzo and Di Massa, 2006 a) to have:

$$T(\theta,\phi) = \int_{-\infty}^{+\infty}\int_{-\infty}^{+\infty} q(x',y')e^{jk(x'sin\theta cos\phi + y'sin\theta sin\phi)}dx'dy' \quad (9)$$

Under the simplified assumption of an infinitesimal ideal probe, the left hand side of equation (9) expressed in its scalar form, gives the antenna radiation pattern at coordinates (θ,ϕ), while the term $q(x',y')$ represents the near-field probed at coordinates (x',y').

If we consider a near-field polar surface of radius a, the following expression (Costanzo and Di Massa, 2006 a) can be derived for the radiation integral:

$$T(\theta,\phi) = \int_0^a \int_0^{2\pi} q(\rho',\phi') e^{jk\rho' sin\theta cos(\phi-\phi')} \rho' d\rho' d\phi' \tag{10}$$

where the coordinates transformations $x' = \rho' cos\phi'$ and $y' = \rho' sin\phi'$ are applied.
The inner integral into relation (10) can be easily recognized as a convolution with respect to the azimuthal variable ϕ', so the convolution theorem (Bracewell, 2000) can be applied to simplify its computation in terms of FFT. By exploiting this convolution property, compact expressions of equation (10) can be derived for the plane-polar, bi-polar and planar spiral configurations, as it will be discussed in the follows.

2.2.1 NF-FF transformation on plane-polar geometry

In the plane-polar configuration (Fig. 6), near-field data are acquired on concentric rings filling a disk of radius a, with sampling steps in the radial and azimuthal directions given by the expressions:

$$\Delta\rho = \frac{\lambda}{2}, \quad \Delta\phi = \frac{\lambda}{2r_o} \tag{11}$$

r_o being the radius of the smallest sphere enclosing the AUT.

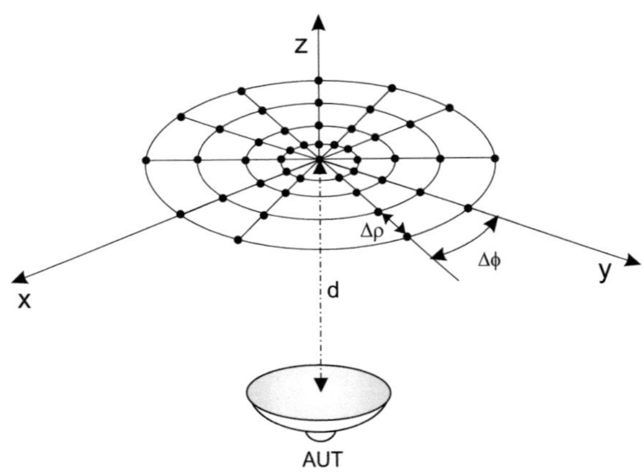

Fig. 6. Plane-polar near-field scanning.

In the presence of polar near-field samples, equation (10) can be expressed in a compact form as (Costanzo and Di Massa, 2006 a):

$$T(\theta,\phi) = \int_0^a \int_0^{2\pi} q_1(\rho',\phi') r(\theta,\phi,\rho',\phi') d\rho' d\phi' \tag{12}$$

where:

$$q_1(\rho',\phi') = \rho' q(\rho',\phi'), \quad r(\theta,\phi,\rho',\phi') = e^{jk\rho' sin\theta cos(\phi-\phi')} \tag{13}$$

The convolution form with respect to the azimuthal variable ϕ' leads to express (13) in terms of FFT as:

$$T(\theta,\phi) = \int_0^a \mathcal{F}^{-1}\left\{\tilde{q}_1(\rho',w)\tilde{r}(\theta,\phi,\rho',w)\right\} d\rho' \tag{14}$$

where the symbol $\mathcal{F}\{..\}$ and the tilde ($\tilde{}$) on the top denote the Fourier transform operator. If we consider a plane-polar near-field data set at coordinates $(m\Delta\rho, n\Delta\phi)$, with $m = 0, ...M-1$, $n = 0, ..., N-1$, M being the number of concentric rings and N the number of sectors, the radiation integral (14) can be numerically implemented as:

$$T(\theta,\phi) = \sum_{m=0}^{M-1}\sum_{n=0}^{N-1} \left[\tilde{q}_1(m\Delta\rho, w)\,\tilde{r}(\theta,\phi,m\Delta\rho,w)\right] e^{j\frac{2\pi n' w}{N}} \tag{15}$$

where the terms: $\tilde{q}_1(m\Delta\rho, w)$ and $\tilde{r}(\theta,\phi,m\Delta\rho,w)$ represent the DFT of the sequences $q_1(..)$ and $r(..)$ with respect to the azimuthal coordinate ϕ'.
The computation scheme given by equation (15) can be summarized by the following steps:

1. multiply the near-field plane-polar samples by the radial coordinate ρ';
2. perform FFT on the result coming from step 1 with respect to the azimuthal coordinate ϕ';
3. perform FFT on the exponential function $e^{jk\rho' sin\theta cos(\phi-\phi')}$ with respect to the azimuthal coordinate ϕ'
4. compute the inverse FFT on the product of results coming from steps 2 and 3;
5. perform summation on the result coming from step 4 with respect to the radial coordinate ρ'.

2.2.2 NF-FF transformation on bi-polar geometry

In the bi-polar geometry, the positions of the near-field samples lying on radial arcs can be completely described in terms of the probe arm length L and the angles α, β, giving the rotations of the AUT and the probe, respectively (Fig. 7).

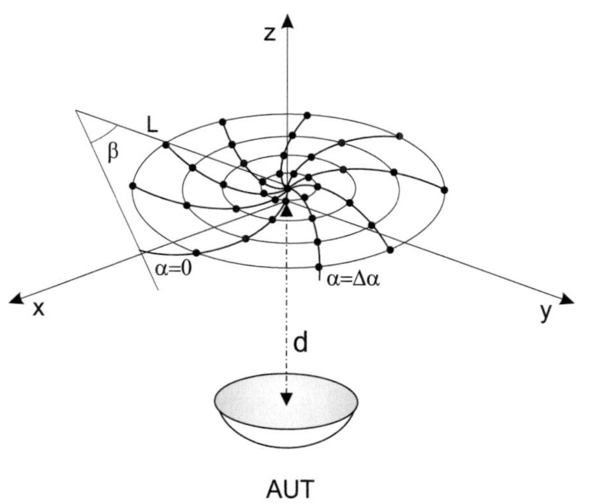

Fig. 7. Bi-polar near-field scanning.

As a consequence of this, a curvilinear coordinate system can be used to describe the scanning grid and the radiation integral (10) can be expressed as (Costanzo and Di Massa, 2006 b):

$$T(\theta,\phi) = L^2 \int_0^{\beta_{max}} \int_{\frac{\beta'}{2}}^{\frac{\beta'}{2}+2\pi} q(\alpha',\beta')\, e^{j2kLsin\theta sin\left(\frac{\beta'}{2}\right)cos\left(\phi-\alpha'+\frac{\beta'}{2}\right)} sin\beta' d\beta' d\alpha' \tag{16}$$

where β_{max} is the maximum angular extent and the following transformations from polar coordinates (ρ, ϕ) to curvilinear coordinates (α, β) are applied:

$$\rho = 2Lsin\left(\frac{\beta}{2}\right), \quad \phi = \alpha - \frac{\beta}{2} \tag{17}$$

The inner integral into relation (16) can be easily recognized as a convolution in the variable α', so the convolution theorem can be invoked to obtain the equivalent form:

$$T(\theta, \phi) = \int_0^{\beta_{max}} \mathcal{F}^{-1}\left\{\tilde{q}_1(w, \beta')\tilde{r}(\theta, \phi, w, \beta')\right\} d\beta' \tag{18}$$

where:

$$q_1(\alpha', \beta') = L^2 q(\alpha', \beta') sin\beta', \quad r(\theta, \phi, \alpha', \beta') = e^{j2kLsin\theta sin\left(\frac{\beta'}{2}\right)cos\left[\left(\phi+\frac{\beta'}{2}\right)-\alpha'\right]} \tag{19}$$

Let us consider a bi-polar scanning grid, with near-field samples located at coordinates $(m\Delta\alpha, n\Delta\beta)$, $m = 0, ...M-1$, $n = 0, ..., N-1$, M being the number of arcs and N the number of measurement points along each arc. Incremental steps $\Delta\alpha$, $\Delta\beta$ coherent with the sampling requirements inherent to the plane-polar configurations are assumed, by imposing relations (11) into expressions (17). Under the above assumptions, the numerical implementation of integral (18) is given as (Costanzo and Di Massa, 2006 b):

$$T(\theta, \phi) = \sum_{n=0}^{N-1}\sum_{m=0}^{M-1}\left[\tilde{q}_1(w, n\Delta\beta)\tilde{r}(\theta, \phi, w, n\Delta\beta)\right] e^{j\frac{2\pi m' w}{M}} \tag{20}$$

where the terms $\tilde{q}_1(w, n\Delta\beta)$ and $\tilde{r}(\theta, \phi, w, n\Delta\beta)$ represent the DFT of the sequences $q_1(..)$ and $r(..)$ with respect to the azimuthal coordinate α'.
The above computation procedure can be summarized by the following steps:

1. multiply the near-field bi-polar data by the term $L^2 sin\beta'$;
2. perform FFT on the result coming from step 1 with respect to the azimuthal coordinate α';
3. perform FFT on the exponential function $e^{j2kLsin\theta sin\left(\frac{\beta'}{2}\right)cos\left(\phi-\alpha'+\frac{\beta'}{2}\right)}$ with respect to the azimuthal coordinate α';
4. compute the inverse FFT on the product of results coming from steps 2 and 3;
5. perform summation on the result coming from step 4 with respect to the angular coordinate β'.

2.2.3 NF-FF transformation on planar spiral geometry

The planar spiral scanning (Costanzo and Di Massa, 2007) is derived from the bi-polar configuration by imposing the simultaneous rotation of the AUT and the measuring probe in terms of angles α' and β', respectively. This gives a samples arrangement at positions described by the coordinates s' and α' (Fig. 8), where:

$$s' = \frac{\rho'}{d}, \quad \alpha' = \phi' + \frac{\beta'}{2} \tag{21}$$

d being the distance between the AUT and the measurement plane.
By applying the coordinates transformation (21) into equation (10), the following expression is derived for the radiation integral (Costanzo and Di Massa, 2007):

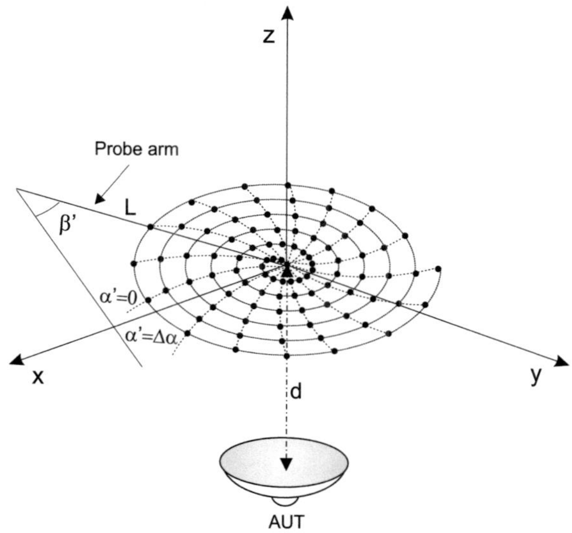

Fig. 8. Planar spiral near-field scanning.

$$T(\theta,\phi) = \int_0^{\frac{\rho_{max}}{d}} \int_{\frac{\beta'}{2}}^{\frac{\beta'}{2}+2\pi} q(s',\alpha') e^{j2kds' sin\theta cos\left(\phi-\alpha'+\frac{\beta'}{2}\right)} d^2 s' ds' d\alpha' \tag{22}$$

A compact form of equation (22) can be written as:

$$T(\theta,\phi) = \int_0^{\frac{\rho_{max}}{d}} \int_{\frac{\beta'}{2}}^{\frac{\beta'}{2}+2\pi} q_1(s',\alpha') r(\theta,\phi,s',\alpha') ds' d\alpha' \tag{23}$$

where:

$$q_1(s',\alpha') = d^2 s' q(s',\alpha'), \qquad r(\theta,\phi,s',\alpha') = e^{j2kds' sin\theta cos\left[\left(\phi+\frac{\beta'}{2}\right)-\alpha'\right]} \tag{24}$$

Following a similar procedure as that applied to the plane-polar and bi-polar configurations, the convolution form of the inner integral into equation (22) is exploited to obtain the following simplified form in terms of FFT (Costanzo and Di Massa, 2007):

$$T(\theta,\phi) = \int_0^{\frac{\rho_{max}}{d}} \mathcal{F}^{-1}\left\{\widetilde{q}_1(s',w)\widetilde{r}(\theta,\phi,s',w)\right\} ds' \tag{25}$$

Let us assume a spiral trajectory with near-field samples located at coordinates $\alpha_m = m\Delta\alpha$, $s_m = \frac{\rho_{mn}}{d}$, $m = 0,..,M-1$, $n = 0,...,N-1$, where $\rho_{mn} = a(\alpha_m + 2\pi n)$, a being the Archimedean spiral parameter, N the number of loops in the spiral arrangement and M the number of samples for each loop.

The above assumptions on the near-field samples distribution lead to express the numerical computation of radiation integral (25) as:

$$T(\theta,\phi) = \sum_{n=0}^{N-1}\sum_{m=0}^{M-1} \left[\widetilde{q}_1(s_{nm},w)\,\widetilde{r}(\theta,\phi,s_{nm},w)\right] e^{j\frac{2\pi m' w}{M}} \tag{26}$$

where the terms $\widetilde{q}_1(s_{nm},w)$ and $\widetilde{r}(\theta,\phi,s_{nm},w)$ denotes the DFT of the sequences $q_1(..)$ and $r(..)$ with respect to the angular variable α'.

A schematic overview of the processing method for far-field computation from near-field samples on planar spiral geometry is reported under Fig. 9.

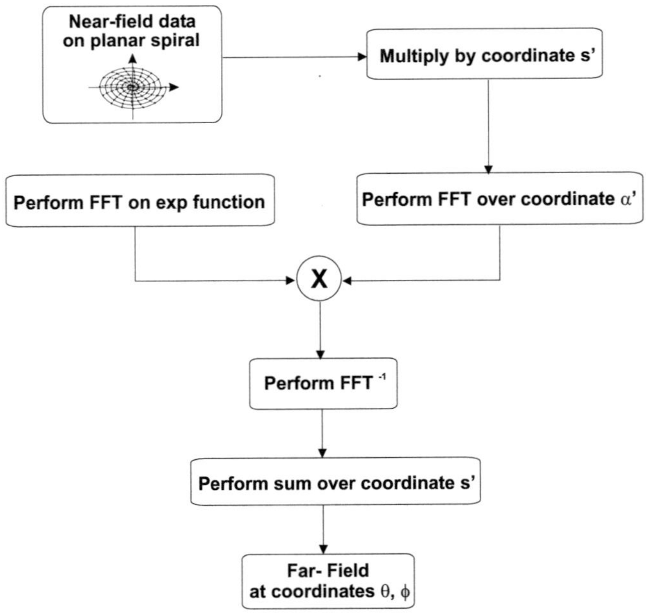

Fig. 9. Flow-chart of NF-FF transformation on planar spiral geometry.

2.2.4 Numerical validations on planar-type NF-FF transformation processes

Numerical simulations are performed on elementary dipole arrays to assess the validity of the NF-FF processing schemes illustrated in the previous paragraphs. As a first example, a near-field bi-polar acquisition is considered on a square array of $21x21$ y-oriented Huyghens sources $\lambda/2$ spaced each others along x and y axes. The array elements are excited with a $20dB$, $n = 2$ Taylor illumination (Elliott, 2003), scanned to an angle $\theta = 15^o$ in the H-plane. A scan plane of radius $a = 10\lambda$, at a distance $d = 6\lambda$ from the AUT, is sampled with angular spacings $\Delta\alpha = 5.2^o$ and $\Delta\beta = 0.38^o$. The normalized amplitude of the simulated near-field is reported under Fig. 10, while the H-plane pattern resulting from the processing scheme is successfully compared in Fig. 11 with the exact radiation pattern coming from the analytical solution.

As a further example, a circular array of 10 y-oriented elementary dipoles $\lambda/2$ spaced is considered, with excitation coefficients chosen to have a main lobe in the direction $\theta = 10^o$ in the H-plane. Simulations are performed on a planar spiral with $N = 20$ loops and $M = 136$ points along each loop, at a distance $d = 10\lambda$ from the AUT. The normalized near-field amplitude is shown in the contour plot of Fig. 12, while the H-plane pattern obtained from the direct transformation algorithm is successfully compared in Fig. 13 with the exact array solution.

3. Hybrid approach for phaseless near-field measurements

The standard near-field approach requires the knowledge of the complex tangential components (both in amplitude and phase) on the prescribed scanning surface. Near-field data are generally collected by a vector receiver and numerically processed to efficiently

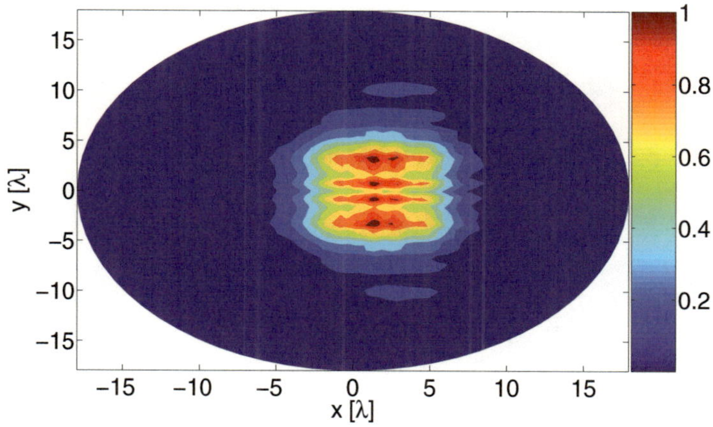

Fig. 10. Normalized bi-polar near-field amplitude for a 21x21 dipole array with Taylor illumination.

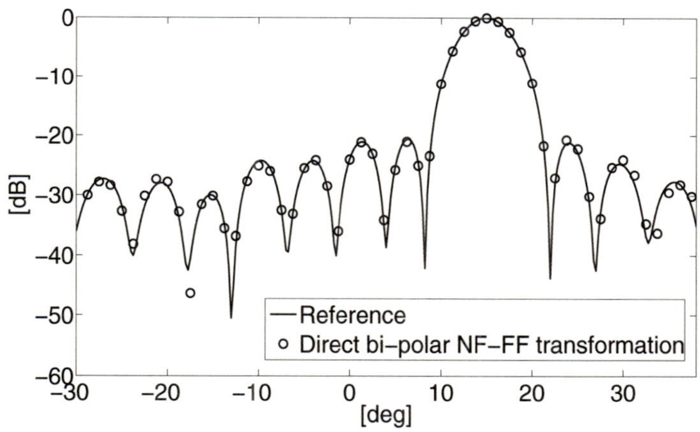

Fig. 11. Co-polarized H-plane pattern for a 21x21 dipole array with Taylor illumination.

evaluate the far-field pattern. The accuracy and performances of NF-FF transformations essentially rely on the precision of the measurement setup and the positioning system, with increasing complexity and cost when dealing with electrically large antennas. As a matter of fact, accurate phase measurements are very difficult to obtain at millimeter and sub-millimeter frequency ranges, unless expensive facilities are used. To overcome this problem, new advanced techniques have been recently developed which evaluate the far-field pattern from the knowledge of the near-field amplitude over one or more testing surfaces (Isernia et al., 1991; 1996). Generally speaking, two classes of phaseless methods can be distinguished, the one based on a functional relationship within a proper set of amplitude-only data (Pierri et al., 1999), the other adopting interferometric techniques (Bennet et al., 1976). In some recent works (Costanzo et al., 2001; Costanzo and Di Massa, 2002; Costanzo et al., 2005; 2008), a novel hybrid procedure has been proposed which combines all the best features of the two kinds of phaseless methods. A basically interferometric approach is adopted, but avoiding the use of a reference antenna as required in standard interferometry. The phase reference is directly obtained from the field radiated by the AUT, which is collected by two probes on two

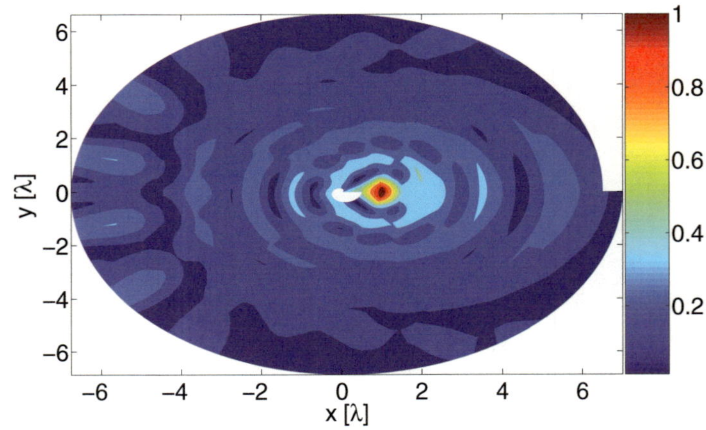

Fig. 12. Normalized bi-polar near-field amplitude for a $21x21$ dipole array with Taylor illumination.

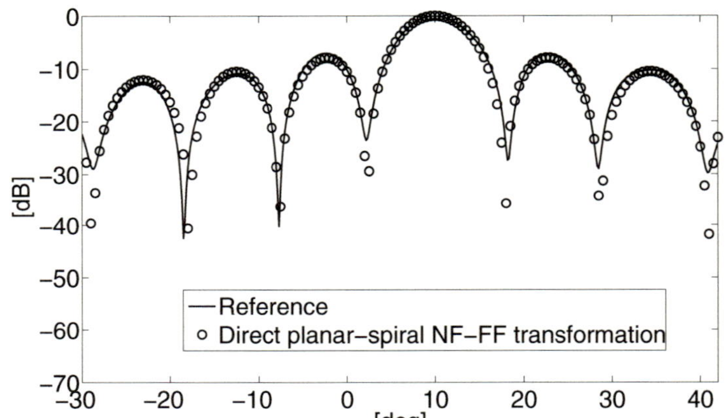

Fig. 13. Co-polarized H-plane pattern for a $21x21$ dipole array with Taylor illumination.

different points along the scanning curve to interfere by means of a simple microstrip circuit (Costanzo et al., 2001; Costanzo and Di Massa, 2002). A certain number of sets of retrieved near-field phase results from the application of the proposed interferometric technique. Each set includes phase values on different measurement points, apart from a constant phase shift to be determined. The union of these sets provides the full near-field phase information along the scanning curve, but a complete characterization obviously requires the evaluation of all unknown phase shifts, one for each set. This problem is solved by taking advantages of the analytical properties of the field radiated by the AUT. In particular, a non redundant representation is adopted which is based on the introduction of the reduced field (Bucci et al., 1998), obtained from the original field after extracting a proper phase function and introducing a suitable parameterization along the observation curve. Following this approach, the radiated field on each scanning line is easily identified from the knowledge of the dimension and shape of the AUT. The procedure is repeated along a proper number of observation curves to cover the whole measurement surface. The proposed approach gives a hybrid procedure placed "half the way" between interferometric techniques and functional relationship based methods. In particular, it takes advantages of the interferometric approach to significantly reduce the number of unknowns in the phase retrieval algorithm. Although the functional to be minimized is highly non-linear, the lower number of unknowns, given by the phase shifts, allows an accurate and fast convergence to the solution. Furthermore, the absence of a reference antenna gives a simpler and more compact measurement setup.

3.1 Theoretical formulation of hybrid phase-retrieval technique

Let us consider an observation curve C over an arbitrary scanning geometry (Fig. 14), with a sampling step $\Delta s = \lambda/2$ and a separation $d = i\lambda/2$ between two adjacent interference points, i being an integer greater than one. Two identical probes simultaneously moving along the measurement curve (Fig. 14) are used to obtain four amplitude information, namely (Costanzo et al., 2001; Costanzo and Di Massa, 2002; Costanzo et al., 2005):

$$|V_1|^2, \quad |V_2|^2, \quad |V_1 + V_2|^2, \quad |V_1 + jV_2|^2 \tag{27}$$

where:

$$V_1 = |V_1| \cdot e^{j\varphi_1}, \quad V_2 = |V_2| \cdot e^{j\varphi_2} \tag{28}$$

are the complex signals on a pair of interference points along C.

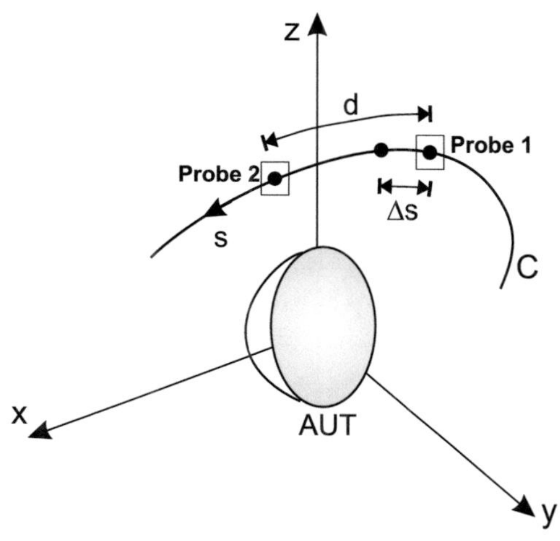

Fig. 14. Observation curve C with probes positions.

Intensity data (27) are processed to give the phase shift $\Delta\varphi = \varphi_1 - \varphi_2$ by means of the following interferometric formula (Costanzo et al., 2001; Costanzo and Di Massa, 2002):

$$\Delta\varphi = tg^{-1}\left[\frac{|V_1 + jV_2|^2 - |V_1|^2 - |V_2|^2}{|V_1 + V_2|^2 - |V_1|^2 - |V_2|^2}\right] \tag{29}$$

Let be:

$$E(s) = |E(s)| \cdot e^{j\varphi(s)} \tag{30}$$

the field radiated by the AUT on the observation curve C, where parameter s denotes the curvilinear abscissa along C (Fig. 14). If we suppose to scan 2N+1 measurement points (N even), the application of equation (29) gives a number of sets of complex near-field data equal to i, namely (Costanzo et al., 2001; 2005):

$$\left[E\left(s_{(1)}\right), E\left(s_{(2)}\right) = \varepsilon\left(s_{(2)}\right) \cdot e^{j\Delta\phi_1}, E\left(s_{(3)}\right) = \varepsilon\left(s_{(3)}\right) \cdot e^{j\Delta\phi_2}, \ldots \right.$$
$$\left. \ldots, E\left(s_{(i)}\right) = \varepsilon\left(s_{(i)}\right) \cdot e^{j\Delta\phi_{i-1}}\right] \tag{31}$$

wherein:

$$\begin{aligned}
s_{(1)} &= \left[-N\frac{\lambda}{2}, (-N+i)\frac{\lambda}{2}, (-N+2i)\frac{\lambda}{2}, \ldots\right] \\
s_{(2)} &= \left[(-N+1)\frac{\lambda}{2}, (-N+i+1)\frac{\lambda}{2}, \right. \\
&\qquad \left. (-N+2i+1)\frac{\lambda}{2}, \ldots\right] \\
&\vdots \\
s_{(i)} &= \left[(-N+i-1)\frac{\lambda}{2}, (-N+2i-1)\frac{\lambda}{2}, \right. \\
&\qquad \left. (-N+3i-1)\frac{\lambda}{2}, \ldots\right]
\end{aligned} \tag{32}$$

The terms $\underline{\varepsilon}\left(s_{(2)}\right), \underline{\varepsilon}\left(s_{(3)}\right), \ldots, \underline{\varepsilon}\left(s_{(i)}\right)$ into expression (31) are known quantities and the phase shifts $\Delta\phi_1, \Delta\phi_2, \ldots, \Delta\phi_{i-1}$ are the unknowns to be determined. If we change $\Delta\phi_1, \Delta\phi_2, \ldots, \Delta\phi_{i-1} \in [-\pi, \pi[$, expression (31) gives the set S_m of all fields compatible with the measured data. The field radiated by the AUT is so given by the intersection $S_m \cap S_A$, where S_A is the set of all fields that the AUT can radiate.
In order to successfully retrieve the unknown phase shifts $\Delta\phi_1, \Delta\phi_2, \ldots, \Delta\phi_{i-1}$, a non redundant representation is adopted which substitutes the original field (30) with the reduced field (Bucci et al., 1998) $F(\xi) = E(\xi) \cdot e^{j\psi(\xi)}$, obtained after extracting a proper phase function $\psi(\xi(s))$ and introducing a suitable parameterization $\xi(s)$ along the observation curve. A proper choice of these parameters leads to approximate the reduced field by a cardinal series of the kind:

$$F(\xi) = \sum_{n=1}^{N'} E(\xi_n) \cdot e^{-j\psi(\xi_n)} \Phi\left[w(\xi - \xi_n)\right] \tag{33}$$

where $\Phi(x)$ is the $\frac{sin(x)}{x}$ function or the Dirichlet function, $\xi_n = \frac{n\pi}{\chi \cdot W}$ are the positions of non-redundant sampling points, while N′ represents the number of non redundant samples falling in the measurement interval.
The above relation, discretized in the M measurement points, say ξ_m, $m = 1, \ldots, M$, can be written in matrix form as (Costanzo et al., 2005):

$$\underline{r} = \underline{\underline{A}} \cdot \underline{s} \tag{34}$$

where $\underline{s}$ is the array of the reduced field values in the non redundant sampling positions and $\underline{r}$ is the corresponding array of the reduced field values at the measuring points . Due to the representation error and the presence of noise usually corrupting measurements, data do not belong in general to the range of matrix $\underline{\underline{A}}$. Consequently, the following generalized solution is adopted:

$$\inf_{\Delta\phi_1,\, \Delta\phi_2,\ldots,\Delta\phi_{i-1}} d\left(S_m, S_A^N\right) \tag{35}$$

The term $d(.,.)$ into equation (35) represents the distance between the two sets, while S_A^N is the set of all reduced field (evaluated at the M measurement points) that the AUT can radiate.
The distance d between the two sets is numerically evaluated by introducing the projector operator $\underline{\underline{P}} = \underline{\underline{A}}\ \underline{\underline{A}}^+$ onto the range of matrix $\underline{\underline{A}}$, $\underline{\underline{A}}^+$ denoting the pseudoinverse of $\underline{\underline{A}}$. Consequently, the near-field phase retrieval involves the finding of:

$$\min_{\Delta\phi_1,\, \Delta\phi_2,\ldots,\Delta\phi_{i-1}} \left\| \underline{r}(\Delta\phi_1,\, \Delta\phi_2, \ldots, \Delta\phi_{i-1}) - \underline{\underline{P}}\, \underline{r}(\Delta\phi_1,\, \Delta\phi_2, \ldots, \Delta\phi_{i-1}) \right\|^2 \tag{36}$$

which can be easily performed by a suitable least-square procedure.

3.2 Experimental validations of hybrid phase-retrieval technique

The hybrid phase-retrieval technique is experimentally validated by designing a multifrequency prototype properly working within X-band. Two rectangular waveguides used as probes are connected to the microstrip circuit in Fig. 15(a) for obtaining the required amplitude information. Measurements are performed on a standard X-band pyramidal horn (Fig. 15(b)) by assuming a cylindrical scanning geometry of $47x85$ points along z and ϕ, respectively, with sampling steps $\Delta z = \lambda/2 = 1.5cm$ and $\Delta\phi = 4.23^o$ at different frequencies.

(a)

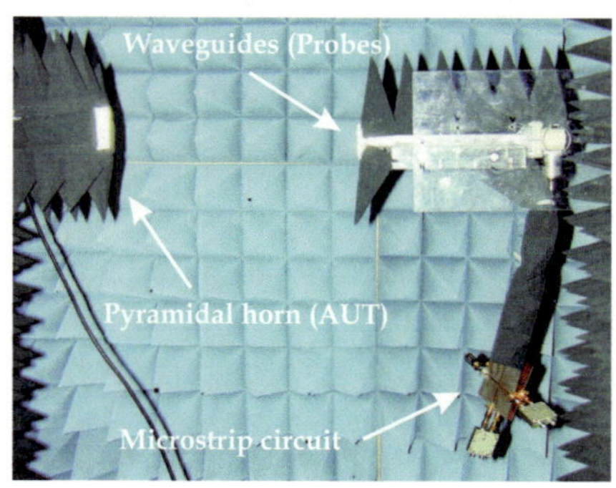

(b)

Fig. 15. (a) Microstrip circuit and (b) test setup for phaseless near-field measurements.

The near-field directly measured at one output of the integrated probe is reported under Figs. 16-17 for both amplitude and phase at two different frequencies, namely $f = 8GHz$ and $f = 10GHz$. The interferometric formula (29) is used in conjunction with the minimization procedure (36) to obtain the retrieved near-field phase, whose agreement with the exact one is illustrated under Figs. 16(b)-17(b) along the cylinder generatrix at $\phi = 90^o$.
The standard NF-FF cylindrical transformation (Leach and Paris, 1973) is then applied to obtain the far-field patterns of Figs. 18-19. In particular, a good agreement between results obtained from direct and retrieved near-field phase can be observed under Figs. 18(b)-19(b) for the H-plane.

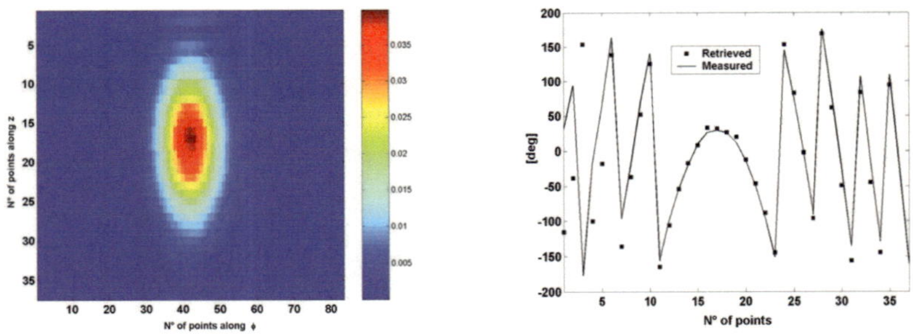

(a) (b)

Fig. 16. (a) Measured near-field amplitude on the cylindrical surface and (b) near-field phase (retrieved and measured) on the cylinder generatrix at $\phi = 90^o$: frequency $f = 8GHz$.

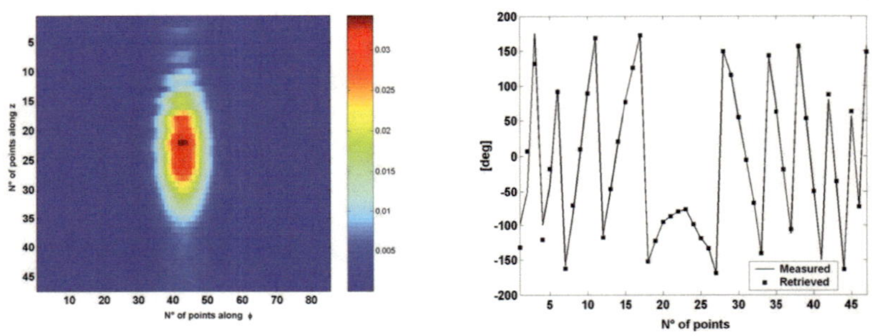

(a) (b)

Fig. 17. (a) Measured near-field amplitude on the cylindrical surface and (b) near-field phase (retrieved and measured) on the cylinder generatrix at $\phi = 90^o$: frequency $f = 10GHz$.

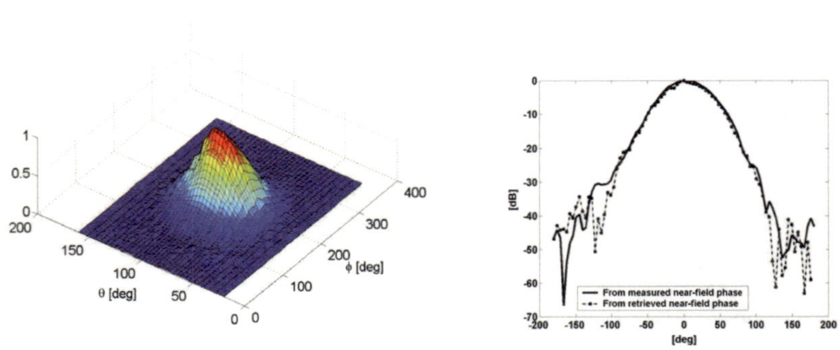

(a) (b)

Fig. 18. (a) 3-d view of radiation pattern and (b) H-plane obtained from exact and retrieved near-field phase: frequency $f = 8GHz$.

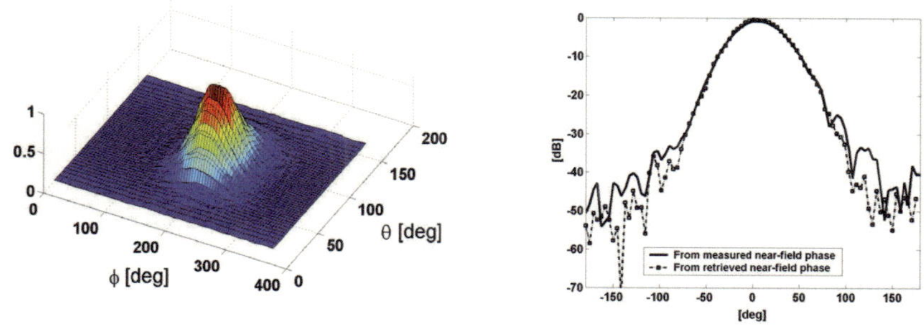

(a) (b)

Fig. 19. (a) 3-d view of radiation pattern and (b) H-plane obtained from exact and retrieved near-field phase: frequency $f = 10GHz$.

4. Conclusion

Innovative techniques for near-field antenna testing have been presented in this chapter. Two primary aspects, namely the reduction of both measurement time and cost setup on one hand, and the accurate near-field phase characterization on the other hand, have been accurately faced. For what concerns the first focus point, accurate and fast near-field to far-field transformations on new strategic geometries of helicoidal, plane-polar, bi-polar and planar spiral type have been presented. On the other hand, the problem of accurate phase retrieval at high operating frequencies has been faced by presenting a hybrid interferometric/functional-kind approach to obtain the antenna far-field pattern from a reduced set of amplitude-only near-field data acquired on a single scanning surface. All discussed procedures have been successfully validated by numerical and experimental tests.

5. References

Abramowitz, M. & Stegun, I. A. (1972). *Handbook of mathematical functions*,Dover, New York.

Bennet, J. C., Anderson, A. P., Mcinnes, P. A. & Whitaker, J. T. (1976). Microwave holographic metrology of large reflector antennas. *IEEE Trans. Antennas Propag.*, Vol. 24, (1976) page numbers (295-303).

Bracewell, R. N. (2000). *The Fourier Transform and Its Applications*, McGraw-Hill, ISBN 0-07-303938-1, Singapore.

Bucci, O. M., Gennarelli, C. & Savarese, C. (1998). Representation of electromagnetic fields over arbitrary surfaces by a finite and nonredundant number of samples. *IEEE Trans. Antennas Propag.*, Vol. 46, (1998) page numbers (351-359).

Costanzo, S., Di Massa, G. & Migliore, M. D. (2001). Integrated microstrip probe for phaseless near-field measurements on plane-polar geometry. *Electronics Letters*, Vol. 37, (2001) page numbers (1018-1020).

Costanzo, S. & Di Massa, G. (2002). An integrated probe for phaseless near-field measurements. *Measurement*, Vol. 31, (2002) page numbers (123-129).

Costanzo, S., Di Massa, G. & Migliore, M. D. (2005). Integrated microstrip probe for phaseless near-field measurements on plane-polar geometry. *IEEE Trans. Antennas Propag.*, Vol. 53, (2005) page numbers (1866-1874).

Costanzo, S. & Di Massa G. (2004). Far-field reconstruction from phaseless near-field data on a cylindrical helix. *Journal of Electromagn. Waves Applicat.*, Vol. 18, (2004) page numbers (1057-1071).

Costanzo, S. & Di Massa G. (2006). Efficient near-field to far-field transformation from plane-polar samples. *Microwave Opt. Tech. Letters*, Vol. 48, (2006) page numbers (2433-2436).

Costanzo, S. & Di Massa G. (2006). Direct far-field computation from bi-polar near-field samples. *Journal of Electromagn. Waves Applicat.*, Vol. 20, (2006) page numbers (1137-1148).

Costanzo, S. & Di Massa G. (2007). Near-field to far-field transformation with planar spiral scanning. *Progress In Electromagnetics Research, PIER*, Vol. 73, (2007) page numbers (49-59).

Costanzo, S. & Di Massa, G. (2008). Wideband phase retrieval technique from amplitude-only near-field data. *Radioengineering*, Vol. 17, (2008) page numbers (8-12).

Elliott, R. S. (2003). *Antenna theory and design*, IEEE Press, ISBN 0-471-44996-2, New York.

Isernia, T., Pierri, R. & Leone, G. (1991). New technique for estimation of farfield from near-zone phaseless data. *Electronics Letters*, Vol. 27, (1991) page numbers (652-654).

Isernia, T., Leone, G. & Pierri, R. (1996). Radiation pattern evaluation from near-field intensities on planes. *IEEE Trans. Antennas Propag.*, Vol. 44, (1996) page numbers (701-710).

Johnson, R. C., Ecker, H. A. & Hollis, J. S. (1973). Determination of far-field antenna patterns from near-field measurements . *Proc. of IEEE*, Vol. 61, (1973) page numbers (1668-1694).

Leach, M. W. & Paris, D. T. (1973). Probe compensated near-field measurements on a cylinder. *IEEE Trans. Antennas Propag.*, Vol. 21, (1973) page numbers (435-445).

Ludwig, A. C. (1971). Near-field far-field transformations using spherical-wave expansions. *IEEE Trans. Antennas Propag.*, Vol. 19, (1971) page numbers (214-220).

Pierri, R., D'Elia, G. & Soldovieri, F. (1999). A two probes scanning phaseless near-field far-field transformation technique. *IEEE Trans. Antennas Propag.*, Vol. 47, (1999) page numbers (792-802).

Wang, J. J. H. (1988). An examination of theory and practices of planar near-field measurements. *IEEE Trans. Antennas Propag.*, Vol. 36, (1988) page numbers (746-753).

Yaghajian, A. D. (1986). An overview of near-field antenna measurements. *IEEE Trans. Antennas Propag.*, Vol. 34, (1986) page numbers (30-45).

16

Numerical Simulations of Seawater Electro-Fishing Systems

Edo D'Agaro
Medical Veterinary Faculty
University of Udine
Italy

1. Introduction

In the last decades, several surveys and research works have reported a decrease in pelagic fish resources in the Mediterranean sea, with the exception of the Adriatic sea. In fact, in this area, an overall decrease of stocks of fish species was reported as opposed to the simultaneous increase in others (Picinetti 2008). Fishing methods that use attractive elements of fish such as light and the electric current are used in many parts of the world. In this regard, the attraction of light, which exploits the phototropism of certain fish species is widely used, for instance, by the famous Japanese method for squid catching or electro-fishing techniques of bluefish in use throughout the Mediterranean. Also in freshwater lakes and rivers is very common to use electro-fishers to attract and capture fish. Regarding the electrical fishing in salt water, various experiments have been carried out to develop this new technique (Kolz,1993; Kurk,1971,1972; Roth et al., 2006). These studies were mainly carried out in the United States, France and Soviet Union (Blabcheton,1971; Diner & Le Men, 1971; Kolz, 1993; Van Harreveld, 1938). The basic elements that must be taken in consideration for the personnel who, for the first time, is preparing to use a sea electric attraction system are, first and foremost, the safety of operators and possible damage to fish. To understand these effects, it is necessary to know some basic principles of electrical circuits and the chemical-physical characteristics of water and fish subjected to different types of current. Regarding the former, it is important the knowledge of circuit features such as the power and characteristics of an electric generator, the current type, shape and use of electrodes (anode and cathode). The application of electric fields in non homogeneous systems consisting of fish and salt water is far more difficult than in freshwater conditions. This point is of fundamental importance and its understatement, in fact, may impair or reduce the efficiency of electrical fishing. Electric fishing is based on the principle of introducing an electric potential gradient in the water body, between one or more cathodes and one anode. The perception of this potential gradient by fish is function of their position towards electrodes and of their conductivity in respect to water's, as well as of temperature, size and species. The potential gradient produces different effects on fishes depending on the intensity and type of current used. Those effects are known and described since the end of 1800 (Van Harreveld, 1938). Currents used in electro-fishing can be continuous (DC), alternate (AC) or pulsed (PDC), depending on environmental characteristics (conductivity, temperature) and fish to be sampled (species, size). The three current types (DC, AC, PDC) produce different effects. Only DC and PDC cause a galvanotaxis reaction, as an active swim towards the anode. With AC this phenomenon is not possible due to the continuous changing in polarity of the electrodes. Fundamental limit to the application of electric fishing in sea water is given by the high conductivity of salted water, that being much greater than animal tissues causes the current to flow around the fish instead of passing through it. In high conductive water, PDC is the mainly used current form, because of the lower power demand, at parity of result, compared to DC (Le Men, 1980; Beaumont et al., 2002), and also causes galvanotaxis in fish (Kurc et al., 1971). Fish in fact swims towards the anode under the effect of the muscle contraction given by each electric impulse (electrotaxis) until narcosis occurs (tetanus) (Beaumont et al., 2002).

2. Electro-fishing theory

2.1 Definition of an electric field

Materials consist of particles characterized by positive electric charges (protons) and negative (electrons), while others have neutral charge (neutrons). In various materials, in particular in metals, electrical charges have the ability to move. In reality, there is not a real movement of electrons, but a transfer of energy through collisions between electrons. The movement of charges, which occurs at a given time, is defined as movement of electric current (I) and is measured in amperes (A). The relationship between the aforementioned variables is as follows:

$$I=Q/t \tag{1}$$

where:
Q=charge in coulombs
I = electrical current in amperes
t = time in seconds.
Table 1 shows the basic terms, definitions and units of measurement of variables used in circuit theory and electric fields.

Term	Symbol	Unit
Electric charge	Q	coulomb
Voltage energy	V	volt
Current load/time	I	ampere
Electric resistance	R	ohm
Energy power/time	P	watts
Energy power*time	W	watt/hour
Resistivity fraction x distance	p	ohm/cm
Conductivity	1/P	µS/cm
Voltage gradient variation		e volts/
Current density		J amp/cm^2
Power density		D watt/cm^3

Table 1. Terms, symbols and unit used in the current field theory

The electric current is made up of a flow of charges which tend to restore a state of neutrality between two electrically charged bodies. If the two bodies become neutral, the current ceases immediately to flow (because there is no more a force of attraction between the two bodies). The circulation of electric current is higher in materials that have a large amount of free electrons as conductors. In this way, the electric current flows from a region with high negative charges to one with positive charges. The electric current (I) is measured with the ammeter. The voltage (V) is defined as the potential difference between two points of the electrical circuit and is measured with a voltmeter. With a voltage V and a current density I, the power P can easily calculated as P = V x I. The electric circuits can be classified into two main types: circuit in series or parallel. In the series circuits, all components (generator, switch and the transformer) form a single path. Instead, the circuits in parallel are divided into branches. If two different charged electrodes are immersed in a liquid, several lines of force are created between the two poles. Along these lines of force flows the electrical current. These lines of force coincide with the current lines (Fig.1).

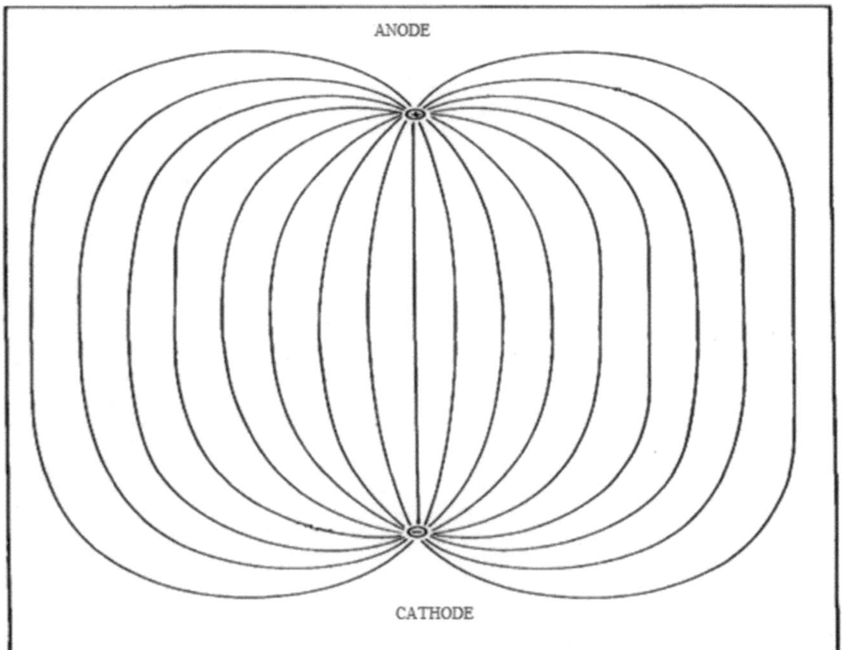

Fig. 1. Force lines are formed between the anode (positive) and cathode (negative) immersed in a liquid

Now, let's take an example of a potential difference of 400 V between the two poles of the field. This potential difference decreases gradually starting from the anode (+) going to the cathode (-) to finally reach the value of 0 volts at the cathode. Consequently, we can see that on the same force line, voltage values varie according to the position. We can also get lines that have the same voltage values. These lines are called equipotential lines (Fig.2).

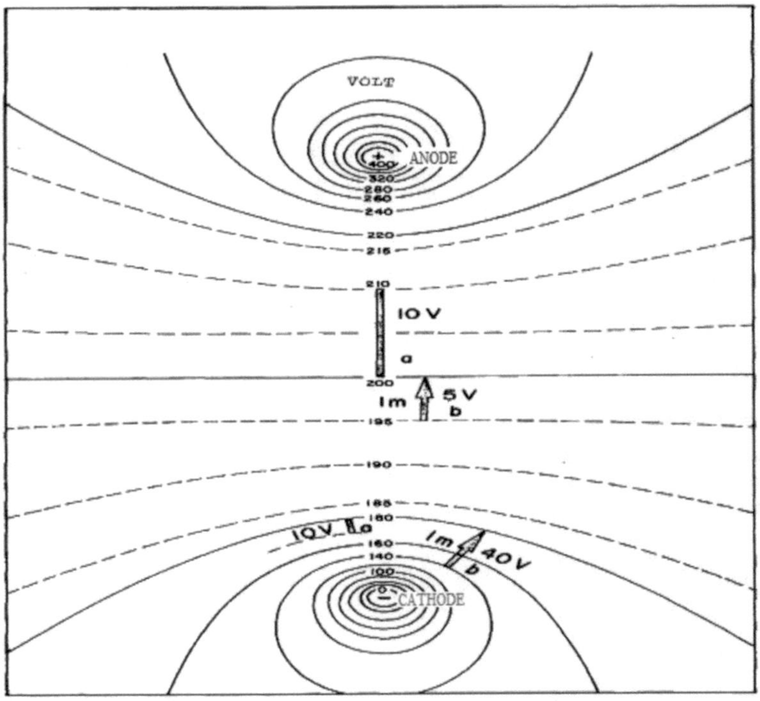

Fig. 2. The equipotential lines are obtained by bringing together points of equal voltage The figure obtained resembles a map in which lines mark the same altitude.

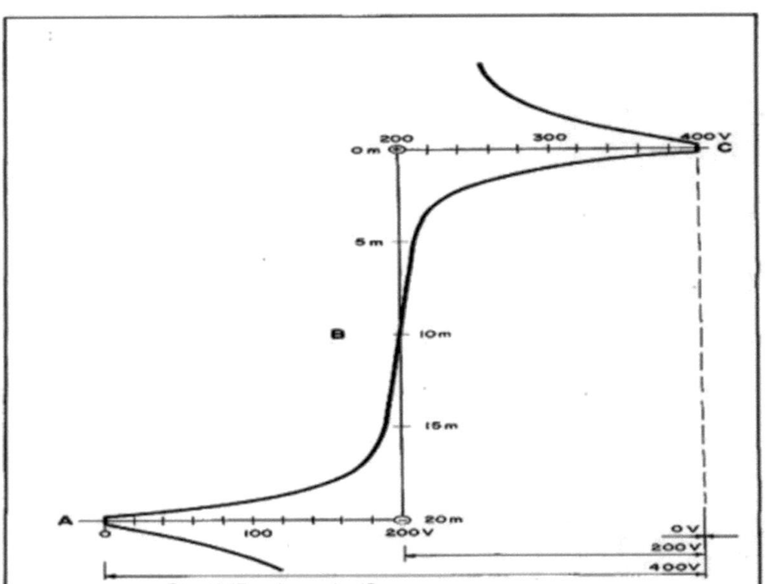

Fig. 3. Voltage curve between the anode (+) and cathode (-) located at a distance of 20 m apart

Potential differences are measured along a line of force (Fig. 3) . The greatest potential difference is obtained at the two electrodes A and C. Approaching the cathode, voltage decreases. For example at point B, midway between the two poles, voltage difference is 200 V. There is a progressive decrease until it reaches the value 0 at the cathode itself. This means that an object placed in an electric field is subjected to a potential difference. This potential difference varies depending on the location of the electric field where the object is placed and is greater in the vicinity of one of the two poles. Inside an electrical conductor, the movement of electrons is slowed down from their original path when the moving electrons collide with others. This phenomenon is called electrical resistance (R). The electrical resistance varies depending on the conductor. In practice, the electrical resistance results in a reduction of the current flow and a loss of energy. The electrical resistance increases in relation to the length of the conductor and decreases with higher cross-section values. If R is the total resistance of a conductor, the formula to determine the value will be:

$$R = \rho\, l / s \tag{2}$$

where:
R = electrical resistance in ohms
l = length of conductor in m
s = section in mm^2 conductor
ρ = coefficient of electrical resistivity
The ratio voltage / current intensity measured in an electrical circuit has a constant value. In fact, being the resistance equal, the change in current intensity is directly proportional to the voltage. This relationship is explained by the second law of Ohm:

$$R = V / I \tag{3}$$

$$I = V / R \tag{4}$$

where:
R = electrical resistance in ohms
V = voltage in volts
I = electric current in amperes
Conductivity is reciprocal of resistance. The conductivity is measured in siemens (S). The conductivity varies for each material. Once known essential elements regarding electrical power and circuits is possible to build a system for electrical fishing.

2.2 Types of current waves

The current is a continuous movement of electricity between two points on a conductor that are at different potential. The different types of electrical current produce different electrical shapes or wave forms.
The three most important type of electric currents are:

- Direct Current (DC)
- Alternating Current (AC)
- Pulsed Direct Current (PDC)

Direct current produces a unidirectional, constant electrical current. DC is a current of equal intensity with a smooth continuous flow that occurs from pole to pole. Strength and direction remain constant.

Alternating Current (AC) is an electrical current in which the direction of current reverses a number of times per second. Alternating current produces a wave form that consists of a sequence of positive and negative waves that are equal, usually sinusoidal, and follow each other alternately at regular time intervals. An alternating current is a current that changes strength and direction of propagation with a time constant. For example, a period lasts 1/50 of a second. Frequency is the number of periods per second. The unit of frequency is the hertz (Hz).

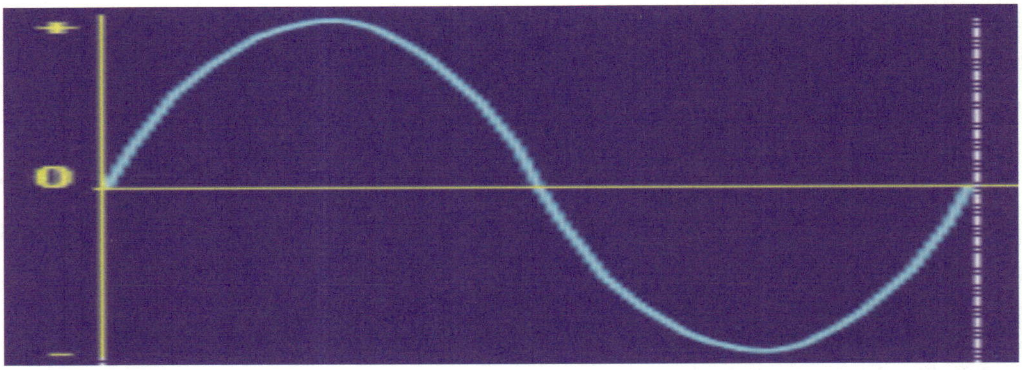

The Pulsed direct Current (PDC) is, in the simplest case, a direct interrupted current. This current flows in the form of pulses.

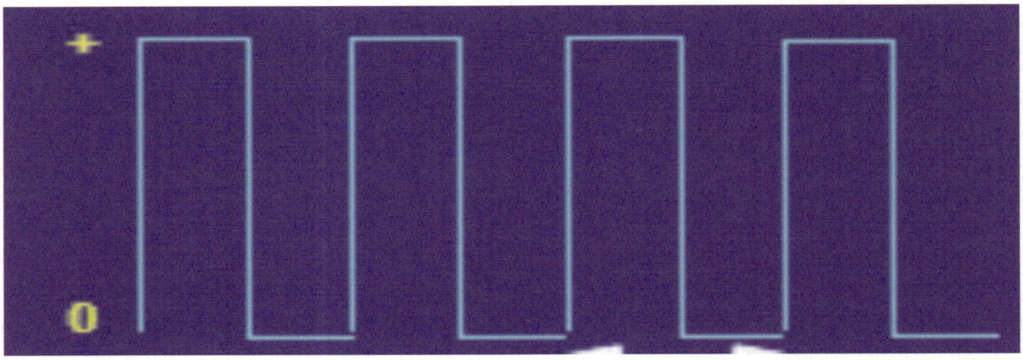

A period (duty cycle), in this instance comprises the pulse duration and pause.

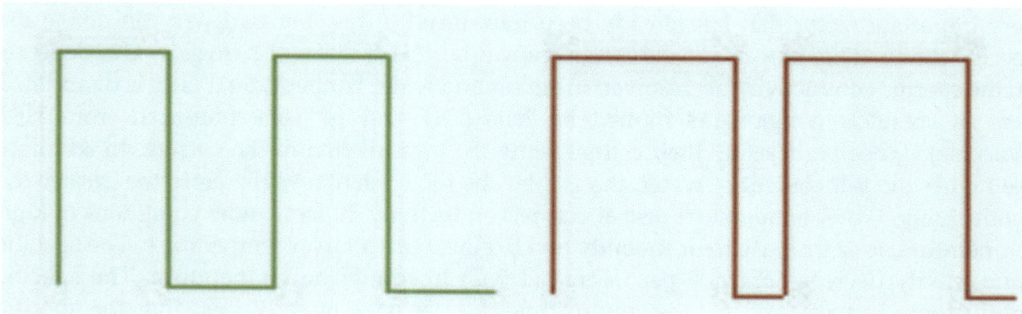

2.3 Electrical fishing systems

Electro-fishing is the use of electricity to capture fish. The essential components of an electrical circuit are:

- The generator. The generator produces electricity. It is usually classified as a voltage source or current source. Conventional circuits are generally used for generating power.
- Conductors. Conductors are used to carry electric current from the generator to the electrodes.
- The transformer. The transformers allow to convert electrical energy into another form of energy (mechanical, thermal, etc.).

The electricity is generated by the generator whereby a high voltage potential is applied between two or more electrodes that are placed in the water. In the case of sea water, the voltage potential is created using a pulsed direct current which produces a unidirectional electrical current composed of a sequence of cyclic impulses. Sometimes you can have more than one cathode and anode. In a fishing system, with a single anode and a cathode, lifting them up from the water opens the circuit. The same is not true in a systems with multiple anodes and cathodes. Being arranged in parallel, their lifting from the water does not break the circuit and therefore does not terminate the action of fishing, at least until then the water is applied to the cathode or anode. However, even if they are applied more anodes, the circuit is opened by lifting the cathode from the water. In the systems for electrical fishing, water and fish are a component of the circuit. The basic requirement of electrical fishing equipment is to transfer energy from water to fish. The resistance of the fish is generally different from that of water. The difference between water resistence and resistance of fish can reduce the energy transmitted and thus the capture efficiency of the equipment. Thus, difficulties encountered in the use of electrical fishing are due mainly by transfer of adequate amounts of energy from the generator to the fish. Most systems are equipped with instruments for measuring the voltage (V) and current intensity (A). Characteristics of the current can be easily changed. In particular, for the PDC, it is possible to change the number of pulses and the pulse width. In electrical circuits there are two types resistances: the resistance inside the system and the load resistance. The maximum efficiency of the system is reached when the internal resistance is equal to the current load. An increase in resistance, causes a loss of power and an increase in tension. The maximum power transfer occurs when the current load is equal to 1, and this happens, as mentioned earlier, when the current load equals the internal resistance. The internal resistance is formed by the cathode, while a variable part, is composed by fish and some water. When the conductivity of the water and fish are the same, all the applied power will be transferred to the fish. The conductivity of sea water varies with the temperature and salinity (Fig. 4). The conductivity of water is a very important factor that has already been introduced in the first part. We can define the specific conductivity of water as the conductivity of a cube of water of 1 cm side. This depends on the specific conductivity of dissolved materials and water temperature. Water is dissociated into its chemical components formed by ions (OH^- and H^+ ions produced from H_2O molecule). These particles by their charge allow the transmission of the current. In addition, the higher the salt content of water, the greater the ion content and therefore the greater the conductivity. Water temperature also affects its conductivity. In fact, under conditions of high temperature, ions increase their mobility and decline with a lower temperature. The specific conductivity decrease of 2.5% per degree (1 ° C) lowering the temperature. The specific conductivity is measured by the conductometric. We have already seen that the specific conductivity is measured in microseconds / cm (microsiemens per cm). The specific resistance and specific conductivity are calculated using the relationship: 1 Ohm x cm = 1.000.000/µS/cm.

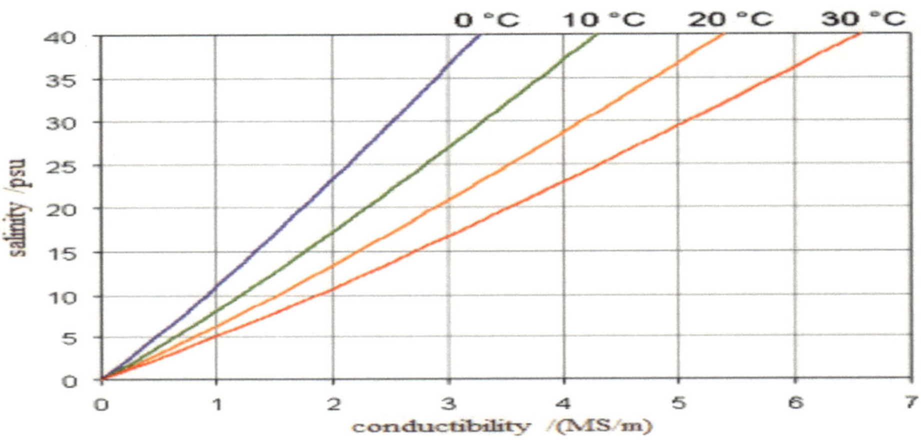

Fig. 4. Effects of salinity and temperature on salt water conductivity

In order to optimize the electro-fishing system in salt water, we should know in advance the average conductivity values of water and fish and water temperature of the area of interest. Figure 5, the horizontal axis indicates the ratio water/ fish conductivity and the vertical axis the percentage of the maximum transfer of power.

The maximum value (100%) is obtained when the ratio water conductivity/fish conductivity is equal to 1. While the conductivity of water is easily determined, this is not the case for fish and therefore, for all practical purposes, it is assumed that the latter is equal to115 µS/cm (0.0115 S/m), as recommended by Miranda and Dolan (2003). The choice of this value, although not exact for all species, is essential for the standardization of electrical fishing. In practice, in waters with low conductivity, there is a decrease in the current voltage (volts), while in waters with high conductivity, there is a reduction in the current density (amperes). The standardization of electrical fishing require precise measurements of the electric field. These can be made using some instruments such as oscilloscopes or meters. In the absence of such instruments, the biologist should observe the behavior of fish, identifying the most appropriate adjustment of the power and pulse. Physical characteristics of the electric field change not only as a function of the current, but also in relation of the shape, size, position, distance and orientation of the electrodes. In all environments and conditions, the goal is

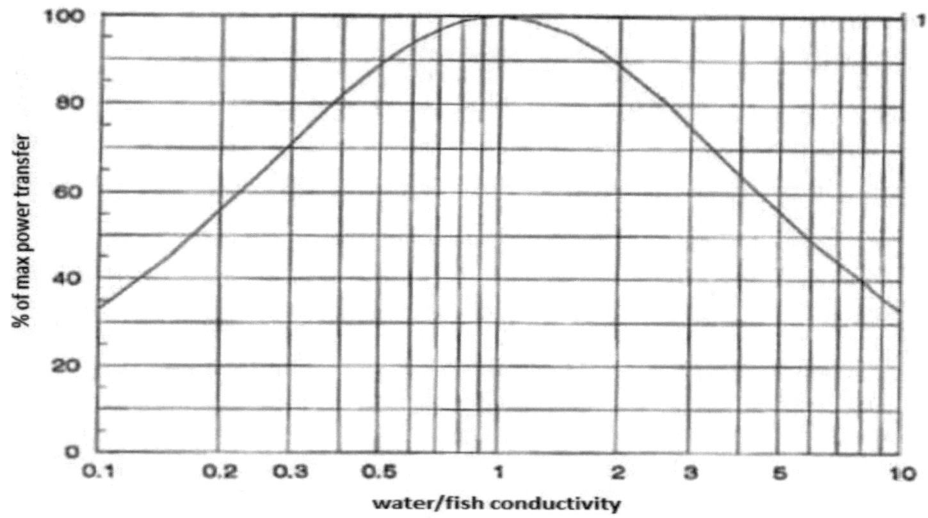

Fig. 5. Effect of fish and water conductivities on maximum power transfer

always the same: to bring the fish to the surface in the vicinity of the operators. In general, the cathode must have an area equal to or greater than the anode, thus avoiding power dissipation at the cathode. Another element that is very important but often overlooked, is the shape of the electrodes. In particular, attention should be paid to the size of the anode which should be of a diameter as large as possible to avoid causing damage to the fish. The increased diameter results in an increase in the size of the electric field which decreases the current intensity in the vicinity of the anode itself. Therefore, these solutions are recommended especially in waters with high conductivity, which require the use of small anode surface to prevent overloading of electrical generators. The anode can have different shapes, and usually the ideal shape is a sphere that ensures a uniform dispersion of energy. However, that solution would be impractical for weight, size and strength. Therefore, a more practical device consists of a chain consisting of 2 cm rings. Reducing the distance between the anode and cathode may be important to increasing the strength of the field. In this case, we need to prevent the contact of the two electrodes in order to avoid damage to the electrical generator. The electrodes are the link between the power generator and water and must, therefore, be located in such a way to allow the unit to operate under optimum conditions. The proportions of the size of the anode and cathode can be changed from 1: 4 to 1: 10. The efficacy is greatest when the electrodes are opposite each other on the side of their larger surface area. Several studies have shown that it is above or close the electrical circuit that the nervous system and muscle of the fish is stimulated.

2.4 Effects of electricity on fish

The two variables that can be modified using the PDC system are the pulse duration or amplitude (typically 5 msec) and the number of pulses per unit time (frequency: number of pulses per second or Hertz). The frequency typically used is 50/60 Hertz. Given the variability of the pulse, this current has a maximum voltage and an verage intensity. To catch fish, both variables are important, although the intensity of the peaks may assume primary importance. Fish are attracted to the anode (positive galvanotassia) probably because the front of the brain seems to carry negative charges. It should be noted, moreover, even if they have the same nervous system, not all species respond similarly to electric fishing and also in the same species, the answer change depending on the size. Larger fish tend to be more vulnerable because of the current pulses intersect both axis cephalo-caudal and along the dorsal-ventral. From this point of view, it is worth noting that short-term treatments reduce the mortality or damage of the skeletal system. Instead, for smaller fish, and in general for all fish, any damage can be caused by the duration and frequency of pulses. These phenomena can be amplified by the special structure of fish skeletal muscle. In particular, it is important the percentage of muscle mass relative to total body mass. Another element that regulates the response of fish to electric applications is the magnitude and nature of the scales. Large and thick flakes, reduce the catchability, by contrast, the small scales are increased. Electrical fishing involves a complex system with a series of interactions between the electric field, water and fish. In fact, the study of electrophysiological responses of fish is based almost exclusively on laboratory experiments performed under controlled conditions. In fact, these experiments are only a part of the real complex natural situations. In this part, the basic reactions of fish in the electric field are discussed.

The typical reactions of fish to electric current are as follows:

- Electro-taxis: forced swimming towards the anode
- Electro-narcosis: muscle relaxation or stunning (fish swims)
- Tetanus: muscle stiffness, immobilization

The PDC causes reactions in the fish which are similar to those produced by a constant current, but, in the case of PDC, effects depend on the frequency (the number of pulses per unit time). The first reaction of fish is spasms and convulsions whose intensity depends on the number of electrical impulses.The second reaction (electro-taxis) depends on the shape of the pulses. During the third reaction (electronarcosis), the swimming motion decreases abruptly and the fish is immobilized. The ultimate goal of a well-conducted electrical fishing is the achievement of electro-taxis, i.e. the stage (or situation), where the fish is oriented toward the anode and swim actively to the electrode. It is also evident that it is important the achievement of the third stage in which the fish can not swim actively. The electric current density is the basic element that influence the reactions of fish. The current density at which the fish is exposed depends mainly on fish body size and its structure of epidermis. Using an electrical fishing equipments in marine waters, we can find that the specific resistance of fish body is smaller than that of water. As illustrated in figure 6, all the lines of force are directed toward the body of the fish. As a consequence of the lower resistance offered by fish compared with the aquatic environment, the electric force lines are concentrated in the body of fish.

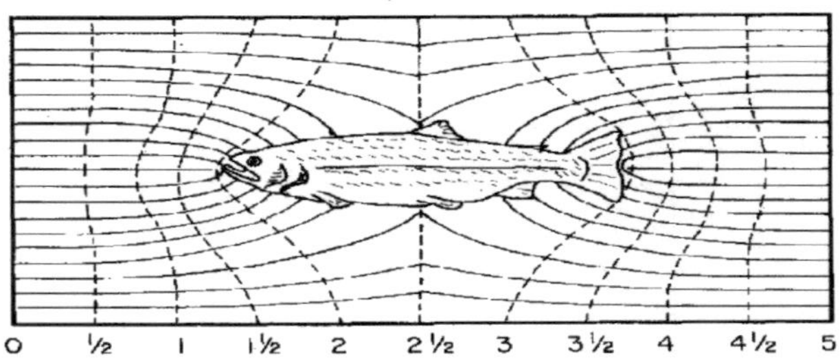

It 's possible to define a minimum value (threshold) for the desired reaction. The current density is measured in A/m^2 (amperes per square meter) or $\mu A/mm^2$ (microamperes per square millimeter). By definition, this is the intensity of current flowing through a unit surface perpendicular to the lines of force of the electric field. This current density required to obtain a specific reaction in the fish is fairly constant and characteristic for each species of fish. By means of laboratory experiments, current density values have been determined for a given species and a given length of fish. This value is the potential difference between the head and tail of the fish. This value is required to activate the physiological reactions of fish. In summary, to obtain a certain reaction, if the length of the body increases, the density of current required decreases being constant the potential difference of the body. In other words, the potential difference of the body necessary to obtain electro-taxis will be reached more rapidly in larger specimens. Furthermore, fish exposed to a potential difference below a threshold value are not attracted and they can escape. Extensive research shows that the application of electrical fishing made as the right criteria is not harmful to fish. Only by applying inappropriate techniques such as voltage too high and for long periods will create serious drawbacks. The physiological reactions of fish to an electric field can be divided into:

- involuntary reaction
- voluntary reaction

The involuntary reaction consists of the first movement or contraction of the fish body. The curvature (bending) of the body is followed immediately by a voluntary backlash in the opposite direction. At this point we have three possible effects on the orientation and movement of fish.

1) a fish is swimming oriented with the head towards the cathode

but after some time, the fish is no longer able to swim. When fish is showing cramps, it stops swimming and voluntary movement is transformed into spasms toward the anode [involuntary reaction].

2) one fish is swimming oriented with the head towards the cathode. The fish shows firstly a spasm and than it makes an half run toward the anode. Note that the reasons for this "half-turn towards the anode are not yet fully understood. After the change of orientation towards the anode, fish fall back into the dynamics of the first effect.

3) The fish is placed perpendicular to the force lines of the current field [position across]. After anodic curve and the new orientation, fish fall back into the dynamics of the first effect.

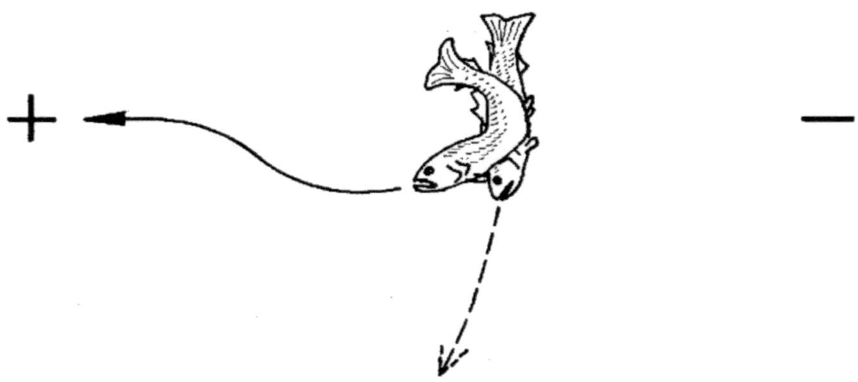

3. Numerical simulations of electro-fishing systems

Generally, data simulation includes all methods that can reproduce the processes of a system in a theoretical fashion. Numerical simulation is the kind of simulation that uses numerical methods to quantitatively represent the evolution of a physical system. It pays much attention to the physical content of the simulation and emphasizes the goal that, from the numerical results of the simulation, knowledge of background processes and physical understanding of the simulation region can be obtained. In practice, numerical simulation uses the values that can best represent the real environment. In the specific, a numerical simulation was used to set up an electro-fishing system to be used in the open sea environment. Subsequently, a laboratory trial was carried out to obtain real electric field values in a confined environment (tank) to validate the theoretical simulation values. The tank trials reproduced the open sea conditions at different distances from the electrodes for a given geometry of electrodes and voltage. Electric field simulations were obtained through a bi-dimensional campistic model of stationary conduction in a non homogenous electric system (fish swimming in sea water). This model can calculate the current density distribution and electric field pattern both in the fish and in water for a given electrode geometry. The numerical model is based on a discrete formulation of the electro-magnetic field equations in stationary conduction conditions and is a module of a software named GAME (Geometric Approach for Maxwell Equations) (Specogna & Trevisan, 2005; Specogna & Trevisan, 2006; Codecasa et al., 2007). It requires to discrete the dominion of interest (made up of fish in marine water) in a couple of reticules one dual of the other. Subsequently, the physical quantities were univocally associated to the geometric nodes of the two complexes. In this way, the geometric aspects at a discrete level are evidenced and the physical laws are directly translated into an algebraic shape without having to discrete equations to the partial derivatives. Coupling then the approximated equations (Ohm's law in the specific case) in a discrete shape, it is possible to write scattered algebraic systems of great dimensions that once resolved supply the solution of the field problem. Such approach is alternative to the classic methodologies such the finite elements, finite differences or side elements and it can be used to study this physical problem in which the mediums are non homogeneous. The model gives output values for the following parameters: electrode current (A), fish head-tail potential difference (V), mean electric field inside the fish (from the mean of discrete portions constituting the fish, V/m) and in the surrounding water (from the mean of values of discrete portions of water near the fish, V/m), values relative to arbitrary sampling points (electric field E, V/m and current density A/m^2). For the Gulf of Trieste (Northern Adriatic Sea), monthly recorded mean values for salinity range from 32.29 to 38.12 psu and for temperature from 6.60 to 24.20°C (Stravisi, 1983). A range of 30 - 40 psu for salinity and of 6 - 25°C for temperature has therefore been considered. On the basis of known relationship between salinity, temperature and conductibility in sea water, at depth 0 m, the considered values of salinity and temperature correspond to the range 2.99 - 5.97 S/m of water conductibility (Stravisi, 1983). Therefore, numerical simulations have been conducted at water conductibility of 3.0, 4.0, 5.0 and 6.0 S/m.

3.1 Numerical simulations of fish in an open sea

The transversal section of the electrodes geometry in sea water (Fig.7) is given by a circular electrode (D =1 m) symmetric to a couple of cathodes far A=10 m from each other and with width 2 m. The anode and cathode are supplied with V_1 and V_2 potentials, respectively. Being the model a stationary conduction bi-dimensional system, its depth is unitary (1 m). The electric field for the described geometry was numerically simulated. The electric field was described in five points (*d1, d2, d3, d4, d5*), which are respectively 2.5, 2.7, 3.2, 4.7, 8.4 m far from the centre of anode and cathode. The electric field intensity which is required to achieve an electro-taxis response at a given distance from electrodes and water conductivity were obtained from bibliographic data (threshold values of 10 V/m for electric field (Beaumont et al., 2002); water conductibility of 3.5 S/m (Beaumont et al., 2002, Le Men, 1980); 40 µA/mm^2 for current density (Beaumont et al, 2002)). The required power of the system was calculated from those values. In the specific, the power transfer theory (*PTT*) as defined by Kolz (1989) and validated by Miranda & Dolan (2003) for pulsed direct current was calculated as:

$$P_f = \frac{P_w}{M_{cp}} \tag{5}$$

$$M_{cp} = \frac{\left(1 + \frac{C_f}{C_w}\right)^2}{4 \cdot \frac{C_f}{C_w}} \tag{6}$$

where P_w is the power applied to water and P_f is the power transferred to fish (µW/cm^3); C_f and C_w are the conductibility of fish (µS/cm) and water, respectively.

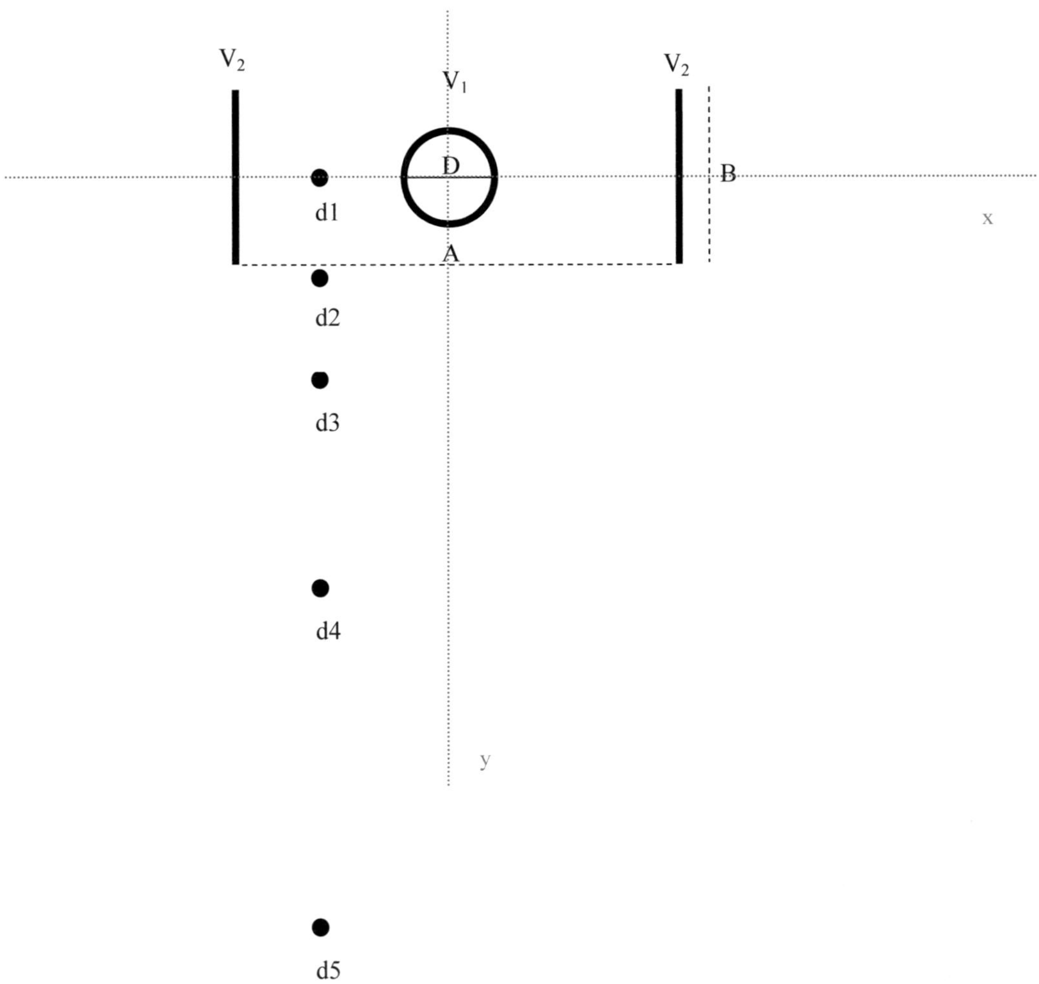

Fig. 7. Transversal section of electrodes in open sea. Dimensions are defined by parameters A, B, D. *d1-d5* are the sampling points in which the electric field has been described.

$$P_w = C_w \left(\frac{V}{D} \right)^2 \tag{7}$$

where V is the voltage at the electrodes and D the distance (cm) between electrodes. The *PTT* has been defined and validated for a uniform electric field, generated by parallel plate electrodes in a tank (Kolz, 1989; Miranda & Dolan, 2003). fish conductivity value was of 115 µS/cm (0.0115 S/m), as recommended by Miranda and Dolan (2003). Using this value to calculate M_{cp}, we obtained the smallest error of estimate. Power density was calculated using the peak voltage (Beaumont et al., 2002; Kolz, 1989) obtaining the maximum power density. Miranda and Dolan (2003) reported a minimum threshold value for power transferred to the fish necessary for narcosis, obtained with *PDC* at 60 Hz, that corresponds to P_f=15 µW/cm³. So, considering this power density and assuming C_f=115 µS/cm, the required P_w is given by:

$$P_w = P_f \cdot M_{cp} \tag{8}$$

The required voltage is obtained from (3), using D=500 cm and with electrodes described earlier. Simulations have been carried out without fish using four water conductivity values (3,4,5,6 S/m). The same simulations have been repeated in presence of fish: single and in a group (30 fish). Fish had a length of 10 cm (single fish and group) and 30 cm (single fish), respectively. Single fish were positioned in the five sampling points (d1-d5) and in the case of a group of fish, the barycentre of the group was centred on the sampling point.
The effect of water conductibility and fish length on the electric field variables were tested using one way ANOVA and Tukey's test as a *post-hoc* test. A group of fish of 30 individuals was used. Levene's test and normality of residuals were carried out to check the ANOVA assumptions. Data analysis was carried out using the statistical package SPSS 14.0. Equipotential surfaces areas were obtained using the software ImageJ and Mathlab from the output files of the *G.A.M.E fish* software. Applying the *PPT* equations, a constant voltage value of about 90 V was obtained. This effect can be explained because P_w/C_w is a constant and is itself multiplied for a constant (D^2). Using several values of water conductivity, voltage values at the electrodes resulted almost constant (Fig. 8).

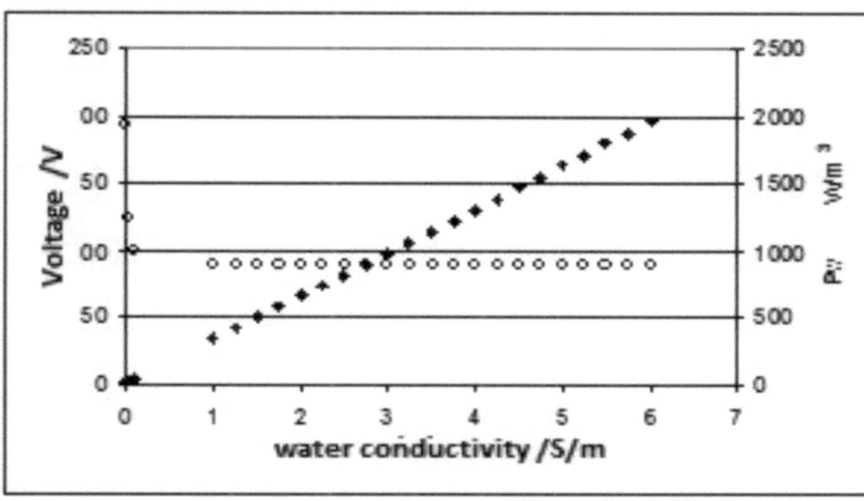

Fig. 8. Voltage (white) and P_w (black) for increasing water conductibility values

Using 90 V voltage at the electrodes, for a water conductivity ranging between 3 and 6 S/m, the electric field intensity values ranged between 15.14 V/m and 1.48 V/m at the *d1* and *d5* positions. The intensity of the field is function of distance but not of the water conductivity (table 1). On the other hand, electric density at the electrodes increased at higher water

power kW	Tension V	Current at electrodes A	Water conductivity S/m	point	Distance from anode m	V/m	A/m²	Mean V
51.75	90	574.99	3	1	2.5	15.14	45.44	37.77
				2	2.7	13.28	39.83	36.55
				3	3.2	9.43	28.3	33.13
				4	4.7	4.44	13.32	27
				5	8.4	1.48	4.43	19.41
69.00	90	766.65	4	1	2.5	15.14	60.58	37.77
				2	2.7	13.28	53.1	36.55
				3	3.2	9.43	37.73	33.13
				4	4.7	4.44	17.76	27
				5	8.4	1.48	5.91	19.41
86.25	90	958.32	5	1	2.5	15.14	75.73	37.77
				2	2.7	13.28	66.38	36.55
				3	3.2	9.43	47.16	33.13
				4	4.7	4.44	22.2	27
				5	8.4	1.48	7.39	19.41
103.50	90	1149.98	6	1	2.5	15.14	90.87	37.77
				2	2.7	13.28	79.65	36.55
				3	3.2	9.43	56.59	33.13
				4	4.7	4.44	26.64	27
				5	8.4	1.48	8.87	19.41

Table 1. Results of numerical simulations of fish and open sea using 90 V at the electrodes (water conductibility between 3.0 and 6.0 S/m in points *d1-d5)*

conductivities. The required power ranged from about 52 kW to 103 kW for 3 - 6 S/m conductivity values (applying 90 V voltage). Assuming a threshold of 10 V/m, the electric field gradient values obtained from the model are suitable to produce electro-taxis until point 3, that is a distance of almost 3 m from the centre of the anode. Fig. 9 shows the distribution of equipotential areas respect to the electrodes. An area of 28.9 m² shows values greater than 9.6 V/m.

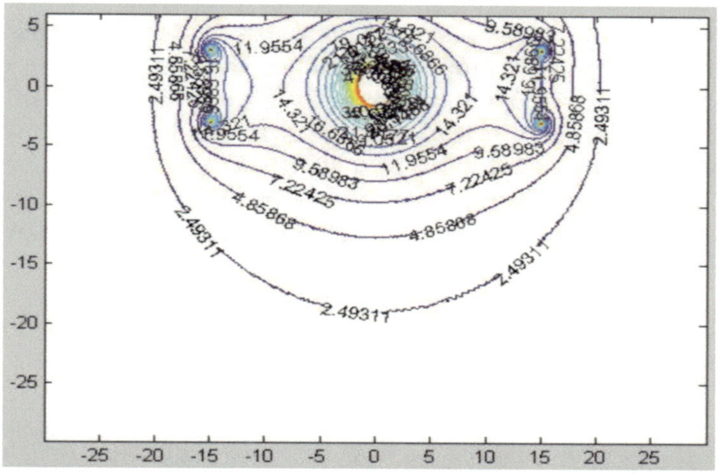

Fig. 9. Electric field distribution and equipotential areas obtained supplying 90 V to the electrodes in open sea

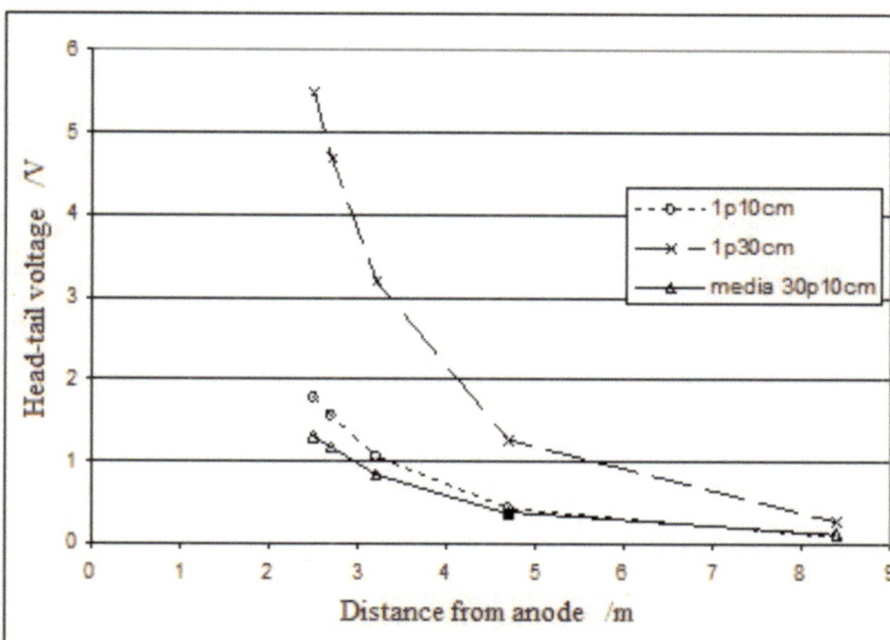

Fig. 10. Head-tail potential difference in fish

Water conductivity had no significant effect on fish parameters: head-tail potential difference, mean, maximum and minimum field inside and outside the fish, for no fish configuration (1 fish 10 cm and 1 fish 30 cm: P=1,000; $F_{3,19}$=0,000; N=20; 30 fish 10 cm: P=1,00; $F_{3,599}$=0,0; N=600). The head-tail potential difference and the field outside the fish decreased with distance (Fig. 10 and 11). This is due to the fact that the electric field is not uniform and its effects are reduced closer to the cathode. Table 2 shows the results of the simulations in open sea in presence of fish. While the mean current field external to the fish is similar using different fish configurations, the internal mean field is greater considering fish groups, with values that are more than double respect to single fish. The mean field inside the fish is greater than the field in the water surrounding the fish (table 2). Fish dimensions do not have a significant effect on the mean field inside the fish ($F_{2,59}$=0.24, P=0.787; N=60). Correlation between mean external and internal field in the fish is positive and significant (R=0,81; P=0.000; N=640). The relationship between the mean field inside fish and in the water is not linear (Fig. 12).

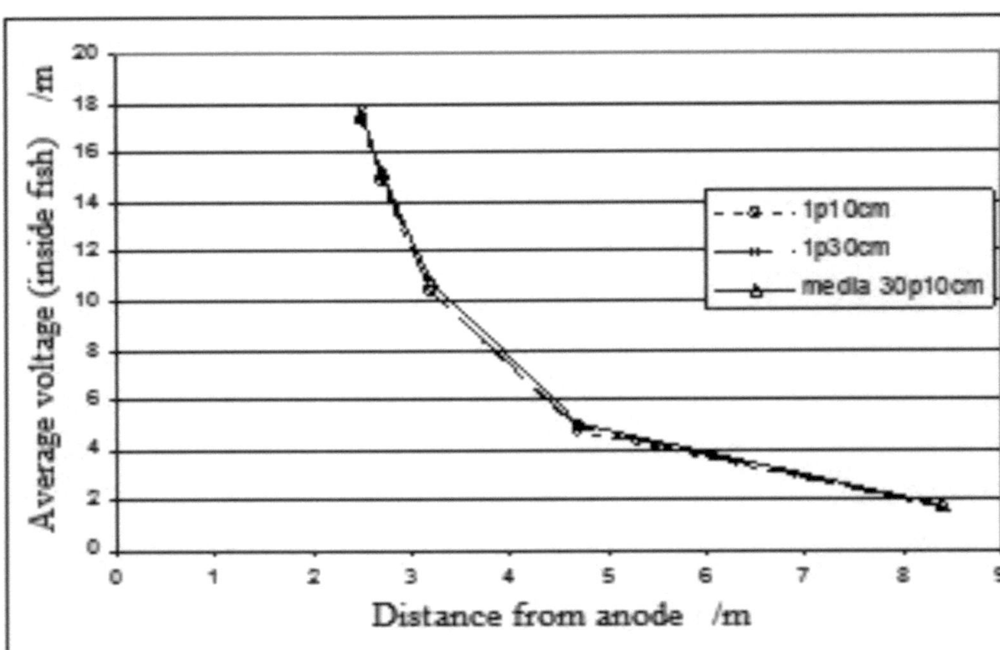

Fig. 11. Mean electric field in the water surrounding the fish

Mean field inside the fish decreased with distance; in the case of single fish (10 and 30 cm) maximum values were obtained 3 m far from the anode (Fig. 12).

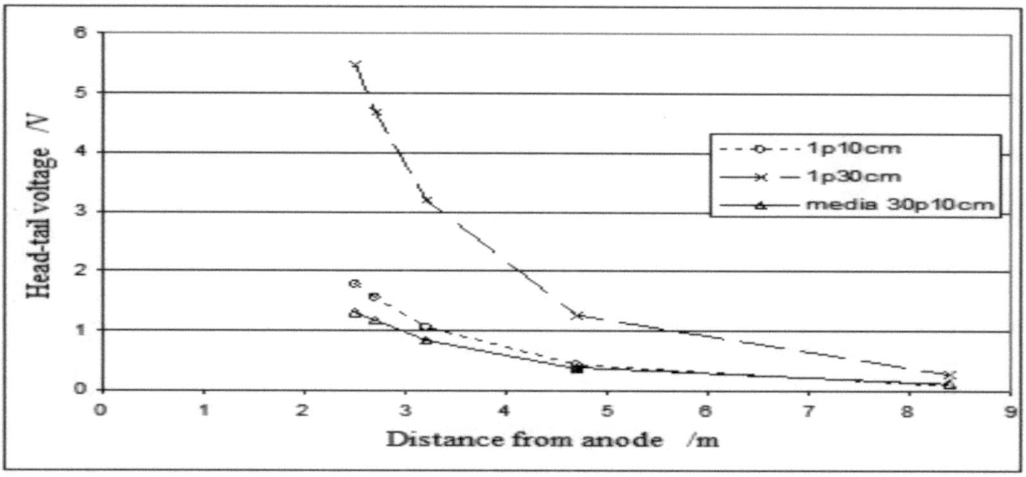

Fig. 12. Mean electric field inside the fish

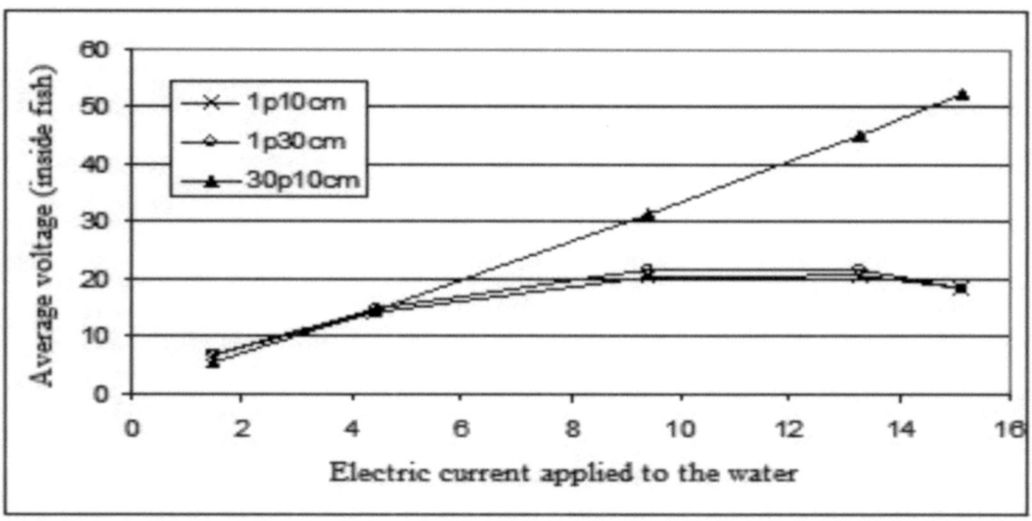

Fig. 13. Mean electric field inside the fish (without fish; water conductivity of 5S/m)

The mean electric field of the water (closed to the fish) increased compared to the same conditions but without fish.

Total n. fish	dim fish (cm)	point	dist from anode (m)	cond water (S/m)	Current at electrodes (A)	power kW	ddp V	E_{man} int V/m	E_{max} int V/m	E_{min} int V/m	E_{max} ext V/m	E_{min} ext V/m	E_{mean} ext V/m
1	10	d1	2.5	3	574.98	51.7	1.78	18.25	19.66	11.43	19.63	13.62	17.39
				6	1149.97	103.5	1.78	18.26	19.68	11.41	19.65	13.61	17.39
		d2	2.7	3	574.98	51.7	1.54	20.43	24.47	14.00	21.65	3.69	14.91
				6	1149.96	103.5	1.54	20.50	24.60	14.10	21.72	3.59	14.92
		d3	3.2	3	574.97	51.7	1.06	20.23	28.22	17.05	19.16	1.31	10.36
				6	1149.94	103.5	1.06	20.35	28.51	17.13	19.25	1.30	10.36
		d4	4.7	3	575.00	51.8	0.42	14.17	18.45	11.80	12.09	0.34	4.75
				6	1150.01	103.5	0.43	14.27	18.62	11.88	12.18	0.34	4.76
		d5	8.4	3	574.99	51.7	0.09	6.63	8.85	5.79	5.17	0.17	1.67
				6	1149.97	103.5	0.09	6.68	8.93	5.83	5.22	0.15	1.68
1	30	d1	2.5	3	574.84	51.7	5.48	18.48	20.15	16.03	20.09	14.96	17.76
				6	1149.68	103.5	5.49	18.49	20.16	16.03	20.10	14.96	17.76
		d2	2.7	3	574.86	51.7	4.67	21.51	23.60	19.24	22.80	4.07	15.15
				6	1149.73	103.5	4.68	21.59	23.72	19.31	22.89	3.98	15.16
		d3	3.2	3	574.90	51.7	3.18	21.52	24.42	19.68	21.76	1.32	10.39
				6	1149.80	103.5	3.18	21.65	24.59	19.78	21.88	1.25	10.39
		d4	4.7	3	574.97	51.7	1.25	14.81	16.96	13.21	13.70	0.34	4.85
				6	1149.94	103.5	1.25	14.92	17.10	13.30	13.79	0.30	4.86
		d5	8.4	3	574.95	51.7	0.26	6.72	7.93	5.92	5.51	0.16	1.67
				6	1149.90	103.5	0.26	6.77	8.00	5.96	5.55	0.15	1.68
30	10	d1	2.5	3	573.57	51.6	1.31	51.92	77.30	40.13	42.66	2.78	17.52
				6	1147.13	103.2	1.31	52.28	78.04	40.36	42.99	2.69	17.57
		d2	2.7	3	573.97	51.7	1.18	45.04	63.02	35.09	37.65	1.95	15.20
				6	1147.92	103.3	1.18	45.36	63.60	35.30	37.93	1.88	15.25
		d3	3.2	3	574.49	51.7	0.82	30.98	46.92	23.72	25.85	1.62	10.80
				6	1148.97	103.4	0.83	31.19	47.37	23.85	26.04	1.56	10.83
		d4	4.7	3	574.88	51.7	0.37	14.35	20.80	10.90	12.01	0.89	5.05
				6	1149.77	103.5	0.37	14.45	20.99	10.96	12.10	0.86	5.06
		d5	8.4	3	574.97	51.7	0.12	5.38	7.87	4.19	4.40	0.23	1.75
				6	1149.93	103.5	0.12	5.42	7.94	4.21	4.44	0.22	1.75

Table 2. Numerical simulations in open sea (water conductivity 3-6 S/m) in presence of fish. For fish in group mean values are shown (N=30). The impressed voltage is 90 V.

3.2 Numerical simulations of fish in a tank

Numerical simulations in a controlled environment have been carried out considering an experimental tank of 2.5 m x 0.7 m; h max 0.6 m. Plate electrodes are positioned on the short sides of the tank and are supplied with a V_1 and V_2 potential, respectively. The dimensions of the electrodes, which are identical and parallel, are 0.6 m x 0.6 m. This configuration permits to obtain a uniform electric field (Holliman and Reynolds, 2002). The same fish configurations used before were also used in the tank simulations (single fish of 10 cm and 30 cm and group of 30 fish of 10 cm). The orientation of fish in the group is the same as in open sea simulation. Single fish are centred in the tank, parallel to the electric field; for the group, the barycentre corresponds to the centre of the tank (Fig. 14).

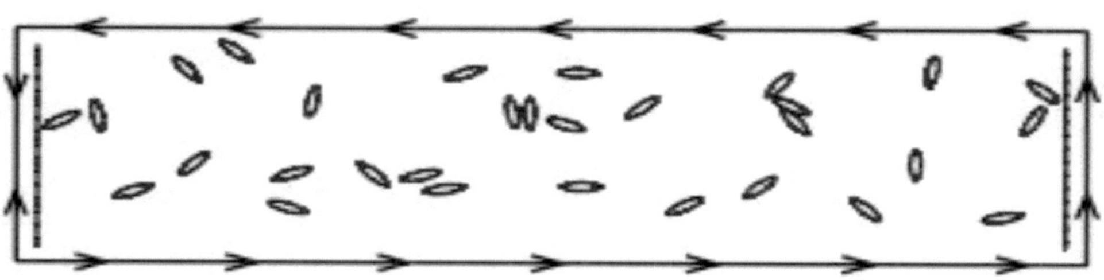

Fig. 14. Lay out of the group of 30 fish in the tank. The two electrodes, supplied with V_1 and V_2 potentials , are parallel and placed at the short sides of the tank.

Tank simulations have been carried out with the same values of V/m obtained from open sea simulations in the five sampling points d_1-d_5. Only values greater than 5 V/m have been considered, which correspond to about half the minimum field intensity required to achieve electro-taxis in sea fish (Le Men, 1980). Water conductibility values were the same as in the open sea simulations: 3.0, 4.0, 5.0, and 6.0 S/m. In the tank simulations, the voltage used at the electrodes was similar to the values obtained in the open sea simulations in the points *d1-d3*. Similarly to the open sea simulations, the work carried out for tanks, showed that the mean current field inside the fish was greater than the field in the water surrounding the fish. Furthermore, fish in groups showed values inside the body grater and more than double respect to single fish. Results of simulations of electric fields for fish reared in a tank are presented in Table 3. In these simulations, a specific voltage was applied at the electrodes to produce voltage gradients which were identical to those obtained in simulations of open sea conditions without fish. As for the open sea, the mean current density inside fish was greater compared to the water close to the fish and for groups of fish compared to single fish. Using a voltage similar to the values obtained in open sea in the points *d1-d3*, the mean electric field inside the fish resulted different between tank and open sea simulations (table 4). In the tank, the electric field inside the fish increased linearly. By contrast, in open sea, the electric field is not uniform and it varies in the three considered sampling points (*d1-d3*). This determines a non linear pattern of the mean field inside the fish compared to the field in the water without fish. The difference between tank and open sea values is higher for the mean field inside the fish but negligible for the field in the water surrounding the fish. Table 5 shows the difference between tank and sea. For single fish, the difference between tank and sea increases for higher field intensities and for fish groups. In each case, electric field mean module inside the fish was always lower in the tank than in open sea. The required power, expressed as the applied voltage at the electrodes is listed in table 5. These values represent the maximum instantaneous required power. Using *PDC* the effective required power, in the time unit, depends on the impulselength and frequency. Therefore, using for example a *PDC* with 60 Hz frequency and 6 msec impulses (duty cycle 36%), the mean required power/sec corresponds to the 36% of the maximum instantaneous power. In practice, in this case, the required power is reduced from 103 kW to less than 40 kW (table 5).

E water V/m	Applied voltage V	Total n. fish	length m	conduc water S/m	current A	ddp V	E_{mean} int V/m	E_{max} int V/m	E_{min} int V/m	E_{max}_ext V/m	E_{min}_ext V/m	E_{mean}_ext V/m
15.1	**36.24**	**1**	**0.10**	3	19.10	1.76	18.05	19.81	11.27	19.72	12.19	17.11
				6	38.20	1.76	18.06	19.83	11.25	19.73	12.17	17.11
			0.29	3	18.89	5.34	18.25	19.70	15.82	19.69	12.99	17.40
				6	37.79	5.34	18.26	19.72	15.82	19.70	12.99	17.41
		30	**0.10**	3	17.59	1.18	44.29	62.19	31.86	38.24	2.40	15.62
				6	35.15	1.18	44.56	62.72	32.02	38.50	2.32	15.66
13.3	**31.92**	**1**	**0.10**	3	16.82	1.55	15.90	17.45	9.93	17.37	10.73	15.07
				6	33.65	1.55	15.90	17.46	9.91	17.38	10.72	15.07
			0.29	3	16.64	4.70	16.07	17.35	13.94	17.34	11.44	15.33
				6	33.28	4.70	16.08	17.36	13.94	17.35	11.44	15.33
		30	**0.10**	3	15.49	1.04	39.01	54.78	28.06	33.68	2.12	13.76
				6	30.96	1.04	39.25	55.24	28.20	33.91	2.04	13.79
9.4	**22.56**	**1**	**0.10**	3	11.89	1.09	11.24	12.33	7.02	12.28	7.59	10.65
				6	23.78	1.09	11.24	12.34	7.01	12.28	7.58	10.65
			0.29	3	11.76	3.32	11.36	12.27	9.85	12.26	8.08	10.83
				6	23.53	3.33	11.36	12.27	9.85	12.26	8.08	10.84
		30	**0.10**	3	10.95	0.74	27.57	38.71	19.84	23.80	1.50	9.72
				6	21.88	0.74	27.74	39.04	19.93	23.97	1.44	9.75

Table 3. Numerical simulations of a tank using different fish configurations. E water (first column) is the current field obtained in points *d1-d3* in the open sea simulation without fish

				ddp	E_{med} int V/m	E_{med} est V/m	% Δ int	% Δ est
Field in water	15,1V/m							
point d1		1fish 10cm	tank	1,76	18,06	17.11	0.20	0.28
			sea	1,78	18,26	17.39		
		1fish 30cm	tank	5,34	18,26	17.41	0.23	0.35
			sea	5,48	18,49	17.76		
		30fish 10cm	tank	1,18	44,51	15.65	7.70	1.91
			sea	1,31	52,21	17.56		
Field in water	13,3V/m							
point d2		1fish 10cm	tank	1,55	15,90	15.07	4.59	-0.15
			sea	1,54	20,49	14.92		
		1fish 30cm	tank	4,70	16,08	15.33	5.49	-0.17
			sea	4,67	21,57	15.16		
		30fish 10cm	tank	1,04	39,20	13.78	6.09	1.46
			sea	1,18	45,29	15.24		
Field in water	9,4V/m							
point d3		1fish 10cm	tank	1,09	11,24	10.65	9.08	-0.29
			sea	1,06	20,32	10.36		
		1fish 30cm	tank	3,33	11,36	10.84	10.27	-0.45
			sea	3,18	21,63	10.39		
		30fish 10cm	tank	0,74	27,71	9.74	3.44	1.08
			sea	0,83	31,15	10.82		

Table 4. Summary comparison values obtained from open sea and tank simulation, for the same field intensity. Only values for water conductivity of 5 S/m are shown. In the last columns, the difference between sea and tank field (internal and external to the fish) values, in percentage on sea values, are reported

Water conductivity S/m	Peak power kW	Mean power at 36% duty cycle kW
3	51.7	18.6
4	69.0	24.8
5	86.2	31.0
6	103.5	37.3

Table 5. Maximum (peak) and mean power required in an open sea electro-fishing system at different water conductivity values (voltage of 90 V and 36% duty cycle)

4. Field testing of electro-fishing systems

The effectiveness of the electro-fishing is affected by several factors as type of current, voltage applied, electrode shape, water conductivity and temperature, distance of fish, size and fish species. The number of pulses per second (pulse frequency) and the time (pulse width) have different effects on different species of fish. In a PDC field, fish body flexes with each pulse, and returns to normal situation. Flexing and straightening movements of fish towards the anode, called electro-taxis. Modern equipments allow complete control over the electrofisher output. These methods of synthesizing waveforms makes it possible to produce virtually any waveform, so it can be selected one that is safest for the fish. It allows to create narrow pulses to achieve the same results as wide ones. An electric field in water can be considered to have three separate areas. The outer peripheral area is a weak field to which the fish is indifferent to. The next area, closer to the electrodes, has a stronger electrical field, but not enough to stun the fish. In this area, the involuntary swimming action will occur and the fish will swim towards the anode. The innermost area has the strongest electrical field, and fish within that area are immobilized. When electro-fishing starts, fish are usually hiding up to three meters away, so high power is required to attract them out of hiding. Fish close to the anode receive a very high head-to-tail voltage. Most fish injuries occur within half a meter from the anode. This is called the zone of potential fish injury. We can minimize the injury by reducing the time the electricity is turned on. The duty-cycle is the percent of on-time. It is a product of the pulse width and the pulse frequency. The duty-cycle can be lowered in three ways: by reducing the pulse width, by reducing the pulse frequency, or by using gated bursts, where the power is off for a period between each burst of pulses. Fish close to an anode with a low duty-cycle are far less likely to be injured than with a high duty-cycle. The way in which voltage and current distribute around electrofisher electrodes is complex. Note that the current density and voltage gradient are highest near the electrodes. The dimensions of the electrodes are very important in determining the voltage distribution around electro-fisher electrodes. The cathode dimension is considered to be infinite. Field testing has confirmed that the mean electric field simulated inside the fish is greater than the nominal field in the water, with a significant effect of orientation of the fish towards the electric field. To collect fish by electrical means we must create an electrified zone of sufficient amplitude to stun fish. The responses of fish to electric fields in water are dependent on the field's intensity. Field intensity can be described by any of three interrelated quantities: voltage gradient, current density or power density. Field intensity is greatest next to the electrodes and decreases to barely perceptible levels as distance from the electrodes increases, even in the area directly between anode and cathode when they are sufficiently separated. Electrofishing fields are nearly always heterogeneous, with field intensity highest at the electrode surface and decreasing geometrically from that surface to barely perceptible levels a few meters away. The outer boundary for each response zone represents the minimum in-water field intensity or threshold for that response. The specific values for these thresholds vary with water conductivity and temperature, electric-field waveform and frequency, and the pertinent electrical and physiological characteristics of the fish, which, considered as a whole, define its effective conductivity. Electrofishing tends to be size selective, larger fish being more vulnerable to capture, has long been established (Reynolds 1996). Larger fish are also more likely to be injured by electrofishing than smaller ones of the same species. Sharber et al. (1994) demonstrated a curvilinear relationship between pulse frequency and injury rate; frequencies of 60 Hz and higher were more damaging than lower frequencies. This relationship has been confirmed repeatedly (McMichael 1993, Dalbey et al. 1996, Ainslie et al. 1998). The likelihood of tetany (forced muscle contraction) also increases with pulse frequency, lending credence to the idea that tetany tends to induce injury. Pulse frequency can often be manipulated on manufactured equipment, In general, operators should reduce pulse frequency to the range of 15-30 Hz, while trying to maintain acceptable catch rate, if injury rate has to be significantly reduced. Pulse duration is related to duty cycle. At a given peak voltage or amplitude, changing pulse duration will change the average voltage (area under the waveform curve), meaning that the fish is subjected to more electrical energy. It is possible that longer pulse duration (e.g., 6-8 ms) contributes more to added stress than injury, compared to shorter pulse duration (e.g., 2-4 ms). Experimental results of sea bass after exposure to electro-fishing in laboratory tanks are presented in Figure 15 and 16. These figures illustrate differences in sea bass fish (two sizes: 10 and 30 cm) in terms of electro-taxis and tetanus threshold values after electrical exposure. Tetanus threshold values decreased significantly ($P<0.05$) for higher frequencies in both sizes while electro-taxis was not influenced by the electrical exposure. It is worth noting that, these values decreased with the fish size. All fish were immobilized during the electrical exposure. However, after 5 minutes, they recovered the opercular movements and swimming ability.

Results of electro-fishing exposure (frequency: 25-75-125 Hz; duty cycle: 5-20-40%) on carcass quality characteristics are reported in Table 6, Fig.15 -16. No effects on carcass quality characteristics were identified for any of the fish exposed to the experimental treatments. Fish were inspected for hemorrhages in the skin, external damage, internal haemorrhaging, blood spotting and damage of the spines. No differences were found after electro-fishing on other carcass quality characteristics (QIM, colour, shear force, rigor mortis).

	Treatments									
	25-5	25-20	25-40	75-5	75-20	75-40	125-5	125-20	125-40	Rse df 18
pH	6.4	6.1	6.4	6.1	6.4	6.2	6.1	6.2	6.3	0.19
Colour:										
L*	34.8	36.4	35.5	36.5	36.1	36.1	35.5	35.8	36.0	2.65
a*	-1.9	-1.6	-1.7	-2.7	-1.5	-1.5	-1.5	-2.5	-1.8	0.16
b*	6.0	7.6	6.3	5.4	5.1	5.1	6.4	6.1	6.5	1.74
Croma	6.3	7.8	7.3	6.7	5.3	5.3	6.6	6	6.7	1.63
Hue angle	107.3	102.2	109.6	107.4	106.9	106.9	105.1	109.8	106.2	15.98
Cooking yield (%)	98.76	98.00	97.96	98.62	99.02	98.93	97.66	97.78	98.10	0.96
Maximum force (N)	9.0	8.5	8.7	9.2	8.3	7.5	8.5	8.9	9.0	4.34
Total amount of work (J)	0.125	0.095	0.122	0.104	0.090	0.088	0.103	0.100	0.101	0.0001

Table 6. Results of electro-fishing exposure on carcass quality characteristics of sea bass

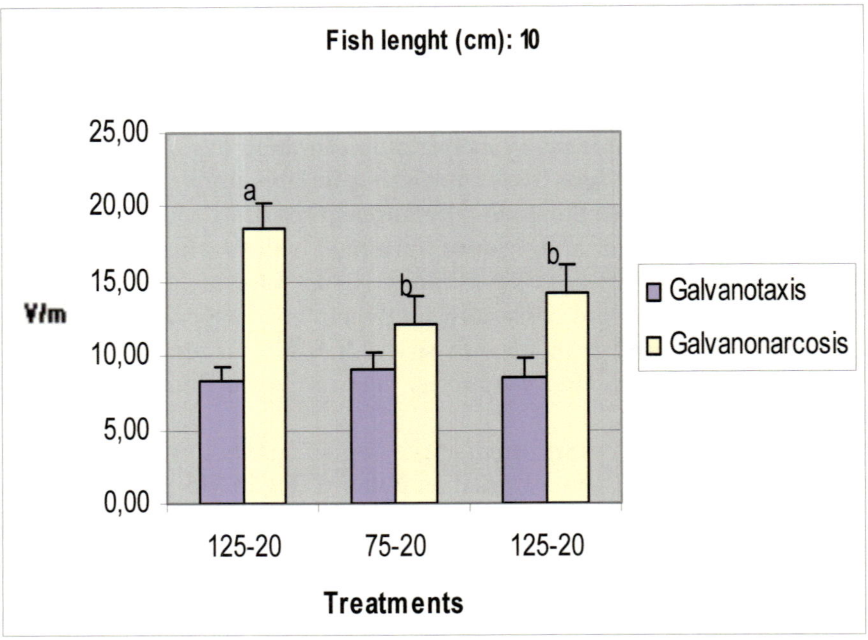

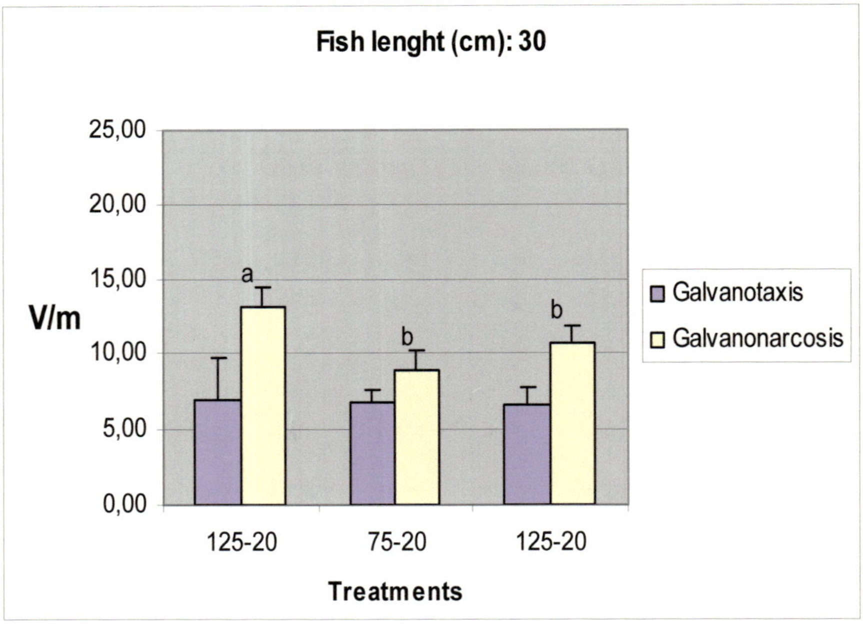

a, b < P<0.05

Fig. 15. 16. Electric-induced electro-taxis and tetanus of sea bass after electro-fishing exposure (frequency:25-75-125 Hz; duty cycle: 20)

5. Conclusions

The main problem in sea water electro-fishing is the high electric current demand in the equipment, brought about by the very high ionic concentration of salt water. The solution of this problem is to reduce the current demand as much as possible by using pulsed direct current, the pulses being as small as possible. For example, if pulse duration is reduced to 1 or 2 milliseconds, and pulse frequency is kept below 30 hertz (pulses per second), this will allow the operator to increase the amplitude, or height, of the pulses with the voltage control. Fish generally respond best when the peak voltage is higher and the average voltage (area under each pulse curve) is lower. If the fish don't respond, then average voltage is increased (i.e., pulse frequency and/or pulse duration) is increased until they do respond. It is usually better to increase frequency first, followed by duration. Ultimately, if none of this may work, the power source (generator) is may be inadequate. In this case, one can experiment with smaller electrodes (reduced surface area) to further reduce the demand for current. The numerical simulations of a non homogeneous electric field (fish and water) permit to estimate the current gradient in the open sea and to evaluate the attraction capacity of fish using an electro-fishing device. An area of about 30 m^2 suitable for electro-taxis is estimated for a voltage of 90 V on a circular anode and two linear cathodes which are 5 m far from the centre of the anode. Tank simulations are, instead, carried out in a uniform electric field, generated by two parallel linear electrodes. The convenience of using an uniform field is given by the need of finding threshold values of current field which are independent from the position of the fish in the tank. Numerical simulations allow to compare the electric field in the water and inside fish. The current field inside fish is resulted smaller in a tank compared to the open sea. This means that, in practice, in the open sea situation, the efficacy of an electro-fishing system is stronger, in terms of attraction area. Numerical simulations carried out using a group of 30 fish, both in open sea and in the tank, showed the presence of a "group effect", increasing the electric field intensity in the water around each fish. In this situation, each single fish has a greater current field compared to a fish group.

6. Acknowledgement

This study was funded by the Region Friuli Venezia Giulia, Innovation Projects 2010.

7. References

Ainslie, B.J. & Post, A.J. (1998). *Effects of pulsed and continuous DC electrofishing on juvenile rainbow trout*. North American Journal of Fisheries Management, 18, 905-918

Beaumont, W.R.C.; Taylor, A.A.L.; Lee, M.J. & Welton, J.S. (2002). *Guidelines for electric fishing best practice*, R&D Technical Report W2-054/TR. Environmental Agency, Bristol, UK.

Blancheteau, M. (1971). *La peche electrique en eau del mer. II - choix du stimulus approprié a la peche a l'electricité en mer*. Rev. Trav. Inst. Pêches Marit., 35(1), 13-20

Hamrin, S.; Heggberget, T.G.; Rassmussen, G. & Salveit, S.J. (1989). *Electrofishing - Theory and practice with* special *emphasis on salmonids*. Hydrobiologia, 173, 9-43

Codecasa, R.; Specogna, R. & Trevisan, R. (2007). *Symmetric Positive-Definite Constitutive Matrices for Discrete Eddy-Current Problems*. IEEE T. Magn., 42 (2), 510-515

Dalbey, S.R.; McMahon, T.E. & Fredenberg, W (1996). *Effect of electrofishing pulse shape and electrofishing-induced spinal injury to long-term growth and survival of wild rainbow trout.* North American Journal of Fisheries Management, 16, 560-569

Diner, N. & Le Man, R. (1971). *La peche electrique en eau del mer: III – Etude du champ electrique necessaire a la taxie anodique du poisson.* Rev. Trav. l'Inst. Pêches Marit., 35(1), 21-34

Kolz, A.L. (1989). *A power transfer theory for electrofishing. In: A.L. Kolz, J.B. Reynolds (Eds), Electrofishing, a power related phenomenon.* U.S. Fish and Wildlife Service, Technical Report, 22, 1-11

Kolz, A.L. (1993). *In water electrical measurements for evaluating electrofishing systems.* U.S Fish and Wildlife Service, Biological Report 11

Kurk, G. (1971). *La peche electrique en eau de mer: I – Peche a l'électricité avec lumiére artificielle et pompe.* Rev. Trav. Inst. Pêches Marit., 35(1), 5-12

Kurk, G.(1972). *Device for electric sea-fishing.* United States Patent Office, N. 3, 693,276

Le Men, R. (1980). *Comportement de poissons marins dans un champ electrique – perspectives d'application a la peche.* Rev. Trav. Inst. Pêches Marit., 44(1), 5-83

McMichael, G.A. (1993). *Examination of electrofishing injury and short-term mortality in hatchery rainbow trout.* North American Journal of Fisheries Management, 13, 229-233

Miranda, L.E. & Dolan, C.R. (2003). *Test of a power transfer model for standardized electrofishing.* T. Am. Fish. Soc., 132, 1179-1185

B.; Slinde, E. & Arildsen, J. (2006). *Pre or post mortem musle activity in Atlantic salmon (Salmo salar). The effect on rigor mortis and the physical properties of flesh,* Aquaculture, 257, 504-510

Sharber, N.G. & Carothers, S.W. (1988). *Influence of electrofishing pulse shape on spinal injuries in adult rainbow trout.* North American Journal of Fisheries Management, 8, 117-122.

Specogna, R. & Trevisan, F.(2005). *Discrete constitutive equations in A-χ geometric eddy-currents formulation.* IEEE T. Magn., 41(4), 1259-1263

Specogna, R. & Trevisan, F.(2006). *Voltage Source in A-χ discrete geometric approach to eddy currents.* Eur. J. Appl. Phys., Vol. 6, 97-101

Stravisi, F. (1983). *The vertical structure annual cycle of the mass field parameters in the Gulf of Trieste.* Boll. Oceanol. Teor. Appl., 1 (3), 239-250

Van Harreveld, A. (1938). *On galvanotropism and oscillotaxis in fish.* J. Exp. Biol., 15, 197-208

17

Numerical Analysis of a Rotor Dynamics in the Magneto-Hydrodynamic Field

Jan Awrejcewicz[1] and Larisa P. Dzyubak[2]
[1]*Technical University of Łódź*
[2]*National Technical University "Kharkov Polytechnic Institute"*
[1]*Poland*
[2]*Ukraine*

1. Introduction

In general, rotating machinery elements are frequently met in mechanical/mechatronical engineering, and in many cases their non-linear dynamics causes many harmful effects, i.e. noise and vibrations. In particular, nonlinear rotordynamics plays a crucial role in understanding various nonlinear phenomena and in spite of its long research history (see for instance (Tondl, 1965; Someya, 1998; Rao, 1991; Gasch et al., 2002; Muszyńska, 2005) and the references therein) it still attracts attention of many researchers and engineers. Since the topics related to nonlinear rotordynamics are broadband and cover many interesting aspects related to both theory and practice, in this chapter we are aimed only on analysis of some problems related to rotor suspended in a magneto-hydrodynamics field in the case of soft and rigid magnetic materials.

The magnetic, magneto-hydrodynamic and also piezoelectric bearings are used in many mechanical engineering applications in order to support a high-speed rotor, provide vibration control, to keep lower rotating friction losses and to potentially avoid flutter instability. There are a lot of publications devoted to the dynamics analysis and control of a rotor supported on various bearings systems. The conditions for active close/open-loop control of a rigid rotor supported on hydrodynamic bearings and subjected to harmonic kinematical excitation are presented in (Kurnik, 1995; Dziedzic & Kurnik, 2002). The methodology for modeling lubricated revolute joints in constrained rigid multibody systems is described in (Flores et al., 2009). The hydrodynamic forces, used in the dynamic analysis of journal-bearings, which include both squeeze and wedge effects, are evaluated from the system state variables and included into the equations of motion of the multibody system. To analyze the dynamic behavior of rub-impact rotor supported by turbulent journal bearings and lubricated with couple stress fluid under quadratic damping the authors of (Chang-Jian & Chen, 2009) have used the system state trajectory, Poincaré maps, power spectrum, bifurcation diagrams and Lyapunov exponents. It was detected the dynamic motion as periodic, quasi-periodic and chaotic types.

In (Zhang & Zhan, 2005; Li et al., 2006) a rotor–active magnetic bearings (rotor–AMB) systems with time-varying stiffness are considered. Using the method of multiple scales a governing nonlinear equation of motion for the rotor-AMB system with 1-dof is transformed to the averaged equation and then the bifurcation theory and the method of detection function are used to analyze the bifurcations of multiple limit cycles of the averaged equation.

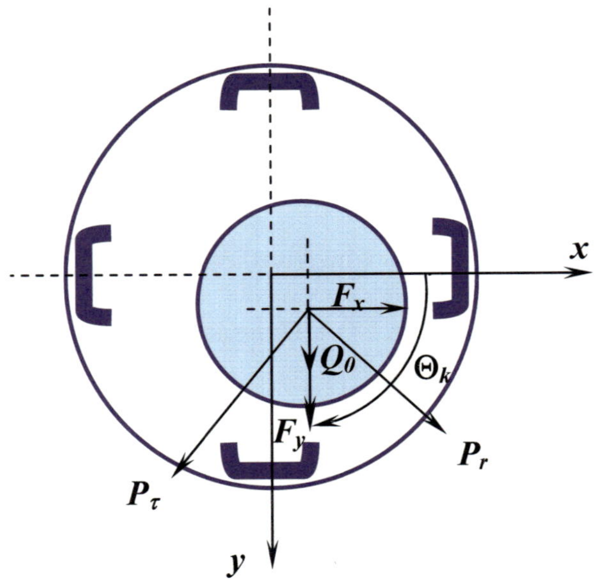

Fig. 1. The cross–section diagram of a rotor symmetrically supported on the magneto–hydrodynamic bearing

In the present chapter 2-dof nonlinear dynamics of the rotor supported on the magneto-hydrodynamic bearing (MHDB) system is analyzed in the cases of soft and rigid magnetic materials. In the case of soft magnetic materials the analytical solutions have been obtained by means of the method of multiple scales (Nayfeh & Mook, 2004). Rigid magnetic materials possess hysteretic properties which are realized in the frames of the present work by means of Bouc-Wen hysteretic model. This model allows simulating hysteretic loops of various forms for systems from very different fields (Awrejcewicz & Dzyubak, 2007). Chaotic regions and the amplitude level contours of the rotor vibrations have been obtained in various control parameter planes.

2. Mathematical model of the rotor suspended in the magneto-hydrodynamic field

Consider a uniform symmetric rigid rotor (Fig. 1) which is supported by a magneto–hydrodynamic bearing system. The four–pole legs are symmetrically placed in the stator. F_k is the electromagnetic force produced by the kth opposed pair of electromagnet coils. This force is controlled by electric currents

$$i_k = i_0 \pm \Delta i_k$$

can be expressed in the form

$$F_k = -\frac{2\mu_0 A N^2 i_0}{\left(2\delta + l/\mu^*\right)^2} \Delta i_k ,$$

where i_0 denotes bias current in the actuators electric circuits, μ_0 is the magnetic permeability of vacuum, A is the core cross-section area, N is the number of windings of the electromagnet, δ is the air gap in the central position of the rotor with reference to the bearing sleeve, l is the total length of the magnetic path, the constant value $\mu^* = B_s/(\mu_0 H_s)$ denotes the magnetic permeability of the core material; the values of the magnetic induction B_s and magnetizing force H_s define the magnetic saturation level. θ_k is the angle between axis x and the kth magnetic actuator. Q_0 is the vertical rotor load identified with its weight, (P_r, P_τ) are the radial and tangential components of the dynamic oil-film action, respectively. Equations of motion of the rotor are represented in the following form (Kurnik, 1995; Dziedzic & Kurnik, 2002; Osinski, 1998)

$$m^*\ddot{x}^* = P_r^*\left(\rho,\dot{\rho}^*,\dot{\varphi}^*\right)\cos\varphi - P_\tau^*\left(\rho,\dot{\varphi}^*\right)\sin\varphi + \sum_{k=1}^{K} F_k^*\cos\theta_k + Q_x^*(t),$$

$$m^*\ddot{y}^* = P_r^*\left(\rho,\dot{\rho}^*,\dot{\varphi}^*\right)\sin\varphi + P_\tau^*\left(\rho,\dot{\varphi}^*\right)\cos\varphi + \sum_{k=1}^{K} F_k^*\sin\theta_k + Q_0^* + Q_y^*(t),$$

$$P_r^*\left(\rho,\dot{\rho}^*,\dot{\varphi}^*\right) = -2C^*\left\{\frac{\rho^2\left(\omega^* - 2\dot{\varphi}^*\right)}{p(\rho)q(\rho)} + \frac{\rho\dot{\rho}^*}{p(\rho)} + \frac{2\dot{\rho}^*}{\sqrt{p(\rho)}}arctg\sqrt{\frac{1+\rho}{1-\rho}}\right\},$$

$$P_\tau^*\left(\rho,\dot{\varphi}^*\right) = \pi C^*\frac{\rho\left(\omega^* - 2\dot{\varphi}^*\right)}{q(\rho)\sqrt{p(\rho)}}.$$

Here m^* denotes the rigid rotor mass, (x^*, y^*) are the Cartesian coordinates of the rotor center; $Q_x^*(t)$, $Q_y^*(t)$ are the external excitation characterizing bearing housing movements. We are considering vibrations of the rotor excited by harmonic movements of the bearing foundation in the vertical direction

$$Q_x^*(t) = 0,\ Q_y^*(t) = Q^*\sin\Omega^* t^*,$$

where Q^* and Ω^* are the amplitude and frequency of the external excitation, respectively. Constant C^* is defined as

$$C^* = \frac{6\mu_s R_c L_c}{\delta_s^2}.$$

Parameters μ_s, δ_s, R_c, L_c denote oil viscosity, relative bearing clearance, journal radius and total bearing length, respectively. (ρ, ϕ) are the polar coordinates, $p(\rho) = 1 - \rho^2$, $q(\rho) = 2 + \rho^2$ are the functions conditional ρ.

To represent the equations of motion in a dimensionless form the following changes of variables and parameters are introduced:

$$t = \omega^* t^*,\ \dot{\varphi} = \frac{\dot{\varphi}^*}{\omega^*},\ \dot{\rho} = \frac{\dot{\rho}^*}{\omega^*},\ x = \frac{x^*}{c^*},\ \dot{x} = \frac{\dot{x}^*}{\omega^* c^*},\ \ddot{x} = \frac{\ddot{x}^*}{\omega^{*2} c^*},\ y = \frac{y^*}{c^*},\ \dot{y} = \frac{\dot{y}^*}{\omega^* c^*},$$

$$\ddot{y}=\frac{\ddot{y}^*}{\omega^{*2}c^*},\ C=\frac{C^*}{m^*\omega^* c^*},\ \Omega=\frac{\Omega^*}{\omega^*},\ Q=\frac{Q^*}{m^*\omega^{*2}c^*},\ Q_0=\frac{Q_0^*}{m^*\omega^{*2}c^*},$$

$$F_k=\frac{F_k^*}{m^*\omega^{*2}c^*},\ P_r=\frac{P_r^*}{m^*\omega^{*2}c^*},\ P_\tau=\frac{P_\tau^*}{m^*\omega^{*2}c^*},$$

where ω^* is the rotation speed of the rotor; c^* is the bearing clearance.
Thus the dimensionless equations of motion take the form

$$\begin{aligned}\ddot{x}&=P_r(\rho,\dot{\rho},\dot{\varphi})\cos\varphi-P_\tau(\rho,\dot{\varphi})\sin\varphi+F_x,\\ \ddot{y}&=P_r(\rho,\dot{\rho},\dot{\varphi})\sin\varphi+P_\tau(\rho,\dot{\varphi})\cos\varphi+F_y+Q_0+Q\sin\Omega t,\end{aligned}\tag{1}$$

$$P_r(\rho,\dot{\rho},\dot{\varphi})=-2C\left\{\frac{\rho^2(1-2\dot{\varphi})}{p(\rho)q(\rho)}+\frac{\rho\dot{\rho}}{p(\rho)}+\frac{2\dot{\rho}}{\sqrt{p(\rho)}}arctg\sqrt{\frac{1+\rho}{1-\rho}}\right\},\ P_\tau(\rho,\dot{\varphi})=\pi C\frac{\rho(1-2\dot{\varphi})}{q(\rho)\sqrt{p(\rho)}}.$$

Here

$$x=\rho\cos\varphi,\ y=\rho\sin\varphi,\ \dot{\varphi}=\frac{\dot{y}x-\dot{x}y}{\rho^2},\ \dot{\rho}=\frac{x\dot{x}+y\dot{y}}{\rho},\ \rho=\sqrt{x^2+y^2},$$

$$\cos\varphi=\frac{x}{\sqrt{x^2+y^2}},\ \sin\varphi=\frac{y}{\sqrt{x^2+y^2}};$$

the magnetic control forces are expressed as follows

$$F_x=-\gamma\dot{x}-\lambda(x-x_0),\ F_y=-\gamma\dot{y}-\lambda(y-y_0),$$

where (x_0,y_0) are the coordinates of the rotor static equilibrium, γ and λ are the control parameters.

3. Soft magnetic materials

In this section, we consider 2-dof dynamics of the rotor in the MHDB system without taking hysteresis into account.

3.1 The non-resonant case

The right-hand sides of Eqs (1) were expanded in Taylor's series and the origin was shifted to the location of the static equilibrium (x_0,y_0) for the convenience of the investigation. The linear and quadratic terms were kept. So, the reformed equations of motion are as follows:

$$\begin{aligned}\ddot{x}+\alpha x-\beta\dot{y}&=-2\hat{\mu}_1\dot{x}+\alpha_1x^2+\alpha_2y^2+\alpha_3x\dot{x}+\alpha_4xy+\alpha_5x\dot{y}+\alpha_6\dot{x}y+\alpha_7y\dot{y},\\ \ddot{y}+\alpha y+\beta\dot{x}&=-2\hat{\mu}_2\dot{y}+\beta_1x^2+\beta_2y^2+\beta_3x\dot{x}+\beta_4xy+\beta_5x\dot{y}+\beta_6\dot{x}y+\beta_7y\dot{y}+F\cos(\Omega t+\tau).\end{aligned}\tag{2}$$

We seek the first-order solution for small but finite amplitudes in the form

$$x = \varepsilon x_1(T_0,T_1) + \varepsilon^2 x_2(T_0,T_1) + \ldots,$$
$$y = \varepsilon y_1(T_0,T_1) + \varepsilon^2 y_2(T_0,T_1) + \ldots, \tag{3}$$

where ε is the small, dimensionless parameter related to the amplitudes and $T_n = \varepsilon^n t$ (n=0, 1) are the independent variables. It follows that the derivatives with respect to t become expansions in terms of the partial derivatives with respect to T_n according to

$$\frac{d}{dt} = \frac{\partial}{\partial T_0}\frac{\partial T_0}{\partial t} + \frac{\partial}{\partial T_1}\frac{\partial T_1}{\partial t} + \frac{\partial}{\partial T_2}\frac{\partial T_2}{\partial t} + \ldots = D_0 + \varepsilon D_1 + \varepsilon^2 D_2 + \ldots,$$

$$\frac{d^2}{dt^2} = \left(D_0 + \varepsilon D_1 + \varepsilon^2 D_2 + \ldots\right)^2 = D_0^2 + 2\varepsilon D_0 D_1 + \varepsilon^2\left(D_1^2 + 2D_0 D_2\right) + \ldots, \text{ where } D_k = \frac{\partial}{\partial T_k}.$$

To analyze the non–resonant case the forcing term is ordered so that it appears at order ε. Thus, we recall in (2) $F=\varepsilon f$, $\hat{\mu}_n = \varepsilon \mu_n$. Substituting (3) into (2) and equating coefficients of similar powers of ε we obtain
Order ε

$$D_0^2 x_1 + \alpha x_1 - \beta D_0 y_1 = 0,$$
$$D_0^2 y_1 + \alpha y_1 + \beta D_0 x_1 = f\cos(\Omega T_0 + \tau). \tag{4}$$

Order ε^2

$$D_0^2 x_2 + \alpha x_2 - \beta D_0 y_2 = -2D_0\left(D_1 x_1 + \mu_1 x_1\right) + \beta D_1 y_1 + \alpha_1 x_1^2 + \alpha_2 y_1^2 +$$
$$\alpha_3 x_1 D_0 x_1 + \alpha_4 x_1 y_1 + \alpha_5 x_1 D_0 y_1 + \alpha_6 y_1 D_0 x_1 + \alpha_7 y_1 D_0 y_1,$$
$$D_0^2 y_2 + \alpha y_2 + \beta D_0 x_2 = -2D_0\left(D_1 y_1 + \mu_2 y_1\right) - \beta D_1 x_1 + \beta_1 x_1^2 + \beta_2 y_1^2 +$$
$$\beta_3 x_1 D_0 x_1 + \beta_4 x_1 y_1 + \beta_5 x_1 D_0 y_1 + \beta_6 y_1 D_0 x_1 + \beta_7 y_1 D_0 y_1. \tag{5}$$

The solution of (4) is expressed in the form

$$x_1 = A_1(T_1)\exp(i\omega_1 T_0) + A_2(T_1)\exp(i\omega_2 T_0) + \Phi_1 \exp\left[i(\Omega T_0 + \tau)\right] + CC,$$
$$y_1 = \Lambda_1 A_1(T_1)\exp(i\omega_1 T_0) + \Lambda_2 A_2(T_1)\exp(i\omega_2 T_0) + \Phi_2 \exp\left[i(\Omega T_0 + \tau)\right] + CC, \tag{6}$$

where CC denotes the complex conjugate of the preceding terms, A_1 and A_2 are the arbitrary functions of T_1 at this level of approximation,

$$\Lambda_n = \frac{\omega_n^2 - \alpha}{\omega_n \beta} i, \; \Phi_1 = \frac{i}{2}\frac{\beta\Omega f}{\left(\alpha - \Omega^2\right)^2 - \beta^2\Omega^2}, \; \Phi_2 = \frac{1}{2}\frac{f\left(\alpha - \Omega^2\right)}{\left(\alpha - \Omega^2\right)^2 - \beta^2\Omega^2}, \; (n=1, 2).$$

ω_n are assumed to be distinct and ω_n^2 are the roots of the characteristic equation

$$\det\begin{pmatrix} -\lambda & 1 & 0 & 0 \\ -\alpha & -\lambda & 0 & \beta \\ 0 & 0 & -\lambda & 1 \\ 0 & -\beta & -\alpha & -\lambda \end{pmatrix} = \lambda^4 + \left(2\alpha + \beta^2\right)\lambda^2 + \alpha^2 = \omega_n^4 - \left(2\alpha + \beta^2\right)\omega_n^2 + \alpha^2 = 0, \tag{7}$$

$$\lambda_{1,2} = \pm i\omega_1\,,\quad \lambda_{3,4} = \pm i\omega_2\,,\quad \lambda_{1,2} = \pm\frac{1}{2}\sqrt{-4\alpha - 2\beta^2 + 2\beta\sqrt{\beta^2 + 4\alpha}}\,,$$
$$\lambda_{3,4} = \pm\frac{1}{2}\sqrt{-4\alpha - 2\beta^2 - 2\beta\sqrt{\beta^2 + 4\alpha}}\,.$$

Substitution of (6) into (5) gives

$$\begin{aligned}
&D_0^2 x_2 + \alpha x_2 - \beta D_0 y_2 = \left[-2i\omega_1\left(A_1' + \mu_1 A_1\right) + \beta\Lambda_1 A_1'\right]\exp\left(i\omega_1 T_0\right) + \\
&\left[-2i\omega_2\left(A_2' + \mu_1 A_2\right) + \beta\Lambda_2 A_2'\right]\exp\left(i\omega_2 T_0\right) + \ldots + CC, \\
&D_0^2 y_2 + \alpha y_2 + \beta D_0 x_2 = \left[-2i\omega_1\Lambda_1\left(A_1' + \mu_2 A_1\right) - \beta A_1'\right]\exp\left(i\omega_1 T_0\right) + \\
&\left[-2i\omega_2\Lambda_2\left(A_2' + \mu_2 A_2\right) - \beta A_2'\right]\exp\left(i\omega_2 T_0\right) + \ldots + CC.
\end{aligned} \tag{8}$$

The terms, which do not influence solvability conditions, are not presented in the last equations and replaced by dots.
To determine the solvability conditions of (8), following to the method of undetermined coefficients we seek a particular solution in the form

$$x_2 = P_{11}\exp\left(i\omega_1 T_0\right) + P_{12}\exp\left(i\omega_2 T_0\right),$$

$$y_2 = P_{21}\exp\left(i\omega_1 T_0\right) + P_{22}\exp\left(i\omega_2 T_0\right) \tag{9}$$

with unknowns P_{11}, P_{12}, P_{21} and P_{22}. Substitution of expressions (9) into (8) and collection of coefficients at $\exp\left(i\omega_1 T_0\right)$ and $\exp\left(i\omega_2 T_0\right)$ yields

$$\left(\alpha - \omega_n^2\right)P_{1n} - i\beta\omega_n P_{2n} = R_{1n}\,,$$

$$i\beta\omega_n P_{1n} + \left(\alpha - \omega_n^2\right)P_{2n} = R_{2n} \qquad \text{(n=1,2)}, \tag{10}$$

where

$$R_{11} = -2i\omega_1\left(A_1' + \mu_1 A_1\right) + \beta\Lambda_1 A_1',\quad R_{12} = -2i\omega_2\left(A_2' + \mu_1 A_2\right) + \beta\Lambda_2 A_2',$$
$$R_{21} = -2i\omega_1\Lambda_1\left(A_1' + \mu_2 A_1\right) - \beta A_1',\quad R_{22} = -2i\omega_2\Lambda_2\left(A_2' + \mu_2 A_2\right) - \beta A_2'.$$

Taking into account the characteristic equation (7), the determinant Δ of the set of linear algebraic equations relative to P_{1n}, P_{2n} (10) is equal to zero

$$\Delta = \begin{vmatrix} \alpha - \omega_n^2 & -i\beta\omega_n \\ i\beta\omega_n & \alpha - \omega_n^2 \end{vmatrix} = \left(\alpha - \omega_n^2\right)^2 - \beta^2\omega_n^2 = 0\,.$$

According to Kronecker-Kapelly's theorem, the set of linear algebraic equations is compatible if and only if the matrix rank of the linear set is equal to the extended matrix rank. Therefore, the solvability conditions are

$$\begin{vmatrix} R_{1n} & -i\beta\omega_n \\ R_{2n} & \left(\alpha - \omega_n^2\right) \end{vmatrix} = 0 \qquad \text{(n=1,2)},$$

otherwise the set of linear algebraic equations (10) has no solutions.
So,

$$R_{1n} = \frac{i\beta\omega_n R_{2n}}{\omega_n^2 - \alpha}$$

and the solvability conditions can be written in the form

$$R_{1n} = \frac{R_{2n}}{\bar{\Lambda}_n} \qquad \text{(n=1,2).} \tag{11}$$

The differential equations to define $A_1(T_1)$ and $A_2(T_1)$ are the consequence of solvability conditions (11)

$$\begin{aligned}
&\left(\beta\Lambda_1 - 2i\omega_1 + \frac{2i\omega_1\Lambda_1 + \beta}{\bar{\Lambda}_1}\right)A_1' + \left(\frac{2i\omega_1\Lambda_1\mu_2}{\bar{\Lambda}_1} - 2i\omega_1\mu_1\right)A_1 = 0,\\
&\left(\beta\Lambda_2 - 2i\omega_2 + \frac{2i\omega_2\Lambda_2 + \beta}{\bar{\Lambda}_2}\right)A_2' + \left(\frac{2i\omega_2\Lambda_2\mu_2}{\bar{\Lambda}_2} - 2i\omega_2\mu_1\right)A_2 = 0.
\end{aligned} \tag{12}$$

It follows from (3), (6) and (12) that the complex solution of the differential set (2) is

$$\begin{aligned}
&x = \varepsilon\left[\exp(-\varepsilon\nu_1 t)a_1\exp(i\omega_1 t) + \exp(-\varepsilon\nu_2 t)a_2\exp(i\omega_2 t) + \Phi_1\exp\left[i(\Omega t + \tau)\right] + CC\right] + O\left(\varepsilon^2\right),\\
&y = \varepsilon\left[\Lambda_1\exp(-\varepsilon\nu_1 t)a_1\exp(i\omega_1 t) + \Lambda_2\exp(-\varepsilon\nu_2 t)a_2\exp(i\omega_2 t) + \Phi_2\exp\left[i(\Omega t + \tau)\right] + CC\right] + O\left(\varepsilon^2\right).
\end{aligned}$$

Then the real solution is as follows

$$\begin{aligned}
&x = \varepsilon\left[\exp(-\varepsilon\nu_1 t)a_1\cos(\omega_1 t + \Theta_1) + \exp(-\varepsilon\nu_2 t)a_2\cos(\omega_2 t + \Theta_2) + 2\operatorname{Im}\Phi_1\sin(\Omega t + \tau)\right] + O\left(\varepsilon^2\right),\\
&y = \varepsilon\left[\operatorname{Im}\Lambda_1\exp(-\varepsilon\nu_1 t)a_1\sin(\omega_1 t + \Theta_1) + \operatorname{Im}\Lambda_2\exp(-\varepsilon\nu_2 t)\times\right.\\
&\left.a_2\sin(\omega_2 t + \Theta_2) + 2\Phi_2\cos(\Omega t + \tau)\right] + O\left(\varepsilon^2\right),
\end{aligned} \tag{13}$$

where $\nu_n = \dfrac{2\omega_n(\mu_1 + \mu_2)}{4\omega_n - \beta\left(\operatorname{Im}\Lambda_n + \dfrac{1}{\operatorname{Im}\Lambda_n}\right)}$, a_n and Θ_n are the real constants.

Figure 2 shows a comparison of the numerical integration of (2) and the perturbation solutions (13). The following parameters of set (2) were accepted for all cases (a). (b), (c) α=1500, β=70, α_1=9.985×10^2, α_2=2×10^3, α_3=7.9588×10^3, α_4= 0.002, α_5= -4.0794×10^3, α_6=4.0002×10^3, α_7=8.0005×10^3, β_1=29.9975, β_2= -0.001, β_3= -4.1594×10^3, β_4= -1.9997×10^3, β_5= -7.9188×10^3, β_6=0.7959, β_7= -0.4083; initial conditions are the following $x(0)=10^{-12}$, $y(0)=10^{-10}$, $\dot{x}(0) = \dot{y}(0) = 0$.
In the case of non-resonant undamped vibrations of the rotor (Fig. 2 (a)) it is accepted for numerical integration that $\hat{\mu}_1$ =0, $\hat{\mu}_2$ =0, F=0. According to (13), the perturbation solution is presented by the expressions

$$x=8.2686044\cdot 10^{-6}\cos(17.2015t)+1.6313956\cdot 10^{-6}\cos(87.2015t),$$

$$y=8.2686044 \cdot 10^{-6} \sin(17.2015t)-1.6313956 \cdot 10^{-6} \sin(87.2015t).$$

Fig. 2 (b) corresponds to the non-resonant damped vibrations of the rotor. For this case $\hat{\mu}_1=0.1$, $\hat{\mu}_2=0.15$, $F=0$. The perturbation solution has the form

$$x=8.2686044 \cdot 10^{-6} \exp(-0.0412t) \cos(17.2015t)+1.6313956 \cdot 10^{-6} \exp(-0.2088t) \cos(87.2015t),$$

$$y=8.2686044 \cdot 10^{-6} \exp(-0.0412t) \sin(17.2015t)-1.6313956 \cdot 10^{-6} \exp(-0.2088t) \sin(87.2015t).$$

For the non-resonant forced damped vibrations of the rotor (Fig. 2 (c)) it is accepted for numerical integration that $\hat{\mu}_1=0.1$, $\hat{\mu}_2=0.15$, $F=0.005$, $\Omega=10$, $\tau=-\pi/2$. The perturbation solution is

$$x=5.8241 \cdot 10^{-6} \exp(-0.0412t) \cos(17.2015t)+1.69495 \cdot 10^{-6} \exp(-0.2088t) \cos(87.2015t) - 2.38095 \cdot 10^{-6} \sin(10t-\pi/2),$$

$$y=5.8241 \cdot 10^{-6} \exp(-0.0412t) \sin(17.2015t)-1.69495 \cdot 10^{-6} \exp(-0.2088t) \sin(87.2015t) + 4.7619 \cdot 10^{-6} \cos(10t-\pi/2).$$

Fig. 2 demonstrates good agreement of the numerical and analytical solutions.

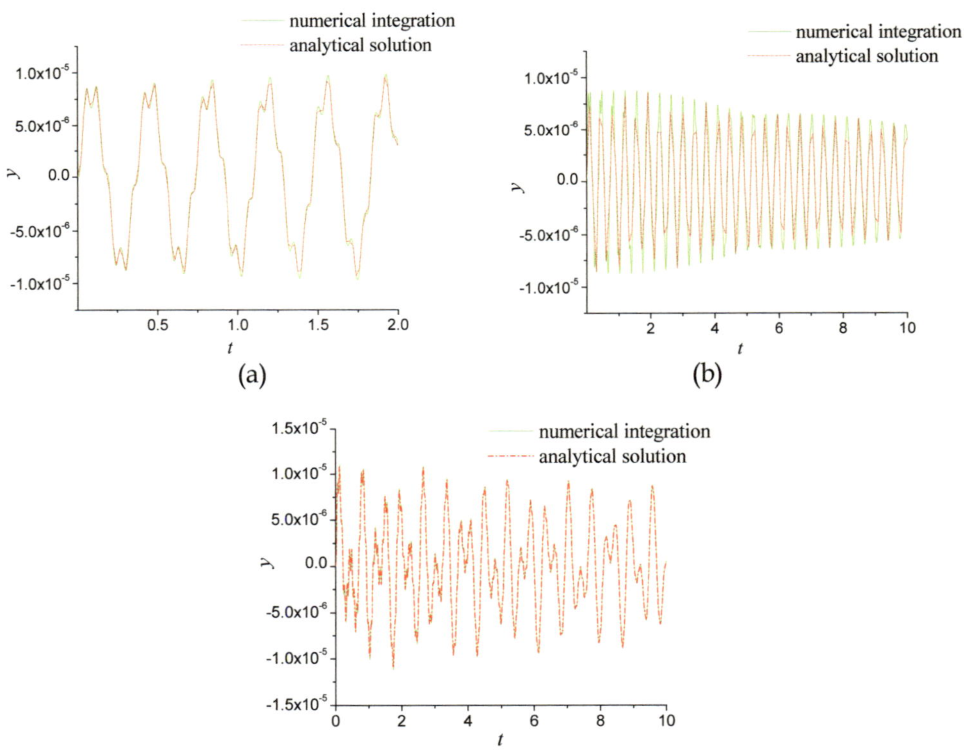

Fig. 2. Comparison of numerical integration (2) and perturbation solutions (13) in the case of (a) nonresonant undamped vibrations of the rotor, (b) nonresonant damped vibrations of the rotor; (c) nonresonant forced damped vibrations of the rotor

3.2 Primary resonance: The cases of no internal resonance and an internal resonance

To analyze primary resonances the forcing term is ordered so that it appears at order ε^2 or in the same perturbation equation as the non-linear terms and damping. Thus, we recall in (2) $F=\varepsilon^2 f$, $\hat{\mu}_n=\varepsilon\mu_n$. Consider the case in which $\Omega\approx\omega_2$. The case $\Omega\approx\omega_1$ is analogous. Let us introduce detuning parameter σ_1 and put $\Omega=\omega_2+\varepsilon\sigma_1$.

Substituting (3) into (2) and equating coefficients of similar powers of ε we obtain

Order ε

$$\begin{aligned} &D_0^2 x_1+\alpha x_1-\beta D_0 y_1=0,\\ &D_0^2 y_1+\alpha y_1+\beta D_0 x_1=0. \end{aligned} \tag{14}$$

Order ε^2

$$\begin{aligned} &D_0^2 x_2+\alpha x_2-\beta D_0 y_2=-2D_0\left(D_1 x_1+\mu_1 x_1\right)+\beta D_1 y_1+\alpha_1 x_1^2+\alpha_2 y_1^2+\\ &\alpha_3 x_1 D_0 x_1+\alpha_4 x_1 y_1+\alpha_5 x_1 D_0 y_1+\alpha_6 y_1 D_0 x_1+\alpha_7 y_1 D_0 y_1,\\ &D_0^2 y_2+\alpha y_2+\beta D_0 x_2=-2D_0\left(D_1 y_1+\mu_2 y_1\right)-\beta D_1 x_1+\beta_1 x_1^2+\beta_2 y_1^2+\\ &\beta_3 x_1 D_0 x_1+\beta_4 x_1 y_1+\beta_5 x_1 D_0 y_1+\beta_6 y_1 D_0 x_1+\beta_7 y_1 D_0 y_1+f\cos\left(\Omega T_0+\tau\right). \end{aligned} \tag{15}$$

The solution of (14) is given in the form

$$\begin{aligned} &x_1=A_1(T_1)\exp(i\omega_1 T_0)+A_2(T_1)\exp(i\omega_2 T_0)+CC,\\ &y_1=\Lambda_1 A_1(T_1)\exp(i\omega_1 T_0)+\Lambda_2 A_2(T_1)\exp(i\omega_2 T_0)+CC, \end{aligned} \tag{16}$$

where $\Lambda_n=\dfrac{\omega_n^2-\alpha}{\omega_n\beta}i$.

Substitution of (16) into (15) yields

$$\begin{aligned} &D_0^2 x_2+\alpha x_2-\beta D_0 y_2=\left[-2i\omega_1\left(A_1'+\mu_1 A_1\right)+\beta\Lambda_1 A_1'\right]\exp(i\omega_1 T_0)+\\ &\left[-2i\omega_2\left(A_2'+\mu_1 A_2\right)+\beta\Lambda_2 A_2'\right]\exp(i\omega_2 T_0)+\\ &A_1^2\left[\alpha_1+\Lambda_1^2\alpha_2+i\omega_1\alpha_3+\Lambda_1\alpha_4+i\omega_1\Lambda_1\alpha_5+i\omega_1\Lambda_1\alpha_6+i\omega_1\Lambda_1^2\alpha_7\right]\exp(2i\omega_1 T_0)+\\ &A_2^2\left[\alpha_1+\Lambda_2^2\alpha_2+i\omega_2\alpha_3+\Lambda_2\alpha_4+i\omega_2\Lambda_2\alpha_5+i\omega_2\Lambda_2\alpha_6+i\omega_2\Lambda_2^2\alpha_7\right]\exp(2i\omega_2 T_0)+ \end{aligned} \tag{17}$$

$$\begin{aligned} &A_1A_2\left[2\alpha_1+2\Lambda_1\Lambda_2\alpha_2+(i\omega_1+i\omega_2)\alpha_3+(\Lambda_1+\Lambda_2)\alpha_4+(i\omega_2\Lambda_2-i\omega_1\Lambda_1)\alpha_5+\right.\\ &\left.(i\omega_2\Lambda_1+i\omega_1\Lambda_2)\alpha_6+(i\omega_1+i\omega_2)\Lambda_1\Lambda_2\alpha_7\ \right]\exp(i(\omega_1+\omega_2)T_0)+\\ &\bar{A}_1A_2\left[2\alpha_1+2\bar{\Lambda}_1\Lambda_2\alpha_2+(i\omega_2-i\omega_1)\alpha_3+(\Lambda_2+\bar{\Lambda}_1)\alpha_4+(i\omega_2\Lambda_2-i\omega_1\bar{\Lambda}_1)\alpha_5+\right.\\ &\left.(i\omega_2\bar{\Lambda}_1-i\omega_1\Lambda_2)\alpha_6+(i\omega_2-i\omega_1)\bar{\Lambda}_1\Lambda_2\alpha_7\ \right]\exp(i(\omega_2-\omega_1)T_0)+\\ &A_1\bar{A}_1\left(\alpha_1+\Lambda_1\left(\bar{\Lambda}_1\alpha_2+\alpha_4+i\omega_1(\alpha_5-\alpha_6)\right)\right)+A_2\bar{A}_2\left(\alpha_1+\Lambda_2\left(\bar{\Lambda}_2\alpha_2+\alpha_4+i\omega_2(\alpha_5-\alpha_6)\right)\right)+CC, \end{aligned}$$

$$
\begin{aligned}
&D_0^2 y_2 + \alpha y_2 + \beta D_0 x_2 = \left[-2i\omega_1\Lambda_1\left(A_1' + \mu_2 A_1\right) - \beta A_1'\right]\exp(i\omega_1 T_0) + \\
&\left[-2i\omega_2\Lambda_2\left(A_2' + \mu_2 A_2\right) - \beta A_2'\right]\exp(i\omega_2 T_0) + \\
&A_1^2\left[\beta_1 + \Lambda_1^2\beta_2 + i\omega_1\beta_3 + \Lambda_1\beta_4 + i\omega_1\Lambda_1\beta_5 + i\omega_1\Lambda_1\beta_6 + i\omega_1\Lambda_1^2\beta_7\right]\exp(2i\omega_1 T_0) + \\
&A_2^2\left[\beta_1 + \Lambda_2^2\beta_2 + i\omega_2\beta_3 + \Lambda_2\beta_4 + i\omega_2\Lambda_2\beta_5 + i\omega_2\Lambda_2\beta_6 + i\omega_2\Lambda_2^2\beta_7\right]\exp(2i\omega_2 T_0) +
\end{aligned}
\tag{18}
$$

$$
\begin{aligned}
&A_1A_2\left[2\beta_1 + 2\Lambda_1\Lambda_2\beta_2 + (i\omega_1 + i\omega_2)\beta_3 + (\Lambda_1 + \Lambda_2)\beta_4 + (i\omega_2\Lambda_2 - i\omega_1\Lambda_1)\beta_5 + \right. \\
&\left.(i\omega_2\Lambda_1 + i\omega_1\Lambda_2)\beta_6 + (i\omega_1 + i\omega_2)\Lambda_1\Lambda_2\beta_7\right]\exp\left(i(\omega_1 + \omega_2)T_0\right) + \\
&\bar{A}_1A_2\left[2\beta_1 + 2\bar{\Lambda}_1\Lambda_2\beta_2 + (i\omega_2 - i\omega_1)\beta_3 + (\Lambda_2 + \bar{\Lambda}_1)\beta_4 + (i\omega_2\Lambda_2 - i\omega_1\bar{\Lambda}_1)\beta_5 + \right. \\
&\left.(i\omega_2\bar{\Lambda}_1 - i\omega_1\Lambda_2)\beta_6 + (i\omega_2 - i\omega_1)\bar{\Lambda}_1\Lambda_2\beta_7\right]\exp\left(i(\omega_2 - \omega_1)T_0\right) + \\
&A_1\bar{A}_1\left(\beta_1 + \Lambda_1\left(\bar{\Lambda}_1\beta_2 + \beta_4 + i\omega_1(\beta_5 - \beta_6)\right)\right) + A_2\bar{A}_2\left(\beta_1 + \Lambda_2\left(\bar{\Lambda}_2\beta_2 + \beta_4 + i\omega_2(\beta_5 - \beta_6)\right)\right) + \\
&\frac{1}{2} f \exp\left(i(\omega_2 T_0 + \sigma_1 T_1 + \tau)\right) + CC.
\end{aligned}
$$

Let $\omega_2 > \omega_1$ for definiteness. We need to distinguish between the case of internal resonance $\omega_2 \approx 2\omega_1$ and the case of no internal resonance, i.e., ω_2 is away from $2\omega_1$. The case $\omega_1 > \omega_2$, $\omega_1 \approx 2\omega_2$ is analogous. When ω_2 is away from $2\omega_1$ the solvability conditions (11) are written in the form

$$
\begin{aligned}
&q_{\omega_1} + \frac{1}{\Lambda_1} p_{\omega_1} = 0, \\
&q_{\omega_2} + \frac{1}{\Lambda_2} p_{\omega_2} + \frac{1}{2\Lambda_2} f \exp\left(i(\sigma_1 T_1 + \tau)\right) = 0,
\end{aligned}
$$

where

$$
q_{\omega_1} = -2i\omega_1\left(A_1' + \mu_1 A_1\right) + \beta\Lambda_1 A_1', \quad q_{\omega_2} = 2i\omega_2\left(A_2' + \mu_1 A_2\right) + \beta\Lambda_2 A_2',
$$

$$
p_{\omega_1} = -2i\omega_1\Lambda_1\left(A_1' + \mu_2 A_1\right) - \beta A_1', \quad p_{\omega_2} = -2i\omega_2\Lambda_2\left(A_2' + \mu_2 A_2\right) - \beta A_2'.
$$

Thus, when there is no internal resonance, the first approximation is not influenced by the non-linear terms; it is essentially a solution of the corresponding linear problem.
Actually, the solutions of the differential equations below

$$
\begin{aligned}
&\left(\beta\Lambda_1 - 2i\omega_1 + \frac{2i\omega_1\Lambda_1 + \beta}{\bar{\Lambda}_1}\right)A_1' + \left(\frac{2i\omega_1\Lambda_1\mu_2}{\bar{\Lambda}_1} - 2i\omega_1\mu_1\right)A_1 = 0, \\
&\left(\beta\Lambda_2 - 2i\omega_2 + \frac{2i\omega_2\Lambda_2 + \beta}{\bar{\Lambda}_2}\right)A_2' + \left(\frac{2i\omega_2\Lambda_2\mu_2}{\bar{\Lambda}_2} - 2i\omega_2\mu_1\right)A_2 = -\frac{1}{2\Lambda_2} f \exp\left[i(\sigma_1 T_1 + \tau)\right]
\end{aligned}
$$

are

$$
A_1(T_1) = \frac{1}{2} a_1 \exp\left(-\nu_1 T_1 + i\Theta_1\right),
$$

$$A_2(T_1)=\frac{1}{2}a_2\exp(-\nu_2T_1+i\Theta_2)+\frac{f(\nu_2-i\sigma_1)}{2\operatorname{Im}\Lambda_2\operatorname{Im}\kappa_2\left(\nu_2^2+\sigma_1^2\right)}\exp\left[i(\sigma_1T_1+\tau)\right],$$

where a_n and Θ_n are the real constants,

$$\nu_n=\frac{2\omega_n(\mu_1+\mu_2)}{4\omega_n-\beta\left(\operatorname{Im}\Lambda_n+\dfrac{1}{\operatorname{Im}\Lambda_n}\right)},\ \kappa_2=-4\omega_2 i+\beta\left(\operatorname{Im}\Lambda_2+\frac{1}{\operatorname{Im}\Lambda_2}\right)i.$$

As $t\to\infty$, $T_1\to\infty$ and

$$A_1\to 0,\ A_2\to\frac{f(\nu_2-i\sigma_1)}{2\operatorname{Im}\Lambda_2\operatorname{Im}\kappa_2\left(\nu_2^2+\sigma_1^2\right)}\exp\left[i(\sigma_1T_1+\tau)\right] \tag{19}$$

according to (16), we obtain the following steady-state response:

$$x_1=\frac{f(\nu_2-i\sigma_1)}{2\operatorname{Im}\Lambda_2\operatorname{Im}\kappa_2\left(\nu_2^2+\sigma_1^2\right)}\exp\left[i(\omega_2T_0+\sigma_1T_1+\tau)\right]+CC,$$

$$y_1=\Lambda_2\frac{f(\nu_2-i\sigma_1)}{2\operatorname{Im}\Lambda_2\operatorname{Im}\kappa_2\left(\nu_2^2+\sigma_1^2\right)}\exp\left[i(\omega_2T_0+\sigma_1T_1+\tau)\right]+CC.$$

Therefore, the real solution is

$$x=\frac{F}{\varepsilon}\frac{1}{\operatorname{Im}\Lambda_2\operatorname{Im}\kappa_2\left(\nu_2^2+\sigma_1^2\right)}\left[\nu_2\cos(\Omega t+\tau)+\sigma_1\sin(\Omega t+\tau)\right]+O\left(\varepsilon^2\right),$$

$$y=\frac{F}{\varepsilon}\frac{1}{\operatorname{Im}\kappa_2\left(\nu_2^2+\sigma_1^2\right)}\left[\sigma_1\cos(\Omega t+\tau)-\nu_2\sin(\Omega t+\tau)\right]+O\left(\varepsilon^2\right),$$

or it can be rewritten in the form

$$\begin{aligned}x&=\frac{F}{\varepsilon}\frac{1}{\operatorname{Im}\Lambda_2\operatorname{Im}\kappa_2\left(\nu_2^2+\sigma_1^2\right)^{1/2}}\sin(\Omega t+\tau+\tilde{\gamma}_1)+O\left(\varepsilon^2\right),\\ y&=\frac{F}{\varepsilon}\frac{1}{\operatorname{Im}\kappa_2\left(\nu_2^2+\sigma_1^2\right)^{1/2}}\sin(\Omega t+\tau+\tilde{\gamma}_2)+O\left(\varepsilon^2\right),\end{aligned} \tag{20}$$

where $\tilde{\gamma}_1=arctg(\nu_2/\sigma_1)$, $\tilde{\gamma}_2=-arctg(\sigma_1/\nu_2)$.
Other situation occurs when the internal resonance $\omega_2\approx 2\omega_1$ exists. Let us introduce detuning parameter σ_2 and put $\omega_2=2\omega_1-\varepsilon\sigma_2$.
Taking into account (11), the solvability conditions for this case become

$$\begin{aligned}&q_{\omega_1}+\frac{1}{\Lambda_1}p_{\omega_1}+\left(q_{\omega_2-\omega_1}+\frac{1}{\Lambda_1}p_{\omega_2-\omega_1}\right)\bar{A}_1A_2\exp(-i\sigma_2T_1)=0,\\ &q_{\omega_2}+\frac{1}{\Lambda_2}p_{\omega_2}+\left(q_{2\omega_1}+\frac{1}{\Lambda_2}p_{2\omega_1}\right)A_1^2\exp(i\sigma_2T_1)+\frac{1}{2\Lambda_2}f\exp(i(\sigma_1T_1+\tau))=0.\end{aligned} \tag{21}$$

Here coefficients $q_{\omega 1}$, $q_{\omega 2}$, $q_{\omega 2-\omega 1}$, $q_{2\omega 1}$ are the expressions in the bracket at the exponents with the corresponding powers (17) and $p_{\omega 1}$, $p_{\omega 2}$, $p_{\omega 2-\omega 1}$, $p_{2\omega 1}$ are the expressions in the bracket at the exponents with the corresponding powers (18):

$$q_{\omega_1} = -2i\omega_1\left(A_1' + \mu_1 A_1\right) + \beta\Lambda_1 A_1', \quad q_{\omega_2} = 2i\omega_2\left(A_2' + \mu_1 A_2\right) + \beta\Lambda_2 A_2',$$

$$q_{2\omega_1} = \alpha_1 + \Lambda_1^2\alpha_2 + i\omega_1\alpha_3 + \Lambda_1\alpha_4 + i\omega_1\Lambda_1\alpha_5 + i\omega_1\Lambda_1\alpha_6 + i\omega_1\Lambda_1^2\alpha_7,$$

$$q_{\omega_2-\omega_1} = 2\alpha_1 + 2\bar{\Lambda}_1\Lambda_2\alpha_2 + \left(i\omega_2 - i\omega_1\right)\alpha_3 + \left(\Lambda_2 + \bar{\Lambda}_1\right)\alpha_4 + \left(i\omega_2\Lambda_2 - i\omega_1\bar{\Lambda}_1\right)\alpha_5 +$$
$$\left(i\omega_2\bar{\Lambda}_1 - i\omega_1\Lambda_2\right)\alpha_6 + \left(i\omega_2 - i\omega_1\right)\bar{\Lambda}_1\Lambda_2\alpha_7,$$

$$p_{\omega_1} = -2i\omega_1\Lambda_1\left(A_1' + \mu_2 A_1\right) - \beta A_1', \quad p_{\omega_2} = -2i\omega_2\Lambda_2\left(A_2' + \mu_2 A_2\right) - \beta A_2',$$

$$p_{2\omega_1} = \beta_1 + \Lambda_1^2\beta_2 + i\omega_1\beta_3 + \Lambda_1\beta_4 + i\omega_1\Lambda_1\beta_5 + i\omega_1\Lambda_1\beta_6 + i\omega_1\Lambda_1^2\beta_7,$$

$$p_{\omega_2-\omega_1} = 2\beta_1 + 2\bar{\Lambda}_1\Lambda_2\beta_2 + \left(i\omega_2 - i\omega_1\right)\beta_3 + \left(\Lambda_2 + \bar{\Lambda}_1\right)\beta_4 + \left(i\omega_2\Lambda_2 - i\omega_1\bar{\Lambda}_1\right)\beta_5 +$$
$$\left(i\omega_2\bar{\Lambda}_1 - i\omega_1\Lambda_2\right)\beta_6 + \left(i\omega_2 - i\omega_1\right)\bar{\Lambda}_1\Lambda_2\beta_7.$$

For the convenience let us introduce the polar notation

$$A_m = \frac{1}{2}a_m \exp\left(i\Theta_m\right), \quad m = 1, 2, \tag{22}$$

where a_m and Θ_m are the real functions of T_1.
Substitution of (22) into (21) yields

$$\begin{aligned}
&\left(a_1' + ia_1\Theta_1'\right) + \nu_1 a_1 + \frac{1}{2\kappa_1}a_1 a_2\left[\varphi + i\psi\right]\exp\left(i\gamma_2\right) = 0,\\
&\left(a_2' + ia_2\Theta_2'\right) + \nu_2 a_2 + \frac{1}{2\kappa_2}a_1^2\left[\zeta + i\eta\right]\exp\left(-i\gamma_2\right) + \frac{f}{\kappa_2\Lambda_2}\exp\left(i\gamma_1\right) = 0.
\end{aligned} \tag{23}$$

In the expressions above the following notations were introduced

$$\varphi = \mathrm{Re}\left(q_{\omega_2-\omega_1} + \frac{1}{\Lambda_1}p_{\omega_2-\omega_1}\right), \quad \psi = \mathrm{Im}\left(q_{\omega_2-\omega_1} + \frac{1}{\Lambda_1}p_{\omega_2-\omega_1}\right), \quad \zeta = \mathrm{Re}\left(q_{2\omega_1} + \frac{1}{\Lambda_2}p_{2\omega_1}\right),$$

$$\eta = \mathrm{Im}\left(q_{2\omega_1} + \frac{1}{\Lambda_2}p_{2\omega_1}\right), \quad \kappa_n = -4\omega_n i + \beta\left(\mathrm{Im}\,\Lambda_n + \frac{1}{\mathrm{Im}\,\Lambda_n}\right)i, \quad n = 1, 2,$$

$$\gamma_1 = \sigma_1 T_1 + \tau - \Theta_2, \quad \gamma_2 = \Theta_2 - 2\Theta_1 - \sigma_2 T_1,$$

ν_1 and ν_2 are defined as in Eq (13).
Separating Eqs. (23) into real and imaginary parts and taking into account that according to (6) Λ_n (n=1,2) is the imaginary value, we obtain

$$a_1' = -\nu_1 a_1 - \frac{a_1 a_2}{2\operatorname{Im}\kappa_1}(\psi\cos\gamma_2 + \varphi\sin\gamma_2),$$

$$a_1\Theta_1' = \frac{a_1 a_2}{2\operatorname{Im}\kappa_1}(\varphi\cos\gamma_2 - \psi\sin\gamma_2), \tag{24}$$

$$a_2' = -\nu_2 a_2 - \frac{a_1^2}{2\operatorname{Im}\kappa_2}(\eta\cos\gamma_2 - \zeta\sin\gamma_2) + \frac{f}{\operatorname{Im}\kappa_2\operatorname{Im}\Lambda_2}\cos\gamma_1,$$

$$a_2\Theta_2' = \frac{a_1^2}{2\operatorname{Im}\kappa_2}(\zeta\cos\gamma_2 + \eta\sin\gamma_2) + \frac{f}{\operatorname{Im}\kappa_2\operatorname{Im}\Lambda_2}\sin\gamma_1 .$$

For the steady-state response $a_n' = \gamma_n' = 0$, therefore $\Theta_1' = \frac{1}{2}(\sigma_1 - \sigma_2)$, $\Theta_2' = \sigma_1$.

Two possibilities follow from (24). The first one is given by (19). It is the solution of the linear problem. Let us find functions a_1 and a_2 of T_1 according to the second possibility. It follows from the first two Eqs. (24) that

$$\frac{4\omega_1(\mu_1 + \mu_2)}{a_2} = -\psi\cos\gamma_2 - \varphi\sin\gamma_2,$$

$$\frac{\operatorname{Im}\kappa_1}{a_2}(\sigma_1 - \sigma_2) = \varphi\cos\gamma_2 - \psi\sin\gamma_2 .$$

So,

$$a_2 = \left(\frac{16\omega_1^2(\mu_1 + \mu_2)^2 + \operatorname{Im}\kappa_1^2\left((\sigma_1 - \sigma_2)^2\right)}{\varphi^2 + \psi^2}\right)^{1/2}. \tag{25}$$

Let us take $\sin\gamma_2$ and $\cos\gamma_2$ using, for example, the formulas by Cramer

$$\cos\gamma_2 = \frac{\Delta_1}{\Delta},\quad \sin\gamma_2 = \frac{\Delta_2}{\Delta},\ \text{where}\ \Delta = \begin{vmatrix} -\psi & -\varphi \\ \varphi & -\psi \end{vmatrix} = \varphi^2 + \psi^2,$$

$$\Delta_1 = -\frac{1}{a_2}\begin{vmatrix} 2\operatorname{Im}\kappa_1\nu_1 & \varphi \\ \operatorname{Im}\kappa_1(\sigma_1 - \sigma_2) & \psi \end{vmatrix} = \frac{1}{a_2}\left(4\omega_1(\mu_1 + \mu_2)\psi + \operatorname{Im}\kappa_1(\sigma_1 - \sigma_2)\varphi\right),$$

$$\Delta_2 = \frac{1}{a_2}\begin{vmatrix} -\psi & 2\operatorname{Im}\kappa_1\nu_1 \\ \varphi & \operatorname{Im}\kappa_1(\sigma_1 - \sigma_2) \end{vmatrix} = \frac{1}{a_2}\left(-\operatorname{Im}\kappa_1(\sigma_1 - \sigma_2)\psi - 4\omega_1(\mu_1 + \mu_2)\varphi\right).$$

Then a biquadratic equation relative to a_1 follows from the last two Eqs. (24)

$$a_1^4\left(\zeta^2 + \eta^2\right) + 4a_1^2\left[-2\omega_2(\mu_1 + \mu_2)a_2(\eta\cos\gamma_2 - \zeta\sin\gamma_2) - \operatorname{Im}\kappa_2\sigma_1 a_2(\zeta\cos\gamma_2 + \eta\sin\gamma_2)\right] +$$

$$4\left[4\omega_2^2(\mu_1+\mu_2)^2+\operatorname{Im}\kappa_2^2\sigma_1^2\right]a_2^2-\frac{4f^2}{(\operatorname{Im}\Lambda_2)^2}=0\,.$$

Finally, we obtain the expression for a_1:

$$a_1=\left[-\frac{p}{2}\pm\left(\left(\frac{p}{2}\right)^2-q\right)^{\frac{1}{2}}\right]^{\frac{1}{2}}, \tag{26}$$

where

$$p=\frac{4a_2}{\zeta^2+\eta^2}\left[-2\omega_2(\mu_1+\mu_2)(\eta\cos\gamma_2-\zeta\sin\gamma_2)-\operatorname{Im}\kappa_2\sigma_1(\zeta\cos\gamma_2+\eta\sin\gamma_2)\right],$$

$$q=\frac{1}{\zeta^2+\eta^2}\left\{4a_2^2\left[4\omega_2^2(\mu_1+\mu_2)^2+\operatorname{Im}\kappa_2^2\sigma_1^2\right]-\frac{4f^2}{(\operatorname{Im}\Lambda_2)^2}\right\}.$$

Thus, the unknown functions in (16) were defined. It follows from (3), (16) and (22) that

$$x=\varepsilon\left[\frac{1}{2}a_1\exp\left[i(\Theta_1+\omega_1T_0)\right]+\frac{1}{2}a_2\exp\left[i(\Theta_2+\omega_2T_0)\right]+CC\right]+O\left(\varepsilon^2\right),$$
$$y=\varepsilon\left[\frac{1}{2}\Lambda_1a_1\exp\left[i(\Theta_1+\omega_1T_0)\right]+\frac{1}{2}\Lambda_2a_2\exp\left[i(\Theta_2+\omega_2T_0)\right]+CC\right]+O\left(\varepsilon^2\right).$$

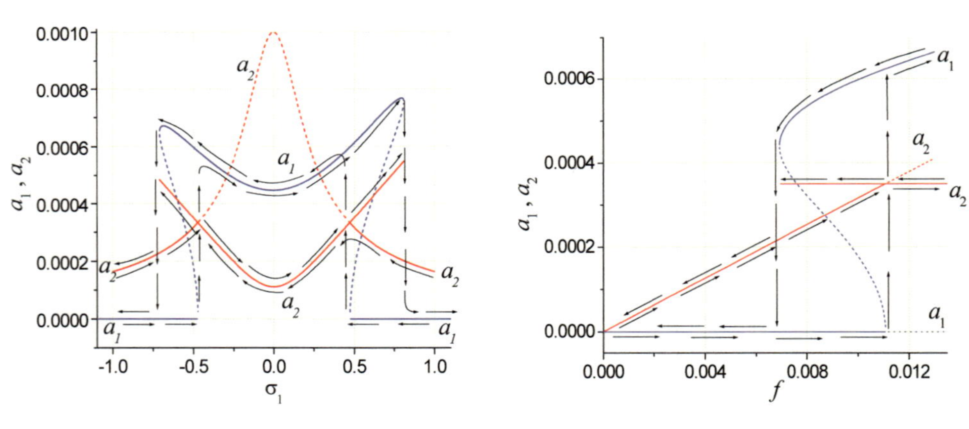

Fig. 3. (a) Frequency-response curves; σ_2=0, $\Omega\approx\omega_2$; (b) amplitudes a_1, a_2 versus the amplitude of external excitation f; $\Omega\approx\omega_2$, σ_1= –0.5, σ_2= 0

Then, the real solution is as follows

$$x = \varepsilon \left\{ a_1 \cos\left[\frac{1}{2}(\Omega t + \tau - \gamma_1 - \gamma_2) \right] + a_2 \cos(\Omega t + \tau - \gamma_1) \right\} + O(\varepsilon^2),$$
$$y = -\varepsilon \left\{ a_1 \operatorname{Im} \Lambda_1 \sin\left[\frac{1}{2}(\Omega t + \tau - \gamma_1 - \gamma_2) \right] + a_2 \operatorname{Im} \Lambda_2 \sin(\Omega t + \tau - \gamma_1) \right\} + O(\varepsilon^2). \quad (27)$$

Here a_1 and a_2 are defined by (25), (26).

Let us consider the expression for a_1 (26). When $\{[(p/2) > 0] \wedge (q > 0)\} \vee [(p/2)^2 < q]$, there are no real values of a_1 defined by (26) and the response must be given by (20). When $[(p/2)^2 > q] \wedge (q < 0)$, there is one real solution defined by (26). Therefore, the response is one of the two possibilities given by (20) and (27). When $[(p/2) < 0] \wedge [(p/2)^2 > q] \wedge (q > 0)$, there are two real solutions defined by (26). Therefore, the response is one of the three possibilities given by (20) and (27).

In Fig. 3 (a) the frequency–response curves are depicted. a_1 and a_2 are plotted as a function of σ_1 for σ_2=0. The dashed line having a peak at σ_1=0 corresponds to a_1=0 and it is a solution of the corresponding linear problem. Arrows indicate the jump phenomenon associated with varying the frequency of external excitation Ω. Perturbation solution obtained is the superposition of two submotions with amplitudes a_1 and a_2 and frequencies ω_1, ω_2 correspondingly. To compare the perturbation and numerical solutions we performed an approximate harmonic analysis of solutions x(t), y(t) obtained numerically. These functions are expanded in Fourier series formed of cosines

$$x(t) = \frac{a_0}{2} + \sum_{k=1}^{\infty} a_k \cos\frac{k\pi t}{T}, \quad a_k = \frac{2}{T}\int_0^T x(t)\cos\frac{k\pi t}{T} dt, \quad k=0,1,2\ldots,$$

where T is the period of integration, $0 \le t \le T$. The coefficients of the Fourier series were calculated approximately. The following parameters of set (2) were accepted: α=200, β= 10 (parameters α=200, β=10 correspond to natural frequencies ω_1=10, ω_2=20, i.e. ω_2=2ω_1), α_1=9.985×10^2, α_2=2×10^3, α_3=7.9588×10^3, α_4= 0.002, α_5= -4.0794×10^3, α_6=4.0002×10^3, α_7=8.0005×10^3, β_1=29.9975, β_2= -0.001, β_3= -4.1594×10^3, β_4= -1.9997×10^3, β_5= -7.9188×10^3, β_6=0.7959, β_7= -0.4083. The perturbation and numerical solutions of (2) are in good agreement.

In Fig. 3 (b) one can see saturation phenomenon. As f increases from zero, a_2 increases too until it reaches the value a_2=3.5×10^{-4} while a_1 is zero. This agrees with the solution of the corresponding linear problem. Then a_2 saves the constant value and a_1 starts to increase. Approximate harmonic analysis demonstrates good agreement of the theoretical prediction presented in Fig. 3 (b) and the corresponding numerical solution of (2).

4. Rigid magnetic materials. Conditions for chaotic vibrations of the rotor in various control parameter planes

In the case of rigid magnetic materials the hysteretic properties of system (1) can be considered using the Bouc–Wen hysteretic model. It was shown (Awrejcewicz & Dzyubak, 2007) that this modeling mechanism for energy dissipation was sufficiently accurate to model loops of various shapes in accordance with a real experiment, reflecting the behavior of hysteretic systems from very different fields. The hysteretic model of the rotor–MHDB system is as follows

$$\ddot{x} = P_r(\rho,\dot{\rho},\dot{\varphi})\cos\varphi - P_\tau(\rho,\dot{\varphi})\sin\varphi - \gamma_m\dot{x} - \lambda_m\left[\delta(x-x_0)+(1-\delta)z_1\right],$$

$$\ddot{y} = P_r(\rho,\dot{\rho},\dot{\varphi})\sin\varphi + P_\tau(\rho,\dot{\varphi})\cos\varphi - \gamma_m\dot{y} - \lambda_m\left[\delta(y-y_0)+(1-\delta)z_2\right] + Q_0 + Q\sin\Omega t, \quad (28)$$

$$\dot{z}_1 = \left[k_z - \left(\gamma + \beta\,\mathrm{sgn}(\dot{x})\,\mathrm{sgn}(z_1)\right)|z_1|^n\right]\dot{x},$$

$$\dot{z}_2 = \left[k_z - \left(\gamma + \beta\,\mathrm{sgn}(\dot{y})\,\mathrm{sgn}(z_2)\right)|z_2|^n\right]\dot{y}.$$

Here z_1 and z_2 are the hysteretic forces. The case $\delta=0$ corresponds to maximal hysteretic dissipation and $\delta=1$ corresponds to the absence of hysteretic forces in the system, parameters (k_z, β, n)$\in R^+$ and $\gamma \in R$ govern the shape of the hysteresis loops.

Conditions for chaotic vibrations of the rotor have been found using the approach based on the analysis of the wandering trajectories. The description of the approach, its advantages over standard procedures and a comparison with other approaches can be found, for example, in (Awrejcewicz & Dzyubak, 2007; Awrejcewicz & Mosdorf, 2003; Awrejcewicz et al., 2005).

The stability of motion depends on all the parameters of system (28), including initial conditions. We traced the irregular vibrations of the rotor to sufficient accuracy in the parametric planes of amplitude of external excitation versus hysteretic dissipation (δ, Q), the amplitude versus frequency of external excitation (Ω, Q), the amplitude versus dynamic oil-film action characteristics (C, Q) and the amplitude versus the magnetic control parameters (γ_m, Q), (λ_m, Q).

It should be noted, that chaos is not found in absence of hysteresis when $\delta=1$. Chaotic vibrations of the rotor are caused by hysteresis and for all chaotic regions presented $\delta\neq 1$. So, in system (28) chaos was quantified using the following conditions

$$\exists t^* \in [t_1,T] : \left\{\left(\left|x(t^*)-\tilde{x}(t^*)\right| > \alpha A_x\right) \vee \left(\left|y(t^*)-\tilde{y}(t^*)\right| > \alpha A_y\right)\right\} \quad (29)$$

⇓ chaotic vibrations in the horizontal direction

⇓ chaotic vibrations in the vertical direction

Here $x(t)$, $\tilde{x}(t)$ and $y(t)$, $\tilde{y}(t)$ are nearby trajectories respectively, A_x and A_y are the characteristic vibration amplitudes of the rotor in the horizontal and vertical direction respectively

$$A_x = \frac{1}{2}\left|\max_{t_1\le t\le T} x(t) - \min_{t_1\le t\le T} x(t)\right|,\quad A_y = \frac{1}{2}\left|\max_{t_1\le t\le T} y(t) - \min_{t_1\le t\le T} y(t)\right|.$$

$[t_1,T]\subset[t_0,T]$ and $[t_0,T]$ is the time interval over which the trajectories are considered. The interval $[t_0,t_1]$ is the time interval over which all transient processes are damped. The parameter α introduced is an auxiliary parameter such that $0<\alpha<1$. αA_x, αA_y are referred to as the divergence measures of the observable trajectories in the horizontal and vertical directions and, with the aid of the chosen parameter α, are inadmissible for the case of regularity of the motion.

If the inequality (29) is satisfied in some nodal point of the sampled control parameter space, then the motion is chaotic (including transient and alternating chaos). The manifold of all such nodal points of the investigated control parameter space defines the domains of chaotic behaviour for the considered system.

Figure 4 (a) displays the regions of rotor chaotic vibrations in (δ, Q) plane. The part of this plane ($10^{-7}<\delta\leq 0.0017$; $0.00125<Q\leq 0.00185$) was sampled by means of an uniform rectangular grid. For this aim two families of straight lines were drawn through dividing points of the axes

$$\delta^{i} = i\Delta\delta \quad (i=0, 1,\ldots, 120),$$

$$Q^{j} = j\Delta Q \quad (j=0, 1,\ldots, 120).$$

Here $\Delta\delta=1.4165\times 10^{-5}$, $\Delta Q=5\times 10^{-6}$.

The time period for the simulation T is of $\dfrac{200\pi}{\Omega}$ in nondimentional time units. During the computations, two thirds of the time period T corresponds to the time interval $[t_0,t_1]$, where transient processes are damped. The integration step size is $0.02\dfrac{\pi}{\Omega}$. Initial conditions of the nearby trajectories are differed less than 0.5% of characteristic vibration amplitudes, e.g. the starting points of these trajectories are in the rectangle ($|x(t_0)-\tilde{x}(t_0)|<0.005A_x$, $|y(t_0)-\tilde{y}(t_0)|<0.005A_y$). The parameter α is chosen to be equal to $\dfrac{1}{3}$.

All domains have complex structure. There are a number of scattered points, streaks and islets here. Such a structure is characteristic of domains where chaotic vibrations are possible. For each aggregate of control parameters there is some critical value of the hysteretic dissipation ($1-\delta_{cr}$) that if ($1-\delta$)<($1-\delta_{cr}$), chaos is not observed in the system considered.

In Fig. 4 (b) chaotic regions for the vertical vibrations of the rotor are depicted in the (Ω, Q) parametric plane ($0.25<\Omega\leq 1.2$; $0.0015<Q\leq 0.0022$). The time period for the simulation T and other numerical integration characteristics are the same as for (δ, Q) parametric plane, $\Delta\Omega=7.91667\times 10^{-3}$, 5.83333×10^{-6}. Numerical experiments show that for the larger hysteretic dissipation the chaotic regions areas are increased.

Figure 5 shows the phase portrait (a), hysteretic loop (b) and Poincaré map (e) of chaotic motion of the rotor. Parameters of motion correspond to the parameters of chaotic region depicted in Fig. 4 (b). The phase portrait (c), hysteretic loop (d) and Poincaré map (f) of the periodic rotor motion are also agree well with the obtained regions of regular/irregular behaviour of the rotor depicted in Fig. 4 (b). The influence of the magnetic control parameters γ_m, λ_m on chaos occurring in the rotor vibrations can be observed in Fig. 6. The (γ_m, Q) (a) and (λ_m, Q) (b) parametric planes were uniformly sampled by120×120 nodal points in the rectangles ($0<\gamma_m\leq 0.09$; $0.00165<Q\leq 0.0019$), $\Delta\gamma_m=7.5\times 10^{-4}$, $\Delta Q=2.08333\times 10^{-6}$; ($450<\lambda_m\leq 630$; $0.00145<Q\leq 0.0025$), $\Delta\lambda_m=1.5$, $\Delta Q=8.75\times 10^{-6}$. The influence of the dynamic oil-film action characteristics on chaos occurring in the rotor motion can be observed in Fig. 7. One can see the restraining of chaotic regions with

decreasing of hysteretic dissipation (1-δ). The (C, Q) parametric plane was uniformly sampled by 120×120 nodal points in the rectangles ($0<C\leq1.5$; $0.0015<Q\leq0.0021$), $\Delta C=0.0125$, $\Delta Q=5\times10^{-6}$ (a) and ($0<C\leq1.5$; $0.0015<Q\leq0.00225$), $\Delta C=0.0125$, $\Delta Q=6.25\times10^{-6}$ (b). The time period for the simulation T and other numerical integration characteristics are the same as for (δ, Q) parametric plane.

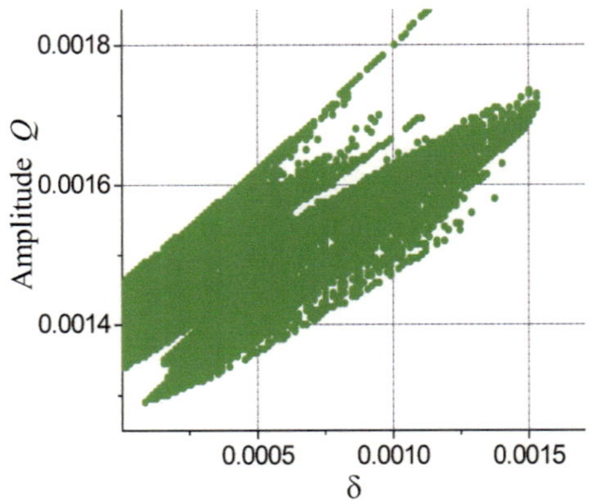

(a)

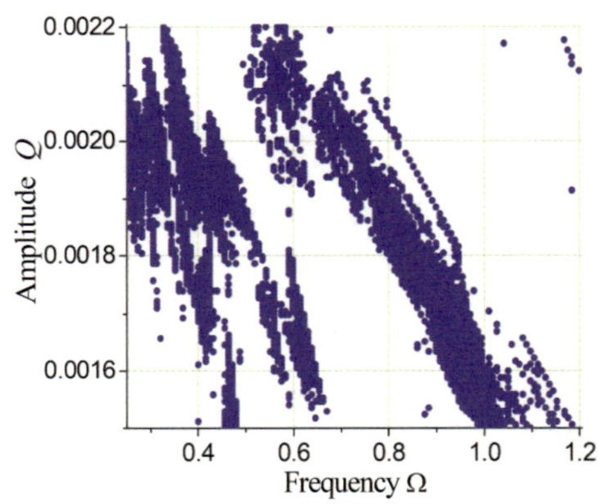

(b)

Fig. 4. (a) The influence of hysteretic dissipation parameter δ on chaos occurring in vertical vibrations of the rotor (28) in the case of rigid magnetic materials. The following parameters are fixed: C=0.03, γ_m=0.001, λ_m=450, k_z=0.000055, γ=15, β=0.25, n=1.0, Ω=0.87, Q_0=0, x_0=0, y_0=0, $x(0)=y(0)=10^{-8}$, $\dot{x}(0)=\dot{y}(0)=0$, $z_1(0)=z_2(0)=0$;
(b) chaotic regions for the vertical vibrations of the rotor in the (Ω, Q) parametric plane with other parameters of the system fixed: δ=0.0001, C=0.2, γ_m=0, λ_m=500, k_z=0.000055, γ=15, β=0.25, n=1.0, Q_0=0, x_0=0, y_0=0, $x(0)=y(0)=10^{-8}$, $\dot{x}(0)=\dot{y}(0)=0$, $z_1(0)=z_2(0)=0$.

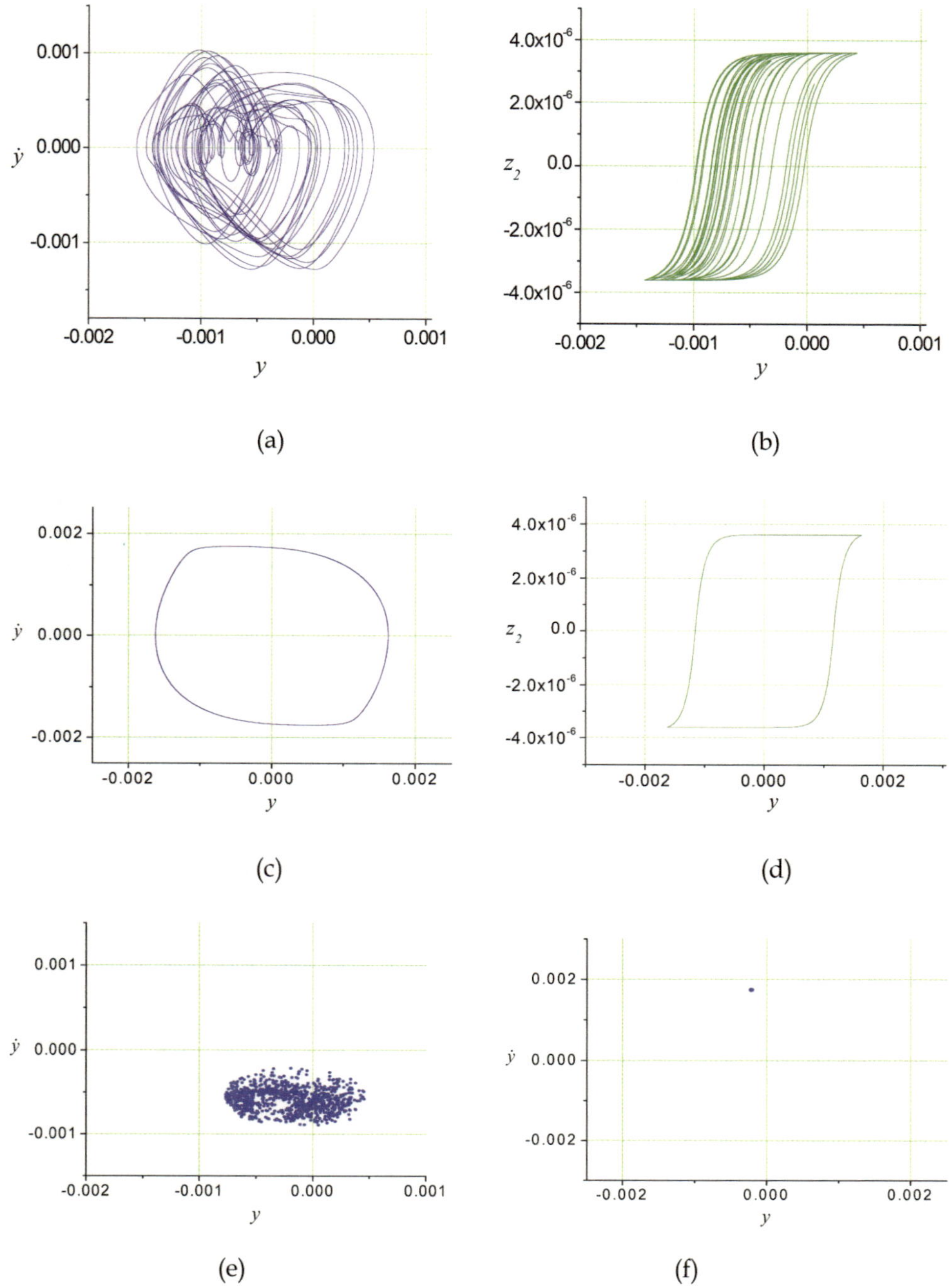

Fig. 5. Phase portraits (a), (c), hysteresis loops (b), (d) and Poincaré maps (e), (f) of the chaotic (a), (b), (e) and periodic (c), (d), (f) rotor motion that agree well with the chaotic/regular regions in Fig. 4 (b). The parameters δ=0.0001, C=0.2, γ_m=0, λ_m=500, k_z=0.000055, γ=15, β=0.25, n=1.0, Q_0=0, x_0=0, y_0=0, $x(0)=y(0)=10^{-8}$, $\dot{x}(0)=\dot{y}(0)=0$, $z_1(0)=z_2(0)=0$ are fixed; (a), (b), (e) Ω=0.87, Q=0.00177; (c), (d), (f) Ω=1.2, Q=0.0017

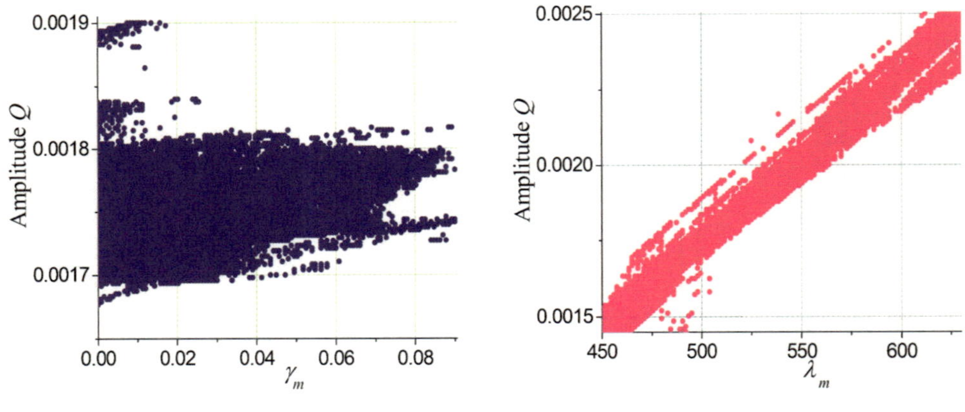

(a) (b)

Fig. 6. The influence of the magnetic control parameters γ_m (a) and λ_m (b) on chaos occurring in vertical vibrations of the rotor (28) in the case of rigid magnetic materials. The parametric planes are depicted at (a) λ_m=500 and (b) γ_m=0 with other parameters of the system fixed: δ=0.000001, C=0.2, k_z=0.000055, γ=15, β=0.25, n=1.0, Ω=0.87, Q_0=0, x_0=0, y_0=0, $x(0)=y(0)=10^{-8}$, $\dot{x}(0)=\dot{y}(0)=0$, $z_1(0)=z_2(0)=0$

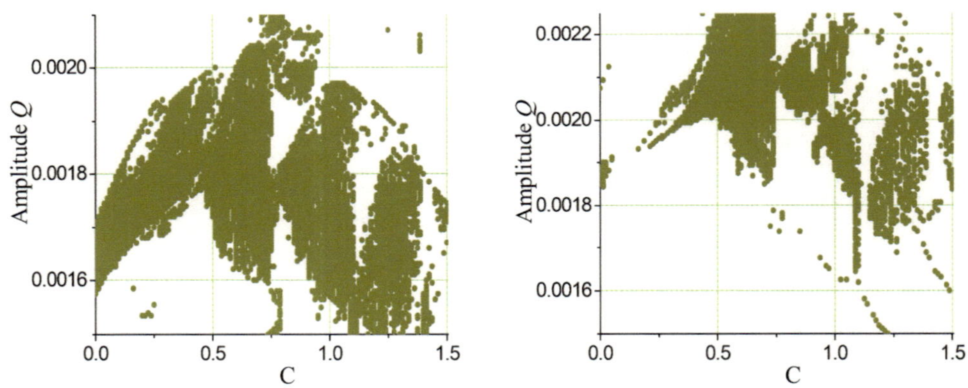

(a) (b)

Fig. 7. The influence of the dynamic oil-film action characteristics on chaos occurring in vertical vibrations of the rotor (28) in the case of rigid magnetic materials. The parametric planes (C, Q) are depicted at (a) δ=0.000001, γ_m=0 and (b) δ=0.001, γ_m=0.03 with other parameters of the system fixed: λ_m=500, k_z=0.000055, γ=15, β=0.25, n=1.0, Ω=0.87, Q_0=0, x_0=0, y_0=0, $x(0)=y(0)=10^{-8}$, $\dot{x}(0)=\dot{y}(0)=0$, $z_1(0)=z_2(0)=0$

In order to see if the rotor chaotic motion is accompanied by increasing of the amplitude of vibration, the amplitude level contours of the horizontal and vertical vibrations of the rotor have been obtained. In Fig. 8 (a) the amplitude level contours are presented in (γ_m, Q)

parametric plane with the same parameters as in Fig. 6 (a). Some "consonance" between the chaotic vibrations regions and the amplitude level contours is observed. At that the amplitudes of chaotic rotor vibrations are greater in comparison to the periodic vibrations. In Fig. 8 (b) the amplitude level contours are presented in (C, Q) parametric plane with the same parameters as in Fig. 7 (a). Although some "consonance" between the chaotic regions of vibrations and the amplitude level contours is observed, it can not be concluded that chaos leads to essential increasing of the rotor vibrations amplitude.

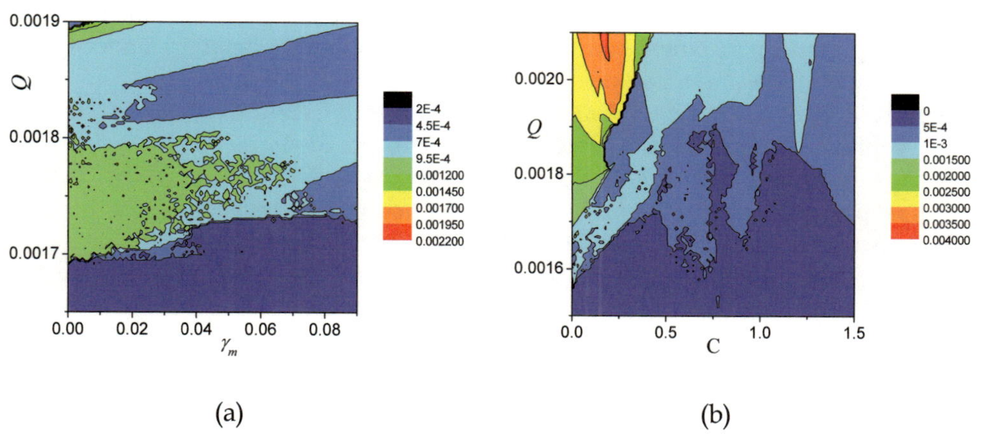

Fig. 8. The amplitude level contours of vertical vibrations of the rotor (28): (a) in the parametric plane (γ_m, Q) that corresponds to Fig. 6 (a); (b) in the parametric plane (C, Q) that corresponds to Fig. 7 (a)

5. Conclusions

2-dof non-linear dynamics of the rotor suspended in a magneto-hydrodynamic field is studied. In the case of soft magnetic materials the analytical solutions were obtained by means of the method of multiple scales. In the non-resonant case the system exhibits linear properties. The perturbation solutions are in good agreement with the numerical solutions. The cases of primary resonances with and without an internal resonance were investigated. The frequency-response curves were obtained. The saturation phenomenon was demonstrated. When the amplitude of the external excitation increases (or decreases), above some critical value the energy pumping between various submotions of the rotor occurs. A comparison of the analytical and numerical solutions based on the approximate harmonic analysis was made.

In the case of rigid magnetic materials, hysteresis was considered using the Bouc-Wen hysteretic model. Using the approach based on the analysis of the wandering trajectories the regions of chaotic vibrations of the rotor were found in various control parameter planes: amplitude of external harmonic excitation versus hysteretic dissipation, versus frequency of external harmonic excitation, dynamic oil-film action characteristics as well as versus the magnetic control parameters. The amplitude level contours of the horizontal and vertical vibrations of the rotor were obtained. Phase portraits and hysteretic loops are in good agreement with the chaotic regions obtained. Chaos was generated by hysteretic properties of the system considered.

6. References

Awrejcewicz, J. & Dzyubak, L. (2007). Hysteresis modelling and chaos prediction in one- and two-dof hysteretic models. *Archive of Applied Mechanics,* No.77, pp. 261-279

Awrejcewicz, J., Dzyubak, L. & Grebogi, C. (2005). Estimation of chaotic and regular (stick-slip and slip-slip) oscillations exhibited by coupled oscillators with dry friction. *Non-linear Dynamics,* No.42(2), pp. 383-394

Awrejcewicz, J. & Mosdorf, R. (2003). *Numerical Analysis of Some Problems of Chaotic Dynamics,* WNT, Warsaw

Chang-Jian, C. W. & Chen, C. K. (2009). Non-linear analysis of a rub-impact rotor supported by turbulent couple stress fluid film journal bearings under quadratic damping. *Non-linear Dynamics,* No.56, pp. 297-314

Dziedzic, K. & Kurnik, W. (2002). Stability of a rotor with hybrid magneto-hydrodynamic support. *Machine Dynamics Problems,* No.26(4), pp. 33-43

Flores, P., Ambrosio, J., Claro, J. C. P., Lancarani, H. M. & Koshy, C. S. (2009). Lubricated revolute joints in rigid multibody systems. *Non-linear Dynamics,* No.56, pp.277-295

Gasch, R., Nordmann, R. & Pfützner, H. (2002). *Rotordynamik,* Springer, Berlin

Kurnik, W. (1995). Active magnetic antiwhirl control of a rigid rotor supported on hydrodynamic bearings. *Machine Dynamics Problems,* No.10, pp. 21-36

Li, J., Tian, Y., Zhang, W. & Miao, S. F. (2006). Bifurcation of multiple limit cycles for a rotor-active magnetic bearings system with time-varying stiffness. *International Journal of Bifurcation and Chaos*

Muszyńska, A. (2005). *Rotordynamics,* CRC Press, Boca Raton

Nayfeh, A. H. & Mook, D. T. (2004). *Non-linear oscillations,* Wiley, New York

Osinski, Z. (Ed.) (1998). *Damping of Vibrations,* A.A. Balkema, Rotterdam, Brookfield

Rao, J. S. (1991). *Rotor Dynamics,* Wiley, New York

Someya, T. (1998). *Journal-Bearing Databook,* Springer, Berlin

Tondl, A. (1965). *Some Problems of Rotor Dynamics,* Chapman & Hall, London

Zhang, W. & Zhan, X. P. (2005). Periodic and chaotic motions of a rotor-active magnetic bearing with quadratic and cubic terms and time-varying stiffness. *Non-linear Dynamics,* No.41, pp. 331-359

18

Mathematical Modeling in Chemical Engineering: A Tool to Analyse Complex Systems

Anselmo Buso and Monica Giomo
Department of Chemical Engineering, University of Padova
Italy

1. Introduction

The essence of engineering modeling is to capture the fundamental aspects of the problem which the model is intended to describe and to understand what the model's limitations as a result of the simplifications are.
Engineering models are therefore not judged by whether they are "true" or "false", but by how well they are suitable to describe the situation in question. It may therefore often be possible to devise several different models of the same physical reality and one can choose among these depending on the desired model accuracy and on their ease of analysis.
Even though in engineering applications the choice of the model can be done among the following :

1. Physical models: small-scale replica of the system or its parts (pilot plant, scale models of buildings, ships models);
2. Analog models (electronic, electric and mechanical devices);
3. Drawing and maps;
4. Mathematical models,

over the past decade there has been an increasing demand for suitable material in the area of mathematical modeling, because they represent a more convenient and economic tool to understand the factors that influence the performance of a system.
Developments in computer technology and numerical solver have provided the necessary tools to increase power and sophistication which have significant implications for the use and role of mathematical modeling.
The conceptual representation of a real physical system can be translated in mathematical terms adopting the usual types of models and their combinations:

- Deterministic models: the relationships between different quantities of different engineering system are given via the continuum equations describing the conservation of mass, momentum and energy and the relevant constitutive equations. The appropriate differential equations are solved for a set or system of process variables and parameters;
- Statistical-Stochastic models: the principle of uncertainty is introduced instead of the possibility of assigning defined values to each dependant variable for a set of values of independent ones. Being the input-output relationships and the structure of elements not precisely known, the use of statistical tools is implemented;

- Empirical models: they are directly connected to the functional relationships between variables and parameters by fitting empirical data, without assigning any physical meaning and consequently any cause to their relationships. Examples of empirical models are those based on polynomials used to fit empirical data by the "least square" method,

or using more recent tools such as neural network and fuzzy logic techniques or fractal theory.

Mathematical models are of great importance in chemical engineering because they can provide information about the variations in the measurable macroscopic properties of a physical system using output from microscopic equations which cannot usually be measured in a laboratory. On the other hand, mathematical models can lead to wrong conclusions or decisions about the system under investigation if they are not validated with experimental tests. Therefore, a complete study of a physical system should integrate modeling, simulation and experimental work.

Computer aided modeling, simulation and optimization permit a better understanding of the chemical process behaviour, saves the time and money by providing the fewer configuration of the experimental work. In addition, computer simulation and optimization can help to improve the performance and the quality of a process and represent a more flexible and cost effective approach in design and operation.

This chapter presents two different examples of developing a mathematical model relevant to two different complex chemical systems. The complexity of the system is related to the structure heterogeneity in the first case study and to the various physical-chemical phenomena involved in the process in the second one.

Specific task is demonstrating how, through the use of information coming from experimental investigations and simulation, it is possible checking the validity of the assumptions made and fine tuning the predictive mathematical model capability.

The possibility of analysing and quantifying the role played by each step of the process is examined in order to define the relevant mathematical expressions. The latter allows getting useful indications about the impact of different operating conditions on the role of each step discussing the improvements in operation (efficiency of the process) brought about by simulation.

Next step focuses on the estimation of the significant parameters of the process. In complex systems the determination "a priori" of some parameters is not always feasible and they are therefore determined as a comparison of experimental and simulation data.

The final result is therefore the availability of a tool, the verified and validated (V&V) mathematical model, that can be used for simulation, process analysis, process control, optimization, design.

2. How to build a mathematical model

The general strategy of analysis of real systems consists of the following steps:

Problem definition

Preliminary we must pick up the essential information related to the case study/project; establish the objectives and related priority; state what is given and what is required. Then, we must analyse the entire process and the system in which it develops to fix the independent and dependent variables. When the process and/or the system is so complex that it is difficult either understand and describe it as a whole, we can break it down into subsystems. They do not necessary have to correspond to any physical parts of the real process; they can be hypothetical elements which are isolated for detailed considerations. After the process has been split up into the elements and each part has been analysed, relationships existing among the subsystems have to be defined and assembled in order to describe the entire process. Through the analysis of the variables and their relationships, it is possible to define a simple and consistent set which is satisfactory for the scope. While doing this, we can simplify the problem by introducing some assumptions so that the mathematical model can be easy to manipulate. These simplifications had to be later evaluated to have assurance of representing the real process with reasonable degree of confidence.

Model development

Defined the problem, we must translate it into mathematical terms.

Models based on transport phenomena principles, the first category of mathematical models mentioned in Introduction, are the common type models used in chemical engineering. The various mathematical levels (molecular, microscopic, multiple gradient, maximum gradient and macroscopic) used to represent the real processes are chosen according to the complexity of the internal detail included in the process description. For engineering purposes, molecular representation is not of much direct use. Microscopic and multiple-gradient models, give a detailed description of processes but they are often excessively complex for practical applications. Maximum-gradient model level may be considered a multiple-gradient model in which the dispersion terms are deleted and only the largest component of the gradient of the dependent variable is considered in each balance. These models are more easy to deal with and generally satisfactory for describing chemical systems Then, macroscopic scale is used to represent a process ignoring spatial variations and considering properties and variables homogeneous throughout the entire system. In this way no spatial gradients are involved in equations and time remains the only differential independent variable in the balances. Mathematical description results greatly simplified, but there is a significant loss of information regarding the behaviour of the systems.

The development of a mathematical model requires not only to formulate the differential or algebraic equations but as well to select appropriate initial and/or boundary conditions. In order to determine the value of the constants which are introduced in the solution of differential equations, it is necessary to fix a set of n boundary conditions for each nth order derivative with respect to the space variable or with respect to time. In particular, boundary conditions can influence the selection of a coordinate system used to formulate the equations in microscopic and multiple-gradient models.

After setting up the model, we must evaluate the model parameters. In the microscopic models, the required parameters are transport properties. Various methods of estimating values for pure components and for mixtures are available in literature. The "effective" parameters, introduced in mathematical models to describe transport phenomena in homogeneous or multiphase systems, are clearly empirical and must be determined for the particular system of interest. In literature predicting relationships only for traditional systems may be available.

If deterministic models cannot be satisfactory applied in developing a model, stochastic or empirical models can be used. These model-building techniques have more limited applications as a consequence of that a lot of the limitations of deterministic models apply also to stochastic and empirical ones. Moreover, the empirical models show additional

limitations due to the fact that they are valid only for the process for which data were collected.
Whatever is the model-building technique adopted, as more complex is the mathematical description of the process, as more difficult is its solution. Therefore the process description shall be a compromise among the required details, the available information on model parameters and the limitations of the available mathematical tools.

Model solving

The goal of this step is to obtain the analytical solution (if this is possible) and/or, failing that, the numerical solution of the model equations, which may include algebraic equations, differential equations and inequalities. For many complex chemical processes the model result is set of nonlinear equation requiring numerical solution. The most common way to deal with this is to use modelling software such as gPROMS , COMSOL, Aspen Custom Builder or other software such as Matlab.

Model verification and validation (V&V)

These actions are essential part of the model building process.
Verification concerns with building the model right. In this step a comparison between the chosen conceptual representation and the outcome of the model is carried out to evaluate its suitability to describe the conception. Verification is achieved through tests performed to ensure that the model has been implemented properly and that the input parameters and logical structure of the model have been correctly represented.
Validation concerns with building the right model. This step grants that the model is in line with the intended requirements with reference to the methods adopted and outcome. Validation is achieved through an interactive process of comparing prediction data to experimental ones and using discrepancies between the values and information coming from comparison to improve the model. This procedure is repeated as many times as desired model accuracy is achieved.

3. Development of a mathematical model to analyze the behavior of a prototype electrochemical reactor

The availability of mathematical modeling is of paramount importance in the development of new equipments to evaluate their performances at operating conditions variations.
On the other hand, referring to systems characterized by either complex structure and/or processes which involve several steps or phases, the settlement of a reliable simulation model leads to the availability of experimental data allowing to check the assumptions taken in the model and to estimate the model parameters. Therefore it is the combination of equipments availability and the development of a specific mathematical model that allows to achieve a good level of process simulation.
In this case study we intend to develop a model allowing to evaluate the performance of a prototype electrochemical reactor for electro-coagulation and electro-flotation processes treating slurry. The reactor is equipped with reciprocating sieve-plates as electrodes. The peculiar characteristic of this reactor means that the fluid-dynamics of the system from "plug flow reactor" to "perfectly mixed reactor" can be varied as a function of the agitation level induced (Buso et al. 1991).
The reactor is a flanged plexi-glass tube, with a diameter of 40 mm and a height of 1060 mm. The column is fitted with an agitation device, consisting of a group of 16 stainless steel plate electrodes, mounted on a central shaft and uniformly distributed, with a space span of 50

mm. Each 6-mm thick plate had a diameter of 400 mm and 106 holes, each 12 mm across. Reciprocating is provided by an electric motor coupled to a gear drive fitted with frequency control, allowing the reciprocating frequency to range from 60 to 120 rpm. A continuously variable eccentric cam regulates reciprocating amplitude up to maximum plate spacing. Slurry is fed through two horizontal jet injectors.

The RPC reactor is a non homogenous system with complex geometric features. The perforated plates, mounted on a central shaft, have a double function: to grant, thanks to their movement, the desired agitation level and, being electrodes, to allow the generation of the electrochemical process. The latter is characterized by having several steps which contribute to define the overall kinetics.

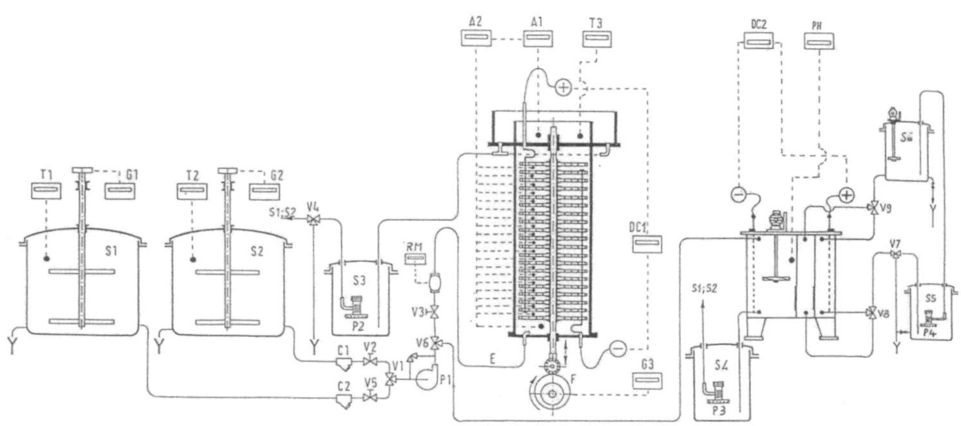

Fig. 1. Schematic representation of the pilot plant. A1,A2 conductivity cells; C1,C2 filters; DC1,DC2 D.C. power supply; E liquid injectors; F variable speed motor; G1÷G3 speed controls; P1÷P4 pumps; PH pH-meter; S1÷S6 storage tanks; T1,T3 thermometers; RM flow meters; V1÷V8 valves.

In this study the fluid-dynamic behaviour of the reactor is analysed by means of the time dependant input technique in the reactor itself, where the plates are not acting as electrodes. Experimental tests are carried out in the pilot plant shown in Fig. 1.

The two tanks, S1 and S2, contain the feed reactor and the relevant tracer which, by means of the 3-ways valve V1 , is injected in the form of step input pulses.

The reactor is treated as system composed of two elements: the "feed zone" and the "reaction zone" comprising the 16 perforated reciprocating plates.

Various models to represent each subsystem can be used. In order to describe the whole system, we must define the relationships existing among the elements. In this case the input-forcing functions for the models proposed to represent the "reaction zone" are given by the outputs of the model adopted to describe the "feed zone", when a STEP change in feed concentration is made.

The "feed zone" is considered to be either a CSTR or a tubular reactor. Its behaviour is represented mathematically in terms of the CSTR model and axial dispersed model, respectively, see Table 1.

The "reaction zone" is represented either by a tubular reactor or by a series of N backflow CSTR. Depending on the constructional features of the stack-plate, the literature suggests different values for the number of stages N (Miyanami et al., 1973, Parthasarathy et al. 1984). With reference to the equipment studied, the space between two neighbouring plates can be considered an ideal mixer, that is N = 16. The N perfectly mixed cells have the same volume and constant net or bulk flow rate $\dot{V}$ at all cross-sections and recirculation flow rate $\dot{F}$ from each cell back to the preceding cell in the chain. The backflow ratio β is defined as $\beta=\left(\dot{F}/\dot{V}\right)$. The mixing between the stages generates imperfection of the chain of several ideal mixers, so the parameter $\gamma=\beta/(1+\beta)$ is determined from the agitation level. Dotted cell (0) and (N+1) are fictitious cells with negligible hold-up or volume, representing the inlet and outlet sections of the column. In the first case system behaviour is represented mathematically in terms of dispersed model, while a backflow cell model is used in the second one.

Moreover, only one model - dispersed or backflow cell - is used to describe the behaviour of the entire system, consisting of the "feed zone" and the "reaction zone" .

The sets of equations proposed for each representation are then solved analytically or using numerical techniques if necessary. The breakthrough curves - (C/C_0) - for the suggested models vary progressively between two threshold conditions : from "plug flow reactor" to "perfectly mixed reactor", simply as a function of the characteristic parameters such as dispersion coefficient E and total flow ratio γ, see Table 1.

The experimental step input response curves are compared with the theoretical ones, obtained from the proposed models in order to determine the controlling parameters.

Parameters values are obtained by applying the methods of moments. (Himmelblau & Bishoff, 1968).

Models which simulate the "feed zone" as tubular reactor may describe the behaviour of different configurations of the "feed zone", as a function of induced mixing level and thus of dispersion coefficient, E. Moreover, the predictive capability can be improved estimating parameters E and γ for the sole "reaction zone".

Mathematical models simulating the whole system as a tubular reactor or a series of backflow CSTR take backmixing between the "feed zone" and the "reaction zone" into consideration, although the estimated parameters are less suitable for modelling reactor behaviour .

This analysis allows to select the most suitable model, according to the "feed zone" geometry and operating conditions range, that is, the agitation level adopted.

Experimental tests in the frequency range 60÷120 rpm and amplitude 0.1÷1.8 cm are carried out to evaluate the effects of the agitation level on fluid-dynamics parameters.

At zero agitation, the liquid velocity has a non-uniform radial profile and the dispersion coefficient is relatively high. As agitation (A·f) is increased, when amplitude A is low, localised agitation improves radial mixing inducing a fluid-dynamic behaviour similar to that found in a plug flow-reactor. The dispersion coefficient decreases to a minimum. If agitation level is further increased, the mixing between the zones of reactor gave rise, until the behaviour of a perfectly mixed reactor is reached. The dispersion coefficient gradually increases.

The dispersion coefficient determined from experimental data is then compared with those estimated by correlations available in literature for single phase flow (Karr et al., 1987; Lounes & Thibault, 1996). Karr's correlation matches the experimental values satisfactory, although it is inadequate when low amplitude and high frequencies are used.

The second aspect that we have to investigate regards the effects of process kinetics on the system behaviour.

Feed zone: CSTR + **Reaction zone:** Dispersed reactor

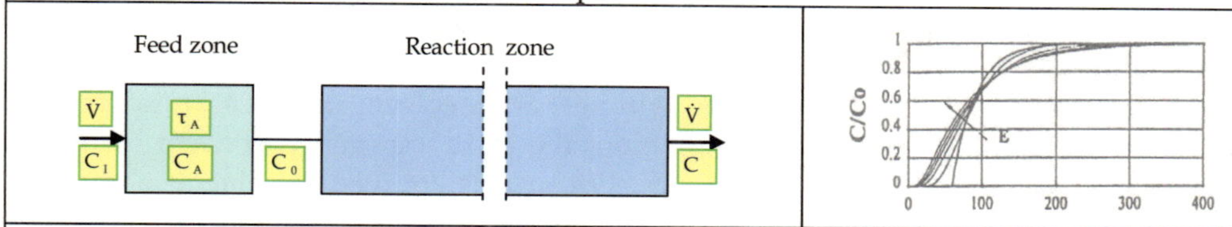

Feed zone: Dispersed Reactor + **Reaction zone:** Dispersed reactor

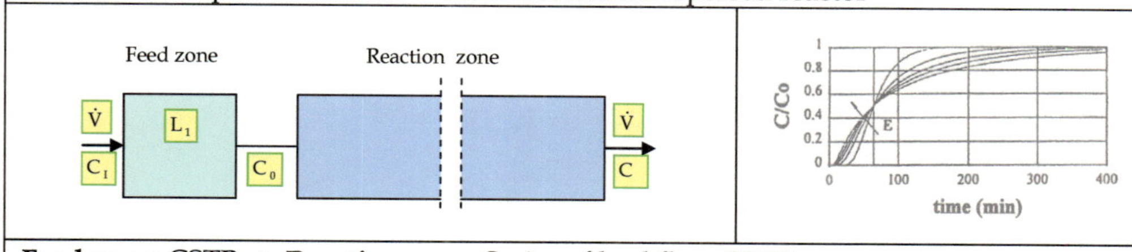

Feed zone: CSTR + **Reaction zone:** Series of backflow CSTR

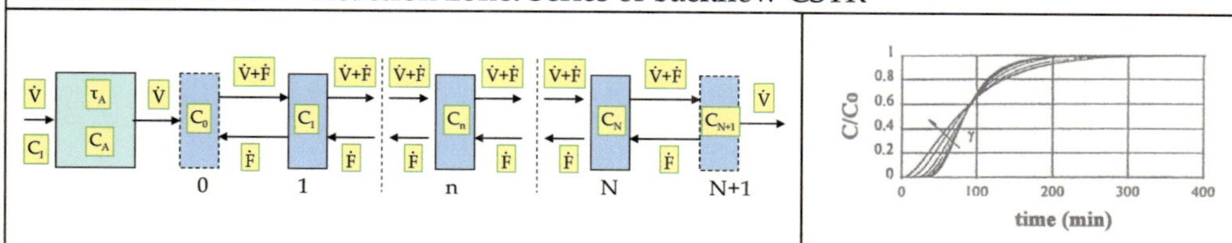

Feed zone: Dispersed Reactor + **Reaction zone:** Series of backflow CSTR

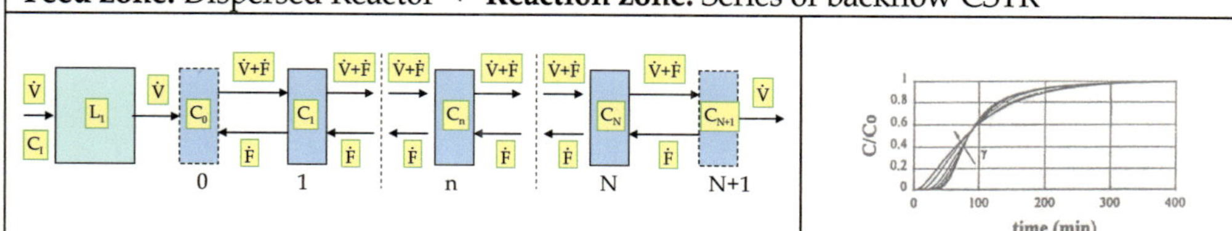

Feed zone + **Reaction zone:** Dispersed Reactor

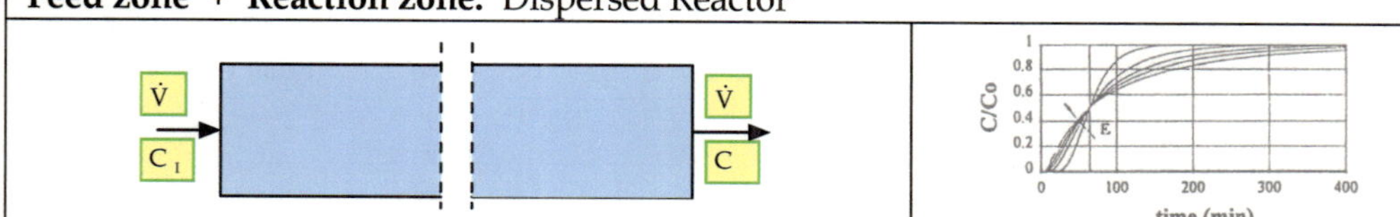

Feed zone + **Reaction zone:** Series of backflow CSTR

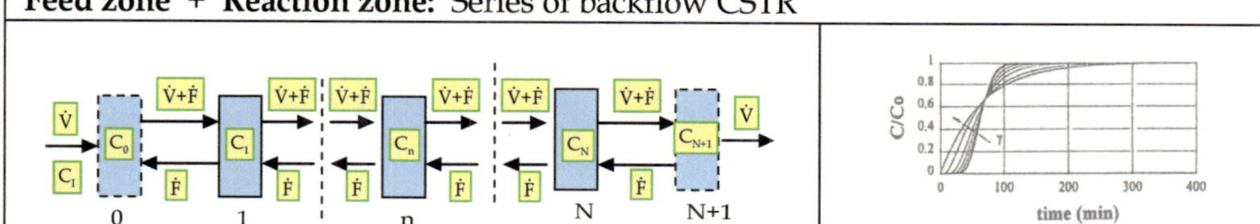

Table 1. Fluid-dynamics simulation. Schematic representations of the RPC reactor and concentration profiles for various values of dispersion coefficient, E, and total flow ratio, γ. C_I dimensionless initial molar concentration; C_0 dimensionless inlet reaction zone molar concentration; C dimensionless exit molar concentration; τ_A mean residence time of CSTR; C_A dimensionless molar concentration in CSTR; L_1 length tubular reactor.

Electrochemical processes on the electrode involve the following steps: diffusion from the bulk toward the electrode surface, adsorption, electron exchange, de-adsorption and diffusion from the electrode to the bulk. These steps contribute to define the overall kinetics. Since in the waste water treatment dilute solutions are involved, the mass transport can be considered the limiting step. In these conditions the mass transport coefficient become the controlling parameter and the process kinetics are determined by the fluid-dynamics behaviour of the solution rather than the electrode characteristics.
In the limiting current conditions, when reactant concentrations fell to zero close to the electrode surface, the flux expression was reduced to (Prentice, 1991):

$$N_j = \frac{60\,\Im_l}{n\,F} = K_m C_\infty \tag{1}$$

where:
C_∞ - bulk ion molar concentration
F - Faraday's constant
$\Im_l$ - limiting current density
K_m - mass transport coefficient
n - number of electrons involved in the reaction
N_j - molar flux of the j-th species
provided that reactant migrations as consequence of the electric field is negligible.
In these conditions, the mass transport coefficient may be determined experimentally by measuring the concentration of solution, C_∞ , and the limiting current density , $\Im_l$, by means of the following:

$$K_m = \frac{60\,\Im_l}{n\,F\,C_\infty} \tag{2}$$

In order to obtain accurate data relevant to the limiting current density, electrochemical characterization of an aqueous solution of potassium iodide, with an excess of sodium sulphate as supporting electrolyte, is carried out using the laboratory apparatus shown in Fig.2, equipped with stainless steel electrodes having the same thickness and distance as those used in the reactor.

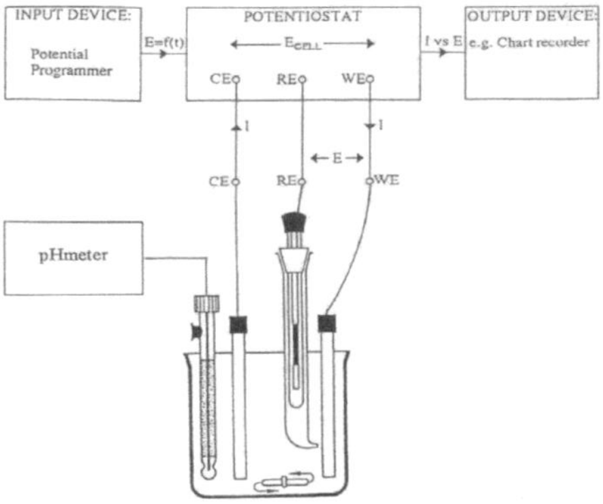

Fig. 2. Electrochemical laboratory apparatus. CE counter- electrode; Re reference electrode WE working electrode.

The main reaction at the anode are:

$$2\,I^- \leftrightarrow I_2 + 2e^- \tag{3}$$

and/or

$$3\,I^- \leftrightarrow I_3^- + 2e^- \tag{4}$$

$$I^- + 3H_2O \leftrightarrow IO^{3-} + 6H^+ + e^- \tag{5}$$

$$2\,H_2O \leftrightarrow O_2 + 4H^+ + 4e^- \tag{6}$$

Current polarisation curves for the potassium iodide solution for various agitation levels are obtained. These curves are then compared with the polarisation curves of the supporting electrolyte solution obtained in the same operating conditions, in order to identify any noise phenomena as a result of undesirable oxidation.

Data obtained allow to define the operating conditions which are used in tests on the reactor where the plates are acting as electrodes.

The same aqueous solution of potassium iodide, with an excess of sodium sulphate as supporting electrolyte is used in batch runs, carried out first on a single cell then on an increasing number of cell, until the whole reactor became involved. In these conditions data collected may be compared with those of the laboratory apparatus results. For each run, polarisation curves are obtained by varying the agitation level within the range 60÷150 rpm. In this way information about the effect of the agitation level on current, in mass transfer controlled regions, can be obtained. In particular, when higher agitation levels are used, the limiting current values increase with the agitation level and the potential range in which the current assumes the limiting value decreases until mass transport become a non-controlling phenomenon (Buso et al., 1997).

In order to analyze the effect of agitation level on mass transport coefficient, K_m, the reactor is completely filled with the solution of potassium iodide and tests are carried out separately, varying the amplitude and frequency of the plate oscillation. The applied potentials are chosen according to the limiting current values previously obtained.

The mass transport coefficient may be evaluated using equation (2) where the limiting current density is expressed through limiting current, $\Im_l$, and total active electrode surface, S. It is therefore possible to estimate the values of the $(K_m S)$ group, simply by measuring limiting current, I_l, and concentration of solution, C_∞. In this way the values of the $(K_m S)$ group are available in the same form used in the mathematical models which describe the behaviour of the electrochemical reactor.

The effect of geometric, fluid-dynamic and physical-chemical variables on the rate of mass transfer may be evaluated through the following controlling dimensionless number relationship:

$$Sh = \psi\,(Re)^{\kappa}\,(Sc)^{\theta} \tag{7}$$

where:

ψ, κ, θ - empirical constant

$(Re) = (A\,f)(d/s)(\rho/\mu)$ - dimensionless Reynolds number

$(Sc)=(\mu/\rho D)$ - dimensionless Schmidt number

$(Sh)=(K_m L/D)$ - dimensionless Sherwood number

A - stroke
d - hole diameter
D - diffusion coefficient
f - frequency
L - characteristic length
s - fractional free flow area
ρ - solution density
μ - solution viscosity.

In this case both the geometry and the solution properties are constant. Equation (7) may be rewritten as follows:

$$K_m S = \xi \, (Re)^{\kappa} \tag{8}$$

$$\xi \, (Re)^{\kappa} = \psi \, (Sc)^{\theta} \left(\frac{DS}{L} \right) \tag{9}$$

According to Reynolds number definition, equation (8) becomes:

$$K_m S = \zeta \, (A\, f)^{\kappa} \tag{10}$$

$$\zeta = \xi \left(\frac{\rho\, d}{s\, \mu} \right)^{\kappa} \tag{11}$$

The values of parameters κ and ζ may be obtained by fitting of experimental data.
In this way we have obtained a dimensionless numbers relationship which allows, according to the electrochemical process of interest, to evaluate the effects of agitation level on mass transfer rates.
Now, we have the information to develop a steady-state reactor model.
With reference to the electrochemical system studied, the reactor may be represented as $N/2$ perfectly mixed cells including cathodes, $N/2$ reactions cells including anodes, feed zone and the fictitious cells relevant to the inlet and the outlet sections of the reactor. Electrochemical process occurs only in cells with anodes, so that, in steady state conditions, the inlet concentration in the "feed zone" and in the "reaction zone" are the same. Therefore, the models proposed for the whole reactor become the more suitable to represent mathematically the system behaviour.
The dispersed model equations and relevant boundary conditions are:

$$0 = -v \frac{\partial c}{\partial z} + \frac{\partial^2 c}{\partial z^2} + \left(\frac{K_m S}{V} \right) \tag{12}$$

$$v\, c\big|_{z=0^+} - E \left.\frac{\partial c}{\partial z}\right|_{z=0^+} = v\, c\big|_{z=0^-} \tag{13}$$

$$\left.\frac{\partial c}{\partial z}\right|_{z=L} = 0 \tag{14}$$

where:

c - ion concentration

v - overall velocity

z - length coordinate through reactor.

The backflow cell model equations are:

$$\begin{aligned}
&\textit{inlet cell} \quad n=1\\
&0=\dot{V}c_0 + \beta\,\dot{V}c_2 - \dot{V}(1+\beta)\,c_1\\
&\textit{anodes} \quad n=2,4,\ldots,16\\
&K_m\,S_a c_n = \dot{V}(1+\beta)\,c_{n-1}+\beta\,\dot{V}c_{n+1}-\dot{V}(1+2\beta)\,c_n\\
&\textit{cathodes} \quad n=3,5,\ldots,17\\
&0=\dot{V}(1+\beta)\,c_{n-1}+\beta\,\dot{V}c_{n+1}-\dot{V}(1+2\beta)\,c_n\\
&\textit{outlet cell} \quad n=18\\
&0=\dot{V}(1+\beta)\,c_{17}+\dot{V}(1+\beta)\,c_{18}
\end{aligned} \tag{15}$$

where:

S_a - total active anode surface

The dispersed model solution was obtained analytically , while the backflow cell model was solved numerically using the Thomas algorithm.

To validate the proposed models, experimental tests are carried out in the pilot plant, especially modified to operate in steady-state conditions. Samples are taken at the inlet, outlet and at various sections of the reactors.

The characteristic parameters of the two models, (E, K_m) and (γ, K_m), are adjusted to give the best fit to the experimental concentration profiles relevant to different operating conditions. Their values are then compared with the output of fluid-dynamic study and electrochemical characterization developed separately, together with those estimated in literature.

A typical comparison of the model outputs and the experimental value are shown in Fig. 3.

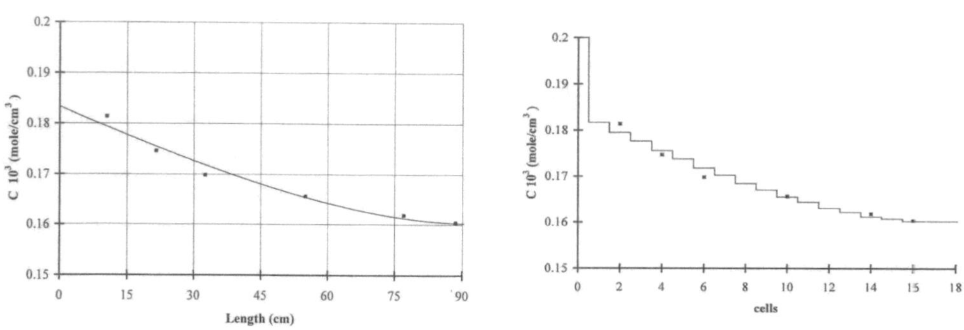

Fig. 3. Concentration profile in the RPC reactor. Comparison of experimental data and predictive profile obtained with dispersed model and backflow cell model.

The good match among the data confirms the predictive capacity of the proposed models. Moreover, it is possible to verify the results of the effects of agitation level on the fluid-dynamic kinetic parameters.
The response solutions of the continuous diffusion and backflow cell models, obtained with the same value of the kinetic parameter $(K_m S)$, are then compared using the Crank method (Roemer & Durbin, 1967). The good match between the characteristic parameters:

$$Pe = \frac{v\,L}{E} = 2.34 \tag{12}$$

$$\Phi = \frac{2N(1-\gamma)}{1+\gamma} = 2.13 \tag{13}$$

determined using E and γ estimated from experimental data, confirms that the diffusion model response approaches that of the backflow cell model.
The methodology proposed provides, for the process of interest, tools to define operating conditions which improve both reduction rates and energy consumption.

4. Development of a mathematical model to analyze the electro-generation of hydrogen peroxide using an oxygen-reducing gas-diffusion electrode

Hydrogen peroxide is a powerful oxidising agent. It finds applications in a wide variety of chemical processes (Brillas et al, 2000; Drogui et al., 2001; Gonzáles-García et al., 2007). Due to the low solubility of the oxygen in aqueous solution, in the electrosynthesis of hydrogen peroxide, electrochemical devices with high specific surface area are required. Gas-diffusion electrodes (GDE) are devices suitable to supply commercially reasonable current densities for practical implementation of this process (Alcaide et al., 2002; Da Pozzo et al., 2005; Lobyntseva et al., 2007).
The availability of mathematical models for optimal design and process control strategy, can improve the use of these devices.
In this case study we intend to develop a model which allows to evaluate the contributions of the transport and reaction steps to the overall electrosyntesis process.
The process of interest occurs at the cathode. In the dilute acidic solution it can be described by the following reaction (Alcaide et al., 2002, 2004, Kolyagin&Kornienko, 2003):

$$O_2 + 2\,H^+ + 2\,e^- \rightarrow H_2O_2 \tag{14}$$

When a GDE is used as cathode, the process involves three phases: the gas phase (O_2), the liquid phase (a dilute acidic solution) and, in the middle, the porous electrode.
The pore space of the electrode is filled partly with liquid and partly with gas. The gaseous component (O_2) must overcome the mass transport resistances in the external gas film and the gas-filled pore volume before it can be absorbed in the liquid phase. Then oxygen diffuses through the flooded part of the pore and is reduced on the electrode surface, forming hydrogen peroxide. This product is transported from the reaction zone through the flooded layer out of the pore and into the liquid bulk.
Due to process complexity, some assumptions shall be taken to develop a model which has to be sufficiently representative and easy to use. Moreover determining "a priori" some parameters will not be an easy task, and therefore it might be necessary to obtain them

through a comparison between experimental data and simulation values. The availability of experimental equipments allows to check the assumptions taken, to determine the parameters and finally to validate the proposed model.

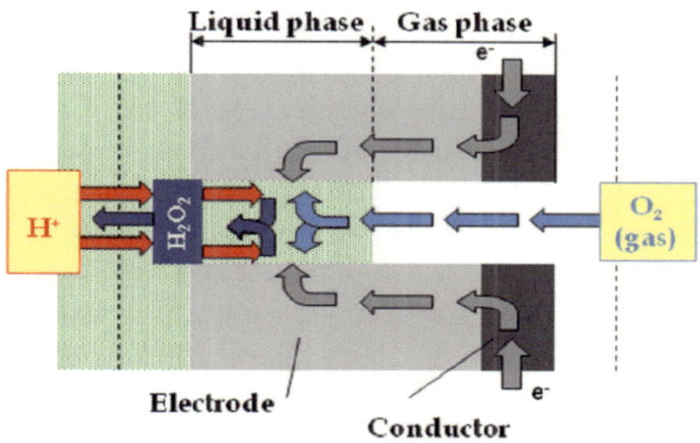

Fig. 4. Gas Diffusion Electrode: schematic representation of the three-phase process.

In this case study, either laboratory equipment and pilot plant are used. In particular, the scheme of the pilot plant is shown in Fig. 5.

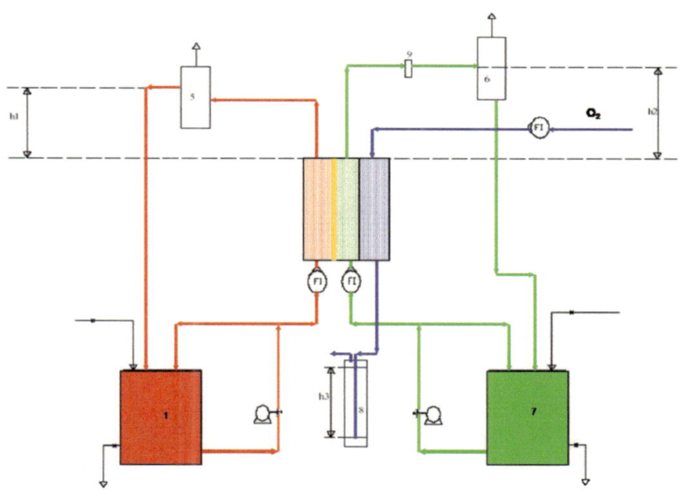

Fig. 5. Schematic diagram of pilot plant. (1) anolyte reservoir; (2) anodic compartment; (3) cathodic compartment; (4) gas chamber; (5) and (6) liquid holders; (7) catholite reservoir; (8) drechsel; (9) tank for the reference electrode; (h_1) anodic circuit head; (h_2) cathodic circuit head; (h_3) gas circuit head.

The anodic solution (0.5 M H_2SO_4) is circulated through the reactor by a centrifugal pump. During the experiments, the feed fluid is partially recycled back to the tank to mix the stored solution. A liquid holder allows to purge the gas generated in working conditions at the anode, according to the following reaction: $H_2O \rightarrow ½ O_2 + 2H^+ + 2 e^-$. A similar flow circuit is arranged to feed the reactor with catholyte (0.07 M NaCl solution). In this case, purging removes the gases generated from hydrogen peroxide degradation or those passing through the cathode into the solution. Liquid holders are placed to ensure the right pressure values

in the anodic and cathodic compartments. Pure O_2 is supplied to the gas chamber in contact with the cathode. A drechsel maintains the correct pressure in the gas chamber.
The electrochemical cell is composed of three separate elements: the side-units act as the anodic and gas compartments, respectively. The anodic solution is fed from the bottom, whereas the gas flows in from the top. In the central unit the electrodes are placed. The anode is made of platinum-coated titanium net and the cathode is a O_2-diffusion electrode. The latter consists of a silver-plated nickel web, covered with layers of VULCAN XC-72 Carbon catalyst on both sides of the assembly and a coating of SAB (Shawinigan Acetylene Black) on the gas-side. This hydrophobic barrier prevents flooding of the electrode. The inter-electrode compartment has lower inlet and upper outlet tubes for catholyte circulation. The cathode compartment is separated from the anode compartment by a cation-exchange membrane.
The process analysis starts with the study of the process kinetic aspects.
Electrochemical processes are generally described by reaction path including several reactions, but often it is possible to choose a single reaction as the one which is controlling the process. In this case we assume that the process can be described only by the reaction (14) while the side reactions (Alcaide et al., 2002; Agladze et al., 2007; Kolyagin & Kornienko, 2003):

$$O_2 + 4\,H^+ + 4\,e^- \rightarrow 2H_2O_2 \tag{15}$$

$$H_2O_2 + 2\,H^+ + 2\,e^- \rightarrow 2H_2O \tag{16}$$

can be considered negligible.
Reaction rate expression, R_{O_2}, is formulated as a first-order equation with reference to oxygen (Brillas&Casado, 2002):

$$R_{O_2} = K\,c_{O_2} \tag{17}$$

In Eq. (4), c_{O_2} is the oxygen molar concentration in the liquid phase. Since the surface overpotential is a large negative value during the process, the exponential term of the anodic portion of reaction (14) in the Butler-Volmer equation can be neglected. In dilute solution, at constant pH value, rate coefficient K is given as:

$$K = \frac{j_0\,a}{nFc^*_{O_2}}\ \exp\left[-\alpha n \frac{F}{RT}(U-U_0)\right] \tag{18}$$

where :

a	- specific electrode surface
$c^*_{O_2}$	- oxygen equilibrium concentration
F	- Faraday constant
j_0	- exchange current density
n	- number of electrons involved in the reaction (14)
R	- gas law constant
T	- temperature
U	- potential
U_0	- open circuit potential
α	- cathodic transfer coefficient.

Pilot plant behaviour is studied in a batch recycle mode of operation.
The model analysis is restricted to the cathodic section, where oxygen reduction for hydrogen peroxide generation occurs. Experimental data, available in literature (Kolyagin & Kornienko, 2003), shown that the pH of the catholyte remains almost constant during electrolysis, indicating that H^+ ion transport from the anodic compartment (through the proton-exchange membrane) is not a limiting step for the process.
The cathodic section is treated as system composed of two elements: the liquid phase reservoir and the cathodic semi-cell, containing the GDE.
For the reservoir, the mixing conditions achieved by partial recirculation of the feed solution allow to consider it a perfectly mixed vessel. Therefore to simulate its behaviour in a batch recycle mode of operation, an unsteady-state perfectly mixed model is used.
In order to analyse the role played by each step of the process, the cathodic semi-cell can be divided into two subsystems: the porous electrode and the cathodic compartment, as shown in Fig.6.

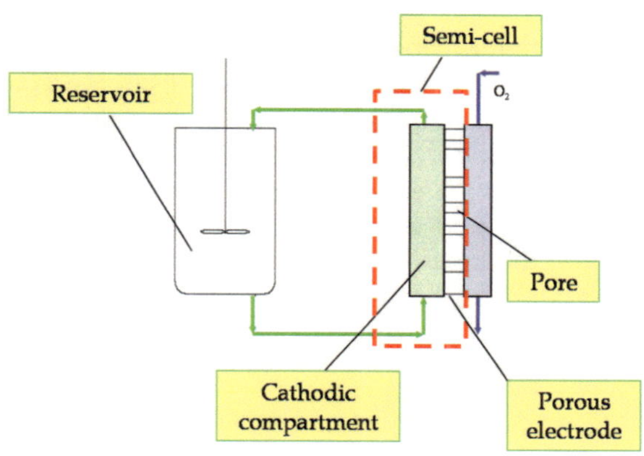

Fig. 6. Schematic representation of the cathodic section.

Porous electrode: considering that the front face of the GDE is in contact with the catholyte and the other face with the gas compartment, each pore of electrode can be represented as a sum of two elements: the gas-filled pore volume and the flooded layer. As a consequence of hydrophobicity of the electrode material, the penetration depth of the liquid phase is assumed to be 50% of the electrode thickness.
In the experimental tests pure oxygen is used. We can assume that no transport limitations in the gas phase occur. Therefore, only the gas-liquid interface condition is considered. At the interface oxygen dissolves in the liquid phase and this process is assumed to be in equilibrium.
In the flooded layer oxygen diffuses and is reduced on the electrode surface, forming hydrogen peroxide. This product moves from the reaction through the flooded layer until the end of the pore. Then it is transported into the liquid bulk.
In order to represent the oxygen and hydrogen peroxide behaviour in the flooded layer, no radial transport limitations are assumed.
Unsteady- state models are developed as a consequence of the fact that experimental runs were carried out in a batch recycle mode of operation.
Water is not taken into account, as it is the excess component in the liquid phase and has no significant influence on the overall process.
Cathodic compartment: this subsystem can be represented as a non homogeneous reactor in which the hydrogen peroxide production occurs on the wall in front of electrode. Its

behaviour may be described using models which keep into account, in different way, the role played by fluid-dynamic conditions on the hydrogen peroxide production.
Two ideal flow models, the CSTR model and the plug flow reactor model, are considered first. They represent two limiting cases of flow patterns: perfect mixing assumes complete uniformity of composition throughout the reactor. At the other extreme, plug flow occurs when fluid velocity is uniform over the entire cross-section of the reactor and there is no intermixing of fluid elements entering the vessel later. The flow patterns found in actual reactors fall between these two extremes. Many models have been suggested (Fahim & Wakao, 1982; Vakao & Kaguei,1982) to represent non-ideal flow conditions, of which one-dimensional dispersion seems to be the most widely used (Trinidad et al., 2006). Therefore, the dispersed model is also applied to represent the chatodic compartment, considering dispersion in the axial direction, characterised by a dispersion coefficient independent of position.
To simulate chatodic compartment behaviour in a batch recycle mode of operation, unsteady-state models are used.
When the whole cathodic section is considered, the dead time of the feed liquid line, due to feed pipes, fittings and flow meter, is added to the mean residence time of the storage tank.
The model of the cathodic section consists of the unsteady-state material balance equations for oxygen and hydrogen peroxide in liquid phase, carried out over the reservoir and the semi-cell. It contains the constitutive equations for the physical-chemical properties of the species involved in the process and the kinetic expression for the reaction as presented above. Moreover it includes the relationships existing among the selected subsystems and the appropriate initial and boundary conditions.
The equations developed to represent mathematically the cathodic section behaviour are the following:

Reservoir

Oxygen

$$V_S \frac{d\, c_{O_2}^{s}}{dt} = \dot{V}\left(c_{O_2}^{R} - c_{O_2}^{S}\right) \tag{19}$$

To define the initial condition we assume that only liquid in the flooded layer can achieve saturation before current supply starts. Therefore:

$$c_{O_2}^{S}\,(0) = 0 \tag{20}$$

In equation (19) :

$c_{O_2}^{S}$ - molar concentration of oxygen in catholyte reservoir

$c_{O_2}^{R}$ - molar concentration of oxygen in cathodic compartment of cell

V_S - volume of chatolyte in the tank

$\dot{V}$ - volumetric flow rate of catholyte

t - time

Hydrogen Peroxide

$$V_S \frac{d\, c_{H_2O_2}^{s}}{dt} = \dot{V}\left(c_{H_2O_2}^{R} - c_{H_2O_2}^{S}\right) \tag{21}$$

To define the initial condition we assume that no hydrogen peroxide is present in the catholyte at the beginning of the process. Therefore:

$$c^S_{H_2O_2}(0) = 0 \tag{22}$$

where:

$c^S_{H_2O_2}$ - molar concentration of hydrogen peroxide in catholyte reservoir

$c^R_{H_2O_2}$ - molar concentration of hydrogen peroxide in cathodic compartment of cell

Cathodic semi-cell

Porous electrode

Flooded layer

Oxygen

$$\frac{\partial c^P_{O_2}}{\partial t} = D_{eff\,O_2} \frac{\partial^2 c^P_{O_2}}{\partial z^2} - R_{O_2} \tag{23}$$

Hydrogen Peroxide

$$\frac{\partial c^P_{H_2O_2}}{\partial t} = D_{eff\,H_2O_2} \frac{\partial^2 c^P_{H_2O_2}}{\partial z^2} - R_{H_2O_2} \tag{24}$$

In equations (23) and (24):

$c^P_{O_2}$ - molar concentration of oxygen in flooded layer of electrode

$c^P_{H_2O_2}$ - molar concentration of hydrogen peroxide in flooded layer of electrode

z - length coordinate through pore.

The rate of consumption of O_2, R_{O_2}, is expressed by equation (17). The rate of production of H_2O_2, $R_{H_2O_2}$, is:

$$R_{H_2O_2} = - R_{O_2} \tag{25}$$

directly derived from the stoichiometry of reaction.

For each components i, the pore diffusion coefficient is related to the molecular diffusion coefficient by the relationship:

$$D_{eff\,i} = \chi D_i \tag{26}$$

where:

χ - tortuosity factor .

To define the initial condition we assume that a flow of oxygen is first established through the cathode up to saturation of the stagnant solution in the flooded layer; then, at time zero, current supply starts and the cathodic solution is circulated through the reactor. The hydrogen peroxide is assumed not to evaporate during the process and the continuity of molar fluxes at the pore exit is accounted for (Varma & Morbidelli,1997).

Oxygen

$$c^P_{O_2}(z,0) = c^{sat}_{O_2} \tag{27}$$

$$c_{O_2}^{P}\ (0,t) = c_{O_2}^{sat} \tag{28}$$

$$-D_{eff\,O_2}\left(\frac{\partial\, c_{O_2}^{P}}{\partial\, z}\right)_{L,t} = K_{mO_2}\left[\left(c_{O_2}^{P}\right)_{L,t} - c_{O_2}^{R}\right] \tag{29}$$

where

K_{mO_2} – oxygen mass transfer coefficient

L – thickness of flooded layer.

Hydrogen Peroxide

$$c_{H_2O_2}^{P}\ (z,0) = 0 \tag{30}$$

$$\left(\frac{\partial\, c_{H_2O_2}^{P}}{\partial z}\right)_{0,t} = 0 \tag{31}$$

$$-D_{eff\,H_2O_2}\left(\frac{\partial\, c_{H_2O_2}^{P}}{\partial\, z}\right)_{L,t} = K_{mH_2O_2}\left[\left(c_{H_2O_2}^{P}\right)_{L,t} - c_{H_2O_2}^{R}\right] \tag{32}$$

where:

$K_{mH_2O_2}$ – hydrogen peroxide mass transfer coefficient.

The oxygen concentration in the liquid phase, $c_{O_2}^{sat}$, is related to the partial pressure in the gas phase, P_{O_2} , by Henry's law:

$$P_{O_2} = H_{O_2}\, c_{O_2}^{sat} \tag{33}$$

where H_{O_2} is the Henry constant. This equation represents the relationship existing among the considered elements: the gas-filled pore volume and the flooded layer.

Cathodic compartment

- *CSTR model*

Oxygen

$$V_R\,\frac{d\, c_{O_2}^{R}}{dt} = \dot{V}\left(c_{O_2}^{S} - c_{O_2}^{R}\right) + n_{O_2} \tag{34}$$

where:

V_R – volume of catholyte in cathodic compartment.

The molar flow rate of oxygen in liquid film, n_{O_2} ,is expressed the linear transport law:

$$n_{O_2} = A\,\varepsilon\, K_{mO_2}\left[\left(c_{O_2}^{P}\right)_{L,t} - c_{O_2}^{R}\right] \tag{35}$$

where:

A – electrode surface

ε – total porosity of electrode.

To define the initial condition we assume that only liquid in the flooded layer can achieve saturation before current supply is started. Therefore:

$$c_{O_2}^{R}\ (0) = 0 \tag{36}$$

Equation (35) represents the relationship existing among the considered elements: flooded layer and cathodic compartment.

Hydrogen Peroxide

$$V_R \frac{d\, c_{H_2O_2}^{R}}{dt} = \dot{V}\left(c_{H_2O_2}^{S} - c_{H_2O_2}^{R}\right) + n_{H_2O_2} \tag{37}$$

The molar flow rate of hydrogen peroxide in liquid film, $n_{H_2O_2}$,is expressed the linear transport law:

$$n_{H_2O_2} = A\, \varepsilon\, K_{mH_2O_2}\left[\left(c_{H_2O_2}^{P}\right)_{L,t} - c_{H_2O_2}^{R}\right] \tag{38}$$

To define the initial condition we assume that no hydrogen peroxide is present in the catholyte at the beginning of the process. Therefore:

$$c_{H_2O_2}^{R}\ (0) = 0 \tag{39}$$

Equation (38) represents the relationship existing among the considered elements: flooded layer and cathodic compartment.

- *Plug- flow reactor model*

Oxygen

$$\frac{\partial\, c_{O_2}^{R}}{\partial\, t} = -\, v\, \frac{\partial\, c_{O_2}^{R}}{\partial y} + \frac{A\, \varepsilon}{V_R}\, K_{mO_2}\left[\left(c_{O_2}^{P}\right)_{L,t} - c_{O_2}^{R}\right] \tag{40}$$

where:

v - velocity

y - length coordinate through cathodic compartment.

According to the above said assumptions, the initial and boundary condition are expressed by the following expressions:

$$c_{O_2}^{R}\ (y,0) = 0 \tag{41}$$

$$c_{O_2}^{R}\ (0,t) = c_{O_2}^{S} \tag{42}$$

Hydrogen Peroxide

$$\frac{\partial\, c_{H_2O_2}^{R}}{\partial\, t} = -\, v\, \frac{\partial\, c_{H_2O_2}^{R}}{\partial y} + \frac{A\, \varepsilon}{V_R}\, K_{mH_2O_2}\left[\left(c_{H_2O_2}^{P}\right)_{L,t} - c_{H_2O_2}^{R}\right] \tag{43}$$

According to the above said assumptions, the initial and boundary condition are expressed by the following expressions:

$$c^{R}_{H_2O_2}(y,0) = 0 \tag{44}$$

$$c^{R}_{H_2O_2}(0,t) = c^{S}_{H_2O_2} \tag{45}$$

- *Dispersed model*

Oxygen

$$\frac{\partial c^{R}_{O_2}}{\partial t} = - v \frac{\partial c^{R}_{O_2}}{\partial y} + E_{O_2} \frac{\partial^2 c^{R}_{O_2}}{\partial y^2} + \frac{A\,\varepsilon}{V_R} K_{mO_2}\left[\left(c^{P}_{O_2}\right)_{L,t} - c^{R}_{O_2}\right] \tag{46}$$

The initial and boundary condition are expressed by the following expressions:

$$c^{R}_{O_2}(y,0) = 0 \tag{47}$$

$$v\, c^{R}_{O_2}\Big|_{y=0} - E_{O_2} \frac{\partial c^{R}_{O_2}\Big|_{y=0}}{\partial y} = v\, c^{S}_{O_2} \tag{48}$$

$$\left.\frac{\partial c^{R}_{O_2}}{\partial y}\right|_{y=h} = 0 \tag{49}$$

where:

h – height of the cathodic compartment of the cell.

Hydrogen Peroxide

$$\frac{\partial c^{R}_{H_2O_2}}{\partial t} = - v \frac{\partial c^{R}_{H_2O_2}}{\partial y} + E_{H_2O_2} \frac{\partial^2 c^{R}_{H_2O_2}}{\partial y^2} + \frac{A\,\varepsilon}{V_R} K_{mH_2O_2}\left[\left(c^{P}_{H_2O_2}\right)_{L,t} - c^{R}_{H_2O_2}\right] \tag{50}$$

The initial and boundary condition are expressed by the following expressions:

$$c^{R}_{H_2O_2}(y,0) = 0 \tag{51}$$

$$v\, c^{R}_{H_2O_2}\Big|_{y=0} - E_{H_2O_2} \frac{\partial c^{R}_{H_2O_2}\Big|_{y=0}}{\partial y} = v\, c^{S}_{H_2O_2} \tag{52}$$

$$\left.\frac{\partial c^{R}_{H_2O_2}}{\partial y}\right|_{y=h} = 0 \tag{53}$$

The availability in literature of suitable data and empirical correlations concerning mass transport in this kind of systems allows to evaluate model parameters, such as physical-chemical properties of the species involved in the process, Henry constant, porosity and tortuosity factor of the electrode and external mass transfer coefficients. The kinetic coefficient, K, can be determined using the equation (18). In order to obtain the required data, experimental runs were carried out in an electrochemical laboratory apparatus. The evaluation of the dispersion coefficient requests the availability of data relevant to the effects of fluid-dynamics on the system behaviour. Normally, for complex systems, these information are obtained by carrying out the work in equipments, where the time dependent input technique is used. Lack of information about the fluid flow within the cathodic compartment, leads to assign to this parameter various values in order to analyse the role that these fluid-dynamics aspects have on the whole system performance.
The model's equations can be solved numerically by g-PROMS software.
In order to validate the model, electrolyses are carried out in the pilot plant above described. The amount of hydrogen peroxide generated is monitored during the experiments.
With reference to the working conditions of experimental tests, the concentration profiles from various proposed models are obtained.
To verify the models, tests are performed varying the dispersion coefficient value in the dispersed model. Results confirm that, increasing the dispersion coefficient, it is possible to change from the behaviour of a "plug flow reactor" to a "perfectly mixed reactor", described by the relevant models.
The comparison between the concentration of hydrogen peroxide at the exit section of the electrochemical cell at the threshold conditions typical of the "plug flow reactor" and "perfectly mixed reactor", allows to define the range in which dispersion coefficient affects the behaviour of the system. At the beginning of electrolysis, the effects of non-ideal flow patterns in the hydrogen peroxide concentration profiles inside the cathodic compartment are striking, as Fig. 7 clearly shows.

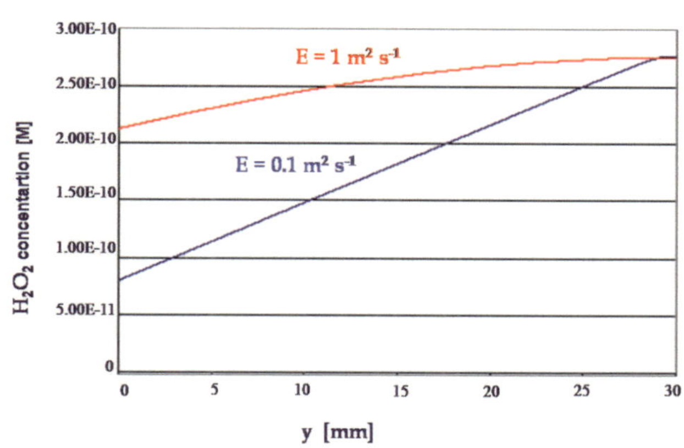

Fig. 7. Simulated hydrogen peroxide concentration profile inside the cathodic compartment . Effect of dispersion.

With increasing time, the effects become more blurred because of recirculation. In these conditions, the system is poorly sensitive to variations in the dispersion coefficient.
The shape of hydrogen peroxide concentration profiles in the flooded layer inside the pore, at various times is a combination of the resistances of the electrochemical reaction and the

diffusion of both components in the liquid phase. In the given working conditions, results of simulation, shown in Fig. 8, highlight that at longer times, more hydrogen peroxide accumulates within the pore. This may become a limiting factor when the contribution of the peroxide decomposition reaction to the overall process is considered.

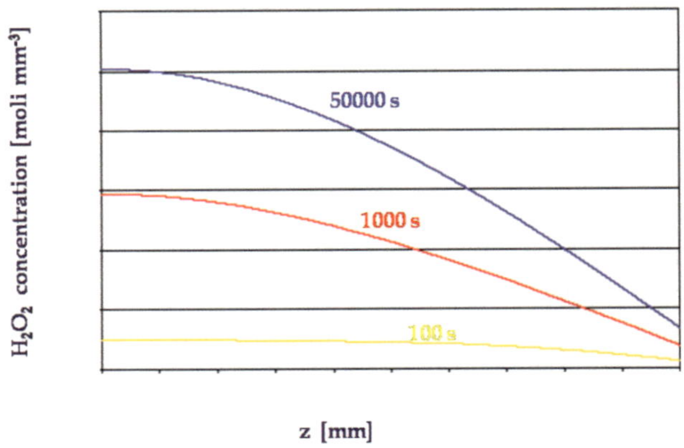

Fig. 8. Simulated hydrogen peroxide concentration profile inside the flooded layer at different times.

Lastly, validation is achieved comparing predictions based on equations (6)÷(40) with the experimental data obtained in the pilot plant (Giomo et al., 2008). Fig.9 shows the results with reference to simulated values obtained from CSTR model.

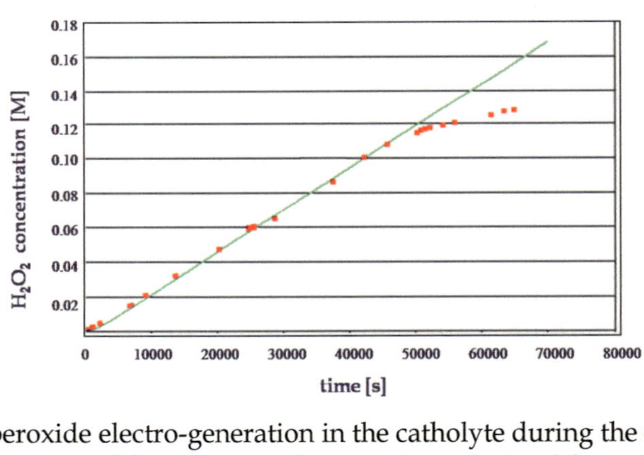

Fig. 9. Hydrogen peroxide electro-generation in the catholyte during the electrolysis. Comparison of experimental data and simulation values obtained from CSTR model.

A good match between simulated and experimental values is observed at the beginning of electrolysis, in accordance with the literature (Da Pozzo et al., 2005). At longer times, the model overestimates hydrogen peroxide production, perhaps due to several factors, e.g., higher rate of side reactions (15) and (16) (Da Pozzo et al., 2005), electrode flooding (Pasaogullari & Wang, 2004), or existence of considerable local overpotential or OH^- concentration values on the cathode surface, followed by H_2O_2 decomposition and H_2O production (Alcaide et al., 2002; Agladze et al., 2007; Kolyagin & Kornienko, 2003), not represented by the first-order kinetic equation used in this first model approach.

5. Conclusion

The two applications presented are basic examples of:

- simulations of the same system by using different models so as to compare their predictive capacity and the limitations of the solution techniques required to solve them;
- splitting the process into the main steps to define the subsystems which allow to analyse those particular attributes of the process that are of interest;
- development of mathematical models for each subsystems which allow to highlight the role played by the single step of the process and the parameters which are controlling its behaviour. The purpose is to obtain a representation of the whole process based on fairly simple representations for the parts;
- design of several laboratory apparatus or pilot plants to analyse the behaviour of subsystems, to obtain information about the essential features of the process and to evaluate the parameters in the model;
- comparison between calculated values and experimental data to evaluate how well the model represents the real process and to check the validity of assumptions made.

6. References

Agladze, G.R. ; Tsurtsumia, G.S.; Jung, B.I.; Kim, J.S. & Gorelishvili, G. (2007). Comparative study of hydrogen peroxide electro-generation on gas-diffusion electrodes in undivided and membrane cells. *Journal of Applied Electrochemistry*, Vol. 37 , No. 3, pp. 375-383, ISSN 1572-8838

Alcaide, F.; Brillas, E. & Cabot, P.L. (2002). Impedance study of the evolution of a HO_2^- generating hydrophobic gas diffusion electrode. *Electrochemistry Communications*, Vol. 4, No. 10, pp. 838-843, ISSN1388-2481

Brillas, E.; Calpe, J.C. & Casado J. (2000). Mineralization of 2,4-D by advanced electrochemical oxidation processes. *Water Research*, Vol. 34, No.8, pp. 2253-2262, ISSN 0043-1354

Buso, A. ; Giomo, M. & Paratella, A. (1991). Multistage Vibrating-Disk Column with concurrent gas-liquid flow. Fluodynamic simulation. *Chemical and Biochemical Engineering Quaterly*, Vol. 5, No. 1-2, pp. 23-33

Buso, A. ; Giomo, M.; Boaretto, L.; Sandonà, G. & Paratella, A. (1997). New electrochemical reactor for waste water treatment: electrochemical characterisation. *Chemical Engineering and Processing*, Vol. 36, No. 4, pp.255-260, ISSN0255-2701

Da Pozzo , A; Di Palma , L.; Merli, C.; Petrucci, E. (2005) An experimental comparison of a graphite electrode and a gas diffusion electrode for the cathodic production of hydrogen peroxide, *Journal of Applied Electrochemistry*, Vol. 35, No. 4, pp. 413-419, ISSN 1572-8838

Drogui, P.; Elmaleh, S. ; Rumeau, M. & Rambau A. ; (2001) Hydrogen peroxide production by water electrolysis: Application to disinfection, *Journal of Applied Electrochemistry*, Vol. 31 , p. 877-887, ISSN 1572-8838

Fahim, M.A. & Wakao N. (1982) *Chemical Engineering Journal*, Vol. 25, p. 1, ISSN....

Giomo, M.; Buso, A.; Fier, P.; Sandonà, G.; Boye, B. & Farnia G. (2008) A small-scale pilot plant using an oxygen-reducing gas-diffusion electrode for hydrogen peroxide electrosynthesis, *Electrochimica Acta*, Vol. 54, No. 2, pp. 808-815, ISSN0013-4686

Gonzáles-García, J.; Bank, C.E.; Sljukic, B. & Compton, R.G. (2007). Electrosynthesis of hydrogen peroxide via the reduction of oxygen assisted by power ultrasound. *Ultrasonics Sonochemistry,* Vol. 14, No.4, pp.405-412, ISSN1350-1477

Himmelblau, D.H., Bishoff, K.B. (1968) *Process Analysis and Simulation,* J. Wiley& Sons, USA

Karr , A. E.; Ramanujam, S; Lo, T. C.; Baird, M.H.I. (1987) Axial mixing and scale-up of reciprocating plate column. *Canadian Journal Chem. Eng.,*Vol. 65, No.3, pp. 373-381, ISSN1939-019X

Kolyagin, G.A. &Kornienko,V.L. (2003). Kinetics of hydrogen peroxide accumulation in electrosynthesis from oxygen in gas diffusion electrode in acid and alkaline solutions. *Russian Journal Applied Chem.,* Vol. 76, No.7, pp. 1070-1075, ISSN1608-3296

Lobyntseva , E.; Kallio, T.; Alexeyeva, N.; Tammeveski, K. & Konturri, K. (2007). Electrochemical synthesis of hydrogen peroxide: Rotating disk electrode and fuel cell studies. *Electrochimica Acta,* Vol. 52,No.25, pp. 7262-7269, ISSN0013-4686

Lounes, M. & Thibault, J. (1996). Axial dispersion in a reciprocating plate column. *Canadian Journal Chem. Eng.* , Vol.74, No.2 , pp.187-194, ISSN1939-019X

Miyanami, K.; Tojo, K. & Yano, T.J. (1973). Liquid–phase mixing in a multistage vibrating-disk column with concurrent gas-liquid flow. *Chemical Engineering Japan,* Vol. 6, No.6, p.518-522

Parthasarathy, P.; Sriniketan, G.; Srinivas, N.S. & Varma, Y.B.G. (1984). Axial mixing of continuous phase in reciprocating plate columns. *Chemical Engineering Science,* Vol. 39, No. 6, pp.987-995, ISSN0009-2509

Pasaogullari U. & Wang, C.Y (2004). Liquid water transport in gas diffusion layer of polymer electrolyte fuel cells. *Journal of Electrochemistry society,* Vol. 151 ,No. 3, pp. A399-406, ISSN1945-7111

Prentice, G. (1991) *Electrochemical engineering principles,* Ed. Prentice-Hall , New Jersey USA

Roemer, M. H. & Durbin L.D. (1967). Transient response and moments analysis of backflow cell model for flow systems with longitudinal mixing. *Industrial and Engineering Chemistry Fundamentals,*Vol. 6, pp. 120-129, ISSN0196-4313

Trinidad , P.; Ponce de Léon , C. & Walsh, F.C. (2006). The application of flow dispersion model to the FM01-LC laboratory filterpress reactor. *Electrochimica Acta,* Vol. 52, No. 2,pp. 604-613, ISSN0013-4686

Vakao, N. & Kaguei S. (1982) *Heat Transfer in Packed Beds,* Gordon and Breach Science, New York USA

Varma , A. & Morbidelli M. (1997) *Mathematical Methods in Chemical Engineering,* Oxford University Press, Oxford, MA, USA

19

Monitoring of Chemical Processes Using Model-Based Approach

Aicha Elhsoumi, Rafika El Harabi,
Saloua Bel Hadj Ali Naoui and Mohamed Naceur Abdelkrim
Unité de Recherche MACS, Ecole Nationale d'Ingénieurs de Gabès
Rue Omar Ibn Elkhatab
Tunisie

1. Introduction

In a chemical plant, a faulty sensor or actuator may cause process performance degradation (e.g. lower product quality) or fatal accidents (e.g. temperature run-away). For complex systems (e.g. CSTR reactors), fault detection and isolation are more complicated for the reason that some sensors cannot be placed in a desirable place. Furthermore, for some variables (concentrations, moles ...), no sensor exists. Therefore, the need for accurately monitoring process variables and interpreting their variations increases rapidly with the increase in the level of instrumentation in chemical plants. Supervision is a set of tools and methods used to operate a process in normal situation as well as in the presence of failures. Main activities concerned with supervision are real time Fault Detection and Isolation (FDI) and Fault Tolerant Control (FTC) to achieve safe operation of the system in the presence of faults. Supervision scheme is illustrated in two parts (see Fig. 1). The present paper deals with the FDI aspect using a model based approach. For reconfiguration or accommodation of the system, FTC methodology can be consulted in (Blanke M. & al., 2006).

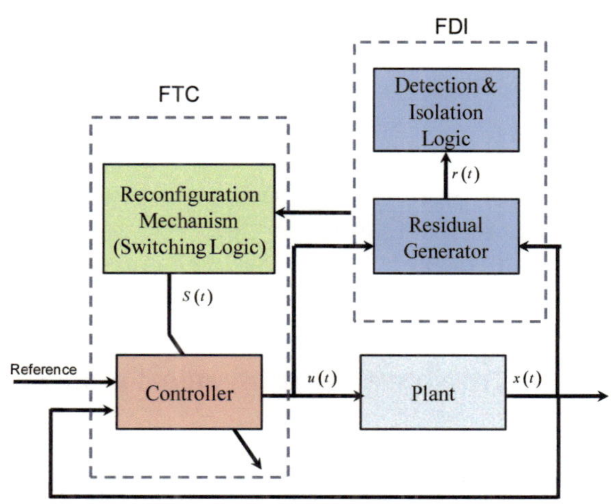

Fig. 1. Supervision scheme in process engineering.

Many researchers tried to find new approaches for performing fault diagnosis (Venkatasubramanian V., 2005), (Samantaray A.K. & al, 2006), (El Harabi R. & al., 2010a) and (El Harabi R. & al., 2010b). Others used existing approaches such the classic ones to develop their performance for new complex systems (Sotomayor O.A.Z. & al., 2005), (Chetouani Y., 2004) and (Venkatasubramanian V., 2003). Several fault diagnosis approaches have been proposed for processes operating mainly in steady-state conditions. The application of these techniques to batch chemical processes are usually challenging, because of their nonlinear dynamics and intrinsically unsteady operating conditions. In addition, complete state and parameters measurements (i.e. products composition) are usually not available (Levenspiel O., 1999). These approaches can be based on a mathematical model (e.g. analytical redundancy methods, observers based methods…) (Edwards C. & al., 2000), (Caccavale F. & al., 2009) or only on historical data (e.g. fuzzy methods, neural approach…) (De Miguela L.J. & al., 2005), (Evsukoffa A. & al., 2005).
Model-based methods consist in the comparison between the measurements of variables set characterizing the behavior of the monitored system and the corresponding estimates predicted via the mathematical model of system. The deviations between measured and estimated process variables provide a set of residuals, sensitive to the occurrence of faults; then, by using the information carried by residuals, faults can be detected (i.e., the presence of one or more faults can be recognized) and isolated (i.e., the faulty components are determined). Among model-based analytical redundancy approaches, observer-based schemes have been successfully adopted in a variety of application fields (Sotomayor O.A.Z. & al., 2005), (Patton R.J & al., 1997), (Frank P.M. & al., 1990). Namely, a model of the system (often called diagnostic observer) is operated in parallel to the process to compute estimated process variables to be compared to their measured values. Application of approaches based on Luenberger and/or Kalman observers to chemical reactors diagnosis are usually designed by resorting to linearized models of the reactor. However, the adoption of linearized models has been proven to work properly for the Continuous Stirred Tank Reactors (CSTRs), mainly operating at steady state, due to their intrinsic unsteady behavior (Rajaraman S. & al., 2006), (Favache A. & al., 2009), (Hsoumi A. & al., 2009), (Han Z. & al., 2005).
The basic idea of this paper concerns use of Luenberger and Kalman observers for modeling and monitoring nonlinear dynamic processes. Furthermore, the generated fault indicators are systematically associated to a specific (sensor, actuator) faults which may affect the system. A Continuous Stirred Tank Reactor with its environment has been selected as an application.
The paper is organized as follows. Section 2 presents a brief review of Fault Detection and Isolation (FDI) in the chemical processes and basic proprieties of linear observers. In the third section, it is shown how the Luenberger and Kalman observers can be used for systematic generation of FDI algorithms. The methodology is applied for online diagnosis of a pilot chemical reactor. Finally, the fourth section concludes the work.

2. Model-based diagnosis methods in the chemical processes

2.1 Review

Due to the frequent and serious accidents that have occurred in the last decades in the chemical industry, the importance of incipient fault detection and diagnosis in complex process plants has become more obvious. The interest to determine the fault occurrence on-line during the chemical reaction justifies the development of fault detection methods. Therefore, extensive reviews of different fault diagnosis methods of chemical process can be found in the literature. As cited above, according to the knowledge and the quality of data available for the process to be monitored, the FDI methods used are mainly based on two approaches: model-based and non-model-based. In this section are consulted only papers related to model based diagnosis applied to the chemical processes.

Model-based methods explicitly use a dynamic model of the process. A pedagogical theory on model based FDI and FTC can be consulted in (Blanke M. & al., 2006). Those methods can be classified into two classes: namely, quantitative model based and qualitative model based. Qualitative model based methods include structural and functional analysis, fault tree analysis, temporal causal graphs, signed directed graphs, etc.. The models can be given under formal format. Quantitative model based methods such as observer based diagnosis, parity space, and extended Kalman filters, etc. strongly rely on the availability of an explicit analytical model to perform the FDI of the process. In (Chetouani Y., 2004) and (Chetouani Y. & al., 2002), the measurements of a set of process variables (from chemical reactor) are compared to the corresponding estimates, predicted via the mathematical model of the system. By comparing measured and estimated values, a set of variables sensitive to the occurrence of faults (residuals) are generated; by processing the residuals. Estimation of monitored process variables requires a model of the system (diagnostic observer) to be operated in parallel to the process. For this purpose, Luenberger observers, Unknown Input Observers and Extended Kalman Filters (UIOEKF) have been mostly used in fault detection and identification for chemical processes. A Luenberger observer is used for sensor fault detection and isolation in chemical batch reactors in (Chetouani Y., 2004), while in (Chetouani Y. & al., 2002), the robust approach is compared with an adaptive observer for actuator fault diagnosis. In (Paviglianiti G. & al., 2007), two different nonlinear observer-based methods have been developed for actuator Fault Diagnosis of a chemical batch reactor. An adaptive observer has been used to build a residual generator able to perform detection of incipient and abrupt faults. This scheme of observer-based diagnosis consists of a bank of two observers for residual generation which guarantees sensor fault detection and isolation in presence of external disturbances and model uncertainties. Since perfect knowledge of the model is rarely a reasonable assumption, soft computing methods, integrating quantitative and qualitative information, have been developed to improve the performance of FD observer-based schemes for uncertain systems. Observer FDI based is well suited for linear or a class of nonlinear dynamic models. Furthermore, such technique is more widely used for sensor and actuator faults detection. Their isolation needs a bank of observers.

The extended Kalman filter (EKF) is employed to estimate both the parameters and states of chemical engineering processes. The basic idea of the adopted approach is to reconstruct the outputs of the system from the measurements by using observers or Kalman filters and using the residuals for fault detection. Two faults in a perfectly stirred semi-batch chemical reactor, occurring at an unknown moment, are experimentally realized. EKF is applied on a two-tank system and a fluid catalytic cracking (FCC) unit in (Huang Y. & al., 2003). In (Porru G. & al., 2000), the fault detection method is based on a test applied to the reaction mass temperature which represents the monitoring parameter. This parameter is considered essential because it is the result of all the faults effects and of the introduced experimental parameters (inlet flow, stirring rate, cooling flow, etc.). Indeed, the reaction mass temperature is the dynamic image in case of fault absence or fault presence. Moreover, this temperature is an accessible measurement in all chemical reactors. A significant number of applications of Kalman filter for fault diagnosis in chemical processes are developed in the literature. Nevertheless, previous knowledge of the process is necessary. Indeed, successful fault detection needs a judicious adjustment of the filter parameters, which expresses the response of the filter to anomalies. Among the model-based approaches, analytical redundancy methods have been mostly used in sensor and actuator fault detection and identification (Paviglianiti G. & al., 2006).

2.2 Linear observers

Fault diagnosis is usually performed to accomplish one or more of the following tasks: fault detection (or monitoring), indication of the fault occurrence; fault isolation, the determination of the exact location of fault and fault identification, estimation of the fault magnitude.

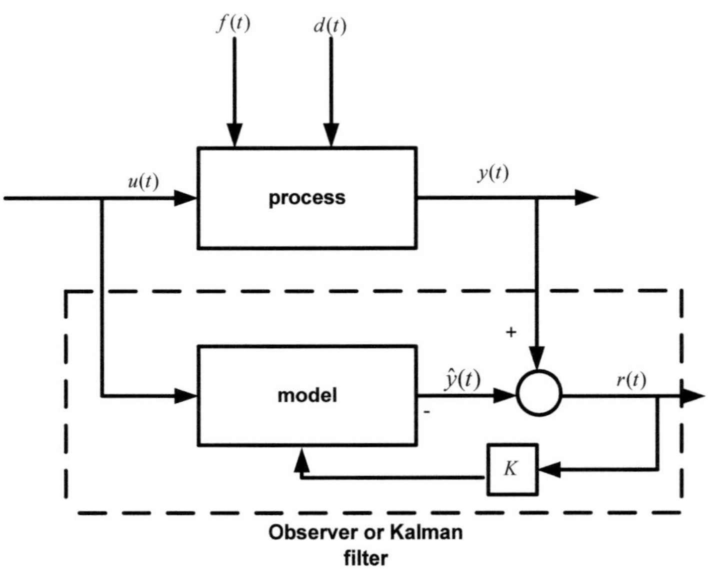

Fig. 2. Scheme of a linear observer

The observer-based diagnosis algorithm generally consists in comparing real measured information with that of nominal behavior as shown in Fig. 2. The difference between these types of information indicates if fault is present or not (detection). This scheme is called a residual generation which will be mentioned in the next paragraph.

2.2.1 Residual generation

Residual generation is the core element of a fault diagnosis system. It consists in estimating the process output by using either a Luenberger observer in a deterministic setting case or a Kalman filter in a stochastic one. Estimation error (or innovation in the stochastic case) is defined as the residual. The main concern of observer-based FDI is the generation of a set of residuals which detect and especially identify different faults. These residuals should be robust in the sense that the decisions are not corrupted by unknown inputs as unstructured uncertainties like process and measurement noise and modeling uncertainties. Observer based fault detection makes use of the disturbance decoupling principle, in which the residual is computed assuming the decoupling of the effects of faults on different inputs.

The basic idea of a linear observer-based residual generator is illustrated in Fig. 2. $u(t)$ and $y(t)$ denote respectively the input and output vectors, $f(t)$ is the vector of faults to be detected and $d(t)$ is the vector of unknown inputs, to which detection system should be insensitive. Variable $\hat{y}(t)$ corresponds to estimated outputs vector, $r(t)$ is residual vector and K is observer gain.

The output estimation error is given by:

$$e_y(t) = y(t) - \hat{y}(t) \tag{1}$$

To provide useful information for fault diagnosis, the residual should be defined as:

$$\begin{cases} r(t) = 0 \text{ (or } r(t) \approx 0\text{), if } f(t) = 0, \\ r(t) \neq 0, \text{ if } f(t) \neq 0 \end{cases} \tag{2}$$

2.2.2 Luenberger observer

An observer is defined as a dynamic system with state variables that are estimated from state variables of another system (Lie Q., 2001). A dynamic process can be described mathematically in several ways. It can be represented in the following form:

$$\begin{cases} \dot{x}(t) = Ax(t) + Bu(t) + Ed(t) + Ff_a \\ y(t) = Cx(t) + Du(t) + Gd + Hf_s \\ x(0) = x_0 \end{cases} \tag{3}$$

where x is the state vector, u is the input, y is the output, d is the disturbances; f_s and f_a are respectively sensor and actuator faults , A , B , C and D are statistic matrix.

Observer based residual generation is simple and reliable to implement in practical applications. In this subsection, the procedure for designing a dedicated observer and the associated residual generator is proposed. A Luenberger observer given by (Lie Q., 2001) is described by:

$$\begin{cases} \dot{\hat{x}} = A\hat{x} + Bu + L[y - \hat{y}] \\ \hat{y} = C\hat{x} + Du \\ \hat{x}(0) = \hat{x}_0 \end{cases} \tag{4}$$

and can be written as follows:

$$\begin{cases} \dot{\hat{x}} = (A - LC)\hat{x} + (B - LD)u + Ly \\ \hat{y} = C\hat{x} + Du \\ \hat{x}(0) = \hat{x}_0 \end{cases} \tag{5}$$

where $\hat{x}$ is the state estimate, $\hat{y}$ is the output estimate and $\hat{x}(0)$ the initial state estimate.

The Luenberger can be considered for residual generator design; here L is the observer gain matrix such that $(A-LC)$ is stable. The state error is defined as:

$$e = x - \hat{x} \tag{6}$$

Hence

$$\begin{aligned}\dot{e} &= \dot{x} - \dot{\hat{x}} \\ &= Ax + Bu - \overbrace{(A-LC)}^{\hat{A}}\hat{x} - \overbrace{(B-LD)}^{\hat{B}}u - Ly \\ &= Ax + Bu - \hat{A}(x-e) - \hat{B}u - LCx \\ &= \hat{A}e + (A - LC - \hat{A})x + (B - \hat{B})u\end{aligned} \tag{7}$$

The matrices $\hat{A}$ and $\hat{B}$ are chosen and the error goes to zero regardless of x and u. So $\dot{e}$ becomes in the following form:

$$\begin{aligned}\dot{e} &= \hat{A}e \\ &= (A-LC)e\end{aligned} \tag{8}$$

The matrix L is to determine. However, if the error converges to zero; observer can be stable, the real part of all eigenvalues of $(A-LC)$ must be negative.
The residual r is the difference between the output and its estimate denoted respectively y and $\hat{y}$:

$$\begin{aligned}r &= y - \hat{y} \\ &= Cx - C\hat{x} \\ &= C(x-\hat{x}) \\ &= Ce\end{aligned} \tag{9}$$

Hence $\dot{e}$ and r expressions, for a system with sensor and actuator faults, are the following:

$$\begin{cases}\dot{e} = (A-LC)e + Ed + Ff_a \\ r = Ce + Gd + Hf_s\end{cases} \tag{10}$$

Residual is influenced by the sensor fault; however $\dot{e}$ depends on the actuator fault.

2.2.3 Kalman filter

Kalman filter is essentially an algorithm for revising the moments of stochastic components of a linear time series model to reflect information about them contained in time series data. A dynamic process can be described mathematically in several ways (Chetouani Y., 2004); let us consider the linear stochastic system; the model can be described with the following discrete form:

$$\begin{cases}x_{k+1} = A_k x_k + B_k u_k + G_k w_k \\ y_k = C_k x_k + D_k u_k + v_k\end{cases} \tag{11}$$

where x_k is the state vector, u_k is the input, y_k is the output, w_k is a zero mean Gaussian noise vector and the corresponding covariance matrix is Q, v_k is the measurement noise which is assumed to be normally distributed with zero mean where R is the covariance matrix associated. A_k, B_k, C_k, D_k are statistic matrices and G_k is the disturbances matrix.
Kalman filter based residual generation can be used with simplicity if the disturbances can be modeled. The following procedure is investigated for designing a simple Kalman filter and generating residuals.
The discrete Kalman filter for the above system can be written in two steps:

- Time update "predict":

The object of this stage is the state estimation by using only the previous state.
Filter application should start with state and state covariance matrix initialization.

$$\begin{cases} x_{0/0} = x_0 \\ P_{0/0} = P_0 \end{cases} \tag{12}$$

In this step, there are two parts:
(Part1) Project the state ahead

$$x_{k/k-1} = A_{k-1} x_{k-1/k-1} + B_{k-1} u_{k-1} \tag{13}$$

(part 2) Project a state covariance matrix ahead

$$P_{k/k-1} = A_{k-1} P_{k/k} A_{k-1}^T + G_{k-1} Q_{k-1} G_{k-1}^T \tag{14}$$

The model of prediction step can be written in the following form:

$$\begin{cases} x_{k/k-1} = A_{k-1} x_{k/k} + B_{k-1} u_{k-1} \\ P_{k/k-1} = A_{k-1} P_{k/k} A_{k-1}^T + G_{k-1} Q_{k-1} G_{k-1}^T \end{cases} \tag{15}$$

Measurement update "correct":
This is the step of reactualization of state estimation with output measurements.
In this step, three parts should be followed:
(part 1) Compute the Kalman gain

$$K_k = P_{k/k-1} C_k^T (C_k P_{k/k-1} C_k^T + R_k)^{-1} \tag{16}$$

(part 2) Update estimate with measurement y_k

$$x_{k/k} = x_{k/k-1} + K_k (y_k - C_k x_{k/k-1}) \tag{17}$$

(part 3) Update the state covariance matrix

$$P_{k/k} = (I - K_k C_k) P_{k/k-1} \tag{18}$$

So the model of this stage has the following form:

$$\begin{cases} K_k = P_{k/k-1} C_k^T (C_k P_{k/k-1} C_k^T + R_k)^{-1} \\ x_{k/k} = x_{k/k-1} + K_k (y_k - C_k x_{k/k-1}) \\ P_{k/k} = (I - K_k C_k) P_{k/k-1} \end{cases} \tag{19}$$

The discrete Kalman filter for the above system can be written as:

$$\begin{cases} x_{k/k-1} = A_{k-1}x_{k/k} + B_{k-1}u_{k-1} \\ P_{k/k-1} = A_{k-1}P_{k/k}A_{k-1}^T + G_{k-1}Q_{k-1}G_{k-1}^T \\ K_k = P_{k/k-1}C_k^T(C_kP_{k/k-1}C_k^T + R_k)^{-1} \\ x_{k/k} = x_{k/k-1} + K_k(y_k - C_kx_{k/k-1}) \\ P_{k/k} = (I - K_kC_k)P_{k/k-1} \end{cases} \tag{20}$$

Then priori and posteriori estimate errors are defined as:

$$\begin{cases} e^- = x_k - \hat{x}_{k/k-1} \\ e^+ = x_k - \hat{x}_{k/k} \end{cases} \tag{21}$$

The posteriori estimate error is used in the present work and can be written in the following expression:

$$\begin{aligned} e_{k+1}^- &= x_{k+1} - x_{k+1/k} \\ &= A_kx_k + B_ku_k + G_kw_k - A_kx_{k/k} - B_ku_k \end{aligned} \tag{22}$$

or A_k, B_k, C_k, D_k and G_k are statistic matrices, so the error expression is :

$$\begin{aligned} e_{k+1}^- &= A(x_k - x_{k/k}) + Gw_k \\ &= A(x_k - x_{k/k-1} - K_k(y_k - Cx_{k/k-1})) + Gw_k \\ &= A(x_k - x_{k/k-1} - K_k(Cx_k + v_k - Cx_{k/k-1})) + Gw_k \\ &= (A - K_kC)(x_k - x_{k/k-1}) + Gw_k - K_kv_k \\ &= (A - K_kC)e_k^- + Gw_k - K_kv_k \end{aligned} \tag{23}$$

The residual r is the difference between output and its estimate denoted respectively y_k and $\hat{y}_k$:

$$\begin{aligned} r &= y - \hat{y} \\ &= Cx_k + v_k - Cx_{k/k-1} \\ &= C(x_k - x_{k/k-1}) + v_k \\ &= Ce_k^- + v_k \end{aligned} \tag{24}$$

So the error e_{k+1} and residual r are given by:

$$\begin{cases} e_{k+1} = (A - K_kC)e_k^- + Gw_k - K_kv_k \\ r = Ce_k^- + v_k \end{cases} \tag{25}$$

For a system with sensor and actuator faults is described as:

$$\begin{cases} x_{k+1} = Ax_k + Bu_k + Gw_k + Ff_a \\ y_k = Cx_k + Du_k + v_k + Hf_s \end{cases} \tag{26}$$

The error and residual have the following forms:

$$\begin{cases} e_{k+1} = (A - K_k C)e_k^- + Gw_k - K_k v_k + Ff_a \\ r = Ce_k^- + v_k + Hf_s \end{cases} \tag{27}$$

The residual is influenced by the sensor fault and the state error, however e_{k+1} depends on the actuator fault.

3. Application to continuous reactor

3.1 Process description

The continuous reactor with heat exchange is defined as the most common type of process equipment to be found in manufacturing plants. It is used in many process operations such as fermentation, chemical synthesis, polymerisation, crystallisation ...etc.

The process to be supervised consists of a reaction vessel, a jacket vessel, an entry and exit feeding pipes, a coolant and products, valves, a stirring system and a heat exchange surface. Jacket is fitted to the reactor vessel by using an external heated transfer coil wrapped around the vessel surface. The reaction takes place within the reactor. A stirring system maintains the mixture among the reactants and products with a good homogeneous degree of physical and chemical properties.

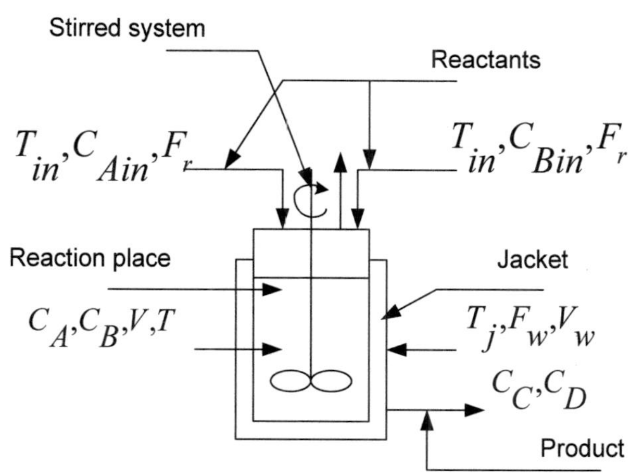

Fig. 3. Scheme of the continuous reactor

Concentration and temperature variables are not in function of the position and they represent average values for all the reactor volume.

The reaction, occurring in the reactor vessel, is an irreversible and very exothermic oxido-reduction (Rajaraman S. & al., 2006), the oxidation of sodium thiosulfate by hydrogen peroxide is given by:

$$Na_2S_2O_3 + 2H_2O_2 \rightarrow \frac{1}{2}Na_2s_2O_6 + \frac{1}{2}Na_2SO_4 + 2H_2O \tag{28}$$

The kinetic reaction law is reported in the literature to be:

$$r_A = -k(T_r)C_A C_B = -(k_0 + \Delta k_0)\exp(-\frac{E_a + \Delta E_a}{RT_r})C_A C_B \tag{29}$$

where k_0 is the pre-exponential factor, C_A and C_B are respectively concentrations of components A and B (A is the $Na_2S_2O_3$ and B is the H_2O_2), E_a is the activation energy, R is the perfect gas constant, Δk_0 and ΔE_a represent uncertainty respectively in the pre-exponential factor and in the activation energy and T_r is the reactor temperature.

A mole balance for species A and energy balances for the reactor and the cooling jacket result in the following nonlinear process model with ($C_A = C_B$):

$$\begin{cases} \frac{dC_A}{dt} = \frac{F_r}{V}(C_{Ain} - C_A) - 2k(t)C_A^2 \\ \frac{dT_r}{dt} = \frac{F_r}{V}(T_{in} - T_r) + 2\frac{(-\Delta H_r) + \Delta(-\Delta H_r)}{\rho C_p}k(t)C_A^2 - \frac{UA + \Delta UA}{\rho C_p V}(T_r - T_j) \\ \frac{dT_j}{dt} = \frac{F_w}{V_w}(T_{jin} - T_j) + \frac{UA + \Delta UA}{\rho_w C_{pw} V_w (T_r - T_j)} \end{cases} \tag{30}$$

This system (30) represents the dynamic reactor comportment. The three equations represent the evolution of three states (C_A : molar concentration of A, T_r: reactor temperature and T_j : cooling jacket temperature). So, state vector can be defined as:

$$x(t) = \begin{bmatrix} x_1 \\ x_2 \\ x_3 \end{bmatrix} = \begin{bmatrix} C_A \\ T_r \\ T_j \end{bmatrix} \tag{31}$$

In this case, the state representation of the studied system is given as:

$$\begin{cases} \frac{dx_1}{dt} = \frac{F_r}{V}(x_1(0) - x_1) - 2k(t)x_1^2 \\ \frac{dx_2}{dt} = \frac{F_r}{V}(x_2(0) - x_2) + 2\frac{(-\Delta H_r) + \Delta(-\Delta H_r)}{\rho C_p}k(t)x_1^2 - \frac{UA + \Delta UA}{\rho C_p V}(x_2 - x_3) \\ \frac{dx_3}{dt} = \frac{F_w}{V_w}(x_3(0) - x_3) + \frac{UA + \Delta UA}{\rho_w C_{pw} V_w}(x_2 - x_3) \end{cases} \tag{32}$$

where the initial state vector is:

$x(0) = \begin{bmatrix} x_1(0) \\ x_2(0) \\ x_3(0) \end{bmatrix} = \begin{bmatrix} C_{Ain} \\ T_{rin} \\ T_{jin} \end{bmatrix}$; $y(t) = Cx(t)$ is the observation vector, $C = I(3)$.

Parameters values are represented in this table:

process parameters	Symbols	Value
feed flow rate	F_r	120 $l.\min^{-1}$
inlet feed concentration	C_{Ain}	1 $mol.l^{-1}$
volume of the reactor	V	100 l
pre-exponential factor	k_0	4.11×10^{-13} $l.\min^{-1}.mol^{-1}$
activation energy	E_a	76534.704
inlet feed temperature	T_{in}	275 K
heat of the reaction	$(-\Delta H_r)$	596619 J.mol^{-1}
density of the reaction mixture	ρ	1000 $g.l^{-1}$
heat capacity of the reacting mixture	c_p	4.2 $J.g^{-1}.K^{-1}$
coolant flow rate	F_w	30 $l.\min^{1}$
overall heat transfer rate	UA	12×10^5 $J.\min^{-1}.K^{-1}$
Volume of the cooling jacket	V_w	10 l
density of coolant fluid	ρ_w	1000 $g.l^{-1}$
heat capacity of the coolant	c_{pw}	4.2 $J.g^{-1}.K^{1}$
inlet coolant temperature	T_{jin}	250 K

Table 1. Process parameter values for CSTR operationThe conversion rate can be given by:

$$x_c = \frac{n_{A0} - n_A}{n_{A0}} = \frac{C_{Ain} - C_A}{C_{Ain}} \tag{33}$$

Figure 4 and Figure 5 depict respectively the concentration evolution of reactant C_A, conversion rate x_c and the temperature profiles of reactor T_r and jacket T_j. The concentration evolution has two phases: a dynamic phase, when the reaction is taken place, and a permanent phase after the end of reaction; when mole number of component A becomes constant. Reaction perfectly takes place so the conversion rate converges rapidly to 1.

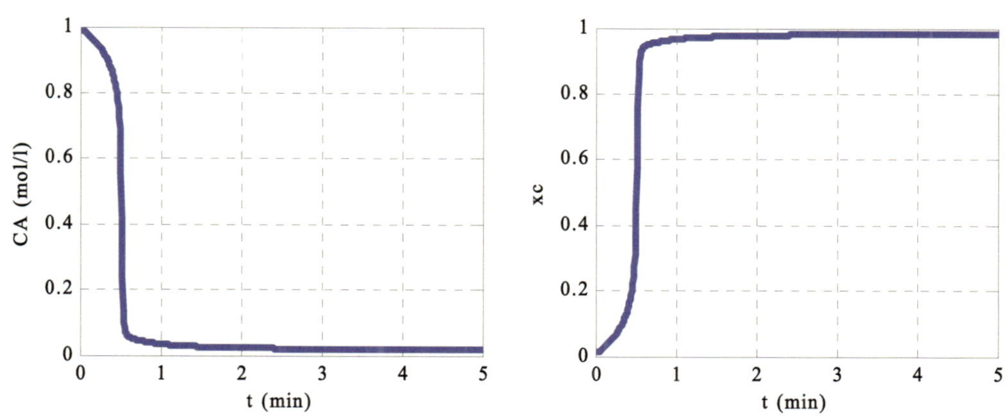

(a) (b)

Fig. 4. (a) Concentration evolution of reactant A (b) Conversion rate evolution

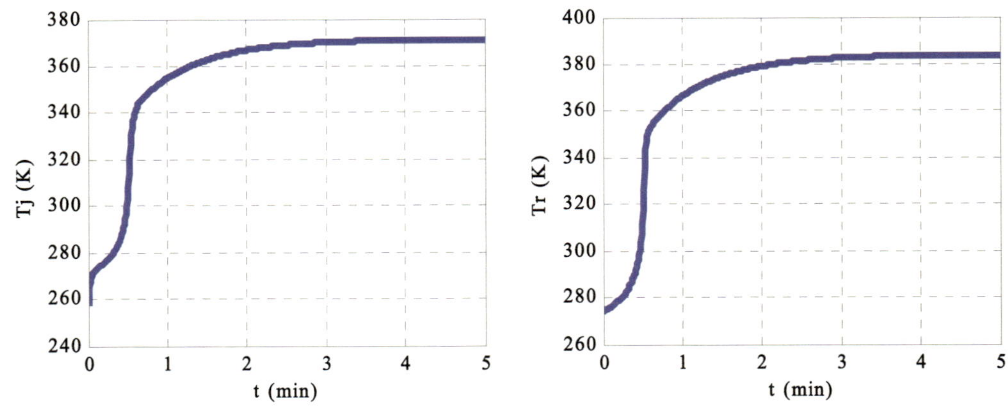

Fig. 5. Trajectories of (a) jacket temperature (b) reactional temperature

Figure 5 shows that the reactor temperature increases with time from 275 K to 385 K. This causes an increase of temperature in the jacket. In this case (exothermic reaction), the jacket presents a cooling coil around the reactor vessel.
From equation (32), the system is a non linear. So, it should be linearized in order to obtain an observer with the form described in section 2.

3.2 Model linearization

The nominal nonlinear model exhibits multiple steady states, of which the upper steady state (i.e. C_A =0.0192076 mol/l; T_r =384.005 K; T_j =271.272 K.), is stable and chosen as a normal operating point.
Hence, system state representation obtained by linearizing the process model (32) around the chosen steady state is:

$$\begin{cases} \dot{x} = Ax + Bu \\ y = Cx \end{cases} \tag{34}$$

$$x = \begin{bmatrix} \Delta C_A \\ \Delta T_r \\ \Delta T_j \end{bmatrix} ; y = \begin{bmatrix} \Delta T_r \\ \Delta T_j \end{bmatrix} ; u = T_{jin} ; C = \begin{bmatrix} 0 & 1 & 0 \\ 0 & 0 & 1 \end{bmatrix} ;$$

$$A = \begin{bmatrix} -125.8815 & -0.0747 & 0 \\ 1.7711e+004 & 6.5538 & 2.8571 \\ 0 & 28.5714 & -31.5714 \end{bmatrix} ; \; B = \begin{bmatrix} 0 \\ 0 \\ 3 \end{bmatrix}$$

Fig. 6 shows evolution trajectories of two outputs ΔT_r and ΔT_j according to time after the linearization around an operating point (without faults and uncertainties).
The linear model of continuous reactor is:

$$\begin{cases} \dot{x} = Ax + Bu + Ff_a \\ y = Cx + Hf_s \end{cases} \tag{35}$$

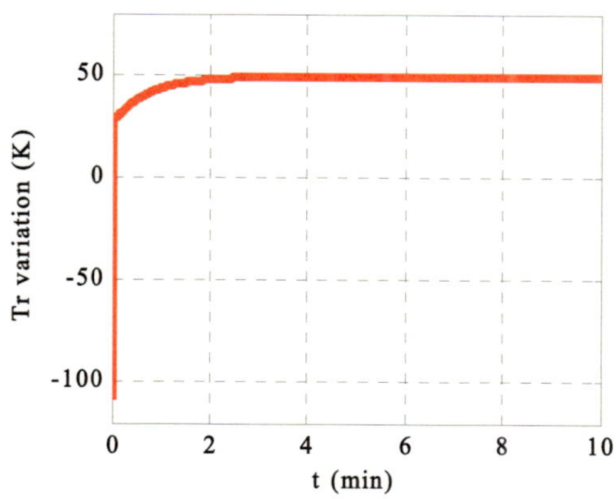

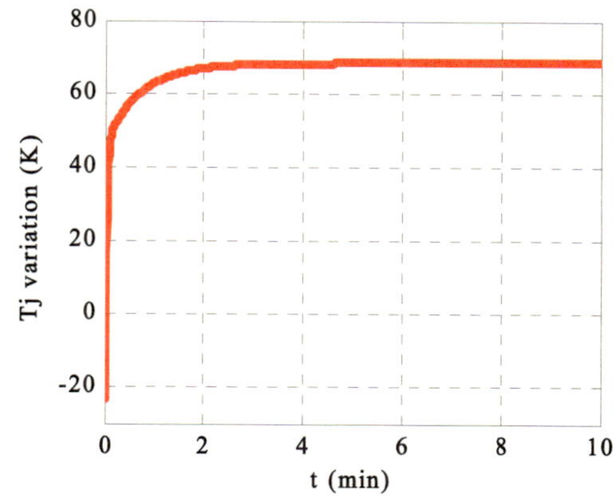

Fig. 6. Output component's evolution around the steady state (respectively T_r and T_j variations)

with $f_s = \begin{pmatrix} f_{s1} \\ f_{s2} \end{pmatrix}$ and f_a are respectively a sensor and actuator fault.

$F = \begin{pmatrix} 0 \\ 1 \\ 1 \end{pmatrix}$ is fault matrix in state expression and $H = \begin{pmatrix} 1 & 0 \\ 0 & 1 \end{pmatrix}$ is an output fault matrix.

3.3 Luenberger based FDI

- In this section the performance of the proposed fault diagnosis is demonstrated through taking the example of non-isothermal CSTR with parametric uncertainties.

The linear model of continuous reactor is:

$$\begin{cases} \dot{x} = (A + \Delta A)x + Bu + Ef_a \\ y = Cx + Hf_s \end{cases} \tag{36}$$

with:

$$u = 250\,;\; A = \begin{bmatrix} -125.8815 & -0.0747 & 0 \\ 1.7711e+004 & 6.5538 & 2.8571 \\ 0 & 28.5714 & -31.5714 \end{bmatrix};\; B = \begin{bmatrix} 0 \\ 0 \\ 3 \end{bmatrix};$$

$$C = \begin{bmatrix} 0 & 1 & 0 \\ 0 & 0 & 1 \end{bmatrix};\quad A + \Delta A = \begin{bmatrix} -32.3012 & -0.0198 & 0 \\ 4.6389e+003 & -1.2541 & 3 \\ 0 & 30 & -33 \end{bmatrix}$$

ΔA is the model uncertainties which are the function of parameter uncertainties ($\Delta k_0 = 5\% k_0$, $\Delta E = 6\% E$, $\Delta(-\Delta H_r) = 5\%(-\Delta H_r)$ and $\Delta UA = 5\% UA$).

$f_s = \begin{pmatrix} f_{s1} \\ f_{s2} \end{pmatrix}$ and f_a are respectively a sensor and actuator fault.

$F = \begin{pmatrix} 0 \\ 1 \\ 1 \end{pmatrix}$ is fault matrix in state expression and $H = \begin{pmatrix} 1 & 0 \\ 0 & 1 \end{pmatrix}$ is an output fault matrix.

A Lunberger observer can be applied to diagnosis of chemical process. Eigenvalues of the closed loop observer are placed at: {-114.9, -1.3687, -34.6304} to determinate observer gain L expressed as: $L = [L_1 \quad L_2]$.

Results obtained are: $L_1 = \begin{bmatrix} -1.3549e-008 \\ -3.4228e-005 \\ 4.2821e-004 \end{bmatrix}$ and $L_2 = \begin{bmatrix} 1.3421e-007 \\ -1.1250e-005 \\ -3.4228e-005 \end{bmatrix}$

3.4 Kalman filter-based FDI

The obtained reactor model is continuous. Hence, for this approach, a step of model discretization should be achieved to make the system applicable by the Kalman filter.
Therefore, the sample time can be chosen $T_e = 0.01s$, depending on the comportment of non linear system.
The obtained descritized model by the Zero-Order Hold method has the following form:

$$\begin{cases} x_{k+1} = A_k x_k + B_k u_k + G_k w_k \\ y_k = C_k x_k + v_k \end{cases} \quad (37)$$

with:

$$A_k = \begin{bmatrix} -0.0821 & -5.8989e-004 & -1.2668e-005 \\ 156.2330 & 1.0489 & 0.0269 \\ 33.5511 & 0.2690 & 0.7227 \end{bmatrix}; B_k = \begin{bmatrix} -1.6941e-007 \\ 4.2393e-004 \\ 0.0256 \end{bmatrix};$$

$G_k = \begin{bmatrix} -3.2482e-006 \\ 4.7426e-004 \\ 1.0139e-004 \end{bmatrix}$; $C_k = C$; w : is a zero mean Gaussian noise vector and the corresponding covariance matrix is $Q = 0.0035$, v_k is the measurement noise which is again assumed to be equal to zero. The matrix G_k is a distribution of model uncertainties in the activation energy ΔE.
The specific equations for the time and measurement updates are presented by:

$$\begin{cases} x_{k/k-1} = A_{k-1} x_{k/k} + B_{k-1} u_{k-1} \\ P_{k/k-1} = A_{k-1} P_{k/k} A_{k-1}^T + G_{k-1} Q_{k-1} G_{k-1}^T \\ K_k = P_{k/k-1} C_k^T (C_k P_{k/k-1} C_k^T)^{-1} \\ x_{k/k} = x_{k/k-1} + K_k (y_k - C_k x_{k/k-1}) \\ P_{k/k} = (I - K_k C_k) P_{k/k-1} \end{cases} \quad (38)$$

with:

$$\begin{cases} x_{0/0} = \begin{bmatrix} 0 \\ 0 \\ 0 \end{bmatrix} \\ P_{0/0} = 1000.I(3) \end{cases}$$

3.5 Simulation results

1. Lunberger-based FDI

a. Fault detection

The purpose of fault detection is to determine whether a fault has occurred in the system.
To accommodate the need to analyze the behavior of the residual signal in more detail, the behavior model is augmented with fault signals and transfer functions from faults to residuals are computed. Commonly, the fault signals are either added or multiplied to the model of the normal behavior and are therefore often referred to as additive and multiplicative faults. For linear systems also multiplicative faults appear as an additive signal after system linearization.
System behavior without faults can be observed by a state estimation with the closed loop system and tests will be used to detect changing in the system outputs behaviors. If fault exists, detection must be achieved; thus, system must have the same behavior estimations.

- Sensor fault detection

Additive and structural sensor fault signals are introduced and their shapes and sizes are given in figure 7.

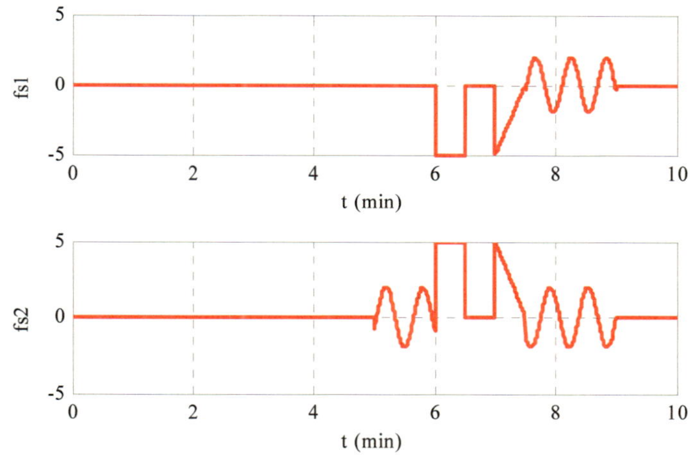

Fig. 7. Sensor faults evolution

Figure 8 represents output and residual system behaviors with sensor faults, where the dashed lines describe the system without uncertainties.
Faults are detected and residuals have the same forms and sizes as faults. When the model contains parameter uncertainties, the detection is achieved but residuals have a smaller size with appearance of some peaks in the time of inversion time.

- Actuator fault detection

This fault has been supposed to have the same form that the first sensor fault multiplies in amplitude by 1.5.
Outputs and residuals trajectories illustrated in Fig.9 show the uncertainties and actuator fault effects on residual behaviors.
Actuator fault is not detectable with the Lunberger observer both without and with uncertainties. The fault effect appears as small disturbances in the output behavior and Lunberger-based approach indicate the non detectability of actuator fault. The fault is detected when its energy is higher than that introduced by the whole uncertainties.

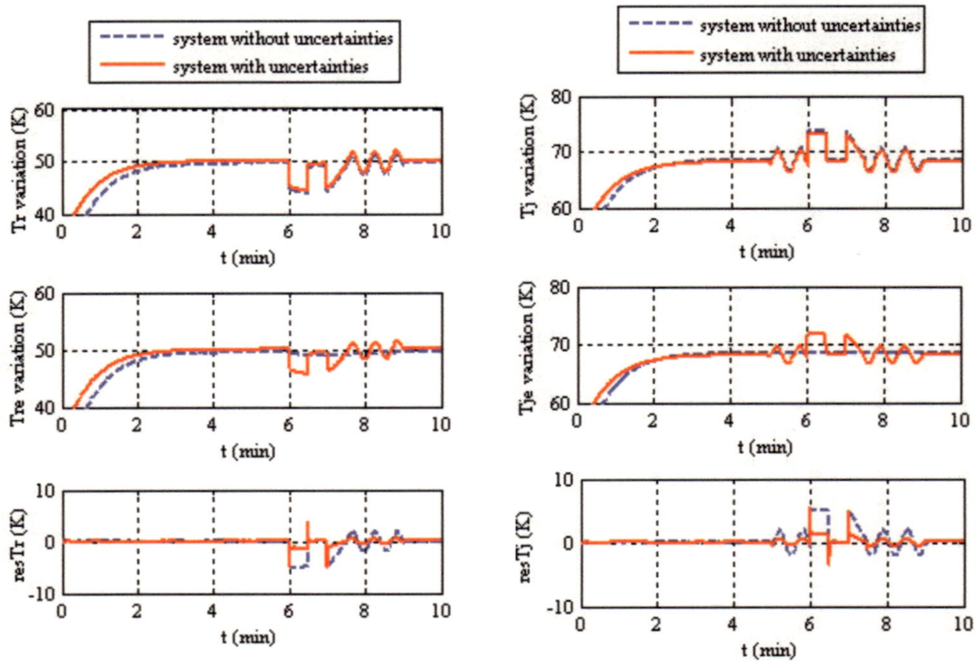

Fig. 8. Residual evolution and estimated temperature in the reactor and in the jacket

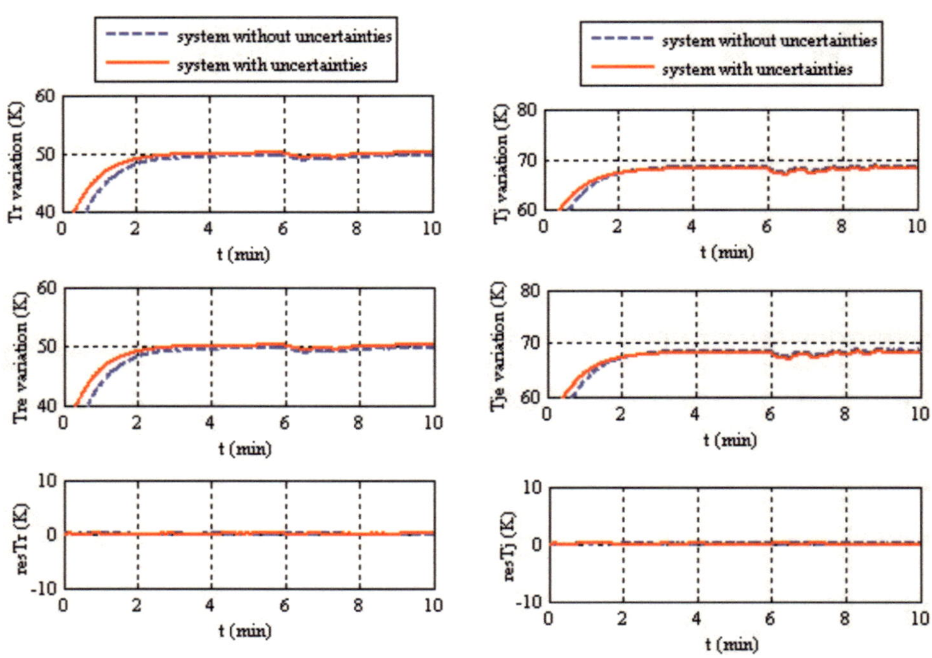

Fig. 9. Residual evolution and estimated temperatures with actuator fault and without/with uncertainties.

- Actuator and sensor faults detection

Figure 10 shows the reaction of the residuals to actuator and sensor fault. Theses test results with two type of faults are similar to the first test results and the effect of actuator fault is always as small disturbances in output behavior.

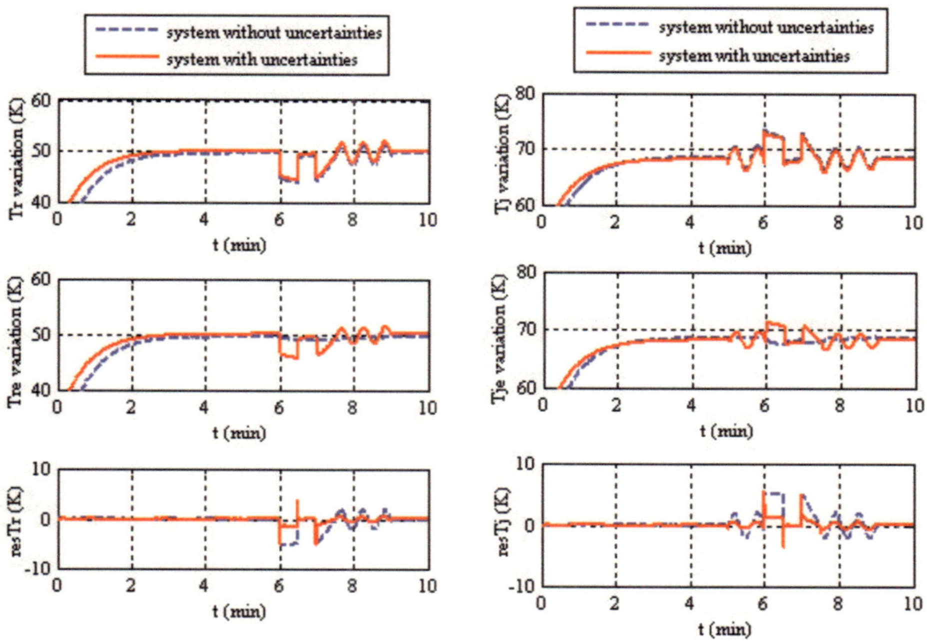

Fig. 10. Residual evolution and estimated temperatures with actuator and sensor faults without uncertainties.

b. Fault isolation

Generally, the isolation purpose is to pinpoint and determine the source or location of a fault. This is mainly done by generating an event consisting of collected pieces of information characterizing the error detected. But if the detection is not achieved, we cannot affirm that the fault does not exist. Hence, a fault can be detected by an approach and not by another; this is related to the approach robustness. Also, the detection can be achieved in spite of fault absence for the reason that some disturbances and measurements noises are detected. In order to distinguish between faults and disturbances, a threshold should be fixed to accept only detected faults which have a size more than double of this threshold.

(1) Choice of threshold:

To fix this threshold, a test with a healthy system (without faults) should be achieved. The threshold is the error between an output and its estimate (residual). Fig.11 shows threshold size in the residuals evolution. The thresholds of normal operation are given with dot lines.

Residuals variation for healthy system is about 2.5e-14. So, a fault can be detected if its size is more than 5e-14. This condition is achieved by proposed sensors and actuator faults. Hence, we can pass to residual evaluation step.

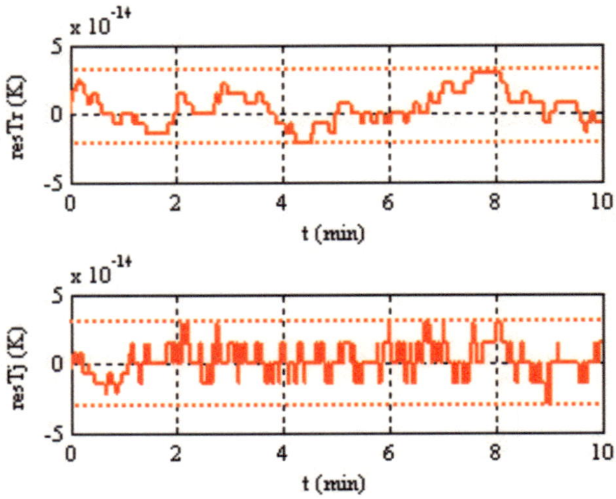

Fig. 11. Residuals behavior for healthy system

(2) Residuals evaluation:

In this step, an incidence matrix from faults to residual can be constructed with residuals in columns and faults in rows. If residual is affected by fault the matrix element is equal to 1 and it is equal 0 otherwise.
For our example, the residual vector is expressed as:

$$r = \begin{pmatrix} 0 & 1 & 0 \\ 0 & 0 & 1 \end{pmatrix}(x - \hat{x}) + \begin{pmatrix} 1 & 0 \\ 0 & 1 \end{pmatrix}\begin{pmatrix} f_{s1} \\ f_{s2} \end{pmatrix} \tag{39}$$

We can conclude that two residuals are affected by two faults. So, a theoretical incidence matrix can be built as the following table:

residual/fault	f_{s1}	f_{s2}	f_a
r_1	1	0	1
r_2	0	1	1

Table 2. Incidence matrix

All rows and columns are different. Consequently, faults are theoretically isolated. However, test shows that experimental residuals are not affected by the actuator fault because the detection is not achieved. So, a second approach must be applied to correct this problem.
2. Kalman filter -based FDI
The system with parameter uncertainties will be considered. Thus results are presented in three tests.
a. System with sensor faults
We consider here system with only sensor faults. Fig.15 shows outputs and residuals evolution. Figure 12 shows that Kalman filter detect the two sensor faults in spite of the presence of parameter uncertainties and residuals have the same forms and size as faults.

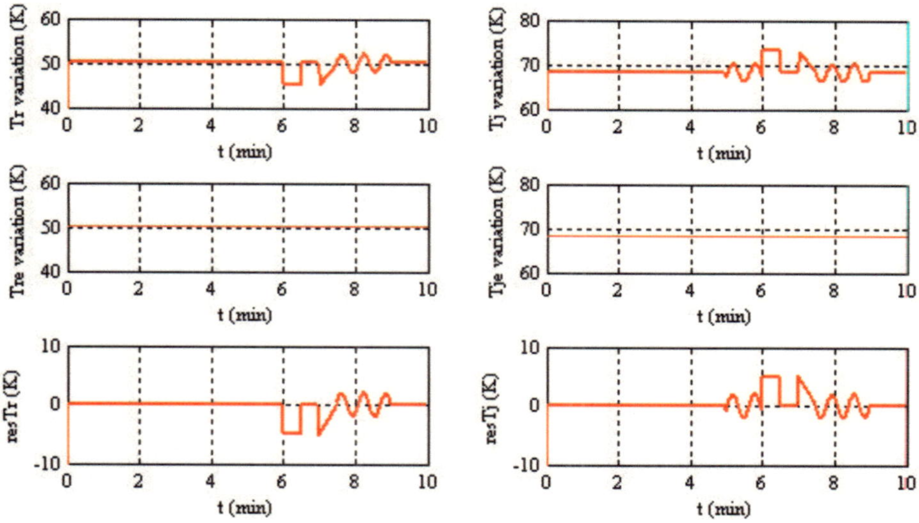

Fig. 12. Residual evolution and estimated temperature in the reactor and the jacket with uncertainties

b. System with actuator fault

Fig.16 illustrates outputs and residuals behavior for system with actuator fault.

Actuator fault is also detected by the filter and the residual size is smaller than fault size (Fig. 13) because of the small effect of this fault in outputs and thereafter in residuals. This effect can be concluded by the flowing expressions:

$$\begin{cases} y = Cx \\ \hat{y} = C\hat{x} \end{cases} \tag{40}$$

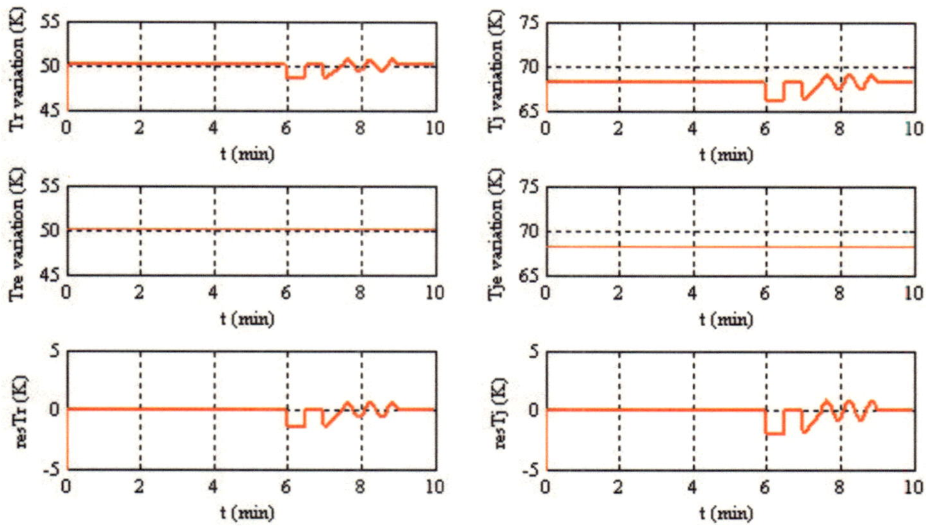

Fig. 13. Residual evolution and estimated temperatures with actuator fault and uncertainties

c. System with actuator and sensor faults

The last test is for system with two types of faults. Fig.17 shows outputs and residuals trajectories for this case.

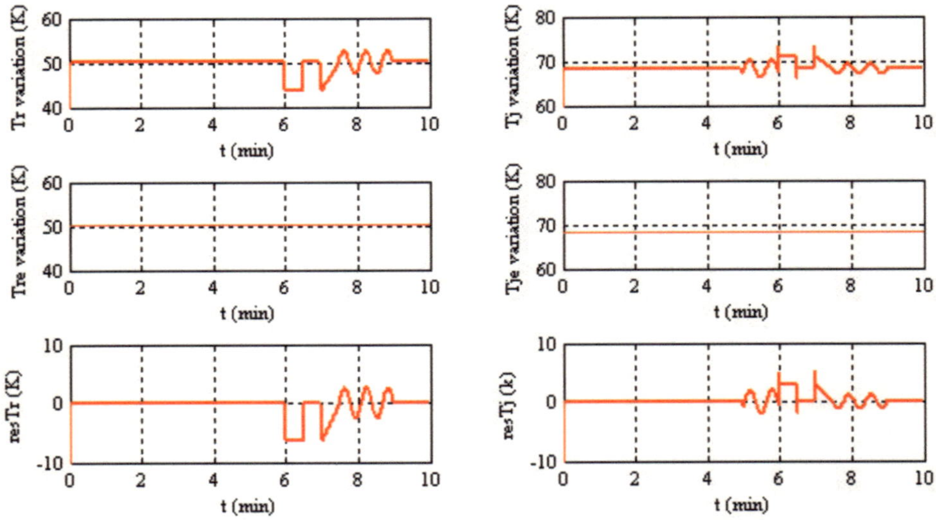

Fig. 14. Residual evolution and estimated temperatures with actuator and sensor faults and without uncertainties

The last test is different from others; residuals are affected by two types of faults. The first residual has the same form of the first sensor fault and the size is an addition of two residuals sizes in previous tests. The same case is with the second residual but residual size is smaller with appearance of peaks because the second sensor fault and that of the actuator have different forms and size.

3.6 Comparison between two approaches

Simulation results demonstrate that Luenberger observer can successfully detect sensor faults for system without uncertainties but for system with uncertainties, generated residuals have the same form of faults with small size. Actuator fault is not detectable by this approach in two cases. These problems are resolved by Kalman filter; two sensors and actuator faults are detected for system with uncertainties. However, for this approach disturbances should be modeled to diagnosis system; this condition can cause problem for complex systems.

4. Conclusion

The fault diagnostic approach in this paper uses linear observers (Lunberger and Kalman filter) to detect and isolate sensors and actuator faults with satisfactory accuracy for chemical reactors with uncertainties. An application on a continuous stirred tank reactor is given to illustrate the proposed scheme. However, this type of observer is particularly unable to diagnosis the real model of complex processes. A generalised Lunberger can be used to resolve this problem. Using robust or adaptive observer, FDI for more general nonlinear systems with uncertainties can be investigated in the future.

5. References

Blanke M., Michel Kinnaert, Jan Lunze, and Marcel Staroswiecki. (2006). *Diagnosis and Fault-Tolerant Control*. Springer Verlag.

Caccavale F., Pierri F., Lamarino M., and Tufano V. (2009). An integrated approach to fault diagnosis for a class of chemical batch processes. Journal of process control, 19:827 – 841, May 2009.

Chetouani Y., Mouhab N., Cosmao J.M., and Estel L. (2002). Application of extended kalman filtering to chemical reactor fault detection. Chemical Engineering Communications, 189:1222 – 1241.

Chetouani, Y. (2004). Fault detection by using the innovation signal: application to an exothermic reaction, Chemical Engineering and Processing, 43, 1579–1585.

De Miguela L. J. and Blàzquez L. F. (2005). Fuzzy logic-based decision-making for fault diagnosis in a DC motor, Engineering Applications of Artificial Intelligence, 18, 423–450.

Edwards C., Spurgeon S. K. and Patton R. J. (2000). Sliding mode observers for fault detection and isolation, Automatica, 36, 541-553.

El Harabi R., Ould Bouamama B., El Koni Ben Gayed M., Abelkrim M.N. (2010a). "Pseudo Bond Graph for Fault Detection and Isolation of an Industrial Chemical Reactor, Part I: Bond Graph Modeling", 9th International Conference on Bond Graph Modeling and Simulation, 11 - 16 Avril 2010, Orlando, Florida, pp. 180-189. ISBN 978-1-61738-209-3.

El Harabi R., Ould Bouamama B., El Koni Ben Gayed M., Abelkrim M.N. (2010b). "Pseudo Bond Graph for Fault Detection and Isolation of an Industrial Chemical Reactor, Part II: FDI System Design", 9th International Conference on Bond Graph Modeling and Simulation, 11 - 16 Avril 2010, Orlando, Florida, pp. 190-197. ISBN 978-1-61738-209-3.

Evsukoffa A. and Gentil S. (2005). Recurrent neuro-fuzzy system for fault detection and isolation in nuclear reactors, Advanced Engineering Informatics, 19, 55–66.

Favache A. and Dochain D. (2009). Thermodynamics and chemical systems stability: The CSTR case study revisited, Journal of Process Control, 19, 371–379.

Frank P. M. (1990). Fault diagnosis in dynamic systems using analytical and knowledge-based redundancy-a survey and some new results, Automatica, 26, 459-474.

Han Z., Li W. and Shah S. L. (2005). Fault detection and isolation in the presence of process uncertainties, Control Engineering Practice, 13, 587–599.

Huang, Y., Reklaitis G.V., and Venkatasubramanian, V. (2003). A heuristic extended kalman filter based estimator for fault identification in a fluid catalytic cracking unit. Ind. Eng. Chem. Res., 42:3361 – 3371.

Hsoumi A., El Harabi R., Bel Hadj Ali S. and Abdelkrim M. N. (2009). Diagnosis of a Continuous Stirred Tank Reactor Using Kalman Filter, International Conference on Computational Intelligence, Modelling and Simulation, (cssim), pp:153-158.

Lie, Q. (2001). Observer-Based Fault Detection for Nuclear Reactor, Massachusetts Institute of Technology.

Levenspiel, O. (1999). Chemical reaction engineering, New York: John Wiley & Sons, 121-123.

Patton R.J. and Chen J. (1997). Observer-Based Fault Detection and Isolation: Robustness and Applications", Control Eng. Practice, 5, 671-682.

Paviglianiti G. and Pierri F. (2006). Sensor fault detection and isolation for hemical batch reactors. In In Proc. Of the IEEE International Conference on Control Application, Munich, Germany.,. In Proc. of the IEEE International Conference on Control Application.

Paviglianiti G. and Pierri F. (2007). Observer-based actuator fault detection for chemical batch reactors: A comparison between nonlinear adaptive and h-based approaches. In Mediterranean Conference on Control and Automation, Athens-Greece, 2007.

Porru G., Aragonese C. and Baratti R. (2000). Alberto servida] monitoring of a CO oxidation reactor through a grey model-based EKF observer. Chemical Engineering Science, 55:331 – 338.

Rajaraman, S., Hahn, J. and Mannan, M.S. (2006). Sensor fault diagnosis for nonlinear processes with parametric uncertainties. Journal of Hazardous Materials, 130, 1–8.

Samantaray A.K., Medjaher K., Ould Bouamama B., Staroswiecki M. and Dauphin-Tanguy G. (2006). Diagnostic bond graphs for online fault detection and isolation, Simulation Modelling Practice and Theory, 14, 237–262.

Sotomayor, O.A.Z., and Odloak, D. (2005). Observer-based fault diagnosis in chemical plants. Chemical Engineering Journal, 112, 93–108.

Venkatasubramanian V., Rengaswamy R., Yin K. and Kavuri S.N. (2003). Areview of process fault detection and diagnosis Part I: Quantitative model-based methods. Computers and Chemical Engineering, 27, 293-311.

Venkatasubramanian V. (2005). Prognostic and diagnostic monitoring of complex systems for product lifecycle management: Challenges and opportunities, Computers and Chemical Engineering, 29, 1253–1263.

20

The Static and Dynamic Transfer-Matrix Methods in the Analysis of Distributed-Feedback Lasers

C. A. F. Fernandes[1] and José A. P. Morgado[2]
[1,2]Instituto de Telecomunicações
[2]Portuguese Air Force Academy
Portugal

1. Introduction

Numerical simulation plays a decisive role in the design of modern optical communication components. However, time efficient and user-friendly numerical techniques that perform simulations in that area are not easily available. In this chapter, an example concerning the use of a numerical simulation method, designated by transfer-matrix-method (TMM), is presented. Although the TMM is a numerical simulation tool especially adequate for the design of distributed feedback (DFB) laser structures in high bit rate optical communication systems (OCS), it represents a paradigmatic example of a numerical method related to heavy computational times.

Nowadays, distributed-feedback lasers are indispensable in high-bit rate OCS (Bornholdt et al., 2008; Sato et al., 2005; Tang et al., 2006; Utake et al., 2009; Wedding & Pöhlmann, 2004; Wedding et al., 2003), where they should present single-longitudinal mode (SLM) operation over the largest range of current injection. In order to assure sufficient intensity modulation bandwidth in high-bit rate systems, the current injected into the laser cavity can assume high values, (Sato et al., 2005; Wedding & Pöhlmann, 2004; Wedding et al., 2003). On the other hand, to fulfill the SLM condition, high mode selectivity and almost uniform intracavity field distributions are demanded. In the context of OCS, DFB lasers with a 90° phase discontinuity near the centre of the cavity[1] are commonly cited in the specialized literature, due to their high mode selectivity, small current bias and zero frequency detuning at threshold condition (Ghafouri-Shiraz, 2003). Their main drawback is related to the high non-uniformity of the field distribution along the cavity, which presents a strong peak near the centre. Above-threshold, this non-uniformity induces important variations of the carrier and refractive-index distributions arising from the spatial hole-burning (SHB) effect, with serious consequences in the laser behavior in the high power regime, namely: increased linewidth (Ghafouri-Shiraz, 2003), multi-mode emission (Morthier, 1997) and less flat laser frequency modulation response (Agrawall & Dutta, 1986). Therefore, a careful and suitable design of the laser emitter, with a rigorous assessment of the electric field distribution along the laser cavity, is crucial in order to reduce the impact of SHB in OCS.

DFB structure analysis can be performed assuming the classical solution of the wave propagation inside periodic structures. The grating of the cavity is responsible for a

---

[1] Generally designated by *quarterly wavelength-shifted* (QWS) or $\lambda/4$ DFB lasers.

coupling between two counter-running waves, which is ruled by a pair of differential equations, usually designated by *coupled-mode equations*. These equations represent the essence of the theoretical analysis of longitudinal modes inside periodic laser structures, whose initial works are attributed to H. Kogelnik and C. Shank (Kogelnik & Shank, 1972). Resonant frequencies and threshold criteria for the oscillation modes have been determined for both index and gain periodicities. However, even in the simplest case - conventional anti-reflexive (AR) coated DFB lasers - the coupled-mode equations must be solved numerically. Since the number of boundary conditions to match is generally high, the procedure will quickly become a tremendous and fastidious task for most of DFB structures. Usually, DFB structures demand the use of simulation tools more flexible than the traditional numerical techniques based on analytical or semi-analytical methods. In this scenario TMM takes place as one of the most popular and useful numerical simulation tools. It is a method that can easily handle with complex periodic structures, both for static and dynamic regimes. The same generic algorithm may be used in a straightforward way for the analysis of any kind of multi-section laser structures, namely, multiple phase-shift (MPS)-DFB (Tan et al., 1995), distributed-coupled coefficient (DCC)-DFB (Ghafouri-Shiraz, 2003; Boavida et al., 2011), corrugation pitch modulated (CPM)-DFB (Fessant, 1997), multi-electrode DFB (Ghafouri-Shiraz, 2003), distributed Bragg reflector (DBR) (Lowery, 1991), vertical cavity (Yu, 2003), etc, as long as the perturbation included in the periodic chain may be described by a transfer matrix. A detailed description of those numerical techniques will be the scope of this work. However, as previously referred, matrix methods are usually very heavy in terms of processing times and so they should be optimized in order to improve their time computational efficiency. The search for adequate strategies aiming at an efficient convergence of the TMM, both for static and dynamic regimes, is crucial and it will be one of the *leit-motiv* of the present study. Accordingly, a convenient approach to TMM suggests an introduction to the coupled wave theory.

2. The coupled wave theory

In a homogeneous, source-free and lossless medium, any time harmonic electric field obeys the vector wave equation

$$\nabla^2 \overline{E} + k_0^2 \cdot n^2 \cdot \overline{E} = 0. \tag{1}$$

In (1) the time dependence, t, of the electric field has been assumed to be $e^{j\omega t}$, with ω the angular frequency, $\overline{E}$ the complex amplitude of the electric field, n the refractive index and k_0 the free space propagation constant. From Maxwell equations it is possible to show that in a semiconductor laser, which has an oscillating lateral and transversal confined electric field, the longitudinal wave propagation obeys the one-dimensional homogeneous wave equation

$$\frac{d^2\overline{E}(z)}{dz^2} + \overline{k}^2(z) \cdot \overline{E}(z) = 0, \tag{2}$$

commonly referred as the *scalar wave-equation*. In (2) $\overline{k}(z)$ is the complex propagation constant related to $\overline{E}$, given by

$$\overline{k}(z) = \beta(z) + jg_u(z), \tag{3}$$

where $\beta(z)$ is the phase propagation constant by unit length and $g_u(z)$ is the amplitude gain by unit length associated with the propagation of the electric field along the cavity. In DFB lasers the corrugation-induced dielectric perturbation along the laser cavity (grating) leads to a periodic Bragg waveguide and, therefore, to the longitudinal dependence of the propagation constants. These are given by

$$\beta(z) \triangleq \frac{2\pi f}{c_\Lambda(z)}, \tag{4}$$

where f is the frequency and $c_\Lambda(z)$ is the propagation velocity of $\bar{E}$ inside the Bragg waveguide, given by

$$c_\Lambda(z) \triangleq \frac{1}{\sqrt{\mu(z)\cdot\varepsilon(z)}}. \tag{5}$$

In (5) μ represents the magnetic permeability, usually given for non-magnetic materials by its value in free space $\mu_0 = 4\pi\times10^{-7}\ \mathrm{H\cdot m^{-1}}$, and ε is material permittivity ($\varepsilon_0 = 8.854\times10^{-12}\ \mathrm{F\cdot m^{-1}}$ for free space). Substituting (5) in (4), it yields

$$\beta(z) = 2\pi f\cdot\sqrt{\varepsilon(z)\cdot\mu(z)} \cong 2\pi f\cdot\sqrt{\varepsilon_0\cdot\mu_0}\,\frac{\sqrt{\varepsilon(z)\cdot\mu_0}}{\sqrt{\varepsilon_0\cdot\mu_0}} \cong k_0\cdot n(z), \tag{6}$$

with the free-space phase propagation constant and the semiconductor refractive index given, respectively, by

$$k_0 \triangleq 2\pi f\cdot\sqrt{\mu_0\cdot\varepsilon_0}\ \ ;\ n(z) \cong \frac{\sqrt{\mu_0\cdot\varepsilon(z)}}{\sqrt{\mu_0\cdot\varepsilon_0}} = \sqrt{\frac{\varepsilon(z)}{\varepsilon_0}}. \tag{7}$$

Assuming that the corrugation has a period Λ, it is implicitly assumed that the refractive index and the amplitude gain are also periodic functions of the same period. Since the length of the laser cavity (commonly hundreds of micrometers) is much longer than Λ (generally, some nanometers), it is possible to represent the waveguide by a Fourier series. In this approach, the Bragg waveguide may be considered a first-order waveguide, leading to

$$n(z) \cong n_0 + \Delta n\cdot\cos\left(2\pi\cdot\frac{z}{\Lambda}+\Omega_\Lambda\right)\ ;\ g_u(z) \cong g_{u0} + \Delta g_u\cdot\cos\left(2\pi\cdot\frac{z}{\Lambda}+\Omega_\Lambda+\theta_\Lambda\right). \tag{8}$$

In (8), where only the first two terms of the series have been considered, n_0 and g_{u0} are the mean values of $n(z)$ and $g_u(z)$, respectively, and Δn and Δg_u are their modulation amplitudes. Ω_Λ is the phase of the periodic variations of the refractive index for z=0 and θ_Λ is the relative phase deviation between the perturbations $n(z)$ and $g_u(z)$. Hereafter, g_{u0} will be designated by α. The period Λ imposes some restrictions to the values that $\beta(z)$ can assume. In Fig. 1 it is schematically shown the propagation of the electric field in a periodic structure, assuming $g_u(z) = 1\mathrm{m}^{-1}$.

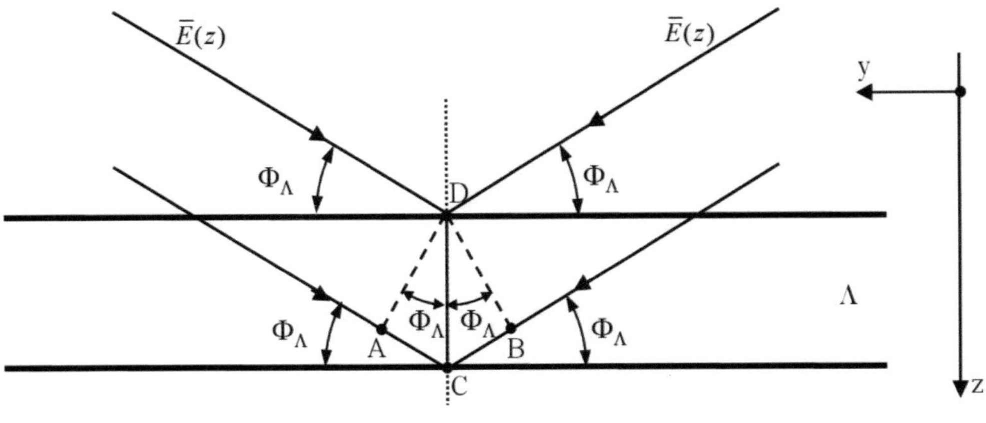

Fig. 1. Electric field propagation in a periodic waveguide, assuming lateral and transversal confinements of $\bar{E}(z)$.

For N_Λ periods, N_Λ reflected waves will be generated. Their positive interference demands that the phase difference between two reflected waves be a multiple of 2π. According to Fig. 1 this means that

$$\beta(z)\cdot\left(\overline{AB}+\overline{BC}\right)=\beta(z)\cdot\left[2\Lambda\cdot\sin\left(\Phi_\Lambda\right)\right]=2m\pi \quad : \quad m=1;2;3\ldots \,. \tag{9}$$

Assuming Φ_Λ =90°, for a first order corrugation it yields $\beta(z)=\pi/\Lambda$. Therefore, the propagation constant is independent of *z*, being known as the *Bragg propagation constant* $\beta_\Lambda=\pi/\Lambda$. Physically, it represents a value in the vicinity of which the propagation constant must be included so that the electric field may propagate along the structure. Related to this value, it may be defined the structure wavelength $\lambda_{\text{struct}}\triangleq 2\pi/\beta_\Lambda=2\Lambda$. This parameter may be related to an oscillator whose frequency is designated by the *Bragg frequency*, which is given by

$$f_\Lambda \triangleq \frac{c}{\lambda_{\text{struct}}\cdot n_0}. \tag{10}$$

In (10) *c* is the free-space velocity. For an oscillator in free-space of the same frequency, the wavelength is known as the *Bragg wavelength*, and it is given by

$$\lambda_\Lambda \triangleq \frac{c}{f_\Lambda}=\lambda_{\text{struct}}\cdot n_0=2\Lambda\cdot n_0. \tag{11}$$

Assuming that $g_u(z)\ll\beta(z)$, $\Delta n\ll n_0$ and $\Delta g_u\ll\alpha$, it is possible, after some algebraic manipulation, to show that

$$\begin{aligned}\bar{k}^2(z)\cong{}&\beta^2(z)+j2\cdot\beta(z)\cdot\alpha+2\cdot\beta(z)\cdot\bar{\kappa}_{R\leftarrow S}\cdot\exp\left[-j\left(2\cdot\beta_\Lambda\cdot z+\Omega_\Lambda\right)\right]+\\&+2\cdot\beta(z)\cdot\bar{\kappa}_{S\leftarrow R}\cdot\exp\left[j\left(2\cdot\beta_\Lambda\cdot z+\Omega_\Lambda\right)\right]\end{aligned} \tag{12}$$

with $\bar{\kappa}_{R\leftarrow S}$ and $\bar{\kappa}_{S\leftarrow R}$ being the coupling coefficients related to the Bragg waveguide, which are given by

$$\bar{\kappa}_{R\leftarrow S} \triangleq \frac{\pi \cdot \Delta n}{\lambda_0} + j \cdot \frac{\Delta g_u}{2} \cdot \exp(-j \cdot \theta_\Lambda) \ ; \ \bar{\kappa}_{S\leftarrow R} \triangleq \frac{\pi \cdot \Delta n}{\lambda_0} + j \cdot \frac{\Delta g_u}{2} \cdot \exp(j \cdot \theta_\Lambda) \tag{13}$$

with

$$\lambda_0 \triangleq \frac{2\pi}{k_0} \ . \tag{14}$$

Considering $\kappa_R \triangleq \pi \cdot \Delta n / \lambda_0$ and $\kappa_I \triangleq \Delta g_u / 2$, it is possible to write the coupling coefficients (13) as

$$\bar{\kappa}_{R\leftarrow S} = \kappa_R + j \cdot \kappa_I \cdot \exp(-j \cdot \theta_\Lambda) \ ; \ \bar{\kappa}_{S\leftarrow R} = \kappa_R + j \cdot \kappa_I \cdot \exp(j \cdot \theta_\Lambda). \tag{15}$$

From (15), it may be seen that the contributions for the coupling coefficients, related to the perturbations in the refractive index or in the gain per unit length, are included in κ_R and κ_I, respectively. Using (12) in (2), it yields

$$\begin{aligned} \frac{d^2\bar{E}(z)}{dz^2} + \beta^2(z) \cdot \bar{E}(z) + j \cdot 2\beta(z) \cdot \alpha \cdot \bar{E}(z) + 2\beta(z) \cdot \left\{ \bar{\kappa}_{R\leftarrow S} \cdot \exp\left[-j(2\beta_\Lambda \cdot z + \Omega_\Lambda)\right] \right\} \cdot \bar{E}(z) + \\ + 2\beta(z) \cdot \left\{ \bar{\kappa}_{S\leftarrow R} \cdot \exp\left[j(2\beta_\Lambda \cdot z + \Omega_\Lambda)\right] \right\} \cdot \bar{E}(z) = 0 \ . \end{aligned} \tag{16}$$

Equation (16) gives the electric field profile considering the global effects of the lateral and transversal confinements and the presence of a corrugation in the laser cavity.
Without corrugation, which is the case of the Fabry-Pérot (FP) lasers, $\bar{\kappa}_{R\leftarrow S} = \bar{\kappa}_{S\leftarrow R} = \Delta n = \Delta g_u = 0$. Therefore, from (16), results

$$\frac{d^2\bar{E}(z)}{dz^2} + \left[\beta^2 + j \cdot 2\beta \cdot \alpha\right] \cdot \bar{E}(z) = 0. \tag{17}$$

Taking into account that in this case $g_u(z) = \alpha \ll \beta(z) = \beta$, it yields

$$\beta^2 + j \cdot 2\beta \cdot \alpha \cong \beta^2 + j \cdot 2\beta \cdot \alpha + \alpha^2 = (\beta + j\alpha)^2 . \tag{18}$$

Being (17) a linear homogeneous ordinary differential equation with constant coefficients, the solution may be written as

$$\bar{E}(z) = \bar{A}(z) \cdot \exp(-j \cdot \beta \cdot z) + \bar{B}(z) \cdot \exp(j \cdot \beta \cdot z), \tag{19}$$

where $\bar{A}(z)$ and $\bar{B}(z)$ are arbitrary complex constants to be determined according to the boundary conditions imposed at the cavity ends.
Let us now assume a DFB laser, that is, a laser with a corrugation inside the cavity, which is responsible for an amount of feedback distributed along the cavity. The solution is seen to be formally identical to the one obtained in (19) but with β replaced by β(z), which is in the vicinity of the Bragg propagation constant so that positive interference should happen. Therefore, it may be assumed that

$$\left|\beta(z) - \beta_\Lambda\right| \ll \beta_\Lambda , \tag{20}$$

with the detuning defined as

$$\delta \triangleq \beta(z) - \beta_\Lambda . \tag{21}$$

According to (20) and (21), (19) may be rewritten as

$$\bar{E}(z) = \bar{R}(z)\cdot \exp(-j\cdot\beta_\Lambda\cdot z) + \bar{S}(z)\cdot \exp(j\cdot\beta_\Lambda\cdot z) , \tag{22}$$

where

$$\bar{R}(z) \triangleq \bar{A}(z)\cdot \exp(-j\cdot\delta\cdot z) \;\; ; \;\; \bar{S}(z) \triangleq \bar{B}(z)\cdot \exp(j\cdot\delta\cdot z) . \tag{23}$$

Equation (22) shows that $\bar{E}(z)$ is the superposition of two counter-running waves, $\bar{R}(z)$ and $\bar{S}(z)$. Using (22) in (16), it is obtained after some algebraic manipulation

$$\begin{aligned} -\frac{d\bar{R}(z)}{dz} + (\alpha - j\delta)\cdot \bar{R}(z) &= j\bar{\kappa}_{R\leftarrow S}\bar{S}(z)\cdot \exp(-j\cdot\Omega_\Lambda) \;\; ; \\ \frac{d\bar{S}(z)}{dz} + (\alpha - j\delta)\cdot \bar{S}(z) &= j\bar{\kappa}_{S\leftarrow R}\bar{R}(z)\cdot \exp(j\cdot\Omega_\Lambda) . \end{aligned} \tag{24}$$

Equations (24) are known as the *coupled-wave equations*. It should be emphasized that (24) is valid for periodic laser cavities as far as the included perturbations are weak. The physical meaning of the coupling coefficients $\bar{\kappa}_{R\leftarrow S}$ and $\bar{\kappa}_{S\leftarrow R}$ is clearly described by (24). They represent the amount of feedback per unit length in the propagation along the cavity. This means that there is a net energy transfer between the two counter-running waves associated to the electric field distribution. The coupling coefficient $\bar{\kappa}_{R\leftarrow S}$ measures the coupling that $\bar{S}(z)$ induces in $\bar{R}(z)$. It is known as the *forward coupling coefficient.* The coupling coefficient $\bar{\kappa}_{S\leftarrow R}$ measures the coupling that $\bar{R}(z)$ induces in $\bar{S}(z)$. It is known as the *backward coupling coefficient.*

In the following, some applications of the coupled-wave theory in the analysis of the threshold regime related to simple laser structures will be considered.

2.1 Threshold analysis of conventional DFB lasers with reflective facets

Let us consider a conventional DFB laser structure, which is a DFB laser with a constant period grating defined by $\Lambda(z) = \Lambda$. The cavity ends (facets) will be defined by their reflectivities, $\hat{r}_1$ and $\hat{r}_2$, at left and right facets, respectively. Without loss of generality, it will be considered hereafter θ_Λ=0. From (15) and (8), it yields

$$\begin{aligned} &\bar{\kappa}_{R\leftarrow S} = \bar{\kappa}_{S\leftarrow R} = \kappa_R + j\cdot\kappa_I \;\; ; \\ &n(z) \cong n_0 + \Delta n\cdot \cos\left[\Psi_\Lambda(z)\right] \;\; ; \\ &g_u(z) \cong \alpha + \Delta g_u \cdot \cos\left[\Psi_\Lambda(z)\right] , \end{aligned} \tag{25}$$

where $\Psi_\Lambda(z) \triangleq 2\beta_\Lambda\cdot z + \Omega_\Lambda$ represents the corrugation phase at *z* coordinate.

Since the forward and backward coupling coefficients are equal, they will be referred as the coupling coefficient and represented by $\bar{\kappa}$. According to (24) the solution of the coupled-wave equations may be written as

$$\begin{aligned}\bar{R}(z) &= \bar{R}_1(z)\cdot\exp(\bar{\gamma}\cdot z)+\bar{R}_2(z)\cdot\exp(-\bar{\gamma}\cdot z)\\ \bar{S}(z) &= \bar{S}_1(z)\cdot\exp(\bar{\gamma}\cdot z)+\bar{S}_2(z)\cdot\exp(-\bar{\gamma}\cdot z)\ .\end{aligned} \tag{26}$$

From (22) and (26), it yields

$$\begin{aligned}\bar{E}(z) &= \left[\bar{R}_1(z)\cdot\exp(\bar{\gamma}\cdot z)+\bar{R}_2(z)\cdot\exp(-\bar{\gamma}\cdot z)\right]\cdot\exp(-j\beta_\Lambda\cdot z)+\\ &+\left[\bar{S}_1(z)\cdot\exp(\bar{\gamma}\cdot z)+\bar{S}_2(z)\cdot\exp(-\bar{\gamma}\cdot z)\right]\cdot\exp(j\beta_\Lambda\cdot z)\ .\end{aligned} \tag{27}$$

In the previous equations, $\bar{R}_1(z)$, $\bar{R}_2(z)$, $\bar{S}_1(z)$, $\bar{S}_2(z)$ and $\bar{\gamma}(z)$ are complex values that are determined according to the boundary conditions imposed at the cavity facets. However, no matter the type of facets considered, it is possible to show that, in order that the solution (27) is non-trivial, the following condition should always be verified

$$\bar{\gamma}^2 = (\alpha - j\delta)^2 + \bar{\kappa}^2. \tag{28}$$

This condition is generally known as *the dispersion equation*. For a cavity with length L and reflecting facets with reflectivities $\hat{r}_1$ and $\hat{r}_2$, respectively, at left and right ends, the boundary conditions at the cavity ends impose that

$$\begin{aligned}\bar{R}(z_1)\cdot\exp\left(-j\bar{\beta}_\Lambda\cdot z_1\right) &= \hat{r}_1\cdot\bar{S}(z_1)\cdot\exp\left(j\bar{\beta}_\Lambda\cdot z_1\right)\\ \bar{S}(z_2)\cdot\exp\left(j\bar{\beta}_\Lambda\cdot z_2\right) &= \hat{r}_2\cdot\bar{R}(z_2)\cdot\exp\left(-j\bar{\beta}_\Lambda\cdot z_2\right).\end{aligned} \tag{29}$$

From (29) and the dispersion equation (28) it is obtained, after some algebraic manipulations

$$\bar{\gamma}L = \frac{-j\bar{\kappa}\cdot L\cdot\sinh(\bar{\gamma}L)}{D}\cdot\left[(\hat{r}_1+\hat{r}_2)\cdot(1-\hat{r}_1\cdot\hat{r}_2)\cdot\cosh(\bar{\gamma}L)\pm(1+\hat{r}_1\cdot\hat{r}_2)\cdot\varsigma^{0.5}\right], \tag{30}$$

with

$$\begin{aligned}\varsigma &\triangleq (\hat{r}_1-\hat{r}_2)^2\cdot\sinh^2(\bar{\gamma}L)+(1-\hat{r}_1\cdot\hat{r}_2)^2\\ D &\triangleq (1+\hat{r}_1\cdot\hat{r}_2)^2-4\cdot\hat{r}_1\cdot\hat{r}_2\cdot\cosh^2(\bar{\gamma}L)\\ \hat{r}_1 &= r_1\cdot\exp\left[j(2\beta_\Lambda\cdot z_1+\Omega_\Lambda)\right]=r_1\cdot\exp\left(\Psi_{\Lambda_1}\right)\\ \hat{r}_2 &= r_2\cdot\exp\left[-j(2\beta_\Lambda\cdot z_2+\Omega_\Lambda)\right]=r_2\cdot\exp\left(\Psi_{\Lambda_2}\right).\end{aligned} \tag{31}$$

In (31) Ψ_{Λ_1} is the corrugation phase at the left facet (z=z_1) and Ψ_{Λ_2} is the symmetric of the corrugation phase at the right facet (z=z_2). Equation (30) represents the threshold condition for the conventional DFB laser. It depends on the coupling coefficient, the cavity length and the reflectivities at both cavity ends. Its solution allows the determination of the detuning, δ, and the gains associated with all modes, α, that are allowed to propagate inside the cavity. For most practical cases it recurs to numerical methods, taking into account that it may be rewritten in a more suitable form as

$$(\overline{\gamma}L)^2 \cdot D + (\overline{\kappa} \cdot L)^2 \cdot \sinh^2(\overline{\gamma}L) \cdot \left(1-\hat{r}_1^2\right) \cdot \left(1-\hat{r}_2^2\right) + \\ +j2(\overline{\kappa} \cdot L).(\hat{r}_1 + \hat{r}_2) \cdot (1-\hat{r}_1 \cdot \hat{r}_2) \cdot (\overline{\gamma}L) \cdot \sinh(\overline{\gamma}L) \cdot \cosh(\overline{\gamma}L) = 0 . \tag{32}$$

The solutions of (32) are seen to depend strongly on the conditions at the cavity ends, through the values assumed for their reflectivities, both in amplitude and phase. This may be problematic as far as the laser characterization is concerned, since due to fabrication limitations the values assumed for the phases in the facet reflectivities are known with a certain degree of uncertainty.

To solve the complex equation (32), Newton-Raphson iteration techniques are generally used, provided the Cauchy-Riemann condition on complex analytical functions are satisfied. In the following paragraphs it is briefly presented a generalization of the usual Newton-Raphson method for the solution of non-linear real equations. Let us then consider the following generic equation of an arbitrary complex function of a complex variable,

$$\overline{W}(\overline{z}) = 0, \tag{33}$$

and let us assume that $\overline{W}(\overline{z})$ is an analytical function, i.e., that it is possible to calculate $d\overline{W}(\overline{z})/d\overline{z}$ in the vicinity of $\overline{z}$. The complex function is described as

$$\overline{W}(\overline{z}) = U(\overline{z}) + jV(\overline{z}). \tag{34}$$

In (34) $U(\overline{z})$ and $V(\overline{z})$ are real functions that represent the real and imaginary parts of $\overline{W}(\overline{z})$, respectively. Taking into account that $\overline{z} = x + jy$, the solution of (34) is equivalent to the solution of the following system of equations

$$U(x,y) = 0 \ ; \ V(x,y) = 0 . \tag{35}$$

The Taylor expansion of (35) in the vicinity of an approximate solution (x_0, y_0) yields to

$$U(x_1,y_1) = U(x_0,y_0) + \left.\frac{\partial U(x,y)}{\partial x}\right|_{x_0,y_0} \cdot (x_1 - x_0) + \left.\frac{\partial U(x,y)}{\partial y}\right|_{x_0,y_0} \cdot (y_1 - y_0) \tag{36}$$

$$V(x_1,y_1) = V(x_0,y_0) + \left.\frac{\partial V(x,y)}{\partial x}\right|_{x_0,y_0} \cdot (x_1 - x_0) + \left.\frac{\partial V(x,y)}{\partial y}\right|_{x_0,y_0} \cdot (y_1 - y_0). \tag{37}$$

From (35), (36) and (37), it yields

$$U(x_1,y_1) \cong 0 \ ; \ V(x_1,y_1) \cong 0 \ , \tag{38}$$

where x_1 and y_1 are in the vicinity of x_0 and y_0. Using (38) in (36) and (37), it is obtained

$$\left.\frac{\partial U(x,y)}{\partial x}\right|_{x_0,y_0} \cdot x_1 + \left.\frac{\partial U(x,y)}{\partial y}\right|_{x_0,y_0} \cdot y_1 = \left[-U(x_0,y_0) + \left.\frac{\partial U(x,y)}{\partial x}\right|_{x_0,y_0} \cdot x_0 + \left.\frac{\partial U(x,y)}{\partial y}\right|_{x_0,y_0} \cdot y_0 \right] \tag{39}$$

$$\left.\frac{\partial V(x,y)}{\partial x}\right|_{x_0,y_0}\cdot x_1+\left.\frac{\partial V(x,y)}{\partial y}\right|_{x_0,y_0}\cdot y_1=\left[-V(x_0,y_0)+\left.\frac{\partial V(x,y)}{\partial x}\right|_{x_0,y_0}\cdot x_0+\left.\frac{\partial V(x,y)}{\partial y}\right|_{x_0,y_0}\cdot y_0\right]. \quad (40)$$

The solutions x_1 and y_1 of the previous system of equations are

$$x_1=x_0+\frac{V(x_0,y_0)\cdot\left.\frac{\partial U(x,y)}{\partial y}\right|_{x_0,y_0}-U(x_0,y_0)\cdot\left.\frac{\partial V(x,y)}{\partial y}\right|_{x_0,y_0}}{\Delta_{\text{Newt}}} \quad (41)$$

$$y_1=y_0+\frac{U(x_0,y_0)\cdot\left.\frac{\partial V(x,y)}{\partial x}\right|_{x_0,y_0}-V(x_0,y_0)\cdot\left.\frac{\partial U(x,y)}{\partial x}\right|_{x_0,y_0}}{\Delta_{\text{Newt}}}, \quad (42)$$

where

$$\Delta_{\text{Newt}}=\left.\frac{\partial U(x,y)}{\partial x}\right|_{x_0,y_0}\cdot\left.\frac{\partial V(x,y)}{\partial y}\right|_{x_0,y_0}-\left.\frac{\partial V(x,y)}{\partial x}\right|_{x_0,y_0}\cdot\left.\frac{\partial U(x,y)}{\partial y}\right|_{x_0,y_0}.$$

Taking into account (34), it is straightforward that[2] $U(x,y)=\Re\left[\bar{W}(\bar{z})\right]$ and $V(x,y)=\Im\left[\bar{W}(\bar{z})\right]$, which yields

$$\frac{d\bar{W}(\bar{z})}{d\bar{z}}=\frac{dU(\bar{z})}{d\bar{z}}+j\frac{dV(\bar{z})}{d\bar{z}}. \quad (43)$$

From $\bar{z}=x+jy$, and (43) one obtains the following equations

$$\begin{aligned}\frac{\partial U(x,y)}{\partial x}&=\frac{dU(\bar{z})}{d\bar{z}}\cdot\frac{\partial\bar{z}}{\partial x}=\frac{dU(\bar{z})}{d\bar{z}}=\Re\left[\frac{d\bar{W}(\bar{z})}{d\bar{z}}\right]\\ \frac{\partial V(x,y)}{\partial x}&=\frac{dV(\bar{z})}{d\bar{z}}\cdot\frac{\partial\bar{z}}{\partial x}=\frac{dV(\bar{z})}{d\bar{z}}=\Im\left[\frac{d\bar{W}(\bar{z})}{d\bar{z}}\right]\end{aligned} \quad (44)$$

$$\frac{\partial U(x,y)}{\partial y}=\frac{dU(\bar{z})}{d\bar{z}}\cdot\frac{\partial\bar{z}}{\partial y}=j\frac{dU(\bar{z})}{d\bar{z}}\;;\;\frac{\partial V(x,y)}{\partial y}=\frac{dV(\bar{z})}{d\bar{z}}\cdot\frac{\partial\bar{z}}{\partial y}=j\frac{dV(\bar{z})}{d\bar{z}}. \quad (45)$$

Replacing (45) in (43), it is obtained

$$\frac{d\bar{W}(\bar{z})}{d\bar{z}}=\frac{\partial V(x,y)}{\partial y}-j\frac{\partial U(x,y)}{\partial y}. \quad (46)$$

---

[2] $\Re[\cdot]$ and $\Im[\cdot]$ are, respectively, the real and imaginary parts of the arguments.

From (46) and (44), it is easily shown that

$$\frac{\partial V(x,y)}{\partial y}=\Re\left[\frac{d\overline{W}(\overline{z})}{d\overline{z}}\right]\;;\;\frac{\partial U(x,y)}{\partial y}=-\Im\left[\frac{d\overline{W}(\overline{z})}{d\overline{z}}\right]. \tag{47}$$

It should be noticed that from (45) and (47) it results

$$\frac{\partial U(x,y)}{\partial x}=\frac{\partial V(x,y)}{\partial y}\;;\;\frac{\partial U(x,y)}{\partial y}=-\frac{\partial V(x,y)}{\partial x}. \tag{48}$$

It is worth noticing that (48) corresponds to the Cauchy-Riemann condition, which states that, in fact, $\overline{W}(\overline{z})$ is an analytical function.
Given the initial guess (x_0,y_0) the numerical iteration process starts. A new value is obtained using (41) and (42) taking into account (44) and (47) and it is used as the initial condition for the next iteration until the difference for the previous guess is within a pre-defined range (for example, less than 10^{-8}). The method is very fast, while strongly dependent on the initial guess. Moreover, it assumes that the analytical description of the complex function $\overline{W}(\overline{z})$ is known. It can be a good option, whereas as the structure under analysis is of moderate complexity. Some examples are given below.

2.2 Threshold analysis of anti-reflective (AR) coated conventional DFB lasers

These lasers avoid the uncertainty related to the phase facets. Starting from (32) and assuming $\hat{r}_1=\hat{r}_2=0,$ it yields

$$j(\overline{\gamma}L)=\pm\overline{\kappa}\cdot L\cdot\sinh(\overline{\gamma}L). \tag{49}$$

There exist two pairs of possible solutions for each oscillation mode (mathematically those solutions correspond to complex conjugates). The solutions, gain and detuning related to the several modes that are allowed to propagate inside the cavity, are symmetrically placed related to the Bragg wavelength, where $\delta L=0.$ Therefore, the laser spectrum is double degenerate. Since there is no solution with null detuning (Agrawall & Dutta, 1986), the SLM operation is prevented. In spite of being the less complex DFB structure, it is useless in the OCS domain.
However, some remarks should be emphasized for this type of laser structures. For a given laser cavity, when the coupling coefficient increases, the normalized amplitude gain decreases or, equivalently, the threshold current will decrease. This is consistent with the fact that a larger coupling coefficient means a stronger optical feedback along the DFB laser structure. Alternatively, a reduction in the threshold gains can be obtained for a fixed coupling coefficient using a longer cavity length, since a larger single pass gain can be more easily achieved.

2.3 Threshold analysis of AR-coated, single phase-shifted (1PS) DFB lasers

As previously referred, a stable SLM operation is not guaranteed in conventional DFB lasers: neither in AR-coated DFB, since the laser spectra is double degenerate, nor in several reflective facets DFB lasers, due to the randomness of the corrugation phase at the laser facets. To overcome this drawback, some alterations should be included in the laser

corrugation. The most popular solution corresponds to the inclusion of a single phase-shift discontinuity in the corrugation.
The laser characteristics are shown to be strongly dependent on the value assumed for the phase discontinuity and on its location inside the cavity (Ghafouri-Shiraz, 2003; Fernandes et al., 2009). It can be shown that one of the most advantageous situations corresponds to a phase-shift of 90° placed near the centre of the cavity. This structure is referred as quarterly-wavelength-shifted (QWS) and it is related to important improvements in the main laser figures of merit near threshold regime defined for OCS.
Based on the coupled-wave theory and after some tedious algebraic manipulations by matching all the boundary conditions (Ghafouri-Shiraz, 2003), the oscillating equation for an AR 1PS-DFB laser with a phase-shift discontinuity ϕ placed at the cavity centre is found, being given by $\left[\overline{\kappa}\hat{\Gamma}\left(1-\exp(\overline{\gamma}L)\right)/\left(\overline{\kappa}^2+\hat{\Gamma}\exp(\overline{\gamma}L)\right)\right]^2=\exp(2j\phi)$ with $\hat{\Gamma}=\alpha-j\delta-\overline{\gamma}$.

Laser structure	Complex equation
AR- DFB	$j(\overline{\gamma}L)=\pm\overline{\kappa}\cdot L\cdot\sinh(\overline{\gamma}L)$
DFB with reflexive facets	$(\overline{\gamma}L)^2\cdot D+(\overline{\kappa}\cdot L)^2\cdot\sinh^2(\overline{\gamma}L)\cdot\left(1-\hat{r}_1^2\right)\cdot\left(1-\hat{r}_2^2\right)+j2.$ $\cdot(\overline{\kappa}\cdot L).\left(\hat{r}_1^2+\hat{r}_2^2\right)\cdot\left(1-\hat{r}_1^2\cdot\hat{r}_2^2\right)\cdot(\overline{\gamma}L)\cdot\sinh(\overline{\gamma}L)\cdot\cosh(\overline{\gamma}L)=0$
AR-1PS DFB	$\left[\overline{\kappa}\hat{\Gamma}\left(1-\exp(\overline{\gamma}L)\right)/\left(\overline{\kappa}^2+\hat{\Gamma}\exp(\overline{\gamma}L)\right)\right]^2=\exp(2j\phi)$
FP	$\hat{r}_1\cdot\hat{r}_2\exp\left(-j\overline{k}L\right)=1$

Table 1. Transcendental equations associated to oscillation conditions in some very simple laser structures.

Table 1 summarizes the equations assumed by the oscillation condition for the DFB lasers described in sections 2.1, 2.2 and 2.3. The first two cases correspond to conventional DFB lasers, i.e., those with perfect periodic corrugations. The first of them is AR-coated type, and it corresponds to (49); the second structure has finite reflectivity facets and it corresponds to (32). The third structure is an AR-coated DFB laser with a single phase-discontinuity ϕ placed in the middle of the cavity. The last row corresponds to a different type of laser: the Fabry-Pérot cavity, the simplest type of optical oscillator. There is no corrugation ($\overline{\kappa}=0$) and the optical feedback that couples the two counter-running waves originates from the laser facets through their reflectivity values, $\hat{r}_1$ and $\hat{r}_2$.

3. The static-TMM

In section 2 the coupled wave theory has been applied to study the oscillation static conditions in several simple laser structures. Different eigen-value equations were obtained by matching different boundary conditions inside the laser cavity. From their solutions the oscillating modes in the cavity may be determined, from which the impacts due to laser parameters may be discussed.
Non-conventional DFB lasers diodes have been successively proposed to be used in OCS as improved alternatives to the QWS-DFB laser diode. These lasers aim to avoid the

degradation of SLM operation with the current injection, by reducing the SHB effect (Agrawall & Dutta, 1986; Ghafouri-Shiraz, 2003; Morthier & Vankwikelberge, 1997). The SHB effect reduction can be achieved, for instance, by optimizing the coupling coefficient profile (Ghafouri-Shiraz, 2003) and/or modulating the corrugation pitch (Fessant, 1997) along the cavity length. However, the search for the improvement in the laser performance leads to the inclusion of additional boundary conditions that makes the static analysis of the modified laser structures based on the couple-wave theory tedious and inadequate, even for situations near the laser threshold regime, where non-linear effects are expected to be negligible.

More flexible methods are then required. It is generally accepted that TMM represents an adequate alternative to evaluate the laser performance in modified laser structures, as long as the included modifications are described in a matricial form. The great flexibility of the method relies on the fact that, in those assumptions, the same algorithm may be straightforward applied to the analysis of several laser structures.

3.1 The threshold regime

Basically, to perform the static-TMM-based model for the laser threshold analysis, the cavity with length L is divided into M concatenated sections, each one being identified by the constancy of its structural parameters. These are, for the m-th section with length L_m: the corrugation period Λ_m, the amount of feedback per unit length $\overline{\kappa}_m$ and the phase of the section grating with respect to the left side of the section Ω_m (Fig. 2).

Each section is described by two counter-propagating electrical field waves, given by their complex amplitudes $\overline{E}_R(z)$ and $\overline{E}_S(z)$, which allow the internal electrical field intensity $\mathrm{E}(t,z)$ to be determined according to

$$E(t,z) \propto \Re\{[\overline{E}_R(z)+\overline{E}_S(z)]\cdot \exp(j\omega t)\} = \Re\{[\overline{E}(z)]\cdot \exp(j\omega t)\}. \tag{50}$$

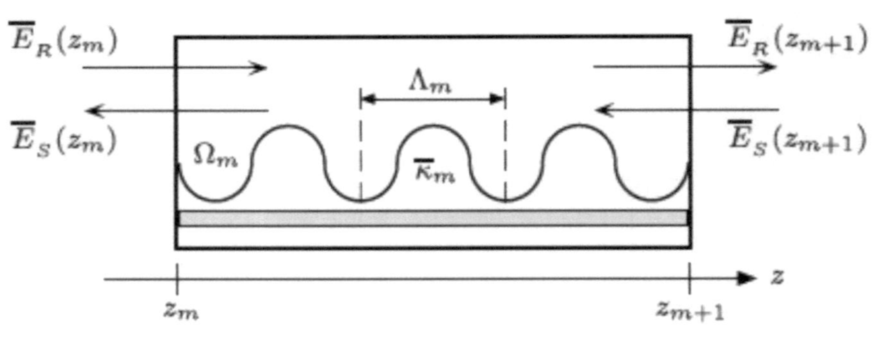

Fig. 2. A schematic diagram for a one-dimensional DFB laser structure section, placed between z_m and z_{m+1} .

From (22), it is obtained

$$\overline{E}(z) = \overline{E}_R(z) + \overline{E}_S(z) = \overline{R}(z)\cdot \exp(-j\cdot \beta_m \cdot z) + \overline{S}(z)\cdot \exp(j\cdot \beta_m \cdot z), \tag{51}$$

where

$$\begin{aligned}\overline{R}(z) &= \overline{R}_{1m}\cdot\exp(\overline{\gamma}_m\cdot z)+\overline{R}_{2m}\cdot\exp(-\overline{\gamma}_m\cdot z)\\ \overline{S}(z) &= \overline{S}_{1m}\cdot\exp(\overline{\gamma}_m\cdot z)+\overline{S}_{2m}\cdot\exp(-\overline{\gamma}_m\cdot z),\end{aligned}\tag{52}$$

with

$$\overline{S}_{1m}=\overline{\rho}_m\cdot\exp(j\cdot\Omega_m)\cdot\overline{R}_{1m}\quad ;\quad \overline{R}_{2m}=\overline{\rho}_m\cdot\exp(-j\cdot\Omega_m)\cdot\overline{S}_{2m}\tag{53}$$

and

$$\begin{aligned}&\overline{\rho}_m\triangleq\frac{j\overline{\kappa}_m}{\alpha-j\delta_m+\overline{\gamma}_m}\quad ;\quad \overline{\gamma}_m\triangleq\sqrt{(\alpha-j\delta_m)^2+\overline{\kappa}_m^2}\\ &\delta_m\triangleq\delta+\pi\left(\frac{1}{\Lambda_1}-\frac{1}{\Lambda_m}\right)\quad ;\quad \beta_m\triangleq\frac{\pi}{\Lambda_m}\end{aligned}\tag{54}$$

$$\Omega_m=\Omega_1+2\sum_{k=1}^{m-1}\left(\frac{\pi}{\Lambda_k}L_k\right);\ 2\le m\le M.\tag{55}$$

In (54) α and δ are, respectively, the gain and the detuning, taking the left section as a reference. Using (53) in (52) it yields

$$\begin{cases}\overline{R}(z)=\overline{R}_{1m}\cdot\exp(\overline{\gamma}_m\cdot z)+\overline{\rho}_m\cdot\overline{S}_{2m}\cdot\exp(-j\cdot\Omega_m)\cdot\exp(-\overline{\gamma}_m\cdot z)\\ \overline{S}(z)=\overline{\rho}_m\cdot\overline{R}_{1m}\cdot\exp(j\cdot\Omega_m)\cdot\exp(\overline{\gamma}_m\cdot z)+\overline{S}_{2m}\cdot\exp(-\overline{\gamma}_m\cdot z)\end{cases}.\tag{56}$$

Assuming a generic m cell, placed between $z=z_m$ and $z=z_{m+1}$, it is obtained from (56)

$$\begin{cases}\overline{R}(z_m)=\overline{R}_{1m}\cdot\exp(\overline{\gamma}_m\cdot z_m)+\overline{\rho}_m\cdot\overline{S}_{2m}\cdot\exp(-j\cdot\Omega_m)\cdot\exp(-\overline{\gamma}_m\cdot z_m)\\ \overline{S}(z_m)=\overline{\rho}_m\cdot\overline{R}_{1m}\cdot\exp(j\cdot\Omega_m)\cdot\exp(\overline{\gamma}_m\cdot z_m)+\overline{S}_{2m}\cdot\exp(-\overline{\gamma}_m\cdot z_m)\\ \overline{R}(z_{m+1})=\overline{R}_{1m+1}\cdot\exp(\overline{\gamma}_{m+1}\cdot z_{m+1})+\overline{\rho}_{m+1}\cdot\overline{S}_{2m+1}\cdot\exp(-j\cdot\Omega_{m+1})\cdot\exp(-\overline{\gamma}_{m+1}\cdot z_{m+1})\\ \overline{S}(z_{m+1})=\overline{\rho}_{m+1}\cdot\overline{R}_{1m+1}\cdot\exp(j\cdot\Omega_{m+1})\cdot\exp(\overline{\gamma}_m\cdot z_{m+1})+\overline{S}_{2m+1}\cdot\exp(-\overline{\gamma}_{m+1}\cdot z_{m+1})\end{cases}.\tag{57}$$

After an algebraic manipulation of (57) it is possible to write $\overline{R}(z_{m+1})$ and $\overline{S}(z_{m+1})$ as functions of $\overline{R}(z_m)$ and $\overline{S}(z_m)$. Finally, using (51) it is obtained

$$\begin{bmatrix}\overline{E}_R(z_{m+1})\\ \overline{E}_S(z_{m+1})\end{bmatrix}=\mathrm{T}(z_{m+1}/z_m)\cdot\begin{bmatrix}\overline{E}_R(z_m)\\ \overline{E}_S(z_m)\end{bmatrix},\tag{58}$$

where the transfer matrix for the m-th section of the one-dimensional DFB laser structure, $\mathrm{T}(z_{m+1}/z_m)$, links the column matrices related to the complex electric fields of the wave solutions at z_m and z_{m+1}. It is given by

$$\mathrm{T}(z_{m+1}/z_m) \triangleq \begin{bmatrix} t_{11}^{m)} & t_{12}^{m)} \\ t_{21}^{m)} & t_{22}^{m)} \end{bmatrix}, \tag{59}$$

where $t_{11}^{m)}, t_{12}^{m)}, t_{21}^{m)}$ and $t_{22}^{m)}$ are given, respectively, by

$$\begin{aligned} t_{11}^{m)} &\triangleq \frac{\xi_m - \bar{\rho}_m^2 \xi_m^{-1}}{\left(1-\bar{\rho}_m^2\right)\zeta_m} \; ; \quad t_{12}^{m)} \triangleq -\frac{\bar{\rho}_m\left(\xi_m - \xi_m^{-1}\right)\cdot \exp(-j\Omega_m)}{\left(1-\bar{\rho}_m^2\right)\zeta_m} \\ t_{21}^{m)} &\triangleq \frac{\bar{\rho}_m\left(\xi_m - \xi_m^{-1}\right)\cdot \exp(j\Omega_m)}{\left(1-\bar{\rho}_m^2\right)\zeta_m^{-1}} \; ; \quad t_{22}^{m)} \triangleq \frac{\xi_m^{-1} - \bar{\rho}_m^2 \xi_m}{\left(1-\bar{\rho}_m^2\right)\zeta_m^{-1}}, \end{aligned} \tag{60}$$

with $\xi_m \triangleq \exp\left[\bar{\gamma}_m(z_{m+1}-z_m)\right]$ and $\zeta_m \triangleq \exp\left[j\beta_m(z_{m+1}-z_m)\right]$. Equations (58) to (60) are a generalization of the TMM presented in (Ghafouri-Shiraz, 2003), in order to allow the inclusion of variations in the grating period of laser structures, such as the CPM-DFB lasers. The fields at both cavity ends are connected by the elementary matrix product

$$\begin{bmatrix} \bar{E}_R(L) \\ \bar{E}_S(L) \end{bmatrix} = \left[\mathbf{T}_{\mathbf{cor}}\right]\cdot \begin{bmatrix} \bar{E}_R(0) \\ \bar{E}_S(0) \end{bmatrix}, \tag{61}$$

where

$$\left[\mathbf{T}_{\text{cor}}\right] \triangleq \prod_{m=M}^{1} \mathrm{T}(z_{m+1}/z_m). \tag{62}$$

Assuming that the field discontinuity is usually small along the plane of the phase-shift, the inclusion of one phase-shift φ placed at $z = z_m$ (Fig. 3) may be described by the following set of equations

$$\bar{E}_R\left(z_m^+\right) = \bar{E}_R\left(z_m^-\right)\cdot \exp(j\cdot\varphi) \; ; \; \bar{E}_S\left(z_m^+\right) = \bar{E}_S\left(z_m^-\right)\cdot \exp(-j\cdot\varphi). \tag{63}$$

The associated matrix is then given by

$$\left[\mathbf{M}_\varphi\right] \triangleq \begin{bmatrix} \exp(j\varphi) & 0 \\ 0 & \exp(-j\varphi) \end{bmatrix}. \tag{64}$$

The matrix given by (64) should be included in the matrix product $\left[\mathbf{T}_{\mathbf{cor}}\right]$ given by (62) at the correspondent z position.

Let us now consider the cavity facet description. The uncertainty in the corrugation length regarding the period of the corrugation is itself a quantification of the uncertainty in the phase-shift related to the facet reflectivity. The left and right facet reflectivities are given, respectively, by

$$\hat{r}_1 \triangleq r_1 \cdot \exp(j\cdot\varphi_1) \; ; \quad \hat{r}_2 \triangleq r_2 \cdot \exp(j\cdot\varphi_2). \tag{65}$$

Fig. 4 represents schematically the counter-running waves at the left facet. Let us consider, firstly, the situation corresponding to $\varphi_1 = \varphi_2 = 0$. For the left facet $(z = 0)$, it yields

$$\bar{E}_R(0^+) = \bar{E}_R(0^-) \cdot t_1 + r_1 \cdot \bar{E}_S(0^+) \;\; ; \;\; \bar{E}_S(0^-) = \bar{E}_S(0^+) \cdot t_1 - r_1 \cdot \bar{E}_R(0^-). \tag{66}$$

In (66) t_1 is the left facet transmitivity. The second equation of (66) may be rewritten as

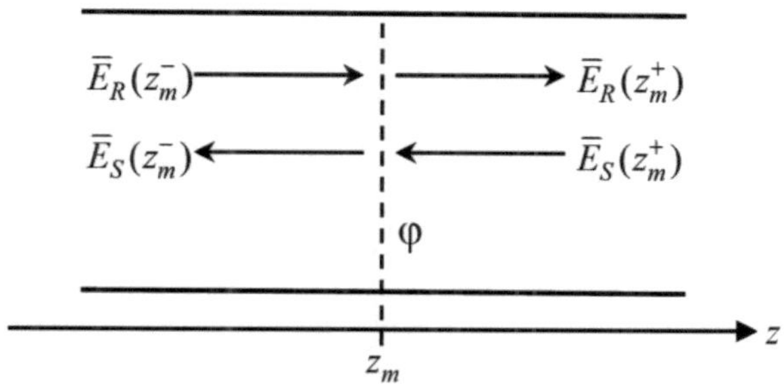

Fig. 3. A simplified schematic diagram of a phase-shift change φ at $z = z_m$ in the DFB laser corrugation.

$$\bar{E}_S(0^+) = \frac{1}{t_1} \cdot \bar{E}_S(0^-) + \frac{r_1}{t_1} \cdot \bar{E}_R(0^-) \,. \tag{67}$$

Substituting (67) in the first equation of (66), it is obtained

$$\bar{E}_R(0^+) = \bar{E}_R(0^-) \cdot \left(t_1 + \frac{r_1^2}{t_1} \right) + \frac{r_1}{t_1} \cdot \bar{E}_S(0^-) \,. \tag{68}$$

Assuming (67), (68) and that $t_1^2 + r_1^2 = 1$, it results

$$\begin{bmatrix} \bar{E}_R(0^+) \\ \bar{E}_S(0^+) \end{bmatrix} = \frac{1}{t_1} \cdot \begin{bmatrix} 1 & r_1 \\ r_1 & 1 \end{bmatrix} \cdot \begin{bmatrix} \bar{E}_R(0^-) \\ \bar{E}_S(0^-) \end{bmatrix}. \tag{69}$$

Therefore, the matrix associated with the left facet, assuming $\varphi_1 = 0$, is given by

$$\left[\mathbf{M}_{r_1} \right] \triangleq \frac{1}{t_1} \cdot \begin{bmatrix} 1 & r_1 \\ r_1 & 1 \end{bmatrix}. \tag{70}$$

In order to include the phase associated with the left reflectivity we should consider a matrix associated with the phase- shift similar to (64). This means that

$$\begin{bmatrix} \bar{E}_R(0^+) \\ \bar{E}_S(0^+) \end{bmatrix} = \left[\mathbf{M}_\varphi \right] \cdot \left[\mathbf{M}_{r_1} \right] \cdot \begin{bmatrix} \bar{E}_R(0^-) \\ \bar{E}_S(0^-) \end{bmatrix} = \begin{bmatrix} \exp(j\varphi) & r_1 \cdot \exp(j\varphi) \\ r_1 \cdot \exp(-j\varphi) & \exp(-j\varphi) \end{bmatrix} \cdot \begin{bmatrix} \bar{E}_R(0^-) \\ \bar{E}_S(0^-) \end{bmatrix}. \tag{71}$$

In the oscillation condition the cavity incoming waves are null $\left(\bar{E}_R\left(0^-\right)=\bar{E}_S\left(L^+\right)=0\right)$, leading to

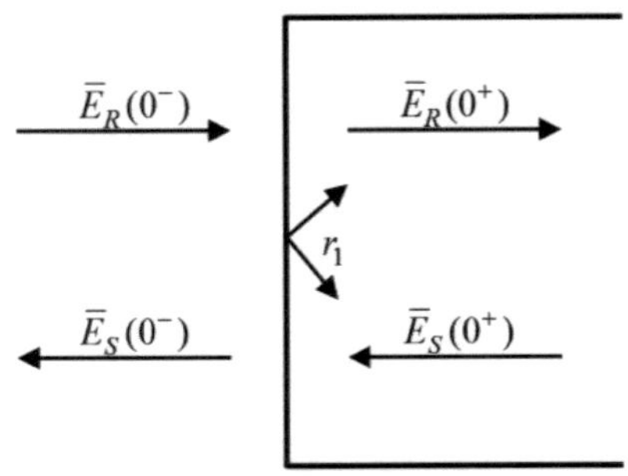

Fig. 4. A simplified schematic diagram of the two counter-running waves at left facet.

$$\bar{E}_R\left(0^+\right)=\frac{1}{t_1}\cdot r_1\cdot\exp(j\varphi)\cdot\bar{E}_S\left(0^-\right)\ ;\ \bar{E}_S\left(0^+\right)=\frac{1}{t_1}\cdot\exp(-j\varphi)\,, \tag{72}$$

which originates

$$\hat{r}_1=\frac{\bar{E}_R\left(0^+\right)}{\bar{E}_S\left(0^+\right)}=r_1\cdot\exp(2\cdot j\cdot\varphi)\,. \tag{73}$$

From (65) and (73) it results that $2\cdot\varphi=\varphi_1$. Therefore

$$\left[\mathbf{M}_{\varphi}\right]\triangleq\left[\mathbf{M}_{\varphi_1}\right]=\begin{bmatrix}\exp\left(j\frac{\varphi_1}{2}\right) & 0\\ 0 & \exp\left(-j\frac{\varphi_1}{2}\right)\end{bmatrix}. \tag{74}$$

Similarly, it could be shown that

$$\left[\mathbf{M}_{\mathbf{r}_2}\right]=\frac{1}{t_2}\cdot\begin{bmatrix}1 & -r_2\\ -r_2 & 1\end{bmatrix}\ ;\ \left[\mathbf{M}_{\varphi_2}\right]=\begin{bmatrix}\exp\left(j\frac{\varphi_2}{2}\right) & 0\\ 0 & \exp\left(-j\frac{\varphi_2}{2}\right)\end{bmatrix}. \tag{75}$$

The matrix $\left[\mathbf{T}_{\text{tot}}\right]$ for the overall cavity (corrugation+facets) will be then given by

$$\begin{bmatrix}\bar{E}_R\left(L^+\right)\\ \bar{E}_S\left(L^+\right)\end{bmatrix}=\left[\mathbf{M}_{\mathbf{r}_2}\right]\cdot\left[\mathbf{M}_{\varphi_2}\right]\cdot\left[\mathbf{T}_{\text{cor}}\right]\cdot\left[\mathbf{M}_{\varphi_1}\right]\cdot\left[\mathbf{M}_{\mathbf{r}_1}\right]\cdot\begin{bmatrix}\bar{E}_R\left(0^-\right)\\ \bar{E}_S\left(0^-\right)\end{bmatrix}=\left[\mathbf{T}_{\text{tot}}\right]\cdot\begin{bmatrix}\bar{E}_R\left(0^-\right)\\ \bar{E}_S\left(0^-\right)\end{bmatrix}, \tag{76}$$

where $\left[\mathbf{T}_{\text{tot}}\right]\triangleq\left[\mathbf{M}_{\mathbf{r}_2}\right]\cdot\left[\mathbf{M}_{\varphi_2}\right]\cdot\left[\mathbf{T}_{\text{cor}}\right]\cdot\left[\mathbf{M}_{\varphi_1}\right]\cdot\left[\mathbf{M}_{\mathbf{r}_1}\right]$. Notice, that in modified DFB structures with axial variations of the coupling coefficient $\bar{\kappa}(z)$, the minimum number of sections to be considered in the static-TMM should be compatible with the assumption of a constant value for the coupling coefficient in each section. The oscillation condition corresponds to the vanishing of the incoming waves $\left(\bar{E}_R\left(0^-\right)=\bar{E}_S\left(L^+\right)=0\right)$. It is stated by the following requirement

$$t_{22}^{\text{total}}(\alpha,\delta)=0, \tag{77}$$

where t_{22}^{total} is the 4th element of the matrix $\left[\mathbf{T}_{\text{tot}}\right]$. The solutions are the mode gain, α, and the detuning, δ, for each mode that is allowed to propagate inside the cavity. For the main mode their values are, respectively, the threshold gain, α_{th}, and the threshold detuning, δ_{th}. Considering a grating with a first-order Bragg diffraction, the mode gain and the detuning can be expressed, respectively, as (Ghafouri-Shiraz, 2003)

$$\alpha(z)=\frac{\Gamma g(z)-\alpha_{\text{loss}}}{2} \quad ; \quad \delta(z)=\frac{2\pi}{\lambda}n(z)-\frac{2\pi\cdot n_g}{\lambda\cdot\lambda_\Lambda}(\lambda-\lambda_\Lambda)-\frac{\pi}{\Lambda(z)}, \tag{78}$$

where α_{loss} is the total loss, n is the effective index, λ is the lasing mode wavelength, n_g is the group effective index and g is the material gain, given by (Ghafouri-Shiraz, 2003)

$$g(z)=A_0\left[N(z)-N_0\right]-A_1\left\{\lambda-\left[\lambda_0-A_2\left(N(z)-N_0\right)\right]\right\}^2. \tag{79}$$

In (79), N is the carrier concentration, A_0 is the differential gain, N_0 is the carrier concentration at transparency $(g=0)$, λ_0 is the peak wavelength at transparency and A_1 and A_2 are parameters used in the parabolic model assumed for the material gain. Using the first-order approximation for the effective index n, one obtains (Ghafouri-Shiraz, 2003)

$$n(z)=n_0+\Gamma\frac{\partial n}{\partial N}N(z), \tag{80}$$

where n_0 is the effective index at zero carrier injection and $\partial n/\partial N$ is the differential index. The photon concentration (S) and N are coupled together through the steady-state carrier rate equation (Ghafouri-Shiraz, 2003)

$$\frac{I}{qV_{act}}=AN(z)+BN^2(z)+CN^3(z)+\frac{v_g g(z)S(z)}{1+\varepsilon_g S(z)}, \tag{81}$$

where I is the injection current, q is the modulus of the electron charge, V_{act} is the volume of the active layer, A is the spontaneous emission rate, B is the radiative spontaneous emission coefficient, C is the Auger recombination coefficient, ε_g is a non-linear coefficient that takes into account saturation effects and $v_g=c/n_g$ is the group velocity.

In a purely index-coupled DFB laser cavity, which is the case in the most of laser structures under analysis, the mutual interaction between the coupled waves can be neglected in the rate of total power change (Ghafouri-Shiraz, 2003; Kapon, et al., 1982). Therefore, the local photon density inside the cavity can be expressed as

$$S(z)\approx\frac{2\varepsilon_0 n(z)ng\lambda}{hc}c_0^2\left[\left|\bar{E}_R(z)\right|^2+\left|\bar{E}_S(z)\right|^2\right], \tag{82}$$

where h is the Planck's constant, and c_0 a dimensionless coefficient that allows the determination of the total electric field at the above-threshold regime, taking into account that the normalization

$$\left|\bar{E}_R(0)\right|^2 + \left|\bar{E}_S(0)\right|^2 = 1 \tag{83}$$

has been imposed in the left cavity end. The boundary conditions at the left facet and (83) allow the calculation of the two counter-running waves, $\bar{E}_R(z)$ and $\bar{E}_S(z)$, at z=0. The use of the TMM allows the calculation of the longitudinal electric field profile. The output power at the right facet can therefore be determined as

$$P = \frac{dw}{\Gamma} v_g \frac{hc}{\lambda} S(L), \tag{84}$$

where d and w are the thickness and width of the active layer, respectively.
From the solutions of the oscillation condition (77), α_{th} and δ_{th} are determined. Using (78) to (80), the carrier concentration at threshold (N_{th}), the effective index at threshold (n_{th}), the threshold wavelength (λ_{th}), and λ_0 are successively evaluated. Threshold current (I_{th}) is then obtained from (81), assuming that S is negligible at threshold. Within this assumption, the z dependence is neglected in the first equation (78), (79) and (80). This is also true in the second equation (81), except for the CPM structures where a z dependence should be included in $\Lambda(z)$.
The number M of cells needed to implement the TMM-threshold analysis of several laser structures is summarized in Table 2.

Laser structure	**Number of cells M**	**Number of Phase-Shifts**	**Remarks**
FP	3	-	$\bar{\kappa}=0;\ \Lambda \to \infty$
AR-Conventional DFB	1	-	$\hat{r}_1 = \hat{r}_2 = 0$
Conventional DFB with reflexive facets	3		$\hat{r}_1, \hat{r}_2 \neq 0$
QWS	5	3	$\hat{r}_1, \hat{r}_2 \neq 0$
MPS	2N+3	N	$\hat{r}_1, \hat{r}_2 \neq 0$
CPM	5	-	$\hat{r}_1, \hat{r}_2 \neq 0$
CPM	Large number	-	$\hat{r}_1, \hat{r}_2 \neq 0$
N layer VCSEL	N+2	-	$\hat{r}_1, \hat{r}_2 \neq 0$

Table 2. Spatial discretization in static TMM for several semiconductor laser structures in the threshold regime.

The first conventional DFB structure is a mirrorless (AR) DFB laser. One single cell is needed for the corrugation description. The first CPM-DFB structure is a symmetric structure with two corrugation periods Λ_o and Λ_c, respectively, for the outer zones, closer to the facets, and for the central zone. For the whole laser description five cells are needed: two cells for the facets, two cells for the outer zones in the corrugation and one cell for the central zone. The second CPM laser corresponds to a linear chirp corrugation, that is, a structure with a continuous change in the corrugation period.

3.2 Above-threshold analysis

In the above-threshold regime, $S(z)$ assumes high enough values to induce important non-uniformities in $N(z)$ and $n(z)$. Despite the SHB effect might be minimized by an adequate design of the DFB structure, the interdependence of $S(z)$, $N(z)$ and $n(z)$ can't be neglected anymore. Therefore, in order to insure a correct evaluation of the above-threshold characteristics, each section shall be divided into several sub-sections. According to (Ghafouri-Shiraz, 2003), for a 500 μm cavity length, about 5000 cells should be considered in order to ensure a reasonable accuracy in the stationary analysis.

The above-threshold calculations follow closely the method described in (Fessant, 1997; Ghafouri-Shiraz, 2003). However, in order to ensure a quick convergence in the evaluations of the laser characteristics, an adequate strategy is proposed.

3.2.1 Lasing-mode analysis

For each bias current I, the numerical above-threshold analysis concerning the lasing-mode is summarized as follows

a. Successive $(G \times G)$ grids are created in the (c_0, λ) plane. The i-th grid is centered at $\left(c_{0_c}^{(i)}, \lambda_c^{(i)}\right)$ and it is enclosed in the region defined by the limits $c_{0_{\min}}^{(i)}, c_{0_{\max}}^{(i)}, \lambda_{\min}^{(i)}$ and $\lambda_{\max}^{(i)}$. For the initial grid $(i=1)$ [3]

$$\lambda_c^{(1)} = \lambda_{th} \tag{85}$$

$$c_{0_c}^{(1)} = \sqrt{\frac{hc\left(I - I_{th}\right) / \left(2q\, V_{act}\, v_g\, g_{th}\, \varepsilon_0\, n_{th}\, n_g\, \lambda_{th}\right)}{\left|\bar{E}_R(0)\right|^2 + \left|\bar{E}_S(0)\right|^2}} = \sqrt{\frac{hc\left(I - I_{th}\right)}{2q\, V_{act}\, v_g\, g_{th}\, \varepsilon_0\, n_{th}\, n_g\, \lambda_{th}}} \tag{86}$$

$$\begin{aligned} c_{0_{\min}}^{(1)} &= c_{0_c}^{(1)} - \Delta c_0^{(1)} \quad ; \quad c_{0_{\max}}^{(1)} = c_{0_c}^{(1)} + \Delta c_0^{(1)} \\ \lambda_{\min}^{(1)} &= \lambda_c^{(1)} - \Delta\lambda^{(1)} \quad ; \quad \lambda_{\max}^{(1)} = \lambda_c^{(1)} + \Delta\lambda^{(1)} \ . \end{aligned} \tag{87}$$

For $G \simeq 10$, $\Delta c_0^{(1)} \triangleq c_{0_c}^{(1)} / 10$ and $\Delta\lambda^{(1)} \triangleq 0.1\ \text{nm}$ seem adequate for most of DFB laser structures. However, a readjustment of $\Delta c_0^{(1)}$ and $\Delta\lambda^{(1)}$ may, occasionally, be necessary in order to prevent an eventual convergence towards a local minimum. This is a critical aspect of the proposed analysis, since an inadequate choice would prevent the numerical convergence.

b. For each one of the G^2 pairs of the i-th grid, $\left(c_{0_k}^{(1)}, \lambda_l^{(1)}\right)$ with $k;l = 1 \ldots G$, equations (79-82) are self-consistently solved in order to determine the material gain, the carrier

---

[3] In (86) it has been taken into account the normalization condition (83).

density, the photon density and the effective index for each one of the *j*-th sub-section, respectively, g_j, N_j, S_j and n_j, with $1 \le j \le M$.

c. Equations (78) are solved in order to determine the lasing-mode gain and detuning for the *j*-th sub-section, respectively, α_j and δ_j. The transfer matrix of the *j*-th sub-section , $\mathrm{T}\left(z_{j+1} / z_j\right)$ is then calculated.

d. Using the TMM , the two counter-running waves at the output of the *j*-th sub-section, $\bar{E}_{R_j}$ and $\bar{E}_{S_j}$, are obtained. For the *M*-th sub-section the discrepancy found between those values and the laser right facet boundary condition is represented by $\varepsilon_{kl}^{(i)}$. This value is evaluated and stored for each pair $\left(c_{0_k}^{(i)}, \lambda_l^{(i)}\right)$ of the *i*-th grid. The error associated to the *i*-th grid is given by $\varepsilon^{(i)} = \min\left(\varepsilon_{kl}^{(i)}\right)$.

e. Whenever $\varepsilon^{(i)} = \varepsilon^{(i-1)}$, the central pair remains the same $\left(c_{0_c}^{(i+1)} = c_{0_c}^{(i)}, \lambda_c^{(i+1)} = \lambda_c^{(i)}\right)$, but new limits are required for the next grid description. The partitions should be reduced considering, for instance: $\Delta c_0^{(i+1)} = \Delta c_0^{(i)} / 10$ and $\Delta\lambda^{(i+1)} = \Delta\lambda^{(i)} / 10$. Whenever $\varepsilon^{(i)} < \varepsilon^{(i-1)}$, the pair associated with $\min\left(\varepsilon_{kl}^{(i)}\right)$ is chosen as the next central pair $\left(c_{0_c}^{(i+1)}, \lambda_c^{(i+1)}\right)$, while c_0 and λ partitions remain unchangeable. For $i=1$, $\varepsilon^{(i-1)}$ is taken as the error associated with the central pair $\left(c_{0_c}^{(1)}, \lambda_c^{(1)}\right)$.

For each one of the G^2 pairs $\left(c_{0_k}^{(i+1)}, \lambda_l^{(i+1)}\right)$, the steps a)-e) are repeated until $\varepsilon^{(i+1)} < \varepsilon_{\min}$, where $\varepsilon_{\min}$ is a preset error value, for instance, less than 10^{-14} (Ghafouri-Shiraz, 2003). Since the gain α_j and the detuning δ_j are *z*-dependent, the lasing characteristics for each bias current are associated with their mean values along the cavity, given by

$$\alpha_{av}(I) = \frac{1}{M}\sum_{j=1}^{M}\alpha_j(I) \quad ; \quad \delta_{av}(I) = \frac{1}{M}\sum_{j=1}^{M}\delta_j(I). \tag{88}$$

Notice that the sequential analysis a) to e) assumes a one-mode propagation laser behavior. This procedure is itself a good assumption, since the present analysis focus on DFB structures that must guarantee SLM operation. Otherwise, different strategies should be adopted.

Finally, when studying the influence of the bias current on the laser characteristics, a considerable CPU time reduction can be achieved if, for each subsequent current, instead of using (85), $\lambda_c^{(1)}$ is taken as the solution found for the previous bias current.

3.2.2 Side-mode analysis

$S(z)$, $N(z)$ and $n(z)$ profiles are settled for each bias current by the lasing-mode profiles obtained in section 3.2.1. At threshold, theses distributions are nearly uniform along the cavity, assuming average values, respectively, 0, N_{th} and n_{th}. The gain mode and detuning associated with the side-mode at threshold, respectively, α_{side} and δ_1, are settled. In the one-mode approximation, the use of (79) leads to

$$\lambda_R(\delta_1) = \frac{2\pi\lambda_B\left(n_{th} + n_g\right)}{\delta_1\lambda_\Lambda + 2\pi n_g + \dfrac{\pi\lambda_\Lambda}{\Lambda_{av}}}, \tag{89}$$

where Λ_{av} is the average grating period given by

$$\Lambda_{av} = \frac{\sum_{m=1}^{M} L_m \cdot \Lambda_m}{L}. \tag{90}$$

This assumption means that $\lambda_R(\delta_1)$ would be the threshold wavelength if δ_1 would correspond to the lasing mode. On the other hand, regarding the side-mode gain, (78) imposes that

$$2\alpha_{\text{side}} = \Gamma g_1 - \alpha_{\text{loss}}, \tag{91}$$

where g_1 is obtained from (82) , making $N(z) = N_{th}$ and $\lambda = \overline{\lambda}_1(\alpha_{\text{side}})$. The parameter $\overline{\lambda}_1(\alpha_{\text{side}})$ should be interpreted as the wavelength in the one-mode approach if α_{side} would correspond to the threshold gain. It will be designated by the *side-mode effective wavelength*. Similarly, for the lasing mode, it is obtained

$$2\alpha_{th} = \Gamma g_{th} - \alpha_{\text{loss}}, \tag{92}$$

where $g_{th} = A_0(N_{th} - N_0)$. Then, from (91) and (92), it can be shown that

$$\overline{\lambda}_1(\alpha_{\text{side}}) = \lambda_{th} + j\lambda_I(\alpha_{\text{side}}); \; \lambda_I(\alpha_{\text{side}}) = \sqrt{\frac{2(\alpha_{\text{side}} - \alpha_{th})}{A_1\Gamma}}. \tag{93}$$

A $(G\times G)$ grid is created in the plane (λ_I, λ_R), adopting a similar procedure as the one described in Section 3.2.1 for the plane (c_0, λ). The initial grid is centered in $\left(\lambda_{I_c}^{(1)}, \lambda_{R_c}^{(1)}\right)$, where $\lambda_{I_c}^{(1)}$ and $\lambda_{R_c}^{(1)}$ are given, respectively, by the second equation (93) and (89). The limits of the initial grid are defined by $\lambda_{I_c}^{(1)} \pm \Delta\lambda_I^{(1)}$ and $\lambda_{R_c}^{(1)} \pm \Delta\lambda_R^{(1)}$. The values $G = 10$, $\Delta\lambda_I^{(1)} \simeq 0.01$ nm and $\Delta\lambda_R^{(1)} \simeq 0.1$ nm seem reasonable for most of the structures but, as previously referred, a readjustment may once in a while be necessary to avoid the mode hopping. Usually $\Delta\lambda_I^{(1)}$ is one order of magnitude lower than $\Delta\lambda_R^{(1)}$ because the difference between the normalized gains for different modes is about one order of magnitude lower than the difference between their normalized detunings.

Successive $(G\times G)$ grids are defined in the wavelength plane, centering the *i*-th grid in $\left(\lambda_{I_c}^{(i)}, \lambda_{R_c}^{(i)}\right)$, and enclosing it in the region defined by the limits $\lambda_{I_c}^{(i)} \pm \Delta\lambda_I^{(i)}$ and $\lambda_{R_c}^{(i)} \pm \Delta\lambda_R^{(i)}$.

Then, for each bias current and pair (k,l) of the i-th grid, i.e. $\left(\lambda_{I_k}^{(i)},\lambda_{I_l}^{(i)}\right)$, the mode gain and detuning for each one of the $j(j=1,....M)$ sub-sections of the cavity are obtained as, respectively

$$\alpha_{\text{side}_{klj}}^{(i)}=\alpha_j(I)+\left(\lambda_{I_k}^{(i)}\right)^2\frac{A_1\Gamma}{2}\ ;\ \delta_{\text{side}_{klj}}^{(i)}=\frac{2\pi}{\lambda_{R_l}^{(i)}}n_j(I)-\frac{2\pi n_g}{\lambda_{R_l}^{(i)}\lambda_\Lambda}\left(\lambda_{R_l}^{(i)}-\lambda_B\right)+\frac{\pi}{\Lambda_j}. \tag{95}$$

In (95) $\alpha_j(I)$ and $n_j(I)$ are, respectively, the lasing-mode gain and the refractive index associated with the j-th subsection for a biasing current I achieved in Section 3.2.1. Besides, Λ_j is the corrugation period of the j-th subsection. Similarly as in Section 3.2.1, steps c)-e) are the sequentially followed. However, the side-mode analysis is quicker than the lasing mode analysis since the step b) is not implemented.

4. The dynamic TMM

In its conventional form, the transfer matrix $\mathrm{T}(z_{m+1}/z_m)$ of a given cell inside the laser cavity expresses the relationship described by (58). In this formulation, a steady-state operation has implicitly been assumed. It is now required to develop a time-dependent implementation of the TMM. As far as the dynamic-TMM is concerned, the increment of time requires updating the travelling-wave amplitudes as they pass through a section. The increment Δt is chosen so that the spatial step size, Δl, is given by the product of the time increment by the group velocity $\left(\Delta l=\Delta t\times v_g\right)$. So, after one increment Δt, the backward wave $\overline{E}_S(z_{m+1},t)$ travels one section to the left, becoming $\overline{E}_S(z_m,t+\Delta t)$, and the forward wave $\overline{E}_R(z_m,t)$ travels one section to the right, being then designated by $\overline{E}_R(z_{m+1},t+\Delta t)$. Assuming that the transfer matrix remains unchanged during the time step, it yields after some simple manipulation of (58) (Lee et al., 1999) that

$$\begin{bmatrix}\overline{E}_R(z_{m+1},t+\Delta t)\\ \overline{E}_S(z_m,t+\Delta t)\end{bmatrix}=\frac{1}{t_{22}^{(m)}}\begin{bmatrix}t_{11}^{(m)}t_{22}^{(m)}-t_{12}^{(m)}t_{21}^{(m)} & t_{12}^{(m)}\\ -t_{21}^{(m)} & 1\end{bmatrix}\times\begin{bmatrix}\overline{E}_R(z_m,t)\\ \overline{E}_S(z_{m+1},t)\end{bmatrix}. \tag{96}$$

Equation (96) forms the basis of the dynamic TMM, where it is assumed that the variations in $\mathrm{T}(z_{m+1}/z_m)$ and in the wave amplitudes occur in a time scale negligible in comparison with the optical frequency. In a multi-electrode DFB model the local variations in carrier, photon and refractive index are taken into account by further dividing the separately pumped sections into subsections each one described by its own matrix $\mathrm{T}(z_{m+1}/z_m)$ (Davis & O'Dowd, 1991, 1992). Obviously, accuracy increases with the number of cells, but it should always be kept in mind that the time computation increases almost quadratically with the number of cells: increasing M decreases the step size Δl and, simultaneously, the time increment Δt.

Dynamic-TMM analysis reinforces the relevance of the questions related to the need of decreasing the heavy simulation times arising from the intensive search for those laser parameters that complies with the boundary conditions of the problem under analysis. For typical lengths of hundred of micrometers and data rate less than about 40 Gb/s, simulation analysis requires no more than $M = 100$ sections to guarantee enough method accuracy (Jia, X. et al., 2007). The model solves self-consistently the carrier and photon rate equations similarly as described in Section 3.1.

5. Simulation results and discussions

As an application example of the TMM it has been chosen a multiple phase-shift DFB laser structure especially designed to provide SLM operation.

5.1 The laser structure

The laser structure is represented in Fig. 5. It is a multi-section AR-coated DFB laser with uniform grating period $(\Lambda_m = \Lambda)$ and uniform coupling coefficient $(\overline{\kappa}_m = \overline{\kappa})$. Three PS discontinuities (φ_i) are located along the DFB laser structure. Their positions are represented by a normalized parameter given by

$$\mathrm{PSP}_i = \frac{z_i}{L} \quad i = 1,2,3, \tag{97}$$

where z_i is the φ_i position.

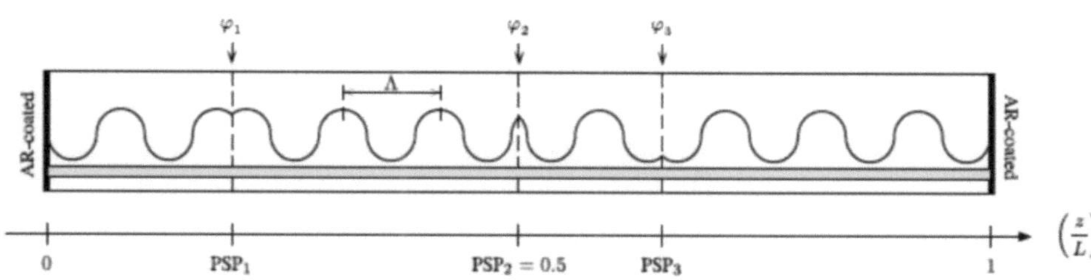

Fig. 5. A simplified schematic diagram of the 3PS-DFB laser structure with non-equal and non-identical 3PS.

A purely index-coupled laser structure assures that $\overline{\kappa}$ is real. For the structure, it has been assumed L=500μm, Λ=227,039 nm, $\Omega_1 = 0$ rad and $\mathrm{PSP}_2 = 0.5$. Two important laser figures of merit in the area of OCS are the normalized mode selectivity σ and the flatness of the electric field distribution along the cavity $\Im$, which are given by

$$\begin{aligned} &\sigma = \alpha \cdot L - \alpha_{th} \cdot L ; \\ &\Im = \frac{1}{L}\int_0^L \left[\mathrm{I}(z) - \mathrm{I}_{av} \right]^2 dz , \end{aligned} \tag{98}$$

where $\mathrm{I}(z)$ is the normalized electric field intensity at an arbitrary position z, which is given by

$$\mathrm{I}(z) = \frac{\left|\overline{E}_R(z)\right|^2 + \left|\overline{E}_S(z)\right|^2}{\left|\overline{E}_R(0)\right|^2 + \left|\overline{E}_S(0)\right|^2} \tag{99}$$

and I_{av} is its average value along the cavity. Notice that according to the normalization condition (83), $I(z)$ is numerically equal to $|\bar{E}_R(z)|^2 + |\bar{E}_S(z)|^2$. For laser structures with $L=500\mu m$ it is generally accepted (Ghafouri-Shiraz, 2003) that a stable SLM operation requires $\sigma \geq 0.25$ and $\Im \leq 0.05$. The laser structural and material parameters used in the simulations are summarized in Table 3.

Laser parameter	Value	Laser parameter	Value
Material Parameters		**Structural parameters**	
Spontaneous emission rate, A	$2.5\times10^{8}\ s^{-1}$	Active layer width, w	1.5 μm
Bimolecular recombination coefficient, B	$1.0\times10^{-16}\ m^{3}s^{-1}$	Active layer thickness, d	0.12 μm
Auger recombination coefficient, C	$3.0\times10^{-41}\ m^{6}s^{-1}$	Cavity length, L	500 μm
Differential gain, A_0	$2.7\times10^{-20}\ m^{2}$	Optical confinement factor, Γ	0.35
Gain curvature, A_1	$1.5\times10^{19}\ m^{-3}$	Grating period, Λ	227.039 nm
Differential peak wavelength, A_2	$2.7\times10^{-32}\ m^{4}$		
Internal loss, α_{loss}	$4.0\times10^{3}\ m^{-1}$		
Effective index at zero injection, n_0	3.41351524		
Carrier density at transparency, N_0	$1.23\times10^{24}\ m^{-3}$		
Differential index, dn/dN	$-1.8\times10^{-26}\ m^{3}$		
Group velocity, v_g	$8.33\times10^{7}\ m\times s^{-1}$		
Nonlinear gain coefficient, ε_g	$1.5\times10^{-23}\ m^{3}$		

Table 3. Summary of laser parameters.

5.2 The structure optimization (threshold situation)

The objective is twofold: to maximize σ and to minimize $\Im$ at threshold. For this purpose, it will be varied, simultaneously and independently, the following set of variables (decision variables): $\bar{\kappa}L$, φ_2, PSP_1, φ_1, PSP_3 and φ_3. The procedure initializes with the boundary values that insure a stable SLM operation according to the selection criteria previously referred, i.e., $\sigma = \sigma_{min} = 0.25$ and $\Im = \Im_{max} = 0.05$. After each step, these values are adjusted by fixing tighter limits, i.e., higher σ and smaller $\Im$. The starting point is a AR QWS-DFB laser structure[4] $(\varphi_1 = 0, \varphi_2 = 90^{\circ}, \varphi_3 = 0)$ with $\bar{\kappa}L = 2$. In the specialized literature these

[4] This phase change corresponds to a quarter wavelength shift and so, the name single $\lambda/4$-shifted DFB also used.

lasers are often associated with high mode selectivity, zero frequency and small current density at threshold. Nevertheless, the highly non-uniform electric field distribution induces local carrier depletion near the centre of the cavity that is responsible for the degradation of the laser performance in the high power regime. In the procedure adopted hereby it will always be assumed that $PSP_1 \leq PSP_2$ and $PSP_2 \leq PSP_3$. The step-by-step procedure can be summarized as follows

Step 1. One PS, (φ_1), is added in the first half of the cavity. The optimization of $\sigma(PSP_1, \varphi_1)$ and $\Im(PSP_1, \varphi_1)$ is performed by varying simultaneously and independently both arguments in their ranges: $0 \leq PSP_1 \leq 0.5$ and $0^\circ \leq \varphi_1 \leq 180^\circ$. It will be assumed as selection criteria that $\sigma(PSP_1, \varphi_1) \geq \sigma_{min}$ and $\Im(PSP_1, \varphi_1) \leq \Im_{max}$. This procedure will lead to the definition of a region in the (PSP_1, φ_1) plane from which a solution is chosen and new boundaries $(\sigma_{min}, \Im_{max})$ are settled;

Step 2. For the new boundaries, another PS, (φ_3), is placed in the second half of the cavity. A similar procedure as the one described in step 1 is adopted, now for $\sigma(PSP_3, \varphi_3)$ and $\Im(PSP_3, \varphi_3)$, assuming $0.5 \leq PSP_3 \leq 1$ and $0^\circ \leq \varphi_3 \leq 180^\circ$.

Steps 1 and 2 are sequentially repeated until no improvements on σ and $\Im$ are achieved. The optima values for the set $(PSP_1, \varphi_1, PSP_3, \varphi_3)$ are found, assuming $\overline{\kappa}L = 2$ and $\varphi_2 = 90^\circ$. New optima boundaries $(\sigma_{min}, \Im_{max})$ are settled.

Step 3. An optimization of $\sigma(\overline{\kappa}L, \varphi_2)$ and $\Im(\overline{\kappa}L, \varphi_2)$ is performed by varying simultaneously and independently both arguments in their ranges: $1 \leq \overline{\kappa}L \leq 3$ and $0^\circ \leq \varphi_2 \leq 180^\circ$. It will be assumed as selection criteria that $\sigma(\overline{\kappa}L, \varphi_2) \geq \sigma_{min}$ and $\Im(\overline{\kappa}L, \varphi_2) \leq \Im_{max}$.

Steps 1, 2 and 3 are repeated until no improvements on σ and $\Im$ are achieved. This means that the best 3PS-DFB laser structure $(PSP_1, \varphi_1, PSP_2 = 0.5, \varphi_2 = 90^\circ, PSP_3, \varphi_3, \overline{\kappa}L)$ is obtained, as far as σ and $\Im$ are concerned. In all steps, and whenever necessary, an argument based on the smallest threshold gain is used in order to decide the best solution.

Fig.6 and Fig.7 show, respectively, the contour maps for $\sigma(PSP_3, \varphi_3)$ and $\Im(PSP_3, \varphi_3)$, when the arguments vary along their entire range, assuming $PSP_1 = 0.127$, $\varphi_1 = 110.7^\circ$, $PSP_2 = 0.5$, $\varphi_2 = 60^\circ$ and $\overline{\kappa}L = 1.7$.

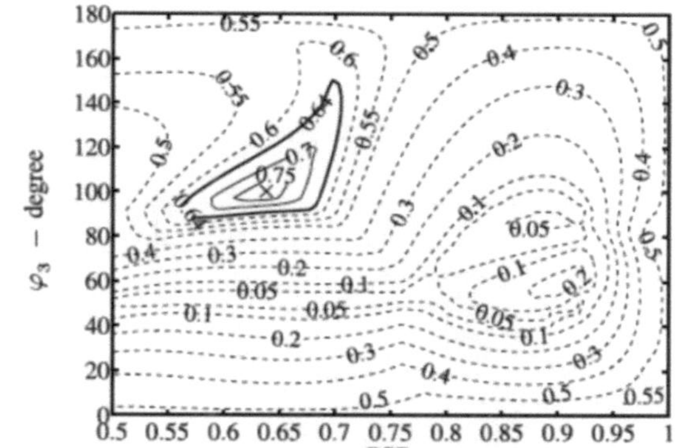

Fig. 6. Contour maps of the mode selectivity in the (PSP_3, φ_3) plane. Values for $\sigma \geq 0.64$ are represented by solid lines.

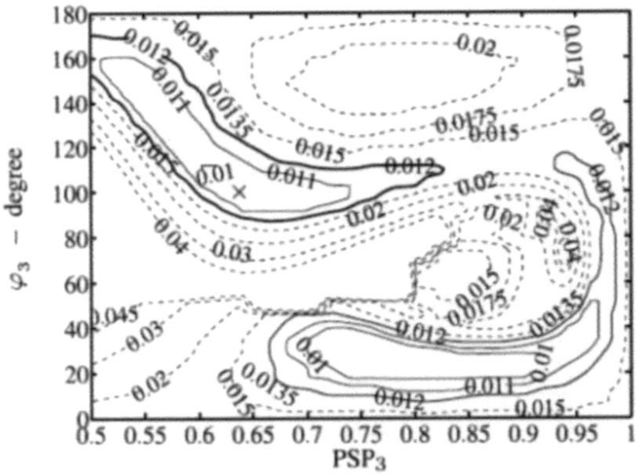

Fig. 7. Contour maps of the flatness in the $(\mathrm{PSP}_3, \varphi_3)$ plane. Values for $\Im \leq 0.012$ are represented by solid lines.

Solid lines enclose all combinations $(\mathrm{PSP}_3, \varphi_3)$ that ensure $\sigma(\bar{\kappa}L, \varphi_2) \geq 0.64$ and $\Im(\bar{\kappa}L, \varphi_2) \leq 0.012$, since $\sigma_{\min} = 0.64$ and $\Im_{\max} = 0.012$ have been settled in the previous iteration. Within all the possibilities, the chosen solution, $(\times)$, is $(\mathrm{PSP}_3 = 0.64, \varphi_3 = 100^{\circ})$, which corresponds to $\sigma_{\min} = 0.78$ and $\Im_{\max} = 0.010$. At the end of the optimization process, the final solution has been found: $\mathrm{PSP}_1 = 0.127$, $\varphi_1 = 110.7^{\circ}$, $\mathrm{PSP}_2 = 0.5$, $\varphi_2 = 60^{\circ}$, $\mathrm{PSP}_3 = 0.64$, $\varphi_2 = 100^{\circ}$ and $\bar{\kappa}L = 1.7$. Besides, the optimized laser structure presents $\alpha_{th} = 1.18$, which corresponds to $I_{th} = 23.4\,\mathrm{mA}$. This value is similar to those reported in (Ghafouri-Shiraz, 2003) for the QWS-DFB and the symmetric 3PS-DFB lasers, respectively, $I_{th} = 19.8\,\mathrm{mA}$ and $I_{th} = 21.8\,\mathrm{mA}$.

Table 4 summarizes the results for $\sigma, \Im$ and $\alpha_{th}L$ achieved for three different laser structures: the optimized 3PS-DFB (asymmetric), the QWS-DFB and the symmetric 3PS-DFB referred in (Ghafouri-Shiraz, 2003). All lasers are AR-type because the random corrugation phases at the laser facets will cause extra difficulty in controlling the laser characteristics.

Laser structure	σ	$\Im$	$\alpha_{th}L$
Asymmetric 3PS-DFB (optimized) $\mathrm{PSP}_1 = 0.127$; $\varphi_1 = 110.7^{\circ}$ $\mathrm{PSP}_2 = 0.500$; $\varphi_2 = 60^{\circ}$ $\mathrm{PSP}_3 = 0.640$; $\varphi_3 = 100^{\circ}$	0.78	0.010	1.18
QWS-DFB	0.73	0.30	0.70
3PS-DFB (Ghafouri-Shiraz, 2003) $\mathrm{PSP}_1 = 0.25$; $\varphi_1 = 60^{\circ}$ $\mathrm{PSP}_2 = 0.50$; $\varphi_2 = 60^{\circ}$ $\mathrm{PSP}_3 = 0.75$; $\varphi_3 = 60^{\circ}$	0.34	0.012	0.78

Table 4. Figures of merit for the symmetric, asymmetric 3PS-DFB and QWS-DFB laser structures.

As far as the flatness is concerned, the 3PS-DFB laser structures are clearly advantageous. This is not surprising, since the inclusion of several PS along the laser cavity flattens the field distribution. However, it is worth noticing that the asymmetric 3PS-DFB structure reaches higher mode selectivity than the other two laser structures.
A threshold analysis has been presented. Nevertheless, one should always bear in mind that the results for a structure presenting an adequate performance at threshold are not conclusive. An above-threshold analysis is essential in order to assess the rate at which the SHB effect deteriorates the laser features with the increasing current.

5.3 The above-threshold analysis

We shall begin with the stationary analysis, but, as we shall refer later, the transient aspects may be determinant, which in fact imposes the need of a dynamic analysis in order to describe adequately the laser performance in the domain of high currents. Both analysis will lead to heavier simulations than the threshold analysis, since the number of cells needed for a correct evaluation of the carrier and photon profiles is deeply increased.

5.3.1 The static-TMM results

Fig.8 shows the photon distribution in the asymmetric structure for different bias currents. It shows the gradual increase of the photon number in the whole structure, due to the stimulated emission. The 3PS-DFB lasers include local maxima other than the central one, leading to flatter distributions than those obtained for the QWS structure. Moreover, both 3PS-DFB lasers show smaller differences between the central photon density and the escaping photon densities at the facets, thus benefitting the laser performance as far as the emitted power is concerned, as it shall be seen later in the light-current stationary characteristics of these structures (Fig. 12).
Fig.9 shows the laser mode selectivity *vs.* current injection. Similar mode discriminations at threshold for the asymmetric 3PS and the QWS at threshold can be seen. Nevertheless, the mode selectivity has a severe reduction with increasing bias current for the QWS case, showing that the laser is strongly affected by the SHB effect. For the symmetric 3PS-DFB laser, it is apparent that the stability related to flatter photon profiles was obtained at an expense of a great reduction in the mode selectivity, while the situation is reverted at high values of biasing currents. Undoubtedly, the best option is the asymmetric 3PS optimized structure.

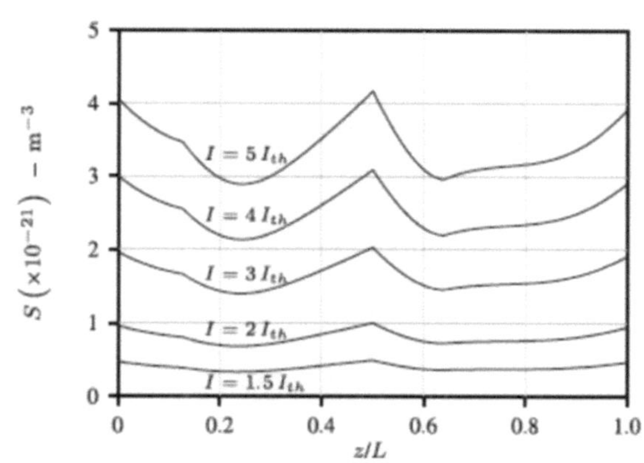

Fig. 8. $S(z)$ in the optimized asymmetric 3PS-DFB laser structure under different biasing currents.

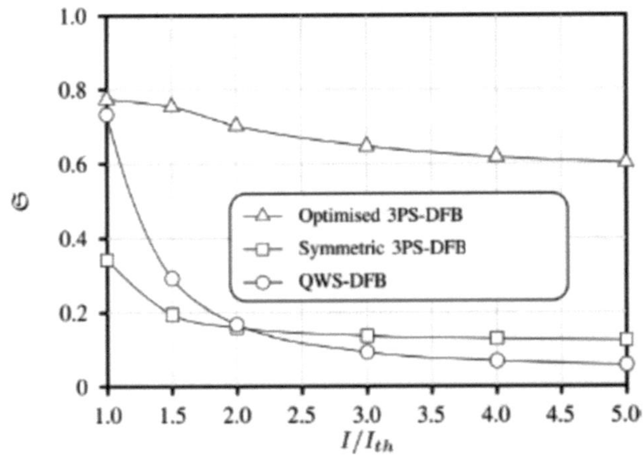

Fig. 9. Mode selectivity *vs.* current injection for the 3 structures under analysis.

Fig.10 focuses on the evolution of the flatness with current injection for the two 3PS-DFB lasers, showing a monotonically decreasing function for both structures. It should be emphasized that the flatness lies in the range defined by the selection criteria for both lasers, which is not definitely the case for the QWS-DFB, since this structure presents high-non uniformities in the photon profile ($\Im = 0.3$ at threshold, and $\Im = 0.079$ for $I = 5 \times I_{th}$). Notice that the QWS-DFB laser flatness falls outside the axis limits.

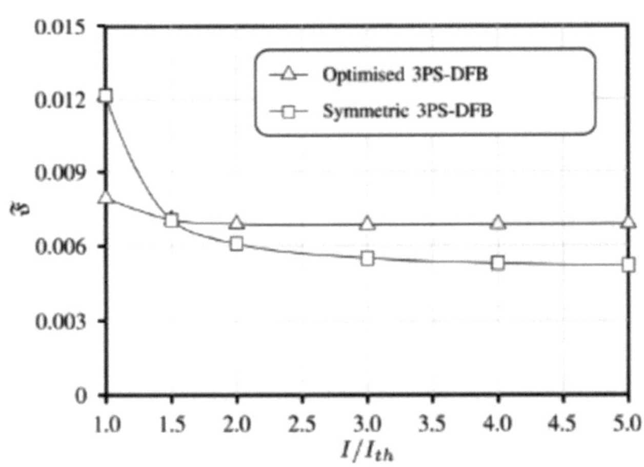

Fig. 10. Flatness *vs.* current injection for the three laser structures under analysis.

A comparative analysis of the three laser structures may be observed in Fig.11 to Fig.14, as far as the emitted power and wavelength are concerned. In the current range $1 \le I / I_{th} \le 5$, relative variations in the emitted wavelengths $(\Delta\lambda / \lambda_{th})$ of 9.4×10^{-4}%, 1.5×10^{-3}% and 5.5×10^{-3}% are observed for the asymmetric, the symmetric and the QWS lasers, respectively (Fig.11). Under similar normalized current injections the asymmetric structure shows larger values for the optical output power, measured at the right facet (Fig.12). This may be explained by the increase of the escaping photon density at right facet related to the induced asymmetry. A similar consequence would be attained using different facet reflectivities at the laser cavity ends (Boavida, et al., 2011).

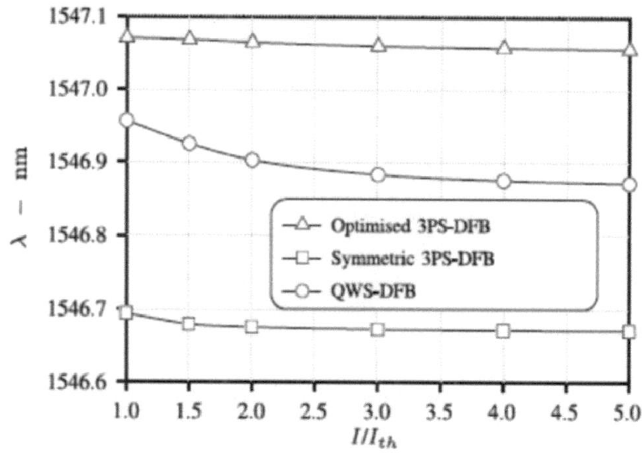

Fig. 11. Lasing wavelength *vs* current injection for the 3 laser structures under analysis.

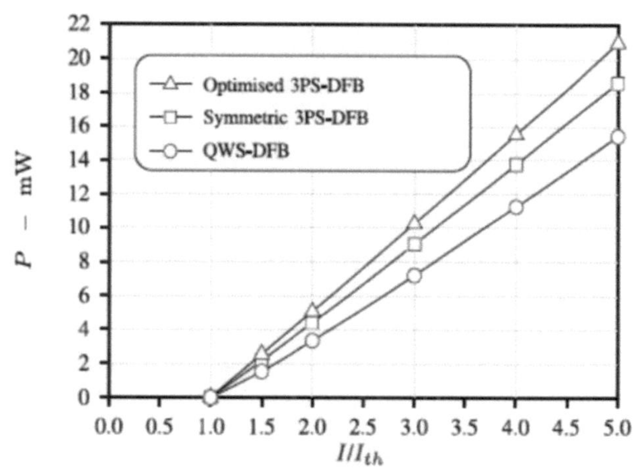

Fig. 12. Emitted power *vs* current injection for the 3 laser structures under analysis.

The measurement of the laser spectral characteristics is a way of checking its single-mode stability. Fig.13 shows the normalized spontaneous emission power for $I = 1.5 \times I_{th}$ and $I = 5 \times I_{th}$, for the asymmetric laser. High values are obtained for the side-mode-suppression ratio (SMSR) for both currents. Besides, it is worth noticing that the "blue-shift" in wavelengths is negligible. The inset of Fig. 10 shows the $\alpha(\delta)$ plot for the modes in the cavity at threshold. The figure points out two possible side-modes that are very close in frequency (encircled by a dashed line), which originates the broadening of the spectrum around 1546.4 nm. Another relevant aspect lies with the fact that, near 1547.7 nm, the spectral amplitude of the dominant mode remains at a high value when the current injection increases, showing no severe mode competition in the high power regime.

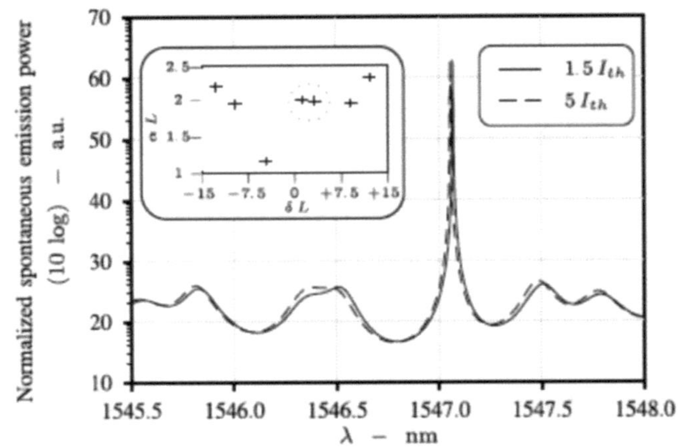

Fig. 13. Above-threshold normalized spontaneous emission spectra under two different biasing current for the asymmetric 3PS-DFB laser structure.

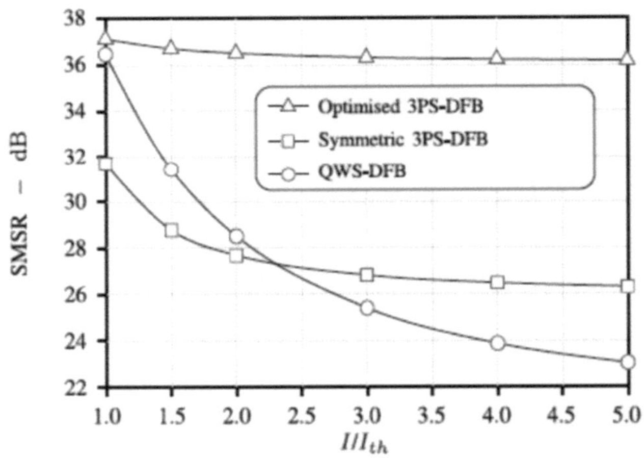

Fig. 14. Side-mode-suppression ratio *vs* current injection for the 3 laser structures under analysis.

This is pin-pointed in Fig.14, where the SMSR of the asymmetric structure is maintained throughout the range of biasing currents under analysis. This is not the case with the two other structures, the SMSR becoming lower than the required 30dB for the SLM operation (Morthier & Vankwikelberge, 1997) over the most part of the current range. As we shall see in next section this will be enhanced in the results obtained from the dynamic-TMM.

5.3.2 The dynamic-TMM results

Fig. 15 illustrates the transient response (emitted power) of the asymmetric 3PS-DFB laser when I is a step-function of $2\times I_{th}$. There is a delay of about 0.25 ns in the output $S(t)$ dynamics and a frequency of the relaxation oscillations of about 4 GHz, which agrees with the result obtained from the approximate expression (Agrawall & Dutta, 1986)

$$f_n \cong \frac{1}{2\pi}\sqrt{\frac{A_0 v_g \Gamma(I - I_{th})}{qLwd}}. \tag{100}$$

This parameter is usually known as the -3dB *modulation bandwidth*. Using the dynamic-TMM for step-like biasing currents, the stationary values can be interpreted as the asymptotic values of the time evolutions.

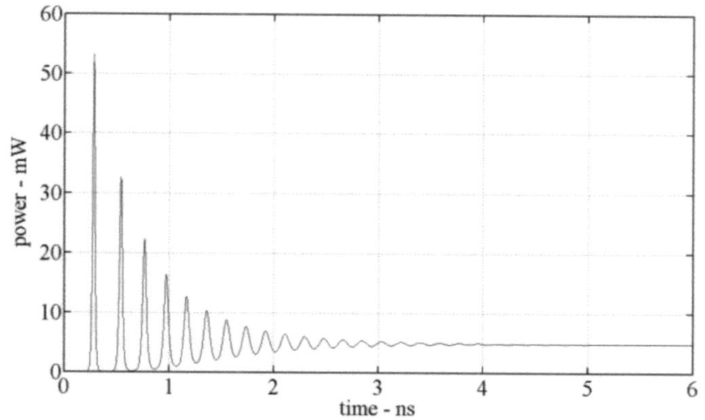

Fig. 15. Transient response of the asymmetric 3PS-DFB laser when the final current is $2 \times I_{th} \cong 46.8$ mA.

Fig. 16 compares the light-current characteristics obtained from the static-TMM with those extracted from the time evolutions obtained using the dynamic-TMM for the three lasers under analysis. Small deviations between the results obtained with the two TMM models are visible for the asymmetric 3PS-DFB laser, especially for high bias current values. This is due to the great difference in the number of sections that are present in the two models: 5000 cells in the static-TMM and only 100 cells in the dynamic-TMM. This may be especially important for the asymmetric structure, since using less than 1000 cells we cannot accurately define the first PS position in the asymmetric 3PS-DFB laser (PSP_1=0.127). However, it must always be kept in mind that

- As referred in Section 4 the time of computation increases almost quadratically with the number M of cells;
- In order to obtain the stationary situation, time evolutions during 1-2 carrier lifetimes (τ_n) should be considered, where

$$\tau_n \cong \left(A + B \cdot N_{th} + C \cdot N_{th}^2\right)^{-1}; \tag{101}$$

- For high currents, the lasing output of unstable lasers experiences transient oscillations that originates from the beating frequency of multiple mode lasing.

This last aspect is referred in (Jia et al., 2007) for the QWS-DFB laser in the transient response to a step-like biasing current whose final state value is $I = 90$ mA. The oscillations in the emitted power arise from beating frequency of multiple mode lasing. The random feature of spontaneous emission is determinant in the transient response of the lasers, especially when the SMSR and the mode selectivity are small, which is the case for the QWS-DFB at high biasing currents. Its influence may be taken into account including Langevin noise sources as additional terms in the rate equations (Coldren & Corzine, 1995). These sources are assumed to be white noise and are small enough to make use of the differential rate equations. The influence of spontaneous emission may be included in the TMM considering extra photon fluxes emerging from each cell to seed the growth of the travelling waves (Davis & Dowd, 1992). Their influence is negligible in DFB lasers that guarantee sufficiently high SMSR in the high power regime. Therefore, since the side-mode is almost completely suppressed in the asymmetric 3PS-DFB, a good dynamic SLM operation is ensured.

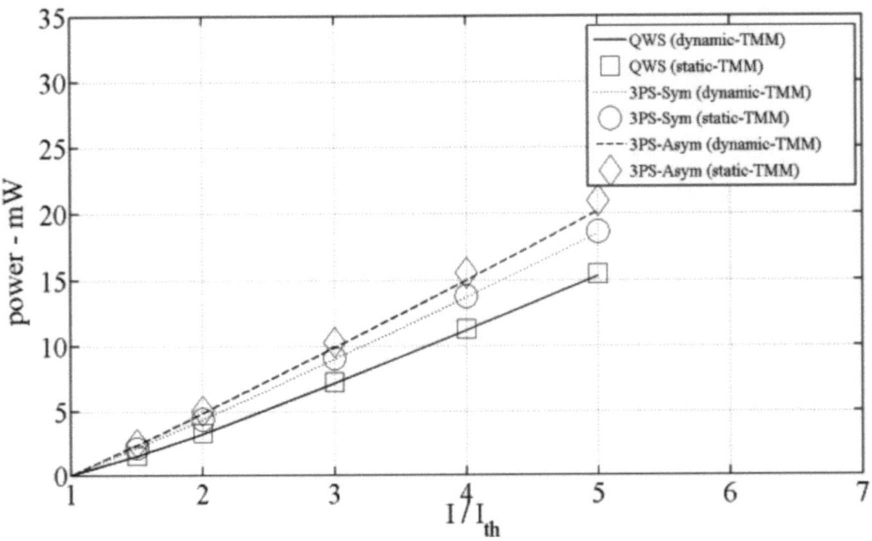

Fig. 16. Light-current stationary characteristics for lasers under analysis obtained using the static and the dynamic TMM.

6. Conclusion

The TMM is described both for static and dynamic analysis. The advantages of the TMM are numerous. Namely: it is not necessary to solve the coupled-mode equations, but instead we need to describe any perturbation in the wave propagation inside the laser cavity by the appropriate transfer matrix. This means that the same model works for several laser structures: FP, DFB, DBR (Kim & Jeong, 2003) or any combination of these; external feedback is easily included; weak or strong coupling can be treated. The model can handle laser amplifiers as well.

The static-TMM has been used for the optimization of a multiple-phase-shifted DFB laser. Above-threshold analysis using both the static-TMM and the dynamic-TMM have demonstrated that indeed the main laser figures of merit of the 3PS-DFB optimized structure exceeded those for the commonly referred QWS-DFB or for other similar multiple-phase-shifted DFB structures presented elsewhere. We may conclude that the TMM, both in its static and dynamic versions, represents itself a powerful tool to be used in the important domain of OCS for the optimization of laser structures especially designed to provide SLM operation.

7. References

Agrawall, G. & Dutta, N. (1986). *Semiconductor Lasers*, (1st Edition), Van Nostrand Reinhold, ISBN: 0-442-20995-9, N.Y.

Boavida, J., Morgado, J. & Fernandes, C. HR-AR, coated DFB lasers with high-yield and enhanced above-threshold performance, *Optics and Laser Technology*, 43, 2011, pp. 729-735.

Bornholdt C., Troppenz, U, Kreissl, J., Rehbein, W., Sartorius, B., Schell, M. & Woods, I. 40Gbit/s directly modulated passive feedback DFB laser for transmission over 320 km single mode fibre, *Proc. 34th European Conference on Optical Communication (ECOC'08)*, Vol. 2, Brussels, Belgium, 2008.

Coldren, L. & Corzine, S. (1995). *Diode Lasers and Photonic Integrated Circuits*, (1st Edition), John Wiley & Sons, Inc., ISBN: 0-471-11875-3), USA.

Davis, M. & O' Dowd, R. A Transfer Matrix-Based Analysis of Multielectrode DFB Lasers, *IEEE Photonics Technology Letters*, Vol. 3, No. 7, 1991, pp. 603-605.

Davis, M. & O' Dowd, R. A New Large-Signal Dynamic Model for Multielectrode DFB Lasers Based on the Transfer Matrix Method, IEEE Photonics Technology Letters, Vol. 4, No. 8, 1992, pp. 838-840.

Fernandes, C,, Morgado, J. & Boavida, J. Optimisation of an asymmetric three phase-shift distributed feedback semiconductor laser, *EPJ AP Applied Physics*, 46, 2009, p.30701.

Fessant, T. Threshold and Above-Threshold Analysis of Corrugation-Pitch Modulated DFB Lasers with Inhomogeneous Coupling Coefficient, , *IEE. Proc. Optoelectron, Pt J*, 144(6), 1997, pp. 365-376.

Fessant, T. Influence of a nonuniform coupling coefficient on the static and large signal dynamic behavior of Bragg-detuned DFB lasers, J. *Ligthwave Techn*. Vol.16, no.3, 1998, pp. 419-427.

Ghafouri-Shiraz, H. (2003). *Distributed Feedback Laser Diodes and Optical Tunable Filters*, (1st Edition), J. Wiley & Sons, ISBN: 0-470-85618-1, Chichester.

Jia, X., Zhong, D., Wang, F., Chen, H. Detailed modulation response analysis on enhanced single-mode QWS-DFB lasers with distributed coupling coefficient, *Optics Communications*, 277, 2007, pp. 166-173.

Kapon, E., Hardy, A. & Katzir, A. The effect of complex coupling coefficients on distributed feedback lasers, *IEEE J. Quantum Electron.*, 18, 1982, pp.66-71.

Kim, Y. & Jeong, J. Analysis of Large-Signal Dynamic Characteristics of 10-Gb/s Tunable Distributed Bragg Reflector Lasers Integrated With Electroabsorption Modulator and Semiconductor Optical Amplifier Based on the Time-Depenedent Transfer Matrix Method, *IEEE Journal of Quantum Electronics*, Vol. 39, No. 10, 2003, pp. 1314-1320.

Kogelnik, H. & Shank, C. Coupled-wave theory of distributed feedback lasers, *J. Appl. Phys.* 43(5), 1972, pp. 2327-2335.

Lee, H., Yoon, H., Kim, Y. & Jeong, J. Theoretical Study of Frequency Chirping and Extinction Ratio of Wavelength-Converted Optical Signals by XGM and XPM Using SOA's, *IEEE Journal of Quantum Electronics*, Vol. 35, No. 8, 1999, pp. 1213-1219.

Lowery, A. Integrated mode-locked laser design with a distributed-Bragg reflector, *IEE-Proceedings*, Pt. J, 138(1), 1991, pp.39-46.

Morthier, G. & Vankwikelberge, P. (1997). *Handbook of Distributed Feedback Laser Diodes*, (1st Edition) Artech House, ISBN: 0-89006-607-8, Norwood.

Sato, K., Kuwahara, S. & Miyamoto, Y. Chirp characteristics of 40-Gb/s directly modulated distributed-feedback laser diodes, *IEEE/OSA J. Lightwave Technology*, Vol. 23, No.11, 2005, pp. 3790-3796.

Tan, P., Ghafouri-Shiraz, H. & Lo, B. Theoretical analysis of multiple-phase-shift controlled DFB wavelength tunable optical filters, *Microwave Opt. Technol. Letters*, 8(2), 1995, pp.72-75.

Tang, J., Lane, P. & Shore, K. High speed transmission of adaptively modulated optical OFDM signals over multimode fibres using directly modulated DFBs, *IEEE/OSA J. Lightwave Technology*, Vol. 24, No. 1, 2006, pp. 429-441.

Utake, A., Otsubo, K., Matsuda, M., Okumura, S., Ekawa, M. & Yamamoto, T. 40 Gbps direct modulation of 1.55-μm AlGaInAs semi-insulating buried-heterostructure distributed reflector lasers up to 85°C, *Proc. 2nd Annual Meeting of the IEEE Photonics Society*, Vol. 1, Antalya, Turkey, 2009.

Wedding, B., Pöhlmann, W., Gross, H. & Thalau, O. 43 Gbit/s transmission over 210 km SMF with a directly modulated laser diode, *Proc. 29th European Conference Optical Communication (ECOC'03)*, Rimini, Italy, 2003, 2003.

Wedding, B. & Pöhlmann, W. 43Gbit/s transmission over 40.5 km SMF without optical amplifier using a directly modulated laser diode, *Proc. 30th European Conf. Optical Communication (ECOC'04)*, Stockholm, Sweden, 2004.

Yu,S. (2003). *Analysis and Design of Vertical Cavity Surface Emitting Lasers*, (1st Edition), Wiley, series in Lasers and applications, ISBN: 0-471-39124-7, New Jersey.

21

Adaptive Signal Selection Control Based on Adaptive FF Control Scheme and Its Applications to Sound Selection Systems

Hiroshi Okumura[1] and Akira Sano[2]
[1]*Research & Development Department, Medical System Division, Shimadzu Corporation*
[2]*Faculty of System Design Engineering, Keio University*
Japan

1. Introduction

Noise pollution is one of the social problems, and many researches on active noise control (ANC) or active vibration control (AVC) have been done (Tokhi & Veres, 2002). Almost all previous studies were interested in suppression of unwanted noise signals. However, actually some necessary signals should not be suppressed but transmitted and only unnecessary noise should be blocked. Therefore, a control method which can selectively attenuate only unnecessary signals is needed.

In this chapter, we will propose a novel control scheme which can transmit necessary signals (Necs) and attenuate only unnecessary signals (Unecs) selectively. The control scheme is named as Signal Selection Control (SSC) scheme.

The purpose of this chapter is to develop two types of the SSC; one is Necs-Extraction Controller which transmits only signals set as Necs, and the other is Unecs-Canceling Controller which attenuates only signals set as Unecs. The Necs-Extraction Controller was proposed by us before (Okumura & Sano, 2009), and the Unecs-Canceling Controller is newly proposed in this chapter. Results of both controllers are the same; both controllers transmit Necs and attenuate Unecs selectively, however, the design concept of each controller is different. When some Necs are known, the Necs-Extraction Controller is suitable and the Necs is set to be transmitted. On the other hand, when some Unecs are known, the Unecs-Canceling Controller is suitable and the Unecs is set to be attenuated. We can choose these two controllers according to the application systems.

The SSC is based on adaptive feedforward (FF) control schemes which were adopted in the fields of ANC and AVC due to its excellent performance of noise attenuation. In this chapter, four adaptive controllers will be introduced and characterized; (i) the filtered-X LMS controller which is a conventional approach in the adaptive FF control field (Burgess, 1981; Widrow et al, 1982), (ii) the 2-degree-of-freedom filtered-X LMS controller (Kuo, 1996, 1999), (iii) the Virtual Error controller which is proposed by one of the authors before (Kohno & Sano, 2005; Ohta & Sano, 2004), and (iv) the 2-degree-of-freedom Virtual Error controller which is also proposed by us before(Okumura & Sano, 2009).

To validate effectiveness of the proposed SSC, two applications to Sound Selection Systems (SSS) are considered as numerical simulations.

(i) First example is an application of the Necs-Extraction Controller to a smart window system of a car, which can transmit only electronic siren sound of ambulance as Necs, but block any other noises such as road noise and engine noise. Purpose of this application is to keep car room silent and safety against car accidents at the same time.
(ii) Second example is another application of the Unecs-Canceling Controller to rotating machinery such as a compressor, which can attenuate only sound of rotating motor as Unecs even when rotating speed is changing, but transmit some abnormal sound of the machinery. Purpose of this application is to keep machinery silence and detectability of machine abnormality at the same time.
Through above two numerical simulations, effectiveness of the proposed Signal Selection Control (SSC) scheme is validated.

2. Sound Selection System

In those two numerical simulations, we consider a double glazed plate system as a Sound Selection System (SSS), and develop its mathematical models.
The structure of a double glazed plate was often employed in ANC field. Two type of approaches were taken; one is 'cavity control' applying acoustic control sources in the air gap between the two plates (Sas et al, 1995; Jakob & Möser, 2003a, 2003b; Kaiser et al, 2003), and the other is 'panel control' applying vibration control sources on the radiating plate (Bao & Pan, 1997, 1998). In the cavity control approaches in which microphones and loudspeakers are usually used to sense and actuate sounds, there must be some large space to place them. Therefore, we will employ the panel control approach to realize the SSS.
For the purpose, we use piezoelectric ceramics to sense and control the vibration of plates by making use of the advantage that piezoelectric ceramics can be used as both actuator and sensor. Besides, due to its simplicity, small size, broad bandwidth, easy implementation, and efficient conversion between electrical and mechanical energy, recently, smart structures with piezoelectric actuator and sensor pairs have collected much attention (Moheimani, 2003).

2.1 Description of the SSS considered in this chapter

Fig. 1 shows the structure of the considered Sound Selection System (SSS). As shown in Fig. 1(a) and Fig. 2, the SSS is a double glazed plate whose distance between two plates is 34mm, and a piezoelectric reference sensor and error sensor are attached on the 1st and 2nd plates to sense each plate's vibration respectively. A piezoelectric actuator is also attached on the 2nd plate to control the 2nd plate's vibration.
Fig. 1(b) describes the position of piezoelectric actuators or sensors on each plate, and the reference sensors, error sensors and control actuators are patched on the same position of each plate's surface (this positioning is so called 'collocation'). There are two patches; one is for actuation or sensing of vibration along one axis, the other is for along the other axis.

2.2 Control scheme of the SSS

Fig. 2 and Fig. 3 show a schematic diagram for adaptive control of the SSS.
As shown in the Fig. 2 and Fig. 3, SSS is a double glazed plate system, and in the SSS, the adaptive SSC operates to control transmitting sound through the double glazed plate by controlling the 2nd plate's vibration using piezoelectric actuator on it, according to information of 1st plate's vibration sensed by piezoelectric sensor on it.

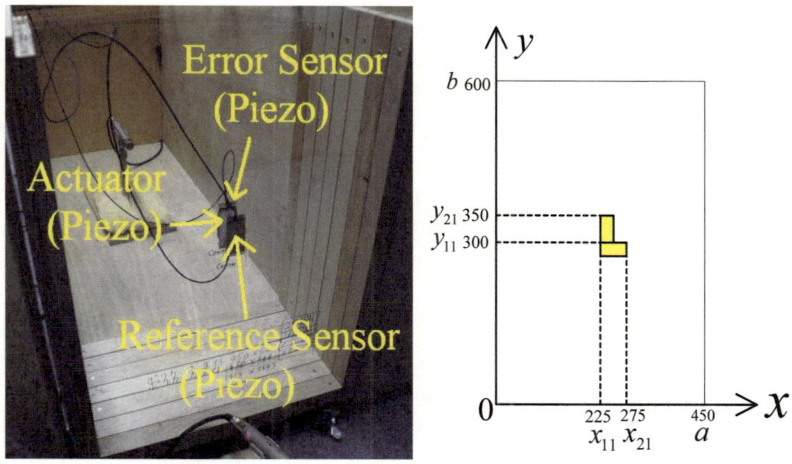

(a) Setup of the SSS (b) Position of actuator and sensor

Fig. 1. Structure of the considered Sound Selection System

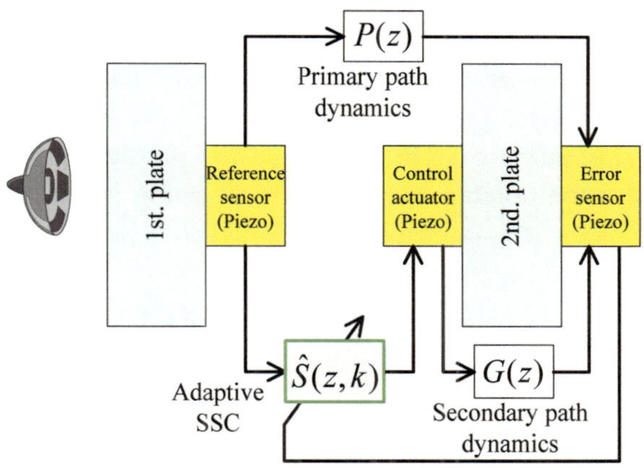

Fig. 2. Schematic diagram of the considered SSS

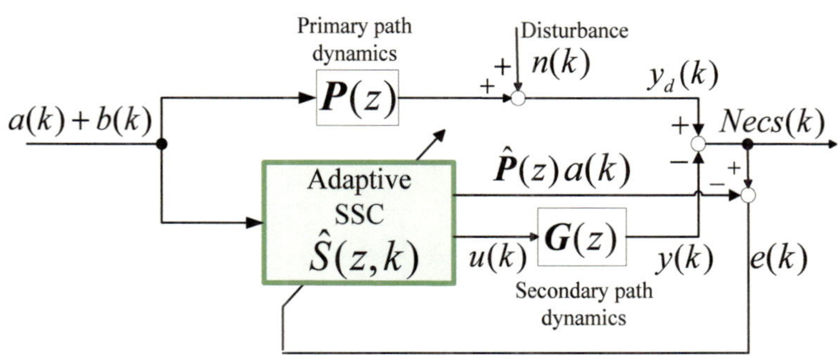

Fig. 3. Block diagram for the proposed Signal Selection Control scheme

A path from the reference sensor to error sensor is referred to as the primary path dynamics $P(z)$, and a path from the control actuator to error sensor as the secondary path dynamics $G(z)$. Let $a(k)$ be necessary signals to be transmitted, $b(k)$ be other unnecessary noise to be suppressed, $n(k)$ the disturbance in the primary path which cannot be sensed by the reference sensor, $u(k)$ the control voltage input to the piezo actuator, $Necs(k)$ the transmitted vibration signal sensed by the error sensor on the 2nd plate, and $e(k)$ the error signal used to adjust the adaptive controller $\hat{S}(z,k)$. $y_d(k)$ and $y(k)$ denote the vibration signal excited in the primary and secondary path dynamics respectively, which are not available separately.

The purpose of the adaptive controller $\hat{S}(z,k)$ is to transmit only necessary sound $a(k)$, but blocks any other unnecessary noises $b(k)$ and disturbances $n(k)$ in the primary path. As mentioned later, $\hat{S}(z,k)$ is referred to as the Signal Selection Controller, and it is composed of an extractor which can extract only desired signals, and of an adaptive controller which can force the error $e(k)$ to zero even when the primary and secondary path dynamics are both unknown and the unknown disturbance $n(k)$ is added to the primary path.

In the section 3, modelling of the primary and secondary path dynamics is described, and in the section 4, design of the adaptive SSC is explained.

3. System modelling for numerical simulations

This section gives the model description for the primary path dynamics $P(z)$ and the secondary path dynamics $G(z)$ in Fig. 2 and Fig. 3.

At first, necessary physical parameters for the plates and piezoelectric ceramics are listed in Table 1 and Table 2, and the notations are used in modeling of the path dynamics. In the Table 2, the conversion factor κ is described as follows (Moheimani & Fleming, 2005).

$$\kappa = \frac{3d_{31}IE_bE_p\left\{\left(\frac{h}{2}+h_p\right)^2-\left(\frac{h}{2}\right)^2\right\}}{2h_p\left[E_p\left\{\left(\frac{h}{2}+h_p\right)^3-\left(\frac{h}{2}\right)^3\right\}+E_b\left(\frac{h}{2}\right)^3\right]} \tag{1}$$

Parameters	Characters	Values	Units
Width	a	0.450	[m]
Height	b	0.600	[m]
Thichness	h	$0.5\text{x}10^{-3}$	[m]
Density	ρ	$1.18\text{x}10^{3}$	[kg/m^3]
Young's modulus	E	$0.21\text{x}10^{10}$	[N/m^2]
Poisson's ratio	υ	0.16	-
Moment of inertia of area	I	$4.7\text{x}10^{-12}$	[m^4]

Table 1. Parameters of the plates (Polycarbonate)

Parameters	Characters	Values	Units
Length	L_p	49.999x10-3	[m]
Width	W_p	24.993x10-3	[m]
Thichness	h_p	0.4549x10-3	[m]
Capacitance	C_p	298.200x103	[F]
Young's modulus	E_p	6.2x1010	[N/m2]
Strain coefficent	d_{31}	-266x10-12	[m/V]
Conversion factor	κ	-9.655x10-6	$[(N \cdot m)/V]$

Table 2. Parameters of the piezoelectric ceramics (PZT)

3.1 Modelling of the primary path dynamics P(z)

The primary path dynamics $P(z)$ is a path from the reference sensor to the error sensor, as shown in Fig. 2. As mentioned above, if the distance between two plates is set to 34mm and the sampling frequency is chosen as 50kHz (0.02ms), then it takes 5 sampling instants for the primary sound to propagate the gap distance. In the case, the primary path dynamics can be expressed as a simple delay and constant multiplication, described as follows.

$$P(z) = p_1 z^{-5}, \quad (0 < p_1 \leq 1) \tag{2}$$

Where z^{-1} means the time delay operator.

3.2 Modelling of the secondary path dynamics G(z)

The secondary path dynamics $G(z)$ is a path from the control actuator to the error sensor, as shown in Fig. 2. A dynamic model of $G(z)$ is described as a transfer function from the control voltage input for the actuator to the error sensor voltage sensing the vibration of the 2nd plate. So, the modeling of $G(z)$ needs analysis how the piezoelectric actuator excites vibration onto the plate by the input voltage and how the piezoelectric sensor detects the vibration.

The plate's equation of motion is described by a distributed parameter system expressed as

$$\rho h \frac{\partial^2 w(x,y,t)}{\partial t^2} + D\left(\frac{\partial^4 w(x,y,t)}{\partial x^4} + \frac{\partial^4 w(x,y,t)}{\partial x^2 \partial y^2} + \frac{\partial^4 w(x,y,t)}{\partial y^4} \right) = F(x,y,t), \tag{3}$$

where $w(x,y,t)$ is the displacement of the plate along z-axis and $F(x,y,t)$ is the external force at the position (x,y) and time t, and D is the bending rigidity. The external force $F(x,y,t)$ by the piezoelectric actuator as the moment is expressed as

$$F(x,y,t) = \frac{\partial^2 M(x,y,t)}{\partial x^2} + \frac{\partial^2 M(x,y,t)}{\partial y^2}, \tag{4}$$

where $M(x,y,t)$ is the moment at the position (x,y) and time t. Thus, the equation of motion is rewritten as

$$\rho h \frac{\partial^2 w(x,y,t)}{\partial t^2} + D\left(\frac{\partial^4 w(x,y,t)}{\partial x^4} + \frac{\partial^4 w(x,y,t)}{\partial x^2 \partial y^2} + \frac{\partial^4 w(x,y,t)}{\partial y^4}\right) = \frac{\partial^2 M(x,y,t)}{\partial x^2} + \frac{\partial^2 M(x,y,t)}{\partial y^2}. \tag{5}$$

Besides, the moment can be expressed by using the actuator voltage input $v_a(t)$ as

$$M(x,y,t) = \kappa v_{ai}(t), \tag{6}$$

where κ is defined by (1), and the subscript i denotes the actuator number in a multi-channel case using multiple actuators.

On the other hand, the piezoelectric sensor generates voltage by its bending deformation, described as

$$v_{sj}(t) = \frac{d_{31}E_p W_p}{C_p} \int_0^b \int_0^a \left(\varepsilon_x + \varepsilon_y\right) dxdy, \tag{7}$$

where $v_{sj}(t)$ is the sensor voltage and subscript j means the sensor number in a multi-channel case using multiple sensors, and ε is the strain of the piezoelectric sensor generated by bending of the plate (Moheimani & Fleming, 2005).

As a result, from (5), (6) and (7), it follows that the transfer function $G(s)$ from the i-th actuator voltage $v_{ai}(t)$ to the j-th sensor voltage $v_{sj}(t)$ is given by

$$G(s) = \frac{V_{sj}(s)}{V_{ai}(s)} = -\frac{\kappa d_{31}E_p W_p\left(\frac{h}{2} + h_p\right)}{C_p \rho h} \cdot \sum_{k=1}^{\infty} \frac{\left(\Psi_{kj} + \Phi_{kj}\right)\left(\Psi_{ki} + \Phi_{ki}\right)}{\left(\int_0^b \int_0^a W_k^2(x,y) dxdy\right)\left(s^2 + 2\varsigma_k \omega_k s + \omega_k^2\right)}, \tag{8}$$

where $V_{ai}(s)$, $V_{sj}(s)$ are the Laplace transform of $v_{ai}(t)$, $v_{sj}(t)$ respectively, $W_k(x,y)$ is the eigen modal function of the plate, and the subscript k denotes the modal number, ς_k, ω_k are the damping ratio and eigen frequency of k-th mode respectively, and Ψ, Φ are calculated from the modal function at the location of the piezoelectric patches along x-axis and y-axis respectively. In adaptive controller design in numerical simulation, we use a truncated model within 30th modes.

Finally, we obtain a discrete-time FIR model $G(z)$ by the impulse invariance method, that is, by sampling the impulse response of the continuous-time model $G(s)$. As a result, $G(z)$ is given as an FIR model expression as

$$G(z) = \sum_{n=0}^{L_g} g_n z^{-n}, \tag{9}$$

where g_n is the impulse response coefficient at n-th sample, and L_g is the filter length of FIR model $G(z)$. g_0 becomes 0 because the transfer function is strictly proper.

It should be noticed that the secondary path dynamics (8) involves parameter uncertainties in its mathematical model, and that is a reason why the adaptive control approach is useful.

4. Design of adaptive Signal Selection Controller

The purpose of the adaptive Signal Selection Controller (SSC) $\hat{S}(z,k)$ for the SSS in Fig. 2 and Fig. 3 is to transmit only the necessary signals (Necs) and cancel any other unnecessary noise (Unecs) and the disturbance. In this section, it will be described how to realize the adaptive SSC $\hat{S}(z,k)$ which is composed of an extractor and an adaptive controller.
In the section 4.1, at first, principle of the adaptive SSC is explained.
And in the section 4.2, design of the extractor which is a component of the SSC is shown.
Next, in the section 4.3, design of the adaptive controller which is another component of the SSC is summarized.
Finally, in the section 4.4, overall structure of the SSC is described.

4.1 Principle of the adaptive Signal Selection Control scheme

Two types of the SSC is introduced; one is Necs-Extraction Controller which transmit only signals set as Necs as shown in Fig. 4, and the other is Unecs-Canceling Controller which attenuate only signals set as Unecs as shown in Fig. 5. Results of both controllers are the same; both controllers transmit Necs and attenuate Unecs selectively, however, the design concept of each controller is different. When some Necs are known, we choose the Necs-Extraction Controller and set the Necs to be transmitted. On the other hand, when some Unecs are known, we choose the Unecs-Canceling Controller and set the Unecs to be attenuated.

4.1.1 Principle of Necs-Extraction Controller

Fig. 4 shows the schematic diagram of the Necs-Extraction Controller.

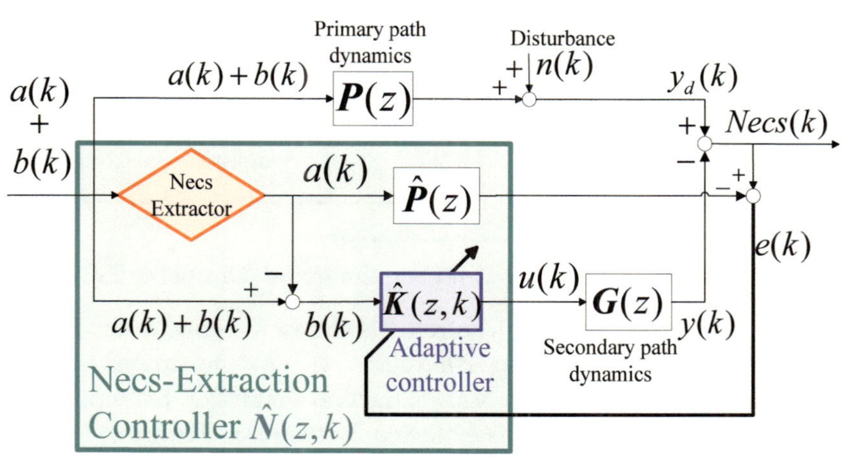

Fig. 4. Schematic diagram of the Necs-Extraction Controller (One of the SSC)

As mentioned, the SSC is composed of an extractor and an adaptive controller. In Fig. 4, $a(k)$ is a necessary signal (Necs), and $b(k)$ is an unnecessary noise (Unecs). $Necs(k)$ is the transmitted vibration signal sensed by the error sensor on the 2nd plate, $e(k)$ is the error signal used to adjust the adaptive controller $\hat{K}(z,k)$, and $\hat{P}(z)$ is an identified model of the primary path dynamics $P(z)$.

The main operations of the Necs-Extraction Controller $\hat{N}(z,k)$ are summarized as follows;

1. The extractor extracts only the necessary signal $a(k)$.
2. Next, $a(k)$ is subtracted from the input signal to the adaptive controller $\hat{K}(z,k)$.
3. Then, $\hat{K}(z,k)$ works to attenuate only the unnecessary signal $b(k)$.
4. Then, $\hat{K}(z,k)$ is adjusted to force $e(k)$ into zero.

The above procedure is executed simultaneously in on-line manner.

The canceling error $e(k)$ is expressed as

$$e(k) = Necs(k) - \hat{P}(z)a(k), \tag{10}$$

therefore, if $e(k) \to 0$ then $Necs(k) \to \hat{P}(z)a(k)$. Thus, if $a(k) \to 0$ then $Necs(k) \to 0$, and if $a(k)$ is the necessary signal then $Necs(k)$ converges to the necessary signal through the primary path dynamics. That is the principle of the proposed Necs-Extraction Controller $\hat{N}(z,k)$.

4.1.2 Principle of Unecs-Canceling Controller

Fig. 5 shows the schematic diagram of the Unecs-Canceling Controller.

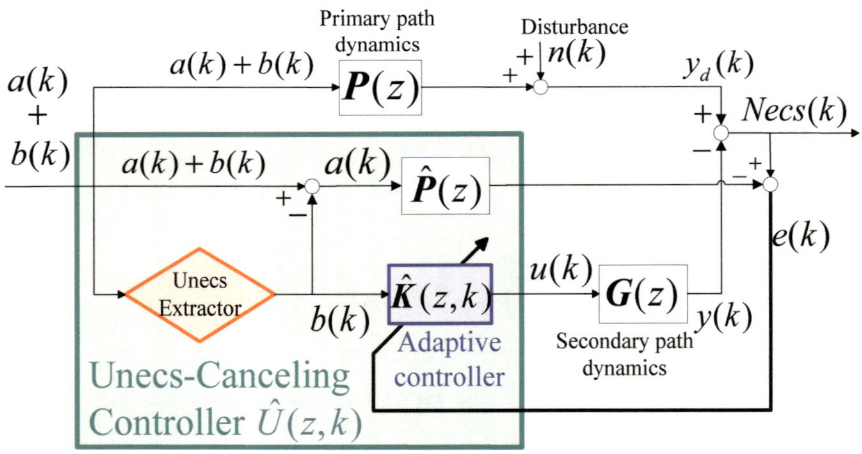

Fig. 5. Schematic diagram of the Unecs-Canceling Controller (One of the SSC)

The principle of the Unecs-Canceling Controller is almost the same as the Necs-Extraction Controller. Difference between two controllers is how to make input signal to the adaptive controller $\hat{K}(z,k)$. In the Necs-Extraction Controller, the input signal $b(k)$ is made by subtraction of $a(k)$ (which is extracted by the Necs Extractor) from $a(k)+b(k)$, however, in the Unecs-Canceling Controller, $b(k)$ is directly made by the Unecs Extractor.

The main operations of the Unecs-Canceling Controller $\hat{U}(z,k)$ are summarized as follows;

1. The extractor extracts only the unnecessary signal $b(k)$.
2. Next, $\hat{K}(z,k)$ works to attenuate only the unnecessary signal $b(k)$.

3. Then, $\hat{K}(z,k)$ is adjusted to force $e(k)$ into zero.

The above procedure is executed simultaneously in on-line manner.

The canceling error $e(k)$ is expressed as same as (10), therefore, if $e(k) \to 0$ then $Necs(k) \to \hat{P}(z)a(k)$. Thus, whether $b(k)$ is exist or not, $b(k)$ is not transmitted and $Necs(k)$ converges to the necessary signal through the primary path dynamics. That is the principle of the proposed Unecs-Canceling Controller $\hat{U}(z,k)$.

In the following sections, we show how to design the extractor extracting only desired signal with varying frequencies, and how to update the adaptive controller $\hat{K}(z,k)$ so that the canceling error can be forced into zero.

4.2 Design of the extractor

The purpose of the extractor is to extract the desired signal by tracking only frequencies of desired signals even in the presence of frequency variations. It should be noticed that Necs Extractor and Unecs Extractor is the same; when the desired signal is Necs $a(k)$, the extractor is named as Necs Extractor, and when the desired signal is Unecs $b(k)$, the extractor is named as Unecs Extractor.

The extractor is a new adaptive filter with tacking ability to selected frequencies, which is composed of a harmonics synthesizer and a judging synthesizer as shown in Fig. 6. The harmonics synthesizer estimates frequency and amplitude of all sinusoidal signals in the input signals. And then, the judging synthesizer judges whether each sinusoidal signal is necessary or not. Depend on the purpose of the extractor, the judging synthesizer should be modified.

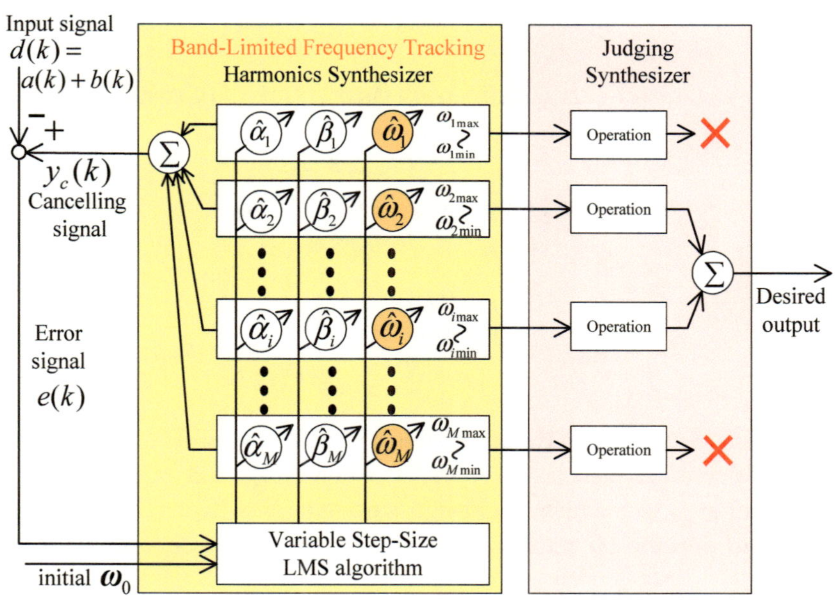

Fig. 6. Schematic diagram of the extractor

The algorithm for the extractor is based on the DXHS algorithm (Shimada et al, 1999), but we improve the operation performance by adding new abilities and functions; (i) improvement of readiness for frequency estimation by introduction of a variable step-size algorithm, (ii) limitation of frequency-estimation bandwidth, and (iii) judging system whether one signal is necessary or not.

The main procedure of the extractor is summarized as follows;

1. Estimation of the amplitudes α, β and frequency ω of each sinusoidal signal composing the input signal $d(k)$ adaptively by using the error signal $e(k) = y_c(k) - d(k)$, where $y_c(k)$ is the canceling signal for $d(k)$ which is the sum of all estimated sinusoidal signal.
2. Judging whether each estimated sinusoidal signal is necessary or not.
3. Synthesizing only necessary signals to be a desired output.

In the Fig. 6, the Extractor estimates M sinusoidal signals, and each estimation bandwidth is limited from $\omega_{\min}$ to $\omega_{\max}$. Then, 2nd and i th signal are judged to be necessary.

The canceling signal $y_c(k)$ is synthesized as

$$y_c(k) = \sum_{i=1}^{M} \left(\hat{\alpha}_i(k)\cos(\hat{\Omega}_i(k)) + \hat{\beta}_i(k)\sin(\hat{\Omega}_i(k)) \right) \tag{11}$$

$$\hat{\omega}_i(k)kT \equiv \hat{\Omega}_i(k) = \hat{\Omega}_i(k-1) + \hat{\omega}_i(k)T, \; (-\pi \le \hat{\Omega}_i(k) < \pi), \tag{12}$$

and the amplitudes and frequencies are estimated adaptively by the adaptation laws as;

$$\hat{\alpha}_i(k+1) = \hat{\alpha}_i(k) - 2\mu e(k)\cos(\hat{\Omega}_i(k)) \tag{13}$$

$$\hat{\beta}_i(k+1) = \hat{\beta}_i(k) - 2\mu e(k)\sin(\hat{\Omega}_i(k)) \tag{14}$$

$$\hat{\omega}_i(k+1) = \tilde{\omega}_i(k) - 2\mu_\omega(k)Te(k) \cdot \left[-\hat{\alpha}_i(k)\sin(\hat{\Omega}_i(k)) + \hat{\beta}_i(k)\cos(\hat{\Omega}_i(k)) \right] \tag{15}$$

$$\tilde{\omega}_i(k) = \begin{cases} \omega_{i\max} & (\omega_{i\max} \le \omega_i(k)) \\ \omega_i(k) & (\omega_{i\min} < \omega_i(k) < \omega_{i\max}) \\ \omega_{i\min} & (\omega_i(k) \le \omega_{i\min}) \end{cases} \tag{16}$$

$$\mu_\omega(k) = (\mu_{\max} - \mu_{\min}) \frac{\left(\sum_{n=k-N}^{k} |e(n)|\right)/N}{\rho + \left(\sum_{n=k-N}^{k} |d(n)|\right)/N} + \mu_{\min}, \tag{17}$$

where μ is a constant step size in the adaptation of amplitudes and $\mu_\omega(k)$ is a variable step size in the adaptation of frequencies given in (17) where $\mu_{\max}$ and $\mu_{\min}$ are maximum and minimum value of step size which are design parameters, ρ is a small positive constant employed to avoid division by zero, and N is the sample number to be used for moving average.

4.2.1 Necs Extractor for ambulance's siren sound

In this chapter, we consider the Necs-Extraction Controller which extracts the siren sound of ambulance. So in this section, design of the judging synthesizer for siren sound is described.

In Japan the siren signal of an ambulance consists of 960Hz sound (pi) and 770Hz sound (po), and the two sounds repeat one after the other at 0.65s cycle. The two frequencies change by the Doppler effect from 900Hz to 1060Hz for pi and from 700Hz to 850Hz for po respectively, when the maximum relative speed against an ambulance is 120km/h. We also consider a situation when another unnecessary noise exists in a band of the varying siren frequencies, for instance, unnecessary sinusoidal noise with 900Hz.

To judge the siren signal, we use the frequency information mainly and amplitude information supplementarily. To be more specific, the frequency information used for siren judgement is as follows;

1. 'pi' is 960Hz sound and 'po' is 770Hz sound.
2. The two sounds vary in the same ratio by the Doppler effect.
3. The two sounds alternate in 0.65s cycle.

The judgement flow is given as follows;

1. Estimate the frequency of likely 'pi' (or 'po').
2. Calculate the frequency of the alternative, that is, 'po' (or 'pi') by using the Doppler effect.
3. If there is a sound 0.65s before whose frequency is a similar one calculated in step 2, it must be the siren signal.
4. Output the signals judged as the siren.

By above four steps, the judging synthesizer judges the siren signals.

4.2.2 Unecs extractor for compressor's motor sound

In this chapter, we consider the Unecs-Canceling Controller which attenuates the rotating motor's sound of a compressor. So in this section, design of the judging synthesizer for compressor's motor sound is described.

In this case, information of rotation order signal can be used. In the case of using AC servo motor, rotation orders like target frequency is sent to the motor. Using this target frequency information, the judging synthesizer can extract only rotating motor sound with tracking to the rotating frequency variation.

4.3 Design of the adaptive controllers

In the Fig. 4 and Fig. 5, the adaptive controller $\hat{K}(z,k)$ needs to update the parameter of the controller itself so that the canceling error $e(k)$ can be forced into zero.

In this section, four adaptive controllers are introduced and characterized; (i) the filtered-X LMS controller which is a conventional approach in the adaptive FF control field (Burgess, 1981; Widrow et al, 1982), (ii) the 2-degree-of-freedom filtered-X LMS controller (Kuo, 1996, 1999), (iii) the Virtual Error controller which is proposed by one of the authors before (Kohno & Sano, 2005; Ohta & Sano, 2004), and (iv) the 2-degree-of-freedom Virtual Error controller which is also proposed by us before (Okumura & Sano, 2009). The following section gives summary for these controllers, brief description about controller (i), (ii) and (iii), and detail information about controller (iv).

4.3.1 Summary for four adaptive controllers

In the fields of ANC and AVC, adaptive feedforward control schemes were adopted due to excellent performance of noise attenuation. Almost previous works employed various type of filtered-x (FX) algorithms (Burgess, 1981; Widrow et al, 1982), but they are not stability-assured

since the canceling error is directly used in adaptive algorithms for updating controller parameters. One of the authors proposed the Virtual Error (VE) approach which does not use the canceling error directly but a virtual error in the adaptation, and is locally stability-assured (Kohno & Sano, 2005; Ohta & Sano, 2004). However, since both FX and VE approaches are used in the feedforward (FF) control, they cannot attenuate the effects of unknown disturbances to the primary path dynamics, which cannot be sensed by a reference sensor.
To attenuate the disturbance noise in the primary path, feedback (FB) control should be additionally employed. Previously we proposed a two degree-of-freedom (2DF) control scheme consisting of an adaptive FF controller and a fixed but robust FB controller (Okumura et al, 2008), but the approach needs nominal information on the secondary path dynamics and the performance sometime becomes degraded due to its model uncertainty. A 2DF control scheme consisting of adaptive FF and FB controllers based on 2DF filtered-X algorithm has also been studied (Kuo, 1996, 1999), but can hardly adjust the two adaptive controllers simultaneously. So, we proposed a novel VE approach for updating all the parameters of the both adaptive FF and FB controllers simultaneously in on-line manner, which is the 2DF Virtual Error controller (Okumura & Sano, 2009).

4.3.2 Filterd-X LMS (FX) controller

Fig. 7 shows block diagram of the filtered-X LMS (FX) controller. And the adaptation law for the controller parameters is as follows (Burgess, 1981; Widrow et al, 1982). (Meanings of characters are described in section 4.3.5, so see detail in the section 4.3.5.)

$$\hat{\theta}_C(k+1) = \hat{\theta}_C(k) + \mu_C e(k) G(z) \xi(k) \quad (18)$$

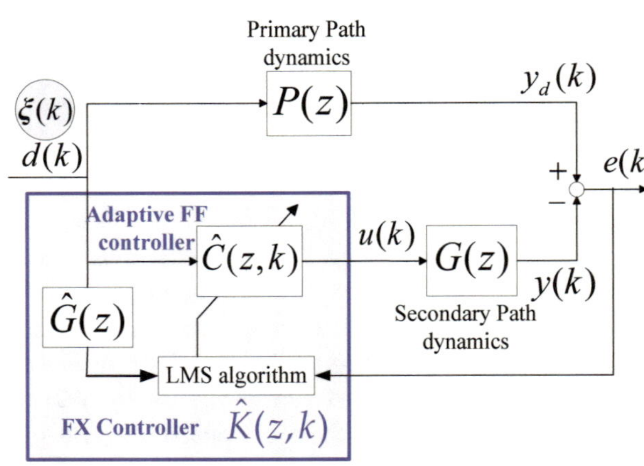

Fig. 7. Block diagram of the filtered-X LMS controller

4.3.3 2-degree-of-freedom filtered-X LMS (2DF-FX) controller

Fig. 8 shows block diagram of the 2-degree-of-freedom filtered-X LMS (2DF-FX) controller. And the adaptation laws for the controller parameters are as follows (Kuo, 1996, 1999). (Meanings of characters are described in section 4.3.5, so see detail in the section 4.3.5.)

$$\hat{\theta}_C(k+1) = \hat{\theta}_C(k) + \mu_C e(k) G(z) \xi(k) \quad (19)$$

$$\hat{\boldsymbol{\theta}}_B(k+1) = \hat{\boldsymbol{\theta}}_B(k) + \mu_B e(k) G(z) \boldsymbol{\eta}(k) \tag{20}$$

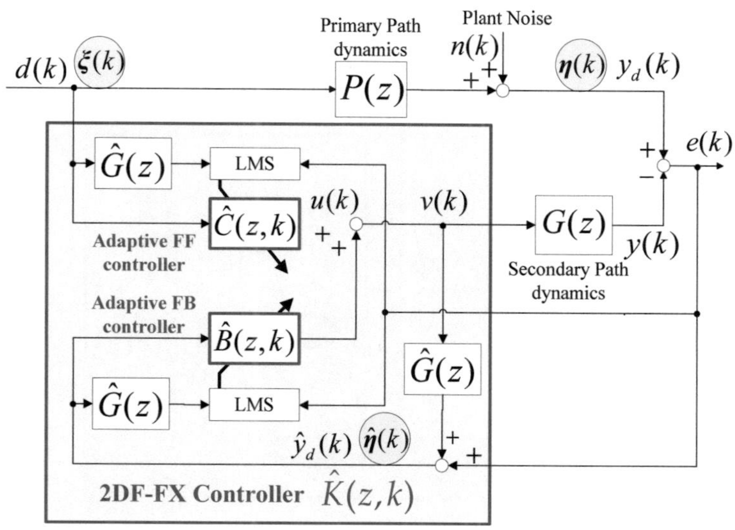

Fig. 8. Block diagram of the 2-degree-of-freedom filtered-X LMS controller

4.3.4 Virtual Error (VE) controller

Fig. 9 shows block diagram of the Virtual Error (VE) controller. And the adaptation laws for the controller parameters are as follows (Kohno & Sano, 2005; Ohta & Sano, 2004). (Meanings of characters are described in section 4.3.5, so see detail in the section 4.3.5.)

$$\hat{\boldsymbol{\theta}}_D(k+1) = \hat{\boldsymbol{\theta}}_D(k) + \mu_D e_A(k) \boldsymbol{\xi}(k) \tag{21}$$

$$\hat{\boldsymbol{\theta}}_H(k+1) = \hat{\boldsymbol{\theta}}_H(k) + \mu_H e_A(k) \boldsymbol{\varsigma}(k) \tag{22}$$

$$\hat{\boldsymbol{\theta}}_C(k+1) = \hat{\boldsymbol{\theta}}_C(k) + \mu_C e_B(k) \varphi(k) \tag{23}$$

4.3.5 2-degree-of-freedom Virtual Error (2DF-VE) controller

The main purpose of the adaptive controller block $\hat{K}(z,k)$ is to force the error signal $e(k)$ into zero even in the presence of uncertainties in the path dynamics and disturbance. In this section, we propose a 2-degree-of-freedom virtual error (2DF-VE) approach to update the parameters of four adaptive filters shown in Fig. 10.

The original version of the virtual error (VE) approach was proposed by one of the authors (Kohno & Sano, 2005; Ohta & Sano, 2004), but it could not treat with the unknown disturbance $n(k)$. In the new VE approach, by introducing the adaptive feedback (FB) controller $\hat{B}(z,k)$, we can also suppress the disturbance effects by $n(k)$. Hence this scheme is referred to as the 2DF-VE algorithm, since it consists of the adaptive feedforward (FF) controller $\hat{C}(z,k)$ and the adaptive feedback (FB) controller $\hat{B}(z,k)$.

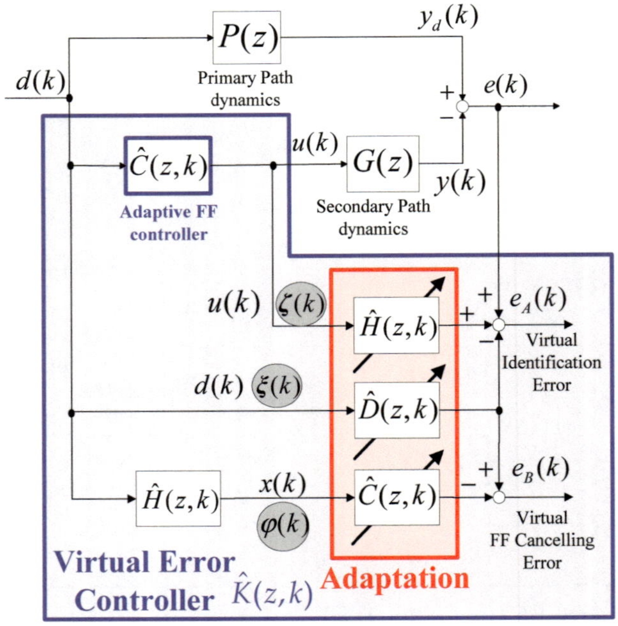

Fig. 9. Block diagram of the Virtual Error controller

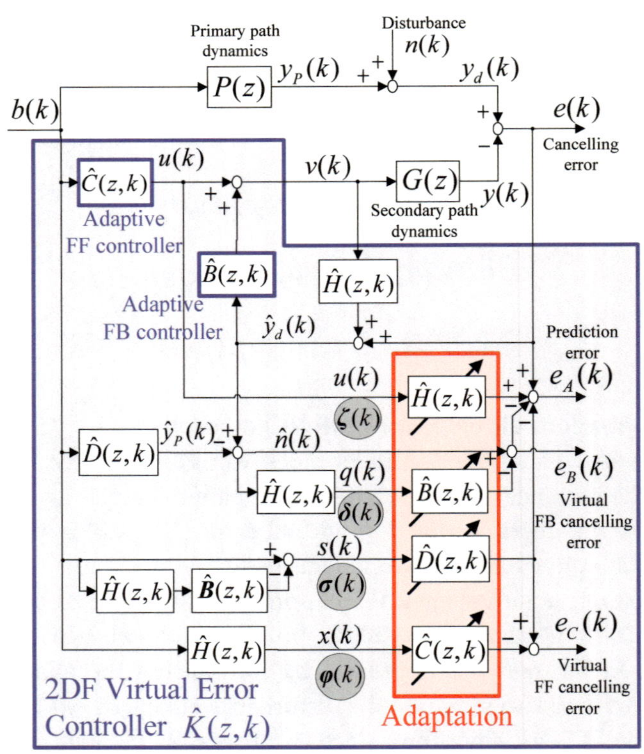

Fig. 10. Block diagram of the 2-degree-of-freedom Virtual Error controller

As shown in Fig. 10, we introduce the virtual FB canceling error $e_B(k)$ and the virtual FF canceling error $e_C(k)$ as well as the prediction error $e_A(k)$ to update the parameters of the four FIR adaptive filters $\hat{B}(z,k)$, $\hat{C}(z,k)$, $\hat{H}(z,k)$ and $\hat{D}(z,k)$, which are given as

$$\hat{D}(z,k) = \hat{d}_1(k)z^{-1} + \hat{d}_2(k)z^{-2} + \cdots + \hat{d}_{L_d}(k)z^{-L_d} \tag{24}$$

$$\hat{H}(z,k) = \hat{h}_1(k)z^{-1} + \hat{h}_2(k)z^{-2} + \cdots + \hat{h}_{L_h}(k)z^{-L_h} \tag{25}$$

$$\hat{B}(z,k) = \hat{b}_1(k)z^{-1} + \hat{b}_2(k)z^{-2} + \cdots + \hat{b}_{L_b}(k)z^{-L_b} \tag{26}$$

$$\hat{C}(z,k) = \hat{c}_1(k)z^{-1} + \hat{c}_2(k)z^{-2} + \cdots + \hat{c}_{L_c}(k)z^{-L_c}. \tag{27}$$

Let the parameter vector of each adaptive filter be defined by

$$\hat{\boldsymbol{\theta}}_D(k) = \left(\hat{d}_1(k), \hat{d}_2(k), \cdots, \hat{d}_{L_d}(k)\right)^T \tag{28}$$

$$\hat{\boldsymbol{\theta}}_H(k) = \left(\hat{h}_1(k), \hat{h}_2(k), \cdots, \hat{h}_{L_h}(k)\right)^T \tag{29}$$

$$\hat{\boldsymbol{\theta}}_B(k) = \left(\hat{b}_1(k), \hat{b}_2(k), \cdots, \hat{b}_{L_b}(k)\right)^T \tag{30}$$

$$\hat{\boldsymbol{\theta}}_C(k) = \left(\hat{c}_1(k), \hat{c}_2(k), \cdots, \hat{c}_{L_c}(k)\right)^T. \tag{31}$$

Let the corresponding regressor vector be defined as:

$$\boldsymbol{\sigma}(k) = \left(s(k-1), s(k-2), \cdots, s(k-L_d)\right)^T \tag{32}$$

$$\boldsymbol{\varsigma}(k) = \left(u(k-1), u(k-2), \cdots, u(k-L_h)\right)^T \tag{33}$$

$$\boldsymbol{\delta}(k) = \left(q(k-1), q(k-2), \cdots, q(k-L_b)\right)^T \tag{34}$$

$$\varphi(k) = \left(x(k-1), x(k-2), \cdots, x(k-L_c)\right)^T. \tag{35}$$

The principle of the 2DF-VE controller is not to force the error $e(k)$ directly into zero, but to force it indirectly by making three virtual errors $e_A(k), e_B(k), e_C(k)$ zero. That is why we call the approach as the virtual error method.

In Fig. 10, $e_A(k)$ is a prediction error, and if the signals have the PE property then the identification of $P(z)$ and $G(z)$ can be completely done. However, the PE property is not required but we only need the convergence of $e_A(k)$ to zero. Therefore, the parameters in $\hat{D}(z,k)$ and $\hat{H}(z,k)$ are adjusted adaptively so that $e_A(k)$ becomes zero. $e_B(k)$ is a virtual FB canceling error, and the parameters of the adaptive FB controller $\hat{B}(z,k)$ are updated to cancel the estimated plant noise $\hat{n}(k)$ so that $e_B(k)$ converges to zero. $e_C(k)$ is a virtual FF canceling error, and the parameters of the adaptive FF controller $\hat{C}(z,k)$ are also updated so that $e_C(k)$ converges to zero. These errors are related with the signals in Fig. 10 and can be expressed as follows:

$$e_A(k) = e(k) - (\hat{D} - \hat{D}\hat{B}\hat{H} - \hat{H}\hat{C})d(k) - e_B(k) \tag{36}$$

$$e_B(k) = (1 - \hat{B}\hat{H})\hat{n}(k) \tag{37}$$

$$e_C(k) = (\hat{D} - \hat{D}\hat{B}\hat{H} - \hat{C}\hat{H})d(k), \tag{38}$$

then it gives that

$$e_A(k) + e_B(k) + e_C(k) = e(k) + (\hat{H}\hat{C} - \hat{C}\hat{H})d(k). \tag{39}$$

If the parameters of $\hat{H}(z,k)$ and $\hat{C}(z,k)$ converge to constants, then it gives that

$$e_A(k) + e_B(k) + e_C(k) = e(k). \tag{40}$$

Therefore, if $e_A(k), e_B(k), e_C(k)$ are separately forced to zero, then it holds that $e(k)$ converges to zero.
To derive the adaptive algorithm which forces the errors $e_A(k), e_B(k), e_C(k)$ separately to zero, we first describe the error systems relating each error with the parameter errors as

$$\begin{aligned} e_A(k) &= (P - \hat{D})s(k) - (G - \hat{H})u(k) + \alpha(k) \\ &= \left[\boldsymbol{\theta}_{D*} - \hat{\boldsymbol{\theta}}_D(k)\right]^T \boldsymbol{\sigma}(k) - \left[\boldsymbol{\theta}_{H*} - \hat{\boldsymbol{\theta}}_H(k)\right]^T \boldsymbol{\varsigma}(k) + \alpha(k) \end{aligned} \tag{41}$$

$$e_B(k) = \left(\frac{1}{\hat{H}} - \hat{B}\right)q(k) + \beta(k) = \left[\boldsymbol{\theta}_{B*} - \hat{\boldsymbol{\theta}}_B(k)\right]^T \boldsymbol{\delta}(k) + \beta(k) \tag{42}$$

$$e_C(k) = \left(\frac{\hat{D} - \hat{D}\hat{B}\hat{H}}{\hat{H}} - \hat{C}\right)x(k) + \gamma(k) = \left[\boldsymbol{\theta}_{C*} - \hat{\boldsymbol{\theta}}_C(k)\right]^T \varphi(k) + \gamma(k) \tag{43}$$

where $\alpha(k), \beta(k), \gamma(k)$ are uncertain terms due to unmodelled dynamics, and the subscript * denotes the true value of each adaptive filter.
As a result, we can derive the robust adaptation laws by using ε_1-modification approach (Narendra & Annaswarny, 1986) as follows;

$$\hat{\boldsymbol{\theta}}_D(k+1) = \left(1 - \gamma_A \left|\frac{e_A(k)}{m_A(k)}\right|\right)\hat{\boldsymbol{\theta}}_D(k) + \frac{\mu_D e_A(k)\boldsymbol{\sigma}(k)}{m_A^2(k)} \tag{44}$$

$$\hat{\boldsymbol{\theta}}_H(k+1) = \left(1 - \gamma_A \left|\frac{e_A(k)}{m_A(k)}\right|\right)\hat{\boldsymbol{\theta}}_H(k) + \frac{\mu_H e_A(k)\boldsymbol{\varsigma}(k)}{m_A^2(k)} \tag{45}$$

$$\hat{\boldsymbol{\theta}}_B(k+1) = \left(1 - \gamma_B \left|\frac{e_B(k)}{m_B(k)}\right|\right)\hat{\boldsymbol{\theta}}_B(k) + \frac{\mu_B e_B(k)\boldsymbol{\delta}(k)}{m_B^2(k)} \tag{46}$$

$$\hat{\boldsymbol{\theta}}_C(k+1) = \left(1 - \gamma_C \left|\frac{e_C(k)}{m_C(k)}\right|\right)\hat{\boldsymbol{\theta}}_C(k) + \frac{\mu_C e_C(k)\varphi(k)}{m_C^2(k)} \tag{47}$$

$$m_A(k+1) = \mu_{mA} m_A(k) + g_A \max\left(\left\|\begin{matrix}\boldsymbol{\sigma}(k)\\ \boldsymbol{\varsigma}(k)\end{matrix}\right\|, 1\right) \tag{48}$$

$$m_B(k+1) = \mu_{mB} m_B(k) + g_B \max\left(\left\|\boldsymbol{\delta}(k)\right\|, 1\right) \tag{49}$$

$$m_C(k+1) = \mu_{mC} m_C(k) + g_C \max\left(\left\|\varphi(k)\right\|, 1\right) \tag{50}$$

where $0 < \mu_m < 1,\ \ g > 0,\ \ \gamma > 0,\ \mu$ is step size, and $\|\bullet\|$ denotes the vector norm. $m(k)$ is the normalizing signal employed to stabilize the adaptation even in the presence of unmodelled dynamics (Ortega & Yu, 1987).

4.4 Overall structure of adaptive signal selection controller

The overall structure of the adaptive Signal Selection Controller in Fig. 4 and Fig. 5 is now given by combining the extractor in Fig. 6 and adaptive controllers $\hat{K}(z,k)$ in Fig. 7~10.
Fig. 11 shows one example of overall Necs-Extraction Controller, which is Fig. 4 type combining Fig. 6 and Fig. 10.

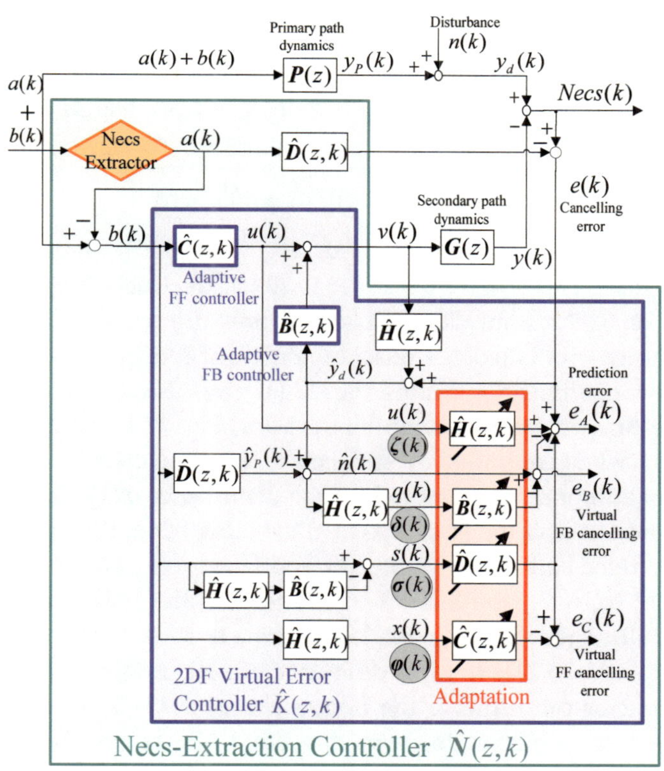

Fig. 11. One example of overall structure for Necs-Extraction Controller

5. Results of numerical simulations

To validate effectiveness of the proposed SSC, two applications to Sound Selection Systems (SSS) are considered as numerical simulations.

5.1 Numerical simulation of Necs-Extraction Control

First example is an application of the Necs-Extraction Controller to a smart window system (SWS) of a car, which can transmit only electronic siren sound of ambulance as Necs, but block any other noises such as road noise and engine noise. Purpose of this application is to keep car room silent and safety against car accidents at the same time.

In the simulation, we compare the results obtained by the four adaptive algorithms: (i) the filtered-X LMS approach (FX-SWS), (ii) the 2DF filtered-X LMS approach (2DF-FX-SWS), (iii) the Virtual Error approach (VE-SWS), and (iv) the proposed 2DF Virtual Error approach (2DF-VE-SWS). In the two filtered-X approaches, the modeling error of 20% in the filtered dynamics is considered. The simulation setup for the proposed method is summarized in Table 3.

Schemes	Design parameters
2DF-VE Controller	$L_d = 1, \mu_D = 0.220, L_H = 20, \mu_H = 0.23,$ $L_b = 5, \mu_B = 0.068, L_C = 30, \mu_C = 1.20,$ $\mu_{mA} = 0.4, g_A = 0.6, \gamma_A = 0.0006,$ $\mu_{mB} = 0.4, g_B = 0.6, \gamma_B = 0.0018,$ $\mu_{mC} = 0.4, g_C = 0.6, \gamma_C = 0.0220$
Extractor	$\mu = 0.03, \mu_{\omega\max} = 16, \mu_{\omega\min} = 4, N = 500, M = 4,$ $\omega = 20 - 650Hz, 650 - 1200Hz, 700 - 850Hz, 870 - 1060Hz$

Table 3. Design parameters of the 2DF-VE-SWS in simulations

In the simulation, it is assumed that the Necs $a(k)$ is set to the siren signal of a passing ambulance car at speed of 60km/h from 10 sec to 20 sec, the Unecs $b(k)$ is set to a unwanted stationary noise of 840Hz sinusoid with sound pressure level (SPL) of 90dB, and the unknown disturbance $n(k)$ is 100Hz sinusoid with SPL of 80dB.

Fig. 12 shows the four simulation results. Fig. 12 (a) gives $Necs(k)$ when uncontrolled, Fig. 12 (b) plots the estimated frequency by the extractor, Fig. 12 (c)-(f) compare the obtained profiles of $Necs(k)$ when controlled by each control approach. As shown in Fig. 12 (c) and (e), the FF control approaches cannot reduce the disturbance $n(k)$, though they can block the Unecs $b(k)$ and transmit the Necs $a(k)$. On the other hand, the proposed 2DF-VE-SWS can successfully reduce both disturbance $n(k)$ and Unecs $b(k)$ and transmit only the Necs $a(k)$, as in Fig. 12 (f), while the 2DF-FX-SWS based on the ordinary filtered-x algorithm cannot obtain stabilized results due to modeling errors as shown in Fig. 10 (d). Note that the scale of the vertical axis in Fig. 12 (d) is different from other figures. Fig. 12 (b) shows that the proposed extractor can estimate the frequencies of $a(k)+b(k)$ correctly, where large variations of the two estimated frequencies around 15 sec are due to passing of the ambulance. Consequently, it is validated that the performance of the proposed method 2DF-VE-SWS is the best in four controllers.

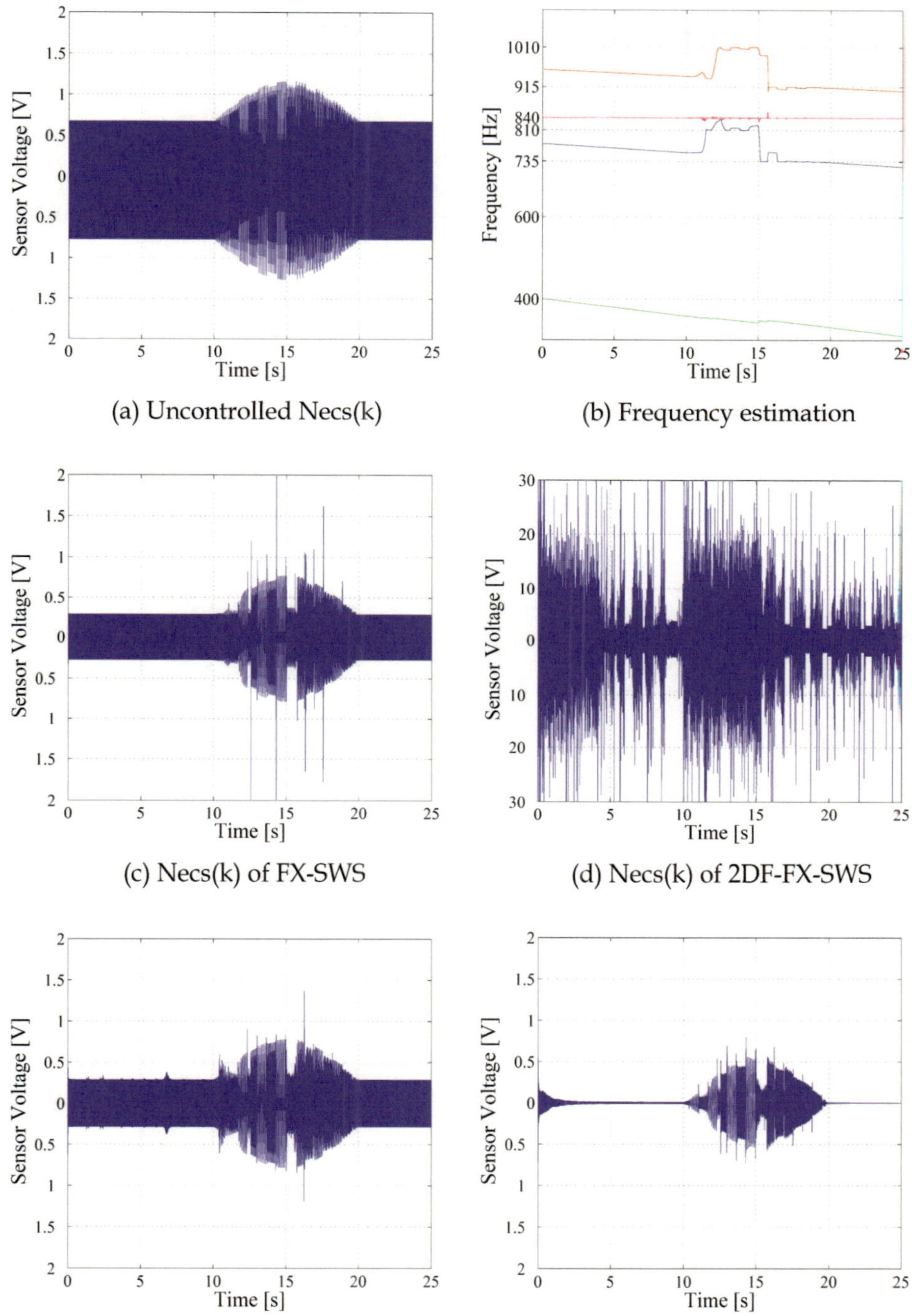

(a) Uncontrolled Necs(k)

(b) Frequency estimation

(c) Necs(k) of FX-SWS

(d) Necs(k) of 2DF-FX-SWS

(e) Necs(k) of VE-SWS

(f) Necs(k) of 2DF-VE-SWS

Fig. 12. Simulation results of four Necs-Extraction Controllers

5.2 Numerical simulation of Unecs-Canceling Control

Second example is another application of the Unecs-Canceling Controller to rotating machinery such as a compressor, which can attenuate only sound of rotating motor as Unecs even when rotating speed is changing, but transmit some abnormal sound of the machinery. Purpose of this application is to keep machinery silence and detectability of machine abnormality at the same time.

In the simulation, we will examine whether the Unecs-Canceling Controller works correctly or not. We consider the case that AC servo motor of a compressor starts to rotate from 0rpm at 0sec, and accelerate to 3600rpm until 10sec, then rotate constantly at 3600rpm after 10sec. Additionally, 240Hz abnormal sound of the machinery occurs from 8sec to 20sec.

And in this simulation, we consider the Unecs-Canceling Controller composed of 2-degree-of-freedom Virtual Error Controller, because the 2DF-VE controller shows the best performance in the simulation of Necs-Extraction Controller in section 5.1.

The simulation setup for the proposed method is summarized in Table 4.

Fig. 13 shows the simulation results. Fig. 13 (a) gives $Necs(k)$ when uncontrolled, Fig. 13 (b) shows the obtained profiles of $Necs(k)$ when controlled by 2DF-VE control approach, Fig. 13 (c) plots the estimated motor rotation speed by the extractor, and Fig. 13(d) describes the cancelling error.

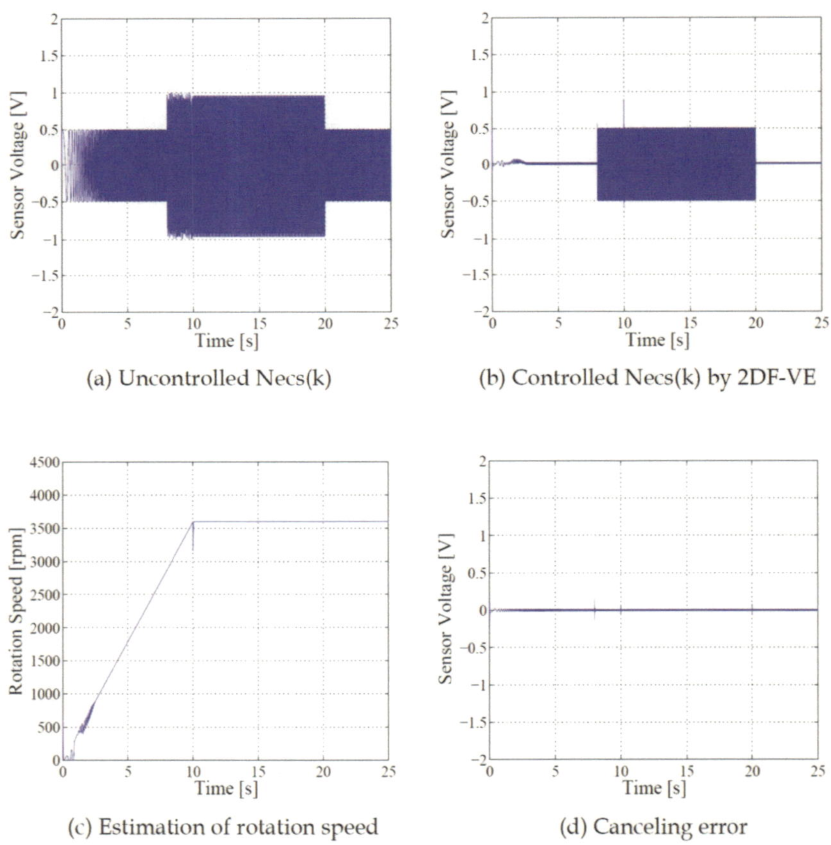

Fig. 13. Simulation results of Unecs-Canceling Controller

As shown in Fig. 13(b), the Unecs-Canceling Controller can attenuate motor sound, and transmit only abnormal sound of machinery from 8sec to 20sec. And Fig. 13(c) shows the good performance of the frequency estimation of the extractor. Besides, Fig. 13(d) shows that adaptation of the 2DF-VE controller is stable and rapid enough even if the frequency of extracting signal varies.
Consequently, it is validated that Unecs-Canceling Controller shows good performance to attenuate only desired signals.

Schemes	Design parameters
2DF-VE Controller	$L_d = 1, \mu_D = 0.220, L_H = 20, \mu_H = 0.23,$ $L_b = 5, \mu_B = 0.068, L_C = 30, \mu_C = 1.20,$ $\mu_{mA} = 0.4, g_A = 0.6, \gamma_A = 0.0006,$ $\mu_{mB} = 0.4, g_B = 0.6, \gamma_B = 0.0018,$ $\mu_{mC} = 0.4, g_C = 0.6, \gamma_C = 0.0220$
Extractor	$\mu = 0.03, \mu_{\omega\max} = 16, \mu_{\omega\min} = 4, N = 500, M = 4,$ $\omega = 0-650Hz, 200-300Hz, 300-600Hz, 600-1000Hz$

Table 4. Design parameters of the Unecs-Canceling Controller in simulations

6. Conclusion

We have proposed a novel control scheme which can transmit necessary signals (Necs) and attenuate only unnecessary signals (Unecs) selectively. The control scheme is named as Signal Selection Control (SSC) scheme.
Proposed control schemes are two types of the SSC; one is Necs-Extraction Controller which transmits only signals set as Necs, and the other is Unecs-Canceling Controller which attenuates only signals set as Unecs.
Besides, in the SSC, we have introduced four types of adaptive controller, and it is validated that the 2-degree-of-freedom Virtual Error controller has the best performance in the four adaptive controllers.
Consequently, effectiveness of both SSC are validated in two numerical simulations of the Sound Selection Systems.

7. Acknowledgment

This work was fully supported by Graduate School of Integrated Design Engineering, Keio University, Yokohama, Japan.

8. References

C. Bao and J. Pan, "Experimental study of different approaches for active control of sound transmission through double walls," *J. Acoust. Soc. Am.* , Vol. 102, No. 3, pp. 1664-1670, 1997.

J.C. Burgess, "Active adaptive sound control in a duct," *J. Acoust. Soc. Am.* , Vol. 70, No. 3, pp. 715-726, 1981.

A. Jakob and M. Möser, "Active control of double-glazed windows Part I: Feedforward control," *J. Applied Acoust.*, Vol. 64, pp. 163-182, 2003.

A. Jakob and M. Möser, "Active control of double-glazed windows. Part II: Feedback control," *J. Applied Acoust.*, Vol. 64, pp. 183-196, 2003.

O.E. Kaiser, S.J. Pietrzko and M. Morari, "Feedback control of sound transmission through a double glazed window," *J. Sound and Vibration*, Vol. 263, pp. 775-795, 2003.

T. Kohno and A. Sano, "Direct adaptive active noise control algorithms in case of uncertain secondary path dynamics, Int. *J. Adapt. Contr. Signal Process.*, Vol. 19, pp. 153-176, 2005.

S.M. Kuo, D.R. Morgan, *Active Noise Control Systems -Algorithms and DSP Implementations-*, Wiley. Interscience, 1996.

S.M. Kuo and D.R. Morgan, "Active noise control: a tutorial review," *Proc. The IEEE*, Vol. 87, No. 6, pp. 943-973, 1999.

S.O. Reza Moheimani, "A survey of recent innovations in vibration damping and control using shunted piezoelectric transducers," *IEEE Trans. Contr. Syst. Tech.*, Vol. 11, No. 4, pp. 482-494, 2003.

S.O. Reza Moheimani and A.J. Fleming, *Piezoelectric Transducers for Vibration Control and Damping*, Springer, 2005.

K.S. Narendra and A.M. Annaswamy, "Robust adaptive control in the presence of bounded disturbances," *IEEE Trans. Automatic Control*, Vol. AC-31, No. 4, pp. 306-315, 1986.

Y. Ohta and A. Sano, "Direct adaptive approach to multichannel active noise control and sound reproduction", *Proc. 2004 American Control Conference*, pp.2895- 2900, Boston, USA, 2004.

H. Okumura, R. Emi and A. Sano, "Adaptive two degree-of-freedom vibration control for flexible plate with piezoelectric patches," *Proc. SICE Annual Conf. 2008*, Tokyo, 1A09-5, pp. 218-221, 2008.

H. Okumura and A. Sano, "Adaptive Necessary Signal Extraction Controll Based on 2DF Virtual Error Approach to Smart Window Systems," *Proc. 48th IEEE Conf. on Desision and Control held jointly with 2009 28th Chinese Control Conf.*, Shanghai, China, ThC06. 4, pp. 5446-5453, 2009.

R. Ortega and T. Yu, "Theoretical results of robustness of direct adaptive controllers," *Proc. IFAC World Congress*, Munchen, 1987.

J. Pan and C. Bao, "Analytical study of different approaches for active control of sound transmission through double walls, *J. Acoust. Soc. Am.*, Vol. 103, No. 4, pp. 1916-1922, 1998.

P. Sas, C. Bao, F. Augusztinovicz and W. Desmet, "Active control of sound transmission through a double panel partition," *J. Sound and Vibration*, Vol. 180, No. 4, pp. 609-625, 1995.

Y. Shimada, Y. Nishimura, T. Usagawa and M. Ebata, "Active control for periodic noise with variable fundamental -an extended DXHS algotithm with frequency tracking ability -," *J. Acoust. Soc. Jpn. (E)*, Vol. 20, No. 4, pp. 301-312, 1999.

O. Tokhi and S. Veres, *Active sound and vibration control -theory and applications-*, The Institution of Electrical Engineers, 2002.

B. Widrow, D. Shur and S. Shaffer, "On adaptive inverse control," *Proc. the 15th Asilomar Conf. Circuits, Syst. Comput.*, Vol. 9, No. 11, pp. 185-189, Pacific Grove, CA1981-11, 1982.

22

Measurement Uncertainty of White-Light Interferometry on Optically Rough Surfaces

Pavel Pavlíček
Palacky University, Faculty of Science, Regional Centre of Advanced Technologies and Materials, Joint Laboratory of Optics of Palacky University and Institute of Physics of Academy of Science of the Czech Republic
Czech Republic

1. Introduction

White-light interferometry is an established method to measure the geometrical shape of objects. A typical setup for white-light interferometry is shown in Fig. 1.

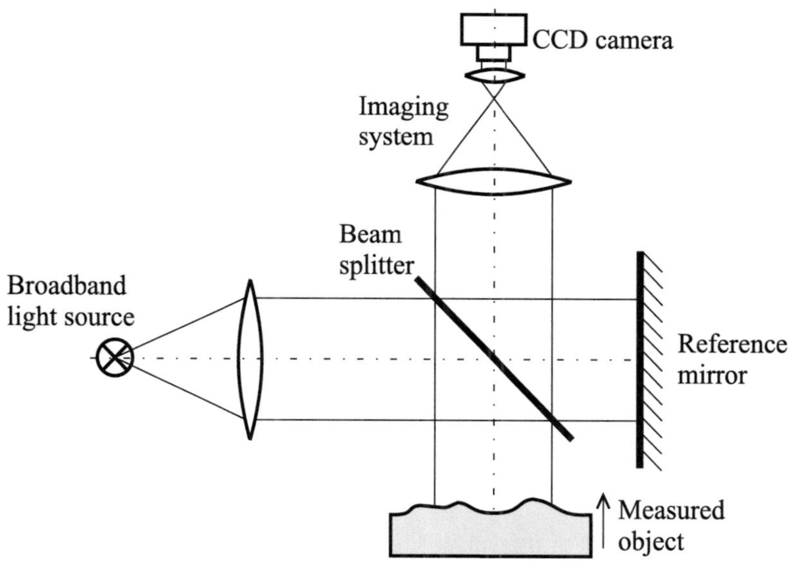

Fig. 1. Schematic of white-light interferometry.

A Michelson interferometer is illuminated by a broadband light source (e.g. light-emitting diode, superluminescent diode, arc or incandescent lamp). At the output of the interferometer, a CCD camera is used as a multiple detector. The measured object is placed in one arm of the interferometer and moved in the longitudinal direction as indicated by the arrow in Fig. 1. The surface of the object is imaged by a telecentric optical system onto the lightsensitive area of the CCD camera. During the moving of the object in the longitudinal direction, a series of images is acquired. From the acquired series, the coherence function (also referred to as correlogram or interferogram) can be extracted for each object point. The maximum of the envelope of the correlogram is assigned to the longitudinal distance of the respective object point (Kino & Chim, 1990; Lee & Strand, 1990). A typical white-light correlogram is shown in Fig. 2.

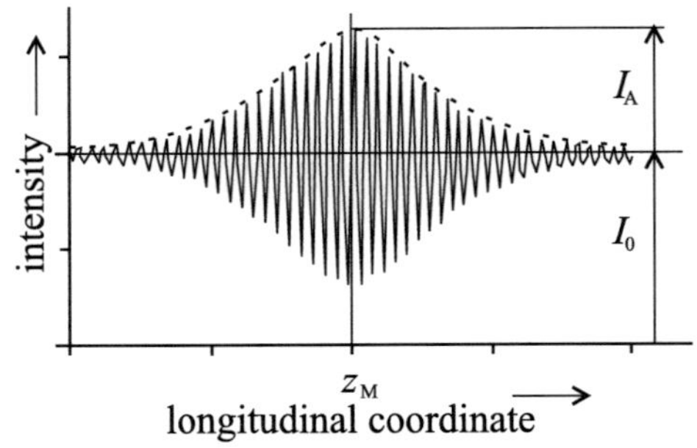

Fig. 2. Typical white-light correlogram.

Unlike to classical interferometry, white-light interferometry can be used for the measurement of the objects with an optically rough surface (Dresel et al., 1992). A surface is regarded as being optically rough when the standard deviation of the height variations within one resolution cell of the imaging system exceeds one-fourth of the wavelength of the used light. The property of the surface to be optically smooth or rough depends not only on the surface roughness but also on the wavelength of the used light and the size of the resolution cell of the imaging system (Häusler et al., 1999). In white-light interferometry on rough surface, the longitudinal distance of the object point is determined from the envelope of the correlogram only. The phase of the correlogram is not evaluated because it is a random quantity. The rough surface of the measured object implies the formation of speckle pattern in the image plane (on the lightsensitive area of the CCD camera).

In this work, we consider two influences that cause the measurement uncertainty: rough surface and the shot noise of the camera. The influence of rough surface on measurement uncertainty was described in our previous work (Pavlíček & Hýbl, 2008). It shows that the measurement uncertainty caused by surface roughness depends on the roughness and the intensity of individual speckle. The measurement uncertainty δz is given by the formula derived by T. Dresel (Dresel, 1991)

$$\delta z = \frac{1}{\sqrt{2}} \sqrt{\frac{\langle I_{\text{obj}} \rangle}{I_{\text{obj}}}} \sigma_h. \tag{1}$$

Here σ_h is the rms roughness of the surface, I_{obj} is the local intensity and $\langle I_{\text{obj}} \rangle$ is the mean intensity of the speckle pattern. The subscript obj emphasizes that the intensities I_{obj}, $\langle I_{\text{obj}} \rangle$ are meant with the shut reference arm (only the object arm is illuminated). Equation (1) indicates that the measurement of the longitudinal coordinate z is more precise for brighter speckles.

The intensity in the speckle pattern is distributed according to the gamma distribution (Parry, 1984)

$$p(I_{\text{obj}}) = \frac{M^M I_{\text{obj}}^{M-1}}{\langle I_{\text{obj}} \rangle^M \Gamma(M)} \exp\left(-\frac{M I_{\text{obj}}}{\langle I_{\text{obj}} \rangle} \right), \tag{2}$$

where $\Gamma(\,)$ is the gamma function. The shape parameter M depends on the rms roughness σ_h and the coherence length l_c of the used light. For a light source with a Gaussian spectrum, the shape parameter M is equal to

$$M = \sqrt{1 + 8\left(\frac{\sigma_h}{l_c}\right)^2}. \tag{3}$$

If the coherence length l_c is long and the rms roughness σ_h is small ($\sigma_h \lesssim \sqrt{8} l_c$), the gamma distribution differs only slightly from the negative exponential distribution (that corresponds to the monochromatic illumination)(Horváth et al., 2002). The coherence length l_c is related to the spectral width of the light source $\Delta\lambda$. For a spectral width $\Delta\lambda$ much lower than the central wavelength λ_0 of the light source, it holds (Pavlíček & Hýbl, 2008)

$$l_c \cong \frac{\sqrt{\ln 2}}{\pi} \frac{\lambda_0^2}{\Delta\lambda}. \tag{4}$$

The spectral width $\Delta\lambda$ in Eq. (4) is defined as full width at half maximum (FWHM).
George and Jain demonstrate that speckle patterns of two different wavelengths become decorrelated if the surface roughness exceeds a certain limit (George & Jain, 1973). A similar effect is observed with the speckle pattern produced by broadband light. If the rms roughness is high and the coherence length is short, the speckle becomes decorrelated. A decorrelated speckle implies a distorted correlogram. An example of a distorted correlogram is shown in Fig. 3.

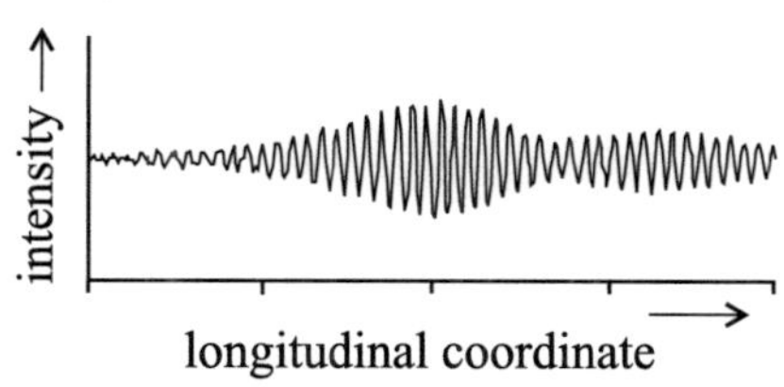

Fig. 3. Distorted white-light correlogram.

The limit beyond which the correlogram becomes distorted was found numerically (Pavlíček & Hýbl, 2008)

$$l_c < 4\sigma_h \sqrt{\frac{\langle I_{obj} \rangle}{I_{obj}}}. \tag{5}$$

The influence of the shot noise on the measurement uncertainty of white-light interferometry is described in (Pavlíček & Hýbl, 2011). The measurement uncertainty δz caused by shot noise is given by

$$\delta z = \sqrt{2} \sqrt[4]{\frac{2}{\pi}} \frac{N_{shot}}{I_A} \sqrt{\Delta z l_c}, \tag{6}$$

where N_{shot} is the intensity of the noise, I_A is the amplitude of the modulation of the correlogram, and Δz is the distance between two subsequent values of the coordinate z_O - the sampling step. The ratio N_{shot}/I_A is the noise-to-signal ratio and the meaning of I_A is shown in Fig. 2. The shot noise is caused by the uncertainty in counting the incoming photons. For a long integration time of the CCD camera (significantly longer than the coherence time of the used light), the photocount distribution can be assumed as Poissonian (Peřina, 1991). Then

$$N_{shot} = \sqrt{I}, \tag{7}$$

where I is the signal. Both N_{shot} and I are expressed in electrons. According to Eq. (7), the intensity N_{shot} of noise is different for each point of the correlogram. For a correlogram with the form as shown in Fig. 2, the intensity N_{shot} of noise in Eq. (7) can be replaced by the mean value $\overline{N_{shot}} = \sqrt{I_0}$. The meaning of the offset I_0 is shown in Fig. 2. The measurement uncertainty caused by the shot noise is then given by

$$\delta z = \sqrt{2}\sqrt[4]{\frac{2}{\pi}}\frac{\sqrt{I_0}}{I_A}\sqrt{\Delta z l_c}. \tag{8}$$

The intensities I_0 and I_A in Eq. (8) are again expressed in electrons.

Until now, the influence of both effects (rough surface and shot noise) have been studied separately. The goal of this work is to find the measurement uncertainty of white-light interferometry influenced by both effects. Similar to (Pavlíček & Hýbl, 2008), the calculations are performed numerically.

2. Assumptions

We understand the measurement uncertainty as the standard deviation of the distribution of the measurement error (the difference between the estimate and the true value). For the calculation of the error caused by surface roughness and shot noise, we take into consideration following assumptions:

1. The surface is macroscopically planar and microscopically rough. The height h_j of the j-th scattering center is a normally distributed random variable with zero mean. The standard deviation of the height distribution is equal to the rms roughness σ_h. The number of scattering centers inside of the resolution cell of the imaging system is n.
2. Because of the different reflectivity of the scattering centers, the amplitude a_j of the light reflected from j-th scattering center is a random variable obeying uniform distribution from 0 to A_M. The resultant amplitude of the light reflected from the measured surface is given by (Goodman, 1984)

$$\hat{A} = \sum_{j=1}^{n} \frac{a_j}{n^{1/2}} \exp(i2kh_j). \tag{9}$$

   We assume that the amplitudes a_j and heights h_j are independent of each other and the amplitudes a_j do not depend on wave number k.
3. The spectral density of the broadband light has Gaussian form

$$S(k) = \frac{1}{2\sqrt{\pi}\Delta k} \exp\left[-\left(\frac{k-k_0}{2\Delta k}\right)^2\right], \tag{10}$$

   where $k_0 = 2\pi/\lambda_0$ is the central wave number and $\Delta k = 1/(2l_c)$ is the effective band width in wave number units (Born & Wolf, 2003). The effective bandwidth Δk can be calculated from the spectral width $\Delta\lambda$ by means of Eq. (4).
4. The noise is a signal-independent normally distributed random variable with zero mean and standard deviation $\overline{N_{shot}}$.

3. Simulation

3.1 Generation of the correlogram

The phasor amplitude of light having passed through the object arm with the rough surface is, according to Eq. (9), given by

$$\hat{A}(k, z_O) = \sum_{j=1}^{n} \frac{a_j}{n^{1/2}} \exp[i2k(z_O + h_j)]. \tag{11}$$

The position z_O of the rough surface is given by the position of the mean value of height distribution as shown in Fig. 4.

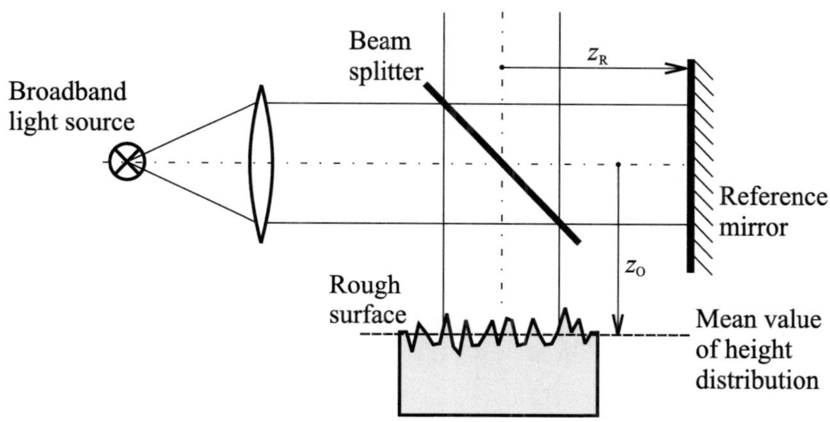

Fig. 4. Object and reference arm of the setup for white-light interferometry.

The phasor amplitude of light having passed the reference arm with the reference mirror is given by

$$\hat{B}(k, z_R) = B \exp(i2kz_R), \tag{12}$$

where B is the amplitude of light in the reference arm and z_R is the position of the reference mirror. The meaning of both the positions z_O and z_R follows from Fig. 4.
The light intensity at the interferometer output is given by

$$I_k(k, z_O - z_R) = |\hat{A}(k, z_O) + \hat{B}(k, z_R)|^2. \tag{13}$$

The subscript k means that I_k is the intensity calculated for the wave number k. To obtain the total intensity at the output of the interferometer, I_k must be integrated over all wave numbers. Because the light components with various wave numbers are not uniformly distributed in the spectrum, I_k must be multiplied by spectral density $S(k)$. Theoretically, the integration should be performed over the whole interval $(-\infty, \infty)$. However, the integration is calculated numerically and therefore we restrict the calculation on a finite interval which corresponds to three standard deviations on each side from the central wave number: $k_{\min} = k_0 - 3\sqrt{2}\Delta k, k_{\max} = k_0 + 3\sqrt{2}\Delta k$

$$I(z_O - z_R) = \int_{k_{\min}}^{k_{\max}} S(k) I_k(k, z_O - z_R) dk. \tag{14}$$

The integration in Eq. (14) is transformed to a sum

$$I(z_O - z_R) = \sqrt{\frac{2}{\pi}} \frac{3}{n_k} \sum_{l=1}^{n_k} \exp\left[-\left(\frac{k_l - k_0}{2\Delta k} \right)^2 \right] I_k(k_l, z_O - z_R) \tag{15}$$

with

$$k_l = \frac{l - 1/2}{n_k}(k_{\max} - k_{\min}) + k_{\min}. \tag{16}$$

In Eqs. (15) and (16), n_k is the number of used wave numbers.
Equation (15) for the intensity I expressed as a function of the coordinate z_O, while the coordinate z_R is constant, describes the correlogram. The correlogram is calculated for n_c points (values of the coordinate z_O). The calculated correlogram is superposed by the noise with normal distribution and a constant (signal independent) standard deviation $\overline{N_{\text{shot}}}$.

$$I_n(z_m) = I(z_m) + N_m \tag{17}$$

with $z_m = m\Delta z$ for $m = 1, ..., n_c$.
The local intensity I_{obj} of the speckle pattern that appears in Eqs. (1), (2), and (5) can be calculated from Eq. (15) for $B = 0$ (the reference arm is shut) and an arbitrary value of z_O. Because the expression for I_{obj} contains no interference term, it does not depend on the coordinate z_O. For simplicity we choose $z_O = z_R$

$$I_{\text{obj}} = \sqrt{\frac{2}{\pi}} \frac{3}{n_k} \sum_{l=1}^{n_k} \exp\left[-\left(\frac{k_l - k_0}{2\Delta k} \right)^2 \right] \left[\left(\sum_{j=1}^{n} \frac{a_j}{\sqrt{n}} \cos(2k_l h_j) \right)^2 + \left(\sum_{j=1}^{n} \frac{a_j}{\sqrt{n}} \sin(2k_l h_j) \right)^2 \right]. \tag{18}$$

The mean intensity of the speckle pattern is given by

$$\langle I_{\text{obj}} \rangle = \langle a_j^2 \rangle. \tag{19}$$

According to Eq. (12), the intensity of the reference beam is

$$I_{\text{ref}} = B^2. \tag{20}$$

Thus the amplitude of the modulation is given by

$$I_A = 2B\sqrt{I_{\text{obj}}} \tag{21}$$

and the noise-to-signal ratio is equal to

$$\text{NSR} = \frac{N_{\text{shot}}}{2B\sqrt{I_{\text{obj}}}}. \tag{22}$$

If the amplitudes $\{a_j\}$ obey uniform distribution from 0 to A_M as postulated in assumption 2 in Sec. 2

$$\langle I_{\text{obj}} \rangle = \frac{1}{3} A_M^2 \tag{23}$$

and

$$\text{NSR} = \frac{\sqrt{3}}{2} \sqrt{\frac{\langle I_{\text{obj}} \rangle}{I_{\text{obj}}}} \frac{N_{\text{shot}}}{A_M B}. \tag{24}$$

The heights $\{h_j\}$, amplitudes $\{a_j\}$ and noise values $\{N_m\}$ used for the simulation are random numbers. The random numbers have been generated by quantum random number generator developed in the Joint Laboratory of Optics (Soubusta et al., 2003).

3.2 Evaluation of the correlogram

The obtained noised correlogram is evaluated to find the "measured" value z_M of the surface. The value z_M is determined from the maximum of the envelope of the correlogram. The meaning of z_M is shown in Fig. 2.

The envelope of the correlogram is calculated using a discrete Hilbert transform. The calculation of the envelope can be described in five steps (Onodera et al., 2005). In the first step, the mean intensity I_0 is subtracted from the correlogram. In this way, the zero mean correlogram is obtained. In the second step, the zero mean correlogram is Fourier transformed. In the third step, the Fourier transform is multiplied by the imaginary unit (i) for positive frequencies and by the negative of the imaginary unit (-i) for negative frequencies. In the fourth step, the result is inversely Fourier transformed. Thus the Hilbert transform of the zero mean correlogram is obtained. The Hilbert transform of the correlogram alters its phase by $\pi/2$. Finally, in the fifth step, the Hilbert transform of the zero mean correlogram is squared and added to the square of the zero mean correlogram itself for each value of z_O. The square root of this sum is the value of the envelope of the correlogram for the given value of z_O.

The position z_M of the maximum of the envelope is estimated by use of the least-squares method (Press et al., 1992). The sought measurement error is the difference between the estimate and the true value. Without the influence of surface roughness and shot noise, the maximum of the envelope would be located at $z_M = z_R$. Therefore, the measurement error is mathematically expressed by

$$\Delta = z_M - z_R. \tag{25}$$

4. Results of the simulation

Here the results of the simulation are presented. The quantities are calculated numerically for n_s speckles, each of them calculated using a set of values $\{h_j\}, \{a_j\}$, and $\{N_m\}; j = 1, 2, ..., n$, $m = 1, 2, ..., n_c$. The sets $\{h_j\}$ have a normal distribution with the standard deviation σ_h. The sets $\{a_j\}$ have a uniform distribution from 0 to A_M and the sets $\{N_m\}$ have a normal distribution with the standard deviation $\overline{N_{shot}}$.

4.1 Distribution of the intensity

First, the attention is given to the intensity distribution in the object arm. Intensity I_{obj} is calculated from Eqs. (15), (13), and (11) with $B = 0$ and $z_O = z_R$. The parameters of the simulation are $n_s = 20\,000$, $n = 200$, $n_k = 200$, $A_M = 1$.

Figure 5 displays the results of the calculated intensity distribution for $\lambda_0 = 820nm$, $\sigma_h = 1.2\mu m$, and three values of spectral width $\Delta\lambda = 10, 38$, and $80nm$.

The numerically calculated results are compared with the solutions obtained from Eq. (2). The gamma distribution described by Eq. (2) is plotted in Fig. 5 with a dashed curve. The numerically obtained results are in good agreement with the analytical solutions as follows from Fig. 5. The variance of the intensity distribution described by Eq. (2) is equal to

$$\text{var}\{I_{obj}\} = \frac{\langle I_{obj}\rangle^2}{M}. \tag{26}$$

The contrast of the speckle pattern is given by (Parry, 1984)

$$C = \frac{\sqrt{\text{var}\{I_{obj}\}}}{\langle I_{obj}\rangle} \tag{27}$$

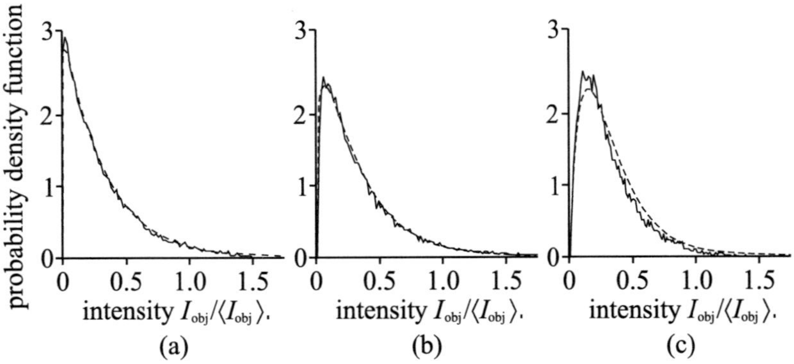

Fig. 5. Intensity distribution for $\lambda_0 = 820nm$, $\sigma_h = 1.2\mu m$. (a) $\Delta\lambda = 10nm$. (b) $\Delta\lambda = 38nm$. (c) $\Delta\lambda = 80nm$.

and from Eq. (26), it follows

$$C = \frac{1}{\sqrt{M}}. \tag{28}$$

In Table 1, the values of contrast C_{num} calculated numerically from Eq. (27) are compared with the values of contrast C obtained by means of Eqs. (3) and (28). Because $A_M = 1$, the mean

$\Delta\lambda(nm)$	$l_c(\mu m)$	$\langle I_{obj}\rangle$	var$\{I_{obj}\}$	C_{num}	C
10	17.8	0.335	0.110	0.99	0.99
20	8.9	0.333	0.106	0.98	0.97
30	5.9	0.333	0.097	0.94	0.93
40	4.5	0.333	0.089	0.90	0.89
50	3.6	0.335	0.081	0.85	0.85
60	3.0	0.334	0.074	0.81	0.81
70	2.5	0.335	0.066	0.77	0.77
80	2.2	0.336	0.062	0.74	0.74

Table 1. Numerically calculated speckle contrast for various spectral widths of the light source ($\lambda_0 = 820nm, \sigma_h = 1.2\mu m$)

intensity $\langle I_{obj}\rangle$ of the speckle pattern is equal approximately to $1/3$ according to Eq. (23). The dependence of the contrast C_{num} on the spectral width $\Delta\lambda$ is plotted in Fig. 6(a). This dependence is an analogy to the dependence of the contrast on the illumination aperture as described in (Häusler, 2005). For comparison, the dependence of the contrast on the illumination aperture is illustrated in Fig. 6(b).

4.2 Distribution of the measurement error

The distribution of the measurement error caused by surface roughness and shot noise is calculated numerically using Eq. (25). The parameters of the simulation are $n_s = 20\,000$, $n_c = 1024$, $n = 200$, $n_k = 200$, $A_M = 1$, $B = 1$. As an example, the distribution of the measurement error is calculated for $\lambda_0 = 820nm$, $\Delta\lambda = 35nm$, $\sigma_h = 0.4\mu m$, $I_{obj} = \langle I_{obj}\rangle$, $\Delta z = \lambda_0/10$, and $N_{shot} = 0.0577$. The relation $I_{obj} = \langle I_{obj}\rangle$ means that only those cases are entered into the statistics when the intensity I_{obj} falls into a certain neighborhood of the mean intensity $\langle I_{obj}\rangle$. The noise-to-signal ratio is equal to NSR $= 0.05$ according to Eq. (24). The results of the calculation are presented in Fig. 7.

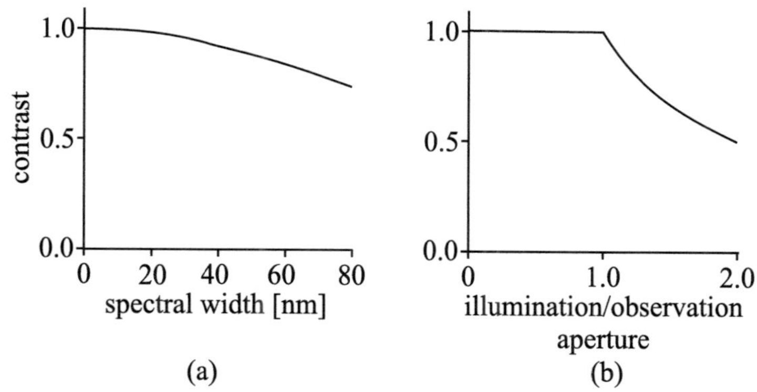

Fig. 6. (a) Speckle contrast as a function of spectral width (numerically calculated data) for $\lambda_0 = 820nm$, $\sigma_h = 1.2\mu m$. (b) Speckle contrast as a function of illumination aperture according to Häusler.

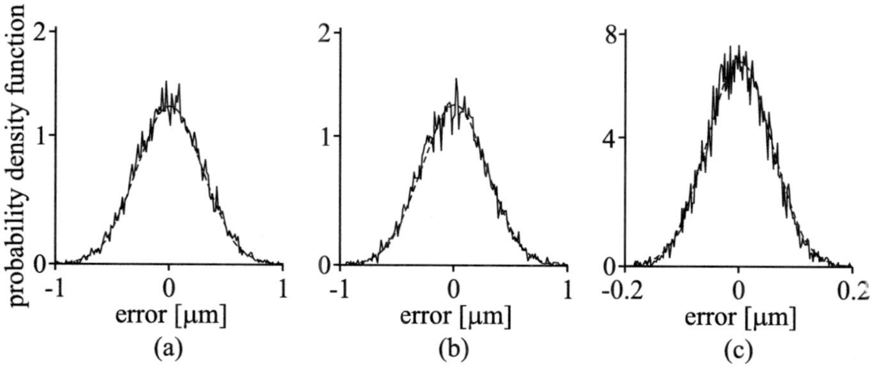

Fig. 7. Distribution of the measurement error for $\lambda_0 = 820nm$, $\Delta\lambda = 35nm$, $\sigma_h = 0.4\mu m$, $I_{obj} = \langle I_{obj} \rangle$, and NSR $= 0.05$. (a) Error caused by surface roughness and shot noise. (b) Error caused by surface roughness only. (c) Error caused by shot noise only.

The distribution of the measurement error for the noised correlogram on rough surface is shown in Fig. 7(a). Figure 7(b) shows the distribution of the measurement error for the correlogram without noise. Finally, the distribution of the measurement error for the noised correlogram on smooth surface is illustrated in Fig. 7(c). It shows up that the distribution of the measurement error tends in all three cases to a normal distribution centered at zero. For comparing, the shape of the normal distribution is plotted by dashed line in Fig. 7. The zero mean of the calculated distribution means that the expected value of the measured coordinate is the mean value of height distribution within the resolution cell. The standard deviation of the calculated distribution is the sought measurement uncertainty. In the given example, the numerically calculated measurement uncertainties are $\delta z = 0.293\mu m$, $\delta z_{rough} = 0.288\mu m$, and $\delta z_{noise} = 0.055\mu m$ for the cases shown in Figs. 7(a), 7(b), and 7(c), respectively.
It is apparent that it holds

$$(\delta z)^2 = (\delta z_{rough})^2 + (\delta z_{noise})^2. \tag{29}$$

This result is to be expected, because the influences of the noise and of the rough surface are independent. A sum of two independent random variables with normal distribution and

the standard deviations equal to σ_A and σ_B, respectively, is a random variable with normal distribution and standard deviation equal to $\sigma = \sqrt{\sigma_A^2 + \sigma_B^2}$.
The numerically calculated measurement uncertainties are compared with the theoretical values calculated from Eqs. (1) and (6). For the abovementioned example, the theoretical results are $\delta z = 0.286\mu m$, $\delta z_{\text{rough}} = 0.283\mu m$, and $\delta z_{\text{noise}} = 0.041\mu m$ which is in a good agreement with the numerical calculations. The numerically calculated value of δz_{noise} is higher than the theoretical prediction. The reason is that the fit is performed on a limited interval of the longitudinal coordinate ($-\sqrt{3/2}l_c < z_O - z_M < \sqrt{3/2}l_c$). The numerical calculations for other values of λ_0, $\Delta\lambda$, σ_h, I_{obj}, Δz, and N_{shot} confirm the validity of Eq. (29).
By comparing the values δz_{rough} and δz_{noise}, it is apparent that the influence of rough surface is significantly higher for "usual" values of spectral width, sampling step and noise-to-signal ratio. However, when white-light interferometry is operated with a narrow-band light source or with an extremely long sampling step, the influence of noise will increase. Equations (1) and (6) enable to compare the influences of both effects.

4.3 Measurement uncertainty

The measurement uncertainty caused by surface roughness and shot noise is calculated as function of the spectral widht $\Delta\lambda$. The parameters of the simulation are $n_s = 10\,000$, $n_c = 1024$, $n = 200$, $n_k = 200$, $A_M = 1$, $B = 1$. Figure 8 shows the result for $\lambda_0 = 820nm$, $\sigma_h = 1.2\mu m$, $I_{\text{obj}} = \langle I_{\text{obj}} \rangle$, and NSR $= 0.05$ as an example.

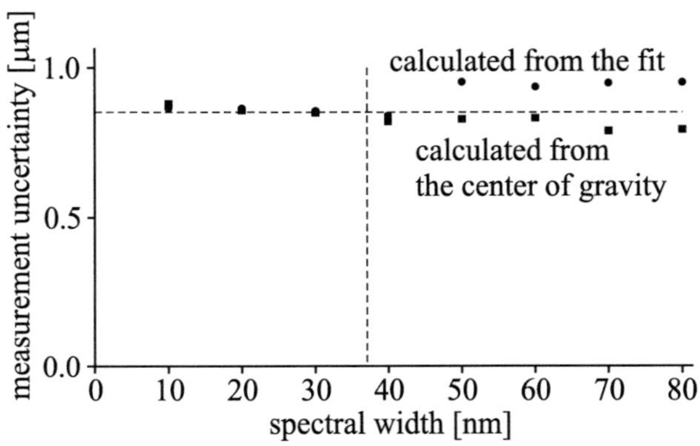

Fig. 8. Numerically calculated measurement uncertainty δz as a function of spectral width $\Delta\lambda$ for $\lambda_0 = 820nm$, $\sigma_h = 1.2\mu m$, $I_{\text{obj}} = \langle I_{\text{obj}} \rangle$, and NSR $= 0.05$.

The circles indicate the values calculated from the fit using the least-squares method. The squares correspond to the values calculated from the center of gravity of the correlogram envelope (Pavlíček & Hýbl, 2008). For small values of the spectral width, both methods yield approximately same results. The numerically calculated measurement uncertainty corresponds to the value calculated using Eqs. (29), (1), and (6). This value is indicated by the horizontal dashed line for the respective values of σ_h, I_{obj}, and NSR. In fact, the line is slightly inclined because the measurement uncertainty caused by shot noise depends on spectral width of the used light according to Eq. (6).
After the spectral width exceeds the spectral width corresponding to the limit coherence length given by Eq. (5), the values calculated from the fit begin to differ from those calculated from the center of gravity. The limit spectral width for the respective values of σ_h and I_{obj} is indicated by the vertical dashed line in Fig. 8. The measurement uncertainty calculated

from the fit begins to increase. The reason is the distortion of the correlogram as shown in Fig. 3. The fitting of the envelope and its evaluation by means of least-squares method is no more as accurate as for an undistorted correlogram. On the other hand, the evaluation of a distorted correlogram by means of the center of gravity is more accurate than that of an undistorted correlogram (Pavlíček & Hýbl, 2008). For a light source with an extremely large spectral width $\Delta\lambda = 120nm$ (other conditions are the same as above), the measurement uncertainty calculated from the center of gravity sinks to $0.770\mu m$.

5. Conclusion

The influence of rough surface and shot noise on measurement uncertainty of white-light interferometry on rough surface has been investigated. It has shown that both components of measurement uncertainty add geometrically. The numerical simulations have shown that the influence of the rough surface on the measurement uncertainty is for usual values of spectral width, sampling step and noise-to-signal ratio significantly higher than that of shot noise. The influence of rough surface prevails over the influence of shot noise. The obtained results determine limits under which the conditions for white-light interferometry can be regarded as usual. For low values of spectral width and high values of sampling step and noise-to-signal ratio, the influence of the noise must be taken into account.

6. Acknowledgement

This research was supported financially by Operational Program Research and Development for Innovations - European Social Fund (project CZ.1.05/2.1.00/03.0058 of the Ministry of Education, Youth and Sports of the Czech Republic).

7. References

Born, M. & Wolf, E. (2003). *Principles of Optics*, Cambridge University Press, Cambridge.

Dresel, T. (1991). *Grundlagen und Grenzen der 3D-Datengewinnung*, Master's thesis, University Erlangen-Nuremberg, Erlangen.

Dresel, T., Häusler, G. & Venzke, H. (1992). Three-dimensional sensing of rough surfaces by coherence radar, *Applied Optics* Vol. 31 (No. 7): 919–925.

George, N. & Jain, A. (1973). Speckle reduction using multiple tones of illumination, *Applied Optics* Vol. 12 (No. 6): 1202–1212.

Goodman, J. W. (1984). Statistical properties of laser speckle patterns, *in* Dainty, J. C. (ed.), *Speckle and Related Phenomena*, Springer-Verlag, pp. 9–75.

Häusler, G., Ettl, P., Schenk, M., Bohn, G. & László, I. (1999). Limits of optical range sensors and how to exploit them, *in International Trends in Optics and Photonics ICO IV*, Vol. 74 Springer Series in Optical Sciences, Springer-Verlag, Berlin, pp. 328–342.

Häusler, G. (2005). Speckle and coherence, *in* Guenther, B. D. (ed.), *Encyclopedia of Modern Optics*, Elsevier, Academic Press, Amsterdam, pp. 114–123.

Horváth, P., Hrabovský, M. & Bača, Z. (2002). Statistical properties of a speckle pattern, *in Proc. SPIE*, Vol. 4888, pp. 99–108.

Kino, G. S. & Chim, S. S. C. (1990). Mirau correlation microscope, *Applied Optics* Vol. 29 (No. 26): 3775–3783.

Lee, B. S. & Strand, T. C. (1990). Profilometry with a coherence scanning microscope, *Applied Optics* Vol. 29 (No. 26): 3784–3788.

Onodera, R., Watanebe, H. & Ishii, Y. (2005). Interferometric phase-measurement using a one-dimensional discrete Hilbert transform, *Optical Rewiev* Vol. 12 (No. 1): 29–36.

Parry, G. (1984). Speckle patterns in partially coherent light, *in* Dainty, J. C. (ed.), *Speckle and Related Phenomena*, Springer-Verlag, pp. 77–121.

Pavlíček, P. & Hýbl, O. (2008). White-light interferometry on rough surfaces – measurement uncertainty caused by surface roughness, *Applied Optics* Vol. 47 (No. 16): 2941–2949.

Pavlíček, P. & Hýbl, O. (2011). Pavlíček, P. Palacky University, Faculty of Science, Regional Centre of Advanced Technologies and Materials, Joint Laboratory of Optics of Palacky University and Institute of Physics of Academy of Science of the Czech Republic, & Hýbl, O. are preparing a manuscript to be called: Theoretical limits of the measurement uncertainty of white-light interferometry.

Peřina, J. (1991). *Quantum statistics of linear and nonlinear optical phenomena*, Kluwer Academic Publishers, Dordrecht.

Press, W. H., Teukolsky, S. A., Vettering W. T. & Flannery B. P. (1992). *Numerical Recipes in C: The Art of Scientific Computing*, Cambridge University Press, Cambridge.

Soubusta, J., Haderka, O., Hendrych, M. & Pavlíček, P. (2003). Experimental realization of quantum random generator, *in Proc. SPIE*, Vol. 5259, pp. 7–13.

23

On the Double-Arcing Phenomenon in a Cutting Arc Torch

Leandro Prevosto[1], Héctor Kelly[1,2] and Beatriz Mancinelli[1]
[1]*Grupo de Descargas Eléctricas, Departamento Ing. Electromecánica, Facultad Regional Venado Tuerto (UTN), Laprida 651, Venado Tuerto (2600), Santa Fe*
[2]*Instituto de Física del Plasma (CONICET), Departamento de Física, Facultad de Ciencias Exactas y Naturales (UBA) Ciudad Universitaria Pab. I, (1428), Buenos Aires Argentina*

1. Introduction

Transferred arc plasma torches are widely used in industrial cutting process of metallic materials because of their ability to cut almost any metal and the very high productivity that can be achieved with this technology (Boulos et al., 1994).

The plasma cutting process is characterized by a transferred electric arc that is established between a cathode, which is a part of the cutting torch, and a work-piece (the metal to be cut) acting as the anode. In order to obtain a high-quality cut, the plasma jet must be as collimated as possible and also must have a high power density. To this end, the transferred arc is constricted by a metallic tube (a nozzle) with a small inner diameter (of the order of one millimeter). Usually, a vortex-type flow with large axial and azimuthal velocity components is forced through the nozzle to provide arc stability and to protect its inner wall. In such case the hot arc is confined to the center of the nozzle, while centrifugal forces drive the colder fluid towards the nozzle walls, which are thus thermally protected. The axial component of the gas flow continuously supplies cold fluid, providing an intense convective cooling at the arc fringes. In addition, the vortex flow enhances the power dissipation per unit length of the arc column, resulting in high temperatures at the arc axis. Since the nozzle is subjected to a very high heat flux, it is made of a metal with a high thermal conductivity (copper is broadly used). The arc current is of the order of ten up to a few hundred amperes, and the gas pressure is several atmospheres. Arc axis temperatures around 15 kK are usual, but larger values, close to 25 kK or even higher, have been reached. A typical configuration of a cutting torch is presented in Fig. 1(a).

The most explored region of plasma in an arc cutting system is the arc column located between the nozzle exit and the work-piece. The experimental data from that region are obtained usually by non-invasive spectroscopic techniques (Girard et at., 2006; Peters et al., 2007; Freton et al., 2002, 2003; Pardo et al., 1999). Recently, also Langmuir probes have been used for plasma diagnostics in this kind of arcs (Prevosto et al., 2008a, 2008b, 2009a). However, due to the smallness of the nozzle bore, and the hostile conditions occurring inside such arcs, access to experimental information about the plasma state inside the nozzle region is out of reach to most plasma diagnostics; thus the published experimental data on the arc column located between the cathode and the nozzle exit are very scarce (Prevosto et al., 2009b). Numerical simulations are usually used to study this region. However, most of the developed numerical simulations are based on the plasma local thermodynamic equilibrium (LTE) assumption (Freton et al., 2002, 2003; Gonzalez-Aguilar et al., 1999), in spite of the fact that substantial deviations from LTE should occur at the arc boundary inside the torch, where the electron density is presumably much lower than that prescribed by the Griem´s criterion for LTE equilibrium (Boulos et al., 1994); and where very high temperature gradients may be present over the last few electron Debye lengths from the nozzle wall. Only recently, a non- local thermodynamic equilibrium (NLTE) modelling of a 200 A oxygen-plasma cutting torch was presented (Ghorui et al., 2007). In this work, it was shown that the electron temperature remained high near the nozzle wall and hence well decoupled from the heavy particle temperature. For instance, an electron temperature of about 12000 K was reported for the arc boundary at the nozzle exit (a value much higher than the heavy particle temperature of about 1000 K close to the inner nozzle wall temperature).

The problem of sheath formation at the plasma boundary is of importance for nearly all applications where the plasma is confined totally or partially to a finite volume by solid walls – as in the case of cutting torch nozzles–(Riemann, 1991). When a plasma is in contact with a negatively biased surface (with a biasing voltage of the order or lower than the floating value), a strong electric field appears between the NLTE plasma and that surface. This sheath becomes positively charged, rejecting electrons from the plasma and attracting ions to the negatively biased wall. The typical thickness of the sheath as compared with the characteristic lengths of the plasma (e.g., ion mean-free-path) determines the collisional degree of the sheath. Three regimes of sheath behavior can appear in high pressure plasmas. There is a collision-dominated (i.e., mobility limited) regime when the sheath thickness is larger than the ion mean free path, a collisionless regime when the sheath is very thin, and a transition regime when both lengths are comparable. For the collision-dominated regime, expressions that describe the sheath have been developed for both the cases of constant ion mean-free-path, and constant ion mobility (Franklin, 2002a; Riemann, 2003; Sheridan & Goeckner, 1995). In the opposite limit, when ion collisions are negligible, Child's law gives a simple description of the sheath (Raizer, 1991). The number of ion mean-free-paths in the sheath needed to cause the transition from the collisionless to the collision-dominated regime for the constant mean-free-path model is only about one-half (Sheridan & Goree, 1991).

For high-pressure weakly ionized plasmas the sheath thickness is usually large compared with the ion mean-free-path, and the sheath is collision-dominated. Such a picture corresponds to the space-charge sheath formed between the NLTE plasma and the nozzle wall inside of a cutting torch because, as it will be shown later, the electron temperature is low. Near the plasma-sheath boundary the electric field accelerating the ions toward the walls is negligible. Thus the fluid velocity of the ions is small as compared to their thermal motion and the collision frequency is independent of the ion fluid velocity. On the other hand, well inside the sheath region, the electric field accelerates the ions to velocities comparable or larger than its thermal speed, and the collision frequency becomes proportional to the ion drift velocity. There is a smooth transition from a constant collision frequency of the ions within the plasma at the sheath edge to an approximately constant mean-free-path of the ions at the sheath region close to the wall where a high electric field exists. A smooth transition between these two ion collision approximations appears where the potential drop over an ion mean-free-path becomes comparable to the ion thermal energy (Sternovsky & Robertson, 2006).

In the normal mode of operation –Fig. 1(a)–, the nozzle is a floating conductor (i.e., it is not electrically connected to any part of the torch electric circuit). However, such operating mode is somewhat unstable. The much higher electrical conductivity of the nozzle as compared with that of the confined arc column would cause instability. Under certain operating conditions (too large arc current, too small gas mass flow, or a nozzle with a too small bore diameter or with a too large length) the level of arc stabilization provided by the vortex flow can be insufficient and the arc, which normally connects the cathode and the work-piece, is broken into two. One of them connects the cathode with the nozzle and the other connects the nozzle with the anode –see Fig. 1(b)–; following the path of smallest electrical resistance. Such type of arc instability is called double-arcing. From a practical point of view, the double-arcing is very undesirable; since the arc roots on the nozzle wall (especially that corresponding to the arc originated from the cathode) usually destroy the nozzle almost instantaneously (Nemchinsky & Severance, 2006). However, in a recent review (Colombo et al, 2009); high-speed images of a "non-destructive" double-arcing with a short duration (< 1 ms) were registered in cutting torches at low gas flow rates.

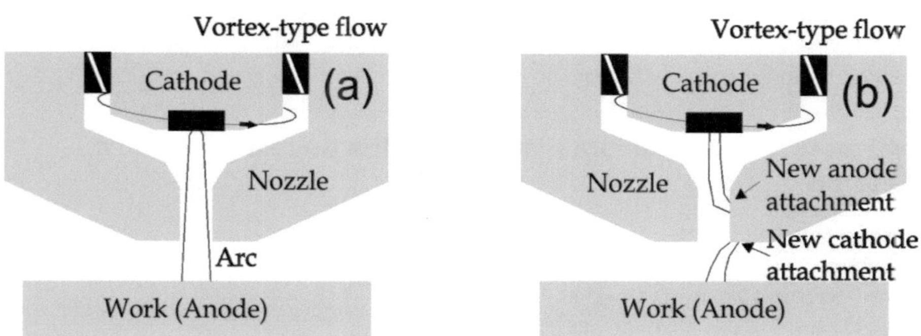

Fig. 1. Normal (a) and double-arcing (b) modes of nozzle operation of transferred arc cutting torch.

The aim of this chapter is to presents a comprehensive study of the double-arcing phenomenon which, as quoted above, is one of the main drawbacks that put limits to increasing capabilities of the plasma arc cutting process. Surprisingly, relatively little has been done to explore and understand this process, keeping in mind that the double-arcing is common not only to arc cutting but to other industrial processes as well. Section 2 presents some hypothesis suggested in the literature on the physical mechanism that triggers the double-arcing in cutting torches. In Section 3, an experimental study carried out by the authors is presented. The starting point for such a study is the analysis and interpretation of the nozzle current-voltage characteristic curve. Since there is no comprehensive theory for interpreting the electron branch in highly collisional plasmas, only the ion branch is analyzed. The influence of the collisions on the physical structure of the plasma-nozzle transition has been considered under the typical assumption of constant ion mean free path. Within this assumption and using an approximate analytical solution for the sheath thickness, the value of the ion flux to the wall is related to the nozzle voltage and the electron temperature and density at the plasma boundary. To describe the plasma composition an appropriate non-equilibrium two-temperature statistical model was used. A physical interpretation on the origin of the double-arcing phenomenon is presented, that explains why the double-arcing (that it is established when the space-charge sheath adjacent to the nozzle wall breaks-down) appears for example at low values of the gas mass flow. A complementary numerical study of the space-charge sheath formed between the plasma and the nozzle wall of a cutting torch is also reported in Section 4. The numerical study corresponds to a collision-dominated model (ion mobility-limited motion) for the hydrodynamic description of the sheath adjacent to the nozzle wall inside of a cutting torch. The model does not assume cold ions so drift-diffusion type equations are used. Also an improved expression for the ion-neutral momentum transfer is employed, instead of the classical ion collision approximations (constant ion mean free path, and constant ion collision frequency). The ion and electron densities, electrostatic potential and ion velocity distributions are calculated inside the sheath. Boundary conditions for the numerical solutions within this sheath are based on experimental plasma data previously obtained by the authors. A physical explanation on the origin of the transient double-arcing (the so called non-destructive double-arcing) in cutting torches is reported in Section 5. Against to the proposed hypothesis (Colombo et al., 2009; Nemchinsky 2009) which assumes a transient arc voltage rise due to dielectric films deposited on the nozzle surface (which are later either carried away by the gas flow or are burned out); the experimental observations suggest that such a phenomenon is related with a strong dynamics of the space-charge sheath contiguous to the nozzle due to the arc power source ripple. Conclusions are summarized in Section 6.

2. On the physical mechanism that triggers the double-arcing in a cutting torch

In practice, a double-arcing event is seen to occur when some of the following conditions are accomplished:
(1) the arc current is too high, and/or
(2) the nozzle bore is too narrow, and/or
(3) the nozzle is too large, and/or
(4) the gas flow is too low and/or
(5) the gas flow does not have enough swirl.
Under conditions (1)-(5), the arc voltage drop inside the nozzle is high, especially when the arc current is highly constricted or the nozzle is large. For example, in a 30 A high-energy density cutting torch as is shown in Fig. 2, the measured electric field value (an average along the nozzle) is about of 11 V/mm, resulting in an arc voltage drop about of 50 V.
Before double-arcing conditions, the total current to the nozzle is zero, since the nozzle is electrically floating. However, as the whole nozzle is at a constant voltage (equipotential), each axial portion of the nozzle surface is facing an arc portion with different plasma voltage. This means that the voltage drop between the arc and the nozzle surface varies in the axial direction, and hence some portions of the nozzle surface can be collecting ions while other axial portions will collect electrons. This situation does not alter the floating character of the nozzle, because the zero current balance is fulfilled not locally (by an ambipolar flux to the nozzle), but globally on the whole body of the nozzle. Furthermore, taking into account the fact that the electrical current is almost carried by electrons, the electron collecting section of the nozzle will be very short compared to the ion collecting section. This implies that the nozzle floating potential must be close to the arc voltage at the nozzle inlet. Hence, the voltage drop between the metallic nozzle and the plasma at the nozzle exit will reach a value very close to the total arc voltage drop inside the nozzle (estimated in the previous example in about 50 V).

It has been suggested in several published works (Nemchinsky, 1998; Prevosto et al, 2009b, 2009c) that the reason for double-arcing is the high voltage drop inside the nozzle. However, the specific mechanism that triggers the double-arcing event is less clear. It was suggested (Nemchinsky, 1998; Nemchinsky & Severance, 2006) that the voltage drop inside the nozzle is concentrated across the gas envelope (i.e., the cold quasi-neutral plasma layer) that separates the hot plasma and the nozzle. In particular, in the above quoted operation conditions–(1) to (5)–, the thickness of the cold envelope could be very low and the plasma voltage drop inside the nozzle will be high. Therefore, the plasma-nozzle voltage drop will also be high (especially at axial positions close to the nozzle exit) and the electric field strength inside the cold envelope could be very close to the threshold value necessary to develop a Townsend avalanche, triggering the double-arcing. However, some experimental results (Prevosto et al., 2009b) suggest that the voltage drop inside the nozzle is concentrated in the space charge sheath formed between the quasi-neutral plasma and the nozzle wall and not in the quasi-neutral plasma, as it was previously suggested. Furthermore, a complementary numerical approach for describing the sheath structure (Prevosto et al., 2009c), suggest a possible breakdown mechanism based on the local electric field strength intensification at the nozzle wall close to the bore exit. This enhanced field could be strong enough to trigger a breakdown even if the average electric field across the sheath is not strong enough. Recently (Nemchinsky, 2009), it was proposed another breakdown mechanism where dielectric films deposited on the nozzle wall would play a key role. Such a mechanism explains the relative ease of double-arcing with worn consumables (cathode and nozzle). However, experimental evidence is required to support (or disapprove) such hypothesis.

3. An experiment to infer the plasma-nozzle sheath structure

3.1 Experimental details

The metallic nozzle that bounds the arc can be considered itself as a large-sized Langmuir probe, and hence it can be used to collect charges from the contiguous plasma (i.e., to build the current-voltage characteristic curve of the nozzle) and therefore to obtain information about the plasma state inside it. The necessary condition for a comprehensive use of the probe (that is: the plasma should not be perturbed sufficiently far away from the probe surface) is fully accomplished since the nozzle-probe behaves as a natural boundary to the arc.

To obtain the current-voltage nozzle characteristic, it was necessary to bias the nozzle (that under normal arc operation remains floating –see Fig. 1(a)–). The nozzle biasing circuit is shown in Fig. 2. Different nozzle bias voltages V_N were obtained using a high-impedance rheostat, and were registered (with respect to the grounded anode) by using a voltage meter. Alternatively, a two-channel digital oscilloscope (Tektronix TDS 1002 B) with a sampling rate of 500 MS/s and a analogical bandwidth of 60 MHz was used to register eventual fluctuations induced by the arc power source ripple. The nozzle current i was calculated from the voltage drop V_0 through a small resistance R_0. Alternatively, the nozzle was disconnected to perform nozzle floating voltage measurements. To determine the plasma floating potential close to the nozzle exit, sweeping electrostatic probes previously developed (Prevosto et al., 2008a) were employed.

Experiments were conducted using a high-energy density cutting torch as is shown in Fig. 2. It consists of a cathode centered above an orifice in a converging-straight copper nozzle without liquid cooling. The cathode was made of copper (7 mm in diameter) with a hafnium tip (1.5 mm in diameter) inserted at the cathode center. A flow of oxygen gas cooled the cathode and the nozzle and was also employed as the plasma gas. The gas passed through a swirl ring to provide arc stability. The nozzle consisted in a converging-straight bore (with a bore radius R_N = 0.5 mm and a length L_N = 4.5 mm) in a copper holder surrounding the cathode (with a separation of 0.5 mm between the holder and the cathode surface). To avoid plasma contamination by metal vapors from the anode, a rotating steel disk with 200 mm in diameter and 15 mm thickness was used as the anode (Ramakrishnan et al., 1997). In this study, the disk upper surface was located at 5 mm from the nozzle exit. The arc was transferred to the edge of the disk, and the rotating frequency of the disk was equal to 29.5 Hz. At this velocity, a well-stabilized arc column was obtained, and the lateral surface of the anode disc was completely not melted. Thus, practically no metal vapors from the anode were present in the arc. A 3-phase transductor type of power supply with a root-mean-square (RMS) ripple value of 7 % was used to run the torch. The ripple level was eventually reduced to 3 % (RMS value) by using a high-impedance inductor choke. The fundamental ripple frequency was in all the cases 150 Hz. The measured arc torch operating conditions were: the arc current I, the chamber pressure (p_{ch}) and the gas mass flow rate ($\dot{m}$). During the experiments the arc current was fixed at 30 A.

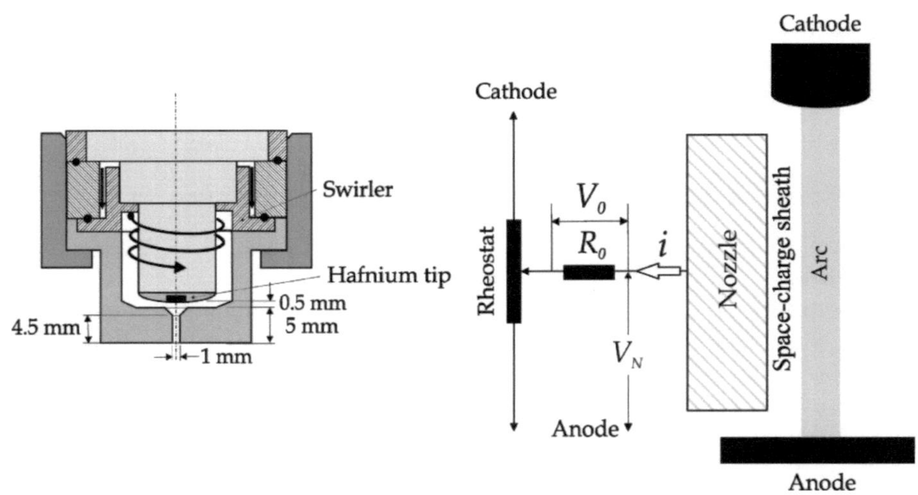

Fig. 2. Scheme of the biasing nozzle circuit and the physical structure of the plasma contiguous to the nozzle surface (right). At the left a schematic of the arc torch indicating several geometric dimensions is also presented.

3.2 Experimental data

A typical current–voltage nozzle characteristic curve (with the electron current considered as positive) based on the voltage meter measurements (i.e., -RMS- values of i and V_N) is shown in Fig. 3. This figure corresponds to $\dot{m} = 0.54\ \mathrm{g\,s^{-1}}$, p_{ch} = 0.65 MPa and a power source ripple level of 3 %. A detail of the ion branch with an enlarged current scale is shown. For comparison purposes the ion branches corresponding to other $\dot{m}$ values have been included in Fig. 3. The intersection points of the ion branches with the zero-current line (i.e., the nozzle floating voltage values) are clearly identified. For the smallest $\dot{m}$ value double-arcing was found for V_N = -155 ± 5 V. Using a well-known relationship between the floating and plasma potential (Raizer, 1997), that establishes that the difference between these two potentials is a linear function of the electron temperature, it is possible to derive the plasma potential. For the electron temperature range of interest (12000 to 16000) K (Prevosto et al., 2008b), and from the plasma floating value at the nozzle exit obtained with the electrostatic probe under this operating condition (= -30 ± 3 V); a plasma potential value of ≈ -22 V was obtained.

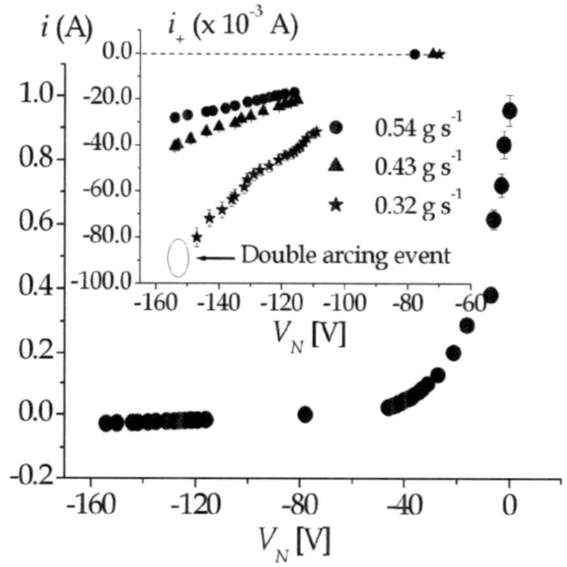

Fig. 3. Nozzle i-V_N characteristic for the largest gas mass flow used. A detail of the ion branches for several gas mass flow values is also shown. Taken from Prevosto et al., 2009b.

From Fig. 3, note also that the largest electron current drained from the arc is relatively small ≈ 1 A, notwithstanding the fact that the size of the nozzle is quite large. This fact reflects the existence of a very low electron density close to the nozzle wall. Also note the great difference between the intensities of the ion and electron collected currents, indicating that in this experimental conditions electron attachment is not significant. These features were common to all the $\dot{m}$ values investigated. Concerning to the ion branches shown in Fig. 3, note that the current drained by the nozzle increases when $\dot{m}$ decreases. Also note that no ion saturation current was found. This behaviour is similar to those presented in wall-stabilized arc experiments with (Hill & Jones, 1979) or without externally imposed axial gas flow (George & Richards, 1968)

3.3 Data interpretation

As quoted before, it has been suggested that the double-arcing is triggered by the high voltage drop inside the nozzle. From Fig. 3 a total voltage drop of 133 ± 5 V can be derived as the voltage breakdown value at the nozzle exit for $\dot{m} = 0.32\,\mathrm{g\,s^{-1}}$. That voltage drop results from a plasma potential of - 22 V minus a nozzle voltage of – 155 V. For the other larger investigated $\dot{m}$ values the nozzle voltage could be lowered up to values very close to the cathode voltage without evidence of any breakdown. According to Paschen's law (Raizer, 1997) the breakdown voltage value depends on the gas layer thickness D times the gas density n_n. A reasonable estimation of n_n at the nozzle exit can be obtained by taking an outer value of 0.1 MPa for the gas pressure and by assuming a heavy particle (gas) temperature T_h close to the estimated nozzle inner wall temperature ($T_h \approx 1000$ K). Therefore, neglecting the plasma pressure (this assumption will be verified later in this chapter) it results $n_n \approx 7.2 \times 10^{24}$ m^{-3}. Using the inferred n_n value and the total voltage drop (133 V) across the gas layer thickness together with the experimentally determined Paschen's law for an oxygen gas (Hackam, 1969), a threshold value $D = 20 \pm 2$ μm was determined at the nozzle exit. This means that for sheath thickness equal or shorter than that threshold breakdown will occur between the arc plasma edge and the nozzle, thus triggering the double-arcing. To relate D with the plasma characteristic it was assumed that D corresponds to the thickness of the electrical boundary layer that appears between the unperturbed plasma and the nozzle wall. Such an assumption will be later verified.

Due to the high operating gas pressure values and the relatively low electron density (n_e) at the plasma boundary, we will also assume that this layer is fully-collisional. When the sheath is collisional and without ionization (because both, the electron density and the thickness of the sheath are small), there is a smooth joining between the plasma and the space-charge layer without the need of introducing a transitional sheath (i.e., the pre-sheath) (Blank, 1968; Franklin, 2003a, 2003b, 2004). The thickness of such a fully-collisional space-charge layer that appears between the nozzle wall and the NLTE plasma in a cutting torch can be approximated in terms of the plasma-wall voltage drop ($\Delta V^{\circ} V_N - V_p$ where V_p is the plasma potential.) as (Sheridan & Goree, 1991)

$$D» 2.2 \times 10^4 \, \Delta V^{3/5} \, n_e^{-1/2} \, T_e^{-1/10} , \qquad (1)$$

where all the physical variables are given in MKS units (T_e is the electron temperature). In NLTE plasmas, when the particle population in the different energy levels is still dominated by electron collisions, the non-equilibrium generalized Saha-equation (van de Sanden et al., 1989) is appropriate to describe the composition of the quasi-neutral plasma. For the first ionization

$$\frac{n_e n_i}{n_n} = 2 \frac{Q_i}{Q_0} \left(\frac{2\pi \, m k \, T_e}{h^2} \right)^{3/2} \exp\left(-\frac{E_I}{k \, T_e} \right) , \qquad (2)$$

(where n_i is the ion density, Q_i and Q_o are the statistical weights of oxygen ions and atoms, m is the electron mass, k is the Boltzmann's constant, h is the Planck's constant and E_I is the ionization energy of the oxygen atoms). Also the neutrality equation can be used for the unperturbed plasma region at the sheath edge,

$$n_e \approx n_i \, . \qquad (3)$$

Employing the derived threshold D value, together with the already calculated neutral gas density ($n_n \approx 7.2 \times 10^{24}$ m^{-3}) and the equations (1) to (3); the plasma values T_e and n_e (evaluated at the sheath edge) at the nozzle exit are $n_e \approx 7.5 \times 10^{19}$ m^{-3} and $T_e \approx 5700$ K. Note that the obtained value for n_e is well below the lower limiting value to apply local thermodynamic equilibrium in accord with Griem's criterion ($\geq 10^{23}\ \mathrm{m}^{-3}$). Also note that in this region the plasma pressure ($kn_e(T_e + T_h) \approx 10\ \mathrm{Pa}$) results much lower than the gas pressure, which justify the assumption made in the estimation of the gas density at the nozzle exit.

The physical picture presented up to now can be used to look for an explanation of the behaviour of the nozzle ion branch characteristic. The ion current (i_+) collected by the nozzle can be written as

$$i_+ = 2\pi R_N\, e \int_{z=0}^{z=L_N} n_{is}\, u_{is}\, dz \tag{4}$$

where z is the coordinate directed along the nozzle wall and the ion density and velocity must be evaluated at the sheath edge. Due to the collisional regime of the sheath, the ion entrance velocity is (Franklin, 2002b)

$$u_{is} \approx u_B \left(\lambda_+ / \lambda_{Ds} \right)^{1/2}, \tag{5}$$

which is lower than the Bohm velocity (u_B). (λ_+ is the collisional ion mean free path and λ_{Ds} is the electron Debye length at the layer entrance). It should be noted that because the sheath thickness depends on the nozzle voltage value –equation (1)–, the presented physical picture suggest that a larger ΔV value produces a thicker sheath and hence the plasma is "probed" at different radial positions producing different current values to the nozzle. This fact explains the lack of saturation in the ion branch. It is interesting to note that, since the expected values of T_e are around 5000-6000 K (according to what was found with the breakdown estimation), the generalized Saha equation (2) predicts a very strong dependence of n_e on T_e, thus resulting in very small variations of T_e that are able to produce large enough variations of n_e that in turn can explain the behaviour of the characteristic. In order to invert equation (4), the z-dependence of the integrand must be known. To do this, the following assumptions were made: 1) a linear variation of the pressure (p) and V_p on z, 2) a constant value for T_e in the axial direction (an average along the nozzle length) at a radial position close to the nozzle wall.

Assumptions 1) and 2) have been shown to be valid in cutting torches (Pardo et al., 1999; Freton et al., 2002; Ghorui et al., 2007). In any case, the obtained solution is almost insensitive to the particular chosen variations of p since the dependence of the integral in equation (4) with n_n is very weak (leading to a dependence of the kind $n_n^{1/8}$). To calculate the electrostatic potential of the plasma it is necessary to know its value in two different axial positions. Both values have been previously inferred from the experiments. For instance for $\dot{m} = 0.32\ \mathrm{g\,s^{-1}}$ the values of V_p are: $V_p(z=L) \approx -22\ \mathrm{V}$ and $V_p(z=0) \approx -70\ \mathrm{V}$ (see Fig. 3). The resulting value of the constant axial electric field in this case is 11 V/mm. From assumption 2) T_e only depends on the radial coordinate r and it can written in a simple form as a polynomial expansion

$$T_e(r) = a_0 + a_1\, r + a_2\, r^2 + \ldots + a_{q-1}\, r^{q-1}, \tag{6}$$

where $a_0, a_1, ..., a_{q-1}$ are q unknown constant numerical coefficients. Then replacing n_e in terms of T_e (evaluated at the sheath edge $T_e(r = R_N - D)$) through Saha equation in equation (1), the z dependence of the sheath thickness D as a function of the quoted unknown q numerical coefficients is found. Hence equation (4) can be integrated for q points of the ion branch characteristic to produce a closed system of equations.

It should be noted that in this kind of cutting torches, the arc is extremely constricted, resulting in high pressures, high current densities and correspondingly high temperatures on the arc axis. So the radiative arc loses are a significant fraction of the electrical power input with a strong contribution in the UV range (Shayler & Fang, 1978). Using the NEC model (Naghizadeh-Kashani et al., 2002) for an atmospheric pressure oxygen plasma, and a copper photoemission coefficient $\gamma_v \approx 10^{-4}$ (Dowell et al., 2006); the maximum photoelectron current from the nozzle surface results ≈ 10 mA. This photoelectron current will not depend on the nozzle voltage, and only could produce a change in the characteristic curves at the vicinities of the nozzle floating voltage value (see Fig. 3). For this reason, the characteristic region near the floating voltage was not considered in the inversion of equation (4). With all these considerations, and using the well-known Chebyshev formula (Noble, 1964) to approximate the integrals of this system of equations, the inversion problem finally can be solved calculating the solution of the $q \times q$ system of equations in terms of the q numerical coefficients in equation (6). Thus the $T_e(r)$ profile that fits the characteristic ion branch in the radial range cover for the D values was found.

In practice for all the studied cases, a linear variation of $T_e(r)$ was found sufficient to fit the characteristic ion branches within the experimental uncertainty (≈ 5%), resulting mainly from statistical fluctuations of the current and voltage RMS values.

In Fig. 4 $D(z)$ for the different $\dot{m}$ values and for the largest nozzle voltage value registered in each characteristic ion branch is presented. It can be seen that for the lowest gas mass flow value ($\dot{m} = 0.32\,\mathrm{g\,s^{-1}}$) an almost constant $D(z) \approx 21\,\mu\mathrm{m}$ results. Note that the gas layer thickness at the nozzle exit value (≈ 20 ± 2 μm) inferred from the voltage breakdown measurement for this case is quite close to the predicted space-charge sheath thickness value (thus supporting the hypothesis of that the voltage drop inside the nozzle is concentrated in the space-charge layer, and not in the quasi-neutral plasma). In the other cases, a more marked increase with z appears in $D(z)$, varying in the range 26 to 30 μm for $\dot{m} = 0.43\,\mathrm{g\,s^{-1}}$ and 27 to 31 μm for $\dot{m} = 0.54\,\mathrm{g\,s^{-1}}$. These values are higher than the sheath thickness value corresponding to the lowest gas mass flow case, which is consistent with the absence of breakdown found in these cases. Concerning the validity of the colisional sheath assumption, the ratio of the sheath thickness to the ion mean free path results $D/\lambda_+ \approx 100$, showing that the above-mentioned assumption is fully satisfied.

In Fig. 5 the radial profiles of T_e corresponding to the registered ion branch characteristics are presented as a function of the radial coordinate measured from the nozzle wall (R_N - r). Fig. 5 shows that the values of T_e for the different $\dot{m}$ values are not very different (4700 to 5700 K), but there appear large and quite different T_e radial gradients. In fact, gradients of the order of 0.9 to 1.1 × 10^8 K m^{-1} for 0.43 to 0.54 g s^{-1} and 1.1 × 10^9 K m^{-1} for 0.32 gs^{-1} are found very close to the nozzle wall, thus supporting the assumption of the lack of LTE.

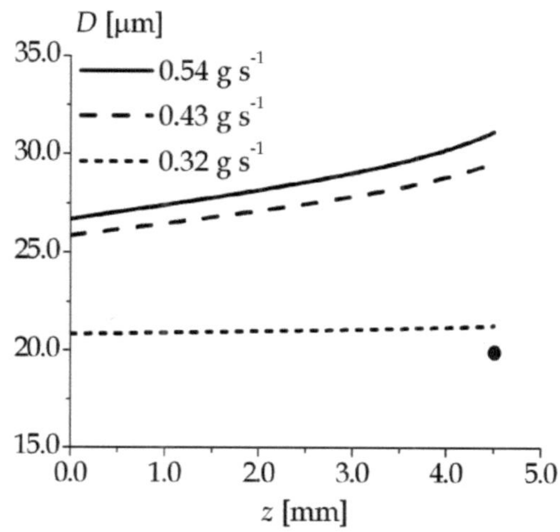

Fig. 4. Sheath thickness along the nozzle wall for the largest nozzle voltage value experimentally registered for each gas mass flow value. For comparative purposes, the black circle indicates the sheath thickness value inferred at the nozzle exit using the voltage breakdown measurement. Taken from Prevosto et al., 2009b.

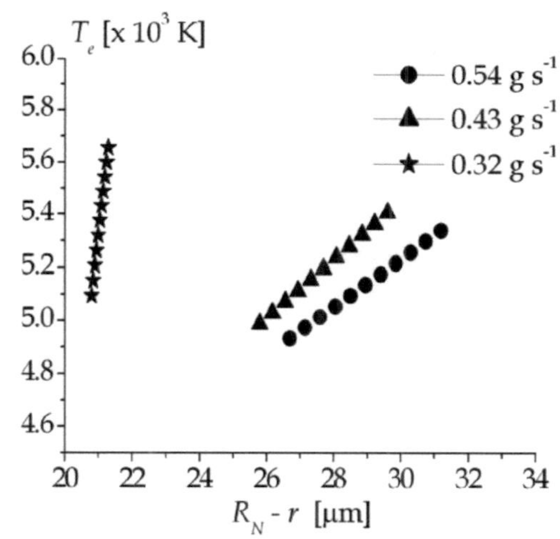

Fig. 5. Radial profiles of the average (along the nozzle wall) plasma electron temperature as a function of the radial position measured from the nozzle wall, for the different gas mass flow values. Taken from Prevosto et al., 2009b.

The spatial distribution of the plasma density is presented in Figs. 6a) and b), for a gas mass flow rate of 0.32 g s^{-1} and 0.54 g s^{-1}, respectively. A steep plasma density radial gradient is shown in Fig. 6a) due to the existence of very large electron temperature radial gradient close to the nozzle wall (see Fig. 5). Less marked plasma density gradients close to the nozzle wall are shown in Fig. 6b) for the largest gas mass flow rate registered. In both figures, the existence of a plasma pressure gradient along the nozzle produces the axial variation in the plasma density.

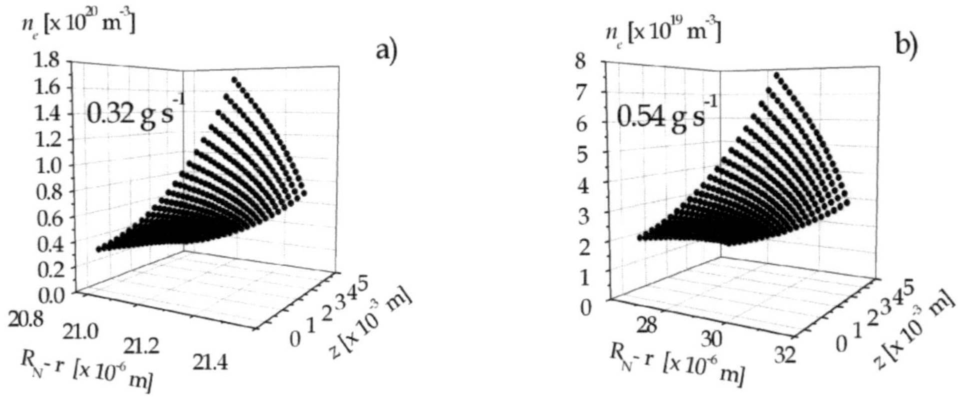

Fig. 6. a) Spatial distribution of the plasma density close to the nozzle wall for the lowest gas mass flow experimentally registered. b) Spatial distribution of the plasma density close to the nozzle wall for the largest gas mass flow experimentally registered. Taken from Prevosto et al., 2009b.

According to the experimental and theoretical results given above by Figs. 3 to 6, the physical structure of the electrical boundary layer is strongly influenced by the gas mass flow rate. The experimental results varying the $\dot{m}$ value show that the current drained by the nozzle increases (see Fig. 3) when the gas mass flow decreases until finally a breakdown appears, (see Figs. 4 to 6), in the sense that the T_e profile critically depends on the $\dot{m}$ value. When the $\dot{m}$ value decreases, very large T_e radial gradients (of the order of 10^9 K m^{-1}) produce (through Saha equation) steep n_e radial gradients over the last few Debye electron lengths from the nozzle wall. As a result, the sheath thickness is almost independent on the ΔV value, producing an almost constant (and thin) sheath thickness along the nozzle for low $\dot{m}$ values. Once the sheath thickness is smaller than the critical value, the space-charge sheath breaks-down leading to double-arcing. A good agreement between the critical value of the D thickness at the nozzle exit inferred from the voltage breakdown (under the Townsend breakdown hypothesis) and the predicted value was found.

4. Numerical model to describe the plasma-nozzle sheath structure at large negative bias voltages

4.1 Collisional sheath model

As quoted in Section 3, when both plasma and sheath are collisional, and when the ionization inside the sheath can be neglected, there is a smooth joining between the plasma and the space-charge layer, thus avoiding the need of the presence of a transitional sheath (the so called pre-sheath). Thus, the sheath edge coincides with the unperturbed quasi-neutral plasma. The model geometry showing the collisional space-charge sheath contiguous to the negatively biased nozzle is sketched in Fig. 7. Since the sheath remains thin as compared with the nozzle bore size (see Fig. 4) a planar geometry is used (y and x are the normal and axial coordinates with respect to the nozzle wall, see Fig. 7). At negative nozzle potentials (of the order or lower than the floating value), the electron density within the positive sheath remains small as compared to the ion density, so ionizations inside the sheath can be ignored. The elastic mean-free-paths for all species are much smaller than the sheath thickness, and therefore the fluid description applies. Steady-state conditions are assumed.

The governing equations (Goldston & Rutherford, 1995) are given by the ion continuity equation

$$\nabla\cdot(n_i \bar{u}_i) = 0 , \tag{7}$$

the electron continuity equation

$$\nabla\cdot(n_e \bar{u}_e) = 0 , \tag{8}$$

the ion momentum equation

$$n_i M(\bar{u}_i\cdot\nabla)\bar{u}_i = -\nabla(n_i kT_h) - en_i\nabla V_p + n_i M(\bar{u}_n - \bar{u}_i)\nu_i , \tag{9}$$

where $\bar{u}_e$ is the electron fluid velocity, M is the ion mass and e the electron charge. The last term of equation (9) represents the drag force due to the collisions between ions and neutrals. $\bar{u}_n$ is the neutral fluid velocity and ν_i the ion-neutral collision frequency for momentum transfer.
The electron momentum equation

$$n_e m(\bar{u}_e\cdot\nabla)\bar{u}_e = -\nabla(n_e kT_e) + en_e\nabla V_p - n_e m\bar{u}_e\nu_m , \tag{10}$$

where ν_m is the effective collision frequency for momentum transfer. Finally, Poisson's equation relates the difference between ion and electron densities within the sheath to the self-consistent potential

$$\varepsilon_0\nabla^2 V_p = -e(n_i - n_e) , \tag{11}$$

where ε_0 is the vacuum permittivity.

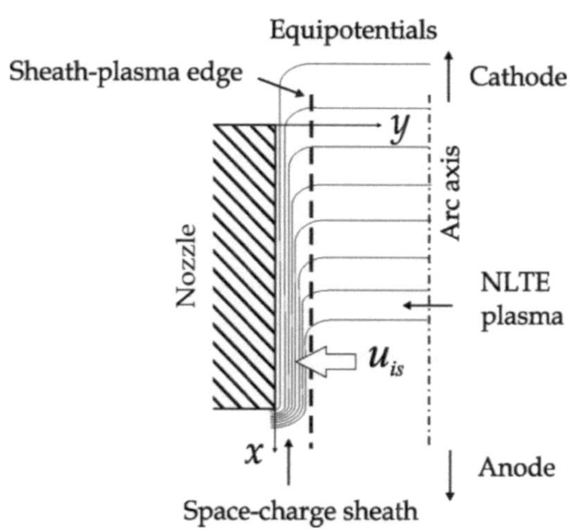

Fig. 7. Schematic of the sheath formed between the NLTE plasma and the nozzle wall. Taken from Prevosto et al., 2009c.

The inertial term can be safely dropped from equation (10) because of the smallness of the electron mass. Considering the Einstein relation equation (10) reduces to the total electron flux (Raizer, 1991)

$$\overline{\Gamma}_e \equiv n_e \overline{u}_e = n_e \mu_e \nabla V_p - D_e \nabla n_e , \tag{12}$$

where the usually small thermo-diffusion term (proportional to $-\nabla T_e$) was neglected in equation (10) as compared to the diffusion term (Raizer, 1991). μ_e and D_e are the electron mobility and diffusion coefficients. If the nozzle potential is sufficiently negative, due to the high mobility of the electrons, oppositely directed high diffusion and drift electron fluxes approximately balance each other to yield a small resultant total electron flux, comparable with (or less than) the ion flux. Hence $\overline{\Gamma}_e \approx 0$ in equation (12) and the electron density inside the sheath obeys the relation

$$n_e = n_{es} \exp\left[\frac{e\left(V_p - V_{ps}\right)}{kT_e}\right], \tag{13}$$

where n_{es} and V_{ps} are the density and the electrostatic potential of the plasma at the sheath-plasma edge. The neutral particles are considered at rest (i.e. $u_i >> u_n$). To close the model, an expression for the ion momentum transfer by elastic collisions must be established. Two special cases are usually treated in the literature (Franklin, 2002a; Riemann, 2003): constant ion mean-free-path and constant ion collision frequency. In the first case, the basic assumption is $e\left|\nabla V_p\right|\lambda_i >> kT_h$, which means that the ion drift velocity is much larger than the ion thermal velocity. Hence the drag force is modeled by $-Mu_i\overline{u}/\lambda_i$, where the ion mean-free-path $\lambda_i \equiv (n_n \sigma)^{-1}$ is constant (σ is the momentum transfer cross section for elastic collisions between ions and neutrals). The collision frequency $\nu_i = u_i/\lambda_i$ depends in this case on the ion fluid velocity. In the opposite limit the assumption $e\left|\nabla V_p\right|\lambda_i << kT_h$ applies. If this condition is satisfied, the ion fluid velocity is much smaller than its thermal speed. The collision frequency of the ions is thus determined by their random thermal motion rather than their fluid velocity and thus $\nu_i = \sqrt{2}\, u_{th} / \lambda_i$. In this relation the ion thermal velocity is given as $u_{th} = \sqrt{8kT_h / (\pi M)}$, and the constant ion collision frequency is independent of the fluid velocity. The factor $2^{1/2}$ is due to the mutual motion of the ions and neutral assuming the same temperature for both species (Boulos et al., 1994). The drag force in this case is given as $-M\nu_i\overline{u}_i$. Both physical approximations assume that the collision cross section is independent of the ion fluid velocity. At high pressures, for strongly collisional sheaths, the constant ion mean-free-path approximation applies close to the wall where the electric field strength is stronger. On the other hand, the constant ion mobility approximation (constant ion collision frequency) is physically more accurate at the sheath-plasma edge (where the electric field is relatively weak). In the transition region, the collision frequency is given by $\nu_i(u_i) = \sqrt{(\nu_\lambda)^2 + (\nu_\nu)^2}$ (Sternovsky & Robertson, 2006) where ν_λ and ν_ν are the ion collision frequencies in the previously quoted approximations. Following this approach, the ion collision frequency can be written as

$$\nu_i(u_i) = \frac{\sqrt{u_i^2 + 2u_{th}^2}}{\lambda_i}. \tag{14}$$

In spite of the collisional nature of the sheath, inelastic electron collisions are very rare and also the electron energy transfer to heavy particles by elastic collisions is small. Therefore, it can be assumed that $T_e \approx$ constant inside the sheath, with a value corresponding to the sheath-plasma edge value.

The model is now closed. In the limit of strong ion-neutral collisions (i.e., the mobility-limited ion motion approximation) the collision parameter D/λ_i is large as was shown in Subsection 3.3. In such circumstances equation (9) is simplified by neglecting the convective term on its left hand side. Combining equations (7), (9), (11), (13) and (14), a system of coupled partial differential equations for describing the mobility-limited ion colisional sheath was obtained.

$$\frac{\partial(n_i u_{ix})}{\partial x} + \frac{\partial(n_i u_{iy})}{\partial y} = 0, \tag{15}$$

$$-\frac{\partial(n_i k T_h)}{\partial x} - e n_i \frac{\partial V_p}{\partial x} - n_i M u_{ix} \nu_i = 0, \tag{16}$$

$$-\frac{\partial(n_i k T_h)}{\partial y} - e n_i \frac{\partial V_p}{\partial y} - n_i M u_{iy} \nu_i = 0, \tag{17}$$

$$\frac{\partial^2 V_p}{\partial x^2} + \frac{\partial^2 V_p}{\partial y^2} = -\frac{e}{\varepsilon_0} n_{is} \left[\frac{n_i}{n_{is}} - \exp\left(\frac{e(V_p - V_{ps})}{k T_e} \right) \right], \tag{18}$$

where the ion collision frequency is given by equation (14). A similar plasma sheath model was presented (Sheridan & Goree, 1991) for a two-fluid ($T_h << T_e$, i.e. cold ions) uniform plasma but under the above quoted extreme collisional approximations. The present model is further complicated by the axial potential drop along the arc column facing the equipotential nozzle (see Fig. 7). Also for large ion temperatures (in this problem T_h is comparable to T_e) the thermal ion flux to the wall cannot be neglected; therefore the diffusive term in equation (9) must be considered.

To solve equations (15)-(18), the appropriate boundary condition (sheath thickness, plasma density and electron temperature at the sheath-plasma edge, arc voltage and gas pressure profiles inside the nozzle) were presented in Section 3. At the nozzle wall ($y = 0$), the voltage of the nozzle is known (V_N). The sheath-plasma edge ($y = D$) coincides with the quasi-neutral plasma, so $n_{is} \equiv n_i \cong n_e$ and the voltage distribution is that of the plasma arc (variable) voltage. Also the radial electric field value at the sheath-plasma edge is very small (Raizer, 1991), hence $\left.\partial V_p/\partial y\right)_{y=D} \approx 0$. The ions enter the sheath from the plasma with a velocity normal to the boundary surface given by $u_{is} \approx u_B\left(\lambda_i/\lambda_{Ds}\right)^{1/2}$. At the nozzle inlet ($x = 0$) and exit ($x = L_n$), open boundary conditions were assumed. So the quantities $\partial u_{ix}/\partial x$, $\partial u_{iy}/\partial x$, $\partial n_i/\partial x$ and $\partial V_p/\partial x$ are conserved through these surfaces.

4.2 Numerical results and discussion

The governing equations (8)-(12) were solved for the electric potential, ion velocity (both components) and for the ion density, by integrating them numerically using a finite difference discretization technique in a 100 × 50 uniform grid. An iterative method was adopted, that continued until the relative difference between two consecutive iterations of all the physical quantities was less than 10^{-5}.

To found the mechanism that triggers the undesirable sheath breakdown, the following torch operation conditions were used: arc current of 30 A, oxygen gas mass flow of 0.32 g s^{-1} and V_n = -155 V. In such conditions, a thin sheath with an almost constant thickness of $D(z)$ = 21 μm (see Fig. 4) was formed between the plasma and the nozzle wall.

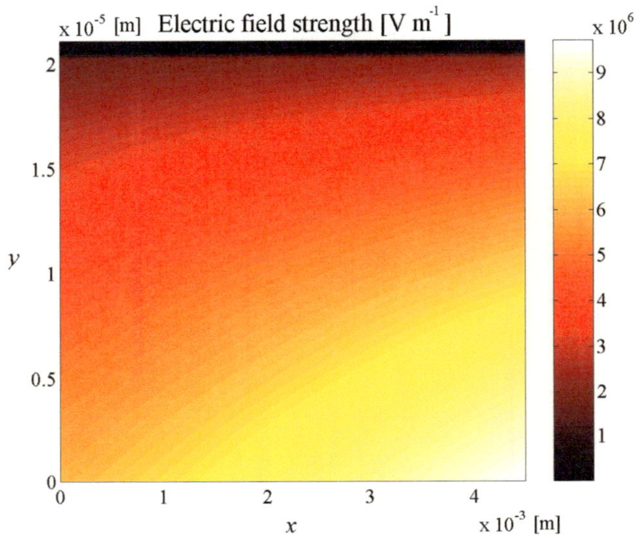

Fig. 8. Spatial distribution of the electric field strength inside the sheath. Taken from Prevosto et al., 2009c.

In Fig. 8, the spatial distribution of the electric field strength is presented. As it can be seen, the electric field value is high, with the largest values along the nozzle wall, varying from 6×10⁶ V m⁻¹ near the nozzle entrance to about 9×10⁶ V m⁻¹ at the nozzle exit. This enhanced value is higher than the average field value across the sheath, and is of the order of the breakdown threshold value. This means that an undesired sheath breakdown could occur close to the nozzle exit even if the average electric field across the sheath is not strong enough.

The spatial distributions of the ion and electron densities inside the sheath are presented in Figs. 9 and 10. As it can be seen in these Figs., n_i drops sharply near the sheath edge and continues decreasing slowly, while the electron density also shows a very steep drop near the sheath edge, with a virtually zero value everywhere inside the sheath. The lack of electrons inside the sheath implies that the electron thermal conduction flux to the nozzle wall can be neglected. The nozzle wall results thus thermally isolated, in spite of the high electron temperature in its adjacency. It was found that both the ion and electron densities decrease when the electrostatic potential decreases. This behavior of n_i is due to the ion acceleration at an almost constant ion flux, while the n_e behavior is due to the fact that the electrons are related with the electric field according to a Boltzmann equation -equation 13-.

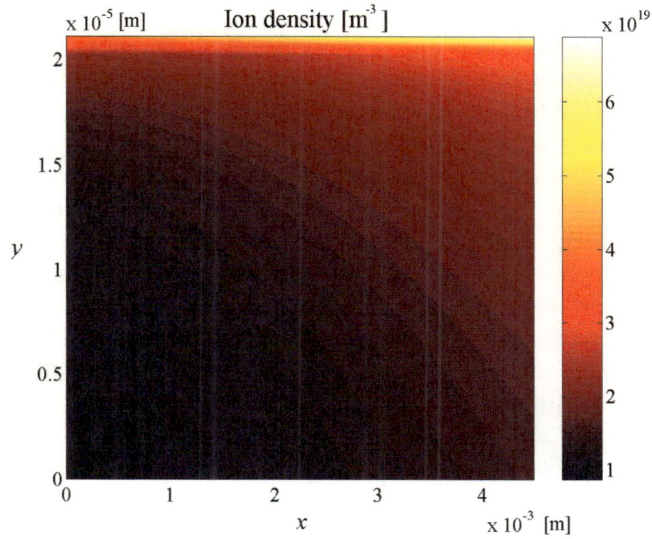

Fig. 9. Spatial distribution of n_i inside the sheath. Taken from Prevosto et al., 2009c.

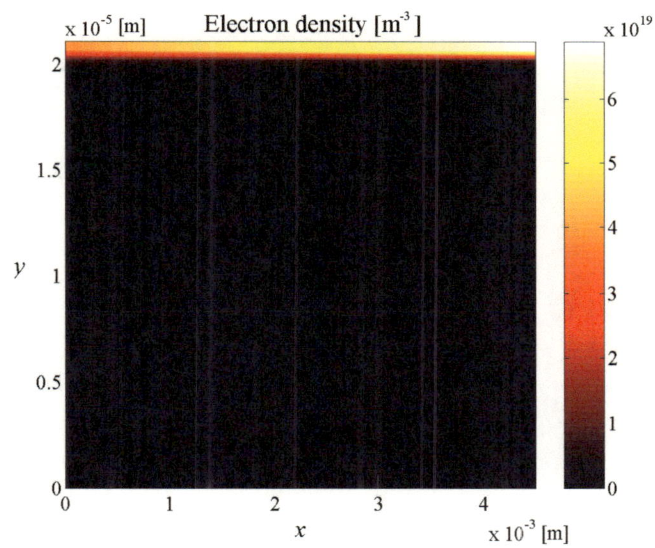

Fig. 10. Spatial distribution of n_e inside the sheath. Taken from Prevosto et al., 2009c.

5. Experimental evidence on the "non-destructive" double-arcing

In Section 1 it was mentioned that a transient (duration < 1 ms), non-destructive, double-arcing in cutting torches was recently identified (Colombo et al, 2009) by using high-speed imaging during the torch piercing phase. Gas flow rates and torch stand-off were set to increase the probability of double arcing. In Colombo's experiment, the sequence of images showed several phenomena that can be associated with the double arcing. In particular, green vapours and silver grey vapours appearing in some of the frames can be correlated with copper (nozzle wall) and hafnium (cathode) vapour emissions, respectively. The emission of copper vapours could be the consequence of an arc attachment to the nozzle, while the hafnium vapours exiting the nozzle could be related to a greater erosion of the hafnium cathode insert in the case of double-arcing due to an arc root attachment instability on the cathode emissive surface. The high-speed double-arcing images have been time-correlated with the oscilloscope waveform of the arc voltage drop between the cathode and the nozzle, and good correspondence was found. The authors then suggested that the non-destructive double-arcing phenomena during piercing probably occur as a consequence of the deposition of a small amount of hafnium oxide on the nozzle orifice wall, which induces a local increase in the radial electric field and hence an increase in the probability of double arcing. When double arcing occurs, rapid (<1 ms) evaporation of hafnium oxide with vapour emission from the nozzle restores the previous and normal arc behaviour. Due to their very short duration, the described phenomena should have a non-destructive character.

Usually, the power sources used for run cutting torches are poorly stabilized and have large ripple factors, with RMS values that can amount to 10 % of the time-averaged arc voltages (Pardo et al, 1999; Prevosto et al., 2008a; 2008b). This is due to the fact that the arc currents in cutting torches are typically large (of the order of 100 A) which difficult an effective filtering of the ripple. If a 3-phase transductor type power supply is used, then the fundamental ripple frequency is 150 Hz and if 3-phase silicon controlled rectifier (SCR) based power supply is used, then the ripple frequency is 300 Hz. The strong oscillatory components in the voltage and arc current should produce in turn, large fluctuations in the plasma quantities that vary at the ripple frequency.

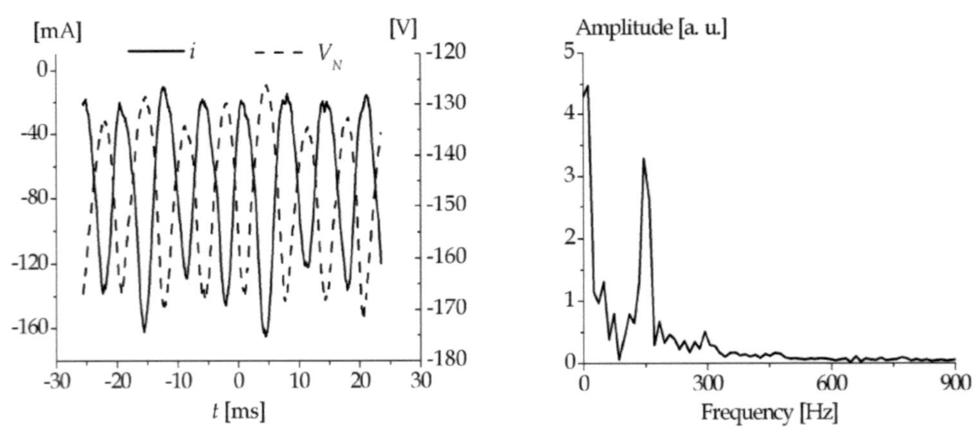

Fig. 11. Ion current and nozzle voltage waveforms for a 7 % RMS ripple level. The Fourier analysis of the ion current waveform is also shown.

Fig. 11 shows a typical V_N and i waveforms corresponding to the torch described in Section 3.1 for $\dot{m} = 0.39\,\mathrm{g\,s^{-1}}$ and a power supply ripple level of 7 %. The gas mass flow value is close to that producing double-arcing in this torch. It can be seen from Fig. 11 (left) that both waveforms exhibit high fluctuation levels, reaching for the ion current signal an amplitude (peak value) of about ≈ 75 % of the time-averaged value. Also, both waveforms are in opposite phase, a fact that could be related to a negative slope of the current-voltage characteristic curve of this kind of arcs. The Fourier analysis of the ion current waveform (fig. 11, right) shows that the signal has a very strong component at 150 Hz, which is the fundamental frequency of the power source ripple.

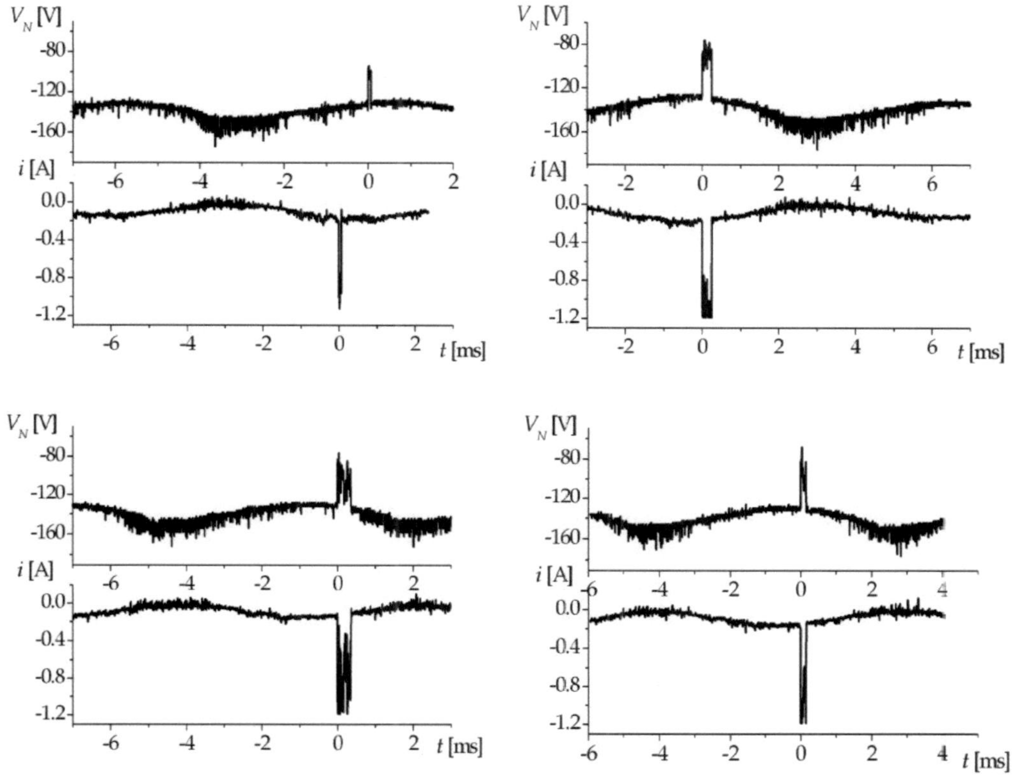

Fig. 12. Sequence of ion current and nozzle voltage waveforms with a reduced time-scale showing arc instabilities associated with the transient double-arcing phenomenon. The arc operation is close to the full-scale double-arcing.

This experimental result shows that the NLTE plasma inside the nozzle of a cutting torch results strongly affected by the arc voltage ripple, and thus it is far from the steady state, as it is usually assumed in the literature (e.g., Gonzalez-Aguilar et al., 1999; Freton et al., 2002; 2003; Ghorui et al., 2007; Zhou et al., 2009, Guo et al., 2010). Such dynamics could explain the mechanism of formation of the non-destructive double arcing; as it is shown with detail in Fig. 12. In these oscillograms (with a reduced time-scale), the ion current and nozzle voltage are shown for the same arc operating conditions (i.e., $\dot{m} = 0.39\,\mathrm{g\,s^{-1}}$ and a ripple level of 7 %). The sequence of images shows marked arc instabilities (during time intervals < 1 ms) that can be associated with the transient double-arcing phenomenon. It should be noted that such instabilities approximately coincides with the negative peak value of the ion current; thus supporting the hypothesis that the "non-destructive" double-arcing phenomenon is related to the plasma dynamics inside the nozzle. Another argument to support this hypothesis is the quite high repeatability of the phenomenon.

6. Final discussion and conclusions

In this work, we have presented a study of the arc plasma-nozzle sheath structure, which is the region where the double-arcing takes place.
The starting point was obtaining a physical interpretation of the RMS current-voltage characteristic of the nozzle that led to predict the thickness of the quoted sheath in terms of the gas mass flow value. Thus, a Towsend-type breakdown of the neutral gas inside the sheath was suggested as the double-arcing trigger. The predicted gas mass flow value that produced a breakdown was in good agreement with the experimental $\dot{m}$ that actually produced double arcing in our torch.
A detailed study of the sheath structure by developing a numerical model for a collisional sheath was also presented. This model allowed obtaining profiles of the electron and ion densities and electric field along the sheath, which confirmed the Towsend-type breakdown of the sheath as the most likely mechanism to produce double-arcing. In particular the breakdown was based on the local electric field strength intensification at the nozzle wall close to the bore exit. This enhanced field could be strong enough to trigger a breakdown even if the average electric field across de sheath is not strong enough.
The proposed mechanism is quite different from that previously found in the literature (Nemchinsky (1998) and Nemchinsky & Severance (2006)), in which it is suggested that the voltage drop inside the nozzle is concentrated across the cold quasi-neutral plasma layer that separates the hot plasma and the nozzle. Note that our hypothesis implies that the thickness of the space-charge layer (where almost all the electric field is concentrated) is shorter than the cold gas envelope (i.e., the electric field cannot penetrate deep inside such envelope), thus the average electric field in the nozzle vicinity rises ($\approx \Delta V/D$). The cold gas envelope hypothesis was recently adopted by Guo et al. (2010). Its thickness was arbitrary defined as the contour corresponding to 7000 K ($\approx$ 0.5 mm). However, the electric field cannot penetrate inside such envelope since the space-charge layer at this temperature value is much smaller than such gas envelope.
A transient (duration < 1 ms), double-arcing in cutting torches –the so called "non-destructive" double-arcing– was recently identified (Colombo et al, 2009) under torch operating conditions close to those producing double-arcing. Similar observations of this phenomenon have been presented in this work. Due to their very short duration the described phenomena can have a non-destructive character. Although the literature proposed hypothesis (Colombo et al., 2009; Nemchinsky 2009) assumes a transient arc voltage rise due to dielectric films deposited on the nozzle surface (which are later either carried away by the gas flow or are burned out); our experimental observations suggest that such a phenomenon is more likely related with the dynamics of the space-charge sheath contiguous to the nozzle due to the arc power source ripple.

7. Acknowledgement

This work was supported by grants from the Universidad de Buenos Aires (PID X108), CONICET (PIP 5378) and Universidad Tecnológica Nacional (PID Z 012). H. K. is member of the CONICET.

8. References

Blank, J. L. (1968). Collision-dominated positive column of a weakly ionized gas. *Phys. Fluids*, 11, 1686.

Boulos, M.; Fauchais, P. & Pfender, E. (1994). *Thermal Plasmas, Fundamentals and Applications*, Vol1, Plenum Press, New York.

Colombo, V.; Concetti, A.; Ghedini, E.; Dallavalle, S. & Vancini, M. (2009). High-speed imaging in plasma arc cutting: a review and new developments. *Plasma Sources Sci. Technol.*, 18, 023001.

Dowell, D. H.; King, F. K.; Kirby, R. E. & Schemerge, J. F. (2006). In situ cleaning of metal cathodes using a hydrogen ion beam. *Phys. Rev. ST Accel. Beams*, 9, 063502.

Franklin, R. N. (2002). What significance does the Bohm criterion have in an active colisional plasma-sheath? *J. Phys. D: Appl. Phys.*, 35, 2270.

Franklin, R. N. (2002). You cannot patch active plasma and collisionless sheath. *IEEE Trans. Plasma Sci.* 30 (2002) 352.

Franklin, R. N. (2003). The plasma-sheath boundary region. *J. Phys. D: Appl. Phys.*, 36, R309.

Franklin, R. N. (2003). There is not such thing as a collisionally modified Bohm criterion. *J. Phys. D: Appl. Phys.*, 36, 2821.

Franklin, R. N. (2004). Where is the sheath edge? *J. Phys. D: Appl. Phys.*, 37, 1342.

Freton, P.; Gonzalez, J. J.; Camy Peyret, F. & Gleizes, A. (2003). Complementary experimental and theoretical approaches to the determination of the plasma characteristics in a cutting plasma torch. *J. Phys. D: Appl. Phys.*, 36, 1269.

Freton, P.;Gonzalez, J. J.; Gleizes, A.; Camy Peyret, F.; Caillibotte, G. & Delzenne, M. (2002). Numerical and experimental study of a plasma cutting torch. *J. Phys. D: Appl. Phys.*, 35, 115.

George, D. W. & Richards, P. H. (1968). Boundary conditions in wall-stabilized arc columns. *Brit. J. Appl. Phys. (J. Phys. D)*, 1, 1171.

Ghorui, S.; Heberlein, J. V. R. & Pfender, E. (2007). Non-equilibrium modelling of an oxygen-plasma cutting torch. *J. Phys. D: Appl. Phys.*, 40, 1966.

Girard, L.; Teulet, Ph.; Razafinimanana, M.; Gleizes, A.; Camy-Peyret, F.; Baillot, E. & Richard, F. (2006). Experimental study of an oxygen plasma cutting torch: I. Spectroscopic analysis of the plasma jet. *J. Phys. D: Appl. Phys.*, 39, 1543.

Goldston, R. J. & Rutherford, P. H. (1995). *Introduction to Plasma Physics*, Institute of Physics Publishing Bristol and Philadelphia IOP.

González-Aguilar, J.; Pardo, C.; Rodríguez-Yunta, A. & García Calderón, M. A. G. (1999). A theoretical study of a cutting air plasma torch. *IEEE Trans. Plasma Sci.*, 27, 264.

Guo, S.; Zhou, Q.; Guo, W. & Xu, P. (2010). Computational analysis of a double nozzle structure plasma cutting torch. *Plasma Chem. Plasma Process*, 30, 121.

Hackam, R. (1969). Total secondary ionization coefficients and breakdown potentials of hydrogen, methane, ethylene, carbon monoxide, nitrogen, oxygen and carbon dioxide between mild steel coaxial cylinders. J. Phys. B (Atom. Molec. Phys.), 2, 216.

Hill, R. J. & Jones, G. R. (1979). The influence of laminar and turbulent flows upon the electrical characteristics of wall-stabilised arcs. *J. Phys. D: Appl. Phys.*, 12, 1707.

Naghizadeh-Kashani, Y.; Cressault, Y. & Gleizes, A. (2002). Net emission coefficient of air thermal plasmas. *J. Phys. D: Appl. Phys.*, 35, 2925.

Nemchinsky, V. A. & Severance, W. S. (2006). What we know and what we do not know about plasma arc cutting. *J. Phys. D: Appl. Phys.*, 39, R423.

Nemchinsky, V. A. (1998). Plasma flow in a nozzle during plasma arc cutting. *J. Phys. D: Appl. Phys.*, 31, 3102.

Nemchinsky, V. A. (2009). A mechanism that triggers double arcing during plasma arc cutting. *J. Phys. D: Appl. Phys.*, 42, 205209.

Noble, B. (1964). *Numerical Methods: 2 Differences, Integration and Differential Equations*. Oliver and Boyd Ltd, Edinburgh.

Pardo, C.; González-Aguilar, J.; Rodríguez-Yunta, A. & Calderón, M. A. G. (1999). Spectroscopic analysis of an air plasma cutting torch. *J. Phys. D: Appl. Phys.*, 32, 2181.

Peters, J.; Heberlein, J. V. R. & Lindsay, J. (2007). Spectroscopic diagnostics in a highly constricted oxygen arc. *J. Phys. D: Appl. Phys.*, 40, 3960.

Prevosto, L.; Kelly, H. & Mancinelli, B. (2008). On the use of sweeping Langmuir probes in cutting arc plasmas–Part I: Experimental results. *IEEE Trans. Plasma Sci.*, 36, 263.

Prevosto, L.; Kelly, H. & Minotti, F. O. (2008). On the use of sweeping Langmuir probes in cutting arc plasmas–Part II: Interpretation of the results. *IEEE Trans. Plasma Sci.*, 36, 271.

Prevosto, L.; Kelly, H. & Minotti, F. O. (2009). An interpretation of Langmuir probe floating voltage signals in a cutting arc. *IEEE Trans. Plasma Sci.*, 37, 1092.

Prevosto, L.; Kelly, H. and Mancinelli, B. (2009). On the physical origin of the nozzle characteristic and its connection with the double-arcing phenomenon in a cutting torch. *J. Appl. Phys.*, 105, 013309.

Prevosto, L.; Kelly, H. and Mancinelli, B. (2009). On the space–charge boundary layer inside the nozzle of a cutting torch. *J. Appl. Phys.*, 105, 123303.

Raizer, Y. P. (1991). *Gas Discharge Physics*. Berlin, Germany: Springer.

Ramakrishnan, S.; Gershenzon, M.; Polivka, F.; Kearny, T. N. & Rogozinsky, M. W. (1997). Plasma generation for the plasma cutting process. *IEEE Trans. Plasma Sci.*, 25, 937.

Riemann, K–U. (1991). The Bohm criterion and sheath formation. *J. Phys. D: Appl. Phys.*, 24, 493.

Riemann, K–U. (2003). Kinetic analysis of the colisional plasma–sheath transition. *J. Phys. D: Appl. Phys.*, 36, 2811.

Shayler, P. J. & Fang, M. T. C. (1978). Radiation transport in wall-stabilized nitrogen arcs. *J. Phys. D: Appl. Phys.*,11, 1743.

Sheridan, T. E. & Goeckner, M. J. (1995). Colisional sheath dynamics. *J. Appl. Phys.*, 77, 4967.

Sheridan, T. E. & Goree, J. (1991). Colisional plasma sheath model. *Phys. Fluids B*, 3, 2796.

Sternovsky, Z. & Robertson, S. (2006). Numerical solutions to the weakly colisional plasma and sheath in the fluid approach and the reduction of the ion current to the wall. *IEEE Trans. Plasma Sci.*, 34, 850.

van de Sanden, M. C. M., Schram, P. P. J. M.;.Peeters, A. G.; van der Mullen, J. A. M. & Kroesen, G. M. W. (1989). Thermodynamic generalization of the Saha equation for a two-temperature plasma. *Phys. Rev. A*, 40, 5273.

Zhou, Q.; Yin, H.; Li, H.; Xu, X.; Liu, F.; Guo, S.; Chang, X.; Guo, W. & Xu, P. (2009). The effect of plasma–gas swirl flow on a highly constricted plasma cutting arc. *J. Phys. D: Appl. Phys.*, 42, 095208.

24

Statistical Mechanics of Inverse Halftoning

Yohei Saika
Gunma National College of Technology
Japan

1. Introduction

For many years, researchers have investigated information science, such as image analysis (Besag, 1974, Winkler, 1995, Cressie, 1993). Especially, image restoration has been studied as a fundamental problem in information science. In a recent development of this field, theoretical physicists have applied statistical mechanics to information based on analogy between statistical mechanics and Bayesian inference via the maximizer of the posterior (MPM) estimate (Nishimori, 2001). In this field, many techniques in statistical mechanics have been applied to various problems. Following the strategy, the present author has applied statistical mechanics to image restoration using the plane rotator model (Saika & Nishimori, 2002) and phase retrieval (Saika & Nishimori, 2005). Recently, statistical mechanical approach for information becomes an established field called as statistical mechanical informatics. Now statistical mechanics has been applied to many problems in various areas, such as information communication and quantum computation.

In print technology, many techniques have been proposed to print images with high quality. Especially, a technique called as digital halftoning (Ulichney, 1987) is essential to convert an original image into a halftone image expressed as a set of black and white dots which are visually similar to the original image through human vision system. A lot of techniques have been proposed for this problem, such as the dither method (Bayer, 1973). On the other hand, the inverse of digital halftoning is called as inverse halftoning and then the purpose is to reconstruct the original image from the halftone image (Miceli, C. M. & Parker, K. J., 1992). A lot of techniques have been proposed. From the practical point of view, Wong (Wong, 1995) has proposed statistical smoothing to inverse halftoning for halftone images. Then, Stevenson (Stevenson, 1995) has constructed the MAP estimation for halftone dithered images.

In this article, we demonstrate recent development of our researches both on theoretical and practical aspects of inverse halftoning for halftone images obtained by the dither and error diffusion methods (Ulichney, 1987). As shown in Fig. 1, our strategy for this problem is based on the analogy between statistical mechanics and the Bayesian inference via the maximizer of the posterior (MPM) estimate (Fig. 2) and is then to propose the statistical mechanical techniques for this problem. First, we construct a Bayesian probabilistic formulation for inverse halftoning utilizing statistical mechanics of the Q-Ising model (Saika, et al., 2009, Saika & Okamoto, 2010). Then, we clarify the statistical performance of the present method using both the Monte Carlo simulation for a set of the snapshots of the Q-Ising model and the analytical estimate via the infinite-range model.

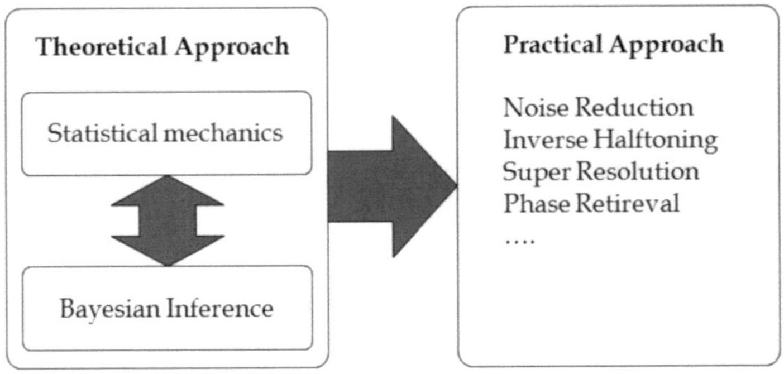

Fig. 1. Statistical mechanical approaches to image processing technology

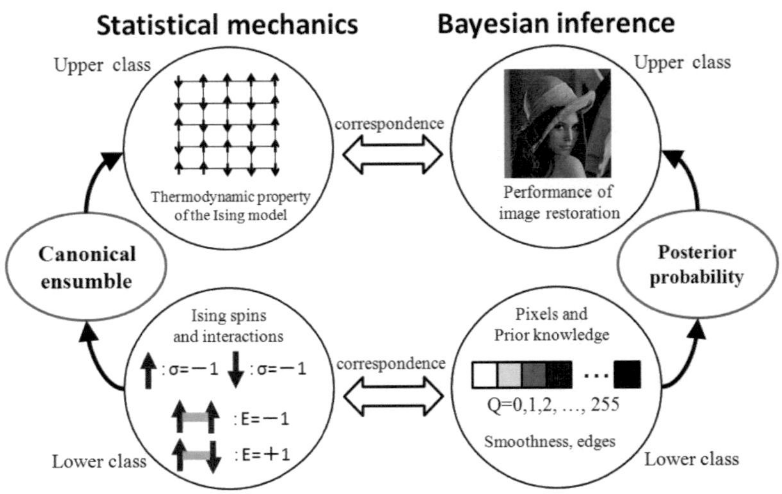

Fig. 2. Analogy between statistical mechanics and Bayesian inference

These estimates clarify that the present method realizes optimal performance around the Bayes-optimal condition. Next, we investigate the practical aspect of this problem by means of the generalized statistical smoothing (GSS) (Saika & Yamasaki, 2007, Saika, et al., 2010a, 2010b) which is regarded as the generalized MAP estimate corresponding to the deterministic limit of the MPM estimate. Using the numerical simulation for several standard images, we clarify that the GSS is a practically useful method for inverse halftoning, if we set parameters both for edge enhancement and generalized parameter scheduling appropriately. From the above studies, we clarify that statistical mechanical approach and its variants serve various powerful tools for clarifying both theoretical and practical aspects of inverse hafltoning.

2. Theoretical apsect of inverse halftoning

In this section, after we show the prescription of statistical mechanics, we then demonstrate the theoretical aspect of our studies (Saika, et al., 2009, Saika & Okamoto, 2010) for inverse halftoning. Especially, we indicate that the framework of statistical mechanics is available of inverse halftoning and that the various techniques in statistical mechanics become powerful tools to clarify the statistical performance of the MPM estimate, such as the Monte Carlo simulation and the analytical estimate via the infinite-range model.

2.1 Prescription of statistical mechanics

In this section, we briefly show that statistical mechanics is useful for the clarification of macroscopic properties of many-body systems using knowledge of microscopic elements.

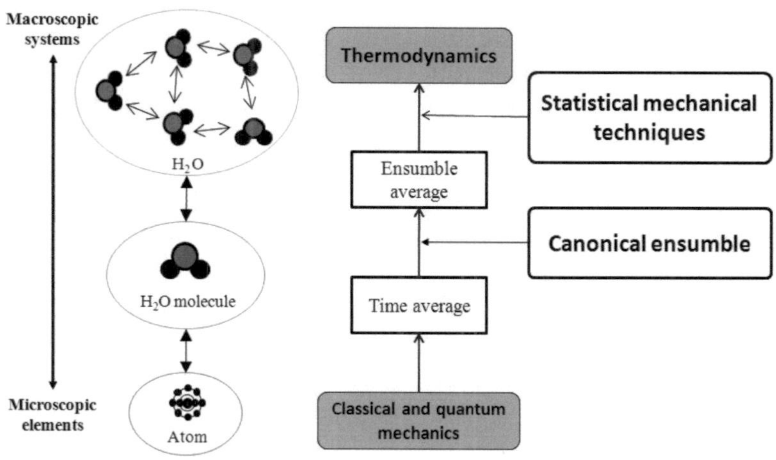

Fig. 3. Prescription of statistical mechanics

As shown in Fig. 3, a goal of statistical mechanics is to clarify the thermodynamic properties of many-body systems starting from the knowledge of interactions between microscopic elements. The general prescription of statistical mechanics is to calculate the thermal average of a physical quantity using the probability distribution

$$\Pr(\{\xi\}) = \frac{1}{Z}\exp[-\beta H(\{S_i\})] \tag{1}$$

for a given Hamiltonian. Here $\{S_i\}$ represents a set of spin states which are regarded as a typical example of the microscopic elements. Here we take the unit of temperature such that Boltzmann's constant k_B is unity. Then, β is the inverse temperature $\beta=1/T$. The normalization factor Z is called as the partition function:

$$Z = \sum_{S_1=\pm1}\sum_{S_2=\pm1}\cdots\sum_{S_N=\pm1} e^{-\beta H(\{S\})} \tag{2}$$

Equation (1) is called the Gibbs-Boltzmann distribution and then $e^{-\beta H}$ is termed the Boltzmann factor. Then, by making use of the Gibbs-Boltzmann distribution, we can estimate the macroscopic quantities, such as the free energy, as

$$\langle A\rangle = \frac{1}{Z}\sum_{S_1=\pm1}\sum_{S_2=\pm1}\cdots\sum_{S_N=\pm1} A(\{S\})e^{-\beta H(\{S\})} \tag{3}$$

utilizing various thermodynamical relations. For instance, the internal energy of the system is obtained by the relation:

$$\langle E \rangle = \frac{1}{Z} \sum_{S_1=\pm1} \sum_{S_2=\pm1} \cdots \sum_{S_N=\pm1} E(\{S\}) e^{-\beta H(\{S\})} = -\frac{\partial}{\partial \beta} \log Z \quad (4)$$

using the partition function.
Then, we briefly show the strategy of statistical mechanics to information science and technology. The basic concept of the statistical mechanics to information is based on the analogy between statistical mechanics and the Bayesian inference via the MPM estimate. Following this strategy, the statistical mechanical formulations have been constructed for various problems in information science and technology, such as image restoration and error-correcting codes. Then, researcheres utilize various statistical mechanical techniques, such as the mean-field theory and its variants including the Bethe approximation. Further, we can use these statistical mechanical techniques to clarify the statistical performance, such as the Monte Carlo simulation and the analytical estimate via the infinite-range model.

2.2 Statistical mechanical formulation for inverse halftoning

In this section, as shown in Fig. 4, we show the statistical mechanical formulation for inverse halftoning using the Bayesian inference via the MPM estimate for a set of snapshots of the Q-Ising model.

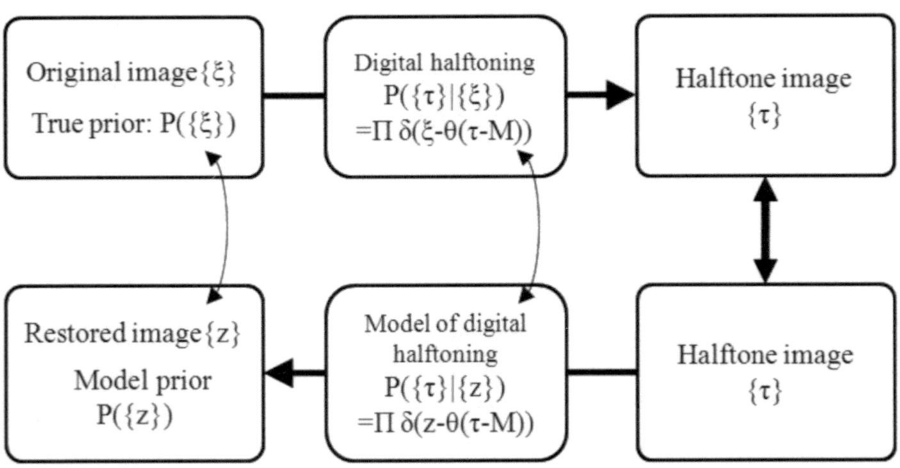

Fig. 4. The reconstruction-based inverse halftoning based on the Bayesian inference.

In this formulation, we first consider the set of original grayscale images $\{\xi_{x,y}\}$ ($\xi_{x,y}$=0,…,255 and x,y=1,…,L) generated by the assumed true prior which is expressed as the probability distribution:

$$\Pr(\{\xi\}) = \frac{1}{Z_s} \exp\left[-\frac{J_s}{T_s} \sum_{x=1}^{L} \sum_{y=1}^{L} [(\xi_{x,y} - \xi_{x+1,y})^2 + (\xi_{x,y} - \xi_{x,y+1})^2] \right] \quad (5)$$

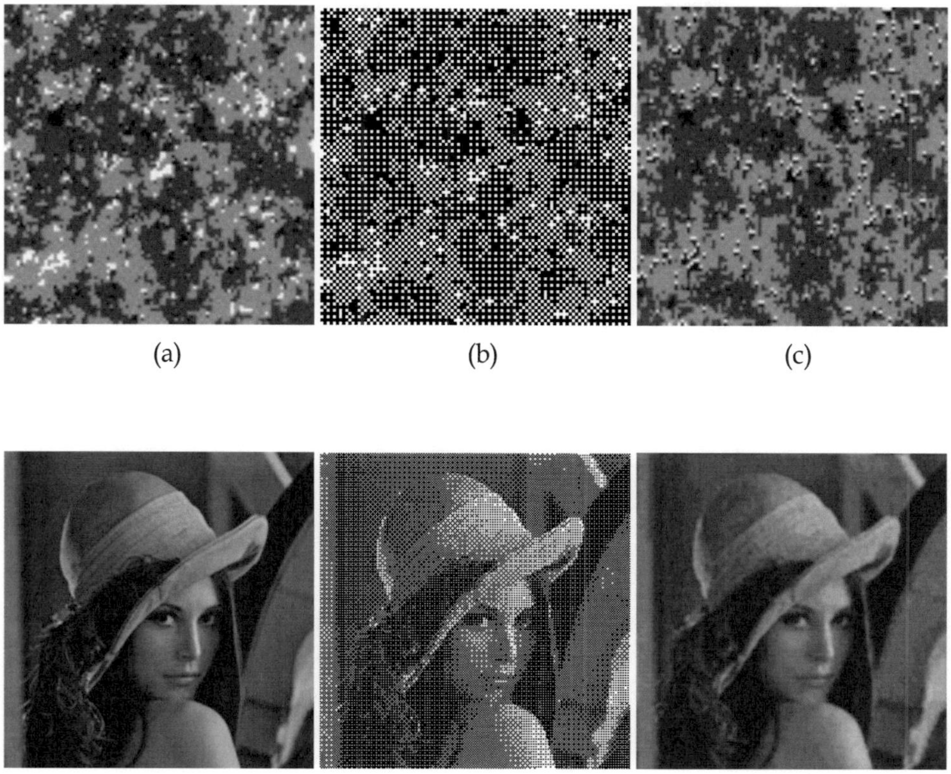

Fig. 5. (a) a snapshot of the 4-level Q-Ising model with 100×100 pixels, (b) a halftone image of (a) converted by the dither method via the 2×2 Bayer-type threshold array, (c) a grayscale image reconstructed from (b) by the MPM estimate under the Bayes-optimal condition, (d) the 256-level standard image "Lena" with 256×256 pixels, (e) a halftone version of (d) converted by the dither method via the 4×4 Bayer-type threshold array, (f) a grayscale image reconstructed from (e) by the MPM estimate when J=5.0.

Here J_s and T_s are parameters to generate grayscale images with smooth structures appearing in natural images. A typical pattern of the original images is shown in Fig. 5(a). On the other hand, when we estimate the performance for realistic images we use the 256-level standard image "Lena" with 256×256 pixels in Fig. 5(d).

Then, in the procedure of digital halftoning, we rewrite each original image $\{\xi_{x,y}\}$ into a halftone image $\{\tau_{x,y}\}$ by using the dither method via the p×p Bayer-type threshold array $\{M_p\}$ in Fig. 5. Here $\tau_{x,y}$= 0, 1 and x, y = 1,…,L. The typical threshold arrays are shown in Figs. 6(a) and (b). These threshold arrays $\{M_p\}$ are generated by using the recurrence relation:

$$\{M_p\} = \begin{bmatrix} 4M_{p/2} & 4M_{p/2} + 2U_{p/2} \\ 4M_{p/2} + 3U_{p/2} & 4M_{p/2} + U_{p/2} \end{bmatrix} \tag{6}$$

$$\{M_2\} = \begin{bmatrix} 0 & 2 \\ 3 & 1 \end{bmatrix} \tag{7}$$

Here U_n is a $n\times n$ matrix whose all elements are unity. Then, the element of the threshold M_p is an integer from 0 to p^2-1. When we rewrite the original image $\{\xi_{x,y}\}$ into the halftone image $\{\tau_{x,y}\}$, we first make a one-to-one correspondence between each pixel of the original image $\{\xi_{x,y}\}$ and the threshold of the Bayer-type threshold array $\{M_p\}$ using the correspondence relation:

$$\xi_{x,y} \leftrightarrow M_{x\%p,y\%p} \tag{8}$$

Here $a\%b$ denotes a surplus which divides a by b. Then, we carry out thresholding at each pixel of the original image $\{\xi_{x,y}\}$ by the corresponding threshold $\{M_p\}$ as

$$\tau_{x,y} = \theta(\xi_{x,y} - M_{x\%p,y\%p} \cdot Q / p^2 - 1/2) \tag{9}$$

Here $\theta(\ldots)$ is the unit-step function which is defined by

$$\theta(x) = \begin{cases} 0 & (x<0) \\ 1 & (x>0) \end{cases}. \tag{10}$$

The halftone images of the original images in Figs. 5(a) and (d) are shown in Figs. 5(b) and (e). These halftone images are visually similar to the original image if we observe them through the human vision system, although the information on the original images is lost through the halftone procedure.

In the procedure of inverse halftoning, we reconstruct the original image so as to maximize the posterior marginal probability. The pixel value at the (x,y)-th pixel of the reconstructed image is given as

$$\hat{z}_{x,y} = \arg\max_{z_{x,y}} \sum_{\{z\}\neq z_{x,y}} \Pr(\{z\} \mid \{\tau\}). \tag{11}$$

The posterior probability in (11) can be estimated based on the Bayes formula:

0	8	2	10
12	4	14	6
3	11	1	9
15	7	13	5

(a)

0	32	8	40	2	34	10	42
48	16	56	24	50	18	58	26
12	44	4	36	14	46	6	38
60	28	52	20	62	30	54	22
3	35	11	43	1	33	9	41
51	19	59	27	49	17	57	25
15	47	7	39	13	45	5	37
63	31	55	23	61	29	53	21

(b)

Fig. 6. (a) the 4×4 Bayer-type threshold array, (b) the 8×8 Bayer-type threshold array

$$\Pr(\{z\}\,|\,\{\tau\}) = \frac{\Pr(\{z\})\Pr(\{\tau\}\,|\,\{z\})}{\sum_{\{\tau\}}\Pr(\{z\})\Pr(\{\tau\}\,|\,\{z\})}. \tag{12}$$

using the assumed model prior and the likelihood. In this study, we assume the model prior which is expressed as the probability distribution:

$$\Pr(\{z\}) \propto \exp\left[-\frac{J}{T_m}\sum_{x=1}^{L}\sum_{y=1}^{L}[(z_{x,y}-z_{x+1,y})^2+(z_{x,y}-z_{x,y-1})^2]\right] \tag{13}$$

so as to enhance smooth structures in the patterns of the reconstructed image. Then, in order to construct the Bayes-optimal solution, we consider the model prior which has the same form as the assumed true prior in (5). Then, we use the likelihood which is expressed as the conditional probability representing the dither method via the Bayer-type threshold array as

$$\Pr(\{z\}\,|\,\{\tau\}) = \prod_{x=1}^{L}\prod_{y=1}^{L}\delta(\tau_{x,y}, \theta(z_{x,y} - M_{x\%p,y\%p}\cdot Q/p^2 - 1/2)) \tag{14}$$

In this study, the reconstructed image is obtained by

$$\hat{z}_{x,y} = \Theta(\overline{z}_{x,y}), \tag{15}$$

where

$$\overline{z}_{x,y} = \sum_{\{z\}} z_{x,y}\Pr\left(\{z\}\,|\,\{\tau^{p^2}\}\right), \tag{16}$$

$$\Theta(x) = \sum_{k=0}^{Q}\theta\left(x-k+\frac{1}{2}\right)-\theta\left(x-k-\frac{1}{2}\right). \tag{17}$$

When we estimate the performance of the present method for the realistic image, we evaluate the mean square error (MSE) defined by

$$MSE = \frac{1}{L^2}\sum_{x=1}^{L}\sum_{y=1}^{L}\left(\hat{z}_{x,y}-\xi_{x,y}\right)^2. \tag{18}$$

Then, when we estimate the statistical performance, we evaluate the MSE averaged over the set of the original images $\{\xi_{x,y}\}$ as

$$MSE = \sum_{\{\xi\}}\Pr(\{\xi\})\frac{1}{L^2}\sum_{x=1}^{L}\sum_{y=1}^{L}\left(\hat{z}_{x,y}-\xi_{x,y}\right)^2. \tag{19}$$

2.3 Statistical performance

In this section, we indicate that the Monte Carlo simulation is useful for clarifying the statitstical performance of the MPM estimate. When we investigate the statistical performance for the set of the snapshots of the Q-Ising model. As shown in Fig. 5(a), we numerically estimate the statistical performance for the set of the snapshots of the Q-Ising model. These images are generated by the assumed true prior expressed by the Boltzmann factor of the Q-Ising model when we set to Q=4 and J_s=T_s=1. Then, each original image is converted into the halftone image by the dither method via the 2×2 Bayer-type threshold array. Then, when we carry out the Monte Carlo simulation, we use the Metropolis algorithm with 20000 Monte Carlo steps.

In order to clarify the statistical performance for the set of the Q-Ising model, we numerically estimate how the MSE depends on the parameter T_m when J=1. As shown in Fig. 7, the Monte Carlo simulations clarify that optimal performance is realized around the Bayes-optimal condition, T_m=T_s. (=1) within statistical uncertainty. This result also means that the optimal performance of the MPM estimate is as well as that of the MAP estimate, if we set the parameters appropriately. Here, we denote the MAP estimate as the $T_m \rightarrow 0$ limit of the MPM estimate.

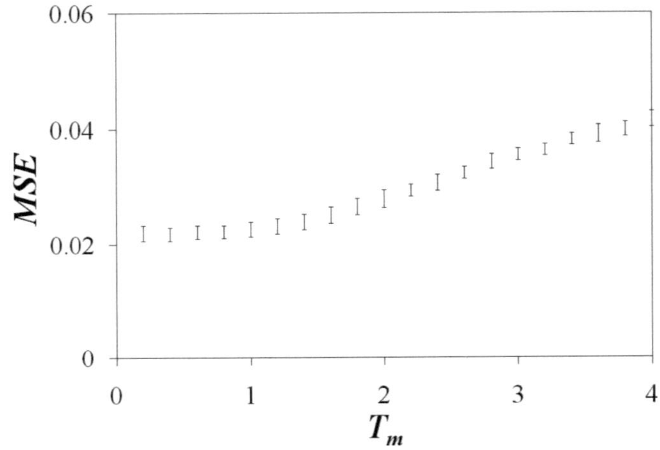

Fig. 7. The MSE as a function of T_m obtained by the Monte Carlo simulation for the set of the snapshots of the Q-Ising model.

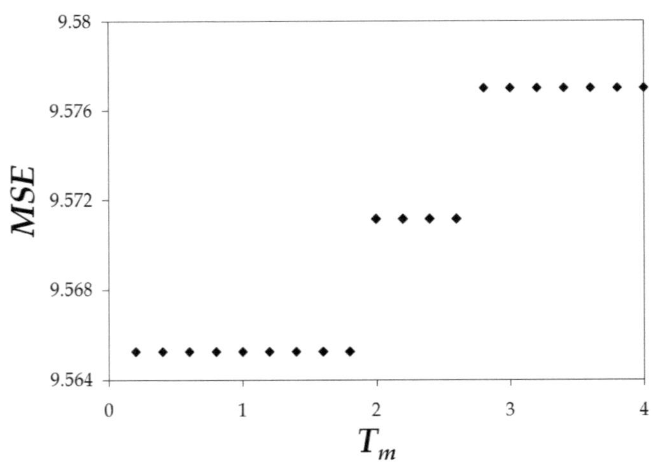

Fig. 8. The MSE as a function of the parameter T_m obtained by the analytical estimate using the infinite-range model.

2.4 Analytical estimate via the infinite-range model

In this section, we clarify that the analytical estimate via the infinite-range model is useful for the estimation of the statistical performance of the MPM estimate averaged over the set of the snapshots of the Q-Ising model. For convenience, we here use the language in the field of statistical mechanics.

In order to estimate the statistical performance, we first introduce the infinite-range versions of the model and true priors:

$$\Pr(\{\xi_i\}) = \frac{1}{Z_s}\exp\left[-\frac{J_s}{T_s}\sum_{i<j}\left(\xi_i - \xi_j\right)^2\right], \tag{20}$$

$$\Pr(\{z_i\}) = \frac{1}{Z_m}\exp\left[-\frac{J_m}{T_m}\sum_{i<j}\left(z_i - z_j\right)^2\right], \tag{21}$$

both of which are assumed to approximate the assumed model and true priors in two dimensions. Then, based on the saddle-point conditions on the free energy (Nishimori, 2001, Saika, et al., 2009), we can derive the self-consistent equations on m_0 and m as

$$m_0 = \frac{1}{Z_s}\sum_{\xi=0}^{Q-1}\xi\exp[\beta_s(2m_0\xi - m_0^2)] \tag{22}$$

$$m = \frac{1}{Z_s}\sum_{\xi=0}^{Q-1}\exp[\beta_s(2m_0\xi - m_0^2)]\left[\frac{\sum_{z=0}^{Q-1}\prod_{k=1}^{L_M^2}\delta(\xi,\theta(z - k\frac{kQ}{L_M^2})\exp[\beta_m(2mz - m_0^2)]z}{\sum_{z=0}^{Q-1}\prod_{k=1}^{L_M^2}\delta(\xi,\theta(z - k\frac{kQ}{L_M^2})\exp[\beta_m(2mz - m_0^2)]}\right] \tag{23}$$

$$Z_s = \sum_{\xi=0}^{Q-1}\exp[\beta_s(2m_0\xi - m_0^2)] \tag{24}$$

using the infinite-range versions of the model and true priors. In above equations, $\beta_s = 1/T_s$ and $\beta_m = 1/T_m$ respectively. By making use of the solutions m_0 and m on the self-consistent equations in (22)-(24), we can estimate the *MSE*:

$$MSE = \frac{\sum_{\xi=0}^{Q-1}\exp[\beta_s(2m_0\xi - m_0^2)]}{\sum_{\xi=0}^{Q-1}\exp[\beta_s(2m_0\xi - m_0^2)]}(\Theta(\hat{z}) - \xi)^2, \tag{25}$$

where

$$\hat{z} = \frac{\sum_{z=0}^{Q-1}\prod_{k=1}^{L_M^2}\delta(\xi,\theta(z - k\frac{kQ}{L_M^2})\exp[\beta_m(2mz - m_0^2)]z}{\sum_{z=0}^{Q-1}\prod_{k=1}^{L_M^2}\delta(\xi,\theta(z - k\frac{kQ}{L_M^2})\exp[\beta_m(2mz - m_0^2)]} \tag{26}$$

which is averaged over the true prior.

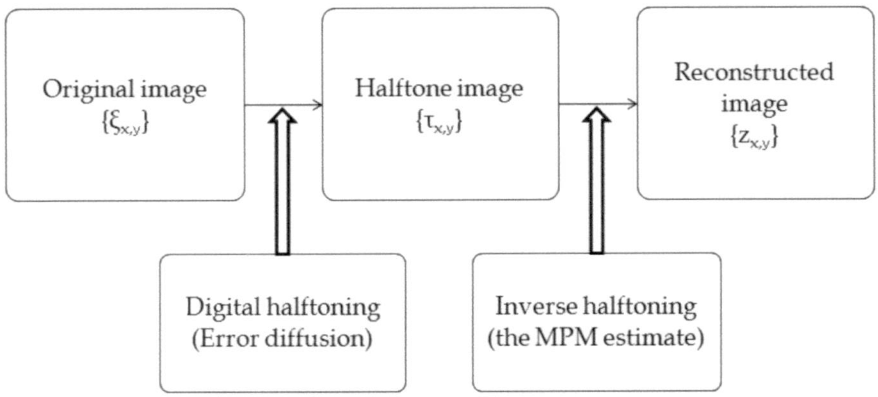

Fig. 9. The general formulation of inverse halftoning for the halftone image converted by the error diffusion method

As shown in Fig. 8, the analytical estimate via the infinite-range model clarifies that the MPM estimate achieves the optimal performance around the Bayes-optimal condition T_m=T_s (=1) without the statistical uncertainty. This shows that the results of the Monte Carlo simulation are qualitatively confirmed by the analytical estimate via the infinite-range model.

2.5 Realistic image

In this section, we indicate that the present method is also available of inverse halftoning for realistic images. Especially, we numerically estimate the performance of the MPM estimate using the Monte Carlo simulation for the 256-level standard image "Lena" with 256×256 pixels. As shown in Fig. 5 (f), we find that the present method is effective for inverse halftoning, if we assume the parameters appropriately.

3. Practical apsect of inverse halftoning

3.1 Generalized statistical smoothing

In this section, we indicate that the practically useful technique can be constructed as the generalized MAP estimate corresponding to the deterministic limit of the MPM estimate. In this article, the technique called as the GSS (Saika & Yamasaki, 2007, Saika et al., 2010a, Saika et al., 2010b) is constructed by introducing the edge enhancement and the generalized parameter scheduling into the MAP estimate. Here we show how to use the GSS to inverse halftoning for the halftone image which is converted by the error diffusion method (Floyd and Steinberg, 1975).

As shown in Fig. 9, we show the general formulation of the GSS to inverse halftoning for the halftone image converted by the error diffusion method. Then, we indicate the performance measure which utilizes the MTF function of the human vision system.

In this formulation, we first consider an original grayscale image $\{\xi_{x,y}\}(\xi_{x,y}=0,\ldots,255, x,y=0,\ldots,L-1)$ on the square lattice. Here the pixel value $\xi_{x,y}$ represents the brightness at the

(x,y)-th site on the square lattice. In this study, we use several 256-level standard image, such as "Lena" with 256×256 pixels in Fig. 10(a). Then, in the procedure of digital halftoning, we convert the original image $\{\xi_{x,y}\}$ into a halftone image $\{\tau_{x,y}\}(\tau_{x,y}=0, Q-1, x,y=0,\ldots,L-1)$ by using the error diffusion method. The block diagram of this method is shown in Fig. 11 and the Floyd-Steinberg kernel is shown in Fig. 12. Then, as shown in Fig. 10(b), the density of the black and white dots of the halftone image approximate the gray levels of the original image and are visually similar to the original image through the human vision system.

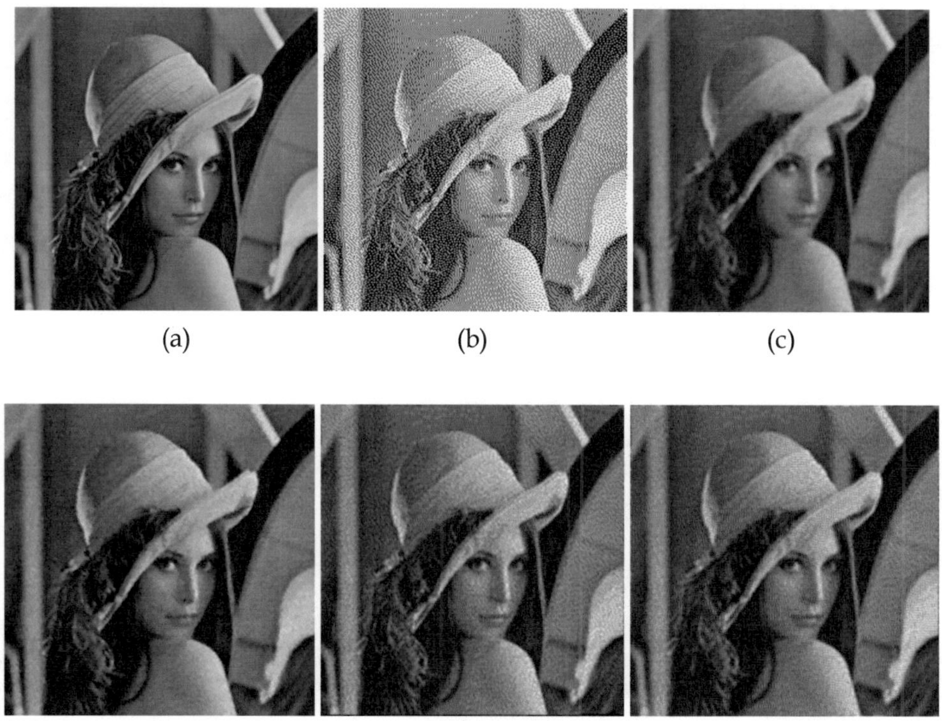

(a) (b) (c) (d) (e) (f)

Fig. 10. (a) the 256-level standard image "Lena" with 256×256 pixels, (b) the halftone image converted from the standard image (a) by the error diffusion using the Floyd-Steinberg's kernel, (c) the restored image due to the GSS when κ=2.5 and D=0 (d) the restored image using the GSS when κ=2.5 and D=25, (e) the restored image obtained by the Gaussian filter, (f) the restored image obtained by the average filter.

Next, we carry out inverse halftoning by using the GSS constructed by introducing both the edge enhancement and the generalized parameter scheduling into the statistical smoothing originally proposed by Wong (Wong, 1995). Here, we construct this method so as to achieve the optimal performance when we observe images through the MTF function of the human vision system. We carry out the GSS by repeating fundamental processes by 5 times. Then, each fundamental process composed of two parts is carried out through pixel by pixel in a raster scan. At the first part, we calculate a mean:

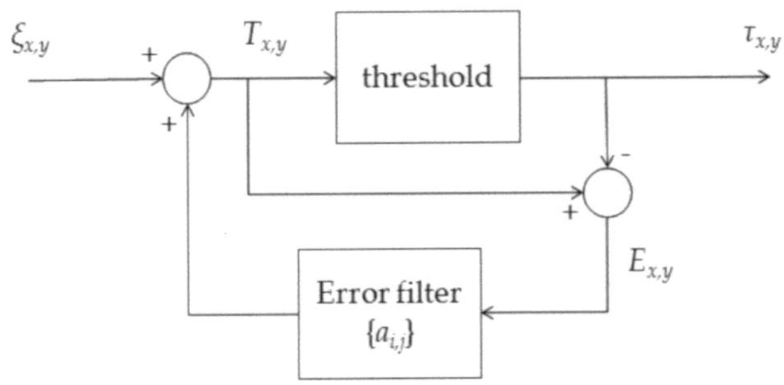

Fig. 11. Block diagram of the error diffusion method, where $\{a_{i,j}\}$ is the kernel of the error diffusion method

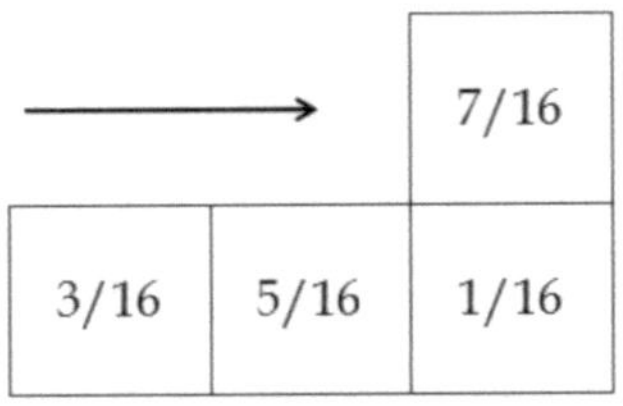

Fig. 12. Floyd-Steinberg's kernel used in the error diffusion method

$$\mu_{m,n} = \sum_{i,j \in R_{m,n}} a_{i,j} x_{i,j}^{\text{old}} \tag{27}$$

which is averaged over the pixels in the region $R_{m,n}$ which includes the (m, n)-th site and the $(m+\delta_x, n+\delta_y)$-sites (δ_x, δ_y=-1,0,1) which hold the condition:

$$| x_{m+\delta_x, n+\delta_y}^{\text{old}} - x_{m,n}^{\text{old}} | < D. \tag{28}$$

Here, D is the threshold to detect edges appearing in original images and should be set respective of the choice of the original image. Then, {ai,j} is the kernel of the conventional Gaussian filter. We note that the present method is regarded as the original statistical smoothing, if D=256. On the other hand, as clearly seen from eq. (28), smoothing does not work if we set to D=0. In this procedure, we then compute a measure $v_{m,n}$ given by the standard deviation:

$$v_{m,n} = \left[\frac{1}{\|R_{m,n}\|} \sum_{(i,j) \in R_{m,n}} \left| x_{i,j}^{\text{old}} - \mu_{i,j} \right|^r \right]^{1/r}. \tag{29}$$

which is averaged over the pixels in the region $R_{m,n}$. Here$\|R_{m,n}\|$is the number of the pixels in the region $R_{m,n}$. Then, the second step of the core process is the smoothing procedure as

$$x_{m,n}^{\text{new}} = \begin{cases} \mu_{m,n} + \gamma v_{m,n} & \text{if } x_{m,n}^{\text{old}} > \mu_{m,n} + \gamma v_{m,n} \\ \mu_{m,n} - \gamma v_{m,n} & \text{if } x_{m,n}^{\text{old}} < \mu_{m,n} - \gamma v_{m,n} \\ x_{m,n}^{\text{old}} & \text{otherwise} \end{cases} \tag{30}$$

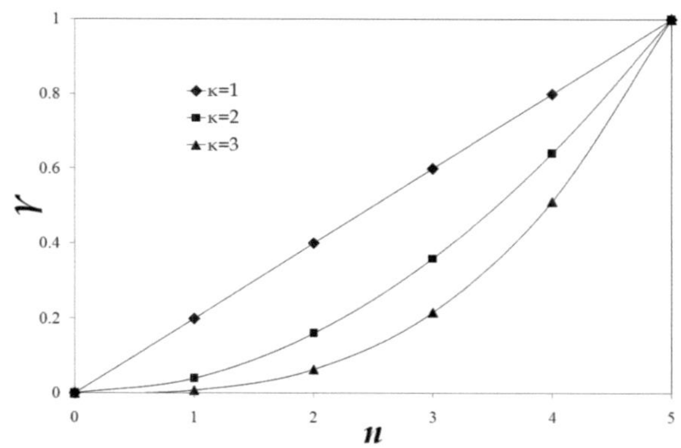

Fig. 13. Generalized parameter scheduling in the GSS.

Here γ is a positive parameter which evolves following the schedule:

$$\gamma = \left(\frac{n}{5}\right)^{\kappa} \tag{31}$$

where n is the positive integer from 1 to 5. This schedule is also shown in Fig. 11. If κ=1, this method is same as the original statistical smoothing proposed by Wong (Wong, 1995). Then, if γ =0, the present method is regarded as the conventional smoothing filter which is characterized by the kernel $\{a_{i,j}\}$.

When we estimate the performance of the GSS for the standard image, as shown in Fig. 14, we use the mean square error between original and reconstructed images both of which are modulated by the MTF function:

$$H(k_x, k_y) = \begin{cases} 5.05\exp\left[-1.38\sqrt{k_x^2+k_y^2}\right]\left(1-\exp\left[-0.1\sqrt{k_x^2+k_y^2}\right]\right) & \\ & (5 \le \sqrt{k_x^2+k_y^2}) \\ 1 & (0 < \sqrt{k_x^2+k_y^2}) \end{cases} \tag{32}$$

which approximates the human vision system. That is, we numerically estimate the performance measure which is expressed as

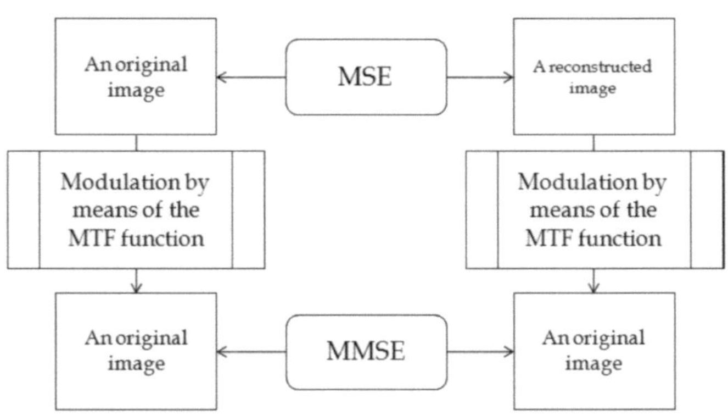

Fig. 14. Performance measure via the MTF function approximating the human vision system

$$MMSE = \frac{1}{L^2}\sum_{x=0}^{L}\sum_{y=0}^{L}\left| \hat{z}_{x,y} - \hat{\xi}_{x,y} \right|^2 , \tag{33}$$

where

$$\hat{z}_{x,y} = \sum_{x=1}^{L}\sum_{Y=1}^{L} \exp[-i(k_x x + k_y y)]\hat{z}_{k_x,k_y} , \tag{34}$$

$$\hat{z}_{k_x,k_y} = z_{k_x,k_y} H(k_x,k_y), \tag{35}$$

$$\hat{z}_{k_x,k_y} = \frac{1}{L^2}\sum_{x=1}^{L}\sum_{Y=1}^{L} \exp[i(k_x x + k_y y)]\hat{z}_{k_x,k_y} \tag{36}$$

For convenience, we note the performance measure as the *MMSE* in the following part of this paper.

3.2 Numerical simulation

In this section, using the numerical simulation for the 256-level standard image "Lena" with 256×256 pixels (Fig. 10(a)), we estimate the performance of the GSS to inverse halftoning for the halftone images converted by the error diffusion method via the Floyd-Steinberg's kernel. When we estimate the performance of the GSS for inverse halftoning, we numerically estimate the *MMSE* between original and reconstructed images.

First, in order to clarify the efficiency of the edge enhancement and the generalized parameter scheduling, we evaluate how the *MMSE* depends on the threshold D for the edge enhancement and the parameter κ for the generalized parameter scheduling. Using the numerical simulation for the 256-level halftone image "Lena" with 256×256 pixels, as shown in Fig. 15, we find that the GSS achieves the optimal performance, if we set to D=25 and κ=2.5 for the 256-level standard image "Lena" with 256×256 pixels. Then, as shown in Figs. 10 (d) and (f), . We also find that the generalized parameter scheduling due to the parameter κ appropriately, and that the GSS reconstructs original image with higher image quality than the conventional average and Gaussian filters.

These results indicate that the performance of the statistical smoothing is improved by introducing appropriate models of the edge enhancement and the generalized parameter scheduling and that the practically useful technique via the GSS can be constructed as the extension of the statistical mechanical method which corresponds to the Bayesian inference via the MPM estimate.

4. Conclusion

In above sections, we have shown our researches on both theoretical and practical aspects of inverse halftoning using the statistical mechanical method and the practical filter via the GSS. First, on the basis of the statistical mechanics of the Q-Ising model, we have investigated the theoretical aspect on inverse halftoning utilizing the Bayesian inference via the MPM estimate. Then, we have investigated the statistical performance using the Monte Carlo simulation for the set of the snapshots of the Q-Ising model. The simulations have found that the optimal performance is realized around the Bayes-optimal condition within statistical

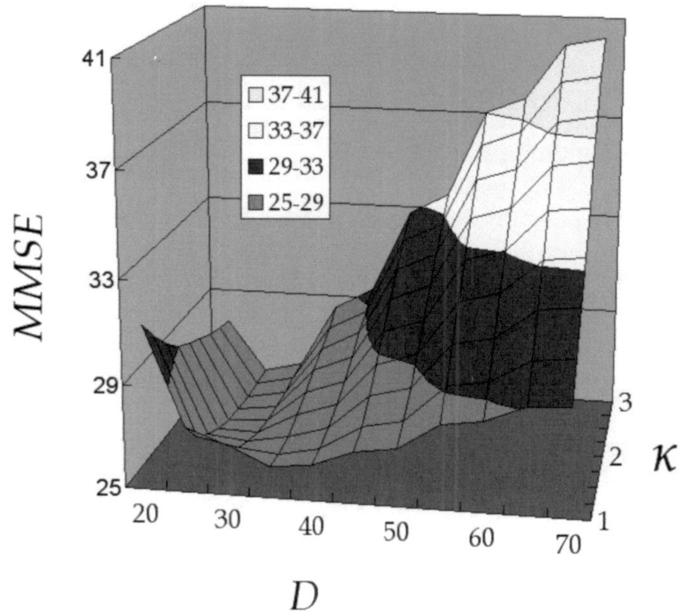

Fig. 15. *MMSE* as a function of the parameter D and κ for the 256-level standard image "Lena" with 256×256 pixels

uncertainty and that it is almost same as the performance of the MAP estimate corresponding to the deterministic limit of the MPM estimate. These results are qualitatively confirmed by the analytical estimate via the infinite-range model. Also we have clarified that the MPM estimate reconstructs original images accurately, if we assume the appropriate model of the true prior. These results have clarified that prior information on original images are important to achieve inverse halftoning with high image quality. Next, we have investigated the practical aspect of inverse halftoning for the halftone image converted by the error diffusion method. In this study, we have constructed the GSS which is regarded as the generalized MAP estimate corresponding to the deterministic limit of the MPM estimate. Here, in order to realize the high performance technique for inverse halftoning, we have proposed the GSS which is constructed by introducing both the edge enhancement and the generalized parameter scheduling into the conventional MAP estimate. Using the numerical simulation for the 256-level standard image, we have clarified that the high performance is achieved by tuning both the threshold for the edge enhancement and the parameter for the generalized parameter scheduling. The above studies have indicated that the theoretical study based on the statistical mechanics gives useful suggestions to construct the practically useful technique based on the MAP estimate.

In the previous researches, we have clarified that the statistical mechanics serves various powerful tools to investigate the problem of inverse halftoning by making use of various techniques, such as the Monte Carlo simulation and the analytical estimate via the infinite-range model, and that the statistical mechanics serves practical and useful techniques based on the MAP estimate. As a future problem, we are going to construct the statistical mechanical techniques based on the Bayesian inference via the MPM estimate by utilizing the knowledge obtained from the practical approach via the GSS for inverse halftoning.

5. References

Bayer, B. E. (1973). An optimum method for two-level rendition continuous tone pictures, *ICC CONF. RECORD*, pp. 11-15, 1973

Besag, J. (1974). Spatal Interaction and Statistical Analysis of Lattice System, *the Journal of the. Royal. Statistics. Society, Series B*, 36(2), pp. 192-236, 1974

Cressie, N. A. C. (1993). *Statistics for Spatial Data*, Wiley, New York, 1993

Floyd, R. W. & Steinberg, L. (1975). Adaptive algorithm for spatioal gray scale, *Proceedings of the SID International Symposium Digest of Technical Papers*, pp. 36-37, 1975

Miceli, C. M. & Parker, K. J. (1992). Inverse Halftoning, *J. Electron Imaging*, Vol. 1, pp. 143-151, 1992

Nishimori, H. (2001). *Statistical Physics of Spin Glasses and Information Processing; An Introduction*, Oxford, London, 2001

Saika, Y. & Nishimori, H. (2002). Statistical Mechanics of Image Restoration by the Plane Rotator Model, *the Journal of the Physical Society of Japan*, Vol. 71, pp. 1052-1058, 2002

Saika, Y. & Nishimori, H. (2005). Statistical mechanical Approaches to the Problem of Phase Retrieval by the Q-Ising Model, *Progress of Theoretical Physics Suppliment*, Vol. 157, pp.292-295, 2005

Saika, Y. & Yamasaki, T. (2007). Generalized Statistical Smoothing to the Problem of Inverse Halftoning for Error Diffusion, *Proceedings of the ICCAS 2007*, pp. 781-784, 2007

Saika, Y.; Inoue, J.; Tanaka, H. & Okada, M. (2009). *Bayes-optimal solution to inverse halftoning based on statistical mechanics of the Q-Ising model, Central European Journal of Physics*, Vol. 7(3), pp. 444-456

Saika, Y. & Okamoto, K. (2010). Probabilistic Modeling to Inverse Halftoning using Edge Preserving Prior, *Proceedings of the SPPRA 2010*, pp. 318-321, 2010

Saika, Y. Sugimoto, K. & Okamoto, K. (2010). Performance Estimation of Generalized Statistical Smoothing to Inverse Halftoning based on the MTF Function of Human Eyes, *Proceedings of the ICA3PP 2010*, pp. 358-367, 2010

Saika, Y., Okamoto, K. & Nakagawa, M. (2010). Generalized Parameter Scheduling and Edge Enhancement in Statistical Smoothing Inverse Halftone Filter, *Proceedings of the CIVS 2010*, pp. 2010, pp. 142-145, 2010

Stevenson, R. (1995). Inverse Halftoning via MAP Estimation, *IEEE Trans. Image Processing*, Vol. 6, pp. 574-583, 1995

Ulchney, R. (1987). *Digital Halftoning*, The MIT Press, Cambridge, Massachusetts, London, England 1987

Winkler, G. (1995). *Image Analysis, Random fields and Dynamic Monte Carlo Methods, A Mathematical Introduction*, Springer-Verlag, Berlin, 1995

Wong, P. W. (1995). Inverse Halftoning and Kernel Estimation for Error Diffusion, *IEEE Trans. Image Processing*, 4, pp. 486-498, 1995

25

A Framework Providing a Basis for Data Integration in Virtual Production

Rudolf Reinhard, Tobias Meisen, Daniel Schilberg, Sabina Jeschke
Institute of Information Management in Mechanical Engineering
RWTH Aachen University
Germany

1. Introduction

Complexity in modern production processes increases continuously. Therefore, the virtual planning of these processes simplifies their realisation extensively and decreases their implementation costs. So far, several institutions have implemented their own simulation tools, which differ in the simulated production technique and in the examined problem domain. On the one hand, there are specialized simulation tools available simulating a specific production technique with exactness close to the real object. On the other hand, there are simulations which comprise production processes as a whole. The latter do not achieve prediction accuracy comparable to the one of specialized tools.

However, both types are commonly applied in university research.

Furthermore most of the applied algorithms in these tools are not yet implemented in commercial tools. Hence, the simulation of a whole production process using these tools is often not realisable due to an insufficient prediction accuracy or the missing support of the asked production techniques. In solving the problem, it is necessary to interconnect different specialized simulation tools and to exchange their resulting data. However, the interconnection is often not achievable because of incompatible file formats, mark-up languages and models used to describe the simulated objects. Therefore, the simulation of a production process as a whole using different simulation tools is hard to realise because of the missing consistency of data and interfaces.

Therefore, results received within a simulation can only be integrated into another one after being checked manually and being adapted to the needs of following simulations, which is both tedious and fault-prone. On the one hand, the huge data volumes being characteristic for simulation processes are not supported by current solutions. On the other hand, the possibilities to adapt a simulation process as a consequence of changes (e.g. integration of a new application, modification of a simulated object) are poorly supported.

In this paper, the architecture of a framework for adaptive data integration is presented, which enables the interconnection of simulation tools of a specified domain. The framework provides generic functionality which, if customised to the needs for a specified domain (e.g. by transformation rules or data interfaces), supports the system to integrate any domain specific application in the process by making use of adaptive integration.

For this purpose, this chapter focus on the integration of data generated during the applications' usage, whereas the applications' link-up technique, which can be handled with the help of modern middleware techniques, will not be stressed. The framework is getting developed within the project "Integrated Platform for Distributed Numerical Simulation", which is a part of the Cluster of Excellence "Integrative Production Technology for High-Wage Countries" at RWTH Aachen University.

2. State of the art

Since the eighties, but at least since the nineties, data integration as well as Enterprise Application Integration (EAI) belongs to the most frequented topics across application boundaries [cf. Halevy et al. (2006)]. Today, a multitude of data integration products can be found which are used in different fields of application. In general, the functionality of those products can be sub-divided into three categories [cf. White (2005)] (cf. figure 1):

- data propagation
- data federation
- data consolidation

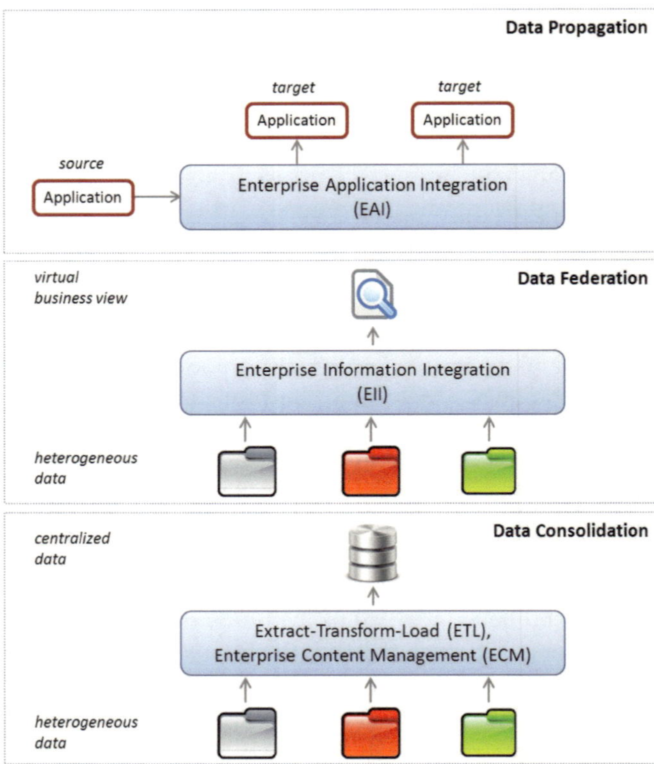

Fig. 1. Main areas of data integration

With regard to the operational section, Data Propagation is applied in order to make use of data on a cross-application basis, which is often realised via data propagation. As already presented in [White (2005)], data propagation mainly focuses on small data volumes like messages and business transactions that are exchanged between different applications. In order to realize EAI, a contemporary architecture concept is used, which was developed in connection with service-based approaches Chappell (2004) and which will be emphasized within this contribution - the so called Enterprise Service Bus (ESB). The basic idea of ESB, which can be compared to the usage of Integration Brokers, comprises the provision of services within a system [Schulte (2002)]. Each service provides a technical or technological functionality with the help of which business processes are supported. All services are connected with each other via the Integration Bus. Transformation services provide general functions in order to transfer data from one format and model into another one. Against that, routing services are used to submit data to other services. Both transformation and routing services are used by adaptors in order to transfer data provided by the Service Bus into the format and the model of an application. Consequently, transformation services support the reuse of implemented data transformations. The advantage of a solution based on the ESB pattern is to be seen in the loose interconnection of several services, whereas the missing physical data interconnection can be regarded as a disadvantage [cf. Rademakers et al. (2008)]: If recorded data has to be evaluated or to be analysed subsequently (e.g. with the help of data exploration techniques like OLAP or Data Mining), it will have to be read out and to be transformed once again. According to this fact, a historic or at least long-term oriented evaluation of data is inconvertible. In order to realize a unified examination on a cross-data basis, other sections belonging to the field of data integration need to be taken into consideration (cf. figure 1). Data Federation, which is examined within the field of Enterprise Information Integration (EII), might serve as one possible solution to enable a unified examination. With the aid of EII, data, which is stored in different data sources, can be unified in one single view [cf. White (2005) and Bernstein et al. (2008)]. This single view is employed by the user to query this virtual, unified data source. The query itself is processed by the EII system by interrogating the underlying, differing data sources. Because of the fact that most EII do not support advanced data consolidation techniques, the implementation will only be successful if the data of the different data sources can be unified and if access to this data is granted (e.g. via query interfaces). Otherwise, techniques belonging to the field of data consolidation, which comprises the integration of differing data into a common, unified data structure, need to be utilised. Extract-Transform-Load (ETL) - a current process with regard to data integration - can be seen as one example of data consolidation [Vassiliadis et al. (2002)]. ETL consists of the following aspects: The extraction of data from one or several - mostly operational - data sources, the transformation of the data format as well as of the data model into a final schema and, finally, the uploading of the final schema to the target data base. The presented sections of data integration (and not just those) have in common that, independent of the type of integration, the heterogeneity of data has to be overcome. In literature, different kinds of heterogeneity are distinguished [cf. Kim et al. (1991) and Goh (1991)]. In this chapter, the types of heterogeneity listed in Leser (2007) will be stressed:

- Technical heterogeneity
- Syntactic heterogeneity
- Data model heterogeneity
- Structural or schema heterogeneity
- Semantic heterogeneity

The problem of technical heterogeneity, which addresses the problem of accessing data, can be handled with the help of modern middleware techniques Myerson (2002). Syntactic heterogeneity, a problem arising as a result of the representation of data (e.g. number formats, character encoding), is solved by converting the existing representation into the required one; in most cases, the conversion is carried out automatically. The handling of data model heterogeneity is more complex, as this kind of heterogeneity can be traced back to data using different data models (e.g. relational database, XML data model, structured text file). Nevertheless, modern data integration solutions provide readers and writers to access data from popular data models like relational databases or XML. Besides that, the support of other data models can be implemented. The combination of both structural and semantic heterogeneity is the most complex form of heterogeneity. Structural heterogeneity addresses the problem of representing data in one data model in different ways, for instance the usage of element attributes versus nested elements in a XML document. Semantic heterogeneity comprises differences in meaning, interpretation and in the type of usage of schema elements or data. Schema and ontology matching as well as mapping methods can be used to find alignments between data schemas as well as to process these alignments. Thereby, an alignment is a set of correspondences between entities of schemas that have to be matched. In the past years, several matching and mapping algorithms have been published [cf. Euzenat et al. (2007)]. However, these methods often focus on database schemas, XML schemas and ontologies without taking into account the background domain specific information [cf. Giunchiglia et al. (2006)]. This chapter will not take a closer look at the last point mentioned. The restriction to a kind of heterogeneity that is predictable via a set of simulation tools restricted beforehand implies a low flexibility that is provided by the corresponding architecture. The user may not employ the specialization of a single tool for a special purpose and is thus forced to disclaim qualified results in a special case.

3. Use case

During procedures like the manufacture of a line pipe, different production techniques are put to use. Within the use case, these techniques are simulated via specialised tools. The use case starts with a simulation of the annealing, the hot rolling as well as the controlled cooling of the components via CASTs, an application developed by Access e.V.. Within a further step, the cutting and the casting will be represented with the help of Abaqus (Dassault Systems), whereas the welding and the expanding of the line pipe will be simulated via SimWeld, a tool which was developed by the Welding and Joining Institute of RWTH Aachen University, and via SysWeld, a software product contrived by the ESI-Group [cf. Rossiter et al. (2007)]. Furthermore, the simulation of modifications in the micro structure of the assembly will be realized by making use of Micress [cf. Laschet et al. (1998)] and Homat [cf. Laschet (2002)], which were both developed by Access e.V.. All in all, the use case contains six different kinds of simulations, each of them based on different formats and models. Apart from that, the project "Integrated Platform for Distributed Numerical Simulation" comprises four additional use cases, on which the requirements directed to the framework are based. Nevertheless, these use cases will not be stressed in the following. The requirements aforementioned were first examined and described in [cf. Schilberg et al. (2009)] and more detailed in [cf. Schilberg (2010)]. Two requirements, which turned out to be central with reference to the framework presented in this paper, are the possibility of Data Propagation and the necessity of a process-oriented Data Consolidation (cf. figure 1). Both of them are used to facilitate a subsequent visualization and analysis of data collected within the process. Another important demand concerns the implementation of the following aspects without having to adapt the application significantly: the illustration of new simulation processes as well as the integration of new simulation tools.

4. The framework's architecture

The framework's architecture is based on the Enterprise Service Bus' (ESB) architectural concept and thus follows the requirements described in section 3. The architecture is illustrated in figure 2 (as described in Chappell (2004)). In order to realise a communication

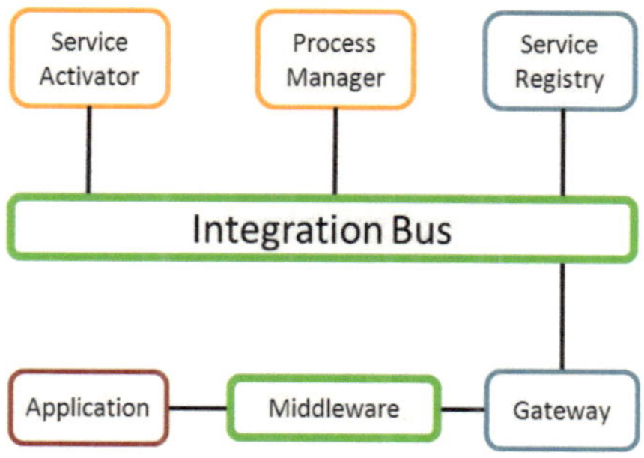

Fig. 2. The system-architecture of the framework

process between the integration server and the applications, a middleware is used that encapsulates the functionality of routing services, which are typical of those ones used in ESB concepts (e.g. within the use case mentioned in section 3, the application-oriented middleware Condor [cf. Thain et al. (2005)] is employed).

Since a service does not provide any capability to communicate over messages it needs a further instance to undertake this task. This instance is the Service Activator. Each Service has its own Service Activator, whereas a Service Activator might also handle several Services. The Service Activator listens to the Integration Bus with the intention to identify any messages containing queries, which could be executed by one of the services the Service Activator cares about. Beside the query itself, the message contains also information about the requirements that need to be fulfilled by the service. In the case there is a query matching the capability of one of the services entrusted to the Service Activator's care, it locks one of its services to process this message and marks it as "in work", so that there is no other service processing this query. The procession's result is getting packed into a message by the Service Activator and is sent to the specified reply queue.

Each process within a simulated production process is managed by the Process Manager. It writes messages containing queries into the Integration Bus' Queue, so that processes can be executed by a service and it cares about the process initiation and eradication. The Integration Bus consists in particular of a queue containing the different queries the Process Manager writes into. The messages are read by at least one Service Activator.

Hence, routing services are not considered in this framework because the integration of standard middleware is straight forward. The framework is employed with the intention of realising an integration level at which service providers, which are directly linked to the Integration Bus, make different services available. Due to the fact that the integration architecture needs to allow the easy substitution of one application by another one, the choice of a service-oriented architecture was helpful, to obtain an adaptable solution. In the following, there will be a concise explanation of the architecture's components.

The services considered in this architecture comprise the following tasks: integration, extraction (both of them act as translators), analysis, transformation and planning. The Integration Services care about the processing of data for the further employment by making use of a particular application. That's why the Service Integration interface needs an own specialised implementation for each integration purpose. The Analysis Service checks the data that has been inserted into the database concerning their current structure as well as its semantics and the structure as well as its semantics requested by the next simulation tool within the simulated production process. Thereby it determines how the current data have to be transformed for the next step. To define the transformation steps needed to prepare the data, in a way that they can be processed by the next simulation tool within the simulated production process, the Analysis Service has to parse the message in order to know which processes are necessary to fulfil the requirements written into the message. Each implementation of the Transformation Service cares about exactly one special aspect in the existing data. This could be for example the indexing of nodes within a geometry. A necessary data model requirement for this purpose is the link between the node objects and "their" geometry object. There are applications starting the indexing for nodes with 0, whereas other applications start it with 1. Furthermore a random number might be determined during the creation of the geometry. By trying to interconnect two of those tools with each other the necessity is obvious to change the index of the existing data such that it can be understood by the next tool. Another example is the conversion of the temperature of a work piece from °C to °F.

In most cases, it is not sufficient to make more than one step to modify output data of one application such that they can be processed by the next application. An important constraint is the order in which these transformations have to be executed as a request exists to obtain a fully automated interconnection of applications on the one hand and the determining of the kind of transformations and their execution order on the other hand. At this point, Planning Services come into consideration.

They determine the kind of Services needed to perform the required operations and how these services have to interact. After their preparation by the appropriate, transformed data they get extracted by an Extraction Service. The Extraction Service cares about the extraction of data, which got recently processed by an application and is meant to get used by another one. In turn, the simulation results are stored within a file with a particular format. In certain cases it might be necessary to modify the input data. This step is called Enrichment.

Since the communication between all components is message driven the question arises, how to activate the adequate service for a certain task. The Process Manager controls the realisation of the current step by an appropriate service instance within a running integration or extraction process. It does not know which functionality can be provided by any service, not about the data a service needs to run. Thus there is the need for an instance having exactly this knowledge. This instance is called Service Registry. It contains information about available services, the functionality each service provides and which input data is required by each service to run properly.

A Gateway always belongs to a single application, which does not possess any capability to communicate with other architecture components over the Message Bus. The Gateway provides access for the architecture components to the application it belongs to and vice versa [Hohpe et al. (2004)]. The described components, in particular the service oriented architecture allow to implement the concept of data integration in an adaptive way. This point will be considered in the following section.

5. Adaptive data integration

The main goal of the adaptive data integration is to overcome the problems of structural and semantic heterogeneity. The adaptive data integration is part of the enrichment process step (cf. section 4), which can be assigned to the extended ETL process being used during the extraction of data. The objective of the extraction process consists in the generation of data in a given data format, taking into account the data model and structure as well as the semantics of this format. Therefore, the implemented enrichment allows the discovery and exploitation of background-specific information. The concept is based upon ontologies and planning algorithms that are usually applied in artificial intelligence. The underlying enrichment process is depicted in figure 3 . In the first instance, the existing data is analysed. The goal of the analysis is the determination of so-called features that are fulfilled by the data. A feature is domain specific, which means that it is expressing a structural or semantic property of the domain. Besides, the analysis step determines features that have to be fulfilled by the data to satisfy the requirements of the specific output format of the extraction process. Subsequent to the analysis, planning algorithms are used to find a data translation that transforms and enriches data in a way that allows for the fulfilment of features needed by the output format. After the planning is finished, the data translation, which is part of the executed step, is processed. The domain-specific data transformation algorithms are stored in transformation services following the ESB architectural concept, whereas the information about existing transformations and features is stored within an ontology. According to Gruber (1993), an ontology is an explicit specification of a conceptualization. In this chapter, the ontology-driven data integration will not be focused due to the limited space, which will not suffice to describe it in a proper way.

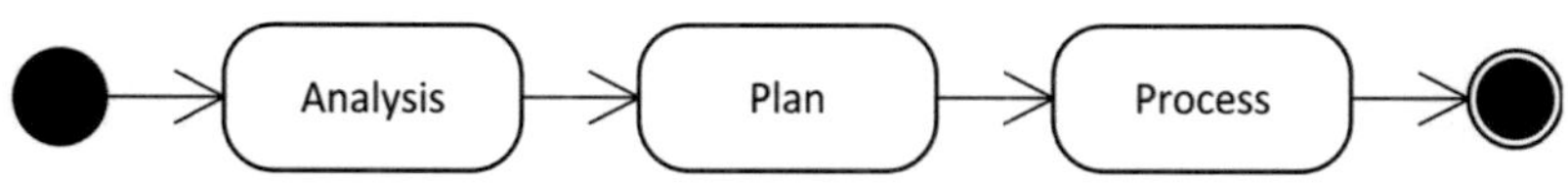

Fig. 3. The Enrichment Process

6. Application of the framework in the use case

Within the domain of the use case described in section 3 and the requirements resulting from the examination of four additional use cases in the domain of FE-simulations, an application has been implemented in parallel to the realisation of the framework. The regarded applications are simulations that use the finite-element-method [cf. Zienkiewicz et al. (2005)]. With regard to the implementation of an application, which is based upon the framework, a domain specific data schema, adaptor services for the integration and extraction process, the transformation service, the data model and the domain ontology have to be provided. An extract of the implementation is presented in figure 4. The domain-specific data schema has been determined by analysing the different input and output formats of the simulations that were employed in the use case. Within this data schema, the geometry of the assembly can be regarded as the central entity. It consists of nodes, cells and attributes. The latter ones exhibit attribute values, which are assigned to individual cells or nodes depending on the class of attributes available in the whole geometry. The integration services, which were specified within the use case, read the geometrical data provided by the simulation, transform it into the central data model and upload the results into the database. In contrast, the extraction services proceed as follows: The geometrical data is read out from the central database and is transformed into the required format. Finally, the data is uploaded into the destination file or into the target database. Because of the prior enrichment, all structural and semantic data transformations have been carried out. Hence, most of the data transformations formerly performed by the adaptors' integration and extraction services are omitted. Integration

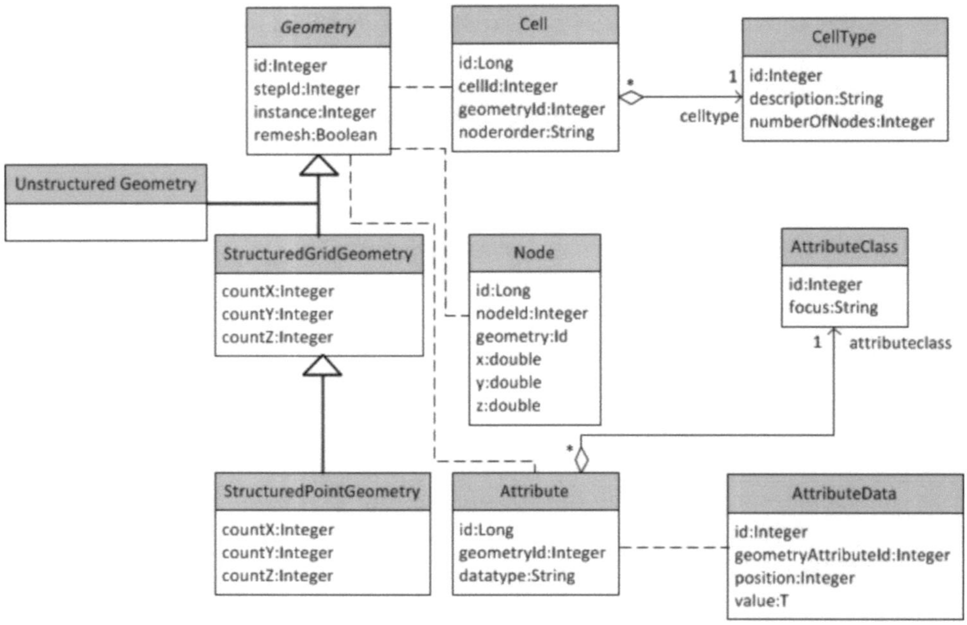

Fig. 4. Extract of the data schema used in the domain of FE-simulation

and extraction service: Most of these service adaptors have been implemented using the Pentaho Data Integrator (PDI). In case that more complex data or binary formats have been given, which can only be read by programming interfaces of the manufacturer, either the PDI functionality have been extended using the provided plug-in architecture or the needed functionality has been implemented using Java or C++. For example, the simulation results generated within the simulation tool CASTS are stored in the Visualization Toolkit (VTK) format [cf. Schroeder et al. (2004)]. Hence, an integration service was implemented, which is based on the programming interface supported by the developers of VTK using the provided functionality of the framework. Furthermore, an extraction service was developed with regard to the Abaqus input format, whereby, in this case, the aforementioned ETL tool PDI was used. Transformation library service: In order to realize the data integration, different sorts of data transformations for FE data were implemented into the application as services, for example the conversion of attribute units, the deduction of attributes from those ones that are already available, the relocating of the component's geometry within space, the modification of cell types within a geometry (e.g. from a hexahedron to a tetrahedron) or the aforementioned re-enumeration of nodes and cells.

7. Conclusion

The development of the framework presented in this chapter can be regarded as an important step in the establishment of digital production, as the framework allows a holistic, step-by-step simulation of a production process by making use of specialized tools. Both, data losses as well as manual, time-consuming data transmissions from one tool to another are excluded by this approach. The suggested framework facilitates the linking of simulation tools, which were, "until now", developed independently from each other and which are specialized for certain production processes or methods, too. Furthermore, the integration of data generated in the course of the simulation is realized in a unified and process-oriented way. Apart from the integration of further simulation tools into an application that was already established, it is essential to extend the domain of simulations reflected upon with additional simulations covering the fields of machines and production. In this way, a holistic simulation of production processes is provided. Thereby, a major challenge consists in generating a central data model, which supports the possibility of illustrating data uniformly and in consideration of its significance in the overall context, which, in turn, comprises the levels of process, machines as well as materials. Due to the methodology presented in this article, it is not necessary to adapt applications to the data model aforementioned. On the contrary, this step is realized via the integration application, which is to be developed on the basis of the framework. Because of the unified data view and the particular logging of data at the process level, the framework facilitates a comparison between the results of different simulation processes and simulation tools. Furthermore, conclusions can be drawn much easier from potential sources of error. This is a procedure, which used to be characterized by an immense expenditure of time and costs. The realization of this procedure requires the identification of Performance Indicators, which are provided subsequently within the application. In this context, the development of essential data exploration techniques on the one side and of visualization techniques on the other side turns out to be a further challenge.

8. Acknowledgement

The approaches presented in this paper are supported by the German Research Association (DFG) within the Cluster of Excellence "Integrative Production Technology for High-Wage Countries".

9. References

J. M. Myerson, The Complete Book of Middleware. Boston, MA, USA: Auerbach Publications, 2002.

A. Halevy, A. Rajaraman, and J. Ordille, "Data integration: the teenage years" in VLDB'2006: Proceedings of the 32nd international conference on Very large data bases, pp. 9-16, VLDB Endowment, 2006.

C. White, "Data Integration: Using ETL, EAI, and EII Tools to Create an Integrated Enterprise" tech. rep., The Data Warehousing Institute, 2005.

D. Chappell, Enterprise Service Bus: Theory in Practice. O'Reilly Media, 2004.

R. W. Schulte, "Predicts 2003: Enterprise service buses emerge" tech. rep., Gartner, 2002.

T. Rademakers and J. Dirksen, Open-Source ESBs in Action. Greenwich, CT, USA: Manning Publications Co., 2008.

P. A. Bernstein and L. M. Haas, "Information integration in the enterprise" Commun. ACM, vol. 51, no. 9, pp. 72-79, 2008.

P. Vassiliadis, A. Simitsis, and S. Skiadopoulos, "Conceptual modeling for etl processes," in DOLAP '02: Proceedings of the 5th ACM international workshop on Data Warehousing and OLAP, (New York, NY, USA), pp. 14-21, ACM, 2002.

W. Kim and J. Seo, "Classifying schematic and data heterogeneity in multidatabase systems" Computer, vol. 24, no. 12, pp. 12-18, 1991.

C. H. Goh, Representing and reasoning about semantic confliicts in heterogeneous information systems. PhD thesis, Massachusetts Institute of Technology, 1997. Supervisor-Madnick, Stuart E.

U. Leser, Informationsintegration : Architekturen und Methoden zur Integration verteilter und heterogener Datenquellen. Heidelberg: Dpunkt-Verl., 1. Auflage, 2007.

J. Euzenat and P. Shvaiko, Ontology matching. Berlin/New York: Springer, 2007.

F. Giunchiglia, P. Shvaiko, and M. Yatskevich, "Discovering missing background knowledge in ontology matching" in Proceeding of the 2006 conference on ECAI 2006, (Amsterdam, The Netherlands, The Netherlands), pp. 382-386, IOS Press, 2006.

U. D. E. Rossiter, O. Mokrov, "Integration des Simulationspaketes SimWeld in FEM-Analyseprogramme zur Modellierung von Schweißprozessen" Sysweld Forum 2007, 2007.

G. Laschet, J. Neises, and I. Steinbach, "Micro-Macrosimulation of casting processes" 4iéeme école d'été de "Modélisation numérique en thermique", vol. C8, pp. 1-42, 1998.

G. Laschet, "Homogenization of the thermal properties of transpiration cooled multi-layer plates" Computer Methods in Applied Mechanics and Engineering, vol. 191, no. 41-42, pp. 4535-4554, 2002.

D. Schilberg and T. Meisen, "Ontology based semantic interconnection of distributed numerical simulations for virtual production" in Industrial Engineering and Engineering Management, 2009. IE EM '09. 16th International Conference on, pp. 1789 -1793, 21-23 2009.

D. Schilberg, Architektur eines Datenintegrators zur durchg"angigen Kopplung von verteilten numerischen Simulationen. PhD thesis, RWTH Aachen University, 2010.

D. Thain, T. Tannenbaum, and M. Livny, "Distributed Computing in Practice: The Condor Experience" Concurrency and Computation: Practice and Experience, vol. 17, pp. 2-4, 2005.

P. Cerfontaine, T. Beer, T. Kuhlen, and C. Bischof, "Towards a flexible and distributed simulation platform" in ICCSA '08: Proceedings of the international conference on Computational Science and Its Applications, Part I, (Berlin, Heidelberg), pp. 867-882, Springer-Verlag, 2008.

G. Hohpe, B. Woolf, Enterprise Integration Patterns, Addisson-Wesley, 2004

T. R. Gruber, "A translation approach to portable ontology specifications" Knowledge Acquisition, vol. 5, pp. 199-220, 1993.

O. C. Zienkiewicz and R. L. Taylor, The Finite Element Method. Basis and Fundamentals. Butterworth Heinemann, 6th ed., 2005.

W. Schroeder, K. Martin, and B. Lorensen, The Visualization Toolkit, Third Edition. Kitware Inc., 2004.

26

Mathematical Modelling and Numerical Simulation of the Dynamic Behaviour of Thermal and Hydro Power Plants

Flavius Dan Surianu
Politechnica University of Timisoara
Romania

1. Introduction

The global economic and social development process has brought about increasing capacities of electric energy production, transportation and distribution. This fact has required both the development of the national power systems and the interconnection of most of them, leading to real expanded continental power systems. But technological development and territorial expansion have generated new problems concerning their running and monitoring. Planning, designing, leading and running such huge systems has turned to very complex activities, indissolubly linked with their operating stability. The problem of power system stability has got new spatial and temporal dimensions implying the reconsideration of the means and methods of analysis through revising and expanding mathematical modelling in order to get a most accurate numerical simulation of the operating regime[1]. The operating experience shows that the synchronism of synchronous generators in networking power plants can be lost even at a few minutes after a disturbance has appeared. In this case the phenomena are much more complex and they refer to slow power oscillations on the interconnecting electric lines among large areas which lead to a decrease in frequency and loss of synchronism among these regions. Such phenomena can appear due to the poor performance of the frequency - exchange power control and the unsatisfactory answer of the slow action of the governing elements as, for example, those of the boilers, turbines, charging valves, feeding pumps, hydro units etc. In this respect, they speak about Long Term Dynamic (LTD) stability or slow phenomena stability[2]. From the point of view of time scale analysis, the phenomena which are manifest in Long Term Dynamic processes are minute long, comprising a part of the time allotted to the variation of consumers` electric loading and the values of the time constants of the boilers and steam turbines as well as those of the primary installations of the hydro units. Therefore it is necessary to increase the number of the system elements whose mathematical modelling has to be considered in simulation, so that the main components of the power system be included starting from the thermal, hydro and mechanical primary installations up to the consumers, including the characteristics of the respective elements and the functional relationships between the input and the output values and the assembly as a whole.

---

[1] (Ernst et al., 2004)
[2] (Hongesombut et al., 2005)

2. The mathematical modelling of the primary installations of a thermal power plant

In Long Term Dynamics, due to the expansion of the time scale analysis, the slow thermal- mechanical processes will appear and influence the behaviour of the electric power system.

2.1 The mathematical modelling of the steam boiler

Two aspects have to be considered in this case: on one hand, it is the realization of the mathematical model, which automatically represents a storing element, inducing an important delay of the output signal and, on the other hand, the determination of the mathematical model of the boiler control system which, from the point of view of automation, is a chain of proportionally integrating and proportionally derivative elements with multiple delays and limitations[3].

The boilers used in thermal power plants are drum type boilers and once-through boilers. In the case of the former, their dynamics is dominated by fuels and air, and for the latter the feed water is dominant on the main parameter, which changes in large limits and can influence the power of the corresponding turbine, namely the pressure of the live steam, p_t.

The boiler aggregate, as a controlled object, having pressure as an output value is considered to be made of two cascaded elements: the combustion chamber and the steam generator (figure 1). In the case of boilers without coal dust hopper there appears a third element, the coal mill (figure 2).

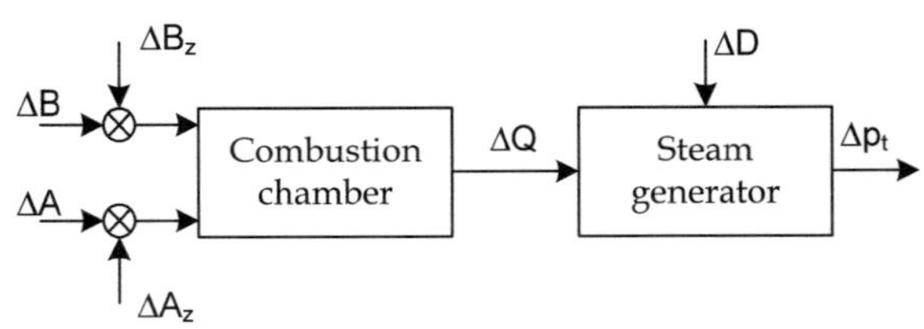

Fig. 1. The diagram of the steam boiler as a controlled object

The controlled value, pressure, changes with the variation of the heat quantity, ΔQ, produced by the combustion chamber, as a result of the modification of the fuel flow rate, ΔB and that of the air, ΔA, at the entry into the combustion chamber. The main disturbances which operate on the steam pressure are the variation of the steam load required by the consumer, ΔD, which acts as an external disturbance and the variation of the fuel flow rate, ΔB_z, which acts as an internal disturbance. The variation of the air flow rate, ΔA_z, although, from a quantitative point of view, having an effect similar with ΔB_z, has got a much less effect on the steam pressure because the air excess in the combustion chamber leads to the increase of heat losses through the evacuated gases, and its excessive reduction determines the increase of losses due to imperfect chemical combustion. Steam pressure, p_t, remains constant if the thermal and mass balance are undisturbed.

[3] (Surianu, 2008)

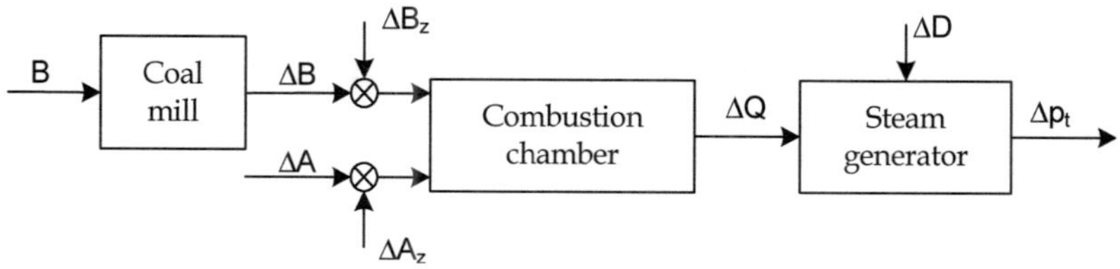

Fig. 2. The diagram of the steam boiler without coal dust hopper

If we consider that the mass balance between the feed water flow rate and steam flow rate is satisfied, the pressure variation process is described approximately through the differential equation:

$$T_a \frac{dp_t}{dt} = D_q - D; \tag{1}$$

where: D_q - is the boiler thermal load; D - is the steam load; T_a [kg/at] – is the accumulation constant. By means of T_a, there can be calculated the boiler inertia time as following:

$$T_p = T_a \frac{p_{tn}}{D_{max}}; \tag{2}$$

For the modern boilers, $T_p = (125 \div 300)$ seconds. If there are used per units related to the boiler nominal values, steam load, D, becomes $d = p_t$ and from expressions (1) and (2) there follows:

$$T_p \frac{dp_t}{dt} = d_q - \dot{m}_t - p_t; \tag{3}$$

where: d_q represents the boiler thermal load in per unit and $\dot{m}_t$ is the steam flow rate, in per unit (p.u.). Expression (3) allows the representation of the steam generator through a transfer function having a first order delay, if the operational operator, $s = \frac{d}{dt}$, is introduced, namely:

$$H_c = \frac{1}{1 + s \cdot T_p}. \tag{4}$$

The mathematical model of the boiler, described by transfer function (4) has got for input value (figure 3) the algebraic sum of the signals of the load and the steam flow rate, $\dot{m}_t$ (if there is no thermo-mechanical control system), or the algebraic sum between the load signal and the load reference signal of the synchronous generator (if there is a thermo-mechanical control system).

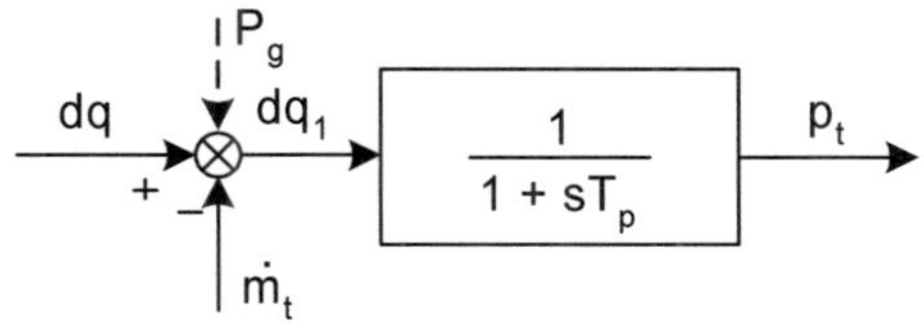

Fig. 3. The diagram of the mathematical model of the steam boiler.

The output value is represented by steam pressure, p_t. This mathematical model has the advantage of simplicity but it implies a more detailed representation of the control system. Though simple, it approximates fairly well the dynamic behaviour of any type of steam generator, both from a quantitative and from a qualitative point of view. As to the combustion chamber, its influence on the dynamic behaviour of the boiler depends on its construction and on the combustion method. The heat evolved by the combustion chamber is determined by the control system of the combustion process, which contains a fuel feeding system and a fuel control. The fuel controller reacts to the steam flow rate and steam pressure and to other parameters depending on its construction and it emits a modification impulse of the fuel flow rate. After emitting the impulse, after a certain period of time, depending on the delay in the fuel feeding system, there starts the modification of thermal load, D_q. In the case of drum type boilers, the modification process of the thermal load can be described by the differential equation:

$$T_c \frac{dD_q}{dt} + D_q = \mu_B \cdot e^{-\frac{t}{T_F}}; \tag{5}$$

where: $T_F = (20 \div 25)$ s is the time constant of the combustion chamber and $T_c = (6 \div 60)$ s is the time constant of the fuel carriage which depends on the control type and on the type of the fuel that is used. The position of the control device of the fuel feeding system has been assigned to μ_B. In the case of once-through boilers, as the dynamics of the boiler is determined by the rapid water-steam flow, the influence of the steam generator is much diminished versus the delay introduced by the water feed pumps, which can be represented by the following transfer function:

$$\mathrm{H_p} = \frac{1}{1 + \mathrm{M} \cdot \mathrm{s}} \tag{6}$$

where: $M = (20 \div 25)$ s represents the time constant of the boiler-water feed pumps[4].

2.2 The mathematical modelling of the steam boiler automation

The automatic control of the steam boiler has to solve a set of problems connected with the synchronous control of more values: load control, combustion control, keeping constant the water level in the drum type boilers, keeping constant steam temperature and negative pressure in the combustion chamber. The control of these values means modelling the types of control equipments, namely the pressure of steam, the fuel and air, the feed water and the temperature. As temperature modifications and control are very slow, their modelling can be neglected. As to the fuel and air control and feed water control equipments, these will determine boiler load D_q. The main components which influence the boiler response being fuel dynamics and the dynamics of the air introduced in the ventilators as well as the response of the feed water pumps and of the associated control equipments, the dynamic dependences will be manifest through two distinct ways: a slow one (fuel-air) and a quick one (water-steam). The two ways have no direct physical correspondence, but they can be used together to simulate either drum type boilers (where the dominant effect on pressure belongs to fuel and air) or once-through boilers (where the boiler load dynamics is

[4] (Surianu, 2009)

dominated by the boiler feed water parameters); there can also be combinations of both effects, depending on the value adopted for a weight factor $0 \le K \le 1$, introduced into the calculation programs, which simulate steam boiler behaviour in dynamic processes. The block diagram of the steam boiler automation is represented in figure 4.

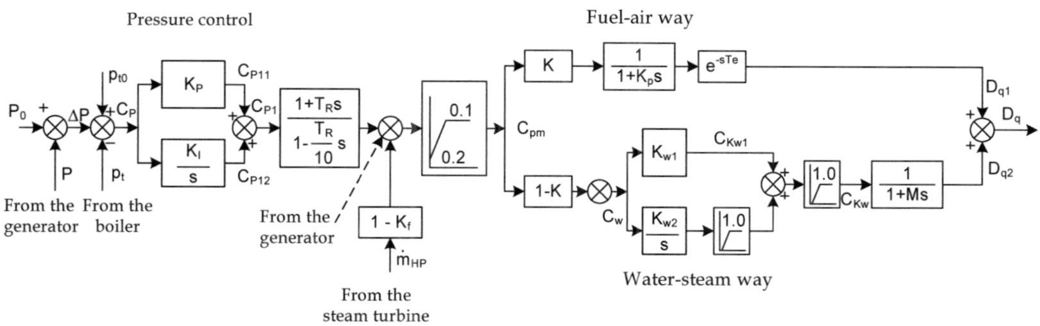

Fig. 4. The block diagram of the steam boiler automation

The pressure control equipments have been represented through a $P-I$ type, followed by a differential control unit (figure 4). At the entrance into the control equipment there has been applied the signal of pressure error at the admission valve versus the pressure reference value, balanced with the load error of the generator. The output signal can be balanced with the generator load signal or with the signal of the turbine steam flow rate, when there is no coordinating thermo-mechanical control system and it has got both superior and inferior limits. Fuel-air dynamics (the case of the drum type boilers) is represented through a delay of $\left(1/(1+T_F \cdot s)\right)$ and $\left(e^{-sT_c}\right)$ type smoothness, due to fuel feed, smoothness that can be neglected if the boiler is fed with burning oil and gas. Water- steam dynamics (the case of the once-through boilers) is simulated through a $P-I$ control unit described by expression$\left(K_{W_1} + K_{W_2} / s\right)$, with a corresponding limitation and by a first order delay function, I, due to the water feed pumps $\left(1/(1+M \cdot s)\right)$, where M is the time constant of the water feed pumps. The action signal of the boiler load, D_q, has been got from adding up the output signals of the two ways (fuel-air and water-steam). The mathematical model described in figure 4 allows simulating automation for both types of boilers, drum type boilers and once-through boilers, through values 1, respectively, 0, assigned to weighting factor K.

2.3 The mathematical modelling of the steam turbine

The changes in the energetic status of a steam turbine can be generated by the following disturbing values:

- Load variations (the electric power and the voltage at the synchronous generator terminals);
- Live steam flow variation (the boiler steam flow);
- Live steam pressure variation (due to the modification of the fuel heating power);
- Live steam flow variation at the turbine's steam bleeding.

2.3.1 The transfer function of the steam turbine

The nominal electric power of the steam turbine-synchronous generator aggregate operating in steady regime is given by the expression:

$$P = M_T \Omega = \eta \cdot \eta_e \cdot D \cdot H \; ; \tag{7}$$

where: η is the real efficiency of the turbine, η_e is the electric energy efficiency, D is the steam flow rate at the entrance of the turbine and H is the enthalpy variation in the turbine[5]. The difference between the instantaneous values of mechanical torque M_T, of the turbine and the synchronous generator electric torque M_G, modifies the aggregate dynamic torque, according to the second principle of Newtonian mechanics:

$$M = M_T - M_G = J\frac{d\Delta\omega}{dt} \, . \tag{8}$$

In the transitory regimes of the electric power systems, the deviations of pulsation versus the synchronous pulsation $(\Delta\omega = \omega - \omega_n)$ do not exceed (20-30) %. In this scale, the characteristics turbine torque-pulsation can be approximated through tangent lines in the point corresponding to the rated speed. In figure 5 there is represented such a family of characteristics having μ as position parameter of the steam admission valve of the speed control system.
In this case, the equation of the characteristic turbine torque-pulsation is expressed in per units as following:

$$M_T = \alpha - \beta \cdot \omega_n \; ; \tag{9}$$

where: α and β are constant coefficients which, according to figure 5, satisfy the expression:

$$\alpha = 1 + \beta \; ; \tag{10}$$

and $\beta = (0.7 \div 1.2)$ for different types of turbines.

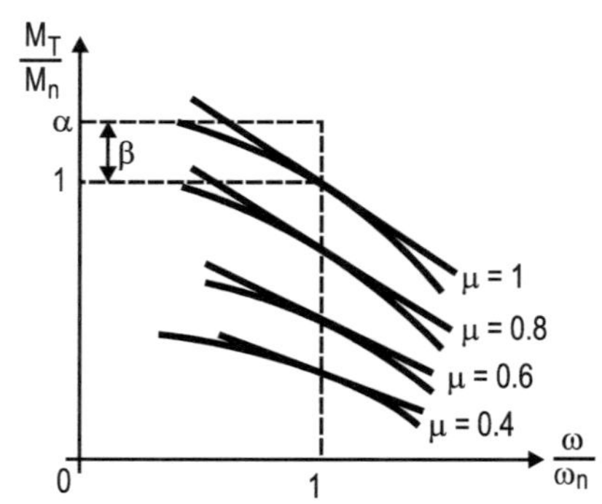

Fig. 5. The diagram of the characteristics turbine torque - pulsation

Experimentally there has been observed that, when the turbine power varies, the slope of the characteristics turbine torque-pulsation varies depending on the torque corresponding to the rated speed, namely:

$$M_T = M_n(\alpha - \beta\omega) \, . \tag{11}$$

---

[5] (Zhiyong et al., 2008)

In expression (11) coefficient $M_n\beta = k\varphi$ is the turbine automatic control coefficient and it is equal with the slope of the characteristic. If the variation of the torque and pulsation in expression (8) are related to the corresponding nominal values, the following result is obtained:

$$\frac{\Delta M}{M_n} = J\frac{\omega_n}{M_n}\frac{d\frac{\Delta\omega}{\omega_n}}{dt}; \tag{12}$$

where: factor $J\omega_n / M_n$ has a temporal dimension and represents the starting time constant or the launching time of the turbine - synchronous generator aggregate, namely:

$$T_l = J\frac{\omega_n}{M_n} = J\frac{\omega_n^2}{P_n}. \tag{13}$$

Launching time, T_l, does not modify proportionally with the machine power as inertia moment J, due to constructive reasons, does not increase proportionally with the increase in the machine power.
Equation (12) can be rewritten in an operational form, as a transfer function H(s), considering the operator $s = \frac{d}{dt}$, namely:

$$H(s) = \frac{1}{T_l \cdot s}. \tag{14}$$

Relation (14) shows that the aggregate behaves like an integral unit whose output value has a linear variation in time, at a step variation of the input value.

2.3.2 The mathematical modelling of the boiler with steam re-heater

The presence of the steam re-heater modifies the behaviour in the case of turbines built with three pressure units. The use of steam re-heater in this case allows increasing the aggregate power and efficiency but it leads to a worsened dynamic behaviour because the steam re-heater follows with some delay the power variations generated by the control valve of the intermediate and low pressure units (IPU+LPU), introducing a dead time in the transmission of the variations of the steam flow rate at the entrance[6]. At the same time, the large volume of steam leads, through pressure release in (IPU+LPU), to large super-adjustments of speed and rapid power variations. This is due to the fact that the contribution to power of (IPU+LPU) is about (70÷80) % of the nominal value while that of the high pressure unit (HPU) is only (20÷30) %. A simplified representation of the turbine-synchronous generator aggregate, having a steam re-heater is given in figure 6.
The steam generated by the boiler flows through HPU, where it releases part of its thermal energy, determining a torque MT_1 at the turbine axis, then flows through the connecting pipe and enters the steam re-heater where it receives an excess of thermal

[6] (Dimo et al., 1980)

energy and from here it flows through the connecting pipe with IPU+LPU, where determines torque MT_2 at the turbine axis. The rotors of units HPU, IPU and LPU being rigidly coupled, the total torque will be the sum of the torques developed in each unit. In the studies of Long Term Dynamic stability the mathematical modelling of the turbine with three pressure units and steam re-heater can be described through the block diagram in figure 7.

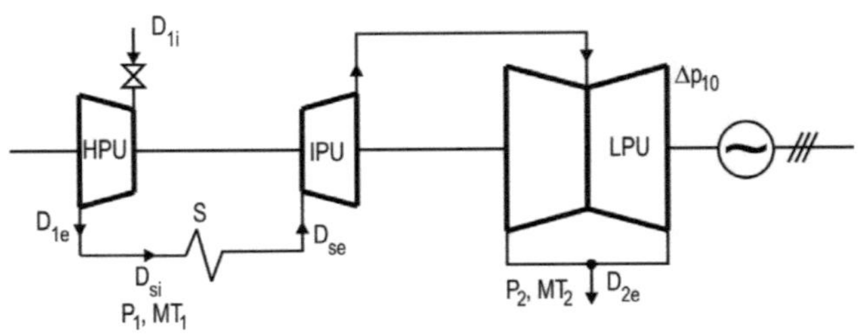

Fig. 6. Block diagram of the boiler with steam re-heater

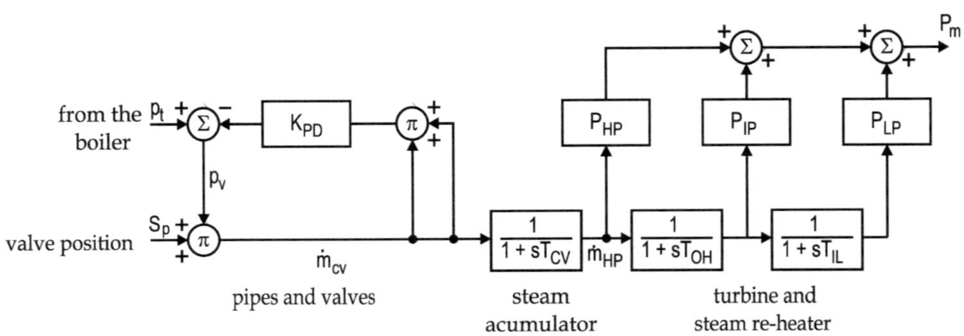

Fig. 7. The block diagram of the steam turbine aggregate.

The input value of the mathematical model of the steam turbine in figure 7 is steam flow rate $\dot{m}_{CV}$, at the output of the assembly of pipes – admission valves – speed governor. The steam flow rate, $\dot{m}_{CV}$, is calculated in per units, multiplying the position signal of the admission valve, S_p, by the pressure at admission valve, p_V , (p_V being calculated through the algebraic summing of the steam pressure given by the boiler with the output value of the proportional reaction given by the assembly of high pressure pipes). There follows:

$$\dot{m}_{CV} = S_p\left(p_t - K_{PD} \cdot \dot{m}_{CV}^2\right); \quad (15)$$

where: K_{PD} is the amplifying factor corresponding to the drop pressure in the high pressure pipes. To the steam flow rate, $\dot{m}_{CV}$, there is applied a delay described by a transfer function with a first order delay $1/(1+sT_{CV})$, where T_{CV} is the steam time constant through pipes and valves, resulting in steam flow rate $\dot{m}_{HP}$ at the entrance of the high pressure unit of the turbine. The steam turbine is modelled through two serially connected first order delay elements representing the delays given by the steam re-heater having time constant T_{OH} and by the steam transfer between the intermediate and low pressure units with time constant T_{IL}, as well as three proportional elements corresponding to the mechanical power weight of the high, intermediate and low pressure units. The generally accepted values[7] of the constants of the mathematical model are given in Table 2. The amplifying factors are given in per units and the time constants, in seconds. The output value of the mathematical model is the mechanical power at turbine axle, P_m, expressed in per units, too.

Aggregate type	K_{PD}	P_{HP}	P_{IP}	P_{LP}	T_{CV} [s]	T_{OH} [s]	T_{IL} [s]
Turbine with 3 units of pressure and steam re-heater	0 ÷ 1	0.3	0.4	0.3	0.1÷0.4	4 ÷ 11	0.3÷0.5

Table 2. The values of the constants of the steam turbine

The mathematical model of the steam turbine represented in the block diagram in figure 7 is described by the following set of algebraic and differential equations:

$$\dot{m}_{CV} = S_p\left(p_t - K_{PD}\cdot \dot{m}_{CV}^2\right);$$

$$\frac{d\dot{m}_{HP}}{dt} = T_{CV}^{-1}\left(\dot{m}_{CV} - \dot{m}_{HP}\right);$$

$$\frac{d\dot{m}_{IP}}{dt} = T_{OH}^{-1}\left(\dot{m}_{HP} - \dot{m}_{IP}\right); \qquad (16)$$

$$\frac{d\dot{m}_{LP}}{dt} = T_{IL}^{-1}\left(\dot{m}_{IP} - \dot{m}_{LP}\right);$$

$$P_m = P_{HP}\dot{m}_{HP} + P_{IP}\dot{m}_{IP} + P_{LP}\dot{m}_{LP}\,.$$

The initial values of the variables are obtained from the pre-disturbance steady state, which results from annulling the derivatives in expression (16), this fact leading to the system of above mentioned algebraic equations. Though, there has to be mentioned that the steam turbine, as an assembly, behaves like a derivative element of first order delay, the modelling described as a transfer function $K_T/(1+sT_T)$, is legitimate if constants K_T and T_T are chosen appropriately. But we consider that such a representation is too general to be valid in the case of interconnecting the steam turbine with the steam boiler upstream and the synchronous generator downstream.

3. The mathematical modelling of the primary installations of a hydro power plant

The theoretical study of the behaviour and stability of hydro power plants is complex and highly difficult due to the large number of variables, to the fact that hydro units cannot be standardized (each of them depending on the geographical situation of the area where it is placed) and to the non-linearity of the hydro power system[8]. That is why the first research works in the field have been directed to realizing the linearity of the system around the

[7] (Surianu, 2009)
[8] (Fraile-Ardanuy et al., 2006)

operating point. In order to be able to analyze the stability of a hydro power plant, this should be theoretically divided into two subsystems: the hydro subsystem (from the reservoir to the turbine) and the electro-mechanical one (comprising the turbine, the admission valves control system and the speed governor). The assembly of the two subsystems is represented in figure 8.

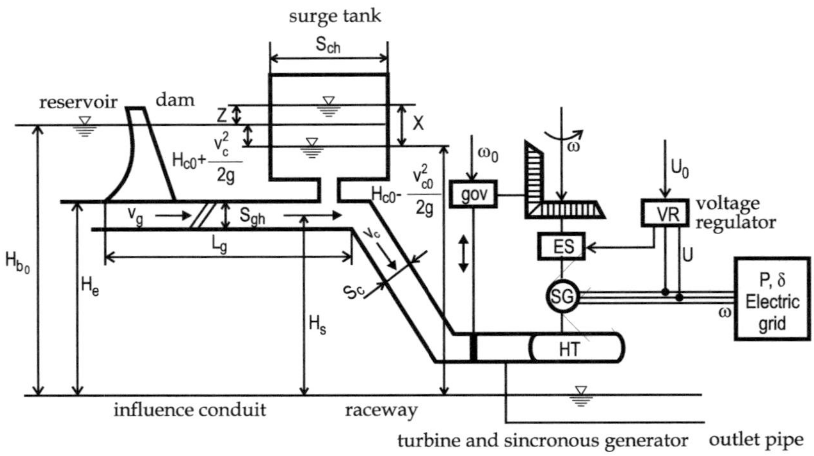

Fig. 8. The block diagram of a hydro power plant.

3.1 The simple mathematical modelling of a hydro power plant

The hydro power plant comprises the reservoir, the influent conduit, the surge tank, the raceway and the hydro turbine. The mathematical modelling of the hydro power plant implies writing the characteristic operating equations for each unit separately, established for common operating conditions and assembling the equations in a mathematical system which is solved at each simulation step. The problem is highly difficult and that is why, for the largest number of the power system stability studies, the modelling of the hydro power plant is reduced to modelling the hydro turbine whose transitory characteristics are deduced from the dynamics of the water in the raceway. The following mathematical model is obtained and it is presented in figure 9.

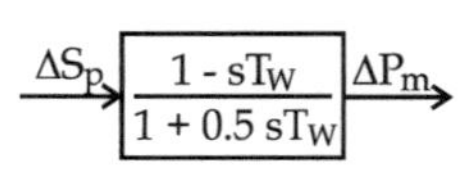

Fig. 9. The ideal model of the hydro turbine

In this mathematical model, the whole hydro power plant is considered practically through the value attributed to constant, T_W, which represents the water launching time or the water time constant. It is associated with the water acceleration time in the raceway between the dam and the turbine and it can be determined with the following expression:

$$T_W = \frac{L \cdot v}{g \cdot H_t} \; ; \tag{17}$$

where: L is the length of the raceway, v is the water speed, g is the gravity acceleration and H_t is the net head of water in the raceway. The longer the net head of water is the shorter the water launching time and, usually, T_W = (0.5 ÷ 7) s. This mathematical model is simple and easy to handle but it is too general and cannot be applied to long raceways.

3.2 The complex mathematical model of the hydro power plant

In order to obtain the complex mathematical model of a hydro power plant[9] we need some explanations and preliminary calculations. Thus:

a. All the values are expressed in per units related to the absolute values corresponding to the operating point in the pre-disturbance steady state.
b. Considering the problem of a hydro unit stability implies that with a relatively short time variation , Δt, all the values vary only in the vicinity of their operating point in steady state, fact accepted physically due to the big inertia of the system and of the corresponding large time constants. This way, the infinitesimal quantities of a rank higher than 2 are neglected and only the first terms in the series development around the steady state point are kept, namely the equations describing the behaviour in time of the different elements of the hydro power plants are smoothed.
c. There are defined the following values for the hydro turbine and hydro unit according to the turbine mechanical, hydro and geometrical parameters. These values are presented in Table 3:

Physical values	Mathematical formula	Observations
Turbine energy value	$\varepsilon = \dfrac{2 \cdot g \cdot H_n}{R^2 \cdot n^2}$	R– turbine radius; n– turbine speed.
Turbine water flow rate value	$\gamma = \dfrac{Q_n}{S \cdot R^3 \cdot n}$	Q_n – nominal flow rate; S – turbine section.
Turbine power value	$\psi = \dfrac{2 \cdot P_{mn}}{\rho \cdot S \cdot R^5 \cdot n^3}$	P_{mn} –nominal mechanical power; ρ – water density.
Turbine efficiency value	$\eta = \dfrac{P_{mn}}{\rho \cdot g \cdot H_n \cdot Q_n}$	H_n – the net head of water.
Relationship among the 4 values	$\psi = \varepsilon \cdot \gamma \cdot \eta$	
Reference section of the turbine	$s_r = \dfrac{S}{R^2}$ where: $S = \pi\left(R^2 - R_n^2\right)$ $S = \pi R_e^2$	S – turbine section; R – turbine radius (Francis, Kaplan turbines); R_e - Pelton turbines.
The maximum water level in the surge tank	$Z = v_{go}\sqrt{\dfrac{L_g \cdot S_g}{g \cdot S_{ch}}}$	S_{ch} –surge tank section; L_g, S_g – geometry of the influent conduit; v_{g0} – water speed.
The time constant of the raceway	$T_g = \sqrt{\dfrac{L_g \cdot S_g}{g \cdot S_{ch}}}$	

Table 3. Basic values for the turbine and the hydro power plant.

[9] (Huimin & Chao, 2006)

3.2.1 The determination of the basic hydro parameters of the hydro turbine

In steady state, if the cavitation is neglected, the hydro behaviour of a turbine is determined by the following expressions:

$$F(\varepsilon,\gamma,\eta)=0 \text{ and } G(\varepsilon,\gamma,A)=0 \; ; \tag{18}$$

which in the spatial Cartesian system represent two surfaces. But, if plan representation is used, we get functions $\varepsilon = f(\gamma)$, with η parameter and $\varepsilon = f(\gamma)$, with A parameter, representing the position of the wicket and the turbine blades. These functions can be represented in plan (ε,γ) according to figure 10. If we consider point P, as the operating point in steady state, the behaviour of the turbine, from the point of view of stability, is wholly determined by two tangent plans in point P, to the surfaces described in expressions (18). But the orientation of each plan is determined by two slopes, then, theoretically, it suffices to know 4 of the slopes to approach any stability problem of the turbine around the point corresponding to the steady state[10]. Practically, these 4 slopes are obtained in per units, as following:

$$t_1=\left.\frac{\delta\gamma}{\delta\varepsilon}\right|_{A_0} \; ; \; t_2=\left.\frac{\partial\gamma}{\partial A}\right|_{\varepsilon_0} \; ; \; t_3=\left.\frac{\delta\eta}{\delta\varepsilon}\right|_{A_0} \; ; \; t_4=\left.\frac{\partial\eta}{\partial A}\right|_{\varepsilon_0} . \tag{19}$$

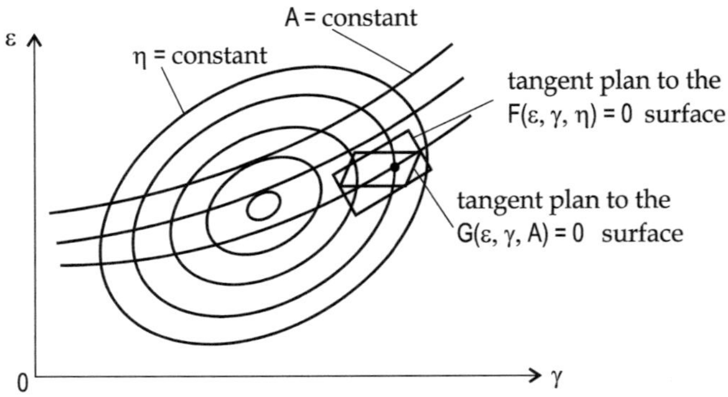

Fig. 10. The diagram of the operating characteristics of the hydro turbine.

The 4 slopes represent the basic hydro values of a hydro turbine. But their values cannot be calculated unless the surfaces which characterize the hydro behaviour of the turbine are expressed analytically. That is why for solving this problem we use statistical data obtained from a large number of turbines of all types (Pelton, Francis, spiral and Kaplan), resulting in variation curves of the basic hydro values depending on the speed value, given in Figure 11. The turbine speed value is defined by the expression:

$$v=n\sqrt{\frac{Q}{s_r\cdot(g\cdot H_n)^{3/2}}} \; ; \tag{20}$$

where: Q – the turbine water flow rate; n – the turbine speed; s_r – the reference section; H_n – the net head of water and g – gravity acceleration.

[10] (Surianu & Dilertea, 2004)

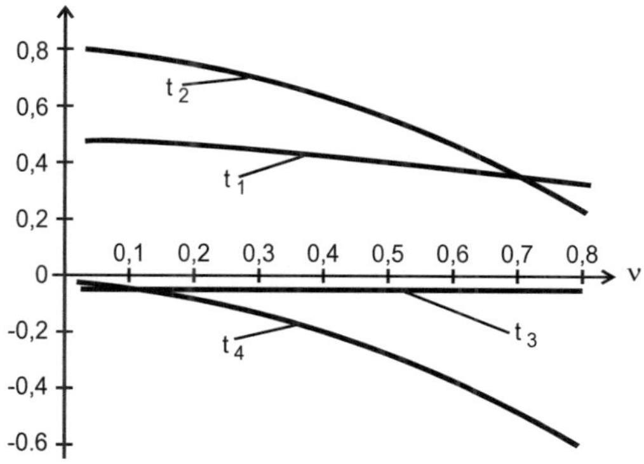

Fig. 11. The statistical relationships among the basic hydro values and speed value v .

By means of the basic hydro values, the following auxiliary hydro values are defined:

$$t_5 = 1 + t_1 + t_3\,;\; t_6 = t_2 + t_4\,;\; t_7 = 1 - 2t_1\,;\; t_8 = t_2 \cdot t_5\,;\; t_9 = 1 - 2t_1 - 2t_3\,;\; t_{11} = -2t_3\,. \quad (21)$$

These values, together with the basic hydro ones define completely the hydro turbine behaviour in terms of stability, the differentials of functions $\gamma_r = f(\varepsilon_r, a)$; $\eta_r = f(\varepsilon_r, a)$; and $\psi_r = \varepsilon_r \cdot \gamma_r \cdot \eta_r$ are expressed as following:

$$d\gamma_r = t_1 \cdot d\varepsilon_r + t_2 \cdot da; \quad d\eta_r = t_3 \cdot d\varepsilon_r + t_4 \cdot da; \quad d\psi_r = t_5 \cdot d\varepsilon_r + t_6 \cdot da. \quad (22)$$

3.2.2 The operating equations of the hydro power plant

The operating equations of the hydro power plant are presented in Table 4, in the order corresponding to the water flow sense, from the water reservoir to the hydro turbine.

Equation type	Mathematical expression
Equation of losses in the influent conduit	$\Delta h_g = 2\Delta q_{V_g}^2$ Δh_g - variation of the water height losses; Δq_{V_g} - variation of the water flow rate.
Equation of the kinetic energy in the point of the surge tank insertion	$\Delta e_{ch} = 2 \cdot \Delta q_{V_g}$
Equation of surge tank filling	$S_{ch}\dfrac{dX}{dt} = Q_{ch}$ S_{ch}- surge tank section; dX- water height variation; Q_{ch}- water flow rate.
Surge tank equation	$T_{ch}\dfrac{dX}{dt} = Q_{ch}$, where: $T_{ch} = \dfrac{S_{ch}\left(H_{bo} - H_{go}\right)}{Q_{V_{go}}}$ T_{ch} - surge tank time constant; H_{bo} - water height in the reservoir; H_{go} - water height in the influent conduit.

Equation type	Mathematical expression
Water flow rate equation	$Q_{ch} = Q_{Vg} - Q_c$ Q_{ch} - water flow rate at the basis of the surge tank; Q_{Vg} - water flow rate in the influent conduit Q_c - water flow rate in the raceway.
Influent conduit equation	$T_{ch} \cdot T_{gi} \frac{d^2X}{dt^2} + 2(c_2 + c_4) T_{ch} \frac{dX}{dt} + X =$ $= -T_{gi} \frac{d\Delta q_c}{dt} - 2(c_2 + c_4)\Delta q_c + (1 + c_2) g \cdot \Delta h_b$ with: $c_2 = \frac{p_0}{h_0}$ and $c_4 = \frac{v_{ch}^2}{2g(H_{b0} - H_{g0})}$ where: $p_0 = \frac{H_{g0}}{Z}$ and $h_0 = \frac{H_{b0} - H_{g0}}{Z}$ T_{gi} - time constant of the influent conduit; c_2 - load loss in the influent conduit in steady state; c_4 - kinetic energy in the point of surge tank insertion; $\Delta h_b = H_{b0} - H_{g0}$, is the water height variation in the reservoir (p.u.).
Equation of specific energy related to the mass in the point of surge tank insertion	$T_{gi} \frac{d\Delta e_a}{dt} + 2(c_2 + c_4)\Delta e_a =$ $= T_{gi} \frac{dX}{dt} + 2c_2 X + 2c_4(1 + c_2) g \Delta h_b$ Δe_a - variation of specific energy related to the mass.
Equation of load losses in the raceway	$\Delta e_c = 2\Delta q_c$ Δe_c – variation of the water energy in the raceway; Δq_c – variation of water flow rate in the raceway.
Water hammer equation in the raceway	$e_p = -T_c \frac{d\Delta q_c}{dt}$, where: $T_c = \frac{\int_0^{L_c} v_{c0} dL_c}{g H_{no}}$ e_p - specific energy related to mass (p.u.) due to the water hammer; T_c - hydro inertia time constant of the raceway.
Equation of the net specific energy related to mass	$\Delta e_k = (1 + h_2)\Delta e_a - 2h_2 \Delta q_c - T_c \frac{d\Delta q_c}{dt}$ Δe_k – variation of net specific energy related to mass; h_2 - load loss in the raceway in steady state.
Equation of the turbine water flow rate	$\Delta q = t_7 \Delta n_r + t_1 \Delta e_k + t_2 \Delta a$ where: $\Delta q_c = \Delta q$ (continuity law)
Equation of the hydro turbine efficiency	$\Delta \eta_r = t_{11} \Delta n_r + t_3 \Delta e_k + t_4 \Delta a$
Equation of the hydro turbine mechanical power	$\Delta p_m = t_9 \Delta n_r + t_5 \Delta e_k + t_6 \Delta a$

Table 4. Operating equations of the hydro power plant in dynamic regime

3.2.3 The expression of the complex mathematical model of the hydro power plant

Starting from the above mentioned equations, there can be written a system of differential and algebraic equations to synthesize the mathematical models of the different elements within the hydro power plant equipped with influent conduit and surge tank and which, together with the equation of rotor (turbine & generator) movement and the equations of the speed control system of the power generating unit characterize completely the behaviour of a hydro power plant in dynamic stability[11].

The set of differential and algebraic equations consists of:

the equation of the water level in the surge tank;
the equation of the net specific energy in the point of surge tank insertion;
the equation of the net specific energy;
the equation of the hydro turbine flow rate;
the equation of the hydro turbine mechanical power.

To make the set of equations easier to approach through integrating the differential equations and solving the algebraic ones, the equations are ranked and displayed in a form to allow applying Runge-Kutta integration methods. Thus, the following system is obtained:

$$\frac{dB}{dt} = -\frac{2(c_2+c_4)}{T_{gi}}B - \frac{1}{T_{gi}T_{ch}}X - \frac{2(c_2+c_4)}{T_{gi}T_{ch}}\Delta q - \frac{1}{T_{ch}}\frac{d\Delta q}{dt} + \frac{1+c_2}{T_{gi}T_{ch}}g\Delta h_b;$$

$$\frac{dX}{dt} = B; \quad \frac{d\Delta e_a}{dt} = B + \frac{2c_2}{T_{gi}}X - \frac{2(c_2+c_4)}{T_{gi}}\Delta e_a + \frac{2c_4(1+c_2)}{T_{gi}}g\Delta h_b;$$

$$\frac{d\Delta q}{dt} = \frac{(1+h_2)}{T_c}\Delta e_a - \frac{2h_2}{T_c}\Delta q - \frac{1}{T_c}\Delta e_k; \; \Delta e_k = \frac{1}{t_1}(\Delta q - t_7 \cdot \Delta n_r - t_2 \cdot \Delta a) \tag{23}$$

$$\Delta p_m = t_9\Delta n_r + t_5\Delta e_k + t_6\Delta a\,.$$

To the set of equations (23) we have added the movement equation of the assembly of rotors (turbine & synchronous generator) and the equations of the speed governor system (SG), which give the values of speed variation Δn_r and the value of the variation of valve position, Δa. Figure 12 presents the block diagram of an operating hydro-mechanical installation equipped with influent conduit and surge tank. Equations (23) and the corresponding block diagram in figure 12 have a general character describing the behaviour of the whole hydro-mechanic installation around the steady state point. If the hydro power plant has no influent conduit and surge tank, equations (23) stay valid but they are particularized through annulling the constants corresponding to these elements, and, in figure 12, the corresponding blocks disappear from the diagram.

3.3 The mathematical modelling of the speed governor

Frequency, as a unique parameter of the electric power system, plays a special role in its reliable and economic operation. If the reactive current component is neglected (for $\cos\ \varphi = 0.8$) there can be stated that the active power losses in the electric power systems are proportional to frequency increased to the power of four:

[11] (Surianu & Barbulescu, 2008)

$$\Delta P_{EPS} \cong K_P \cdot f^4 \; ; \tag{24}$$

and then an increase in frequency leads to increasing power losses, and a decrease in frequency leads to a diminished consumers` productivity. There has also to be mentioned that keeping frequency at a constant level is a "must" in the case of the interconnection of large power systems, frequency variations being incompatible between partners.
In real circumstances, frequency is not kept strictly constant, but variable in pre-established limits, slightly depending on disturbance, which in this case is represented by the active power variation (ΔP) consumed in electric power systems. That is why there are realized static characteristics of the speed to allow a univocal distribution of the disturbing values on the power units set in parallel, either in the same power plant or in different points of the power system.

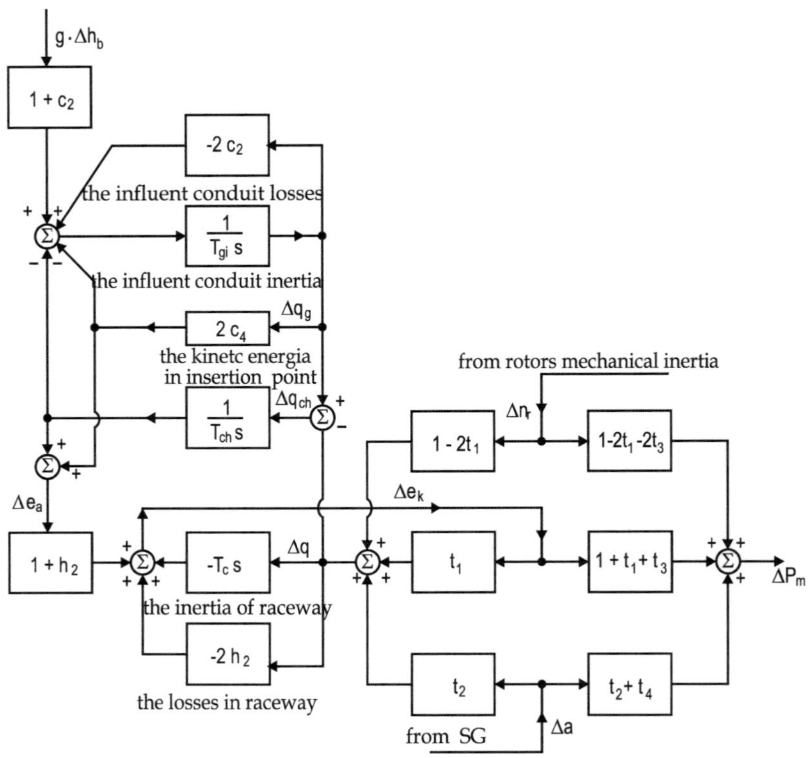

Fig. 12. The block diagram of a hydro-mechanical installation equipped with influent conduit and surge tank.

3.3.1 The block diagram and the mathematical models for the speed governors of the thermal and hydro power plants

The speed control of the power units is realized by means of turbine automatic control systems, namely speed governors (SG). To make possible univocal distribution and necessity based modification of the disturbing values distribution, the automatic control of speed is a static one, with offset characteristics between (1 – 7) %. There are a large number of SG types, with mechanical, electrical, electronic elements with which turbines are equipped[12], but no matter the type, SG's mainly consist of the following elements: a measuring element for speed (or frequency), amplifying elements (servo-engines) which take over the shifting of the pendulum and shift the heavy control units of the turbine, and reaction devices which insure the control stability and quality of transitory processes. From Long Term Dynamics studies there have been chosen two different general models to describe SG behaviour for thermal, respectively hydro-mechanical installations, these types being described in the block diagram in figure 13.

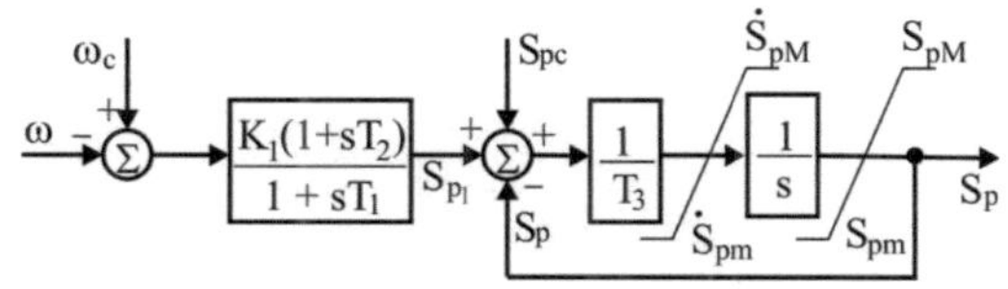

a) thermal installations;

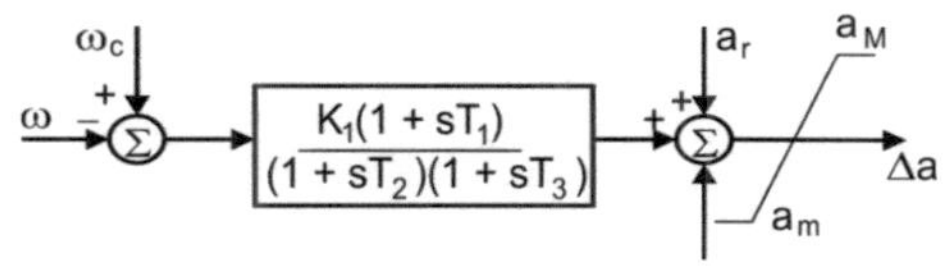

b) hydro installations

Fig. 13. The diagrams of general SG models:

The equations which describe SG behaviour in figure 13 are:
for the thermal model:

$$\frac{dS_{p1}}{dt} = \frac{1}{T_1}\left(K_1\omega_c - K_1\omega - S_{p1} - K_1 T_2 \frac{d\omega}{dt} \right); \quad \frac{dS_p}{dt} = \frac{1}{T_3}\left(S_{pc} + S_{p1} - S_p \right); \tag{25}$$

with :

$$S_{pm} \le S_p \le S_{PM}\,; \; \dot{S}_{pm} \le \dot{S}_p \le \dot{S}_{PM}\,.$$

for the hydro model:

$$\frac{dz}{dt} = \frac{1}{T_1}\left(\omega_c - \omega - z - T_2 \frac{d\omega}{dt} \right); \quad \frac{da_1}{dt} = \frac{1}{T_3}\left(K_1 \cdot z - a_1 + K_1 T_2 \frac{dz}{dt} \right); \tag{26}$$

with:

$$\Delta a = a_r + a_1\,; \; a_m \le \Delta a \le a_M\,.$$

To equations (25) and (26) the movement equation of rotors is added.
As to the values of the coefficients in equations (25) and (26), these can have the following values: $T_1 = (0.2 - 2.8)$ s; $T_2 = (0 - 1.0)$ s; $T_3 = (0.025 - 0.15)$ s; $K_1 = (10; 15; 25)$; $\dot{S}_{pm} = -0.1$ p.u./s;

---

[12] (Hanmandlu et al., 2006)

$\dot{S}_{PM} = 0.1$ p.u./s; $S_{pm} = 0.0$ p.u.; $S_{PM} = 1.0$ p.u.; $a_m = 0.1$ p.u.; $a_M = 1.1$ p.u.

3.4 Numerical simulations of the primary installations of the power plants

For the numerical simulation of power plants in dynamic regimes, the mathematical models of the components of the primary installations have to be assembled according to their causal links and there have to be written the corresponding systems of equations. Conceiving the algorithms and writing the calculation programs for each type of power plant and, finally applying them to real operating power plants turns hypotheses to certainty[13].

3.4.1 The model of the primary installations of a thermal power plant

Based on the mathematical models of the elements of a thermal power plant, there has been conceived an assembly operating block diagram of the thermal unit of a power plant. It is represented in figure 14. The diagram allows modelling both types of primary installations, either those provided with drum type boilers or those with once-through boilers.

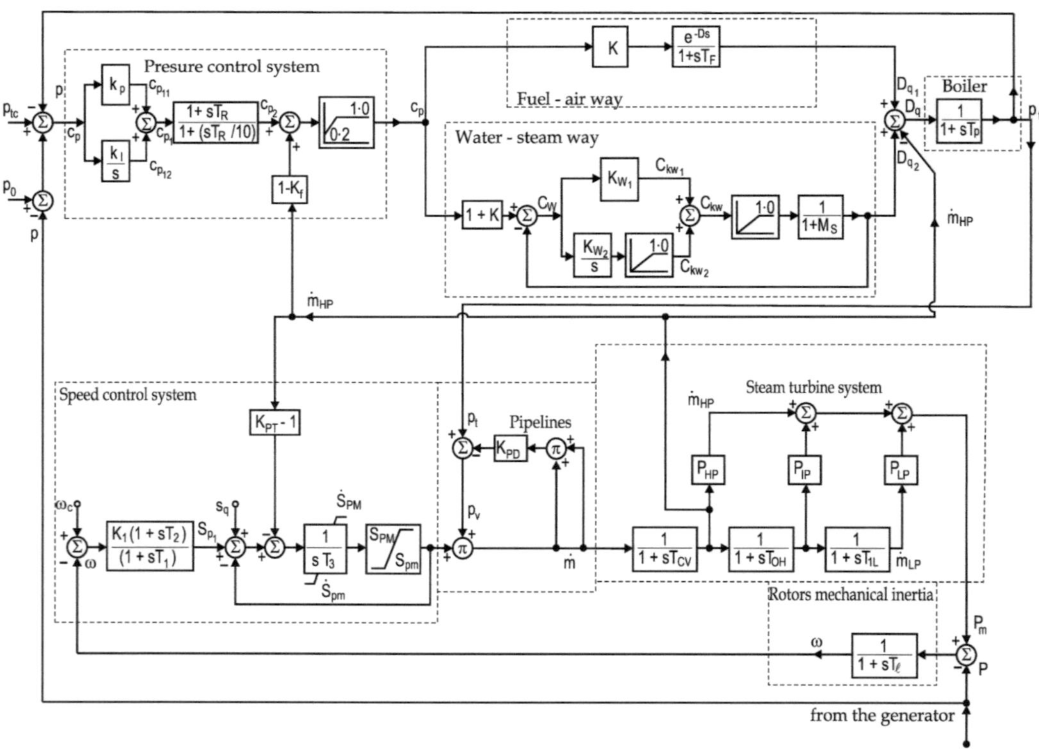

Fig. 14. The operating block diagram of the primary installations of a thermal power plant

The assembly operation is described by a set of algebraic and differential equations which are added to the inequalities of the corresponding limitations, as following:

[13] (Surianu, 2009)

$$C_p = P_0 + p_{tc} - P - p_t \,;\; C_{p11} = K_p \cdot C_p \,;$$
$$\frac{dC_{p12}}{dt} = K_I C_p \,;$$
$$C_{p1} = C_{p11} + C_{p12};$$
$$\frac{dG}{dt} = -\frac{10}{T_R} G + \frac{10}{T_R} C_{p1};$$
$$C_{p2} = G + T_R \frac{dG}{dt};$$
$$C_{pm} = C_{p2} + \left(1 - K_f\right)\dot{m}_{HP};$$
$$\frac{dp_t}{dt} = \frac{1}{T_p} D_q - \frac{1}{T_p} p_t;$$
$$\frac{d\omega}{dt} = \frac{1}{T_L} P_m - \frac{1}{T_L} P;$$
$$\frac{dS_{p1}}{dt} = \frac{1}{T_1}\left(K_1\omega_c - K_1\omega - S_{p1} - K_1 T_2 \frac{d\omega}{dt} \right);$$
$$\frac{dS_P}{dt} = \frac{1}{T_3}\left(S_{pc} - S_{p1} - S_p\right) - \left(K_{PT} - 1\right)\dot{m}_{HP};$$

$$0.2 \le C_{p2} \le 1.0;$$
$$\frac{dD_{q1}}{dt} = \frac{K(t - T_c)}{T_F} C_{pm} - \frac{1}{T_F} D_{q1};$$
$$C_w = (1 - K)C_{pm} - D_{q2};$$
$$C_{kw1} = K_{w1} C_w;$$
$$\frac{dC_{kw2}}{dt} = K_{w2} C_w;$$
$$0.0 \le C_{kw2} \le 1.0;$$
$$C_{kw} = C_{kw1} + C_{kw2};$$
$$0.0 \le C_{kw} \le 1.0;$$
$$\frac{dD_{q2}}{dt} = \frac{1}{M} C_{kw} - \frac{1}{M} D_{q2};$$
$$D_q = D_{q1} + D_{q2} - \dot{m}_{HP};$$
$$\dot{S}_{pm} \le \dot{S}_p \le \dot{S}_{pM};$$
$$S_{pm} \le S_p \le S_{pM};$$
$$p_V = p_t - K_{PD} \cdot \dot{m}_{CV}^2;$$
$$\dot{m}_{CV} = S_p \cdot p_V;$$
$$\frac{d\dot{m}_{HP}}{dt} = \frac{1}{T_{CV}}(\dot{m}_{CV} - \dot{m}_{HP});$$
$$\frac{d\dot{m}_{IP}}{dt} = \frac{1}{T_{OH}}(\dot{m}_{HP} - \dot{m}_{IP}); \qquad (27)$$
$$\frac{d\dot{m}_{LP}}{dt} = \frac{1}{T_{IL}}(\dot{m}_{IP} - \dot{m}_{LP});$$
$$P_m = P_{HP} \cdot \dot{m}_{HP} + P_{IP} \cdot \dot{m}_{IP} + P_{LP} \cdot \dot{m}_{LP}.$$

3.4.2 The model of the primary installations of the hydro power plant

The operational block diagram for the primary installations of a hydro power plant has been presented in figure 12 and the equations corresponding to the mathematical model are expressions (23). If to this block diagram there is added the general representation of SG and the block corresponding to the mechanical inertia of the assembly of the turbine & synchronous generator rotors, we get the complete operational block diagram in figure 15.
The equations describing the operation of the primary installations of the hydro power plants equipped with speed governors are:

$$\frac{dB}{dt} = -\frac{2(c_2 + c_4)}{T_{gi}} B - \frac{1}{T_{gi}T_{ch}} X - \frac{2(c_2 + c_4)}{T_{gi}T_{ch}} \Delta q - \frac{1}{T_{ch}} \frac{d\Delta q}{dt} + \frac{1 + c_2}{T_{gi}T_{ch}} g\Delta h_b;$$

$$\frac{dX}{dt} = B; \quad \frac{d\Delta e_a}{dt} = B + \frac{2c_2}{T_{gi}} X - \frac{2(c_2 + c_4)}{T_{gi}} \Delta e_a + \frac{2c_4(1 + c_2)}{T_{gi}} g\Delta h_b;$$

$$\frac{d\Delta q}{dt} = \frac{(1 + h_2)}{T_c} \Delta e_a - \frac{2h_2}{T_c} \Delta q - \frac{1}{T_c} \Delta e_k;$$

$$Q = Q + \Delta q\,; \quad \Delta e_k = \frac{1}{t_1}(\Delta q - t_7 \Delta n_r - t_2 \Delta a)\,;$$

$$E_k = E_k + \Delta e_k\,; \quad \Delta p_m = t_5 \Delta e_k + t_9 \Delta n_r + t_6 \Delta a\,; \quad (28)$$

$$P_m = P_m + \Delta p_m\,; \quad \frac{d\omega}{dt} = \frac{1}{T_l}\Delta p_m - \frac{1}{T_l}\Delta p\,;$$

$$\Delta n_r = \omega_c - \omega\,; \quad \frac{dz}{dt} = \frac{1}{T_1}\left(\omega_c - \omega - z - T_2 \frac{d\omega}{dt}\right);$$

$$\frac{da_1}{dt} = \frac{1}{T_3}\left(K \cdot z - a_1 + KT_2 \frac{dz}{dt}\right);$$

$$\Delta a = a_r + a_1\,; \quad a_m \le \Delta a \le a_M\,.$$

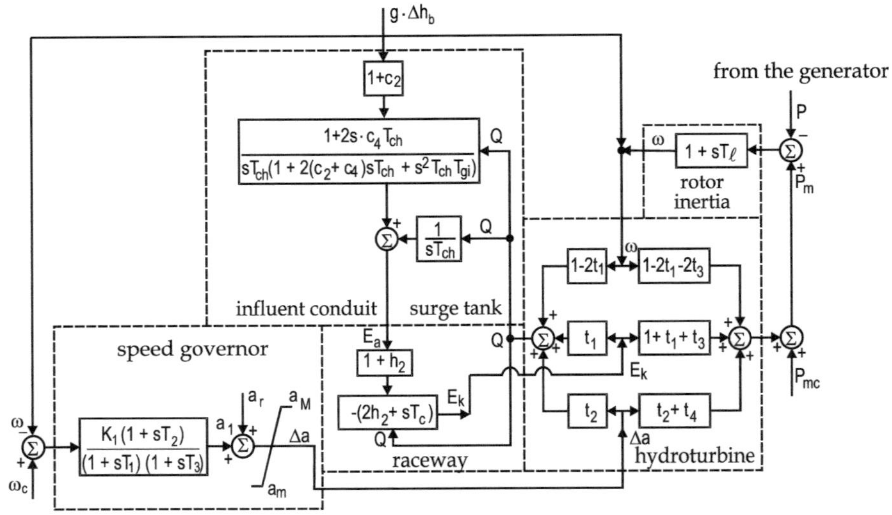

Fig. 15. The operating block diagram of the primary installations of a hydro power plant

3.4.3 Applications and the interpretation of the results of the computer simulation of thermal and hydro primary installations

For simulating the dynamic processes in power plants, using the mathematical models of the primary thermal and hydro installations, there have been conceived two calculation programs, named THERMO and HYDRO, whose flow charts are described in figure 16, a and b. The programs have been written in DELPHI. They have aimed at studying the way in which the systems of equations satisfy the initial conditions corresponding to a pre-disturbance steady state and they allow the calculus of the initial values of variables. We have studied the way in which the models respond to a given disturbance, the adjustment of the models according to the response to disturbances as well as checking the stability of the mathematical models having in view the possibility of linking them to the mathematical models of the synchronous generators and electric networks[14]. The validity of the mathematical models has been demonstrated by applying them to the operating parameters of two real big power installations of the electric power system of Romania. These installations belong to Thermal Power Plant Mintia, equipped with six power units of 210 MW each and Hydro Power Plant Raul Mare, equipped with two power units of 167.5 MW each. The analysis of the components has been made for a single power unit of each type.

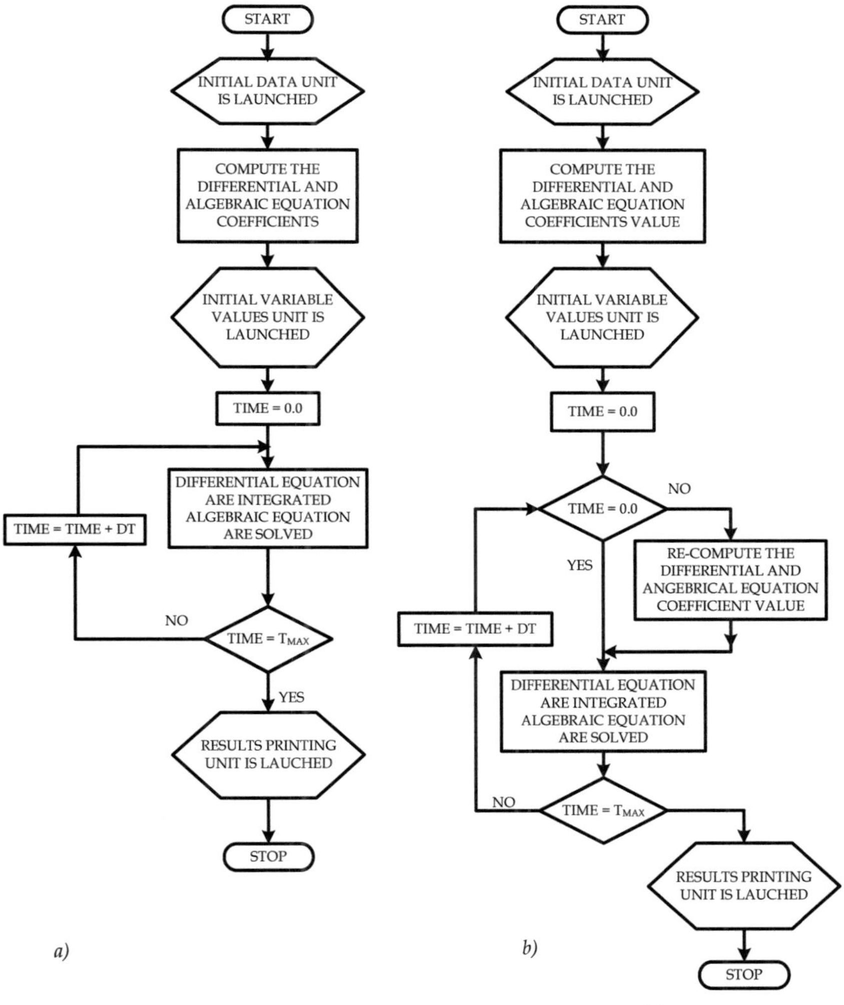

Fig. 16. The flow charts of the calculation programs. a) THERMO; b) HYDRO

By means of THERMO there has been analyzed the response in time of a thermal-mechanical installation equipped with a once-through boiler at a sudden electric load increase of 5 % at the synchronous generator terminals. There has been considered the boiler having a nominal steam pressure of $p_t = 140\ at$ and a normal steam flow rate of $\dot{m}_t = 630\ t / h$, supplying with steam an assembly turbine & synchronous generator of a power

[14] (Surianu, 2009)

unit having a nominal electric power $P_n = 210\ MW$ and operating at an electric power $P = 0.8 \cdot P_n$. The launching time of the assembly is $T_l = 6.5s$ at the nominal frequency, $f = 50\ Hz$. The boiler inertia time constant is $T_p = 300\ s$, and the principal automation constants of the boiler on the feed water way are: $K_{w1} = 1.5$; $K_{w2} = 0.5$; $M = 5$ s. The turbine with three pressure units and re-heater has got the following parameters: $T_{CV} = 0.5$ s, $T_{OH} = 7$ s; $T_{IL} = 0.4$ s; $P_{HP} = 0.3$; $P_{IP} = 0.4$; $P_{LP} = 0.3$. The analysis of the dynamic evolution of the thermal-mechanical system has been made for a time of 100 s, with an increasing step of $\Delta t = 1$ s. All the values have been written in per units. In Figure 17, there have been presented synthetically the main thermal - mechanical installations of Thermal Power Plant Mintia, Romania to which dynamic simulation has been applied and the results of the dynamic behaviour analysis are represented in Figure 18, having an operating once-through boiler.

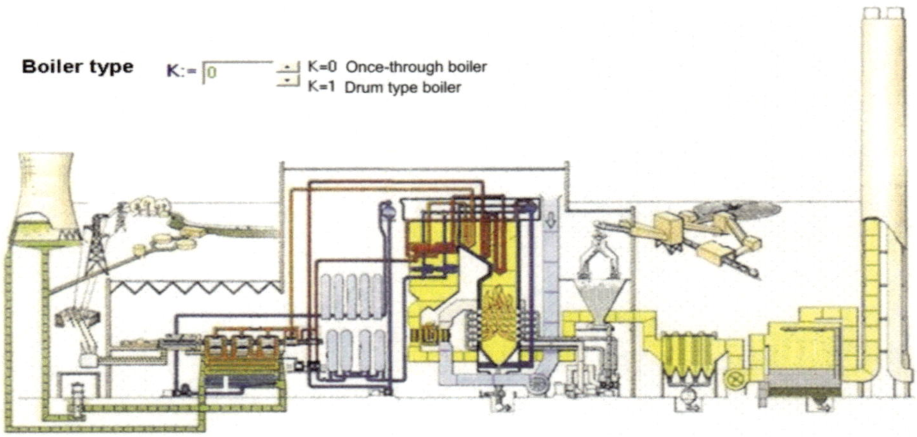

Fig. 17. Representation of the main thermal-mechanical installations of the power plant

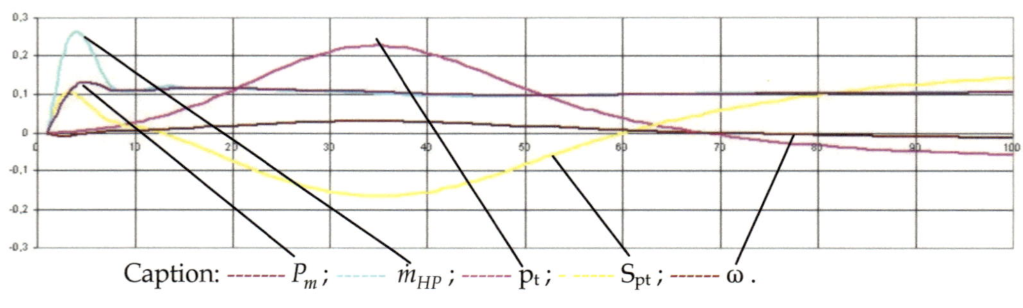

Fig. 18. The diagram of the simulation of the dynamic behaviour of the thermo-mechanical installations of Thermal Power Plant Mintia, Romania

Analyzing the curves obtained, there has been observed that at a sudden increase in the power necessity of the power system, there starts opening the steam admission valves, S_{pt}. Thus the steam flow rate at the turbine increases rapidly, $\dot{m}_{HP}$ and the mechanical power, P_m, starts increasing. Steam pressure p_t varies slowly due to the oscillatory movement of the steam admission valve and the big inertia of the primary fuel feeding installation. The slow pressure oscillation at the admission valve is longer than 100 seconds. In the first five seconds after the disturbance moment, the pulsation, ω, slightly decreases due to the increase in electric power, which determines a retarding torque at the synchronous generator axle coupled to the steam turbine. After this decreasing tendency, the pulsation recovers slowly at a relatively constant value, a little bit higher than the initial one, and after 60 seconds, due to the action of the speed governor, the initial speed is reached, simultaneously with reaching the balance of the mechanical power with the electric one. The analysis of the dynamics of the thermo-mechanic installations for a period of 100 seconds points out the stabilization tendency of the thermo-mechanic operating system through a damped oscillatory process of all the thermal and mechanical values.

For modelling the dynamic behaviour of a hydro power station using the HYDRO program, we have considered Hydro Power Plant Raul Mare, Romania, equipped with a Francis turbine defined by the following parameters: nominal mechanical power, $P_{mn} = 167.5\ MW$, $f = 50\ Hz$, nominal pulsation $n_0 = 52.36\ rad/s$, reference radius $R = 1.425\ m$ and unit launching time, $T_l = 7.5\ s$. For the nominal speed value, $v_0 = 0.408\ m/s$, obtained from nominal water flow rate $Q = 127\ m^3/s$, there have been obtained the turbine angular parameters operating in nominal regime, $t_1 = 0.47;\ t_2 = 0.6;\ t_3 = -0.03;\ t_4 = -0.23$. The hydro power plant has the following structure: an influent conduit of length $L_g = 18.400\ m$ and section $S_g = 18.8\ m^2$, a surge tank of section $S_{ch} = 109\ m^2$ and a raceway of length $L_c = 812\ m$ and section $S_c = 31.2\ m^2$. The water height in the reservoir is $H_{b0} = 980\ m$ and the water height in the influent conduit, $H_{g0} = 13.37\ m$, resulting the head of the water in the surge tank, $H_{k0} = 966.63\ m$, a net head of water in the raceway, $H_k = 474.5\ m$ and a load loss in raceway, $h_2 = 16.33\ m$. The water speed in the influent conduit, in nominal regime is $v_{g0} = 3.52\ m/s$ and in the raceway, $v_{c0} = 4.07\ m/s$. The elements of the hydro assembly have the following inertia time constants: $T_{gi} = 6.7\ s$; $T_{ch} = 99\ s$ and $T_c = 1.15\ s$. The steady state pre-disturbance consists of the hydro power plant operating at electric power $P = 134.05\ MW$ and a net head of water in the raceway of $H_n = 474.5\ m$.

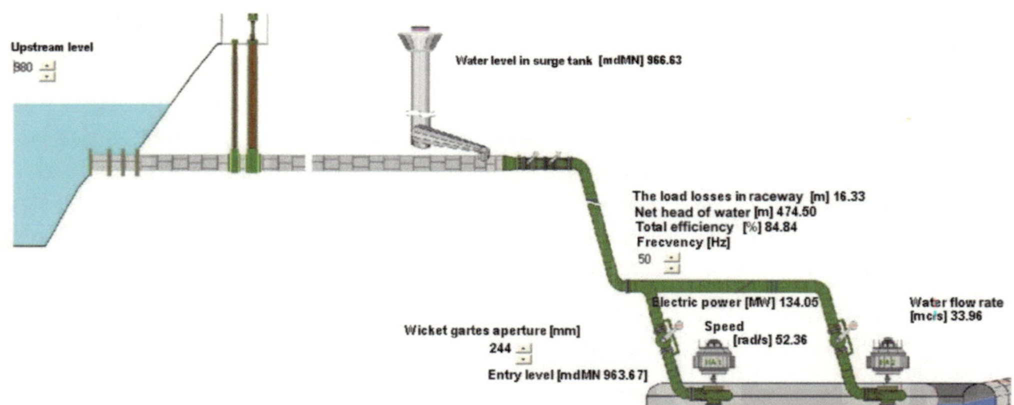

Fig. 19. The diagram of the main hydro-mechanic installations of the hydro power plant

The dynamic behaviour of the hydro-mechanic installation has been analyzed for a disturbance consisting of 10% increase of electric power versus the steady state at the synchronous generator's terminals, represented by the hydro power station operating with a single generating unit loaded with 80 % of the nominal power. There has been studied the evolution in time of the mechanic and hydro values on an interval of 200 seconds, with a time incremental step of $\Delta t = 1\,s$. In Figure 19 there are presented synthetically the main hydro-mechanic installations of the hydro power plant to which the dynamic simulation is applied. The results of the dynamic behaviour are represented in Figure 20. There has been observed that a sudden increase in the electric power required at the terminals of the synchronous generator results in a rapid decrease in speed, n, due to the appearance of a strong braking couple. The speed governor registers the speed decrease and initiates the opening of the wicket gates. At the beginning, the wicket gates open very quickly and mechanical power P_m increases, surpassing the value of the electric power, this fact leading to the appearance of an accelerating mechanical torque and, this way, speed n starts increasing. But as soon as the wicket gates open an increase in water flow rate Q of the turbine is registered and this cannot be compensated by the water leaking through the dam, through the influent conduit and water level, H_k, in the surge tank starts decreasing, leading to a diminishing of the net head of water and, correspondingly, to a decrease in the net specific energy, E_k.

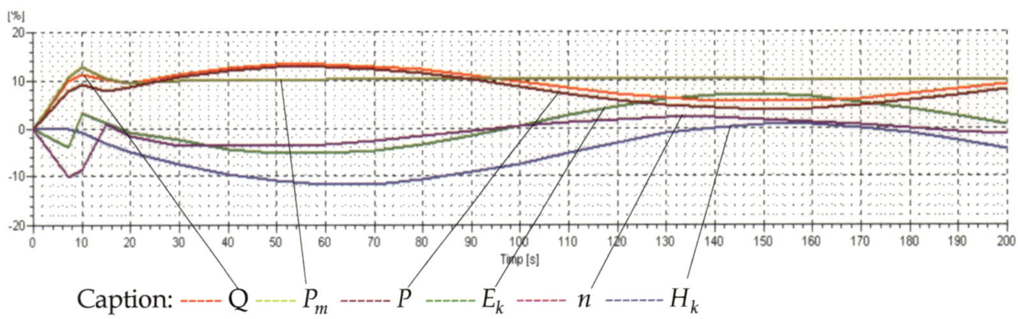

Fig. 20. Mathematical simulation of the dynamic behaviour the hydro-mechanic installations of Hydro Power Plant Raul Mare, Romania

This dynamic process in the hydro power plant, due to its big inertia, is produced much more slowly than the control dynamic process given by the speed governor which now, registering the speed increase, initiates the closing of the wicket gates and reduces the mechanical power under the value of the electric one. The speed decreases and re-starts opening the wicket gates but, as the water level in the surge tank is diminished and the net head of water is shorter, in order to get the corresponding mechanical power, there is needed a bigger water flow rate on a longer period of time. After having balanced the powers, the closing of the wicket gates is initiated, this leading to an increase in the water level of the surge tank and in the corresponding net specific energy.

4. Conclusions

The analysis of the simulation results has shown concordance with the evolution of the dynamics of thermal and hydro-mechanic primary installations in real circumstances. The simulation represents realistically the physical phenomena both in pre- disturbance steady state and in the dynamic processes following the disturbances in the electric power system. These models have proved to be useful for experts to draw up contiguities leading to optimum operating regimes and appreciate the necessary measures to be taken in critical circumstances. They also provide instruments for the operating regimes and for further studies concerning the expansion of the existing electric power systems.

5. Referances

Dimo, P.; Constantinescu, J.; Pomarleanu, M; Radu, I. (1980). Determination of the Power Systems Behaviour in Long Term Dynamics, Produced by Successive Perturbations in System, *Energetica Revue*, Vol. 28, No. 10-11, November, 1980, pp. 443-448

Ernst, D.; Glavic, M. & Wehenkel, L. (2004). Power Systems Stability Control: Reinforcement Learning Framework, *IEEE Transactions on Power Systems*, Vol.19, No.1, (February 2004), pp. 427–435, ISSN: 0885-8950

Fraile-Ardanuy, J.; Wilhelmi, J.R.; Fraile-Mora, J.J. & Perez, J.I. (2006). Variable-speed hydro generation: operational aspects and control, *IEEE Transaction on Energy Conversion*, Vol. 21, No. 2, (June 2006), pp. 569 – 574, ISSN: 0885-8969

Hanmandlu, M., Goyal, H. & Kothari D.P. (2006). An Advanced Control Scheme for Micro Hydro Power Plants, *International Conference on Power Electronics, Drives and Energy Systems, (PEDES '06)*, December 2006, pp. 1-7. ISBN: 0-7803-9772-X, New Delhi, India

Hongesombut, K.; Mitani, Y.; Tada, M.Y.; Takazawa, T.& Shishido, T. (2005). Object-Oriented Modelling for Advanced Power System Simulations, *IEEE Power Tech Conference*, pp. 1–6, ISBN: 978-5-93208-034-4, St. Petersburg, Russia, June 27-30, 2005

Huimin G.; Chao W. (2006). Effect of Detailed Hydro Turbine Models on Power System Analysis, *Power Systems Conference and Exposition (PSCE'06) IEEE PES*, pp. 1577-1581, ISBN: 1-4244-0177-1, Atlanta, USA, October 28-November, 1, 2006

Surianu F.D.; Dilertea F. (2004). Using "HYDRO" Mathematical Model in Simulating Dynamic Behaviour of Hydro Mechanical Equipment of Hydro Power Plant Raul Mare- Retezat, *Scientific Bulletin of the "Politehnica" University of Timisoara, Romania, Transactions on Engineering*, Vol.50 (64), No.1-2, (November 2005), pp. 553-560, ISSN: 1582-7194

Surianu F.D.; Bărbulescu C. (2008). Complete Dynamic Behaviour Mathematical Modelling of Hydro Mechanical Equipment. Case study: Hydro Power Plant Raul Mare-Retezat, Romania, *WSEAS Transactions on Power Systems*, Volume 3, Issue 7, August, 2008, pp. 517-526, ISSN 1790-5060

Surianu F.D. (2008). Experimental Determination and Numerical Simulation of the Dynamic Insulation of a Large Consumer Unit, *Proceedings of WSEAS International Conference on Electric Power Systems, High Voltages, Electric Machines, (POWER'08)*, November, 2008, pp. 239-246, ISBN 978-960-474-026-0, Venice, Italy

Surianu, F.D. (2009). *Modelling and Identification of Power System Elements.* (in Romanian) Orizonturi Universitare, ISBN: 978-973-638-457-8, Timisoara, Romania.

Zhiyong, H; Renmu, H.& Yanhui, X. (2008). Effect of steam pressure fluctuation in turbine steam pipe on stability of power system, *Third International Conference on Electric Utility Deregulation and Restructuring and Power Technologies (DRPT 2008)*, pp. 1127-1131, ISBN: 978-7-900714-13-8, Nanjuing, China, 6-9 April, 2008

Numerical Simulations of the Long-Haul RZ-DPSK Optical Fibre Transmission System

Hidenori Taga
National Sun Yat-Sen University
Taiwan

1. Introduction

Return-to-zero differential phase shift keying (RZ-DPSK) is a promising modulation format for the long-haul large capacity optical fibre transmission system, and it demonstrated a superior performance compared to the conventional intensity-modulation direct-detection (IM-DD) system experimentally (Cai et al., 2006; Inoue et al., 2004; Rasmussen et al., 2004). For the IM-DD based long-haul system, dispersion map is a commonly used technology to improve the transmission performance (Bergano, 2005). The dispersion map was developed to compromise following two incompatible conditions: close to zero dispersion is preferred from the point of the waveform distortion due to the chromatic dispersion, while a finite dispersion is required to reduce the nonlinear degradation due to the optical fibre. The dispersion map realizes close to zero end-to-end dispersion while keeping the finite local dispersion by combining positive and negative dispersion fibre in the transmission line. For example, the positive dispersion fibre is a standard single mode fibre (SMF), and the negative dispersion fibre is a non-zero dispersion shifted fibre (NZDSF). For the long-haul IM-DD system, so-called "block type" dispersion map is the most popular style. For this block type dispersion map, both the positive and negative dispersion fibres are combined to compose one dispersion block of several hundred to one thousand kilometres, and an entire long-haul system is composed of several dispersion blocks (Bergano, 2005).
Even though the block type dispersion map is effective to improve the performance of the conventional IM-DD based system, it was reported that the performance of the long-haul 10Gbit/s RZ-DPSK system with the block type dispersion map using the NZDSF and the SMF showed performance degradation near the system zero dispersion wavelength (Dupont et al., 2007; Moh et al., 2007; Vaa et al., 2004). It is a strange feature of the RZ-DPSK transmission system, because the conventional IM-DD system shows better performance near the system zero dispersion wavelength rather than the other wavelengths. Then, this chapter has been intended to clarify the reason why the long-haul RZ-DPSK system shows such behaviour using the numerical simulations.
Section 2 describes the method of the numerical simulations. The simulator is using the standard calculation scheme of the long-haul optical fibre transmission. It solves the nonlinear Schrödinger equation using the split-step Fourier method (Agrawal, 2006). Using this simulator, the transmission performance of the long-haul RZ-DPSK system is evaluated, and the difference between the block type and block-less type maps is compared in section 3. The results obtained through the simulation agree to the experimental results

qualitatively, and the validity of the simulation program is confirmed (Taga, 2007). In section 4, a little more detail of the transmission performance of the block type dispersion map is investigated. By reducing number of the dispersion blocks in the system, the performance is simulated, and it is confirmed that smaller number of the dispersion blocks improves the system performance without changing any system parameters (Taga, 2008). In section 5 and 6, the transmission performance of the long-haul RZ-DPSK system using an advanced optical fibre is simulated. For the IM-DD based long-haul system, the dispersion flattened fibre (DFF) is developed to improve the transmission performance, and it was already installed in the Pacific Ocean (Bakhshi, 2004). The DFF should also be effective to improve the transmission performance of the RZ-DPSK based system, and a comparison of the long-haul system using the conventional NZDSF and the DFF is conducted (Taga, 2009). The difference between the block type and block-less type dispersion map using the DFF is also investigated (Taga & Chung, 2010). Finally, this chapter is concluded.

2. Simulation method

There are various methods for the numerical simulation of the optical pulse propagation. For the simulation of the optical fibre communication system, optical pulse propagation described by the nonlinear Schrödinger equation should be calculated, and the split-step Fourier method is generally used for the calculation (Agrawal, 2006). In this section, the simulation technique using the split-step Fourier method is briefly explained.

2.1 Split-step Fourier calculation

The numerical simulator solved the coupled nonlinear Schrödinger equations using the split-step Fourier method. The equation used for the simulation is

$$\frac{\partial A_j}{\partial z} + \frac{i}{2}\beta_{2j}\frac{\partial^2 A_j}{\partial T^2} - \frac{\beta_{3j}}{6}\frac{\partial^3 A_j}{\partial T^3} + \frac{\alpha_j}{2}A_j = i\gamma_j\left(\left|A_j\right|^2 + 2\sum_{k\neq j}\left|A_k\right|^2\right)A_j \tag{1}$$

where A is the amplitude of the electrical field of the optical signal, z is the distance in the fibre, T is the time, β_2 is the second-order group velocity dispersion (GVD) coefficient, β_3 is the third-order GVD coefficient, α is the fibre loss coefficient, γ is the nonlinear parameter of the fibre, and the subscripts j and k are the channel number. The split-step Fourier method calculates this equation through two steps. The first step calculates the linear part while ignoring the nonlinear terms. As the linear part contains partial differentiations, the calculation utilizes the Fourier transform to convert the differentiations in the time domain into the frequency multiplications in the frequency domain. Using the Fourier transform and inverse Fourier transform, the partial differentiations are calculated in the frequency domain and converted back to the time domain. The second step calculates the nonlinear part while ignoring the linear terms. Repeating these two steps, the optical pulse propagation within the optical fibre can be calculated numerically.

It is known that the sprit-step method generates spurious tones in the frequency domain if the step length is set uniform (Bosco et al., 2000). Therefore, the fibre step length for the split-step calculation was set to nonuniform, and it was expanded exponentially from the initial length of 100 metres. The reason to expand the step length exponentially is the fact that the transmission loss of the fibre decays the optical signal power exponentially. Then, the product of the signal power and the fibre step length becomes constant, and it could maintain the effect of the fibre nonlinearity in each calculation step.

2.2 Q-factor calculation

In general, transmission performance of the digital communication system is evaluated by the bit-error rate (BER). The optical fibre communication system is no exception. Therefore, the numerical simulation needs a functionality to evaluate the transmission performance by the BER. A Monte-Carlo scheme is the straightforward way to evaluate the BER, but it requires large number of simulated bits to evaluate small BER. It takes long time to simulate large number of bits, and the Monte-Carlo method is not efficient to obtain small BER values. Then, a Q-factor is calculated through the simulation to evaluate the transmission performance. The definition of the Q-factor is (Personick, 1973)

$$Q = \frac{|\mu_1 - \mu_0|}{\sigma_1 + \sigma_0} \tag{2}$$

where μ_1 and μ_0 are the averaged value of "1" bits and "0" bits, respectively, and σ_1 and σ_0 are the standard deviation of "1" bits and "0" bits, respectively. Fig. 1 shows the relationship of these parameters and the intensity eye diagram of the received optical signal schematically. The Q-factor is related to the BER through the equation

$$BER = \frac{1}{2} erfc\left(\frac{Q}{\sqrt{2}}\right) \tag{3}$$

Therefore, it is possible to obtain the BER from the Q-factor. As a matter of fact, the Q-factor is widely used for evaluating the transmission performance of the optical fibre communication system (Bergano et al., 1993).

For the DPSK system, however, it is impossible to obtain the intensity eye diagram like shown in Fig. 1 through the numerical simulation. Therefore, a method to use the phase eye diagram to calculate the Q-factor was proposed (Wei et al., 2003). For this scheme, the optical signal phase is directly calculated from the optical field. The difference of the phase is defined as the phase difference between two sampling points separated by one bit period, and it is plotted between 3π/2 and -π/2. Then, the averaged value and the standard

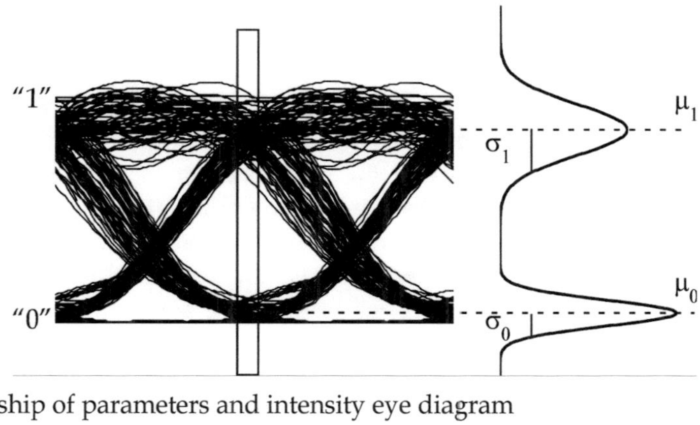

Fig. 1. Relationship of parameters and intensity eye diagram

deviation of "π" phase and "0" phase can be calculated. The Q-factor can be defined similar to equation (2) as

$$Q = \frac{|\mu_\pi - \mu_0|}{\sigma_\pi + \sigma_0} \quad (4)$$

where μ_π and μ_0 are the averaged value of "π" phase bits and "0" phase bits, respectively, and σ_π and σ_0 are the standard deviation of "π" phase bits and "0" phase bits, respectively. Fig. 2 shows the relationship of these parameters and the phase eye diagram of the received optical signal schematically. Using this Q-factor, it becomes possible to estimate the transmission performance of the simulated DPSK system.

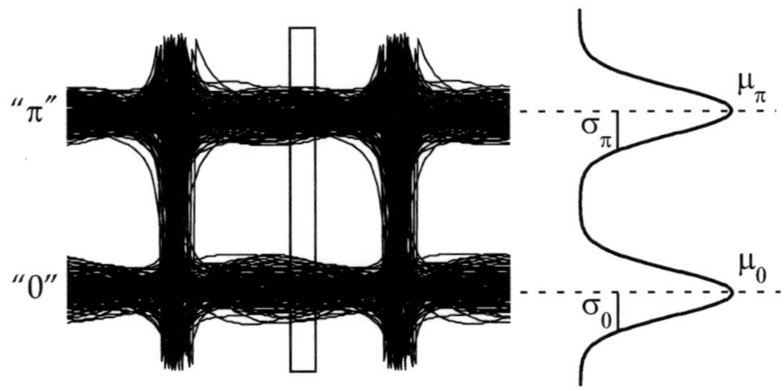

Fig. 2. Relationship of parameters and phase eye diagram

3. Comparison of block type and block-less type dispersion map

The long-haul RZ-DPSK transmission system showed significantly different behaviour between the block type dispersion map and the block-less type dispersion map (Dupont et al., 2007; Moh et al., 2007; Vaa et al., 2004). It is important to clarify the reason why the RZ-DPSK transmission system showed such behaviour. Numerical simulations have been conducted to clarify this issue.

3.1 Simulation model

Fig. 3 shows a schematic diagram of the simulation model. Thirty-two optical transmitters (TXs) with the signal wavelengths ranged between 1543.8 to 1556.2 nm were used. The channel separation was set to 0.4 nm. The bit rate and the pattern of the transmitters were 10 Gb/s and 2^9 De Brujin sequence, respectively. A Mach–Zehnder modulator (MZM) was assumed to generate the PSK signal, and the waveform applied for the two arms of the MZM was a raised cosine with the non-return-to-zero (NRZ) format. The RZ waveform was applied after the PSK modulation, and the waveform was also raised cosine. The pulse duty ratio was 50 %. The multiplexer (MUX) did not have any wavelength-selective function, and the modulated pattern of each transmitter was randomized at the output of the MUX. Three different sets of the initial pattern at the output of the MUX was simulated in order to reduce the pattern-dependent cross phase modulation (XPM) impact (Essiambre & Winzer, 2005), and the obtained results were averaged over these three sets.

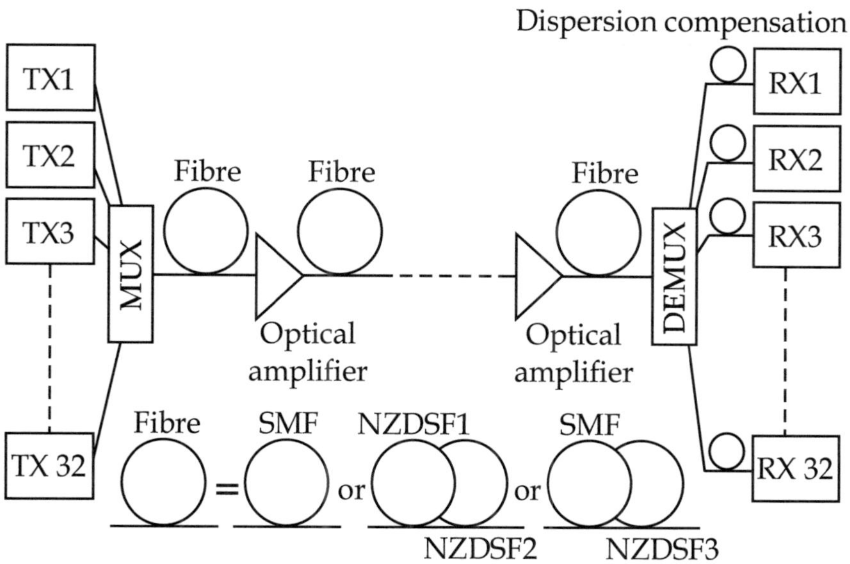

Fig. 3. A schematic diagram of the simulation model

The output power and the noise figure of the optical amplifier repeater were set to +11 dBm and 4.5 dB, respectively. The amplifier spontaneous emission (ASE) noise generated by the repeater had a random complex electrical field, and it was added to the complex electrical field of the optical signal. The repeater span length was 100 km, and the number of the repeaters was 63. The wavelength-dependent gain of the repeater was ignored in the simulation.

The optical demultiplexer (DEMUX) had the first-order Gaussian shape with the bandwidth of 0.1 nm. The cumulative chromatic dispersion for each channel was compensated at the receiving end, and the residual dispersion after dispersion equalization was set to 100 ps/nm. The Q-factor was calculated for each channel.

Two different dispersion maps were simulated. The first one was the conventional block type dispersion map, and the second one was the block-less type map. Both maps used the NZDSF and the SMF, but the parameters of the fibres were slightly different for each map. Table 1 summarizes the parameters of those fibres (Moh et al., 2007). The block type map comprised eight NZDSF spans and one SMF span to compose one block, and the SMF span was placed in the centre of the block (i.e., fifth span). Each NZDSF span comprised NZDSF1 and NZDSF2. The differences of these two fibres were the effective area and the dispersion slope. The block-less type map comprised hybrid spans except for both ends of the transmission line. The hybrid span was composed of the SMF and the NZDSF, while only the SMFs were used for both ends. Fig. 4 shows the cumulative dispersion at 1550 nm of these two maps. While the block type map compensated the cumulative dispersion periodically, the block-less type map compensated the cumulative dispersion only at both ends. The averaged zero dispersion wavelength of both maps was set to 1550 nm, and the transmission distances were 6300 km for the block type map and 6360 km for the block-less type map.

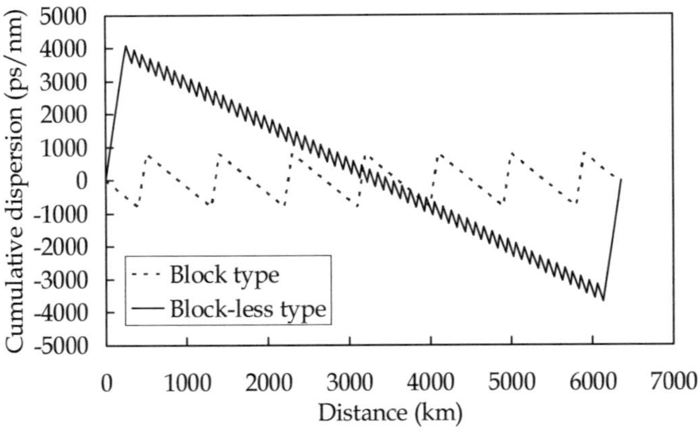

Fig. 4. Dispersion maps of the simulated systems

	Block type			Block-less type	
	NZDSF1	NZDSF2	SMF	SMF	NZDSF3
Length (km)	50	50	100	25	75
Loss (dB/km)	0.21	0.21	0.18	0.18	0.21
Chromatic dispersion (ps/nm/km)	-2.0	-2.0	16.0	16.0	-7.0
Dispersion slope (ps/nm^2/km)	0.10	0.06	0.06	0.06	0.08
Effective area (≅m^2)	70	50	100	100	50
Nonlinear refractive index	2.6×10^{-20}				

Table 1. Fibre parameters used for the simulation

3.2 Simulation results

Fig. 5 shows a comparison of two dispersion maps. The obtained Q-factors are shown as a function of the signal channels. For the block type map, the Q-factor is degraded near the centre channels, while there is not a significant dependence upon the channels for the block-less type map. The averaged Q-factors were 12.3 and 13.7 dB for the block type map and the block-less type map, respectively. These results qualitatively agree the experimental result (Moh et al., 2007) because it showed a performance dip near the centre channels for the block type map and the performance improvement for the block-less type map.

Then, to examine the reason of the performance improvement of the block-less type map, the effects of the self phase modulation (SPM) and the XPM were evaluated. Fig. 6 (A) and (B) show the performance without the SPM or the XPM of the block type map and the block-less type map, respectively. As shown in Fig. 6 (A), the performance of the block type map was greatly improved when the SPM was ignored especially near the centre channels, while the improvement was small when the XPM was ignored. From this result, it can be said that the SPM caused the performance degradation near the centre wavelength channels of the block type map. On the other hand, as shown in Fig. 6 (B) for the case of the block-less type map, the performance improvement caused by ignoring the SPM was limited compared to the block type map, and the improvement was not channel dependent. In addition, the performance was almost identical when the XPM was ignored. The averaged Q-factors without the SPM for the block type map and the block-less type map were 13.8 and 14.6 dB, respectively. The averaged Q-factors without the XPM for the block type map and the block-less type map were 12.9 and 13.7 dB, respectively

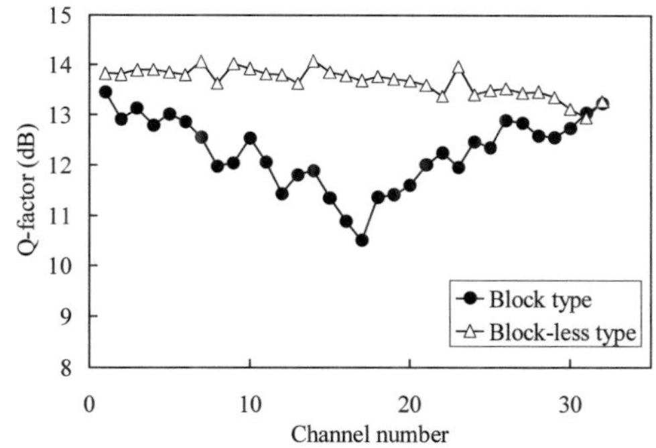

Fig. 5. Simulated transmission performance of the block type and block-less type map

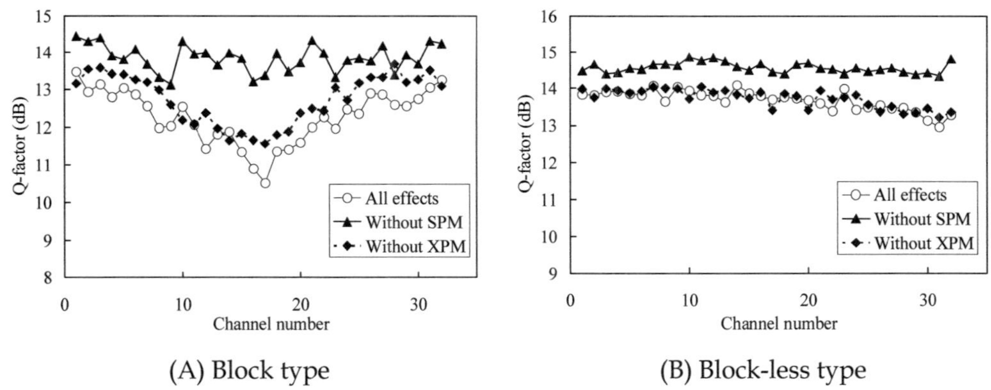

Fig. 6. Impact of the SPM and XPM for the block type and block-less type map

Two conclusions can be drawn from these results. The first conclusion is the SPM causes the wavelength-dependent degradation for the block type map, and the degradation is significant in the region close to the system zero dispersion wavelength. The second conclusion is the XPM plays a relatively minor role of the performance degradation of the block type map while it has virtually no effect for the block-less type map. It can be concluded that the block-less type dispersion map reduces the impairments of both the SPM and the XPM for the long-haul RZ-DPSK transmission compared to the block type dispersion map, and improves the system performance.

4. Impact of number of dispersion blocks

Comparing the block type map and the block-less type map, one notable difference between them is number of zero-crossing points of the cumulative dispersion along the transmission distance. This is due to number of dispersion blocks in the system. Therefore, in this section, the effect of number of dispersion blocks upon the transmission performance of the long-haul RZ-DPSK system is studied. At first, the system performance of the block type dispersion map was evaluated as a function of the transmission distance. Then, the system performances of several different block type dispersion maps were evaluated as a function of number of dispersion blocks in the system.

4.1 Simulated dispersion maps

The model used for this study was the same as the previous study, and it is shown in Fig. 3. The simulated block type dispersion maps were using NZDSF1, NZDSF2, and SMF shown in Table 1. The output power and the noise figure of the optical amplifier repeater were set to +11 dBm and 4.5 dB, respectively. The repeater span length was 100km, and the total transmission distance was 6300 km.

Number of dispersion blocks was adjusted by changing the position of the SMF span in the transmission line. Then, different style of the dispersion maps was realized whereas the fibre parameters were kept identical. Fig. 7 shows these maps. Number of dispersion blocks was one to seven corresponding to the number of dispersion map. This means Map 1 has one dispersion block, Map 2 has two dispersion blocks, and so on.

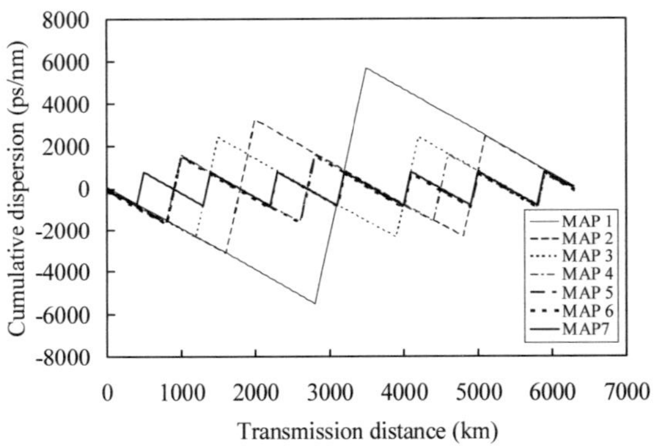

Fig. 7. Dispersion maps with different number of dispersion blocks

4.2 Transmission distance dependency

At first, the system performance of Map 7 was evaluated as a function of the transmission distance. Fig. 8 shows the results. The horizontal axes shows the channel number, and the vertical axes shows the relative Q-factor for each transmission distance. The relative Q-factor is defined as the difference from the value of channel 32. As seen in this figure, the performance dip near the system zero dispersion wavelength became obvious when the transmission distance was increased. This tendency implies that large number of dispersion blocks causes the performance degradation near the system zero dispersion wavelength. Then, the effects of the SPM and the XPM were investigated. Fig. 9 (A) and (B) show the transmission distance dependency without the SPM and the XPM, respectively. As shown in Fig. 9 (A), there is not any significant dip when the SPM effect was ignored, while the degradation near the centre channels was obvious for Fig. 9 (B). These results imply that large number of dispersion blocks combined with the SPM degrades the performance of the RZ-DPSK signal near the system zero dispersion wavelength.

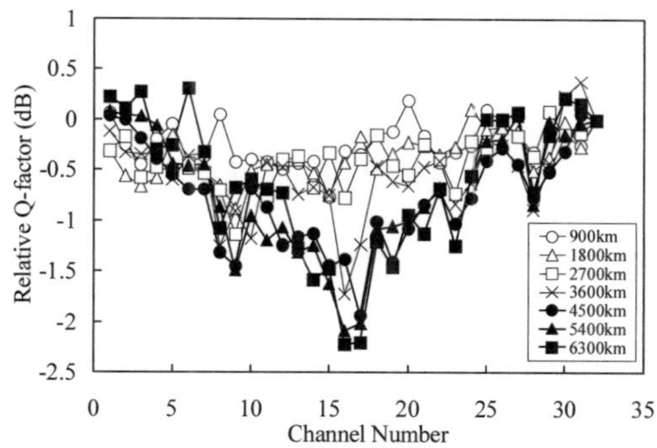

Fig. 8. Relative channel performance as a function of the transmission distance

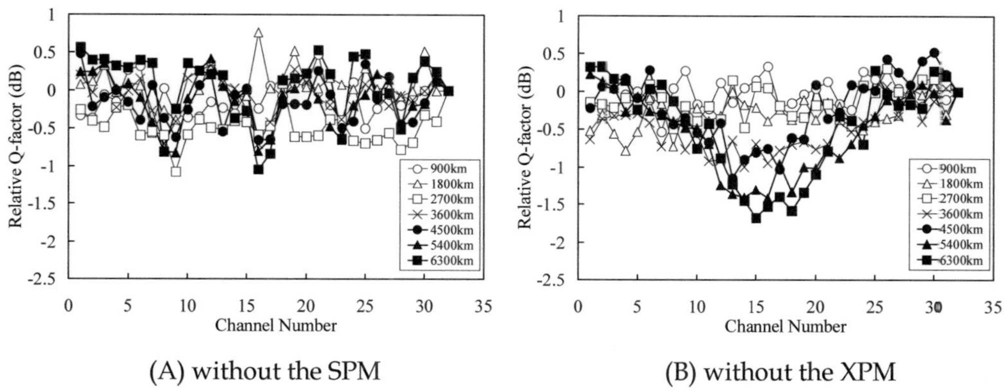

Fig. 9. Relative channel performance as a function of the transmission distance without the SPM and the XPM

4.3 Number of dispersion blocks dependency

Next, the system performance of several different block type dispersion maps shown in Fig. 7 was evaluated. Fig. 10 shows the results. As seen in the figure, the performance dip near

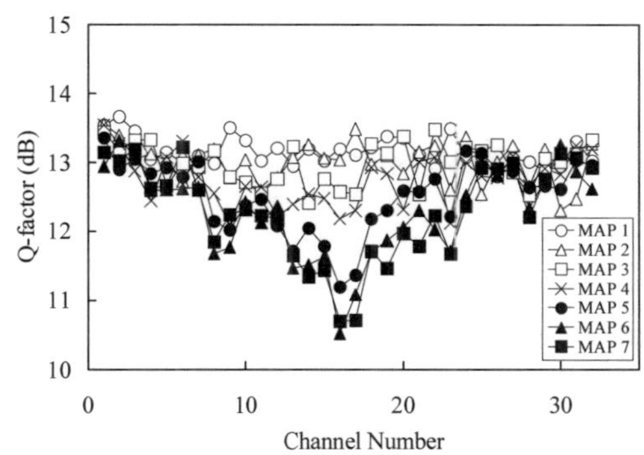

Fig. 10. Transmission performance of different number of dispersion blocks

the centre channels became significant when number of dispersion blocks was increased. This tendency clearly shows that large number of dispersion blocks causes the performance degradation near the system zero dispersion wavelength. Then, the effects of the SPM and the XPM were investigated. Fig. 11 (A) and (B) show the dispersion map dependency without the SPM and the XPM, respectively. As shown in Fig. 11 (A), there is not any significant dip when the SPM effect was ignored, while the degradation near the centre channels was obvious for Fig. 11 (B). These results show that large number of dispersion blocks combined with the SPM degrades the performance of the RZ-DPSK signal near the system zero dispersion wavelength.

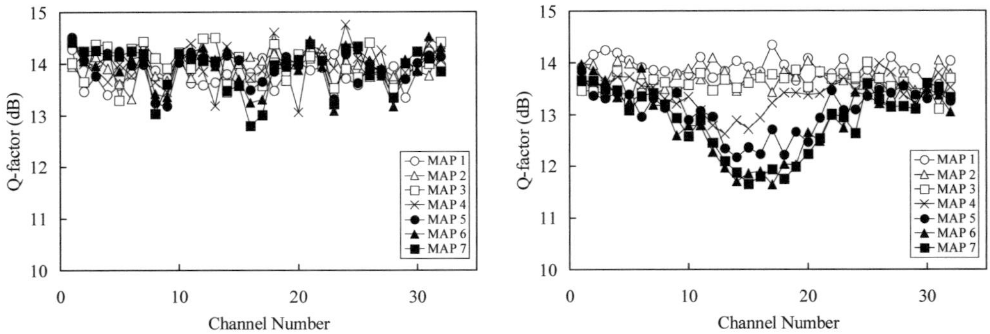

(A) without the SPM (B) without the XPM

Fig. 11. Transmission performance of different number of dispersion blocks without the SPM and the XPM

5. Comparison of dispersion flattened fibre and non-zero dispersion shifted fibre

The DFF is a well-known solution to improve the performance of the long-haul IM-DD system, but there are not enough studies to characterize the transmission performance difference between the DFF and the NZDSF for the RZ-DPSK based system. In this section, a comparative study of the long-haul RZ-DPSK system performance using the DFF and the NZDSF is conducted.

5.1 Simulation model

Fig. 12 shows a schematic diagram of the simulation model. Ninety-six optical TXs were employed, and the signal wavelengths were ranged from 1540.5 nm to 1559.5 nm with 0.2 nm channel separation. The bit rate and the pattern were 10 Gbit/s and 2^9 De Brujin sequence, respectively. The PSK signal was assumed to be generated by a MZM, and the waveform applied for the two arms of the MZM was a raised cosine with the NRZ format. The RZ waveform was applied after the PSK modulation, and the waveform was also raised cosine. The pulse duty ratio was 50 %. The MUX did not have any wavelength selective function, and the modulated pattern of each transmitter was randomized at the output of the MUX. Three different sets of the initial pattern at the output of the MUX were used for the simulation to reduce the pattern dependent XPM impact (Essiambre & Winzer, 2005), and the obtained results were averaged over these three sets.

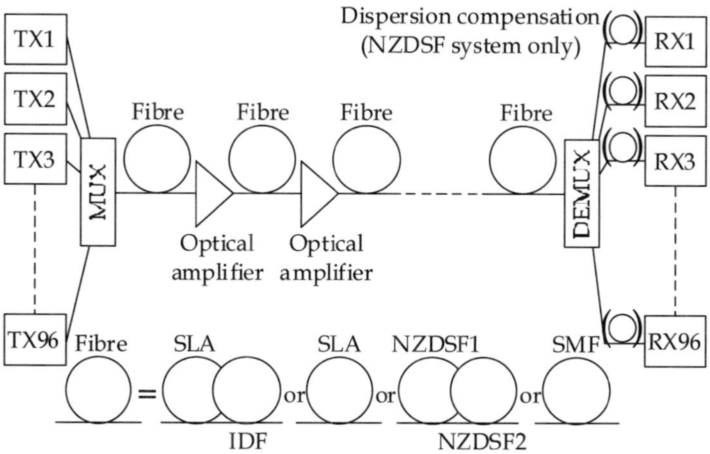

Fig. 12. A schematic diagram of the simulation model

The optical DEMUX had the second-order Gaussian shape, and the 3dB bandwidth of the DEMUX was 0.1 nm. As the relative dispersion slope of the SLA and the IDF was the same, the cumulative dispersion of all signal channels after the transmission was equal to zero for the DFF system. On the other hand, the cumulative dispersion of each channel was equalized to be 100 ps/nm for the NZDSF system after the DEMUX.
The transmission line comprised optical amplifier repeaters and fibres. The noise figure of the optical amplifier repeater was set to 4.5 dB. The ASE noise generated by the amplifier had a random complex electrical field, and it was added to the complex electrical field of the optical signal. The amplifier spacing was 100 km. The wavelength dependent gain of the optical amplifier was ignored in the simulation.
The fibre span comprised the DFF or the NZDSF. The DFF was composed from the super large area fibre (SLA) and the inverse dispersion fibre (IDF) (OFS), and there were two types of the NZDSF. The parameters of the fibres are summarized in Table 2. The DFF span loss was 21.1 dB and the NZDSF span loss was 21.0 dB. Fig. 13 shows the dispersion map of the DFF system and the NZDSF system. The block-less type map was employed. Three different wavelengths, 1540.5, 1550, and 1559.5 nm were shown in the figure to show the difference between the fibres clearly. Both maps had pure positive fibre spans in the centre of the system, and the span length of this section was 96 km for the DFF system and 100 km for the NZDSF system. Thus, the total transmission distance was 6272 km and 6300 km for

	DFF		NZDSF		
	SLA	IDF	NZDSF1	NZDSF2	SMF
Length (km)	65	35	50	50	100
Loss (dB/km)	0.19	0.25	0.21	0.21	0.18
Chromatic dispersion (ps/nm/km)	20.0	-44.0	-2.0	-2.0	16.0
Dispersion slope (ps/nm^2/km)	0.06	-0.132	0.10	0.06	0.06
Effective area (m^2)	106	30	70	50	72
Relative dispersion slope	0.003	0.003	-	-	-
Nonlinear refractive index	2.6×10^{-20}				

Table 2. Fibre parameters of the DFF and the NZDSF

the DFF system and the NZDSF system, respectively. The positive dispersion fibre used for the DFF system was the SLA, and that for the NZDSF system was the SMF.

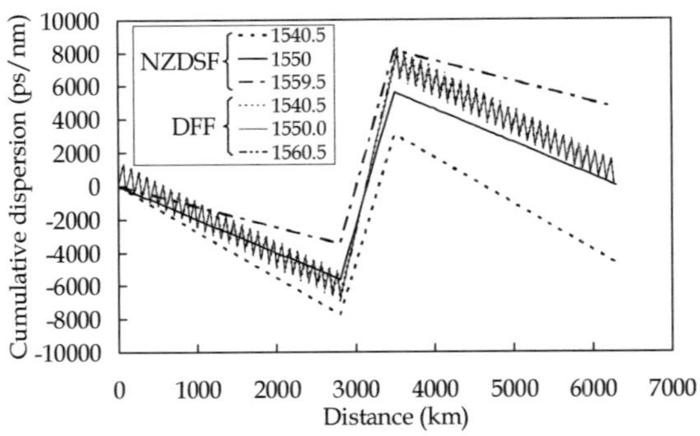

Fig. 13. Dispersion maps of the DFF and the NZDSF systems

5.2 Comparison of the dispersion flattened fibre and the non-zero dispersion shifted fibre based system

At first, the system performance was evaluated as a function of the repeater output power. Fig. 14 shows the results. The horizontal axis shows the repeater output power, and the vertical axis shows the averaged Q-factor of ninety-six channels. As seen in the figure, when the repeater output power was smaller than +14 dBm, the performance of both systems was similar. This result shows that the difference of the fibre parameters did not have so significant impact on the transmission performance when the optical fibre nonlinearity was not dominant. The performance was improved as the repeater output power was increased up to +18 dBm for the DFF system and up to +16 dBm for the NZDSF system. This result clearly shows that the DFF had smaller transmission impairment caused by the optical fibre nonlinearity than the NZDSF. When the repeater output power was +16 dBm, averaged Q-factors for the DFF system and the NZDSF system were 13.9 dB and 12.6 dB, respectively. There was 1.3 dB performance difference between the DFF and the NZDSF systems when the repeater output power was set to the optimum value of the NZDSF system. Furthermore, when the repeater output power was +18dBm, averaged Q-factor for the DFF system was improved to 14.9 dB. Therefore, the DFF system had 2.3 dB performance advantage against the NZDSF system when the system was operated under the optimum condition.

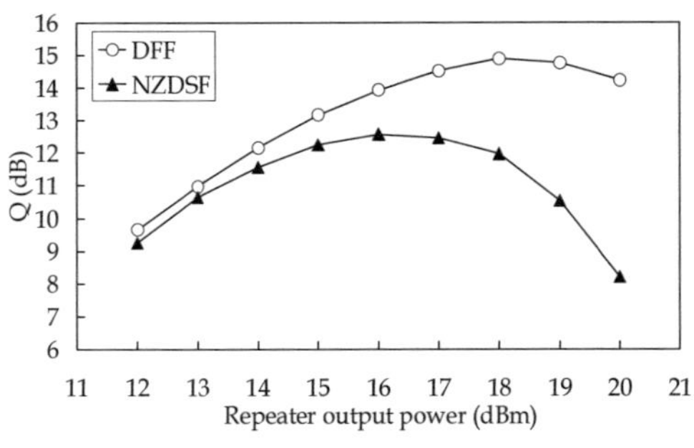

Fig. 14. Repeater output power dependency of the DFF and the NZDSF system

Fig. 15 shows channel dependence of the Q-factor for the DFF system and the NZDSF system. Fig. 15 (A) shows +14dBm repeater output power, and Fig. 15 (B) shows +16dBm repeater output power. The DFF system showed slightly improved performance than the NZDSF system in Fig. 15 (A), and it showed clearly better performance in Fig. 15 (B). In addition, Fig. 16 shows the comparison at the optimum repeater output power. The DFF system at +18 dBm repeater output power showed superior performance than the NZDSF system at +16 dBm. These results show that the DFF is effective to improve the transmission performance of the long-haul RZ-DPSK system, but the repeater output power should be high enough to fully utilize the advantage of the DFF.

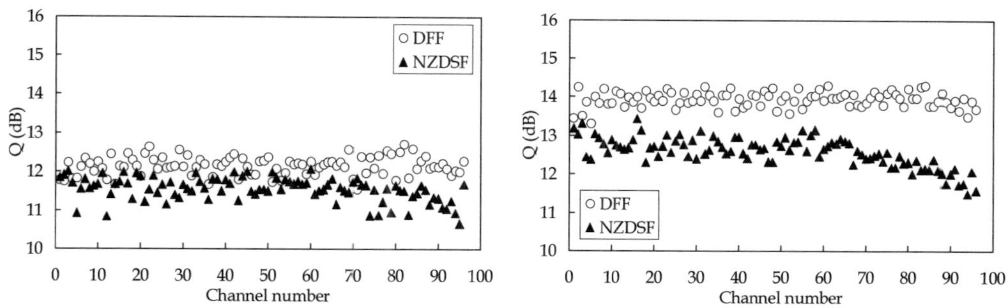

(A) +14 dBm repeater output power (B) +16 dBm repeater output power

Fig. 15. Transmission performance of 96 channels with the DFF and the NZDSF system

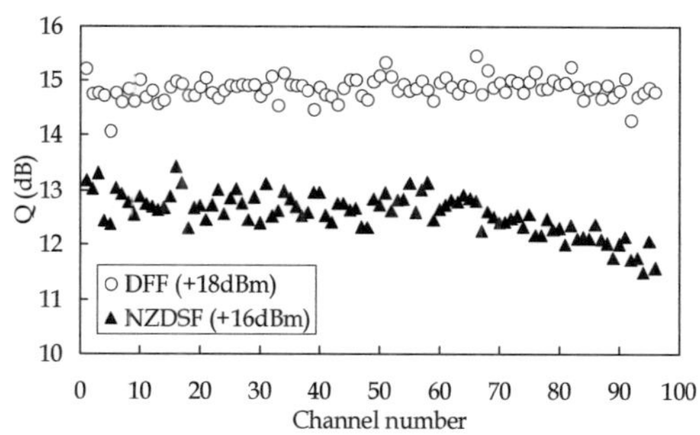

Fig. 16. Transmission performance of 96 channels with the optimum repeater output power

As mentioned above, the DFF system exhibited 2.3 dB performance improvement compared to the NZDSF system when the repeater output power was optimized. The reason of this 2.3 dB advantage could be explained in two steps. Firstly, there is 2 dB difference of the optimum repeater output power. This difference could be justified by the effective area difference between the SLA and NZDSF1. As the effective areas of the SLA and the NZDSF1 are 107 μm^2 and 70 μm^2, respectively, the difference of the effective area in dB scale is 1.8 dB, and this could cause 2 dB difference of the optimum power level. Roughly speaking, 2 dB improvement of the repeater output power improves the optical signal to noise ratio of 2 dB, and it can improve the Q-factor of 2 dB. Secondly, remaining 0.3dB discrepancy could be attributed to channel dependent degradation of the NZDSF system at +16 dBm repeater output power. As shown in Fig. 15 (B), channel performance of the NZDSF system above the system zero dispersion wavelength clearly exhibits gradual degradation when the channel wavelength becomes longer. Actually, if the average Q-factor of the NZDSF system is calculated using only fourty-eight shorter wavelength channels (i.e., channel 1 to 48), the average is improved to 12.8 dB.

6. Impact of number of dispersion blocks for the dispersion flattened fibre based system

As discussed in section 4, for the NZDSF based system, the block type dispersion map is not optimum for the RZ-DPSK format and number of dispersion blocks changes the transmission performance significantly. This implies that the transmission performance of the DFF based system is also affected significantly by the number of dispersion blocks. Therefore, this section focuses on this issue whether the block type dispersion map causes the performance degradation of the DFF based RZ-DPSK system.

6.1 Simulation model

The simulation model used for this study was similar to that of the previous section, and it is shown in Fig. 12. The DFF parameters and span configuration was the same, and each DFF span had negative chromatic dispersion of -240ps/nm. The cumulative negative dispersion was compensated by the SLA only span. To compose the block type dispersion map, one dispersion block comprised nine DFF spans and one SLA only span. The SLA only span was placed at the sixth span. The span length of the SLA only span was 108km. There were six dispersion blocks, and the total transmission distance was 6048km.

Six different dispersion maps were used for the simulation. Number of dispersion blocks was changed for each map. Map 1 had one dispersion block, Map 2 had two dispersion blocks, and so on. Map 1, 2, 3, and 6 had uniform dispersion blocks while Map 4 and 5 had two different block lengths within the system. Fig. 17 shows the dispersion maps used for this study. Note that the difference was only the position of SLA only span, and the physical parameters of the fibres were identical.

6.2 Number of dispersion blocks dependency

Fig. 18 shows the performance of ninety-six channels after 6048km transmission as a function of the repeater output power. As seen in the figure, for small repeater output power of below +14 dBm, there was not any significant difference between the maps, but the performance of map 6 became inferior than the others when the repeater output power was increased above +16 dBm. These results clearly indicate that the nonlinear penalty of the system strongly depends on the dispersion map design.

Fig. 19 shows the average Q-factor of ninety-six channels as a function of the repeater output power and the dispersion map. It is obvious that increasing the number of dispersion blocks leads to performance degradation in higher repeater output power (i.e., higher nonlinear regime). Regarding dispersion map design, the tendency is the same as the NZDSF based system, and it is favourable for the DFF system to reduce number of dispersion blocks to improve the performance.

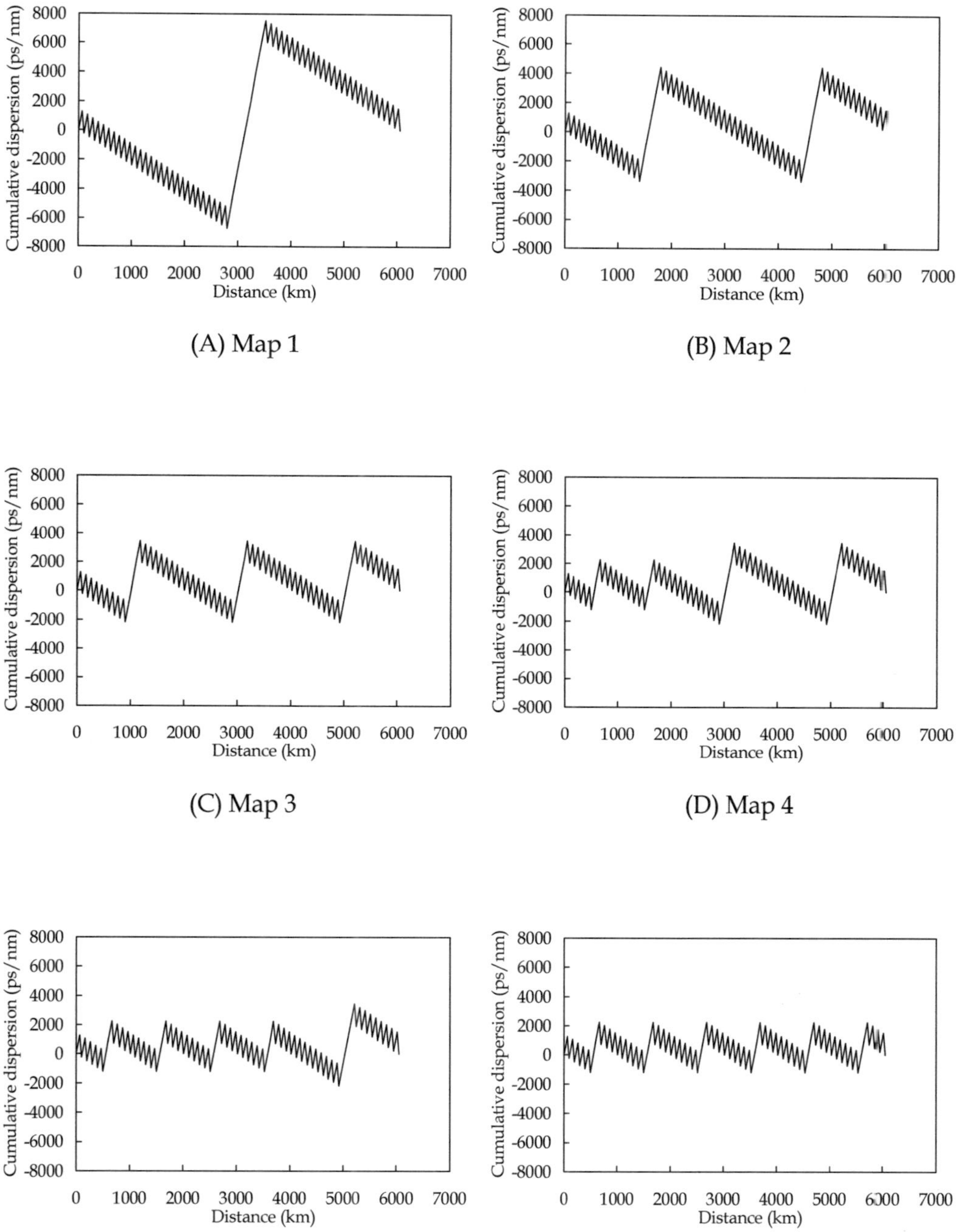

(A) Map 1

(B) Map 2

(C) Map 3

(D) Map 4

(E) Map 5

(F) Map 6

Fig. 17. Dispersion maps

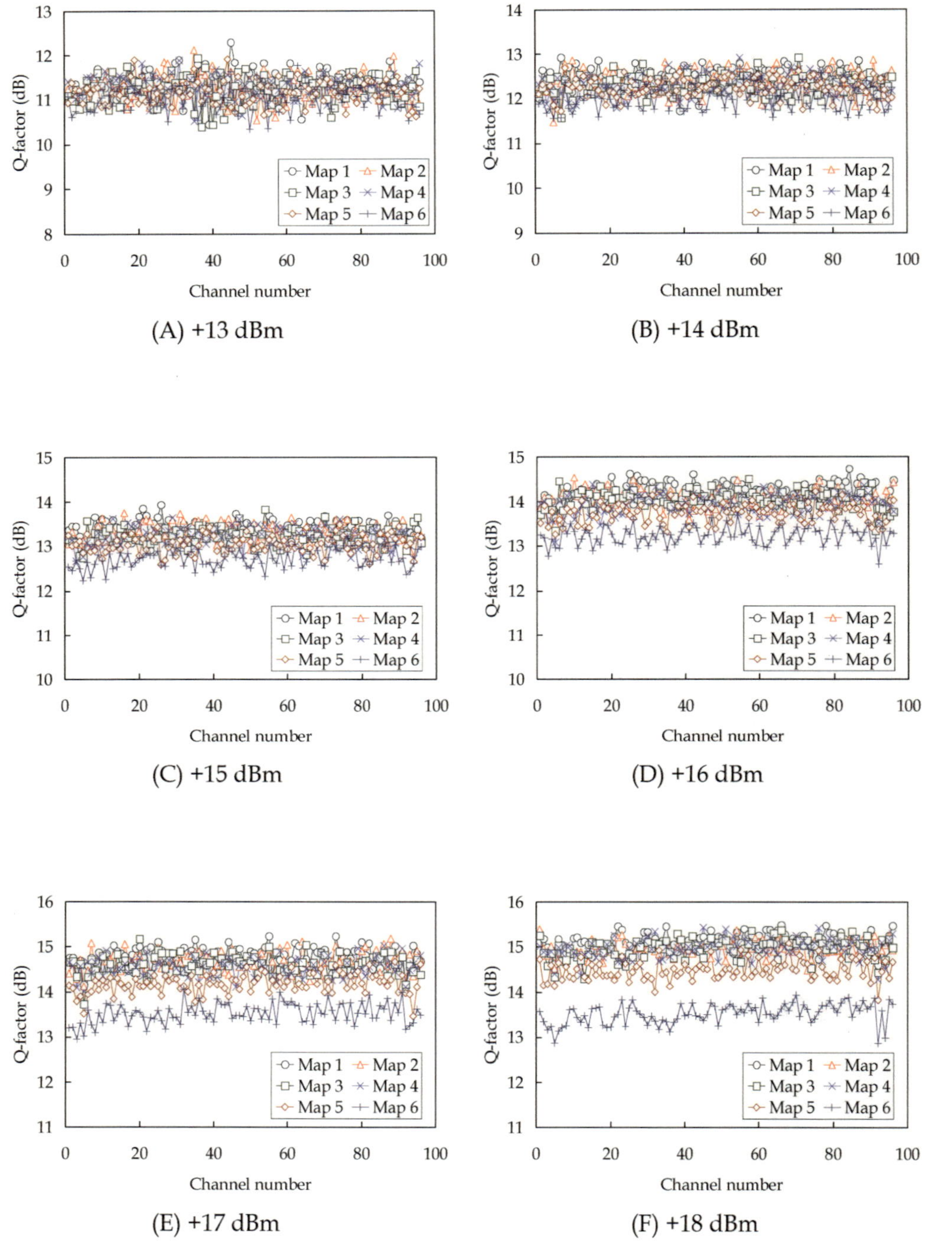

Fig. 18. Transmission performance of 96 channels as a function of the repeater output power

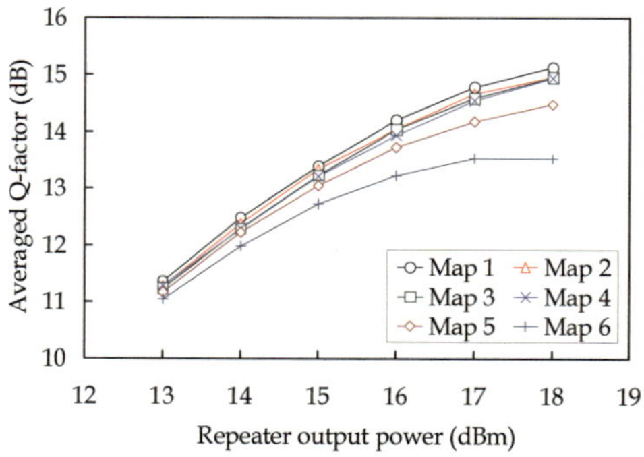

Fig. 19. Repeater output power dependency of different dispersion map

7. Conclusion

In this chapter, the transmission performance of the long-haul RZ-DPSK system with respect to the dispersion map design was discussed using the numerical simulations. The block type dispersion map could not realize better performance than the block-less type dispersion map either using the NZDSF or the DFF for the RZ-DPSK transmission. The reason of the performance degradation for the block type map was pointed out to be the SPM, and it was also confirmed experimentally (Wang & Taga, 2010). This proved the appropriateness of the numerical simulations for the long-haul RZ-DPSK based optical fibre communication system.

8. Acknowledgment

This work is supported partially by National Science Council 99-2221-E-110-030-MY3 and partially by Aim for the Top University Plan of the National Sun Yat-Sen University and Ministry of Education, Taiwan, R.O.C.

9. References

Agrawal, G. P. (2006). *Nonlinear Fiber Optics (Fourth Ed.)*, Academic Press, ISBN 978-0-12-369516-1, San Diego, California, USA

Bakhshi, B.; Manna, M.; Mohs, G.; Kovsh, D. I.; Lynch, R. L.; Vaa, M.; Golovchenko, E. A.; Patterson, W. W.; Anderson, W. T.; Corbett, P.; Jiang, S.; Sanders, M. M.; Li, H.; Harvey, G. T.; Lucero, A. & Abbott, S. M. (2004). First Dispersion-Flattened Transpacific Undersea System: From Design to Terabit/s Field Trial, *Journal of Lightwave Technology*, Vol.22, No.1, (January, 2004), pp. 233-241

Bergano, N. S.; Kerfoot, F. W. & Davidsion, C. R. (1993). "Margin measurements in optical amplifier system, *IEEE Photonics Technology Letters*, Vol.5, No.3, (March, 1993), pp. 304-306

Bergano, N. S. (2005). Wavelength division multiplexing in long-haul transoceanic transmission systems, *Journal of Lightwave Technology*, Vol.23, No.12, (December 2005), pp. 4125-4139

Bosco, G.; Carena, A.; Curri, V.; Gaudino, R.; Poggiolini, P. & Benedetto, S. (2000). Suppression of spurious tones induced by the split-step method in fiber systems simulation, *IEEE Photonics Technology Letters*, Vol.12, No.5, (May, 2000), pp. 489–491

Cai, J.-X.; Nissov, M.; Anderson, W.; Vaa, M.; Davidson, C. R.; Foursa, D. G.; Liu, L.; Cai, Y.; Lucero, A. J.; Patterson, W. W.; Corbett, P. C.; Pilipetskii, A. N. & Bergano, N. S. (2006). Long-haul 40 Gb/s RZ-DPSK transmission with long repeater spacing, *Proceedings of Optical Fiber Communication Conference*, paper OFD3, Anaheim, California, USA, March 5-10, 2006

Dupont, S.; Marmier, P.; Mouza, L. d.; Charlet, G. & Letellier, V. (2007). 70 x 10 Gbps (mixed RZ-OOK and RZDPSK) upgrade of a 7224km conventional 32 x 10 Gbps designed system, *Proceedings of European Conference of Optical Communication (ECOC)*, Paper 2.3.5, Berlin, Germany, September 16-20, 2007

Essiambre, R.-J. & Winzer, P. J. (2005). Fibre nonlinearities in electronically pre-distorted transmission, *Proceedings of European Conference of Optical Communication (ECOC)*, Paper Th3.2.2, Glasgow, Scotland, September 25-29, 2005

Inoue, T.; Ishida, K.; Tokura, T.; Shibano, E.; Taga, H.; Shimizu, K.; Goto, K. & Motoshima, K. (2004). 150km repeater span transmission experiment over 9,000klm, *Proceedings of European Conference of Optical Communication (ECOC)*, paper Th4.1.3, Stockholm, Sweden, September 5-9, 2004

Mohs, G. ; Anderson, W. T. & Golovchenko, E. A. (2007). A New Dispersion Map for Undersea Optical Communication Systems, *Proceedings of Optical Fiber Communication Conference and Exposition and The National Fiber Optic Engineers Conference*, paper JThA41, Anaheim, California, USA, March 25-30, 2007

OFS, Available from:<http://www.ofsoptics.com/resources/UWOceanFiber-fiber-115.pdf>

Personick, S. D. (1973). Receiver Design for Digital Fiber Optic Communication Systems, I & II, *The Bell System Technical Journal*, Vol.52, No.6, (July-August, 1973), pp. 843–886

Rasmussen, C.; Fjelde, T.; Bennike, J.; Liu, F.; Dey, S.; Mikkelsen, B.; Mamyshev, P.; Serbe, P.; Wagt, P. v. d.; Akasaka, Y.; Harris, D.; Gapontsev, D.; Ivshin, V. & Reeves-Hall, P. (2004). DWDM 40G Transmission Over Trans-Pacific Distance (10 000 km) Using CSRZ-DPSK, Enhanced FEC, and All-Raman-Amplified 100-km UltraWave Fiber Spans, *Journal of Lightwave Technology*, Vol.22, No.1, (January 2004), pp. 203-207

Taga, H.; Shu, S.-S.; Wu, J.-Y. & Shih, W.-T. (2007). A theoretical study of the effect of the dispersion map upon a long-haul RZ-DPSK transmission system, *IEEE Photonics Technology Letters*, Vol.19, No.24, (December, 2007), pp. 2060–2062

Taga, H.; Shu, S.-S.; Wu, J.-Y. & Shih, W.-T. (2008). A theoretical study of the effect of zero-crossing points within the dispersion map upon a long-haul RZ-DPSK system, *Optics Express*, Vol.16, No.9, (April, 2008), pp. 6163-6169

Taga, H. (2009). A theoretical investigation of the long-haul RZDPSK system performance using DFF and NZDSF, *Optics Express*, Vol.17, No.8, (April, 2009), pp. 6032-6037

Taga, H. & Chung, W.-H. (2010). Impact of dispersion map design upon transmission performance of long-haul RZDPSK system using dispersion flattened fiber, *Optics Express*, Vol.18, No.8, (April, 2010), pp. 8332-8337

Vaa, M.; Golovchenko, E. A.; Mohs, G.; Patterson, W. & Pillipetskii, A. (2004). Dense WDM RZ-DPSK transmission over transoceanic distances without use of periodic dispersion management, *Proceedings of European Conference of Optical Communication (ECOC)*, Paper Th4.4.4, Stockholm, Sweden, September 5-9, 2004

Wang, H. M. and Taga, H. (2010), An Experimental Study of XPM and SPM Upon a Long-Haul RZ-DSPK Transmission System With a Block-Type Dispersion Map, *Journal of Lightwave Technology*, Vol.28, No.22, (November, 2010), pp. 3220-3225

Wei, X.; Liu, X. & Xu, C. (2003). Numerical simulation of the SPM penalty in a 10-Gb/s RZ-DPSK system, *IEEE Photonics Technology Letters*, Vol.15, No.11, (November, 2003), pp. 1636–1638